SIXTH EDITION

Death and Dying, Life and Living

Charles A. Corr

*Southern Illinois University
Edwardsville*

Clyde M. Nabe

*Southern Illinois University
Edwardsville*

Donna M. Corr

*St. Louis Community College
at Forest Park*

 WADSWORTH
CENGAGE Learning™

Australia • Brazil • Japan • Korea • Mexico • Singapore • Spain • United Kingdom • United States

WADSWORTH
CENGAGE Learning™

Death and Dying, Life and Living, **Sixth Edition**
Charles A. Corr, Clyde M. Nabe, Donna M. Corr

Publisher: Michele Sordi

Assistant Editor: Magnolia Molcan

Editorial Assistant: Trina Tom

Managing Technology Project Manager: Amy Cohen

Marketing Manager: Sara Swangard

Marketing Assistant: Melanie Cregger

Marketing Communications Manager: Linda Yip

Project Manager, Editorial Production: Mary Noel

Creative Director: Rob Hugel

Art Director: Vernon T. Boes

Print Buyer: Rebecca Cross

Permissions Editors: John Hill, Bob Kauser

Production Service: Carol O'Connell, Graphic
    World Inc.

Text Designer: John Edeen

Photo Researcher: Sam Marshall

Cover Designer: Andy Norris

Cover Image: Peter Adams/Stone/Getty Images

Compositor: Graphic World Inc.

© 2009, 2006 Wadsworth, Cengage Learning

For product information and technology assistance, contact us at
Cengage Learning Customer & Sales Support, 1-800-354-9706.

For permission to use material from this text or product, submit all
requests online at **cengage.com/permissions.**
Further permissions questions can be e-mailed to
permissionrequest@cengage.com.

Library of Congress Control Number: 2008920143

ISBN-13: 978-0-495-50646-1

ISBN-10: 0-495-50646-X

Wadsworth
10 Davis Drive
Belmont, CA 94002-3098
USA

Cengage Learning is a leading provider of customized
learning solutions with office locations around the globe,
including Singapore, the United Kingdom, Australia, Mexico,
Brazil, and Japan. Locate your local office at: **international
.cengage.com/region.**

Cengage Learning products are represented in Canada by
Nelson Education, Ltd.

For your course and learning solutions, visit **academic
.cengage.com.**

Purchase any of our products at your local college store or at
our preferred online store **www.ichapters.com.**

Printed in Canada
1 2 3 4 5 6 7 12 11 10 09 08

We dedicate this sixth edition of *Death and Dying, Life and Living* to the memory and the legacy of three individuals who contributed in extraordinary ways to understanding and care for persons who are coping with life-threatening illness, dying, and bereavement:

Dame Ciccly M. Saunders (1918–2005)
Dr. John D. (Jack) Morgan (1933–2005)
Senator Jack D. Gordon (1922–2005)

Death is no enemy of life; it restores our sense of the value of living. Illness restores the sense of proportion that is lost when we take life for granted. To learn about value and proportion, we need to honor illness, and ultimately to honor death.

—A. W. Frank, *At the Will of the Body* (2002, p. 120)

How do we learn to die?

We live in a world that panics at this question and turns away. Other civilizations before ours looked equally at death. They mapped the passage for both the community and the individual. They infused the fulfillment of destiny with a richness of meaning. Never perhaps have our relations with death been as barren as they are in this modern spiritual desert, in which our rush to a new existence carries us past all sense of mystery. We do not even know that we are parching the essence of life of one of its wellsprings.

—F. Mitterand, Foreword, in M. de Hennezel, *Intimate death: How the dying teach us to live* (1998, p. vii)

About the Authors

Charles A. Corr, Ph.D., CT, has taught courses on death and dying, children and death, and related subjects at Southern Illinois University Edwardsville since 1975. Since 1978, he has been a member of the Association for Death Education and Counseling (Board of Directors, 1980–1983) and the National Hospice and Palliative Care Organization (NHPCO). Dr. Corr is a long-time member and former chairperson (1989–1993) of the International Work Group on Death, Dying, and Bereavement. Currently, he is also a member of the Board of Directors of The Hospice Institute of the Florida Suncoast, a member of the Leadership Advisory Council of the Children's Project on Palliative/Hospice Services (ChiPPS) of the National Hospice and Palliative Care Organization, and a member of the Executive Committee of the National Donor Family Council. His publications include three dozen books and booklets, such as *Helping Children Cope with Death: Guidelines and Resources* (2nd ed., 1984), *Childhood and Death* (1984), *Adolescence and Death* (1986), *Handbook of Adolescent Death and Bereavement* (1996), as well as 5 books co-edited with Donna Corr and over 100 book chapters and articles published in professional journals. Dr. Corr's professional work has been recognized by the Association for Death Education and Counseling (ADEC) in an award for Outstanding Personal Contributions to the Advancement of Knowledge in the Field of Death, Dying, and Bereavement (1988) and in its Death Educator Award (1996); by Children's Hospice International (CHI) in an award for Outstanding Contribution to the World of Hospice Support for Children (1989) and in the establishment of its Charles A. Corr Award for Lifetime Achievement (Literature) (1995); by The Dr. Robert Fulton CDEB Founder's Award from the Center for Death Education and Bioethics at the University of Wisconsin–La Crosse for Outstanding University Teaching, Research, Publication, and Professional Service in the Field of Death, Dying and Bereavement (2007); and by Southern Illinois University Edwardsville in Research Scholar (1990), Outstanding Scholar (1991), and Kimmel Community Services (1994) awards.

The Reverend Clyde M. Nabe, Ph.D., has taught courses on death and dying since 1976 at Southern Illinois University Edwardsville. He is an Episcopal priest and has been priest-in-charge in several missions and parishes. Dr. Nabe's research and publications have focused on issues in medical ethics, philosophy of religion, and comparative religion.

Donna M. Corr, R.N., M.S. in Nursing, has worked as a nurse with open heart, kidney transplant, oncology, and hospice patients. For 17 years, she was a faculty member (rising from Instructor to Professor) in the Nursing Faculty of St. Louis Community College at Forest Park, St. Louis, Missouri, and then a Lecturer for two semesters at Southern Illinois University Edwardsville. Her publications include 5 books co-edited with Charles Corr: *Hospice Care: Principles and Practice* (1983), *Hospice Approaches to Pediatric Care* (1985), *Nursing Care in an Aging Society* (1990), *Sudden Infant Death Syndrome: Who Can Help and How* (1991), and *Handbook of Childhood Death and Bereavement* (1996), as well as two dozen book chapters and articles published in professional journals. Books edited by Donna and/or Charles Corr have received five Book of the Year Awards from the *American Journal of Nursing*.

Brief Contents

Contents

CHAPTER 3
Changing Attitudes toward Death   44

CHAPTER 4
Death-Related Practices and the American Death System   62

CHAPTER 5
Cultural Differences and Death 95

PART THREE   Dying
127

CHAPTER 6
Coping with Dying 128

PART FIVE Developmental Perspectives 317

PART SIX   Legal, Conceptual, and Moral Issues   451

CHAPTER 16
Legal Issues   452

Preface

We offer the sixth edition of *Death and Dying, Life and Living* as a new contribution to ongoing human conversations about death, dying, and bereavement. In his allegory "The Horse on the Dining-Room Table" (our Prologue in this book), Richard Kalish wrote that we cannot magically make death disappear from our lives nor can we erase completely the sadness and other forms of distress associated with it. However, we can talk, share insights and attitudes, learn from each other, and strive together to cope more effectively with dying, death, and bereavement. Constructive interactions such as these help us lead more productive lives in the face of death.

In the interval since the fifth edition of this book was published, new encounters with death have occurred, new issues have come to the fore, new insights and attitudes have emerged, and much that is of enduring value has evolved and matured. We have worked diligently to incorporate these and other death-related developments in this new edition.

❦ Features

This book can be used as a primary textbook for undergraduate and graduate courses in death, dying, and bereavement; as a supplementary text in related courses; and as a general resource in this field. Individual instructors and other readers can easily adapt the contents of this book to their own needs and preferences. In particular, different parts of the book can be studied in any order, and most chapters within a specific section can be read on their own. Instructors can request a copy of the *Instructor's Manual with Test Bank* (ISBN: 0495596272), which provides suggestions about how to use this book, educational resources (from organizations, printed materials, guest speakers, and audiovisuals), detailed guides for each chapter, and an extensive test bank. Instructors can also obtain the electronic version of the test bank—ExamView (ISBN: 0495596280). It contains all the test items found in the test bank portion of the *Instructor's Manual with Test Bank* and enables you to create customized tests up to 250 items in print or online. In addition, the companion website for this text—accessible at academic.cengage.com/psychology/corr—provides tutorial quizzes, review material, and more for students, as well as materials that can help simplify instructors' course preparation. For any or all of these materials, instructors should contact their local Cengage sales representative.

Each of the seven parts in this book opens with a short introduction, and every chapter begins with a bulleted list of Objectives and a representative vignette or case study. Each chapter closes with a brief Summary, a Glossary, some Questions for Review and Discussion, a list of Suggested Readings, and selected Web Resources, which include some useful search terms and suggested Internet sites. In addition to the text, two Appendices identify and provide annotated descriptions of books on death-related topics for children and adolescents, along with a source from which to obtain copies of or ongoing information about such publications.

The following features distinguish our work in this book:

1. A careful exploration of the main features of *death-related experiences* in our society, examined in terms of *changing encounters with death, changing attitudes toward death,* and *changing practices associated with death* within the *American death system*

2. An emphasis on *coping with death-related experiences*—instead of merely reporting how individuals *react* to death-related encounters, we strive for an appreciation of the *efforts made to manage* those encounters and to integrate their implications into ongoing living

3. The use of a *task-based approach* to explain coping—by individuals and by communities—with life-threatening illness and dying, with loss and grief, with funeral and memorial rituals, and as a bereaved child, adolescent, or adult

4. Sensitivity to a *developmental perspective,* which considers death-related issues in ways that emphasize experiences of individuals within four different eras in the human life course: as children, as adolescents, as young and middle-aged adults, and as older adults

5. An emphasis on *cultural differences* within American society that recognizes distinctive modes of death-related encounters, attitudes, and practices typically found in Americans of Hispanic/Latino, African, Asian or Pacific Island, and American Indian or Alaskan Native backgrounds

6. A practical orientation that highlights *helping with death-related experiences*—helping others; helping oneself; and helping through families, social groups, institutions, and communities

7. An appreciation of *moral, ethical, religious, and spiritual values* not only in debates about controversial issues such as assisted suicide and euthanasia but also throughout the book as an essential framework for such topics as care of the dying, support for the bereaved, and helping children and adolescents

8. Recognition of *important lessons about life and living*—lessons about limitation and control, individuality and community, vulnerability and resilience, and quality in living and the search for meaning—that can be learned from the study of death, dying, and bereavement

❦ New to This Edition

A number of reviewers and instructors who have used this book as a basis for classroom or distance learning courses asked us not to change its basic structure. We have accepted that advice for this edition and have kept the book's overall structure unchanged. However, we have undertaken significant alterations in the internal organization of two chapters. The first of these occurs in Chapter 9, where the central sections on mourning have been revised to provide a more accurate reflection of some important changes in how experts have recently been thinking about this subject. The second alteration draws on another suggestion from reviewers, namely, that we clarify the role of Chapter 20, which has been reorganized to make clear that its purpose is to take one specific disease context to use as an example and illustration of the underlying structure and themes of this book. We have also changed the title of Chapter 15 to "Older Adults," to reflect the increasing vitality of individuals in our society who are 65 years of age and older. That led us to relabel Chapter 14 as "Young and Middle-Aged Adults."

Throughout this sixth edition, we report the most recent statistical data currently available from the National Center for Health Statistics (NCHS) and other sources. This includes final data for 2004 on numbers of deaths, death rates, and causes of death for the population as a whole in Chapter 2; for four selected cultural and racial groups in Chapter 5; and for children, adolescents, young and middle-aged adults, and older adults in Chapters 12 through 15. We also provide the most recent NCHS data available on average life expectancy and location of death in Chapter 2, as well as on accidental deaths and homicide in Chapter 4. In Chapter 2, we also include a new figure on cancer-related deaths from the American Cancer Society.

Beyond that, we draw on the latest data from the U.S. Census Bureau concerning selected cultural and racial groups in Chapter 5, and concerning hospitals, long-term care facilities, and home health care programs in Chapter 8. Also in Chapters 8 and 12 we report the most recent data on hospice programs from the National Hospice and Palliative Care Organization. These data include the interesting fact that hospice programs cared for approximately one-third of all Americans who died in 2005 even while they discharged alive nearly 200,000 patients.

In addition, we provide recent data from: the American Association of Suicidology in Chapters 13 (concerning adolescents), 15 (concerning older adults), and 17 (concerning the American population as a whole); the United Network for Organ Sharing in Chapter 16 concerning organ and tissue donation and transplantation; the Oregon Department of Human Services in Chapter 18 on physician-assisted suicide under the Oregon Death with Dignity Act; the Centers for Disease Control and Prevention in Chapter 20 concerning HIV and AIDS in the United States; and UNAIDS in Chapter 20 concerning experiences with HIV and AIDS around the world.

In addition to updating the text in these many ways, we have also revised and expanded its contents in many other important respects. For example, in Chapter 1 we added mention of some new patterns in formal death education programs in secondary schools, along with comments on the "virtual autopsy." In Chapter 2, we take note of research reporting that although "The United States spends considerably more money on health care than the United Kingdom . . . [still] US residents are much less healthy than their English counterparts" (Banks, Marmot, Oldfield, & Smith, 2006, p. 2037), and we also include a new box on threats of epidemic in the twenty-first century. In Chapter 3, we include a description of some ways in which an Amish community mourned after the killings of young children at Nickel Mines Amish School on October 2, 2006. In Chapter 4, in addition to new data on deaths involving accidents and homicide, we added mention of Hurricane Katrina and its effects after it came ashore in the New Orleans area on August 29, 2005, along with new boxes on mass murders and suicide terrorists. In Chapter 5, we take note of several research reports urging caution in generalizing about minority groups in our society and calling for research that is more nuanced and more sensitive to differences within such groups. We tried to follow that advice in our own comments on these groups.

In our discussions of dying in Part Three, Chapters 6–8 (like many others in this new edition) identify several new books about personal coping with life-threatening illness and about ways to help those engaged in such coping. Chapter 6 mentions Avery Weisman's concept of "middle knowledge," while Chapter 8 includes two of Art Buchwald's unique comments on hospice care and the results of new research reports showing that hospice care has actually extended life for some persons, saved money for Medicare, and received good evaluations from bereaved family members, as well as important recent developments in hospice and palliative care for infants, children, and their family members.

In Part Four, we reorganized and expanded the discussion of grief and mourning in Chapter 9 to take account of recent developments in how those important experiences are understood. This includes new sections on how mourning is being newly interpreted by some contemporary theorists, stages of grief (including two new boxes on that subject), meaning reconstruction, fixed end points, opportunities for growth and transformation, and complicated grief reactions or prolonged grief disorder. In Chapter 10 we refer to the death of Barbaro, the thoroughbred racing horse, in January 2007, and in Chapter 11 we mention a new way to dispose of cremains and some recent efforts to use the World Wide Web in mourning.

In Part Five, we devote four full chapters to developmental perspectives, more than any other comparable book in our field. In this new edition, Chapters 12–15 are enriched with new statistical data, new reference citations, and new entries in their Suggested Readings sections. Chapter 12 also has information from a recent report on underlying factors that may predispose some infants to Sudden Infant Death Syndrome. In addition, we modified the titles of Chapters 14 and 15, along with many of their internal headings to clarify that the former is concerned with young and middle-aged adults (for the most part, those who are 25–44 and 45–64, respectively), while the latter has to do with older adults (those 65 years and older, a growing segment of our society).

In Part Six, we altered the primary headings in Chapter 16 to guide readers more easily to discussions of "Advance Directives for Health Care," "Definition, Determination, and Certification of Death," "Organ, Tissue, and Body Donation," and "Disposition of One's Body and Property." The section on "Organ, Tissue, and Body Donation" has also been reorganized and rewritten extensively to take account of recent developments in this field, such as who can donate or authorize donation, "donor rights" legislation, and "first-person consent" registries in several states. In addition to updated statistical data, Chapter 17 includes a new box on a child's reactions to her father's completed suicide and another on "Warning Signs of Suicide" that complements an existing box on practical ways to help individuals who might be contemplating suicide. Chapter 18 identifies some of the many books published about the death of Terri Schiavo, describes recent developments in euthanasia practices in the Netherlands, documents events associated with the Oregon Death with Dignity Act through 2006, reports the decision by the U.S. Supreme Court overturn a former U.S. Attorney General's attempt to interfere with the practice of that Act, and takes note of the release from jail of Dr. Jack Kevorkian on June 1, 2007. In Chapter 19, there is a new box for critical reflection on the shooting deaths of 33 persons at Virginia Tech University on April 16, 2007, and their implications for personal security in our society.

As already explained, Chapter 20 has been extensively reorganized to clarify its goal. In this chapter, we use one specific disease entity to illustrate the basic themes and underlying structural features of this book. Those themes have been described earlier in this Preface; they are also set forth in the introduction to Part Seven and in the Prologue to Chapter 20. Information is provided in Chapter 20 about the development and current status of the HIV/AIDS epidemic in the United States and about the central features of the larger pandemic around the world.

Among many other distinctive features in this sixth edition of *Death and Dying, Life and Living,* there are 16 new, updated, or significantly revised boxes among a total of 90 boxes, 40 tables (25 of which have updated information), 8 figures (2 with updated information), almost 400 new references in a total of nearly 2,200 entries, and 116 photos, cartoons, and other images. In this edition, most boxes have been newly divided into two types: "Personal Insights" that report significant perspectives from individuals and "Focus On" pieces that explore a specific subject or set of resources. Other boxes, set off in a distinctive format and layout, are now identified as "Issues For Critical Reflection" and are designed to stimulate discussion on 19 important topics (four of these are completely new, while two others add new information for this edition). We have also again worked diligently to simplify and clarify the text of this sixth edition, to make its tone even more personal, and to update its factual base.

One important feature of our distinctive effort in Part Five to devote four full chapters to developmental perspectives on death, dying, and bereavement involves the identification and description of books on these topics for young readers. Accordingly, in Chapter 12 we revised the box on books about death-related topics for children (Focus On 12.2) to identify 69 titles. Annotated descriptions and complete bibliographical information for these and a wide range of other books (a total of 192 titles—many new to this edition) are provided in Appendix A. Similarly, in Chapter 13 the box on books about death-related topics for adolescents (Focus On 13.1) now identifies 37 titles, with annotated descriptions and complete bibliographical information for these and many other books (a total of 94 separate titles) in Appendix B. We believe these two boxes and their related appendices are the most thorough and helpful sources of information about death-related literature for young readers available from any textbook (and perhaps from any other book-length source) in our field. In Chapter 14, there also are new entries in the box (Focus On 14.1) on books about bereavement experiences during young and middle adulthood.

❧ Acknowledgments

We are grateful to all who have shared their personal and/or professional life experiences with us and who have helped us learn many of the important lessons about death, dying, and bereavement that we seek to describe in this book. We want to thank all who helped in the preparation of this sixth edition, especially Reyna Paez and her family who contributed an important box to Chapter 17, and Dr. Ashley Harvey of Colorado State University who asked us a significant question about comparative death rates. Our thanks also go to many others who are credited in the text for the boxes, photos, and images that they helped us obtain and that are such important features of this book.

We are indebted to all of the many reviewers who helped us on previous editions of this book: Patrick Ashwood, Hawkeye Community College; David Balk, now of Brooklyn College; Thomas Blank, University of Connecticut; Bryan Bolea, Grand Valley State University; Sandra Brackenridge, Idaho State University; Brookes Cowan, University of Vermont; Gerry Cox, University of Wisconsin–La Crosse; Kenneth Curl, University of Central Oklahoma; Craig Demmer, Lehman College CUNY; Kenneth Doka, The College of New Rochelle; Nancy Falvo, Clarion University of Pennsylvania; Mal Goldsmith, Southern Illinois University Edwardsville; Nancy Goodloe, Baylor University; Judy Gray, Tidewater Community College; Bert Hayslip, Jr., University of North Texas; Gary Heidinger, Roane State Community College; Joseph Heller, California State University, Sacramento; Clayton Hewitt, Middlesex Community Technical College; Dean Holt, Pennsylvania State University; Elizabeth Kennedy, University of Akron; Patricia LaFollette, Florida State University; Susan Lamanna, Onondaga Community College; Daniel Leviton, University of Maryland; Jean G. Lewis, Austin Peay State University; Martha Loustaunau, New Mexico State University; Debra Mattison, University of Michigan; Jude Molnar, Fairmont State College; Sarah O'Dowd, Community College of Rhode Island; Thomas Paxson, Southern Illinois University Edwardsville; Velma Pomrenke, University of Akron; Constance Pratt, Rhode Island College; James Rothenburger, University of Minnesota; Randy Russac, University of North Florida; Rita Santanello, Belleville Area College; Raymond L. Schmitt, Illinois State University; Pamela Schuetze, SUNY College at Buffalo; Brett Smith, University of Kentucky; Dorothy Smith, State University of New York, Plattsburgh; Gordon Thornton, Indiana University of Pennsylvania; James Thorson, University of Nebraska, Omaha; Mirrless Underwood, Greenfield Community College; J. B. Watson, Stephen F. Austin State University; Robert Wrenn, University of Arizona; and Richard Yinger, Palm Beach Community College.

We owe a particular debt of gratitude to four experienced classroom instructors who took part in the review processes for this new edition (although their names were unknown to us until our work on this project was nearly completed): Gerry Cox of the University of Wisconsin–La Crosse, Bert Hayslip Jr. of the University of North Texas, Gary Heidinger of the Roane State Community College–Oak Ridge Campus, and Pamela Schuetze, SUNY College at Buffalo. It is extremely helpful to receive insightful and constructive comments from knowledgeable educators who teach courses in this field in a variety of institutions and contexts across the United States. We greatly appreciate their willingness to share their insights and ideas to help make this book stronger.

At our publisher, we thank Dr. Michele Sordi and her colleagues. We also express our gratitude to Carol O'Connell at Graphic World, Inc., who was both efficient and cooperative in the production of this edition.

Although we have worked diligently to provide accurate, up-to-date knowledge about death, dying, and bereavement, neither we nor anyone else could claim to have covered every aspect of this extraordinarily broad field of study. For that reason, we encourage readers to pursue additional opportunities that are available to them for further study and research on these subjects. We welcome comments and suggestions for improvements that we might make in this book, because we know that imperfections are inevitable in as large and sweeping an enterprise as this project and in a field that often changes rapidly and has many ramifications. Such comments or suggestions—along with outlines or syllabi for courses in which this book has been used, as well as references and other supplementary materials—can be sent to us by e-mail at **charlescorr@mindspring.com** or **c8813nabe@verizon.net.**

Charles A. Corr
Clyde M. Nabe
Donna M. Corr

Prologue

The Horse on the Dining-Room Table

by Richard A. Kalish

I struggled up the slope of Mount Evmandu to meet the famous guru of Nepsim, an ancient sage whose name I was forbidden to place in print. I was much younger then, but the long and arduous hike exhausted me, and, despite the cold, I was perspiring heavily when I reached the plateau where he made his home. He viewed me with a patient, almost amused, look, and I smiled wanly at him between attempts to gulp the thin air into my lungs. I made my way across the remaining hundred meters and slowly sat down on the ground—propping myself up against a large rock just outside his abode. We were both silent for several minutes, and I felt the tension in me rise, then subside until I was calm. Perspiration prickled my skin, but the slight breeze was pleasantly cool, and soon I was relaxed. Finally I turned my head to look directly into the clear brown eyes, which were bright within his lined face. I realized that I would need to speak.

"Father," I said, "I need to understand something about what it means to die, before I can continue my studies." He continued to gaze at me with his open, bemused expression. "Father," I went on, "I want to know what a dying person feels when no one will speak with him, nor be open enough to permit him to speak, about his dying."

He was silent for three, perhaps four, minutes. I felt at peace because I knew he would answer. Finally, as though in the middle of a sentence, he said, "It is the horse on the dining-room table." We continued to gaze at each other for several minutes. I began to feel sleepy after my long journey, and I must have dozed off. When I woke up, he was gone, and the only activity was my own breathing.

I retraced my steps down the mountain—still feeling calm, knowing that his answer made me feel good, but not knowing why. I returned to my studies and gave no further thought to the event, not wishing to dwell upon it, yet secure that someday I should understand.

Many years later I was invited to the home of a casual friend for dinner. It was a modest house in a typical California development. The eight or ten other guests, people I did not know well, and I sat in the living room—drinking Safeway Scotch and bourbon and dipping celery sticks and raw cauliflower into a watery cheese dip. The conversation, initially halting, became more animated as we got to know each other and developed points of contact. The drinks undoubtedly also affected us.

Eventually the hostess appeared and invited us into the dining room for a buffet dinner. As I entered the room, I noticed with astonishment that a brown horse was sitting quietly on the dining-room table. Although it was small for a horse, it filled much of the large table. I caught my breath, but didn't say anything. I was the first one to enter, so I was able to turn to watch the other guests. They responded much as I did—they entered, saw the horse, gasped or stared, but said nothing.

The host was the last to enter. He let out a silent shriek—looking rapidly from the horse to each of his guests with a wild stare. His mouth formed soundless words. Then in a voice choked with confusion he invited us to fill our plates from the buffet. His wife, equally disconcerted by what was clearly an unexpected horse, pointed to the name cards, which indicated where each of us was to sit.

The hostess led me to the buffet and handed me a plate. Others lined up behind me—each of us quiet. I filled my plate with rice and chicken and sat in my place. The others followed suit.

It was cramped, sitting there, trying to avoid getting too close to the horse, while pretending that no horse was there. My dish overlapped the edge of the table. Others found other ways to avoid physical contact with the horse. The host and hostess seemed as ill at ease as the rest of us. The conversation lagged. Every once in a while, someone would say something in an attempt to revive the earlier pleasant and innocuous discussion, but the overwhelming presence of the horse so filled our thoughts that talk of taxes or politics or the lack of rain seemed inconsequential.

Dinner ended, and the hostess brought coffee. I can recall everything on my plate and yet have no memory of having eaten. We drank in silence—all of us trying not to look at the horse, yet unable to keep our eyes or thoughts anywhere else.

I thought several times of saying, "Hey, there's a horse on the dining-room table." But I hardly knew the host, and I didn't wish to embarrass him by mentioning something that obviously discomforted him at least as much as it discomforted me. After all, it was his house. And what do you say to a man with a horse on his dining-room table? I could have said that I did not mind, but that was not true—its presence upset me so much that I enjoyed neither the dinner nor the company. I could have said that I knew how difficult it was to have a horse on one's dining-room table, but that wasn't true either; I had no idea. I could have said something like, "How do you feel about having a horse on your dining-room table?", but I didn't want to sound like a psychologist. Perhaps, I thought, if I ignore it, it will go away. Of course I knew that it wouldn't. It didn't.

I later learned that the host and hostess were hoping the dinner would be a success in spite of the horse. They felt that to mention it would make us so uncomfortable that we wouldn't enjoy our visit—of course we didn't enjoy the evening anyway. They were fearful that we would try to offer them sympathy, which they didn't want, or understanding, which they needed but could not accept. They wanted the party to be a success, so they decided to try to make the evening as enjoyable as possible. But it was apparent that they—like their guests—could think of little else than the horse.

I excused myself shortly after dinner and went home. The evening had been terrible. I never wanted to see the host and hostess again, although I was eager to seek out the other guests and learn what they felt about the occasion. I felt confused about what had happened and extremely tense. The evening had been grotesque. I was careful to avoid the host and hostess after that, and I did my best to stay away altogether from the neighborhood.

Recently I visited Nepsim again. I decided to seek out the guru once more. He was still alive, although nearing death, and he would speak only to a few. I repeated my journey and eventually found myself sitting across from him.

Once again I asked, "Father, I want to know what a dying person feels when no one will speak with him, nor be open enough to permit him to speak, about his dying."

The old man was quiet, and we sat without speaking for nearly an hour. Since he did not bid me leave, I remained. Although I was content, I feared he would not share his wisdom, but he finally spoke. The words came slowly.

"My son, it is the horse on the dining-room table. It is a horse that visits every house and sits on every dining-room table—the tables of the rich and of the poor, of the simple and of the wise. This horse just sits there, but its presence makes you wish to leave without speaking of it. If you leave, you will always fear the presence of the horse. When it sits on your table, you will wish to speak of it, but you may not be able to.

"However, if you speak about the horse, then you will find that others can also speak about the horse—most others, at least, if you are gentle and kind as you speak. The horse will remain on the dining-room table, but you will not be so distraught. You will enjoy your repast, and you will enjoy the company of the host and hostess. Or, if it is your table, you will enjoy the presence of your guests. You cannot make magic to have the horse disappear, but you can speak of the horse and thereby render it less powerful."

The old man then rose and, motioning me to follow, walked slowly to his hut. "Now we shall eat," he said quietly. I entered the hut and had difficulty adjusting to the dark. The guru walked to a cupboard in the corner and took out some bread and some cheese, which he placed on a mat. He motioned to me to sit and share his food. I saw a small horse sitting quietly in the center of the mat. He noticed this and said, "That horse need not disturb us." I thoroughly enjoyed the meal. Our discussion lasted far into the night, while the horse sat there quietly throughout our time together.

Learning about Death, Dying, and Bereavement

Life and death are two aspects of the same reality. To see this fact represented in graphic form, look at the image on page 2 of this book. You can decipher its meaning by rotating the image one-quarter turn clockwise and then one-quarter turn counterclockwise from its original position. Clearly, one could not properly understand one aspect of this image ("life") without also grasping something about its second aspect ("death"). Similarly, we believe that learning about death, dying, and bereavement is an important way of learning about life and living, and the reverse is equally true. Just as every human being is inevitably involved in learning about life and living, we suggest that each person is also engaged in a process of learning about death, dying, and bereavement. In this book, we pursue that process in a deliberate and explicit way.

Our Prologue, Richard Kalish's allegory, "The Horse on the Dining-Room Table," teaches us that it is desirable to talk about death together, to share insights and attitudes, to try to learn from each other, and to strive to cope more effectively in the face of death. But how do we begin?

One good place to start is with some preliminary remarks about education in the field of death, dying, and bereavement. Thus, in Chapter 1 we examine some concerns that lead people to study death-related subjects, how this type of education is conducted, its four principal dimensions, and its six central goals. These introductory remarks are a kind of warm-up for the main event, which follows in the remainder of this book. Some readers might prefer to bypass this warm-up by jumping directly to the central work of this book and returning later to Chapter 1. Others will benefit from these preparatory comments about certain aspects of the project ahead.

CHAPTER 1

Education about Death, Dying, and Bereavement

The Grief Center of Texas

Objectives of This Chapter

◆ To explore the *nature* and *role* of education about death, dying, and bereavement (commonly called *death education*)

◆ To examine *concerns* that lead people to the study of death-related subjects

◆ To look briefly at *how* death education *is conducted*

◆ To describe *four dimensions* of death education

◆ To identify *six main goals* of death education

◆ To point out some *things we can learn about life and living* by studying death, dying, and bereavement

Death and life: two dimensions of the same reality. To interpret the drawing, rotate the image one-quarter turn clockwise, then one-quarter turn counterclockwise from its original position.

🍒 A Student Studies Death, Dying, and Bereavement

When they learned she was reading children's books for a college class, Ellen Johns' friends began to tease her. But they stopped their teasing when she asked them: "How would YOU explain death to a 7-year-old child?"

Ellen was an education major in college who had taken a course on death and dying as an elective. She was seeking practical guidance about what she could say or do if she ever had a bereaved child in one of her classes. She also realized that some of her special education students might be in precarious health or even be seriously hurt in an accident. And she was concerned about the implications of school violence for children.

So Ellen was glad when her college course gave her a chance to read books about death-related topics that had been written for young children. She discovered that there was quite a large body of this literature (see Focus On 12.2, Appendix A, & Corr, 2004a). Ellen especially liked the simplest stories, like *The Dead Bird* (Brown, 1958), in which some children find a dead bird while they are playing, touch its cold, stiff body, and act out a ceremonial burial. Ellen also identified books about bereavement in childhood (see Corr, 2004b) and a variety of other death-related topics involving grandparents, pets, spirituality, parents, and siblings and child friends (see Corr, 2004c-e; Corr, 2007b; Corr, in press b).

Ellen's studies also led her to examine familiar children's stories like "Little Red Riding Hood" in an effort to determine what they were teaching about death. She was surprised to find that there were at least three different versions of the ending of this well-known story (see Focus On 1.1 & Bertman, 1974). In the original version, the story ends when *the wolf eats Little Red Riding Hood* (as he had previously eaten her grandmother). Do you remember the story ending that way when you first read it? Or perhaps you recall the woodsman in the second example who intervened with his ax (low technology) *after the wolf had gobbled up Little Red Riding Hood*. Or maybe you remember how a hunter came on the scene with his gun (high technology) in the third example *before the wolf could eat our heroine*.

Ellen was amazed that a story about what might happen when a child does not listen to warnings from her parents could convey such different messages about death. In the first example, Little Red Riding Hood is eaten by the wolf (she dies); in the second example, Little Red Riding Hood is swallowed up but then brought back to life (at the expense of the wolf's life); in the third example, Little Red Riding Hood is in grave peril but is saved from death (while the wolf dies). Ellen realized that a key issue is the validity and value of the message any story is conveying.

Ellen's project helped her think about what her professor called "death education." She was impressed by the many ways in which educators could work cooperatively with parents, counselors, religious leaders, and others to prepare children for sad situations or to help them when they were coping with any type of loss and grief.

What Really Happened to Little Red Riding Hood?

EXAMPLE 1:

The Wolf, seeing her come in, said to her, hiding himself under the bed-clothes:

"Put the custard and the little pot of butter upon the stool, and come and lie down with me."

Little Red Riding-Hood undressed herself and went into bed, where, being greatly amazed to see how her grandmother looked in her night-clothes, she said to her:

"Grandmamma, what great arms you have got!"

"That is the better to hug thee, my dear."

"Grandmamma, what great teeth you have got!"

"That is to eat thee up."

And, saying these words, this wicked wolf fell upon Little Red Riding-Hood, and ate her up.

Source: From Lang, 1904, p. 66.

EXAMPLE 2:

"The better to EAT you with," said the wolf. And he sprang from the bed and ate Little Red Riding Hood up.

A passing woodsman stepped into the house to see how Little Red Riding Hood's grandmother was feeling. And when he saw the wolf, he said, "Ah ha! I've found you at last, you wicked old rascal!" He lifted his ax, and with one blow, killed him. Then he cut the wolf open and out stepped Little Red Riding Hood and her grandmother.

They thanked the woodsman for what he had done. Then all three sat down and ate the cake and the butter and drank of the grape juice which Little Red Riding Hood had brought.

Source: From Jones, 1948.

EXAMPLE 3:

"THE BETTER TO EAT YOU WITH, MY DEAR," cried the wolf. He pushed back the covers, and jumped out of the bed. Then Little Red Riding Hood saw that it was the big wolf pretending to be her grandmother!

At that moment a hunter passed the house. He heard the wolf's wicked voice and Little Red Riding Hood's frightened scream. He burst open the door. Before the wolf could reach Little Red Riding Hood, the hunter lifted his gun to his shoulder, and killed the wicked wolf. Little Red Riding Hood was very happy and she thanked the kind hunter.

Grandmother unlocked the door and came out of the closet, where she had been hiding. She kissed Little Red Riding Hood again and again. And she thanked the hunter for saving them both from the big wolf. They were all so happy that they decided to have a party right then and there. Grandmother gave the hunter and Little Red Riding Hood a big glass of fresh milk, and took one herself. They ate up all the cake and fruit that Little Red Riding Hood had brought to her grandmother. And they all lived happily ever after.

Source: From Anonymous, 1957.

🍂 Concerns Leading People to the Study of Death-Related Subjects

During the 1960s and early 1970s, people often said that death was a *taboo topic* in American society, a subject that was somehow not acceptable for scholarly research, education, and public discussion (Feifel, 1963). In effect, a fundamental and defining aspect of human life had largely been removed from investigation and critical study. It was as if death needed to be quarantined in order not to infect the way in which people wished to think about and live out their lives.

Not surprisingly, eventually there was a reaction to prohibitions like this. New initiatives by modern pioneers like Herman Feifel (1959, 1977b), Elisabeth Kübler-Ross (1969, 1997), and Cicely Saunders (DuBoulay, 1984) encouraged behavioral scientists, clinicians, and humanists to pay attention to these topics. Thoughtful people began to study death-related behavior, develop new programs of care for the dying and the bereaved, and conduct research on attitudes toward death. This began the development of what has been called the *death-awareness* movement or *thanatology* (from *thanatos,* the Greek word for *death,* + *-ology* = a science or organized body of knowledge) (Doka, 2003). We prefer (as indicated in the title of this book) to think of this body of knowledge as focused on life and living considered from the perspective of death, dying, and bereavement or, as Kastenbaum (2004a, p. 19) has defined it, as "the study of life—with death left in."

As this movement developed, books like this one were published, instructors began to offer courses on death and dying (Corr & Corr, 2003c), and people like you became involved in this subject. We can think of several *concerns that helped death education thrive.* Do any of the following apply to you?

It might be because of *the work you are already doing,* perhaps as a nurse, a social worker, or a counselor. Or because *you are preparing to enter some profession or vocation in which you may be asked to help people who are coping with death, dying, or bereavement* like education (as was the case for Ellen Johns), the ministry, medicine, or volunteer service through a hospice organization.

Perhaps you came to the study of death education because your personal concerns were more direct or more pressing. You might be *dealing with the aftermath of an unresolved encounter with death in your own life.* Or you might be *struggling to cope with a current death-related experience in your life.* Death education often interests people who have experienced the death of a loved one in the past or whose close relative or friend is presently trying to meet the challenges of a terminal illness. Sometimes an individual in a class may be living with a life-threatening condition. All of these people may want to use the information and other resources that death education provides to help them cope with their own experiences. If this is true for you, your feelings may be tender, and you may be vulnerable to added pain. For this reason, *death education needs to develop a special sensitivity to and compassion for its participants,* to make a special effort to care for those who engage in this study (Attig, 1981).

Of course, education is different from counseling, and a classroom is not really an appropriate context for individual therapy. Education alone may not be sufficient to address the needs of individuals who are unable to cope with difficult personal experiences by themselves. If you are in this situation, it may be desirable to seek a referral for personal counseling or therapy. Also, if you have recently experienced a major loss in your life and do not find comfort in a dispassionate, educational approach to death-related topics, you might choose to postpone enrolling in a course on death and dying until some later time. Our point is that the classroom environment may not meet all needs at all times.

Maybe you are simply *curious about some subject or issue in the field of death, dying, and bereavement.* People become interested in this field as a result of publicity about social phenomena such as media reports of mass deaths, stories about homicide committed by juveniles, or debates about physician-assisted suicide. Curiosity of this type might or might not be joined to *a desire to prepare for personal experiences that might arise in the future.* For example, some students have said to us: "No important person in my life has yet died. But my grandparents are getting pretty old." These students are aware that life is fragile, but they are not content simply to wait until events demand a response under pressure. They prefer to seize the initiative ahead of time in order to prepare themselves (as much as possible) to cope with the death of loved ones and friends. Individuals such as this realize that no human life is ever completely "death free."

❦ What Is Death Education Like?

How Is Death Education Conducted?

Death education may be conducted formally or informally (Corr & Corr, 2003c). *Formal or planned death education* is usually associated with programs of organized instruction of the kind that are found in schools, colleges, graduate education, professional workshops, and volunteer training programs (Corr, 2004f; Noppe, 2007). These formal programs may be of many types. For example, one imaginative resource that can be used with children to teach about grief and mourning in primary school classrooms or grief support groups (and with adults to encourage open discussions with such children) is *Lessons from Lions: Using Children's Media to Teach about Grief and Mourning* (Adams, 2006). This slim booklet provides an outline for discussion along with 10 slides from the Disney movie, *The Lion King*, with each slide encouraging conversation on specific key points.

Early examples of formal death education in secondary schools typically focused directly on the subjects of death, dying, and bereavement (Stevenson, 2004). In recent years, however, it seems that such courses are often more likely to emphasize such topics as: Coping with Loss (including bereavement and grief, but in which "death" is a secondary element); Suicide and Suicide Prevention (aimed more directly at students than earlier programs developed for faculty, staff, and parents); Violence and Violence Prevention (in which loss and grief are typically addressed as factors contributing to violence); or Crisis Counseling courses for school counselors and teachers, as well as agency-based counselors (R. W. Stevenson, personal communication, February 9, 2007). One report described how a school health education program involved adolescents in normalizing and encouraging family discussions about end-of-life choices (in this case, especially about organ and tissue donation) in

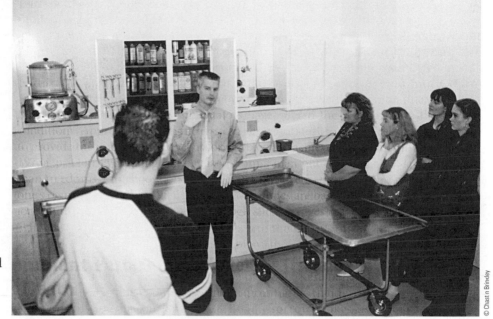

High school students could learn by visiting a funeral home.

© Chast n Brindley

a non-crisis context (Waldrop, Tamburlin, Thompson, & Simon, 2004). One of the main goals of this book is to support programs of formal death education however they may be organized.

Informal or unplanned death education is more typical and more widespread, although it may not always be recognized for what it is. Most human beings first learn about loss, sadness, and coping in the arms of a parent or guardian and through interactions within a family or similar social group (Gilbert & Murray, 2007). They also learn about death, dying, and bereavement from their own experiences, from the people whom they meet throughout their lives, and from events in which they take part. Travel, the media (especially television), and many other sources contribute raw materials and insights to a lifelong process of informal death education that may take place almost without one's notice. In addition, the Internet can also contribute to informal death education. For example, if you search on the Internet for the phrase *virtual autopsy,* you will be led to two different types of sites. Some of these sites offer information about radiological imaging technology that can be used to examine mummies and other dead bodies. The advantage of these techniques is that they can determine causes of death in a bloodless, minimally invasive way that does not involve damage to the corpse in question. Other sites linked to the phrase "virtual autopsy" offer case examples of death scenarios, ask the reader to identify their causes, and then explain the actual causes of these deaths. Both of these types of sites can help educate medical students, those interested in anatomy, researchers, and individuals who are merely curious about death-related issues.

Visiting a cemetery can be a "teachable moment."

Courtesy of Kevin A. Corr

Opportunities for informal death education also emerge naturally from *teachable moments*. These are the unanticipated events in life that offer important occasions for developing useful educational insights and lessons, as well as for personal growth. For example, the vignette near the beginning of this chapter explains that when Ellen Johns explored death-related literature for children, she realized that these books and others like them depicted many different situations in which children might encounter loss or death. A natural disaster, an act of violence like the horrific events of September 11, 2001, or the mass killings at Virginia Tech on April 16, 2007, barely avoiding an auto accident, the death of a pet, or the funeral of a loved one are only a few of the many instances in which teachable moments thrust themselves into the middle of life and offer important opportunities for informal death education for both children and adults.

Four Dimensions of Death Education

We recognize *four central dimensions of death education*. These dimensions relate to what people know, how they feel, how they behave, and what they value (Corr, 2003b). They are the cognitive, affective, behavioral, and valuational dimensions of death education—distinguishable but interrelated aspects of this educational process.

Death education is most obviously a *cognitive* or intellectual enterprise because it provides factual information about death-related experiences and tries to help us understand or interpret those events. For example, death education offers facts about death-related encounters (see Chapter 2), insights into the American death system and cultural differences among Americans (see Chapters 4 and 5), and information about topics like suicide (see Chapter 17). Also, death education identifies new ways of organizing or interpreting the data of human experience. Such a cognitive reorganization took place in the early 1980s, when some physicians recognized that they were diagnosing a relatively rare form of skin cancer (Kaposi's sarcoma) in an unusually high number of young adult men, a cancer that had hitherto been confined largely to a specific group of elderly males. This realization helped identify a new disease and cause of death, acquired immunodeficiency syndrome (AIDS) and human immuno-deficiency virus (HIV) (see Chapter 20).

The *affective* dimension of death education has to do with feelings, emotions, and attitudes about death, dying, and bereavement (see Chapter 3). In this regard, death education attempts to sensitize those who are not bereaved to the depth, intensity, duration, and complexities of grief and mourning following a death. For example, many bereaved persons have told us that it appears insensitive and arrogant to them when someone who is not bereaved says, "I know how you feel." How could that be true of someone who has not experienced their loss? To the bereaved, such statements (however well intentioned they may be) seem to diminish the uniqueness and poignancy of their loss. In addition, in our society many people still seem to think—wrongly—that a few days or weeks may be more than adequate to "forget" or "get over" the death of an important person in one's life. In fact, mourning a significant death in one's life is far more like an ongoing process of learning to live with one's loss than it is like solving a problem once and for all (see Chapter 9). Sharing and discussing grief reactions and mourning responses are important parts of the affective dimension of education in the field of death, dying, and bereavement.

Death education also has a *behavioral* dimension as it explores why people act as they do in death-related situations, which of their behaviors are helpful or unhelp-ful, and how they could or should act in such situations. In our society it seems that much behavior, both public and private, seeks to avoid contact with death, dying, and bereavement. Often, that is because people do not know what to say or what to do in such situations. They pull back from the dying and the bereaved, leaving people alone in very stressful circumstances, without support or companionship at a time when sharing and solace may be most needed. In fact, a better understanding of the needs of those who are coping with dying and/or bereavement (see Chapters 6 and 9) demonstrates that there is much that individuals and social organizations can do to be helpful in such situations (see Chapters 7–8 and 10–11). Above all, this behavioral education points out the great value embodied in the *simple presence* of a caring person, someone who does not so much talk to those who are coping with death and loss, but who *truly listens* to them. Death education can help us develop skills in interacting with such persons.

In its *valuational* dimension death education can help to identify, articulate, and affirm the basic values that govern human lives. Life as we know it is inextricably bound up with death. *We would not have this life as we know it if death were not one of its essential parts.* Life and death, living and dying, attachments and loss, happiness and sadness—neither alternative in these and many other similar pairings stands alone in human experience. Death provides an essential (and inescapable) perspective from which humans can try to achieve an adequate understanding of their own lives (see Chapter 19).

Reflecting on values is closely related to many of the death-related challenges that confront us as we move forward in the 21st century: terrorism and the threat of nuclear warfare, epidemics and their prevention, famine and malnutrition, dislocation of populations, capital punishment, abortion, assisted suicide, euthanasia, and all of the quandaries posed by modern medicine and its complex technologies. Values also come sharply into focus when adults are asked what they will tell children about death. Education in this field shows that death should not be hidden from children, that life should not be portrayed as an unending journey without shadows or tears (see Chapter 12). Hiding death from children, even if we really could do that, will not prepare them to cope effectively with future losses, a common part of human life. It is far better to introduce children to the realities of life and death in ways that are appropriate to their developmental level and capacities, and with the support of mature values that will enable them to live wisely and cope with death constructively.

❧ Six Goals of Death Education

Education that is well planned always has in mind some general goals and specific objectives that it hopes to accomplish for and with its participants. For example, college courses are commonly designed to encourage critical thinking in order to help individuals judge for themselves the value, meaning, and validity of subjects they address. Education about death, dying, and bereavement incorporates these broad aims and typically links them to more limited purposes (Corr, 1995c, 2003b; Wass, 2004).

We were challenged to think about our own goals shortly after we first began teaching a course on death and dying. With no advance notice, we received the letter reproduced in Personal Insights 1.1 from a person who had not been in our course and whom we did not know. We appreciated Mrs. Koerner's comments about our course, but we were also a bit perplexed: How should we evaluate her remarks? Should we really take credit for teaching people how to die, as Mrs. Koerner seemed to think we were doing? That letter challenged us to think about what we want to accomplish in our courses. In returning to this issue from time to time, we have come to recognize six basic goals in this type of education.

The first goal of education about death, dying, and bereavement is *to enrich the personal lives* of those to whom it is directed. In the end, as the ancient Greek philosopher Socrates is reported to have said, "The really important thing is not to live, but to live well" (Plato, 1948 [*Crito*, 48b]). Death education contributes to this goal by helping individuals to understand themselves more fully and to appreciate both their strengths and their limitations as finite human beings. A second goal of death education is *to inform and guide individuals in their personal transactions with society.* It does this by making them aware of services that are available and options that they

A Letter to a Teacher in a Course on Death and Dying

October 16, 1975

Dear Dr. Corr,

Want to thank you for your course "Death and Dying."

Not having been in your classroom, you might wonder what prompts me to write this letter.

My mother was one of the most dedicated Christians we in our lives have ever known.

She became very ill and it took 54 days, in and out of an Intensive Care Unit, for her to die.

Doc and I spent as much time as humanly possible at her side.

One day she looked at me with her beautiful soft brown eyes and said, "Why didn't anyone teach me how to die? We are taught at our mother's knee how to live but not how to die."

Hope your course will help people through this experience because we will all have a turn unless the Rapture comes first.

God bless you,

Dr. and Mrs. S. Koerner

might or might not select in such matters as end-of-life care or funeral practices and memorial rituals.

A third goal of death education is *to prepare individuals for their public roles as citizens.* In this way, death education helps to clarify important social issues that face society and its representatives, such as advance directives in health care, assisted suicide, euthanasia, and organ and tissue donation (see Chapters 16 and 18). A fourth goal of death education is *to help prepare and support individuals in their professional and vocational roles.* Those whose work involves teaching about death, caring for the dying, or counseling the bereaved can benefit from the perspectives offered by a well-grounded death education (Dickinson, 2006).

A fifth goal of death education is *to enhance the ability of individuals to communicate effectively about death-related matters.* Effective communication is essential when addressing death-related topics that may be difficult for many people (Strickland & DeSpelder, 1995). A sixth goal of death education is *to assist individuals in appreciating how development across the human life course interacts with death-related issues.* Children and adolescents, as well as young, middle-aged, and older adults, face issues that are dissimilar in many ways and cope with them differently when they confront death, dying, and bereavement (see Chapters 12–15).

A teen volunteer talks about hospice care at a community meeting.

🌱 What Are Some of the Things We Can Learn about Life and Living by Studying Death, Dying, and Bereavement?

As you read this book, we suggest that you ask yourself what you are learning about death, dying, and bereavement, as well as what that is teaching you about life and living. For ourselves, we have come to see that life and death, living and dying, are inexorably intertwined. That explains the title of this book and our basic conviction that the study of death-related topics inevitably and simultaneously teaches us about life and living.

For example, studying death, dying, and bereavement soon reminds us that we humans are finite, limited beings. This realization clearly impacts on how we live our lives, for we learn that although there are many things in life that we can control, there are many others that we cannot. Death-related education reveals some specific things we can *control*, even as it shows many of the *limitations* that make our control less than complete.

Further, when studying death-related topics we recognize that in the end it is always an individual person who must deal with these particularized experiences: no one else can die our death or experience our grief. These events are marked out by their unique individuality. However, studying death, dying, and bereavement also reveals to us that being human means being involved in community and being inescapably linked to other persons. Thus, we learn that life and death involve both *individuals* and *communities*.

Again, although we often prefer to ignore our inevitable mortality, both life and death make our vulnerability to pain and suffering all too obvious. Still, death education helps us realize that this vulnerability is not the same as helplessness. We learn that most human beings have powerful coping capacities and are amazingly resilient. In fact, some persons respond to death-related challenges in ways that can be ennobling and even awesome. Thus, human beings find themselves located between *vulnerability* and *resilience.*

Beyond this, our studies of death-related topics reveal the importance of *quality in living* and *the human search for meaning.* One man who was facing his own imminent death founded an organization called "Make Today Count" (Kelly, 1975). In so doing, he implicitly recommended that *we all should try to make every day in our lives count* by striving to maximize the quality of our own lives right now and by appreciating that life can be good even though it is transient. When death challenges the value of life, death education shows that humans work hard to find sources of inspiration and religious or philosophical frameworks within which enduring meaning can be established. Thus, *quality in living* and the *search for meaning* are significant issues for those who are coping with death as well as for those who are simply living their day-to-day lives.

We mention these particular themes here because you will sometimes easily find them in this book, while at other times they will be below the surface of our explorations. In that sense, these four themes (control/limitation; individual persons/community; vulnerability/resilience; quality in living/the search for meaning) are subtexts throughout this book. You can enrich your studies of the subjects in this book if you will occasionally *stop to dig below the surface of the text,* take time to reflect on what you are reading, and bring to the surface themes like these—as well as others that you may find.

🌰 Summary

In this chapter, we examined education about death, dying, and bereavement. We considered some reasons why individuals did or might become interested in this type of education. We mentioned formal death education of the type represented by this book, as well as informal death education that is most evident in what we called *teachable moments.* We explored four central dimensions of death education (cognitive, affective, behavioral, and valuational). We looked at six goals for this type of education, and we asked what we could learn about life and living through the study of death, dying, and bereavement. All of this reminds us of the main lesson from the Prologue to this book: human beings cannot magically make death, loss, and grief disappear from their lives, but they can profitably study these subjects and share insights with each other as a way of learning to live richer, fuller, and more realistic lives.

Glossary

Death education: teaching and learning about death-related subjects, such as dying and bereavement

Dimensions of death education: *cognitive* (concerned with information about death-related subjects, as well as organizing and interpreting the data of death-related experiences); *affective* (feelings, emotions, and attitudes about death-related subjects); *behavioral* (how one does, could, or should act in death-related situations); *valuational* (identifying, articulating, and affirming basic values related to death and life)

Formal death education: planned and organized instruction involving death-related topics

Informal death education: death-related education that emerges from everyday experiences and interactions, including messages from society, the media, the Internet, parents, and other adults

Teachable moments: unanticipated life events offering important occasions for developing educational insights and lessons, as well as for personal growth

Questions for Review and Discussion

1. This book is part of an effort to improve education about death, dying, and bereavement. Would you recommend this type of education to a friend or relative? Why or why not?

2. What is it in your own life that brought you to the study of death, dying, and bereavement?

3. What do you think you might learn about death, dying, and bereavement from reading this book? About life and living?

4. What do you think you might learn from sharing what you are studying with others? (If you wish to share what you learn from such exchanges with the authors of this book, please e-mail us at: charlescorr@mindspring.com or c8813nabe@verizon.com.)

5. The Prologue to this book is "The Horse on the Dining-Room Table" by Richard A. Kalish. The Epilogue is "Calendar Date Gives Mom Reason to Contemplate Life" by Elizabeth Vega-Fowler. Read these pieces now if you have not already done so. What did you learn from each of them? What similarities and differences do you see in the lessons that these authors want to teach us?

Suggested Readings

This list and those at the end of each chapter in this book focus almost exclusively on book-length publications. Among these, general resources in the field of death, dying, and bereavement include:

Balk, D., Wogrin, C., Thornton, G., & Meagher, D. (Eds.). (2007). *Handbook of Thanatology: The Essential Body of Knowledge for the Study of Death, Dying, and Bereavement.*

Bryant, C. D. (Ed.). (2003). *Handbook of Death and Dying* (2 vols.).

Corr, C. A., Morgan, J. D., & Wass, H. (Eds.). (1994). *Statements about Death, Dying, and Bereavement by the International Work Group on Death, Dying, and Bereavement.*

Doka, K. J. (Ed.). (2007c). *Death, Dying and Bereavement* (4 vols.) [Vol. 1, The Human Encounter with Death; Vol. 2, Developmental Perspectives; Vol. 3, Illness, Dying and Death; Vol. 4, Loss and Grief.]

Howarth, G., & Leaman, O. (Eds.). (2001). *Encyclopedia of Death and Dying.*
Kastenbaum, R. (Ed.). (2003). *Macmillan Encyclopedia of Death and Dying.*

Full bibliographical data for these publications appear in the References at the end of this book. Journal articles and other literature can be accessed via the Internet, using the search terms provided at the end of each chapter.

Selected Web Resources

Some useful search terms include: DEATH EDUCATION; FORMAL EDUCATION; INFORMAL EDUCATION; TEACHABLE MOMENTS; VIRTUAL AUTOPSY

Visit the book companion website for *Death & Dying, Life & Living, Sixth Edition,* at academic.cengage.com/psychology/corr for all URLs and live links to the following *organizational and other Internet sites:*

About.com (multiple topics)

Association for Death Education and Counseling (ADEC)

Center for Death Education and Bioethics, University of Wisconsin–La Crosse

King's University College Centre for Education about Death and Bereavement

National Center for Death Education, Mount Ida College

PART TWO
Death

Gordon Allport once said that in some ways each of us is like *every* other human being, in other ways each of us is only like *some* other human beings, and in still other ways each of us is like *no* other human being (J. W. Worden, personal communication, April 22, 2001). In studying death, dying, and bereavement, it helps to sort out these various aspects: the universal, the particular, and the uniquely individual. Part Two examines the particular: contemporary experiences with death in the United States.

Human beings always live within particular *social and cultural* frameworks. Of course, not every individual or group shares every aspect of the experiences that characterize a society as a whole. Thus, specific individuals and members of distinct groups within the United States have their own unique experiences with life and death. This leads us, in the chapters that follow, to describe both the broad context of American society and representative examples of many cultural and racial differences that can be found within that general framework.

Human beings also live within particular *historical* frameworks. Thus, the patterns of experience with death within contemporary American society differ from the experiences of individuals who lived in earlier periods in the United States.

(And, of course, the death-related experiences of people living in other countries may be very different from those of most Americans, now or in the past.)

In the four chapters that follow, we examine *death-related experiences* in terms of three key components:

◆ *encounters with death*
◆ *attitudes toward death*
◆ *death-related practices*

These three components are specific aspects of *the totality of human experience*, each shaping the others and each being shaped by the others. In everyday human experience, encounters, attitudes, and practices are so closely intertwined as to be almost impossible to tell apart. We discuss them in separate chapters to facilitate individual analysis: death-related encounters in Chapter 2, attitudes toward death in Chapter 3, and death-related practices in Chapter 4.

In Chapter 5 we sketch some specific *cultural differences* within our society. By contrast with the earlier portrait of mainstream American society in Chapters 2 through 4, this profile in Chapter 5 helps make us more sensitive to cultural, racial, and other differences between individuals and social groups in the United States.

CHAPTER 2

Changing Encounters with Death

© Michael Grecco/Stock, Boston

Objectives of This Chapter

◆ To define *death-related encounters* as a component of *death-related experiences*

◆ To identify principal features of death-related encounters in the United States early in the 21st century:
  1. Death rates (and differences related to gender, class, infant mortality, and maternal mortality)

2. Average life expectancy
3. Causes of death (communicable versus degenerative diseases)
4. Dying trajectories, their duration and shape
5. Location of death

◆ To indicate how these features of death-related encounters have changed over time in the United States

◆ To describe six factors associated with these changes:

1. Industrialization (including transportation and communication)
2. Public health measures
3. Preventive health care
4. Cure-oriented medicine
5. The nature of contemporary families
6. Lifestyle

❧ Bryan Lee Curtis Shares His Encounter with Death

Bryan Lee Curtis asked a local newspaper to publish two photographs. One photo, taken just before his 34th birthday, shows Curtis with his 2-year-old son when both seemed to be in striking good health; the second, *taken just nine weeks later* and reprinted on this page, shows him less than three hours before his death, with his wife and son at his bedside (Landry, 1999a). Curtis wanted these photographs published to inform people about the dangers of smoking and to encourage changes in attitudes, behaviors, and values related to smoking.

Curtis' death was caused by advanced lung cancer that had spread to his liver and that resulted from his 20-year habit of smoking. He had begun smoking at age 13, eventually building up to a habit of more than two packs of cigarettes a day. His addiction was so strong that he was unable to quit smoking until just a week before his death when the ravages of his illness made it impossible for him to continue.

The newspaper had been concerned that readers would respond negatively to these poignant pictures. In fact, readers were overwhelmingly positive in their

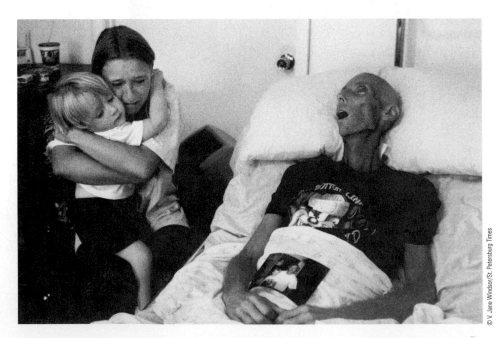

Bryan Lee Curtis on the day of his death about 9 weeks after his diagnosis.

© V. Jane Windsor/St. Petersburg Times

comments; they understood very well the message that Curtis was trying to communicate. As a result, the story of Bryan Lee Curtis and his pictures appeared on websites around the world and were widely reprinted (DeGregory, 2000; Landry, 1999b; Noack, 1999).

❧ Encountering Death in America Today

Death-related experiences include encounters with death, attitudes toward death, and death-related practices. In this chapter, we examine *death-related encounters* in the United States by considering some typical ways in which Americans *encounter or meet up with death* soon after the beginning of the 21st century. Significant features of these encounters are not always obvious, nor are they the only ways in which humans have interacted or might interact with mortality. Earlier peoples did not encounter death as we do at the present, nor do many peoples in other parts of the world today. For that reason, we indicate throughout some of the ways in which these features have changed over time in the United States.

Demographic statistics can teach us a lot about contemporary encounters with death (Hinde, 1998; Newell, 1989; Preston, Heuveline, & Guillot, 2001; Rowland, 2003; Swanson & Siegel, 2004; Yaukey & Anderton, 2001). For example, the National Center for Health Statistics (NCHS) reported that there were 2,397,615 deaths in the United States in 2004 (the year for which most recent data are available as this chapter is written; see Table 2.1), 50,673 less than the total number of deaths in 2003. These deaths, occurring in a total population that the U.S. Census Bureau (2004) has estimated to be approximately 288.2 million, help to shape our present and future attitudes toward death, as well as our death-related practices and our broader experiences with life and living. However, it is difficult for us to grasp a number as large as one on the order of 2.4 million deaths and we cannot study all of their aspects simultaneously. Thus we concentrate in this chapter on outlining five central features within the broad patterns of death-related encounters in our society.

❧ Death Rates

In general, death rates are determined by choosing some specific group of people and dividing the number of those in the group who die during a particular time period by the total population of the group. For instance, the overall death rate for males of all races in the United States in 2004 was determined by dividing the number of deaths among these males (1,181,668) by the total number of males in the entire population. Usually, a death rate is expressed as some number of deaths per 1,000 or 100,000 persons. According to the National Center for Health Statistics (see Table 2.1), crude or unadjusted death rates in 2004 were 816.5 per 100,000 for the entire population of the United States, 817.6 for males, and 815.4 for females (all of which round out to 8.2 per 1,000). In the same year, "the age-adjusted death rate [which takes the aging of the population into account] was 800.8 deaths per 100,000

TABLE 2.1
Number of Deaths and Death Rates (per 100,000 population) by Age and Gender: United States, 2004

Age	All Races, Both Sexes		All Races, Male		All Races, Female	
	Number	Rate	Number	Rate	Number	Rate
All ages	2,397,615	816.5	1,181,668	817.6	1,215,947	815.4
Under 1 Year[a]	27,936	685.2	15,718	753.7	12,218	613.4
1–4 Years	4,785	29.9	2,649	32.4	2,136	27.3
5–9 Years	2,888	14.7	1,645	16.4	1,243	13.0
10–14 Years	3,946	18.7	2,354	21.7	1,592	15.4
15–19 Years	13,706	66.1	9,678	91.0	4,028	39.9
20–24 Years	19,715	94.0	14,909	138.0	4,806	47.3
25–29 Years	18,771	96.0	13,554	135.6	5,217	54.5
30–34 Years	22,097	107.9	14,805	143.2	7,292	72.0
35–39 Years	31,944	151.7	20,485	193.8	11,459	109.3
40–44 Years	53,418	231.7	33,192	289.5	20,226	174.5
45–49 Years	77,927	352.3	48,514	444.4	29,413	262.5
50–54 Years	99,770	511.7	62,649	657.0	37,121	372.7
55–59 Years	121,163	734.8	73,400	917.3	47,763	562.7
60–64 Years	143,534	1,140.1	84,632	1,411.0	58,902	893.6
65–69 Years	171,984	1,727.4	98,455	2,125.1	73,529	1,381.2
70–74 Years	227,682	2,676.4	124,436	3,279.2	103,246	2,191.0
75–79 Years	310,746	4,193.2	160,308	5,173.5	150,438	3,488.7
80–84 Years	373,484	6,717.2	173,361	8,179.0	200,123	5,816.6
85 yrs & over	671,793	13,823.5	226,650	15,031.1	445,123	13,280.3
Not stated	346	—	274	—	72	—

[a]Death rates for "Under 1 year" (based on population estimates) differ from infant mortality rates (based on live births); see Table 2.3 for infant mortality rates.

Source: Miniño et al., 2007.

standard population, representing a decrease of 3.8 percent from the 2003 rate and a record low historical figure" (Miniño, Heron, Murphy, & Kochanek, 2007, p. 1). Age-adjusted death rates for males in 2004 were 955.7 and 679.2 for females. For the most part, we provide unadjusted death rates in this book; age-adjusted death rates are offered in connection with comparisons between subgroups in the population such as those given in Chapter 5.

Death rates can only be determined if one has access to a fund of demographic data. These data derive from birth, death, and census records, which are familiar features of modern society. Where those records are absent or have not been maintained carefully, as in the past or in many poor and not well-organized societies today, statistical accuracy gives way to more or less imprecise estimates.

Changing Death Rates in the United States

Studies of international data on death rates have long shown that Americans—and, in general, those who reside in other developed societies around the world—have many advantages in their encounters with death (Preston, 1976). Although the total number of deaths in the United States in 2004 is impressive on its own, we can point out some notable advantages for those living in American society in the 21st century without going beyond our own borders simply by comparing current U.S. death rates with those at the beginning of the 20th century.

Just over 100 years ago, death rates were considerably higher than they are today—in the United States and in most industrialized nations of the world, as shown in Table 2.2. In 1900, the death rate for the entire American population of approximately 76 million people was 17.2 deaths per 1,000 in the population. By 1954, that rate had dropped to 9.2 per 1,000 (U.S. Bureau of the Census, 1975). That was a decline of nearly 47 percent in only 54 years—a stunning change unparalleled in any other period in human history. Still, as Table 2.2 shows, by 2004 the overall American death rate had dropped even lower, to approximately 8.2 per 1,000.

It is increasingly difficult to continue to reduce overall death rates as they get lower and lower. We can see this just by contrasting a decline of nearly 47 percent from 1900 to 1954 with a decline of about 10.9 percent from 1954 to 2004. Thus, in recent years overall death rates in the United States have tended to level out and may be approaching a minimum level below which they are not likely to go.

Reductions in overall death rates have a significant impact on encounters with death. Above all, they mean that most living Americans are likely to have fewer encounters with natural death than did our great-grandparents. The typical American alive today will have lived through fewer deaths of family, friends, and neighbors than did his or her ancestors at the same time of life. Not surprisingly then, when death actually does occur, it seems a stranger, an alien figure that has no natural or appropriate place in human life (see Personal Insights 2.1).

TABLE 2.2
Death Rates by Gender and Age, All Races, per 1,000 Population: United States, 1900 and 2004

	1900			2004		
	Both Sexes	Males	Females	Both Sexes	Males	Females
All ages	17.2	17.9	16.5	8.2	8.2	8.2
Under 1 year	162.4	179.1	145.4	6.9	7.5	6.1
1–4 years	19.8	20.5	19.1	0.3	0.3	0.3
5–14 years	3.9	3.8	3.9	0.2	0.2	0.1
15–24 years	5.9	5.9	5.8	0.8	1.1	0.4
25–34 years	8.2	8.2	8.2	1.0	1.4	0.6
35–44 years	10.2	10.7	9.8	1.9	2.4	1.4
45–54 years	15.0	15.7	14.2	4.3	5.4	3.1
55–64 years	27.2	28.7	25.8	9.1	11.3	7.1
65–74 years	56.4	59.3	53.6	21.6	26.4	17.6
75–84 years	123.3	128.3	118.8	52.8	63.9	45.2
85 yrs & over	260.9	268.8	255.2	138.2	150.3	132.8

Source: Miniño et al., 2007; U.S. Bureau of the Census, 1975.

Differences in Changing Death Rates: Gender and Class

Substantial declines in death rates throughout the 20th century were found in nearly every segment of the population in the United States. But this is not the whole story. Death rates can be examined more closely in terms of some significant variables, the most prominent of which are gender, race, and social class (Field, Hockey, & Small, 1997; Guthke, 1999; Hoyert, Singh, & Rosenberg, 1995; Kitagawa & Hauser, 1973; Stillion, 1985). Weaver and Rivello (2007) have also recently argued that "social capital," defined as situations involving "a community . . . where a spirit of trust prevails, where crime and violence are low, where resources are accessible to support healthy lives and lifestyles, and where the sick receive needed care" (p. 33), has a strong, inverse effect on mortality rates. We will consider racial and cultural differences in Chapter 5. Here, we focus on gender and class differences.

In terms of gender differences, death rates for males in the United States in 1900 were higher at 17.9 per 1,000 population than those for females at 16.5 per 1,000 population (see Table 2.2). By 2004, however, male and female death rates in our society were very nearly equal at about 8.2 per 1,000. Here females have lost an important advantage that they had formerly held.

PERSONAL INSIGHTS 2.1

On Being Notified of a Death in Our Society Today

This is all new to me. I know there are others like myself who have led semi-charmed lives and often find themselves saying, "No one close to me has ever died." Even the aunt you treasured when you were nine waits to die until you're thirty-one and haven't seen her in eleven years. It's a death cushion. The tragedy, the devastation, the dropping to your knees in anguish never comes. You are spared.

This story is about not being spared. It's about when the tragedy, the devastation, the dropping to your knees in anguish comes. It's about reaching the brink of acceptance and then being slammed by death in ways you couldn't possibly have fathomed.

I keep going back to that moment with the beeper cradled in my palm as if it were the present because I haven't accepted much since. I sometimes run it all backward, subtracting each thing that happened by the week, by the day, by the hour . . . but I can never seem to erase the first phone call.

The one that comes with a ring of camouflage—could be the dry cleaners, could be the finance department trying to verify something on your expense report, could be the security guard downstairs notifying you that your lunch order has arrived.

Or it could be the trapdoor that drops you into your first hard lesson in death, American style.

Source: Shine, 2000, p. 15.

In terms of class or societal differences, it is well recognized that a "social inequality of death" exists in the sense that members of the least advantaged socioeconomic classes tend on average to have higher death rates than members of middle and upper socioeconomic classes within the same society (Blane, 1995; Goldscheider, 1971). The reason for this is that those who are better off economically are likely to have the advantages of better education, housing, nutrition, access to health care, and financial resources (Marmot, 2004; Marmot & Wilkinson, 2005). This part of the story is perhaps obvious, although there may be some subtler differences within and between members of various socioeconomic classes. One of the most important factors producing this disparity is that the U.S. Census Bureau (DeNavas-Walt, Proctor, & Mills, 2004) has estimated that approximately 45 million individuals, or 15.6 percent of the U.S. population, were without health insurance coverage in 2003. In fact, the United States (compared with other industrial nations) is the only country that does not provide health insurance to all of its citizens.

Differences in Changing Death Rates: Infant and Maternal Mortality

Huge differences in U.S. death rates are found over time among infants and children. At the start of the 20th century, the very young in the United States were far more likely to die than they are today (Preston & Haines, 1991). Overall death rates for infants—newborns and children under 1 year of age—were nearly 24 times higher in 1900 than in 2004: 162.4 versus 6.79 infant deaths per 1,000 live births. This is a major reduction in infant death rates in just over 100 years.

The United States was the richest country in the world at the beginning of the 20th century and remains so in the 21st century. However, in 2004 there still were 27,936 infant deaths in the United States. And in 2003, 25 other countries with a population of at least 2.5 million had lower infant death rates than those in the United States, ranging from Hong Kong, Singapore, and Japan with rates of 2.3, 2.7, and 3.0 infant deaths per 1,000 live births, respectively, to Ireland, the United Kingdom, and Cuba, with rates of 5.1, 5.3, and 6.3 infant deaths per 1,000 live births, respectively (Hamilton et al., 2007). Some (but not all) of these countries are comparatively small and have relatively homogeneous populations, but it appears that a variety of factors combine to influence infant mortality rates, many of which result in a high percentage of low birth weight infants in our society. For example, a UNICEF report released on February 14, 2007 (Associated Press, 2007), ranked the United States 20th among 21 wealthy countries (Britain was ranked 21st) in a survey of child welfare because of high levels of inequality and child poverty, along with poorly developed services to families with children. The bottom line is that, "The position of the United States relative to other countries remains unfavorable in terms of IMRs [infant mortality rates]" (Hamilton et al., 2007, p. 355). (For additional information on infant mortality rates and death rates for children under 1 year of age, see Table 2.3 in this chapter and Table 12.2 in Chapter 12.)

Decreases in infant death rates directly affect not only infants who would have died if past conditions had continued to prevail but other members of society as well. For example, parents in 1900 were far more likely to be confronted by the death of one of their children than were parents in the latter half of the century (Rosenblatt, 1983; Uhlenberg, 1980). Also, youngsters in 1900 were far more likely to encounter the death(s) of one or more of their brothers or sisters than are children today.

Further, pregnancy and birth are not only life threatening for babies; they are also life threatening for their mothers. Death rates among pregnant women and women in the process of giving birth or immediately after childbirth were much higher in the United States in 1900 than they are today. Maternal death rates of 608 per 100,000 live births in 1915 had been reduced to 7.1 by 1995 (U.S. Bureau of the Census, 1998) but rebounded to 13.1 in 2004 (Miniño et al., 2007). This overall reduction is a substantial achievement, but the 2004 figures are more than twice the maternal death rate in countries like Norway and Switzerland and are significantly higher than the goal of not more than 3.3 maternal deaths per 100,000 live births that the United States had hoped to reach by the year 2000. Moreover, although there were only 540 maternal deaths in the United States in 2004, experts estimate that about half of those deaths were preventable. In particular, young mothers and those who view pregnancy as risk free or whose pregnancy is unintended or unwanted may fail to seek proper care that might prevent or treat complications leading to death.

Of course, death is always a greater threat to vulnerable populations than to those who are healthy and well-off. Death rates shortly after the beginning of the 20th century were high for the sick, the weak, and the aged, and they continue to be high for similar groups today. Today, death rates for nearly every vulnerable group are much lower than they were in times past. Those who are most vulnerable to death today are not as fortunate as their less vulnerable contemporaries, but as a group they are far better off than their counterparts were in 1900. Many deaths are

TABLE 2.3
Number of Infant, Neonatal, and Postneonatal Deaths and Mortality Rates per 1,000 Live Births by Age, Race, and Hispanic Origin: United States, 2004

Age	All Races		White Non-Hispanic		Black Non-Hispanic		Hispanic[a]	
	Number	Rate	Number	Rate	Number	Rate	Number	Rate
Under 1 year (= infant mortality)	27,936	6.8	13,046	5.6	8,221	13.0	5,321	5.9
Under 28 days (= neonatal mortality)	18,593	4.5	12,354	3.9	5,646	9.5	3,354	3.8
28 days–11 months (= postneonatal mortality)	9,343	2.3	5,713	1.9	2,878	4.8	1,589	1.8

[a]Persons of Hispanic origin may be of any race.
Source: Miniño et al., 2007; Hamilton et al., 2007.

now avoided that would have taken place in our society in the past or that might still take place in other societies today.

🍒 Average Life Expectancy

Average life expectancy is closely related to death rates and is another significant feature in the changing patterns of encounters with death. Note that *life span* (the maximum length of life for individuals or the biological limit on length of life in a species) should not be confused with *life expectancy* (an estimate of the average number of years a group of people will live) (Yin & Shine, 1985). Here, we speak only of life expectancy (not life span) and we express that as an average figure.

One author (Thorson, 1995, p. 34) dramatized the fact that life expectancy figures are averages by imagining "a sample of ten people, six of whom died by age 1 and the rest of whom lived full lives of eighty years." In this group, the six infants lived less than a total of 6 years, whereas the other four people lived a total of 320 years. To say that 32.6 years (6 + 320 ÷ 10) was the average life expectancy for all ten individuals in this odd group would misrepresent both the whole cohort and each of its subpopulations.

Projected average life expectancy for all individuals born in the United States in 2004 rose to a record high of 77.8 years (Miniño et al., 2007). For all males the average life expectancy in 2004 was 75.2 years versus 80.4 for females; for all whites the figure was 78.3 versus 73.1 for all blacks. In the same year, record high projected average life expectancies were reached for white and black males (75.7 years and 69.5 years, respectively), as well as for white and black females (80.8 years and 76.3 years, respectively). Also, the gender gap in average life expectancy for the population as a whole narrowed from 6.4 years in 1995 to 5.2 years in 2004, while the racial differential between the white and black populations narrowed from 6.9 years to 5.2 years.

Average life expectancy identifies the average remaining length of life that can be expected for individuals of a specific age. For example, an American who was already 20 years of age in 2004 could expect to live an additional 58.8 years on average, a 40-year-old person could expect to live an average of 39.9 additional years, and a 60-year-old person could expect to live an average of 22.5 additional years.

During the 20th century, overall average life expectancy in the United States increased from fewer than 50 years to 76.7 years. This is a gain of more than 50 percent in a period of only 100 years! To put this another way, not until the latter portion of the 20th century in the United States and in some other industrialized countries did the average human life expectancy exceed the biblical promise of "three score and ten" (that is, 70 years). Of course, even in the 19th century and at other times, some individuals lived beyond the estimated averages (see, for example, Focus On 2.1). That is the whole point of averages: many individuals in a group exceed the average figure and many others do not reach it.

In general, average life expectancy increased rapidly in the United States during the 20th century because of a major decrease in the number of deaths occurring during the early years of life. When more individuals survive birth, infancy, and childhood, average life expectancy for the population rises. As time passes, however, it becomes more and more difficult to reduce death rates (especially during infancy

Two Epitaphs from New Hampshire

Sacred to the Memory of Amos Fortune
who was born free in Africa
a slave in America, he purchased
liberty, professed Christianity,
lived reputably, died hopefully
Nov. 17, 1801 Aet. 91.

Sacred to the Memory of Violate
by purchase the slave of Amos Fortune
by marriage his wife, by her
fidelity his companion and solace
She died his Widow
Sept. 13, 1802 Aet. 73.

Source: From Mann & Greene, 1962, p. 37.

and childhood) and to extend average life expectancy. When it is increasingly difficult to lower death rates among the young, improvements in death rates among mature adults and the elderly have a more modest impact on increases in overall average life expectancy. Most of the early and relatively easy victories have already been won in the campaign to lower death rates and increase average life expectancy. The battles that lie ahead are much more difficult. Their complexity is suggested by a report that although "The United States spends considerably more money on health care than the United Kingdom . . . [still] US residents are much less healthy than their English counterparts" (Banks, Marmot, Oldfield, & Smith, 2006, p. 2037). In any event, the rate of increase in average life expectancy in the United States has slowed in recent years (Glannon, 2002; Miller, 2002; Smith, 1995).

One last point to note is that as average life expectancy increases, it is the elderly who are more and more perceived by individuals in our society as the dying—so much so that in our society death is exclusively associated in many people's minds with the aged. Table 2.1 shows that just over 73 percent of all deaths in the United States in 2004 involved those who were 65 years of age or older.

❦ Causes of Death: Communicable versus Degenerative Diseases

A third distinguishing factor in death-related experiences has to do with *causes of death*. Around 1900 in the United States, the largest number of deaths resulted from infectious or *communicable diseases* (see Table 2.4). These are acute diseases that can be transmitted or spread from person to person (Ewald, 1994; Morse, 1993).

TABLE 2.4
The Ten Leading Causes of Death, in Rank Order, All Races, Both Genders: United States, 1900 and 2004

Rank	Cause of Death	Death Rates per 100,000 Population	Percent of All Deaths
1900			
	All causes	1,719.1	100.0
1	Influenza and pneumonia	202.2	11.8
2	Tuberculosis (all forms)	194.4	11.3
3	Gastritis, duodenitis, enteritis, etc.	142.7	8.3
4	Diseases of the heart	137.4	8.0
5	Vascular lesions affecting the central nervous system	106.9	6.2
6	Chronic nephritis	81.0	4.7
7	All accidents	72.3	4.2
8	Cancer (malignant neoplasms)	64.0	3.7
9	Certain diseases of early infancy	62.6	3.6
10	Diphtheria	40.3	2.3
2004			
	All causes	816.5	100.0
1	Diseases of the heart	222.2	27.2
2	Cancer (malignant neoplasms)	188.6	23.1
3	Cerebrovascular diseases	51.1	6.3
4	Chronic lower respiratory diseases	41.5	5.1
5	Accidents (unintentional injuries)	38.1	4.7
6	Diabetes mellitus	24.9	3.1
7	Alzheimer's disease	22.5	2.8
8	Influenza and pneumonia	20.3	2.5
9	Nephritis, nephrotic syndrome, and nephrosis	14.5	1.8
10	Septicemia	11.4	1.4

Source: Miniño et al., 2007; U.S. Bureau of the Census, 1975.

Earlier cultures experienced sporadic waves of these communicable diseases. From time to time, epidemics of such diseases as influenza, cholera, scarlet fever, measles, smallpox, and tuberculosis would run through human communities. Perhaps the most famous of these epidemics, at least for Europeans, was the black (bubonic) plague of the 14th century, which killed nearly

25 million people in a total European population much smaller than that of today (Gottfried, 1983).

Communicable diseases are often accompanied by observable symptoms like diarrhea, nausea, vomiting, headache, fever, and muscle ache. In cultures where vaccines and/or antibiotics were not or are not available—and in many undeveloped or poverty-stricken portions of the world today—those providing physical care for people with communicable diseases mainly dealt (or still deal) with these symptoms rather than with their underlying causes. They tried to isolate the ill person to minimize the likelihood of spreading the disease. They also offered or continue to offer such things as shelter from the elements, a warm fire, a place to rest, hot food (chicken soup!), and a cool cloth to wipe a feverish brow.

Today, relatively few people in developed countries die of communicable diseases—with the notable exception of deaths associated with influenza and pneumonia, septicemia, and infection by the human immunodeficiency virus (HIV) and acquired immunodeficiency syndrome (AIDS). Still, in recent years there has been growing concern about potential threats from other communicable diseases such as bird flu, meningitis, and West Nile virus (a form of encephalitis carried by birds and spread by mosquitoes) that was first discovered in North America in the summer of 1999 when it killed nine people in the New York City area (Garrett, 1995) (see Issues for Critical Reflection #1). Of special interest is a possible resurgence in the lethal potential of drug-resistant communicable diseases such as tuberculosis (e.g., Platt, 1995), which might become particularly dangerous in environments like hospitals and nursing homes where ill and potentially vulnerable people live together in close quarters. There also has been much concern about the possibility that some people might use biological agents in terrorist acts (Cordesman, 2005; Miller, Engelberg, & Broad, 2001; Tucker, 2001).

In our society today, the largest numbers of death result from the long-term wearing out of body organs, a deterioration associated with aging, lifestyle, and environment. In other words, people in our society die mostly of a set of chronic conditions or causes called *degenerative diseases.* In fact, the four leading causes of death in the United States (diseases of the heart, malignant neoplasms [cancers], cerebrovascular diseases, and chronic lower respiratory diseases [formerly called chronic obstructive pulmonary diseases or COPD]) all fall into the category of degenerative diseases. Two of these degenerative diseases (heart disease and cancer) alone accounted for more than half of all deaths in our society in 2004, despite the fact that death rates from both of these causes have been in gradual decline for some years (Miniño et al., 2007). (For additional information on leading causes of death in the United States, consult the interactive website http://www.cdc.gov/ncipc/wisqars/.)

Deaths produced by degenerative diseases have their own typical characteristics. For example, vascular diseases (coronary attacks, strokes, embolisms, aneurysms, and so on) sometimes cause quick, unanticipated deaths. Nevertheless, although the outcome or exposure of the underlying condition may be sudden (as is suggested by the term *stroke*), these diseases themselves usually develop slowly over time and generally produce a gradual (but often unnoticed) debilitation. When such debilitation does not occur, the first symptom may be a dramatic, unexpected, almost instantaneous death. Such a death may be relatively painless—in one's sleep or after a rapid onset of unconsciousness. However, deaths resulting from degenerative diseases are

#1 Threats of Epidemics in the Twenty-First Century

Early in the 1980s, the appearance of the human immunodeficiency virus (HIV) alerted people that an infectious disease could once again become a significant factor in human mortality, even in the developed world— something that had not occurred in many years and even decades (see Chapter 20). In fact, infection with the HIV rapidly turned into an epidemic, and then a pandemic. (An *epidemic* affects a large number of individuals within a specific locale or population group during a specific period of time. A *pandemic* affects a majority of persons over a larger geographical area during a specific period of time.) Since the beginning of the HIV epidemic, other infectious diseases have emerged as possible new epidemics, bringing with them the threat of fatal consequences.

For example, in 2003 a strain of influenza virus first found among birds in Asia began to spread and was reported in England in 2007 (Cowell, 2007). Since 2003, the number of persons infected with this strain has continued to increase. While the actual number of persons so far infected has remained small (256), the mortality rate for this group is extraordinarily high (159 or 62%) (Eckert, 2007). Some estimates suggest that were the virus to mutate further, allowing human-to-human transmission, millions of persons could become infected within months. In the 1918–1920 flu pandemic, half a million people died from the disease in the United States. According to one report, "if a 1918–1920 pandemic hits the US today, nearly two million people would die and 30 percent of the country's 300-million people would be infected" (Zaheer, 2007). Meltzer, Cox, and Fukuda (1999) estimated that this size pandemic would cost from $71–166 billion, 80% of which would be due to deaths resulting from the disease. Such a pandemic would also put a severe strain on health care resources, making treatment that much more difficult.

Tuberculosis is another infectious disease that threatens to reach epidemic proportions. Since 1985, the number of cases of tuberculosis in the United States has risen by 14% (Simone & Dooley, 1994). In particular, a strain of the bacillus causing tuberculosis has developed which is resistant to several of the drugs typically used to treat the disease. New York City experienced an epidemic of this multidrug-resistant strain in the 1990s. It cost nearly $1 billion to control that epidemic (National Institute of Allergy and Infectious Diseases [NIAID], 2005). The World Health Organization has labeled multidrug-resistant tuberculosis a global emergency since 2 to 3 million people die every year from it. Persons with weakened immune systems, those suffering from poor nutrition, and those who are advanced in age are most vulnerable to the disease, but worldwide, tuberculosis is the leading cause of death among young adults and women of child-bearing age (NIAID, 2005). The mortality rate associated with multidrug-resistant tuberculosis is high, nearly 70% (Simone & Dooley, 1994). As a result, in May of 2007 public health authorities were alarmed when a man diagnosed with extreme drug-resistant tuberculosis flew internationally on commercial airlines.

A third possible source of an epidemic is the *Staphylococcus aureus* bacterium. It too has evolved a strain resistant to many of the drugs used for many years to control it. *Staphylococcus aureus* infections most typically have been found in health care institutions. However, recently new strains of

(continued)

the bacterium (community-acquired strains) have appeared outside of these institutions. These latter forms have more serious effects, including some deaths. While less virulent forms of the community-acquired bacillus cause blisters and cellulitis which are easy to treat, the newer strains attack internal organs and infect the blood stream. These infections can overwhelm the heart or destroy lung tissue, leading to death (Voyich et al., 2005). As a result, it has recently been reported that, "Invasive MRSA [methicillin-resistant *Staphylococcus aureus*] infection affects certain populations disproportionately. It is a major public health problem primarily related to health care but no longer confined to intensive care units, acute care hospitals, or any health care institution" (Klevins et al., 2007, p. 1763).

What each of these situations demonstrates is that there are infectious diseases which threaten human communities, even those with well-developed health care systems, and that new forms of treatment will have to be developed in the face of the ever-evolving environments of infectious agents if epidemics and pandemics are to be prevented or controlled. This will all require heavy investments, both monetary and creative.

more often slow and may be quite painful—even heart attacks do not necessarily lead to "easy" or "quick" deaths.

Many people know something about leading causes of death in our society. Still, it is surprising to discover inadequacies in what is thought to be known (Largo, 2006). Consider the example of cancer, currently the second leading cause of death in our society. In fact, cancer is really a collection of diseases, each of which involves malignant cells that reproduce aggressively and each with its own distinctive characteristics and mortality rate. When we have asked students to identify the leading cancer cause of death for males and for females, they most often reply that it is prostate or colon cancer for males and breast cancer for females. In fact, since the early 1950s for males and the mid-1980s for females, the leading cancer cause of death for members of both genders has been lung cancer (see Figure 2.1)! Thus, in 2004 in the United States, 89,630 males died of cancer of the lung, bronchus, and trachea by comparison with 29,004 males who died of prostate cancer, while 68,461 females died of cancer of the lung, bronchus, and trachea by comparison with 40,954 who died of breast cancer (Miniño et al., 2007). High numbers of deaths from lung cancer are a particularly ironic outcome for women who have been told by cigarette advertising, "You've come a long way, baby." ("And, if so, why are they still calling us 'baby'?" one female student asked.) Interestingly, in February 2007 the R. J. Reynolds Tobacco company launched a new cigarette, "Camel #9," marketed to women with the slogan, "Light and Luscious" (Anonymous, 2007c). Is this another contribution to lung cancer in females?

Age-Adjusted Cancer Death Rates,[a] Males by Site, United States, 1930–2003

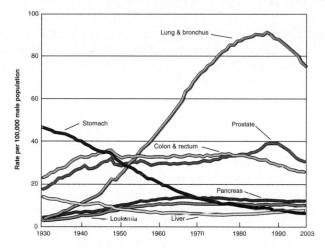

[a]Per 100,000, age-adjusted to the 2000 U.S. standard population. Note: Due to changes in ICD coding, numerator information has changed over time. Rates for cancers of the liver, lung and bronchus, and colon and rectum are affected by these coding changes.

Source: U.S. Mortality Public Use Data Tapes 1960–2003, U.S. Mortality Volumes 1930–1959, National Center for Health Statistics, Centers for Disease Control and Prevention, 2006. American Cancer Society, Surveillance Research, 2007.

Age-Adjusted Cancer Death Rates,[a] Females by Site, United States, 1930–2003

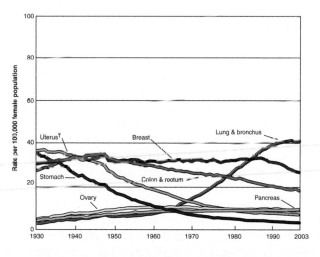

[a]Per 100,000, age-adjusted to the 2000 U.S. standard population. †Uterus cancer death rates are for uterine cervix and uterine corpus combined. Note: Due to changes in ICD coding, numerator information has changed over time. Rates for cancers of the lung and bronchus, colon and rectum, and ovary are affected by these coding changes.

Source: U.S. Mortality Public Use Data Tapes 1960–2003, U.S. Mortality Volumes 1930–1959, National Center for Health Statistics, Centers for Disease Control and Prevention, 2006. American Cancer Society, Surveillance Research, 2007.

FIGURE 2.1
Cancer Death Rates by Gender and Site, United States, 1930–2003.

Source: From *Cancer Facts and Figures 2007*, pp. 2, 3, by the American Cancer Society. Copyright © 2007, American Cancer Society, Inc. www.cancer.org. Reprinted with permission.

🐦 Dying Trajectories

Different causes of death are typically associated with different patterns of dying called *dying trajectories* (Glaser & Strauss, 1968). Their differences are marked primarily by duration and shape. *Duration* in the dying trajectory refers to the time involved between the onset of dying and the arrival of death. This is the so-called living-dying interval, which Pattison (1977) described as including an "acute crisis phase" (one that often involves rising anxiety generated by the critical awareness of impending death), a "chronic-living-dying phase" (which may contain a variety of potential fears and challenges), and a "terminal phase" (which is likely to emphasize issues concerning hope and concerns about different types of death). *Shape* in the dying trajectory designates the course of the dying process, whether one can predict how that process will advance, and whether death is expected or unexpected. Some dying trajectories involve a swift or almost instantaneous onset of death, while others last a long time; some can be anticipated, others are ambiguous or unclear (perhaps involving a series of remissions and relapses), and still others give no advance warning at all (see Figure 2.2).

Most communicable diseases are characterized by a relatively brief dying trajectory. The period from the onset of the infection until its resolution, either in death or in recovery, is usually short—measured in days or weeks. (HIV infection is a notable exception to this pattern; beginning as a communicable disease, it often develops into the chronic complications of AIDS, which in many ways resemble degenerative diseases in their overall pattern; see Chapter 20.)

Dying trajectories associated with degenerative diseases are likely to be very different from those linked to communicable diseases. In general, the former are lengthier, sometimes much lengthier; are often far less predictable; and may be linked with long-term pain and suffering, loss of physical control over one's body, and/or loss of one's mental faculties. Diseases with dying trajectories of this type include motor neuron disease (for example, amyotrophic lateral sclerosis, often called "ALS" or "Lou Gehrig's disease"), Alzheimer's disease, Parkinson's disease, muscular dystrophy, and multiple sclerosis.

Consider the case of cancer as an example of a degenerative disease often displaying a complicated dying trajectory. Cancer is one of the most dreaded diseases in our culture, despite the fact that it is much less often a fatal diagnosis and much less typically a disease with a prognosis of imminent death than it was 25 years ago. Perhaps much of the fear of cancer has to do with the dying processes that we associate with this disease. Familiar images of cancer usually involve suffering, pain, and discomfort for a long period. These images have been reinforced by the popular media and by the personal stories of a number of prominent individuals (see Focus On 6.1 in Chapter 6). Nevertheless, this is not an entirely appropriate depiction of cancer. Not all cancers are fatal, some do not involve much pain or discomfort, some can be "cured" either outright or at least in the sense that intervention leads to survival for five years or more, and much depends on family history and individual circumstances.

The effects of therapeutic interventions, such as those available to treat some degenerative diseases, may complicate differences in the duration of dying trajectories. When such interventions are successful, they may restore quality and long life

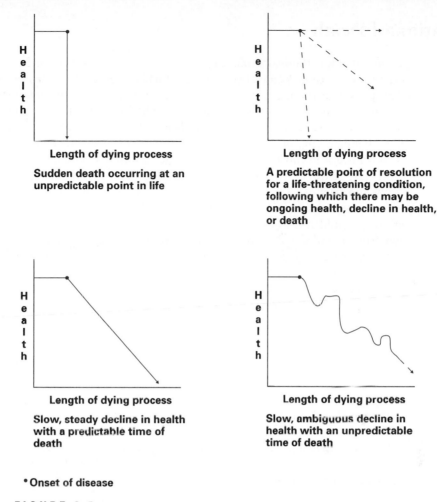

Sudden death occurring at an unpredictable point in life

A predictable point of resolution for a life-threatening condition, following which there may be ongoing health, decline in health, or death

Slow, steady decline in health with a predictable time of death

Slow, ambiguous decline in health with an unpredictable time of death

• **Onset of disease**

FIGURE 2.2
Some Contrasting Dying Trajectories.

to persons with such diseases. Alternatively, an intervention may halt the advance of the disease and leave affected individuals to live out the balance of their lives in a partially debilitated or handicapped condition. Other interventions may only be able to slow (not halt or bring to a stop) the progress of a degenerative disease or prolong the dying of people with the disease. This prolongation of living/dying may be measured in terms of weeks, months, or even years.

The relative prominence of degenerative diseases in the United States today alters American experiences with dying and death. Although death is less frequently encountered in our society, when it does occur it is often associated with a protracted and ambiguous dying trajectory. On one hand, this may provide more time for individuals to say their good-byes, get their affairs in order, and prepare for death. On the other hand, experiences with dying from degenerative diseases often drain physical, emotional, social, spiritual, and financial resources.

❦ Location of Death

Imagine that it is the year 1900. You are at the bedside of a loved one who is dying. You are *in that person's home,* because that is where perhaps as many as 80 percent of all people in the United States die in 1900: in their own beds (Lerner, 1970). You and your loved one are surrounded by sights, sounds, smells, and people that are familiar. Hospitals or other sorts of health care institutions are not the places where people living in 1900 encounter death. (This is also true of many encounters with death in most developing countries around the world in the early years of the 21st century). In 1900, only people who have no personal resources or no family and friends to care for them are likely to be found in public hospitals as they approach death. In 1900, those who have the personal or economic resources certainly would not want to leave the comforts of home—their own bed, their own friends and family—to go somewhere else to die. By contrast, more than 68 percent of people in today's United States die *in a public institution* of some sort (usually a hospital or long-term care facility)—in a strange place, in a strange bed, and surrounded mostly by strangers (see Table 2.5).

In 1900, you and other members of the family would have been the primary health care providers. What you provide to the dying person is largely palliative care—that is, care for distressing symptoms. If there is fever, you apply a cool cloth along with frequent washings. If the dying person is hungry, you prepare familiar, favorite foods. If the dying person grows frightened, you hold his or her hand, sit with him or her, read or recite words of comfort, and share your love.

When death is near, you also are near, in the same or a nearby room. After death, you clean and clothe the body—the last act of love in a lifelong drama. The

TABLE 2.5
Location of Death: United States, 2004

	Number	Percentage	Number	Percentage
Total			2,401,400[a]	100.0
Hospital, clinic, or medical center				
Inpatient	903,953	37.64		
Outpatient	178,837	7.45		
Dead on arrival	24,641	1.03		
Total			1,107,431	46.12
Hospice facility			10,326	0.43
Nursing home/long-term care			530,818	22.10
Decedent's home			586,564	24.42
Other place			159,415	6.63
Place unknown			6,846	0.29

[a] Data include deaths of nonresidents of the United States.

Source: CDC, 2006e.

body might well be left in the bed while friends and neighbors "visit." Or perhaps the body is placed in a coffin (sometimes handmade by you and other family members—another last action for the deceased) and laid out in the parlor for a wake or visitation. After the funeral, the body is lowered by the family into a grave that you have helped to dig in a nearby family plot or churchyard. As a mark of special honor, the family fills in the grave. The struggles of one family to do this are well depicted in William Faulkner's novel *As I Lay Dying* (1930).

In this situation, death is familiar. Most people have seen, heard, and been touched by the death of a family member. Children also are included in these situations. If grandmother is dying in her bed at home, children participate by talking and sitting with her, or helping with small chores. Children are present during the wake (since it is held in the home) and the funeral. Death is not a stranger in these children's lives.

All these customs have changed for most (but not all) Americans. In 1949, 49.5 percent of all deaths in our society occurred in some sort of health care institution (mainly in a hospital). By 2004, more than 68 percent of all deaths in the United States took place in an institution: over 46 percent in a hospital or medical center, and more than 22 percent in some sort of long-term care facility (see Table 2.5). In recent years, there has been a modest shift away from hospitals into nursing homes and private residences, but still the vast majority of deaths in our society now occur in public institutions. In general, what happened in our society during the last half of the 20th century is that death for many has gradually been moved out of the mainstream of life. In turn, families have more and more become spectators at a family member's death, rather than participants or primary caregivers. When many Americans die today, they are away from the people they know best and with whom they have shared personal, long-term histories. This is not a criticism of professional caregivers; our point is only to note that they are not the same people who would have provided care in the past. When there is an absence of long-term relationships with the person who is dying, those who are providing care may be unaware of his or her personal interests, values, needs, and preferences. This is one reason why many contemporary Americans report that they fear dying more than death. It is also one reason why there has been so much recent interest in advance directives as an effort to ensure that one's voice will be heard and respected when critical decisions are made in end-of-life care (see Chapter 16).

Because dying now often occurs outside the home, death is unknown, or at least not well known, to many of us. In these circumstances, family members may not be present at the moment of death in our society. Except among certain groups (for example, some Mormons, Orthodox Jews, and Amish), the last loving actions—cleaning and dressing the body—for most persons who die in our society are performed by strangers: nurses, nurses' aides, and funeral directors. The body is most likely taken from the place where death occurred to a funeral home. There, after preparation, the family may see the body dressed, arranged, made up. In many ways, the actual event of death is hidden or removed from the lives of most people. Also, at many cemeteries today families are taken from the gravesite before the casket is lowered into the grave, or the last separation may take place at a chapel near the cemetery entrance and at a distance from the gravesite. All of these customs can force family members into the helpless, empty inertia of mere observers.

In short, direct, personal encounters with many facets of natural human death have been diminished in our society. Care for the dying and of the dead has been

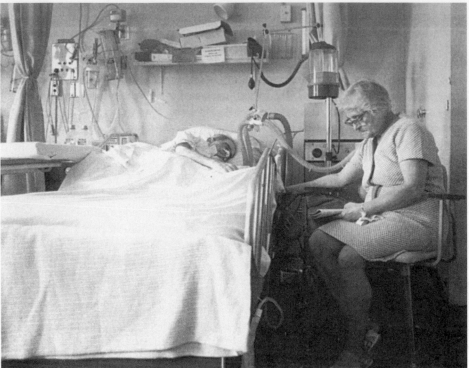

Sitting, waiting, and anticipating in a high-tech medical setting.

moved away from the family and out of the home for many in our society (although this situation is changing somewhat with the support of programs like hospice). Thus, few may experience the moments immediately before, at the time of, or directly after the death of someone they love. For all others, death is increasingly distanced—some would say estranged or made alien—from the mainstream of life's events.

❦ What Factors Helped Bring about These Changing Encounters with Death?

This section examines six factors related to changing encounters with death. Death rates, for example, had already begun to decrease in a noticeable way in the middle to latter half of the 19th century. What was happening that could account for that decrease?

The earliest and most important factor was *industrialization* in the late 18th and 19th centuries. This historical and social phenomenon had several immediate consequences. Among them were increased production of food, better clothing, and better housing, all of which supported a healthier population. That is, industrialization led to improvements in the environment and in the general standard of living. In turn, that meant death became a less familiar visitor in human lives.

Industrialization also brought about the development of more effective means of communication (for example, telegraph and telephone) and more effective means of transportation (for example, rail systems, better highways, more efficient trucking)—which, in turn, changed patterns of encounters with death. For instance, now when crops fail in one place, that fact can be made known to people in other areas, surpluses from elsewhere can be moved to that place, and malnutrition and starvation can be alleviated or eliminated. High death rates from hunger and malnutrition in some poor societies in recent years have exposed deficiencies in these aspects of those societies. Food shipped from other parts of the world has gone to waste when inadequate port or distribution facilities prevent it being taken to where it is most needed.

The second major factor in reducing death rates involved *public health measures* that first achieved significance in the 19th and early 20th centuries. For example, threats posed by many communicable diseases (such as cholera, typhoid, encephalitis, and malaria) were reduced by a better understanding of their vectors or how they were transmitted (for example, by mosquitoes or rats) and the subsequent control of those vectors. In addition, Pasteur's discovery in the late 19th century that communicable diseases are caused by microbial agents led to isolation of those with communicable diseases (quarantine), separation of drinking water sources from sewage, and other improvements in basic sanitation. These actions contributed to declining death rates and helped in the prevention of morbidity and mortality in the society as a whole.

When industrialization and public health measures first led to a decline in death rates in the United States, fewer people died, but young people—infants in particular—continued to die at high rates. Nutrition and preventive health measures for individuals had to be better understood before overall death rates, and particularly deaths in infancy, could be reduced further. When such measures were pursued in increasingly effective ways, there were significant gains in average life expectancy during the late 1930s and 1940s.

The third major factor working to reduce death rates in our society is *preventive health care for individuals* (Cohen, 1989). This is most evident in techniques like vaccination, whereby an individual can be inoculated or infected in a controlled way with an illness (Allen, 2007). The purpose of the vaccination procedure is to permit the individual's own immune system to build up defenses to future attacks by the illness. These preventive measures originated in 1798, when Jenner introduced a vaccination for smallpox. However, it took nearly a century for another such advance: the introduction by Louis Pasteur in 1881 of a vaccination for anthrax (Wehrle & Top, 1981). Beginning around the end of the 19th century, the number of available vaccines increased rapidly, although advances occurred at irregular intervals. These vaccines protected more and more persons from deadly—often childhood—diseases, thus quickly helping to increase average length of life. Other methods of preventive health care for individuals include the use of media to circulate advice on healthy diet and exercise, warnings against the health-related dangers of tobacco use, and efforts to persuade pregnant women not to drink alcoholic beverages or use illegal drugs.

All of these factors were influential in changing encounters with death before the fourth major variable, *the rise of modern cure-oriented medicine,* which first gained significance in the second quarter of the 20th century. By this time, the hospital had begun to be a major contributor to health care. The biomedical model of disease had become dominant with its tendencies to emphasize cure over prevention. Physicians were now important in providing health care, and health care had become curative in many key ways. To provide this sort of health care, special technologies were developed, many

Copyright © Stefan Verwey

of which are quite expensive. Thus, they are localized in particular places, mainly hospitals. Health care in our society is usually not delivered to where the sick person is; rather, the person with disease is delivered to the place where health care is provided.

Medicine had now become an important factor in reducing death rates and in accelerating changes that had begun much earlier. Especially since the introduction of successful antibiotics (that is, antimicrobial agents such as penicillin)—largely a post–World War II (after 1945) phenomenon—modern medicine contributed to improvements in death rates and average life expectancy of contemporary peoples, at least in the industrialized nations. Along with earlier factors, modern cure-oriented medicine has affected both overall death rates and infant death rates, although the latter have not improved (declined) as quickly as the former and only approached their current levels in the late 1950s and 1960s.

A fifth factor that is also significant in how death is encountered and experienced in our society has to do with *the nature of contemporary families*. When families were large, extended social groups who generally lived near each other and had members (especially women) who stayed at home, many members could be counted on to take part in caring for the ill, the dying, the bodies of the dead, and the bereaved. When

38   PART TWO   Death

families are smaller, more obliged to have all of their adult members work out of the home, more scattered throughout the country or the world, and with members who are generally less connected to each other—and especially when family and other kinship groups are shattered or nonexistent, as is the case for many single and homeless individuals in our society—then encounters with dying, death, and bereavement occur in quite a different way. Religious communities and friendly neighbors might have taken up some of this slack, but for many in our mobile, secular, and impersonal society those ties are also less typical, less strong, and less available.

A sixth factor that influences how death is encountered and experienced in our society, one that has been attracting increasing attention in recent years, is *lifestyle*. The ways in which we live our lives often have a direct influence on when and how we die. In fact, a seminal article (McGinnis & Foege, 1993) using mortality data for deaths in 1990 established that *nearly half of all deaths in the United States arise from or are associated with underlying causes that are, in principle, preventable.* Recently, that conclusion has been supported by another group of researchers (Mokdad, Marks, Stroup, & Gerberding, 2004; see Table 2.6) who make essentially the same point using mortality data for 2000. Commenting on this recent study, McGinnis and Foege (2004, p. 1264) wrote: "The estimates [by Mokdad et al.] would suggest that diet/physical activity patterns are now in fact likely greater contributors to mortality than tobacco is (and, in retrospect, probably were in 1990) and are most likely increasing in their impact."

For example, the story of Bryan Lee Curtis near the beginning of this chapter clearly demonstrates the harmful effects of using tobacco products. Smoking is the major factor that has led to lung and bronchial cancers becoming the leading cancer causes of death among both men and women in our society (see Figure 2.1). Worse

TABLE 2.6
Underlying Causes of Preventable Deaths in the United States, 1990 and 2000

Actual Cause	1990 Number, Percentage		2000 Number, Percentage	
Tobacco	400,000	19%	435,000	18.1%
Poor diet and physical inactivity	300,000	14%	400,000	16.6%
Alcohol consumption	100,000	5%	85,000	3.5%
Microbial agents	90,000	4%	75,000	3.1%
Toxic agents	60,000	3%	55,000	2.3%
Motor vehicle	25,000	1%	43,000	1.8%
Firearms	35,000	2%	29,000	1.2%
Sexual behavior	30,000	1%	20,000	0.8%
Illicit drug use	20,000	<1%	17,000	0.7%
Total	1,060,000	50%	1,159,000	48.2%

Source: Mokdad et al., 2004.

yet, smoking also influences heart disease and numerous other harmful conditions (Kessler, 2001), so much so that the Surgeon General felt obliged to issue a report on *The Health Consequences of Smoking* (U.S. Department of Health and Human Services, 2004). Similarly, eating high-cholesterol foods predisposes us to heart and circulatory problems. Also, ingesting large amounts of alcohol and sweetened beverages, along with consumption of other high-sugar foods and lack of regular exercise, helps to explain the increasing rates of obesity and diabetes among Americans. Thus, the National Center for Health Statistics (2004) has reported data from the 1999–2002 National Health and Nutrition Examination Survey that show that 30 percent of adults 20 years of age and over (over 60 million people) have a body mass index (BMI) of 30 or greater and thus are classified as obese, whereas another 35 percent are classified as overweight (BMI≥25). (BMI = weight in pounds divided by height in inches, and again divided by height in inches, then multiplied by 703; many BMI calculators are available on the Internet.) Beyond that, 16 percent of all children and teens ages 6 to 19 (over 9 million individuals) are overweight. Moreover, the American Heart Association (Associated Press, 2004) recently estimated that more than 10 percent of U.S. children ages 2 to 5 are overweight, up from 7 percent in 1994. As a result, the Surgeon General issued a *Call to Action to Prevent and Decrease Overweight and Obesity* (U.S. Department of Health and Human Services, 2001a), the Institute of Medicine (2004) published a report on *Preventing Childhood Obesity: Health in the Balance,* and a recent study appearing in the *New England Journal of Medicine* (Olshansky et al., 2005) reported that obesity has already begun to stall the long-term trend toward increases in average life expectancy. In addition, whether or not we practice safe driving techniques affects the prevalence of deaths from motor vehicle accidents. Finally, lack of exercise, misuse of firearms, certain forms of risky sexual behavior, and illicit drug use all contribute to early and avoidable deaths.

These six factors—some going back centuries, others gaining prominence in recent years—seem to be the most prominent variables that influence overall encounters with death in our society. As a result of factors like these, death has been removed in numerous important ways from the home and from the mainstream of contemporary living. In addition, death is all too often encountered without some of the community supports that might have been in place in the informal familial and other social networks of times past. Of course, this does not mean that death no longer comes into our world in any form; the issue is *the form death takes* when it does come into our world. For example, when death rates (especially those associated with birth and infants) are as low as they now are in the United States, potential parents can decide to have fewer offspring and to delay first pregnancies since they are less fearful than parents in earlier times that death will disrupt their plans. Other individuals may be all too complacent about their own use of tobacco and alcohol products, their poor diet, their lack of physical exercise, or the importance of having their children vaccinated. The form that death takes in our society depends on certain variables, such as the most prevalent causes of death, the dying trajectories we encounter, the location in which death occurs, and how our family, our ethnic group, and our local community are or are not able to rally to support individuals experiencing dying, death, and bereavement.

We will all die, sooner or later. And we will all have encounters with death, dying, and bereavement during our lives. What this chapter has shown is that those encounters will typically be different for us than in times past in our own country or currently in many other parts of the world. Our encounters with death in the United States today are an important component in a special set of experiences. In many ways, these death-related experiences represent desirable improvements over the lot of other human beings; in other ways, they have less favorable implications. We will explore further aspects of those changing experiences with death in subsequent chapters.

❧ Summary

In this chapter, we learned about *contemporary encounters with death*, especially those found in the United States and in other developed countries. We examined those encounters both in themselves and as they differ from mortality patterns in our society in the past or in developing countries in other parts of the world at present. In the United States today, death rates are lower overall, average life expectancy is longer, people die most often from degenerative rather than communicable diseases, typical dying trajectories are quite different from what they once were, and more people die in institutions than at home. In addition, we examined six variables or principal factors that are correlated with these changes in death-related encounters: industrialization, public health measures, preventive health care for individuals, modern cure-oriented medicine, the nature of contemporary families, and lifestyle.

Glossary

Average life expectancy: an estimate of the average number of years a group of people will live

Communicable diseases: diseases that can be transmitted or spread from person to person

Cure-oriented medicine: medical science and health care primarily designed to cure, reverse the course, or halt/slow the advance of disease or other life-threatening conditions

Death rates: numbers of deaths among members of a given population group divided by the total number of those in the group; usually expressed as some number of deaths per 1,000 or 100,000 individuals

Degenerative diseases: diseases that typically result from long-term wearing out of body organs, typically associated with aging, lifestyle, and environment

Dying trajectories: patterns of dying or the ways in which dying plays out, typically distinguished by *duration* (the time between the onset of dying and the arrival of death) and *shape* (the course of the dying, its predictability, and whether death is expected or unexpected)

Encounters with death, dying, and bereavement: ways in which we confront or meet up with death-related events

Extended family: a large kinship group whose members often live near each other

Industrialization: the organization of labor, especially manufacturing, into industries; often involving mechanization versus hand labor

The living-dying interval: the period between the onset of dying and the arrival of death; described by Pattison as including an "acute crisis phase," a "chronic-living-dying phase," and a "terminal phase"

Location of death: the physical place in which death occurs, for example, in a home or public institution

Preventive health care: medical and health care primarily designed to prevent or minimize the likelihood of acquiring disease or putting one's life at risk

Public health measures: community actions to protect or improve the health of society's members, for example, to combat threats posed by communicable diseases, provide safe drinking water, and dispose of sewage, garbage, and other contaminants

Questions for Review and Discussion

1. Two types of statistical data can be used to illustrate changes in encounters with death in American society: death rates and average life expectancy. How have these sets of data changed over the last hundred years in the United States? How have these changes affected your encounters with death, dying, and bereavement?

2. People in American society a hundred years ago often died of communicable diseases; today they often die of degenerative diseases. How do we distinguish these two types of causes of death, and what are the patterns of dying that are associated with them typically like? How might these different causes of death affect your encounters with death, dying, and bereavement?

3. This chapter noted changes in the locations that people typically die in American society. Think about how encounters with death are likely to be different when a person dies at home and when a person dies away from home (for example, in an institution like a hospital or nursing home). How will these changes in location affect the encounters with death of the person who is dying and of those who are his or her survivors?

Suggested Readings

The basic materials for demographic studies of mortality are found in:

Centers for Disease Control and Prevention (CDC). *Morbidity and Mortality Weekly Report.* Provides current information and statistics about disease. See www.cdc.gov.

National Center for Health Statistics (NCHS). This agency of the CDC offers various publications; among these, the *National Vital Statistics Reports* summarize preliminary and final mortality data. See also the NCHS home page at www.cdc.gov/nchs.

National Safety Council. *Injury Facts.* Published annually. See www.nsc.org.

U.S. Bureau of the Census. (1975). *Historical Statistics of the United States, Colonial Times to 1970, Bicentennial Edition.*

U.S. Census Bureau. *Statistical Abstract of the United States.* Published annually; reflects data from a year or two earlier. See also the census bureau's Web page at www.census.gov.

Selected Web Resources

Some useful search terms include: AVERAGE LIFE EXPECTANCY; COMMUNICABLE DISEASES; CURE-ORIENTED MEDICINE (OR CURATIVE CARE); DEATH ENCOUNTERS (OR DEATH-RELATED ENCOUNTERS OR ENCOUNTERS WITH DEATH); DEATH RATES (OR MORTALITY RATES); DEGENERATIVE DISEASES; DYING TRAJECTORIES; FAMILY (SIZE/STRUCTURE); INDUSTRI-ALIZATION; INFANT MORTALITY RATES; LIFESTYLE; THE LIVING-DYING INTERVAL; MATERNAL MORTALITY RATES; LOCATION OF DEATH (OR PLACE OF DEATH); PREVENTIVE HEALTH CARE; PUBLIC HEALTH

Visit the book companion website for *Death & Dying, Life & Living, Sixth Edition,* at academic.cengage.com/psychology/corr for all URLs and live links to the following *organizational and other Internet sites:*

Centers for Disease Control and Prevention (CDC)

Epidemiology of Dying and End-of-Life Experiences

National Center for Health Statistics (NCHS)

National Safety Council

U.S. Census Bureau

World Health Organization

C H A P T E R   3

Changing Attitudes toward Death

© AP Photo/Kentucky New Era, Peter Wright

Objectives of This Chapter

◆ To explain the concept of an "attitude" and to show how death-related *attitudes* interact with death-related *encounters* as part of our overall death-related *experiences*

◆ To describe the notion of "death anxiety" and interest in understanding that notion

◆ To identify four basic categories of death-related concerns and responses found in individuals

◆ To sketch a theory of five dominant social patterns in Western attitudes toward death

◆ To illustrate the role that attitudes play in death-related experiences through examples taken from contemporary Amish life in North America and from the New England Puritans of the 17th century

🍂 Amish Attitudes toward Death

John Stolzfus bore one of the most common names in the Old Order Amish community in eastern Pennsylvania where he had lived all of his life. The Stolzfus family traced its roots through 18th-century immigrants from Alsace and then back to Swiss origins in the 16th-century Anabaptist movement. The Anabaptists were persecuted in Europe for their rejection of infant baptism (on the grounds that children come into the world without a knowledge of good and evil, and thus do not need to be baptized as infants to remove sin). No Amish (whose name comes from their founder, Jacob Ammann) remain in Europe today, but an estimated 180,000 live in 24 states in the United States and in the Canadian province of Ontario (Hostetler, 1994; Kraybill, 2001; Zielinski, 1975, 1993).

As a member of a close-knit Amish community, John Stolzfus centered his life on religious beliefs and practice, a large extended family, and work on a farm. The Old Order Amish are known for their distinctive dress. The men wear plain, dark clothes fastened with hooks and eyes, broad-brimmed hats, and full beards without mustaches, and the women dress in bonnets and long, full dresses. Members of this community use horse-drawn buggies instead of automobiles, espouse pacifism, and reject many modern devices (such as high-line electricity and tractors with pneumatic tires).

These are the outward expressions of a slow-changing culture that is determined to follow its understanding of biblical injunctions. Its central guidelines include: "Be not conformed to this world" (Rom. 12:2) and "Be ye not unequally yoked together with unbelievers" (2 Cor. 6:14). Amish society essentially turns inward to community to worship God, moderate the influences of humanity's evil circumstances, and preserve values in ethical relationships through obedience and conformity. As Kraybill has written (2001, p. 28), "Amish faith has not been separated from daily living; it penetrates their entire way of life." The Amish blend together an emphasis on oral tradition, shared practical knowledge, closeness to nature, respect for elders, striving for self-sufficiency, and smallness in social scale. Usually, 25 to 35 households in geographical proximity form a congregation or church district and take turns in hosting biweekly religious services in their homes.

The Stolzfus family rose with the sun and went to bed shortly after nightfall. As a child, John was assigned chores that contributed to meeting his family's needs. This type of work continued during his school years, with different responsibilities appropriate to his age, growth, and maturity. John's schooling did not extend beyond the eighth grade because the Amish find that sufficient for the lives they have chosen to lead. They are wary that additional formal education might only tend to subvert their traditional beliefs and values. Like most of his peers, at the age of 16 John experienced *rumspringa*, a "running around" coming-of-age ritual in which the strict rules of Amish community life are temporarily lifted while the individual decides whether or not to be baptized (Shachtman, 2006). After that, he was baptized at the age of 18 into his local church district, thereby making a formal commitment to the church. One November day soon after, he married a young woman from the same community.

At first, the young couple lived with John's family, and he continued to work on their farm. Eventually, through a small inheritance from a relative and with some financial help from their families, John and his wife bought a small piece of land to farm on their own. The birth of their first three children, building their own house, and the great communal activity of raising a large barn on their farm all marked a productive period in John's life.

Shortly after the birth of their fifth child, John's first wife died. Relatives helped with the care of the children and with work on the expanding farm until John found one of his wife's unmarried cousins who was willing to marry him and take on the role of mother for his existing children and for the additional children they would have together. After that, life went on for many years in a quiet and steady way. Eventually, the offspring from both of John's marriages grew up and were themselves married. John and his second wife became respected members of their community, he as a deacon or minister to the poor in the church, and she for her work in church groups and for her quiet presence at community gatherings.

In time, after what he thought of as a good life, John began to decline in vigor and in his ability to get around. In accordance with Amish custom, a small house (called a "grandfather house") was built next to the main farmhouse, and John retired there. After his retirement, John concentrated on reading his beloved Bible, whittling simple wooden toys, and spending time with his second wife, their children, and their grandchildren. When he could no longer get out of bed, both John and other members of his community realized that his death was not far off. Gradually, Amish neighbors of all ages began to come by to pray together and say good-bye one last time. John spoke openly of his coming death and used these visits to encourage others to prepare for and calmly accept their own deaths. At the age of 82, John Stolzfus died peacefully one night in his own bed, as one of his daughters sat quietly in a nearby rocking chair and two of his grandchildren slept in their own beds in the same room.

John's body was embalmed by a non-Amish funeral director and then returned to the home, where male family members dressed his body in traditional white garments (Bryer, 1979). The body was placed in a six-sided wooden coffin that had been made ready a few weeks before, and the coffin was laid out in the central room of the house on top of several planks and two sawhorses covered by a plain sheet. Friends helped with many of these arrangements and made sure that those who had known John were notified of his death. That evening, the next day, and the following evening, other members of the community came to the house to bring gifts of food and to offer practical, emotional, and spiritual support to John's family. Several people took turns sitting with the body through the night until the grave could be dug and other preparations made for the funeral. In keeping with the whole of his life, John Stolzfus' funeral was a simple event, a familiar ritual that involved members of the community in the services, the burial, a communal meal afterward, and a recognized pattern of consolation activities during the following weeks and months. No one was shocked or surprised by this death or by its surrounding events. Experience, tradition, and shared attitudes had prepared individuals and the community as a whole to support each other and to contend with the cycles of life and death in their midst. (For a real life example of Amish mourning after traumatic deaths, see Focus On 3.1.)

Amish Mourning after Traumatic Deaths

On October 2, 2006, Charles Carl Roberts IV invaded the one-room Nickel Mines Amish School in southeastern Pennsylvania. Freeing adult women and boys, Roberts eventually shot ten girls, killing five of them and wounding the others before he took his own life.

The response of the Amish community to this horrific event was seen as remarkable by many Americans. That community responded by shunning publicity and asking the media to refrain from "close-up gawking and picture taking" (Levin, 2006, p. 4A). Instead, they released a statement through the state police that said in part, "We don't know or understand why this happened, but we do believe that God allowed this to happen" (Levin & Hall, 2006, p. 3A). Most remarkable perhaps was the lack of anger on the part of the community, together with a powerful support system for the primary mourners and the community itself in the face of such tragedy.

Four qualities of Amish life were prominent in the ways in which the people of this community coped with these events (Hampson, 2006, p. 3A):

◆ Believing that the world is basically evil, they accepted God's plan, however mysterious or painful it may be, and trusted that the dead children were now in heaven.
◆ Acting on the Christian injunction to turn the other cheek and to love one's enemies, the Amish bowed to their suffering and made efforts to console bewildered members of Roberts' family.
◆ Following a general practice of not acting in ways that emphasize one's individuality, the Amish did not rush to speak to the media or show much emotion publicly.
◆ Working closely together and helping each other as is typical of this community, members of the community acted *as a community* to prepare for the series of wakes, funerals, and burials for the five dead children, and to provide meals for those who would attend. They also demolished the school building in which the shootings occurred and built a new school for their children on nearby land owned by a member of the community.

In all of this, the Amish provided distinctive examples of acting out a specific form of religious faith, a willingness to forgive those who have done them harm, and a painstaking effort at reconciliation.

Religious faith and the community itself provided needed support, and demonstrate why this community does not rely on professionals from outside the community for assistance with their losses.

🍎 The Interplay of Death-Related Encounters and Attitudes

In Chapter 2, we examined how death-related events thrust themselves into human life. The *encounters* that we have with these events constitute one central component of our death-related experiences. In the present chapter, we explore a second key aspect of those experiences: our *attitudes* toward death. According to the *Oxford English Dictionary,* the term *attitude* arose in art. Originally it meant the disposition or posture of a figure in statuary or painting. That definition led to the notion that a posture of the body could be related to a particular mental state. From there, the term *attitude* came to be associated with some "settled behaviour or manner of acting, as representative of feeling or opinion" (*Oxford English Dictionary,* 1989, vol. 1, p. 771).

In other words, an attitude is a way of presenting oneself to or being in the world. If one's bodily posture (one's attitude) includes an upraised fist, a general tenseness, and a facial grimace as one leans toward another person, that posture itself will affect how that particular encounter develops. Compare such an attitude with one that includes open arms, a smile, and a generally relaxed body. Good examples of attitudes expressed in everyday behavior include offering to shake hands when one meets another person or spreading one's arms wide and hugging or kissing the cheek of an individual as a form of greeting. Both of these behavioral patterns indicate friendliness, lack of hostility, and the absence of a weapon in one's grasp. Attitudes like these influence one's encounters by predisposing the person who is being greeted to a friendly or cordial response. Thus, one's way of being in the world, or how one meets the world, often influences the kinds of encounters one has and how those encounters are likely to develop. It also works the other way around; one's encounters influence one's own bodily postures and habits of mind.

This means that we human beings *contribute* to our experiences. We are not merely passive receivers of information. We shape and form our knowledge of what is happening, depending on our prior beliefs and feelings. We meet the world from a particular stance, in specific ways. The Amish do this in their special ways, and the Puritans (whom we will discuss at the end of this chapter) did it in theirs; everyone does it in some way or other. Thus, a central issue relating to attitudes concerns the ways in which patterns of belief and feeling enter into what we think and do, especially as our attitudes become dispositions or habitual ways of thinking about and acting in the world.

This is true both for attitudes in general and for those that are specifically related to death. That is, death-related attitudes are both products and determinants of many of our encounters with the world (see Issues for Critical Reflection #2). They dispose us favorably to some types of death-related encounters, while leaving us not so favorably disposed—or even negatively disposed and actively hostile—to others. At the same time, events around us help in their own ways to shape our knowledge and understanding of the world. Death-related encounters certainly play an important role in shaping death-related attitudes. As we learned in Chapter 2 for instance, unlike the example of John Stolzfus, most people in the United States today die in a hospital or other institution. As a result, their deaths may be physically removed from the presence of family members and friends. That makes such deaths remote from their survivors. Most Americans today do not often confront death directly, a circumstance that can contribute to and support a belief that death is, or should be, invisible. But think of this situation also the other way around. If one's habitual way of behaving in the face of someone else's stress is to withdraw because it creates discomfort, then one is likely to stay away from the hospital where someone is dying. In this way, *attitudes* toward death (for example, "death is stressful—stay away from stressful situations") influence encounters. The attitudes that one holds may tend to encourage one to withdraw or become remote from encounters with death.

ISSUES FOR CRITICAL REFLECTION

#2 Why Should We Try to Integrate Encounters and Attitudes with Death?

This chapter develops various pictures of attitudes toward dying, death, and bereavement. This is part of our overall effort to examine the death-related encounters, attitudes, and practices that, taken together, make up our experiences with death, dying, and bereavement. To that end, it is helpful to integrate what is said in Chapter 3 about death-related attitudes with what was discussed in Chapter 2 about death-related encounters (and eventually with our descriptions of death-related practices in Chapter 4). Our basic premise is that encounters affect attitudes and attitudes affect encounters. As a result, examining the two together now can enrich our understanding of how these two aspects of our experience of dying, death, and bereavement interweave in specific ways. For instance, Ariès (whose views are described later in this chapter) suggested that in contemporary society, when someone dies, one can hardly tell that anything has happened. Society does not pause in its ongoing rhythms of work and play (as it would in a situation like that described by what Ariès called "tame death"). Except for a brief funeral period in our society (and this

typically involves only the closest associates of the dead person), the surface of societal life often goes on largely as usual. As a result, death is hidden (not visible, therefore not encountered), and this is compatible with an attitude of seeing it as forbidden.

But of course this works the other way around, too. That is why, for example, Ariès remarked that with the medicalization of Western society, death is no longer seen as entirely natural. As people turned increasingly to institutional care of the dying, death again became hidden from ordinary view. Some individuals in our society have even undertaken extraordinary intervention measures designed to forestall death—some of which may also prolong their dying. These changing and more limited encounters with death helped to support the view that death was unnatural, even indecent. Studying the content of Chapters 2 and 3 together in this way—integrating their separate arguments and implications—can allow death-related encounters and attitudes to be placed back together, and the full complexity of their interweavings as components of death-related experiences can be better appreciated.

🍒 Death-Related Attitudes

Death Anxiety

In recent years, much research on death-related attitudes has had to do with matters related to *death anxiety* (e.g., Neimeyer, 1994; Neimeyer & Van Brunt, 1995; Neimeyer, Wittkowski, & Moser, 2004). Results of these studies are interesting, especially when repeated reports confirm the plausibility of their conclusions. For example, in many studies women report higher death anxiety than men. It is not clear precisely whether women really are more anxious than men about death or whether women are simply more open than men in discussing their attitudes toward emotionally intense subjects. Many studies also note that older adults appear to report less death anxiety than some younger persons, such as adolescents, and individuals with strong religious convictions report less death anxiety than those who do not share such a value framework. Death anxiety has also been examined in terms of other demographic (e.g., occupation, health status, and experience with death) and personality (e.g., psychopathology) factors, but results are more mixed. Death anxiety may not be linear (that is, increasing or decreasing steadily as life goes on) but may vary with life accomplishments and past or future regrets (Tomer & Eliason, 1996). It also may not be easy to change people's anxieties about death.

Death anxiety is a complex and still not fully understood subject. Moreover, the efforts of researchers to measure various forms of death anxiety, to determine the variables that do or do not influence such anxiety, and to compare different population groups in terms of their death anxieties face several difficulties. For example, many of these studies seem to have assumed that: (1) death anxiety does exist (in all humans and all respects, or just in some?); (2) individuals will be both willing and able to disclose their death anxieties; and (3) adequate instruments and methodologies are available to identify and measure death anxieties. In fact, whereas Becker (1973) argued that awareness of individual mortality is the most basic source of anxiety, Freud (1959c, p. 289) believed that humans could not really be anxious about their own deaths because "It is indeed impossible to imagine our own death ... at bottom nobody believes in his own death, or ... in the unconscious every one of us is convinced of his own immortality." Further, however much or little an individual may be anxious about death, most of the research on this subject depends upon self-reports (in response to questionnaires, interviews, projective tests), usually taken on a one-time basis from conveniently accessible groups like college students (for example, Thorson, Powell, & Samuel, 1998). Researchers conducting these studies are sensitive to questions of interpretation, such as: How valid or reliable are such reports? Are they representative or taken out of context? In particular, if one's score on a death anxiety scale is low, does that indicate low death anxiety or high denial and active repression of scary feelings? Note that the familiar distinction between *fears* (attitudes or concerns directed to some specific focus) and *anxieties* (attitudes that are more generalized and diffuse or less particularized in their objects) is set aside in most of this research.

Still, instruments for studying death anxiety have improved since the early Death Anxiety Scale (Templer, 1970; see also Lonetto & Templer, 1986) involving 15 short statements that one endorses as true or false to a number of more recent measures described in the *Death Anxiety Handbook* (Neimeyer, 1994). There also have been efforts (for example, Neimeyer & Van Brunt, 1995) to encourage greater sophistication and effectiveness in this field.

Death-Related Concerns and Responses

One way to move forward in our thinking about death-related attitudes might be to pay attention not merely to aversive attitudes (such as anxiety, denial, distancing, fear) but to more accepting attitudes as well. For example, Focus On 3.2 reproduces a playful, humorous parody of a grammar lesson—one that was part of a municipal celebration in Mexico of the Day of the Dead. It is also useful to sort out death-related attitudes in terms of the specific heart of their concern. For example, the word *death* is often used to designate, not the situation or state of being dead, but the *process of dying* or coming to be dead. Thus, when we say, "John had a very difficult death," we are likely referring not to the fact of his death but to the manner of his dying. Alternatively, the word *death* sometimes refers primarily to the *aftermath of a death*. Thus, one might say, "Mary is finding John's death to be quite hard." These different ways of speaking reveal that death-related attitudes can center on one or more of the following: (1) attitudes about *my own dying*; (2) attitudes about *my own death*; (3) attitudes about *what will happen to me after my death*; and (4) attitudes related to *the dying, death, or bereavement of someone else* (Choron, 1964; Collett & Lester, 1969).

My Own Dying Attitudes (which include beliefs, feelings, values, postures, and dispositions to action) are frequently directed to *my own dying*. Such attitudes among contemporary Americans commonly reflect fears and anxiety about the possibility of experiencing a long, difficult, painful, or undignified dying process, especially in an alien institution under the care of strangers who might not respect one's personal needs or wishes. People who hold these attitudes often express a preference that their dying might occur without any form of distress, without prior knowledge, and in their sleep. Some even try hard not to think about their death, whereas others set out in proactive ways to prepare an advance directive (see Chapter 16) to try to ensure that their dying process will not be unduly and painfully prolonged.

FOCUS ON 3.2

Conjugating Death

Yo muero	*I die*
Tú falleces	*You perish*
El sucumbe	*He succumbs*
Nosotros expiramos	*We expire*
Vosotros os petateais	*You kick the bucket*
Ellos se pelan	*They check out*
Y todos felpamos	*And we all bite the dust*

Source: Garciagodoy, 1998, p. 295.

In other societies or among individuals who are guided by a different set of concerns, many people hold attitudes that lead them to fear a sudden, unanticipated death. For such individuals, it is important to have time to address what some have called "unfinished business" by expressing to their loved ones such sentiments as "Thank you," "I love you," "I am sorry for anything I might have done to hurt you," "I forgive you for anything you might have done to hurt me," or simply, "Good-bye"—a contraction for "God be with you" (Byock, 2004). Others may wish to have enough time and awareness to "get ready to meet their Maker" or otherwise prepare themselves for death through meditation and a special positioning of the body (see Personal Insights 3.1). Many want to satisfy personal concerns about how their goods will be distributed after their deaths. Some individuals who find value in setting an example for others or bearing suffering for some altruistic or religious motive may even look forward to their dying with courage and some degree of anticipation. Attitudes toward my own dying are at the heart of each of these examples.

PERSONAL INSIGHTS 3.1

The Death of a Tibetan Buddhist Teacher

In . . . 1983, Kyabje Ling Rinpoche, senior tutor to His Holiness the Dalai Lama . . . suffered the first in a series of small (strokes). On Christmas Day of that year, four of the disciples spontaneously gathered together at Ling Rinpoche's house in the foothills of the Himalayas. While sitting in his downstairs room rejoicing over their chance meeting, they were informed that he had just passed away . . . He was eighty-one years old.

In death, Ling Rinpoche's exceptional spiritual attainment was made quite evident. He died . . . in a special meditation posture modeled on the posture the Buddha assumed at *parinirvana* [his passage from this world]. In the Tibetan tradition, the body of a dead person is left on the deathbed for at least three days in order to allow the stream of consciousness to leave the body peacefully. Several techniques can be utilized during the death experience if one is an accomplished meditator. With these techniques, the body does not show any signs of deterioration as long as the consciousness remains in it. . . . Ling Rinpoche maintained a technique called the Meditation on the Clear Light of Death for a total of thirteen days. The Swiss disciple who cared for him during the last weeks of his life visited his room daily to make sure everything was satisfactory. She confirmed that during this entire time Ling Rinpoche's face remained beautiful and flesh-toned, and his body showed none of the normal signs of death.

His Holiness the Dalai Lama was so moved by the spirituality of his personal teacher that he decided to have Ling Rinpoche's body embalmed instead of cremated. Today the statue holding the remains of Kyabje Ling Rinpoche may be viewed at the palace of the Dalai Lama in Dharamsala.

Source: From Blackman, 1997, pp. 73, 75.

My Own Death A second category of death-related attitudes is primarily concerned with death itself, specifically *my own death*. Here the main issue is about how my death will impact what I am experiencing right now. For example, those who find life difficult or filled with hardships might look forward to its ending, to the simple cessation of the tribulations they are now experiencing—whatever happens after death. Such persons might reject difficult, painful, or expensive interventions along with those perceived as likely to be ineffective. Alternatively, suppose that I value life very highly—including my relationships with those I love. In that case, I might resist my death with all possible means at my disposal because it will result in my losing what is so important to me. In either of these cases, the main focus of concern is on my death itself and its immediate implications for me (and not on what happens after death or for what is happening or may happen to others).

What Will Happen to Me after My Death? A third category of death-related attitudes concerns *what will happen to me after my death*. Here the central concerns have to do with what the consequences or aftereffects of death will mean for the self. For some, that might involve anxiety about the unknown. For others, it might include a fear of judgment or punishment after death. For still others, it might depend upon anticipation of or hope for a heavenly reward for a lifetime of hard work, upright living, or faithfulness. In a similar way, many see death itself as merely a bridge or passage to another life in which, for example, the conditions of their existence might be improved over this present life or in which a reunion might be achieved with a loved person who had died earlier. All of these attitudes have primarily to do with some outcome or result for the self that is thought to follow my own death.

The Dying, Death, or Bereavement of Someone Else The death-related attitudes we have examined thus far all involve attitudes held by an individual about his or her experiences prior to, at the time of, and after his or her own death. A fourth set of death-related attitudes is principally concerned not with the self but with the *dying, death, or bereavement of someone else*. For example, I might be mainly concerned about the implications for me of someone else's dying or death. I might worry that I will not be sufficiently strong and resourceful to see an ill or dying person whom I love through the challenges and losses that he or she faces. Or perhaps I look forward to taking care of someone who so frequently cared for me in the past. If so, I might make arrangements to keep that person at home with me, rather than permitting him or her to enter some institutional care setting. Equally, I might be concerned about impending separation from someone whom I love. If the dying individual is a disagreeable person or is experiencing great difficulty in his or her struggles, I might anticipate the relief that will be associated with that person's death. Or I might be fearful about how I will be able to go on with living after someone else upon whom I depend is gone.

Alternatively, it might be the implications for someone else of my dying or death that are of primary concern to me. For example, I might be concerned about the burdens that my illness and dying are placing upon those whom I love. Or I might

Sentiments in an early 20th-century memorial card.

be worried about what will happen to loved ones after I am gone or how my death will affect plans and projects that I had previously pursued. With these concerns in mind, some individuals strive to remain alert as long as they can so that they can spend more time with those they love. Others make provisions to support their survivors-to-be. Still others redouble efforts to complete their prized projects or at least to take them as far as they can.

Some Implications of Death-Related Attitudes

Two major implications of our discussion of death-related attitudes are that such attitudes vary greatly and that humans can exert some influence over their own death-related attitudes. In terms of *variation in death-related attitudes,* it is common to hear talk of fears and anxieties in attitudes about death. Certainly, these are familiar elements or aspects of death-related attitudes, perhaps because dying, death, and bereavement represent something sharply different from or even opposed to the everyday life we now know. Thus, if we ask ourselves what most bothers or frightens us about the implications of death, or what are some of the ways in which we would *most not like to die,* it is not surprising that fears and anxieties should quickly rise to the surface. However, death-related attitudes need not always center on fear or anxiety. In general, humans may adopt a broad range of attitudes, feelings, and emotions concerning death and its implications, just as they can have many different attitudes about various aspects of life and living.

In terms of the *influence that humans can exert over death-related attitudes,* humans are able to reflect upon their own and other possible attitudes, select with some degree of freedom the attitudes that they wish to hold, and change their attitudes in light of new encounters or additional reflection on matters related to death. That is why many epitaphs, such as the following one from an 1830 grave marker in Connecticut (Jones,

1967, p. 148), encourage individuals to develop what are thought to be appropriate attitudes toward death and life:

> Remember me as you draw nigh,
> As you are now, so once was I.
> As I am now, so must you be,
> Prepare for death and follow me.

More recently, two expert commentators have offered these remarks on the human condition: "Appreciation of finiteness can serve not only to enrich self-knowledge but to provide the impulse to propel us forward toward achievement and creativity" (Feifel, 1977a, p. 11); "Everything can be taken from a man but one thing: the last of the human freedoms—to choose one's attitude in any given set of circumstances, to choose one's own way" (Frankl, 1984, p. 86). Our attitudes are basic to human life and behavior, but they can be changed—even though such changes may not be easy to make.

Five Dominant Patterns in Western Attitudes toward Death

Historians, sociologists, and anthropologists also have contributed to our understanding of the richness and complexity of death-related attitudes. Philippe Ariès (1974b, 1981, 1985), a French cultural historian, developed an insightful and instructive account of Western attitudes toward death over a period of several centuries up to our contemporary period. He found five dominant patterns of these attitudes and linked them more or less to specific historical time frames. His historical analysis may or may not be convincing; in any event, it is not important for our purposes here. Instead, in this section we briefly describe some of the central components of Ariès' five patterns. What comes out of this work is a greater awareness of that richness and complexity of death-related attitudes—in this case, mainly large-scale social and cultural attitudes—we mentioned previously.

Ariès named his five patterns of attitudes toward death *tame death, death of the self, remote and imminent death, death of the other,* and *death denied* (some others have called this last pattern *forbidden death*). They can be briefly described as follows:

- *Tame death*: Death is familiar and simple; that is, it is regarded as inevitable and no attempt is made to evade it. Persons who are dying typically calmly await their deaths, usually surrounded by loved ones and members of the community, all of whom wait peacefully for the end. In other words, death is a public event. A major of focus of attention is the community; it is deeply affected by the loss of one of its necessary participants. (Compare the death of John Stolzfus in the vignette near the beginning of this chapter.) Death is also seen as a sort of sleep; either one is awakened at some point to eternal bliss, or one remains eternally asleep.
- *Death of the self*: The focus of attention is on the one who dies. Death produces great anxiety in that person because it is believed that one is either rewarded or punished in his or her future state. (This much is found in the

example of the New England Puritans described in the next section.) For Ariès, death of the self involves a final testing period, and what one does at this moment determines what will happen to one after death (and indeed the meaning of one's whole life). Several religious traditions have some such belief. For instance, some Jews believe that it is important at the moment of death to recite the Shema ("Hear, O Israel: the LORD is our God, the LORD alone, You shall love the LORD your God with all your heart, and with all your soul, and with all your might"—Deuteronomy 6:4, 5). Muslims are taught that invoking the Divine Name at the moment of death can be salvific (Jonker, 1997; Kassis, 1997). And some Buddhists hold that chanting the name of Amitabha Buddha at this point in one's life will ensure that one will end up in the Pure Land after death (Yeung, 1995). In the West, this attitude once led to the development of a formal *ars moriendi,* an art of dying well (Kastenbaum, 1989a).

◆ *Remote and imminent death*: One's attitude toward death is basically highly ambivalent. Death is viewed as a wholly natural event (not a supernatural one), but still great effort is made to keep it at a distance. It is both natural and dangerous, inviting and repelling, beautiful and to be feared.

◆ *Death of the other*: Here, the main focus of attention is on the survivors. Death primarily involves the breaking of relationships. For survivors, it results in an intolerable separation from the one who dies. Feelings and behaviors may go nearly out of control (wailing, keening, throwing oneself in the grave, etc.). For the one who dies, death is primarily a period of waiting to be rejoined with loved ones in some other state.

◆ *Death denied/forbidden death*: Death is seen as being dirty or indecent (even "pornographic"—see Gorer, 1965a). Thus, it is offensive to die in public. Dying persons are therefore more or less isolated from the rest of the community. The very fact that the person is dying is denied, both to that person and to those around her or him. Emotions, both before and after the death, are to be kept hidden, and thus mourning may be seen as morbid or even pathological (Ariès, 1974a).

It can be instructive to look at these five patterns as independent categories or snapshots of social attitudes. In fact, however, as Ariès admitted, they overlap each other, both within cultural/historical periods and even within individual persons. Further, when one studies the basic components of each of these patterns, it becomes apparent that these are not just Western patterns. Rather, some components of each of them can be found in almost all cultures (for examples demonstrating this, see Chapter 5).

❦ The Puritans of Seventeenth-Century New England

The critical role of attitudes in shaping the character of experiences with death can be illustrated in one final example: that of the Puritans of 17th-century New England. We selected this example because it draws upon a historical group in the United States and because their views differ in so many ways from some prominent contemporary death-related attitudes. This example also reminds us once again that the patterns Ariès has described are not strictly sequential; one pattern does not simply replace another; different groups may emphasize different attitudinal patterns (or different aspects of a pattern).

The Puritans originated as a reformist group within the Church of England. Those Puritans who came to America searched for a new land in which they would be free to uphold their beliefs and practice their religion as they wished. The New England Puritans established thriving settlements in various colonies, but their presence was particularly notable in Massachusetts during the middle and latter portions of the 17th century. Here, they emphasized the importance of preaching and conversion through an intense personal experience.

For the Puritans, everything that existed or happened was part of a divine purpose. At the same time, they viewed human history since Adam and Eve as one long descent into ever-deepening depravity. In this situation, no human being could be truly worthy of salvation, nor could any good works earn the favor of God's grace. Nevertheless, the Puritans believed that God, in His infinite mercy and love, had chosen a select and predetermined few for salvation.

The great question for each individual Puritan was whether he or she was a member of God's holy elect. No one could ever have confident knowledge concerning the answer to that question. To think that one did have such knowledge would be to think that one understood the all-knowing mind of God. More likely, to believe that one was assured of salvation was good evidence that one had actually succumbed to the seductive falsehoods of Satan. Confidence in the "sure and certain hope of resurrection to eternal life" was simply not open to the Puritans.

Nevertheless, fear of death and the question of personal salvation preoccupied individual Puritans, in ways not found among the Amish. Each Puritan struggled continuously with his or her conscience to discern, in the midst of innumerable signs of personal depravity, at least some indicators or "marks" that he or she might be among the chosen few. Thus, Puritanism was "a faith marked by a never-ending, excruciating uncertainty . . . [in which] the Puritans were gripped individually and collectively by an intense and unremitting fear of death, while simultaneously clinging to the traditional Christian rhetoric of viewing death as a release and relief for the earth-bound soul" (Stannard, 1977, pp. 75, 79). For the Puritans, one must constantly recognize one's own utter and total depravity, while at the same time praying earnestly for a salvation that one is helpless to secure.

Puritan preachers dwelt vividly on the contrast between the potential terrors and bliss of the afterlife. Those who were not among the elect were subject to the eternal torment of the damned. Those who actually were among the elect were themselves troubled by lack of certainty even up to the very moment of death. Thus, as Stannard (1977, p. 89) has argued, "The New England Puritans, despite their traditional optimistic rhetoric, were possessed of an intense, overt fear of death—the natural consequence of what to them were three patently true and quite rational beliefs: that of their own utter and unalterable depravity; that of the omnipotence, justness, and inscrutability of God; and that of the unspeakable terrors of Hell."

These attitudes toward death among the New England Puritans had implications not only for individual adults but also for children and for society as a whole. The Puritan worldview combined a deep love of children with a strong sense of their depravity and sinful pollution (so different, in this latter regard, from the Amish). Also, the era of the Puritans in New England was a time when infants and children actually were at great risk of dying, and when parents gave birth to many children in the expectation that few would remain alive to care for them in the hour of their own deaths. Perhaps for both these reasons, in their personal relationships with their children Puritan parents were advised to maintain an attitude of "restraint and even aloofness, mixed with . . . an intense parental effort to impose discipline and encourage spiritual precocity" (Stannard, 1977, p. 57).

Puritan children were constantly reminded of the likelihood that they might die at any moment. They were threatened with the dangers of personal judgment and damnation in which even their own parents might testify against them. The expectation of reunion with parents after death was denied to them. They were also reminded of the guilt they would bear if through sinfulness they should bring harm to their parents. In this vein, books for children, including even the *New England Primer* (1727/1962) from which they learned the alphabet, were designed to remind young readers of the imminence and possible consequences of death. How different this attitude is from those of today, or even from 19th-century emphases, such as that expressed in one of the famous McGuffey's readers (1866), which stressed the eternal reunion of children and parents after death for a new life in heaven (Minnich, 1936a, 1936b; Westerhoff, 1978).

Burial practices are a particularly good indicator of death-related attitudes among the New England Puritans. At first, absence of ceremony and restraint of emotion reflected the Puritan reaction to the excesses of "papist" practices. That is, the corpse was regarded as a meaningless husk, burial was swift and simple, and excessive displays of sadness or grief were discouraged. Funeral sermons were not delivered at the time of burial and were not very different from other forms of preaching.

In the latter half of the 17th century, however, Puritan society in New England underwent many changes that threatened the prospects for its holy mission. Several important early leaders died (e.g., John Winthrop, Thomas Shepard, John Cotton, and Thomas Hooker), while a civil war in England and an ensuing official doctrine of religious toleration isolated the New England Puritans in their emphasis on doctrinal righteousness. Also, growing immigration and mercantilism in America produced an increasingly complex society in which the Puritan community declined in numbers and significance.

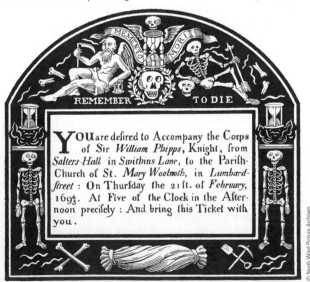

A Puritan view of death: An invitation to the funeral of Sir William Phipps (1651–1695).

In reaction, the embattled New England Puritans developed more and more elaborate funeral practices. Gloves were sent to friends and acquaintances as a form of invitation to the funeral, church bells were rung on the day of the funeral, a funeral procession conducted the coffin to the burial ground, and those who returned to the church or home of the deceased after the burial were given food and distinctively designed, costly funeral rings as tokens of attendance. As the deaths of Puritan leaders and community pillars were experienced, prayer was conducted at the funeral, and funeral sermons took on the form of eulogies. Gravestones carved with elaborate verses praising the moral and religious character of the deceased began to mark the sites of burial. Clearly, a special set of attitudes toward death existed in Puritan New England, shaped by deeply held beliefs and implemented in earnest practice.

❦ Summary

In this chapter, we examined attitudes toward death—clusters of beliefs, feelings, habits of thought, behaviors, and underlying values. In so doing, we saw that individuals may have a variety of concerns and responses to death—including those that focus on one's own dying, the death of oneself, what will happen to the self after death, and the dying, death, or bereavement of another—and that they can have some influence over those concerns and responses. We also saw different sets of social attitudes toward death in Ariès' account of five dominant patterns across Western history (tame death, death of the self, remote and imminent death, death of the other, and death denied) and in two specific examples (the Amish in America today and the New England Puritans of the 17th century). Patterns of death-related attitudes across history, in the United States today, and in individual Americans can be strikingly different and diverse. Such patterns have changed before; they can, and will, change again. None is the eternal essence of how human beings everywhere and throughout all time think about, feel about, or behave in the face of death.

Glossary

Ars moriendi: literally, the "art of dying," a practice that focused on what one should do to die well

Death anxiety: concerns or worries related in some way to death

Death attitude: a more or less settled way of being in the world, presenting oneself to the world, behaving, or acting that reflects some belief, opinion, or feeling related to death

Forbidden death: a death-related attitude that views death as offensive and unacceptable, something to be denied and hidden from public view; a phrase from Ariès

Pornography of death: a death-related attitude much like forbidden death, implying that death is dirty and indecent, and yet somehow titillating and intriguing; a phrase from Gorer

Tame death: a death-related attitude that views death as familiar and simple, a public event mainly affecting the community; a phrase from Ariès

Questions for Review and Discussion

1. Think about how this chapter described attitudes toward death, dying, and bereavement. How do attitudes differ from encounters (as discussed in Chapter 2)? How were your attitudes affected by your encounters (either directly or through the media) with the terrorist attacks on America of September 11, 2001, or with some other major death-related event(s)?

2. This chapter described in some detail two specific sets or patterns of attitudes regarding death: those of the present-day Amish and those of the Puritans in 17th century New England. Note similarities and differences in these sets of attitudes. How did or do the attitudes of these two groups affect their encounters with death, dying, and bereavement?

3. Think about the four categories of death-related concerns and responses described in this chapter: attitudes about your own dying, your death, what will happen to you after death, and the dying, death, or bereavement of someone you love. Which of these categories is most important to you at this point in your life? What in particular is happening in your life that leads you to select this specific category of death-related attitudes as most significant? What are your chief concerns within this category?

4. Philippe Ariès described five dominant patterns of attitudes toward death found in Western societies. Which of the five patterns seems most familiar to you? Which aspects of each of the five patterns can you find in your own experience?

Suggested Readings

For depictions of various attitudes toward death in America, as well as in Western art, literature, and popular culture, see:

Bertman, S. L. (1991). *Facing Death: Images, Insights, and Interventions.*

Crissman, J. K. (1994). *Death and Dying in Central Appalachia: Changing Attitudes and Practices.*

Enright, D. J. (Ed.). (1983). *The Oxford Book of Death.*

Farrell, J. J. (1980). *Inventing the American Way of Death: 1830–1920.*

Geddes, G. E. (1981). *Welcome Joy: Death in Puritan New England.*

Hostetler, J. A. (1994). *Amish Society* (4th ed.).

Isenberg, N., & Burstein, A. (Eds.). (2003). *Mortal Remains: Death in Early America.*

Jackson, C. O. (Ed.). (1977). *Passing: The Vision of Death in America.*

Kraybill, D. M. (2001). *The Riddle of Amish Culture* (2nd ed.).

Mack, A. (Ed.). (1974). *Death in American Experience.*

Shachtman, T. (2006). *Rumspringa: To Be or Not to Be Amish.*

Siegel, M. (Ed.). (1997). *The Last Word: The New York Times Book of Obituaries and Farewells—A Celebration of Unusual Lives.*

Stannard, D. E. (1977). *The Puritan Way of Death: A Study in Religion, Culture, and Social Change.*

Weir, R. F. (Ed.). (1980). *Death in Literature.*

Zielinski, J. M. (1993). *The Amish across America* (rev. ed.).

Selected Web Resources

Some useful search terms include: ARS MORIENDI; DEATH ANXIETY; DEATH AT-TITUDES (OR DEATH-RELATED ATTITUDES); DEATH DENIAL; FORBIDDEN DEATH; PORNOGRAPHY OF DEATH; TAME DEATH

Visit the book companion website for *Death & Dying, Life & Living, Sixth Edition,* at academic.cengage.com/psychology/corr for all URLs and live links to the following *organizational and other Internet sites:*

American Anthropological Association

American Psychological Association

American Sociological Association

BELIEVE: Religious Information Source website (multiple topics)

Death Clock

Death Studies **(published by Taylor & Francis)**

Illness, Crisis & Loss **(published by Baywood Publishing Co., Inc.)**

Mortality **(published by Taylor & Francis, Ltd.)**

Omega, Journal of Death and Dying **(published by Baywood Publishing Co., Inc.)**

Pennsylvania Dutch Country Welcome Center (PaDutch.com)

CHAPTER 4

Death-Related Practices and the American Death System

© Robert Galbraith/Reuters/Corbis

Objectives of This Chapter

◆ To identify death-related *practices* as a component of death-related *experiences*

◆ To explain the concept of a "death system" in any society, including its elements and functions

◆ To describe selected examples of death-related practices in the United States:

   1. Human-induced death associated with accidents, homicide, terrorism, war and genocide, the Holocaust, and the nuclear era

2. Death and language, as illustrated in contrasts between language about death and death-related language

3. Death as presented in the media, both in news reports (vicarious death experiences) and in entertainment (fantasized death and violence)

❧ September 11, 2001

September 11, 2001, was a clear, fall day on the East Coast of the United States of America. It was also a day that was to be filled with horror, large-scale death and injury, and massive destruction of property.

On that Tuesday morning, many people went to work at the 110-story towers of the World Trade Center in New York City and at the Pentagon in Arlington, Virginia. About the same time, crews and passengers boarded commercial airliners in Boston, suburban Washington, D.C., and Newark for flights to California.

Shortly after takeoff, hijackers commandeered four commercial airliners, each with a full load of fuel for a transcontinental flight. The hijackers took over these flights, removed their pilots, and diverted the planes to their own ends. At 8:45 A.M., one plane was flown directly into the north tower of the World Trade Center about 20 stories below the top of the building. Eighteen minutes later, a second plane crashed into the south tower in a similar way. Shortly thereafter, about 9:30 A.M., a third plane crashed into the southwest side of the Pentagon. On the fourth plane, some of the passengers joined together to resist the terrorists, fought with them, and prevented them from carrying out their intended plans (to crash into the White House or the Capitol in Washington, D.C., or perhaps Camp David in Maryland). As a result of that struggle, this last plane crashed in western Pennsylvania, southeast of Pittsburgh, shortly after 10:00 A.M. (Kashurba, 2006; Morgan, 2006).

About 10:00 A.M., the south tower of the World Trade Center collapsed as a result of the structural damage that it had suffered from being hit by the airliner and especially from the intensity of the subsequent fire fed by jet fuel. Approximately 29 minutes later, the north tower also collapsed. Later, four other buildings in the World Trade Center complex and a nearby Marriott hotel also collapsed.

Some 248 passengers and crewmembers aboard the four airliners (including 19 terrorists) died in these events, along with 126 killed at the Pentagon. Approximately 2,800 people died at the scene of the World Trade Center disaster, including workers at the offices, shops, and restaurants in the complex, visitors, and more than 340 firefighters and police officers who rushed into the buildings or set up nearby command posts in their efforts to save lives and help out. In New York City many bodies were consumed by the fires or buried under massive rubble that was only gradually removed from the scene. Some bodies were identified through DNA testing; many other families were never able recover the bodies of their loved ones.

❧ The Death System in Every Society

In this chapter, we turn to *death-related practices* as the third key element in our general portrait of *experiences with death in our society.* Our goal is to supplement what we have already learned about *death-related encounters* in Chapter 2 and *death-related attitudes* in Chapter 3, and to show how encounters and attitudes affect practices. To do this we began with an encounter with death that could hardly have been imagined before it took place and that has drastically affected American attitudes and practices: the events of September 11, 2001. Of course, there are a bewildering variety of death-related practices in the United States, too many to explore adequately in a single chapter. We also cannot fully separate practices from encounters and attitudes. One way to organize and provide context for the death-related practices selected for discussion in this chapter is to consider them in terms of the concept of a "death system."

Kastenbaum (1972, p. 310) defined a death system as the "sociophysical network by which we mediate and express our relationship to mortality." He meant that every society works out, more or less formally and explicitly, a system that it interposes between death and its citizens, one that interprets the former to the latter. The presence of such systems—which are easily recognizable by most members of a society when attention is drawn to them—reflects the existence and importance of social infrastructures and processes of socialization in human interactions with death, dying, and bereavement (Fulton & Bendiksen, 1994; Parsons, 1951; Seale, 1998). According to Kastenbaum (1972), each societal death system has its own constitutive elements and characteristic functions (see Focus On 4.1).

Some type of death system is found *in every society.* It may be formal, explicit, and widely acknowledged in some of its aspects, even while it is largely hidden and often unspoken in other aspects. As Blauner (1966) has shown, many small, primitive, tribal societies must organize many of their activities around death's recurrent presence. In large, modern, impersonal societies such as in the developed countries of North America and Western Europe, the social implications of death are often less disruptive, less prominent, and more contained—at least until shocking events such as natural disasters highlight them (see Issues for Critical Reflection #3).

As it actually operates, the death system in contemporary American society appears to act in many important ways to keep death at a distance from the mainstream

Death practices are always embedded within specific cultural contexts.

Elements and Functions of a Societal Death System

Elements of a death system include:

◆ *People*—individuals whose social roles are more or less directly related to death, such as life insurance agents, medical examiners and coroners, funeral directors, lawyers, and florists
◆ *Places*—specific locations that have a death-related character, such as cemeteries, funeral homes, health care institutions, and the "hallowed ground" of a battlefield or disaster
◆ *Times*—occasions that are associated with death, such as Memorial Day, Good Friday, or the anniversary of a specific person's death
◆ *Objects*—things linked to death, such as death certificates, hearses, obituaries and death notices in newspapers, weapons, tombstones, and a hangman's gallows or electric chair
◆ *Symbols*—objects and actions that signify death, such as a black armband, a skull and crossbones, certain organ music, and certain words or phrases ("Ashes to ashes, dust to dust . . .")

Functions of a death system are:

◆ *To give warnings and predictions,* as in sirens or flashing lights on emergency vehicles or media alerts concerning the likelihood of violent weather, an earthquake, or a terrorist act
◆ *To prevent death,* as in the presence of police or security officers, systems of emergency medical care, or the Department of Homeland Security in the federal government
◆ *To care for the dying,* as in modern hospice programs and some aspects of hospital services
◆ *To dispose of the dead,* as in the work of the funeral industry, along with cemeteries and crematories
◆ *To work toward social consolidation after death,* as in funeral rituals or self-help groups for the bereaved
◆ *To help make sense of death,* as in the case of many religious or philosophical systems
◆ *To bring about socially sanctioned killing* of either humans or animals, as in training for war, capital punishment, and the slaughtering of livestock for food

Source: Based on Kastenbaum, 1972.

of life and to gloss over many of its harsh aspects. That is, our death system often acts to support death denial. The problem with this is that we may have "created systems which protect us in the aggregate from facing up to the very things that as individuals we most need to know" (Evans, 1971, p. 83). However, other aspects of our death system draw attention to death and respond to its appearances. For example, note the

Natural disasters take many forms. Hurricanes, tornadoes, earthquakes, floods, wildfires, blizzards, and other natural disasters can present major challenges to societal death systems. One of the worst natural disasters in the United States in recent years took place on August 29, 2005. On that day, Hurricane Katrina came ashore just east of New Orleans with hurricane-force winds extending for 120 miles.

Portions of the American death system functioned extremely well. For example, the National Hurricane Center provided advance warnings of the storm's likely track, and Coast Guard helicopters rescued many people stranded by flood waters in New Orleans and elsewhere. However, the overall responses by local, state, and federal officials were severely criticized for mismanagement and lack of leadership. In any event, this monster storm caused over 1,800 deaths (with some bodies still remaining unidentified as this is written) and over $80 billion dollars worth of damage, making it the costliest Atlantic hurricane in history.

Eight months earlier, a disaster with even larger impact took place outside the United States on December 26, 2004, when an earthquake occurred off the northwest coast of the Indonesian island of Sumatra. This earthquake created a tsunami that first hit the shores in Indonesia and Thailand near the epicenter of the earthquake. The tsunami then traveled across the Indian Ocean and eventually came ashore in countries thousands of miles away, including Sri Lanka and India. It has been estimated that this tsunami caused more than 185,000 deaths and left more than 42,000 missing among both native peoples and visitors. The impact of this deadliest tsunami in recorded history, along with its concomitant widespread destruction, while it would overwhelm the death system of any society, proved particularly challenging in the mostly poor and remote areas of the world where it did the greatest damage.

There was no early warning system in the Indian Ocean that might have alerted authorities in affected countries and perhaps have allowed them to mobilize their populations to prevent death on this massive scale by escaping from beachfront and low-lying areas. Such a system is available in the Atlantic and Pacific Oceans and would have been a key element of a regional death system in the area. In the circumstances, governments, nongovernmental organizations, and individuals from many countries could only mobilize to create an improvised *"worldwide* death system" to cope with the consequences of a disaster of this extraordinary magnitude.

Postage stamps have been used to draw public attention to life-threatening illnesses.

Reacting to Hurricane Katrina's devastating destruction.

© Ross Taylor/Getty Images

concern for a leading cause of death expressed by the U.S. Postal System in the design of the stamps reproduced on page 66.

The key point here is that every society has some system for coping with the fundamental challenges that death presents to human existence. Thus, it is helpful to the study of death, dying, and bereavement to examine the nature of a society's death system and the ways in which it functions.

❦ The American Death System and the Events of September 11, 2001

The September 11, 2001, attack occurred within the continental United States and struck at some of the most prominent symbols of American economic and military power in the form of the World Trade Center towers and the Pentagon (The Editors of *New York* Magazine, 2001). Like terrorist attacks throughout the world with which many people have had to learn to cope and to live with for a long time, this one killed and injured innocent men, women, and children. Included were individuals of many ethnic backgrounds, cultures, races, and religions, as well as citizens from more than 80 countries around the world, as diverse as Australia, Bangladesh, Germany, Great Britain, India, Israel, Mexico, Pakistan, and South Korea (Bumiller, 2001; *St. Petersburg Times,* 2001c). The attack also raised homicidal terrorism to a new level within the United States, exceeding in its scope other terrorist incidents affecting Americans at home or abroad.

On September 11, many Americans seemed surprised that terrorists would or could attack the United States directly. In fact, for some time knowledgeable observers had expected some type of terrorist action on American soil. Unfortunately, elements of the American death system did not provide specific *warnings and predictions* that might have prevented any or all of these events. For example, it would have been important to know that some suspicious individuals had gained entry into the United States, that some of them were taking flying lessons (but not expressing interest in takeoff and landing procedures), and that some terrorist circles had been expressing interest in using commercial airliners as weapons. For many reasons, this very important function of sounding warnings, making specific predictions, communicating information effectively, and acting on that information to protect the country was not successful. Many failures of intelligence and coordination have been identified in the report of the National Commission on Terrorist Attacks (2004; see also Kean & Hamilton, 2006) and are detailed by former Senator Bob Graham (2004) as a result of his work as co-chair of the House/Senate Joint Inquiry into Intelligence Community Activities Before and After the Terrorist Attacks of September 11, 2001.

Still, on September 11 itself other elements of American society and its death system did almost immediately spring into action. Some passengers on one of the planes joined together to try to overcome their hijackers and frustrate the goals of the terrorists (see Beamer, 2002). Others used cell phones to try to warn outsiders about what was happening. Still others who could do so left messages for a loved one on an answering machine like the one that Brian Sweeney, a 38-year-old passenger on United Airlines flight 175 that crashed into the World Trade Center's south tower, left for his wife, Julie:

> Hey, Jules, it's Brian. I'm on a plane and it's hijacked and it doesn't look good. I just wanted to let you know that I love you and I hope to see you again. If I don't, please have fun in life and live your life the best you can. Know that I love you and no matter what, I'll see you again. (*St. Petersburg Times*, 2001b)

Our death system was evident in its more formal aspects when many firefighters, police officers, and others rushed to the scenes of the tragedy and ran into burning buildings in an attempt to *prevent death* and save lives—only to lose their own lives when the buildings collapsed. In addition, the Federal Aviation Administration immediately grounded all airplanes in the United States to forestall a further attack from the air and to make it difficult for co-conspirators to leave the country. The FBI began to scrutinize selected telephone conversations for congratulatory calls, sought out material witnesses and others who might have been involved in this terrorist conspiracy, and began to trace the sources of funding that it required. Hospitals and rescue workers prepared to *care for the injured and the dying,* while pathologists and funeral directors set out to *dispose of the dead* in appropriate ways by removing bodies from the scene, identifying them, and preparing them for disposition. Unfortunately, disposing of the dead was a very long and difficult process that ultimately was only partly successful in recovering and identifying the dead (Kastenbaum, 2004b).

In the days after September 11, there was powerful support for *social consolidation,* along with long-drawn-out stress and uneven government response. Mayor Rudy Giuliani of New York and other political and religious leaders moved to extend and coordinate many of these efforts. Individuals and communities faced significant challenges in trying to *help make sense of death* in these circumstances. Many Americans came together in memorial services and around rallying symbols, such as the phrase "United We Stand" or the song "God Bless America." Counselors advised how adults should speak to children about these events, and President George W. Bush spoke to the nation and to the world about American perceptions of these events as an attack not only on the United States but also on the civilized world. The Congress approved a new cabinet-level Department of Homeland Security.

Finally, as Kastenbaum (2004b) has noted, there was a quick shift from perceiving ourselves as victims of killing to outraged warriors. The president mobilized American military power and the international political community in an attempt to root out and bring to justice those who were behind the conspiracy that culminated on September 11. These events also led to some *socially sanctioned killing*—for instance, through the U.S. invasion of Afghanistan and the overthrow of its Taliban leaders because they supported al-Qaida. Subsequently, the U.S. also mounted an invasion of Iraq as a result of the belief—which has since been questioned (e.g., Mueller, 2006a, 2006b)—that the then-leader of that country, Saddam Hussein, was a supporter of Islamist terrorism and a threat to the world.

The September 11 attack resulted in many challenges to personal safety and security for Americans at home and abroad. These challenges did not completely overwhelm the American death system, but they did impact it significantly. Above all, these events mobilized American society in many ways and at many different levels—local, state, national, and international. In 2004 the National Commission on Terrorist Attacks issued a report describing systemic deficiencies that contributed to the September 11 attack and offering recommendations to improve our intelligence and homeland security operations. After much debate, legislation was passed by the Congress and signed by the president to create a cabinet-level post of director of national intelligence and to implement many of the National Commission's recommendations.

🐾 Human-Induced Death

During the 20th century, American society witnessed an enormous increase in the numbers of deaths that human beings visited upon themselves and others. In part, this is the result of an increase in the number of people who are alive. A population explosion such as the last century witnessed inevitably results in more deaths no matter what else happens. However, it may also lead to more tension and stress that may increase interpersonal violence in response. In many instances, such violence results in premature death. In this section, we examine *human-induced deaths* associated with accidents, homicide, terrorism, war and genocide, the Holocaust, and the nuclear era. (Other examples of human-induced death, such as suicide, assisted suicide, and euthanasia, will be examined in Chapters 17 and 18.)

Accidents

Accidents or *unintentional injuries* are the fifth leading cause of death in the United States for the population as a whole, and the leading cause of death among all persons aged 1 to 44 (Miniño et al., 2007; National Safety Council, 2007). In 2004, 112,012 Americans died in accidents, representing approximately 4.7 percent of all deaths that year. If one assumes that each accidental death affects an average of just ten survivors, over 1 million persons were affected by such deaths in the United States in 2004. The death rate for accidents in the United States in 2004 was 38.1 per 100,000. In addition, 9 million people suffered disabling injuries. Among the fatalities, 44,933 of the deaths, or just over 40 percent, involved motor vehicles. (Compare this large number of deaths with the 848 combat deaths in Iraq in the same year. This latter number of deaths was a legitimate matter of concern to many Americans; yet the much larger number of deaths from automobile accidents every year seems to have little impact on American attitudes.)

Death rates for accidents declined by more than one-quarter during the period 1979–1992, but those rates have been gradually increasing ever since. The decline seems to have resulted from educational efforts that have urged Americans to become more safety conscious in their driving practices—for example, by driving more carefully, wearing seatbelts, and not driving after consuming alcoholic beverages. Along with this new awareness, accidents have moved from the fourth to the fifth leading cause of death in our society, largely as a result of shifts in the relative importance of other causes of death. In recent years, increases in numbers of accidental deaths in our society appear to be related to an expanding population and an upsurge in fast-paced, stress-filled lifestyles in our highly developed technological society.

The National Safety Council (NSC) reviews all forms of accidental injuries and deaths, along with many other types of human-induced injuries and deaths in its annual report, *Injury Facts* (2007). The NSC also offers on its Web site (http://www.nsc.org/lrs/statinfo/odds.htm) a chart reviewing the odds of dying from such causes in the most current year for which data are available or over one's lifetime. (For a diagrammatic version of the NSC chart [based on 2003 data], see Anonymous, 2006b.)

Mothers Against Drunk Driving (MADD) sponsors billboards to draw attention to injuries and deaths from motor vehicle accidents.

Motor vehicle accidents are among the most significant causes of deaths in our society, affecting members of every societal subgroup—males and females, young and old, Caucasian Americans and African Americans, Hispanic Americans, Asian and Pacific Island Americans, and American Indians. Within these larger populations, the behaviors of some more specific groups of people increase their susceptibility to this form of death. For example, individuals 15 to 24 years of age consistently have the highest death rates from motor vehicle accidents (26.3 deaths per 100,000 in 2004; see Miniño et al., 2007), and mortality rates from vehicular accidents remain historically much higher for males than for females.

These deaths contrast with some basic assumptions about mortality patterns in contemporary society. For example, in automobile accidents it is adolescents and young adults who are most likely to die, not the elderly. Also, these deaths are most often sudden, unexpected, and violent. Frequently, the person killed is badly disfigured in the accident, perhaps even burned. The scenario may go like this: a knock on the door (or a telephone call) by a police officer leads to the announcement that someone is dead (Iserson & Iserson, 1999). Disbelief and denial may follow: "He (or she) had just driven to a movie! How could death have intervened?" If the body is disfigured, survivors may never see it again. If not, and if the person is delivered to a hospital for stabilization, then attempts at emergency intervention or determination of death—sometimes followed by requests to authorize organ, tissue, or eye donation—may pose unexpected challenges to shocked family members. An air of unreality may pervade the experience. Grief and mourning following such a death are often complicated.

Homicide

Homicide (now termed "assault" in the new international system of classifying and coding causes of death) is an act by one human being that is intended to or actually does kill another human being. In the United States in 2004, there were 17,357 homicide deaths with an overall death rate of 5.9 per 100,000 (Miniñeo et al., 2007). The good news is that homicide has declined from 11th leading cause of death for the population as a whole in 1990 to only 15th in 2004, largely as a result of shifts in the relative importance of other causes of death. The bad news is that numbers of deaths from homicide have been trending gradually upward since the late 1980s (with a sharp spike in 2001 resulting from deaths associated with the September 11 attack on America). To this, one can add that numbers and rates of homicide death in the United States are extraordinarily high for a developed society in the 21st century. In fact, contemporary American society has the dubious distinction of leading the industrial West in both the number and rates of homicide (Seltzer, 1994).

The distribution of homicide deaths varies widely across the population. Perhaps the most disturbing features of the demography of homicide are its prominence as a cause of death among the young and among males. (See Chapter 5 for comments on homicide in selected racial and cultural groups.) For at least the last decade, the highest rates of homicide deaths have been found among Americans who are 15 to 24 years old (12.2 deaths per 100,000, followed directly by those 25 to 34 years of age (11.2 deaths per 100,000). In 15- to 24-year-olds, homicide is currently the second leading cause of death (exceeded only by accidents and followed by suicide). After young adulthood, homicide as a leading cause of death generally declines with increasing age.

In terms of gender, males in the United States are far more likely than females to be both the perpetrators and the victims of homicide. Homicide is especially prominent as a cause of death among males in American society, with approximately 3.6 male deaths from homicide to each female death from the same cause in recent years. Homicide is also a leading cause of death among African Americans who die from this cause at a ratio of nearly 1.5 to 1 when compared with Caucasian Americans (nearly 1.9 to 1 if only males in these two groups are compared). Furthermore, more than 72 percent of all homicide deaths in the United States involve individuals between the ages of 15 and 44.

Two features that stand out in any analysis of American homicide deaths can lead to better understanding of this subject. First, approximately 50 percent of all homicides occur between family members or acquaintances (Seltzer, 1994). A corollary of this is that in 90 percent of all homicides the victims and the assailants are of the same race. A second prominent feature of homicide in our society is that it is heavily correlated with the use (or misuse) of firearms.

What we learn from the data on homicide is that it is a significant component—even though it has been declining in overall importance—in American behaviors and encounters with death. Increasingly, homicide is the cause of deaths in groups that have not typically been thought of as vulnerable to death—notably adolescents and young adults. In addition, some homicide deaths appear utterly capricious and therefore meaningless, as when a stray bullet from a drive-by shooting or carjacking strikes someone uninvolved in that activity. All of these factors help to explain why homicide intrudes in a forceful way on many contemporary Americans' thinking about death.

Nevertheless, in a sense homicidal behavior is overplayed in its significance in discussions of death in the American death system. For example, the popular media have tended to seize on and give disproportionate attention to selected examples of violence and homicide, such as those involving school shootings. Thus, most Americans are familiar with the shootings at Columbine High School in Littleton, Colorado, in April 1999, and at Virginia Tech University in Blacksburg, Virginia, in April 2007, that combined both mass murder and educational contexts. While much is known about these incidents, there is much yet to learn about them and much to do to minimize their likelihood (Lazenby et al., 2007; Newman, 2004; see also Issues for Critical Reflection #4 in this chapter and Issues for Critical Reflection #18 in Chapter 19).

One point to keep in mind about homicides in schools is that they are very atypical experiences. As Fox and Levin (2006, p. 131) have observed, "Despite the school violence hype and panic, schools actually are the safest place for our kids to be." In fact, the annual report from the U.S. Departments of Education and Justice, *Indicators of School Crime and Safety: 2003* (DeVoe et al., 2003, p. v), stated that, "In each school year from 1992 to 2002, youth ages 5–19 were at least 70 times more likely to be murdered away from school than at school." A similar report for 2004 (DeVoe et al., 2004) made essentially the same point. We may have a distorted picture of school violence in general and homicide in particular because, as one commentator (Twomey, 2001, p. 14A) noted, "the news media report crime, particularly violent crime, far out of proportion to its actual occurrence."

The basic facts to keep in mind about homicide in the American death system are that since 1992 it has been declining in relative importance as a leading cause of

Although rare, several mass murders occurring in educational institutions that appear to most Americans to be safe environments have taken place in the United States during the last half century. For example, on August 1, 1966, Charles Whitman, a student at the University of Texas at Austin, climbed up a 27-story tower on campus and used a rifle to kill 14 people and wound 31 others before being shot dead by police.

A second example involving adolescent killers occurred at Columbine High School in Littleton, Colorado, on April 20, 1999. Two students there, Eric Harris and Dylan Klebold, used multiple weapons to kill 12 students, one teacher, and themselves, while also wounding a number of others.

In a third example, the largest mass killing in U.S. history occurred on April 16, 2007, when a disgruntled student, Cho Seung-Hui, killed 32 people and himself, while also wounding many others on the campus of Virginia Tech University in Blacksburg, Virginia.

Fox (2007; see also Fox & Levin, 2005, 2006) observed that, "Seven of the eight largest mass shootings in modern U.S. history have occurred in the last 25 years." He also pointed out that these shootings are a subset of mass murders. Fox defined mass murders as events "in which four or more people are killed in the same episode," to distinguish them from serial killings which occur over time.

Fox suggested that several changes in our society may have contributed to the rise of these tragic events.

- We are a more mobile and rootless society, often living in locations where we have no friends or extended family to fall back on.

- More of us live in urban areas where we may not even know our nearest neighbors.
- Many of us have lost access to once-familiar features of traditional communities, such as stable marriages or partnerships, extended families, and religious institutions, that might previously have provided support and acted as moderating influences on our behavior.
- We are an open, democratic society, vulnerable in many ways, while at the same time we stress individual rights, aggressive competition, and immediate gratification, with little compassion for those who do not succeed (however that is to be defined).
- More of us have easier access to firearms, especially to powerful, semiautomatic weapons, along with knowledge and training in how to use them.

Fox also described typical characteristics of the (mainly male) perpetrators of these mass shootings as including the following:

- They often have a long history of frustration and failure, and a diminished ability to cope with life's disappointments.
- They externalize blame, frequently complaining that others didn't give them a chance or are not fairly treating their ethnic, racial, or gender group.
- They commonly lack emotional support from friends or family and are often described as "loners."
- They generally suffer a precipitating event or major disappointment they view as catastrophic.
- They have access to weapons that are powerful enough to satisfy their need for revenge.

death in the overall American population, but that a significant number of homicide deaths still do occur in our society. Homicide is far too often a cause of death in the United States for its present levels to be regarded as acceptable. Americans must strive to prevent or minimize instances of homicidal violence in our society. To do so, we need to set aside erroneous and misleading perceptions of homicide in the United States and come to understand this important death-related phenomenon and its causes in accurate, factual terms.

Beyond the fact that some instances of homicidal violence are particularly shocking and traumatic, nearly all homicides result in sudden and unexpected death with only a short transition from the act of violence to the death. Consequently, this type of death presents special problems for survivors: they are faced with an unexpected death in circumstances that might be unclear, traumatic, and often involve some social stigma. Even if the agent is identified, this may not help. In fact, it may further complicate the grief of survivors when the agent is a family member, friend, or peer, and when the homicide has been deliberately perpetrated on innocent people. Also, legal proceedings against the agent may be complex, and families of victims are often deliberately shut out of or kept at a distance from such proceedings. A sense of outrage, fed by impressions of injustice and lack of control, may complicate their mourning (Bucholz, 2002; Magee, 1983).

Terrorism

Terrorism is a difficult subject to address. Although some have argued that identifying what will be called terrorism depends to some extent on one's point of view (Martin, 2003; Player, Skipper, & Lambert, 2002), others have asserted that "terrorism simply means deliberately and violently targeting civilians for political purposes" (Richardson, 2006, p. 4). According to Richardson, terrorists seek three things: *revenge* for perceived or actual hurts to themselves or to some community with which they identify and to redress a perceived sense of humiliation; *renown* in the form of publicity, attention, and glory for the individual and the cause, a kind of notoriety that is essentially conferred on them by their community and their adversaries; and *reaction*, which might involve surrender or widespread repression by their opponents since either demonstrates their strength and communicates their message.

In any event, terrorism plays a large role in many people's thinking when they reflect on contemporary encounters with death, dying, and bereavement. This is not an entirely new phenomenon, to be sure. The term *terrorism* can be traced back at least to the French Revolution (Anonymous, 2002), but acts that might be called terrorist ones can be found even in the ancient world. What has changed recently is the frequency and magnitude of terrorist acts. Before the Industrial Revolution and its concomitant scientific and technological creations, no single act could destroy thousands of lives and millions of dollars worth of property in a few seconds. Although there is already a large body of literature on this subject (e.g., Benjamin & Simon, 2002; Carr, 2002; Jenkins, 2003; Laqueur, 2003; Lewis, 2003), this is still a new death-related reality with which people in the 21st century will have to deal for the foreseeable future. We will explore terrorism here by reflecting on its perpetrators and their goals, the means used, and the implications for death, dying, and bereavement.

Perpetrators of Terrorism and Their Goals Three broad categories of terrorism can be identified by distinguishing between terrorist acts carried out by individuals, groups, or states. In examples of *individual terrorism,* one person characteristically engages in an act that harms or kills others and destroys property, often acting as a lone agent or perhaps with the support of one or two other individuals. Frequently, this is done to express anger or frustration with those who are targeted or in an effort to mobilize the larger society to rectify some perceived wrong or to act in some other desired way. For example, Timothy McVeigh, with the help of Terry Nichols, bombed the Alfred P. Murrah Federal Building in Oklahoma City on April 19, 1995, killing 169 people and injuring more than 500 others (Linenthal, 2001; Michel & Herbeck, 2001). Similarly, the so-called Beltway Snipers (John Allen Muhammad and Lee Boyd Malvo) terrorized the Washington, D.C., area for three weeks in October of 2002, killing ten people and injuring three others. Individual terrorism of this type (along with group terrorism) is most often the tactic of an agent who perceives himself or herself to be weaker than her or his opponent.

Group terrorism is practiced when a formally or informally organized group of people attempts to do harm for religious, political, or ideological reasons to those whom it perceives as its opponents. Well-known examples of this behavior have been seen in the actions of radical Catholic and Protestant factions in Northern Ireland, Palestinian organizations in the Middle East, and Chechen separatists or their sympathizers who seized a theater in Moscow in October 2002 and who took control of a school in southern Russia in September of 2004. Group terrorism has become a frequent occurrence in Iraq since the overthrow of the Hussein regime in 2004. Since then, various factions have targeted both foreign and Iraqi people, both military and civilians, with violence, using techniques such as roadside bombs, sniper, mortar, or grenade attacks, and kidnappings. Efforts like these can have many different goals, for example, to force outsiders to leave the country, to overthrow what is perceived as a puppet regime, to lay claim to political power, or to try to set up a separate state.

State-supported terrorism is a strategy most often employed by a political administration against its own or a neighboring population. Terrorism of this type may be explicitly undertaken or only tacitly supported by a government. This sort of terrorism is generally employed by a stronger side against a weaker group in an effort to coerce them into certain behaviors or to remove them from the society, by either forced emigration or extermination. For example, Saddam Hussein employed terrorist tactics (in the form of poison gas) against some Kurdish communities in Iraq in 1988, and the Nazis in Germany in the late 1930s and early 1940s acted to eliminate many groups of persons they blamed for various problems or believed to be hostile to their goals. More recently, in 1994 the Rwandan government called on everyone in its Hutu majority population to murder everyone in the Tutsi minority (Gourevitch, 1998).

Means Employed by Terrorists Terrorists employ a wide variety of violent means, which may or may not put the terrorists themselves at risk. For example, Timothy McVeigh, engaged in a form of terrorism that involved *acting at a distance.* He used a truck bomb that did not require his actual presence at the scene of the action when the harmful event occurred and did not put him directly at risk of harm. More recently in Iraq, roadside bombs ("improvised explosive devices" or IEDs, as they are called) and hit-and-run attacks using mortars or rocket-propelled grenades are similar *acts-at-a-distance.* Americans and American interests have been frequently

© Pedro Armestre/AFP/Getty Images

Sudden and horrendous losses produced by terrorist acts can occur anywhere, anytime.

and for some time the victim of this type of terrorism: for example, car bombs that detonated outside American embassies in Kenya and Tanzania within minutes of each other in 1989; a bomb in a parking garage beneath the World Trade Center on February 26, 1993; a car bomb at a U.S. military headquarters in Riyadh, Saudi Arabia, in 1995; and a truck bomb that exploded outside the Khobar Towers barracks in Dharan, Saudi Arabia, in 1996. These acts together killed over 200 people and wounded thousands more, many—but not all—of whom were Americans.

By contrast, some terrorist acts require *the direct presence of the perpetrator.* These include the behavior of snipers or kidnappings with the typical aim of achieving some political (rather than merely economic) goal. These acts frequently are planned to allow for the possibility of escape from immediate retribution, even though they may put the life of the individual terrorist at risk.

In addition, individuals and groups have engaged in acts of *terrorism through self-destruction* in which the death and devastation they seek to cause is achieved through the sacrifice of the terrorists' own lives (Gambetta, 2006). Best known in examples of *suicide bombings,* this has been a familiar form of terrorism in Israel over many years. It was the tactic used in 2000 when an American destroyer, the *USS Cole,* was

Members of the global Salafi jihad were generally middle-class, educated young men from caring and religious families, who grew up with strong positive values of religion, spirituality, and concern for their communities. . . . The Core Arabs, who grew up in core Arab lands, came from a communal society and belonged to one of the most communal of all religions. They were isolated when they moved away from their families and friends and became particularly lonely and emotionally alienated in this new individualistic environment. The lack of spiritualism in a utilitarian culture was keenly felt. Underemployed and discriminated against by the local society, they felt a personal sense of grievance and humiliation. They sought a cause that would give them emotional relief, social community, spiritual comfort, and cause for self-sacrifice. Although they did not start out particularly religious, there was a shift in their devotion before they joined the global jihad, which gave them both a cause and comrades.

. . . Their education was modern . . . and they were not "brainwashed" into fanaticism through a madrassa education. Most became more devout before joining the jihad. Contrary to most writing on terrorists, the large majority of the individuals examined were married and most had children. Yet they were willing to sacrifice themselves for the cause. . . .

Most were from very well-to-do backgrounds and led lives more consistent with rising expectations than relative deprivation. The Core Arabs were so well-off that their families sent them to study abroad, where their radicalization began. In their host countries, they were alienated, underemployed, and perhaps discriminated against, and therefore in a situation of relative deprivation. . . .

Just before they joined the jihad, the prospective mujahedin were socially and spiritually alienated and probably in some form of distress. They would not have been the best candidates to form a tightly cohesive group, whose members were willing to perform the ultimate sacrifice in the name of what the group stood for. Yet, this is exactly what happened. (Sageman, 2004, pp. 96–98)

Suicide terrorists are *not* primarily from religious cults whose members are uneducated, isolated from society, and easily brainwashed into pursuing delusional aspirations. Nor are suicide terrorists mainly from criminal gangs whose members are motivated by youthful impulsiveness, personal satisfaction in harming others, or the antisocial habits of a life of crime. Nor are suicide terrorists drawn from the ranks of the mentally ill, individuals so depressed that they cannot hold a job, enjoy life, or otherwise lead productive lives and thus seek to die as an end in itself.

In general, suicide attackers are rarely socially isolated, clinically insane, or economically destitute individuals, but are most often educated, socially integrated, and highly capable people who could be expected to have a good future. The profile of a suicide terrorist resembles that of a politically conscious individual who might join a grassroots movement more than it does the stereotypical murderer, religious cult member, or everyday suicide. (Pape, 2005, p. 200)

Most of the prospective al-Qaeda recruits were from the middle or upper class, nearly all of them from intact families. They were largely college-educated, with a strong bias toward the natural sciences and engineering.

(continued)

Few of them were products of religious schools; indeed, many had trained in Europe or the United States and spoke as many as five or six languages. They did not show signs of mental disorders. Many were not even very religious when they joined the jihad. (Wright, 2006, p. 301)

The popular claims that suicide terrorists are desperate or crazy are not consistent with any of the research on the subject. Suicide terrorists do not act alone; they are selected, trained, supervised, and encouraged by a group. Moreover, those who do the selecting from among the many volunteers competing for the honor consistently argue that they do their best to ensure that those who are selected are psychologically sound. . . . The truth is that suicide terrorists are not crazy in any meaningful sense of the word." (Richardson, 2006, p. 117)

attacked in Yemen by a small boat loaded with explosives. It was the approach employed on September 11, 2001, when hijackers flew three commercial airliners into buildings (see Issues for Critical Reflection #5). And finally, in Iraq acts of terrorism carried out by radical Islamists through suicide bombing have become familiar in recent years.

Implications of Terrorism for Death, Dying, and Bereavement Acts of terrorism most often employ violent means that result in traumatic losses (for more on this subject, see Chapter 9). Typically, they bring about sudden death, injuries that may lead to subsequent death or disability, and damage (often localized, sometimes widespread) to property. Death, disability, and destruction may be primarily aimed at official representatives of the perceived opponent but often are indiscriminate or heedless of harm visited on others. Deaths associated with terrorism are characteristically sudden, unexpected, violent, and represent a form of human behavior that often appears repugnant in its careless disregard of human life. A single act of terrorism may cause multiple deaths and mutilation, and may have directly threatened the lives of those who survive its effects. Bereavement and grief associated with such deaths is usually complicated. Individuals have little or no time to prepare for such deaths. Bodies may be destroyed, leaving survivors little or nothing to bury. Their grief is compounded by the knowledge that other human beings were the deliberate agents of these deaths. They agonize over why the terrorist act was not prevented or what could have been done to mitigate its consequences. They are grimly aware that the terrorists often acted with clear indifference both to those who would be harmed by their acts and to other innocent people who might become involved. Personal security and safety are challenged by such acts, as are common assumptions about life and the world. In addition, survivors may feel abandoned by a social system that often is unable to either find or prosecute the perpetrators.

War and Genocide

In recent years, *war and genocide* have led to *socially sanctioned death* involving large numbers of people both as perpetrators and as victims. To arrange for and bring about large numbers of deaths requires extensive and systematic organization, involving legal, economic, military, and political structures, sometimes along with educational and scientific research structures. For example, the Chinese have killed more than 1 million Tibetans since 1950 (Ingram, 1992), and repressive regimes have killed at least thousands and sometimes millions of citizens in countries like Cambodia (Kampuchea) and Myanmar (Burma). Similarly, certain regions of the Balkans have witnessed an "ethnic cleansing" that killed or dispossessed large numbers of people. The example of Rwanda in 1994 has already been noted. More recently, the Sudanese government has apparently been supporting an ongoing genocide conducted by Arab militias designed to kill an entire race of Black African citizens in the western Darfur region of the country. Best estimates are that since early 2003 over 400,000 people have been killed and more than 2 million displaced or made homeless despite the fact that all of the groups involved are Muslims (www.darfurgenocide.org; www.savedarfur.org).

The number of deaths arising from outright war and other violent conflicts is astonishing. For example, World War I (1914–1919) saw at least 9 million soldiers killed in combat or dead from combat injuries (Elliot, 1972), the Korean War (1950–1953) produced 1 million deaths among combatants, and it has been estimated that nearly 62 million people were killed by the Soviet regime in the 70 years after 1917 (Glover, 1999). In the Balkans during the 1990s, not only were many people killed, but rape, torture, and enslavement of men and women were used as systematic instruments of terror. Three Bosnian Serbs were found guilty by a

Terrorism and war play significant roles in contemporary death systems.

United Nations war crimes tribunal in February 2001 of crimes against humanity for such acts committed during 1992 and 1993 (*St. Petersburg Times*, 2001a). More recently, since coalition forces invaded Iraq in March 2003, by November 2007 nearly 3,900 American military personnel had died and well over 28,000 had been wounded, along with countless other casualties among Iraqis and citizens of other countries. Deaths and injuries like these affect both military personnel in Iraq and Afghanistan and family members at home (for two examples, see Henderson, 2005; Raddatz, 2007).

Numbers of people killed in wars often do not include civilian deaths, which are notoriously difficult to identify. Generals count dead combatants on both sides because that is important for them to know or at least to estimate accurately. The number of civilians killed (sometimes downplayed or dismissed as "collateral damage") is of lesser interest—unless, of course, one is among or somehow connected to those civilians. Also, figures on civilian deaths may even be hidden for a variety of reasons—for instance, to avoid evidence of war crimes.

Even if we could obtain accurate figures for deaths associated with war and genocide, how could we possibly make sense of them? How can we grasp the deaths of huge numbers of people, often in far-off locations? Many individuals have found the death of a single beloved person to be incomprehensible and unintelligible. How to make sense of the deaths of thousands or millions may well elude our imaginations (Elliot, 1972). An important danger here is that we may become accustomed or desensitized to the numbers of these sorts of deaths. They are so unimaginable that we may stop trying to comprehend them. But that may make us even more vulnerable to accepting them as tolerable.

The Holocaust

During World War II, what became under the Nazis a systematic program to eliminate whole classes of people from the face of the earth can still be regarded as unique for its scope and political or ideological basis (Bauer, 1982; Dawidowicz, 1975; Pawelczynska, 1979; Reitlinger, 1968). The Nazis slaughtered 6 million European Jews and millions of others during the late 1930s and early 1940s.

The Nazi program of genocide was fueled by a particular ideology (not only politics or economics or even military considerations). According to the Nazis' perverted philosophy, members of the Jewish "race"—along with whole categories of other people, such as gypsies, Jehovah's Witnesses, and homosexuals—were classified as *Untermensch* or subhuman. At first, this led to outbursts of anti-Semitism, loss of civil and human rights, relocation and ghettoization, and shipment to "concentration camps." Inhabitants in many of these camps soon became a slave labor force working on behalf of the German war effort, although this did not protect them from extremely harsh living and working conditions, inadequate rations, and brutal pressures of all sorts that led to large numbers of deaths. At the same time, random violence, terror, and crude forms of systematic killing were implemented both within and outside the camps in areas that fell under Nazi control. Ample and adequate documentation of these horrors is available from both firsthand witnesses (for example, Kulka, 1986; Langbein, 1994; Levi, 1986) and later historians (Gilbert, 1993).

In 1941, a decision was made to go further (Browning, 2004): the "final solution" was to eradicate the Jews from all areas within Nazi control. In search of efficiency, relatively crude methods of killing—bludgeoning, hanging, and shooting people to death; machine gunning and burying them in mass graves; and using engine exhaust gasses to suffocate those who were being transported in closed vans to locations where their bodies were burned or interred—were replaced by the infamous gas chambers and crematories of the "extermination camps" *(Vernichtungslager)*. The term itself is significant: one kills a human being, but one exterminates a less-than-human pest.

This final stage of *the Holocaust* occurred above all in occupied Poland, especially at a former military barracks on the edge of the city of Auschwitz (Oswiecim)—whose gate still today proclaims the infamous and cruelly ironic motto, "*Arbeit macht frei*" ("Work makes one free")—and its newly constructed satellite about two miles away in the countryside at Birkenau (Brzezinka). Here, in the words of the camp commander (Hoess, 1959, p. 160), was developed "the greatest human extermination center of all time." And here (but elsewhere also), cruel and hideous experiments were undertaken under the guise of medical research (Lifton, 1986; Michalczyk, 1994).

According to the most authoritative calculations, at Auschwitz/Birkenau alone "the number of victims was at least 1.1 million, about 90 percent of whom were Jews from almost every country in Europe," although with slightly different data and assumptions "the number of Jewish victims killed in the camp would rise to about 1.35 million, with the total number of Auschwitz victims reaching about 1.5 million" (Piper, 1994, pp. 62, 72). All of these deaths took place from the time when the first prisoners arrived (June 14, 1940)—and especially after September 1941, when the use of cyanide gas was first tested—until January 27, 1945, when the Soviet army

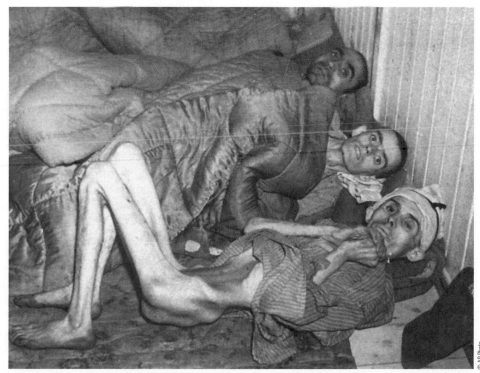

Prisoners at the liberation of a Nazi concentration camp.

liberated the camp and freed some 7,000 remaining prisoners. Toward the end, it is reported that some 80 percent of the people (mainly women, children, and the elderly) who arrived at Auschwitz/Birkenau in the daily transports (which tied up railroad equipment desperately needed by the German military for the war effort) went directly to their deaths from the notorious "selections" held at rail side as they arrived at the camp.

Nothing like this had been seen in the world previously. To visit Auschwitz many years after the Holocaust is to confront an enormous incongruity between what is in many ways an ordinary, even banal, setting, and innumerable images of horror that endure as a reminder of the dark side of human capacity (Corr, 1993b; Czarnecki, 1989). Perhaps that is why some writers (such as Czech, 1990; Gilbert, 1993) have employed the techniques of chronology and cartography to depict the horrors of the Holocaust in impersonal, dispassionate ways, whereas others (such as MacMillan, 1991; Wiesel, 1960) have used literary forms to convey in imaginative and evocative ways messages about the Holocaust that are not effectively transmitted in other forms. And there have been impressive accounts of what was involved in survival and resistance within the death camps of the Holocaust (Des Pres, 1976; Langbein, 1994).

The basic lesson for all to draw from these horrible events—like many fundamental morals—is simple: "We have the choice between the Holocaust as a warning and the Holocaust as a precedent" (Bauer, 1986, p. xvii). Although some have sought to deny the facts of the Holocaust (Lipstadt, 1993), its reality and implications continue to resonate within the North American death system (Novick, 1999). Consider just a few examples: the book *Schindler's List* (Keneally, 1982; see also Crowe, 2004) and Steven Spielberg's Oscar-winning movie (1993) of the same title; the dedication in 1993 of the U.S. Holocaust Memorial Museum in Washington, D.C. (tel. 202-488-2642; www.ushmm.org); the founding in 1994 of the Survivors of the Shoah Visual History Foundation in Los Angeles (tel. 818-777-7802; www.vhf.org); and the many institutions listed in the annual directory of the Association of Holocaust Organizations (Shulman, 2005).

It is important to note that the horrific numbers of state-sanctioned deaths discussed in this section were not limited to Nazi Germany's actions. Josef Stalin is estimated to have ordered the deaths of 10,000,000 kulaks in the 1930s, and Mao Ze Dong's orders are estimated to have led to the deaths of 30,000,000 Chinese during his "Great Leap Forward" in 1959–1961. These two national leaders' state-sanctioned civilian mass murders were largely due to "ideologically induced starvation" (Skidelsky, 2004, p. 18). When put alongside the German Holocaust, a picture emerges of the 20th century as having set precedents for mass murder that would have been unimaginable before then.

The Nuclear Era

From its outset, *the nuclear era* introduced a form of socially sanctioned death and an ongoing death-related threat for which there is no adequate historical precedent. Nuclear power was first unleashed on July 16, 1945, at the Trinity test site in New Mexico. It became a new force for death at Hiroshima on August 6, 1945, when an estimated 100,000 people died in a single flash of light and, again, 3 days later at Nagasaki, when 50,000 more died in the second atomic bombing. In both Japanese cities, mass death from the blast and heat of the bomb was joined for the first time to the lingering effects of radiation, secondary effects that are believed to have caused deaths equal in number to those killed outright.

What was unique at Hiroshima was the instantaneous quality of the first large-scale wave of deaths and the fact that they resulted from a single nuclear "device." Also distinctive were the lingering effects of radiation and the unparalleled destructive potential of nuclear weapons. The scope and character of this new way of encountering death have challenged the best efforts of reporters (such as Hersey, 1948; Lustig, 1977) and scholars (such as Lifton, 1964, 1967) to understand and articulate their implications. The use of nuclear power at Hiroshima and Nagasaki has also led to debates about the moral, political, and other aspects of using such weapons (such as Alperovitz, 1995; Lifton, 1982; Lifton & Mitchell, 1995; Maddox, 1995).

In both the Holocaust and Hiroshima, as well as in various terrorist assaults, women, children, and the elderly were killed as readily as men in the military. During World War II in particular, saturation bombing and other methods of waging war intentionally blurred the distinction between combatants and noncombatants (Grayling, 2006). These techniques were employed as much to destroy civilian morale as to damage specific military targets. At Hiroshima and Nagasaki, that strategy was carried further in such a way that life itself seemed to come under a threat against which there was no adequate defense.

Since 1945, the lethal potential of nuclear weapons has been magnified many times over, along with their accuracy and modes of delivery (Arkin & Fieldhouse, 1985). Death and destruction can now be brought down on humankind in a degree and form that is far beyond the wildest dreams—or nightmares—of human beings over nearly the whole of recorded history.

The level of tension associated with nuclear weapons declined somewhat with the dissolution of the Soviet Union in 1991 and subsequent efforts to destroy some warheads and their delivery systems. However, there are new worries that economic difficulties in Russia and elsewhere may lead to problems with remaining nuclear weapons. Furthermore, many are now concerned about nuclear threats from terrorist groups or rogue governments who might construct so-called "suitcase bombs" or crash planes into nuclear reactors (Allison, 2004). And since 2001, the international community has struggled with how to discourage nations (notably, North Korea and Iran) who seek to develop their own nuclear weapons from doing so. As a result, the University of Chicago's Bulletin of the Atomic Scientists' Doomsday Clock moved to five minutes until midnight on January 17, 2007, representing the closest the world has been to total destruction since 1990 (Anonymous, 2007b).

The nuclear era has also revealed another face as nuclear power has become a source of much needed energy supplies. Here, the initial appearance is benign and welcome; and in many ways it has remained so. However, accidents in nuclear reactors at Three Mile Island in Pennsylvania in 1979 (Walker, 2004) and at Chernobyl in Ukraine in 1986 have shown that even a peaceful source of nuclear energy can pose a real threat to humankind. Explosion, fire, and local irradiation, however lethal they may be to the surrounding territory, are nothing compared to the airborne radiation and long-term contamination of land, water, food supplies, and people of the type that followed the 1986 events at Chernobyl. (The last reactor at Chernobyl was finally shut down as an active power plant in 2000.)

How are these dangers associated with nuclear weaponry and nuclear power to be kept in check? How should they be balanced against legitimate needs for self-defense and sources of energy to sustain quality in living? More broadly, what does it mean to live under the nuclear shadow? For some, it seems the subject does not bear thinking about; they simply put it out of their minds through techniques of dissociation and denial. For others, the power of the threat and the difficulty of doing anything about it diminish their joy in living and their sense of promise for the future. For all, it is a new and unprecedented dimension of death-related experiences in the early years of the 21st century.

Looking back, Lifton and Mitchell (1995, p. xi) wrote, "You cannot understand the twentieth century without Hiroshima." We would say that death-related experiences in the 20th century cannot be understood without considering the various forms of human-induced death examined in this section. In particular, terrorism, war and genocide, the Holocaust, and the beginning of the nuclear era must be taken into account. All of these involve mass death. Terrorism, war, and genocide most often have to do with ideological, religious, and political conflict. The Holocaust resulted from a perverted ideology, and the nuclear era reflected a new technology. In each case, the results have involved what Leviton (1991a, 1991b) called "horrendous death," a transformation in both the quantity and the quality of human encounters with death that remains momentous and without parallel even now in the 21st century. Kastenbaum (2004b) described this as "death writ large" and suggested that it calls for a "*macrothanatology*," which he defined as "the story of deaths (a) that occur on a large scale, and/or (b) through complex and multidomain processes that are difficult to place within a simple cause-and-effect frame" (p. 376).

Death and Language

One way in which a society and its death system try to control and influence how death is experienced is evident in language patterns and practices. Both *language about death* and *death-related language*—which may seem to point to the same thing, but are in fact quite distinct—reflect strong social messages concerning appropriate emotions and behaviors regarding death.

Language about Death

In the contemporary American death system (and in the death systems of some other societies as well), many people often go to great lengths to avoid saying words like *dead* and *dying*. In place of this direct language, individuals commonly employ *euphemisms*—that is, they substitute a word or expression with comparatively pleasant or inoffensive associations for language that they view as harsher or more offensive, even though the latter ways of speaking might more precisely designate what is intended. Thus, people don't die; they merely "pass away." In principle, euphemisms are pleasing ways of speaking; in practice, they usually involve underlying attitudes that seek to "prettify" language to make it appear more delicate, "nice," or socially acceptable and to avoid seeming disagreeable, impolite, or nasty. Using euphemisms is not necessarily undesirable in itself, but it can become so when it is excessive or when it reflects an unwillingness to confront the realities of life and death directly. A brief survey of "sympathy cards" ("She's not dead, she's just sleeping") can illustrate this point.

Euphemisms that relate to death are familiar to most users and students of language (Neaman & Silver, 1983; Rawson, 1981). They arise in many contexts. Long before recent interest in "thanatology" (itself a euphemism for death-related studies), these figures of speech were recognized by scholars (for example, Pound, 1936). Terms like "kicked the bucket" (originally, a graphic description of one way of committing suicide by hanging) or "bought the farm" are euphemistic descriptions of death. The "dearly departed" have been "called home," "laid to rest," or "gone to their reward." Much the same is true for those who "conk out," who are "cut down," or whose "number is up." Anyone who is "on his last legs" has "run the good race," "is down for the long count," and "it's curtains." The precise status of those who are "no longer with us" is not quite clear.

Professional caregivers sometimes say that they "lost" a patient or that the individual "expired." Such language always has some original foundation. One has lost the company of a spouse or friend who has died; the spirit or last breath has gone out of the person who expired. But those who use such expressions today are usually not thinking of such linguistic justifications. They are most often simply unwilling to speak directly. Hence, the hyperbole of bureaucratic health care, which twists death into the contortions of "negative patient care outcome," or the ways in which counterespionage agencies talk about "terminating with extreme prejudice" instead of speaking about killing.

The change in labels from "undertaker" (a word that the *Oxford English Dictionary* traces back to 1698 in England) to "mortician" (a term originating in America in 1895 with roots in the Latin word *mors* or death) to "funeral director" or "funeral services practitioner" reflects both a euphemistic tendency and a broadened vocational scope.

Language may be more effective as a vehicle for accurate communication when people speak directly in ways that are neither excessively camouflaged nor brutal. Consider the state to which our society has come in trying to express in ordinary language what veterinarians do to very sick or infirm pets. Among many people to whom we speak, such animals are not simply "killed" or "euthanized." Rather, they are "put to sleep." What does that convey to young children—who may then be urged to stop asking annoying questions and take a nap? It is very challenging to try to express the same point in some other way in colloquial but effective English. Some say that animals are "put out of their misery" or "put down." Does that help explain things?

Euphemisms are not solely linked to death. On the contrary, they are ways to stand back from or cover over all sorts of taboo topics. Consider, for example, common expressions for genital organs or excretory functions. Both the New England Puritans of the 17th century and adherents of the Romantic Movement in the United States during the 19th century firmly censored talk about sexuality even as they readily spoke of death (usually for moral or religious purposes). In the 21st century, it often seems that people have simply inverted these attitudes and practices so as to be tongue-tied about death but all too unrestrained in talking about sex.

Direct speech and candor are not always desirable. Frankness can be admirable or out of place; the same is true for avoidance. Both overemphasis and underemphasis, whether on sexuality or on death, are equally unbalanced postures. Both distort and demean central realities of life. Still, as Neaman and Silver (1983, pp. 144–145) noted some time ago, contemporary American society is special:

> At no other time in history has a culture created a more elaborate system of words and customs to disguise death so pleasantly that it seems a consummation devoutly to be wished. . . .
>
> The motives for euphemizing death are in many ways similar to those for disguising our references to pregnancy and birth. Great superstition surrounded these events, as did great distaste and a sense of social impropriety. Propelled by these feelings, we have attempted to strip death of both its sting and its pride—in fact to kill death by robbing it of its direct and threatening name. The terms change and the euphemisms grow, but the evasion of the word "death" survives.

Linguistic attempts to avoid talking about death are more than detours around the unpleasant. Euphemisms become problematic whenever they are not held in check or counterbalanced by personal experience. Most euphemisms originated in a rich soil of experiential contact with death. As death-related encounters have become increasingly less frequent and more limited in much of American society (see Chapter 2), these essential roots of language have dried up. The problem with an overabundance of euphemisms in recent American talk about death is that they reveal and themselves contribute to a kind of distancing or dissociation from important and fundamental events of life itself.

Death-Related Language

One might conclude from the preceding that death-related language is simply absent from most ordinary speech. Such a conclusion would be "dead wrong." In talk about actual events pertaining to death and dying, it is quite common for language about death to be avoided. But in a curious and paradoxical reversal, *death-related language* is frequently employed in talk about events that have nothing to do with actual death and dying (see, for example, Partridge, 1966; Wentworth & Flexner, 1967; Weseen, 1934).

Most people in contemporary American society speak quite openly about dead batteries, dead letters, a deadpan expression, a dead giveaway, deadlines, and being dead drunk. Everyone knows people who are dead tired, dead on their feet, dead certain, a deadbeat or dead broke, deadly dull, deadlocked, dead to the world in sleep, or scared to death. Marksmen who hit the target dead center have a dead eye or are dead shots. Gamblers recognize a "dead man's hand" (aces and eights, all black cards; the hand that Wild Bill Hickok was holding when he was shot dead), while truckers "deadhead" back home with an empty vehicle. Parents may be "worried to death" about children who "will be the death" of them. Those who are embarrassed may "wish they were dead" or that they "could just die." Orville Kelly (1977, p. 186), a man with a life-threatening illness, reported encountering a friend who said, "I'm just dying to see you again."

Similarly, in today's society when one has nothing else to do one may be said to be killing time. There is quite a difference between a lady-killer who is dressed "fit to kill" and a killjoy. And most contemporary Americans know what it means to "die on base," "flog a dead horse," or "kill the lights." To "kill a bottle of whiskey" leaves us with a "dead soldier." To be "dead as a doornail" is to be as hammered into insensitivity as was the nail head driven into the center of doors against which knockers were once struck before doorbells came into prominence. Good comedians "slay" their audiences, who "die of laughter"; poor comedians "die on their feet."

In these and many, many other similar phrases, death-related language emphasizes and exaggerates what is said. To be dead right is to be very right, completely or absolutely right, the most right one can be. Death-related language dramatizes or intensifies a word or phrase that might have seemed too weak on its own to convey the intended meaning or depth of feeling. It trades on the ultimacy and finality of death to heighten in the manner of the superlative.

Placing this familiar use of death-related language alongside common euphemisms teaches interesting lessons about linguistic practices in the contemporary American death system. Death language is frequently avoided when Americans speak of death itself, but it is often employed (sometimes with enthusiasm) when they are not speaking directly about death. In fact, language is powerful; naming can influence the reality we experience. Perhaps that is why death-related language is easily employed in "relatively safe situations" that have nothing to do with death itself, but just the reverse is the case when one uses euphemisms that seek to soften death or allude to it obliquely.

🎃 Death and the Media

The media play an important role in the contemporary American death system, as is evident in news reports and entertainment programs. As we saw in Chapter 2, many Americans have limited personal experience with natural human death. However, most people in the United States have experienced in a vicarious or secondhand way thousands of violent or traumatic deaths. One estimate is that "by the time the average child graduates from elementary school, she or he will have witnessed at least 8,000 murders and more than 100,000 other assorted acts of violence. Depending on the amount of television viewed, our youngsters could see more than 200,000 violent acts before they hit the schools and streets of our nation as teenagers" (Huston et al., 1992, pp. 53–54). These vicarious experiences come to us through news and entertainment services provided by newspapers and magazines or on the radio, but it is television and other electronic media that appear to be most influential.

Vicarious Death Experiences: News Reports in the Media

On September 11, 2001, and in the days immediately following, television was perhaps at its best in informing the American public about a horrific, death-related event. It had hard news to report and graphic images to share. However, that was a high point that is not always typical of the media in general or television in particular. For example, human-induced deaths are pervasive on televised evening news reports as in scenes of death and destruction from the ongoing conflict in Iraq or from natural disasters like the Asian tsunami in late December 2004. In these and other media reports, homicide, accidents, war, and other forms of traumatic death and violence are staple "newsworthy" events. Hence the slogan, "If it bleeds, it leads" (Kerbel, 2000).

In fact, routine televised accounts of violence and war often generate a kind of psychological immunity in the general public to the impact of death. Experiencing violent death in these vicarious ways often does not seem to have the same impact as being there in person. Watching someone being shot to death on a smaller-than-life-size television screen is quite different from direct participation in the event.

These media deaths are distant or remote for most people, and death itself may remain outside our actual experience despite frequent vicarious encounters with its surrogates.

A flip side of this issue arises when government and the media actually hide some deaths from view. As part of an official policy, the remains of persons killed in the war in Iraq and Afghanistan have been forbidden to be shown arriving back in the United States. This attempt to hide war deaths from the public by limiting what the media can show can lead to a failure to grasp the full reality of those military actions. (A counterexample is the practice in which the "News Hour with Jim Lehrer" on PBS shows pictures of service members when their deaths are made official and pictures become available.)

One reason for the remote or distanced quality of these newsworthy events is that they are *a highly selective portrait of death and life* in today's society and around the world. Anything "newsworthy" is by definition out of the ordinary. We know this and can recognize the truth in the words of one expert commentator (Krugman, 2001, p. 16A) who observed that "the media, and especially news channels that have to keep people watching all day, thrive on hype." As a result, the news media are preoccupied with the deaths of special persons or with special sorts of death. They depict death in a selective, distorted, and sensationalized way to individuals in a society that has less and less contact with natural human death. Ordinary people who die in ordinary ways are not newsworthy; they are tucked away in death announcements on the back pages of a newspaper or silently omitted from the television news. Television in particular is heavily focused on stories that can be accompanied by dramatic visual images.

One exception to the rules of newsworthiness are the brief notices that report the fact of an individual's death, names of survivors, and plans (if any) for funeral or burial services (Johnson, 2006). Typically, these *death announcements* (sometimes called *obituaries*) appear in small type (a source of complaint among some elderly or visually impaired readers), in alphabetized columns, near the classified advertisement section in newspapers. This location is not surprising, since death announcements are essentially public notices often paid for by survivors and usually arranged through funeral directors. Like the classified ads, which they resemble, death announcements record ordinary events of everyday life. They differ greatly from the news stories that the media run without charge to mark the deaths of prominent persons.

The selectivity implicit in what is thought to be newsworthy carries with it a curious kind of reassurance. It encourages people to comfort themselves with thoughts like these: because I am not a very special person and because I do not expect to die in any very special way, I can distance myself from the staple fare of death in newspapers and on television, and thus from unpleasant associations with death.

The specialized and highly selective drama of death in media news reports is abstract and insubstantial; it lacks the definite shape, feelings, texture, and concreteness of one's own life. Having been shocked by so many out-of-the-ordinary, newsworthy events, people often become thick-skinned, passive spectators, hardened against the personal import of death. It becomes just one more among many distant and unusual phenomena paraded before us in a regular, unending, and not always very interesting series.

Moreover, the unusual modes of death reported so selectively in the media may themselves come to be seen as ordinary or typical. For example, extensive and highly dramatized coverage of tragic school shootings in our society has led many to believe death is common in our high schools when, in fact, schools are among the safest places for children in America (DeVoe et al., 2003, 2004). By contrast with these dreadful events in which a small number of deaths have been blown out of proportion, one's own death—which is not perceived as anything like these second-hand events—may come to appear less likely and less proximate.

Fantasized Death and Violence: Entertainment in the Media

The distortion of death in news reports is compounded in many entertainment programs in the media. Death and violence are ever present in American entertainment media—on television and in movies, video games, and music lyrics (Wass, 2003). But this is typically a very unrealistic presence. Think of cowboy, war, or gangster movies, police or military shows and science fiction fantasies on television, battles with alien invaders in video games, and the language of much "gangsta rap."

What is most remarkable about the typical portrayal of death in these media is that it is usually very unrealistic or *fantasized*. Those who die are unimportant people or "bad guys." Heroes and heroines repeatedly survive extreme peril, whereas actors die one week only to reappear unharmed the next. Violent fantasies of a very graphic nature are acted out—but suffering, grief, and other consequences of this violence and death are mostly noticeable for their absence. Murders take place, but audiences are chiefly interested in whether their perpetrator can be identified. Killings occur, but they usually satisfy a sense of poetic justice, and their consequences are not of much interest. The realities of death, dying, and bereavement are rarely apparent. Thus, as a result of their research on American film, Schultz and Huet (2000, p. 137) concluded: "In American film, death is distorted into a sensational stream of violent attacks by males, with fear, injury, further aggression, and the absence of normal grief reactions as the most common responses."

A committee of the American Academy of Pediatrics (AAP, 1995) studied this matter and related research. It concluded that "American media are the most violent in the world, and American society is now paying a high price in terms of real-life violence" (p. 949). Some reject a cause-effect link between media violence and violence in real life, but the AAP has noted that a majority of researchers in the field (for example, Comstock & Paik, 1991; Eron, 1993; Strasburger, 1993) are convinced that such a link has been firmly established. Thus, the AAP (1995, p. 949) concluded that "although media violence is not the only cause of violence in American society, it is the single most easily remediable contributing factor."

Children's cartoons on television also illustrate this very special vision of death, although they may often be more benign than many of the examples just cited. These cartoons validate our point by simplifying the complexities of other entertainment forms. Since it is assumed that attention spans in an audience of children are short and distraction is always likely, the plot must be gripping and it must continually reassert its hold over viewers (Minow & LaMay, 1995). Thus, television cartoons frequently emphasize lively action, as in cats chasing mice or dogs chasing cats, which may improperly reinforce a perception in some children that death is temporary.

In the well-known *Road Runner* cartoon series, Wile E. Coyote relentlessly pursues the flightless bird only to be caught over and over again in his own traps. He is repeatedly the apparent victim of horrible death experiences, but he usually enjoys an instant resurrection and in the end he always survives. In other words, *he never dies; he just keeps getting killed.* Destruction is followed so rapidly by delight, joy, and renewed activity that there is no time for grief. The cartoon is about the ongoing action of an endless chase. It is not really about death, although inevitably it communicates many messages about that subject.

In the latter part of the 20th century, death became an even more vivid presence in adult entertainment. Earlier, no one ever bled when shot or stabbed in a movie. Fistfights erupted in saloons, six-guns blazed away, actors staggered against walls and crumpled in death—but all the while their clothes were clean and their hats usually remained firmly on their heads. By contrast, the movie *Saving Private Ryan* (1988) was widely praised as an accurate portrait of the real horrors of war because it showed lost limbs and ghastly wounds. Of course, shock and horror in the media are often excessive. Graphic representations of blood, gore, and crashing automobiles are now standard fare in much that passes for contemporary entertainment. So much artificial blood and apparent mayhem can make today's movie and television viewers jaded. It is no longer easy to surprise or impress them, or even to catch and hold their attention.

More recently, many video games designed for children and adults have traded on various forms of violence and death involving fantasy figures or replicas of real human beings to capture the interest of their audiences. Late in 2004, a new video game that could be downloaded from the Internet (for a suitable fee) even allowed the player to assume the role of Lee Harvey Oswald in the act of assassinating President John F. Kennedy! President Kennedy's brother, Senator Edward Kennedy, is reported to have described this video as "despicable." It is certainly an extraordinary example of its genre, but not at all unique in contributing to a widespread desensitization to the realities of violence and death (see Personal Insights 4.1). Again, death has been distorted through a process of selectivity and fantasization.

Clearly, selectivity is unavoidable in reporting the news or telling a story, and fantasy is neither unhealthy nor undesirable in itself. The games, songs, and fairy tales of childhood have long been full of fantasy and death, and children have coped without major difficulty. Two factors have been central: (1) the way in which the violence and death—and their real-life consequences—are (or are not) presented and (2) a firm grasp by the audience on the essential distinction between fantasy and reality.

The problem in our society is a looser grip on the realities of life and death, coupled with increasing violence and gore. Selectivity, distortion, and fantasy become dangerous in media depictions of death when they substitute for or supplant a balanced appreciation of life.

Electronic Representations of Violence and Death

Nothing is more common in the postmodern world than the replication of the violence of interactive video games and Internet images. In a world of semblances, people die by violence but their deaths are and are not understood as real. Violence is envisaged as simultaneously actualizing and derealizing death. If all is semblance, a game, death's finality is fictive, undecidable. . . . When school children kill their teachers and classmates we are convinced that they have been overcome by the images in which they are immersed, that they reenact the virtual murders they witness hour after hour on video and TV monitors. How real for them is the difference between pulling a trigger on a gun and clicking a mouse? They learn afterward—in the flesh, so to speak, and always too late—that these dead and wounded bodies are not only images, that the images are surfaces of vulnerable flesh.

Source: Wyschogrod and Caputo, 1998, p. 303.

🍎 Summary

In this chapter, we focused on selected examples of death-related practices in the United States and throughout the world in order to complement our discussions of death-related encounters and attitudes in Chapters 2 and 3. We introduced the concept of a societal "death system" and the example of the terrorist attacks in the United States on September 11, 2001, to show how the American death system mobilized itself in response to a particularly difficult challenge. We then examined a series of examples that showed the contemporary American death system in operation. For instance, we offered an account of various forms of human-induced deaths, including deaths associated with accidents, homicide, terrorism, war and genocide, the Holocaust, and the nuclear era. Throughout, we indicated how these events changed human encounters with death and have had important ongoing implications up to the present time. Next, we considered American linguistic practices, noting that many individuals use euphemistic language to avoid talking about death as such, even as they use death-related language to discuss topics that are not at all related to death. Finally, we identified highly selective and fantasized portraits of death and violence in the media (in both news reports and entertainment).

These death-related practices, along with many others that we explore throughout this book, demonstrate that it is not correct to conclude as some (such as Gorer, 1965a; Kübler-Ross, 1969) have done that ours is merely a "death-denying society," one from which death has largely been exiled as a social or public presence. The evidence presented in this chapter suggests that it is more defensible to argue (as do Dumont & Foss, 1972; Weisman, 1972) that death-related practices in the United States are neither simply death denying nor death accepting. These practices and the American death system express both types of attitudes—sometimes separately, sometimes simultaneously—along with other attitudes as well.

Glossary

Accidents: unintentional injuries

Death-related language: speech that employs language about death to describe or intensify talk about subjects that have nothing to do with death

Death-related practices: familiar routines, procedures, and actions that follow from or are related to death-related encounters and actions

Death system: the formal or informal structure that every society employs to mediate between death and its members; composed of specific elements designed to perform particular functions

Euphemism: language that substitutes a word or expression that is thought to be less distasteful or offensive for one more exactly descriptive of what is intended

Fantasized death: unrealistic portraits of death (in the media)

Genocide: the annihilation or attempted annihilation of an entire race of people

The Holocaust: the attempt by the Nazis during the late 1930s and early 1940s to completely destroy or annihilate the Jewish people

Homicide: the action of one human being that kills another human being

Human-induced death: death resulting from the actions or inactions of human beings

Language about death: speech about topics like death, dying, and bereavement

The nuclear era: the period from July 1945 to the present during which the splitting of the atom unleashed a new form of power that can be used for weapons or as a source of energy

Socially sanctioned killing and/or death: societal actions that are intended to bring about killing and/or death among their own members or among members of other societies, for example, war or genocide

Terrorism: the use of extreme violence to kill, coerce, or intimidate others

Questions for Review and Discussion

1. This chapter described selected examples of death-related practices in the United States in recent years. On a theoretical level, how do death-related *practices* join with death-related *encounters* and *attitudes* to make up a mosaic of death-related *experiences* in our society? Are our descriptions of death-related practices in our society representative of your experiences within that society?

2. This chapter introduced the concept of a *death system* and its five elements: people, places, times, objects, and symbols. Think about the death system you live within. What elements (that is, what people, places, and so on) of this system have you encountered?

3. In the 20th century, violence has become an ever-larger factor in encounters with death. What role (if any) have accidents, homicide, or terrorism played in your encounters with death? Think about a specific example of an accidental death, a homicide, or a terrorist assault. How, if at all, did that event affect your attitudes and behaviors?

4. Can you think of additional examples of pertinent speech patterns as you read or discussed the sections on language about death and death-related language in this chapter?

Suggested Readings

On terrorism and violence, consult:

Allison, G. (2004). *Nuclear Terrorism: The Ultimate Preventable Catastrophe.*
Combs, C. C., & Slann, M. (2002). *Encyclopedia of Terrorism.*
Kushner, H. W. (2002). *Encyclopedia of Terrorism.*
Martin, G. (2003). *Understanding Terrorism: Challenges, Perspectives, and Issues.*
National Commission on Terrorist Attacks. (2004). *The 9/11 Commission Report: Final Report of the National Commission on Terrorist Attacks upon the United States.*
Stevenson, R. G., & Cox, G. R. (Eds.). (2007). *Perspectives on Violence and Violent Death.*

Among the many historical, biographical, and literary accounts related to the Holocaust, see:

Bauer, Y. (1982). *A History of the Holocaust.*
Czarnecki, J. P. (1989). *Last Traces: The Lost Art of Auschwitz.*
Czech, D. (1990). *Auschwitz Chronicle, 1939–1945.*
Dawidowicz, L. S. (1975). *The War against the Jews 1933–1945.*
Gutman, I., & Berenbaum, M. (Eds.). (1994). *Anatomy of the Auschwitz Death Camp.*
Pawelczynska, A. (1979). *Values and Violence in Auschwitz: A Sociological Analysis.*
Reitlinger, G. (1968). *The Final Solution: The Attempt to Exterminate the Jews of Europe 1939–1945* (2nd rev. ed.).
Wiesel, E. (1960). *Night.*

On the beginning of the nuclear era and some of its implications, see:

Arkin, W., & Fieldhouse, R. (1985). *Nuclear Battlefields.*
Hersey, J. (1948). *Hiroshima.*
Lifton, R. J. (1967). *Death in Life: Survivors of Hiroshima.*
Lifton, R. J. (1979). *The Broken Connection.*

For euphemisms and death-related language, consult:

Neaman, J. S., & Silver, C. G. (1983). *Kind Words: A Thesaurus of Euphemisms.*

Selected Web Resources

Some useful search terms include: ACCIDENTS; DEATH PRACTICES (OR DEATH-RELATED PRACTICES); DEATH-RELATED LANGUAGE; DEATH SYSTEM; EUPHEMISMS; FANTASIZED DEATH; GENOCIDE; THE HOLOCAUST; LANGUAGE ABOUT DEATH; THE MEDIA AND DEATH; THE NUCLEAR ERA (ALSO CHERNOBYL, HIROSHIMA, NAGASAKI, THREE MILE ISLAND); SOCIALLY SANCTIONED DEATH; TERRORISM

Visit the book companion website for *Death & Dying, Life & Living, Sixth Edition,* at academic.cengage.com/psychology/corr for all URLs and live links to the following *organizational and other Internet sites:*

Association of Holocaust Organizations

Concerns of Police Survivors (COPS)

Federal Bureau of Investigation, Uniform Crime Reports

Mothers Against Drunk Driving (MADD)

National Organization for Victim Assistance (NOVA)

National Organization of Parents of Murdered Children, Inc. (POMC)

Survivors of the Shoah Visual History Foundation

Tragedy Assistance Program for Survivors (TAPS)

U.S. Department of Homeland Security

U.S. Holocaust Memorial Museum (Washington, D.C.)

CHAPTER 5

Cultural Differences and Death

© Kathy McLaughlin/The Image Works

Objectives of This Chapter

In Chapters 2 through 4 we have given a broad account of experiences with death, dying, and bereavement—describing death-related encounters, attitudes, and practices, along with prominent features of the contemporary death system in the United States. This account has uncovered the general background shared by all individuals in American society (Corr & Corr, 2003a). Everyone living in the United States today is compelled, to one extent or another, to interact with our society's death system. For example, some official designated by the larger society must declare a person to be dead—no matter who that person may be.

But this story is incomplete. In fact, the United States is not a single, homogeneous entity with only one death system and one universal set of death-related encounters, attitudes, and practices. On the contrary, our society embraces within its boundaries a kaleidoscope of cultural, social, racial, ethnic, and religious groupings, each of which may display important differences in some aspects of its death-related experiences. This chapter addresses some of these differences as we pursue the following objectives:

◆ To demonstrate how *cultural differences affect death-related experiences*

- To describe some specific patterns of death-related *encounters* in four selected cultural groups in the United States: Hispanic Americans, African Americans, Americans who trace their backgrounds to Asian countries or the Pacific Islands, and American Indians and Native Alaskans

- To explore some death-related *attitudes* within these four groups
- To illustrate some death-related *practices* within these four groups

❦ A Happy Funeral

A charming picture book for young readers entitled *The Happy Funeral* (Bunting, 1982) describes two young Chinese-American sisters who are preparing to take part in their grandfather's funeral. When their mother first tells May-May and Laura about their grandfather's death, she says that he is going to have a happy funeral. The girls are puzzled by that concept. "It's like saying a sad party. Or hot snow. It doesn't make sense" (p. 1).

May-May and Laura are perplexed, and they are unclear about many of the events that follow. Although they loved their grandfather and are clearly expected to be participants in this community event, the girls have not had much experience with death and funerals. They are insiders to the community, but outsiders in many ways to what is about to happen. Above all, they do not expect to be happy at their grandfather's funeral.

At the funeral home, bunches of flowers are everywhere and incense sticks burn in front of Grandfather's casket. There are many gifts for Grandfather's "journey to the other side," such as a map of the spirit world, some food, and half a comb (Grandmother keeps the other half, to be rejoined when she is reunited with her husband after her own death). A cardboard house, play money, and pictures of various objects (for example, a drawing of Chang, the big black dog that Grandfather had when he was a boy, and a picture of a red car with a silver stripe of the kind that Grandfather never was able to have in this life) are burned, with the idea that they will become real when they turn into smoke and rise to the spirit world.

At the funeral service in the Chinese Gospel Church, there are more flowers and a big photograph of Grandfather framed in roses. The adults talk about Grandfather's fine qualities and the many good things that he did. Some of the adults cry and Laura feels a big lump in her throat when she realizes how tiny Grandmother is and that she is even older than Grandfather. After the ceremony, a woman gives a small candy to each of the mourners "to sweeten your sorrow" (p. 22). Then Grandfather's casket is put in a glass-sided car, and his photograph is propped on the roof of one of the two flower cars. With a marching band playing spirited music, the cars parade throughout the streets of Chinatown.

At the cemetery, Grandfather's casket is placed on a wooden table next to a big hole in the ground. The minister says that Grandfather is going to his spiritual reward, but Laura tries to think of him flying the wonderful kites that he used to make. During all of these events, Laura alternates between warm memories and feelings of sadness, between smiles and tears. Eventually, she realizes that although she and May-May were not happy to have their grandfather die, his funeral really was a happy one because he was ready for his death and he left a good legacy through his well-lived life and everyone's fond memories of him. Mom "never said it was happy for us to have him go" (p. 38).

❦ The Significance for Our Topic of Studying Cultural Differences

As we noted in the introduction to this chapter, thus far we have discussed American society as if it were a single culture. To demonstrate the limits of that view, think about the term *culture*. Thomas (2001, p. 40) suggested the following definition: "Culture is a unified set of values, ideas, beliefs, and standards of behavior shared by a group of people; it is the way a person accepts, orders, interprets, and understands experiences throughout the life course." This definition should help us realize that, in fact, America is a society made up of *many cultures.* As a result, members of American society do not all approach events in their lives from exactly the same cultural stance. In this chapter, therefore, we study minority cultural groups within American society in order to help us:

◆ Appreciate the diversity *within American society and between American cultures*

◆ *From that appreciation,* develop a richer understanding of persons *whose encounters, attitudes, and practices may differ from those of persons in the dominant culture*

◆ Learn more about ourselves *by comparing and contrasting our experiences with those described in this chapter*

One result of achieving a better understanding and appreciation of ourselves and others within American society is to put us in a position to provide more sensitive and appropriate care (as professionals, volunteers, or fellow human beings) to those who are coping with dying, death, and bereavement. This last point about caring for each other is particularly important. One way to demonstrate the tie between our study of various minority cultures and our provision of care is to reflect on what Thomas (2001, p. 42) wrote in the following passage: "Communication about end-of-life issues is the key to understanding and making rational decisions." Anything that gets in the way of good communication can impede both rational decision making and, in turn, the provision of good care (Mazanec & Tyler, 2003; Ward, 2003). One such impediment is the assumption that all human beings—or for that matter that even all Americans—operate out of the same culture.

Following the structure of Chapters 2–4 in this book and the way in which U.S. government sources identify and organize statistical data, we describe in this chapter encounters with death, attitudes toward death, and death-related practices in *four prominent American cultural groups:* Hispanic Americans, African Americans, Asian and Pacific Island Americans, and American Indians and Native Alaskans. We have chosen to focus on these particular groups because individuals from these groups are those whom readers are most likely to meet. (Those who might wish to go beyond these limits can do so by drawing on the Suggested Readings at the end of this chapter.) In general, descriptions of *encounters* with death within these minority

People of different backgrounds and cultures may turn to each other for support in coping with death-related issues.

The Hospice of the Florida Suncoast

groups are the most reliable because they draw on demographic data gathered by the National Center for Health Statistics. By contrast, careful research on death-related *attitudes* and *practices* typically depends on a sampling of some members of a specific group. Such studies usually warn that the population sample is limited in size or makeup and thus does not support broad generalizations about the group as a whole. Our report of such studies is essentially a series of snapshots of attitudes and practices within these groups. There is much room for you, as a reader of this book, to supplement this chapter (see Issues for Critical Reflection #6).

Throughout this chapter, we note that none of the cultures that we study here is itself monolithic or homogeneous. As a result, when specific populations are studied, the persons participating in the study may not be representative of the whole minority culture; often, they are mostly representative of some subgroup within the minority culture. Thus, among Americans of Hispanic/Latino origin, there are Puerto Ricans, Mexican Americans, Cuban Americans, and persons with backgrounds from Central and South American countries. That these are quite different cultures may be obvious; that they are not homogeneous can be demonstrated by the debate among persons from these cultures as to whether and for whom terms like *Hispanic, Latino,* and *Chicano* are the best descriptors. (We recognize that some members of this broad group prefer one descriptor over the others, but we feel obliged throughout this chapter to follow the ways in which the National Center for Health Statistics categorizes subgroups in the U.S. population.) In addition, among African Americans, there are American-born, Caribbean-born, and African-born persons (Rodgers, 2004). Also, Asian Americans may trace their ancestries to very different societies, including China, Japan, Kampuchea (Cambodia), Korea, Thailand, and Vietnam, or to the Pacific Islands (e.g., Hawaii and Samoa). Finally, among American Indians (sometimes called Native Americans, or as in Canada, "First Nation Peoples"), there are hundreds of distinct groupings (e.g., Navajo, Zuni, Dakota, Seminole, and Crow); individual American Indians can trace their ancestral homes to nearly every part of the North American continent. It is both naïve and prejudicial to think of these many subgroups within our four primary ones as essentially interchangeable or wholly like the others within the primary group.

Thus the reader should keep in mind *the need to avoid the danger of stereotypes.* Everyone discussed in this chapter is simultaneously an American, a member of some particular cultural group (or subgroup), and an individual person. No one of them in his or her death-related experiences is completely identical to any other individual—even to other members of his or her own cultural group, because like all human beings, each is a *unique individual.*

❦ Hispanic Americans

According to projections by the U.S. Census Bureau (2005) based on the 2000 census, in 2004 Hispanics were the largest minority group in the United States, consisting of just over 41.3 million persons, or 14.1 percent of the total population (see Table 5.1). This is an increase of just under 84.4 percent from the 1990 census count of 22.4 million Hispanic Americans (Guzman, 2001). However, this needs careful qualification. Population counts in the 2000 census describe the resident population of the 50 United States. Residents of the Commonwealth of Puerto Rico and the U.S. Island Areas (the U.S. Virgin Islands, Guam, American Samoa, and the Commonwealth of the Northern Mariana Islands) are counted separately and are not included in totals given in Table 5.1. These U.S. resident figures for 2000 reflected very important real changes (mainly increases) in the population, as well as significant alterations in the census process. Real changes in the Hispanic-American population during the 1990s resulted from high immigration (especially among people of Mexican origin) and high birth rates. Alterations in the census process involved census coverage and the census questionnaire itself (for example, the new questionnaire asked, "Is this person Spanish/Hispanic/Latino?"). Perhaps more importantly, individuals responding to the 2000 census were permitted to classify themselves in more than one racial or cultural category—reflecting the so-called Tiger Woods description, whereby this famous golfer insists on describing himself as "Caublinasian" to reflect the ethnic blend in his ancestry of Caucasian, black, American Indian, and Asian. Further, to speak of a "Hispanic" American is to point to a cultural category, not a racial one. In fact, Hispanic Americans may be of any race. Therefore, in the 2000 census some individuals (e.g., those with parents of different races) who were formerly classified solely in a particular racial category

TABLE 5.1
Resident Population: United States, 1900 and 2004

	1900[a]		2004[b]	
	Number	Percentage	Number	Percentage
Total population	75,994,000	100.0	293,655,000	100.0
Male	38,816,000	51.1	144,537,000	49.2
Female	37,178,000	48.9	149,118,000	50.8
Hispanic or Latino (of any race)[c]	(NA)		41,322,000	14.1
Non-Hispanic White	(NA)		197,841,000	67.4
One race only:	(NA)		289,217,000	100.0
Caucasian Americans	66,809,000	87.9	236,058,000	81.6
African Americans	8,834,000	11.6	37,502,000	13.0
Asian Americans and Pacific Islanders	(NA)		12,832,000	4.4
American Indians[d]	(NA)		2,825,000	1.0
Two or more races	(NA)		4,180,000	1.5

[a]Excludes Alaska and Hawaii.

[b]Excludes individuals living in the Commonwealth of Puerto Rico and the U.S. Island Areas who are counted separately. Note also that in the 2000 census individuals could report more than one race, as well as "Hispanic"; as a result, numbers within categories for 2004 may add to more or less than the total population given above.

[c]Persons of Hispanic origin may be of any race; not included in data for the total population.

[d]Includes Aleuts and Eskimos.

Source: U.S. Census Bureau, 2005.

(solely as Caucasian Americans, African Americans, etc.) may have chosen to add a second such category or also to classify themselves as Hispanic. All of this reinforces our concerns about conceptual and methodological problems in carrying out research on Hispanic Americans, problems that have led some (e.g., Duarté-Vélez & Bernal, 2007) to recommend focusing on narrower groups within this diverse population, defined perhaps by social, cultural, and contextual factors, as well as more traditional gender and developmental variables.

Nevertheless, although the present figures may be in part an artifact of the new processes and classification system used in the 2000 census, the Hispanic portion of the American population (not including the more than four million Hispanics who are counted separately in the Commonwealth of Puerto Rico) has clearly been growing over the past decades and is now widely recognized to be the largest minority group in American society.

Within the Hispanic-American population recorded in the 2000 census, approximately 58.5 percent were of Mexican origin, 9.6 percent originated in Puerto Rico, 3.5 percent were Cuban Americans, and some 28.4 percent had other origins (mostly in Central America, South America, and the Dominican Republic) (U.S. Census Bureau, 2004). (Note that by 2007, the Mexican-American portion of this group is likely to have become even larger.) Some people of Hispanic origin are recent immigrants, others have lived in the continental United States for generations, and all Puerto Ricans have been U.S. citizens since 1917.

Hispanic-American Encounters with Death, Dying, and Bereavement

Efforts to study numbers of deaths and death rates among Hispanic Americans face special difficulties. In the United States, most of the data collected on death rates come from records in county offices. Such records depend upon death certificates, which provide separate spaces to record the race and the specific Hispanic origin of the individual who has died (see Figure 16.1). Much depends, therefore, on the accuracy of the person who fills out the death certificate and on reliable information from his or her sources. Nevertheless, these are the best data available and the foundation for all that follows here.

Within the United States, data on *numbers of deaths* show that there were 122,416 deaths of Hispanic Americans in 2004 (see Table 5.2). This figure is strikingly low—it amounts to about 5.1 percent of all deaths in the United States in 2004 within a group that represents about 14.1 percent of the total population. As a result, the Hispanic-American, *age-adjusted death rate* of 586.7 per 100,000 in 2004 was significantly lower than that of the non-Hispanic, Caucasian ("Anglo") death rate of 797.1.

One might expect that several factors contribute to these relatively low numbers of deaths and death rates among Hispanic Americans, such as the fact that there is a comparatively large proportion of young persons within the Hispanic-American community, Hispanic-American immigrants may have been (self) selected for their general good health, and some Hispanic Americans may return to their country of origin to die or when they are seriously ill.

TABLE 5.2
Deaths and Age-Adjusted Death Rates (per 100,000 U.S. Standard Population) by Specified Race or Hispanic Origin and Gender: United States, 2004

	Both Sexes	Age-Adjusted Death Rates[a]	Male	Age-Adjusted Death Rates[a]	Female	Age-Adjusted Death Rates[a]
All origins[b]	2,397,615	800.8	1,181,668	955.7	1,215,947	679.2
Caucasian Amercans, Non-Hispanic	2,056,643	797.1	1,007,266	949.0	1,049,377	677.5
African Americans, Non-Hispanic	287,315	1,044.7	145,970	1,291.5	141,345	869.4
Hispanic origin[c]	122,416	586.7	68,544	706.8	53,872	485.9
Asian and Pacific Island Americans[d]	40,533	443.9	21,298	534.7	19,235	375.5
American Indians and Native Alaskans[e]	13,124	650.0	7,134	758.1	5,990	557.9

[a]"Age-adjusted death rates are constructs that show what the level of mortality would be if no changes occurred in the age composition of the population from year to year. . . . Also age-adjusted death rates are better indicators of relative risk when comparing mortality . . . between sex or race subgroups of the population that have different age compositions" (Miniño et al., 2007, p. 1).

[b]Figures for origin not stated are included in "all origins" but are not distributed among specified origins.

[c]Persons of Hispanic origin may be of any race; these data should be interpreted with caution since race and Hispanic origin are reported separately on death certificates and because of inconsistencies between reporting Hispanic origin on death certificates and on censuses and surveys.

[d]Includes Chinese, Filipino, Hawaiian, Japanese, and Other Asian or Pacific Islander.

[e]Includes Aleuts and Eskimos.

Source: Miniño et al., 2007.

This picture is likely to change as the Hispanic-American population ages, as more of its members are born within the United States, and as it increasingly integrates itself into mainstream American society. Also, like members of many other cultural groups, especially those dominated by immigrants, as Hispanic Americans adjust to their surrounding culture in the United States, they often take on many of the characteristics of that culture, further confounding claims about that which is distinctive in Hispanic-American experiences with death, dying, and bereavement (Rosenwaike & Bradshaw, 1988, 1989; Salcido, 1990; Soto & Villa, 1990). Nevertheless, in 2002 *infant mortality rates* among Hispanic Americans of 5.6 per 1,000 live births were slightly better than comparable rates (5.8) for non-Hispanic, Caucasian infants (Anderson & Smith, 2005). Also Hispanic-American maternal mortality rates of 8.5 per 100,000 live births were lower than similar rates for non-Hispanic, Caucasian Americans (9.8) or for the U.S. population as a whole (13.1) (Miniño et al., 2007).

Among *causes of death*, there are significant differences between the Hispanic and non-Hispanic populations in the United States. For example, two leading causes of death—heart disease and cancer—accounted for 51.3 percent of all deaths in 2004 for the non-Hispanic, Caucasian population, but only 42.7 percent of deaths in the Hispanic population (Miniño et al., 2007). Similarly, although chronic lower respiratory diseases, Alzheimer's disease, and influenza and pneumonia rank as 4th, 6th, and 8th leading causes of death, respectively, for the non-Hispanic, Caucasian population, they rank only 8th, 16th, and 9th, respectively, as leading causes of death among Hispanic Americans.

By contrast, homicide is the seventh leading cause of death among Hispanic Americans, whereas it ranks only as 16th for the non-Hispanic population (Anderson & Smith, 2005). In general, homicide—and to a lesser extent HIV infection—is an especially significant cause of death for young Hispanic-American males. Not surprisingly, in a population with a large proportion of young persons one is likely to find a larger proportion of deaths due to causes that are more prevalent at younger ages. Nevertheless, differences in homicide rates among different Hispanic-American communities suggest that other factors are also at work, such as poverty and other socioeconomic variables.

Hispanic-American Attitudes toward Death

When we turn to attitudes (and practices) associated with death, dying, and bereavement, it quickly becomes apparent that there is much less information available for study. Thus, what we present in this chapter are merely snapshots of four minority cultures. We have mostly chosen to include recent studies for these snapshots so that readers can get a sense of what is being learned by current research on these four groups. We begin our series of snapshots with those describing Hispanic-American attitudes.

◆ *Importance of family:* Beginning with Kalish and Reynolds' work and continuing through the present, several studies have indicated that family plays an influential role in shaping Hispanic-American attitudes. Thus, Kalish and Reynolds (1981) described Mexican-American families in their study as tightly knit and as striving to maintain a strong locus of emotional support in the family unit. This assertion was reinforced by Thomas (2001), who reported that Hispanic Americans place high value on being cared for by family members (see also Cox & Monk, 1993; Delgado & Tennstedt, 1997a). In fact, Thomas reported that Hispanic elders stress that the family should be involved extensively in both planning and providing care. Not to do so may be seen as not fulfilling one's responsibilities (Cox & Monk, 1993). And in a study of Puerto Rican sons providing care for ill parents, Delgado and Tennstedt (1997b) reported that these men took on this role out of a "sense of responsibility."

◆ *The role of religion:* Religion is another significant influence shaping Hispanic-American attitudes. In their study of Mexican Americans in Los Angeles, Kalish and Reynolds (1981) found that 90 percent of their participants were Roman Catholic. In fact, the dominant religion among all Hispanics in the United States still is Roman Catholicism (Clements et al., 2003; Cox & Monk, 1993). As a result, this church's teaching and rituals are likely to play significant roles in how Hispanic Americans think about and approach dying and death.

◆ For some Mexican Americans, *pre-Hispanic religious beliefs and rituals* also continue to be significant. One belief shared by many Hispanic Americans

Hispanic Americans tending the grave of a loved one.

is the continuous relationship between life and death (Clements et al., 2003; Munet-Vilaró, 1998). This means that death is seen as a complement to life as part of an ongoing cycle; the two are not seen as utter opposites as they are by many persons in the dominant culture. This belief may play a role in how Hispanic Americans look on living wills and "Do not resuscitate" (DNR) orders, as well as their willingness to consult hospice services.

◆ *Fatalism and anticipatory grief:* Munet-Vilaró (1998) reported that Puerto Rican parents of children with leukemia tended to see the disease as a "death-sentence" and were "fatalistic" about its outcome, even in the face of countervailing evidence. She believed that this attitude helped the parents and children prepare for an eventual death. Also, Grabowski and Frantz (1993) suggested that this attitude helped to ease the intensity of grief for those adopting it (for a different view of "anticipatory grief," see Chapter 9).

Death-Related Practices among Hispanic Americans

◆ *Care of the dying:* As in many other cultures, caregivers for relatives among Hispanic Americans are most often female (Cox & Monk, 1993; Delgado & Tennstedt, 1997a; Gelfand et al., 2001). Although such care can be stressful for the person providing it, Cox and Monk found that most of these caregivers did not seek formal assistance for their stress. They concluded that "reluctance to use such programs may be attributed to a cultural resistance to sharing familial problems with outsiders or to admitting that caring for a parent or spouse is too demanding" (p. 98). This suggestion is compatible with our earlier note that typically in a Hispanic-American culture, family members are firmly expected to provide such care; not to do so is seen as failing in one's responsibilities to the family. These sorts of reasons may also help to explain why Hispanic Americans resist using nursing homes for family members. Of course, as Hispanic Americans become more acculturated to the dominant culture (more women working, for instance), the ability of family members to provide such care may be undermined (Delgado & Tennstedt, 1997a).

◆ *Presence at death:* Some studies have suggested that some Hispanic Americans find value in being with a dying relative, so that any unresolved conflicts can be worked on. However, Iwashyna and Chang (2002) found that fewer Mexican Americans now die at home. In such circumstances, the constraints of institutions that provide care for dying persons may make it more difficult to realize this value.

◆ *Grieving practices:* Hispanic-American mourning practices include an open expression of grief, but this typically differs by gender. "Although it is not unusual to hear women wailing loudly, calling out the name of the deceased, and fainting, machismo . . . plays a significant part in the lack of emotional response of adult Latino men. Latino men are expected to 'be strong' for the family and usually do not grieve openly" (Clements et al., 2003, p. 21).

◆ *After-death rituals:* Rituals focused around death take a variety of forms among Hispanic Americans. Some of them are much like the dominant culture's, including open caskets, a requiem mass in the church, and a procession to the burial site (Clements et al., 2003). But there are also some rituals more specific to a Hispanic culture. See, for example, the practices described in a children's book in Personal Insights 5.1.

◆ Other Hispanic-American rituals have *religious roots.* Thus, Roman Catholics may have a novena (usually in the home). A novena includes a nine-day period after the funeral in which the rosary (a specific series of prayers) is

---

PERSONAL INSIGHTS 5.1

A Mural for Mamita/Un Mural Para Mamita

A Mural for Mamita/Un Mural Para Mamita (Alexander, 2002) is a book for children about a young girl, her family, and their entire neighborhood as they plan a memorial service. The service is to be a fiesta in tribute to the girl's grandmother who had recently died after a long illness. As the proprietor of the local *bodega,* Mamita was well known and greatly loved in the neighborhood. The girl's special contribution to this commemorative event is a brilliant mural painted on the side of Mamita's store. Hispanic-American traditions are affirmed as the family and the extended community join in this tribute to a central figure in their lives. Also notable are the ways in which the adults emphasize that this event is a celebration of Mamita's life, freely include the young girl in these events, and allow her to give full reign to her creative expression of love for her grandmother. This book is unusual because its text appears in both English and Spanish.

said in the deceased person's name. During the time of the novena, the house may be kept closed, allowing the family an undisturbed period for mourning (Grabowski & Frantz, 1993; Munet-Vilaró, 1998).

◆ Another ritual specifically found in Mexican-American communities *is the Day of the Dead* (Garciagodoy, 1998). This ritual traces its ancestry both to Roman Catholic tradition (it occurs on November 2, Roman Catholicism's Feast of All Souls) and to pre-Hispanic Mexican traditions. Family altars may be cleaned, food may be offered to the spirits of the dead, and the family may visit the cemetery to put flowers on the grave of the deceased (Munet-Vilaró, 1998).

◆ *Variations in mourning:* Finally, Shapiro (1995) provided a lengthy description of the mourning of a Puerto Rican woman ("Carmen") in Boston. In that description, the Hispanic-American belief in the continuing relationship between the survivors and the deceased is fully apparent. Carmen, the daughter of the deceased woman, reported dreams in which her mother appeared and spoke to her. She was both comforted and disturbed by these

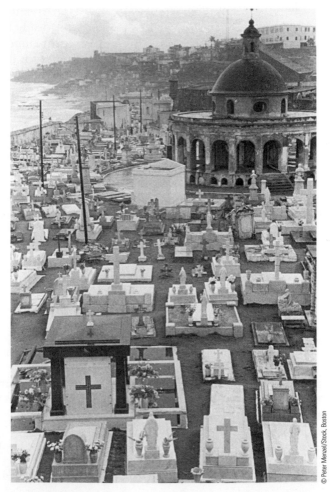

Memorials for those who have died are framed by culture: a cemetery in San Juan, Puerto Rico.

visits. Two younger children also reported that their mother "continued to be a physical presence in the household," although they found such experiences frightening. Older siblings, too, reported that they experienced spiritual visitations by their mother, but they found these to be understandable manifestations of their mother's spirit. Thus, although different family members responded to such experiences in a variety of ways, what is revealed here overall is that "Puerto Rican culture is more comfortable than the secular American culture with the idea that the deceased continues to exist in the family as a spiritual presence" (Shapiro, 1995, p. 169). To be unaware or insensitive to these beliefs and practices may significantly interfere with the open communication necessary to understand and provide good care to members of this culture.

African Americans

African Americans are the second largest minority group among residents of the United States, consisting of an estimated 37.5 million persons, or almost exactly 13 percent of the total population (see Table 5.1). African Americans are linked in many ways by origins on the African continent, the history of slavery and slave trading, and experiences of discrimination. Slavery itself was a practice with many death-related implications. These included the killings involved in taking individuals prisoner and removing them from their tribal homes, suffering and death during transport to the New World, harsh living and working conditions on this side of the Atlantic, and all that is entailed in being treated as objects who could become the property of others. That background influences many aspects of contemporary African-American experiences with death in America. As Kalish and Reynolds (1981) wrote, "To be Black in America is to be part of a history told in terms of contact with death and coping with death" (p. 103).

African-American Encounters with Death, Dying, and Bereavement

In terms of *numbers of deaths,* non-Hispanic African Americans experienced 287,315 deaths in 2004, or almost 12 percent of all deaths in the United States in that year (see Table 5.2). These deaths result in *age-adjusted death rates* of 1044.7 per 100,000 in the standard population for non-Hispanic African Americans, higher than those for the U.S. population as a whole and for all of the subgroups listed in Table 5.2. Much the same is true for non-Hispanic African-American males and females.

It is only fair to add that relative disadvantages in death rates for African Americans may not have resulted simply from ethnicity. Many minority groups in American society are disadvantaged in their socioeconomic standing, and such disadvantages almost always reveal themselves in higher death rates (Benjamin, 1965; Blane, 1995). One decade-long study of 530,000 individuals confirmed that employment status, income, education, occupation, and marital status—as well as race—all have "substantial net associations with mortality" (Sorlie et al., 1995, p. 949). Poverty, inadequate access to health care, and higher incidences of life-threatening behavior have direct and unhappy implications for death rates. Because racial, cultural, and socioeconomic factors of this sort are so complex and closely intertwined, it is difficult to identify or rank causal factors that influence death rates for African Americans as a group. Still, correlations between membership in some subgroups within this population and the statistical likelihood of dying at an earlier age than many members of other subgroups or than Caucasian Americans are evident.

One can describe the situation facing African Americans today in various ways. For example, estimated *average life expectancy* for an African-American infant born in 2004 is 5.2 years lower than for a Caucasian-American infant (73.1 years versus 78.3 years). In fact, until old age, African Americans have notably higher death rates than their Caucasian counterparts and are at greater risk of dying from most causes. In terms of some African-American subgroups, however, things may be much different. For example, McCord and Freeman (1990) demonstrated that African-American males living in Harlem, an area of New York City, are less likely to reach the age of 65 than men living in Bangladesh, one of the poorest countries in the world. As these authors wrote, the "situation in Harlem is extreme, but it is not an isolated phenomenon. . . . Similar pockets of high mortality have been described in other U.S. cities" (p. 176).

In terms of *causes of death*, in 2004 there were nearly as many deaths of non-Hispanic African Americans from homicide (8,135) as there were homicide deaths among non-Hispanic Caucasian Americans (8,643)—even though the Caucasian-American population is more than 7 times larger than the African-American population (Miniño et al., 2007). For males in these groups, there were more deaths from homicide among African-Americans (6,839) than there were among their counterpart Caucasian-American (6,302). As a result, age-adjusted death rates for homicide were much higher in 2004 among African Americans than among Caucasian Americans (21.1 versus 3.6 per 100,000) and the disparity is even greater for African-American males by contrast with Caucasian-American males (37.1 versus 5.3 per 100,000). Further, homicide is the leading cause of death among African-American males between the ages of 15 and 24. To be young, African American, and male in our society is to find oneself at unusual risk for death by homicide in comparison with all other Americans. Although African Americans can find some comfort in the fact that their age-adjusted death rates from suicide are lower than those of Caucasian Americans (9.0 versus 12.3 per 100,000), deaths from suicide appear to be increasing among young, African-American males. Clearly, further study of cultural variables that appear to mitigate suicide risk in this population is desirable (Utsey et al., 2007).

Infant mortality rates were 2.4 times higher among African Americans in 2004 than among Caucasian Americans—13.8 versus 5.7 deaths per 1,000 live births (Miniño et al., 2007). Although infant mortality rates have declined significantly for both African Americans and Caucasian Americans during the past 40 years, differences in infant mortality rates between these two groups have actually increased (for many complex reasons), and the present disparity between them is projected to continue through the first decade of the 21st century (Singh & Yu, 1995).

On a related point, although *maternal death rates* at the time of childbirth have decreased dramatically for all Americans over the past 100 years, in 2004 they were more than 3.7 times higher among African Americans than among Caucasian

Americans (Miniño et al., 2007). That is, the 214 maternal deaths among African Americans resulted in a maternal death rate of 34.7 per 100,000 live births, whereas the 300 maternal deaths among Caucasian Americans yielded a maternal death rate of 9.3. Also, there is a higher incidence of and lower survival rates with cancer among African Americans (Polednak, 1990). Finally, according to federal reports, whereas mortality from breast cancer fell among Caucasian-American women between 1989 and 1992, it actually rose among African-American women *(St. Louis Post-Dispatch,* 1995).

These differences do not themselves directly reveal the underlying factors from which they result. Still, in studies in which other factors were held constant, some aspects of these death rates and lower life expectancies were found to be more directly related to education and socioeconomic status than to race or ethnicity (Polednak, 1990). This finding is not surprising. For instance, Powell-Griner (1988) reported that higher risks of infant mortality are associated with illegitimacy, blue-collar families, inadequate prenatal care, and low birth weight. Quite often, these factors are not unrelated to each other; where they are added together, they are likely to converge in a way that puts an infant at higher risk of premature death (Plepys & Klein, 1995).

Din-Dzietham and Hertz-Picciotto (1998) reported another disturbing finding: the disparity between infant mortality rates among African Americans and Caucasian Americans is not decreased by maternal educational level. Although completing 12 years of education reduced the risk of infant mortality in both groups, further education reduced the risk only among Caucasian Americans. This results in the disparity in infant mortality rates between African Americans and Caucasian Americans actually increasing with more maternal education.

In addition, as early as 1986 it was noted that "Blacks and Hispanics comprise a disproportionately high percentage of AIDS cases" (Institute of Medicine, 1986, p. 102). Despite the fact that HIV disease in 2004 was only the 20th leading cause of death for the American population as a whole, it remained among the ten leading causes of death for African-American males and females from middle adolescence through young and middle adulthood. More specifically, HIV/AIDS was the leading cause of death for African-American females ages 25–34 in 2004 and the second leading cause of death for African-American males ages 35–44 in the same year (Miniño et al., 2007). Thus, deaths associated with HIV infection represent a major inequality related to racial and cultural differences in American society.

Lastly, in a study of *location of death,* Iwashyna and Chang (2002) found that more African Americans die outside of their homes (that is, in a hospital or nursing care facility) than do Caucasian Americans. (This result has not been supported by other studies [for instance, Owen et al., 2001]. That these different studies report very different findings reveals in a quite specific manner two problems we pointed to previously with current work on cultural groups outside of the dominant one: these studies are marred by the small size and the particularity of the samples studied.) In any case, Iwashyna and Chang also reported that the difference they identified between African Americans and Caucasian Americans in location of death does "not appear to be mediated by differences in age, sex, income . . . education structure of these groups, nor by differences in the particular causes of death" (p. 115). They offered a series of possible explanations for this difference but admitted that they found none of them wholly convincing. Whatever the reasons for this difference, as we noted in Chapter 2, when persons die in some institutional setting rather than at home, the actual encounters with dying and death among family members and friends are likely to be reduced.

African-American Attitudes toward Death

◆ *Importance of family:* Systematic study of attitudes associated with death, dying, and bereavement among African Americans is not extensive, even after nearly 40 years of work in this field. Kalish and Reynolds (1981) published one early report about such attitudes among African Americans in Los Angeles in 1976. They found that individuals in the study relied on friends, church associates, and neighbors for support when dealing with these issues. The implication was that family relationships were not as important among African Americans as they were among other groups in their study. (In retrospect, it appears that one reason for the relative lack of importance of family among African Americans in the Kalish and Reynolds study may have been that the individuals they studied had moved to Los Angeles in recent years and thus may not have had many family members available to them locally from whom they could obtain support and help.)

The view that family support is not important to African Americans in coping with death-related situations has not been supported by other, more recent studies. For instance, in their study comparing African-American to Caucasian-American caregivers of persons with Alzheimer's disease,

An elderly man with a life-threatening illness being supported at home by his extended family.

Owen et al. (2001) found that 53 percent of the African-American patients died at home, whereas only 38 percent of the Caucasian-American patients did so. African-American patients were also significantly less likely than Caucasian-American patients to die in a nursing home. In her study of African Americans, Thomas (2001) also found resistance to placing a relative in a nursing home. And Clements et al. (2003) claimed that the African-American family is an important support system for grieving persons. What these recent studies suggest is that African Americans do place a strong emphasis on the family in providing care for both dying persons and those who are grieving.

Hayslip and Peveto (2004) carried this point further by examining the impact of cultural change on death-related attitudes. Their results support the view that for African Americans and other minority cultural groups in the United States, by contrast with Caucasian Americans, there has developed a greater focus on family and relationships, a shift toward more interest in being informed about one's own terminal prognosis, and a more personal approach to funeral and mourning observances.

♦ *Suspicion of the medical community:* Several studies (Owen et al., 2001; Tschann, Kaufmann, & Micco, 2003; Waters, 2001) have reported that African Americans exhibit a mistrust of the medical community. Waters (2001) found that the African Americans in her study believed that they received less health care than did Caucasian Americans, and they believed that they would not receive all of the appropriate health care they needed if they wrote a living will. Some participants traced this distrust of the medical community to the legacy of the Tuskegee syphilis experiment (see Focus On 5.1). This has

FOCUS ON 5.1

What Was the Tuskegee Syphilis Study?

The Tuskegee syphilis study was conducted by the United States Public Health Service, beginning in 1932. It was intended to study the consequences of syphilis infection in African Americans as compared to that same infection in Caucasian Americans. Researchers recruited 399 poor African-American sharecroppers in Alabama for the study. The participants were not informed of the nature of their disease; they were simply told that they had "bad blood." The men initially received the only known treatments for the infection. However, since the results of the study at this point were unimpressive, treatment was halted in order to study the progress of the disease until the participants died. Even after penicillin became available in the mid-1940s and was shown to be effective in treating the disease, the men were left untreated. Finally, in 1972, after the study was exposed in the press, the study was halted. Approximately 100 of the men died of the disease over the course of the study. (For more information on the Tuskegee study, see Jones, 1992.)

raised concerns among health care providers and stimulated some efforts to be more culturally sensitive in the delivery of health care (Dula, 1994; Koenig & Gates-Williams, 1995).

Death-Related Practices among African Americans

◆ *Advance directives and organ donation:* Several studies (e.g., Owen et al., 2001; Thomas, 2001; Tschann et al., 2003; Waters, 2001) have reported that doubts among African Americans about their treatment by the health care system may account, at least in part, for this group's resistance to making advance plans, either for treatment at the end of life or for after death. These and other accounts (e.g., Barrett, 2006; Greiner et al., 2003; Minniefield et al., 2001; Wasserman et al., 2006) have also reported that African Americans are less likely to use hospice services, agree to terminate life supports, or donate organs after death (see also Chapter 16 on this last point).

◆ *Mourning practices:* In times of grief, African Americans in the Kalish and Reynolds study (1981) saw themselves as freely expressive and regarded funerals as important (see also Hines, 1986). Similarly, the study group held funeral directors in high regard. Another author (Jackson, 1980) argued

---

PERSONAL INSIGHTS 5.2

Langston Hughes: As Befits a Man

I don't mind dying—
But I'd hate to die all alone!
I want a dozen pretty women
To holler, cry, and moan.

I don't mind dying
But I want my funeral to be fine:
A row of long tall mamas
Fainting, fanning, and crying.

I want a fish-tail hearse
And sixteen fish-tail cars,
A big brass band
And a whole truck load of flowers.

When they let me down,
Down into the clay,
I want the women to holler:
Please don't take him away!
Ow-ooo-oo-o!
Don't take daddy away!

> *Source:* "As Befits Man," from *The Collected Poems of Langston Hughes* by Langston Hughes, edited by Arnold Rampersad with David Roessel, Associate Editor, © 1994 by The Estate of Langston Hughes. Used by permission of Alfred A. Knopf, a division of Random House, Inc.

Sunflowers and Rainbows for Tia: Saying Goodbye to Daddy

In the book *Sunflowers and Rainbows for Tia: Saying Goodbye to Daddy* (Alexander-Greene, 1999), a 10-year-old African-American girl named Tia describes how she, her 7-year-old twin brothers, her mother, and her grandparents feel when her Daddy dies suddenly. Tia tells about her sadness and grief, along with her fears that Mama might also die and leave the children alone. Tia also explains how people came over to the house to express their love for Daddy, support her family, and bring food to share. She makes clear that it helped her to be involved in many of the preparations for Daddy's funeral and to take part in that ritual. In particular, Tia was comforted when she was allowed to bring Daddy's favorite sunflowers to the ceremony and a big rainbow shone through the clouds on the way to the cemetery.

that African Americans use the funeral as a moment in which recognition can be provided for the deceased person's ability to stand up to others and (in the case of males) for the individual's masculinity (see Personal Insights 5.2). Thus, what happens at the funeral (how many persons are present, the appearance of the casket, etc.) can be quite important (Holloway, 2003). Personal Insights 5.3 offers an example taken from a children's book of what family and friends meant to an African American child when her father died abruptly.

◆ *The importance of storytelling:* Rodgers (2004) studied the mourning practices of several African-American widows in the Northwest. She emphasized the central importance of storytelling in these women's handling of their grief. Tracing this emphasis back to the oral traditions of their African heritage, Rodgers suggested that "storytelling was at the heart of every widow's description of her lived bereavement experience" (p. 12). In the telling of their stories, Rodgers found that the women took on the roles of the various persons in the story, using different tones and accents in their voices, as well as hand and body gestures and facial expressions to make the story live. Such vivid enactments of their stories were helpful to them in their mourning processes. Beyond this, Rosenblatt and Wallace (2005a; 2005b) have shown how often narratives of grieving African Americans feature themes of racism in the lives of deceased family members.

❦ Asian and Pacific Island Americans

Asian and Pacific Island Americans are individuals who trace their origins back to various countries in Asia or to the Pacific islands. Together, they are the third largest minority group among residents of the United States, consisting of 12.8 million persons or 4.4 percent of the total population (see Table 5.1). The largest of the Asian-

American communities are Chinese Americans (constituting approximately 24 percent of the total), followed by Filipino Americans (18 percent), Asian Americans from India (16.4 percent), Vietnamese Americans (11 percent), and Korean Americans (10.5 percent). Differences between Asian and Pacific Island communities complicate research on many death-related topics (Else et al., 2007; Leong et al., 2007).

Asian and Pacific Island American Encounters with Death, Dying, and Bereavement

Numbers of deaths among Asian Americans and Pacific Islanders in the United States in 2004 are given in Table 5.2. Taken together, these add up to 40,533 deaths, about 1.7 percent of all deaths for that year in a population that now totals more than 2.5 times that share of the U.S. resident population.

Age-adjusted death rates in the Asian-American and Pacific-Island-American community as a whole were 443.9 per 100,000, lower than similar rates for all of the subgroups in the U.S. population listed in Table 5.2. Although the three leading *causes of death* among both Asian Americans and Caucasian Americans are cancer, heart disease, and cerebrovascular disease, cancer leads the list for Asian Americans while heart disease is ranked first among Caucasian Americans (see also Anderson & Smith, 2005).

Infant mortality rates for Asian Americans vary slightly among subgroups, with the lowest rates found among Chinese Americans and the highest rates among Filipino Americans. Nevertheless, infant mortality rates of 3.8 per 1,000 for Asian Americans as a whole are and have been for some time significantly lower than those for Caucasian Americans, Hispanic Americans, African Americans, and Native Americans (Anderson & Smith, 2005).

Lauderdale and Kestenbaum (2002) carefully reviewed mortality statistics in the United States between 1990 and 1999 for persons 65 and older among six Asian-American groups: Chinese, Indian, Japanese, Korean, Filipino, and Vietnamese. Because this study was based on enrollees in Medicare Part B, it had a large sample size (varying from 116,000 for Indian males to 737,000 for Chinese females)—unlike most of the other studies cited in this chapter. Results revealed that Asian-American men and women 65 years of age and older consistently have lower mortality rates than the comparable Caucasian population. This disparity could not be linked to socioeconomic status, the relation within each subgroup of immigrant to U.S.-born persons, or the mortality levels in the countries of origin. Even the Vietnamese, who of all the subpopulations studied had more persons with incomes below the poverty level, not only upheld the advantage of the other groups in mortality rates but also in fact proved to have the greatest advantage.

Asian and Pacific Island American Attitudes toward Death

◆ *Communication issues:* Kalish and Reynolds (1981) found members of the Japanese community in Los Angeles to insist on maintaining control over communication. Thus, even when members of this community were dying and in distress, they were often quite restrained in communicating what they were feeling to health care providers. This sort of restraint is influenced by another attitude found among many Asian Americans: the belief that talking about bad things may actually produce them (Braun et al., 2001; Thomas, 2001). This belief may help to explain why death is something of a taboo subject among some Chinese Americans (Eisenbruch, 1984; Tanner, 1995). It also probably plays a role in what several studies—among Japanese Americans (Hirayama, 1990), Cambodian Americans (Lang, 1990), and Chinese Canadians (Tong & Spicer, 1994)—have shown, namely, that family members may prefer that dying persons not be told that they are dying (Thomas, 2001).

◆ *Decision making:* Many Asian-American cultures are patriarchal and hierarchical (McQuay, 1995). In our context, this means that there is some specific person, usually the oldest male or at least an older member of the family (Blackhall et al., 1995; Crowder, 2000; Tong & Spicer, 1994), who is expected to make any decisions about the care of family members.

◆ *Physician-assisted suicide:* Braun et al. (2001) studied attitudes toward physician-assisted suicide among several Asian-American groups in Hawaii. The attitudes of these groups tended to be associated with religious factors and their acculturation to the dominant culture. Thus, first-generation Filipinos, who were primarily Roman Catholic, saw euthanasia and suicide as prohibited acts. However, Filipinos who had worked in health care believed that withholding futile treatment and providing pain medication, even when that suppressed respiration, were acceptable.

Of the five groups studied, Filipinos and native Hawaiians were most resistant to physician-assisted suicide. Thus, Braun et al. (2001) reported that native Hawaiians (who have the worst health status and the shortest life expectancy of the groups studied) distrusted the health care system, fearing that they do not receive appropriate care from it. Chinese-American and Japanese-American participants in the study approved of physician-assisted suicide by large numbers (in fact, by larger numbers than the Caucasians in the study).

◆ *Attitudes toward funerals:* Crowder (2000) studied Chinese funerals in San Francisco. She reported that there were disagreements within the Chinese community about the appropriateness of various traditional customs. These disagreements tended to occur between those who were more acculturated to the dominant culture and those who were more recent immigrants to the United States. However, most Asian Americans believe that funeral rituals are very important; they are believed to help maintain healthy relationships between the living and the dead (Crowder, 2000; Hirayama, 1990; Kalish & Reynolds, 1981; McQuay, 1995). As Crowder wrote about the participants in her study: "For the Chinese, funerals are major life passage rituals. . . . Ancestor worship . . . is the cornerstone of Chinese cultural belief, social structure and religious practice. With death, a family member can be a beneficial ancestor, and funerals are the ritual means of accomplishing this transition" (p. 452).

Death-Related Practices among Asian and Pacific Island Americans

◆ *Mourning customs:* Kalish and Reynolds (1981) reported on the mourning customs of Japanese Americans in Los Angeles and found them to be quite conservative. For instance, they found that few members of this group believed that remarriage, or even dating after the death of a spouse, was appropriate.

Korean Americans mourning the death of their loved one.

◆ *Blending Western and non-Western elements in Asian-American funeral rituals:* Crowder (2000) provided a lengthy description of Chinese funerals in San Francisco. As one of the largest enclaves of Chinese Americans in the United States, San Francisco's Chinatown provides a cross section of this culture. As Crowder reported, since this Chinatown is situated in the midst of a larger urban center, people living here have to adapt traditional customs to the expectations and legal boundaries for behavior set by the larger community. Therefore Chinese funerals in this context are often a melding of rituals that can be traced to non-Western settings (usually from the country of origin) with Western ones. This blending of traditions can also be found in Samoan-American funerals, which bring together Samoan tradition, elaborate Christian ceremony, and the realities of a new environment, and which usually include the giving of gifts in the form of both money and fine Samoan mats (King, 1990).

◆ *One description of a Chinese-American funeral:* Crowder (2000) identified five components present in a Chinese-American funeral that she observed (compare this description with the vignette near the beginning of this chapter). First, there was a visit to the mortuary. At this visit, the family lined up in hierarchical order (oldest son first, and so on) to receive visitors. The casket was placed among other items: food offerings and a paper house, paper people ("servants"), and paper money. All of these last items were to be burned at the gravesite. Second, on the next day after the visit, the funeral proper occurred at the mortuary. At the funeral she observed, a Methodist minister conducted the service. Then everyone "paid their last respects," and the attendees lined up in order for the procession. Third, as the procession began to leave the mortuary, a Western band began to play. As the procession moved through

Chinese Americans tending the grave of a loved one.

© Ting-Li Wang/The New York Times

Chinatown, "spirit" money (plain paper) was thrown from the hearse, in part, it is believed, to ward off spirits who might interfere with the corpse. Fourth, at the gravesite, after the casket had been lowered into the grave, flowers were thrown into the grave and the paper house, "servants," and money were burned. Fifth, the funeral party then retired to a "longevity" banquet. This banquet provides support and reintegration for the mourners.

◆ *Gravesite visits:* Since many Asian-American communities believe in a continued interaction between the living and the deceased, and that the well-being of living descendents is at least partly related to the care taken on behalf of deceased ancestors, many members of such groups visit gravesites on a frequent basis and care for such sites to express their ongoing concern and care for their ancestors (Hirayama, 1990).

🌱 American Indians and Native Alaskans

Readily available information about death-related experiences among American Indians and Native Alaskans (or Native Americans, a population group that includes Aleuts and Eskimos for statistical purposes) is limited, not always reliable, and not easily subject to generalization. There are hundreds of American Indian tribal groups in the United States and Canada, varying in size from fewer than 100 members (for example, Picuris Pueblo in New Mexico) to the Cherokee and Navajo, with more than 729,000 and nearly 300,000 members, respectively (U.S. Census Bureau, 2005). Each American Indian group has its own set of death-related encounters, attitudes, and patterns of behavior.

Official estimates place the total population of American Indians who reside in the United States at approximately 2.8 million persons, or about 1 percent of the total population (see Table 5.1). However, not all American Indians live within a tribal group or on tribal lands, where data about their death-related experiences can easily be located and identified. In fact, an estimated 55–60 percent of American Indians live in urban areas in North America, where they may be invisible in many ways to an external observer (Thompson & Walker, 1990). Also, more than 20 years ago it was reported that there are some 6.7 million additional individuals who claim partial American Indian ancestry (U.S. Congress, 1986). For all of these reasons, generalizations about death, dying, and bereavement may be particularly inappropriate or hazardous for this relatively small but very heterogeneous portion of American society.

American Indian and Native Alaskan Encounters with Death, Dying, and Bereavement

In terms of *numbers of deaths,* there were 13,124 deaths among American Indians and Native Alaskans in 2004 (see Table 5.2), just one-half of 1 percent of all deaths in the United States that year, yielding an *age-adjusted death rate* of 650.0 per 100,000. Still, these are aggregate figures, subject to all of the limitations just noted. Death is likely to be encountered in quite different ways in different American Indian groups.

Historically, *causes of death* among American Indians have most often involved communicable diseases, diabetes mellitus, and chronic liver disease and cirrhosis, as well as accidents and suicide (Anderson & Smith, 2005). As some of these causes have become less significant and the average life expectancy of most American Indians has increased, heart disease and cancer have become more important as leading causes of death in these groups. Available research indicates that both American Indian males and females have lower rates than other groups for all disease sites combined; however, females have increased rates of cervical cancer. Overall, American Indians also have the least favorable survival rates from cancer.

American Indian *infant mortality rates* of 8.1 per 1,000 are substantially higher than those for Caucasian Americans, Hispanic Americans, and Asian Americans although not as high as those for African Americans (Anderson & Smith, 2005). Trends in these rates for all American cultural groups appear to be affected mainly by maternal education and family income. Among all cultural groups, American Indian infants are at highest risk of dying of sudden infant death syndrome (Iyasu et al., 2002; Singh & Yu, 1995).

The study of specific American Indian groups has also produced important information. For instance, Long (1983) reported that alcohol abuse leads to a death rate from alcohol-related cirrhosis of the liver among Crow Indians at 8 to 9 times the rate of such deaths among Caucasians in the Northwest. Long also reported that the deaths due to homicide among the Crow occur at a rate 2 to 8 times the national average.

In many American Indian groups, automobile accidents are a significant factor in death rates. For example, Mahoney (1991) found high death rates from automobile accidents among American Indian populations in New York State, nearly double the overall rate in the United States. The largest portion (73.7 percent) of these deaths occurred among males (Mahoney, 1991). Carr and Lee (1978) found motor vehicle accidents to be the leading cause of death among Navajo males and the second leading cause among females on the reservation. Campbell (1989) made a similar report concerning American Indians in Montana. Olson et al. (1990) also reported that deaths due to motor vehicle crashes were exceptionally high among American Indian children in New Mexico. Finally, Long (1983) reported that among Crow Indians, automobile accidents are the major cause of death. She also wrote that the majority of these accidents involve alcohol abuse.

However, high vehicular death rates among American Indian populations may in part be attributed to their living in areas where people live far apart from one another and where roads are often in poor condition. In these circumstances, increased motor vehicle use is necessary but also more dangerous, given the condition of the roads. All this is compounded when poverty and alcoholism are additional contributing factors. Thus, Bachman (1992) argued that what appear to be high homicide rates in some American Indian communities are influenced by such factors as the historical experience of a kind of internal colonialism, social disorganization, cultural conflicts, a subculture of violence, economic deprivation, and abuse of alcohol and drugs. In fact, when socioeconomic status and other cultural factors are controlled, it appears that "racial differences in homicide rates decrease substantially" (Holinger et al., 1994, p. 20).

Suicide among American Indians has been the subject of competing reports (see Chapter 17). The National Center for Health Statistics (Miniño et al., 2007) lists suicide as the eighth leading cause of death among all American Indian populations in 2004, accounting for 404 deaths and a death rate of 12.8 per 100,000. Clearly, this subject deserves careful study in specific native populations (Alcántara & Gone, 2007; Olson & Wahab, 2006).

American Indian and Native Alaskan Attitudes toward Death

♦ *Attitudes toward death:* Many commentators (e.g., Brown, 1987; Hultkrantz, 1979) have suggested that American Indians tend to view life and death not in a linear but in a circular or interwoven fashion in which death is regarded as part of life. This belief is illustrated both in some American Indian legends (see Personal Insights 5.4 for example) and in several children's books with American Indian perspectives (see Personal Insights 5.5).

Nevertheless, death-related attitudes of specific American Indian groups may range from acceptance without anxiety to a high level of fear. For example, Carr and Lee (1978) reported that among Navajos, death taboos "favor bringing the sick into the hospital to die rather than permitting them to die at home" (p. 280) so that the home will not be polluted by the experience of death. Differences in these American Indian perspectives reinforce the point that each American Indian group and even each individual American Indian may have a distinctive set of attitudes toward death—to which others must be sensitive and respectful.

♦ *Communication issues:* Thomas (2001) reported that some American Indians believe that talking about dying and death may cause it to happen. This often results in little discussion about advance directives. Long's (1983, p. 123)

PERSONAL INSIGHTS 5.4

Why Do People Die? A Navajo Legend

When they [the Navajo people as the "Origin Legend" describes early events in their emergence into this world] reached the mainland, they sought to divine their fate. To do this someone threw a hide-scraper into the water, saying: "If it sinks we perish, if it floats, we live." It floated and all rejoiced. But Coyote said: "Let me divine your fate." He picked up a stone, and saying, "If it sinks we perish; if it floats we live," he threw it into the water. It sank, of course, and all were angry with him and reviled him; but he answered them saying: "If we all live, and continue to increase as we have done, the earth will soon be too small to hold us, and there will be no room for the cornfields. It is better that each of us should live but a time on this earth and then leave and make room for our children." They saw the wisdom of his words and were silent.

Source: From Matthews, 1897, p. 77.

analysis of mourning patterns among Crow children noted that Crow culture values "self-reliance, individual independence, and a 'keeping to oneself.'" This latter value is realized in action by not imposing one's opinions or feelings on others. This led the mourning children in Long's study to display a flattening of their emotional grief responses and an avoidance of sharing or acknowledging what they were feeling. In this way, Long found that these values can produce a difficult mourning period for the grieving child. They also can lead caretakers to misinterpret what is happening in the survivor.

◆ *Survivor actions and the post-death journey:* Clements et al. (2003) reported that some Navajos believe that what survivors do after the death of the person can affect the deceased person's journey into the next world. Thus, post-death rituals assume great importance for these persons.

Death-Related Practices among American Indians and Native Alaskans

◆ *Caring for the dying:* In Canada, people from remote areas who have acute life-threatening illnesses or long-term chronic illnesses are normally referred for treatment in urban tertiary-care hospitals. For First Nation peoples, one effect of this practice is to remove them from their home communities and to locate death in the alien cultural environment of an urban hospital. A report from Winnipeg (Kaufert & O'Neil, 1991) described ways in which trained native interpreters acted as mediators for Cree, Ojibway, and Inuit patients who were terminally ill: (1) as language translators; (2) as cultural informants who could describe native health practices, community health issues, and cultural perspectives on terminal illness and postmortem rituals to clinical staff; (3) as interpreters of biomedical concepts to native peoples; and (4) as patient and community advocates—for instance, by

Four Children's Books with American Indian Perspectives

Four books for children emphasize American Indian convictions about the intertwining of life and death across time and across generations. *The Great Change* (Horn, 1992) and *Beyond the Ridge* (Goble, 1993) each describe death as a moment of transition from life on earth to a life in the spirit world. In *The Great Change* an American Indian grandmother explains to her 9-year-old granddaughter, Wanba, that death is not the end, but the Great Change. As she says, "We need death in order to have life." Death is part of the unbreakable Circle of Life in which our bodies become one with Mother Earth while our souls or spirits endure. Similarly, *Beyond the Ridge* describes an elderly Plains Indian woman who experiences the afterlife believed in by her people. At her death and as her body is prepared according to their custom, the woman makes the long climb up a difficult slope to see the Spirit World beyond the ridge.

Annie and the Old One (Miles, 1971) uses humor to reinforce the appropriateness of acknowledging that death is part of life. In this book, her grandmother (the Old One) tells a 10-year-old Navajo girl, "When the new rug [that the girl's mother is weaving] is taken from the loom, I will go to Mother Earth." To forestall that outcome, Annie misbehaves in school in the hope that her mother will have to stop weaving to go talk with her teacher. She also releases the goat and the sheep from their pen so the adults will have to spend time to round them up. Annie even tries to unravel the weaving in secret. When the adults realize what is going on, Annie's grandmother explains that we are all part of a natural cycle, one that includes both death and life. Finally, Annie recognizes that she cannot hold back time and she is ready herself to take part in the weaving.

My Grandmother's Cookie Jar (Miller, 1987) revolves around Grandma's special cookie jar, which is shaped like an Indian head. Although the cookie jar is a little scary to her granddaughter, her anxieties fall away when Grandma removes its headdress, reaches inside, and takes out a cookie. Then, as they share the cookies from the jar each evening, Grandma tells stories of her Indian people of long ago. The stories make Indian ways, Indian pride, and Indian honor come alive for the little girl. But one day, Grandmother is gone and Grandfather gives the Indian head to the girl. He tells her it is full, not of cookies but of Grandma's love and her Indian spirit heritage. He says that some day the girl will have children of her own and put cookies in the jar. And the girl knows that when she tells Grandma's stories with each cookie, she will be keeping Grandma's spirit alive and the spirit of those who went before her.

enabling patients to return to their communities to spend their final days with their families.

◆ *Hopi mourning:* As an example of American Indian practices associated with mourning, there are several studies of Hopi experiences. One study was of a man in San Francisco (Hanson, 1978). A death of a family member was followed by his having "auditory hallucinations." Officials at a local psychiatric authority judged this to represent psychosis. However, Hanson's agency returned the young man to his reservation, where he could participate in tribal rituals related to the burial of the dead. His hallucinations stopped. As Hanson remarked, "Practices that are difficult to understand are usually interpreted as indicators of psychopathology by the dominant society" (p. 20). However, they might simply represent another culture's way of mourning. In another study, Shen (1986) reported on a second grieving Hopi male who also experienced hallucinations related to the death of his father.

These sorts of experiences are not only found among Hopi males. Hopi women, too, have been reported to experience paranormal experiences as part of the mourning process (Matchett, 1972). In cases described by Matchett, the experiences allowed the beholder to converse with, describe in visual detail, and even struggle with the figure that appeared to her or him.

◆ *How grief is expressed:* In terms of grief and its expression, one report (Preston & Preston, 1991) points out that the Cree people living east of James Bay in the province of Quebec regard death as "at once a commonplace event and one with much significance" (p. 137). Because they place great value on personal autonomy and competence, the Cree strive not to interfere in the lives of others. "The ideal for Cree grieving is an immediate, shared, emotional release, with mutual support for those most at loss and perhaps at risk. But the release of crying and support is soon followed by a return to outward self-reliance and composure, though the inward, private feelings may still be strong" (Preston & Preston, 1991, p. 155).

◆ *Post-death rituals:* Many American Indian groups have distinctive bereavement rituals (e.g., Walker & Balk, 2007). For example, Clements et al. (2003) described Navajo post-death rituals as follows: "The deceased's relatives and friends have 4 days after the death [to complete] cleansing and preparation of the body, burial, mourning, and disposing of the deceased's belongings by giving them away to others or by destroying them (often by burning). . . . The body is washed, and the face is painted with *chei* (i.e., a war paint made of soft red rock . . . mixed with sheep fat) and white corn to protect the deceased on the journey [to the next world]. The deceased is clothed in his or her best clothing and blessed with corn pollen. The deceased's hair is tied with an eagle feather to symbolize a return home. Traditionally, the deceased was buried in the family's hogan . . . and then the hogan was abandoned. . . . On the morning of the fourth day . . . the deceased's relatives and friends wash themselves as a symbol of cleansing themselves of the event of the burial" (p. 23).

Tanacross Athabaskans (of east central Alaska) include a funeral and a *memorial potlatch* among their after-death rituals (Simeone, 1991). The funeral involves preparing the corpse, building a coffin and grave fence, and conducting a Christian religious service. Nonrelatives assume the work of preparing the body and building the funeral structures because the spirit of the dead person is thought to be dangerous to relatives. However, it is relatives who prepare a three-day ceremony involving feasting, dancing, singing, oratory, and a distribution of gifts (such as guns, beads, and blankets) on

Grilling salmon in preparation for a Native-American funeral feast in British Columbia.

© Museum of History & Industry/Corbis

the last night to those who have fulfilled their obligations. This ceremony is the memorial potlatch, which "marks the separation of the deceased from society and is the last public expression of grief" (Simeone, 1991, p. 159). One reason to distribute gifts is to objectify and personalize the grief of the hosts. Through the whole potlatch ceremony, social support is provided and strong emotions of grief are given legitimate expression in the Tanacross Athabaskan community, but the larger social context is one that contains grief in a culture that values emotional reserve.

❦ Summary

In this chapter, we examined death-related encounters, attitudes, and practices among Hispanic Americans, African Americans, Americans who trace their backgrounds to Asian countries or the Pacific Islands, and American Indians and Native Alaskans. In so doing, we tried to be careful to respect differences between and within these groups, to reflect the present state of our imperfect knowledge about these groups, and to avoid stereotypes. Without going beyond the four groups selected for analysis in this chapter, we noticed the rich diversity of death-related experiences within American society. Each of these groups is both a part of the larger society in which we all share and a distinct entity with its own unique death system. Normally, membership in such a cultural group is a matter of birth and socialization; individuals do not usually have an opportunity to choose such membership. Also, it can be difficult to overcome ethnocentric tendencies in which one is inclined to draw on long-standing experiences of one's own group as the norm and other groups as outsiders who vary from that norm. However, everyone can learn from the various cultural groups that exist in the United States. Taking part in the death-related practices of such groups (when outsiders are permitted to do so), reading about their attitudes and rituals, and sharing personal experiences (for example, through discussions in a course on death and dying) can enrich us, both as individuals and as citizens in a multicultural society. In the list of suggested readings that follows, we identify some resources for additional cultural research in the field of death, dying, and bereavement both within and beyond North America, and we occasionally cite examples of such work throughout this book.

Glossary

African Americans: Americans whose cultural origins trace back to the Black cultures of the African continent (especially in West African nations)

American Indians (sometimes called Native Americans or "First Nation Peoples"; for statistical purposes, this group often includes Alaskan Natives): Americans whose cultural origins trace back to the indigenous populations of North America

Asian Americans: Americans whose cultural origins trace back to the Asian continent

Cultural differences: distinctive features arising from a unified set of values, ideas, beliefs, and standards of behavior shared by a group of people

Hispanic Americans: Americans whose cultural origins trace back to countries in which the dominant language is Spanish (e.g., Cuba, Mexico, and Puerto Rico, as well as Central and South American countries)

Pacific Island Americans: Americans whose cultural origins trace back to the Pacific Islands (e.g., Hawaii and Samoa)

Questions for Review and Discussion

1. This chapter showed us at least four different, more particularized death systems operating within the overarching American death system. What major factors do you note as unique to each of the four groups described? What major factors do you note as similar among each of the four groups described?

2. What do you judge to be key relationships between death-related encounters and attitudes, on one hand, and death-related practices, on the other, in any one or more of the four population groups discussed in this chapter?

3. Focusing on your own ethnic, religious, familial, or economic background, can you identify a particular death-related encounter, attitude, or practice that you have had to explain or defend to someone who does not share your background? What was it about the death-related encounter, attitude, or practice that seemed unusual to the person who did not share your background? Why did it seem unu-

sual to that person? How did you explain the origins of the encounter, attitude, or practice?

Suggested Readings

Book-length studies of cultural differences and of different cultural experiences with death within American society include:

Braun, K., Pietsch, J., & Blanchette, P. (Eds.). (2000). *Cultural Issues in End-of-Life Decision Making.*

Churn, A. (2003). *The End is Just the Beginning: Lessons in Grieving for African Americans.*

Cosby, B., & Poussaint, A. F. (2007). *Come On, People: On the Path from Victims to Victors.*

Hayslip, B., & Peveto, C. A. (2004). *Shifts in Attitudes Toward Death, Dying, and Bereavement.*

Irish, D. P., Lundquist, K. F., & Nelson, V. J. (Eds.). (1993). *Ethnic Variations in Dying, Death, and Grief: Diversity in Universality.*

JanMohamed, A. B. (2004). *The Death-Bound-Subject: Richard Wright's Archaeology of Death.*

Leininger, M. (1995). *Transcultural Nursing: Concepts, Theories, and Practices* (2nd ed.).

McGoldrick, M., Pearce, J. K., & Giordano, J. (Eds.). (1982). *Ethnicity and Family Therapy.*

Mindel, C. H., Habenstein, R. W., & Wright, R. (1988). *Ethnic Families in America: Patterns and Variations* (3rd ed.).

Parry, J. K. (Ed.). (1990). *Social Work Practice with the Terminally Ill: A Transcultural Perspective.*

Parry, J. K., & Ryan, A. S. (Eds.). (1995). *A Cross-Cultural Look at Death, Dying, and Religion.*

Radin, P. (1973). *The Road of Life and Death: A Ritual Drama of the American Indians.*

Rosenblatt, P. C., & Wallace, B. R. (2005b). *African American Grief.*

For examples of reports on death-related experiences outside North American society, see:

Abrahamson, H. (1977). *The Origin of Death: Studies in African Mythology.*

Brodman, B. (1976). *The Mexican Cult of Death in Myth and Literature.*

Counts, D. R., & Counts, D. A. (Eds.). (1991). *Coping with the Final Tragedy: Cultural Variation in Dying and Grieving.*

Danforth, L. M. (1982). *The Death Rituals of Rural Greece.*

Field, D., Hockey, J., & Small, N. (Eds.). (1997). *Death, Gender and Ethnicity.*

Garciagodoy, J. (1998). *Digging the Days of the Dead: A Reading of Mexico's Dias de Muertos.*

Goody, J. (1962). *Death, Property, and the Ancestors: A Study of the Mortuary Customs of the LoDagaa of West Africa.*

Hockey, J. L., Katz, J., Small, N., & Hockey, J. (Eds.). (2001). *Grief, Mourning and Death Rituals.*

Kalish, R. A. (Ed.). (1980). *Death and Dying: Views from Many Cultures.*

Kurtz, D. C., & Boardman, J. (1971). *Greek Burial Customs.*

Lewis, O. (1970). *A Death in the Sanchez Family.*

Morgan, J. D., & Laungani, P. (Eds.). (2003). *Death and Bereavement around the World: Vol. 2, Death and Bereavement in the Americas.*

Morgan, J. D., & Laungani, P. (Eds.). (2004). *Death and Bereavement around the World: Vol. 3, Death and Bereavement in Europe.*

Morgan, J. D., & Laungani, P. (Eds.). (2005). *Death and Bereavement around the World, Vol. 4, Death and Bereavement in Asia, Australia, and New Zealand.*

Parkes, C. M., Laungani, P., & Young, B. (Eds.). (1997). *Death and Bereavement across Cultures.*

Rosenblatt, P. C., Walsh, P. R., & Jackson, D. A. (1976). *Grief and Mourning in Cross-Cultural Perspectives.*

Scheper-Hughes, N. (1992). *Death without Weeping: The Violence of Everyday Life in Brazil.*

Selected Web Resources

Some useful search terms include: AFRICAN AMERICANS AND DEATH; ALASKAN NATIVES AND DEATH; AMERICAN INDIANS AND DEATH; ASIAN AMERI-CANS AND DEATH; CULTURAL DIFFERENCES; ETHNICITY AND DEATH; HISPANIC AMERICANS AND DEATH; NATIVE AMERICANS AND DEATH; PACIFIC ISLAND AMERICANS AND DEATH

Visit the book companion website for *Death & Dying, Life & Living, Sixth Edition,* at academic.cengage.com/psychology/corr for all URLs and live links to the following *organizational and other Internet sites:*

Association of Asian Pacific Community Health Organizations

Duke Institute on Care at the End of Life, Duke University Divinity School

Ethnic Elders Care

National Alliance for Hispanic Health

National Black Women's Health Imperative

National Center for Health Statistics (NCHS)

National Minority AIDS Council

National Native American AIDS Prevention Center

U.S. Census Bureau

PART THREE

Dying

In an extended sense of the word, every living thing can be said to be *dying or* moving toward death from the moment of its conception. However, this stretches the meaning of the word *dying* so far as to make it useless for most customary purposes. Even if we are all dying in some broad sense, some of us are more actively dying than others. In Chapters 6–8, we examine the special situation of those living persons who are closely approaching death—the situation more properly designated as *dying*.

Some people act as if individuals who are dying are already dead or are as good as dead. This is incorrect, unhelpful, and often hurtful. *Dying persons are living human beings;* they remain living persons as long as they are dying. Thus, we emphasize two points here: (1) dying is a special situation in living, not the whole of life; and (2) death is the outcome of dying, not its equivalent.

Some ask, when does dying begin: when a fatal condition develops, when that condition is recognized by a physician, when knowledge of that condition is communicated to the person involved, when that person realizes and accepts the facts of his or her condition, or when nothing more can be done to reverse the condition and to preserve life (Kastenbaum, 2006)? It is not clear whether any or all of these elements are sufficient to define the state of dying. The situation reminds us of a remark attributed to the English statesman Edmund Burke (1729–1797) that it is difficult to determine the precise point at which afternoon becomes evening, even though everyone can easily distinguish between day and night.

For that reason, it is more helpful to focus not on *when dying begins,* but on *what is involved in dying.* Thus, in Chapter 6, we explore *coping with dying,* together with two types of theoretical models designed to help us understand such coping. In Chapter 7, we investigate *ways in which individuals can help persons who are coping with dying.* And in Chapter 8, we look at *how our society has tried to respond to the needs of dying persons,* including the ways in which our society has organized formal programs to care for those who are coping with dying. Here we give special attention to hospice programs and what they offer for end-of-life care.

CHAPTER 6
Coping with Dying

© Spencer Grant

Objectives of This Chapter

An individual with a life-threatening illness or someone who is in the process of dying is first of all *a person, a living human being*. We emphasize this fact because it is fundamental to all that follows: *people who are dying are living human beings*. There may be much that is distinctive or special about individuals with life-limiting conditions or life-threatening illnesses, and particularly about those who are actively dying. That is be-

cause the *pressures of dying* often underscore the *preciousness of living*. However, like all other living persons, those who are dying have a broad range of needs and desires, plans and projects, joys and sufferings, hopes, fears, and anxieties.

Dying is a part (but only one part) of our experiences of life and living; death does not take place until life, living, and dying have ended (McCue, 1995). One cannot already be dead and yet still be dying. To be dead is to be through with dying; to be dying is still to be alive.

Dying persons are not merely individuals within whom biochemical systems are malfunctioning. That is important, but it is not the whole story. Dying is a human experience, and human beings are more than mere objects of anatomy and physiology. If they were merely those sorts of objects, we would not need to pay any attention to the other dimensions of dying persons.

In fact, each person who is dying is a complex and unique entity, intermixing physical, psychological, social, and spiritual dimensions (Saunders, 1967). Psychological difficulties, social discomfort, and spiritual suffering may be just as powerful, pressing, and significant for a dying person as physical distress. To focus on any one of these dimensions alone is to be in danger of ignoring the totality of the person and overlooking what matters most to him or her. To avoid that danger, in this chapter we investigate a series of issues that relate to dying persons and those who are involved with such persons in pursuit of the following objectives:

◆ To define *coping* and explain some of its key elements

◆ To describe *coping with dying*, keeping in mind that such coping typically involves more than one person

◆ To explain the concepts of *dying trajectories* and *awareness contexts*

◆ To explore two types of models—one based on *stages*, the other on *tasks*—that have been proposed to explain what is involved in coping with dying

🌿 One Family Coping with Life-Threatening Illness and Dying

Josephina Ryan was 63 when she first felt a small lump in her right breast. Until that awful moment in the shower, Jo thought she had been very fortunate in her life. She and Matt had met when he was stationed in her native Philippines. After their marriage and return to the States, the Ryans had five sons and a daughter, now all well established in their own lives and careers. Three of the boys and Christy were married, and they had given their parents six grandchildren between them. Jo had enjoyed raising her children and then returning to her career as a third-grade teacher. Matt was coming up to retirement as a high school principal. He had been very fortunate five years ago when an early diagnosis and surgery had cured him of prostate cancer. After Matt's retirement, they were anticipating spending more time visiting their children and grandchildren, while also traveling to various places with Elderhostel.

When Matt was diagnosed with prostate cancer, it was as if he had been hit over the head with a club. He was stunned and just didn't seem to know what to do. Jo was the strong one throughout that ordeal. She took a brief leave of absence from teaching, coordinated Matt's medical care, kept in touch with all the kids, and was a gentle rock on which Matt could lean. Still, it did help that the testing and the surgery went by pretty fast, and Matt experienced no postoperative complications.

Jo had feared breast cancer, because it had taken her mother and her aunt several years ago. So Jo had been relieved when her family physician had given her a clean bill of health six months ago after her annual physical exam. But now it seemed like maybe it really was her turn.

Still, her first thoughts were about Matt and the kids, not herself. Christy was a strong person, but Jake and Patrick still turned to Mom when they encountered tough times. And, except for Tom and his wife, they all lived far away. There were just so many things to think about!

Jo's biopsy shocked the Ryans. They had to decide quickly about treatment. A partial mastectomy and what the physicians called a "prophylactic" combination of radiation and chemotherapy seemed to kill all the malignant cells, but the nausea, hair loss, and other side effects were really hard to bear. Matt looked just like a lost child during this time, as if he were wandering through life but not recognizing any familiar landmarks.

Afterward, Jo and Matt did have some good times together. They sincerely hoped "the terrors" (as they called them) were all gone. But not many months later (or so it seemed), it looked as if the cancer had only gone into hiding temporarily and was roaring back with a vengeance. Jo's physicians were unsure whether this was a new disease or a recurrence of the old one. In any event, it must have lurked silently for a while to account for its rapid development and spread. There were more tests, new diagnoses, and several rounds of treatment, but the cancer kept spreading.

Toward the end, Jo could hardly leave her bed. Prayer was comforting for the Ryan family, but it was truly a difficult time for Jo and Matt and all those who loved them.

❦ Coping

The American humorist Josh Billings (1818–1885) is reported to have observed that "life consists not in holding good cards but in playing those you do hold well." How we play our cards, particularly in response to life's major challenges, is a metaphor for how we cope, as Matt and Josephina Ryan learned during their own struggles. To understand issues related to coping with dying, it will help us first to clarify what coping means and what it involves.

A Definition of Coping and Its Central Elements

The term *coping* has been defined as "constantly changing cognitive and behavioral efforts to manage specific external and/or internal demands that are appraised as taxing or exceeding the resources of the person" (Lazarus & Folkman, 1984, p. 141; compare Monat & Lazarus, 1991).

This definition can help us to understand both coping with living and coping with dying by:

◆ Focusing on *processes* of coping, with special reference to their changing character—thus emphasizing that coping involves activity and is not static

◆ Directing attention to *efforts* that are central to coping, whatever one is thinking or doing to cope—not only as affective traits that characterize internal feeling states—and reminding us that these efforts may take many forms (cognitive, behavioral, or others)

- Underlining attempts *to manage* a situation, to live or get along with it as best one can
- Linking coping to efforts addressing *specific demands* (wherever or however they originate) *that are perceived as stressful* (Note two corollaries: unperceived demands are usually not stressful; also, because perceptions may change, coping processes may adjust to new perceptions.)
- Referring to efforts undertaken in response to *demands that are appraised as taxing or exceeding the resources of the person,* and thus distinguishing coping from routine, automatized, adaptive behaviors that do not involve an effortful response
- Taking care *not to confuse coping processes with their outcomes*

In short, coping includes any efforts to manage stressful demands, however successful or unsuccessful such efforts might be. Coping does not necessarily seek to *master* stressful demands. A coping person may try—more or less successfully—to master a particular situation but often is content to accept, endure, minimize, or avoid stressful demands.

Moos and Schaefer (1986) extended our understanding of coping by grouping coping skills into three separate categories (see Table 6.1): (1) *appraisal-focused coping* centers on how one understands or appraises a stressful situation; (2) *problem-focused coping* relates to what one does about the problem or stressor itself; and (3) *emotion-focused coping* involves what one does about one's reactions to the perceived problem. We prefer to call this last type of coping *reaction-focused coping* so as not to limit it to feelings alone (see Chapter 9, p. 213). In any event, a person's coping may emphasize any one or all of these focal perspectives, and, as Moos and Schaefer (1986, p. 13) observed, "the word *skill* underscores the positive aspects of coping and depicts coping as an ability that can be taught and used flexibly as the situation requires."

Coping as Learned and Dynamic Behavior

Coping is central to the response one makes to any situation that is perceived as stressful (Corr & Doka, 2001). Such situations might involve almost any aspect of life or death: a death or a significant loss of any type (the ending of a relationship, failing to succeed in some endeavor, being fired from a job, a divorce, and so forth), as well as happier events, such as winning the lottery, taking up a new challenge in life, getting married, or having a baby. Any situations like these might be perceived as stressful. How they are perceived depends upon the individual. How the individual responds to such situations will have much to do with how he or she has learned to respond (Corr & Corr, 2007a).

In thinking about coping with loss, Davidson (1975, p. 28) wrote: "We are born with the *ability* to adapt to change, but we all must *learn* how to cope with loss." As individuals move through life, they observe how others around them cope with separation, loss, and endings—the "necessary losses" (Viorst, 1986) that none of us can avoid, such as a child's discovery that his or her parents are not superhuman or an adult's observations of elderly parents who are becoming less able to care for themselves. Often, we try out in our own lives strategies we have watched others use in coping, or we simply rely on methods that have proved satisfactory to us in

TABLE 6.1
Coping: Three Focal Domains and Nine Types of Skills

Appraisal-Focused Coping

1. *Logical analysis and mental preparation:* Paying attention to one aspect of the crisis at a time, breaking a seemingly overwhelming problem into small, potentially manageable bits, drawing on past experiences, and mentally rehearsing alternative actions and their probable consequences
2. *Cognitive redefinition:* Using cognitive strategies to accept the basic reality of a situation but restructure it to find something favorable
3. *Cognitive avoidance or denial:* Denying or minimizing the seriousness of a crisis

Problem-Focused Coping

4. *Seeking information and support:* Obtaining information about the crisis and alternate courses of action and their probable outcome
5. *Taking problem-solving action:* Taking concrete action to deal directly with a crisis or its aftermath
6. *Identifying alternative rewards:* Attempting to replace the losses involved in certain transitions and crises by changing one's activities and creating new sources of satisfaction

Emotion-Focused Coping

7. *Affective regulation:* Trying to maintain hope and control one's emotions when dealing with a distressing situation
8. *Emotional discharge:* Openly venting one's feelings and using jokes and gallows humor to help allay constant strain
9. *Resigned acceptance:* Coming to terms with a situation and accepting it as it is, deciding that the basic circumstances cannot be altered and submitting to "certain" fate

Source: From "Life Transitions and Crises: A Conceptual Overview," by R. H. Moos and J. A. Schaefer. In R. H. Moos and J. A. Schaefer (Eds.), *Coping with Life Crises: An Integrated Approach,* pp. 3–28. Copyright 1986 Plenum Publishing Corporation. Reprinted with permission of Springer Science and Business Media.

the past. Some of us have little choice in the ways in which we are able to cope: the situation does not present us with many alternatives. Sometimes we can do little about the source of the stress and must focus mainly on our reactions to that situation. In any case, each individual tries to acquire a repertoire of skills that facilitate coping with challenges in life, responding to needs, and helping that person adapt in satisfactory ways.

One popular book, *Who Moved My Cheese?* (Johnson, 1998), tried to depict how individuals cope with challenges and loss. Some people when confronted with an object that blocks their forward journey speed up their engines and charge full speed ahead, crashing into and perhaps through the barrier. Other persons who encounter a roadblock back away and try to find some way around it. Others simply remain stationary, not moving forward, not seeking a way around. Still other people go off in some different direction, seeing the roadblock as something that cannot be overcome and that demands some other road be taken.

In seeking to understand coping, it is important to know *how individuals who are coping perceive their situation and what they are actually thinking or doing in specific contexts of stressful demands* (Hinton, 1984; Silver & Wortman, 1980). One must ask what this particular person is actually thinking or doing as the stressful encounter unfolds, not what people in general do in similar situations, and not even what that individual might do, should do, or usually does in such circumstances. As we observed in the vignette near the beginning of this chapter, Matt and Jo Ryan each reacted to and coped with their spouse's life-threatening illness in different ways. Also, because coping involves shifting processes as the relationship between the person and his or her environment changes, different forms of coping may be undertaken at different times. For example, defensive responses may give way to problem-solving strategies. Thus, what is critical is the actual focus of the individual's coping at any given time.

All of the ways in which one learns to cope are not likely to be of equal value. Some ways of coping are useful in most situations. Some have value in certain situations but not in others. Some merely seem to be effective even though they actually are counterproductive. Some ways of coping may be satisfactory to one person but hurtful to others. The better we learn to cope with past and present losses, the more likely we will be able to cope effectively with future losses.

In each particular situation, we can ask: What does the individual perceive as stressful? How is the individual coping with that stress? Why is he or she coping in this particular way? These questions apply to coping with dying as well as to coping with all other challenges in living. For that reason, although there are significant differences between death and other sorts of stressors or losses, how one copes with the "little deaths" (Purtillo, 1976) and other stressful challenges throughout life may be indicative of how one is likely to cope with the large crises involved in death itself.

Coping with Dying: Who Is Coping?

Coping with dying typically involves more than a single individual. When we reflect on such coping, most often we think immediately of the ill person, the principal actor who is at the center of the coping challenge. That is where we should always begin, but we should not end there because coping with dying is not solely confined to ill and dying persons. Coping with dying is also a challenge for others who are drawn into such situations. These include the family members and friends of the dying person (Grollman, 1995b). They also involve volunteer and professional caregivers who attend to the dying person and must face his or her death, as one surgeon has made clear (Chen, 2006).

Confronting imminent death and coping with dying are experiences that resonate deeply within the personal sense of mortality and limitation of all who are drawn into these processes. A family member who says to a dying person, "Don't die on me," may be conveying anguish at the pending loss of a loved one. A caregiver who says, "I hope we won't lose Mr. Smith tonight," may be expressing frustration at his or her inability to prevent the coming of death or concern with the consequences that Mr. Smith's death will bring for the caregiver. In the case of families, it is especially important to note that people who are coping with dying do so not only as particular, unique individuals but also as members of a family system, and as members of society—all of which influence their coping (Rosen, 1998). For example, a conflicted relationship between a parent and a child or between two siblings who have fought for years may generate special issues that need to be addressed in the context of coping with dying.

The Hospice of the Florida Suncoast

Dying persons still care for and can be cared for by others.

Coping with dying is usually multifaceted. It involves more than one person, and thus involves more than one set of perceptions of what is going on, more than one set of motivations, and more than one way of coping. Those who wish to understand coping with dying need to identify *each person* who is involved in that activity and listen carefully to what his or her coping reveals (Kessler, 2000). Only by empathetic listening can we hope to understand what the coping means for each individual in each particular situation. Only by striving to understand each individual's coping efforts can we hope to appreciate how he or she is interacting in the shared dynamic of the situation. Sensitivity to outward behaviors, to underlying feelings, and to key variables is essential in such listening. (See Focus On 6.1 for examples of literature on coping with dying.)

🐛 Dying Trajectories and Awareness Contexts

Glaser and Strauss (1965, 1968) described two key variables in coping with dying. They are the nature of the dying trajectory and the degree to which those who are involved are aware of and share information about dying. These variables describe both the individual situation and the social context within which coping with dying takes place.

All dying persons do not move toward death at the same rates of speed or in the same ways. Processes of dying or coming to be dead have their own distinctive characteristics in each individual case. As we saw in Chapter 2, Glaser and Strauss (1968) suggested that we should understand *dying trajectories* in terms of two principal characteristics: duration and shape (see Figure 2.2). Some dying

Selected Descriptions of Coping with Life-Threatening Illness

Albom, M. (1997). *Tuesdays with Morrie: An Old Man, A Young Man, and Life's Greatest Lesson.*

Armstrong, L., & Jenkins, S. (2001). *It's Not About the Bike: My Journey Back to Life.*

Barnard, D., Towers, A., Boston, P., & Lambrinidou, Y. (2000). *Crossing Over: Narratives of Palliative Care.*

Broyard, A. (1992). *Intoxicated by My Illness and Other Writings on Life and Death.*

Buchwald, A. (2006). *Too Soon to Say Goodbye.*

Chen, P. W. (2006). *Final Exam: A Surgeon's Reflections on Mortality.*

Cousins, N. (1979). *Anatomy of an Illness as Perceived by the Patient: Reflections on Healing and Regeneration.*

Craven, M. (1973). *I Heard the Owl Call My Name.**

Fanestil, J. (2006). *Mrs. Hunter's Happy Death: Lessons on Living from People Preparing to Die.*

Faulkner, W. (1930). *As I Lay Dying.**

Frank, A. W. (2002). *At the Will of the Body: Reflections on Illness* (new ed.).

Gunther, J. (1949). *Death Be Not Proud.*

Hanlan, A. (1979). *Autobiography of Dying.*

Hunter, E. [aka Ed McBain]. (2005). *Let's Talk: A Story of Cancer and Love.*

Jury, M., & Jury, D. (1978). *Gramps: A Man Ages and Dies.*

Kelly, O. (1975). *Make Today Count.*

Mack, S. (2004). *Janet and Me: An Illustrated Story of Love and Loss.*

MacPherson, M. (1999). *She Came to Live Out Loud: An Inspiring Family Journey Through Illness, Loss, and Grief.*

Mandell, H., & Spiro, H. (Eds.). (1987). *When Doctors Get Sick*

Quindlen, A. (1994). *One True Thing.**

Rauschi, T. M. (2001). *A View from Within: Living with Early Onset Alzheimer's.*

Rosenthal, T. (1973). *How Could I Not Be Among You?*

Ryan, C., & Ryan, K. M. (1979). *A Private Battle.*

Schwartz, M. (1999). *Morrie: In His Own Words.*

Sontag, S. (1978). *Illness as Metaphor.*

Tolstoy, L. (1884/1960). *The Death of Ivan Ilych and Other Stories.**

Webster, B. D. (1989). *All of a Piece: A Life with Multiple Sclerosis.*

Weisman, M.-L. (1982). *Intensive Care: A Family Love Story.*

Wertenbaker, L. T. (1957). *Death of a Man.*

Zorza, V., & Zorza, R. (1980). *A Way to Die.*

*Titles marked with an asterisk are fiction.

trajectories involve an up-and-down history of remission, relapse, remission, and so on—often in a rather unpredictable way. Other dying trajectories make relatively steady progress toward death. In some cases, the dying trajectory may be completed in a very brief, even instantaneous, span of time; in other cases, it may be slow, extending over a period of weeks, months, or even years as in the growing incidence of Alzheimer's disease and other end-of-life situations involving dementia (Hebert et al., 2003).

Obviously, there are variations on these simple patterns. For example, the time when death will occur or the moment when the process will resolve itself so that its ultimate outcome becomes clear may or may not be predictable. We may know that the person will die, when the death will occur, and how it will take place, or we may be unclear about one or more of these points.

Awareness contexts have to do with social interactions among those who are coping with dying. Glaser and Strauss (1965) argued that once a person in our society is discovered to be dying, the relationships between that person and his or her close associates and health care providers can take at least four basic forms.

1. *Closed awareness* is a context in which the person who is dying does not realize that fact. The staff, and perhaps also the family, may know that the person is dying, but that information has not been conveyed to the dying person, nor does he or she even suspect it. Many have thought (and some still do) that it is desirable not to convey diagnostic and prognostic information to dying persons. In fact, this sort of knowledge usually cannot be hidden for long. Communication is achieved in complex, subtle, and sometimes unconscious ways, and awareness is likely to develop at several levels. For example, changes in one's own body associated with progression of the disease, along with alterations in the behaviors of others or changes in their physical appearance, often lead to gradual or partial recognition that all is not well.

2. *Suspected awareness* identifies a context in which the ill person may begin to suspect that he or she has not been given all of the information that is relevant to his or her situation. For a variety of reasons—for example, tests, treatments, or other behaviors that do not seem to correspond with the supposed problem—the person who is ill may begin to suspect that more is going on than is being said. This may undermine trust and complicate future communications.

3. *Mutual pretense* describes a context that was once (and may still be) quite common, in which the relevant information is held by all the individual parties in the situation but is not shared between them. In other words, mutual pretense involves a kind of communal drama in which everyone involved acts out a role intended to say that things are not as they know them to be. "It is the horse on the dining-room table," as Kalish told us in the Prologue to this book. As mutual pretense is lived out, it may even be conducted so as to cover over embarrassing moments when the strategy of dissembling or evading the truth fails temporarily. This is a fragile situation; one slip can cause the entire structure to collapse. Mutual pretense requires constant vigilance and a great deal of effort. Consequently, it is extremely demanding for everyone involved.

4. *Open awareness* describes a context in which the dying person and everyone else realizes and is willing to discuss the fact that death is near. Those who share an open awareness context may or may not actually spend much time discussing the fact that the person is dying. On some occasions, one or the other person may not want to talk about it right then. After all, as has aptly been said, "No one is dying 24 hours a day." But there is no pretense; when persons are ready and willing to discuss the realities of the situation, they are able to do so.

These are four different types of awareness contexts; they are not steps in a linear progression from inhibition to openness. The point is that social interactions and coping with dying are likely to be affected by awareness contexts. Each awareness context brings with it some potential costs and some potential benefits. At some moments, for example, the anxiety and grief of the family member (or staff person) raised by the oncoming death of a loved one may make discussion of that event too difficult to endure. Avoidance of reality can get some people through a difficult moment and thus, in certain circumstances, may be a productive way of coping for that moment.

In general, however, open awareness allows for honest communication if participants are ready for such interaction. It permits each involved person to participate in the shared grief of an approaching loss. Important words of concern and affection can be spoken (Byock, 2004). Ancient wounds can be healed. Unfinished business—between the dying person and his or her family members, friends, or God—can be addressed. These benefits come at the cost of having to admit and face powerful feelings (such as anger, sadness, and perhaps guilt) and recognized facts (e.g., tasks not completed, choices unmade, and paths not taken). This can be quite difficult and painful. Nevertheless, for many persons these costs are preferable to those associated with lack of openness. Always, one balances costs against benefits in both the short and long run.

With these understandings of coping, dying trajectories, and awareness contexts in mind, we turn next to two types of models that have been proposed to explain coping with dying.

🌱 Coping with Dying: A Stage-Based Approach

The best-known model of coping with dying is the *stage-based model* put forward by the Swiss-American psychiatrist Dr. Elisabeth Kübler-Ross (Gill, 1980; Kübler-Ross, 1997). In her book *On Death and Dying* (1969), Kübler-Ross reported the results of a series of interviews that focused on psychosocial reactions in persons who were dying. She developed a theoretical model of five stages in such reactions (see Table 6.2). Kübler-Ross understood these stages as "defense mechanisms" that "will last for different periods of time and will replace each other or exist at times side by side" (p. 138). In addition, she maintained that "the one thing that usually persists through all these stages is *hope*" (p. 138).

In other words, Kübler-Ross argued that dying persons are people who are in a stressful situation. Because they are living persons, like people in other stressful

TABLE 6.2
Kübler-Ross's Five Stages in Coping with Dying

Stage	Typical Expression
Denial	"Not me!"
Anger	"Why me?"
Bargaining	"Yes me, but . . ."
Depression	
Reactive	Responding to past and present losses
Preparatory	Anticipating and responding to losses yet to come
Acceptance	Described as a stage "almost void of feelings"

Source: Based on Kübler-Ross, 1969.

situations, they employ or develop a number of different ways of responding to their situation. So dying persons may cope by withdrawing, or by becoming angry, or by finding what has occurred in their lives up to now that might make death acceptable. One major point to be underlined again is that *different people cope in different ways at different times and in different contexts.*

Kübler-Ross's stages had an immediate attractiveness for many who read about or heard of this model. Her work helped to bring dying persons and issues involved in coping with dying to public and professional attention. She also made it possible for others to go beyond her initial report. In particular, her model identified common patterns of psychosocial responses to difficult situations, responses with which we are all familiar. In addition, it drew attention to the human aspects of living with dying, to the strong feelings experienced by those who are coping with dying, and to what Kübler-Ross called the "unfinished business" that many want to address. Kübler-Ross said that her book is "simply an account of a new and challenging opportunity to refocus on the patient as a human being, to include him in dialogues, to learn from him the strengths and weaknesses of our hospital management of the patient. We have asked him to be our teacher so that we may learn more about the final stages of life with all its anxieties, fears, and hopes" (p. xi).

Nevertheless, there are significant difficulties in accepting Kübler-Ross's model as first presented. Research by others (e.g., Metzger, 1979; Schulz & Aderman, 1974) does not support this model. In fact, since the initial appearance of this model in 1969, there has been no independent confirmation of its validity or reliability, and Kübler-Ross advanced no further evidence on its behalf before her death in August 2004. On the contrary, many clinicians who work with the dying have found this model to be inadequate, superficial, and misleading (e.g., Pattison, 1977; Shneidman, 1980/1995; Weisman, 1977). Widespread acclaim in the popular arena contrasts with sharp criticism from scholars and those who work with dying persons (Klass, 1982; Klass & Hutch, 1985; see also Issues for Critical Reflection #7).

One serious and thorough evaluation of this stage-based model raised the following points: (1) the existence of these stages as such has not been demonstrated; (2) no

#7 What Can We Learn from the Legacy of Elisabeth Kübler-Ross?

Elisabeth Kübler-Ross died on August 24, 2004 (Kessler, 2004). After her death, reflection on the legacies that we inherit from her life and work is appropriate (Kramer, 2005). Some see her theoretical framework, an account of five "stages" experienced by dying persons as set forth in her book, *On Death and Dying* (1969), as her main bequest to others. But at least as important are her lectures, presentations, and other publications that captured the attention of a broad range of audiences. Her workshops in which she taught about the skills involved in being a good care provider for oneself and for others are another significant part of her legacy. And there are many who have been interested in her thoughts about out-of-body experiences and the afterlife.

In general, though, perhaps the most significant lessons that will endure from the work of Elisabeth Kübler-Ross can be found in the brief Preface (p. xi) to her 1969 book (Corr, 1993a). The first of these lessons appears when Kübler-Ross asked her readers to "refocus on the patient as a human being." She meant by this to point out that *those who are coping with dying are still alive* and often have, as she often said, "unfinished business" that they want and need to address. They are not (yet) dead and they deserve to be acknowledged as vital and still active.

The second lesson appears when Kübler-Ross calls upon her readers to "include [the patient] in dialogues, to learn from [that person] the strengths and weaknesses of our ... management of" his or her illness and interests. This lesson is not just about patients, but includes anyone who is coping with dying.

Its main application, however, is to all of the individuals—professionals, volunteers, family members, and friends—who set out to help anyone engaged in such coping. In this lesson, Kübler-Ross drew attention to the fact that *none of us can be an effective care provider unless we listen actively to those we seek to serve and identify with them in their own tasks and needs.*

The third lesson highlights our need to ask those who are coping with dying "to be our teacher so that *we* may learn more about the final stages of life with all its anxieties, fears, and hopes." The crux of this lesson is *our need to learn from those who are dying and coping with dying to come to know ourselves better* (as limited, vulnerable, finite, and mortal, but also as resilient, adaptable, interdependent, and lovable).

In turn, these are lessons about all who are dying and coping with dying; about becoming and being a provider of care; and about what we all need to live our own lives in the most authentic ways.

evidence has been presented that people actually do move from stage 1 through stage 5; (3) the limitations of the method have not been acknowledged; (4) the line is blurred between description and prescription; (5) the totality of the person's life is neglected in favor of the supposed stages of dying; and (6) the resources, pressures, and characteristics of the immediate environment, which can make a tremendous difference, are not taken into account (Kastenbaum, 2006). And we can add a seventh point: Kübler-Ross' theory assumes or at least suggests that we can describe the way in which all human persons respond to stress, independently of any social or cultural influence. But in fact, our social and cultural milieux are essential components influencing how we respond, and even think about responding, to stress. As we noted briefly in Chapter 5, different cultures have different expectations, values, and practices which influence how their members will respond to stress. To leave these out of one's theory is to provide an inadequate account of actual human experience.

If one thinks for a moment about the traits that Kübler-Ross has described as stages, one can see that they are so broadly formulated that they actually designate a variety of reactions. For example, "denial" can describe the following range of responses: (1) I am not ill; (2) I am ill, but it is not serious; (3) I am seriously ill, but not dying; (4) I am dying, but death will not come for a long time; or (5) I am dying and death will come shortly (Weisman, 1972). Similarly, "acceptance" may take the form of an enthusiastic welcoming, a grudging resignation, or a variety of other responses. In addition to noting that there may be orders of denial and of acceptance, Weisman pointed out that denial may have positive value when it permits ill persons to take part in therapy and sustain hope. Further, Weisman proposed the concept of "*middle knowledge*" according to which individuals may sometimes affirm or at other times deny the closeness of death. If this is true, then the important question is not "Does the patient accept or deny death?," but rather "When, with whom, and under what circumstances does the patient discuss the possibility of death?"

In addition, when Kübler-Ross speaks about the trait of "depression," one wonders if she meant sadness, not clinical depression, which is a psychiatric diagnosis of illness and not a normative coping process. Further, we know that there are many ways, not just five, in which to react to dying or any other important event in life.

Moreover, there is no reason to think that the particular five ways identified by Kübler-Ross are linked together as *stages* in a larger process. To some extent, Kübler-Ross agreed with this latter point, insofar as she argued for fluidity, give-and-take, the possibility of experiencing two of these responses simultaneously, or an ability to jump around from one stage to another. This suggests that the language of "stages," with its associated implications of linear progression and regression, is not really appropriate for a cluster of disconnected coping strategies. Stage theories are attractive because they are usually relatively simple, straight-lined, predictable, and culminating in a clear end, but that does not make them necessarily valid or reliable.

Another problem with this model—for which its author is not wholly responsible—is that many people have misused it. There is some irony in this fact. After all, Kübler-Ross set out to argue that dying persons are mistreated when they are objectified—that is, when they are treated as a "liver case" or as a "cardiac case." Unfortunately, since the publication of *On Death and Dying*, some people have come to treat dying persons as a "case of anger" or a "case of depression," others have told ill persons that they have already been angry and should now "move on" to bargaining or depression, and still others have become frustrated by those whom they view as "stuck" in the dying process. (But if I am stuck in the dying process, does that mean I cannot die?) Misusing the Kübler-Ross stage model in ways like these simply forces those who are coping with dying into a pre-established framework that reduces their individuality to little more than an instance of one of five categories (anger, or depression, or . . .) in a schematic

Copyright © Stefan Verwey

process. That is why Rosenthal (1973, p. 39), when he was coping with his own dying, wrote, "Being invisible I invite only generalizations."

All these points suggest that the language of stages and the metaphor of a linear theory (*first* one denies, *then* one is angry, *then* one bargains, etc.) are simply not adequate as a basis for explaining coping with dying. Also, it is not enough to say that a person is "in denial" or has "reached acceptance" if one is to understand that individual in more than a superficial and potentially misleading way.

Perhaps it would be better simply to speak of a broad range of responses to the experience of dying. Essentially, this is what Shneidman (1973a, p. 7) meant by what he called a "hive of affect," a busy, buzzing, active set of feelings, attitudes, and other reactions, to which a person returns from time to time, now expressing one posture (e.g., anger), now another (e.g., denial). The person may return to the hive and experience the same feelings again and again, sometimes simultaneously, sometimes one day after another, sometimes with long intervals in between.

❦ Coping with Dying: A Task-Based Approach

Why Suggest a Task-Based Model?

A *task-based model* of coping with dying seeks to avoid metaphors that emphasize a passive or merely reactive way of understanding such coping. As Weisman (1984) noted, coping involves more than an automatic response or a defensive reaction. Also, a posture of defense is largely a *negative* one; it channels energy into avoiding problems, rather than achieving some kind of adaptive accommodation. That may be useful initially and sometimes on later occasions—for example, as a way of obtaining time in which to mobilize personal or social resources. However, *coping is, or at least can be, an active process, a doing with a positive orientation that seeks to resolve problems or adapt to challenges in living.*

Tasks are work that can be undertaken in coping with dying. When one is coping with dying, like all other work, one can always choose not to take on a particular task. One can proceed with a task, leave it for another time, or work on it for a while and then set it aside. In the face of a series of tasks, one can choose to undertake all or none of them, to attempt this one or that one. The main point is that choice implies empowerment.

Tasks are not merely *needs*. They cannot be reduced to and may include more than needs, even if needs often underlie the task work that one undertakes. The term *task* identifies what a person is trying to do in his or her coping, the specific effort that he or she is making to achieve what is required or desired. Focusing on the language of "needs" often shifts the focus to what others might do to help. Assistance from others in support of an individual's coping tasks can be important and may even be necessary, but it usually ought to take second place to one's own coping efforts.

We explore a task-based model to show that individuals who are coping with life-threatening illness and dying are actors, not just re-actors. They can decide how to cope with their experiences in various ways. This puts the central emphasis on the active efforts that are, at least in principle, open to the person coping with dying. Even when such efforts are not possible in practice (for example, when an individual is unconscious), a task-based model encourages others to see things from the individual's point of view and to arrange or modify their efforts accordingly. This is critical to appreciate the complexity, richness, and variability of the human experiences of living with life-threatening illness and coping with dying.

A Task-Based Model for Coping with Dying

Corr (1992a) proposed that four primary areas of task work can be identified in coping with dying. Clues to the identity of these areas of task work come from the four dimensions in the life of a human being: the physical, the psychological, the social, and the spiritual. These four areas of task work are listed in Table 6.3, along with some suggestions about the basic types of tasks in coping with dying that might be associated with each area. Recall, however, that coping involves individualized responses to concrete situations. If so, full understanding of coping with dying must reflect the specific tasks undertaken by each individual who is coping.

TABLE 6.3
Four Areas of Task Work in Coping with Dying

Areas of Task Work	Basic Types of Tasks in Coping with Dying
Physical	To satisfy *bodily needs* and to minimize *physical distress*, in ways that are consistent with other values
Psychological	To maximize *psychological security, autonomy*, and *richness*
Social	To sustain and enhance those *interpersonal attachments* that are significant to the person concerned, and to sustain selected *interactions with social groups within society or with society itself*
Spiritual	To address issues of *meaningfulness, connectedness*, and *transcendence* and, in so doing, to foster *hope*

Source: Based on Corr, 1992a.

Physical Tasks Physical tasks are associated with bodily needs and physical distress—that is, coping with such matters as pain, nausea, or constipation, and satisfying such needs as hydration and nutrition. *Bodily needs* are fundamental to maintaining biological life and functioning. As Maslow (1971) argued, satisfaction of fundamental bodily needs is usually the indispensable foundation on which the work of meeting other needs can be built. In addition, *physical distress* cries out for relief both for its own sake and in order that the rest of life can be appreciated and lived well. For example, individuals who are experiencing intense pain, severe nausea, or active vomiting are unlikely to be capable of rich psychosocial or spiritual interactions at the same time.

Note, however, that humans can and sometimes do choose to subordinate bodily needs and physical distress to other values. For example, martyrs have endured torture for the sake of spiritual values, and some individuals have been known to sacrifice their own lives for the sake of protecting those whom they love. More simply, individuals who are dying may choose to accept a slightly higher degree of pain or discomfort to be able to stay at home, rather than entering an institution in which constant supervision by skilled professionals could achieve a higher standard in the management of distressing physical symptoms. Others who are offered the support of in-home services may prefer to be in an institution, where they have less fear of being alone, falling, and lying unattended for hours.

Psychological Tasks A second area of task work in coping with dying concerns psychological security, autonomy, and richness. Like the rest of us, individuals who are coping with dying seek a sense of *security* even in a situation that in many ways may not be safe. For example, if they are dependent on others to provide needed services, they may need to be assured that those providers are reliable.

Also, most individuals who are coping with dying wish to retain their *autonomy*, insofar as that is possible. Autonomy means the ability to govern or be in charge of one's own life (*auto* = self + *nomous* = regulating). In fact, no one has control over the whole of one's life; each person is limited and all are interdependent in a host of ways. Autonomy designates the shifting degrees and kinds of influence that individuals are able to exercise within everyday constraints. Nevertheless, for most persons, it is important to retain some degree of self-government. Some wish to make the big decisions in their lives on their own; others simply wish to designate who should make decisions on their behalf. Some turn over much of the management of their own bodies to professionals, even while they retain authority over some symbolic decisions. An outsider cannot say in advance how autonomy will or should be exercised; that would undercut the very notion of *self*-regulation (Gaylin & Jennings, 2003).

For many people, achieving a sense of security and autonomy contributes to a *psychological richness in living* (see Personal Insights 6.1). Many who are near the end of life still appreciate opportunities for a regular shave and haircut, to have their hair washed and set, to use a special bath powder, or to dress in a comfortable and attractive way. Some dying persons may find it important to their psychological well-being to have a taste of a favorite food or to continue a lifelong habit of drinking a glass of wine with meals. The issues involved here refer to *personal dignity and quality in living*.

Social Tasks   A third area of task work in coping with dying concerns two interrelated aspects of social living. Each of us is involved in attachments to other individual persons as well as in relationships to society itself and to its subordinate groups.

PERSONAL INSIGHTS 6.1

Fantasy on a Summer Afternoon

*One day when I was sailing
    quietly up the bay
I listened very intently
And thought I heard a seagull say,
    "You've never had it so good,
    You've never had it so good."
And I thought, "You don't do so
badly soaring up there in the blue."
Then I passed a wise old pelican
    standing sentinel on a pile.
He blinked his beady eyes and said,
    "But it only lasts a little while,
    But it only lasts a little while."
And what he said is true.*

Source: Dr. Alfred King. Reprinted with permission of The Hospice of the Florida Suncoast.

Just because you have a life-threatening illness doesn't always mean you can't continue to enjoy a favorite activity.

One set of social tasks has to do with sustaining and enhancing the *interpersonal attachments* valued by the coping person. Dying individuals often narrow the scope of their interests. They may no longer care about international politics, their former duties at work, college or professional sports, or a large circle of friends. Instead, they may increasingly focus on issues and attachments that involve a progressively smaller number of individuals now perceived as most important in their lives. In this way, they gain freedom from responsibilities now judged to be less compelling or more burdensome than before. The scope of their social interests and concerns has shifted to fit their new priorities.

There is no obvious set of interpersonal tasks on which each person *must* focus. Only the individual can decide which attachments he or she values, and these decisions may alter as one lives through the process of coping with dying. However, autonomy is restricted in a fundamental way if the significance of each attachment is not a matter of individual decision making.

A consequence of this interpersonal dimension of coping with dying is that each person involved will have at least two sets of tasks: one conducted on his or her own behalf and another conducted in relation to the interests of others who are involved. For example, a dying person may face some tasks related to his or her own concerns and others related to the concerns of family members or caregivers. The person may choose to decline further efforts at cure because they are too burdensome and offer too little promise of help; in so doing, that person may be obliged to help family members or caregivers accept this decision and become reconciled to its implications for how soon death will arrive. Similarly, family members may have tasks related to their own concerns, as well as tasks related to their responsibilities to assist the dying person. For themselves, they may seek rest or relief from the burdens of caregiving; for the ill person, it may be important for them to be available to provide companionship and a sense of security. Although only the individual can decide the relative importance of these often-conflicting tasks, it is usually helpful if the dying person and his or her support persons can discuss these matters openly.

A second set of social tasks has to do with *interactions with social groups within society or with society itself*. Society seeks to protect its citizens from harm, to prohibit certain types of behavior, to ensure that property is correctly handed over to legitimate heirs, and to offer certain sorts of assistance and benefit. Social groups may have their own religious and cultural rituals, expectations, and prohibitions. Like all events in living, dying implicates people in social systems. These systems are constructed and implemented by individuals, but they represent the interests of the group. Social tasks in coping with dying include interacting with social systems as may seem desirable or necessary, responding to demands that society and its organizations continue to make (for example, hospital bills and income taxes may still need to be paid), and drawing on social resources as needed (for example, to obtain hospital equipment, transportation, or "Meals on Wheels" services from charitable organizations).

Spiritual Tasks The spiritual area of task work in coping with dying is more difficult to describe than the other three areas, for several reasons. One is that there is little agreement about just what is meant by "spiritual" (Klass, 2006; Stanworth, 2003). Most would agree that "spiritual" concerns are not merely limited to or identified with "religious" concerns. If spiritual and religious concerns were thought to be identical, that would suggest that someone without a religious connection has no

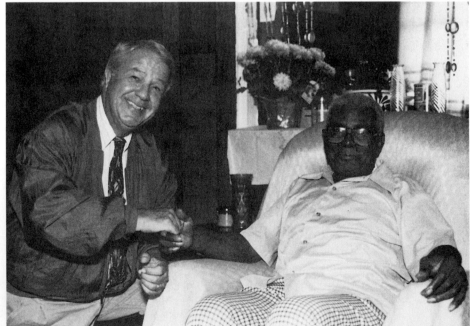

A chaplain visiting a patient at home.

The Hospice of the Florida Suncoast

spiritual tasks to work on. However, this belief is untrue and therefore unhelpful. It might even lead caregivers to miss or to ignore important clues about certain crucial tasks with which a dying person is struggling.

Second, modern societies, including North American societies, are increasingly made up of many subcultures, and this is true spiritually, too. Roman Catholics and Muslims, Baptist Protestant Christians and Hindus, Buddhists and Unitarians, Dakota and Zuni Native Americans, atheists and agnostics—these and a large number of others (and variations on all of these) may be found among those whose spiritual tasks we are trying to understand as part of their coping with dying. However, we cannot be expected to know and to understand all of these traditions and positions on spiritual issues.

One helpful way to approach the spiritual concerns of dying persons (and those around them) is to identify common themes running through this area of task work (Doka, 1993b; Lattanzi-Licht, 2007). Spiritual issues typically involve one or more of the following concerns, which are thus significant components of spiritual task work in coping with dying (Klass, 1988):

Meaningfulness: People who are coping with dying may seek to identify, recognize, or formulate meaning for their lives, for death, for suffering, and for being human. Several types of questions may be pressing in these circumstances: Is my life meaning-full (and often this means worth-full)? If I must die, what does that mean for the value of my having lived? Why is there so much suffering associated with my dying or with my loved one's dying? What does it mean to be human (and when, if ever, does one stop being human, even if life is still present in some form)? These questions are thrusts toward wholeness and integration, and away from fragmentation (Nabe, 1987).

Connectedness: Illness, and perhaps especially life-threatening illness, threatens to break those connections that lend coherence to one's life. For example, one can feel disconnected from one's body (why won't it do what I want it to do?), from other persons (why can't they understand how much pain I am in?), and from whatever one holds the transcendent to be (where is God in all this?). It is often important for a person in this situation to reestablish broken connections or to maintain and deepen existing connections. There are psychological and social components to this work, but the spiritual aspect goes deeper or underlies these other dimensions because (again) it is tied to the search for meaning and integrity.

Transcendence: In addition, people working on spiritual tasks are often looking toward a transcendent level or source of meaning and connection. "Transcendence" refers here to that which goes beyond (though it may also be found in) the ordinary, and especially to that which is of ultimate, surpassing worth. This concern is often tied to issues of *hope* (Groopman, 2004). Religious people may work to enrich and deepen their connections with a god or some basic reality (the Atman or the Tao) and may seek to realize some religious hope (to be absolved of sin, or to overcome metaphysical ignorance, or to achieve eternal bliss). Nonreligious people may also focus on transcendent hopes—for example, to find their place in a reality that is more than just the individual's moment in the life of the universe, to become one with the elements, to continue to contribute to the life of the society through one's creations, students, and descendants even after one has died.

The focus of hope may change over time, and how one acts on one's hopes depends on the individual and his or her culture, history, environment, and condition (see, for instance, Tong & Spicer, 1994). One person may be focused primarily on personal aspirations (will I achieve nirvana, will I meet God face to face?), whereas another person may be more concerned about the welfare of the group (will my descendants continue to contribute to the ongoing life of the group?).

Spiritual task work is as varied and multiform as is task work in the other three areas. And spiritual tasks are irreducibly individual; one Protestant Christian's spiritual tasks are not necessarily (indeed, are seldom) the same as another Protestant Christian's spiritual tasks. That this is the case is important both for gaining a proper understanding of spiritual task work and for helping persons cope with their spiritual tasks.

An Observation on This Task-Based Model This outline of four areas of task work in coping with dying described areas of potential task work. These areas are general categories of tasks for everyone who is coping with dying (not just the dying person). We pointed out that tasks may or may not be undertaken and that some may be more or less necessary or desirable. We also indicated that individuals need not take up any specific task or set of tasks. On the contrary, a task-based model is intended precisely to foster empowerment and participation in coping with dying. This means each individual person will and should be allowed to decide which tasks and sets of tasks are important *to that person*. Another point to consider is that although individual tasks of this sort may be completed, it is never possible to finish all of the task work that confronts an individual. For the dying person, work with tasks ends with death; for those who live on, these and other tasks may arise in coping with bereavement. These areas of task work may also serve as guidelines for helping those who are coping with dying, as we will see in Chapter 7.

Different Tasks in Different Contexts

In reflecting on tasks in coping with life-threatening illness, Doka (1993a) took note of the fact that human life is always temporal and sequential. There are befores, nows, and laters in all of our experiences. Accordingly, a good model of coping with dying ought to throw light on challenges that arise from what has already happened in dying, what is in the process of taking place, and what is yet to come (see also Stedeford, 1984). Doka addressed this by describing how coping tasks might differ across *five phases* in living with a life-threatening illness:

◆ The *prediagnostic phase* is associated with initial indicators of illness or disease: will I ignore these indicators (by hoping that things will get better and "it" will go away on its own), try to minimize my affective responses to their presence, decide to investigate their significance (and, if so, how? Will I ask family members or friends to tell me what to do, turn to a medicine man or traditional healer, seek out medical or other professional sources of advice for investigation or diagnosis of the potential problem)? All of these involve tasks of recognizing possible danger or risk, trying to manage anxiety or uncertainty, and developing and following through on a health-seeking strategy.

◆ The *acute phase* of a life-threatening illness is that period in which one might try to understand the disease, maximize health and lifestyle, foster coping strengths and limit weaknesses, develop strategies to deal with issues created by the disease, arrange for cure-oriented interventions, explore effects of the diagnosis on one's sense of self and others, ventilate feelings and fears, and/or incorporate the reality of the diagnosis into one's sense of past and future.

◆ The *chronic phase* of living with a life-threatening illness involves tasks like managing symptoms and side effects, carrying out health regimens, preventing and managing health crises, managing stress and examining coping, maximizing social support and minimizing isolation, normalizing life in the face of disease, dealing with financial concerns, preserving one's self-concept, redefining relationships with others throughout the course of the disease, continuing to ventilate feelings and fears, and finding meaning in suffering, chronicity, uncertainty, and decline.

◆ If death does not occur, the *recovery phase* still does not free the person from a need to cope. As Doka (1993a, p. 116) noted, task work is ongoing even here because "recovery does not mean that one simply returns to the life led before. Any encounter with a crisis changes us. We are no longer the people we once were." Tasks in the recovery phase include dealing with the aftereffects of illness and anxieties about recurrence, reconstructing or reformulating one's lifestyle, and redefining relationships with caregivers (think of Matt Ryan after the successful treatment of his prostate cancer in the vignette near the beginning of this chapter).

◆ The *terminal phase* is the time in which an individual is faced with a new set of tasks such as dealing with ongoing challenges arising from the disease, its side effects, and treatments; dealing with caregivers and (perhaps) deciding to discontinue cure-oriented interventions or turning to interventions designed to minimize discomforting symptoms; preparing for death and saying good-bye; preserving self-concept and appropriate social relationships; and finding meaning in life and death (this was Jo Ryan's situation after the recurrence of her cancer in the vignette near the beginning of this chapter).

Doka's exploration of changing phases and tasks seeks to be sensitive to the many human—physical, psychological, social, and spiritual —aspects of coping with life-threatening illness. It also brings to the fore three critical factors that influence all coping activities: (1) the wide variety of social and psychological variables (cultural, social, and personal) that enter into processes of coping with life-threatening illness and dying; (2) the developmental context within which the individual confronts this challenge (which we explore in Part Five); and (3) the nature of the disease, its trajectory and effects, and its treatment.

🐦 What Do We Now Know about Coping with Dying?

Kastenbaum and Thuell (1995, p. 176) observed that "strictly speaking, there are no scientific theories of dying, if by 'theory' we mean a coherent set of explicit propositions that have predictive power and are subject to empirical verification. There are distinctive theoretical approaches, however, each of which emphasizes a particular range of experience and behavior." The three approaches that Kastenbaum and

Thuell examined are Glaser and Strauss's account of dying trajectories and awareness contexts, the stage-based schema advanced by Kübler-Ross, and the task-based model proposed by Corr.

In the end, Kastenbaum and Thuell called for a contextual theory of dying, one that "would help us to understand the changing person within his/her changing socio-environmental field" (p. 186). Such a theory "would not be a reductionistic approach that attempts to explain complex multilevel phenomena in a simple way," nor would it be "an over-rationalized logico-deductive model that ignores the power of spirit, emotion and relationships" (p. 186). What these authors seem to have in mind is a kind of active model or evolving narrative that would integrate all of the relevant dimensions of all of the relevant individuals who find themselves drawn together in a process of coping with dying. Until that goal is achieved, the insights and theoretical frameworks described in this chapter represent the major contributions to this field thus far and define the present state of our knowledge (see Corr et al., 1999).

❦ Summary

In this chapter, we explored coping with dying. In so doing, we sought to describe coping processes in ways that do justice to their many elements and to the many individuals involved in such coping. Coping with dying is a part of coping with living, even though dying presents special issues and challenges. We considered dying trajectories and awareness contexts, as well as stage-based and task-based models for explaining coping with dying. Also, we insisted that any adequate account of coping with dying must refer to the whole human being, to each individual human being, and to all who are involved.

Glossary

Awareness contexts: social interactions among those who are coping with dying arising from the types of communication about the facts of the situation; Glaser and Strauss described closed, suspected, and open awareness, as well as mutual pretense

Coping: changing efforts made to manage perceived stressors; coping strategies are often learned from past experience or role models; coping can apply to dying, loss, or any challenging situation in life; coping may involve an individual, his or her family members, and any care providers who may be implicated in the situation

Dying trajectories: patterns of dying or the ways in which dying plays out, typically distinguished by *duration* (the time between the onset of dying and the arrival of death) and *shape* (the course of the dying, its predictability, and whether death is expected or unexpected)

Five phases in coping with life-threatening illness: according to Doka, these are the prediagnostic, acute, chronic, recovery, and terminal phases

Hope: expectations that one looks forward to based on faith and trust; Kübler-Ross said that hope usually persists throughout her five stages of coping with dying;

Corr indicated that hope is primarily associated with spiritual tasks in coping with dying

A stage-based model of coping with dying: describes "stages" in how those coping react to and attempt to manage their stressors; Kübler-Ross identified five of these stages (denial, anger, bargaining, depression, and acceptance)

A task-based model of coping with dying: describes areas of "task work" in coping with dying; Corr identified four areas of such task work: physical (addressing bodily needs and physical distress); psychological (concerned with security, autonomy, and richness or dignity in living); social (relating to interactions with other individuals or social groups); and spiritual (involving meaningfulness, connectedness, and transcendence)

Questions for Review and Discussion

1. Think about some moment in your life when you were quite ill. What was most stressful for you at that time? If you felt fear, what were the sources of your greatest fears? What did you want other people to do for or with you at that time? Now try to imagine yourself in a similar situation, only adding that the illness is a life-threatening one. What would be similar or different in these two situations?

2. One central notion in this chapter is the concept of coping. In what ways in the past have you coped with stressful situations? Choose someone you know well and reflect on how he or she copes with stress. What strengths and limitations do you note in your own ways of coping and in this other person's methods of coping?

3. In our analysis of dying trajectories, awareness contexts, a stage-based model, and a task-based model, which seemed to you to be most (or least) innovative, interesting, and helpful?

4. If you think about the coping processes of dying persons as involving tasks, how might this model of coping affect your understanding of a dying person? How might it affect your interactions with dying persons?

Suggested Readings

Researchers, scholars, and clinicians have written about various aspects of coping with dying in:

Ahronheim, J., & Weber, D. (1992). *Final Passages: Positive Choices for the Dying and Their Loved Ones.*

Doka, K. J. (1993a). *Living with Life-Threatening Illness: A Guide for Patients, Families, and Caregivers.*

Heinz, D. (1999). *The Last Passage: Recovering a Death of Our Own.*

Kübler-Ross, E. (1969). *On Death and Dying.*

Lynn, J., & Harrold, J. (1999). *Handbook for Mortals: Guidance for People Facing Serious Illness.*

Oliver, S. L. (1998). *What the Dying Teach Us: Lessons on Living* (rev. ed.)

Staton, J., Shuy, R., & Byock, I. (2001). *A Few Months to Live: Different Paths to Life's End.*

Tobin, D. (1999). *Peaceful Dying: The Step-by-Step Guide to Preserving Your Dignity, Your Choice, and Your Inner Peace at the End of Life.*

Selected Web Resources

Some useful search terms include: AWARENESS CONTEXTS; COPING; DYING TRAJECTORIES; HOPE; STAGES IN DYING; TASKS IN COPING WITH DYING

Visit the book companion website for *Death & Dying, Life & Living, Sixth Edition,* at academic.cengage.com/psychology/corr for all URLs and live links to the following *organizational and other Internet sites:*

American Self-Help Group Clearinghouse

Care Planner: A Decision Support Tool for Seniors, Caregivers, Family, Friends, and Professionals

Make-A-Wish Foundation of America

National Mental Health Association

National Self-Help Clearinghouse

CHAPTER 7

Coping with Dying: How Individuals Can Help

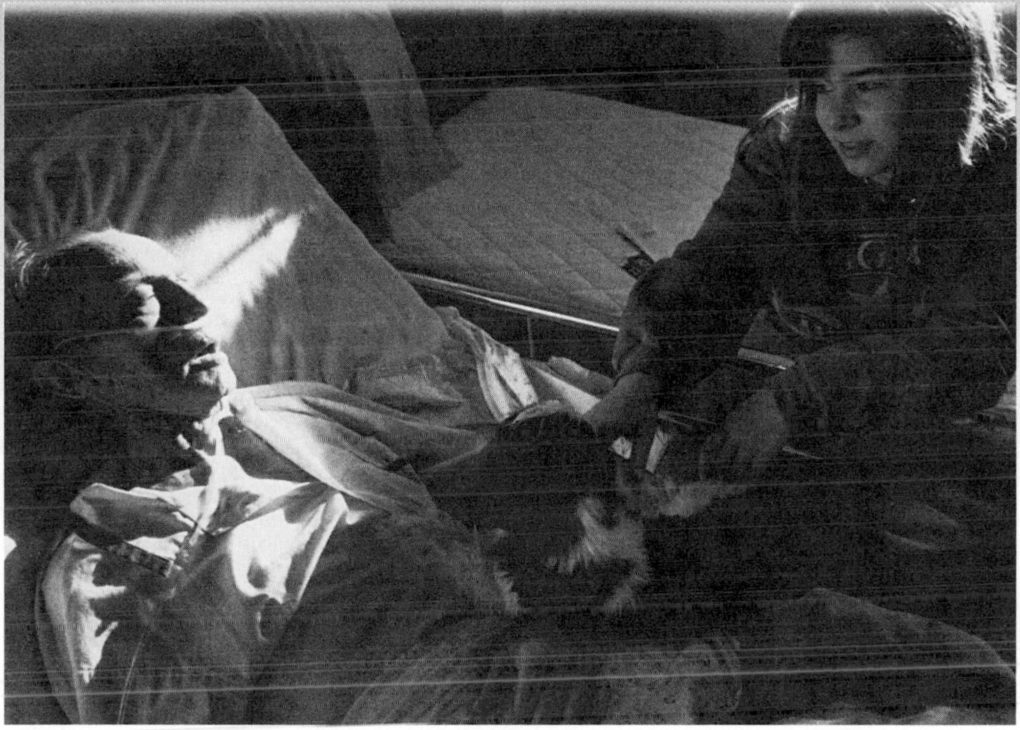

© Joel Gordon/Design Conceptions

Objectives of This Chapter

- To show that helping persons who are coping with dying requires both human presence and the specialized expertise of professionals
- To explore four primary dimensions of care (physical, psychological, social, and spiritual)
- To show how coping tasks, when properly understood, can become guidelines for helpers
- To consider the importance of effective communication
- To draw attention to stress and burnout among helpers, and to explain how they can take care of themselves
- To focus, once again, on the centrality of hope

Individuals Who Helped One Family Cope with Life-Threatening Illness and Dying

Just as Josephina Ryan had helped her husband Matt when he was threatened by prostate cancer, Matt tried to be there for Jo when she experienced a new bout with the cancer that would eventually take her life. But Matt admitted right away that he just didn't know how to be very helpful. He struggled to keep up with practical matters like cleaning the house, doing the laundry, and putting food on the table, but he wasn't good at such chores and his spirits had suffered a hard blow. Jo knew that Matt meant well and she tried to pitch in whenever she could, but her energy level was declining. It was hard to watch Matt wander around the house aimlessly, and she worried about what would happen to him after she was gone.

The Ryans' children tried to help as much as they could. Most of the burden fell on the oldest son, Tom, and his wife, since they lived in town. They helped with some of the household chores and took Matt to shop and do other errands. It helped Matt to get out of the house and to see Tom's children, but he always worried about Jo back at the house. In fact, Jo wasn't very good at first at accepting help from Tom and his wife or from the Ryans' other children when they would fly into town for short visits. She had always been the capable, competent mother in the family doing for others. Her cultural background and personality didn't make it easy for her to let others take over that role, and the children complained that she was pushing them away just when they knew she must need help.

Even if Jo had been more open to accepting help, many of the friends and neighbors to whom they might have turned didn't know how to help in really useful ways. Some offered unhelpful advice or empty clichés, while others just withdrew in confusion. The Ryans were fortunate, however, in their long-standing friendship with Sharon and Bill Applegate. Both of the Applegates were retired, Sharon from her work as a nurse's aide and Bill from his position as assistant principal and coach in Matt's high school. Sharon pitched in to help Jo with basic, practical care. She knew that activities like helping to wash and bathe people made them feel better, while also preventing sores and other complications associated with confinement to a bed. Before Jo became bed bound, Sharon showed Matt and Tom how to help her get around to exercise stiff muscles and how to transfer her to a wheelchair. Later, she gave them advice on moving and positioning Jo in bed. Sharon also devised little jobs for the grandchildren to help out and suggested activities that they could undertake as "junior helpers."

Bill also helped by just spending time with Matt and taking over some practical chores like cutting the lawn that Matt seemed unable to contemplate any longer. When they were together, Matt and Bill didn't actually talk very much, especially about Jo, but Matt seemed to appreciate his presence, and Bill made sure to let Matt know that they could discuss whatever he wanted to talk about. This whole illness thing and the prospect of Jo's dying made Matt feel very isolated and overwhelmed. Bill's interest helped to make things seem a bit less awful. Sometimes Bill could tell Sharon or others in the family what was on Matt's mind and suggest things they could also do to help.

Jo's death was very sad for Matt and the whole Ryan family, just as it was for Sharon and Bill. But the Applegates were gratified at the funeral when Matt told them that Jo's last wish had been to be at home as long as possible before her death. He knew that wouldn't have been possible without their help, and he wanted them to know how grateful he was for their support in helping him to do everything that could be done for his wife and his family. "You made a very bad time just a little bit better," he said, "and for that, I'll always be grateful."

❧ Caring for Persons Who Are Coping with Dying: Human and Professional Tasks

Caring for persons who are coping with dying is not an activity to be carried out only by people who are specially trained to do so (Goldman, 2002; Golubow, 2001; Wolfelt & Yoder, 2005). Certainly, dying persons and others who are coping with dying are people with special needs, some of which can best or perhaps only be met by individuals with special expertise. For example, a dying person may need a physician's prescription for narcotic analgesics or a sacramental act by a member of the clergy. However, much of the care required is not related to special needs; it involves fundamental concerns common to all living human beings, even though they are concerns that may take on a special intensity under the pressures of coping with dying.

For example, dying persons need to eat, they need to exercise their bodies, minds, and spirits, and they need above all to be *cared about, not just cared for.* For most of the 24 hours in each day, the care that dying persons need is not specialized care. This care can be provided by any of us. A hand held, a grief or joy shared, and a question listened to and responded to: these are human moments of caring, and they can be offered by any human being who is willing and able to care. In short, "the secret of the care of patients is still caring" (Ingles, 1974, p. 763; see also Peabody, 1927).

Frank (2002, pp. 45–49) has written about this in the following way:

> The common diagnostic categories into which medicine places its patients are relevant to disease, not to illness. They are useful for treatment, but they only get in the way of care. . . . Caring has nothing to do with categories; it shows the person that her life is valued because it recognizes what makes her experience particular. One person has no right to categorize another, but we do have the privilege of coming to understand how each of us is unique. . . . Terms like pain or loss have no reality until they are filled in with an ill person's own experience. Witnessing the particulars of that experience, and recognizing all its differences, is care.

Persons who are dying are most likely to be concerned about such matters as being abandoned, losing control over their own bodies and lives, and being in overwhelming pain or distress. Dame Cicely Saunders, founder of St. Christopher's Hospice in London and initiator of the modern hospice movement, is reported (Shephard, 1977) to have said that dying persons ask three things of those who care for them: (1) "*Help me*" (minimize my distress); (2) "*Listen to me*" (let me direct things or at least be heard); and (3) "*Don't leave me*" (stay with me; give me your presence).

It is important to recognize the many ways in which we can help those who are coping with dying. Sometimes, what helpers can do is simple and obvious, not dramatic and world-shaking (see Personal Insights 7.1). But even when we cannot do something specific to help, all of us—professionals and nonprofessionals alike—can offer an "empathetic presence" by listening to and staying with dying persons and their significant others. This is the lesson that Sharon and Bill Applegate learned as they helped Jo and Matt Ryan.

To provide adequate care for the dying, we must address the many fears, anxieties, desires, and tasks of dying persons. The same applies to family members and friends of the dying person—those significant others who are also coping with dying. We may be more or less successful in meeting these responsibilities because of pressures of limited time, energy, information, or resources. But if we are serious about providing good care, we ought not to fail to address these needs because of lack of understanding or attention to what is needed by those who are coping with dying. In this chapter, we provide information about and draw attention to ways in which help can be provided to those who are coping with dying.

Dimensions of Care

There are *four primary dimensions of care* for those who are coping with dying: physical, psychological, social, and spiritual (Saunders, 1967; Woodson, 1976). Here, we consider each of these in turn, with special attention to their application

---

PERSONAL INSIGHTS 7.1

The Tale of the Stranded Starfish

As a man walked a desolate beach one cold, gray morning he began to see another figure, far in the distance. Slowly the two approached each other, and he could make out a local native who kept leaning down, picking something up and throwing it out into the water. Time and again he hurled things into the ocean. As the distance between them continued to narrow, the man could see that the native was picking up starfish that had been washed upon the beach and, one at a time, was throwing them back into the water. Puzzled, the man approached the native and asked what he was doing.

"I'm throwing these starfish back into the ocean. You see, it's low tide right now and all of these starfish have been washed up onto the shore. If I don't throw them back into the sea, they'll die up here from lack of oxygen."

"But there must be thousands of starfish on this beach," the man replied. "You can't possibly get to all of them. There are just too many. And this same thing is probably happening on hundreds of beaches all up and down this coast. Can't you see that you can't possibly make a difference?"

The local native smiled, bent down and picked up another starfish, and as he threw it back into the sea he replied, "Made a difference to that one!"

Source: Author unknown.

---

to dying persons. These dimensions are also relevant to others who are coping with dying: family members and friends of the dying person, as well as professional and volunteer helpers/caregivers.

Physical Dimensions

For many dying persons, one of the most pressing needs is the control of *physical pain or distress.* When pain is present, it must be properly studied and carefully understood (Melzack & Wall, 1991; Wall, 2002; Wall & Melzack, 1994). One can distinguish between at least two sorts of pain: acute pain and chronic pain.

Acute pain is a form of pain that is essential to human life. Those who do not feel acute pain—for example, when they touch a hot stove—are in danger of serious harm. When individuals are ill, physicians often obtain the information they need to make an accurate diagnosis by eliciting careful, specific descriptions of pain or distress. For instance, acute pain associated with kidney stones guides both diagnosis and treatment. Thus, acute pain is not always or completely undesirable, given our present human condition. In fact, it may make possible enhancement of both the quality and the quantity of our lives. Of course, dying persons may experience acute pain, too. They may develop symptoms—including physical pain—that may or may not be directly related to the illness that threatens their lives. In this regard, Saunders reminded caregivers that a toothache hurts just as much when you are dying (*Until We Say Goodbye,* 1980).

Chronic pain, however, does not serve any of these constructive functions. Chronic pain does not assist in diagnosis because the diagnosis has already been made. Nor does chronic pain protect the person from dangers in the environment. It is just there, always there. Sharp or dull, constant or intermittent, chronic pain forms the backdrop of whatever the person is doing at the moment. When it is intense, it can become the whole focus of attention of those experiencing such pain (LeShan, 1964).

In life-threatening illness, chronic pain is often associated with a disease that will lead to death. Proper care of the dying person must involve efforts to manage or at least to diminish distress arising from chronic pain—whatever its origin. It may not always be possible to eradicate chronic pain totally, but even to reduce such pain from agony to ache is a notable achievement. Care of the dying has shown that chronic pain can be controlled or at least greatly diminished in most cases (Doyle et al., 2003; Saunders et al., 1995; Twycross, 1994; Twycross & Wilcock, 2002). Needless pain in end-of-life care is a tragedy when good research has taught so much about the nature of pain and the role of analgesics and other therapeutic modalities in its management (Melzack, 1990). Appropriate medications and supportive therapy can see to it that chronic pain need not so fill the consciousness of dying persons that they can pay attention to nothing else but their pain.

The challenge for therapeutic interventions is to select just the right medication(s) to meet the need(s) of the individual, to achieve just the right balance of responses to requirements (without under- or overmedication), and to employ an appropriate route of administration. The philosophy of pain management in end-of-life care has often emphasized administration of medications via oral routes (in liquid, tablet, or capsule form) to avoid the pain of injections. However, both injections and suppositories have been recognized as appropriate in certain cases (for instance, when rapid results achievable by injections are required or when individuals are nauseated and cannot swallow). More recently, these have been supplemented by slow-release analgesic tablets, long-term continuous infusion devices (similar to those used for insulin by some diabetics), transdermal patches and specially formulated creams, and patient-controlled analgesia (whereby individuals have some measure of control and autonomy in administering their own medications, often resulting in less overall medication than might otherwise have been employed).

Drug therapy is not the *only* method of controlling chronic pain. As research leads to a better understanding of the nature of disease, it is evident that most pain has a psychological component. Thus, McCaffery and Beebe (1989, p. 7) wrote, "Pain is whatever the experiencing person says it is, existing whenever the experiencing person says it does." That is, *pain is distress as an individual perceives it.* Pain management may seek to alter the threshold or the nature of that perception, just as it may block the pathways or the effects of a noxious stimulant. Biofeedback, guided imagery, meditation, therapeutic touch, and techniques of self-hypnosis may also assist persons to control their pain or to manage its effects. Also, constructive psychological support may encourage individuals to relax and keep muscles and joints active, thereby helping to lessen the degree of physical pain that occurs when a person remains immobile. These therapies are not in opposition to, but can work alongside, medications and other interventions.

When drug therapies are used, long-standing research has demonstrated that many dying persons, including long-term patients with far-advanced cancer, can tolerate large doses of strong narcotics without becoming "doped up" or "knocked out" (Twycross, 1979b, 1982). The goal is not total anesthesia (unconsciousness), but rather analgesia (an insensibility to pain). This goal can be achieved in most cases by choosing the correct medication(s) for the situation and by carefully titrating or balancing dosages against the nature and level of pain (Storey, 1996; Twycross & Lack, 1989). (In extreme cases, medications can also be used to achieve "terminal sedation," but these instances are rare, they require very careful assessment, and they involve critical ethical decision making for this therapy of last resort [National Ethics Committee, Veterans Health Administration, 2007]).

If the right drug is used and the dose is titrated or calibrated to the precise level needed to control pain—and *no further*—then the pain is well managed. The right drug is crucial. Pain may arise from a variety of sources—for example, direct damage to tissue, inflammation, or pressure. Each source of pain and each route of transmission may require its own appropriate medication. Also, each drug must be selected in terms of the needs of an individual patient, its method of administration, the time intervals at which it will be given, and potential problems with side effects or interactions with other drugs the person may be taking. For example, some drugs like the narcotic Demerol are quick acting and potent, which makes them useful for dealing with episodes of acute pain. However, such a drug may not retain its efficacy long enough to suit someone with chronic pain. If so, a dying person for whom it is prescribed may be in pain again in two or three hours, well before the next dose is administered. This is *not* effective pain control. Morphine and some other strong narcotics have proven their effectiveness in end-of-life care because their effects last long enough to manage chronic pain until the next dose.

Addiction does not occur, even when strong narcotics are prescribed in high doses for dying persons. This has been shown by well-established research (for example, Twycross, 1976) and should now be well known. The psychological "high" and subsequent cravings for steadily escalating doses that characterize addiction are not found. This may have to do with ways in which medications are administered and absorbed in the body: they can be given by mouth in single doses or as a timed-release medication. If necessary, intravenous injections or infusions can be used.

Dying persons may become *physically dependent* on strong narcotics, but that also occurs in other situations—for example, in the use of steroids. Here, *dependence* means only that one cannot withdraw the drug abruptly or while it is still required without harmful side effects. Such physical dependence without underlying emotional disorder is easily terminated and has long been recognized not to constitute an additional problem (Anonymous, 1963). Otherwise, it is as if the body uses the drug to deal with the pain it is experiencing, and it signals when the drug or dose is not correct. Too small or too weak a dose allows pain to return; too large or too powerful a dose induces drowsiness.

Once individuals learn that their pain really can and will be well managed, the dose provided can often be reduced because they no longer are fearful and tense in the face of *expected* pain (Twycross, 1994; Twycross & Wilcock, 2002). Effective drug therapeutics provides a sense of security that reduces anxiety. Addressing such psychosocial components of pain can lower the threshold of analgesia and may make it easier to manage discomfort. Thus relaxation may actually allow individuals to tolerate more pain and accept a lower drug dose.

Dying persons may also experience other physical symptoms that can be just as distressing as or even more distressing than physical pain (Saunders & Sykes, 1993). These symptoms include constipation (a common side effect of narcotics), diarrhea, nausea, and vomiting. Sometimes there is weakness or reduction in available energy, loss of appetite, or shortness of breath. Similarly, loss of hair, dark circles around the eyes, and changes in skin color may also be matters of concern to those who place high value on self-image and how they present themselves to others. Also, if someone sits or lies in bed for long periods, skin ulcers or pressure sores can become a potential source of added discomfort and risk for infection. Reducing this source of distress has always been a concern of effective care for the dying (Kemp, 1999).

Dehydration illustrates an issue that is frequently encountered in dying persons (Zerwekh, 1983; see also Gallagher-Allred & Amenta, 1993). An intravenous infusion might be used, but that method adds another source of pain to the burdens of ill persons at the end of life. Also, it may overload with fluid a body that is weak and whose organ systems may no longer be functioning effectively. Often, small sips of juice or other fluids, ice chips, or flavored mouth swabs may be enough to maintain quality of life. This shows that effective care for dying persons must address all of their distressing physical symptoms and must do so in ways suited to their current situation. Such care may require intervention on the part of physicians, nurses, and other professional caregivers, but family caregivers and significant others also have important roles to play in these situations, especially when they are shown how to be most helpful to the ill person and their own physical needs (e.g., exhaustion) are met.

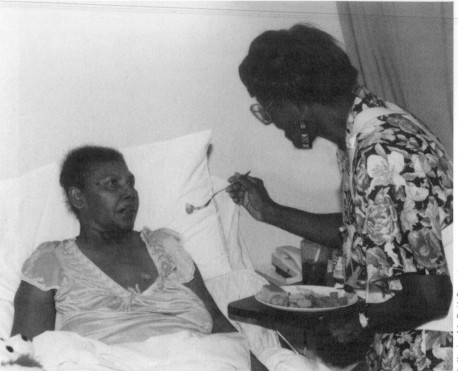

The Hospice of the Florida Suncoast

Sharing a meal has both physical and psychological benefits.

Psychological Dimensions

Another set of concerns revolves around *psychological dimensions* and tasks in coping with dying. Care providers may be even more uncomfortable working with these concerns than with those having to do with physical dimensions in dying persons. It is difficult to be with someone in physical pain, but we may be even more uneasy in the face of so-called negative feelings. Nevertheless, someone who is dying is likely to express these sorts of feelings at one time or another. Such a person may experience anger and sadness, anxiety and fear. In the face of such feelings, people often wonder what is the right thing to say or to do.

Frequently, there is no specific or universal right thing to say or to do, but that does not mean there is *nothing* to say or to do. In fact, one can say and do many things to be helpful. Often, the most helpful thing is simply to be present and listen, making sure that whatever one does say is true, reliable, supportive, and caring (Zerwekh, 1994). To hunt for some way to make all fear, anger, or sadness disappear is to begin a hopeless search. These feelings are real, and they must be lived through.

A student once told us that she believed someone informed of a prognosis of impending death would become sad or depressed, an emotion she thought of as undesirable. She said she would seek any means to prevent it from occurring, or if it did occur, to end it. This is unrealistic. If someone is given unhappy news—of any sort—sadness is a likely and *appropriate* response. Furthermore, some people—including many professional caregivers—too quickly identify sadness with depression. But to realize that one is going to die is to be faced with a loss—and in the face of loss, human beings grieve.

Anger is another feeling that may be particularly discomforting. Anger is often viewed as a destructive emotion, rather than an understandable reaction when one's needs are frustrated or one is hurt, a reaction that can be expressed constructively or destructively. Those who are coping with dying often feel lots of anger. They may be angry because of the losses they are experiencing and because others—apparently for no good reason—are enjoying happy, healthy, and satisfying lives. Further, because of physical or other restrictions, a dying person's anger may be limited in the ways in which it can be expressed. Not surprisingly, strong feelings may be projected onto others—that is, directed at whatever or whoever is most readily available, whether or not that is appropriate.

This sort of anger needs to be identified, acknowledged, and expressed. Feelings like this cannot simply be made to go away. Feelings are real; one cannot just stop feeling what one is feeling. Nor is it reasonable to expect that strong feelings should always be suppressed. For example, anger and an outpouring of adrenaline go together; the anger must be worked off, much like the physical rush of adrenaline. When a helper is the object of growls, complaints, or screaming, it may not be very consoling to realize that there is usually nothing personal in such expressions of anger and other strong feelings—but that is often the case.

In such situations, it may be important to *learn to be comfortable with one's own discomfort.* That is, our task as helpers is not to discover the magical "right" thing to say to make dying persons no longer have such feelings. Letting them talk about why they feel as they do and giving them "permission" to do so through bodily or verbal cues— *really listening to them*—may be the most helpful thing one can do (Nichols, 1995).

In addition, many dying persons have reported that for someone to say to them "I know how you feel" is *not* helpful. For one thing, this is almost certainly not true. Most individuals have not really been in the situation of the other person to whom such a remark is made, and no one can really experience the feelings of another individual. Also, such a remark is often perceived (rightly or wrongly) as an attempt to minimize or trivialize the feelings of the person to whom it is addressed.

How can people who are experiencing "negative" feelings be helped? If this question means, How can someone make them stop having those feelings?, the question may say more about our discomfort with their feelings and our need to end that discomfort than it does about the needs of those who are coping with dying. Two things should be noted here. First, *outsiders cannot make anyone feel different or better.* Second, *that may often be an inappropriate goal.* Dying people must live with and through their feelings, just as they must live with and through all of the rest of their life experiences. They can be helped to do that by assistance in identifying their feelings, by acknowledgment of their feelings as appropriate to their particular situations (if that is, in fact, the case), and by permission for them to vent or share their feelings.

There are no magic formulas here. There are no cookbooks for the right behaviors or statements. Nevertheless, what does seem to help people who are coping with dying is for someone to listen to them and to take seriously what they are

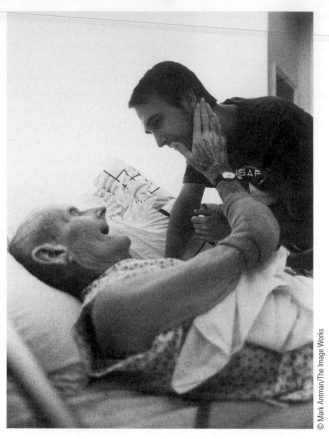

Reaching out to touch can be an important part of care.

© Mark Antman/The Image Works

feeling. This is one thing that can be done to help. Helpers can *be present* to such persons (physically, emotionally, existentially) and can *listen attentively* to what they say (see Personal Insights 7.2). If helpers turn off their own internal monologues, if they stop hunting around for the "right" response, and if they just *listen empathetically,* that can help (Wooten-Green, 2001). It helps because it says to the dying person, loudly and clearly, "You matter; you and your feelings are real and important to me." It also helps to hear what the dying person needs, rather than what others think the person needs. *Compassion* or *empathy,* which reaches out to understand and feel along with the other person, is quite different from *pity,* which commiserates with the other individual from a hierarchical and distant standpoint. As Garfield (1976, p. 181) wrote years ago, "The largest single impediment to providing effective psychosocial support to the terminal patient is the powerful professional staff distinction between 'US' and 'THEM.'"

Something else that can be done to help, at least in many instances, is to *touch the person.* Some people are uncomfortable with physical touch. As Hall (1966) noted in his analysis of what he called "proxemics," such people keep a fairly large personal space around themselves, and they may resent and resist intrusion by others into that space. However, sickness may break down some of these barriers. For example, a body massage may be *psychologically* helpful. Often, it is helpful for a friend or concerned person to touch one's wrist or arm, hold one's hand, or give a hug. Not everyone responds favorably to this; each person is an individual with personal expectations and values. Helpers must respect the dying person's values on this point. Seeking permission might be desirable. But for many persons who are coping with dying, gentle touch is psychologically healing.

Many of the psychological tasks of dying persons can be helped by anybody, whether that person is a professional caregiver or not, although some preparation and training may help (Parkes et al., 1996). If there are psychological dimensions of coping with dying that run deeper and that interfere with the individual's quality in living, a professional counselor or therapist may be helpful. Similarly, those who are especially competent to assist with psychological tasks might be called on for help

On Being a Good Listener

If I am a good listener, I don't interrupt the other nor plan my own next speech while pretending to be listening. I try to hear what is said, but I listen just as hard for what is not said and for what is said between the lines. I am not in a hurry, for there is no preappointed destination for the conversation. There is no need to get there, for we are already here; and in this present I am able to be fully present to the one who speaks. The speaker is not an object to be categorized or manipulated, but a subject whose life situation is enough like my own that I can understand it in spite of the differences between us. If I am a good listener, what we have in common will seem more important than what we have in conflict.

This does not mean that I never say anything, but I am more likely to ask questions than to issue manifestos or make accusations.

Source: Westphal, 1984, p. 12.

One of our most difficult duties as human beings is to listen to the voices of those who suffer. The voices of the ill are easy to ignore, because those voices are often faltering in tone and mixed in message, particularly in their spoken form before some editor has rendered them fit for reading by the healthy. These voices bespeak conditions of embodiment that most of us would rather forget our vulnerability to. Listening is hard, but it is also a fundamental moral act. . . . [Moreover] in listening for the other, we listen for ourselves. The moment of witness in the story crystallizes a mutuality of need, when each is for the other.

Source: Frank, 1995, p. 25.

when coping with dying is accompanied by clinical depression, confusional states, or specific forms of mental illness (Stedeford, 1978, 1984). After all, if the goal is to provide whatever care is needed to make this time in life as good as possible, the lesson must be that no particular expertise or mode of care should be looked on as irrelevant just because the person happens to be dying.

There is no evidence that coping with dying on its own is associated with psychiatric problems such as suicidal tendencies (Brown et al.,1986). Thus, Stedeford (1979, pp. 13–14) suggested that, as a general rule in the care of those who are coping with dying, "sophisticated psychotherapy is not as necessary as are sensitivity, a willingness to follow the patient rather than lead him, some knowledge of the psychology of dying, and the ability to accept the inevitability of death." In the end, we are best able to help a dying person or anyone coping with dying when we are able to begin to cope with the reality of our own mortality and our prior experiences with profound losses. Not to do so often complicates our ability to help because it may fail to appreciate whose needs are being addressed. The fundamental criterion for all aspects of caring for dying persons and their family members is that *caring must be made relevant and must be seen to be relevant to the needs and tasks of the person whom one is trying to help.* Caregivers must always ask, "What is the relative value of the various available methods of treatment *in this particular patient?"* (Cade, 1963, p. 3).

Social Dimensions

Social dimensions in coping with dying are often just as pressing as physical and psychological dimensions. These social dimensions are expressed, first, in the special relationships that most individuals form with one or more people who occupy cherished roles in their lives. It is to these special people that one brings one's intimate achievements and tribulations. Within these relationships individuals seek safety and security. In their shelter, one makes plans, works through problems, and defines that which is meaningful. Here love is expressed most basically in the sharing of two or more lives. Often, it is sufficient merely to be in the company of such special persons to feel a bit better and less beset by the problems of living.

Individuals who are coping with dying can be helped when the relationships that they value are fostered and encouraged. When energy levels are low, they may not be able to sustain all of the relationships that once were important to them. Their circle of personal involvements may change its shape, size, or character, and those who are coping with dying may want to be shown how to uphold the most significant of these relationships. They will want to continue to give care to and to receive care from the special people in their lives. Sensitivity to the identities of these special people, to the nature of their attachments with the person who is coping with dying, and to ways in which such relationships can be maintained and nurtured is an important part of caring and helping.

Reading to a person from sources that interest that individual is a form of social caring.

The Hospice of the Florida Suncoast

Social dimensions also include concerns about one's role and place in the family, in the workforce, and in the community at large. For example, economic concerns may be very important. In our society, many people worry about how their families will survive economically, given the costs of health care and the disappearance of the income that the dying person had formerly provided. There are other concerns, too: Will that project I started at work be completed? What will happen to my business (clients, customers, stockholders, employees, students, parishioners)? How will my spouse be able to cope with being a single parent of young children? Who will take care of my aged parents or aging spouse?

These types of questions arise for many who are dying. One responds in helpful ways to these concerns, first by allowing those who are coping with dying to talk about their concerns, and then by being an advocate for such persons. That is, one can listen and try to help these people find resources that may be of assistance with their specific (or not so specific) problems. Sometimes advocacy involves acting on behalf of or in place of others to try to serve their needs. Often, advocacy means enabling or empowering individuals to act for themselves in seeking to satisfy their requirements. Note that it can be disempowering to take over the work of coping from the other person; it may be sufficient to help that person recognize his or her options and think about ways to go about accomplishing personal tasks. Social roles offer an excellent opportunity for people to assert and maintain autonomy. Social workers, family therapists, counselors, and lawyers are often able to help in areas of social tasks.

Spiritual Dimensions

Dying persons often face a variety of *spiritual tasks.* Many of these tasks concern a search for meaning, for establishing, reestablishing, and maintaining connectedness with oneself, other persons, and with what the person perceives as the transcendent (Longaker, 1998; see also Chapter 6 in this book). It is important to note that the spiritual dimensions of a person's life are not separate from but rather often underlie and run through physical, psychological, and social dimensions.

Caregivers cannot *provide* meaning or connectedness for another individual, nor can they *give* to such individuals an experience or understanding of the transcendent. When asked, one may share one's convictions with others. But when dying persons ask spiritual questions, they may not be interested in our responses. Instead, they are often striving to "tell their own stories" or "sing their own songs" (Brady, 1979).

When we first sat with people and they would raise spiritual issues, we guardedly began to answer them. Sometimes these persons just looked at us and appeared to listen to us; sometimes they went on talking right over our replies. When we stopped talking, they continued with their own thoughts on these matters. Eventually, we learned that individuals often ask questions about what matters to them spiritually as a way of articulating these issues in their own minds. Talking was a way of developing their own thinking, and perhaps they were attempting to determine whether we would allow them to spin out their own answers. Again, what is usually being asked for is for someone to be present, to be empathic, to listen, and to *travel with them on their journey* (Ley & Corless, 1988; Zlatin, 1995).

The Hospice of the Florida Suncoast

Praying or meditating with someone coping with dying can be spiritually valuable.

Helpers can assist in this process. People find meaning, connectedness, and an experience of the transcendent in a variety of ways (Binkewicz, 2005). Among these are objects (sacred books, a volume of poetry, photographs, icons, sculptures); places (a mosque, a cabin in the woods, one's own home); ritual actions (having a text read, receiving a sacrament, praying, having others lay their hands on you); communities—that is, specific groups of people (a church choir or a support group); particular times (the month of Ramadan, Yom Kippur, Christmas, one's own or a loved one's birthday, an important anniversary in the person's life); teachings and ideas (including perhaps a statement of faith, such as the Apostles' Creed for Christians, the Shahada for Muslims, or the Shema for some Jews); and specific persons (a shaman, rabbi, imam, or family member—perhaps one's child). By attentively asking and listening, caregivers can explore what an individual finds of help and then can arrange either to bring the person to whatever or whoever that might be or to bring it to the person (Mazanec & Tyler, 2003). In this way, a caregiver can help to support the dying person on his or her (*not the caregiver's*) spiritual journey. Spiritual quests are rarely if ever completed, even up to the moment of death. Seeking out meaning, fostering connectedness, and grounding hope can be enriched and deepened throughout the entirety of a person's life. A caregiver's role is to support and sustain this ongoing process.

An important avenue of support for the dying person struggling with spiritual issues may be to enhance that individual's opportunities for creativity (Bertman, 1999; Bolton, 2007; Romanoff & Thompson, 2006). For example, one hospice has developed a rich program that offers creative opportunities in music, literature, drama, visual arts, and metalsmithing (Bailey et al., 1990). Artistic endeavors of this sort reflect specifically human qualities in coping with living and dying. They can be undertaken in diverse settings (in institutions or in homes) where helpers can work together with those who are coping with dying to realize meaning and connectedness.

One last word really has to do with all of the dimensions in which one might seek to help a person who is coping with dying. Because the person has dealt with an issue once does not mean that the issue is now settled. The issue may arise again. Questions like, "Who is going to see to it that my child gets a good education?" or "What does my dying at 26 mean?" are likely to be revisited again and again. Helpers need to be ready to listen to the person, wherever he or she is today, *at this moment.* There is no fixed goal at which the dying person or anyone who is coping with dying—along with those who are listening to that person—has to arrive. Though it may be unwise to put off a question or request—death is always an unexpected visitor—still one can rest assured that as long as there is life there will always be more questions, needs, desires, and concerns. No one ever finishes *all* of the business of life, if for no other reason than that each moment lived brings *new* business.

🐛 Tasks as Guidelines for Helping

One reason why we stress a task-based approach to coping with dying in this book is to identify guidelines for helping those who are coping with dying. We can develop such guidelines by focusing on specific tasks that the dying person or other persons affected by his or her dying (a family member, lover, friend, or caregiver) are pursuing. A helper (whether a professional or layperson) can facilitate and assist these persons with their task work. Of course, a person may not wish to have this sort of assistance. Or it may be that the individual is attempting to carry out his or her perceived tasks through some behavior (e.g., suicide) that is morally or legally unacceptable to the one who is asked to help. One person's choices of how to live out his or her life do not necessarily always impose obligations on others.

Careful observation of the ways in which the individual who is coping with dying perceives and responds to potential tasks can shape specific approaches in helping (see Focus On 7.1). For example, a dying person may express a need to get in contact with an estranged relative. That might lead a helper to assist in making a telephone call or in writing a letter, or it might become appropriate (if the dying person so wishes) for the helper to make the first contact as an intermediary with the estranged relative.

For a family member caring for a dying person at home, the helper might provide some temporary respite or relief from the physical burdens of care or some time off for psychological or social rejuvenation. The helper might offer to take over some of the physical care to provide the family caregiver with some time for uninterrupted sleep or rest. Or the helper might just sit with the dying person so that the family caregiver can leave the confines of the house to shop, see a movie, or seek some other form of rejuvenation. A perceptive helper might offer to take young children out for a day in the park so that a dying person and his or her spouse might have time alone together.

Rosen (1998; and see also Davies et al., 1995) described experiences of families who are facing the death of one of their members. According to Rosen, these experiences form a process consisting of a preparatory phase from the time when

Five Themes for Caring and Some Practical Suggestions

THEMES	PRACTICAL SUGGESTIONS
1. **Remember** that you are a different person than the other individual.	Be cautious in supplying answers that you find meaningful—each person has unique experiences and must find his or her own meanings. If asked for your perspectives, do not speak as one who has and intends to give absolute truth, but rather as one who has found some perspectives meaningful in light of your life experiences.
2. **Recognize** that to be facing one's death or the death of a loved one is a profound experience that to some degree involves tasks that each individual must carry out for himself or herself.	Be authentically present: this means to be with the person in that particular moment, paying attention to his or her tasks. Listen to what the person who is coping with dying has to say about his or her particular, individual life experiences, including his or her successes, struggles, and failures, as well as his or her search for meaning; allow that person a safe space in which to come to understand those life experiences and that search for meaning. Try to understand the experiences of the other person by carefully listening and then imagining what it is to be that other person at this particular moment. Be attentive to the clues—subtle or obvious—as to what that person wants from you at this particular moment, for example, whether he or she wants to be alone or accompanied (by you or by someone else). Accept silence as a form of presence, too; recognize your discomfort with that silence, and resist the impulse to fill it with chatter or teaching.
3. **Respect** the meaning and values of those for whom you are providing care.	Avoid making judgments about the other person's meanings and values. Keep in mind that none of us can fully comprehend what the other's life experiences are and have been, and that none of us is infallible in our own knowledge or understanding.
4. **Reinforce** the person's decision-making capacity and support his or her actual decisions.	Ask questions that help the individual clarify his or her preferences, desires, values, and needs, and help the person make choices based on his or her responses to your questions. Be an advocate for the person with other care providers in seeking to realize his or her decisions.
5. **Reminisce** with the person about his or her life and meaning.	Elicit stories from the person about his or her life experiences. Allow the person to reminisce and support the person as he or she remembers and repeats these stories. Record these stories so that they may be shared. Make available to the person (and significant others) poems, songs, readings, rituals, or prayers that are important to the individual and that help in the process of remembrance—thus supporting the development of meaning.

Source: Adapted from Colorado Collaboration on End-of-Life Care (no date).

symptoms first appear through the initial diagnosis, a middle phase of living with the reality of the fatal illness and its associated caregiving tasks, and a final phase of accepting the imminent death and concluding the process of saying farewell (compare this with Doka's account of five phases in living with a life-threatening illness in Chapter 6 on pp. 148–149). There are many ways of helping such families at different points in this process. For example, Rosen recommended that helpers make use of a three-generation family tree (a genogram) to identify the family's structure, history, and relationships (see McGoldrick & Gerson, 1985, 1988). This family tree provides a kind of road map for helping by portraying the interpersonal dynamics within the family and the internal resources that helpers might seek to mobilize. Rosen also showed how literary and cinematic materials might be used to help families, as well as practices ("rituals") with which they are familiar and specific suggestions ("coaching") to direct their attention and energies to tasks that they need to address. One caution in these approaches to helping is that the strategies and tactics used by the helper must be carefully adapted to the specific characteristics of the family in question and to its cultural or ethnic background.

These are only a few examples. The principle is that *coping tasks can become guidelines for helpers if these tasks always are appreciated in their concrete, specific, and individual circumstances.* For example, as they talk together, a dying person and a helper might agree upon a number of coping tasks that could be undertaken. An astute helper will then make it possible for the dying person to determine which (if any) task(s) should be undertaken first and when, and even to change those decisions as time passes. This enhances the autonomy of the dying person and acknowledges the measure of control that he or she still retains at a time when so much may be out of control. Here the helper fosters a sense of security even when much is not safe in the dying person's life.

Individuals who are coping with dying may surprise us with their choices of tasks that are important to them at any given moment. They may be more concerned to have a beloved pet in their company than to permit visits from some human beings who are not very close friends. They may still be preoccupied with how they look or with a diet program. They may find more comfort in talking to a hospital janitor than to a psychiatrist. They may be more grateful to someone who cleans their eyeglasses, gives them a back rub, or trims their ingrown toenails than to the chaplain who offers spiritual advice. They may be more interested in one last taste of a fast-food hamburger and French fries—what the British describe as "a little of what you fancy" (Willans, 1980)—than in the carefully planned nutritional meals from the dietary department.

This range of reactions simply reminds us once again that dying persons are living human beings. They need to sing their own songs, to live out their own lives in ways that they find appropriate and not be "killed softly" by somebody else's song. This is not to imply that helpers should be merely passive. One can suggest things to do, offer options, and provide opportunities. Sometimes it is important to urge people rather strongly to do something they do not want to do but would serve their needs in ways they may not yet have realized or appreciated. Experienced caregivers learn when to be a bit insistent in matters like this and when to back off. However, in the end, decision making must rest primarily with the person being helped, not with the helper.

Helpers of all types need to listen to and be guided by the dying persons; otherwise, they are merely imposing their own agenda on the other person. When one learns that someone is coping with dying, strong feelings well up, and one's urge may be to try to make everything right again. Although that is frequently not possible, one should not conclude that nothing is possible. As long as an individual is alive, it is always possible to do something to improve the quality of his or her life. For this, we must move toward (not away from) the person who is coping with dying.

What one does is not always or even mainly of primary importance. What counts is that one's actions show that one cares. Often, the action can be something simple and concrete. The gesture may not be accepted; it may not even be acknowledged. Dying persons (like everyone else) can be grumpy or exhausted. For those who care, that will not matter too much, because the gesture is made for the sake of the other person, not for one's own sake.

Just as one should begin with the person to be helped wherever he or she is, not where the helper thinks that person should be, so too helpers should begin with themselves wherever they are, with their own talents, strengths, and limitations. Sharing honest emotions or feelings of uncertainty can be a good way to start. Laughing, listening in an interested and nonjudgmental way, and just silently being present are often appreciated. Avoiding insensitive clichés is a good idea (Linn, 1986). Offering help in specific and practical ways is desirable. Conveying one's own sense of hope, fostering opportunities for growth (Byock, 1997), and sharing (often in nonverbal ways) one's conviction that the life of the other person is and has been meaningful in one's own life can be an eloquent form of caring. Holding a dying person's hand and crying with that person speaks volumes when words are not really possible.

Differences in age need not be a barrier to effective communication.

The Hospice of the Florida Suncoast

🍂 Effective Communication

In the past, our death system often advised us not to speak candidly to dying persons about their diagnoses and prognoses (e.g., Oken, 1961; recall our discussion of closed awareness contexts in Chapter 6). It was thought that candor would undercut hope and the will to live or even encourage people to end their own lives. There is, in fact, no evidence that this did or does take place. Even so, the key issue in *effective communication* is whether specific acts of communication are responsive to the needs of dying persons and are carried out in a thoughtful and caring way. The content of the communication may not be as important as the ways in which it is expressed and understood. One can brutalize a vulnerable person with the truth, just as one can harm with falsehood.

For the most part, our death system now encourages speaking with greater candor to dying persons about their diagnoses and prognoses (Novack et al., 1979). In part, this came about because people realized that "communication about end-of-life issues is the key to understanding and making rational decisions" (Thomas, 2001, p. 42). Accordingly, anything that gets in the way of such communication can impede both such rational decision making and, in turn, the provision of good care (Fallowfield et al., 2002). Also, society began to place increased emphasis on informed consent and patients' rights (Annas, 2004; President's Commission, 1982; Rozovsky, 1990). Consent to professional intervention or any sort of supportive treatment cannot be freely given unless it is based on information needed to understand the current situation, the nature of the proposed intervention, and its likely outcome(s). Even in the direst of situations, the necessary information can be provided in a caring manner and consent obtained in ways that foster the dignity of all who are involved.

Two good examples of how to enhance effective communication in coping with dying are available. Buckman (1992b) offered a set of suggestions about how to break bad news (see Table 7.1). Never an easy task, it is essential both for the person who needs to know about his or her own situation and for the helper who needs to convey information and confirm that he or she can be relied on in this way. The steps suggested in Table 7.1 are not necessarily a universal scenario, but they do point to a larger literature on preparing helpers to communicate effectively (for example, Buckman, 1992a; Cassell, 1985; Faulkner, 1993).

In addition, Callanan and Kelley (1992; see also Sanders, 2007) explored what they call "nearing death awareness." This concept recognizes that communications from dying persons are too often dismissed as empty or enigmatic expressions of confusion. Instead, Callanan and Kelley argue that such communications may actually reflect either (1) special awareness of the imminence of death and efforts to describe what dying is like as it is being experienced by the individual or (2) expressions of final requests about what is needed before the individual can experience a peaceful death. These alternatives draw attention to a special set of communicative tasks undertaken by dying persons and, once more, stress the indispensable role of *active listening*.

Effective communication is an important part of fostering hope and quality in living when individuals are coping with dying. It is also important in self-care and in obtaining assistance in meeting the needs of helpers themselves. How one

TABLE 7.1 How to Break Bad News: A Six-Step Protocol	
Step 1	Start carefully: Get the physical context right; if humanly possible, speak face-to-face, in an appropriate setting, and with attention to who should be present.
Step 2	Find out how much the person already knows: Listen for intellectual understanding, communicative style, and emotional content.
Step 3	Find out how much the person wants to know: Determine at what level the person wants to know what is going on; offer willingness to explore matters further in the future.
Step 4	Share the information: Start from the person's point of view; have an agenda with desired objectives; share information in small chunks, in plain, nontechnical language; check reception frequently; reinforce and clarify information frequently; check communication levels; listen for the person's concerns; blend your agenda with that of the person.
Step 5	Respond to the person's feelings: Identify and acknowledge the person's reactions.
Step 6	Plan for the future and follow through.

Source: Based on Buckman, 1992a.

communicates with those one is trying to help can become a model for all helping interactions. The challenge in helping others appears on two basic levels: (1) to keep company with the dying and with others who are coping with dying—even when that requires one to be comfortable with one's own discomfort and to do nothing more than to sit quietly together in silence; and (2) to learn how to identify and respond effectively to the particular physical, psychological, social, and spiritual tasks that are part of a specific individual's coping with dying. The challenge in helping oneself lies in learning to use effective communication to find greater satisfaction in the helping role and to seek from others the professional and personal support that all helpers need.

❦ Helping Helpers: Stress, Burnout, and Self-Care

A task-based approach to coping with dying reminds helpers that they also have their own coping to consider and that self-care is essential in effectively managing stress and preventing caregiver burnout (Corr, 1992c; Grollman, 1995). Helpers, whether they are family members, volunteers, or professionals, are also human beings with needs and limitations. One does not have to be dying to be important.

Helpers must not overburden their own resources. Otherwise, they may become unable to give any further assistance. The best helpers are those who operate from a foundation in a rich and satisfying life of their own, not from a sense that they are overwhelmed by stressors and problems of their own (Larson, 1993).

In the videotape *The Heart of the New Age Hospice* (1987), one woman with a life-threatening illness described the foundation for helping others in the following way: "Duty without love is preposterous. Duty with love is acceptable. Love without duty is divine." Helpers cannot operate solely from their own need to be needed. They must care about those whom they are helping, but their love must also include themselves. The best helpers are those who can also take care of themselves and who take time to meet their own needs. In other words, helpers must strive for a balance between too much involvement and too much distance in their interactions with the needs of others (International Work Group on Death, Dying, and Bereavement, 2006; Papadatou, 2000; Vachon, 2007). The desired balance, often called "detached concern" (Larson, 1993) or "detached compassion" (Pattison, 1977), involves entering into the situation of the person being helped in a way that enables the helper to continue to function effectively in the helping role. Such a posture must be achieved in individual ways by each helper and certainly requires considerable self-awareness. Nouwen (1972) made this point by suggesting that caregivers must recognize that they are "wounded healers."

Stress and burnout in helpers have been the subject of much study (for example, Selye, 1978b). One interesting finding is that stress more often arises from the situation within which one is working and the colleagues with whom one works than from the fact that one is working with dying persons and others who are coping with dying (Vachon, 1987, 1997). In each case, then, one must carefully examine the specific sources of stress and the mediators that may modify that stress in various ways (Friel & Tehan, 1980). Thoughtful programs to address stress include such elements as careful staff selection, training, supervision, and support. When such a program is coupled with the development of an individual philosophy of care and attention to one's own needs for care (whether self-care or care from others), helping those who are coping with dying need not be more stressful than many other activities in our society (Harper, 1994; LaGrand, 1980; Lattanzi, 1983, 1985).

Many of the basic elements in an effective program of managing stress and taking care of oneself are found in a series of suggestions set forth in Table 7.2 and in what Selye (1978a, p. 70) called "a kind of recipe for the best antidote to the stresses of life":

> The first ingredient . . . is to seek your own stress level, to decide whether you're a racehorse or a turtle and to live your life accordingly. The second is to choose your goals and make sure they're really your own, and not imposed on you. . . . And the third ingredient to this recipe is altruistic egoism—looking out for oneself by being necessary to others, and thus earning their goodwill.

Good helpers need to evaluate their own strengths and weaknesses (see Personal Insights 7.3), as well as being open to suggestions and support from other persons—even from the dying person or the family they are helping. Indeed, when dying persons are freed from the burden of distressing symptoms and made to feel secure, they can often be very thoughtful and sensitive in caring for those around them. In short, none of us is without needs in coping with someone else's mortality or with our own mortality. We all can benefit from help as we look to our own tasks in coping.

TABLE 7.2
Suggestions for Stress Management and Self-Care

Be proactive: *Effective intervention begins with good prevention.*

Take charge: *Adopt an active strategy of coping focused on one or more of the following—your appraisal of the stressful situation and its sources, what you can do about the situation, or what you can do about your own reactions to the situation.*

Set limits: *Seek a dynamic balance between demands and resources; limit time and involvements with those you are helping.*

Compartmentalize: *Put some physical and psychological distance between your home life and your work life.*

Develop a stress-hardy outlook:
   Strive to view potentially stressful situations as challenges—that is, as opportunities for growth rather than as threats.
   Strive to balance your commitments to work, family, and friendships.
   Strive to develop the conviction that life's experiences are—within limits—within your control (and a sense of humor that helps to keep stress and striving in perspective).

Practice the art of the possible: *Do what you can even though there is always much that you cannot do; be patient and creative.*

Improve your communication and conflict-resolution skills: *Stress often arises when you are caring and compassionate but do not know what to say or what to do.*

Rejuvenate yourself: *Employ techniques of exercise, relaxation, and meditation in self-care because stress is unavoidable.*

Know yourself: *Befriend yourself; be gentle with your inner discomforts.*

Maintain and enhance your self-esteem: *Develop a positive view of your skills and yourself; doing good can help you to feel good; recognizing your commitment to meaningful work can help you feel better about yourself.*

Strengthen your social support: *Encouragement, support, and feedback can enhance self-esteem and your sense of self-efficacy.*

Source: Based on Larson, 1993.

❧ Hope

This brings us to the subject of *hope*. Sometimes it is said that there is no more hope for dying persons, that they are hopeless cases, and that working with the dying must be a hopeless endeavor. Such assertions reveal a narrow understanding of the role that hope plays in human lives (Corr, 1981; Cousins, 1989). We hope for all sorts of things. I hope that someone will (continue to) love me. He hopes that he can have his favorite food for dinner tonight. She hopes to be able to see her sister again. Many of us hope to live as long as we possibly can. Some dying persons

On Facing and Understanding One's Limitations

Once you face and understand your limitations,
you can work with *them instead of having them*
work against you and get in your way,
which is what they do when you ignore them,
whether you realize it or not.
And then you will find that, in many cases,
your limitations can be your strengths.

Source: Hoff, 1983, pp. 48–49.

hope to live until a special birthday, a holiday, or the birth of a new grandchild. Many hope for an outcome grounded in their spiritual convictions. Perhaps we all hope that our own situation and the situations of those we love will be at least a little bit better while we are dying and after our deaths. Here, hope for a cure may give way to hope for a good dying process and death (Webb, 1997). Helpers hope that their interventions will make a difference even in a life that may soon be over. Until death comes, most of us hope that whatever it is that is making us uncomfortable will be reduced or removed from our lives. This last hope—like many other hopes that we may entertain—cannot always be realized. Still, it is only one hope among many.

Few situations in life are ever completely hopeless. So when someone says, "This situation is hopeless," it may just signify a failure of imagination. Often, it represents the point of view of an outsider (for example, a care provider) and his or her judgment that there is no likelihood of cure for the person in the situation. Usually, this type of statement indicates that the speaker has focused exclusively on a single hope or a narrow range of hopes that cannot be realized in a specific set of circumstances. It would be far better to appreciate the therapeutic potential of hope. This is a serious point, but it has also been suggested in the following lighthearted way: "After all, hope contains no mono or polyunsaturated fats, cholesterol, sugars, artificial sweeteners, flavors or colors; it's classified as 'generally recognized as safe' by the FDA and is a known anticarcinogen" (Munson, 1993, p. 24).

In fact, "hope, which centers on fulfilling expectations, may focus on getting well, but more often focuses on what yet can be done" (Davidson, 1975, p. 49). Hope is a characteristically human phenomenon (Veninga, 1985). But it is fluid, often altering its focus to adapt to changes in the actual circumstances within which we find ourselves. Again, we must listen carefully to each individual—including hope in those who are trying to help people cope with dying—to determine the object of his or her hope. We must also distinguish between hope, which is founded in reality, and unrealistic wishes, which merely express fanciful desires.

❦ Summary

In this chapter, we explored ways in which individuals, whether professionals or laypersons, can contribute to helping those who are coping with dying. We considered four primary dimensions in such care (physical, psychological, social, and spiritual), and we drew on a task-based model to suggest guidelines for helping both others and oneself. We ended with some comments on effective communication, helping helpers, and hope.

Glossary

Active listening: making oneself available to another without interference from one's own concerns; being fully attentive to the needs and concerns of the other

Acute pain: distress in any dimension of an individual's life that is characteristically time limited, although it may recur; may be mild, moderate, or intense

Addiction: a form of habitual dependence upon analgesics (e.g., narcotic drugs) characterized by psychological "highs" and a subsequent craving for steadily escalating doses

Burnout: a condition in which a helper has given so much to others that the helper becomes used up, overwhelmed, exhausted, and unable to function effectively to assist others

Chronic pain: distress in any dimension of an individual's life that is characteristically ongoing and not time limited; may be mild, moderate, or intense

Compassion: "feeling with" another person, involving presence, active listening, and empathy; to be contrasted with "pity," which always implies a "looking down upon"

Dependence: reliance upon drugs or other supports that does not necessarily imply the features of addiction; requires that the drug or other support be terminated or withdrawn in a phased fashion (not "cold turkey") to avoid undesirable side effects

Detached concern or detached compassion: a way of entering into the situation of the person being helped that enables the helper to continue to function effectively in the helping role

Effective communication: interactions whose specific acts are responsive to the needs of the other and are carried out in a thoughtful and caring way; both the content of the exchange and the ways in which it is expressed and understood are important

Empathetic presence: making oneself available to a person in distress; characterized by active listening, empathy, and compassion

Four dimensions of care for individuals who are coping with dying:

Physical: designed to address bodily pain or other sources of corporeal distress (e.g., constipation, diarrhea, nausea, vomiting, dehydration, loss of energy or appetite, shortness of breath, skin ulcers or bedsores, sleeplessness); therapeutic interventions may involve carefully selected medications balanced to need and administered in appropriate ways, often coupled with other modalities, such as positioning in bed or in a chair

Psychological: designed to address emotional or cognitive distress; extreme forms may involve confusional or psychotic states and clinical depression or other forms of mental illness

Social: designed to address interpersonal tensions or difficulties, as well as problems with social groups or organizations; interventions may involve advocacy either to empower individuals to act on their own behalf or to speak or act for them

Spiritual: designed to assist individuals in their search for meaning, for establishing, reestablishing, and maintaining connectedness with oneself, other persons, and with what the person perceives as the transcendent; often facilitated by empathetic presence

Hope: expectations that one looks forward to based on faith and trust; may involve many different prospects; should not be excluded from those who are coping with dying

Nearing death awareness: communications from dying persons that reflect either (1) special awareness of the imminence of death and efforts to describe what dying is like as it is being experienced by the individual or (2) expressions of final requests about what is needed before the individual can experience a peaceful death

Stress: hardship or adversity that imposes pressure or strain, in this case associated with death-related issues

Questions for Review and Discussion

1. Think about some moment in your life when someone you loved was quite ill or dying. What was most stressful for you at that time? What did you do or what might you have done that you now think was helpful or unhelpful to the person who was ill or dying?

2. In this chapter, we described four dimensions or aspects of care for the dying: physical, psychological, social, and spiritual. Think about someone you know who was or is dying (or use the example of the Amish man described in Chapter 3 or Jo and Matt Ryan whom we described in Chapter 6 and again near the outset of this chapter). In the case that you select, how did these four dimensions or aspects of care show up?

3. In this chapter, we pointed out that effective communication is or can be important both for dying persons and for those who are helping such persons. Why is communication important for the dying and their helpers? What makes for effective communication among such people? What is an example from your own experience of poor communication? Of good communication?

4. In this chapter, we suggested that hope is or can be important both for dying persons and for those who are helping such persons. How can hope be important for those who know they will soon be dead or for those who know that the person for whom they are caring will soon be dead? What does hope mean to you?

Suggested Readings

The lives and viewpoints of two women who have been pioneers in care of the dying are described in:

Clark, D. (Ed). (2002). *Cicely Saunders—Founder of the Hospice Movement. Selected Letters 1959–1999.*

DuBoulay, S. (1984). *Cicely Saunders: The Founder of the Modern Hospice Movement.*

Gill, D. L. (1980). *Quest: The Life of Elisabeth Kübler-Ross.*

Kübler-Ross, E. (1997). *The Wheel of Life: A Memoir of Living and Dying.*

Saunders, C. (2003). *Watch with Me: Inspiration for a Life in Hospice Care.*

For guidance on ways in which to help persons who are coping with dying, see:

Berzoff, J., & Silverman, P. (Eds.). (2004). *Living with Dying: A Comprehensive Resource for Health Care Professionals.*

Buckman, R. (1992a). *How to Break Bad News: A Guide for Health Care Professionals.*

Buckman, R. (1992b). *I Don't Know What to Say: How to Help and Support Someone Who Is Dying.*

Byock, I. (1997). *Dying Well: The Prospect for Growth at the End of Life.*

Callanan, M., & Kelley, P. (1992). *Final Gifts: Understanding the Special Awareness, Needs, and Communications of the Dying.*

Cassell, E. J. (1985). *Talking with Patients: Vol. 1, The Theory of Doctor-Patient Communication; Vol. 2, Clinical Technique.*

Cassell, E. J. (1991). *The Nature of Suffering and the Goals of Medicine.*

Davies, B., Reimer, J. C., Brown, P., & Martens, N. (1995). *Fading Away: The Experience of Transition in Families with Terminal Illness.*

Kemp, C. (1999). *Terminal Illness: A Guide to Nursing Care* (2nd ed.).

Kuhl, D. (2002). *What Dying People Want: Practical Wisdom for the End of Life.*

Landay, D. S. (1998). *Be Prepared: The Complete Financial, Legal, and Practical Guide for Living with a Life-Threatening Condition.*

Mace, N. L., & Rabins, P. V. (1999). *The 36-Hour Day: A Family Guide to Caring for Persons with Alzheimer's Disease, Related Dementing Illnesses, and Memory Loss in Later Life* (3rd ed.).

Nouwen, H. (1994). *Our Greatest Gift: A Meditation on Dying and Caring.*

Parkes, C. M., Relf, M., & Couldrick, A. (1996). *Counseling in Terminal Care and Bereavement.*

Quill, T. (1996). *A Midwife Through the Dying Process: Stories of Healing and Hard Choices at the End of Life.*

Rosen, E. J. (1998). *Families Facing Death: A Guide for Health Care Professionals and Volunteers* (rev. ed.).

Sanders, M. A. (Ed.). (2007). *Nearing Death Awareness: A Guide to the Language, Visions, and Dreams of the Dying.*

Saunders, C. M., & Sykes, N. (Eds.). (1993). *The Management of Terminal Malignant Disease* (3rd ed.).

Twycross, R. G. (1994). *Pain Relief in Advanced Cancer.*

Twycross, R. G., & Wilcock, A. (2002). *Symptom Management in Advanced Cancer* (3rd ed.).

Wall, P. (2002). *Pain: The Science of Suffering.*

Werth, J. L., & Blevins, D. (Eds.). (2006). *Psychosocial Issues near the End of Life: A Resource for Professional Care Providers.*

Wooten-Green, R. (2001). *When the Dying Speak: How to Listen to and Learn from Those Facing Death.*

Support for family and other helpers is discussed in:

Corr, C. A. (1992c). *Someone You Love Is Dying: How Do You Cope?*

Grollman, E. A. (1980). *When Your Loved One Is Dying.*

Harper, B. C. (1994). *Death: The Coping Mechanism of the Health Professional* (rev. ed.).

Larson, D. G. (1993). *The Helper's Journey: Working with People Facing Grief, Loss, and Life-Threatening Illness.*

Selected Web Resources

Some useful search terms include: ADDICTION; BURNOUT; COMPASSION; DEPENDENCE; DIMENSIONS OF CARE; EFFECTIVE COMMUNICATION; EMPATHY; HOPE; PAIN (ACUTE AND CHRONIC); STRESS

Visit the book companion website for *Death & Dying, Life & Living, Sixth Edition,* academic.cengage.com/psychology/corr for all URLs and live links to the following *organizational and other Internet sites:*

Americans for Better Care of the Dying

Association for Clinical Pastoral Education

Association for Professional Chaplains

Caring Connections

Family Caregiver Alliance

Growth House (multiple topics and links)

National Alliance for Caregiving

National Family Caregivers Association (NFCA)

Pain.com

CHAPTER 8

Coping with Dying: How Communities Can Help

Hospice Care

usa 33

1998

© AP Photo/U.S. Postal Service

Objectives of This Chapter

◆ To explore *formal programs of care* in the United States that are involved in helping individuals who are coping with dying

◆ To comment on *the importance of recognizing and responding to the needs of persons who are coping with dying*, with specific reference to evidence of shortcomings among caregiving institutions and *growing awareness of the need for better end-of-life care*

◆ To examine the *hospice philosophy* in order to identify ten principles or desirable

elements in an institutional program of care for those who are coping with dying

◆ To describe the historical development and practical roles in contemporary society of four specific institutions that offer care for individuals who are coping with dying: *hospitals,* which focus on *acute care; long-term care facilities,* which focus on *chronic care; home health programs,* which focus on *home care;* and *hospice programs,* which focus on *end-of-life care*

◆ To explain similarities and differences between *hospice care* and *palliative care*

🐦 Social Institutions That Helped One Family Cope with Life-Threatening Illness and Dying

Some of the care that Matt and Josephina Ryan needed was provided by a local hospital. Each was diagnosed and received initial treatment there, and both were seen for a time in the hospital's outpatient clinics after their initial surgeries. Matt was fortunate that he needed no further care other than regular follow-up observations. Unfortunately, Jo's situation was more complicated, especially when she faced the demands of her advanced illness. For a while a community home health care program helped by providing regular visits from nursing personnel during daytime and weekday hours.

Nevertheless, as her health declined, Jo's needs grew, and she was unwilling at that time to remain at home because she was afraid of what might happen and did not want to have her family members take on what she perceived as the burdens of her care.

At that point, the security of a local nursing home that had cared for her mother before her death seemed to offer Jo a good alternative. She liked the slower pace of the nursing home and even made some friends there. But as time went on, Jo found that many of the residents were older than her; some seemed confused and were unable to sustain a relationship. Matt had always been unsure about whether it was a good idea to have Jo stay in any type of facility, and he very much missed her at home. The last straw came when one of the residents unwittingly frightened the children of their son, Tom, and his family visited less often after that.

Jo felt very much alone and overwhelmed by her problems until someone suggested that she talk with a representative of a local hospice program. That led to a transfer to the hospice inpatient unit. The support of the hospice team for Jo and her family helped minimize sources of distress and improve their quality of life. Jo's pain and other symptoms were now managed effectively; both her physical condition and her spirits improved greatly. Jo felt that she had almost miraculously regained control of her life.

Ultimately, with support from the hospice home care team, Jo was even able to go home to be with Matt and her family for several months. In the end, with help from the hospice team, she died in her own bed at home.

🐦 Recognizing and Responding to the Needs of Persons Who Are Coping with Dying

"What people need most when they are dying is relief from distressing symptoms of disease, the security of a caring environment, sustained expert care, and assurance that they and their families will not be abandoned" (Craven & Wald, 1975, p. 1816). This single sentence itemizes many of the concerns of those who are dying and what they need from institutional programs of care.

During the 1960s and 1970s, some caregivers began to wonder whether care provided to those who were dying was properly recognizing and responding to their needs. Studies conducted in Great Britain (e.g., Hinton, 1963; Rees, 1972), Canada (e.g., Mount et al., 1974), and the United States (such as Marks & Sachar, 1973) confirmed that the answer was no. Two points seemed to be central: (1) caregivers did not always realize or acknowledge the level of pain and other forms of distress being experienced by individuals who were dying, and (2) caregivers did not always have or believe that they had at their disposal effective resources to respond to the needs of those who were dying. In practice, this meant that those who were dying were often told: "Your pain cannot be as bad as you say it is"; "You can't really be feeling like that"; "You will just have to get hold of yourself"; "We cannot offer stronger dosages of narcotic analgesics or you will risk becoming addicted"; "We have to save the really strong medications until they are truly needed"; "There is nothing more that we can do."

It is unfortunate when caregivers who want to help do not have the resources to do so. Thus, many were grateful when new forms of narcotic analgesics became available for use to help dying persons. But it is tragic when the needs of those who are dying are not recognized and when that is compounded by inadequate understanding or misguided fears about whether or how to mobilize available resources to meet those needs.

New perspectives were required on several key points, including:

◆ The situation of those who are coping with dying (Noyes & Clancy, 1977; Pattison, 1977)

◆ The nature of pain when one is dying (LeShan, 1964; Melzack & Wall, 1991; Wall & Melzack, 1994)

◆ Appropriate therapeutic regimes for those who are dying, which involve carefully selected narcotics, other medications, and complementary therapeutic interventions (Melzack et al., 1979; Melzack et al., 1976; Twycross, 1976, 1979a)

◆ The value of holistic, person-centered care and interdisciplinary teamwork (Corr & Corr, 1983; Saunders & Sykes, 1993)

◆ Ways in which the social organization of programs serving those who are coping with dying affect the care provided (Saunders, 1990; Sudnow, 1967)

These new elements are all embodied in the hospice philosophy; they have been implemented in hospice and palliative care programs. Some of these elements have also been incorporated in other programs of care for those who are coping with dying.

During the 1990s, increasing interest in end-of-life care was evident in a growing body of literature (e.g., Webb, 1997) and a study commissioned by the Institute of Medicine (Field & Cassel, 1997). Evidence from large-scale research studies identified ongoing deficiencies in end-of-life care. A key study provided quantitative data from controlled, clinical research conducted in five teaching hospitals in the United States (SUPPORT Principal Investigators, 1995). The SUPPORT (Study to Understand Prognoses and Preferences for Outcomes and Risks of Treatments) project examined end-of-life preferences, decision making, and interventions in a total of 9,105 adults hospitalized with one or more of nine life-threatening diagnoses. The two-year first phase of the study observed 4,301 patients and documented substantial shortcomings in communication, overuse of aggressive cure-oriented treatment at the very end of life, and undue pain preceding death. The two-year second phase of the study compared the situations of 4,804 patients randomly assigned to intervention and control groups with each other and with baseline data from Phase 1. Physicians with the intervention group received improved, computer-based, prognostic information on their patients' status. Moreover, a specially trained nurse was assigned to the intervention group in each hospital to carry out multiple contacts with patients, families, physicians, and hospital staff in order to elicit preferences, improve understanding of outcomes, encourage better attention to pain control, facilitate advance care planning, and enhance patient-physician communication.

The SUPPORT study used the following criteria to evaluate outcomes: the timing of written "Do not resuscitate" (DNR) orders; patient and physician agreement (based on the first interview between them) on whether to withhold resuscitation; the number of days before death spent in an intensive care unit either receiving mechanical ventilation or comatose; the frequency and severity of pain; and the use of hospital resources. Results were discouraging. Phase 2 intervention "failed to improve care or patient outcomes" (p. 1591) and led the investigators to conclude

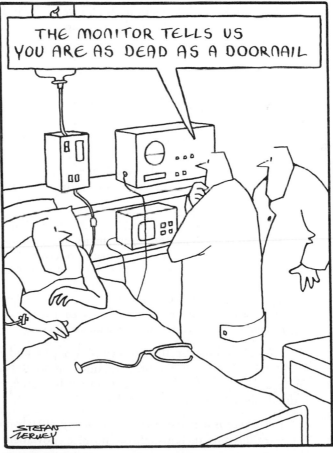

that "we are left with a troubling situation. The picture we describe of the care of seriously ill or dying persons is not attractive" (p. 1597). This is disheartening in light of the scope of the study, its capacity to measure targeted outcomes, the careful design of its interventions, the existence of a well-established, professional knowledge base and models within our health system for this type of care, and the degree of ethical, legal, public, and policy-making attention recently directed to issues related to end-of-life decision making and quality of care. Unfortunately, some similar results have been confirmed by other studies drawing on the SUPPORT project (e.g., Krumholz et al., 1998).

Another study, "Living and Healing During Life-Threatening Illness" (Supportive Care of the Dying: A Coalition for Compassionate Care, 1997), used a qualitative methodology involving focus groups at 11 selected sites in Catholic health care systems across the United States. A total of 407 participants ranging in age from 18 to 93 were brought together between March and June 1996, in small groups of 3 to 10 persons organized in one of five categories: persons with life-threatening illnesses; personal/family caregivers; bereaved persons; professional caregivers; and community members. The overall results of the study suggested that health care systems in our society needed to change in important ways if they were to serve the needs of persons who are coping with dying. Clearly, there is much to be done at all levels—by individuals, professionals, and communities, as well as by health care organizations and systems—to improve end-of-life care in our society.

❧ Hospice Philosophy and Principles

Both the Canadian Hospice Palliative Care Association (www.chpca.net; Ferris et al., 2002) and the National Hospice and Palliative Care Organization (www .nhpco.org; 2006b) in the United States have established standards for hospice care. Drawing on work by NHPCO, Connor (1998, pp. 3–4) defined "hospice care" as:

> [A] coordinated program providing palliative care to terminally ill patients and supportive services to patients, their families, and significant others 24 hours a day, seven days a week. Comprehensive/case managed services based on physical, social, spiritual, and emotional needs are provided during the last stages of illness, during the dying process, and during bereavement by a medically directed interdisciplinary team consisting of patients/families, health care professionals and volunteers. Professional management and continuity of care is maintained across multiple settings including homes, hospitals, long term care and residential settings.

We can summarize the hospice philosophy and its central principles in the following ten points. When properly understood and correctly applied, these principles can become the key elements in guiding any practical program of care for individuals who are coping with dying.

1. *Hospice is a philosophy, not a facility—one whose primary focus is on end-of-life care.* In England, the hospice movement began by building its own

facilities. This reflected the social situation and health care system in a particular country at a specific time. Going outside existing structures in this way is one classic route for innovation. However, it is not the facility in which hospice care is delivered that is essential; the main points are the principles that animate services and the quality of the care itself. That philosophy of care—outlook, attitude, approach—is the central point, along with a focus on persons who are coping with dying (Egan & Labyak, 2001).

2. *The hospice philosophy affirms life, not death.* Dying is a self-limiting condition. Individuals can and will die by themselves, without assistance from others. As Art Buchwald (2006, p. 9) wrote from his hospice bed, "Dying isn't hard. Getting paid by Medicare is." Seriously, the challenging work is supporting life, not allowing people to die or bringing about death. Helping a person to live may be especially difficult when that person is close to death and is experiencing distress in dying. Processes of dying often impose special pressures on quality in living. The key point is to affirm life, to care for and about persons who are coping with dying because they are living and struggling with these special pressures.

3. *The hospice philosophy strives to maximize present quality in living.* Hospice is a form of palliative or symptom-oriented care that tries to minimize discomfort. Without abandoning interest in cure, hospice care is focused on other forms of caring when cure is no longer a reasonable expectation. This is not merely the opposite of "active treatment" (an inaccurate phrase that usually is used to mean cure-oriented treatment), for that would make it merely some passive mode of care. In fact, "the care of the dying patient is an active treatment peculiar to the dying patient" (Liegner, 1975, p. 1048; reprinted 2000, p. 2426). Thus, hospice and other desirable programs of care for those coping with dying embody an active and aggressive mode of care whose focus is on the alleviation of distressing symptoms, as well as on prospects for personal growth at the end of life, even when the underlying condition from which distress arises cannot be halted or reversed (Byock, 1996). As Saunders (1976, p. 674) observed, this is "the unique period in the patient's illness when the long defeat of living can be gradually converted into *a positive achievement in dying*" (our italics).

4. *The hospice approach offers care to the patient-and-family unit.* This means that both the dying person and those whom he or she regards as "family" form the unit receiving care and helping to give care. Hospice care seeks to provide a sense of security and the support of a caring environment for all who are involved in coping with dying—ill persons together with their families, friends, and other involved persons (Egan, 1998; Stedeford, 1987). The principle here is the importance of family-centered care for those who are coping with dying.

5. *Hospice is holistic care.* Recognizing that people being served are persons, whole human beings, hospice care assists them in working with their physical, psychological, social, and spiritual tasks. It seeks to enhance quality in living in each of these dimensions. Good end-of-life care is holistic in nature (Lloyd-Williams, 2003).

The Hospice of the Florida Suncoast

Art therapy can stimulate creativity even in persons who are coping with life-threatening illness.

6. *Hospice offers continuing care and ongoing support to family members coping with dying, death, and loss both before and after the death of someone they love.* Care for family members and friends is relevant before the death of the person they love as well as after that event. Good end-of-life care is intended to have a positive impact on these individuals (Christakis & Iwashyna, 2003). We will return to this topic in Chapters 10 and 11 when we discuss how to help the bereaved.

7. *The hospice approach combines professional skills and human presence through interdisciplinary teamwork.* Special expertise in end-of-life care and in the management of distressing symptoms is essential. Expert medical and nursing care are critical. However, the availability of human companionship is equally important. Professional caregivers can offer human presence, but it is often a special gift of hospice volunteers. Appropriate use of one's expertise and one's presence is dependent upon being available and actively listening to understand correctly the needs of dying persons and their family members. Interdisciplinary teamwork demands respect for the special skills and abilities of others, time to exchange information and insights, and a certain amount of "role blurring" in assisting all whom the hospice program is serving. Interdisciplinary—not multidisciplinary—teamwork is essential to good end-of-life care in any programmatic setting.

8. *Hospice programs make services available on a 24-hour-a-day, 7-day-a-week basis.* Hospice seeks to recreate caring communities to help dying persons and their families. Wherever such communities already exist naturally and whenever dying persons and their families are not experiencing

significant distress, there may be no need for formal hospice programs. When and where a need does exist, these programs must be available around the clock, just as a caring community is—perhaps through phone contacts or the ability to have a caregiver come to the dying person's bedside wherever that person may be. Good end-of-life care does not take holidays or go off duty.

9. *Participants in hospice programs give special attention to supporting each other.* Caring for those who are coping with dying or bereavement and working within the structure of an interdisciplinary team can be stressful. Thus, hospice programs offer both formal and informal programs of support for their own staff members and volunteers. This is important in any program that seeks to offer effective end-of-life care.

10. *The hospice philosophy can be applied to a variety of individuals and their family members who are coping with a life-threatening illness, dying, death, or bereavement.* In its modern usage, hospice care was originally mainly concerned with illnesses like cancer and their implications, especially for older adults. But the hospice philosophy need not be restricted to these conditions or to specific settings and institutions. To benefit from the hospice philosophy, there must be time and opportunity to bring services to bear upon the tasks of the patient-and-family unit. Thus, hospice and other forms of optimal end-of-life care require some advance notice that dying has begun and death is imminent (in a matter of days, weeks, or months), some willingness to accept the benefits and restrictions of the hospice philosophy, and an opportunity to mobilize services in particular circumstances. Given these conditions, the hospice philosophy has been applied in recent years to a broad range of diseases at the end of life (such as HIV/AIDS and end-stage renal, cardiac, and Alzheimer's disease) and to situations involving children and adolescents.

❧ Four Programs of Care for Persons Who Are Coping with Dying

Near the beginning of this chapter, we described the experiences of Jo Ryan and her family. We can understand those experiences more fully and come to better appreciate ways in which hospice principles can be put into practice in any setting by examining the development, role, and principal functions of the caregiving programs that Jo encountered, especially during the last, difficult parts of her life. Programs of this sort are typically associated with an institution and are always based in some physical facility, but it is the services they offer to persons who are coping with dying that are really critical. The relevant institutions here are hospitals or medical centers, long-term care facilities (often called nursing homes), home health care programs, and hospice programs. Each of these institutions specializes in a particular type of care, but all play some role in caring for individuals who are coping with dying.

Acute Care: Hospitals

In the United States today, most people receive most of their acute medical care in hospitals, and more than 46 percent die there. As a result, hospitals play a major role in shaping the end of life in American society (Kaufman, 2006).

Hospitals have an ancient origin. The word *hospital* is derived from the medieval Latin *hospitale,* meaning a place of "reception and entertainment of pilgrims, travellers, and strangers" (*Oxford English Dictionary*, 1989, vol. 7, p. 414). In the ancient world, the original hospitals took in pilgrims, travelers, the needy, the destitute, the infirm, the aged, and the sick or wounded. Such institutions were usually associated with some type of religious fraternity or community.

As Western culture became more urbanized, hospitals began to change. A division of labor began to characterize Western society. Specialization in carrying out tasks became the normal method of operation. No longer did one institution perform many basically different functions; instead, separate institutions now undertook separate functions. These changes were more or less complete by the end of the 19th century.

In the United States up to the 19th century, care of the sick and dying occurred mainly at home and was provided mainly by family members. Hospitals played virtually no role in such care. In fact, in 1800 there were only two private hospitals in the United States, one in New York and one in Philadelphia (Rosenberg, 1987).

Of course, even in that society, there were persons who were too sick to be cared for at home or who had no one at home to take care of them. If such persons were also poor and could not afford to hire someone to take care of them, they ended up in an *almshouse.* Almshouses were charitable public institutions that housed the insane, the blind, the crippled, the aged, the alcoholic, travelers, and ordinary workingmen with rheumatism, bronchitis, or pleurisy. These diverse types of people were freely mixed together. Almshouses most often had large wards, which were usually crowded. Sometimes more than one person had to sleep in a single bed. Because they were usually not well funded, almshouses were typically dark, stuffy, and unpleasant places. Few people entered them voluntarily.

Modern hospitals began to be organized around the beginning of the 19th century. From the outset, they were advocated mainly as having an *educational* function and were not perceived as being primary agents of medical care. These early hospitals had little to offer and were avoided by anyone who could do so because they were often viewed as "unnatural" and demoralizing. Thus, the physician V. M. Francis (1859, pp. 145–146) wrote just before the outbreak of the Civil War that "the people who repair to hospitals are mostly very poor, and seldom go into them until driven to do so from a severe stress of circumstances. When they cross the threshold, they are found not only suffering from disease, but in a half-starved condition, poor, broken-down wrecks of humanity, stranded on the cold bleak shores of that most forbidding of all coasts, charity."

Also, until the middle of the 19th century, care provided inside a hospital was usually no better than care that could be obtained elsewhere. Hospital care mainly involved reporting of symptoms by the patient and "treatment" of such symptoms (usually without much ability to affect their underlying causes) as well as that could be done. This mostly meant allowing the body to heal itself, and in particular not interfering in that process. Basically, what a good hospital provided was a place to rest, shelter from the elements, and decent food.

The Civil War in the United States during the 1860s brought major changes. For one thing, the understanding of disease changed. Up to this time, as Rosenberg (1987, pp. 71–72) has written, the body was seen as "a system of ever-changing interactions with its environment. . . . Every part of the body was related inevitably and inextricably to every other." Health and disease were seen "as general states of the total organism. . . . The idea of specific disease entities played a relatively small role in this system of ideas and behavior." However, disease now began to be seen as involving specific entities and predictable causes. In the 1860s, Pasteur and Lister contributed to the germ theory of disease. This dramatically changed Western culture's understanding of what caused disease and what could be done to treat disease. Henceforth, science with its theories and technology would change the face of modern medicine. Human bodies were seen as complex machines, disease was thought of as a breakdown in the body's machinery, and therapy involved "fixing" the "malfunctioning part"—or, as we have seen in many cases in the last 30 years, replacing that part. As Rosenberg (1987, p. 85) has written, "This new way of understanding illness necessarily underlined the hospital's importance."

The Civil War itself also taught new ideas. Cleanliness, order, and ventilation were discovered to be of great help in bringing about a return to health. For the first time in American history, people (mostly soldiers) of all social classes experienced care in (military) hospitals. Attitudes toward the hospital were changing.

Immediately after the Civil War, many new hospitals were built. In 1873, there were 178 hospitals in the United States; this number had increased to 4,359 by 1909 (Rosenberg, 1987). Health care—and as a result, dying—was moving into hospitals. (It is interesting to note as an aside that according to Rosenberg [1987, p. 31], one Philadelphia almshouse surgeon complained in 1859 that "dead bodies were often left in the wards and placed directly in coffins while the surviving patients looked on." Some persons believed that this was very hard on the surviving patients and more or less recommended that such happenings should be hidden from public view. Here is a germ of the idea that Ariès [see Chapter 3] found arising in our time: the denial of death.) After the Civil War, people increasingly died in hospitals.

This fact produced tension for health care providers and health care recipients alike. As Rosenberg (1987, p. 150) wrote, "Ordinary Americans had . . . begun to accept the hospital. . . . Prospective patients were influenced not only by the hope of healing, but by the image of a new kind of medicine—precise, scientific, and effective." Consequently, hospitals were now expected to be places for the curing of specific diseases. The body's malfunctioning part was to be worked on, made functional, and then the person would get on with his or her life. In this context, death is an unhappy reminder that "scientific" medicine is not always effective—if *effective* is taken to mean capable of producing a cure. In this sort of hospital and according to this medical outlook, death is an anomaly, something abnormal. To the health care provider, death may seem to result from personal ineffectiveness. He or she was not able to "fix" the part in the body that was the problem. Thus, death is perceived to involve a kind of failure.

By the end of the 19th century, "moribund patients were systematically transferred to special rooms" (Rosenberg, 1987, p. 292). In some places, whole wards or units were set aside for those who were not expected to recover—out of sight and, to the degree possible, out of mind.

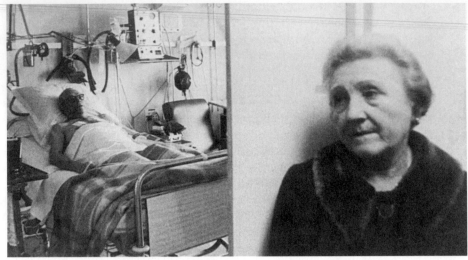

Contemporary acute health care institutions can intensify feelings of separation and powerlessness.

In the 1960s, specific criticisms began to be directed toward the hospital's care (or lack of effective care) for dying persons. The hospital in our culture is largely an *acute care,* short-term facility. Its purpose is mainly to treat specific diseases and to return people to society with more or less the same functional capacity they had before they became ill. Put simply, hospitals are dominated by medical professionals who see themselves as involved in curing people (Starr, 1982). This is why so many of our hospitals are now called "medical centers" or "health centers."

In our culture, acute care is an expensive business. Diagnostic tools become ever more precise—and costly. The stethoscope is an inexpensive diagnostic tool; the CAT scanner is not. An appendectomy is a relatively inexpensive procedure; a kidney or heart/lung transplant is not. To permit someone to spend time in a hospital when no therapy leading to a cure is available may seem to waste bed space and the time and energy of busy caregivers who have been specially trained in the techniques of cure-oriented intervention. In its historical context, this claim seems to make sense. No wonder economists and health planners became involved in the 1980s in an attempt to make the use of the hospital's expensive services more economically efficient (Stevens, 1989). Consequently, some hospitals were forced to go out of business, reducing their total numbers from nearly 7,000 in 1980 to 5,764 in 2003 (U.S. Census Bureau, 2005). Still, Medicare benefits for in-patient hospital services in 2003 totaled approximately $113.6 billion.

However, economic efficiency ought not and must not be the sole criterion for acute care institutions. In particular, humane care of dying persons may require bringing additional values into consideration, as Jo Ryan learned when she was in the hospital.

Chronic Care: Long-Term Care Facilities

Another type of institution that Jo Ryan and her family experienced and in which many people die in the United States is the long-term care facility or nursing home. Before the 1930s, there were no long-term care facilities in this country (Moroney &

Kurtz, 1975). They arose as the hospital became more and more an acute care facility and as urbanization helped change the nature of the family from an extended model or group of various relatives living in the same community to a nuclear model usually restricted to husband, wife, and minor child or children who often lived at a distance from other kin. Also, as average life expectancy increased, many Americans no longer expected to work until just days or hours before their death. They were either unable to work or, for various reasons, they decided to retire from work well before their deaths. Many of these people required assistance in caring for themselves and in activities of daily living as they lived out the remainder of their lives. In this, they joined a group of *younger people with chronic diseases or other handicapping conditions* who also experienced problems in taking care of themselves.

These factors led to a situation in which long-term, chronic disability and illness increased while care for people with these conditions became less available. Long-term care facilities fill this gap in care. In general, they provide a place to live, help with the routine activities of ordinary daily living, and some level of assistance or skilled nursing care. Long-term care facilities usually do not provide intensive physician care.

Developing mechanisms to offer financial assistance to those who become ill toward the end of their lives played an important part in the expansion of long-term care facilities, especially after the passage of the Social Security Act of 1935. With funding available from the personal savings of individuals, from their relatives, from government, and from health insurance and a retirement package (most often provided as a non-salary benefit by employers), potential providers of care began to think about offering services to this newly defined population. Primary sources of payment for services to residents of long-term care facilities who are 65 years of age and older now include Medicaid, Medicare, and private sources (such as private insurance, the resident's own income, family support, social security benefits, and retirement funds).

Until the 1980s, most hospitals did not think of themselves as profit-seeking enterprises. By contrast, many long-term care facilities have sought both to provide a service and to be a profitable business. This puts some pressure on long-term care facilities, for the sort of care they provide—labor-intensive, round-the-clock care—is expensive. In practice, this has meant that most of those who work in long-term care facilities are nurse aides, thus controlling costs and increasing profits by reducing costs of labor. Since long-term care facilities often experience high staff turnover, training of new persons, even when such training is minimal, must be constantly repeated. For both the care provider and the person who is being cared for, this often means that new faces and personalities must be met and learned. This can make the care provided feel discontinuous and uncertain.

There are several different types of long-term care facilities. (Contact the American Health Care Association at 800-628-8140 or www.ahca.org for a free copy of its pamphlet, "A Consumer's Guide to Nursing Facilities.") Perhaps the best-known are *skilled nursing facilities* in which professional nurses provide 24-hour care following orders from each resident's physician and guiding bedside care delivered by nursing assistants and aides. These facilities primarily serve individuals experiencing chronic health conditions that render them unable to care for themselves or perform activities of daily living. For example, those in advanced stages of Alzheimer's disease may display disorientation, memory loss, wandering, and combativeness— all of which require constant supervision. Some skilled nursing care facilities serve special populations such as ventilator-dependent patients. In the United States in 2003, there were 14,838 skilled nursing facilities with nearly 1.3 million beds (U.S. Census Bureau, 2005). In addition to private insurance or out-of-pocket payments, Medicare is the primary source of funding for skilled nursing care. Medicare benefits provided $16.4 billion dollars in 2003 for services offered by skilled nursing facilities (U.S. Census Bureau, 2005).

Other long-term care facilities range from intermediate care facilities to those that offer more basic forms of residential care. Members of this broad group of assisted living facilities may be described in different ways in different locations or regions of the country. Also, they may offer different levels of services within the same institutional complex. For example, in *intermediate care facilities,* nursing assistants or aides provide most of the care under the supervision of a professional nurse and with medical guidance or consultation. These facilities serve a segment of the elderly population who require nursing care, together with younger persons who have chronic illnesses or handicapping conditions. Such individuals need assistance with activities of daily living, such as feeding, bathing, and moving around. Some individuals who are confined to a bed or wheelchair need additional help to deal with infirmities and to avoid the development of pressure sores (which can lead to infections) and other debilitating complications. In addition to private insurance or out-of-pocket payments, joint federal and state Medicaid programs are the primary source of funding for these types of long-term care services.

Finally, there are *residential care facilities,* sometimes called independent living facilities, retirement communities, shelter care facilities, or board-and-care homes. These facilities offer a place to live and to obtain basic meals, economies of scale in purchasing, and some companionship for those who are poor, alone, and in need of some attention on more than a short-term basis. Typically, they offer no formal nursing services.

Individuals in long-term care facilities can generally be divided into two groups: "short stayers," who mostly come from hospitals and who either are rehabilitated and return home or who die within a relatively short period of time; and "long stayers," who are in the facility for months or years until they die. The fact that long-term care facilities discharge approximately 30 percent of their residents each year indicates the importance of their rehabilitative role. The occupancy rate in most long-term care facilities is quite high. Residents in many of these facilities may be very dependent; many are quite elderly, chronically ill, confused, even emotionally disturbed. Such individuals most often lack an available caregiver in the community; they may be single, widowed, childless, and, in general, less well-off economically than the rest of the population. Although long-term care facilities provide services to persons needing quite different sorts of care—from those needing brief, intensive rehabilitation to those who are incontinent, mentally impaired, seriously disabled, or very old and very frail—it is the long-term, chronically disabled persons who more and more often occupy beds in long-term care facilities.

In 2000, it is estimated that approximately 1.6 million persons 65 years of age or older were residents in long-term care facilities in the United States (U.S. Census Bureau, 2005). These residents were overwhelmingly Caucasian American (nearly

90 percent) and female (approximately 75 percent). They represented only about 4.5 percent of all individuals in that age group. Thus, the notion that to be old in the United States means to be in a nursing home is a misperception; most older adults in our society (over 95 percent of the nearly 35 million Americans who are 65 years of age or older) do not live in long-term care facilities. Still, the pressure on long-term care facilities is likely to grow as our population ages and most residents come to need long-term institutional care.

Our society seems content with relatively low overall levels of staff education and compensation in many long-term care facilities. This state of affairs appears to indicate that we do not value properly the increasing importance of such facilities. Nevertheless, many people who work in long-term care prefer the slower and more orderly routines of these facilities, along with opportunities to develop long-term personal relationships within them, by contrast with the more hectic pace and rapid patient turnover in acute care (although much of this may not be accurate when long-term care facilities are understaffed).

Many long-term care facilities operate with high standards and quality services for their residents. Still, there are periodic outcries in the media, in the public, and from legislative bodies about the quality of care provided in nursing homes and other long-term care facilities. Many people are dissatisfied with the quality of care in long-term care facilities, and we are all familiar with aged relatives who plead, "Don't send me to a nursing home."

Quality of living and dying in long-term care facilities can be measured in various ways. One indicator is found in limited contacts between residents and those outside the institution, a situation in which some residents may have no visitors or only a few perhaps on an irregular basis. For many, this suggests

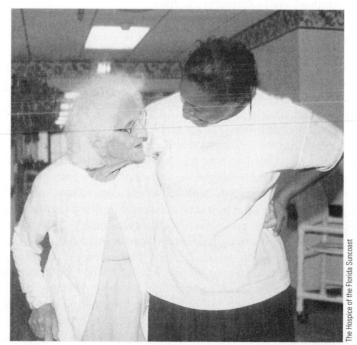

The Hospice of the Florida Suncoast

Long-term care can build caring relationships.

disengagement from or diminishment of external social networks. It has also been argued that there is too much isolation when one is dying in a long-term care facility and insufficient attention to bereavement needs of the institutional community, although that may be changing (Shield, 1988). Because of an acute illness or for other reasons, some individuals are transferred from long-term care facilities to acute care hospitals shortly before they die (Bottrell et al., 2001; Travis et al., 2001). Nevertheless, approximately 22 percent of all deaths in the United States in 2004 took place in a long-term care facility or nursing home.

Long-term care facilities provide services that Americans apparently want or need: someone (else) to take care of long-term, chronically disabled, and sometimes dying people. This may be a choice we are comfortable making. For example, this sort of institutional program was well suited at least for a time to the needs of Jo Ryan and her family. However, an institution designed for long-term care and chronic illness may not be well suited to the requirements of dying persons.

Jo Ryan eventually needed a level and type of service that her nursing home was not able to provide. Situations of this sort contribute to a stereotype often associated with dying persons: alone, afraid, seriously disabled, in unrelieved distress, uncared for, and perhaps uncared about. This stereotype is probably unfair in terms of the actual care provided in many long-term care facilities, but it looms large in the minds of many who may or may not have experienced these institutions with family members or friends. In other words, like hospitals, long-term care facilities do not always provide a comfortable institutional model for dying in our society. Still, both hospitals and long-term care facilities have improved their responses to dying persons in recent years and in many cases have associated themselves with hospice principles or programs of care (Cassarett et al., 2001; Henderson et al., 2003; NHPCO, 2001; Zerzan et al., 2000).

Home Care: Home Health Care Programs

Home health care programs have a long history as part of the health care systems in many societies. Such programs can be found in the district nurse structure in England and the Victorian Order of Nurses (VON) in Canada. In the United States, many city and county public health departments, the Visiting Nurse Association (VNA), and private home care agencies provide home care services.

The rapid growth of home health care in the United States during the last two decades has responded to new needs, together with changes in society and in its health care system. For example, the arrival of HIV infection and AIDS, along with a growing number of frail or confused elders, created new demands for home care. Also, in the 1980s a large number of mental health patients were relocated from psychiatric and other institutions to the community. More recently, federal and other third-party payers placed limitations on inpatient funding (in the form of, for example, "diagnostic-related groups" that capped payment for specific health conditions at a fixed amount), which pressured acute care institutions to discharge patients earlier (often much earlier) than had been previous practice. Some of the factors behind the growth in home health care, such as the desire to limit rising costs in health care by keeping individuals out of expensive institutions as much as possible, are similar to those that gave impetus to the modern hospice movement.

In any event, home health care has expanded in many forms, whether it is provided by traditional home health agencies, new home care agencies in the private sector, or newly developed home care departments of hospitals.

Unlike the other three institutions considered in this chapter, home health care programs are not distinguished by a specific kind of illness. All home health care is essentially a form of skilled nursing care (with supplementation in many cases from social workers, counselors, clergy, pharmacists, physical therapists, homemakers, personal care attendants, dieticians, physicians, occupational therapists, speech therapists, or audiologists). Also, all home health care can be addressed to problems arising from a wide variety of illnesses or conditions. The distinctive feature of this form of care is *the location in which it is provided;* home health care programs deliver their services *in the patient's own home.* For the most part, Medicare, Medicaid, and personal financial resources pay for home health care in our society.

Most home health care programs do offer care for dying persons, although they are not primarily or exclusively committed to providing that type of care. Indeed, some staff members in home health care programs have developed broad experience and expertise in caring for dying persons. As caregiving institutions, however, home health care programs usually do not claim specialized expertise in end-of-life care. Most home health care programs that offer skilled nursing care now make services available on a 24-hour-a-day, 7-day-a-week basis. Some home health care programs also offer a multidisciplinary team approach to care, but that may become problematic when third-party payers will not reimburse for some types of services, such as spiritual or emotional care. In those circumstances, the home health care program must either depend upon the expertise of its skilled nurses to assess and respond to general family and environmental concerns, or leave additional needs to other community agencies. In short, much home health care is based on diagnostic categories and funding that relate to a desire to control costs, not necessarily to patient or family needs. Of course, these are broad generalizations.

In 2000, there were approximately 8,400 home health care programs in the United States serving approximately 1.4 million patients (U.S. Census Bureau, 2004). Approximately 45 percent of these programs were owned by their proprietors, about 42 percent were voluntary nonprofit agencies, and about 13 percent were under government or other ownership. Medicare benefits for home health services in 2003 totaled approximately $5.5 billion (U.S. Census Bureau, 2005).

In recent years, a variety of economic, organizational, and other factors have impacted home health care programs in our society. Although many new home health care programs have been started, some have gone out of business. Others have added a hospice component to their services or may have incorporated some aspects of the hospice philosophy of care in their work. In some settings, a hospice patient who shows improvement may be discharged to a home health care program until his or her condition worsens and he or she is readmitted to hospice care.

End-of-Life Care: Hospice Programs

Hospice programs are the newest addition to the health care system in our society, one that Jo Ryan experienced near the end of her life. As Jo's situation indicates, hospice programs have already become a major way of caring for those who are coping with dying. In our society, hospice programs now provide an essential service in a cost-effective manner for many individuals. They do this by operating out of a distinctive philosophy of care (as already noted) and by delivering most of the care they offer in the homes of those they serve. For this reason, the term *hospice* may be more appropriately used as an adjective to describe a type of care rather than as a noun to identify a place. To appreciate this distinction, we must see how hospice programs developed.

In addition to drawing on age-old human traditions of caring for the dying, hospice programs trace their roots back to medieval institutions that offered rest and support for weary travelers (Stoddard, 1992). In their modern sense, hospice programs offer care for those who are in the final stages of the journey of life. Services are designed primarily to provide care for those who are dying or who have no reasonable hope of benefit from cure-oriented intervention, along with their family members.

One can trace modern hospice care to institutions run by religious orders of nuns in Ireland and England. However, the great impetus came from Dame Cicely Saunders, who founded St. Christopher's Hospice in southeast London in 1967 (DuBoulay, 1984). Originally a nurse, Dame Cicely retrained as a social worker after injuring her back, and then as a physician to pursue her goal of developing and offering better care to the incurably ill and dying. She worked out her views at St. Joseph's Hospice in the East End of London during the 1950s and did research there on medications for the management of chronic pain in those who are dying. Later, she went outside the National Health Service (NHS) in England to found St. Christopher's as a privately owned inpatient facility to implement her theories of clinical practice, research, and education in care of the dying.

At first, it was thought that innovations of this sort could only be undertaken in independent, purpose-built, inpatient facilities. However, in England this original hospice model was later followed by inpatient facilities built with private money and then turned over to the NHS for operation, and eventually by inpatient units within some NHS hospitals (Ford, 1979; Wilkes et al., 1980). England has also seen the development of hospice home care teams designed to support the work of general practitioners and district nurses (Davies, 1999), as well as hospital support teams that advise on the care of the dying in acute care hospitals (Dunlop & Hockley, 1998) and programs of hospice day care (Wilkes et al., 1978). This development is both similar to and different from the growth of hospice care in North America and elsewhere around the world (Clark, 2007; Clark et al., 2005).

Canadian efforts in this field began in the mid-1970s with the development of what were called "palliative care services" at the Royal Victoria Hospital in Montreal and St. Boniface General Hospital in Winnipeg. (The name for these services was apparently chosen at least in part because the word *hospice* in French refers to a home for the destitute; subsequently, the Canadians have most often chosen to speak of "hospice palliative care.") Typically, these services included an inpatient unit based in a large acute care teaching hospital, a consultation service, a home care service, and a bereavement follow-up program (e.g., Ajemian & Mount, 1980). Currently, a broad variety of nearly 500 different programs and services offer hospice palliative care across Canada. There also are several provincial associations in the country and the national Canadian Hospice Palliative Care Association (www.chpca.net).

In the United States, hospice care began in September 1974 with a community-based home care program in New Haven, Connecticut (Foster, Wald, & Wald, 1978; Friedrich, 1999; Lack & Buckingham, 1978). Since that time, hospice care has spread across the country (Connor, 2007). In 2006, the National Hospice and Palliative Care Organization (NHPCO, 2007a) estimated there were more than 4,500 operational hospice programs in all 50 states, the District of Columbia, Puerto Rico, and Guam. (For additional information about hospice services, or to find out how to contact a local hospice program, call the Hospice Helpline at 800-658-8898, or contact the National Hospice and Palliative Care Organization, 1700 Diagonal Road, Suite 625, Alexandria, VA 22314; 703-837-1500; fax 703-837-1233; www.nhpco.org. Another referral source is www.hospicedirectory.org.)

Hospice programs in the United States in 2006 represented a wide variety of organizational models (NHPCO, 2007a). Most were independent freestanding agencies; others were hospital based, divisions of home health agencies, or based in long-term care facilities and other institutions. Approximately 49 percent of hospice programs in the United States were nonprofit in character, 46 percent were for-profit, and 5 percent were government organizations. An estimated 19.6 percent of American hospice programs have their own inpatient facility.

In 1982, funding for hospice care was approved as a Medicare benefit (Miller & Mike, 1995). This benefit emphasized home care for elders who qualified for Medicare. Admission criteria typically required a diagnosis of terminal illness, with a prognosis of fewer than six months to live, and the presence of a primary caregiver in the home (although this last requirement no longer applies in most hospice programs). Reimbursement rates are organized in four basic categories: a regular, daily, home care rate (of $130.79 per day as of October 1, 2006); a general inpatient rate (roughly $581.82 per day); $135.30 for short-term respite care; and $763.36 for continuous in-home care (providing for the presence of a trained hospice staff member in specified blocks of time). Each of these rates usually increases over time and is adjusted to take into account different costs in different geographical areas.

Two things are notable about the Medicare hospice benefit, which pays for 83.7 percent of hospice services (other hospice funding sources include managed care or private health insurance, Medicaid, and charitable donations). First, as a federal funding program it emphasizes home care and shifts reimbursement from a retrospective, fee-for-service basis to a prospective, flat-rate basis. Thus, the hospice program receives the amount specified in the regular home care rate for each day in which a dying person is enrolled in its care, regardless of the services it actually provides to that person on any given day.

Second, all monies provided under the Medicare hospice benefit (except for those paid to an attending primary physician) go directly to the hospice program. Thus the program is responsible for designing and implementing each individual plan of care. No service is reimbursed unless it is included in that plan of care and approved by the hospice team, which gives the hospice program an incentive to hold down costs and only to provide care that is relevant to the needs of an individual patient and family unit.

The Medicare hospice benefit, which has essentially become a model for other forms of reimbursement for hospice services in the United States, is a desirable option for the individuals who qualify (for additional information about this benefit consult the Medicare Learning Network at www.cms.hhs .gov/MLNProducts/downloads/hospice_pay_sys_fs.pdf). This benefit is available in all U.S. hospice programs (nearly 93 percent) that have qualified for Medicare certification. This benefit is subject to change by federal legislation, but it is presently broader than other Medicare benefits and is intended to cover all of the costs of the care provided. Although it does incorporate upper limits on reimbursement to a hospice program, these are expressed in terms of program averages and total benefit days for which the program will be reimbursed, not in figures that apply to any particular individual. In fact, as long as a person has been accepted into a Medicare-certified hospice program and continues to qualify for its services, the law prohibits involuntary discharge—whether or not funds are still flowing for reimbursement. Medicare benefits for hospice services in 2003 totaled approximately $7.2 billion (U.S. Census Bureau, 2005). Hospice care is also covered by Medicaid in 43 states and the District of Columbia, as well as by 82 percent of managed care plans and most private insurance plans.

Some have thought that hospice care in the United States has been too closely identified with death. For example, under the Medicare guidelines a patient who enters hospice care must accept the fact that he or she is dying and must agree to forego cure-oriented interventions (although that individual retains the right to withdraw from hospice care at any point). This may be one reason why some minority groups in the United States with strong sanctity-of-life values, such as African Americans, appear to underutilize opportunities for hospice care.

A child's expression of gratitude to a hospice program after her mother's death.

NHPCO (2007a) estimates that in 2006, hospice programs served over 1,300,000 patients, an increase of 100,000 over 2005. In 2006, approximately 870,000 Americans died while receiving hospice care—approximately 36 percent of all Americans who died that year—220,000 were discharged alive, and 210,000 individuals admitted in 2006 carried over into 2007. In 2006, 74.1 percent of hospice patients were able to die in a place that they called home—a private residence, a nursing home, or other residential facility—by contrast with the general population for whom nearly half die in an acute care medical facility (see Table 2.5 in Chapter 2). Average length of enrollment in hospice care in 2006 was 59 days; median length of service was 20.9 days.

Hospice patients in 2006 were described by NHPCO (2007a) as follows:

◆ About 55.6 percent were female and 44.4 percent male.

◆ Over 64 percent of patients were 75 years of age or older.

◆ Nearly 81 percent were Caucasian Americans; 19.1 percent were members of minority communities, including African Americans (8.2 percent), Asian or

Pacific Island Americans (1.8 percent), American Indians or Alaskan Natives (0.3 percent), and individuals who identified themselves multiracial or were otherwise classified (8.8 percent).

◆ Leading diagnoses on admission were advanced cancer (44.1 percent); end-stage heart disease (12.2 percent); debility unspecified (11.8 percent); dementia including Alzheimer's disease (10.0 percent); lung disease (7.7 percent); other significant diagnoses on hospice admission included stroke or coma, end-stage kidney disease, motor neuron diseases, end-stage liver disease, and HIV/AIDS.

Nearly 96 percent of all hospice care hours were provided in patients' homes, and volunteers contributed an estimated 400,000 hours to hospice programs in 2006. In light of the fact that 28 percent of all Medicare costs go toward care of people in their last year of life and almost 50 percent of those costs are expended in the last 2 months of life, hospice care at home often substitutes for more expensive hospitalizations.

Approximately 18 percent of American hospice programs are already providing care for infants, children, and their families, with another 2 percent planning to do so. For example, NHPCO's ChiPPS program (Children's Project on Palliative/Hospice Services) and other parallel initiatives have greatly improved attention paid to pediat-

Hospice care recognizes that all types of volunteers can play a part in good care— even animals!

The Hospice of the Florida Suncoast

ric palliative care in recent years. ChiPPS itself has developed a free electronic newsletter for professionals (available at www.nhpco .org/pediatrics), a *Compendium of Pediatric Palliative Care* (NHPCO, 2000), and an *Education and Training Curriculum for Pediatric Palliative Care* (NHPCO, 2003). Similar education curricula have been published by The Initiative for Pediatric Palliative Care (2003) and the End-of-Life Nursing Education Consortium (ELNEC, 2003). The Children's Hospice and Palliative Care Coalition has established online support sites in both English and Spanish (www.PartnershipforParents.org; www.PadresCompadres.org) for parents who are coping with challengesassociated with a life-threatening illness in a child through diagnosis, treatment, death, and bereavement. There is also a substantial body of literature in the field of pediatric palliative care for a wide variety of readers (e.g., Armstrong-Dailey & Zarbock, in press; Carter & Levetown, 2004; Corr & Corr, 1985a; Duncan et al., 2007; Field & Berhman, 2003; Goldman et al., 2005; Hilden & Tobin, 2003; Himelstein et al., 2004; Huff & Orloff, 2004; Orloff & Huff, 2003).

It should also be noted that hospice programs provide bereavement care to an average of two family members per hospice patient. In addition, the vast majority (93.9 percent according to NHPCO statistics) of hospice programs provide bereavement services to their communities with community members receiving approximately 16.5 percent of all hospice bereavement services.

Hospice principles have been implemented in different ways in different situations (Saunders & Kastenbaum, 1997). These differences have to do with the needs of particular societies, and especially the structure of their health care and social services systems. In the United States, the hospice emphasis on home care fits with efforts to minimize inpatient care and to encourage home care as more appropriate and more economical. The hospice movement has also made efforts to reach out to underserved groups and to expand access to hospice services (Jennings et al., 2003), to emphasize the importance of cultural diversity (Infeld et al., 1995; NHPCO, 2007b), to build alliances with academic institutions and other community organizations (e.g., Roscoe et al., 2004), and to reflect on the heritage and future of the hospice movement (Corless & Foster, 1999; Parkes, 2007b).

Four recent studies have reported important results about hospice care in the United States.

- The first study (Connor et al., 2007) employed a retrospective statistical analysis of 4,493 patients with five types of cancer and congestive heart failure, a sample of 5 percent of the entire Medicare beneficiary population for 1998–2002. The study concluded that "the mean survival was 29 days longer for hospice patients than for nonhospice patients" (p. 238). In this cohort, medications and other aspects of hospice care intended to manage distressing symptoms and improve quality of life not only did not hasten death, they actually extended length of life in ways that might be especially important to patients and their family members.

- The second study (Taylor et al., 2007) demonstrated that hospice care reduced Medicare costs by an average of $2309 per hospice patient and showed that there would be further cost savings for seven out of ten patients if they had longer enrollments in hospice care. This study concluded that "more effort should be put into increasing short stays as opposed to focusing on shortening long ones" (p. 1476).

- The third study (Teno et al., 2004) reported on evaluations by family members of care received by their loved ones. This study concluded: "Family members of patients receiving hospice services were more satisfied with overall quality of care: 70.7% rated care as 'excellent' compared with less than 50% of those dying in an institutional setting [that is, in a hospital or nursing home] or with home health services" (p. 88).

- The fourth study (Rhodes et al., 2007) examined bereaved African-American family members who reported that what they perceived as disparities in care provided for their loved ones by contrast with care provided to other patient populations decreased when they enrolled in hospice programs.

❦ Hospice Care and Palliative Care

Just as the word *hospice* (in its various forms) has its own history and meaning, so too do the words *palliative* and *palliation* (and related terms). Originally, "to palliate" meant "to cover with . . . a cloak" (*Oxford English Dictionary*, 1989, vol. 11, p. 101). This meaning can be seen in the practice of covering the casket at a funeral with a cloth called a "pall." In health care, "to palliate" means "to alleviate the symptoms of a disease without curing it." Thus, treatment of the common cold is a kind of palliation or palliative care. Although there is no cure for the common cold (or for many other everyday maladies), when individuals have a cough and cold, aspirin, decongestants, antihistamines, antiexpectorants, medications to dry up unwanted secretions, and other interventions (including rest and nutritious food) are often employed to improve quality. In short, symptoms are palliated until the virus that causes the cold works through its own biological trajectory and reaches its natural limits, while the body's own resources rally to repel the invader and restore the person to a healthier condition. Meanwhile, even though cure is not offered, most people are grateful that their distress is at least partially relieved. In all its forms, palliative care means addressing symptoms rather than underlying causes (Twycross, 2003).

As we have already seen, hospice care is a form of palliative care—one that is addressed primarily to distressing symptoms in dying persons or those with a life-threatening condition who are nearing the end of their lives. In terms of linguistic usage, it might have been more accurate to keep the phrases *palliative care* and *hospice care* separate and to treat the latter as a type or subspecies of the former. In fact, at one point in the history of the hospice movement (and perhaps in some contexts today), they were regarded as if they meant essentially the same thing. Thus the World Health Organization (1990, p. 11) regards palliative care as:

> The active total care of patients whose disease is not responsive to curative treatment. Control of pain, of other symptoms, and of psychological, social and spiritual problems, is paramount. The goal of palliative care is achievement of the best quality of life for patients and their families.

Recently, many in the medical community have adopted the phrase *palliative care* and used it in ways that are both broader and narrower than the phrase *hospice care*. *Palliative care* or *palliative medicine* is now used mainly to designate a type of medical care that addresses the relief of distressing symptoms (Doyle et al., 2003; Morrison & Meier, 2004). However, that need not necessarily imply the full scope and interdisciplinary team approach that typify hospice care (O'Connor, 1999). For example, in this sense of palliative care, there may be no spiritual care, home care visits, bereavement services, or volunteers. In this narrowed meaning of the adjective *palliative*, primary emphasis is on the role of the physician, pain and symptom management, and, most often, on hospital-based care (Morrison et al., 2005). Nevertheless, as Quill (2007, p. 1912) has noted: "The palliative care movement continues to grow dramatically in the United States. Most academic medical centers now have palliative care consultation services, and other hospitals are launching such programs at an increasing rate."

How this develops will depend on physician education, institutional structures, and reimbursement policies through managed care programs (NHPCO & the Center to Advance Palliative Care in Hospitals and Health Systems, 2001).

At the same time, this meaning of the phrase *palliative care* may be broader than that of *hospice care* because the former phrase is not necessarily limited to end-of-life care. In this sense, palliative care may apply to many physician-centered efforts to manage pain and other distressing symptoms with or without reference to their origin or their relationship to dying and death. In its richest sense, this meaning of palliative care can bring important resources of pain and symptom management (some of which originated in and have been adapted from the work of the hospice movement) to a broad range of patients; in its most superficial sense, this usage of palliative care may mean little more than traditional forms of physical and psychosocial care.

These are not merely arbitrary shifts in linguistic usage. There are many competing forces behind them. On the one hand, for example, some have chafed at the limits imposed by regulations governing hospice care and by what they perceive to be a "death sentence" that some associate with the word *hospice*. On the other hand, there has been a desire to introduce care of distressing symptoms early in the disease process ("to move hospice care upstream," as the saying goes), to fill empty beds in acute care hospitals, and to have an option available for patients and families who want to stop aggressive cure-oriented interventions.

🍂 An Institutional Recapitulation

Within the American death system, as we have seen in this chapter, four institutions currently care for most persons who are coping with dying.

1. *Hospitals* of all sorts (general hospitals, specialized medical or psychiatric institutions, and tertiary-care trauma centers or teaching hospitals) provide *acute care,* emphasizing assessment and diagnosis of illness and disease together with cure-oriented interventions for reversible or correctable conditions. Most hospitals offer a wide variety of medical services through their own internal facilities, such as emergency departments, medical or surgical wards, and intensive care units, or through outpatient departments and clinics. Physicians also offer some types of care in their offices, in community clinics, and in various specialized centers. Most of these services are not primarily designed for dying persons. Still, a significant portion of hospital-based care is directed toward the last six months of life (Jacobs et al., 2002). Also, just over 46 percent of all deaths in our society in 2004 occurred in hospitals or were brought to these institutions for confirmation and certification of death (see Table 2.5 in Chapter 2). In 1998, 2.6 of every 100 discharges from acute care hospitals resulted from death, which mostly took place in emergency departments and acute care units (Popovic & Kozak, 2000).

2. *Long-term care facilities or nursing homes* offer *long-term care*—that is, custodial, nursing, and rehabilitative care for individuals with chronic illnesses

and other disabling conditions. Such institutions do not merely serve the elderly, nor are more than a very small percentage of the elderly in our society residents of such institutions at any one time. Approximately 22 percent of all deaths in our society in 2004 occurred in long-term care facilities (see Table 2.5 in Chapter 2).

3. *Home health care programs* of many types (services of county and municipal health departments, the Visiting Nurse Association, private home health care agencies, and home care departments of hospitals) deliver *home care* chiefly in the form of skilled nursing and ancillary care. This care is provided to many different kinds of clients, some of whom may be dying.

4. *Hospice programs* offer *end-of-life care* for dying persons and their families. In our society, that care is most likely to take place in the home, but it may also be delivered in a hospital, a long-term care facility, or a hospice inpatient unit under the supervision of a hospice team, or via a hospice day care program (Corr & Corr, 1992a). Hospice programs in the United States originally offered care primarily to elderly cancer patients, but that is no longer the case. Currently, cancer diagnoses apply to less than half of U.S. hospice admissions. In fact, hospice principles are now being applied to care of persons with AIDS (O'Neill et al., 2003), individuals with motor neuron diseases like amyotrophic lateral sclerosis (ALS or Lou Gehrig's disease), persons with Alzheimer's disease and other forms of dementia (Corr et al., 2004), and other adults who are coping with various life-threatening conditions such as end-stage heart, lung, or kidney disease. In recent years, hospice programs and other agencies have also been leaders in sponsoring and developing programs of pediatric palliative care for children, adolescents, and their family members. As a result of these many developments, hospice programs currently care for approximately one-third of all people who die in our society.

❦ Summary

In this chapter, we examined ways in which our society provides care for individuals who are coping with dying through formal programs and institutions. We did this by identifying ten principles in the hospice philosophy to serve as a model for such care. Also, we described the historical development of care and its current practice in hospitals, long-term care facilities, home care programs, and hospice programs. We also added some comments on the relationship between hospice care and palliative care.

Glossary

Acute care: services that diagnose and treat specific diseases, thus halting or slowing their progression; ideally, acute care seeks to return an individual to full health, that is, to approximately the same functional capacity possessed when the person became ill

Chronic care: services for individuals who need rehabilitation or who cannot perform activities of daily living

End-of-life care: services for persons who are within weeks or months of death, together with their family members

Home care: nursing and other ancillary services delivered to individuals in their places of residence; not distinguished by any specific kind of illness

Home health programs: organizations that deliver home care services

Hospice care: services designed to implement the hospice philosophy; a form of palliative care offered near the end of life

Hospice philosophy: an outlook, attitude, or approach to care that affirms life and attempts to maximize present quality in living for patient and family units who are coping with dying

Hospice programs: organizations that deliver hospice services by offering holistic care to dying persons and their family members using an interdisciplinary team across multiple settings and made available on a 24/7 basis

Hospitals: organizations that deliver acute care services; often called "medical centers" or "health centers"

Interdisciplinary teamwork: services offered by an organized group of professional caregivers and volunteers working together to plan and implement care; typically involves a certain amount of "role blurring" by contrast with multidisciplinary teamwork in which members of specialized health care professions work largely independently with loose coordination

Long-term care facilities: institutions that deliver chronic care services; may be residential care, intermediate care, or skilled nursing care facilities

Nursing homes: (see long-term care facilities)

Palliative care: services designed to relieve distressing symptoms of a disease without curing their underlying causes

Questions for Review and Discussion

1. Think about the situation of Jo Ryan as described in the vignette near the beginning of this chapter. Try to focus in particular on her experiences at different points in time: when she first discovered the small lump in her right breast, when she was told that she needed a mastectomy, when she developed cancer again some time later, when she received services from a community home health care program, when she was admitted to a nursing home, when she was transferred to a local hospice inpatient unit, when she went home to be with her family, and when she neared the end of her life. What types of care did Jo need at any or all of these different points in her life? What programs of care were best suited to her needs at these different points?

2. This chapter discussed several different types of care, including that provided by hospitals, long-term care facilities, home health care programs, and hospice programs. Think about being a person with a life-threatening illness (perhaps you can think about someone you know, such as a relative or a friend). What might be the advantages and limitations of being cared for by each of these programs?

3. How would you describe the essential elements in the hospice philosophy of care? Why do you think those elements were implemented (at least at first) in

different ways in England, Canada, and the United States? Could hospice-type principles be implemented in other institutions (for example, hospitals, long-term care facilities, or home health care programs) in the United States?

4. What sorts of experiences (if any) have you had with hospice programs or with other forms of palliative care?

Suggested Readings

Hospice and palliative care principles are set forth in many books, such as:

Beresford, L. (1993). *The Hospice Handbook: A Complete Guide.*

Connor, S. R. (1998). *Hospice: Practice, Pitfalls, and Promise.*

Doyle, D., Hanks, G. W. C., Cherny, N. I., & Calman, K. (Eds.). (2003). *Oxford Textbook of Palliative Medicine* (3rd ed.).

Ellershaw, J., & Wilkinson, S. (2003). *Care of the Dying: A Pathway to Excellence.*

Ferrell, B. R., & Coyle, N. (Eds.). (2005). *Textbook of Palliative Nursing* (2nd ed.).

Field, M. J., & Cassel, C. K. (Eds.). (1997). *Approaching Death: Improving Care at the End of Life.*

Jaffe, C., & Ehrlich, C. H. (1997). *All Kinds of Love: Experiencing Hospice.*

Jesse, G., Taylor, M., & Kurent, J. E. (2002). *A Clinician's Guide to Palliative Care.*

Lattanzi-Licht, M., Mahoney, J. J., & Miller, G.W. (1998). *The Hospice Choice: In Pursuit of a Peaceful Death.*

Lipman, A. G., Kenneth, C., Jackson, I., & Tyler, L. S. (Eds.). (2000). *Evidence-based Symptom Control in Palliative Care: Systemic Review and Validated Clinical Practice Guidelines for 15 Common Problems in Patients with Life-limiting Disease.*

Lynn, J., Schuster, J. L., & Kabcenell, A. (2000). *Improving Care for the End of Life: A Sourcebook for Health Care Managers and Clinicians.*

Randall, F., & Downie, R. S. (1999). *Palliative Care Ethics: A Companion for All Specialties* (2nd ed.).

Randall, F., & Downie, R. (2006). *The Philosophy of Palliative Care: Critique and Reconstruction.*

Saunders, C. M., Baines, M., & Dunlop, R. (1995). *Living with Dying: A Guide to Palliative Care* (3rd ed.).

Smith, S. A. (2000). *Hospice Concepts: A Guide to Palliative Care in Terminal Illness.*

Stoddard, S. (1992). *The Hospice Movement: A Better Way of Caring for the Dying* (rev. ed.).

Twycross, R. G. (2003). *Introducing Palliative Care* (3rd ed.).

Victoria Hospice Society, Cairns, M., Thompson, M., & Wainwright, W. (2003). *Transitions in Dying and Bereavement: A Psychosocial Guide for Hospice and Palliative Care.*

Watson, M., Lucas, C., Hoy, A., & Back, I. (Eds.). (2005). *The Oxford Handbook of Palliative Care.*

Webb, M. (1997). *The Good Death: The New American Search to Reshape the End of Life.*

Hospice and palliative care principles are applied to situations involving children in:

Armstrong-Dailey, A., & Zarbock, S. (Eds.). (In press). *Hospice Care for Children* (3rd ed.).

Bearison, D. J. (2006). *When Treatment Fails: How Medicine Cares for Dying Children.*

Brown, E. (with Warr, B.). (2007). *Supporting the Child and the Family in Paediatric Palliative Care.*

Carter, B. S., & Levetown, M. (Eds.). (2004). *Palliative Care for Infants, Children, and Adolescents: A Practical Handbook.*

Corr, C. A., & Corr, D. M. (Eds.). (1985a). *Hospice Approaches to Pediatric Care.*

Field, M. J., & Berhman, R. E. (Eds.). (2003). *When Children Die: Improving Palliative and End-of-Life Care for Children and Their Families.*

Hilden, J. M., & Tobin, D. R. (with Lindsey, K.). (2003). *Shelter from the Storm: Caring for a Child with a Life Threatening Condition.*

Huff, S. M., & Orloff, S. (Eds.). (2004). *Interdisciplinary Clinical Manual for Pediatric Hospice and Palliative Care.*

Orloff, S., & Huff, S. (Eds.). (2003). *Home Care for Seriously Ill Children: A Manual for Parents.*

For developments in medicine, hospitals, and long-term care facilities, consult:

Bennett, C. (1980). *Nursing Home Life: What It Is and What It Could Be.*

Gubrium, J. F. (1975). *Living and Dying at Murray Manor.*

Kaufman, S. R. (2006). *And a Time to Die: How American Hospitals Shape the End of Life.*

Moss, F., & Halamanderis, V. (1977). *Too Old, Too Sick, Too Bad: Nursing Homes in America.*

Rosenberg, C. E. (1987). *The Care of Strangers: The Rise of America's Hospital System.*

Shield, R. R. (1988). *Uneasy Endings: Daily Life in an American Nursing Home.*

Starr, P. (1982). *The Social Transformation of American Medicine.*

Stevens, R. (1989). *In Sickness and in Wealth: American Hospitals in the Twentieth Century.*

Selected Web Resources

Some useful search terms include: ACUTE CARE; CHRONIC CARE; END-OF-LIFE CARE; HOME HEALTH CARE; HOME HEALTH PROGRAMS; HOSPICE CARE; HOSPICE PHILOSOPHY; HOSPICE PROGRAMS; HOSPITALS; INTERDISCIPLINARY TEAMWORK; LONG-TERM CARE FACILITIES; NURSING HOMES; PALLIATIVE CARE

Visit the book companion website for *Death & Dying, Life & Living, Sixth Edition,* at academic.cengage.com/psychology/corr for all URLs and live links to the following *organizational and other Internet sites:*

American Academy of Hospice and Palliative Medicine

American Association of Homes and Services for the Aging

American Health Care Association

American Hospice Foundation

American Hospital Association

Canadian Hospice Palliative Care Association

The Catholic Health Association of the United States

The Center to Advance Palliative Care

Children's Hospice and Palliative Care Coalition

Children's Project on Palliative/Hospice Services (ChiPPS)

End-of-Life Nursing Education Consortium

Hospice and Palliative Nurses Association

Hospice Association of America

HospiceDirectory.org

Hospice Foundation of America

The Initiative for Pediatric Palliative Care

National Association for Home Care

National Hospice and Palliative Care Organization

Partnership for Parents/Padres Compadres

Promoting Excellence in End-of-Life Care, The Practical Ethics Center at the University of Montana

VA Hospice and Palliative Care (VAHPC) Initiative, U.S. Department of Veterans Affairs

PART FOUR

Bereavement

"Two-sidedness is a fundamental feature of death. . . . There are always two parties to a death; the person who dies and the survivors who are bereaved" (Toynbee, 1968a, p. 267). In fact, as we saw in Part Three, the situation is even more complicated than this would suggest. Prior to death, issues in coping with dying concern not only the person who is dying but also his or her family members, friends, and care providers (whether professionals or volunteers). All of these individuals, except the person who dies, are survivors-to-be. For each of these individuals, "a person's death is not only an ending; it is also a beginning" (Shneidman, 1973a, p. 33).

In Part Four we examine the experiences of these bereaved persons. Nearly everyone has encountered some sort of loss in his or her own life, so we all know something about experiences of loss. In that sense, loss is one of the really fundamental experiences in human life. But there are many kinds of loss. Our special concern in Chapters 9 through 11 is with death-related losses and their consequences. In Chapter 9, we explain key elements and variables in the *experiences of persons who are coping with loss and grief*. In Chapter 10, we offer practical advice for *individuals who are trying to help bereaved persons*. And in Chapter 11, we turn to *ways in which communities within our society have organized themselves to help the bereaved*.

CHAPTER 9

Coping with Loss and Grief

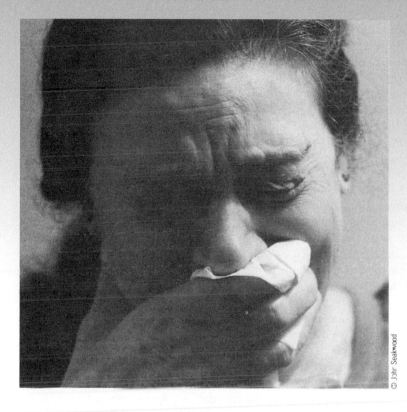

© John Seakwood

Objectives of This Chapter

◆ To clarify the nature of death-related experiences of loss and grief, the language and concepts employed to understand them, and efforts involved in coping with them

◆ To define the key concepts of *loss* and *bereavement*

◆ To explain *grief* itself and *five critical variables* that influence an individual's grief

◆ To define the term *mourning* as it is used in this book

◆ To examine interpretations of normal or uncomplicated *mourning*, such as:

1. Those involving *phases or tasks*
2. Those involving *processes: the dual process model, meaning reconstruction, and continuing bonds*

◆ To contrast depictions of mourning as involving fixed end points with accounts of opportunities for growth and transformation

◆ To describe grief and mourning in relationship to the following variables: *gender, families, anticipated losses, traumatic losses,* and *complicated grief reactions*

🌰 One Woman Experiencing Her Losses

Stella Bridgman was in her early 40s when her 18-year-old son took his own life. His death was the tragic and unfortunate ending to a troubled history involving chemical dependency (starting with marijuana and beer, but escalating to hard liquor, cocaine, and crack) and difficulties at home, in school, and with his part-time job.

Even though her son had a history of erratic and self-destructive behavior, it was a tremendous shock to Stella when she found his body. Her pain was sharp-edged and very powerful. "It was like being punched in the stomach," she said later. Stella experienced a great sense of sadness in losing someone who had been a central part of her life for so many years and whose own life had sprung from her very body. She was also very hurt that her son could reject her (as she viewed it) in this brutal way and spurn the very life that she had given him.

At the same time, Stella was furious at her son for doing this to her and to his 15-year-old sister. She also experienced guilt as she asked herself over and over again whether there was anything in addition to what she had already been doing that she might have done to prevent his death.

The death of her son was not the first loss that Stella had experienced. Her father had died in a distant war when she was a little child; she had not really known him. Her mother, a heavy smoker, had developed lung cancer at a relatively early age and died after a difficult illness a little more than 10 years ago. That was the first death that seemed to have real significance in her life.

The death of her husband in a fiery automobile accident 5 years later was another harsh experience that left Stella with two young children, a small sum of money from insurance and savings, and no job. She had never anticipated that possibility. All the widows she had known were elderly women. Stella turned to her church, became very protective of her children, and rejoined the workforce.

Eventually, Stella did marry again, to a widower whom she met at a church social activity, but her son disliked his new stepfather and the three siblings who came with him into the new "blended" family.

Each of the major deaths in her life had a different impact on Stella. When her mother died, Stella felt as if she was experiencing the death of her past. She found it hard to go forward without the support of the parent who had always been with her. When her first husband died, Stella felt as if it was the death of her present life, a way of living with which she had become comfortable both before and after her mother's death. But the suicide of her son was like the death of her hopes for the future. Could she cope with this new blow on top of all the others? And could she pull all of her energies together one more time and once again find the strength to live on for herself and for her daughter?

Stella asked over and over: "What did I do?" "Why did this happen?" and "How can I go on?"

🌰 Loss and Bereavement

To love is to give "hostages to fortune" (Bacon, 1625/1962, p. 22). Everyone who experiences love or who forms an attachment to another runs the risk of losing the loved person or object and suffering the consequences of loss. If so, then "to grieve is to pay ransom to love" (Shneidman, 1983, p. 29).

Of course, it is in loving that a person shares with others and enriches his or her life. Attachments are those very special, enduring relationships through which individuals satisfy fundamental needs (Bowlby, 1969–1980; Parkes et al., 1993). Stella Bridgman loved the father she had never known, her mother, her two husbands, her own children, and her second husband's children. Not to love in these ways would be to cut oneself off from the rewards of human attachment—to restrict and impoverish one's life. In other words, the only alternative to experiencing the pain of loss would be to have nothing in our lives that is worth losing. Or as Brantner (in Worden, 1982, p. xi) said so aptly: "Only people who avoid love can avoid grief. The point is to learn from it and remain vulnerable to love." To learn about grief and mourning, we begin with some thoughts about loss and bereavement.

Loss

There are *many types of losses* that occur throughout human lives (Hooyman & Kramer, 2006; Viorst, 1986). For example, I may break up with someone I love, be fired or laid off from my job, have to leave my home and relocate, misplace a prized possession, fail in some competition, have a body part amputated, or experience the death of someone close to me. What these and other significant losses all have in common is that the individual who loses something is separated from and deprived of the lost person, object, status, or relationship. This is the *primary loss*—the termination of the attachment or relationship; *secondary losses* are those that follow from a primary loss.

Children, too, can face different levels and types of challenges and losses.

The Hospice of the Florida Suncoast

Death-related losses inevitably involve endings, separations, and other losses, as is evident in the example of Stella Bridgman. What any death will mean to those who live on depends on the losses it involves for those individuals and the ways in which they interpret those losses. For example, death may mean the end of the time I share with my spouse or partner, a separation from one of my parents, or the loss of my child. Death may even involve a relief from a painful attachment or from the suffering of a dying person (Elison, 2007; Elison & McGonigle, 2003). However I interpret a death-related loss, it is likely to involve at least some challenges and pain for me because that loss will impact and alter my life in important ways. Even if I am able to view death in the framework of a possible afterlife and eventual reunion with the loved one, or as a transition of the person who died into a realm of ancestors who continue to interact with us, I will still be a person who has been left behind and I am now no longer able to enjoy the direct, physical presence of the person who died. Moreover, losses through death may sometimes be complicated—for example, when dying is long and difficult, or when death is sudden, unexpected, or traumatic.

Losses that are not related to death can also be complicated in their own ways (Harvey, 1998). Such losses may be as hurtful as those arising from death, or perhaps even more hurtful in some cases. For example, about half of all marriages in the United States now end in divorce. When that happens, there is often one spouse who wishes to terminate the relationship, another who does not wish to do so or who is less determined on that outcome, and perhaps a third person (such as a child) who is involved in what is happening and directly affected by its implications but not immediately able to influence what is taking place. Each of these individuals will experience different types of losses in the divorce. As in death, there is always loss in divorce, but there may also be elements of deliberate choice, guilt, and blame that are not always associated with a death. Divorce may also be complicated by theoretical (if not practical) opportunities for reconciliation and the inevitable implications of subsequent life decisions by all who are involved in the aftermath of the event. Note that we mention divorce here as only one example of the many types of loss humans may experience that do not involve death itself and yet are quite powerful.

Often, as we reflect on our lives, we can identify individuals or objects whose loss would mean a great deal to us. However, sometimes the meaning and value of the lost person or object is only fully appreciated after the loss has taken place. In any event, to understand the implications of any experience of loss, we must look back to the *underlying relationships and attachments* on which it is founded.

Bereavement

The term *bereavement* refers to the state of being bereaved or deprived of something. In other words, bereavement identifies the objective situation of individuals who have experienced a loss of some person or thing that they valued (Corless, 2001). Three elements are essential in all bereavement: (1) a relationship or attachment with some person or thing that is valued; (2) the loss—ending, termination, separation—of that relationship; and (3) an individual who is deprived of the valued person or thing by the loss.

Both the noun *bereavement* and the adjective *bereaved* derive from a verb, *reave,* which means "to despoil, rob, or forcibly deprive" (*Oxford English Dictionary,* 1989, vol. 13, p. 295). Thus, a bereaved person is one who has been deprived, robbed, plundered, or stripped of someone or something that he or she valued. In principle, the losses experienced by bereaved people could be of many kinds; in fact, this language is most often used to refer to the situation of those who have experienced a loss through death. In other words, our language tends to assume that bereavement is about death and that death always entails a more or less brutal loss of someone or something that is important to the bereaved person.

Grief

We address here three questions about grief: (1) What is grief?; (2) How does grief relate to disease, depression, and guilt?; and (3) Is grief typically a normal and healthy reaction to loss?

What Is Grief?

Grief is the term that indicates one's reactions to loss. When one suffers a significant loss, one experiences grief. The word *grief* signifies one's reactions, both internally and exter-

Loneliness is a frequent companion to loss (an illustration from *Tear Soup*, see Personal Insights 10.2).

Illustration © Taylor Bills. Reprinted with permission of Grief Watch

nally, to the impact of the loss. The term arises from the grave or heavy weight that presses on bereaved persons (*Oxford English Dictionary,* 1989, vol. 6, pp. 834–835). Not to experience grief for a significant loss is an aberration. It would suggest that there was no real attachment prior to the loss, that the relationship was complicated in ways that set it apart from the ordinary, or that one is suppressing or hiding one's reactions to the loss.

The term *grief* is often defined as *the emotional reaction to loss.* One needs to be careful in speaking that way. As Elias (1991, p. 117) noted, "broadly speaking, emotions have three components, a somatic [i.e., bodily or physical], a behavioral and a feeling component." As a result, "the term *emotion,* even in professional discussions, is used with two different meanings. It is used in a wider and in a narrower sense at the same time. In the wider sense the term *emotion* is applied to a reaction pattern which involves the whole organism in its somatic, its feeling and its behavioral aspects. . . . In its narrower sense the term *emotion* refers to the feeling component of the syndrome only" (Elias, 1991, p. 119).

Grief clearly does involve feelings, and it is certainly appropriate to think of the affective or feeling dimensions of grief. Anyone who has personally experienced grief or who has encountered a grieving person will be familiar with the outpouring of feelings that is a prominent element of most grief. However, it is also important to recognize that *one's reactions to loss are not merely a matter of feelings.* Grief is broader, more complex, and more deep-seated than this narrower understanding of emotions and emotional reactions to loss might imply (Doka, 2007b; Rando, 1993).

Grief can be experienced and expressed in numerous ways (Worden, 2002). These include physical, psychological (affective/cognitive), and behavioral dimensions, represented by:

◆ *Physical sensations,* such as hollowness in the stomach, a lump in the throat, tightness in the chest, aching arms, oversensitivity to noise, shortness of breath, lack of energy, muscle weakness, dry mouth, or loss of coordination

◆ *Feelings,* such as sadness, anger, guilt and self-reproach, anxiety, loneliness, fatigue, helplessness, shock, yearning, emancipation, relief, numbness, or a sense of depersonalization

◆ *Thoughts or cognitions,* such as disbelief, confusion, preoccupation, a sense of the presence of the deceased, paranormal ("hallucinatory") experiences, or dreams of the deceased

◆ *Behaviors,* such as sleep or appetite disturbances, absentmindedness, social withdrawal, loss of interest in activities that previously were sources of satisfaction, crying, avoiding reminders of the deceased, searching and calling out, sighing, restless overactivity, or visiting places and cherishing objects that remind one of the deceased

Grief can also have social and spiritual dimensions, such as:

◆ *Social difficulties* in interpersonal relationships or problems in functioning within an organization

◆ *Spiritual searching* for a sense of meaning, hostility toward God or a higher power, turning to one's value framework, or perhaps realizing that it is inadequate to cope with this particular loss

To think of grief solely as a matter of feelings is to risk misunderstanding and missing this full range of reactions to loss (see Personal Insights 9.1).

As we seek to grasp the full meaning of grief, we should also note reports that grief can be associated with increased risk of illness or morbidity in bereaved persons (Glick et al., 1974). Other reports (for example, Martikainen & Valkonen, 1996; Steinbach, 1992) suggest that grief may also be a factor in the death of some bereaved persons.

How Does Grief Relate to Disease, Depression, and Guilt?

We can learn more about grief by comparing and contrasting it with three other phenomena: disease, depression, and guilt.

First, some writers (such as Engel, 1961) have noted that there are many similarities between *grief and disease.* For example, a significant loss may affect a bereaved person's ability to function, at least temporarily. Also, metaphors of healing are commonly employed to describe the processes and time required to overcome this impaired functioning. However, there are important distinctions between grief and disease that need to be kept in mind. Grief is a "dis-ease," a discomforting disturbance

Auden on Grief

Stop all the clocks, cut off the telephone,
Prevent the dog from barking with a juicy bone,
Silence the pianos and with muffled drum
Bring out the coffin, let the mourners come.
Let aeroplanes circle moaning overhead
Scribbling on the sky the message HE IS DEAD,
Put crêpe bows round the white necks of the public doves,
Let the traffic policeman wear black cotton gloves.
He was my North, my South, my East and West,
My working week and my Sunday rest,
My noon, my midnight, my talk, my song;
I thought that love would last for ever: I was wrong.
The stars are not wanted now: put out every one;
Pack up the moon and dismantle the sun;
Pour away the ocean and sweep up the wood;
For nothing now can ever come to any good.

Source: "Stop All The Clocks," copyright 1940 W. H. Auden
and renewed 1968 by W. H. Auden, from *Collected Poems,* by
W. H. Auden. Used by permission of Random House, Inc.

of everyday equilibrium, but it is not a "disease" in the sense of a sickness or morbid (unhealthy) condition of mind or body. In fact, most grief is an appropriate and healthy reaction to loss.

Second, sadness and other common manifestations of grief do resemble some of the symptoms associated with the diagnosis of *clinical depression.* Again, however, grief is a healthy reaction to loss, whereas clinical depression is a mental disorder or disease. Thus, Freud (1959a) long ago recognized the difference between mourning and what he called "melancholia." By mourning, Freud was pointing to the normal processes associated with grief; melancholia is his language for the illness state of depression.

Both grief and clinical depression may involve an experience of being pressed down upon and a withdrawal from the world. However, clinical depression is a complicated or pathological form of grieving characterized by angry impulses toward the ambivalently "loved" person, impulses that are turned inward toward the self (Clayton et al., 1974). Normal grief reactions do not include the loss of self-esteem commonly found in most clinical depression. As Worden (2002, pp. 21–22) observed, "Even though grief and depression share similar objective and subjective features, they do seem to be different conditions. Depression overlaps with bereavement but is not the same. Freud believed that in grief, the world looks poor and empty while in depression, the person feels poor and empty." Other research on grief and depression (e.g., Schneider, 1980; Zisook & DeVaul, 1983, 1984, 1985) confirms that they are, in fact, different types of experiences. Thus, Stella Bridgman was beset by her loss and grief, but she was not clinically depressed.

Third, *guilt* may be part of the total grief reaction, but it is important to disentangle issues of guilt from the larger grief experience and address them separately. *Grief* is the broad term for reactions to loss; *guilt* refers to thoughts and feelings that assign blame (often self-blame), fault, or culpability for the loss. Guilt experienced by bereaved persons may be realistic or unrealistic. Suggestions of guilt may arise from one's role (e.g., that of parent and protector) or from something that one believes he or she should or could have done or not done. For example, even though Stella Bridgman knew that her son had brought on himself many of his own difficulties and finally his death, she agonized over whether she could not or should not have found some way to help him more. Eventually, she realized that she had done all she could and that her son was ultimately responsible for taking his own life.

Unrealistic guilt may be part of a process of *reality testing* induced by a loss in which a temporary acceptance of blame may in the long run prove to be one way of confirming that there was, in fact, nothing that the bereaved person could have done to prevent the death. By contrast with clinical depression, when guilt is experienced during bereavement, "it is usually guilt associated with some specific aspect of the loss rather than a general, overall sense of culpability" (Worden, 2002, p. 21).

Is Grief Typically a Normal and Healthy Reaction to Loss?

Ordinary, uncomplicated grief is a healthy, normal, and appropriate reaction to loss. As May (1992, p. 3) has written:

> Grief is neither a disorder nor a healing process; it is a sign of health itself, a whole and natural gesture of love. Nor must we see grief as a step towards something better. No matter how much it hurts—and it may be the greatest pain in life—grief can be an end in itself, a pure expression of love.

A similar point has been made by Lindstrom (2002, p. 20) in the following observation: "To be able to think in terms of past, present, and future, to love and to grieve, is part of the human existential plight and dignity. Grief may add meaning and perspective to one's life just as shadows give depth to a landscape."

Bereaved persons may not be at ease with their situation or with themselves, but they are not, on that ground alone, diseased or depressed in any medical or psychiatric sense. Although encounters with death, grief, and bereavement may not be very frequent or ordinary experiences for many people, the fact that they are *unusual* does not mean that they are *abnormal* or alien in the way disease is foreign to health. Stella Bridgman had experienced several deaths in her life. Each was difficult and demanding in its own way, but in each case she came to realize that her grief was normal and fully warranted by her encounter with loss.

For these reasons, in this book we speak of *signs* or *manifestations* of grief, not *symptoms*. Symptoms are indicators of disease, but bereavement and grief simply are not states of disease from which symptoms would arise. Bereavement and grief may be unusual and daunting, but they are not in themselves abnormal, morbid, or unhealthy.

Some people say that if they were to die their friends should have a party and not be sad. This ignores or misrepresents the nature both of grief and of human attachments. It tells people that they ought not to be experiencing what they actually are experiencing or what they may need to experience. Honest reactions to loss are real; they cannot be turned on and off at will. All human beings react to significant losses; few have much control over what those reactions will be right after an important loss. In addition, loss always has social implications for those who go on living (Osterweis et al., 1984). When I love someone, I experience joyful feelings and other reactions that I usually need and want to express. When I lose someone I have loved, I also have feelings and other grief reactions, and I usually need to express or give vent to those reactions, too.

Moreover, after a death only part of our grief is for the person who died. In large measure, our grief is for ourselves as people who have been left behind:

> When someone you love has died, you tend to recall best those few moments and incidents that helped to clarify your sense, not of the person who has died, but of your own self. And if you loved the person a great deal . . . your sense of who you are will have been clarified many times, and so you will have many such moments to remember. (Banks, 1991, p. 43)

That is why we experience grief even after a slow, lingering, or painful death when we believe that the dying person has been released from distress and is at last at rest. It is also why we encounter grief even when our religious beliefs and theology assure us that the dead person has gone on to a new and better life. Whatever else has happened, as bereaved persons we have experienced a real loss. It is not selfish or improper to react to that loss with grief; it is simply a realistic human reaction.

We have already noted that experiences of bereavement and grief may be more and more unusual or infrequent in a society in which average life expectancies have been greatly extended and death seems less often to enter our lives. However, these changes in our encounters with death should not lead us to view bereavement and grief as *abnormal* parts of life. Loss, death, and grief are normal and natural parts of human life. Because they may be unusual in our experience and are typically associated with a sense of being out of control, it often appears to bereaved persons that they are losing their minds. This is rarely true. *Reacting and responding to loss is a healthful process, not a morbid one.* It may take courage to face one's grief and to permit oneself to experience one's reactions to significant losses, but ultimately this is done in the interests of one's own welfare (Fitzgerald, 1995; Tatelbaum, 1980).

Of course, loss and grief can befall individuals who already have a psychiatric or physical illness, as well as those who are in good health. Hence, in all cases the appropriateness of one's grief must be assessed on an individual basis. *Grief is very much an individualized phenomenon,* unique in many ways to each particular loss and griever. The same griever is likely to react in different ways to different losses; different grievers are likely to react in different ways to the same loss. *Because there is no universal reaction following any given loss, one person's grief should not be construed as a standard by which others should evaluate themselves.* To keep this in mind is to be sensitive and open to the very broad range of manifestations associated with loss. In this way, various normal reactions to loss will not be confused with pathology and the abnormalities of disease.

It is true that loss can sometimes lead to complicated grief reactions that would constitute a disorder warranting therapeutic intervention. We return to the subject of complicated grief reactions at the end of this chapter.

🍂 What Makes a Difference in Bereavement and Grief?

Five critical variables influence experiences of bereavement and grief:

1. The *nature of the prior attachment* or the *perceived value* that the lost person or thing has for the bereaved individual

2. The *way in which the loss occurred* and the *concurrent circumstances* of the bereaved person

3. The *coping strategies* that the bereaved individual has learned to use in dealing with previous losses

4. The *developmental situation of the bereaved person*—that is, how one's being a child, adolescent, adult, or elderly person influences one's grief and mourning (Corr, 1998a)

5. The *nature of the support that is available to the bereaved person after the loss* from family members, friends, other individuals, and social institutions (Parkes, 1975b; Sanders, 1989)

We explore the first three of these factors in this chapter, along with the family context for grief. We will discuss social support in Chapters 10 and 11, and we will consider developmental issues in Part Five.

Prior attachments are not always what they seem to be. The full import of a relationship may not be appreciated until it is over. Some relationships are dependent, abusive, ambivalent, distorted, or complicated in many ways. Almost all relationships are multidimensional. A person whom I love is likely to be significant in my life in many ways—for example, as spouse or partner, helpmate, homemaker, sometime enemy, lover, competitor, parent of my children, guide in difficult times, breadwinner, critic, comforter. Each of these dimensions influences my grief experience and may represent a loss that will need to be mourned. Special difficulties may be associated with the death of a person for whom there were or are ambivalent feelings.

The way in which the loss takes place and the circumstances of the bereaved person are also critical to how we experience grief. As for the way in which the loss takes place, some losses (like the suicide of Stella Bridgman's son and losses associated with violence or unexpected natural disasters) occur in sudden, shocking, or traumatic ways (Doka, 1996b). Some losses can be foreseen or predicted; others cannot. Some losses occur gradually and allow time for preparation; others are drawn out and difficult. Some losses are untimely and run contrary to what we expect in the natural order of things; others fit more easily into our sense of the overall patterns of life. In general, deaths that are "off time"—that occur much before or long after our expectations might have prepared us for them—are likely to be among those we find most difficult (Rando, 1984).

In addition to the characteristics of the loss itself, *the circumstances that surround the bereaved person at the time of the loss* are also influential in shaping the overall bereavement experience. For example, a person who is physically healthy, mentally in top form, and generally at ease with life may be in better condition to cope with loss than someone who is simultaneously beset with a variety of physical, mental, and other challenges in living. By contrast, Shakespeare (*Hamlet,* IV,

Deaths that are unexpected (like those on September 11th) are hard to bear.

© Reuters NewMedia Inc./Corbis

v: 78) wrote that "when sorrows come, they come not like single spies, but in battalions" and according to a popular saying "it never rains but it pours." What these quotations mean is that losses often do (or at least seem to) compound each other, transforming what might otherwise have been a brief, gentle shower into an extended torrential onslaught. Some losses take place at a time in one's life when other burdens or challenges are heavy. Others are complicated because they are part of a series of losses following rapidly one after another that impact a single individual. Still other losses involve many deaths at the same time, as in the deaths of several members of an extended family in a single fatal accident. The events of September 11, 2001, also uncovered complications arising from multiple deaths in a large-scale disaster. For example, many of the men killed at the World Trade Center in New York City were married and relatively young (in their 20s, 30s, and 40s). A significant number of their wives were pregnant at the time. As a result, when their husbands died these women were left on their own to face the problems of pregnancy and giving birth.

In Chapter 6, we pointed out that throughout their lives *different individuals are likely to develop different types of coping strategies.* These are our constantly changing efforts to manage perceived stressors. Each of these coping strategies may be more or less effective. Once a significant loss or death occurs, we are likely to cope in ways that make use of the repertoire of coping strategies and skills that we previously acquired. Thus, despite all of the differences between death and other losses in life, it is often a good rule of thumb to ask how someone has coped with other losses earlier in his or her life to predict how that person is likely to cope with death and bereavement (Shneidman, 1980/1995). Developing new and more effective coping skills requires more time and energy than are usually available in the immediate aftermath of a death or other significant loss. Thus, Stella Bridgman at first did not believe that her coping skills were adequate to enable her to cope with the loss and grief arising from the suicide of her son.

🍂Mourning: Orienting Ourselves

Paying close attention to Stella Bridgman's experiences in the vignette near the beginning of this chapter alerts us to important distinctions between grief and mourning. For example, Stella is described as being deeply impacted in a variety of ways by the death of her son. This was a very difficult loss for Stella and her grief was intense. Unlike earlier death-related losses she had experienced, however, in this case Stella had not yet moved forward very much with her mourning.

Language about Mourning

We think of mourning in this book as an essential process for those who are trying to cope with loss and grief, one that is equally important in helping such persons find a way to go forward with healthful living and adapt to the new world in which they find themselves. As such, mourning has two complementary forms or aspects. It is both an *internal, private, or intrapersonal process*—our inward struggles to cope with or try to manage both the loss and our grief reactions to that loss; and an *outward, public, or interpersonal process*—the overt, visible, and shared expression of grief, together with efforts to obtain social support. Some authors (such as Wolfelt, 1996, as well as Neimeyer and Attig who are discussed later in this chapter) who prefer to emphasize the distinction between these two aspects use terms like *grieving* for the intrapersonal dimension of coping with loss and reserve the term *mourning* for the interpersonal aspects or social expression of grief. We prefer a single term to designate both aspects of mourning, and we use that term to refer to the interactions of the personal and social dimensions of human beings. In this chapter, we concentrate on intrapersonal or intrapsychic dimensions of mourning; we will examine public or interpersonal aspects of mourning more closely in Chapters 10 and 11.

Another way to grasp the meaning of the term *mourning* is to consider the words of Jesus in the Sermon on the Mount: "Blessed are those that mourn, for they shall be comforted." But bereavement, loss, and grief are a burden; how can they be a blessing? The blessing in the experience of bereavement can only be in the capacity to mourn and grow through the loss. As Shneidman (1980/1995, p. 179) wrote: "Mourning is one of the most profound human experiences that it is possible to have. . . .The deep capacity to weep for the loss of a loved one and to continue to treasure the memory of that loss is one of our noblest human traits."

Interpretations or Theories of Mourning

One important difficulty encountered as one begins to reflect on and try to understand human responses to loss is that those responses are complex, personal, and culturally influenced. This insight is one that recent literature on grief and mourning has begun to face in new ways. Until several years ago, there was a standard model of what was going on when people responded to loss. Doka (2007b) traces this model back to an article by Freud (1959a) in which he argued that people responding to loss have to "work through" their grief, which in his view meant the emotions they experienced as a result of the loss. From this, the dominant model for what is going on in responses to loss is that there is a certain amount of "grief work" which must be lived through, acted out, and expressed if mourning is to be "completed" in some acceptable manner, and that grief work has to do with the emotions associated with loss.

The attempt to organize the human experience of mourning into a fairly straightforward picture led in early studies to a theoretical framework or model

As we have learned, Kübler-Ross (1969) proposed a theory of five stages in coping with dying. Despite criticisms noted in Chapter 6 and other serious misgivings about this theory, the notion of "five stages" caught hold in the popular mind and remains alive in some forms of medical and other education. In addition, some who have not noticed its original limited application have gone on to try to force this theoretical schema (which originated in interviews with terminally ill adults who were aware of their impending deaths) on to other populations (e.g., children) and other anticipated losses, as well as post-death bereavement situations, despite the lack of justification for making such applications.

Recently, Maciejewski, Zhang, Block, and Prigerson (2007) sought to offer an empirical justification for a slightly different theory of five stages of grief, which they claimed to have observed as they studied individuals who were processing the death of someone close. Drawing on retrospective interviews with a deliberately limited and selected population of 233 subjects bereaved through natural causes (largely composed of older adult, white, females who most often had experienced the death of a spouse), these authors argued that they identified four sets of sequential responses to loss by death—disbelief, yearning, anger, and depression. They also claimed that acceptance was the dominant *initial* reaction. According to these authors, "[D]isbelief decreased from an initial high at 1 month postloss, yearning peaked at 4 months postloss, anger peaked at 5 months postloss, and depression peaked at

6 months postloss. Acceptance increased throughout the study observation period" (p. 297). As a result, the authors concluded that, "The 5 grief indicators achieved their respective maximum values in the sequence (disbelief, yearning, anger, depression, and acceptance) predicted by the stage theory of grief" (p. 297). Because the maximum values for all five grief indicators occurred within a six-month period, the authors concluded that these "stages" and this period of time describes the "normal" course of grief.

However, there is much evidence to show that these five are not the only obvious reactions to loss through death (consider Elison's [2007] emphases on relief at the death of her abusive husband and in many other situations). Nor can they be taken to be the whole story when we look carefully at reactions beyond an initial six-month period (e.g., at anniversaries and other key moments). Furthermore, the focus in this study on a theory that describes a uniquely linear process does not fit with reports from many bereaved persons who describe experiences of grief as a spiraling, circular process. Evidence for this latter point has been around for a long time; Personal Insights 9.3 reproduces a poem first published in 1977, which makes this point in a particularly poignant and ironic way. Finally, *grief reactions* do not reflect the full scope of bereavement experiences, which also involve *mourning responses*.

All of this gives us much to think about as we turn to factors that make a difference in bereavement and grief, and then to an account of mourning later in this chapter.

which set out from several assumptions: (1) that there is some universal human pattern to how human beings respond to loss; and (2) that pattern can be best understood as a series of normative stages or phases which successful mourners work through toward some goal of completion. As a result of these assumptions, for many years the dominant way of thinking about mourning has been to struggle to describe and uncover these stages or phases in a manner that will clarify how grief work is lived through (Corr & Corr, 2007b; see also Issues for Critical Reflection #8).

Recently however, this whole model has been questioned, both in terms of its basic assumptions and in terms of its adequacy (Doka, 2007b; Jordan & Neimeyer, 2007). Thus it is now suggested that responses to loss are more personal (there is no universal pattern), that they are affected by cultural norms and expectations, and that those responses involve much more than the emotions experienced when a loss occurs (Rosenblatt, 2007). In fact, these responses include cognitive, affective, behavioral, and spiritual components (a point we touched on earlier in our comments about grief reactions), all interacting together in often complex, inevitably personal ways. And these responses always occur within some specific cultural milieu which in turn frames the personal responses in particular ways. We do well to keep these thoughts in mind as we examine different interpretations and implications of what goes on in mourning.

❦ Mourning: Interpretations Involving Phases or Tasks

We begin our exploration with two well-known theories that describe phases and tasks in mourning.

Phases in Mourning

Drawing on work by Bowlby (1961, 1969–1980), Parkes (1970b, 1996) proposed *a phase-based theory* to provide a broad description of *four phases in mourning:* (1) shock and numbness, (2) yearning and searching, (3) disorganization and despair, and (4) reorganization (see Table 9.1). These phases are said to be elements in an overall process of *realization*—making real in one's inner, psychic world what is already real in the outer, objective world.

TABLE 9.1
Phase-Based and Task-Based Interpretations of Mourning

Four Phases (Bowlby/Parkes)	Four Tasks (Worden)
Shock and numbness	To accept the reality of the loss
Yearning and searching	To work through the pain of grief
Disorganization and despair	To adjust to an environment in which the deceased is missing
Reorganization	To emotionally relocate the deceased and move on with life

Source: From Parkes, 1970b, 1996; Worden, 2002.

Shock and numbness are often found among the initial reactions to loss, although they may also recur at other times as one works through one's grief again and again in different circumstances or at a later date. One is shocked or stunned at the impact of the loss. One feels dazed or detached, as if one has been knocked off the familiar balance of one's life, is now overloaded by news of the death, and is unable to absorb or take in anything else. Some have said the effect is like being encircled by an invisible protective shield, a kind of "psychic numbing" or "psychic closing off." Many people also experienced reactions like these in connection with public tragedies like the events of September 11, 2001. Those who are shocked and numbed find it difficult to take care of basic needs like nutrition, hydration, or making decisions. This is a natural defense against bad news and unwanted pain. It is almost always a passing or transitory condition, although it may recur from time to time.

Yearning and searching represent an effort to return to things as they once were. As the pain of grief penetrates the dissolving barriers of shock and one realizes the magnitude of one's loss, one is unwilling to acknowledge the loss or relinquish what no longer exists. One *yearns* or pines for a time that is now gone and finds oneself falling into familiar patterns of setting his place at the table or expecting her to come up the driveway at 6:00 P.M. *Searching* is triggered by a glimpse across a crowded room of someone who resembles him, by a passing whiff of her perfume, by the strains of "our" song (Parkes, 1970b). In fact, yearning and searching are doomed to failure after a death. As the title of the novel, *You Can't Go Home Again* (Wolfe, 1940), says, the past is simply no longer available as it once was. Grasping that fact is to realize the depth, extent, and finality of the bereaved person's loss.

Disorganization and despair are reactions to the inability to bring the past back to life. If the past is truly gone, who am I now? Am I still a wife or a parent? If one of my children has died, should I subtract that child from the total number of my children (see Personal Insights 9.2)? These are questions of self-identity, as well as practical questions of everyday living. Who will now prepare dinner, care for our children, bring home the paycheck? How can we comfort each other when we are both hurting from the death of our child? Should I sell the house and move to the town where the rest of my family lives? It is difficult to answer these and other questions, hard to concentrate on so many new challenges, and easy to become distracted or bewildered in the face of so many new demands. Much that was previously taken for granted has been called into question. Getting through just a few moments, an hour, or one day at a time may be very demanding. Those who are disorganized and disoriented struggle to find a way to go forward.

Reorganization is seen when one can begin to pick up the pieces of one's life again and start to shape them into some new order. Life is never the same after a significant loss or death; some differences are always irrevocable. One has to find a new way of living as a person who now is no longer attached in the way in which he or she once was. "New normals" must be developed for future living. Most bereaved persons do achieve some reorganization in their lives. It is a heroic accomplishment in the highly individual struggle to develop and define a new mode of living.

Some writers offer five (Weizman, 2005), seven (Kavanaugh, 1972), or ten (Westberg, 1971) phases in their models of mourning. Others prefer to combine yearning/searching and disorientation into a three-phase model: (1) shock; (2) a period of intense or active grieving; and (3) reestablishment of physical and mental balance (Gorer, 1965b; Tatelbaum, 1980). Similarly, Rando (1993) described three broad phases in mourning: avoidance, confrontation, and accommodation. The number of phases in these models is not as important as whether they are useful in helping us to understand the experiences of mourning.

Phase-based models of mourning are essentially broad generalizations about common elements in (some? most?) mourning. As such, one must be quite cautious in applying them to individual mourners. It has also been argued (e.g., Wortman & Silver, 1989, 2001) that models based on particular populations (such as elderly widows) may not apply very well beyond the group(s) from which they originated. Some have also thought that phase-based theories of mourning seem to describe a rigid, linear schema in which one phase is said to follow another in sequence. That leads to talk about how much time is appropriate for mourning and to suggestions that mourners will "go through" these phases almost in a passive way, without doing anything else. This is like thinking of mourning as an experience in which a dirty automobile is hooked up to an automatic car wash machine, dragged through the process without exerting any effort, and turned out "clean" at the end. These are criticisms like those we saw of the stage-based theory of coping with dying in Chapter 6 (and see Personal Insights 9.3).

Tasks in Mourning

Worden (2002) recommended that we think of mourning in terms of *tasks,* rather than stages or phases. He suggested *a task-based theory* involving *four tasks in mourning:* (1) to accept the reality of the loss; (2) to work through the pain of grief; (3) to adjust to an environment in which the deceased is missing; and (4) to emotionally relocate the deceased and move on with life (see Table 9.1). A task-based model of this sort has the important advantage of emphasizing that mourning is an

The Five Stages of Grief

The night I lost you
someone pointed me towards
the Five Stages of Grief.
Go that way, they said,
it's easy, like learning to climb
stairs after the amputation.
And so I climbed.
Denial was first.
I sat down at breakfast
carefully setting the table
for two. I passed you the toast—
you sat there. I passed
you the paper—you hid
behind it.
Anger seemed more familiar.
I burned the toast, snatched
the paper and read the headlines myself.
but they mentioned your departure,
and so I moved on to
Bargaining. What could I exchange
for you? The silence
after storms? My typing fingers?
Before I could decide, *Depression*
came puffing up, a poor relation
its suitcase tied together
with string. In the suitcase
were bandages for the eyes
and bottles of sleep. I slid
all the way down the stairs
feeling nothing.
And all the time Hope
flashed on and off
in defective neon.
Hope was a signpost pointing
straight in the air.
Hope was my uncle's middle name,
he died of it.
After a year I am still climbing,
though my feet slip
on your stone face.
The treeline
has long since disappeared;
green is a color

(continued)

I have forgotten.
But now I see what I am climbing
towards: *Acceptance*
written in capital letters,
a special headline:
Acceptance,
its name is in lights.
I struggle on,
waving and shouting.
Below, my whole life spreads its surf,
all the landscapes I've ever known
or dreamed of. Below
a fish jumps: the pulse
in your neck.
Acceptance. I finally
reach it.
But something is wrong.
Grief is a circular staircase.
I have lost you.

Source: Pastan, 1978, pp. 61–62.

active process (Attig, 1991, 1996b), which is similar in some ways to the description of task-based models for coping with dying that we discussed in Chapter 6. Here, examining each of these four tasks in mourning provides another way of understanding some of the basic dynamics of mourning and their complexities.

Worden's first task involves efforts *to accept the reality of the loss.* These efforts may not be apparent in initial grief reactions, but they underlie all of the long-term work of mourning. When confronted by the death of someone one loves, people often feel an immediate sense of unreality. "It can't be true," they say, or "This can't be happening to me." As a temporary or transitional reaction to a significant change in our lives, this is wholly understandable. Nevertheless, making one's loss real and coping with one's grief involve acknowledging and accepting the reality of the death.

To fail to accept the reality of the loss is to move toward delusion and the bizarre. For example, Queen Victoria of England had the clothes and shaving gear of her dead husband (Prince Albert) laid out daily long after his death. Efforts like this are really extreme attempts to suspend living at the precise moment of death so as not to face its harsh implications. They also represent attempts to stay connected to that person without changing one's life. However, wishing that life could resume at some future moment—unchanged from the way it was in the past—is at best unrealistic.

According to Worden, bereaved persons also face a second task in mourning: *to work through the pain of grief.* As Parkes (1996, p. 191) has written, "Anything that continually allows a person to avoid or suppress this pain can be expected to prolong the course of mourning." Productive mourning acknowledges that the pain encountered during bereavement is essential and appropriate. The challenge is to find ways of experiencing this pain that are not overwhelming for the particular individual.

Often, the intensity of a bereaved person's pain and its tendency to consume the whole of his or her universe decline gradually as healthy mourning proceeds. One mother said: "It had to. You simply couldn't live with that level of pain."

Pain is hurtful, both to individuals and to those around them. Not surprisingly, many try to avoid the pain of grief. Some turn to drugs or alcohol to shroud their distress, but that may only drive it underground in their bodies and psyches. Some people literally try to run away from their grief by fleeing the place where the loss occurred. Others attempt to wipe out all memory and traces of the deceased to be relieved of the task of facing the pain of grief after a loss. Ultimately, this strategy of coping through flight is futile. "Sooner or later some at least of those who avoid all conscious grieving break down—usually with some form of depression" (Bowlby, 1969–1980, Vol. 3, p. 158).

A society that is uncomfortable with expressions of grief may encourage bereaved persons to flee from grief's pain by distracting them from their loss or assuring them that the loss was really not all that significant. The wrongheaded message here is that people should not "give in" to grief, an experience that people giving this message may see as morbid and unhealthy. Sometimes, society reluctantly acknowledges that individuals may need to mourn, but then tells them—for example, by commenting that they have "broken down" with grief—that they should only do so alone and in private. Prohibiting people from tasks they need to accomplish—and may need help to learn to accomplish—is often hurtful to the individuals in question and to society itself. Mourning is in principle a healthy and healthful process.

The third of Worden's mourning tasks is *to adjust to an environment in which the deceased is missing*. Parkes wrote, "In any bereavement it is seldom clear exactly what is lost" (1987, p. 27). Bereaved individuals often need to engage in a voyage of discovery to determine the significance of the now-severed relationship, to identify each of the various roles that the deceased played in the relationship, and to adjust to the fact that the deceased is no longer available to fill such roles. This is difficult; a bereaved person might try to ignore this task or withdraw from its requirements. But life calls us forward. Young children need to be changed, bathed, and fed whether or not a spouse has died. Someone must put food on the table and wash the dishes. Adhering to a posture of helplessness is usually not a constructive coping technique—especially not as a long-term or permanent stance. For many bereaved, developing new skills and taking on roles formerly satisfied by the deceased are productive ways of adjusting to loss and growing after a death (Jozefowski, 1999).

Worden describes the fourth task of mourning as one that asks the bereaved person *to emotionally relocate the deceased and move on with life*. Both aspects of this task need careful attention. "Emotional relocation" does not suggest that those who are bereaved should "forget" the deceased person and erase his or her memory. That is neither possible nor desirable (Volkan, 1985). Similarly, "moving on with life" means finding some healthful way to live one's life without the presence of the person who died. That does not necessarily involve investing in another relationship—for example, through remarriage or deciding to have another child. Options of this sort are not open to all bereaved persons. Even when a bereaved person enters into a new relationship, it is important to recognize that no two relationships are ever the same. No new relationship, whatever it may be, will ever be identical to or play the exact same role in the person's life as the one that has now ended.

Clearly, death changes relationships. To think that is not true is to delude oneself. Thus, Worden's fourth task of mourning calls upon the bereaved person to modify or restructure the relationship with or the investment in the deceased in ways that remain satisfying but that also reflect the changed circumstances of life and death. Perhaps for this reason, Worden (1996, pp. 15-16) once observed that, "The task facing the bereaved is not to give up the relationship with the deceased, but to find a new and appropriate place for the dead in their emotional lives—one that enables them to go on living effectively in the world." As a result, in that context he described his fourth task in a slightly different way: "To relocate the dead person within one's life and find ways to memorialize the person."

Satisfying Worden's fourth task would lead a bereaved person to reconceive his or her own personal identity, to restructure his or her relationship with the deceased person in the light of the loss that has taken place, to avoid becoming neurotically encumbered by the past in ways that diminish future quality in living, and to remain open to new attachments and other relationships. Symbols and symbolic gestures can be important in this fourth task (see Personal Insights 9.4).

PERSONAL INSIGHTS 9.4

Four Widows on Emotionally Relocating Their Deceased Husbands and Moving on with Life

Each one of four widows dealt with her wedding ring in a different way after her husband died. One removed her ring and put it away in her jewelry box. "We were married until death parted us," she said. "Now I am no longer married to him." She did not mean that she no longer loved her former husband, but she wanted to emphasize through her actions that death had separated them and that the separation was a permanent one.

A second widow continued to wear her wedding ring on the third finger of her left hand. She knew her husband was dead, but she wanted to emphasize that she still felt connected to him. She felt very content with the legacy of her long, happy, and fulfilling marriage, and she did not intend to look for another husband or a new relationship with another man.

A third widow moved her wedding ring from the third finger of her left hand to her right hand. She did not want to take it off completely or hide it away because it was an important heirloom from her grandmother. Also, she sought an outward sign both to show that she thought of herself as no longer married while also maintaining some tangible indicator of a continuing bond with her deceased husband.

A fourth widow removed her husband's wedding ring before his body was buried. She had a jeweler refashion it, along with her own wedding ring, into a new piece of jewelry, a pendant that she wore around her neck every day. She said, "Now I have a new relationship with my deceased husband, and my lovely pendant symbolizes that new relationship."

Source: Based on Corr, 2001a.

Worden's task-based theory reflects an interpretation of coping (here, mourning) as, in principle, a proactive way of striving to manage one's loss and grief. The efforts involved in those tasks can enable the bereaved person to regain some measure of control over his or her life. Worden (2002, p. 27) wrote that the tasks of mourning "do not necessarily follow a specific order," even though "there is some ordering suggested in the definitions."

Mourning: Interpretations Involving Processes

Accounts of mourning as involving processes focus on what a mourner can do, at least potentially, in responding to loss and developing a new way of living for the future. Such accounts include: the dual process model; descriptions of meaning reconstruction; and emphases on continuing bonds.

The Dual Process Model

The dual process model of Stroebe and Schut (1999) is centered on an oscillation between two complementary sets of coping processes: (1) one that is *loss oriented* or concerned primarily in coping with loss; and (2) the other that is *restoration oriented* or concerned primarily in coping with "restoration" (see Figure 9.1). *Loss-oriented processes* involve the intrusion of grief into the life of the bereaved, grief work, the breaking of bonds or ties to the deceased, and overcoming resistance to change. *Restoration-oriented processes* include attending to life changes, doing new things, and avoiding or distracting oneself from grief. Note that "restoration" in this model is not about trying to make real once again the mourner's former world of lived experiences

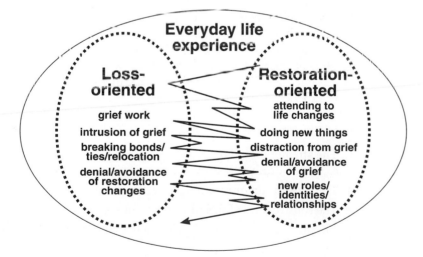

FIGURE 9.1
A Dual Process Model of Coping with Bereavement
From M. Stroebe and H. Schut. Reprinted by permission.

(which no longer exists) or the old assumptive world (which has also been shattered or at least rudely shaken by the loss). Rather, it has to do with efforts to adapt to the new world in which bereaved persons find themselves (Parkes, 1993). What is restored, according to this model, is not a past mode of living, but the ability to live productively in the present and future.

In other words, the dual process model posits an interaction or interplay between two sets of dynamic and interrelated processes in coping with bereavement. "Working through" one's loss and the grief reactions to the primary loss is thought to represent only one side of this duality; addressing secondary losses and new challenges is the other. The dual process model also suggests that emphases in coping with bereavement may differ from: (1) one cultural group to another; (2) one individual to another; and (3) one moment to another. The main point is that some processes in mourning are more focused on coping with loss itself, whereas other mourning processes are more focused on moving forward with healthy living. Thus, this model emphasizes the effort coping requires of bereaved persons, the potentially active nature of mourning, and the complexity of the processes involved.

Meaning Reconstruction

Human beings typically seek to find or construct meaning in their lives, and this often becomes a particularly pressing concern when one has suffered a significant loss. Thus an emphasis on "meaning making" or "making sense of loss" (Davis & Nolen-Hoeksema, 2001) is another way of thinking about or another interpretation of what is involved in mourning. For example, Neimeyer (e.g., 1998, 2000, 2001, 2007) has written about the importance for bereaved persons of engaging in a process of reconstructing meaning in their lives and has asserted that, "meaning reconstruction in response to a loss is the central process in grieving" (1998, p. 110). (Note that Neimeyer and some others prefer to speak of grieving and grievers, rather than mourning and mourners.)

Individual grievers engage in meaning reconstruction at different times, in different ways, and in different connections with their cultures and communities. Some may be able to move on with their lives without doing much beyond dealing with their feelings and practical matters, perhaps because their losses fit into already-existing meaning frameworks (Braun & Berg, 1994). Other bereaved persons, especially those who have experienced violent or traumatic losses, may find it quite difficult to engage in reconstructing meaning in their lives (Davis et al., 2000).

According to Neimeyer (2000, pp. 552–555) meaning reconstruction includes:

1. The attempt to find or create new meaning for the life of the survivor, as well as for the death of the loved one
2. The integration of meaning, as well as its construction
3. The construction of meaning as an interpersonal, as well as personal, process
4. The anchoring of meaning making in cultural, as well as intimate, discursive contexts
5. The development of tacit and preverbal, as well as explicit and articulate meanings
6. The processes of meaning reconstruction, as well as its products

Two prominent ways in which one might seek to reconstruct meaning after an important loss include: (1) developing a benign or favorable account of its significance, often achieved through religious, philosophical, or spiritual frameworks ("He's with his God now"; "She's finally at peace"); or (2) focusing on some positive benefits that apply to those left behind ("I'm now a more sensitive and caring person"; "We're closer together and more focused on family"). Of course, these are only two examples of how bereaved persons might seek to reconstruct meaning in their lives. Each may do so in his or her own ways and at his or her own pace. As a result, advocates of this approach to interpreting mourning argue that it "challenges the notion that grief unfolds in predictable patterns over time" (Holland et al., 2006, p. 183).

According to Neimeyer (2007, pp. 195, 199, 203), three principles at the heart of processes of meaning reconstruction are: (1) "Grieving entails reaffirming or reconstructing a world of meaning that has been challenged by loss"; (2) "Adaptation to bereavement typically involves redefining, rather than relinquishing, a continued bond with the deceased"; and (3) "Narrative methods can play a role in restoring or re-storying a sense of autobiographical coherence that has been disrupted by loss." Attig (2000) also emphasizes narratives in his view that bereaved persons are challenged to move from "loving in presence" to "loving in separation." For Attig (1996b), this challenge has to do with "relearning the world," a set of processes that involve simultaneously finding and making meaning on many levels. These processes include grieving individually, within our families, and within our communities and cultures, in ways that "engage with several of the great mysteries of life in the human tradition" and that allow us to "make a multifaceted transition from loving in presence to loving in absence" (Attig, 2001, p. 34).

Continuing Bonds

Drawing on research with bereaved children, spouses, and parents, as well as other sources, Klass, Silverman, and Nickman (1996; see also Field, 2006) noted the importance for many bereaved persons of their efforts to maintain an ongoing connection to the individual who has died. These connections involve continuing bonds with an internal representation of that individual. This bond is not static but dynamic. It involves negotiating and renegotiating the meaning of the loss over time. It develops in ways that allow the deceased to remain a transformed or changed but ongoing presence in the inner lives of the bereaved. Connections of this type "provided solace, comfort and support, and eased the transition from the past to the future" (p. xviii).

According to these authors, "the continuing bond has been overlooked or undervalued in most scholarly and clinical work" (p. xvii), and there has been "little social validation for the relationship people reported with the deceased or absent person" (p. xviii). Nevertheless, they believe continuing bonds involve new and altered relationships that reflect "the reality of how people experience and live their lives" (p. xix). They are aspects of normal mourning processes and do not represent psychopathology (recall our discussions of misunderstandings of Hopi mourners on pp. 121–122). Stroebe and Schut (2005) have suggested that the key issue is whether continuing or relinquishing bonds to the deceased is helpful or harmful, in what ways or under what circumstances, and for whom.

Anderson (1968, p. 5) touched on continuing bonds in a different way when he observed that "death ends a life, but it does not end a relationship." If this is true,

©Jerry Berndt/Stock, Boston

Family members need each other and can help each other in their grief.

then mourning also involves "enriched remembrance" (Cantor, 1978; see Personal Insights 9.5, which contains many interesting insights even though we would not wish to speak of outcomes of mourning in terms of healing and completion). The concept of "enriched remembrance" involves efforts to restructure the relationship so as to carry its legacy forward with the bereaved person into his or her new modes of living. In this way, effective mourning frees the bereaved to live meaningful lives in their new situation—without wholly abandoning what they have lost.

Other reports have come from some bereaved persons who have sensed the continued presence of the deceased in their lives or have from time to time received after-death communications. Most often, these individuals have found comfort in these extraordinary or paranormal experiences (see, for example, pp. 106–107 in Chapter 5; also LaGrand, 1997, 1999, 2001, 2006). One challenge in mourning is to decide what such experiences might mean and to find ways to integrate them into healthful, ongoing living.

Important Characteristics of These Descriptions of Processes in Mourning

Descriptions of *processes* in mourning share a sense of dynamism—open, ongoing processes in finding ways to cope with loss and adapt to the new world in which those who are bereaved find themselves. They do not reduce to rigid phases or

When Is Mourning Complete?

The emotional pain caused by loss suffered does not move toward forgetfulness. It moves, rather, in the direction of enriched remembrance; the memory becomes an integral part of the mourner's personality. The work of mourning has been completed when the person (or cherished thing) no longer appears as an absence in a barren world but has come to reside securely within one's heart. Each of us must grieve in his or her own manner and at his or her own pace. For many people, one year seems to bring completion. Others require much more or much less time. Periodic waves of grief are often felt for the remainder of one's life. The mourning process must be given the freedom to find its own depth and rhythm; it cannot be artificially accelerated. A loss, like a physical wound, cannot heal overnight. There is no way to hurry the stages of tissue growth and there is no way to speed up the healing process of mourning. But, when mourning has been completed, the mourner comes to feel the inner presence of the loved one, no longer an idealized hero or a maligned villain, but a presence with human dimensions. Lost irreversibly in objective time, the person is present in a new form within one's mind and heart, tenderly present in inner time without the pain and bitterness of death. And once the loved one has been accepted in this way he or she can never again be forcefully removed.

Source: From (with minor adaptations) *And a Time to Live: Toward Emotional Well-Being During the Crisis of Cancer,* by R. C. Cantor, pp. 66–67. Copyright © 1978 by Harper & Row, New York. Reprinted by permission of the author.

stages, and they are not compatible with so-called "normative" preset time frames. Rather they fit best with narratives or stories of personal journeys after loss. The mourning processes we have described look beyond loss itself to the future. They emphasize how very much restoring equilibrium in one's life, finding or reconstructing meaning in living, and developing healthy bonds with the person who died is an individual project, even as it is clearly affected by those around us, our societies, and our cultures.

❧ Mourning as a Potentially Transformative Experience

Our explorations of mourning have produced a number of important lessons. Now we bring some of those lessons together under two questions raised by our study: Are there *fixed end points* in mourning, and are there *opportunities for growth and transformation* in this experience?

Fixed End Points

However mourning is interpreted, its goal has often been described as leading to *recovery, completion,* or *resolution* (Osterweis et al., 1984; Parkes & Weiss, 1983). These terms have fallen into disfavor among contemporary scholars and writers. For example, to *recover* from one's grief seems to suggest that grief is a bad situation like an illness or disease. It also seems to imply that once one is recovered or "healed," one could be essentially unchanged by the experience. Also, *recovery, completion,* and *resolution* all seem to suggest *a fixed end point for mourning,* a once-and-for-all closure after which there is or should be no more mourning. If that were true, mourning would have a set outcome in both principle and time.

Fixed end points are often said to be the goal of mourning. Typically, they are linked to the views of Freud (1959a)—although that link has been questioned by some (e.g., Rando, 1993; Siggins, 1966) as a misstatement of his position—or at least with much psychoanalytic theory, which stresses detachment or withdrawal (decathexis) of emotional attachment from the deceased. Paying attention to continuing bonds in bereavement rejects the view that mourning should involve little more than detachment, "letting go of," or "forgetting" the deceased.

Fixed end points in bereavement may also be assumed without question, partly because they seem to fit neatly with rigid stage- or phase-based theories of mourning and partly because of our desire to assign a specified time period—for example, several weeks or months, one year—as being necessary or sufficient for mourning. "Time heals," we are frequently told. (This adage fits nicely with comparisons between bereavement and physical wounds.) However, this is really not accurate. Time alone does not heal (Smith, 2004c). We have to do more than just "wait it out." What really counts is how that time is used on the individual journey that is mourning. The central issue is the nature of the activities that constitute productive mourning and where they actually do lead those who are bereaved. As one observer commented (S. J. Fleming, personal communication, 9/28/95), "It is not the time we have to use, but the use we make of the time we have."

Previously, we criticized views of grief and mourning as disease states. Here, talk about "recovery" seems equally unsuitable unless one uses that term to mean not a return to a former, pre-death way of living, but a movement forward to a new way of living in the aftermath of loss (Balk, 2004). If that is so, mourning is more than coming back; it is also learning to go forward (Stearns, 1988). Many, if not most, mourners are resilient and find that their lives do improve, but they also can and likely will re-mourn their losses as they find themselves in different places in their future lives (Bonanno, 2004; Dutton & Zisook, 2005).

Opportunities for Growth and Transformation

The possibility of growing and becoming a better person through mourning is analogous to the possibility of growing through coping with dying. Thus, it has been observed that in the Chinese language the term for "crisis" is represented by two symbols, one for "danger" and the other for "opportunity" (see the image on page 235).This is interesting, but one should not think of "opportunity" here as a good chance to seek advantages or benefits; rather, the sense is that of a crucial point at which new (perhaps dangerous) things may begin. In this sense,

Chinese symbol for "crisis."

Courtesy of Linda Riley

PERSONAL INSIGHTS 9.6

A Bereaved Father Reflects on His Growth after the Death of His Son

I am a more sensitive person, a more effective pastor, a more sympathetic counselor because of Aaron's life and death than I would ever have been without it. And I would give up all of those gains in a second if I could have my son back. If I could choose, I would forgo all the spiritual growth and depth which has come my way because of our experiences, and be what I was fifteen years ago, an average rabbi, an indifferent counselor, helping some people and unable to help others, and the father of a bright happy boy. But I cannot choose.

Source: Kushner, 1981, pp. 133–134.

---

dying and bereavement both involve dangerous opportunities. They are, or can be, transformative experiences, challenges whose outcome may leave us better or worse off. Note, however, that even for positive growth in a bereaved person after a death, the price that one pays may be heavy (see Personal Insights 9.6).

As a rough guideline or rule of thumb, we might say that mourning is advancing satisfactorily when the bereaved individual is able to think of the deceased person without the same intensity of pain that was previously experienced. Evidence of this ability is usually apparent when the bereaved individual can once again take up tasks of daily living and can invest in life. For most people, this takes much more time than our society is usually willing to concede, although for some it may not take as long. Certainly, the first year of bereavement—with all of its anniversaries, special days, and moments that remind the bereaved individual again and again of the absence of the deceased and the loss that has been experienced—is a time of special challenge for the bereaved, a period when "anniversary reactions" may be especially prominent. But there is nothing magic in a single year—a second year of bereavement may be even more difficult as it drives home the finality of the first year's experiences (Clayton, 1973, 1974; Glick et al., 1974; Parkes, 1970a).

Perhaps it is better to say with Worden (2002, p. 47): "There is a sense in which mourning can be finished, when people regain an interest in life, feel more hopeful, experience gratification again, and adapt to new roles. There is also a sense in which mourning is never finished." Bereaved persons who are asked, "When did your grief end?" or "When was your mourning over?" often respond: "Never." A bereaved person may rebound from the initial impact of loss and acute grief, or from subsequent eruptions of renewed grief, while never fully getting done with all that mourning involves in learning to live with the same loss and grief.

If mourning really is an individual journey, then it need not have a single, fixed outcome for all bereaved persons. Instead, for at least many bereaved individuals mourning will involve coping with loss and its aftermath, addressing the urgent demands of acute grief, carrying forward the legacy of the relationship in an appropriate way into the new post-death life, and learning to develop and live with "new normals" throughout the rest of the person's life. To these ends, several writers (e.g., Ashenburg, 2004; Bosticco & Thompson, 2005; Gilbert, 2002; Harvey, 1995; Hedtke & Winslade, 2004) have stressed the importance for mourners of narratives or "the drive to story" as a way of making order in disorder or finding meaning in the meaningless.

Bereaved persons who are successful in these processes become *survivors* in the full sense of that word (Corr, 2003a). They have not only survived or lived on after the death of someone they loved, but beyond that, they have coped with their losses and their grief reactions in constructive ways, and they have managed to adjust and reshape their lives to fit into the new world into which their loved one's death rudely thrust them. For many, this is a heroic and awesome achievement.

❦ Grief, Mourning, and Gender

Until recently, much of the research on adult bereavement has been based on women. Reasons for this emphasis include the fact that there are many more widows than widowers, and women are often more willing than men to discuss or share their grief. However, further study of bereaved women and more recent attention to bereaved men has led to contrasting views on grief, mourning, and gender.

For example, there is one view that the way (many? all?) women experience and express their grief and cope with their losses constitutes a "feminine model." An extension of this view is to claim that this feminine model is the "conventional" or right way to grieve. One example of this point of view is provided by Staudacher (1991, p. 3), who argued that "there is only one way to grieve. That way is to go through the core of grief. Only by experiencing the necessary emotional effects of your loved one's death is it possible for you to eventually resolve the loss." In this view, experiencing and expressing emotion—often coupled with a willingness to reach out and accept help—are thought to be essential to healthy bereavement. This is partly about the grief reactions that one has, but the real emphasis is on how those reactions are expressed and on how one copes with loss and grief. For example, in Chapter 5 we reported on some American-Indian groups that seemed to favor explicit expression of grief (although with some limitations in the ways and time frames in which that expression occurred). However one describes this way of living out one's bereavement, among the dominant groups in our society it is often characteristic of bereaved women.

For Staudacher, this description of grief and mourning processes in (many) women has become normative. This so-called feminine way of responding to loss and grief is thought to be the "conventional" or only appropriate way; it is what everyone ought to do. As a result, bereaved men are thought to be disadvantaged because they are seen as ignoring their feelings, hiding from their grief, being unwilling to share their emotions, and refusing offers of help. In short, gender favors women in grief. Women mourn correctly, and men need to learn to follow that pattern of mourning.

An alternative to this "feminization of grief" is a contrasting theory of "masculine grief" (Golden, 1996; Lund, 2000; Martin & Doka, 1996, 1998). For example, masculine grief might be said to focus on feelings of anger and guilt, suppressing other emotional responses and hiding vulnerability, an emphasis on thinking about the loss (versus feeling), a desire for solitude, being reluctant to share grief or seek help, valuing self-reliance, assuming the role of protector, seeking to solve practical problems or engage in physical actions, and immersing oneself in work. According to this second view of grief, mourning, and gender, men have their own ways of coping with loss and bereavement, and they ought to be permitted to proceed according to this "masculine" option.

A third view claims that although patterns of grief and mourning may often be related to gender, they are not determined by it. Martin and Doka (2000) now contrast what they had formerly called "feminine" and "masculine" patterns in grief as "intuitive" versus "instrumental" grieving styles, respectively. According to this view, *intuitive* grievers emphasize experiencing and expressing emotion, whereas *instrumental* grievers focus on practical matters and problem solving. The important point for Martin and Doka is this: *the issue is not really one of gender, but of style.* Women and men often express their reactions to loss and cope with their grief in different ways because they have been socialized to perceive themselves and their roles in different ways. But that tendency is not ironclad. All women have not been socialized in a single, rigid way, nor have all men been socialized in a single, contrasting way. Individuals of both genders have different backgrounds, personalities, and ways of living out their lives. As a result, some women are instrumental grievers, and some men are intuitive grievers. The characters of the cold, distant mother and the warm, supportive father in the novel and film *Ordinary People* (Guest, 1976) illustrate this point well. Thus a man who grieves by expressing rather than repressing his emotions is not being "effeminate," nor is a woman being "masculine" or not being feminine if she does not share her grief. Such judgments by others merely add another layer of stress to the many difficulties with which bereaved persons are already trying to cope.

Perhaps the most important point in this discussion of grief, mourning, and gender is to legitimize individuality in coping with loss and grief, even as we seek to identify shared patterns among various groups of bereaved persons whose members may or may not be of a specific gender.

❦ Grief, Mourning, and Families

Grief has most often been understood in everyday life and studied in the professional literature as an individual reaction to loss. Until recently, not much attention had been given to the role(s) of families or other similar social groups in bereavement (Brabant, 1996; Shapiro, 1994). In this section, we ask four questions: (1) How are families significant in their members' bereavement?; (2) How do families differ in the ways in which they affect their members' bereavement?; (3) Do families grieve as a unit?; and (4) Do families as a unit cope with loss and grief?

The answer to our first question is that, at a minimum, grief within a family "consists of the interplay of individual family members grieving in the social and relational context of the family, with each member affecting and being affected by the others" (Gilbert, 1996, p. 271). This means that a family system (whatever one may identify as one's "family" and however it may be constituted) almost always provides a context that will influence its members' experiences of loss, grief, and mourning.

Second, families are different in the ways in which they affect their members' bereavement. To the degree that they are able or wish to, families socialize or prepare their members to value relationships, acknowledge losses, express grief, and mourn. However, each family views death-related encounters, attitudes, and practices in its own specific way. Each family also forms relationships within its unit in its own way. For example, extremely enmeshed families will entangle their members very closely with each other, whereas disengaged families do not offer much support to their members. Some families allow their members considerable freedom in how they express grief and mourning; other families expect all members to express grief and mourning in the same way. In Chapter 5, we also noted

Grief is expressed in different ways within a family.

© Laurent Van der Stockt/Gamma Presse

that some Hispanic-American families encourage women to express grief freely, but expect men to be stoic and impassive. Other family characteristics that may be relevant to the grief of members include whether the family system engages in open communication or secrecy, the availability of extended family, the family's social and economic resources, the prior role and functioning of the deceased member in the family system, and the existence of conflicted or estranged relationships at the time of death (Walsh & McGoldrick, 2004b). In short, families may be permissive or restrictive and supportive or unsupportive in how they expect and tolerate expressions of grief and mourning by their members.

Families also differ in their place in a family developmental life cycle (McGoldrick & Walsh, 2004). Losses may occur at different points in what systems theorists portray as a three-generational family life cycle (Carter & McGoldrick, 1988):

◆ To unattached young adults who are between families
◆ To young couples who are joining together and creating new family units through marriage
◆ To families with young children
◆ To families with adolescents
◆ To families who are launching children and moving on
◆ To families in later life

Each of these family types is likely to be coping with different developmental challenges. For example, a new couple may be struggling with issues of commitment to their new family system, whereas an established couple who are launching children and moving on may be coping with unaccustomed issues of personal and family identity. For a new couple, questions that arise might include: "Can each of us accommodate our previous independence to make a go of our new family unit?" or "Can we work together to become parents and bring children into the world?" By contrast, a couple that is moving on after launching children might ask: "Can we re-adjust ourselves to take advantage of the opportunities of our new empty nest?" or "Do we still have parental roles to fulfill now that our children have moved away?" In short, families at different points in their life cycle may have different strengths and limitations to make available to their bereaved members. Such families may be affected in different ways and by different sorts of losses.

A third question is whether families grieve as a unit. This goes beyond thinking of families only as the context for each of their members' individual grief and mourning. Shapiro (1994) has argued that grief is a family process, but Montgomery and Fewer (1988) contend that this confuses individual and family-level properties. According to Montgomery and Fewer, responses to loss are found in families, and families engage in the public or interpersonal processes of mourning, but families do not do the intrapersonal processes of experiencing loss and grief—perhaps for the simple reason that families are not persons. That is why one can often observe significant differences in the grief and mourning of individual family members. Gilbert (1996, p. 273) agrees with this view when she writes: "Families do not grieve. Only individuals grieve. This is done in a variety of contexts, one of which is the family."

Still, it is clear that major losses such as death do bring disorder into family systems, and families must cope with that disruption. Thus, the answer to our fourth question is that bereaved families do engage in a type of systemic coping with loss and grief. Death affects the often-unspoken set of assumptions about how life ought to be, well-established roles and relationships, and everyday responsibilities and routines. These and other aspects of family life must be reconsidered and reconstructed (Lamberti & Detmer, 1993). In addition, since loss and grief can "have an effect across the boundaries separating one generation from the next," there may be a "multigenerational ripple effect" from a significant death (Detmer & Lamberti, 1991, p. 366).

Following a death, Walsh and McGoldrick (2004b) have argued that two major tasks confront family members and family units: (1) to share acknowledgment of the reality of death and to share the experience of loss; and (2) to reorganize the family system and to reinvest in other relationships and life pursuits. (Note that each of these combines two of the mourning tasks for individuals described by Worden and restates them in family systems terminology; compare Walsh & McGoldrick, 1988.) Acknowledging the reality of death and sharing the experience of loss involve recognition of the loss and its implications, sharing grief reactions, and tolerating individual differences within the family system. Reorganizing the family system requires family members to reconstruct what the family means to them and their sense of identity as a family. In addition, family members must reapportion or abandon activities and roles formerly assigned to the deceased. Reinvestment, as we noted earlier in this chapter, involves restructuring or transforming the relationship with the deceased so as to allow family members to maintain a sense of connection with that person and with their past even as they move toward the future. Open, honest, and supportive communication within the family system is essential to all of these tasks. Family rituals or shared ways of dealing with issues that bring members together, such as memorialization practices, commemorative activities, or prayer, are often useful (Bowen, 1991; Imber-Black, 1991; Kissane & Bloch, 2002; Nadeau, 1998).

🌛 Anticipatory Grief and Mourning

The concept of *anticipatory grief* was first introduced by Lindemann (1944) and has since been the subject of numerous inquiries (e.g., Aldrich, 1963; Fulton & Fulton, 1971; Fulton & Gottesman, 1980; Rando, 1986c, 2000; Siegel & Weinstein, 1983). Broadly speaking, anticipatory grief refers to grief experiences that take place prior to but in connection with a significant loss that is expected to take place but has not yet occurred—for example, grief that occurs in advance of, but somehow still in relation to, impending death. A forewarning of death is a necessary condition for anticipatory grief, but the heart of the matter is the grief reaction to the anticipated, but not yet actually realized, loss. Edgar Allan Poe provided a clear example of anticipatory grief and mourning in describing his reactions (on more than one occasion) to his wife's anticipated death (see Personal Insights 9.7). Another example appears in a report describing anticipatory grief in children who are facing death (Sourkes, 1996).

Rando (1986c, p. 24) originally defined anticipatory grief as "the phenomenon encompassing the processes of mourning, coping, interaction, planning, and psychosocial reorganization that are stimulated and begun in part in response to the awareness of the impending loss of a loved one and the recognition of associated losses in the past, present, and future." This very broad definition includes both grief reactions

An Extract from a Letter by Edgar Allan Poe of January 4, 1848

"You say—'Can you *hint* to me what was the terrible evil' which caused the irregularities so profoundly lamented?' Yes; I can do more than hint. This 'evil' was the greatest which can befall a man. Six years ago, a wife, whom I loved as no man ever loved before, ruptured a blood-vessel in singing. Her life was despaired of. I took leave of her forever & underwent all the agonies of her death. She recovered partially and I again hoped. At the end of a year the vessel broke again—I went through precisely the same scene. Again in about a year afterward. Then again—again—again & even once again at varying intervals. Each time I felt all the agonies of her death—and at each accession of the disorder I loved her more dearly & clung to her life with more desperate pertinacity. But I am constitutionally sensitive—nervous in a very unusual degree. I became insane, with long intervals of horrible sanity. During these fits of absolute unconsciousness I drank, God only knows how often or how much. As a matter of course, my enemies referred the insanity to the drink rather than the drink to the insanity. I had indeed, nearly abandoned all hope of a permanent cure when I found one in the death of my wife. This I can & do endure as becomes a man—it was the horrible never-ending oscillation between hope & despair which I could not longer have endured without the total loss of reason. In the death of what was my life, then, I receive a new but—oh God! how melancholy an existence."

Source: From *The Letters of Edgar Allan Poe*, 1948, vol. 2, p. 356.

and mourning processes; refers equally to past, present, and future losses, incorporates a shifting time frame as the dying person moves toward death; and encompasses the perspectives of both the dying person and his or her survivors-to-be.

One problem with this definition is that the adjective *anticipatory* would seem to be inappropriate since the grief in question is not limited solely to future or expected losses. A second problem is that the noun *grief* is inexact since the definition includes both grief and mourning. For those reasons, Rando (1988a) first argued that although the phenomenon of anticipatory grief is real, the term itself is a misnomer. Subsequently, she decided to shift to the phrase *anticipatory mourning* in the title of a later book, *Clinical Dimensions of Anticipatory Mourning* (Rando, 2000).

In any event, it seems clear, for example, that when a husband is dying, a wife may realize that she has already lost the help that he used to give her around the house (a past loss), that she is currently losing the vigorous ways in which he used to express his love for her (a present or ongoing loss), and that she will soon lose the comfort of his presence and the shared retirement that they had planned together (an expected or anticipated loss). Each of these losses may generate its own grief reaction, and each may stimulate a mourning process in which one tries to cope with that loss and its associated grief reaction. However, these experiences need not be inconsistent with maintaining the loving ties that characterize an attachment between two living people. After all, partners often experience other losses—a job, a beloved home, a loved parent or friend—but continue to love each other through the loss.

In response to criticisms of the concept of anticipatory grief (e.g., Fulton, 2003), it has been suggested that it would be useful to distinguish between anticipatory grief and anticipatory mourning (Corr, 2007a). From this perspective, anticipatory grief would be understood more narrowly as including only reactions to losses that have not yet occurred and are not yet in process—losses that have not yet moved from expectation to reality. Anticipatory mourning would designate efforts to cope with those anticipated losses and their related grief. Losses that have already been realized would be subject to familiar processes of grief and mourning, although they take place prior to a death and do not involve anticipation. As such, all of these pre-death experiences are components of a larger context of reacting to and coping with dying (Corr & Corr, 2000). Like everything that goes on prior to a death, these experiences have a bearing on what happens afterwards but cannot be expected to take the place of post-death grieving and mourning.

❧ Traumatic Loss and Death

A death or loss is properly termed *traumatic* when its circumstances include certain objective elements, such as "(a) suddenness and lack of anticipation; (b) violence, mutilation, and destruction; (c) preventability and/or randomness; (d) multiple death; and (e) the mourner's personal encounter with death, where there is either a significant threat to personal survival or a massive and/or shocking confrontation with the death and mutilation of others" (Rando, 1993, pp. 568–569). All of these, as we have seen, apply to the losses experienced by the attack on America on September 11, 2001, the Asian tsunami in December 2004, Hurricanes Katrina and Rita in August and September 2005, and the Virginia Tech shootings in April 2007.

First, when the loss or death is *sudden and unanticipated,* its shock effects tend to overwhelm a mourner's capacity to cope (Rando, 1996). There is no opportunity to say good-bye and finish unfinished business (Doka, 1996b; Straub, 2000). Because the event does not seem to make sense, there is often an obsessive effort to reconstruct events so as to comprehend and prepare for them in a retrospective way. Also, traumatic events are often accompanied by intense emotional reactions (fear, anxiety, and a sense of vulnerability and loss of control) and increased physiological arousal (stimulation/excitement). Further, trauma is often followed by major secondary losses, such as having no body to view to confirm the death, a need to rescue others or attend to the wounded, and the demands of legal inquiries.

Second, *violence, mutilation, and destruction* in traumatic events may produce feelings of terror, fear, and anxiety. These feelings may be accompanied by a sense of vulnerability, victimization, and powerlessness. There may also be fantasies of grotesque dying and aggressive thoughts of revenge, as well as a need to go over and over the events of the trauma (Rynearson, 2001).

Third, when a traumatic event is perceived as *preventable,* mourners view it as one that could have been avoided. It appears to be a willful or irresponsibly negligent event as well as an unprovoked violation. As a result, victims of trauma may become angry, outraged, and frustrated. Hence, they strive intensely to find the cause of the event, fix responsibility, and impose punishment. When a traumatic event is perceived as *random,* its unpredictability and uncontrollability can be terrifying. To ward off such terror, mourners and victims often blame themselves for such events, choosing that alternative as a way to defend themselves against the perception that events in the world are truly random and unpredictable, that they cannot be protected against.

Fourth, experiencing *multiple deaths or losses* in a traumatic encounter—especially when they occur simultaneously or in rapid succession—can produce a form of *bereavement overload* (Kastenbaum, 1969) in which mourners find it difficult to sort out and work through their losses, grief reactions, and mourning processes for each individual tragedy. Multiple deaths and losses are often part of public tragedies, which have their own special qualities (Corr, 2003a; Lattanzi-Licht & Doka, 2003), as in the case of the catastrophes that occurred on September 11, 2001.

Fifth, a mourner's *personal encounter with death* in a traumatic event can involve a significant threat to personal survival or can follow a massive or shocking confrontation with the death and mutilation of others. In the former instance, one is likely to experience fear, terror, heightened arousal, a sense of abandonment and helplessness, and increased vulnerability; in the latter instance, horrifying sensory stimuli (sights, sounds, smells) often produce reactive phenomena, such as nightmares, flashbacks, and intrusive images or memories.

One or more of these five objective elements can usually be found in any traumatic event, whether the event is a *human-induced victimization* (as in the events of September 11, 2001, or the Virginia Tech shootings in April 2007, as well as in cases of rape, battering, incest, other criminal assaults, robbery, torture, and terrorism or war-related atrocities) or *a natural disaster* (as in instances of life-threatening disease, serious accidents, hurricanes, tornadoes, earthquakes, tsunamis, and flash floods). These events result in loss or death that is outside the ordinary range of human experience and that is usually associated with intense fear, terror, and a sense of helplessness (Zinner & Williams, 1999). Many have linked the stress response syndromes that result from traumatic events to *post-traumatic stress disorder* (PTSD)—whose basic symptom categories include re-experiencing the traumatic event, avoiding stimuli associated with the traumatic event or numbing of general responsiveness, and increased physiological arousal. Against this, others have argued that they constitute a distinct form of complicated grief, but that claim remains controversial as we will see in the following section of this chapter.

Traumatic events have been reported to shatter our *assumptive world,* the "strongly held set of assumptions about the world and the self which is confidently maintained and used as a means of recognizing, planning, and acting" (Parkes, 1975a, p. 132). In her book *Shattered Assumptions,* Janoff-Bulman (1992) described an assumptive world as "a conceptual system, developed over time, that provides us with expectations about the world and ourselves" (p. 5). She argued that the fundamental assumptions held by most people in their assumptive worlds are: "The world is benevolent"; "The world is meaningful"; and "The self is worthy." She contended that such beliefs are broad, but not foolhardy, assumptions because they "afford us the trust and confidence that are necessary to engage in new behaviors, to test our limits" (p. 23).

A child looks over the ruins of her home destroyed by wildfire.

If we consider traumatic events in terms of their effect on our fundamental assumptions, "in the end, it is a rebuilding of this trust—the reconstruction of a viable, non-threatening assumptive world—that constitutes the core coping task of victims" (Janoff-Bulman, 1992, p. 69). As we noted earlier, this is the path from being merely a *victim* (in this case, of a traumatic event) to becoming a *survivor* in the full sense of that word—someone who not only survives the death but who also survives the bereavement by living in a healthy way after the loss (Corr, 2002b, 2003a; O'Hara, 2006). Such a path to survivorship is a challenging form of meaning reconstruction discussed previously because mourners need to cope with the traumatic aspects of the encounter, as well as the loss and grief found in all bereavement (Beder, 2005; Kauffman, 2002). Thus, Janoff-Bulman (1992) described survivors who have coped effectively with traumatic events and challenges to their fundamental convictions and assumptive worlds in the following ways:

> These survivors recognize the possibility of tragedy, but do not allow it to pervade their self- and worldviews. . . .
> [For such survivors] the world is benevolent, but not absolutely; events that happen make sense, but not always; the self can be counted on to be decent and competent, but helplessness is at times a reality. . . .
> There is disillusionment, yet it is generally not the disillusionment of despair.
> Rather, it is disillusionment tempered by hope. . . .

[In the end, this view] involves an acknowledgment of real possibilities, both bad and good—of disaster in spite of human efforts, of triumph in spite of human limitations. (pp. 174–175)

Without in any way minimizing the suffering involved in traumatic losses, Calhoun and Tedeschi (2006; see also Calhoun & Tedeschi, 1999; Tedeschi & Calhoun, 1995, 2007; Tedeschi et al., 1998) have also stressed the possibility of posttraumatic growth, particularly when assisted by an "expert companion"—someone who possesses scholarly knowledge of bereavement, grief, and trauma, clinical training, and an awareness of limitations and ambiguity in the face of issues associated with traumatic losses.

❧Complicated Grief Reactions

Thus far in this chapter, we have taken the view that the human experiences of grief and mourning are—at least for the most part—normal and healthy. Still, all human processes can become distorted and unhealthy. We take up the subject of complicated grief here because we want to contrast it with previous discussions of "healthy, uncomplicated grief" and because complicated grief is important in itself for the relatively small group of people who experience it. These people experience an excessive form of grief that can overwhelm them in a persistent way and trap them in unproductive, maladaptive behavior. In short, talk of "complicated grief" refers to grief reactions or mourning processes that are not only unusual but also abnormal in the sense of being deviant and unhealthy. (Note that many, but not all, discussions of this topic in the literature do not make the distinction between grief and mourning that we have used throughout this book.) The adjective "complicated" has been chosen by recent writers to avoid the term "pathological," which has come into disfavor as too judgmental in tone (Volkan, 1970, 1985).

Complicated grief reactions have long been recognized in a general way (e.g., Demi & Miles, 1987). Like many other writers, Worden (2002) identified four types of complicated grief reactions:

◆ *Chronic grief reactions,* which are prolonged in duration and do not lead to an appropriate outcome, as when individuals become aware that they are not making progress in getting back into living again

◆ *Delayed grief reactions,* in which grief at the time of the loss is inhibited, suppressed, or postponed, not surfacing again until later, when it most often appears as an excessive reaction to a subsequent loss or other triggering event

◆ *Exaggerated grief reactions,* which are excessive and disabling in ways that may lead to the development of a phobia or irrational fear, to physical or psychiatric symptoms, or to aberrant or maladaptive behavior

◆ *Masked grief reactions,* in which individuals experience symptoms or behaviors—including the complete absence of grief (Deutsch, 1937)—that cause them difficulty but that they do not recognize as related to the loss

In general, complicated grief reactions seem to develop as a result of difficulties in the relationship with the deceased (e.g., ambivalent, dependent, or narcissistic relationships); the circumstances of the death (e.g., uncertainty about or unwillingness to accept the fact of death, or a situation of multiple or traumatic losses); the bereaved person's own history or personality (such as a history of depressive illness, a personality that employs withdrawal to defend against extremes of emotional distress or does not tolerate dependency feelings well, or a self-concept that includes being the "strong" one in the family); or the social factors that surround the experience (e.g., when a loss is disenfranchised as socially unspeakable or socially negated, or when a social support network is absent).

More recently, Parkes (2006b, p. 2) argued that "numerous clinical studies have supported the existence of complicated grief, which is usually seen as taking two forms: an inhibited or delayed form and a chronic or persistent form." He added that, "Of the two, the chronic form is the most frequent."

Nevertheless, Parkes (2006b, p. 2; see also 2007a) added the following comment:

> Despite this evidence, the authors of the DSM [the *Diagnostic and Statistical Manual of Mental Disorders*] have consistently rejected including pathological or complicated grief as a psychiatric diagnosis on the grounds that it has not been clearly distinguished from, on the one hand, uncomplicated grief and, on the other, the other psychiatric disorders that can be triggered by bereavement, most notably Clinical Depression.

Not surprisingly, in recent years there have been several efforts to define more carefully the precise meaning of the phrase "complicated grief" (now sometimes called "prolonged grief disorder") and to provide empirical data that would establish it as a distinct clinical entity. These efforts are ongoing and are likely to involve future developments. For the moment, they can be represented by a "Symposium on Complicated Grief" organized by Parkes (2006a) in which leading advocates in this area (Prigerson & Maciejewski, 2006, p. 11) proposed that complicated grief be recognized as a distinct entity within a new DSM category of Attachment Disorders. According to them, a diagnosis of "complicated grief" is appropriate for a relatively small group of individuals who meet the following criteria:

◆ Criterion A. Chronic and disruptive yearning, pining, and longing for the deceased

◆ Criteria B. The person must have four of the following eight remaining symptoms at least several times a day or to a degree intense enough to be distressing and disruptive:

1. Trouble accepting the death

2. Inability to trust others

3. Excessive bitterness or anger related to the death

4. Uneasiness about moving on

5. Numbness/detachment

6. Feeling life is empty or meaningless without the deceased

7. Envisioning a bleak future

8. Feeling agitated

◆ Criterion C. The above symptom disturbance must cause marked and persistent dysfunction in social, occupational, or other important domains

◆ Criterion D. The above symptom disturbance must last at least six months

More recently, these authors have preferred to speak of "prolonged grief disorder" rather than "complicated grief disorder," but their overall goals remain as does their argument for including some version of this disorder in the DSM (Prigerson, Vanderwerker, & Maciejewski, in press).

Critics of the construct of "complicated grief," such as Bonanno (2006) and some contributors to the Parkes symposium (2006a), argue that it risks stigmatizing, pathologizing, and medicalizing a normal if difficult bereavement experience, thereby turning familiar supportive work on the part of family members and friends over to secularly trained professionals, and that complicated grief rather than being an internal reality is an externally imposed social role with cultural and historical origins. Efforts to define and defend the concept of complicated grief will need to take account of such criticisms, clarify its relationship to traumatic grief and posttraumatic stress disorder (see Ehlers, 2006), and find its place within existing understandings of grief and mourning.

It is important for helpers to be alert to potential complications in grief and mourning, and to obtain appropriate assistance that would help to untangle complications in grief reactions. However, because of the inevitable individuality of grief reactions, professional assessment is often required both to distinguish idiosyncratic but healthy grief reactions from complicated and unhealthy grief reactions and to intervene in useful therapeutic ways (Figley, 1999; Jacobs, 1999; Naparstek, 2005; Rando, 1993).

❦ Summary

In this chapter, we began an examination of central elements involved in the human experiences of loss, bereavement, grief, and mourning. We focused on variables that affect those experiences, paying special attention to how one understands grief and its many manifestations. We then described a series of interpretations of mourning, including theories involving phases or tasks, processes (the dual process model, meaning reconstruction, and continuing bonds), and contrasting views of whether mourning leads to fixed end points or offers opportunities for growth and transformation. After that, we explored issues related to gender and families, anticipatory grief and mourning, traumatic loss and death, and complicated grief reactions.

Glossary

Anticipatory grief and mourning: experiences of grief and mourning occurring prior to but in connection with a significant loss that is expected to take place

Assumptive worlds: conceptual systems that provide individuals with expectations about the world and themselves to guide planning and acting; Janoff-Bulman asserted that the fundamental convictions held by most people are: "The world is benevolent"; "The world is meaningful"; and "The self is worthy"

Attachments: relationships through which individuals satisfy fundamental needs

Bereavement: the objective situation of individuals who have experienced a loss of some person or thing that they valued; involves three key elements—a *relationship or attachment* with some person or thing that is valued, the *loss* of that relationship, and an *individual* who is deprived of the valued person or thing by the loss

Complicated grief reactions or complicated mourning: grief reactions or mourning processes that are abnormal in the sense of being deviant and unhealthy, thereby overwhelming bereaved persons, leading to maladaptive behavior, and inhibiting progress toward satisfactory outcomes in mourning; Worden identified four types: *chronic, delayed, exaggerated,* or *masked* grief reactions

Continuing bonds: Dynamic and ongoing connections that allow the deceased to remain a transformed but ongoing presence in the inner lives of the bereaved and that are comforting

Enriched remembrance: Cantor's phrase for efforts in mourning to restructure the relationship with the lost person (or object) so as to carry its positive legacies forward into the bereaved individual's new modes of living

Families or family systems: almost always provide a key context that influences their members' experiences of loss, grief, and mourning; may be enmeshed or disengaged, permissive or restrictive, supportive or unsupportive in such matters

Five variables that influence experiences of bereavement and grief: the nature of the prior attachment; the way in which the loss occurred and the concurrent circumstances of the bereaved person; coping strategies used by the bereaved person; the developmental situation of the bereaved person; the nature of the support available to the bereaved person

Grief: the term that indicates one's reactions to loss; these reactions may be *physical, psychological* (emotional, cognitive), *behavioral, social,* or *spiritual* in nature

Grief work: processes of coping with loss and grief; equivalent to *mourning* as that term is used in this book

Grieving: a term used by some writers to designate the internal or intrapsychic aspects of what we identify in this book as *mourning;* we prefer to think of *grieving* as "processes of experiencing and expressing grief"

Guilt: thoughts and feelings that assign blame (often self-blame), fault, or culpability for a loss or death

Interpretations or theories of mourning:

  Phases in mourning: describes mourning as a series of phases; the Bowlby/ Parkes model proposed four phases (shock and numbness; yearning and searching; disorganization and despair; reorganization); other writers have proposed three phases (shock, a period of intense or active grieving, and reestablishment of physical and mental balance, in one version; avoidance, confrontation, and accommodation, in another version) or a larger number of phases

  Processes in mourning: describes mourning as involving processes; the dual process model proposed by Stroebe and Schut described two basic processes (loss-oriented processes and restoration-oriented processes)

  Tasks in mourning: describes mourning as involving a series of tasks; Worden suggested four tasks (to accept the reality of the loss; to work through the pain of grief; to adjust to an environment in which the deceased is missing; to emotionally relocate the deceased and move on with life)

Intuitive versus instrumental grieving: Martin and Doka's terms used to contrast two extremes in a spectrum of grieving styles; *intuitive* emphasizes experiencing and expressing emotion, *instrumental* focuses on practical matters and problem solving; formerly, these might have been contrasted as "feminine" (or "conventional") versus "masculine" styles, but the point to note is that this is essentially a matter of style, not gender

Loss: to be separated from and deprived of a valued person, object, status, or relationship; may involve death or other types of endings or terminations; *primary losses* involve the ending of a basic attachment; *secondary losses* are those that follow from a primary loss

Meaning reconstruction: efforts to make sense of loss by finding or creating new meaning in the death of the loved one and in the new life of the bereaved person

Melancholia: Freud's term for clinical depression

Mourning: responses to loss and grief involving efforts to cope with or manage those experiences and to learn to live with them by incorporating them into ongoing living; includes both *internal or intrapsychic* and *external or interpsychic* processes; sometimes called *grief work* or *grieving* (see above); some writers confine *mourning* to external or social expressions of grief and rituals used in coping with bereavement

Outcomes of mourning: many laypersons and theoreticians speak of *recovery, completion,* or *resolution;* we believe that mourning does not lead to fixed end points or closure; rather, we prefer to think of mourning as a process that may never be completely finished but is moving forward constructively if it is helping to manage grief reactions effectively, to incorporate the loss into one's life, and to enable the bereaved person to go forward with healthy, productive living by developing "new normals" to guide that living

Realization: a term used by Parkes to describe what is involved in "making real" all of the implications of loss; "making real" in one's inner, subjective world that which is already real in the outer, objective world

Survivors (of bereavement): individuals who have found their way to healthy living after a death

Traumatic losses: losses and deaths that include objective elements such as suddenness and lack of anticipation; violence, mutilation, and destruction; preventability or randomness; multiple deaths; and the mourner's personal encounter with death, where there is either a significant threat to personal survival or a massive or shocking confrontation with the death and mutilation of others

Uncomplicated grief reactions: healthy, normal, and appropriate reactions to loss

Victims (of bereavement or trauma): individuals who have been victimized (hurt, harmed, "reaved") by loss

Questions for Review and Discussion

1. Think of a time when you experienced the loss of some person or thing that was important in your life. What made this an important loss for you? How might it

have been different if you had lost a different person or thing, or if the loss had occurred in a different way?

2. How did you react to that loss? Try to be as complete as possible in developing this description of your reactions to the loss, including beliefs, feelings, and behaviors (actions).

3. How did you cope with that loss? What helped you to cope with that loss or to integrate it into your ongoing living? What was not helpful? Why was it not helpful?

Suggested Readings

Introductory descriptions of loss, grief, and mourning appear in:

Davidson, G. W. (1984). *Understanding Mourning: A Guide for Those Who Grieve.*
Freeman, S. J. (2005). *Grief and Loss: Understanding the Journey.*
Viorst, J. (1986). *Necessary Losses.*
Westberg, G. (1971). *Good Grief.*

Additional analyses of bereavement appear in the following:

Attig, T. (1996b). *How We Grieve: Relearning the World.*
Calhoun, L. G., & Tedeschi, R. G. (Eds.). (2006). *The Handbook of Posttraumatic Growth: Research and Practice.*
Center for the Advancement of Health. (2004). Report on Bereavement and Grief Research [Special issue.] *Death Studies, 28(6).*
Doka, K. J. (Ed.). (2007a). *Living with Grief: Before and After the Death.*
Freud, S. (1959a). *Mourning and Melancholia.*
Klass, D., Silverman, P. R., & Nickman, S. L. (Eds.). (1996). *Continuing Bonds: New Understandings of Grief.*
Martin, T., & Doka, K. J. (2000). *Men Don't Cry, Women Do: Transcending Gender Stereotypes of Grief.*
Nadeau, J. (1998). *Families Make Sense of Death.*
Neimeyer, R. A. (Ed.). (2001). *Meaning Reconstruction and the Experience of Loss.*
Osterweis, M., Solomon, F., & Green, M. (Eds.). (1984). *Bereavement: Reactions, Consequences, and Care.*
Parkes, C. M. (1996). *Bereavement: Studies of Grief in Adult Life* (3rd ed.).
Parkes, C. M. (Ed.). (2006a). Symposium on Complicated Grief . *Omega, Journal of Death and Dying, 52(1).*
Parkes, C. M. (2006c). *Love and Loss: The Roots of Grief and Its Complications.*
Rando, T. A. (Ed.). (2000). *Clinical Dimensions of Anticipatory Mourning: Theory and Practice in Working with the Dying, Their Loved Ones, and Their Caregivers.*
Raphael, B. (1983). *The Anatomy of Bereavement.*
Sanders, C. M. (1989). *Grief: The Mourning After.*
Stroebe, M. S., Hansson, R. O., Stroebe, W., & Schut, H. (Eds.). (2001). *Handbook of Bereavement Research: Consequences, Coping, and Care.*
Stroebe, M. S., Hansson, R. O., Stroebe, W. & Schut, H. A. (Eds.). (2007). *Handbook of Bereavement Research and Practice: 21st Century Perspectives.*

Selected Web Resources

Some useful search terms include: ANTICIPATORY GRIEF AND MOURNING; ASSUMPTIVE WORLDS; ATTACHMENTS; BEREAVEMENT; COMPLICATED GRIEF REACTIONS OR COMPLICATED MOURNING (CHRONIC, DELAYED, EXAGGERATED, MASKED); CONTINUING BONDS; DEPRESSION; ENRICHED REMEMBRANCE; GRIEF; GRIEF WORK; GRIEVING; GUILT; LOSS; MEANING RECONSTRUCTION; MELANCHOLIA; MOURNING; OUTCOMES OF MOURNING; SURVIVORS; TRAUMATIC LOSS, UNCOMPLICATED GRIEF REACTIONS

Visit the book companion website for *Death & Dying, Life & Living, Sixth Edition,* at academic.cengage.com/psychology/corr for all URLs and live links to the following *organizational and other Internet sites:*

American Association of Retired Persons (AARP)

Living with Loss: Hope and Healing for the Body, Mind and Spirit **(published by Bereavement Publishing, Inc.)**

Centre for Grief Education, Melbourne, Victoria, Australia

Genesis Bereavement Resources

Grief Digest **(published by the Centering Corporation)**

GriefNet, Rivendell Resources

Living with Loss Foundation

MedlinePlus (multiple topics)

National Grief Support Services, Inc.

U.S. National Institute of Mental Health, National Institutes of Health

CHAPTER 10

Coping with Loss and Grief: How Individuals Can Help

Courtesy of Ron Olshwanger

Objectives of This Chapter

◆ To identify *five fundamental needs* of bereaved persons

◆ To describe *some unhelpful messages* often directed to bereaved persons

◆ To explain the concept of *disenfranchised grief and mourning*

◆ To discuss some implications of *animal deaths and pet loss*

◆ To offer some *constructive suggestions for helping* the bereaved

◆ To point out *ways individuals can help bereaved persons with cognitive, affective, behavioral, and valuational tasks in mourning*

◆ To introduce *Widow-to-Widow programs* and the *Stephen Ministry*

◆ To identify and explain *ten principles for facilitating uncomplicated grief*

❦ Individuals Who Helped One Woman during Her Mourning

When her mother died after a long, lingering illness, Stella Bridgman (see Chapter 9) turned for consolation to her husband, to some relatives and friends who lived nearby, and to her church. They provided enough help to her so that she was able to resume a normal life.

But then her first husband died, and it got much worse after her teenage son took his own life. Many of her friends and associates withdrew from her and were not helpful. They felt uncomfortable in the presence of her intense distress, and she felt that she was being badly treated and even stigmatized by some of the ways in which they regarded her because of her association with a death by suicide.

Some people tried to tell Stella that they knew what she was feeling, but she did not find that helpful. Many people would not mention her son's name because they thought that would only make Stella feel bad. They found it especially difficult to talk about the way he had ended his life. Mostly, people tried to avoid Stella and steer clear of any reminders of her loss.

When others withdrew from her, Stella felt isolated and lonely. When others tried not to mention her son's name, Stella perceived this as compounding her initial loss. By not even talking about her son, she feared that people were erasing all mention and memory of his life. Above all, Stella felt hurt by these actions of people from whom she had expected assistance and support.

Stella did find one or two people who really helped her. Each of these people simply gave her a hug, lent her an ear in person or by telephone, and just remained available to Stella. In their presence, Stella knew she didn't have to be careful about what she said or the feelings she expressed. None of them behaved as if he or she needed to have Stella "get over" her grief. One good friend occasionally brought food or came over to cook nutritious meals with Stella. Another encouraged Stella to talk about her losses and to go out for walks with her.

Stella knew the story of Job from the Bible. So she was sensitive to the differences between the very proper church elder who told her that "God never gives us burdens heavier than we can bear" and the young clergyperson who was wise enough to be silent when Stella needed to express her anger at God for letting these tragedies befall her.

❦ Fundamental Needs of Bereaved Persons

Davidson (1984) has written that bereaved persons need five things: social support, nutrition, hydration, exercise, and rest. Among these, social support is most frequently mentioned, and it is often a major post-death variable in determining complicated versus uncomplicated grief. In Chapter 9, we saw that the variables that make a difference in bereavement and grief include the nature of the prior attachment, the way in which the loss occurred and the concurrent circumstances of the bereavement, the coping strategies that the individual has learned to use in dealing with previous losses, the developmental situation of the bereaved person, and the

Friends can help grieving persons by encouraging them to exercise (an illustration from *Tear Soup*—see Personal Insights 10.2).

nature and availability of support for the bereaved person after the loss. Only the last of these—social support—is open to alteration after a death has occurred (see Morgan, 2001). Therefore, it is the main subject of this and the following chapter.

In the videotape *Pitch of Grief* (1985), an experienced hospice bereavement volunteer observes that the single thing that can most help a bereaved person is the "presence of a caring person." It is not as important what such a person says or does—although there are better and worse things that one might say or do—as that the person does care and is available (Donnelley, 1987). As we have seen throughout this book, listening is a way of giving oneself to the other, of putting aside one's own concerns to let the other talk about his or her concerns (see Personal Insights 10.1).

The other factors mentioned by Davidson are often ignored in the literature on bereavement. Individuals who are bereaved may experience a disinterest in food and a general loss of appetite. They may also lack energy or the ability to concentrate on the tasks required to prepare nourishing meals. That is one reason why many communities have traditions in which friends and neighbors bring food and drink to the bereaved. In addition to not nourishing themselves properly, bereaved persons sometimes contribute to their own dehydration and poor nutrition by consuming empty calories or drinking too much alcohol, which dehydrates them.

Similarly, bereaved persons need exercise and rest. Some bereaved persons experience insomnia or other disruptions in sleep patterns, whereas others sleep

Listen

When I ask you to listen to me,
And you start giving me advice,
You have not done what I asked.
When I ask that you listen to me,
And you begin to tell me why I shouldn't feel that way,
You are trampling on my feelings.
When I ask you to listen to me,
And you feel you have to do something to solve my problems,
You have failed me, strange as that may seem.
Listen: All that I ask is that you listen,
Not talk or do—just hear me.
When you do something for me
That I need to do for myself,
You contribute to my fear and feelings of inadequacy.
But when you accept as a simple fact
That I do feel what I feel, no matter how irrational,
Then I can quit trying to convince you
And go about the business
Of understanding what's behind my feelings.
So, please listen and just hear me
And, if you want to talk
Wait a minute for your turn—and I'll listen to you.

Source: By an anonymous author, as appeared in
St. Louis Post-Dispatch, September 19, 1998, p. D3.

continually without ever feeling really rested. Healthy exercise and a good night's sleep can contribute to a productive mourning process.

Those who seek to help bereaved persons can do much to see that they obtain adequate nutrition, hydration, exercise, and rest.

❦ Unhelpful Messages

All too often, our society conveys unhelpful messages to bereaved persons. Typically, these are clustered around: (1) attempts to minimize the loss that has been experienced; (2) admonitions not to feel (or, at least, not to express in public) the strong grief reactions that one is experiencing; and (3) suggestions to get back to living promptly and not disturb others with one's grief and mourning (Baugher, 2001).

The first of these clusters of messages may involve the following sorts of statements:

- "Now that your baby has died, you have a little angel in heaven." (But my pregnancy was not intended as a way of making heavenly angels.)
- "You can always have another baby," or "You already have other children." (But neither of these will replace the baby who died.)
- "You're still young, you can get married again." (But that will not bring back my first spouse or lessen the hurt of my loss.)
- "You had a good, long marriage." (But that only makes me feel all the more keenly the pain of what I have lost.)
- "After all, your grandfather was a very old man." (But that made him all the more dear to me.)

From the standpoint of the bereaved, these messages seem to suggest that the loss was really not all that important or that the deceased person was not truly irreplaceable. One related implication is that bereavement and grief should not be perceived by the individual as such difficult experiences. Another implication is that friends and relatives of the bereaved person, or society as a whole, need not permit the grief-related needs of the bereaved persons to change their daily routines very much.

The second cluster of messages to bereaved persons seeks to suppress the depth or intensity of the grief they are experiencing. For example, such individuals will be told:

- "Be strong," or "Keep a stiff upper lip."
- "You'll be fine," "Don't be upset," "Put a smile on your face."
- "You're the big man or woman of the family now."
- "Why are you still upset? It's been . . . [4 weeks, 6 months, a year]."
- "What you need to do is to keep busy, get back to work, forget her."

In fact, no one can simply stop experiencing what he or she is experiencing. Feelings and all of the other reactions to a significant loss are real. These grief reactions need to be lived with and lived through. They only change in their own ways and at their own pace. The underlying theme of this second cluster of messages is that it is not good for bereaved individuals to experience some feelings or other grief reactions. Even when grief reactions are acknowledged in principle, it will often be suggested to bereaved persons that they should not experience their reactions in certain (especially public or powerful) ways. The principal theme in such messages is that these ways of experiencing one's grief are unacceptable to those around the bereaved person. In other words, the real message is that your grief is making me or us uncomfortable, and that is inappropriate.

The third set of messages is really a variant of the first two. It arises from the common practice in American society of what has been called "oppressive toleration." That is the view that people can do or say whatever they wish (or, in this case, experience and express grief in any ways they might want to), as long as they do not disturb others. Accordingly, it is often made clear to bereaved persons in more or less subtle ways—and often in ways that are not very subtle at all—that if they insist, they can grieve as they wish, but in so doing they must take care not to bother those around them or disrupt the tranquility or happiness of society in general. This viewpoint is reflected in business practices that permit a bereaved person to take 1 or 2 days off work but then expect that individual to come back to work ready to function as if nothing had happened (Fitzgerald, 1999; Wolfelt, 2005b).

Thus, when people in our society speak of the "acceptability" of grief, they usually mean its acceptability to the group, not to the bereaved person. When President Kennedy was assassinated and when President Reagan died, American society applauded their widows for the way they dealt with their bereavement in public—not least because they presented a stoic facade to society and to the media, which we could admire but not be disturbed by. Of course, Mrs. Kennedy faced a sudden, violent death of her husband, whereas Mrs. Reagan had long anticipated the death of her husband from Alzheimer's disease. Nevertheless, it was widely ignored that the examples of these two widows may not have been relevant to or workable for most bereaved people and may have been particularly unhelpful for those having trouble expressing reactions to their losses.

❦ Disenfranchised Grief and Mourning

Often, the unhelpful messages that we have just described are not merely examples in which individuals have failed in the ways in which they tried (or did not try) to help bereaved persons. Usually, these deficiencies reflect specific social or cultural contexts in which a societal death system conveys to its members—whether in formal and explicit ways or through more informal and subtle messages—its views about what is thought to be socially acceptable or appropriate in bereavement. Social norms of this sort are often hurtful to bereaved individuals when the society and its members *disenfranchise* their grief and bereavement experiences.

Disenfranchised grief is "the grief that persons experience when they incur a loss that is not or cannot be openly acknowledged, publicly mourned, or socially supported" (Doka, 1989b, p. 4). To disenfranchise grief is to indicate that a particular individual does not have a right to be perceived or to function as a bereaved person. The important point here is that disenfranchised grief is not merely unnoticed, forgotten, or hidden; it is socially disallowed and unsupported.

According to Doka (1989b, 2002a), grief can be disenfranchised in three primary ways: either the relationship or the loss or the griever is not recognized. Doka also added that some types of deaths, such as those involving suicide or AIDS, may be "disenfranchising deaths" in the sense that they either are not well recognized or are associated with a high degree of social stigma. We witnessed that possibility in the case of a death by suicide in the vignette about Stella Bridgman near the beginning of this chapter.

Relationships are disenfranchised when they are not granted social approval. For example, some unsuspected, past, or secret relationships might not be publicly recognized or socially sanctioned. These could include relationships between friends, co-workers, in-laws, or ex-spouses (Scott, 2000)—all of which might be recognized in principle but not in connection with bereavement—as well as relationships that are often not recognized by others as significant, such as extramarital affairs or same-sex relationships. Folta and Deck (1976, p. 235) argued that devaluing of these relationships results from an emphasis in American society on kin-based relationships and roles: "The underlying assumption is that the 'closeness of relationship' exists only among spouses and/or immediate kin." This assumption is incorrect. Thus, Folta and Deck concluded "rates of morbidity and mortality as a result of unresolved grief may be in fact higher for friends than for kin" (p. 239).

Losses are disenfranchised when their significance is not recognized by society. These might include perinatal deaths, losses associated with elective abortion, or the loss of body parts. Such losses are often dismissed or minimized, as when one is simply told, "Be glad that you are still alive." Similarly, those outside the relationship may not appreciate the death of a pet even though it may be an important source of grief for anyone, regardless of age—child, adolescent, adult, or elder. Also, society often fails to recognize losses that occur when dementia blots out an individual's personality in such a way that significant others perceive the person they loved to be psychosocially dead, even though biological life continues.

Grievers are disenfranchised when they are not recognized by society as persons who are entitled to experience grief or who have a need to mourn. Young children and the very old are often disenfranchised in this way, as are mentally disabled persons (Kauffman, 2004).

In addition to these *structural elements of bereavement* (relationships, losses, and grievers), Corr (1998b, 2002a) has argued that the *dynamic or functional elements of bereavement* (grief and mourning) may also be disenfranchised. For example, a bereaved person might be told by society that the way he or she is

Just lending a shoulder to cry on can provide important loving care to a grieving person.

© Stan Honda/AFP/Getty Images

experiencing or expressing grief is inappropriate, or that his or her ways of coping with the loss and the grief reactions are unacceptable. Some grief reactions and some ways of mourning are rejected because they are unfamiliar or make others in society uncomfortable.

However it occurs, "the problem of disenfranchised grief can be expressed in a paradox. The very nature of disenfranchised grief creates additional problems for grief, while removing or minimizing sources of support" (Doka, 1989b, p. 7). Many situations of disenfranchised grief involve intensified emotional reactions (e.g., anger, guilt, or powerlessness), ambivalent relationships (as in cases of abortion or between persons who were once but who no longer are lovers), and concurrent crises (such as those involving legal and financial problems). *Disenfranchisement* may remove the very factors that would otherwise facilitate mourning (such as a role in planning and participating in funeral rituals) or make it possible to obtain social support (e.g., through time off from work, speaking about the loss, receiving expressions of sympathy, or finding solace within some religious tradition).

🍎 Animal Deaths and Pet Loss

Deaths of animals, especially pets or companion animals, provide examples of losses that are often not well appreciated and may be disenfranchised. Exploring these losses briefly can reinforce much of what we have previously indicated about bereavement while also leading to useful lessons for helpers and preparing us to help bereaved persons with their tasks in mourning.

As we know, children may have their first encounters with death in cases involving wild or domestic animals. We see this in *Charlotte's Web* (White, 1952), a story in which a young girl named Fern (and later a spider named Charlotte) saves a pig named Wilbur who is the runt of his litter from various threats to his life. A different example of the death of an animal and its effect on many admirers was evident in the case of Barbaro—a celebrated thoroughbred racing horse who won the Kentucky Derby in 2006. When Barbaro broke several bones in his right hind leg 2 weeks later in the Preakness Stakes, many people followed closely the various attempts to save his life and bring him back to health, only to be saddened when he had to be euthanized on January 29, 2007.

Pets or companion animals may give unconditional love to a child who finds the world to be sometimes harsh and scary. Since most pets have much shorter life expectancies than do humans, animals often provide opportunities for children and others to learn about loss, sadness, and death (Kaufman & Kaufman, 2006). As a result, pet loss is a familiar subject in death-related books for children (Corr, 2004d). Companion animals may also help children, adolescents, and other humans learn about the responsibilities of caring for another living creature and thereby enhance their self-esteem (Rynearson, 1978). Some animals provide guide services for the disabled, help to guard individuals in dangerous circumstances, comfort those who are lonely and isolated, and bring a spark of joy to residents in long-term care facilities who may otherwise have only limited social contacts outside the institution. When relationships like these are important in one's life,

Courtesy of Donna M. Corr

Bonding between a child and her dog provides security to both.

the death or loss of an animal can have a powerful impact on the humans involved (Planchon et al., 2002; Ross & Baron-Sorenson, 2007).

Some people fail to appreciate or even dismiss the importance of close attachments with animals. This attitude can lead to actions—even well-intentioned ones—that make the bereavement experience more difficult. For example, in a story for young readers called *The Accident* (Carrick, 1976), a dog is buried too quickly after a truck kills it. His parents had thought to spare their young son from the burdens of the sad event by burying the dog in the child's absence. They failed to recognize the child's need to share in this important ritual, to act out his love and grief, and to assuage his guilt for not being sufficiently attentive to the dog's whereabouts as they walked together along the highway. Similarly, in books like *Mustard* (Graeber, 1982) and *I'll Always Love You* (Wilhelm, 1985), bereaved children teach adults useful lessons when they turn down opportunities to get a new animal too soon after the death of a beloved pet.

The importance of death-related losses involving pets to the humans who are their companions is evident in the existence of organizations like the Association for Pet Loss and Bereavement (P.O. Box 106, Brooklyn, NY 11230; tel. 718-382-0690; www.aplb.org) and the International Association of Pet Cemeteries & Crematories (5055 Route 11, P.O. Box 163, Ellenburg Depot, NY 12935; tel. 518-594-3000; www.iaopc.com), as well as in the growing number of pet cemeteries in the United States and other efforts to memorialize deceased animals (Spiegelman & Kastenbaum, 1990). Loss and grief may also be felt deeply in situations such as when a human being is no longer able to care for an animal and must turn it over to someone else, cannot pay for expensive veterinary services that it would need, must give it up entirely when relocating to new living quarters or to an institution, or faces difficult choices when a sick or feeble animal must be euthanized (Stewart,

Memorializing companion animals provides a measure of solace.

© Maggie Steber/Stock, Boston

1999). The problem is that this type of grief may be intense, even though there are few, if any, well-recognized and widely accepted structures to assist in coping with such loss and grief (Carmack, 2003; Sife, 2005; Toray, 2004; Wolfelt, 2004b; Wrobel & Dye, 2003).

We can learn from this several lessons that really apply not only to pet loss, but to all losses: (1) it is the relationship that is really central to appreciating the loss, not the object of the relationship (in this case, the animal in question); (2) the nature of the death or loss and the way it occurred will affect the bereavement; and (3) the circumstances of the bereaved person—both developmental (child, adolescent, adult, or elder) and situational (e.g., living alone, in a supportive family, or in an institution; having prior bereavement experiences or not)—are also critical. As for helpers, individuals confronted by the death or loss of a pet can be helped and supported, if others will take time to recognize the value of the relationships they have enjoyed with their companion animals, appreciate the challenges they face and the losses they have experienced, and explore with them their resulting needs (Adamec, 2000; Butler & Lagoni, 1996; Harris, 1998; Lagoni et al., 1994; Straub, 2004).

CHAPTER 10   Coping with Loss and Grief: How Individuals Can Help   **261**

🍎 Some Constructive Suggestions for Helping

Despite the foregoing, we are not as individuals condemned to hurt bereaved persons or to fail to help them. We can avoid disenfranchising their grief and bereavement, and we can be helpful to them in many ways. For example, after the sudden and unexpected death of his 10-year-old daughter Rachel, one father drew the following lessons for bereaved persons from his experiences (Smith, 1974, pp. 35–40):

1. Don't blame yourself for what has happened.
2. Don't be brave and strong.
3. Don't try to run away.
4. Don't feel that you owe it to the dead child to spend the rest of your life tied to the place in which he or she lived.
5. Don't feel sorry for yourself.

For helpers, Smith (1974, pp. 47–52) had the following advice:

1. Immediately after a death, *do something specific to help* (e.g., notify those who need to be told on the family's behalf, answer the telephone or free family members from other chores that may appear meaningless to them), or make known in other practical ways your willingness to help.
2. Respect preferences that the family may have to be alone.
3. Assist in practical ways through the time of the funeral (e.g., help with meals, cleaning, transportation).
4. In the difficult time after the funeral, do not avoid contact with the bereaved.
5. Act normally and mention the name of the deceased person in ways that would have been natural before the death.
6. Permit the bereaved to determine how or when they do or do not wish to talk about the deceased person.
7. Don't try to answer unanswerable questions or to force your religious or philosophical beliefs upon vulnerable bereaved persons.
8. Don't say, "I know how you feel"—no matter how much it may seem to be so, that is never true unless you have walked in the same path.
9. Be available, but allow the bereaved to find their own individual ways through the work of mourning.

Friends are often hesitant and may feel inadequate in approaching someone who is grieving a significant loss. Still, it is better to try to help than to do nothing. In making an effort to help, it is usually a good idea to try to avoid clichés or empty platitudes (Linn, 1986). Sometimes it may be enough to tell the bereaved person: "I don't know what to say to you," or "I don't know what to do to help," but also "What can I do for you right now?" And it can often be most helpful just to sit with or even cry with the bereaved person (see Personal Insights 10.2).

Tear Soup

A book called *Tear Soup: A Recipe for Healing After Loss* (Schwiebert & DeKlyen, 1999) tells the story of "an old and somewhat wise woman whom everyone called Grandy" (p. 1) who has just suffered a big loss in her life. Grandy faces her loss by making "tear soup," filling a soup pot over and over again with her tears, feelings, memories, and misgivings. She knows that the work of making tear soup must be done alone, is typically messy, and "always takes longer … than anyone wants it to" (p. 6). The resulting broth is bitter and making it is difficult work, but it has to be done.

Tear Soup affirms all of the feelings and experiences that bereaved people encounter, including their anger at God because they do not understand why this terrible loss has occurred and do not know where God is when they are feeling so all alone. The book rejects foolish advice like telling bereaved persons that if only they had true faith they would be spared their deep sadness, anger, and loneliness. Instead, Grandy continued to trust God and she "kept reminding herself to be grateful for ALL the emotions that God had given her" (p. 29).

Tear Soup notes that people in our society are often not very helpful to the bereaved. They are eager to fix things and feel helpless when they cannot do that—so they want to know when this will all be over. Sometimes those who one might have thought were one's friends just drop out of sight and stay away. Even worse are individuals who take it on themselves to show the bereaved person how to make tear soup the "correct" way! Grandy teaches us that real help only comes from those special people who can be present and just listen. Their caring presence does not require the bereaved person to be careful about what is said and does not try to talk that person out of whatever he or she is feeling.

Tear Soup also speaks favorably of "special soup gatherings" in which bereaved persons can share stories that lead to both laughter and additional tears, and "where it's not bad manners to cry in your soup or have second helpings" (p. 37). Finally, *Tear Soup* holds out the hope of a day when one can eventually find it OK to eat something other than tear soup all the time. This does not mean Grandy is completely finished with her tear soup, but the hard work of making it is done and she knows she will survive—even as she keeps a portion of the soup in the freezer to taste a little from time to time.

Source: Based on Schwiebert and DeKlyen, 1999. (Note: Images from *Tear Soup* are reproduced in this book on pp. 213, 254, and 310.)

🌱 Helping Bereaved Persons with Tasks in Mourning

"For all bereaved, the central issue in any helping encounter is to learn to build a life without the deceased" (Silverman, 1978, p. 40). One value of Worden's (2002) account of tasks in mourning that we discussed in Chapter 9 is that those tasks can be adopted by individuals who are helping the bereaved as ways of determining how their assistance might most usefully be offered. However, Worden's tasks are specifically formulated as projects for the bereaved. They need to be adapted to serve as guidelines for helpers. We do that here by exploring ways to help bereaved persons with tasks that involve what they know or believe (cognitive tasks), their emotions or how they feel about their loss (affective tasks), how they act (behavioral tasks), and what they value (valuational tasks).

Throughout this process, helpers need to keep one important caution in mind. At a time when so much in a bereaved person's life is out of control and when he or she is so vulnerable to strong feelings, reactions, and pain, outsiders need to be careful not to take over the bereaved person's tasks of mourning and subtly (or not so subtly) shape them in their own ways (Wolfelt, 2005a). Barring outright pathology—which might be identified as involving direct harm that a person is doing to himself or to others—bereaved persons must be permitted to lead the way in their mourning (read Personal Insights 10.1 again). This is what Manning (1979) meant by the title of his book *Don't Take My Grief Away from Me*.

Helping with Cognitive Tasks

Everyone who is bereaved asks questions about what happened. All bereaved persons have a *need for information*. Knowing the facts about what happened is an essential step in making the event real in one's inner world. That is why many bereaved persons go over and over the details of the circumstances in which a death occurred. Outsiders often become impatient with this process. They ask: "What difference does it make if the car that hit her was blue or red? Isn't she still dead?" But that misses the point. Only when a bereaved person can fill in details like this in a personal intellectual mosaic can he or she grasp the reality of its pattern. Until then, the loss seems blank, devoid of color, unlike life, unreal, and untrue. Cognitive and other tasks may be especially important (and sometimes difficult) for bereaved persons who are used to exercising a high degree of control over their environment. Cognitive tasks may also be difficult for bereaved individuals whose social roles (e.g., as a clergyperson, counselor, physician, or other identified helper) make it hard for them to seek information and assistance from others.

Providing prompt, accurate, and reliable information is a key role for helpers. One day, when Arthur Smith (1974) was 600 miles away from home at a clergy conference, he was called to the telephone. His wife's voice simply said, "Rachel died this morning." Smith later wrote, "There is no other way to tell someone that a loved person has died" (p. 8). But in the circumstances, Smith's first reaction was to scan in his mind the list of sick and elderly persons in his parish who might have died. Failing to identify anyone with that name, he asked, "Rachel who?" The deep silence that followed signaled the moment in which Smith began to face the almost inconceivable fact of his daughter Rachel's death and his great loss.

Information is particularly important when the death is unexpected, untimely, traumatic, or self-inflicted. Anything that adds to the shocking qualities of a loss contributes to a sense of unreality. Protests quickly arise: "Surely, this cannot be happening"; "This sort of thing doesn't happen here"; "This must be some kind of bad dream." Information is often urgently requested: about possible survivors, the cause of the losses, recovery of bodies, and so forth. Sometimes requests for additional information really cannot be answered and are not meant to be answered. Often, they actually are efforts to test reality, to obtain confirmation over and over again that the death has in fact occurred, and perhaps also to confront the hard truth that it will not or may not ever be adequately explained. Testing reality is one way in which bereaved persons move from shock and confusion to other processes of coping constructively with their loss(es) and grief.

For example, even though the ultimate cause of death remains unknown in cases of sudden infant death syndrome (SIDS), it is important that a "syndrome" or pattern of events can be identified. The postmortem examination and associated investigation on which an appropriate diagnosis of the syndrome rests are critical as a basis for assuring bereaved parents that they did not bring about or in any way cause the death of their child and that nothing could have been done by anyone to prevent the death (see Focus On 12.1 in Chapter 12).

Helping with Affective Tasks

Helpers can also assist bereaved persons with affective or emotional reactions to the loss. These reactions typically include both feeling and somatic (bodily) components. Most bereaved persons have a *need to express their reactions to a loss or death.* To do this, they may require assistance in identifying and articulating feelings and other reactions that are strange and unfamiliar to them (Mannino, 1996; Zeitlin & Harlow, 2001). Some bereaved persons find it difficult to acknowledge or explain their grief reactions. They ask questions of themselves and of others like: "What is happening to me?" "Why is my body reacting in these strange ways?" "Why am I experiencing such odd emotions or such a roller coaster of feelings?" Informed and sensitive helpers can give names to the affective reactions that the bereaved are experiencing. Helpers can also assist in finding appropriate ways to express strong feelings and other reactions. Appropriate ways are ones that are safe for both the bereaved person and for others who may become involved.

Often, what is most needed is the company of a caring person who can acknowledge the expression and validate the appropriateness of the emotional reactions. For example, many bereaved persons have found comfort in reading *A Grief Observed,* the published version of the notebooks in which C. S. Lewis (1976) wrote out his feelings and the kaleidoscope of reactions that he experienced after the death of his wife. He originally wrote only for himself as a way of giving release to his grief, but his description has rung so true with other bereaved persons that his little book provides the normalization and reassurance many desperately need. This model of writing out one's thoughts, feelings, and other reactions to loss has been followed with good results by many bereaved persons who keep a journal or other record of their bereavement experiences (Hodge, 1998; Lattanzi & Hale, 1984). There is an extensive body of writings by bereaved persons (see Focus On 14.1 in Chapter 14), together with books intended to help the bereaved in these matters (e.g., Grollman, 1977; Rando, 1988a; Sanders, 1992; Tagliaferre & Harbaugh, 1990).

Helping with Behavioral Tasks

Bereaved persons very often need to act out their reactions to a loss. This behavioral aspect of grief frequently takes the form of activities that reflect a need to *mark or take notice of the death through some external event or action.* For example, nowadays we often see impromptu roadside markers at the sites of motor vehicle accidents (Clark & Cheshire, 2004; Clark & Franzmann, 2006; Haney et al., 1997; Reid & Reid, 2001; we discuss this subject more fully in Chapter 11). Another type of behavioral task in bereavement can be observed in *commemorative activities that are designed to remember the life of the deceased or the legacy that he or she has left behind.* One widow described the value of commemorative activities in her comments about letters of condolence that she received from others who had known her deceased husband, even from individuals who were strangers to her (see Personal Insights 10.3; see also Haley, 2001). The goal of these commemorative activities is to preserve at least in some small measure the memory of the person or thing that has been lost. This may be realized in more or less formal or public ways, but it always involves some act or outward behavior. For example, one might plant a tree in memory of one who has died. This seems to be particularly appropriate because it involves the nurturing of new life in a way that can be revisited from time to time.

Survivors may mark the site of a death in personally meaningful ways.

Courtesy of Clyde M. Nabe

Simpler forms of commemoration include attending a wake or funeral, since a prominent part of funeral ritual (see Chapter 11) has to do with commemoration and memorialization of the deceased. Other commemorative gestures might involve putting together a scrapbook of pictures and memories, designing and executing a collage that symbolizes the life of the deceased, writing a poem about the person who has died, or tracing his or her place in a family tree. The point is not so much how the commemoration is accomplished as that something is done to take note of the life that has now ended and its meaning or impact beyond itself.

Condolence Letters

People dread writing letters of condolence, fearing the inadequacy of their words, the pain they must address, death itself. And few people realize, until the death of someone close, what a benediction those letters are.

The arrival of letters about George was a luminous moment of each day. They made me cry. They made me feel close to him. They gave me the sense that the love he inspired in others embraced me. The best were the longer, more specific ones, the ones that mentioned something the writer cherished in George, or recounted some tale from his past that I was unaware of. Others were inexpressibly poignant. At one time I would have avoided writing any such letter, thinking it unkind to dwell on a subject that was the source of such pain, that I would be rubbing salt into a wound. But now I know that it is not unkind. There is so much joy mixed in with the pain of remembering.

Source: Reprinted from *Rebuilding the House,* by Laurie Graham (Viking Penguin, 1990), copyright Laurie Graham, 1990. Reprinted with permission.

Helping with Valuational Tasks

A fourth area for helping the bereaved has to do with *a need to make sense out of the loss.* The process of finding or making meaning is essential for all human beings, as we have explained in Chapter 9 (see also Cox et al., 2004b; Lamm, 2004). In death and loss, that which had been accepted as a basis for meaning in one's life may have been severely challenged. Mourning initiates the processes of reinvigorating old value frameworks or seeking to construct new ones to take account of the changed realities in our lives.

An example of a parent struggling to find meaning in a difficult loss is found in the book *When Bad Things Happen to Good People* (Kushner, 1981). In this book, Rabbi Harold Kushner described some of the challenges involved in coping with his son's unusual, progressive illness (progeria) and death at a young age. Kushner also focused on the task of finding or making meaning out of the events in his family's life. The conclusions he adopted—mainly that God is not responsible for the bad things that happen to us—have been a source of consolation to many bereaved people.

Some people have such faith or trust in their basic values that they can incorporate a loss directly or at least be patient until meanings begin to clarify themselves. Others must ask repeatedly the ultimate question: Why? Some ways of making meaning are idiosyncratic; many are widely shared among human beings. Some bereaved persons find consolation in the convictions they share with a religious community; others turn to a personal philosophy or set of spiritual beliefs. Sometimes answers from any or all of these sources are not readily available. Almost all human beings need some conviction that life truly is worth living even when death has taken someone who is loved.

Programs Designed to Facilitate One-to-One Intervention to Help the Bereaved

Beyond these guidelines for helping bereaved persons with their tasks of mourning, there are several programs in our society that seek to prepare individuals to help the bereaved in one-to-one relationships. A good example of community-based programs that seek to foster *one-to-one helping relationships* is the Widow-to-Widow program, which began in the Boston area (Silverman, 1986, 2004, 2007). Focusing on a public health perspective and the pivotal idea of bereavement as *transition* (in this case, from wife to widow), this program turned to widows themselves to ask how they viewed and dealt with their needs. As a result, the Widow-to-Widow program was established on the premise—later called *mutual help*—that those who had themselves been bereaved might be in the best position to help others in similar situations. The program was distinguished by the fact that help was offered to every newly widowed person in a community, not only to those who sought it out. Potential helpers (individuals who had been widowed at least two years) gathered to develop their own strategies and procedures with the help of a consultant. The program itself helped to define many of the basic ways of helping bereaved persons. As Silverman (1986, p. 210) noted, "mutual help generally has an advantage over professional help since it does not treat a person as ill and has an image-enhancing emphasis on learning from peers." Emphases on mutual help can also be found in support groups for the bereaved whose leaders are experienced bereaved persons, rather than professionals, such as The Compassionate Friends (see Chapter 11).

Other examples of supportive one-to-one helping relationships for the bereaved are those provided by the clergy, church visitors, faith-based social committees, and parish nurses. A prominent example of a faith-based program that seeks to foster such one-to-one relationships is found in the Stephen Ministry (named after a person in the Christian scriptures, Acts 6–8, who provided care to suffering persons). The Stephen Ministries organization (2045 Innerbelt Business Center Drive, St. Louis, MO 63114-5765; tel. 314-428-2600; www.stephenministries.com) identifies itself as a Christian, transdenominational ministry that provides leadership training through seven-day courses, print and other resources, and ongoing support for Stephen Leaders in enrolled congregations and other organizations. In turn, the leaders prepare members of their organization to be Stephen Ministers who provide direct one-to-one care to troubled individuals. Since its inception in 1975, this program estimates that it has served more than 9,000 congregations in more than 100 Christian denominations in all 50 states, 9 Canadian provinces, and 21 other countries. This program also estimates that it has trained more than 50,000 Stephen Leaders and more than 450,000 Stephen Ministers to serve the needs of persons who are hurting in various ways. Stephen Ministers and members of Widow-to-Widow programs seek to make themselves available to bereaved persons on an individual basis in ways that are consistent with the helping guidelines outlined in this chapter.

🐦 Facilitating Uncomplicated Grief: Grief Counseling

Thus far, we have been describing suggestions for "walking alongside" the bereaved person as a fellow human being or fellow griever (see Personal Insights 10.4). This reflects our view that grief and mourning are most often normal and uncomplicated. They are adequately served by caring and thoughtful individuals and by the social programs that we have described. Professional intervention is not normally required although it may be helpful.

When professional intervention is indicated, Worden (2002) has proposed an important distinction between *grief counseling* and *grief therapy.* The former has to do with helping or facilitating the work of bereaved persons who are coping with normal or uncomplicated grief and mourning; the latter designates more specialized techniques used to help people with abnormal or complicated grief reactions. In helping bereaved persons, one must remain alert for manifestations of complicated grief reactions (Cox et al., 2004a). When those appear, individuals should be referred to appropriate resources for grief therapy (Rando, 1993; Sprang & McNeil, 1995). However, one must not misinterpret normal grief reactions as abnormal or pathological reactions, which would be to misunderstand bereaved persons and to over-professionalize the help they need.

Most often, grief counseling takes the form of a one-to-one intervention with bereaved persons. As such, it can be offered by anyone who is properly prepared and qualified for this work. As a professional intervention to help persons who are coping with uncomplicated grief and mourning, grief counseling might be offered by psychologists, social workers, clergy, nurses, physicians, counselors, and funeral directors. It is important to note, however, that not all professionals are equally

---

PERSONAL INSIGHTS 10.4

For a Time of Sorrow

I share with you the agony of your grief,
    The anguish of your heart finds echo in my own.
I know I cannot enter all you feel
    Nor bear with you the burden of your pain;
I can but offer what my love does give:
    The strength of caring,
    The warmth of one who seeks to understand
    The silent storm-swept barrenness of so great a loss.
This I do in quiet ways,
    That on your lonely path
    You may not walk alone.

Source: From *Meditations of the Heart,* by Howard Thurman. Copyright © 1953, 1981 by Anne Thurman. Reprinted by permission of Beacon Press, Boston.

competent as grief counselors. Also, there has been a recent controversy in the literature about whether or not formal grief counseling is actually effective (or perhaps even harmful) and, if so, for whom (Allumbaugh & Hoyt, 1999; Jordan & Neimeyer, 2003; Larson & Hoyt, 2007a, 2007b; Neimeyer, 2000). Productive grief counseling grows out of caring communities, to which it adds formal understanding of experiences in bereavement and mourning as well as skill in helping individuals with their own coping or problem-solving processes. For such counseling, Worden (2002) identified the following ten principles as guidelines. Many of these principles are also relevant to nonprofessional ways of helping the bereaved.

1. *Help the Bereaved Person Actualize the Loss.* In contrast to the sense of unreality that often accompanies bereavement, this principle recommends an effort "to come to a more complete awareness that the loss actually has occurred and that the person is dead and will not return" (Worden, 2002, pp. 56–57). This is one reason why it is so important to identify the bodies of those killed in plane crashes, natural disasters, war, or terrorist attacks, as was demonstrated so vividly after the collapse of the World Trade Center towers on September 11, 2001. Also, one can simply assist those who are bereaved to talk about their losses. Empathic listening and open-ended questions encourage repeated review of the circumstances of the loss, as do visits to the gravesite. Immediate family members may be familiar with these details and can often become impatient with their repetition. However, as Shakespeare wrote in *Macbeth* (IV, iii: 209), bereaved persons need to "give sorrow words." A caring helper can aid this important process of growing in awareness of loss and in appreciation of its impact. Still, one must not push the bereaved too forcefully or too quickly to grasp the reality of a death if it appears that they are not yet ready to deal with it. One must follow his or her own cues (see Personal Insights 10.5; but note how even this very sensitive expression of grief and mourning assumes a framework in "the stages of grief").

2. *Help the Bereaved Person to Identify and Express Feelings.* Many bereaved individuals may not recognize unpleasant feelings like guilt, anxiety, fear, helplessness, or sadness, or they may be unable to express their feelings and other reactions to loss in ways that facilitate constructive mourning. A helper can aid bereaved persons to be aware of their reactions to loss and then enable those reactions to find an appropriate focus. For example, some persons may find themselves blaming caregivers who were unable to prevent the death. Some may be angry at others who are also bereaved but who appear not to be very affected by the death. Still others are angry at themselves for what they have or have not done. Finally, some people are angry (and this is often difficult to admit) at the deceased for dying and leaving the bereaved person behind to face many problems. Thus, Caine (1975) berated her deceased husband for leaving her unprepared, as she felt, to cope with many challenges in life and to raise their children alone.

    Questions like "What do you miss about him?" and "What don't you miss about him?" may help the person find some balance between positive and negative feelings. Unrealistic guilt that may be experienced as part of the overall grief reaction may respond to reality testing and lead to the realization that "We did everything we could have done." Many (but not all)

A Letter to My Family and Friends

Thank you for not expecting too much from me this holiday season.

It will be our first Christmas without our child and I have all I can do coping with the "spirit" of the holiday on the radio, TV, in the newspapers and stores. We do not feel joyous, and trying to pretend this Christmas is going to be like the last one will be impossible because we are missing one.

Please allow me to talk about my child if I feel the need. Don't be uncomfortable with my tears. My heart is breaking and the tears are a way of letting out my sadness.

I plan to do something special in memory of my child. Please recognize my need to do this in order to keep our memories alive. My fear is not that I'll forget, but that you will.

Please don't criticize me if I do something that you don't think is normal. I'm a different person now and it may take a long time before this different person reaches an acceptance of my child's death.

As I survive the stages of grief, I will need your patience and support, especially during these holiday times and the "special" days throughout the year.

Thank you for not expecting too much from me this holiday season.

Love,

A bereaved parent

Source: From "A Letter to My Family and Friends" in M. Cleckley, E. Estes, and P. Norton (Eds.), *We Need Not Walk Alone: After the Death of a Child,* Second Edition, p. 180. Copyright © 1992 The Compassionate Friends. Reprinted with permission.

bereaved persons may need to be gently encouraged to express, rather than repress, their sadness and crying. Recognizing strong feelings like anger and blame may help grievers begin to put them into perspective and move on. Similarly, it can be comforting to acknowledge that one did do some positive things prior to the death and may still be able to act in some effective ways even at a time when other things are unsettled or out of control. However, grievers must find their own comfort and forgiveness; helpers only facilitate the process and must try to do so with sensitivity and care.

3. *Assist Living without the Deceased.* The helper can assist bereaved persons to address problems or make their own decisions. Because it may be difficult to exercise good judgment during acute grief, bereaved persons are often advised not to make major life-changing decisions at such times, such as those involved in selling property, changing jobs, or relocating. Thus, a central lesson in Judy Blume's novel for young readers, *Tiger Eyes* (1981), is the realization that moving from Atlantic City (where her father was killed in the holdup of his 7-Eleven store) to live with her aunt in Los Alamos was ultimately not a productive way for a teenage girl, her mother, and her younger brother to cope with their grief and with each other.

Nevertheless, the role of the helper is not to take over problems and decision making for the bereaved. Therefore, when issues arise concerning the making of independent decisions (such as how to deal with sexual needs in bereavement, which may range from needs to be touched or held to problems in attaining intimacy with a new person), the helper's main role is only to assist the person in the process of making decisions. This is often best accomplished in a validating and nonjudgmental way. Enabling the bereaved to acquire new and effective coping skills empowers those who may perceive themselves to be powerless in their bereavement.

4. *Help Find Meaning in the Loss.* Finding meaning in the death of a loved one or in any other important loss in one's life is very much an individual project for a bereaved person, as we noted in Chapter 9. Helpers cannot simply assign meanings to a significant loss or determine what that loss will mean for the individual. Nevertheless, helpers can assist individuals as they search for a meaning that they can live with or reassign meanings to the changed world in which they now live. Some people find comfort in religious or spiritual convictions that assure them in particular terms or in a general way that some meaning does exist. Others explain why a loss occurred in terms of the way the deceased person had behaved. Still others view losses as events from which they themselves can learn something. Even when a satisfactory reason cannot

Children and adolescents need someone to grieve with, too.

The Hospice of the Florida Suncoast

be assigned to a loss, many find meaning in activities related to the manner of the death that took the loved one away from them. For example, many establish a memorial or a scholarship in the name of the deceased person, whereas others lobby to minimize handgun violence or drunk driving so that their loved one's death will not have been in vain and in the hope of preventing similar deaths in the future that seem so senseless and unnecessary.

5. *Facilitate Emotional Relocation of the Deceased.* This principle is not only or not always about encouraging the bereaved to form new relationships (see Personal Insights 9.4 in Chapter 9). As time passes, that may be appropriate. However, it is important not to do so too quickly in ways that inhibit adequate mourning. The central point of this principle is to "help survivors find a new place in their life for the lost loved one, a place that will allow the survivor to move forward with life and form new relationships" (Worden, 2002, p. 64). This principle (along with others in this list) is well illustrated by "linking objects" that facilitate recognition of loss, expression of grief, restructuring of relationships, and ongoing connectedness. Thus for one son, attending a final game at a baseball stadium (Comiskey Park) in Chicago that was about to be closed revived important recollections of good times with his father, helped him experience and express his grief in ways he had previously avoided, and gave him precious memories to take with him into the future (Krizek, 1992). Restructuring relationships with the deceased does not overthrow, supplant, or dishonor the dead; it encourages bereaved persons to live as well as possible in the future and to live as well as any deceased person who loved and cared for them would have wanted them to live.

6. *Provide Time to Grieve.* It takes time in a rich, many-faceted relationship to restructure attachments and to close doors on aspects of the past that are now over. Intimate relationships develop on many levels and have many ramifications. Mourning, if it is to be adequate to the loss, can be no less complex. Some people regain equilibrium in their lives and quickly return to familiar routines. They may be impatient with a bereaved person who is moving more slowly or finding it more difficult to deal with his or her loss and grief. They may not appreciate how arduous it is to deal with critical anniversaries or the time around 3 to 6 months after the death, when so much support offered during the funeral and the early days of bereavement is no longer readily available. Effective helpers may need to be available over a longer period of time than many people expect, although actual contacts need not always be very frequent.

7. *Interpret "Normal" Behavior.* Many bereaved persons feel that they are "going crazy" or "losing their minds." This is because they may be experiencing things that they usually do not experience in their lives and they may, at least temporarily, be unable to function as well as they have in the past. Help in normalizing grief reactions can be provided by others who are knowledgeable about or experienced with bereavement. Reassurance will be welcomed that unusual experiences, such as extraordinary experiences ("hallucinations"?) or a preoccupation with the deceased, are common in bereavement and as a rule do not indicate that one is actually going crazy. Encouragement of this sort guides and heartens the bereaved in their time of travail.

Joining with others in a ritual to memorialize a loss can contribute to a healthy mourning process.

8. *Allow for Individual Differences.* This is a critical principle for helpers. The death of any one person affects each of his or her loved ones in different ways. Each bereaved person is a unique individual with his or her own relationships to the deceased and his or her own personality and coping skills. Each person mourns in his or her own ways. Help in appreciating the individuality of grief reactions and mourning processes is especially important for families or other groups who lose a member. It is even more critical when two parents try to understand the ways in which each of them may be reacting differently to the death of their child. Just as helpers need to respect the uniqueness of each bereaved person whom they seek to assist, so too bereaved persons should respect the individuality of grief and mourning in other persons who have been impacted by the same loss.

9. *Examine Defenses and Coping Styles.* By drawing the attention of bereaved persons in a gentle and trusting way to their own patterns of coping, helpers may enable the bereaved to recognize, evaluate, and (where necessary) modify their behaviors. This is the gentle work of suggesting different ways

of coping, not so much directly as by enabling the bereaved person (sometimes through a joint effort) to assess his or her own thoughts and behaviors. Questions such as "What seems to help get you through the day?" or "What is the most difficult thing for you to deal with?" may assist the bereaved person to understand how he or she is coping.

10. *Identify Pathology and Refer.* Most people who engage in helping the bereaved are not prepared to deal with complicated grief reactions on their own because most of us do not possess the specialized skills and expertise of a qualified grief therapist (Rando, 1993; Sanders, 1989; Sprang & McNeil, 1995). However, helpers and counselors can remain alert for manifestations of complicated grief and can play an important role in referring those who need them to appropriate resources. This referral is not a failure; it is a responsible recognition of one's own limitations.

🐦 Summary

In this chapter, we reviewed some of the many ways in which individuals can help those who are coping with loss and grief. We noted and explained examples of unhelpful messages to the bereaved, introduced and clarified the concept of disenfranchised grief, and suggested that losses involving animals and pets are often not well appreciated and may be disenfranchised. We also identified helpful ways in which to assist bereaved persons with tasks in mourning. This sort of assistance essentially constitutes a program for "befriending" the bereaved. We then described the Widow-to-Widow program and the Stephen Ministry as examples of community-based and faith-based programs that prepare individuals to help the bereaved on a one-to-one basis. Further, because the principles underlying professional grief counseling are similar to those that guide everyone who tries to help bereaved persons cope with uncomplicated grief and mourning, we explained ten principles for facilitating uncomplicated grieving.

Glossary

Disenfranchised grief: grief or mourning that persons experience when they incur a loss that is not or cannot be openly acknowledged, publicly mourned, or socially supported

Disenfranchisement: may apply to relationships, losses, grievers, grief, or mourning

Five fundamental needs of bereaved persons: social support, nutrition, hydration, exercise, and rest

Grief counseling: helping bereaved persons who are coping with normal or uncomplicated grief and mourning

Grief therapy: helping bereaved persons who are coping with abnormal or complicated grief reactions

Helping bereaved persons with:

  Affective tasks: assisting with efforts to express emotions and feelings associated with a loss or death in a constructive way

Behavioral tasks: assisting with efforts to mark or take notice of a death through some external event or deed, as well as with commemorative activities designed to remember the life of the deceased or the legacies of that life

Cognitive tasks: assisting with efforts to obtain information about the loss or death

Valuational tasks: assisting with efforts to make sense out of the loss

One-to-one intervention to help the bereaved: programs that draw on those who have previously been bereaved or on trained laypersons to help bereaved persons

Pet loss: death, loss, or ending of a relationship with a pet or companion animal

The Stephen Ministry: a Christian, transdenominational program that provides leadership training and support for helpers who provide direct, one-to-one care to troubled individuals

Unhelpful messages often addressed to bereaved persons: typically, these involve attempts to minimize the loss, admonitions not to feel or express in public strong grief reactions, and suggestions to get back to living promptly and not disturb others with one's grief and mourning

Widow-to-Widow programs: mutual help programs in which those who have previously been bereaved (peers) assist newly bereaved persons on a one-to-one basis

Questions for Review and Discussion

1. Think of a time when you experienced the death of someone you loved or the loss of something important in your life. What did you want others to do with or for you at that time?

2. Bereaved persons often report that some individuals were not helpful to them in their bereavement. Think of a time when you needed or sought help from other persons and did not receive it. What factors (e.g., persons, circumstances) prevented you from receiving the help you needed or sought?

3. Think of the losses that you experienced or that you observed (either directly or through the media) others experience in connection with the events of September 11, 2001. What types of losses did you notice, and what were the main characteristics of those losses?

Suggested Readings

For advice about helping oneself or others in grief, see:

Adams, C. A. (2003). *ABC's of Grief: A Handbook for Survivors*.
Attig, T. (2000). *The Heart of Grief: Death and the Search for Lasting Love*.
Fitzgerald, H. (1995). *The Mourning Handbook: A Complete Guide for the Bereaved*.
Grollman, E. A. (Ed.). (1981). *What Helped Me when My Loved One Died*.
Kushner, H. S. (1981). *When Bad Things Happen to Good People*.
Lewis, C. S. (1976). *A Grief Observed*.
Moffat, M. J. (1982). *In the Midst of Winter: Selections from the Literature of Mourning*.

Neimeyer, R. A. (1998). *Lessons of Loss: A Guide to Coping.*
Rando, T. A. (1988b). *How to Go on Living when Someone You Love Dies.*
Schiff, H. S. (1986). *Living through Mourning: Finding Comfort and Hope When a Loved One Has Died.*
Schwiebert, P., & DeKlyen, C. (1999). *Tear Soup: A Recipe for Healing after Loss.*
Smith, H. I. (1999). *A Decembered Grief: Living with Loss when Others Are Celebrating.*
Smith, H. I. (2004a). *Grievers Ask: Answers to Questions about Death and Loss.*
Smith, H. I., & Jeffers, S. L. (2001). *ABC's of Healthy Grieving: Light for a Dark Journey.*

Guidance for professional helpers is provided in the following:

Becvar, D. S. (2003). *In the Presence of Grief: Helping Family Members Resolve Death, Dying, and Bereavement Issues.*
Buell, J. (2006). *The Emotional First Aid Manual.*
Cook, A. S., & Dworkin, D. S. (1992). *Helping the Bereaved: Therapeutic Interventions for Children, Adolescents, and Adults.*
Crenshaw, D. A. (1995). *Bereavement: Counseling the Grieving throughout the Life Cycle.*
Doka, K. J. (Ed.). (1989a). *Disenfranchised Grief: Recognizing Hidden Sorrow.*
Doka, K. J. (Ed.). (2002a). *Disenfranchised Grief: New Directions, Strategies, and Challenges for Practice.*
Hansen, A. (2004). *Responding to Loss: A Resource for Caregivers.*
Hanson, J. C., & Frantz, T. T. (Eds.). (1984). *Death and Grief in the Family.*
Hooyman, N. R., & Kramer, B. J. (2006). *Living through Loss: Interventions across the Life Span.*
Jeffreys, J. S. (2005). *Helping Grieving People—When Tears are Not Enough: A Handbook for Care Providers.*
Rando, T. A. (1984). *Grief, Dying, and Death: Clinical Interventions for Caregivers.*
Rando, T. A. (1993). *Treatment of Complicated Mourning.*
Sanders, C. M. (1992). *Surviving Grief . . . and Learning to Live Again.*
Sprang, G., & McNeil, J. (1995). *The Many Faces of Bereavement: The Nature and Treatment of Natural, Traumatic, and Stigmatized Grief.*
Stewart, M. F. (1999). *Companion Animal Death: A Practical and Comprehensive Guide for Veterinary Practice.*
Thompson, N. (Ed.). (2002). *Loss and Grief: A Guide for Human Service Practitioners.*
Walsh, F., & McGoldrick, M. (Eds.). (2004a). *Living beyond Loss: Death in the Family* (2nd ed.).
Walter, T. (1999). *On Bereavement: The Culture of Grief.*
Webb, N. B. (Ed.). (2004). *Mass Trauma and Violence: Helping Families and Children Cope.*
Weizman, S. G. (2005). *About Mourning: Support and Guidance for the Bereaved.*
Worden, J.W. (2002). *Grief Counseling and Grief Therapy: A Handbook for the Mental Health Practitioner* (3rd ed.).

Selected Web Resources

Some useful search terms include: DISENFRANCHISED GRIEF; GRIEF COUNSELING; GRIEF THERAPY; PET LOSS; STEPHEN MINISTRY; TASKS IN MOURNING; WIDOW-TO-WIDOW PROGRAMS

Visit the book companion website for *Death & Dying, Life & Living, Sixth Edition,* at academic.cengage.com/psychology/corr for all URLs and live links to the following *organizational and other Internet sites:*

American Counseling Association

Association for Clinical Pastoral Education

Association for Pet Loss and Bereavement

Association for Professional Chaplains

International Association of Pet Cemeteries & Crematories

National Mental Health Association

Petloss.com

Samaritans International

Stephen Ministries

Widowed Persons Service (WPS), American Association of Retired Persons (AARP)

CHAPTER 11

Coping with Loss and Grief: Funeral Practices and Other Ways Communities Can Help

© Vincent Laforet/*The New York Times*

Objectives of This Chapter

◆ To explain the role of ritual and community support in helping individuals cope with life crises

◆ To describe four types of community programs designed to help persons who are coping with loss and grief, including:
   1. Funeral practices and memorial rituals
   2. Aftercare programs in the funeral industry
   3. Hospice bereavement follow-up programs
   4. Support groups for the bereaved

Social Institutions That Provided Support during One Woman's Mourning

Stella Bridgman (see Chapters 9 and 10) found consolation at her son's funeral. Although his life in recent years had seemed so troubled, she was surprised that so many of his friends, schoolmates, and co-workers came to the visitation. They told her about what he had meant to them and about their memories of helpful things he had done. When her son was buried next to his father, Stella believed he was finally at peace.

At the funeral and for many months afterwards, the aftercare specialist at the funeral home checked in with Stella from time to time, gave her short pamphlets on loss and grief, suggested some books that she could read, and was available whenever she had questions. Although her son had not been in hospice care, the aftercare specialist referred her to a local hospice bereavement program so that she might also draw on the resources it had to offer.

Four months after her son's death, Stella felt that she was only now experiencing the full impact of his loss. With the encouragement of the aftercare specialist, a friend took her to a meeting of a local chapter of The Compassionate Friends, an international organization offering support groups for bereaved parents. Stella had heard about this group, but she had thought that it would be too intimidating to go to a meeting on her own. She wondered: Will the group be alien or welcoming? Will it be helpful or not? What if my reactions overwhelm me or I just cannot tolerate the group experience? What if I am physically or emotionally unable to drive home? The presence and support of her friend helped to reduce many of these anxieties.

The group did not draw back when Stella expressed her pain, anger, guilt, and other strong feelings. Members of the group permitted her to give vent to such feelings, and they acknowledged the normalcy of her reactions. Group members also recognized the appropriateness of her questions and validated her experiences as a bereaved parent.

At one meeting, Stella said she felt like she was going crazy. Members of the group agreed that they had often felt that way, too. Stella expressed amazement that other bereaved parents could speak of their dead children without collapsing in tears. How could they go forward with their lives, get through the holidays, and even find it possible to laugh once in a while? Stella tried to tell herself that if these people had also walked "in the valley of the shadow of death" and were now able to find some way to live on, perhaps she could, too. But she could not see how to do that yet.

Over time, just by being themselves, these other bereaved parents showed Stella that one can survive horrendous loss and cope effectively with grief reactions, that life can once again become livable. Also, without needing to offer her any advice, the members of the group served as role models and provided Stella with options from which she might choose in determining how to live her own life.

Life Crises and Rituals

Rituals play important roles in the lives of most human beings. Anthropologists and others have studied ritual for nearly a century using various definitions of the key term. For example, Mitchell (1977, p. xi) described *ritual* as "a general word for corporate symbolic activity." The corporate or communal symbolic activity involved in ritual generally has two components: it involves *external (bodily) actions,* such as gestures, postures, and movements, which symbolize interior realities; and it is *social*—that is, the community is usually involved in ritual activity (Douglas, 1970).

One can identify ritual practices of this sort in all human societies. Van Gennep (1961) emphasized the links between ritual and *life crises* or important turning points in human life, such as childbirth, initiation into adulthood, marriage, and death. Because crises involve a significant change or disruption in human life, they threaten the invasion of chaos. As a result, crises are "dangerous opportunities," as we noted in Chapter 9. Ritual can contribute some degree of ordering or orientation to such events. To the extent that ritual achieves that goal, it helps make the unfamiliar more familiar by providing guidance as to how one should act in these unusual (but not always unanticipated) circumstances. In other words, ritual seeks to "tame" the strange or the unusual experiences in human life to some degree.

Since death is one of the most imposing invasions of disorder and chaos in human life, it is not surprising that throughout history humans have made efforts to bring order into lives that have been affected by death (Bendann, 1930; Puckle, 1926). Archaeologists and anthropologists believe that some of the most ancient artifacts they have discovered had something to do with rituals associated with death and burial. Also, as one moves forward from prehistoric to more recent times, rituals associated with death are found in every societal death system. As Margaret

An American ritual for military personnel who have died includes presenting a flag to the bereaved.

© C.J. Gunther/AFP/Getty Images

Mead (1973, pp. 89–90) wrote: "I know of no people for whom the fact of death is not critical, and who have no ritual by which to deal with it."

Nevertheless, many individuals in our society make efforts to avoid ritualized practices and appear to act as if they have no need for ritual. They do not come to graduation ceremonies, for example, or they try to avoid attending funerals. As a result, some have suggested that American society is making an effort to do away with all ritualized behavior. That is hardly accurate. In fact, evidence of the felt need for ritual at key moments in our lives can be found in the actions of numerous individuals and communities in our society. For example, the death of a member of the military, a police officer, or a firefighter is often followed by formal and elaborate funeral, burial, and memorial activities. Officers attend the funeral in full-dress uniforms, flags are folded in precise ways and presented to surviving family members, buglers may play "Taps," and a firing squad may fire a volley into the air in a deliberate way. Similarly, sports teams often wear black armbands after the death of a teammate and a jersey may be "retired" in honor of that individual. In some communities, the death of a prominent or specially admired member may lead to flags being flown at half-staff and a moment of silence being observed at a social activity. Even small social groups, such as a few friends or family members, may be driven to erect an informal roadside memorial to mark the spot at which a loved one or close friend was killed in a motor vehicle accident (Clark & Cheshire, 2004; Clark & Franzmann, 2006; Everett, 2002; Haney et al., 1997; Reid & Reid, 2001). In these and numerous other examples, we find that many bereaved people do not suffer alone and in silence. Instead, they take action to draw attention to what has

A private roadside memorial . . . replaced by a standardized state memorial.

(right and left) Courtesy of Clyde M. Nabe

#9 Some Criticisms of Roadside Memorials and Responses

Roadside memorials originally arose in Latin-American culture. They have appeared in the southwestern United States (Texas, New Mexico, and Arizona) for nearly 200 years, and in recent decades their use has spread throughout the country (including Alaska and Hawaii).

Collins and Rhine (2003) studied these memorials and reported that they usually appear at the site of a traffic fatality but can be found also at sites where drownings, homicides, or suicides have occurred. Roadside memorials most frequently appear when there has been a sudden and violent death of a younger person, and they may be on public or private land. Those who are bereaved apparently spontaneously place their roadside memorials as near as possible to the site where the death occurred. Indeed, such bereaved persons often use the memorial to mark the site as "sacred" to them in some sense; this is clear particularly when some religious symbol (usually a cross) is used as part of the marker. However, Collins and Rhine also found that many other objects have been used as parts of these memorials, such as "flowers, notes, poems, photos, music tapes, CDs, scarves, pinwheels, balloons" and when young children were the victims, "teddy bears, dolls, toys, or sports equipment" (pp. 230–231).

The memorials are not uncontroversial. Collins and Rhine identified four main criticisms of them. The first concerns maintenance of the right-of-way along the road. Because these memorials may interfere with that maintenance, some states remove them, whereas other states offer to replace the spontaneous memorial with a state-sanctioned one. State-approved memorials are often plainer and less personal than the spontaneous ones erected by the bereaved individuals. (One example of the difference between these two forms of memorials can be seen in the photos on p. 282.)

A second objection to these memorials concerns safety issues. Some claim that roadside memorials are distracting to drivers and thus constitute a danger at the very site that the marker indicates is one where a death has occurred. (It should be noted that Collins and Rhine found that most people who erect roadside memorials do not intend their markers to serve as a warning to other persons.) However, as Collins and Rhine remarked, these memorials are usually small and are easily overlooked, and as potential distractions they are of less significance compared with the number and size of the advertisements we commonly encounter alongside our roadways.

Other people find roadside memorials to be a form of visual pollution. Given the sorts of objects placed at these sites, some people find these memorials to be aesthetically displeasing. However, Collins and Rhine found that most people they interviewed were inclined to be sensitive to the grief of the bereaved and accept some visual "blight" for their sake.

The last criticism Collins and Rhine identified concerned the fact that the memorials are frequently located in public space and on public property. Since they also often use religious symbols as part of the marker, some people have argued that this is a violation of the separation of church and state. Those who oppose roadside memorials erected by private individuals suggest that any such marker should be placed there by the state, presumably with no religious symbols. But such state-approved markers can seem sterile and not very empathetic to the grief of those who have been bereaved by a death.

happened, to let their loss and their grief be known, to speak to the public, and to engage the community in their mourning—whether or not the community always approves of their actions (see Issues for Critical Reflection #9).

However, not every instance of ritual is equally valuable or effective for all bereaved persons or for all communities. Many cultural groups have their own rituals (see Chapter 5 for some examples). Persons who are not members of those groups may not find comfort in such rituals, partly because they do not understand the meaning of the various components of the ritual. Even members of such a group may find little solace in the ritual because it represents views they do not hold or fails to address what they are experiencing.

In the next four sections of this chapter, we offer:

◆ A description of typical elements in contemporary American funeral practices

◆ Brief comments on contrasting views concerning the value of these practices

◆ An analysis of three central tasks associated with such rituals

◆ An account of the roles of cemeteries and selected memorial activities in helping bereaved persons

🌿 Typical Elements in Contemporary American Funeral Practices

Funeral practices in the American death system can take many forms. In this section, we describe these practices in a general way, while remaining aware that they may differ depending on religious, cultural, and ethnic perspectives, or simply because of local customs. Typical elements usually found in many contemporary American funeral practices are:

◆ Removal of the body from the place of death

◆ Preparing the body for viewing or final disposition

◆ A viewing of the body

◆ A funeral service

◆ Delivery of the body for final disposition

◆ In-ground burial or aboveground entombment in a mausoleum or crypt

As we learned in Chapter 2, most people in the United States today die in some type of public institution. When that occurs, staff members typically notify the family if they are not already present, help make arrangements to clean and care for the body until those who need to do so can arrive, assist in making contact with a local funeral director, and organize the removal of the body from the place of death. Members of a hospice or home care team often do much the same when a death occurs at home.

It has been noted that many Americans are not very familiar with the work of funeral service personnel. In fact, their role is fairly straightforward. To begin with, they usually transport the body to a funeral home, while arranging for a death certificate to be properly completed and exchanged for a permit to bury the body or otherwise dispose of it. In some cases involving "direct disposition," the funeral director may simply transport the body to a crematorium or to another appropriate destination (such as the anatomy department of a local medical school) for donation to medical education and research. In all of these cases, efforts will be made to show respect for the body as the remains of someone valued as a human being and to act in accordance with the religious or philosophical beliefs that an individual and his or her social group hold about life and death (Ball, 1995; Habenstein & Lamers, 1974; Kephart, 1950).

Most bodies in the American death system are washed, embalmed, dressed, and prepared by funeral service personnel for a "viewing," "visitation," or "wake," as it may variously be described. In some cultural groups family members or representatives of the group may carry out or take part in this work. *Embalming* grew in popularity in the United States after the Civil War as a practice that made it possible to ship dead bodies back home for burial from distant battlefields (Mayer, 1996). The most celebrated example of this occurred in the case of Abraham Lincoln, whose body was shipped by rail from Washington, D.C., where he was assassinated, to Springfield, Illinois, for burial. This journey took place during a warm part of the year when rapid decomposition of the body was likely, especially as the funeral train made many stops along the way to serve the needs of grief-stricken Americans. If normal biological processes of decomposition had not been delayed, Mr. Lincoln's body would have become an object of social repugnance long before the train reached its destination.

Embalming today involves the removal of blood and other bodily fluids from a corpse and their replacement with artificial preservatives that may help to retard decomposition and color the skin. Embalming may or may not be accompanied by efforts to restore the cosmetic appearance of the corpse. No state law or federal regulation requires embalming to be done, unless certain conditions are present. For instance, embalming may be required if the body is to be transported on a common carrier, such as a train or airplane.

In the contemporary American death system, embalming is mainly practiced to permit viewing of the body during a wake or visitation in some public gathering (e.g., at a funeral home) or in cases of a funeral with an open casket (Iserson, 1994; Raether, 1989). Advocates of embalming argue that it prevents the spread of disease by disinfecting the corpse and neutralizing contaminants in discarded blood and bodily fluids. Of course, much the same could be achieved by direct cremation, immediate burial in a sealed container, or refrigerating the body. In fact, embalming is most often undertaken to slow decay in the bodily tissues of the corpse. This provides time for relatives and friends of the deceased to gather from a distance in a large and dispersed society, and it makes possible viewing of the body once they have come together.

During a *visitation* or *viewing* in our society, the casket containing the body is often open, either fully or at least so as to reveal the upper half of the body. In some instances, the casket may be closed—sometimes as a matter of preference, at other times because of the condition of the corpse. Typically, mourners approach the casket, sometimes to say a brief prayer or for a moment of reflection. Often, they return again and again to the casket to stare at, touch, or kiss the dead body. They seem to be saying final farewells and impressing a last image into their minds, even as the cold, rigid, and non-lifelike features of the corpse convey to them in a silent but forceful way the realities of its differences from a living body. As they come

Taking part in funeral rituals can help oneself and others in coping with loss and grief.

together for a visitation or funeral, participants often find themselves sharing stories about the deceased or reminiscing in ways that help locate and secure that person (and themselves) in the history and memory of the community of those who were touched by the deceased person.

Following a funeral or religious service, *disposition or disposal of bodies* in the United States is typically carried out in one of the following ways: burial in the ground; entombment in some sort of crypt, vault, or mausoleum above the ground; cremation and subsequent disposition of the remains of that process; or donation to a medical or other institution for dissection or other similar purposes, such as scientific research or professional education (Habenstein & Lamers, 1962; Iserson, 1994).

In-ground burial is still the most common form of body disposal in the United States. Generally, the body is buried within several days of the death, although some groups such as Orthodox Jews and Muslims seek to bury prior to sundown on the day of the death or at least within 24 hours. The amount of time between death and burial in our society is usually related to the time needed to prepare the body, make necessary arrangements, and—above all—gather together family members and other important persons from distant parts of the country. *Entombment* in some type of aboveground structure is essentially a variant on in-ground burial.

In the case of burial, the classic picture of this mode of disposition of the body in America would describe a formal procession of vehicles from a funeral home or place of worship to a cemetery, followed by a gathering of mourners around the casket at the burial site, brief prayers or last words about the deceased, lowering of the casket into a grave, individual tossing of symbolic shovelfuls of dirt over the casket, and filling in of the grave. In recent years, formal processions of vehicles have diminished, mourners are likely to be encouraged to leave the gravesite before the casket is lowered into a vault or grave liner (a concrete form placed within the grave that is designed to protect the casket and prevent settling of the ground), the vault is sealed closed, and the grave is filled in with dirt and covered with grass. Sometimes, cemeteries have built chapels and prefer that the last rites be performed there, rather than at the gravesite. These practices mainly have to do with allocation of workload among the cemetery's personnel and a desire not to risk upsetting mourners as workers go about such activities as enclosing the casket within a vault or grave liner, lowering it into the grave, and refilling the grave.

Cremation is often popularly thought of as an alternative to embalming, viewing, and a funeral, but it may also follow those activities as a step between them and final disposition. The process involves placing the body in some sort of container and reducing its size through the application of intense heat (Jupp, 2006; Prothero, 2001). The container need not be a casket; crematories typically only require that the body be turned over to them in an enclosed, rigid, combustible container, which can be handled easily and safely. The body and its container are then heated to 1,600–1,800 degrees Fahrenheit for a period of 2 to 2 ½ hours. Because most of the human body is water, the water evaporates. At the high temperatures reached during cremation, the rest of the soft tissues are consumed by spontaneous combustion. The effect of this process is to reduce the size of bodily remains in a rapid and significant fashion. The residue is primarily ash and those fragments of dense bone that have not been vaporized by heat. When these remains have cooled, they are collected and then usually ground up or pulverized into a coarse powder. Subsequently, the person responsible for the cremated remains or *cremains* may choose what to do with this residue. For example, the cremains may be scattered over water or enclosed in an urn or other permanent container. The urn may then be kept by the bereaved, buried in the ground, or placed in a niche (a small compartment) in a mausoleum-like columbarium. In recent years, some have arranged for a portion of the cremains to be flown into space or permanently entombed under water as part of artificial reef structures (consult Eternal Reefs, tel. 1-888-423-7333 or www.eternalreefs.com).

Sloane (1991, p. 220) observed that "the most remarkable changes in the American cemetery industry in the last forty years have been the resurgence of entombment as an important method of disposal and the steady, recently spectacular, rise of cremation." Entombment in an aboveground space may reflect such variables as soil conditions (e.g., a high water table as in some parts of New Orleans), which make in-ground burial difficult or impossible, a desire to save land space, or a preference for final disposition in a structure that is enclosed, dry, heated, and air conditioned.

In the United States in 2004, 1,858 crematories conducted 740,695 cremations. That figure represented nearly 30.9 percent of the nearly 2.4 million deaths in our society in 2004. The proportion of deaths involving cremation has been increasing each year recently. That proportion is projected to increase to over 38 percent by the year 2010 and to over one-half of all deaths by the year 2025 (Cremation Association of North America, 2007; www.cremationassociation.org). The largest numbers of cremations took place in the states of California, Florida, and New York.

Some contemporary Americans prefer to *donate their bodies for teaching or research purposes.* If so, arrangements usually must be made well ahead of time with the receiving institution because there does not seem to have been a shortage of such donations in our society in recent years. Also, careful preservation of the body is important for this purpose, and the techniques required to prevent decay are considerably more stringent than those used in a typical embalming procedure. Thus,

Typical Cost Items for Funeral Services and Merchandise

SERVICE	INCLUDES
Basic services of funeral director and staff, and overhead costs	Having personnel available 24 hours a day, 365 days a year to respond to initial call; conducting arrangements conference; planning the funeral; consulting with family and clergy; shelter of remains; preparing and filing necessary notices; obtaining necessary authorizations and permits; coordinating with cemetery, crematory, and other third parties; plus a proportionate share of basic overhead costs (e.g., facility maintenance, equipment and inventory costs, insurance and administration expenses)
Embalming	Usually not required by law, but may be necessary if certain funeral arrangements (e.g., viewing, delay before funeral, transportation of the body over a long distance, and with certain diseases) are selected
Other preparation of the body	For example: restoration, cosmetology, washing and disinfection, manicuring
Transfer of deceased to the funeral home	Usually based on a stipulated distance, with added charges beyond that distance
Use of facilities and staff for viewing	At the funeral home first day; each added day
Use of facilities and staff for funeral ceremony	At the funeral home; at another location or facility

(continued)

the receiving institution will usually have a formal protocol for body donation and will typically require access to the body shortly after death. Following use of the body for scientific or educational purposes, the elements that remain may be cremated or buried by the institution or returned to next of kin for similar disposition.

An alternative to a traditional funeral is a *memorial service*. Essentially, memorial services incorporate many of the practices that have already been described, but without the presence of a body. Memorial services might be held when a body has been lost at sea or is otherwise unavailable, when the body has been immediately cremated and the cremains scattered, when the body has been donated for medical research or education, or in other similar situations. *Memorial societies* in North America encourage memorial services as a way to reduce costs and to turn away from what they

Typical Cost Items for Funeral Services and Merchandise

SERVICE	INCLUDES
Use of facilities and staff for memorial service	At the funeral home, including folders, book, and acknowledgment cards; at another location; not including these printed materials
Use of equipment and staff at graveside services	
Use of vehicles	Hearse; service/utility car; limousine
Pastoral services; music	
Cemetery plot and/or other charges	
Forwarding/receiving of remains to/from another funeral home	

MERCHANDISE	INCLUDES
	Casket, outer burial container (vault or grave liner), cremation urn, register books, acknowledgment cards, memorial folders, flowers, clothing

SOME ALTERNATIVES:

Direct cremation (basic services of funeral director and staff, proportionate share of overhead costs, removal of remains, transportation to crematory, necessary authorizations, and cremation). Also, alternative containers made of materials like fiberboard or composition materials.

Immediate burial plus casket (basic services of funeral director and staff, proportionate share of overhead costs, removal of remains, transportation to cemetery). With or without casket provided by purchaser.

Source: Based on Canine, 1999, and general price list (effective January 1, 2005) from Costigan-O'Neill Funeral Home, Inc., Pawtucket, Rhode Island.

regard as an inappropriate emphasis on the corpse (Carlson, 1998; Morgan & Morgan, 2001). They do not favor embalming, caskets, and all of the other elements needed to prepare a body for viewing. Instead, they prefer services without the presence of a body that focus on commemorating the life of the person through music, poetry, readings, and personal testimonials.

Although the Federal Trade Commission regulates the funeral industry, we cannot provide a single list of accurate prices for funeral services and associated merchandise because costs vary greatly across the country and by individual funeral home. The simplest way to determine cost is to ask a local funeral home for its price list or to draw

Selected National Resources for Information on Funerals and Related Matters

Cremation Association of North America
401 N. Michigan Avenue, Suite 2200
Chicago, IL 60611
312-245-1077
www.cremationassociation.org

Funeral Consumers Alliance
33 Patchen Road
South Burlington, VT 05403
800-765-0107; www.funerals.org

International Association of Pet Cemeteries & Crematories
5055 Route 11, P.O. Box 163
Ellenburg Depot, NY 12935
518-594-3000; www.iaopc.com

International Cemetery and Funeral Assn.
1895 Preston White Drive, Suite 220
Reston, VA 20191
800-645-7700; 703-391-8400
www.icfa.org

International Order of the Golden Rule
13523 Lakefront Drive
St. Louis, MO 63045
800-637-8030; 314-209-7142
www.ogr.org

Jewish Funeral Directors of America
Seaport Landing 150 Lynnway, Suite 506
Lynn, MA 01902
781-477-9300; www.jfda.org

Monument Builders of North America
3158 S. River Road, Suite 224
Des Plaines, IL 60018
800-233-4472; 847-803-8800
www.monumentbuilders.org

National Catholic Cemetery Conference
710 N. River Road
Des Plaines, IL 60016
847-824-8131; www.ntriplec.com

National Funeral Directors Association
13625 Bishop's Drive
Brookfield, WI 53005-6607
800-228-6332; 414-789-1880
www.nfda.org

National Funeral Directors and Morticians Assn.
3951 Snapfinger Parkway, Suite 570
Decatur, GA 30035
800-434-0958; 404-286-6680
www.nfdma.org

National Selected Morticians
5 Revere Drive, Suite 340
Northbrook, IL 60062
800-323-4219; 847-559-9569
www.nsm.org

Neptune Society
Local contacts in CA, FL, NY, OR, WA
www.neptunesociety.com

up with a funeral director a "pre-need" plan (Bern-Klug et al., 2000). Preplanning is offered by almost all funeral homes in the United States as a way to design a specific plan that suits an individual and to determine what it will cost. In Focus On 11.1, we identify some of the main cost elements that enter into the price of funeral services in the United States. Additional information on American funeral practices can be obtained from local sources (such as funeral homes, memorial societies, cemeteries, crematories) and from the national organizations listed in Focus On 11.2.

One last point about the work of American funeral directors concerns the roles that some of them assume in responding to mass disasters as members of a Disaster Mortuary Operational Response Team (DMORT, 1998). As temporary federal employees in this capacity, DMORT team members establish temporary morgue facilities; assist with victim identification using latent fingerprints, forensic dental pathology, or forensic anthropology methods; and conduct the processing, preparation, and disposition of human remains. The importance of this work was evident in the efforts of a DMORT team following the events of September 11, 2001 (Hazell, 2001).

❧ Contrasting Views Concerning the Value of Contemporary American Funeral Practices

In our large and heterogeneous society, there is a long and diverse history of comments on the value of contemporary American funeral practices. Three basic viewpoints seem to dominate:

◆ Abolish these post-death rituals: This view argues that American funeral and memorial practices represent a kind of fantasized flight from reality (Mitford, 1963, 1998); such rituals should be abandoned; time, energy, and money invested in funerals should be used in some other way.

◆ Modify these rituals: This view holds that typical American funeral practices are overly lavish and expensive; they should be replaced by other social rituals after death, such as less ostentatious *memorial services* conducted without the presence of the body and often held 2 or 3 weeks after the death (Carlson, 1998; Irion, 1991; Morgan & Morgan, 2001); this viewpoint would substitute one form of ritual for another but is not opposed to all death-related ritual.

◆ Continue traditional rituals with minor alterations: This view maintains that these rituals help people make sense of, and bring order out of, what is potentially a disruptive, stressful, chaotic encounter with death (Manning, 2001; Raether, 1989), and they serve a constructive role in grief work (Howarth, 1996; Romanoff & Terenzio, 1998).

Interestingly, existing research on these topics reports both criticisms of the funeral industry from clergy (e.g., Fulton, 1961; Kalish & Goldberg, 1978), together with much satisfaction among the general public (Bolton & Camp, 1987; Fulton, 1978; Kalish & Goldberg, 1980; Marks & Calder, 1982). Hyland and Morse (1995) noted that widespread public regard for the comfort offered by funeral service personnel is a striking achievement when one takes into account that most of these services are provided by strangers in circumstances of great stress for the bereaved and during what is usually a relatively short period of contact. Also, research by Canine (1999) concluded that the vast majority of respondents who work in the funeral industry put "service to families" as their first priority. On the basis of this evidence, it cannot be maintained that there is widespread social dissatisfaction with funeral rituals within the American death system or that funeral service practitioners do not act without having the interests of society in mind. Of course, specific individuals and groups must decide about their own participation in funeral rituals and their assessments of these rituals' value. Clearly, opinions may differ in this sensitive area, both on the role of funeral rituals in general and on whether or not a particular funeral ritual provided a useful service in a specific instance.

In the following section, we offer an analysis of three basic tasks that ought to inform productive funeral rituals. Through this analysis, we hope to come to a better understanding of the nature and purposes of funeral rituals and other commemorative activities. We also want to help you determine for yourself whether these rituals are effective in serving significant needs in your life. To that end, note that in planning or taking part in a funeral or other memorial ritual of any kind, it is always appropriate to ask: what do these gestures, these actions, or these words mean or suggest? This question may be difficult to pose when a person is stricken with grief. A better time to think through the rationale for what you might desire in any post-death ritual is before the ritual is needed. Preplanning that takes account of the individual and social tasks to which funeral and memorial rituals can contribute can be helpful in providing a funeral that successfully meets individual, familial, and societal needs.

❧ Three Tasks Associated with Funeral Rituals

Scholarly work by anthropologists and sociologists (Durkheim, 1954; Fulton, 1995; Goody, 1962; Malinowski, 1954; Mandelbaum, 1959) uses the language of *functions* to explain funeral rituals. In this book we encourage proactive approaches in which bereaved and other vulnerable individuals can work to regain control over lives that have been impacted by death. Thus, we prefer to interpret funeral and other memorial rituals through a *task-based approach.* Therefore, we propose that these rituals should help bereaved persons themselves and society in general carry out the following three tasks: (1) to dispose of the body of the deceased in appropriate ways; (2) to contribute to making real the implications of the death; and (3) to assist in reintegration and meaningful ongoing living (Corr, Nabe, & Corr, 1994). We use these tasks here to explain and evaluate elements of funeral and memorial rituals.

Disposition of the Body

The first task to which funeral rituals should contribute is *to dispose of the body of the deceased in appropriate ways.* To fail in this task is to risk violating both social attitudes and community health—not to mention doing harm to oneself. As Staples (1994, p. 255) has written: "The rituals of grief and burial bear the dead away. Cheat those rituals and you risk keeping the dead with you always in forms that you mightn't like. Choose carefully the funerals you miss." In all societies, the manner in which ritual disposition is accomplished requires respect for the body as the remains of someone valued as a human being. Thus, most humans are uncomfortable with allowing a corpse simply to be discarded or left lying around (Iserson, 1994). In addition, dealing with a dead body necessitates behavior in accordance with the religious or philosophical beliefs that an individual and his or her society hold about life and death (Ball, 1995; Kephart, 1950). Disrespect for either of these

Funeral rituals can be important outlets for grief.

can result in serious conflict, as dramatized in Sophocles' *Antigone*. In that play, Antigone is concerned that the body of her dead brother must be buried; by contrast, King Creon is concerned that burial of the body will improperly show respect for a rebellious subject.

The question of how to dispose of a human body appropriately in contemporary American society is remarkably complex. Since the United States is a large and diverse society, one finds within it a wide range of religious or philosophical beliefs about the nature of the person, the universe, or any afterlife. Together with or apart from such beliefs, custom is often the guiding force in what many Americans do about disposition of dead bodies. For example, decisions about embalming, a "visitation" (with or without a "viewing" of the body), whether to have a religious or nonreligious funeral or memorial service, cremation, and committal of the body or its cremains to earth burial are often made largely on the basis of the beliefs to which one adheres or the customary practices with which one is familiar. The key point in all of these decisions is the felt need to dispose of human bodies in what is viewed as a respectful and appropriate manner.

Making Real the Implications of Death

A second task addressed by funeral and memorial rituals is *to contribute to making real the implications of death*. Sometimes this is described as seeking "realization" or achieving "separation" from the deceased. This task may not be as easy as it might seem to someone who is not personally involved in the process. In fact, disentangling realistic and unrealistic or symbolic and literal elements in bereavement shortly after a death is difficult for many persons.

Gordon Parks: The Funeral

After many snows I was home again.
Time had whittled down to mere hills
The great mountains of my childhood.
Raging rivers I once swam trickled now
                    like gentle streams.
And the wide road curving on to China or
            Kansas City or perhaps Calcutta,
Had withered to a crooked path of dust
Ending abruptly at the country burying ground.
Only the giant who was my father
                    remained the same.
A hundred strong men strained beneath his coffin
When they bore him to his grave.

That is why it is so important to identify any part of the remains of a deceased person, as was made clear in the strenuous efforts to recover body parts from the rubble of the World Trade Center towers after September 11, 2001. That also explains comments from some bereaved persons in New York City who described others as lucky because at least they had a body to bury. If a bereaved individual is unable to accomplish this task of making real the implications of death, that person's life may be disrupted in some serious ways. Thus, it may be useful to engage in actions that help in the process of recognizing the permanent separation of the dead from the living (in this life, at least).

The funeral can be of assistance in this process of psychological separation of the bereaved from the deceased (Turner & Edgley, 1976). Some have argued that seeing the dead body may help to make the death real. They bolster this argument with comments to the effect that bereaved persons often face special challenges in realization when there is no body—for example, when it has been lost at sea, never returned from combat, or consumed in a horrific explosion or fire. Even the presence of some token remains in a closed casket, so it seems, can be helpful to the bereaved (see Personal Insights 11.2).

If in fact funeral ritual is to help with making real the implications of death, then presumably some of the actions and events associated with it should point to the permanence of the separation of the dead from the living. Some have criticized contemporary American funeral practices as failing to support this separation from the deceased. For example, it has been argued that the use of cosmetics and the expensive linings of caskets both seem to promote an image of life rather than of death (Harmer, 1963, 1971; Mitford, 1963, 1998). If it is important to help the bereaved make the death real for themselves, then contributing to the appearance that the dead person is "asleep," head on a pillow, lying on a mattress, surrounded

A Wife's Description of What Was Recovered after the Death of Her Husband

My most enduring memory of my husband, Ronald Breitweiser, will be his final words to me, "Sweets, I'm fine, I don't want you to worry, I love you." Ron uttered those words while he was watching men and women jump to their deaths from the top of Tower One. Four minutes later, his Tower was hit by United Flight 175. I never spoke to my husband, Ron, again.

I don't really know what happened to him. I don't know whether he jumped or he choked to death on smoke. I don't know whether he sat curled up in a corner watching the carpet melt in front of him, knowing that his own death was soon to come, or if he was alive long enough to be crushed by the buildings when they collapsed. These are the images that haunt me at night when I put my head to rest on his pillow.

I do know that the dream I had envisioned, that I so desperately needed to believe—that he was immediately turned to ash and floated up to the heavens—was simply not his fate. I know this because his wedding band was recovered from ground zero with a part of his left arm. The wedding band is charred and scratched, but still perfectly round and fully intact. I wear it on my right hand, and it will remain there until I die.

Source: Kristen Breitweiser, Co-chairperson of the September 11 Advocates, Testimony on September 18, 2002, before the House/Senate Joint Inquiry into Intelligence Community Activities before and after the Terrorist Attacks of September 11, 2001 (as cited in Graham, 2004, p. 171).

by beautiful bed linens, may be counterproductive—or so we are told. The tension that seems to be operating here may be between the task of making real the implications of a death and the desire to offer the bereaved a final, comforting "memory image" of the body of their loved one. Perhaps the challenge is to achieve both of these goals in satisfactory ways.

Some critics (such as Morgan & Morgan, 2001) have argued that many aspects of contemporary American funeral practices draw too much attention to the *body* itself. On this view, making real the implications of death is concerned primarily with taking leave of the *person* as part of an overall process of restructuring relationships with that person. Because a person is not only a body, or so this argument goes, it is the loss of the person, not his or her body, that is the primary concern. In this sense, the gathering of family and friends is a social validation of significant relationships and the reality of the death.

Issues involved in realization and separation also arise at the place of burial. Sometimes mourners are encouraged to leave the gravesite before the body is lowered into the grave. In other cases, cemeteries have encouraged mourners to perform any last rites and take leave of the body at a chapel on their grounds, rather than at the gravesite. One can understand some of the motivations behind these practices, such as to allow the cemetery employees to complete their work at their own pace and out of sight of tense mourners, but sending mourners away also distances them from the realities of the death and may thus run counter to the desired work of making real the implications of the death.

A second set of criticisms has been directed toward costs involved in much contemporary funeral practice (Arvio, 1974; Bowman, 1959). Airtight or watertight metal caskets are expensive objects. Critics have asked: what real purposes are served by such elaborate merchandise? Even if they prevent the body from decaying—and they surely do not when one considers that they could only inhibit the work of aerobic, not anaerobic, bacteria—why is that important?

Answers to these questions seem to reside at the psychological rather than the economic level of mourning. Some persons have argued that spending money for a funeral and burial allows mourners to feel satisfaction in having shown respect and love for the person who has died. After all, expenditures involved in buying a casket and paying the associated costs of a funeral and burial are said to be the third highest financial outlay that most people will make during their lives, exceeded only by the purchase of a house and an automobile. In this sense, expenses associated with a funeral can be seen as a kind of "going-away" present or final gesture of love toward the deceased. At least indirectly, this expenditure may support the realization that the dead person has in fact left the community of the living.

Purchases associated with funerals also represent to some people the last gift or service that they can make to the person who has died. In addition, the conviction that the body will be "protected from the elements" may provide some psychological satisfaction to the bereaved. This may be true whether or not the merchandise or services actually do accomplish what the buyer thinks they will accomplish. After all, much of what is going on here—especially in its psychological components—is really designed to serve the needs of the living (Jackson, 1963). As one funeral director wrote, "Unlike the fast food restaurant, where value is determined solely by cost, the value of death rituals should be determined by the comfort and consolation they provide to the bereaved" (Weeks, 2001, p. 188).

Reintegration and Ongoing Living

Death and Disintegration The death of someone we love leads to disintegration, a breaking apart of the world as it has been known and understood. Thus, there is a third task facing the bereaved: *to achieve a new integration and thereby to promote meaningful ongoing living.* For many persons, funeral practices and other activities after a death can play important roles in beginning this process. The disintegration experienced by bereaved persons may occur at one or more of four levels. First, people who experience the death of an important person in their lives often experience various kinds of *disintegration at the individual level.* They may feel a loss of integrity or wholeness within themselves. They may ask, "Am I going crazy?" Sleep patterns, eating patterns, and health concerns all may be disrupted by the death of a loved person. In short, customary ways in which individuals live in the world and their familiar sense of their own identity can be shredded by a death. The individual then faces the task of pulling himself or herself back together, usually with a somewhat altered if not wholly new identity.

Second, the impact of death may also be evident in *disintegration at the family level.* The death of a person has many meanings for those closest to that person. It may have economic repercussions for the family as a whole, such as the loss of the deceased's income, the loss of an owner of property, and the loss of the person who typically handled certain financial transactions. Death also has consequences for the ways in which those closest to the deceased person relate to each other and to the rest of the world. Members of the family may experience disruptions in their relationships with one another. They may have to renegotiate how they stand in their relationships to each other (how will siblings relate to each other now that the parent has died?) and to the family unit (who will be responsible for which tasks?). Some bereaved individuals may lose part of their social identity as the relative (spouse, child, or parent) of the person who died. Death can exacerbate old tensions within a family, just as it may create new tensions. All of these effects are forms of family disintegration associated with death. They impose on members the task of reintegrating the family unit (Friedman, 1980; Goldberg, 1973).

Third, almost all deaths also have implications for *disintegration at the social level.* This is most obvious when a public figure or someone of great social standing dies, such as a president or a celebrity, but the death of any person is likely to cause some measure of social disintegration. Who will make the decisions that person

People often come together in spontaneous memorials, as in this one for victims of September 11.

© Reuters NewMedia Inc./Corbis

used to make? Who will take over the work associated with that person's job? Who will have to drive more often in the carpool? The structures of society—the whole civic or national society in some cases, but some level of society (the business or school or church) in most cases—will have to be reworked so that society can once again function as an integrated unit.

Fourth, *disintegration at the spiritual level* can involve tasks that are intellectual and perhaps most pressingly emotional. How does one make sense of a world in which this person is no longer present? As a residue of the dying period, there may be anger, frustration, and even despair. For many, this includes an anxiety about or a sense of being alienated from whatever the person holds to be transcendent (e.g., God). If the person has certain religious beliefs, those beliefs may be severely challenged ("How could God allow her to die such a painful death?"). Other beliefs may also produce uncertainty and anxiety: what has happened to the loved person now that she is dead? The tasks here concern reconfiguring one's understanding of how the world operates and also renegotiating one's relationship to whatever the person conceived the transcendent to be.

Achieving a New Integration In bringing people together, funeral and related rituals can help to begin the process of *reintegration at the individual level.* Mourners need not see themselves as simply alone. The tasks they need to perform can be accomplished, in part through the aid of persons drawn to their sides by the funeral. Though mourners may feel overwhelmed by the grief and disorientation they are experiencing, they are not simply powerless or adrift on wholly uncharted seas. They cannot change the fact that a death has occurred, but they can, with the assistance of relatives, friends, and others, decide how to respond to that fact and how to regain some measure of control over the course of their lives.

After a death in contemporary American society, the most obvious sign of *renewed integration at the family level* is often seen in the physical or geographical drawing together of persons who ordinarily see little of each other in their everyday lives. In our society, families are frequently scattered among several towns or states. A funeral is one moment when they are reintegrated, certainly physically, but also

Allowing children to take part in memorial activities can help them cope with loss and remember important people in their lives.

Courtesy of Karen M. Corr

often psychologically and emotionally. Sometimes families are heard to remark half jokingly that they only seem to get together (in all of these senses) on the occasion of a funeral.

In some cultural groups, the funeral and other rituals associated with a death go on for months or even years (at different levels of activity during those periods). A good example of this is the Jewish tradition of rending one's clothes (*Keriah*), reciting the prayer for the dead (*Kaddish*), and organizing activities in specified ways for particular periods (Lamm, 2000). As Gordon (1974, p. 101) has written: "Judaism recognizes that there are levels and stages of grief and so it organizes the year of mourning into three days of deep grief, seven days of mourning [*shivah*], thirty days of gradual readjustment [*Sh-loshim*], and eleven months of remembrance and healing." In practices such as these, the support system is there, again and again, to assist the bereaved in finding their way through the period of crisis and into the new world that they are entering—a world without the dead person in it.

By contrast, for many individuals in our society, the funeral takes place only a matter of days after the death. After that, participants scatter again, and for many people there is no agreed-upon or designated path through the wilderness of grief and mourning. Integration may be hard to achieve under such circumstances. (Their awareness of the limitations of typical funeral practices in our society may have been part of the motivation that has led many funeral directors to develop "aftercare" programs of support for the bereaved, which we discuss later in this chapter.) In any event, the most important considerations in this situation are how individuals make use of funeral ritual and how they follow up on the beginnings represented by that ritual.

For *reintegration at the social level,* funeral rituals can help to provide a sense that the society is not going to fall apart because of a death. This has been seen in the funerals of many national leaders, like Presidents Kennedy (1963), Reagan (2004), and Ford (2006), but also in the ways in which the funeral and other post-death activities associated with the death of Diana, Princess of Wales, in 1997, brought together people both locally and around the world. The public rituals of these funerals gave testimony to the ongoing viability of the community and provided opportunities for individuals to rededicate themselves to working on behalf of a better society in the future (Andersen, 1998; Greenberg & Parker, 1965; Wolfenstein & Kliman, 1965).

Reintegration at the spiritual level is accomplished for those who hold certain spiritual or religious beliefs if the funeral can help bereaved individuals begin to answer their questions about the meaning of the death. Funeral rituals can also help firmly locate the bereaved in a supportive faith community. Most religious traditions have established recognized rituals to help the bereaved in these ways. These rituals offer many believers reassurance about the continued support of God or some value framework in this life and even after it. Whether or not persons have those types of beliefs, the deceased person can be located and secured in the history and memory of the community of those who were touched by that individual through the sharing of stories about the person at a funeral or memorial service.

A funeral, then, can help bereaved persons begin to overcome the individual, family, social, or spiritual disintegration experienced after a death. Achieving a full measure of this type of integration may take much effort and a long time. A funeral, as we typically know it in the United States today, may not go very far toward accomplishing this task, but it can be a beginning.

🦟 Cemeteries and Selected Memorial Activities

Funeral rituals are not the only formal ways in which communities in the American death system try to support and assist persons who are coping with loss and grief. In addition to a visitation, the funeral, and burial or some other form of disposition of the remains, other *memorial activities* typical of our society are found in cemeteries, memorial sculpture, memorial photography, and the use of the World Wide Web in mourning.

Activities following a death in America have gradually evolved into what has been called a distinctively American way of death (Coffin, 1976; Fales, 1964; Farrell, 1980). To begin with, *cemeteries* serving many groups in American society have developed over time:

◆ From frontier graves, domestic homestead graveyards, churchyards, potter's fields, and town or city cemeteries (such as the New Haven Burying Ground in Connecticut) especially typical of the 17th and 18th centuries

◆ Through what were originally 19th-century rural cemeteries (like Mount Auburn in the Boston area) and lawn-park cemeteries (like Spring Grove in Cincinnati)

◆ To memorial parks in the 20th century (like Forest Lawn in the Los Angeles area) (Kastenbaum, 1989b; Sloane, 1991)

One Native-American form of memorialization: Erecting a "burial canoe" overlooking a river well known to tribal members.

© Lee Snider/The Image Works

A similar history, distinguished in its particulars by the unique character of the African-American community, has been documented for African-American burial sites (Holloway, 2003; Wright & Hughes, 1996).

Many American cemeteries are privately owned, whereas others have national (such as those for veterans), public (municipal or county), or religious owners. In the last 100 to 150 years, many cemeteries have stressed an esthetic layout, even a picturesque or pastoral landscape. Some have become major tourist attractions—for example, Forest Lawn Memorial Park in Glendale, California, which has been the object of both literary satire (Huxley, 1939; Waugh, 1948) and scholarly study (French, 1975; Rubin et al., 1979; Zanger, 1980). Recently, American society has also witnessed rapid growth in the number of cemeteries for beloved pets or companion animals (Spiegelman & Kastenbaum, 1990). The diversity and changing character of American cemeteries reflect different attitudes associated with death and bereavement. Still, all cemeteries provide an exclusive place for disposing of a body or other remains, a unique location to which bereaved persons can return to acknowledge the reality of the death, and a special context in which they can maintain a connection with the individual who died (Bachelor, 2004; Francis et al., 2005).

A second dimension of memorial activities can be observed in the history of *memorial sculpture*. That history is linked to the evolution of cemeteries, in which wooden or stone markers have given way to marble, granite, and bronze (Forbes, 1927; Gillon, 1972). Some of these markers have been quite plain (providing, for example, only the name and dates of birth/death for the deceased). Others have included artistic icons and three-dimensional sculpture. In times past, grave markers often displayed elaborate and interesting epitaphs (see Personal Insights 11.3 for one example; also, Coffin, 1976; Mann & Greene, 1962, 1968; Meyer, 1992; Reder, 1969; Wallis, 1954). Recently, for esthetic reasons and to keep down maintenance costs, grave markers have largely taken the form of flush-to-the-ground plaques. Whatever their form, however, these markers commemorate a life and take note of its ending. Another type of memorial sculpture in American cemeteries is found in

---

PERSONAL INSIGHTS 11.3

Benjamin Franklin's Epitaph

*The body of Benjamin Franklin, Printer
(like the cover of an old book,
Its contents torn out
And stripped of its lettering and gilding)
Lies here, food for the worms.
Yet the work shall not be lost,
For it shall (as he believed) appear once more
In a new and most beautiful edition*

*Corrected and Revised
By the Author.*

---

religious or abstract objects of art as centerpieces in the landscape, together with mausoleums, tombs, and other aboveground structures (Keister, 2004).

A third area of memorialization, *memorial photography*, developed with the invention and increasingly widespread use of photographic technology from the 19th century onward. Memorial photographs enable those who are bereaved to retain a tangible memento of the person and the funeral of the deceased (Burns, 1990). They include snapshots taken by relatives, as well as images created and preserved by professional photographers. More recently, some people have used videotaping as a way to memorialize a life at the moment of its ending and to establish commemorative links to the past. Further advances in technology have led to the development of ways to memorialize on the World Wide Web those who have died (De Vries & Roberts, 2004).

Some are uneasy with the idea of memorial photography (e.g., Lesy, 1973). However, the extent of this practice and its many variations—such as those depicted in *The Harlem Book of the Dead* (Van der Zee et al., 1978)—testify that it serves the needs of many individuals. In fact, memorial photography can help many bereaved persons simultaneously to distance themselves from the dead, acknowledge the implications of their loss, and carry with them an image of the deceased as they move on in their own lives (Ruby, 1987, 1991, 1995). This directly parallels the three tasks for funeral ritual described in this chapter. Contrasting attitudes toward memorial photography illustrate tensions between practices that individuals perceive as helpful in their mourning and public lack of understanding or discomfort with such practices. Efforts to achieve a new understanding of funeral and memorial ritual may help to ease these tensions in our society.

A fourth area of contemporary mourning rituals has developed recently as a result of possibilities arising from the World Wide Web. For example, some individuals have posted tributes to their loved ones who have died (De Vries & Rutherford, 2004; Jones, 2004; Roberts, 2004). Others have used their computer skills to find new ways to express or share their grief reactions and to make connections that might enable them to find some measure of solace. GriefNet (www.griefnet.org) is one of the best known websites serving this last purpose, along with some of the other resources listed at the ends of the three chapters in this Part.

❧ Aftercare Programs in the Funeral Industry

As indicated by the title of a recent book, many funeral service personnel have come to think of *aftercare* as what they might do *When All the Friends Have Gone* (Weeks & Johnson, 2001). From this perspective, "aftercare" includes any assistance and support offered to the bereaved after the funeral is over and their family members and friends have returned to the familiar patterns of their own lives. Although strictly speaking the term is not limited to the work of funeral services practitioners, "aftercare" has come to have a specific meaning within the funeral services industry. As Johnson and Weeks (2001, p. 5) observed:

> Funeral home aftercare may be defined as an organized way to maintain a helpful and caring relationship with clients, offer continuing services to client families beyond the expected body disposition and accompanying rituals, and provide death, loss, and grief education to both clients and the community.

Aftercare in the funeral industry has its roots in the ongoing concern of some funeral directors for the welfare of the bereaved family members of their clients who prior to their deaths had been friends and neighbors in local communities. In this, funeral directors were attuned to the bereavement needs of members of their communities and were willing to offer their empathic presence to the bereaved. Described by Johnson and Weeks as an informal or *"casual" level of aftercare,* this is the first of what they regard as four possible levels of aftercare (see Table 11.1). It involves simply listening while bereaved persons tell their stories, helping them complete paperwork for various bureaucracies and entitlements, and providing basic literature (often in pamphlet form) on grief and bereavement. No extra staff are required and costs are minimal.

As aftercare programs became more formalized within the funeral industry during the 1980s, their design and implementation varied greatly in keeping with the needs of the communities being served and the resources they commanded. Thus, Table 11.1 distinguishes three additional formal levels of aftercare based largely on the personnel involved; their training, personal qualities, and professional skills; the materials they use; the funding they require; and the activities in which they become engaged. (Note that when aftercare programs include community education and other services to the public at large they are no longer confined to activities following a specific death and thus go beyond care *after* death.) Because aftercare is a relatively recent development in the funeral industry, one knowledgeable member

TABLE 11.1
Levels and Characteristics of Funeral Home Aftercare Programs

Program Level	Staff	Activities	Cost
Casual (informal)	No extra staff	Visiting, chance meetings, sharing booklists, brochures	Minimal
Fundamental (formal)	Extra staff but no extensive training	Telephone calls, newsletters, socials, dinners, travel	Moderate
Standard (formal)	Extra staff with specific training in bereavement issues	Support group sponsorship/facilitation, lending library, special holiday programs, community education, cards on special days	Substantial
Premier (formal)	Extra staff: master's degree or higher with concentration on counseling and grief/loss issues	Individual counseling, children's programs, in-service training, community advisory boards, spokesperson for media	Substantial to unlimited

Source: From *When All the Friends Have Gone* by O. D. Weeks and C. Johnson (Eds.), p. 9. Copyright © 2001 Baywood Publishing Co. Reprinted with permission.

of that industry has noted that "the territory of aftercare is being charted and created through experience and experimentation" (Miletich, 2001, p. 33).

There are some concerns about liability issues for funeral homes that get involved in aftercare (an uncharted area) and about whether it is appropriate for aftercare personnel to describe themselves as "counselors" or "therapists" unless they are otherwise so qualified or licensed in their state. Nevertheless, however aftercare may be defined or described, it has been estimated that nearly 50 percent of all funeral homes in the United States are currently offering some form of aftercare. As we saw in the vignette near the beginning of this chapter, after the death of her son, Stella Bridgman benefited from the services of an aftercare coordinator. Thus aftercare is a growing reality in the contemporary American death system as an aspect of community support and assistance for persons who are coping with loss and grief.

❦ Bereavement Follow-up in Hospice Programs

Hospice programs in the United States are required to provide support and counseling for the family members of those whom they serve. This service arises directly out of the hospice philosophy of holistic care, which requires it to address the needs of both the dying person and his or her family members. This care for both the ill person and his or her family members begins at the moment of admission to a hospice program. After a death, hospice care is no longer needed by the dying person, but family members must continue to cope with many old problems, and they must also address new challenges. Consequently, *bereavement follow-up services* are an essential component of hospice work (Arnold et al., 2004a, 2004b).

Not all families need or accept bereavement follow-up from a hospice program. Some may have resources of their own that are adequate to cope with bereavement, whether or not those same resources were sufficient to cope with dying. Moreover, hospice programs do not wish to disable surviving families by making them dependent on hospice services for the remainder of their lives (and few hospice programs would have the resources to sustain such a commitment). Thus, hospice bereavement follow-up is a transitional service designed to assist those family members who wish help in coping with loss and bereavement, usually offered during the first 12 to 18 months after the death of a loved one. Issues that go beyond the capacities of this sort of support, either in their character or duration, would ordinarily require specific evaluation and would likely be referred to professional counseling or therapy.

Programs of bereavement follow-up in hospice care are commonly organized around a detailed plan of care for those who have been identified through careful assessment as key persons in bereavement (Arnold et al., 2004b). This plan of care is initiated prior to a patient's death, although there will usually be a reassessment of needs at that point. The plan of care typically encourages participation by family members and staff in meaningful funeral services and rituals. Subsequently, the remainder of the follow-up program is most often conducted through mail, telephone, or personal contacts at regular intervals. Care is addressed to specific needs of the bereaved, such as information about typical patterns or problems in bereavement, grief, and mourning; acknowledgment and validation of feelings and other grief reactions; guidelines for self-care; suggestions about ways in which to undertake or to join in commemorative and memorialization activities; and a shared conviction that life remains worth living.

Newsletters, cards or letters, individual counseling, annual memorial services, and other social activities are familiar components of hospice bereavement follow-up. Hospice programs also frequently establish support groups for the bereaved or work cooperatively with community organizations that provide such services. In addition, hospice programs typically offer their bereavement services to all members of the community whether or not they cared for the person who died—as we saw in the case of Stella Bridgman. Approximately 16.5 percent of all individuals served by hospice bereavement care are community members who did not otherwise receive hospice care (NHPCO, 2007a). Many of the actual services in hospice bereavement follow-up are carried out by experienced volunteers who have been selected and trained for such work and who are supported by professionals in this field (Parkes et al., 1996). This is especially true when fiscal and staffing pressures impose limitations on hospice bereavement services (Demmer, 2003).

❦ Support Groups for the Bereaved

Support groups for the bereaved take many forms (Hopmeyer & Werk, 1994; Wasserman & Danforth, 1988). One type of support group helps bereaved persons mainly through talks and lectures by experts on a variety of practical problems. Groups of this sort try to show their members how to cook nourishing meals when they are alone, do small repairs around the home, complete income tax returns, invest their money, and so on. One group of funeral homes has named their groups of this type their LIFT program, which stands for "Living Information for Today." Another type of support group focuses on entertainment and social activities, such as holiday parties, visits to restaurants, or bus tours to nearby attractions. Both of these types of groups, whether they emphasize guidance in solving various types of problems or social activities, can be and are meaningful for many bereaved persons. However, they do not take as their principal concern the work of addressing the central issues of grief and mourning.

Support groups whose main concern is to help individuals cope with loss and grief offer support in the broadest sense, but their primary benefits result from the assistance that members of the group give to each other (mutual aid) and from the opportunities that these groups provide for bereaved individuals to help themselves with grief work and tasks of mourning (self-help). An illustration depicting the mutual aid offered by a group known as Parents of Murdered Children (POMC), a national organization with local chapters throughout the country, appears in Figure 11.1. Many groups that function in similar ways have sprung up throughout the United States in recent years in response to a wide variety of loss experiences (see Focus On 11.3; also, Hughes, 1995; Pike & Wheeler, 1992). These endeavors may be local and undertaken for a limited period, ongoing or open-ended projects of a community agency, chapters of a national organization, or groups sponsored by an aftercare or hospice program (Zulli, 2001). Stella Bridgman found one of these support groups to be of great help in her bereavement.

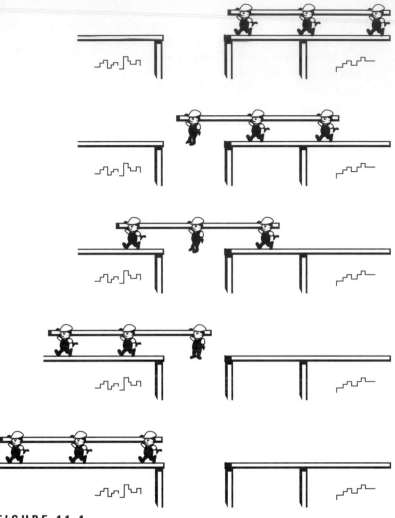

FIGURE 11.1
How POMC Helps

Principles and Practices in Bereavement Support Groups

The very existence and rapid increase in number of bereavement support groups shows that many bereaved persons need or seek assistance beyond what is readily available to them in their own family or everyday community. By and large, however, what is sought from these groups is not professional counseling or therapy—it is help from others who have shared a similar loss experience. Thus, the main purpose of these groups is "to provide people in similar circumstances with an opportunity to share their experiences and to help teach one another how to cope with their problems" (Silverman, 1980, p. 40).

Selected Examples of Bereavement Support Organizations

ORGANIZATION	DESCRIPTION
American Association of Suicidology 4201 Connecticut Avenue NW, Suite 310 Washington, DC 20008 202-237-2280; www.suicidology.org	An information clearinghouse that supplies literature about suicide and local referrals to those bereaved by suicide
Association for Pet Loss and Bereavement P.O. Box 106 Brooklyn, NY 11230 718-382-0690; www.aplb.org	Provides support and guidance to all who have experienced the death of a pet or companion animal
Bereaved Parents of the USA P.O. Box 95 Park Forest, IL 60466 708-748-9184 (fax); www.bereavedparentsusa.org	A national support group with many local chapters serving bereaved parents, grandparents, and siblings
The Candlelighters Foundation 7910 Woodmont Avenue, Suite 460 Bethesda, MD 20814 800-366-2223; www.candlelighters.org	An international network of support groups for parents of children who have or have had cancer
The Compassionate Friends (TCF) P.O. Box 3696 Oak Brook, IL 60522-3696 877-969-0010; 630-990-0010 www.compassionatefriends.org	An international support group with numerous local chapters serving bereaved parents and siblings
Concerns of Police Survivors (COPS) P.O. Box 3199, S. Highway 5 Camdenton, MO 65020 800-784-COPS (2677); 573-346-4911 www.nationalcops.org	A support group for law enforcement officers and their family members who are affected by death and bereavement
Make Today Count National Office Mid-America Cancer Center 1235 E. Cherokee Springfield, MO 65804 800-432-2273 (8:00 A.M.–4:30 P.M., Mon–Fri)	A national support group for individuals who are living with life-threatening illness and for their family members
Mothers against Drunk Driving (MADD) 511 E. John Carpenter Freeway, Suite 700 Irving, TX 75062 800-GET-MADD (438-6233); 214-744-6233 www.madd.org	Support and advocacy on behalf of those who have been victimized by drunken-driving offenses
National Donor Family Council (NDFC) 30 E. 33rd Street New York, NY 10016 800-622-9010; 212-809-2210 www.donorfamily.org	A national resource for information, support, advocacy, and education about organ/tissue donation and transplantation

(continued)

Selected Examples of Bereavement Support Organizations

ORGANIZATION	DESCRIPTION
National Hospice and Palliative Care Organization 1700 Diagonal Road, Suite 300 Alexandria, VA 22314 800-658-8898; 703-837-1500; www.nhpco.org	A resource for information about and referral to local hospice programs and related services
National Organization for Victim Assistance (NOVA) 1757 Park Road, NW Washington, D.C. 20010 800-TRY-NOVA (879-6682); 202-232-6682 www.try-nova.org	A referral resource for local victim assistance services, plus a 24-hour telephone crisis counseling service
National SIDS Resource Center 2070 Chain Bridge Road, Suite 450 Vienna, VA 22182 703-821-8955; www.sidscenter.org	A source of information about sudden infant death syndrome and referrals to local organizations and support groups for those affected by SIDS
Parents of Murdered Children (POMC) 100 East Eighth Street, Suite B-41 Cincinnati, OH 45202 888-818-POMC (7662); 513-721-5683 www.pomc.com	Support for those bereaved by homicide
Parents Without Partners, Inc. 401 N. Michigan Ave. Chicago, IL 60611 301-588-9354; www.parentswithoutpartners.org	Services for single parents and their children
SHARE—Pregnancy and Infant Loss Support, Inc. National Office, St. Joseph Health Center 300 First Capitol Drive St. Charles, MO 63301-2893 800-821-6819; 636-947-6164 www.nationalshareoffice.com	A national mutual-help group for parents and siblings who have experienced miscarriage, stillbirth, or early infant death
Sudden Infant Death Syndrome Alliance 1314 Bedford Avenue, Suite 210 Baltimore, MD 21208 800-221-7437; 410-653-8226; www.sidsalliance.org	An alliance of organizations involved in research and services related to sudden infant death syndrome
THEOS (They Help Each Other Spiritually) International Office 322 Boulevard of Allies, Suite 105 Pittsburgh, PA 15222-1919 412-471-7779	Support and education for the widowed and their families
Tragedy Assistance Program for Survivors (TAPS) 1621 Connecticut Ave., NW, Suite 300 Washington, D.C. 20009 800-959-TAPS (8277); www.taps.org	Support and assistance to all members of the armed services and their family members who are impacted by death and bereavement

Groups of this sort take a variety of forms. They may be time limited or ongoing. They may admit new members at any time or close themselves to additional members once the group has been formed. They may focus their work on all sorts of bereavement or organize themselves around a specific type of loss. They may be led by a bereaved person serving as an experienced volunteer or by a professional facilitator (McNurlen, 1991; Yalom & Vinogradov, 1988).

The question of *leadership* is important, and it highlights the profound differences between grief support groups and therapy groups. These differences arise from the fact that support groups are designed to help otherwise healthy individuals cope with uncomplicated grief reactions, whereas therapy groups are intended to correct psychosocial disorders in individuals who need to restructure their lives in some significant way. Members of grief support groups come together voluntarily because of the difficulties they are facing in coping with a shared life experience (McNurlen, 1991). Prior to their encounter with loss, such individuals were generally functioning normally. They do not seek to be changed in that, but they do want help in coping with losses that have taxed (often, overtaxed) their capacities.

Some bereavement groups do not permit leadership posts to be held by non-bereaved persons; others assign leadership functions to a professional facilitator (Klass & Shinners, 1983). Always, however, real, substantive expertise in bereavement groups is not perceived as hierarchical; it is found in the members themselves. Thus, members are encouraged to become involved with each other outside the group, and topics for discussion within the group are those that members bring up and choose to share. The focus in the group is not on offering solutions or giving advice but on the process of helping itself—talking about problems, exploring situations, and sharing experiences. This process is often guided by principles such as those in the "Serenity Prayer" (see Personal Insights 11.4), which is a frequent component of group ritual. Support groups for the bereaved combine elements of both self-help and mutual aid; one must help oneself, but one does so with the support of others in the group.

Support groups for the bereaved usually have more or less explicit rules or values, such as that confidentiality and a nonjudgmental attitude are to be maintained, advice is not to be given, opportunities are made available for all to speak, side conversations are prohibited, everyone has the right to pass or remain silent,

PERSONAL INSIGHTS 11.4

The Serenity Prayer

God, give us grace
to accept with serenity
the things that cannot be changed,
courage to change the things
that should be changed,
and the wisdom to distinguish
the one from the other.

Source: Sifton, 2003, p. 7.

members respect each other's experiences and viewpoints, and meetings start and end on time. Safety issues are a matter of particular concern in groups for vulnerable people. Support groups usually prohibit "putdowns" or evangelization; they are also sensitive to the need to refer for individual counseling or therapy any persons who disrupt the work of the group or who might endanger themselves.

Helping Factors in Bereavement Support Groups

Most bereavement support groups are organized around eight helping factors (McNurlen, 1991; Yalom, 1995). Explaining these factors recalls the characteristics of The Compassionate Friends group that helped Stella Bridgman after her son's death.

◆ *Helping factor 1.* Identification Bereavement support groups are founded on the shared experience of their members (Borkman, 1976). This shared experience is the basis for a bond through which group members can find *identification* with one another. In the group, bereaved individuals find that they no longer are or need be alone. Although they may feel stigmatized or marked out by their loss experiences from so many others in the world, within the group they discover that others share similar experiences and that members of the group can learn from each other (Wrobleski, 1984).

◆ *Helping factor 2.* Universality Despite all of the uniqueness and individuality of the experience of loss, there is a degree of *universality* found in support groups. In the group, individuals can recognize that they are not alone in their experiences and reactions. Those whom society views as different, shuns, or even stigmatizes because of what has happened to them can be helped by knowing that members of the group do not view them as "bad" or "wrong."

Sharing experiences of grief is one part of a bereavement support group's work (an illustration from *Tear Soup,* see Personal Insights 10.2).

Illustration © Taylor Bills. Reprinted with permission of Grief Works

◆ *Helping factor 3*. Catharsis Within the group, long-repressed, pent-up feelings can be let out for as long as necessary. Some people come to bereavement support groups shortly after their loss experience; others join many years later. Whatever the timing, new and old members typically are grateful to the group for permitting them to vent and share such feelings. They need *catharsis* and find opportunity for it in the group.

◆ *Helping factor 4*. Guidance Individuals also meet other bereaved people within the group from whom they can obtain *guidance* on how they might conduct their own lives after their loss. The group offers such guidance, not primarily through lectures, presentations, or advice, but by providing a forum in which members can describe, exemplify, and live out their experiences with loss and grief. This exchange may or may not validate an individual's personal experiences, but as experiences are shared, important information, guidance, and reassurance are conveyed. For example, most bereaved persons welcome information about grief and mourning processes. Many need to know more about the specific types of losses they have experienced and that may define the nature of the group—for example, about parental bereavement, about homicide and its implications, or about sudden infant death syndrome. Some may need guidance about the social stigma associated with certain kinds of death, such as suicide or AIDS.

◆ *Helping factor 5*. Instillation of hope A dimension of the group experience that is especially significant for many bereaved persons is the interaction between new members and those who have been participants for some time. Coming to know people who are further along in their grief work permits newer members to witness ways in which their more experienced colleagues are managing both their grief and the rest of their lives. Insofar as this demonstrates that things can get better and have gotten better for others, hope is renewed that one's own life might also get better. This *instillation of hope* must be drawn from the group processes by the individual; it cannot simply be injected or imposed from outside.

◆ *Helping factor 6*. Existential issues Bereavement support groups often address *existential issues* involving large questions such as those concerned with the fairness of life, the benevolence of God, or the basic goodness of the universe. These are questions involved in meaning reconstruction that we discussed in Chapter 9. Answers to such profound questions can seldom be given to a person from someone else. More likely, one discovers that one must work out one's own answers or ways of living with such issues and questions, or even with an absence or incompleteness of answers. What a support group can provide in response to these questions is a safe place to recognize that the existential issues raised by loss, grief, and bereavement are legitimate and real, and that different people respond to them in different ways.

◆ *Helping factor 7*. Cohesiveness The bonding among members in a bereavement support group creates a safe, caring environment in a world that—after a significant personal loss—may appear in so many ways to be unsafe and uncaring. *Cohesiveness* or basic trust develops among members in most support groups, arising from two features of the group experience: the experiences that members share as bereaved persons and the discovery by hurt and vulnerable people that they can help each other simply by sharing their own great losses and pain. "Sharing of experience is the fundamental concept that distinguishes the mutual help experience from other helping exchanges. . . . The essence of the process is mutuality and reciprocity" (Silverman, 1980, p. 10).

◆ *Helping factor 8.* Altruism Another sort of empowerment is related to *altruism* or giving to others, which is often experienced by those who remain in a bereavement support group for an extended period. As they move into leadership roles or find different ways to share with others what they have obtained from their own experiences both in bereavement and within the group, senior members also may find new rewards for themselves. Klass (1985b, 1988) called this the great secret of bereavement support groups: in giving to others, one receives for oneself. Giving and receiving help reciprocally to enhance one's self-esteem. Those who make the transition from intense vulnerability in an early meeting to shared ownership of the group at a later point often interpret their newfound ability to help others as an important element in finding meaning in the life and death of their loved one (Klass, 1985a).

Help Outside the Group

Although the main work of support groups for the bereaved occurs within their meetings, that is not the whole of what they have to offer. This point is often neglected. Established, ongoing bereavement support groups like The Compassionate Friends usually set up a network of referral sources for identifying potential new members. Mail or telephone contacts with such individuals may be among the earliest expressions of support that reach a bereaved person.

Sometimes it is enough for the bereaved to know that a support group is available "in case I really need one." That knowledge may be supplemented by regular mailings of a newsletter, which is another mode of support and reassurance that additional help is within reach. Groups may also generate announcements about their activities or reports about loss and grief in the local media. Together with annual memorial events, educational conferences, and public service endeavors, these are other forms of support that reach beyond the boundaries of the group itself.

🌱 Summary

In this chapter, we examined ways in which communities in the American death system have organized specific social programs to offer support and assistance to persons who are coping with loss and grief. This supplements our discussion in Chapter 10 of how individuals can help bereaved persons in one-to-one relationships. In this chapter, we began with an analysis of life crises and rituals. Next we described typical funeral practices in our society today, together with some alternative views of the value of those practices. After that, we offered an analysis of three tasks that organized funeral rituals should help bereaved persons and society with: to dispose of the body in socially approved ways, to make real the implications of a death, and to begin to move toward reintegration and meaningful ongoing living. Individuals and communities who know the options that are available to them among funeral rituals can decide for themselves whether (and, if so, how) any specific funeral practice or associated ritual helps them accomplish these tasks. We added to this analysis a brief exploration of American cemeteries, memorial sculpture, memorial photography, and memorial activities involving the World Wide Web. Then we considered three other social programs for helping the bereaved within our contemporary death system: aftercare programs in the funeral industry, hospice bereavement follow-up programs, and support groups for the bereaved.

Glossary

Aftercare programs: informal and formal programs of support for individuals coping with loss and grief, usually offered by funeral service practitioners after the funeral and disposition are completed; may include providing death education to the community

Bereavement support groups: organized meetings that combine elements of self-help and mutual aid for those who are coping with loss and grief

Burial (in-ground burial): disposition of the body (or of its "cremains") by placing it first in a casket and then in the ground, usually in a cemetery and often within a vault or grave liner designed to protect the casket and prevent settling of land

Cremains: cremated remains, that is, ash and bone resulting from cremating a body

Cremation: a process of reducing the size of the body by subjecting it to intense heat, resulting in ashes and some bone fragments (which may then be ground up or pulverized)

Disposition of the body: removing the body of the deceased from the society of the living

Embalming: removal of blood and bodily fluids from a corpse, together with their replacement with artificial preservatives intended to retard decomposition and color the skin; mainly intended to permit viewing of the body during a wake or visitation; required by law only in limited circumstances, such as when the body is to be transported on a common carrier

Entombment: disposition of the body or its remains by placing them in a mausoleum, crypt, or other aboveground, tomblike structure

Funerals or funeral services: formal services to mark a death and celebrate a life with the body present in an open or closed casket; may be religious, humanist, or secular in nature

Hospice bereavement follow-up programs: hospice services for family members; in particular, services offered after the death of a hospice patient or to community members experiencing loss

Life crises: major turning points in one's life course, such as birth, marriage, or death; typically involving some degree of disorientation resulting from a combination of danger and opportunity

Making real the implications of death: helping the bereaved to grasp the import of the death; often implemented through formal activities of separation from the deceased

Memorial activities: activities intended to commemorate the life or legacy of someone who has died

Memorial services: formal services to mark a death and celebrate a life without the presence of a body; may be held several weeks after a death; need not follow any prescribed format

Reintegration: pulling (back) together the bereaved individuals, family, or society disintegrated by a death

Ritual: corporate or communal symbolic activity, usually involving external (bodily) actions and social participation; designed to contribute order or orientation when crises disrupt life

Support groups for the bereaved: these take many forms, ranging from groups that emphasize assistance with practical problems and groups whose concerns are primarily social, to groups that seek to help individuals cope with loss and grief through mutual aid and self-help

Questions for Review and Discussion

1. Think about rituals (activities involving symbolic external or bodily actions by a community) that you have experienced either in your own private life or in various public events. What purpose(s) do you think these rituals were intended to serve? Why did the persons involved choose to engage in those specific ritual actions?

2. Suppose someone you love has died. What types of activities would you want to have included in a funeral or memorial service? What might or might not be helpful for you at such a moment? Reflect on your answers here and compare them to an actual funeral or memorial service you have attended (or, if you have not attended such an event, think about what you have heard others say about such events).

3. Many bereaved persons report that they found help in their grief from funeral home aftercare programs, hospice bereavement follow-up programs, or bereavement support groups. Why might that be so? What do you think we could learn from these programs and groups in our own efforts as individuals to help the bereaved? Have you had any personal contact with any of these programs? Why do these programs exist?

Suggested Readings

Information about what happens to human bodies after death is provided by:

Iserson, K. V. (1994). *Death to Dust: What Happens to Dead Bodies?*
Roach, M. (2003). *Stiff: The Curious Lives of Human Cadavers.*

Various aspects of American funeral and mourning practices are examined in:

Canine, J. D. (1999). *What Am I Going to Do with Myself when I Die?*
Carlson, L. (1998). *Caring for the Dead: Your Final Act of Love.*
Holloway, K. F. C. (2003). *Passed On: African American Mourning Stories, a Memorial.*
Howarth, G. (1996). *Last Rites: The Work of the Modern Funeral Director.*

Jupp, P. C. (2006). *From Ashes to Dust: The History of Cremation in Britain.*

Laderman, G. (2003). *Rest in Peace: A Cultural History of Death and the Funeral Home in Twentieth Century America.*

Lynch, T. (1997). *The Undertaking: Life Studies from the Dismal Trade.*

Manning, D. (2001). *The Funeral: A Chance to Teach, a Chance to Serve, a Chance to Heal.*

Mayer, R. A. (1996). *Embalming: History, Theory, and Practice* (2nd ed.).

Mitford, J. (1998). *The American Way of Death Revisited.*

Morgan, E., & Morgan J. (2001). *Dealing Creatively with Death: A Manual of Death Education and Simple Burial* (14th rev. ed.).

Prothero, S. (2001). *Purified by Fire: A History of Cremation in America.*

Shaw, E. (1994). *What to Do when a Loved One Dies: A Practical and Compassionate Guide to Dealing with Death on Life's Terms.*

Cemeteries, memorial photography, and other memorial practices are explored in:

Bachelor, P. (2004). *Sorrow and Solace: The Social World of the Cemetery.*

Francis, D., Kellaher, L., & Neophytu, G. (2005). *The Secret Cemetery.*

Keister, D. (2004). *Stories in Stone: The Complete Guide to Cemetery Symbolism.*

Meyer, R. E. (Ed.). (1992). *Cemeteries and Gravemarkers: Voices of American Culture.*

Ruby, J. (1995). *Secure the Shadow: Death and Photography in America.*

Sloane, D. C. (1991). *The Last Great Necessity: Cemeteries in American History.*

Wright, R. H., & Hughes, W. B. (1996). *Lay Down Body: Living History in African-American Cemeteries.*

Concerning aftercare, hospice bereavement support, and self-help groups, see:

Arnold, B., Bruno, S. M., Corr, C. A., Eisemann, L., & Sunter, S. (2004a). *Bereavement Program Training Series* (4 vols.).

Arnold, B., Bruno, S. M., Corr, C. A., Eisemann, L., & Sunter, S. (2004b). *Bereavement Program Development Series* (2 vols.).

Hughes, M. (1995). *Bereavement and Support: Healing in a Group Environment.*

Wasserman, H., & Danforth, H. E. (1988). *The Human Bond: Support Groups and Mutual Aid.*

Weeks, O. D., & Johnson, C. (Eds.) (2001). *When All the Friends Have Gone: A Guide for Aftercare Providers.*

Wolfelt, A. (2004a). *The Understanding Your Grief Support Group Guide: Starting and Leading a Bereavement Support Group.*

Selected Web Resources

Some useful search terms include: AFTERCARE PROGRAMS; BEREAVEMENT FOLLOW-UP; BEREAVEMENT HELPING FACTORS; BEREAVEMENT SUPPORT GROUPS; BURIAL; CREMAINS; CREMATION; DEATH RITUALS; DISPOSITION OF THE BODY; EMBALMING; ENTOMBMENT; FUNERALS; HOSPICE BEREAVEMENT FOLLOW-UP PROGRAMS; LIFE CRISES; MEMORIAL SERVICES; MEMORIALIZATION; RITUAL; SUPPORT GROUPS FOR THE BEREAVED

Visit the book companion website for *Death & Dying, Life & Living, Sixth Edition*, at academic.cengage.com/psychology/corr for all URLs and live links to the following *organizational and other Internet sites*:

Self-help, body disposition, and funeral resources:

American Cryonics Society

American Self-Help Group Clearinghouse

Cremation Association of North America

Funeral Consumers Alliance of America

Thefuneraldirectory.com (multiple topics)

Funeralplan.com

National Funeral Directors Association

National Self-Help Clearinghouse

Bereavement support resources:

Concerns of Police Survivors (COPS)

Mothers Against Drunk Driving (MADD)

National Organization for Victim Assistance (NOVA)

Parents of Murdered Children, Inc. (POMC)

SHARE—Pregnancy and Infant Loss Support, Inc.

Sudden Infant Death Syndrome Alliance

Tragedy Assistance Program for Survivors (TAPS)

PART FIVE

Developmental Perspectives

In much of this book, we describe what is common to all or is at least widespread in contemporary American experiences of death. These common factors include death-related encounters, attitudes, and practices that involve and affect nearly everyone in our society, as well as experiences of coping with dying or bereavement in which many or all share, regardless of age or developmental status. However, in addition to sharing in a common human community, each human being is also a member of a distinctive developmental subgroup or cohort. In the four chapters that follow, we consider death-related subjects from this latter perspective: *development across the life course.*

The merits of a developmental perspective first became evident in studies of childhood. Subsequently, it was recognized that developmental processes continue throughout the human life course. Still, more is known about some eras and some aspects of human development than about others.

Many thinkers, such as Freud (1959b), Jung (1970), Havighurst (1953), Bühler (1968), and Neugarten and Datan (1973), have contributed to our understanding of human development. Among such thinkers, Erikson (1963, 1968) is especially well known for describing eight distinguishable eras (sometimes called ages, periods, or stages) in human development (see Table V.1 on p. 318).

According to Erikson, a predominant psychosocial issue or central conflict characterizes each era in the development of an individual ego. These developmental conflicts involve a struggle between a pair of alternative orientations, opposed tendencies, or attitudes toward life, the self, and other people. Successful resolution of each of these developmental struggles results in a leading virtue, a particular strength or quality of ego functioning.

Developmental theorists argue that each normative conflict has a time of special prominence in the life course. Because this timing is controlled by development, not chronology, it only roughly correlates with age. According to developmental theory, failure to resolve the tasks of one era leaves unfinished work for subsequent eras. In other words, a developmental perspective asserts that: (1) developing individuals strive to integrate aspects of their inner lives and their relationships with the social world; (2) the integrative tasks undertaken in this effort depend on the different crises or turning points that unfold as development proceeds; and (3) the way in which the integration is or is not managed determines the individual's present quality of life, potential for future growth, and residual or unresolved work that remains to be achieved.

Erikson's model is not the only developmental framework that might enrich our study of death, dying, and bereavement, and many have noted some of its limitations or added to its details (e.g., Kail & Cavanaugh, 2006; Newman & Newman, 2005; Papalia, Olds, et al., 2006).

The model is limited in its application to different cultural groups, it may apply equally to both sexes only in societies that give equal options to men and women (Gilligan, 1982; Levinson, 1996), and it tends to describe individuals independently of familial or other systemic contexts (McGoldrick, 1988). Still, a developmental perspective does provide an important frame of reference from which to investigate death-related experiences.

In Chapters 12 through 15, we adopt a developmental perspective to appreciate the fact that "death is one of the central themes in human development throughout the life span. Death is not just our destination; it is a part of our 'getting there' as well" (Kastenbaum, 1977, p. 43).

Our question here is: how or in what ways are death-related experiences distinctive during the principal eras of human development? Chapters 12 through 15 organize answers to that question around four developmental cohorts: children, adolescents, young and middle-aged adults, and older adults. We emphasize the chapters on childhood and adolescence because: (1) many subjects in other parts of this book are already closely associated with young, middle, and older adults; (2) there is so much that is distinctive in children's interactions with death; and (3) death-related issues in adolescence (which are also distinctive in many ways) are often overlooked or obscured by being merged into discussions of childhood or adulthood.

TABLE V.1
Principal Eras in Human Development

Era	Approximate Age	Predominant Issue	Virtue
Infancy	Birth through 12–18 months	Basic trust vs. mistrust	Hope
Toddlerhood	Infancy to 3 years	Autonomy vs. shame and doubt	Will or self-control
Early childhood; sometimes called play age or the preschool period	3–6 years	Initiative vs. guilt	Purpose or direction
Middle childhood; sometimes called school age or the latency period	6 years to puberty	Industry vs. inferiority	Competency
Adolescence	Puberty to about 21 or 22 years	Identity vs. role confusion	Fidelity
Young adulthood	21–22 to 45 years	Intimacy vs. isolation	Love
Middle adulthood or middle age	45–65 years	Generativity vs. stagnation and self-absorption	Production and care
Older adulthood; sometimes called maturity, old age, or the era of the elderly	65 years and older	Ego integrity vs. despair	Renunciation and wisdom

Note: All chronological ages given here are approximate.
Source: Based on Erikson, 1963, 1968.

CHAPTER 12
Children

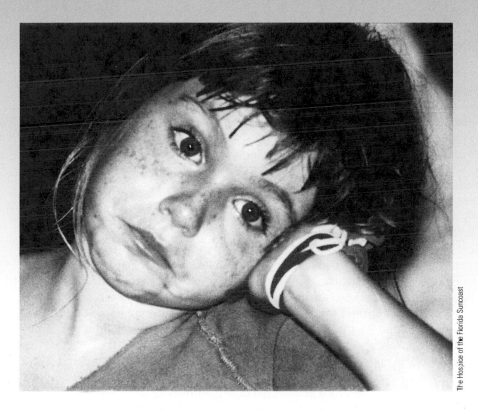

The Hospice of the Florida Suncoast

Objectives of This Chapter

◆ To illustrate some issues that often arise for children within the contemporary American death system

◆ To continue our discussion of children and their distinctive developmental tasks

◆ To describe typical encounters with death in the United States during childhood

◆ To examine research on the development of death-related concepts and attitudes during childhood

◆ To identify key issues for children who are coping with life-threatening illness and dying

◆ To explore central issues for children who are coping with bereavement and grief

◆ To establish principles for helping children cope with death, dying, and bereavement

It is important to note that much still remains to be learned about children and issues related to death, dying, and bereavement. In the current state of our knowledge, we cannot always draw distinctions in death-related matters that parallel divisions between the various developmental eras in childhood. Moreover, the National Center for Health Statistics (NCHS) provides mortality data in age-related categories and formats that do not always match developmental theorists' distinctions among the various eras within childhood and adolescence. Thus, in this chapter we address childhood as a whole, emphasizing throughout what is unique and distinctive about this period and drawing finer developmental distinctions whenever we can.

❦ One Child and Death

In the film, *And We Were Sad, Remember?* (1979), a young girl named Allison is awakened during the night by the sound of a telephone call from her father to her mother. He is calling from a hospital in another town to report that his mother has just died. After the call, Allison's mother explains that Grammie's heart had stopped and she is dead. Allison's mother says that she will drive to Grammie's home tomorrow, and asks whether Allison and her younger brother, Christopher, would like to go with her to Grammie's funeral. She explains what a funeral is and Allison says that she wants to attend. When Christopher wakes, Allison asks him if he would also like to go with her to the "fumeral."

A day or two later, Allison's father tells her he has arranged for her and Christopher to stay with an adult friend during the funeral and to have a fun adventure. Allison replies that her mother had told her she could go to the funeral. She insists that she wants to attend and urges him to let her do so. He is quite reluctant, finally agreeing only that he will think about it and decide later. Allison says that whenever he talks like that, it usually means "no."

When the family and friends are all gathered at Grammie's home, Allison and her cousin get into an argument while they are playing with their dolls and acting out a scene involving illness and death. Allison wants to cover the doll that has "died" with a blanket. Her cousin replies that she has been told that dying is like going to sleep. If so, the doll will still need to breathe and it won't be able to do so if the blanket covers its face. The children take their dispute to Allison's father, who only tells them to stop fighting, put the dolls away, and get ready for bed. When Allison insists that he settle their disagreement, he replies in exasperation: "Little girl, you don't have to worry about that for a hundred years!"

❦ Children, Developmental Tasks, and Death

At one time in Western society, children were essentially thought of as miniature adults (Ariès, 1962). After infancy, when they became able to move about more or less independently, their clothing and much of their behavior were expected to be modeled along adult lines. As sensitivity to developmental differences grew, that viewpoint was abandoned in most Western societies, although the Amish (whom we met in the vignette near the beginning of Chapter 3) still follow some of these practices. Now childhood is seen as different from other eras in human development, and additional distinctions are made between different eras within childhood.

According to this view, *childhood* is the period from birth to puberty or the beginning of adolescence (*Oxford English Dictionary,* 1989)—roughly, the first 10 to 12 years of life. Within this period, most developmental theorists (like Erikson, 1963, 1968) divide childhood itself into *four distinguishable developmental eras*: infancy, toddlerhood, early childhood (also called the play age or preschool period), and middle childhood (also called the school age or latency period). (Note that the term *child* can also include the unborn fetus; thus, some writers (e.g., Newman & Newman, 2005; Papalia et al., 2005) identify the prenatal period extending from conception to birth as the very first era in the human life course.) *Normative developmental tasks within childhood* are to develop *trust* versus mistrust in infancy, *autonomy* versus shame and doubt in toddlerhood, *initiative* versus guilt in early childhood, and *industry* versus inferiority in middle childhood (see Table V.1).

According to this account, infants who develop a sense of basic trust will become *confident and hopeful* because they will believe that they can rely on people and the world to fulfill their needs and satisfy their desires. Toddlers—often depicted as willful agents in the "terrible twos"—who develop their own legitimate autonomy and independence will learn *self-control* and establish a balance between self-regulation and external dictates. In early childhood, the developmental conflict between initiative and guilt will appear in the form of a challenge to cultivate one's own initiative or desire to take action and pursue goals, but to balance that with the moral reservations that one has about one's plans. Combining spontaneity and responsibility in this way promotes a sense of *purpose or direction* in a child's life. In middle childhood, the developmental conflict between industry and inferiority involves developing one's capacities to do productive work, thereby achieving a sense of *competence* and self-esteem rooted in a view of the self as able to master skills and carry out tasks.

Normative development varies, of course, within specific groups of children. Some youngsters advance in these developmental processes more rapidly than others. Some are delayed in their development by various physical or psychosocial factors, such as congenital anomalies, mental or emotional disabilities, or extreme conditions involving starvation or war. Some are influenced more than others by the social, cultural, economic, or historical contexts in which they find themselves. In short, human development is not an absolutely uniform, lockstep process. In particular, although chronological or age markers (which are relatively easy to determine and appear to be objective) are often used to mark out and evaluate a child's development, in fact, development is not primarily a matter of chronology but one of physical, psychosocial, and spiritual maturation. Thus, some persons who are adult in age and body remain at the developmental level of a young child and must in many ways be appreciated and treated primarily with the latter perspective in mind. Nevertheless, broad normative patterns in childhood development are influential in typical types of death-related encounters, understandings, and attitudes during childhood.

❧ Encounters with Death during Childhood

"'The kingdom where nobody dies,' as Edna St. Vincent Millay once described childhood, is the fantasy of grown-ups" (Kastenbaum, 1973, p. 37). The realities of life during childhood include both deaths of children and deaths of others that are experienced by children (Corr, 1995a).

Deaths of Children

Children between birth and 9 years of age make up 13.7 percent of the total U.S. population. In 2004, this group experienced 35,609 deaths (see Table 12.1), down by more than 1,500 deaths per year from 1998. In 2004, these deaths represented approximately 1.5 percent of the more than 2.4 million deaths in the United States.

Infant Deaths More children die during infancy than throughout the remainder of childhood. In 2004, 27,936 infants died during their first year of life in the United States (see Table 12.1). This is a decrease of 89 deaths from 2003 but is only one death less than the total number of infant deaths in 1999. In general, there has been

TABLE 12.1
Number of Deaths during Childhood by Age, Race or Hispanic Origin,[a] and Sex: United States, 2004

	Under 1 Year			1–4 Years			5–9 years		
	Both Sexes	Males	Females	Both Sexes	Males	Females	Both Sexes	Males	Females
All origins[b]	27,936	15,718	12,218	4,785	2,649	2,136	2,888	1,645	1,243
Caucasian Americans, total	18,231	10,265	7,966	3,363	1,878	1,485	2,043	1,178	865
Non-Hispanic Caucasian Americans	13,046	7,399	5,647	2,458	1,365	1,093	1,573	914	659
Hispanic Americans[c]	5,321	2,948	2,373	947	535	412	487	273	214
African Americans	8,494	4,769	3,725	1,164	641	523	685	372	313
Asian or Pacific Island Americans[d]	822	447	375	161	80	81	107	67	40
American Indians and Alaskan Natives[e]	389	237	152	97	50	47	53	28	25

[a]Data for specified groups other than Caucasian Americans and African Americans should be interpreted with caution because of inconsistencies between reporting race and/or Hispanic origin on death certificates and on censuses and surveys.

[b]Figures for origin not stated are included in "all origins" but not distributed among specified origins.

[c]Includes all persons of Hispanic origin of any race.

[d]Includes Chinese, Filipino, Hawaiian, Japanese, and Other Asian or Pacific Islander.

[e]Includes Aleuts and Eskimos.

Source: Miniño et al., 2007.

a slow but steady decline or at least a kind of plateauing in the number of infant deaths in our society over a period of many years. About half of all infant deaths in 2004 were the result of five principal causes: congenital malformations (20%), disorders related to short gestation and low birth weight (17%), sudden infant death syndrome (SIDS; 8%), newborns affected by maternal complications of pregnancy (6%), and unintentional injuries (accidents; 4%) (Hamilton et al., 2007). These five have been the leading causes of deaths during infancy for some time, despite the major reduction in deaths from sudden infant death syndrome that has occurred since 1988 (see Focus On 12.1).

FOCUS ON 12.1

Sudden Infant Death Syndrome

Sudden infant death syndrome, or SIDS, is and has been for many years the leading cause of death in infants from 1 month to 1 year of age (Corr & Corr, 2003b). Officially, SIDS is "the sudden death of an infant under one year of age which remains unexplained after a thorough case investigation, including performance of a complete autopsy, examination of the death scene, and review of the clinical history" (Willinger et al., 1991, p. 681). Typically, a healthy baby dies suddenly and tragically with no advance warning. A death of this sort shocks our sensibilities because it involves a very young child and because it runs counter to the general pattern of our encounters with death.

Some cases of SIDS may not be correctly diagnosed—for example, when it is not possible to conduct a thorough case investigation. Nevertheless, formal identification of this entity as a *syndrome* and its recognition by the World Health Organization as an official cause of death is significant in many ways. A syndrome is a recognizable pattern of events whose underlying cause is unknown. Whenever that pattern is identified, we know that the infant's death did not result from child abuse or neglect and that nothing could have been done ahead of time to prevent the death. The American Academy of Pediatrics (AAP, 2006) has recently suggested ways to distinguish SIDS deaths from those caused by child abuse.

Since there has been no way to screen for an unknown cause of death, SIDS deaths have been thought to be unpreventable. Thus, it has been said that the first symptom of SIDS is a dead infant. SIDS strikes across all economic, ethnic, and cultural boundaries and is not distinguishable from risk factors that put all babies in danger. The only demographic variable that appears to be critical for SIDS is the fact that it occurs only in infancy—with a noticeable peak in incidence around 2 to 4 months of age and during the colder months of the year. This suggests some associations with infant development and environment, but does not explain SIDS.

In the early 1990s, the American death system mobilized itself in new ways to reduce the risk of SIDS. New research (e.g., Dwyer et al., 1995) suggested that infants might be at less risk for SIDS if they were placed on their backs (supine) or sides for sleep, rather than on their stomachs (prone). This recommendation ran contrary to familiar advice that favored sleeping prone to reduce the risk that an infant might regurgitate or spit up fluids, aspirate

(continued)

Sudden Infant Death Syndrome

them into an airway, and suffocate. Researchers now believe that any risk of suffocating in this way is far less than that of SIDS.

Accordingly, as early as 1992 the American Academy of Pediatrics concluded it was likely that infants who sleep on their backs and sides are at less risk for SIDS when all other circumstances are favorable (for example, sleeping on firm mattresses and without soft toys nearby). Even though the reasons for that are not yet fully understood, the AAP (1992, p. 1120) recommended that "healthy infants, when being put down for sleep be positioned on their side or back." Subsequently, in June 1994 the federal government initiated the "Back to Sleep" campaign (Willinger, 1995). Dramatic and sustained reductions in SIDS deaths followed. The numbers of these deaths fell from approximately 5,400 deaths in 1990 to 2,246 in 2004, a reduction of over 58 percent.

As a result of dramatic declines in numbers of SIDS deaths during the past 10–15 years, two separate task forces of the AAP (1996, 2000a) have reaffirmed the recommendation that positioning infants on their backs for sleep is the preferred position. A third, more recent AAP task force (2005, p. 1245) has withdrawn approval for sleeping on an infant's side, noting that "the AAP no longer recognizes side sleeping as a reasonable alternative to fully supine [on back] sleeping." A change in sleep position alone will not settle all problems with SIDS, but it is significant that this ongoing reduction in infant deaths has continued for so many years.

Much attention has been given to the need for additional research on understanding the causal mechanisms behind SIDS (Daley, 2004). In 2006, Paterson and colleagues pointed to brainstem abnormalities and preliminary neurochemical evidence as possibly helping to understand some infants' vulnerability to SIDS (see also Weese-Mayer, 2006). (Further information about SIDS can be obtained from the SIDS Alliance [1314 Bedford Ave., Suite 210, Baltimore, MD 21208; tel. 800-221-7437 or 800-638-7437, www.sidsalliance. org] or from the National SIDS Resource Center [2070 Chain Bridge Road, Suite 450, Vienna, VA 22182; tel. 703-821-8955, www.sidscenter.org]).

The overall death rate for all children under 1 year of age in the United States in 2004 was 6.85 per 1,000 in the estimated population (see Table 12.2). The more precise infant mortality rate (based on live births) was 6.79 per 1,000 in 2004 (see Table 2.3 in Chapter 2), down from a rate of 6.95 in 2002 and 6.84 in 2003 (Hamilton et al., 2007). Within overall death rates for infants in 2004, rates for African-American children (12.85 per 1,000) remain more than twice as high as those for Caucasian Americans (5.74) or for Hispanic Americans (5.87). And, as we noted in Chapter 2, the United States—the richest country on earth—still has an infant mortality rate higher than that of two dozen other industrialized countries in the world.

TABLE 12.2
Death Rates (per 100,000 in the specified population group) during Childhood by Age, Race or Hispanic Origin,[a] and Sex: United States, 2004

	Under 1 Year[b]			1–4 Years			5–9 Years		
	Both Sexes	Males	Females	Both Sexes	Males	Females	Both Sexes	Males	Females
All "origins"[c]	685.2	753.7	613.4	29.9	32.4	27.3	14.7	16.4	13.0
Caucasian Americans, total	574.0	631.6	513.6	27.0	29.4	24.4	13.4	15.1	11.6
Non-Hispanic Caucasian Americans	564.4	625.2	500.7	26.8	29.0	24.4	13.5	15.2	11.6
Hispanic Americans[d]	586.9	636.5	535.1	27.3	30.2	24.3	12.6	13.8	11.3
African Americans	1,284.7	1,414.2	1,149.9	44.8	48.6	40.9	21.6	23.1	20.1
Asian or Pacific Island Americans[e]	418.3	443.1	392.2	21.3	20.7	22.0	11.8	14.7	8.8
American Indians and Alaskan Natives[f]	899.0	1,076.0	715.4	54.4	55.3	53.4	19.6	20.3	18.8

[a]Data for specified groups other than Caucasian Americans and African Americans should be interpreted with caution because of inconsistencies between reporting race and/or Hispanic origin on death certificates and on censuses and surveys.

[b]Death rates for "under 1 year" (based on population estimates) differ from infant mortality rates (based on live births); for infant mortality rates see Table 2.3.

[c]Figures for origin not stated are included in "all origins" but not distributed among specified origins.

[d]Includes all persons of Hispanic origin of any race.

[e]Includes Chinese, Filipino, Hawaiian, Japanese, and Other Asian or Pacific Islander.

[f]Includes Aleuts and Eskimos.

Source: Miniño et al., 2007.

Deaths of Children after Infancy In 2004, 4,785 children between the ages of 1 and 4 years died in the United States, along with 2,888 children between 5 and 9 years of age. In both cases, accidents, congenital malformations, malignant neoplasms (cancer), and homicide (assault) were the leading causes of these deaths (see Table 12.3). In fact, accidents are the leading cause of death in all of childhood after the first year of life, with motor vehicle accidents becoming proportionately more prominent in later childhood deaths. Throughout childhood, congenital malformations decline in relative significance as leading causes of death, whereas cancer and homicide increase in relative significance. By 1992, human immunodeficiency virus (HIV) infection had become the seventh leading cause of death for children 1 to 4 years of age as well as for those between 5 and 14 years of age (Kochanek & Hudson, 1994). In 2004, however, HIV infection no longer appeared among the ten leading causes of death in these two age groups (Miniño et al., 2007), and public health officials were taking note of the significant achievement whereby AIDS deaths among infants as a result of mother-to-child transmission of the HIV have been all but eliminated in our society (Mofenson et al., 2006).

Among American children who die, there are significant differences between Caucasian Americans and members of other American racial and cultural groups, as well as between males and females (see Tables 12.1 and 12.2). For example, as might be expected, *numbers of deaths* in children between 1 and 4 years of age and between 5 and 9 years of age are much larger among Caucasian Americans than they are among African Americans, Hispanic Americans, Asian and Pacific Island Americans, or American Indians. However, *death rates* are especially high among African-American and American-Indian children in these age groups. Moreover, in general, numbers of deaths and death rates are noticeably higher for male children than they are for females. Further, after infancy, deaths resulting from homicide and HIV infection are disproportionately prevalent among African-American children. All

TABLE 12.3

Numbers of Deaths and Death Rates (per 100,000) during Childhood for the Five Leading Causes of Death in Specified Age Groups, Both Genders, All Races: United States, 2004

Rank	1–4 Years of Age			5–9 Years of Age		
	Cause of Death	Number	Rate	Cause of Death	Number	Rate
	All causes	4,785	29.9	All causes	2,888	14.7
1	Accidents (unintentional injuries)	1,641	10.3	Accidents (unintentional injuries)	1,126	5.7
2	Congenital malformations, deformations, & chromosomal abnormalities	569	3.6	Malignant neoplasms	526	2.7
3	Malignant neoplasms (cancer)	399	2.5	Congenital malformations, deformations, & chromosomal abnormalities	205	1.0
4	Assault (homicide)	377	2.4	Assault (homicide)	122	0.6
5	Diseases of the heart	187	1.2	Diseases of the heart	83	0.4

Source: Hamilton et al., 2007; Miniño et al., 2007.

these statistics clearly illustrate the social inequality of death within the contemporary American death system. It is especially hazardous to be an infant, a male child, and an African-American child in our society—and those hazards are compounded when poverty is introduced as an additional variable.

Deaths of Others Experienced by Children

That children experience the deaths of others is also a reality of life in our society. No reliable data are available concerning the frequency or patterns of these death-related encounters, and it appears that many American adults often undervalue the prevalence and importance of this type of death for children. In fact, children may encounter the deaths of a grandparent, parent, sibling, other relative, classmate, friend, neighbor, teacher, pet, or wild animal. In any of these cases, encountering the death of a significant other can be an important experience for a child, having special meaning for his or her subsequent development.

Loss experiences differ for individual children. For example, a deceased grandparent or parent might not have lived with or spent much time with a particular child. As a result, a child might not perceive the death of that individual as a very important loss. By contrast, the death of a cherished pet, a childhood friend, or a caring neighbor might be a significant event in a child's life.

In addition, children within different cultural, ethnic, and socioeconomic communities in the United States may encounter death in different ways. For example, all too many American children are direct or indirect casualties of familial and community violence (Groves et al., 1993; Kozol, 1995; Nader, 1996), either as immediate victims or as witnesses of violence that may involve multiple losses and traumatic deaths—such as those that occurred on September 11, 2001.

Moreover, although few American children directly experience deaths from starvation, civil disruption, or war, they may witness graphic reports of such deaths on television. Think of just five examples in which children were exposed to extensive television coverage of death and destruction: the results of the terrorist attacks on the World Trade Center in New York City and the Pentagon in the Washington, D.C., area on September, 11, 2001; the ongoing conflict in Iraq beginning in March 2003; the effects of the Asian tsunami in late December 2004 and early 2005; the devastation along

Memorializing children who died as a result of abuse.

the U.S. Gulf Coast caused by Hurricanes Katrina and Rita in August and September 2005; and the Virginia Tech shootings in April 2007.

Further, several years ago Diamant (1994) drew on a study by the American Psychological Association to show that children in the United States who watch 2 to 4 hours of television per day will have witnessed fantasized versions of 8,000 murders and 100,000 acts of violence by the time they finish elementary school. Because such fantasized depictions of death and violence are not real, adults often dismiss them as unimportant. However, they may be important in the minds of young children, especially those children who have little direct experience with natural human death that would enable them to put into perspective these surrogate deaths in the media.

The point to emphasize is that children are exposed to these and other death-related events, whether or not adults or society recognize that fact (Slaughter & Lyons, 2003). Curious children are unlikely to ignore such events completely. What is more likely is that the ways in which a child acknowledges and deals with death-related events may not be obvious to adults in their environment. This was evident in the vignette near the beginning of this chapter, when Allison's father failed to understand and respond in helpful ways to her needs. Those who wish to help children in our society need to be sensitive to the many implications of encounters with death during childhood.

To appreciate the ways in which children experience death, we will examine two additional topics associated with children's encounters with death: the development of death-related concepts and the development of death-related attitudes in childhood.

❦ The Development of Death-Related Concepts in Childhood

Systematic study of the development of children's understandings of death began in the 1930s (Anthony, 1939, 1940; see also Anthony, 1972; Schilder & Wechsler, 1934). Since that time, numerous research reports on this subject have been published in English alone (Speece & Brent, 1996; Stambrook & Parker, 1987). We focus here on a classic report by Nagy (1948/1959), which is typical of these studies, as well as more recent work by Speece and Brent (1996).

The Work of Maria Nagy

To learn about children's understanding of the concept of death, Maria Nagy (1948/1959) examined 378 children living in Budapest just before World War II. The children were 3 to 10 years of age, 51 percent boys and 49 percent girls, ranging from dull normal to superior in intelligence level (with most falling in the "normal" range). Nagy's methods were as follows: children in the *7-to-10-year-old range* were asked to "write down everything that comes into your mind about death" (1948, p. 4); children in the *6-to-10-year-old range* were asked to make drawings about death (many of the older children also wrote explanations of their creations); and discussions were held with *all of the children,* either about their compositions and drawings, or (in the case of 3- to 5-year-olds) to get them to talk about their ideas and feelings about death. Because of the war, Nagy's results were not published until 1948; they appeared again in 1959 in a somewhat revised form.

Nagy's results (1948, p. 7) suggested three major developmental stages: (1) "The child of less than five years does not recognize death as an irreversible fact. In death it sees life"; (2) "Between the ages of five and nine death is most often personified and thought of as a contingency"; and (3) "In general only after the age of nine is it recognized that death is a process happening in us according to certain laws." Nagy wrote that because "the different sorts of answers can be found only at certain ages, one can speak of stages of development" (1948, p. 7), although she later added that "it should be kept in mind that neither the stages nor the above-mentioned ages at which they occur are watertight compartments as it were. Overlapping does exist" (1959, p. 81). Brief descriptions of each of these stages, using Nagy's own characterizations, illustrate her results.

Stage 1: There Is No Definitive Death In the first stage of children's conceptual development, Nagy believes that "the child does not know death as such" (1948, p. 7). Either the concept of death has not been fully distinguished from other concepts or its full implications have not yet been grasped. For this reason, *death is not seen as final*; life and consciousness are attributed to the dead. One way in which this occurs is when death is understood either as a departure or a sleep—that is, in terms of continued life elsewhere (departure) or as a diminished form of life (sleep). In Nagy's view, this denies death as a clear and unambiguous concept.

A second way in which the finality of death is not fully grasped is when children "no longer deny death, but . . . are still unable to accept it as a definitive fact" (p. 13). Such children cannot completely separate death from life; they view death as a gradual, transitional process (between dying and being buried or arriving in heaven) or as a temporary situation in which links with life have not yet been completely severed. To Nagy, this means that life and death are either held in simultaneous relation or they are interpreted as being able to change places with one another repeatedly. In short, although death exists, it is not absolutely final or definitive.

It is important to note that Nagy's description of children who have not grasped the finality or definitiveness of death does not necessarily imply blissful ignorance. Even when death is interpreted as a kind of ongoing living somewhere else, separation from someone who is loved and consequent changes in the child's life may still be painful. A child does not have to grasp fully the finality of death or the complete cessation of bodily activities to react to separation from the dead person.

Stage 2: Death = A Person According to Nagy, in this second stage *death is imagined as a separate person* (such as a grim reaper, skeleton, ghost, or death angel), or else *death is identified with the dead themselves* so that the children did not distinguish between death and dead persons. Nagy interpreted this concept as a *personification of death,* which means that the existence and definitiveness of death have been accepted, although, because of children's strong aversion to the thought of death, death is depicted as a person or reality that is outside or remote from them. In this way, death is conceived of as final, but avoidable or not inevitable and not universal. Those caught by the external force do die; those who escape or get away from the clutches of that force do not die. Later researchers (e.g., Gartley

& Bernasconi, 1967; Kane, 1979; Koocher, 1973, 1974) emphasized the theme of death's *avoidability* in this stage rather than its personification (which may only be a child's concrete way of representing the avoidability of death through the device of an external figure). Children who focused on avoiding death made comments like the following when they were asked what they think of death and dying: "You have to get sick before you die, so I am never going to get sick and I'll never have to die" (Adler, 1979, p. 46).

Other children have made clear that they are not satisfied with the simple fact of death as disappearance. They want to know where and how the deceased person continues to live. This curiosity may lead children to speculate about the nature of life in the grave. Because these theories are based on the child's limited life experiences, they may combine keen insight and misinterpretations, as well as feelings of anxiety and fear about what is going on.

Stage 3: The Cessation of Corporal Life In this third stage, Nagy believed children recognize that death is a process operating within us. Such children view death as both *final and universal,* an aspect of life that is inevitable and not avoidable. Nagy suggested that this reflects a realistic view of both death and the world.

The Work of Mark Speece and Sandor Brent

After reviewing the literature and conducting their own research on children's understandings of death, Mark Speece and Sandor Brent (1984, 1996) concluded that the concept of death is not a simple, uncomplicated notion. It embraces a number of distinguishable sub-concepts, each of which is a central aspect in children's concepts of death. Speece and Brent identified *five principal sub-concepts,* some with subordinate components or elements (see Table 12.4).

Universality as a component in the concept of death involves the recognition that *all living things must eventually die.* This is complex, challenging children to bring together three closely related notions: all-inclusiveness, inevitability, and unpredictability. *All-inclusiveness* concerns whether or not the concept of death applies to every living thing ("Does everyone die?"); this points to the fact that no living thing is exempt from death. *Inevitability* has to do with the necessity with which death applies to living things ("Does everyone have to die?") and points to the fact

---

TABLE 12.4
Subconcepts Embraced by the Concept of Death

Universality
  All-inclusiveness
  Inevitability
  Unpredictability
Irreversibility

Nonfunctionality

Causality

Noncorporeal continuation

Source: Based on Speece and Brent, 1996.

that death is ultimately unavoidable for all living things, regardless of its specific causes. *Unpredictability* relates to the timing of death. If death is all-inclusive and inevitable, one might conclude its timing would be certain and predictable—but that is not the case. In fact, anyone might possibly die at any time. Children and others often shy away from acknowledging the personal implications of this aspect of the universality of death.

Two additional sub-concepts, irreversibility and nonfunctionality, are both aspects of the finality of death. *Irreversibility* has to do with the transition from being alive to being dead and to the state that results from death. So, once the physical body of a living thing is dead, it can never be alive again—barring miraculous or magical events and explanations. Medical resuscitation can apply only to a kind of boundary region between being alive and being dead, not to the state of death in which life in a physical body is irreversibly absent. *Nonfunctionality* means that death involves the complete and final cessation of all of the life-defining capabilities or functional capacities (whether external and observable or internal and inferred) typically attributed to a living physical body (Barrett & Behne, 2005).

In addition to universality, irreversibility, and nonfunctionality, Speece and Brent drew attention to two additional sub-concepts: causality and noncorporeal continuation. According to these authors, the sub-concept of *causality* involves comprehending the events or conditions that really do or can bring about the death of a living thing. This sub-concept responds to questions like "Why do living things die?" and "What makes living things die?" It asks children to achieve a realistic understanding of the external and internal events or forces that might bring about death—as opposed to magical thinking, which suggests that bad behavior or merely wishing could cause someone to die (Fogarty, 2000).

The final component in the concept of death—which Speece and Brent term *noncorporeal continuation*—is reflected in children's efforts to grasp or articulate their understanding of some type of continued life apart from the physical body that has died. This is seen when children ask: "What happens after death?" and "Where does your soul or spirit go when you die?" Another example appears in the reflections of an 11-year-old girl whose experiences of living with HIV infection prompted her to write, "If only I could talk to someone in Heaven, then they could tell me how it is there, what things there are to do there, and what I should bring" (Wiener et al., 1994, p. 12). Research by Brent and Speece (1993) has shown that children and adults commonly say that some type of continued life form—often, though perhaps not always, a mode of personal continuation—exists after the death of the physical body. This continuation may take many forms, such as the ongoing life of a soul in heaven without the body or the reincarnation of a soul in a new and different body. Speece and Brent pointed out that many researchers have been disdainful of children's "beliefs in an afterlife" or systematically unwilling to enter into non-naturalistic aspects of the concept of death.

On the basis of their review of the literature on children's concepts of death, Speece and Brent (1996) concluded, "most studies have found that *by seven years of age* most children understand each of the key bioscientific components—Universality, Irreversibility, Nonfunctionality, and Causality" (p. 43; emphasis added). This conclusion needs to be evaluated in light of Speece and Brent's caution that "age by itself explains nothing. It is rather a convenient general, omnibus index of a wide range of loosely correlated biological and environmental variables."

Further, although some researchers (e.g., Lonetto, 1980; Schilder & Wechsler, 1934) have maintained that children recognize that death is possible for all other people before they apply it to themselves, Speece and Brent thought it more likely that most children understand their own personal mortality before they understand that all other people die.

Some Comments on Children's Understandings of Death

The work of Nagy and other researchers who have studied the development of death-related concepts in childhood exposes key elements in the concept of death, such as finality, avoidability versus inevitability, external versus internal forces, and universality. Much of this work has had the great advantage of fitting easily within larger theories or models of developmental psychology, such as those of Jean Piaget (1998; see also Piaget & Inhelder, 1958; Table 12.5). For example, Nagy's characterization of the earliest stages in her account of children's concepts of death agreed with Piaget's observations about an egocentric orientation and several other characteristics of what he calls preoperational thought—such as *magical thinking* (in which all events are explained by the causal influence of various commands, intentions, and forces; see Fogarty, 2000), *animism* (in which life and consciousness are attributed to objects that others think of as inanimate), and *artificialism* (in which it is believed that all objects and events in the world have been manufactured to serve people, a belief that Wass [1984] describes as directly opposed to animism). Similarly, the universality and inevitability that characterize Nagy's final stage conform to Piaget's account of objectivity, generality, and propositional thinking in what he calls the period of formal operations. This finding suggests that children's understandings involve a development or maturation in their capacity to form more and more abstract concepts of subjects like death.

However, research in this field has been plagued by methodological problems, such as lack of precision and agreement in the terms and definitions used for various components of the concept of death, as well as lack of reliable and valid standardized measures for these components. The ensuing literature has not unfairly been characterized as consisting of a "confusing array of results" (Stambrook & Parker, 1987, p. 154). Often, commentators have oversimplified their results, made them more rigid than originally suggested, or applied them uncritically. Many commentators have generalized from studies of particular groups of children (such as Nagy's Hungarian children, who were examined before World War II and before the advent of new cultural forces like television) to other groups of children without taking into account historical or cultural variables in different populations. Speece and Brent (and others, such as Kenyon, 2001; Lazar & Torney-Purta, 1991) have suggested that better research and more nuanced appreciation of results could follow from recommendations to distinguish, standardize, and operationalize key sub-concepts within the concept of death.

Adults striving to gain insight into children's understanding of death, to teach children about death, or to provide empathic support to children who are coping with death, must attend to at least four principal variables: developmental level, life experiences, individual personality, and patterns of communication and support (Kastenbaum, 1977).With respect to *development,* cognitive development is not the only relevant variable; maturation is a multidimensional process that applies

TABLE 12.5
Piaget's System of Cognitive Development

Period and Stage[a]	Life Period[b]	Some Major Characteristics
I. Period of sensorimotor intelligence	Infancy (0-2)	"Intelligence" consists of sensory and motor actions. No conscious thinking. Limited language.[c] No concept of reality.
II. Period of preparation and organization of concrete operations		
1. Stage of preoperational thought	Early childhood (2-7)	Egocentric orientation. Magical, animistic, & artificialistic thinking. Thinking is irreversible. Reality is subjective.
2. Stage of concrete operations	Middle childhood/ preadolescence (7–11/12)	Orientation ego-decentered. Thinking is bound to concrete. Naturalistic thinking. Recognizes laws of conservation and reversibility.
III. Period of formal operations	Adolescence and adulthood (12+)	Propositional and hypo-deductive thinking. Generality of thinking. Reality is objective.

[a]Each stage includes an initial period of preparation and a final period of attainment; thus, whatever characterizes a stage is in the process of formation.

[b]There are individual differences in chronological ages.

[c]By the end of age 2, children, on the average, have attained a vocabulary of approximately 250–300 words.

Source: From "Concepts of Death: A Developmental Perspective" by H. Wass. In H. Wass and C. A. Corr (Eds.), *Childhood and Death,* p. 4. Copyright © 1984 Hemisphere Publishing Corporation. Reprinted with permission.

to all aspects of a child's life—physical, psychological, social, and spiritual. *Life experiences* are a critical but not yet well-studied factor, even though the quantity and quality of a child's encounters with death are likely to be influential in his or her understanding of death. Each child's *individual personality* will be a powerful variable in the ways he or she can and does think about death. And the death-related thoughts that a child shares with others will depend on his or her ability and willingness to *communicate,* together with the *support* and comfort that he or she receives from those others.

A good example of this effect is seen in quite different challenges that are presented to a child when he or she is asked to explain two simple sentences: "You are dead" and "I will die" (Kastenbaum, 2000; Kastenbaum & Aisenberg, 1972). The first sentence applies to another person at the present time; the second refers back to the speaker but at some unspecified time in the future. The issues involved in grasping these two sentences are partly conceptual, but they also relate to the potential threat implied in the second sentence and the child's ability to grasp a future possibility. When children strive to understand the concept of death and its various sub-concepts, those who have experienced a healthy development, who are able to draw on a fund of constructive personal experiences, whose self-concept is stable and well formed, who communicate openly, and who have adequate support from the adults around them are likely to find themselves in a different and more advantageous position by comparison with children who do not have these resources.

Clearly, children do not always think of death as adults do. However, that does not mean they have no concept of death. For example, children who think of death as sleep have *an understanding of death* through which they try to make sense of their experiences—however undifferentiated that understanding may be from other concepts and however inadequate it may seem in the light of some adult standard. As Kastenbaum and Aisenberg (1972, p. 9) noted, "Between the extremes of 'no understanding' and explicit, integrated abstract thought there are many ways by which the young mind can enter into relationship with death." A good way to gain insight into children's understandings of death is to listen carefully to the many questions they ask about this subject (Corr, 1995b, 1996).

The basic lesson from research by Nagy and others is that children do make an active effort to grasp or understand death. Nagy (1948, p. 27) added an important corollary: "To conceal death from the child is not possible and is also not permissible. Natural behavior in the child's surroundings can greatly diminish the shock of its acquaintance with death." Allison's father in the vignette near the beginning of this chapter had not learned this lesson.

❦ The Development of Death-Related Attitudes in Childhood

Children living in the United States today receive many messages about death. These messages come from the societal death system that surrounds the children and expresses itself, in particular, through the media; their parents, family members, and other persons with whom they come into contact; and their own life experiences. Messages such as these often tell children that death is not an acceptable topic for discussion and that children are not permitted to take part in death-related events. Not all societies have transmitted this kind of message to children. For example, as we learned in Chapter 3, among the New England Puritans in colonial America (Stannard, 1977) and in contemporary Amish society (Hostetler, 1994; Kraybill, 2001), children were or are expected to take part in both the happy and sad events in a family's life. Any other alternative would have seemed or would still seem undesirable and impracticable.

Death-related situations and experiences may be new to many children in American society, but new experiences need not be overwhelming unless children have been led to view them that way. Nor are such experiences out of bounds from the inquiring mind of a child. The claim that "the child is so recently of the quick that there is little need in his spring-green world for an understanding of the dead" (Ross, 1967, p. 250) does not describe the authentic lives of children in our society. In fact, there is ample evidence in everyday interactions with children and in the scholarly literature (going back as far as the 1920s and 1930s—e.g., Childers & Wimmer, 1971; Hall, 1922; Koocher et al., 1976; Schilder & Wechsler, 1934) that *normal, healthy children do have thoughts and feelings about death; they are curious about this subject.*

The specific form of any one child's attitudes toward death, as toward any other significant subject, will relate to the nature of the child's encounters with death and to the developmental, personal, and societal forces that help to shape the child's interpretation and response to a given experience. Even young infants who have little experience or conceptual capacity give clear evidence of separation anxiety. Older children who had no role in a parent's death may nevertheless blame themselves if they believe that something they said or did was somehow magically related to the death. In short, attitudes toward death are complex, even in childhood, and may derive from many sources (Wass & Cason, 1984). To show this, we describe here two arenas in which death-related attitudes are apparent during childhood.

Death-Related Games

Long-standing research has demonstrated that death themes are pervasive in children's play in many societies throughout history (e.g., Opie & Opie, 1969). For example, Maurer (1966) suggested that the game of peek-a-boo is a classic death-related game in childhood. From the child's egocentric perspective, what happens in this game is that the external world vanishes and then suddenly reappears. As a child focuses on the (apparent) disappearance of the world, he or she may become tearful; its reappearance will often produce delight. From a young child's perspective many experiences like this involve attitudes that are (at least) quite similar to those associated with death.

Further, Rochlin (1967) reported research on children's play activities demonstrating "that at a very early age well-developed mental faculties are functioning to defend oneself against the realization that life may end" (p. 61). Children appear to recognize that their lives might be changed in important ways by death and act on that recognition in the fantasy world of their play. Rochlin's research focused especially on children's games concerned with action, violence, and at least the potential for death. He concluded that "death is a matter of deep consideration to the very young child . . . thoughts of dying are commonplace . . . behavior is influenced by such thoughts" (p. 54). This is not a point to dismiss lightly, since play is the main work of a child's life.

Rhymes, Songs, Humor, and Fairy Tales

Death-related themes appear frequently in children's rhymes and humor. For example, many have sung a little ditty in which "the worms crawl in, the worms crawl out." Others will be familiar with "Ring around the Rosie," but they may not have realized that it is an English song arising from a plague and describing the roseate skin pustules of disease, as a result of which "we all fall down." Even lullabies, like "Rock-a-Bye Baby," are filled with falling cradle themes (Achté et al., 1990), and the child's prayer, "Now I lay me down to sleep," is a petition for safekeeping against death and other hazards of the night.

Children's fairy tales, whether oral or written, are also chock-full of references to death (Lamers, 1995). Little Red Riding Hood and her grandmother are eaten by the wicked wolf in the original version of the story, not saved by a passing woodsman or hunter before or after they find themselves in the wolf's stomach (see Focus On 1.1 in Chapter 1; Bertman, 1984; Dundes, 1989; Zipes, 1983). The Big Bad Wolf who pursues the three little pigs with threats to huff and puff and blow their houses down dies in a scalding pot of hot water when he falls down the last chimney.

Hansel and Gretel (who were left to die in the forest by their parents because there was not enough food) trick the wicked witch and shut her up in the hot oven where she planned to cook them. The wicked stepmother orders the death of Snow White and demands her heart as proof. A gentle kiss may awaken Sleeping Beauty from a state of coma, but the false bride in "The Goose Girl" is put into a barrel lined with sharp nails and rolled until she is dead (Lang, 1904).

Death-related humor and stories of this sort are not necessarily morbid or unhealthful for children. Bettelheim (1977) argued that they are, in fact, wholesome experiences in which children can work through fears and anxieties related to death in safe and distanced ways. *Death is not absent from the fantasy world of childhood.* Its familiar presence debunks the view that children are simply unfamiliar with death-related thoughts and feelings. Indeed, in our society today the very powerful force of television entertainment programs repeatedly suggest that the way in which people usually come to be dead is by being killed, that only "bad" guys really die, and that death itself is not permanent (see Chapter 4).

❦ Children Who Are Coping with Life-Threatening Illness and Dying

Children coping with life-threatening illness and dying frequently experience anxiety. As they acquire information about their condition, their self-concept is likely to change in discernible ways, and they are apt to share an identifiable set of specific concerns associated with dying.

Anxiety in Ill and Dying Children

Vernick and Karon's (1965) answer to the question, "Who's afraid of death on a leukemia ward?" was *everyone*—children, family members, and professional caregivers. This finding suggests a basis for coming together and sharing with children. However, when Waechter (1971) first began to study ill and dying children, she found many parents and caregivers who did not share with children accurate information about their diagnoses and prognoses. Waechter investigated the attitudes of these children by creating four matched groups of 6- to 10-year-olds: children with chronic disease for which death was predicted; children with chronic disease with a good prognosis; children with brief illness; and nonhospitalized, well children. During an interview, each child was given a projective test (a set of pictures for each of which the child was to develop a story) and a test to measure general anxiety.

Waechter demonstrated that anxiety levels in fatally ill children were much higher than those for either of the other two groups of hospitalized children or for the well children. Also, the fatally ill children expressed significantly more anxiety specifically related to death, mutilation, and loneliness than did other ill children. This was true even though the fatally ill children had not been formally informed of their prognosis. Other studies of ill and dying children have reported similar findings (e.g., Spinetta & Maloney, 1975; Spinetta et al., 1973; and Waechter, 1984, in the United States; and Lee et al., 1984, in China).

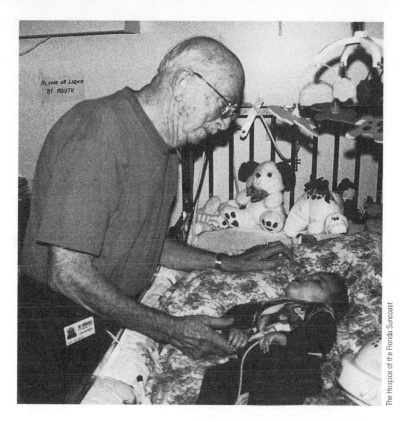

Visiting a sick child.

Acquiring Information and Changing Concepts of Self

A different approach was taken by Bluebond-Langner (1977, 1978), who used the methodology of cultural anthropology to identify keen awareness of their situation in hospitalized, terminally ill children with leukemia. Bluebond-Langner identified five stages in the children's process of acquiring information (see the left-hand column in Table 12.6). The sobering—and really not very surprising—lesson from this portion of Bluebond-Langner's study is that children pay attention to important experiences in their lives, and acquire information from people and events that impact very closely on them.

Bluebond-Langner's research went one step further. She noted that acquisition of information was coordinated with parallel shifts in self-concept. As the children obtained information, they applied it to a changing understanding of themselves (see the right-hand column in Table 12.6). According to Bluebond-Langner, changes in self-concept were associated with events in the illness process and the information available to the children. Critical points here are the timing of these changes in relationship to external events and the children's ability to integrate and synthesize information arising from their experiences to form new self-concepts.

Children learn from their experiences, from other children, and from the ways in which adults treat them. How could it be otherwise? What they learn is not only abstract information; it has meaning and significance for them. As suggested by

TABLE 12.6
The Private Worlds of Dying Children

Stages in the Process of Acquiring Information	Changes in Self-Concept
1. I have a serious illness.	1. From diagnosis (prior to which I had thought of myself as well) to awareness that I am seriously ill.
2. I know the drugs that I am receiving, when and how they are being used, and their side effects.	2. At the first remission, to the view that I am seriously ill—but will get better.
3. I know the purposes of treatments and procedures.	3. At the first relapse, to the view that I am always ill—but will get better.
4. I understand that these treatments, procedures, and symptoms fit together to identify a disease in which there is a cycle of relapses and remissions (i.e., the medicines do not always last as long or work as well as they are supposed to) (does not include death).	4. After several more remissions and relapses, to the view that I am always ill—but will never get better.
5. I understand that the cycle of disease is finite, has an end, and that end is death—there is only a limited number of drugs, and when they stop working, I will die soon.	5. After the death of a leukemic peer, to the realization that I am dying.

Source: Adapted from *The Private Worlds of Dying Children,* by M. Bluebond-Langner, pp. 166, 169. Copyright © 1978 Princeton University Press.

Alexander and Adlerstein (1958), the central point may be not so much the content of death conceptions as their significance for the individuals in question. We will pursue this point in Chapter 13. Here we need only observe that children's concepts of death are intimately associated with ways they feel about and interpret both themselves and the world around them.

Issues for Ill and Dying Children

Many advances have taken place in recent years in understanding pain and other distressing symptoms and in their management in different types of life-threatening childhood illnesses (see, for example, Goldman, 1998; McGrath, 1998). The increased understanding has led to official policy statements on care for children with life-threatening illnesses from the International Work Group on Death, Dying, and Bereavement (1993; www.iwgddb.org), the Association for Children with Life-Threatening or Terminal Conditions and Their Families in Britain (1995; www.act.org.uk), the World Health Organization (1998; www.who.int), and the American Academy of Pediatrics (2000a; www.aap.org). Nevertheless, many studies have confirmed deficiencies in the management of pain and other distressing symptoms in many children who are dying, even as they have offered guidelines for better care (e.g., Hurwitz et al., 2004; McCallum et al., 2000; Wolfe et al., 2000a).

Ill and dying children often have psychosocial needs focused around the importance of love and security with freedom from pain, freedom from deep-seated feelings of anxiety or guilt, a sense of belonging, a feeling of self-respect, and understanding of self (Masera et al., 1999; Morgan & Murphy, 2000). From a developmental standpoint, Waechter (1984) noted that many preschool children with a life-threatening illness have principal concerns about the causality of their illness, threats to body image, treatment procedures, and fears of dying, whereas school-age children most often have concerns about the future, education and social relationships, body image, and issues related to hospitalization and procedures. Not surprisingly, much of their anxiety focuses on safety (from pain or other forms of distress, intervention procedures, bodily assault) and security (both within themselves and in relationship to family members, peers, and other important persons) (Attig, 1996a; Sourkes, 1995). Stevens (1998) put much of this more simply by proposing that the emotional needs of dying children will be: (1) those of all children regardless of health; (2) those arising from the child's reaction to illness and admission to a hospital; and (3) those arising from the child's concept of death.

Many of the concerns of dying children emphasize quality in living and the immediate or present-tense implications of various sorts of threats to quality in living (Zimmerman, 2005). These issues fit with the tendency of many children to live in the moment. Moreover, it is important to recognize that cure rates for many illnesses that were once highly lethal for children have changed so dramatically in recent years that for many children the challenge has changed from coping with dying to living with a serious or life-threatening illness (Adams & Deveau, 1993; Doka, 1996a; Koocher & O'Malley, 1981; Spinetta & Deasy-Spinetta, 1981). Thus it has been argued that the work of contemporary pediatric oncologists is guided by the motto "Cure is not enough" and by an emphasis on quality in living among survivors of childhood cancer (Schwartz et al., 1994). Issues that are often central for survivors—or, as some prefer to say, "graduates"—of a life-threatening illness in childhood are: (1) normalization or incorporating the disease experience into one's life history; (2) learning to live with uncertainty—which may lead to a heightened sense of vulnerability, overprotectiveness by adults, or a transformation of personal priorities, values, and goals; (3) learning to live with compromise and the ongoing repercussions of disease; and (4) overcoming stigma in social contexts (Ruccione, 1994). It is important also to assess and respond appropriately to the spiritual needs of children (Davies et al., 2002).

Similar concerns are found in children with chronic conditions, such as cystic fibrosis (e.g., Bluebond-Langner, 1996; Bluebond-Langner et al., 2001), as well as in children whose experiences with HIV infection and AIDS have turned into coping with a long-term life-threatening or life-limiting condition (Dane, 1996). In many ways, these situations can be as difficult as coping with acute dying. Thus, one 12-year-old girl had the following to say about contending with the uncertainties posed by HIV infection: "Living with HIV and knowing that you can die from it is scary. . . . I think it is hardest in this order: Not knowing when this will happen. . . . Not knowing where it will happen. . . .Worrying about my family. . . . What will happen to my stuff and my room? . . . Thinking about what my friends will think" (Wiener et al., 1994, p. 24).

Children Who Are Coping with Bereavement and Grief

There once was a scholarly debate about whether children are able to mourn after a death (see, for example, Furman, 1973). This debate rests on a failure to distinguish between grief and mourning, together with an absence of adequate models for childhood mourning. Children certainly experience grief (i.e., react to loss). They may cry, get angry, become depressed, have trouble sleeping, regress in their behavior, or react in other ways to loss.

However, children do not react to loss or express their reactions as adults do (Wolfenstein, 1966). For example, bereaved children may not display their feelings as openly as many adults do, and they may immerse themselves in activities of everyday life such as play and school instead of withdrawing into preoccupation with thoughts of the deceased person (Romond, 1989). As a result, children's grief reactions may be *more intermittent in character* than those of many adults and thus *longer in duration* (Worden, 1996). In this way, children may be "dosing" themselves with their grief and mourning, that is, allowing themselves to experience their grief reactions and their efforts to cope for a while, but then turning away when that becomes overwhelming or when other concerns attract their attention. For bereaved children, it is also important to ask how normative developmental tasks influence encounters with loss, and vice versa: can children feel secure when they are coping with loss and grief? Does healthy development help them in such coping? In ways like these, there may be major differences between bereaved adults and children.

The real issue for bereaved children is not so much whether they are able to mourn, but the nature of their reactions and responses to loss. That is, what are the central concerns that are likely to preoccupy bereaved children? And what are the tasks of mourning that children face in coping with loss and grief?

Issues for Bereaved Children

Three central issues are likely to be prominent in the grief experiences of bereaved children and may apply to the perceived or real termination of any relationship for children: (1) did I cause it (death or some other form of loss) to happen; (2) is it going to happen to me; and (3) who is going to take care of me? The egocentricity of these issues is obvious. When a child does not rightly understand the causality involved in a loss, perhaps because of ignorance or magical thinking, it is not surprising that issues of origin and endangerment should present themselves.

The death of a parent or other caring adult may especially evoke the first and third of these issues. For example, if Mommy says in exasperation one day, "You'll be the death of me," and is later killed in a car accident, a child may be anxious about whether the latter event fulfilled the promise of the former. Similarly, when there is widespread discussion of a large-scale trauma, such as happened on September 11, 2001, or nightly media reports about deaths in Iraq, children may

Squib, a young owl, has lost his piece (peace) and is sad.

wonder about potential threats to themselves. And when children's welfare depends in so many ways on parents and other adults, we can understand why the death of an important person might lead a child to be anxious about who will now provide the care that he or she needs (Donnelly, 1987; Silverman, 2000). As a result, many children who have experienced the death of a parent strive to maintain an emotional connection with the deceased parent by talking to that individual or holding on to symbolic linking objects such as pictures or gifts (Silverman et al., 1992).

If someone dies in the family and a child perceives that Daddy (or the doctor or others) did not or could not prevent that sad event, then the child may be concerned that he or she could experience the same unhappy fate. The death of a sibling or other child may be especially difficult since it strikes so close to the child's own self and may rob the bereaved child of emotional support from caregivers (Davies, 1998; Stahlman, 1996; Toray & Oltjenbruns, 1996). A sibling or playmate is equally a companion, competitor, and alter ego. Experiencing such a person's death during childhood may have short-term outcomes in aggressive and attention-seeking behaviors (McCown & Davies, 1995), as well as long-term effects throughout the individual's childhood and later life (Donnelly, 1988; Rosen, 1986; Schuurman, 2003).

It has long been known that bereaved children especially need support, nurturance, and continuity in their lives. In fact, the Harvard Child Bereavement Study established a more detailed list of children's bereavement needs (Worden, 1996). These include:

- ◆ Adequate information—clear and comprehensible information about an impending death (whenever that is possible) and certainly after a death has occurred
- ◆ Fears and anxieties addressed—to know that they will be cared for and to experience consistent discipline
- ◆ Reassurance that they are not to blame
- ◆ Careful listening—in the form of someone who will hear them out and not minimize their concerns
- ◆ Validation of their feelings—including respect for and safe ways to express individual reactions in their own ways
- ◆ Help with overwhelming feelings—especially when sadness, anger, anxiety, and guilt are intense
- ◆ Involvement and inclusion—both before and after a death, with preparation and without being forced to join in
- ◆ Continued routine activities—in the form of age-appropriate activities, such as play and school
- ◆ Modeled grief behaviors—through adults who can share their own grief and mourning, and show how to experience and express these in constructive ways
- ◆ Opportunities to remember—both after a death and throughout life

Children respond to bereavement experiences in ways that suit their particular developmental situation (Fleming, 1985; Furman, 1974; Silverman et al., 1992; Silverman & Worden, 1992a). For example, children who do not appreciate the finality of death may wonder what sort of activities are undertaken by the deceased, who is thought to be somehow alive in a different way or in a different place. By contrast, children who appreciate that death involves irreversibility and nonfunctionality may ask very concrete questions about what happens to a dead body when it stops working.

In their actions, bereaved children may delay beginning their grief work or revealing it to others. In their efforts to cope, children may appear to turn away from death from time to time—for example, to play games, watch television, or to go off to school. To adults, this may seem to display lack of awareness, comprehension, or feeling. More likely, it simply involves a short attention span, a failure to realize that the loss is permanent, or a temporary defense against being overwhelmed by the implications of the loss. Usually, strong feelings of anger and fears of abandonment or death are evident in the behaviors of bereaved children. Also, as we noted earlier, children often play death games as a way to work out their feelings and anxieties in a relatively safe setting. Such games are a familiar part of the lives of children; in them, a child can stand safely aside from the harm that comes to the toys or imaginary figures.

Worden (1996) also noted a "late effect" of bereavement in which a significant minority (though certainly not all) of the school-age children in the Harvard Child Bereavement Study were found to be encountering more difficulties at two years after the death of a parent than they were at earlier times (four months and one year after the death). This finding is closely correlated with the family context of the child and especially with the functioning of the surviving parent. The lesson here seems to be the importance of being sensitive to the possibility of both ongoing issues for a bereaved child and those that may only arise at later point in the child's bereavement. The death of a significant person in a child's life does not necessarily lead to complicated grief and mourning, but it can have a long-term impact through a sense of emptiness and the ongoing "presence" of the absent person.

Another distinguishing feature of childhood bereavement is seen in children who may talk to those around them, even to strangers, as a way of watching for reactions and seeking clues to guide their own responses. By contrast with adults who may withdraw into themselves and limit communication when they are mourning, children often ask questions over and over again—"I know that Grandpa died, but when will he come home?"—as a way of testing reality and confirming that what they have been told has not changed. Some questions from children baffle adults: "Where is dead?"; "When you die and go to heaven, what do you do there all day?"; "If Grandpa died and went up to heaven, why is he buried down in the ground?" When viewed from the developmental and experiential perspective of a child, these are quite logical efforts to interpret the meaning of what has happened.

Tasks in Mourning for Bereaved Children

Ill children, dying children, and children who are bereaved may all experience grief. They are all children who are responding to the events and the losses that have occurred or are occurring in their lives. Mourning is the task work involved in attempting to cope with or learn to live with loss and grief. In a bereaved child the work of mourning will be superimposed on basic developmental tasks. Throughout childhood, mourning tasks may need to be addressed again and again in appropriate ways at different developmental levels and in different contexts. Thus, an individual child may mourn the death of his or her mother, her absence in the months and years that follow, what that subsequently means for being different from schoolmates who have a living mother, and his or her inability to draw on the absent mother's support or to share achievements with her in later school years. Reworking losses and grief responses in this way is quite consistent with maturational processes. Healthy mourning integrates losses in ways that shake off unhealthy obstacles and facilitate ongoing living (Furman, 1973, 1974). Worden (1996) identified four tasks of mourning that apply to bereaved children, although he noted that these tasks "can only be understood in terms of the cognitive, emotional, and social development of the child" (p. 12). According to Worden, these tasks are: (1) to accept the reality of the loss; (2) to experience the pain or emotional aspects of the loss; (3) to adjust to an environment in which the deceased is missing; and (4) to relocate the dead person within one's life and find ways to memorialize the person. This task-based account of mourning is quite similar to the adult model from Worden (2002) that we examined in Chapter 9 (with the possible exception of the way in which the fourth task is phrased here, a new phrasing which seems to reflect the great importance for children of maintaining some sense of the presence in one's life of the now-dead person). Instead of pursuing it here, we turn to another, earlier task-based model of mourning in children first proposed by Fox

(1988a, 1988b; see also Trozzi & Massimini, 1999), who identified the following four tasks as central to productive mourning in children:

- The first of these tasks is *to understand and try to make sense out of what is happening or has happened;* for this task, children seek information about the death and its circumstances, as well as ways of interpreting or coming to understand its meaning.

- The second task is *to express emotional and other strong reactions to the present or anticipated loss;* this involves the identification and validation of feelings and other strong reactions to loss that the child may be experiencing for the first time, as well as finding appropriate ways that are not hurtful to the child or others to express such reactions.

- The third task is *to commemorate the life that has been lost through some formal or informal remembrance;* typically, this involves large-muscle activity (such as running, jumping, or otherwise doing something) and some form of memorializing or remembering the life that was lived.

- The fourth task is *to learn how to go on with living and loving;* this often involves a child's need for permission to find ways to go on with healthy living in the aftermath of a significant loss; it always depends on successfully integrating loss and living.

This schema reminds us that bereavement has many dimensions and that children do strive to find effective ways of managing loss and grief.

Baker and his colleagues (Baker & Sedney, 1996; Baker et al., 1992) built on Fox's task-based schema by noting that children's mourning tasks may shift over time in their focus and relative significance. Early tasks are likely to involve an emphasis on trying to understand what has happened and children's needs to protect themselves and their family. Middle-phase tasks usually emphasize emotional acceptance, reevaluation of the relationship (memories and connections), and slowly learning to tolerate painful and ambivalent feelings. Late tasks typically center on forming a new sense of personal identity, constructing a durable internal relationship to the dead person, investing in new relationships, returning to normative developmental tasks and activities, and coping with periodic resurgences of pain.

❦ Helping Children Cope with Death, Dying, and Bereavement

In this section, we organize guidelines for helping children cope with death, dying, and bereavement in four clusters: some general suggestions; a proactive program of education, communication, and validation; helping ill or dying children; and helping bereaved children.

Some General Suggestions

The basic principle in helping children cope with death is more a matter of attitude than one of technique or easily definable skills. As Erikson (1963, p. 269) wrote: "Healthy children will not fear life if their elders have integrity enough not to fear death." Unfortunately, adults often adopt tactics that attempt to insulate children from death-related events, avoid such topics, and deny the finality of death (Becker & Margolin, 1967). In so doing, they block children's efforts to acquire information, express their feelings, obtain support, and learn to cope with sadness and loss.

At the very least, children deserve assistance from their elders in dealing with challenges presented by death. Katzenbach (1986, p. 322) identified the reason why this is so quite pointedly when he wrote:

> Do you know the sensation of being a child and being alone? Children can adapt wonderfully to specific fears, like a pain, a sickness, or a death. It is the unknown which is truly terrifying for them. They have no fund of knowledge in how the world operates, and so they feel completely vulnerable.

Death-related challenges, including those associated with the unknown and a child's sense of vulnerability, *will* arise, and children *will* attempt to deal with them. The only responsible option open to adults is to make available their knowledge, experience, insights, and coping resources to children (McCue & Bonn, 1996; Nussbaum, 1998). As LeShan (1976, p. 3) has written: "A child can live through *anything,* so long as he or she is told the truth and is allowed to share with loved ones the natural feelings people have when they are suffering" (see Issues for Critical Reflection #10).

Adults cannot face death for their children or live on their behalf, but adults can prepare children to do this for themselves and can often walk alongside, at least part of the way. "Part of each child's adventure into life is his discovery of loss, separation, non-being, death. No one can have this adventure for him, nor can death be locked in another room until a child comes of age" (Kastenbaum, 1972, p. 37).

Helping children cope with death is an ongoing process, not a unique event that occurs only at one specific point in time. Children often return over and over to issues that concern them. Such issues need to be readdressed as children confront different developmental and situational challenges. It is part of their continuing maturation and socialization, which is carried out in a natural and effective manner when it draws on ordinary events in living and teachable moments, together with children's own questions and initiatives. Adults can also strive to create opportunities for constructive dialogue with and between children. For example, summer camps for children who share an illness (such as cancer) have been shown to help establish relationships that last well beyond the camp sessions and that supplement in constructive ways relationships with healthy peers (Bluebond-Langner et al., 1991).

Adults may need to make special efforts to help children cope with death in a society that has limited experience with natural human death and whose death system all too often inhibits constructive interactions between children and death. This entails accepting certain related responsibilities (Corr, 1984a), such as:

◆ Undertaking preparation—by initiating a reflective analysis (which no person ever fully completes) of one's own thoughts and feelings about death, and by becoming familiar with basic principles in the body of knowledge that has been developed in this area

◆ Responding to real needs in children (rather than those adults project on them)

In our society, adults often wonder if they should talk to children about death, what they should say, and how they should act with children in death-related situations. These questions arise in many ways: should we discuss death with children or teach them about loss and grief even before a death takes place; what should we say to children after a death occurs; should we take children to funeral services? Perhaps the most difficult of all questions of this type arise in situations in which adults (parents, family members, or care providers) are challenged by a child who has a life-threatening illness and who is facing his or her imminent death.

One recent contribution to these discussions (Kreicbergs et al., 2004) described a study of Swedish parents whose child had died from cancer between 1992 and 1997. Among the 561 eligible parents, 429 reported on whether they had talked about death with their child. Results showed that more than a quarter of those who did not talk with their child about death regretted that they had not done so. Similar regrets

were reported by nearly half of the parents who had sensed that their child was aware of his or her imminent death. By contrast, among the parents who had talked with their child about death, "No parent in this cohort later regretted having talked with his or her child about death" (p. 1175).

The implications of this study suggest that, despite all of the challenges involved in talking to a child about death and even in the very demanding circumstances of a child facing his or her imminent death, it is most often better to go ahead with such conversations. The main reason for this is that, as Rabbi Earl Grollman has often said, "Anything that is mentionable is manageable." Opening a line of communication with children is preferable to allowing them to try to cope on their own with incomplete or improperly understood information and the demons of their own imaginations. In addition, a child who is able to have his or her concerns addressed in a thoughtful and loving way is a child who has someone he or she can trust when there is a need to look for a source of support.

- ◆ Communicating effectively
- ◆ Working cooperatively—with children, with other adults, and with relevant institutions in American society, such as educational and religious organizations

Cooperative work with and by children is well illustrated by one child (Gaes, 1987) who wrote *My Book for Kids with Cansur.* Helping can flow from children to adults as well as from adults to children.

A Proactive Program of Prior Preparation

Whenever possible, one helps children best by preparing them ahead of time to cope with issues associated with sadness and loss (Metzgar & Zick, 1996). The key elements in a proactive program of prior preparation are education, effective communication, and validation. In terms of *education,* adults can explore with children a relatively safe encounter with death, such as a dead bird found in the woods or a dead fish from the school aquarium (Stevenson & Stevenson, 1996b). "Teachable moments" that are not highly charged with personal feelings can represent good beginnings for adult–child dialogue (Carson, 1984). Children can also "try out" adult rituals by acting out various sorts of memorializing practices, as in one story about classmates who planted a tree in memory of their teacher's dead son (Simon, 1979). (Note that a child's beloved pet may present quite a different and much less "safe" situation than one arising from a strange, wild animal; see Butler & Lagoni, 1996; Tuzeo-Jarolmen, 2006.)

An extensive body of death-related literature is now available to be read with or by children at all developmental and reading levels (for an annotated list of selected examples, see Focus On 12.2 and Appendix A; see also: Corr, 2000a, in press a, Rudman et al., 1993). Also, there is literature for parents, educators, and others who are helping children cope with death (see Focus On 12.3), and in some areas there may be workshops or college courses on issues related to children and death (Corr, 1980, 1984b, 1992b, 2002c). Suggestions on how to use these resources are offered in Focus On 12.4. The underlying principle is that "any subject can be taught effectively in some intellectually honest form to any child at any stage of development" (Bruner, 1962, p. 33). This is well illustrated in an annotated bibliography of children's books about the Holocaust (Rudin, 1998).

FOCUS ON 12.2

Selected Literature for Children about Death, Dying, and Bereavement

Annotated descriptions and complete bibliographical information are provided in Appendix A for the following examples and many other books for preschool and primary school children.

PICTURE AND COLORING BOOKS FOR PRESCHOOLERS AND BEGINNING READERS

About the deaths of pets and other animals:

Breebaart, J., & Breebaart, P. (1993). *When I Die, Will I Get Better?*
Brown, M. W. (1958). *The Dead Bird.*
Fox, M. (1994). *Tough Boris.*
Harris, R. H. (2001). *Goodbye Mousie.*
Hemery, K. M. (2000). *Not Just a Fish.*
Krasny, L., & Brown, M. (1998). *When Dinosaurs Die: A Guide to Understanding Death.*
O'Toole, D. (1988). *Aarvy Aardvark Finds Hope.*
Puttock, S., & Bartlett, A. (2001). *A Story for Hippo: A Book about Loss.*

About the deaths of grandparents, parents, and other adults:

Ewart, C. (2003). *The Giant.*
Fassler, J. (1971). *My Grandpa Died Today.*
Hemery, K. M. (1998). *The Brightest Star.*
Hodge, J. (1999). *Finding Grandpa Everywhere.*

(continued)

Selected Literature for Children about Death, Dying, and Bereavement

About the deaths of grandparents, parents, and other adults: *(continued)*
 Shriver, M. (1999). *What's Heaven?*
 Woodson, J. (2000). *Sweet, Sweet Memory.*
 Zolotow, C. (1974). *My Grandson Lew.*

About dying and the deaths of siblings, peers, and other children:
 Connolly, M. (1997). *It Isn't Easy.*
 Dean, A. (1991). *Meggie's Magic.*
 Muñoz-Kiehne, M. (2000). *Since My Brother Died/Desde Que Murió Mi Hermano.*
 Raschka, C. (2007). *The Purple Balloon.*
 Schlitt, R. S. (1992). *Robert Nathaniel's Tree.*
 Schwiebert, P. (2007). *Someone Came before You.*
 Weir, A. B. (1992). *Am I Still a Big Sister?*
 Yeomans, E. (2000). *Lost and Found: Remembering a Sister.*

About coping with fears and loss:
 Blackburn, L. B. (1991). *I Know I Made It Happen: A Gentle Book about Feelings.*
 Carney, K. L. (1997). *Together We'll Get through This!*
 Doleski, T. (1983). *The Hurt.*
 Mellonie, B., & Ingpen, R. (1983). *Lifetimes: A Beautiful Way to Explain Death to Children.*

STORYBOOKS AND OTHER TEXTS FOR PRIMARY SCHOOL READERS

About the deaths of pets and other animals:
 Graeber, C. (1982). *Mustard.*
 Johnson, J. (1998). *Remember Rafferty: A Book about the Death of a Pet . . . for Children of All Ages.*
 Parker, M. B. (2002). *Jasper's Day.*
 Tamberino, S. S. (2001). *Grunt.*
 Weigelt, U. (2003). *Bear's Last Journey.*

About the deaths of grandparents, parents, and other adults:
 Alexander, A. K. (2002). *A Mural for Mamita/Un Mural Para Mamita.*
 Alexander-Greene, A. (1999). *Sunflowers and Rainbows for Tia: Saying Goodbye to Daddy.*
 Barron, T. A. (2000). *Where Is Grandpa?*
 Bosak, S. V. (2003). *Something to Remember Me By.*
 Bunting, E. (1982). *The Happy Funeral.*
 Bunting, E. (2000). *The Memory String.*
 Copeland, K. M. (2005). *Mama's Going to Heaven Soon.*
 Dickerson, J. G. (1995). *Grandpa's Berries: A Story to Help Children Understand Grief and Loss.*
 Douglas, E. (1990). *Rachel and the Upside Down Heart.*
 Evarts, D. M. (1998). *The Butterfly Bush: A Story about Love.*
 Godfrey, J. (1996). *The Cherry Blossom Tree: A Grandfather Talks about Life and Death.*

(continued)

Selected Literature for Children about Death, Dying, and Bereavement

About the deaths of grandparents, parents, and other adults: *(continued)*
Hanson, R. (2005). *A Season for Mangoes.*
Klein, L. (1995). *The Best Gift for Mom.*
Lowden, S. G. (1993). *Emily's Sadhappy Season.*
McLaughlin, K. (2001). *The Memory Box.*
McNamara, J. W. (1994). *My Mom Is Dying: A Child's Diary.*
Miles, M. (1971). *Annie and the Old One.*
Newman, L. (1995). *Too Far Away to Touch.*
Plourde, L. (2003). *Thank You, Grandpa.*
Powell, E. S. (1990). *Geranium Morning.*
Santucci, B. (2002). *Anna's Corn.*
Simon, N. (1979). *We Remember Philip.*
Tiffault, B. W. (1992). *A Quilt for Elizabeth.*
Vogel, R. H. (2002). *The Snowman.*
Wrenn, E. (2001). *The Christmas Cactus.*
Zebrowski, M. (2002). *Babka's Serenade.*

About the deaths of siblings, peers, and other children:
Alexander, S. (1983). *Nadia the Willful.*
Bunting, E. (1999). *Rudi's Pond.*
Coerr, E. (1977). *Sadako and the Thousand Paper Cranes.*
Cohn, J. (1994). *Molly's Rosebush.*
Keough, P. (2001). *Remembering Our Baby: A Workbook for Children Whose Brother or Sister Dies before Birth.*
Rosen, M. (2004). *Michael Rosen's Sad Book.*

About confronting fears and about events following a death:
Goldman, L. (2006). *Children Also Grieve: Talking about Death and Healing.*
Hemery, K. M. (2001). *The Healing Tree.*
Holmes, M. M. (2000). *A Terrible Thing Happened.*
Johnson, J. (2001). *The Very Beautiful Dragon.*
Reeder-Bey, V., & Wilburn, A. M. (2000). *My Grandma has AIDS: Annisha's Story.*

Contact the **Centering Corporation** (P.O. Box 4600, Omaha, NE 68104-0600; 402-553-1200; fax 402-553-0507; www.centering.org; e-mail to **Centeringcorp@aol.com**) for additional information about death-related literature for children, or to purchase any of the books listed in this chapter and Appendix A.

Effective education and prior preparation in all forms depend on *effective communication.* Here, the central guideline is "take your cues from the children, answer what they want to know, what they are asking about, in their terms" (Bluebond-Langner, 1977, p. 64). Doka (1996a) suggested organizing one's approach around three questions: what does a child need to know; what does a child want to

Selected Literature for Adults about Children and Death

Corr, C. A., & Corr, D. M. (Eds.). (1996). *Handbook of Childhood Death and Bereavement.* A wide-ranging resource for understanding and helping children in their encounters with death and bereavement.

Christ, G. H. (2000). *Healing Children's Grief: Surviving a Parent's Death from Cancer;* **Davies, B.** (1998). *Shadows in the Sun: The Experiences of Sibling Bereavement in Childhood;* **Silverman, P. R.** (2000). *Never Too Young to Know: Death in Children's Lives;* **Worden, J. W.** (1996). *Children and Grief: When a Parent Dies.* Four expert authors guide professionals in understanding and helping bereaved children.

Grollman, E. A. (1990). *Talking about Death: A Dialogue between Parent and Child* (3rd ed.). Principles for helping children, a passage to be read with a child, and guidelines for responding to questions.

Emswiler, M. A., & Emswiler, J. P. (2000). *Guiding Your Child through Grief;* **Fitzgerald, H.** (1992). *The Grieving Child: A Parent's Guide;* **Johnson, J.** (1999). *Keys to Helping Children Deal with Death and Grief;* **Schaefer, D., & Lyons, C.** (2002). *How Do We Tell The Children? A Step-by-Step Guide for Helping Children Two to Teen Cope when Someone Dies;* **Trozzi, M., & Massimini, K.** (1999). *Talking with Children about Loss.* Five practical books offer useful advice for parents and other helpers.

know; and what can a child understand? Each of these requires careful listening, a process through which adults strive to grasp the real concerns of a child and to avoid responding with unnecessary, misleading, or unhelpful information. By employing language that is meaningful to children, one can minimize confusion of the sort generated by a priest in Agee's *A Death in the Family* (1969), who tried to explain that God had taken the children's father because he had had an "accident." The priest was using this word to mean a fatal automobile mishap, but the children understood it to mean a loss of bladder control, and the adults never realized how foolish and perhaps frightening their message about God's responses to wetting your pants seemed to the children.

Effective communication avoids euphemisms and inaccurate or inconsistent answers because they so easily lead children into misunderstandings that may be more disturbing than the real facts (Romano-Dwyer & Carley, 2005). Help in choosing the right words is provided by *What Does that Mean? A Dictionary of Death, Dying and Grief Terms for Grieving Children and Those Who Love Them* (Smith & Johnson, 2006). Effective communication is also dependable: the child must be able to rely on what is said, even if it is not the whole of the available truth. Honesty encourages trust, the basis of all comforting relationships. Thus it is better to admit what one does not know rather than to make up explanations that one really does not believe. After all, even good communication can be limited, fallible, and subject to error, as in the case of the children who were eager to attend a funeral to see the "polar bears" who would, so they thought they had heard, carry the casket (Corley,

Some Guidelines for Adults in Using Death-Related Resources with Children

1. *Evaluate the book or other resource yourself before attempting to use it with a child.* No resource suits every reader or every purpose.
2. *Select resources, topics, and approaches that suit the needs of the individual child.* To be useful, any resource must meet the needs of a particular child.
3. *Be prepared to cope with limitations.* Every resource is likely to have both strengths and limitations. Adapt existing resources to individual purposes.
4. *Match materials to the capacities of the individual child.* Stories, pictures, music, play, drawing, and other options must suit the child's abilities. For example, in using literature, determine the child's reading or interest level. Direct a precocious child to more advanced materials; direct some older children to less challenging titles or invite them to join in partnership with an adult to assess the suitability of simpler materials for younger readers (Lamers, 1986, 1995) so their abilities are not directly challenged by materials that are too difficult for them.
5. *Read or work along with children.* Seize opportunities for rewarding interactions and valuable "teachable moments" from which all can profit (Carson, 1984). Show interest in the child, provide interpretations as needed, and learn from the child.

1973; see also Brent, 1978). Although this piece of miscommunication is delightful in some ways, it reminds us that children may not always correctly grasp what they are told. To minimize misunderstandings about death, adults should try to communicate effectively, and they should check to determine what a child has grasped by asking the child to explain what he or she understood from the message.

Adults must also consider that children communicate in many ways and at many levels (Kübler-Ross, 1983). They might use: (1) symbolic nonverbal communication—which might take place through artwork of various types; (2) symbolic verbal communication—in which indirect comments about imaginary friends or anthropomorphized figures may really have to do with the child's own concerns; and (3) nonsymbolic verbal communication—which most resembles literal interchanges between adults. Symbolic communication through art or other media may be particularly important for deep-seated or emotionally charged concerns in young children who lack many verbal skills (Furth, 1988). This was evident in the case of one 6-year-old child who, while he was dying, drew a series of pictures of ships—smaller and less colorful ships on a progressively darker background as the illness advanced (Grove, 1978).

Validation is a third important element of prior preparation, as well as of support for ill, dying, and bereaved children. Metzgar and Zick (1996) link this to an

Copyright © Stefan Verwey

American-Indian belief that says: *If you give something a name and a shape, you can have power over it. However, if it remains nameless and shapeless, it will continue to have power over you.* Children who are striving to cope with death-related encoun- ters need validation for their questions, concepts, language, and feelings. Adults can validate these and other aspects of children's death-related experiences by acknowledging them for what they are in a nonjudgmental way. Acknowledgment gives permission to explore what is confused and not yet well articulated. Sharing in such a process is empowering; correcting or "fixing" it is likely to be mistaken and harmful.

Helping Ill or Dying Children

The following principles for communication with ill or dying children provide a solid foundation for helping (Stevens, 1998):

1. First, determine the child's own perception of the situation, taking into account his or her developmental level and experience.
2. Understand the child's symbolic language.

3. Clarify reality and dispel fantasy.

4. Encourage expression of feelings.

5. Promote self-esteem through mastery of age-appropriate tasks and activities.

6. Make no assumptions about what the situation will entail; be open to what each encounter can teach; do not underestimate the child's ability to master life's challenges creatively and with humor and dignity.

Perhaps the best programs of care for ill and dying children (and their family members) are those that rely on *the principles of pediatric hospice or palliative care.* The early impetus for the development of programs like these came from a project on home care for dying children and their families in Minnesota (Martinson, 1976) and the establishment of Helen House in Oxford, England (Worswick, 2000). In both cases, the emphasis was on a holistic program of child- and family-centered care (Davies & Howell, 1998). The Minnesota project demonstrated that for some children and families it was both feasible and desirable to take a child home to die. To do this, most families needed preparation for what they might expect to encounter, guidance on how to respond, and support to mobilize their own resources, as well as supplementary assistance to provide needed services. In a parallel way, Helen House confirmed the importance of skilled respite care for families facing the difficult challenges of one or more children with a chronic, life-limiting, or life-threatening illness. Key points in all of this are the recognition by parents of their need for pediatric palliative care, their willingness to enter into such care, and their evaluations of the services received (Bluebond-Langner et al., 2007; Contro et al., 2002; Wolfe et al., 2000b).

More recently, programs of *pediatric palliative care* have applied hospice principles to a wide variety of situations involving children with life-limiting or life-threatening conditions (Armstrong-Dailey & Zarbock, in press; Corr & Corr, 1985a, 1985b, 1985c, 1988, 1992b). This has been achieved in many different ways (e.g., at home, through respite care, or in a medical facility) and with various types of staffing (e.g., hospital, hospice, or home care personnel) (Davies, 1999; Himelstein et al., 2004; Howell, 1993). Applying these principles during pregnancy, at the time of birth (Sumner et al., 2006), and in neonatal intensive care units (Siegel, 1982; Siegel et al., 1985; Whitfield et al., 1982) demonstrates that it is not the setting that is critical but the focus on holistic care for the ill child and on family-centered care for parents, siblings, and involved others (Stevens, 1993).

The needs of children who are approaching the end of their lives, as well as those of their families, have now been well documented (e.g., American Academy of Pediatrics, 2000a; Field & Berhman, 2003). Children's Hospice International (www.chionline.org; info@chionline.org; tel. 800-24-CHILD or 703-684-0330) and the ChiPPS project (Children's Project on Palliative/Hospice Services; www.nhpco.org/pediatrics) of the NHPCO (tel. 703-837-1500) have acted as advocates on behalf of these children and families. Training curricula have been published to prepare individuals for this work (Education Development Center, 2003; End-of-Life Nursing Education Consortium [ELNEC], 2003; NHPCO, 2003), along with a manual on how to develop a home-based support program for children and adolescents with life-threatening conditions (NHPCO, 2004a). Moreover, a number of books have been published to guide both parents and professional providers in the delivery of this type of care (e.g., Brown, 2007; Carter & Levetown, 2004; Goldman et al., 2005; Hilden & Tobin, 2003; Huff & Orloff, 2004; Orloff & Huff, 2003). And numerous publications have focused on the development of partnerships with ill children, good communication, attending to the preferences of children and their families, and what is involved in the implementation of hospice-like principles in oncology and other forms of pediatric care (e.g., Hinds et al., 2005; Solomon et al., 2005; Wolfe et al., 2000a; Young et al., 1999, 2003).

A useful supplement to the services involved in pediatric care is found in *Ronald McDonald House* programs in many communities. These programs provide economical, convenient, and hospitable places where families can stay while a child is receiving treatment in a pediatric medical facility. This service minimizes family disruption, reduces financial and logistical burdens (such as those involving travel, finding lodging, preparing food, and doing laundry), and permits constructive interactions (if not formal counseling) both within and among families who are facing difficult challenges in childhood illness.

Helping Bereaved Children

The task-based models described earlier for understanding bereaved children (Corr & Corr, 1998; Fox, 1988a, 1988b; Trozzi & Massimini, 1999; Worden, 1996) provide a natural agenda for adults who are helping individual children. All bereaved children need information as a foundation for effective grief work (Goldman, 1999; 2006). They may need to know about death itself or about the facts surrounding a specific death, or they may need information about common reactions to loss or about coping with death and grief. Adults can provide such information and, in so doing, share their own grief and model good coping strategies. For example, in one of its policy statements, the American Academy of Pediatrics (AAP, 2000a) has pointed out the constructive role that pediatricians can play in helping parents and other adults in matters of childhood bereavement. Schools, religious institutions, and other community resources can also be helpful (e.g., Fitzgerald, 2003). To do this, they must—above all—try to view the loss from the child's perspective.

For example, adults often fail to appreciate the importance to a child of the death of a friend or pet (Butler & Lagoni, 1996; Lagoni et al., 1994; Toray & Oltjenbruns, 1996; Tuzeo-Jarolmen, 2006). Also, bereaved adults may all too easily overlook a child's grief on the death of a sibling (Davies, 1998). In each case, it is the relationship in all of its many dimensions—companion, buffer, protector, comforter—that is most important to the child. Adults do well to honor these losses rather than brush them aside as trivial. Respect for the child's experiences can be expressed in attention, honesty, avoidance of euphemisms, support, and (wherever possible) encouragement of the child's involvement in the death and subsequent memorialization.

In all deaths, good memories are as important to bereaved children as they are to adults (Christ, 2000; Jewett, 1982). When possible, one should strive to lay down a fund of such memories before loss or death occurs and help a child while someone else is dying (Smith, 2000). Even when that is not possible, as in cases of unanticipated death, an adult might work with a child after a death to develop and articulate the elements of a legacy that the child can carry forward into the future—for example, by examining a scrapbook or photo album depicting the life of the deceased, or by sharing events from that life in which the child might not have participated. Helping bereaved children might also include assembling a memorial collage, donating to a worthy cause, or planting a living memorial.

In recent years, some have questioned whether children should take part in funeral and burial practices (Corr, 1991; Weller et al., 1988). Suggestions like Grollman's (1967, p. 24) that "from approximately the age of seven, a child should be encouraged to attend" have been misinterpreted to support the viewpoint of Allison's father near the outset of this chapter that children under the age of 7 should be prohibited from attending funerals. In fact, research (Fristad et al., 2001; Silverman & Worden, 1992b) has shown that taking part in bereavement rituals can help children with their grief work.

A basic rule is that no child should be forced to take part in any experience that will be harmful (Emswiler & Emswiler, 2000). However, harm need not occur when adults act on themes underlying all of the suggestions we are describing: prior preparation, support during the event, and follow-up afterward. The child should be told ahead of time what will occur at the visitation, funeral, or burial; why we engage in these activities; and what his or her options are for participation. If the child chooses to take part in some or all of these activities, a caring adult should attend to his or her needs during the event. This adult must not be wholly absorbed in personal grief and must be free to accompany a child who might need to arrive late or leave early. After the event, adults should be available to discuss with the child his or her reactions or feelings, answer any questions that might arise, and share their own responses to what has taken place.

Concerns about disruptive behavior by children are no more unique to funerals and burials than they are to graduations and weddings. They can be addressed by

A "teachable moment" can take place when a young child is allowed to take part in his grandparent's visitation.

Courtesy of Charles A. Corr

providing a special time for children to come to the funeral home when adults are not present or by limiting the roles of the children at the funeral service or burial to those that are appropriate to their interest in and tolerance for public ritual. As Crase and Crase (1976, p. 25) noted: "The wise management of grief in children revolves around the encouragement and facilitation of the normal mourning process while preventing delayed and/or distorted grief responses."

Support groups for bereaved children can assist normal mourning processes after a death (Bacon, 1996; Heiney et al., 1995; Hughes, 1995; Pfeffer et al., 2002; Zambelli & DeRosa, 1992). Two good models are found in The Dougy Center: The National Center for Grieving Children and Families (3909 S.E. 52nd Avenue, Portland, OR 97286; tel. 503-775-5683; www.dougy.org) in the United States and Winston's Wish in Cheltenham, England (The Clara Burgess Centre, Bayshill Road, Cheltenham, UK GL50 3AW; www.winstonswish.org.uk). *The Dougy Center,* founded in December 1982 by Beverly Chappell (Chappell, 2001; Corr & the Staff of the Dougy Center, 1991), operates groups for children as young as ages 3 to 5 (Smith, 1991) and as old as 19, including groups focused on the death of a parent or caregiver; a brother, sister, or close friend; suicide; and homicide. It also offers concurrent groups for parents or other adult caregivers of the children being served. *Winston's Wish,* founded in 1992 by Julie Stokes (2004), offers a distinctive program of residential weekends (Stokes & Crossley, 1995), along with groups for families affected by suicide, services to schools, national training programs, an interactive Web site for adolescents, and a national helpline in England. Both programs offer a wide range of helpful publications and other resources.

Each of these programs is firmly grounded in its respective communities. Both emphasize that grief is a natural reaction to loss—for children as well as for adults. For that reason, both programs try hard not to stigmatize the bereaved children and adults whom they serve. Their goal is to offer supportive and preventive care. They honor the natural capacity to mourn in each individual and try to be available to each child and to trust his or her mourning process. Essentially, they walk alongside each child and uphold the vision that he or she will once again be able to find a way in life—even while remaining alert for signs of complicated grief and mourning processes.

Many other support groups for bereaved children see themselves as functioning in a more traditional counseling role and adopt a more structured, time-limited agenda for group meetings (e.g., Hassl & Marnocha, 2000). A body of literature describing activities that can be used with bereaved children in all of these programs is available for adult helpers (e.g., McWhorter, 2003; Whitney, 1991).

Children may also be affected by traumatic death in the form of a homicide, suicide, or mass death caused by a natural disaster or some other form of violent or catastrophic event (Cohen et al., 2006; Lareca et al., 2002; Nader, 1996; Osofsky, 2004; Requarth, 2006). For example, the terrorist attacks on the World Trade Center and the Pentagon on September 11, 2001, led professionals to observe the reactions of some very young children (Schechter et al., 2002) and ways in which other children coped with their experiences through art (Goodman & Fahnestock, 2002).

Especially when groups of children are involved in traumatic events, it is often important to consider programs of *postvention.* This term, coined by Shneidman (1973b, 1981), was originally applied to interventions designed "to mollify the

Allowing children to participate in a memorial ritual—for instance, by releasing balloons in memory of someone who has died—can assist them in their mourning.

aftereffects of the event in a person who has attempted suicide, or to deal with the adverse effects on the survivor-victims of a person who has committed suicide" (1973b, p. 385). However, the concept of postvention and other forms of assistance for children have since been expanded to apply to interventions before and after the fact that focus on children immediately or indirectly affected by a broad range of traumatic losses (Goldman, 2001, 2004).

Principles for postvention with children include: (1) beginning the intervention as soon as possible; (2) implementing a comprehensive and coordinated plan involving affected persons and using relevant resources in the community; (3) providing supportive and caring assistance; (4) anticipating resistance or an unwillingness to cooperate from some persons; (5) expecting individual variations in the nature and timing of traumatic responses; (6) being alert for exaggerated responses that may place an individual's life or health in jeopardy; (7) identifying and changing potentially harmful aspects of the immediate environment; and (8) addressing long-term issues (Leenaars & Wenckstern, 1996). Ideally, postvention and all other programs of crisis intervention for children should be based on prior planning in schools and communities (Klicker, 2000; Lerner et al., 2003; Rowling, 2003; Stevenson, 2001). Such programs should be led by a professional who is well grounded in the principles of child development, in issues of coping with loss and grief, and in the special features of crises and trauma. Where group approaches are inappropriate or insufficient for a particular child, individual psychotherapy will be indicated—even for a very young child (Lieberman et al., 2003; Webb, 2002).

Summary

In this chapter, we studied interactions between children and death in our American death system. We described distinctive developmental tasks of childhood as background for exploring death-related experiences during childhood. In particular, we noted that death rates among infants and toddlers are high, mainly arising from congenital malformations, disorders related to short gestation, sudden infant death syndrome, and accidents; in preschool and school-age children, death rates are much lower, resulting more often from accidents and diseases like cancer. We paid special attention to children's efforts to develop an understanding of the concept of death and its principal sub-concepts, as well as to the development of death-related attitudes in childhood.

Next, we explored children's efforts to cope with life-threatening illness, dying, and bereavement. That led us to discuss how to help children cope with death, dying, and bereavement, which included some general suggestions, a proactive program of prior preparation (involving education, effective communication, and validation), and specific remarks about helping ill, dying, and bereaved children. We also identified a number of useful resources for helping children cope with death.

Glossary

Animism: a view that attributes life and consciousness to objects usually thought of as inanimate

Artificialism: a view in which it is believed that all objects and events in the world have been manufactured to serve people

Causality: understanding the events or conditions that do or can bring about the death of a living thing

Developmental eras in childhood: infancy, toddlerhood, early childhood (also called the play age or preschool period), and middle childhood (also called the school age or latency period)

Irreversibility: once a thing is dead it cannot become alive again (barring miracles)

Magical thinking: a view in which all events are explained by the causal influence of various commands, intentions, and forces

Noncorporeal continuation: the view that some form of life continues after the death of the physical body

Nonfunctionality: a dead body can no longer act in ways like a live body

Normative developmental tasks in childhood: to develop *trust* versus mistrust in infancy, *autonomy* versus shame and doubt in toddlerhood, *initiative* versus guilt in early childhood, and *industry* versus inferiority in middle childhood

Pediatric palliative (or hospice) care: the application of palliative/hospice principles to situations involving children and their family members

Postvention: after-the-fact interventions for individuals affected by traumatic loss

A stage-based theory of the development of children's understandings of death: according to Maria Nagy, in stage 1 there is no definitive death (i.e., death = a form of life = sleep or departure and living elsewhere); in stage 2, death is personified and contingent or avoidable; in stage 3, death is a process operating within us (i.e., the cessation of corporeal life = final and universal)

Sub-concepts involved in the concept of death: according to Mark Speece and Sandor Brent, these sub-concepts are universality (which itself encompasses all-inclusiveness, inevitability, and unpredictability), irreversibility, nonfunctionality, causality, and noncorporeal continuation

Universality: a sub-concept in which death is understood as applying to everyone, not to be avoided (all living things must eventually die), and yet unable to be predicted as to its timing

Questions for Review and Discussion

1. The vignette near the beginning of this chapter depicted a father who did not respond in very helpful ways to the death-related concerns of his daughter, Allison. How would you have responded or have wanted him to respond to those concerns?

2. What types of death-related losses did you experience during childhood? What did they mean to you?

3. Try to remember a time when you were a child and you were seriously ill or you experienced an important loss. What were your most significant concerns about that illness or loss? Or perhaps you know a child who has been in such a situation. If so, what were his or her most significant concerns?

4. If you were asked to recommend to adults how they could help children cope with death, what would you suggest? How would your recommendations differ (if at all) for different children or different losses?

Suggested Readings

General resources on children and death include:

Adams, D. W., & Deveau, E. J. (Eds.). (1995). *Beyond the Innocence of Childhood* (3 vols.).

Corr, C. A., & Corr, D. M. (Eds.). (1996). *Handbook of Childhood Death and Bereavement.*

Concerning life-threatening illness in childhood, consult:

Armstrong-Dailey, A., & Zarbock, S. (Eds.). (In press). *Hospice Care for Children* (3rd ed.).

Bearison, D. J. (2006). *When Treatment Fails: How Medicine Cares for Dying Children.*

Corr, C. A., & Corr, D. M. (Eds.). (1985a). *Hospice Approaches to Pediatric Care.*

Sourkes, B. M. (1995). *Armfuls of Time: The Psychological Experience of the Child with a Life-Threatening Illness.*

Zimmerman, J. (2005). *From the Heart of a Bear: True Stories of the Faith and Courage of Children Facing Life-threatening Illness.*

To understand bereavement and grief in childhood, consult:

Davies, B. (1998). *Shadows in the Sun: The Experiences of Sibling Bereavement in Childhood.*

Doka, K. J. (Ed.). (1995). *Children Mourning, Mourning Children.*

Doka, K. J. (Ed.). (2000). *Living with Grief: Children, Adolescents, and Loss.*

Silverman, P. R. (2000). *Never Too Young to Know: Death in Children's Lives.*

Sjöqvist, S. (Ed.). (2006). *Still Here with Me: Teenagers and Children on Losing a Parent.*

Worden, J. W. (1996). *Children and Grief: When a Parent Dies.*

For helping children cope with loss and grief, see:

Christ, G. H. (2000). *Healing Children's Grief: Surviving a Parent's Death from Cancer.*

Emswiler, M. A., & Emswiler, J. P. (2000). *Guiding Your Child through Grief.*

Fiorini, J. J., & Mullen, J. A. (2006). *Counseling Children and Adolescents through Grief and Loss.*

Fitzgerald, H. (1992). *The Grieving Child: A Parent's Guide.*

Goldman, L. (1999). *Life and Loss: A Guide to Help Grieving Children.*

Goldman, L. (2006). *Children Also Grieve: Talking about Death and Healing.*

Grollman, E. A. (1990). *Talking about Death: A Dialogue between Parent and Child* (3rd ed.).

Johnson, J. (1999). *Keys to Helping Children Deal with Death and Grief.*

Marta, S. Y. (2003). *Healing the Hurt, Restoring the Hope: How to Guide Children and Teens through Times of Divorce, Death, and Crisis with the RAINBOWS Approach.*

Monroe, B., & Kraus, F. (Eds.). (2004). *Brief Interventions with Bereaved Children.*

Schaefer, D., & Lyons, C. (2002). *How Do We Tell the Children? A Step-by-Step Guide for Helping Children Two to Teen Cope When Someone Dies* (3rd ed.).

Smith, H. I. (2004b). *When a Child You Love is Grieving.*

Stokes, J. A. (2004). *Then, Now and Always—Supporting Children as They Journey through Grief: A Guide for Practitioners.*

Trozzi, M., & Massimini, K. (1999). *Talking with Children about Loss: Words, Strategies, and Wisdom.*

Turner, M. (2006). *Talking with Children and Young People about Death and Dying* (2nd ed.).

Webb, N. B. (Ed.). (1999). *Play Therapy with Children in Crisis: Individual, Group, and Family Treatment* (2nd ed.).

Webb, N. B. (Ed.). (2002). *Helping Bereaved Children: A Handbook for Practitioners* (2nd ed.).

For teaching children about death and other school-related issues, see:

Deaton, R. L., & Berkan, W. A. (1995). *Planning and Managing Death Issues in the Schools: A Handbook.*

Fitzgerald, H. (1998). *Grief at School: A Guide for Teachers and Counselors.*

Gordon, A. K., & Klass, D. (1979). *They Need to Know: How to Teach Children about Death.*

Klicker, R. L. (2000). *A Student Dies, A School Mourns: Dealing with Death and Loss in the School Community.*

Lerner, M. D., Volpe, J. S., & Lindell, B. (2003). *A Practical Guide for Crisis Response in Our Schools: A Comprehensive School Crisis Response Plan* (5th ed.).

Stevenson, R. G. (Ed.). (2001). *What Will We Do? Preparing a School Community to Cope with Crises* (2nd ed.).

Stevenson, R. G., & Stevenson, E. P. (Eds.). (1996b). *Teaching Students about Death: A Comprehensive Resource for Educators and Parents*.

Selected Web Resources

Some useful search terms include: ANIMISM; ARTIFICIALISM; CAUSES OF DEATH IN CHILDHOOD; CHILDREN AND DEATH; COGNITIVE DEVELOPMENT; CONCEPTS OF DEATH OR UNDERSTANDINGS OF DEATH; DEVELOPMENTAL ERAS IN CHILDHOOD; DEVELOPMENTAL TASKS IN CHILDHOOD; MAGICAL THINKING; NONCORPOREAL CONTINUATION; NONFUNCTIONALITY; PEDIATRIC PALLIATIVE OR HOSPICE CARE; POSTVENTION; TASKS IN MOURNING

Visit the book companion website for *Death & Dying, Life & Living, Sixth Edition*, at academic.cengage.com/psychology/corr for all URLs and live links to the following *organizational and other Internet sites:*

American Academy of Pediatrics

American School Counselor Association

Association for Children with Life-Threatening or Terminal Conditions and Their Families

Association for the Care of Children's Health

Candlelighters Childhood Cancer Foundation

Children's Hospice International

Children's Project on Palliative/Hospice Services (ChiPPS) of the National Hospice and Palliative Care Organization

The Dougy Center: The National Center for Grieving Children and Families

The Initiative for Pediatric Palliative Care

National Sudden Infant Death Syndrome Resource Center

Sudden Infant Death Syndrome Alliance

Winston's Wish

CHAPTER 13

Adolescents

Ever Get A Pal Smashed?

TAKE THE KEYS.
CALL A CAB.
TAKE A STAND.

FRIENDS DON'T LET FRIENDS DRIVE DRUNK

Ad Council U.S. Department of Transportation

Courtesy of the Ad Council (U.S. Department of Transportation)

Objectives of This Chapter

◆ To define and interpret adolescence and its developmental tasks

◆ To describe typical encounters with death in the United States during adolescence

◆ To discuss death-related attitudes during adolescence

◆ To identify key issues for adolescents who are coping with life-threatening illness and dying

◆ To explore central issues for adolescents who are coping with bereavement and grief

◆ To examine issues concerning homicide and suicide among adolescents

◆ To discuss principles for helping adolescents cope with death and bereavement

Some High School Students Encounter Death and Grief

That April was a tragic time at Central High School. On the third of the month, Tom Adkins and three other boys from Central were killed when a train at a railroad crossing hit the car in which they were riding. The engineer of the train reported that the car ignored the warning lights and drove around the crossing gates. Neither the train's whistle nor its emergency brakes had been able to prevent the high-speed crash. People said, "Isn't this awful! I can't believe this happened."

Two weeks later, Anthony Ramirez, the star kicker and senior cornerback on the football team, shot himself. Anthony was a good student and was well liked by his teachers and other students. He came from a middle-class family in which the parents and three children seemed closely knit and concerned about each other. That evening the rest of the family had gone to a basketball game in which Anthony's younger brother was playing. It was a bit unusual but not worrisome when Anthony chose to stay at home, saying that he had to study for a test. When the family came home they found Anthony in the garage lying in a pool of blood alongside his father's old hunting rifle, which he had used to end his life. There was no note.

During the postmortem investigation, it turned out that many people were aware of some of what was going on in Anthony's life, but no one knew enough to grasp how badly he really felt. Some of Anthony's friends realized that he always used humor to laugh off inquiries about his feelings and to keep people from getting to know the real person inside his popular image. Anthony's girlfriend acknowledged that their relationship had recently ended but said that she had not recognized how hard he had taken her rejection. Anthony's teachers and coaches talked about the pressures to excel that he always seemed to impose on himself; one remembered an angry outburst followed by a long sullen period occasioned by what Anthony regarded as a bad grade. Anthony's parents and siblings spoke of their own recent preoccupations and their wish that they had realized how depressed he must have been. People said, "If only I had known."

Four days before the end of the month, two freshman girls at Central, Whitney Portman and Shawan Miller, were walking home from the store when they found themselves in the middle of a gang fight. The territories of two youth gangs overlapped near the intersection where the two girls were walking, and a dispute had developed over which group had "rights" to sell drugs on that corner. An exchange of insults led to some scuffling and a flare-up of tempers. Some members of one gang ran into a nearby house, got some weapons, and began shooting when they came out. Whitney and Shawan were shot—they were simply two more victims of the neighborhood in which they lived. One of the girls died, the other was critically wounded. People said, "What can we do to stop this violence?"

The Definition and Interpretation of Adolescence

In our society, *adolescence* is an "in-between" or transitional period in human development between childhood and adulthood. At one time in American and other societies—and in some societies or cultural groups today—there was no such in-between period. Coming-of-age rituals marked a direct and relatively abrupt division between the era of childhood and the reality of adult responsibilities (Ariès, 1962). By contrast, our society has interposed a complex, evolving, and rather special developmental stage between the primary school years and the complete recognition of adult status.

The term *adolescence* derives from a Latin root *(adolescentia)* that refers to the process or condition of growing up and that designates a "youth" or person in the growing age (*Oxford English Dictionary*, 1989). In contemporary usage, an adolescent is someone who is no longer thought to be merely a child but who is not yet fully recognized as an adult. Thus, adolescents are normally expected to take on more advanced responsibilities than children and are usually accorded special privileges: educational programs for adolescents differ from those for children, and, as they mature, adolescents are ordinarily thought fit to take on work and wage-earning responsibilities, to qualify to drive a motor vehicle, to vote, to drink alcoholic beverages, and to get married.

It is not accurate simply to equate adolescence with the teenage years. As we noted in Chapter 12, chronology on its own is not an accurate indicator of developmental eras. In fact, most agree that the preteen phenomenon of puberty marks the beginning of the adolescent era. In adopting this marker, however, one must recognize three facts: individuals arrive at puberty at different times (with females typically becoming pubescent at an earlier age than males); puberty itself is more a series of related events than a single moment in time; and it is a historical reality that over the past 150 years the onset of puberty has come earlier in each generation (Kail & Cavanaugh, 2006; Newman & Newman, 2005).

The close of adolescence is less easily designated. In general, the principal developmental task of adolescence is the achievement of individuation and *the establishment of a more or less stable sense of personal identity* (see Table V.1). If so, then adolescence may end when an individual leaves home and his or her family of origin, takes up a career, or gets married. However, the phenomena of leaving and returning home (perhaps repeatedly) are well known in our society (Goldscheider & Goldscheider, 1999), and these events clearly depend on a variety of individual, cultural, and economic factors, not development alone. Thus, Conger and Peterson (1984, p. 82) aptly observed that adolescence is a physical, social, and emotional process that "begins in biology and ends in culture." Still, to speak too readily of the end of adolescence may be to focus solely on the negative or "closing off" side of the story without necessarily reflecting the positive development of *fidelity* or faithfulness—to self, to ideals, and to others—that Erikson (1963) proposed as the principal virtue to be achieved in adolescent development.

Apart from the definition of adolescence and despite the fact that it has been the subject of study for more than 100 years (e.g., Hall, 1904), there continue to be long-standing disagreements among scholars about how to interpret this era and how to characterize the adolescent experience (Bandura, 1980; Weiner, 1985). For example, psychoanalytic perspectives have typically highlighted "storm and stress"—focusing on change, turbulence, and difficulties in adolescent life (see the right-hand image on p. 365). Anna Freud (1958, p. 275) even wrote, "To be normal during the adolescent period is by itself abnormal." By contrast, empirical research by Offer and his colleagues (e.g., Offer, 1969; Offer & Offer, 1975; Offer et al., 1981; Offer et al., 1988) has produced reports in which large numbers of adolescents from

Lawrence Shlcs

To many adults, adolescents appear to be sometimes good "team players" and sometimes definitely not.

different cultures describe themselves as relatively untroubled, happy, and self-satisfied (see the left-hand image on this page). On the basis of their review of available empirical research, Offer and Sabshin (1984, p. 101) observed that almost all researchers who have studied representative samples of adolescents "come to the conclusion that by and large good coping and a smooth transition into adulthood are much more typical than the opposite." The voices of adolescents in the published literature (e.g., Kalergis, 1998) confirm this depiction of adolescence.

An evolving, transitional period in the life course such as adolescence clearly presents challenges to its interpreters. Responses to these challenges color much that is said about the adolescent era. The danger is that adolescence is "the world's most perfect projective device for adults" (Offer et al., 1981, p. 121; see also Bandura, 1980).

🍂 Developmental Tasks in Early, Middle, and Late Adolescence

However one interprets adolescence as a whole, *three specific developmental subperiods* have been identified in this era: *early, middle, and late adolescence* (Blos, 1941, 1979; see Table 13.1). *Early adolescence* (beginning around age 10 or 11 for most individuals and lasting until around age 14) involves decreased identification with parents, increased affinity with peers, fascination with hero figures, and growing interest in sexuality. Early adolescence usually centers on efforts to separate from dependency on parents in order to establish new personal ideals and interpersonal relationships.

TABLE 13.1
Tasks and Conflicts for Adolescents by Maturational Phase

Phase I, Early Adolescence	Age:	11–14
	Task:	Emotional separation from parents
	Conflict:	Separation (abandonment) vs. reunion (safety)
Phase II, Middle Adolescence	Age:	14–17
	Task:	Competency/mastery/control
	Conflict:	Independence vs. dependence
Phase III, Late Adolescence	Age:	17–21
	Task:	Intimacy and commitment
	Conflict:	Closeness vs. distance

Source: Fleming and Adolph, 1986, p. 103.

Middle adolescence or "adolescence proper" (roughly ages 14–17) involves developing autonomy from parents, experimenting with "possible selves" or alternative self-concepts, and forging a distinctive, mature identity. Blos (1979) maintained that in striving to gain greater skill at being independent and self-governing, middle adolescents experience a "second chance" or second individuation process. That is, middle adolescents can develop personal or individual resourcefulness by considerably reorganizing the values internalized from their parents, overcoming the egocentrism of childhood and early adolescence, and making choices about the roles and responsibilities they will assume in life.

Late adolescence (roughly ages 17–21 or 22) is ideally the era of stable character formation. For Blos (1979), this involves meeting four distinct challenges: achieving closure in the second individuation process, attaining personal strength by coping successfully with traumatic life events, establishing historical continuity by accepting one's past and freeing oneself for growth and maturity, and resolving one's sexual identity.

This three-part developmental understanding is helpful in appreciating many death-related experiences during the adolescent era.

❦ Encounters with Death during Adolescence

The National Center for Health Statistics (NCHS) publishes demographic data on numbers of deaths and death rates after early childhood in both 10-year age groupings (5–14 and 15–24 years of age) and 5-year age groupings (10–14, 15–19, and 20–24 years of age). Neither of these formats is consistent with our overall definition of adolescence or with the developmental sub-periods within adolescence that we have outlined. Nevertheless, these data are all that we have available, and they reveal many aspects of typical encounters with death during the adolescent era. In this chapter, we focus mostly on data related to individuals who are 10–14 and 15–19 years of age, but we also mention data for those who are 20–24 years of age and for the broader group of those who are 15–24 years of age when it seems appropriate and useful.

Deaths and Death Rates among Adolescents

Adolescents between the ages of 10 and 19 make up 14.4 percent of the total population of the United States; individuals between the ages of 20–24 add another 7.1 percent of our population. In 2004 in the United States, there were 3,946 *deaths of adolescents* between the ages of 10–14, 13,706 deaths of individuals between the ages of 15–19, and 19,715 deaths of those between the ages of 20–24 (see Table 13.2). Together, these deaths represented about 1.6 percent of the nearly 2.4 million deaths in the country for that year. *Death rates* for these age groups in 2004 were 18.7 per 100,000 for those 10–14 years of age, 66.1 for those 15–19 years of age, and 94.0 for

TABLE 13.2
Number of Deaths during Adolescence, by Age, Race or Hispanic Origin,[a] and Sex: United States, 2004

	10–14 Years			15–19 years			20–24 years		
	Both Sexes	Males	Females	Both Sexes	Males	Females	Both Sexes	Males	Females
All origins[b]	3,946	2,354	1,592	13,706	9,678	4,028	19,715	14,909	4,806
Caucasian Americans, total	2,857	1,727	1,130	10,450	7,267	3,183	14,563	11,039	3,524
Non-Hispanic Caucasian Americans	2,247	1,350	897	8,346	5,636	2,710	11,338	8,381	2,957
Hispanic Americans[c]	618	383	235	2,141	1,662	479	3,287	2,714	573
African Americans	899	516	383	2,680	2,019	661	4,369	3,317	1,052
Asian or Pacific Island Americans[d]	116	69	47	316	221	95	450	315	135
American Indians and Alaskan Natives[e]	74	42	32	260	171	89	333	238	95

[a]Data for specified groups other than Caucasian Americans and African Americans should be interpreted with caution because of inconsistencies between reporting race and/or Hispanic origin on death certificates and on censuses and surveys.

[b]Figures for origin not stated are included in "all origins" but not distributed among specified origins.

[c]Includes all persons of Hispanic origin of any race.

[d]Includes Chinese, Filipino, Hawaiian, Japanese, and Other Asian or Pacific Islander.

[e]Includes Aleuts and Eskimos.

Source: Miniño et al., 2007.

those 20–24 years of age (see Table 13.3). These rates are slightly lower than death rates for the same age groups in 2002 and much lower than death rates for every other age group in the population except young children. In other words, as a group adolescents die in fewer numbers and at lower rates than do infants and adults in our society. As can be seen from Tables 13.2 and 13.3, overall numbers of deaths and death rates in our society rise with increasing age for all adolescents, regardless of gender, race, or ethnicity, with the sole exception of the oldest American Indian females in this group. Increasing numbers of deaths and higher death rates are especially notable as one moves beyond early adolescence to the middle and later years in this era.

TABLE 13.3
Death Rates (per 100,000 in the specified population group) during Adolescence, by Age, Race or Hispanic Origin,[a] and Sex: United States, 2004

	10–14 Years			15–19 Years			20–24 Years		
	Both Sexes	Males	Females	Both Sexes	Males	Females	Both Sexes	Males	Females
All origins[b]	18.7	21.7	15.4	66.1	91.0	39.9	94.0	138.0	47.3
Caucasian Americans, total	17.4	20.6	14.2	64.4	87.1	40.4	88.3	129.1	44.3
Non-Hispanic Caucasian Americans	17.4	20.4	14.3	63.4	83.4	42.4	87.2	126.6	46.3
Hispanic Americans[c]	16.3	19.8	12.7	64.2	96.5	29.7	87.3	130.9	33.9
African Americans	25.3	28.6	21.9	81.4	121.0	40.7	138.8	210.1	67.0
Asian or Pacific Island Americans[d]	12.7	14.7	10.6	34.7	47.2	21.5	43.3	59.9	26.3
American Indians and Alaskan Natives[e]	24.5	27.5	21.5	87.0	112.5	60.7	116.6	161.2	68.9

[a]Data for specified groups other than Caucasian Americans and African Americans should be interpreted with caution because of inconsistencies between reporting race and/or Hispanic origin on death certificates and on censuses and surveys.

[b]Figures for origin not stated are included in "all origins" but not distributed among specified origins.

[c]Includes all persons of Hispanic origin of any race.

[d]Includes Chinese, Filipino, Hawaiian, Japanese, and Other Asian or Pacific Islander.

[e]Includes Aleuts and Eskimos.

Source: Miniño et al., 2007.

Leading Causes of Death among Adolescents

Following NCHS formats, Table 13.4 provides data on numbers of deaths and death rates for all persons 10–14, 15–19, and 20–24 years of age who died in the United States in 2004 in terms of the *five leading causes* of their deaths. Several observations arise from these data. First, 71.9 percent of all deaths among American adolescents between 10–24 years of age occur from accidents, homicide, and suicide—and for that reason each played a role in the vignette near the beginning of this chapter.

Second, numbers of deaths from these three causes rise significantly in the transition from youngsters 10–14 years of age to those in the two older age groups. In fact, in both of these older age groups accidents, homicide, and suicide lead all other causes of death. That fact—that human-induced causes should occupy all three leading positions in a ranking of causes of death—is unique to these two age groups; for all other eras in human development, there is at least one disease-related or natural cause among the three leading causes of death.

TABLE 13.4

Numbers of Deaths and Death Rates (per 100,000) during Adolescence for the Five Leading Causes of Death in Specified Age Groups, Both Genders, All Races: United States, 2004

Rank	10–14 Years			15–19 Years			20–24 Years		
	Cause of Death	Number	Rate	Cause of Death	Number	Rate	Cause of Death	Number	Rate
. . .	All causes	3,946	18.7	All causes	13,706	66.1	All causes	19,715	94.0
1	Accidents (unintentional injuries)	1,540	7.3	Accidents (unintentional injuries)	6,825	32.9	Accidents (unintentional injuries)	8,624	41.1
2	Malignant neoplasms (cancer)	493	2.3	Assault (homicide)	1,932	9.3	Assault (homicide)	3,153	15.0
3	Intentional self-harm (suicide)	283	1.3	Intentional self-harm (suicide)	1,700	8.2	Intentional self-harm (suicide)	2,616	12.5
4	Assault (homicide)	207	1.0	Malignant neoplasms (cancer)	731	3.5	Malignant neoplasms (cancer)	978	4.7
5	Congenital malformations, deformations and chromosomal abnormalities	184	0.9	Diseases of the heart	366	1.8	Diseases of the heart	672	3.2

Source: CDC, National Vital Statistics System, National Center for Health Statistics, Mortality Statistics Branch (www.cdc.gov/nchs/datawh/statab/unpubd/mortabs.htm); Hamilton et al., 2007.

Third, human-induced deaths such as those involving accidents, homicide, and suicide most often occur quickly and unexpectedly, and they are frequently associated with trauma or violence. A large majority of all deaths among adolescents are likely to possess these characteristics. For relatives and friends of those who die in these ways, these deaths are likely to be perceived not only as untimely but also shocking in a way that is especially associated with sudden and unanticipated disaster (Podell, 1989). For other adolescents who survive the death of a friend or classmate who dies suddenly, unexpectedly, and perhaps traumatically, deaths that human beings cause or help to bring on themselves and others may have long-term implications for individuation and developmental tasks (Bradach & Jordan, 1995). For example, an adolescent's sense of competence and intimacy might be threatened by remorse arising from carelessness leading to an accidental death, guilt from perceived failure to save a friend from suicide, or anxiety from the homicidal death of a peer.

Fourth, the largest portion of all deaths from accidents or unintentional injuries noted in Table 13.4 results from motor vehicle accidents. Deaths associated with motor vehicles accounted for well over 75 percent of all accidental deaths in this age group. Like deaths arising from homicide and suicide, accidental deaths (especially those associated with motor vehicles) are perceived by many adults as preventable. For that reason, family members and friends often find themselves angry at the behaviors that led to such deaths and anguished over what might have been done to forestall such outcomes.

Fifth, as early as 1988, human immunodeficiency virus (HIV) infection had become the sixth leading cause of death in the United States among persons 15–24 years of age (late adolescents and early adults), and it remained the seventh leading cause of death in 2004 among individuals 20–24 years of age. In view of the long period of asymptomatic infection that typically characterizes the trajectory of HIV infection (see Chapter 20), this statistic is noteworthy. It contrasts with the fact that many who become infected with HIV during their adolescent years are not likely to die until they are well into adulthood. Further, HIV infection is 3 to 5 times more prevalent among African-American and Hispanic-American adolescents than among their Caucasian-American counterparts.

Sixth, in recent years many deaths among late adolescents who are members of the military have taken place in connection with wars and conflicts in Iraq and Afghanistan. To view the faces of some of these young people on the PBS program, *The News Hour with Jim Lehrer,* is a particularly poignant experience. Often violent and sudden, deaths like these are difficult for their peers in those countries, as well as for relatives and friends back home.

In summary, today adolescents in America and in many other developed societies are mostly healthy persons. Relative to other developmental groups, they enjoy a very low death rate. The reason is that, as a group, adolescents have survived the hazards of birth, infancy, and early childhood, and they have not lived long enough to experience the degenerative diseases that are more characteristic of later adulthood.

Two Variables in Deaths of Adolescents: Gender and Race

Useful contrasts can be drawn among adolescents by gender and by race. Tables 13.2 and 13.3 contrast deaths and death rates among adolescent males with those of adolescent females in the United States for 2004. Differences are obvious. Significantly more adolescent males than females die each year. Roughly the same differences apply to accidental deaths in this cohort, but the difference is more than 6:1 for deaths associated with either homicide or suicide.

When we compare adolescent deaths and death rates among various racial and cultural groups in our society, other important differences emerge (see Tables 13.2 and 13.3). For example, although there are many more deaths of Caucasian Americans in these age groups by contrast with deaths among African Americans, African Americans die at far higher rates. Numbers of deaths in 2004 among younger adolescents (those 10–14 years of age) are much lower for American Indians, Asian and Pacific Island Americans, and Hispanic Americans. Death rates among younger adolescents are lowest for Asian and Pacific Island Americans, higher among Hispanic Americans and Caucasian Americans, and significantly higher among American Indians, but still not as high as those for African Americans. Caucasian Americans are somewhat more likely to die in accidents or from suicide, whereas African Americans are far more likely to die from homicide, diseases of the heart, and HIV infection.

Among all adolescents 15–19 years of age, males are almost 2.5 times more likely to die than females (Table 13.2). Among non-Hispanic Caucasian Americans, this gender differential is only 2.2, but it rises to nearly 3.1 among African Americans in this age group. Differences in death rates between Caucasian-American males and females are at ratios of nearly 3:1 for accidents and HIV infection, more than 4:1 for homicide, and almost 6:1 for suicide. By contrast, differences in death rates between African-American males and African-American females are at ratios of less than 2:1 for diseases of the heart, just over 2:1 for HIV infection, almost 4:1 for accidents, almost 8:1 for homicide, and more than 8:1 for suicide.

Deaths of Others Experienced by Adolescents

There are few reliable sources of data concerning the *deaths of others that are experienced by adolescents*. One early study of more than 1,000 high school juniors and seniors (middle adolescents) reported that 90 percent of those students had experienced the death of someone they loved (Ewalt & Perkins, 1979). In nearly 40 percent of this sample, the loss involved the death of a friend or peer who was roughly their own age. Ewalt and Perkins concluded that "adolescents have more experience with death and mourning than has been assumed" (p. 547). In 20 percent of the sample, the students had actually witnessed a death. A similar study found that when asked to identify their "most recent major loss," 1,139 late adolescent (average age = 19.5) college and university students in New York State reported that the death of a loved one or a sudden death (number = 328) was the most common loss among a total of 46 different types of losses (LaGrand, 1981). Even more recently, Christ, Siegel, and Christ (2002) have pointed out that, "In the United States, more than 2 million children and adolescents (3.4%) younger than 18 years have experienced the death of a parent." Clearly, it is not correct to think that contemporary adolescents have no experience with death and bereavement.

In addition, adolescents encounter deaths involving grandparents; neighbors, teachers, and other adults; siblings and friends; peers and slightly older youths in the military; pets and other animals; and celebrities and cultural heroes with whom they identify (Noppe & Noppe, 2004). Adolescence is also the first era in the human life course in which an individual can experience the death of his or her own offspring. Adolescents also report that they encounter a wide variety of loss-related experiences that do not involve death but may nevertheless be very painful, such as the ending of friendships or loving relationships (LaGrand, 1981, 1986, 1988).

Many experiences with death and other losses may have special significance for an adolescent's developmental tasks. For example, early adolescents who are striving to achieve emotional emancipation from parents may experience complications in those efforts if a parent (or a grandparent to whom they are especially close or who is their surrogate parent) should suddenly die. Such an adolescent may feel abandoned by these adult deaths and may find it hard to attain a feeling of safety in these circumstances.

Similarly, middle adolescents who are seeking to achieve competency, mastery, and control at a time when they enjoy some sense of autonomy may experience a threat to their newfound independence if a friend or other member of their own generation should die (see Personal Insights 13.1). The likelihood that the death of another adolescent will be sudden, unexpected, traumatic, and often violent may enhance the threat to the surviving adolescent's own prospects and security. Adolescents who have carried over from childhood the "tattered cloak of immortality" (Gordon, 1986) or who maintain a "personal fable" (Elkind, 1967) of invulnerability may be shaken when confronted by the death of a person of their own age and similar circumstances (Noppe & Noppe, 2004).

Further, late adolescents who are working to reestablish intimacy and commitment with those who are significant in their lives may feel thwarted and frustrated when they encounter the death of a person of a younger generation—for example, a younger brother, sister, friend, or their own child. Dedicating themselves to a relationship with a person of this sort and achieving the closeness that it can involve are stymied when the other person in the relationship dies. Such deaths may rebuff in a disturbing and disempowering way the older adolescent's efforts to reach out to others.

In addition, many adolescents in our society were impacted by the events of September 11, 2001, and responded in their own unique ways (Noppe et al., 2006). Also, adolescents are more likely than children to recognize and understand large-scale perils, such as global tensions, the threat or reality of war, and terrorism. As well, many adolescents are sensitive to violence at home, in their schools and communities, and in the world at large; ongoing jeopardy associated with nuclear weapons and power plants; and problems involving the environment, such as acid rain, destruction of the world's rain forests, depletion of the ozone layer in the atmosphere, the so-called greenhouse effect involving climatic warming, population growth, and waste disposal.

🍒 Death-Related Attitudes during Adolescence

Given the great diversity among adolescents in our society and the breadth of issues associated with death, we should not be surprised to find a wide variety of death-related attitudes held by adolescents. We can begin to examine such attitudes among adolescents in the contemporary American death system by suggesting some of the many factors that influence them.

Who's Andrea?

The spring day dawned crisp and clear on the desert. A beautiful morning . . . sun shining brightly, cheery children shouting and laughing as they bound toward school whilst slowly wakening commuters tap their fingers in rhythm to the FM beat, contemplating the successes of the impending day. It is February the third, a Wednesday, and a wonderful time to be alive.

It is also the anniversary of a devastating event in the life of Marsha, my wife, and I. An endless 2,192 days ago we last hugged our daughter Virginia, an interminable 52,608 hours since we consoled her and swore that everything would be all right. A millennium since we felt her warm touch. When she died, a piece of us died with her. We will never forget her, even when it seems everyone else has.

On most occasions, when we seek to speak to her spirit, we visit the site of the accident that took her life. Today, however, our memories guide us to her resting-place, so that we may place a flower and reaffirm how much we still love and miss her. To speak through our hearts to a daughter who will forever remain 15 years old.

Her remains reside in a quiet, peaceful columbarium on church grounds that few others know about. It is the perfect foyer to heaven. But what is this? Another visitor has already been here, placed a flower, and left a note! Does someone else remember her? As we peer at the words on the tattered paper, authored by "Andrea," it seems as if God Himself has sensed our feelings of abandonment and sent the message.

As we journey home, one question continues to confound us; just who is Andrea? Neither of us can recall a friend of Virginia's named Andrea. Is Andrea really God incognito, or simply a distraught young woman mourning the loss of her friend? One thing is for certain, Andrea, whomever she is, represents validation that Virginia made a difference while she lived on earth. She touched someone so deeply that even 6 years after her death she is remembered, mourned, missed and loved by someone other than her parents and family. It seems a fitting legacy to the days when she walked on the very ground that Andrea, the two of us, and the rest of humanity walk upon today.

Andrea's handwritten note:

Ginny,
I love-n-miss you very much and know someday we will see each other again. Your always close in my mind-n-heart. With Love, Andrea.

Source: David Stanton, 1999. Reprinted with permission.

For *adolescent understandings of death,* researchers generally agree that before or by the beginning of the adolescent era individuals with normal cognitive development are capable of grasping the concept of death and its principal sub-concepts (see Chapter 12). Most adolescents in Western society are well into what Piaget and

Inhelder (1958) called the period of formal operations, which is characterized by propositional and hypothetical-deductive thinking, generality of concepts, and an objective view of reality (Keating, 1990).

However, it is not enough merely to note that adolescents are *capable* of thinking in ways characteristic of adults. Noppe and Noppe (1991, 1996, 1997) have suggested that *adolescent understandings of death may be influenced by ambiguities or tensions arising from biological, cognitive, social, and emotional factors.* First, rapid *biological* maturation and sexual development is associated in many adolescents with an awareness of inevitable physical decline and ultimate death. This tension is represented in high-risk behaviors among many adolescents who seek to defy or "cheat" death (Bachman et al., 1986). Although "the majority of adolescents engage in some risk-taking behavior but do not experience tragic consequences" (Gans, 1990, p. 17), this behavior is particularly hazardous in a world of high-powered automobiles, readily available drugs and firearms, eating disorders, binge drinking, and HIV (Bachman et al., 1986; Bensinger & Natenshon, 1991; Wechsler et al., 1994). Adolescents conflicted by such challenges and possibilities may have reason to look fondly at what they seem to have lost in moving on from the more restricted, apparently simpler, world of childhood.

Second, in searching for one's own identity and reevaluating parental values, an adolescent's newly developed *cognitive* capacities are challenged to take into account the inevitability of death. Thoughts about death in the abstract may or may not coexist with awareness of its personal significance for an individual adolescent (Corr, 1995d). Looking bravely into what the future holds, adolescents may glimpse both positive and negative possibilities. In the end, they must come to appreciate that although there is much they can do to influence the shape of their futures, it is also true that many things are beyond their control.

Third, changing *social* relationships with family members and peers carry potential for both enrichment and isolation. As their relationships enlarge in scope, especially by moving outside of their family of origin, adolescents are challenged to create a viable social life and to avoid a "social death" (Noppe & Noppe, 1991, 1996). A new peer group offers a context in which an adolescent can be comfortable in his or her new identity, but it also imposes scrutiny and its own demands for conformity. This is further complicated when the chosen peer group is a gang that devotes some of its energies to violent behavior and strife with others. Also, in many adolescent peer groups, transient interpersonal difficulties can become sources of anguish and despair. For many adolescents, this may be compounded by moving into new academic and cultural settings, and by specific ethnic influences that may encourage or inhibit certain kinds of public behaviors, such as the expression of grief and other reactions to loss.

Fourth, adolescent *feelings* about development and death are likely to be closely intertwined. Achieving autonomy and individuation during the adolescent years is not only a matter of abandoning parent–child attachments begun in infancy. The real challenge for developing adolescents is to reformulate and make qualitative changes in such attachments, even as they develop new peer group attachments. All of this can involve threats to an adolescent's sense of self-esteem and purpose in life. Developmental feelings of loss and grief—the fear of losing oneself—coexist in many adolescents with feelings of being intensely alive.

The very broad range of adolescent attitudes toward death is reflected in the entertainment media that are so much a part of the lives of many adolescents and preadolescents. For example, video games often involve animated simulations of violence and death, as do movies that are popular with teenagers and young adults. Death-related themes are also prominent in the fast-changing music scene familiar to most adolescents (see Attig, 1986; Plopper & Ness, 1993). When we asked some adolescents to identify songs they knew that contain death-related themes, they suggested (among many): "Hold On" by the punk band Good Charlotte (an antisuicide lyric); "I'll Be Missing You" by Puff Daddy and Faith Evans; Reba McIntyre's "He Gets It from You" and Tim McGraw's "Live Like You Were Dying" from country music; "Tears in Heaven," an older song by Eric Clapton (about the death of his son); and many titles from the gangsta rap scene, such as "Many Men (Wish Death)" by 50 Cent, "Murder Was the Case" by Snoop Dogg, and "Life after Death" by Notorious B.I.G. No doubt, many who turn their attention to this musical genre will be able to think of numerous other, more current titles. Beyond that, it is perhaps worthwhile to note a comment by one adolescent who said she does not always listen to the lyrics so much as the music itself. Still, death in many of its forms (not only violence or suicide) is widely present in these lyrics and other media directed to adolescents.

A central element in an adolescent's sense of vulnerability or invulnerability has to do not merely with surrogate experiences arising from various aspects of their culture, such as movies, television, and music, but with *lessons learned—or not learned—by adolescents from their own life experiences.* The inability or unwillingness of many adolescents to recognize the personal implications of mortality may have much to do with the limits of adolescent experience and the perspectives that dominate much of adolescent life. This theory is confirmed by an analysis of factors that enter into well-known driving patterns in middle and late adolescence (Jonah, 1986). Two elements are of greatest significance: (1) adolescent drivers may simply not perceive risks inherent in their behaviors (such as the likelihood that an accident might occur or that it might result in serious consequences) and thus may inadvertently put themselves into situations fraught with danger; and (2) adolescent drivers may perceive positive utility or value in taking certain risks, such as seizing control over one's life by acting independently, expressing opposition to adult authority and conventional society, coping with anxiety or frustration, or gaining acceptance from a peer group. We saw both of these elements in the vignette near the beginning of this chapter when Tom Adkins and his friends tried (unsuccessfully) to outrun a train with their car.

Tolstoy captured the sense of invulnerability found in some adolescents in his classic novella *The Death of Ivan Ilych* (1884/1960, p. 131). As Ivan is dying in midlife, he thinks of his youth: "The syllogism he had learnt from Kiezewetter's Logic: 'Caius is a man, men are mortal, therefore Caius is mortal,' had always seemed to him correct as applied to Caius, but certainly not as applied to himself." In other words, mortality for the young Ivan Ilych was an abstraction, whose personal force and relevance to his own life becomes apparent to him only many years later as he is dying.

However, not all adolescents can put aside threats related to death. In one study (Alexander & Adlerstein, 1958), participants were asked to say the first word that came into their minds in response to a series of stimulus words that included death-related words. Responses were measured in terms of the speed with which they were offered and by association with decreased galvanic skin resistance (increased perspiration or sweating). Participants aged 5–8 and 13–16 had high death anxiety scores when compared with the scores of 9- to 12-year-olds. The researchers concluded that death has "a greater emotional significance for people with less stable ego self-pictures" (p. 175).

This seems to suggest that death-related threats have greatest personal significance at times of transition in human development and, within adolescence, at times of decreased stability and self-confidence. This is consistent with a report that death anxiety is highest in teenagers and most closely associated with fears of loss of bodily integrity and decomposition (Thorson et al., 1988). For many individuals, early adolescence is a time of little sense of futurity and a high degree of egocentrism (Elkind, 1967). Thus, a key variable in adolescent attitudes toward death may be the level of maturity that the adolescent has achieved (Maurer, 1964), with greater maturity being associated with "greater sophistication and acknowledgement of the inevitability of death as well as with enjoyment of life and altruistic concerns" (Raphael, 1983, p. 147).

In short, many adolescents tend to live in the moment and may not appreciate personal threats associated with death. The key issue for these adolescents may not arise directly from their capacity to think about death but rather from ways in which the significance of death-related concepts is or is not related to their personal lives. This may not apply to adolescents who have broad and personal experiences with death. For example, some adolescents who have been prepared for and supported in their work as hospice teen volunteers have learned important lessons from those activities (Benham, 2005; see also Personal Insights 13.2). In general, however, most adolescents struggle to grasp the personal significance of death by confronting a paradox: they want to keep their feelings in perspective and distance themselves from intense death-related experiences, while at the same time they attempt to find meaning in abstract concepts of death by applying them in ways that have personal reference and meaning.

❧ Adolescents Who Are Coping with Life-Threatening Illness and Dying

Because dying and adolescence are both transitional experiences, Papadatou (1989, p. 28) has wisely noted that, "it could be argued that seriously ill adolescents experience a double crisis owing to their imminent death and their developmental age." In particular, dying adolescents need to live in the present, to have the freedom to try out different ways of coping with illness-related challenges, and to find meaning and purpose in their lives and in their deaths (Stevens & Dunsmore, 1996a). For most adolescents, effective coping with a life-threatening illness requires information about the disease, involvement in the planning of treatment, and participation in decision making (Cassileth et al., 1980; Dunsmore & Quine, 1995; Freyer, 2004).

Among individuals 15–24 years of age, cancer is the fourth leading cause of death (third among females), followed at a distance by heart disease, congenital malformations, chronic lower respiratory diseases, HIV infection, cerebrovascular diseases, and influenza and pneumonia.

The needs and reactions of adolescents associated with life-threatening illness and dying have been described in a variety of ways (Adams & Deveau, 1986; Waechter,

Two Experiences as a Teen Hospice Volunteer

In my first volunteer experience with hospice, I served as a teen mentor to a 12-year-old boy with a life-threatening illness. . . . This disease . . . limited his physical activity. As a teen mentor, I provided emotional support for this boy by helping him identify his other interests and by taking his mind off his illness. I visited him weekly and often assisted with homework, took him fishing, or simply talked with him about life. It was a truly incredible feeling to see him smile and to know that I made a difference in his life. Realizing that I contributed to the life of another, I gained a greater satisfaction with my own life, as well as a greater appreciation for its many gifts. . . .

One of the greatest challenges I encountered in my work with the terminally ill was through my unique friendship with a 107-year-old hospice patient named Joe, and having that friendship come to an end in November 1998. It was indeed a challenge to grow close with Joe, knowing that our time together would be short. I overcame this challenge by focusing on Joe's life—a century of memories, history, and accomplishments. Each time I visited with Joe I was guaranteed to learn something new, whether it was a history lesson or a lesson on life. I felt that Joe, like all terminally ill patients, should live until he died, so I brought him lunch on occasion and shared pictures with him. When the time came for Joe to pass on, it was extremely difficult to focus on life amidst oxygen machines and tube feedings, yet I continued to hold his hand through it all. On one of Joe's last evenings, he told a friend and I that we were "the best gifts a man could ask for," and that he would never forget us. It was at that moment that the familiar hospice message, "Every day is a gift," truly touched me. From Joe, I learned to cherish this gift of life and to help other hospice patients do the same by offering my compassion during the last stages of their lives.

Source: Copyright © 2000 by Education Development Center, Inc. Reprinted with permission Corace, B., "End-of-Life Care: A Personal Reflection." In *Innovations in End-of-Life Care: Practical Strategies and International Perspectives,* Volume 2, M. Z. Solomon, A. L. Romer, K. S. Heller, and D. E. Weissman (Eds.). Larchmont, NY: Mary Ann Liebert Publishers, 2000, 81–82. This essay was originally published in Volume 2, Number 4 of the online version of *Innovations in End-of-Life Care* at www.edc.org/lastacts.

1984). Perhaps one useful rule of thumb is the reminder that adolescents "are not so much afraid of death as of the dying" (Stevens & Dunsmore, 1996a, p. 109). Having a life-threatening illness begins a pattern of loss for adolescents, leading to experiences of loss or alteration in their sense of themselves as "pre-diagnosis persons"; body image; lifestyle (e.g., a perception of being in control and not unreasonably vulnerable may turn into one of vulnerability and overprotectiveness by adolescents and the adults around them); everyday school activities; independence; relationships with parents, siblings, and friends; and sense of certainty about the future.

Stevens and Dunsmore (1996a) drew on their extensive work with ill and dying adolescents to observe that early adolescents with a life-threatening illness are likely to be especially concerned about physical appearance and mobility. They are also likely to rely on authority figures. Middle adolescents typically focus on what the illness will mean for their ability to attract a girlfriend or boyfriend, on emancipation from parents and authority figures, and on being rejected by peers. Late adolescents may be most concerned with how the illness will affect their lifestyle and their plans for a career and relationships.

Life-threatening diseases impact both the ill adolescent and those who are involved with that adolescent. We see this in two examples of sibling reactions to such situations: a poem by an Australian adolescent (Personal Insights 13.3) and a chronicle of

---

PERSONAL INSIGHTS 13.3

Only a Sibling

How do you tell someone you love
You don't want them to die
How can I try to be normal
I know I will cry

How do I cope with my anger
At life, at God and sometimes even at you
How can I put a smile on my face
While my insides are ripping in two

How can I tell you I'm frightened
Of the skeleton my brother's become
Tired and thin from your battle
A war that I'm scared cannot be won

How can I tell you I love you
When all our lives it's going unsaid
How do I stop you from drowning
When the water's already over my head

Every wince stabs me too, with pain
Why cannot I tell anyone how I feel
When I feel like I'm going insane

How can I think of my future
When it's possibly a future without you there
Why do I feel so damn helpless
And my problems too insignificant to share

How do I tell you big brother
That I'm scared of what's happening to you
Why cannot anyone seem to understand
That your dying is killing me too.

Source: From "Only a Sibling," by Tammy McKenzie (nee McGowan), CanTeen Newsletter. Copyright © 1992 CanTeen Australia Ltd. Reprinted with permission.

the challenges facing healthy adolescents whose ill sibling is coping with cystic fibrosis (see Table 13.5). The challenge for both ill adolescents and those around them is to learn how to live with progressive, life-threatening diseases (Koocher & O'Malley, 1981; Spinetta & Deasy-Spinetta, 1981). This requirement places great demands on individual and familial resources and on processes of communication within the family, especially when the dying trajectory is drawn out. Not surprisingly, adolescents need defenses in such situations and often seek to play an active role in coping with the challenges they face (Dunsmore & Quine, 1995; Spiegel, 1993). Beyond good symptom management, adolescents need to be involved in their care and not treated as younger children. For this, adolescents need to be given accurate information about their situation in a caring way and to be assured, in fact not just in words, that their views and concerns will be taken into account in deciding upon the interventions they are to receive and the ways in which those interventions will be delivered (Stevens & Dunsmore, 1996b). For most adolescents, it is also important to live out their lives in their own ways and to maintain valued involvements with peers, school, and families—the ordinary milieu of adolescent life (Corr, 2002d). Programs of palliative/hospice care for children and adolescents (mentioned in Chapter 12) can be especially useful in this regard.

TABLE 13.5
Well Siblings' Views of Cystic Fibrosis and Their Own Sibling's Condition

Disease Trajectory	Well Siblings' Views
Diagnosis	A serious illness
First year following diagnosis	
First annual examination	A condition one does things for
Months/years following first annual examination (without a major exacerbation)	
First major exacerbation	A disease, not merely a condition
Succeeding exacerbations and other illnesses, with periodic hospitalizations	A series of episodes of acute illness and recovery
Frequent exacerbations, episodes of other diseases, and hospitalizations	Questions emerge about cure, course of the disease, control of it, and efficacy of treatment
Development and increase in complications	Chronic, progressive, incurable disease that shortens the life span (This view does not apply to one's own sibling—at least not in the near future.)
Increased deterioration	Chronic, progressive, incurable disease that shortens the life span (In some cases this view now applies to one's own sibling.)
Terminal phases	Chronic, progressive, incurable disease that shortens the life span (In all cases this view now applies to one's own sibling.)

Source: From "Living with Cystic Fibrosis: The Well Sibling's Perspective," by M. Bluebond-Langner, *Medical Anthropological Quarterly,* 5(2), June 1991, American Anthropological Association. Reprinted by permission.

Papadatou (1989, p. 31) offered one guiding thought to helpers who wish to approach adolescents and their families when they are coping with life-threatening illness: "We must also believe that we are not helpless or hopeless, but have something valuable to offer: an honest and meaningful relationship that provides the adolescent with a feeling that we are willing to share his journey through the remainder of his life."

🌑 Adolescents Who Are Coping with Bereavement and Grief

As noted earlier in this chapter, adolescents may experience bereavement through the death of many different types of individuals whom they view as significant in their lives. Not surprisingly, these individuals may even include celebrities whom they admired, such as Kurt Cobain, the grunge rocker who took his own life; Eazy-E (Eric Wright), the gangsta rapper and cofounder of the group N.W.A., who died of AIDS; Selena, the Tejano singer, who was shot to death; or Aaliyah, who was killed in a plane accident. Perhaps the most prominent feature in all adolescent grief is reflected in the title of an article in a professional journal (Christ et al., 2002): "Adolescent grief: 'It never really hit me . . . until it actually happened.'" Loss and grief frequently often are particularly shocking within the vibrant, complex, and developing context of adolescence.

In recent years, an emerging body of research has developed on adolescent bereavement (e.g., Balk, 1991a; Balk & Corr, 2001). Specific studies have mainly focused on adolescents who have experienced the deaths of a sibling or parent (e.g., Balk, 1991b; Fleming & Balmer, 1996). Surprisingly little attention has been given to the death of an adolescent's friend (Oltjen-bruns, 1996; Servaty-Seib & Pistole, 2007) or pet, or to experiences of bereaved adolescent parents (Bar-nickol et al., 1986; Welch & Bergen, 2000), even though each of these can involve a very close relationship and thus have a powerful impact on an adolescent.

Adolescents need support from their peers when they are coping with loss and grief.

Among the key variables that appear to be most prominent in adolescent bereavement are self-concept, developmental maturity, and depression. For example, two studies of bereaved siblings (Balk, 1990; Hogan & Greenfield, 1991) reported that high *self-concept* scores were correlated with lower intensity of grief, less depression, fear, loneliness, and confusion, while lower self-concept scores tended to correlate with more of these difficult implications. An ongoing attachment to the deceased sibling was also identified in the lives of many bereaved adolescents (Hogan & DeSantis, 1992).

In terms of *developmental maturity*, a study of sibling bereavement among Canadian adolescents reported that while older bereaved adolescents experienced more psychological distress, younger bereaved adolescents experienced more physiological distress (Balmer, 1992). In these adolescents, the increased psychological distress associated with greater developmental maturity was likely to be relatively transient, perhaps because older adolescents (by contrast with their younger peers) were more likely to talk with friends about their bereavement and to find social support.

Among other Canadian high school students, parental death led to more *depression* in bereaved versus nonbereaved adolescents, adolescents without religious beliefs, and those with lower scores of perceived social support (Gray, 1987).

In general, "perhaps the most salient feature of adolescent adjustment following death is the *resiliency* evidenced by the bereaved participants in the face of traumatic loss" (Fleming & Balmer, 1996, p. 153; emphasis added). This is supported by research on bereaved college students showing that *hardiness* was inversely associated with grief misery, while closeness to the deceased was a significant predicator of *personal growth* after the death (Mathews & Servaty-Seib, 2007). All of this suggests that bereavement during adolescence does not of itself predispose to ongoing psychological difficulties; it may actually help many adolescents to become more emotionally and interpersonally mature. However, bereavement may be problematic for vulnerable adolescents by reinforcing conditions they bring to their experience that predispose them to difficulty.

One special feature of adolescence is that, "Adolescents are apt to think that they are the discoverers of deep and powerful feelings and that no one has ever loved as they love" (Jackson, 1984, p. 42). If so, adolescents may assume that their grief is similarly unique and incomprehensible—to themselves and to others. Consequently, adolescents may only express their grief in brief outbursts or may actively suppress it because they fear loss of emotional control and do not want to be perceived by others as being out of control. However, some bereaved adolescents can reach into themselves in powerful ways to express their grief, as illustrated by the comments of one hospice teen volunteer about the death of her own grandfather (see Personal Insights 13.4).

Bereaved adolescents appear to be helped in coping with their grief by activities that reduce stress (playing a musical instrument, keeping busy, or releasing pent-up emotions); their own personal belief systems; support from parents, other relatives, or friends; and professionals or mutual support groups who can normalize grief reactions (Balk, 1991c; Balk & Hogan, 1995; Hogan & DeSantis, 1994). Complications may arise as a result of ambivalent relationships with the deceased or with other survivors; a tendency of some adolescents to idealize the deceased, which may complicate mourning with guilt and self-blame; a possibility that the relationship or the grief may be unacknowledged or disenfranchised by society; the intense, if sometimes relatively transitory, quality of adolescent feelings; the desire to fit in and not be different from peers; or lack of support from peers and adults.

PERSONAL INSIGHTS 13.4

A Hospice Teen Volunteer and the Death of Her Grandfather

My grandfather was diagnosed on January 13, 2000, with cancer of the colon, spleen, and lymph nodes. He died one month later on February 12. Needless to say, there was an extremely limited time period between his diagnosis and death in which we could prepare for the dreaded reality of the situation. However, since I have been trained as a hospice volunteer, I have learned that death can be approached as a celebration of life. I feel that I was able to celebrate my grandfather's life with him during the final moments that we did have together, and for that I am thankful. When I visited him two weeks before he died, Grandpa and I talked a lot, and I would simply sit by his bedside and hold his hand. Although it grew increasingly difficult for him to speak to us, he reminisced with me about a few of his early childhood memories, and commented on the incredible change that has taken place in the morals and values from his generation to mine. He told me how proud he was of me, and how he so hoped to know where Michael [her brother] and I would be going to college. Shortly after we had to go home . . . he grew so weak that he could no longer talk on the phone with me. To make up for that lack of communication, I e-mailed my grandpa every day until he died. My grandma printed out each of the e-mails and read them to him in his bed. I told him how much I loved him, how proud I was to be his granddaughter, and how much he had taught me, growing up. Grandpa and I had been writing letters back and forth for the past ten years. I have kept each of his letters and put them into an album. I will forever cherish those precious letters, as they allow me to remember the special times and conversations I had with my grandfather.

Source: Copyright © 2000 by Education Development Center, Inc. Reprinted with permission. Tibbetts, E., "Learning to Value Every Moment." In *Innovations in End-of-Life Care: Practical Strategies and International Perspectives,* Volume 2, M. Z. Solomon, A. L. Romer, K. S. Heller, and D. E. Weissman (Eds.). Larchmont, NY: Mary Ann Liebert Publishers, 2001, 78–79. This essay was originally published in Volume 2, Number 4 of the online version of *Innovations in End-of-Life Care* at www.edc.org/lastacts.

As in coping with life-threatening illness and dying during adolescence, bereavement for adolescents involves a double crisis in which situational tasks overlay and in many respects parallel normal developmental tasks (Sugar, 1968). For bereaved adolescents, in other words, experiences involving protest or searching, disorganization, and reorganization (as we described in Chapter 9) are often intertwined with normative developmental tasks of establishing emotional separation, achieving competency or mastery, and developing intimacy. If one accepts Coleman's (1978) account of "focal theory"—which holds that most adolescents cope with stressors by concentrating on resolving one crisis at a time—it follows that the double crisis of adolescent bereavement (without further complications, such as a traumatic death, a suicide, or the death of one's own child) is especially challenging both for young copers and for their helpers, who may be trying to determine which aspects of adolescent coping emerge from development and which from bereavement (Corr, 2000b; Garber, 1983).

This perspective suggests that adolescent mourning may not exactly parallel similar processes in adults. Paradoxically, adolescent mourning is likely to be both continuous and intermittent, encompassing as it typically does both grief that comes and goes and an overall process that may involve an extended period of time (Hogan & DeSantis, 1992). In personal relationships and in their social systems, adolescents' bereavement is likely to involve secondary losses and incremental grief. We need to learn more about the role of family dynamics and long-term consequences of death for adolescent development (Balmer, 1992; Hogan & Balk, 1990; Lattanzi-Licht, 1996; Martinson et al., 1987; Meshot & Leitner, 1993).

☙ Adolescents, Homicide, and Suicide

Homicide and Adolescents

Following accidents, homicide is the second leading cause of death among adolescents, one that has been increasing in relative significance in recent years and one characterized by significant gender and ethnic differences. In 2004, homicide was only the fifteenth leading cause of death for the population as a whole, but it remained the second leading cause of death for middle and late adolescents. In terms of absolute numbers, there were 5,085 homicide deaths in 2004 in our society among individuals 15–24 years of age—29.3 percent of all homicide deaths in the entire country that year in a group that represents only 16.6 percent of the total population (see Table 13.4). The death rate from homicide in this age group in 2004 was 12.2 per 100,000.

During the period from 1960 to 1990, the United States experienced a tripling or quadrupling of homicide rates among middle and late adolescents overall. In addition, homicide rates were significantly higher for males as contrasted with females in this age group, and for African Americans as contrasted with Caucasian Americans. In other words, like suicide, *homicide among adolescents is far more a male than a female phenomenon*—by a ratio of approximately 3 to 1. However, unlike suicide, *homicide is far more an experience of African Americans than Caucasian Americans.* In this latter comparison, death rates from homicide for African Americans are nearly 6 times those for Caucasian Americans.

Since 1991, there has been a downward trend in homicide deaths in the United States for the population as a whole (see Chapter 4). Nevertheless, in 2004, homicide remained the leading cause of death for African-American males 15–24 years of age and the second leading cause of death for African-American females in the same age group. From an international standpoint, youth homicide rates are far higher in the United States than in any other country in the world (Fingerhut & Kleinman, 1989).

Homicide among adolescents is complex in both its implications and its origins (Busch et al., 1990). Homicide and other forms of trauma have negative effects on a variety of adolescent populations. Foremost among these are the people who are killed, the *primary victims* of the violence (some of whom may be "innocent

© Michael Siluk/The Image Works

Adolescents and the means to produce violence can lead to lethal behavior.

bystanders," such as the two girls in the vignette near the beginning of this chapter). In addition, adolescent homicide can have negative effects on a broad range of *secondary victims,* such as relatives, friends, those who witness such violence, and even perpetrators of homicides themselves (Shakoor & Chalmers, 1991). This experience may be especially significant for the individuation and developmental tasks of surviving adolescents (Bradach & Jordan, 1995).

Homicide is a phenomenon especially (although not exclusively) prevalent in urban settings (Ropp et al., 1992). As a general rule, most perpetrators and victims of adolescent homicide are likely to come from the same ethnic or racial background, leading to the observation that this type of death is primarily intramural in character (Barrett, 1996). Firearms are involved in the majority of homicide deaths (Fingerhut et al., 1991). In each of these respects, homicide involving adolescents is essentially an extreme form of violence undertaken or experienced by adolescents in their own homes, schools, or communities (American Psychological Association, 1993; National Research Council, 1993; U.S. Department of Health and Human Services, 2001b). Dysfunctional home environments along with violent communities beset by gang and drug-induced criminal activities are settings of real and chronic danger for many poor urban youth in American society (Kozol, 1995). The interplay between homicide and social structure is apparent in reports of lethal violence in the Latino community in Chicago (Block, 1993) and in declining rates of both homicide and suicide resulting from restrictive licensing of handguns in the District of Columbia (Loftin et al., 1991).

Adolescent homicide involving middle-class, socially advantaged, suburban, Caucasian Americans (including females) has recently been brought to public attention by media coverage of school shootings in our society, especially through the widely publicized tragedy at Columbine High School in Littleton, Colorado, in April 1999 and a similar event at Virginia Tech University in Blacksburg, Virginia, in April 2007 (see Issues for Critical Reflection #4 in Chapter 4 and #18 in Chapter 19). In fact, events like these are relatively rare and do not take away from the fact that schools are among the safest places for children in our society, a fact that has recently been confirmed by an official U.S. government report (DeVoe et al., 2004).

What the existence of school-related violence and death does point out is that even in such settings death can intrude in ugly ways.

In fact, it is urban, African-American and Hispanic-American males who are most at risk for becoming perpetrators or victims of adolescent homicide. In the words of Holinger and colleagues (1994, p. 182), "Youth homicide most often involves poverty and the apparently related interpersonal, domestic, and gang-related violence; victims and perpetrators share similar characteristics. Character disorders (e.g., impulse control, sociopathic problems) appear common to both victims and perpetrators of youth homicide." One important feature of adolescent homicide is that it typically occurs in contexts of peer and social influence (Barrett, 1996). Violent adults often act alone; violent adolescents usually act in groups. In some adolescent peer groups, violent behavior seems to be accepted, encouraged, and even regarded as a kind of rite of passage into the group (see Issues for Critical Reflection #11).

The far-reaching implications of adolescent homicide in many communities in America have led some (e.g., Fingerhut & Kleinman, 1989; Sullivan, 1991) to conclude that such homicide should be regarded not principally as a criminal

ISSUES FOR CRITICAL REFLECTION
#11 What Is the Relationship between Gangs and Violence in Our Society?

Modern urban society has produced a particularly lethal combination for adolescents: gangs and violence (especially violence related to the use of firearms). However, most careful studies leave uncertain just how significant the relationship between these factors really is (Nakaya, 2005). For instance, although so-called youth gangs get much attention from the media, there is not much agreement on just what constitutes a "gang." California and Florida law state that three persons can constitute a gang; other states say that there need be only two persons (Myers, 2000). And although some gangs are organized (with names, colors, and hand signals), others are not. One media report (Anonymous, 2001a) claimed that there were 1,300 gangs in Los Angeles. But given the vagueness of deciding what is a gang and what is not, this claim may be exaggerated (Myers, 2000). One consistent finding is that the largest numbers of gang members come from African-American and Latino-American communities, mostly in poor, urban areas (Anonymous, 2001a; Komro, 1999; Myers, 2000).

It is also possible that gang activity is in fact declining (Myers, 2000). What has changed and may give the impression of more gang activity is an increase in the use of violence, especially the use of firearms (Anonymous, 2001a; Komro, 1999; Myers, 2000). One study (Galea et al., 2002) of the 11,133 firearms-related deaths in New York City from 1990–1998 reported that more than a third (36.8 percent) were of persons 15–24 years old. Finally, Komro (1999) reported that among males in this age group, the firearms-related homicide rate is three times the overall homicide rate. What the admittedly conflicting evidence does seem to indicate is that violence among young persons, especially males, is a large social problem, at least in poor urban areas of the United States.

justice issue but rather as *a public health crisis*. Barrett's (1996) review of attempts to explain adolescent homicide revealed them to be as numerous as the multitude of economic, political, racial, sex role, and other factors that appear to be associated with these behaviors. Such explanations include the disputed claim that there is a subculture within some African-American ghetto communities that models and sanctions violence; "black rage" theories that violence results from inadequate ability on the part of younger, nonwhite males to control impulses and cope with anger arising from economic deprivation, poverty, and discrimination; the ready availability of alcohol, drugs, and cheap handguns in America; and the failures of many social institutions, often coupled with what appears to be lack of interest in or a punitive attitude toward "difficult" adolescents.

These and other explanations for the startling level of homicide among American adolescents go beyond our scope in this book. Clearly, there is much that American society and its death system need to do to reduce levels of violence among adolescents and to bring down both the number and rate of homicide deaths in this group. In light of the complexities of both adolescent homicide and suicide, no simple solution is likely to be found (Prothrow-Stith & Spivak, 2004). Holinger and colleagues (1994) synthesized their research on suicide and homicide among adolescents in four central recommendations: (1) gun control to limit the ready availability of firearms; (2) public education concerning the origins of these behaviors, together with what is already known about treatment and prevention strategies; (3) better training of professionals; and (4) more and better research on etiology and treatment. Barrett (1996) proposed similar recommendations, along with a multilevel program of empowerment on the part of religious institutions and local communities; renewed assumption of responsibility on the part of African-American and Hispanic-American adult males; active involvement by parents and educational institutions in the constructive socialization of youth; systematic education about the risk of lethal confrontations and the development of skills in conflict management; reformation of correctional systems; and advocacy of policies of social justice to ameliorate poverty and social distress.

Suicide and Adolescents

Suicidal behavior among adolescents has attracted long-standing attention (e.g., Lester, 1993; Peck et al., 1985; Stillion & McDowell, 1996) for two primary reasons: (1) to many, adolescence seems to be a healthy and productive era during which the individual evolves from child to adult and finds important openings to the future; and (2) during the period between 1960 and 1990, suicide rates among middle and late adolescents increased significantly—more rapidly than for any other age cohort during the same period (Holinger et al., 1994; Maris, 1985).

During the last half of the 1990s, however, suicide rates for middle and late adolescents 15–24 years of age in the United States displayed a downward trend. Between 1990 and 1995, suicide rates ranged from a low of 13.0 to a high of 13.8 per 100,000 in this age group. In 1996, these rates declined to 12.0 suicides per 100,000, and they continued to decline during the last years of the 20th century to reach a new low of 9.9 per 100,000 in 2002. Since that time, suicide rates among adolescents 15–24 years of age have since increased slightly to 10.4 per 100,000 in 2004 (see McIntosh, 2006 and Table 17.1). Suicide was the cause of death of 4,316 persons between the ages of 15–24 in 2004. Along with 283 deaths during the same year that were identified as caused by suicide in early adolescents 10–14 years of age, there is ample reason for concern about youth suicide.

In addition to the fact that the suicide rate for adolescents increased more rapidly than that of any other age group during the period 1960–1990, "the second important characteristic of adolescent suicidal behavior is the dramatic sex difference in suicide attempts versus completions" (Stillion & McDowell, 1996, p. 119). According to reliable estimates, the vast majority (about 75 percent) of all adolescent suicide attempters are female, whereas the largest majority (approximately 85 percent) of adolescent suicide completers is male. These and other disparities in suicidal behavior among adolescents—for example, between female and male attempters, between male and female completers, between late and middle adolescents, and between Caucasian-American and African-American adolescents—suggest that we still have much to learn to understand more clearly the dynamics behind such phenomena.

It may seem paradoxical that self-inflicted death should have become the third leading cause of death among adolescents, in an era of human development that is often perceived by outsiders to be satisfying and promising. In fact, as we saw in the example of Anthony Ramirez in our vignette near the beginning of this chapter, suicide is often chosen by adolescents who do not share the rosy view of their situation that may be held by others, who are overburdened by stresses, who are unable to identify constructive options to resolve their problems, or who are depressed that life is good and promising for others (Jurich & Collins, 1996).

Suicidal behavior in adolescents and others is often complex; it may arise from many factors (Allberg & Chu, 1990; Kirk, 1993; see also Chapter 17 in this book). For that reason, one should not oversimplify the situation of adolescents who attempt or complete actions that may end their lives. Still, we often can identify adolescents who are at risk for suicide (Garrison et al., 1991). Prominent factors include inadequacies or alterations in relationships between adolescents and significant others, such as parents and family members, peers, schoolmates, or co-workers; potent pressures among adolescents to conform to peers; inexperience in coping with problems; and dysfunctional behavior. All of these factors are associated with ineffective communication, inadequate coping skills, and the specific problems of developing adolescents. In addition, there is evidence to support the claim that gay and lesbian youth are at high risk for suicidal behavior (Gibson, 1994). This might be due to a variety of factors, including the attitudes of many members of our society toward gay and lesbian persons. More broadly, adolescents "who experience a wide gulf between who they are and who they want to become are at risk for low self-concepts, self-hatred, depression, and suicidal behavior" (Stillion, McDowell, & May, 1989, p. 194). Such adolescents may be unable to express their needs, solve their personal problems, or obtain the assistance that they require.

Adolescents who can neither resolve their problems nor put them into a larger perspective can become isolated and depressed. Since depression is frequently associated with feelings of helplessness and hopelessness, such adolescents may become desperate (Cobain, 2007). Self-destruction may appear to them to be their only available option. *Most often, this does not reflect a wish to be dead.* In fact, like others, many suicidal adolescents are ambivalent in their feelings about life and death and may be unclear about the personal finality of death. What may be most significant in such adolescents is their *overpowering urge to escape from a stressful life situation* (Berman, 1986; Berman & Jobes, 1991).

© Mark Antman/The Image Works

Depressed adolescents who feel that their lives are going nowhere may turn to life-threatening behavior.

Adolescents who are ambivalent about ending their lives often attempt to communicate their need for help in some way or other. For example, they may begin to give away cherished possessions or speak vaguely about how things would be better if they were no longer around. However, these may not be very effective ways of getting across the desired message. After all, the ability to achieve effective communication is directly related to an ability to cope with problems. An adolescent who can describe his or her problems to others has usually made an important step toward managing them. Nonetheless, those to whom an adolescent tries to communicate his or her feelings may not recognize such messages as cries for assistance because many adolescent communications are exaggerated, because this particular message may be obscure, or because those who are living healthful lives may be unable or unwilling to grasp the desperation associated with the message.

Even when outsiders cannot prevent adolescents from attempting or completing suicide, much can be done to minimize the likelihood of such behaviors (Westefeld et al., 2006). Efforts to increase self-esteem, foster the ability to make sound decisions, and enhance constructive coping skills in adolescents are all desirable. School-based education and intervention programs for teachers, counselors, parents, and adolescents are designed to teach about warning signs of suicide and practical strategies for offering help, such as peer counseling and crisis intervention (Berkovitz, 1985; Leenaars & Wenckstern, 1991; Poland, 1989; Ross, 1980, 1985; Stevenson, 2001; Stevenson & Stevenson, 1996a). The important thing about such programs is that the individuals to whom they are addressed are ideally positioned to identify and assist adolescents who might engage in suicidal behavior.

Some have been concerned that education about suicide may produce the very behaviors it is designed to minimize. This is one version of the so-called "contagion theory," whereby it is thought that mentioning suicide is likely to infect the hearer with a tendency to engage in this behavior. In recent years, this concern has been associated with "cluster" or "copycat" suicides—that is, situations in which the example of others or reports in the media seem to have established models for troubled youth. In fact, no reliable evidence supports these views (Ross, 1985; see also Chapter 17 in this book).

What is dangerous for adolescents is anything they might perceive as giving approval to life-threatening behaviors, not knowledge about suicide or about the suicidal behavior of others (Berman, 1988; Davidson & Gould, 1989). This danger is precisely what is not found in education that is frank about the negative consequences of suicidal behavior. Such education teaches adolescents that *suicide is a permanent solution to a temporary problem.* As Art Buchwald (2006, p. 37) wrote in his distinctive humorous way: "Don't commit suicide, because you might change your mind two weeks later." Effective education about suicide mobilizes resources for resolving problems in other ways and directs attention to the great pain that is a common and widespread legacy of adolescent suicide. Talking about suicide in a constructive educational format is far more likely to clear the air and minimize suicidal behavior than to suggest or encourage such behavior (Stillion & McDowell, 1996).

Crisis intervention programs offer a useful model of intervention to minimize suicidal behaviors in adolescents and others (Fairchild, 1986; Hatton & Valente, 1984). Such programs are directed precisely at those who are ambivalent about ending their lives. They encourage such persons to initiate telephone contact with the helping agency. Many of the volunteers who respond to such contacts are themselves adolescents who have been selected, trained, supervised, and supported in such work (Valente & Saunders, 1987). These volunteers offer a caring presence, an attentive companion during what is most often a limited period of crisis, a helper who can evaluate needs and aid in identifying alternative strategies for resolving problems, and a guide to additional resources for further assistance.

One area of adolescent suicide that is not well understood has to do with those who are left behind when someone completes a suicide (Valente & Sellers, 1986). Grief following the suicide of an adolescent is likely to be intense. This applies to all who are so bereaved but especially to adolescent peers: "Adolescent suicide is a particularly toxic form of death for peers who are left behind" (Mauk & Weber, 1991, p. 115). Adolescent peer bereavement is frequently complicated by feelings of guilt, rejection, frustration, anger, and failure. Quite often, it is also overlaid by societal disapproval, labeling, and stigma—all of which add to the burdens of grief and mourning. Adolescents who endure such experiences deserve sensitivity, care, and support in their bereavement. They should also be helped to celebrate and commemorate the life of their deceased friend (Rubel, 1999). *Postvention programs*, designed to address the specific needs of early and middle adolescents (Hill & Foster, 1996) or later adolescents in college settings (Rickgarn, 1994, 1996), are useful both as interventions after a suicide or other traumatic death and as forward-looking preventive efforts designed to minimize self-destructive behavior in the future.

❧ Helping Adolescents Cope with Death and Bereavement

Adolescents can be helped in their efforts to cope with death through education and preparation prior to the fact (both while they are adolescents and in their earlier childhood) and through support and constructive intervention at the time of and after a death.

Education and Prior Preparation

Parents and other adults influence adolescent coping with death through the foundations they lay down in childhood and the environments they help to create in which adolescents function. Open lines of communication, sharing of thoughts and feelings, role modeling, and other constructive socialization processes enable adolescents to feel secure in themselves and to find satisfaction in the rewards of living, even as they also take account of issues related to loss and death.

McNeil (1986) suggested the following guidelines for adult communications with adolescents about death:

1. Take the lead in heightened awareness of an adolescent's concerns about death and in openness to discussing whatever he or she wishes to explore.
2. Listen actively and perceptively, with special attention to the feelings that appear to underlie what the adolescent is saying.
3. Accept the adolescent's feelings as real, important, and normal.
4. Use supportive responses that reflect acceptance and understanding of what the adolescent is trying to say.
5. Project a belief in the worth of the adolescent by resisting the temptation to solve his or her problems and by conveying an effort to help the adolescent find his or her own solutions.
6. Take time to enjoy the company of the adolescent and to provide frequent opportunities for talking together.

Communications of this sort can be supplemented by proactive programs of death education in secondary schools (e.g., Crase & Crase, 1984; Rosenthal, 1986; Stevenson & Stevenson, 1996a) and at the college level (e.g., Corr, 1978). An extensive body of death-related literature is directed toward and can be helpful to middle school, high school, and other young readers (see Focus On 13.1 and Appendix B; see also Lamers, 1986). Also, principles set forth in literature for adults about children and death (as suggested in Chapter 12) may be relevant to adolescents, with suitable modifications, and there is literature for adults that deals directly with adolescents and death (e.g., Corr & Balk, 1996; Corr & McNeil, 1986). In all programs of education and support for adolescents, careful attention must be paid to the goals that one seeks to achieve and to the needs and experiences of adolescents. In her account of processes in designing a course on death, dying, and bereavement for adolescents, Rosenthal (1986) advised educators to make decisions about possible topics, objectives, materials, methods, and evaluation procedures in terms of three primary aspects of death-related education for adolescents: information, self-awareness, and skills for helping. The important thing is to reach out and make constructive contacts with vulnerable adolescents before they become isolated and alienated.

Support and Assistance after a Death

After the death of Diana, Princess of Wales, in 1997, one father is reported to have told one of her son's classmates: "It will be your duty never to mention her. . . .You must pretend that nothing has happened and just carry on"

Selected Literature for Adolescents about Death, Dying, and Bereavement

Annotated descriptions and complete bibliographical information are provided in Appendix B for the following examples and many other books for middle school and high school readers.

About life-threatening illness and confronting death in various ways as a young person:
Calvert, P. (1994). *Writing to Richie.*
Coburn, J. B. (1964). *Annie and the Sand Dobbies.*
Deaver, J. R. (1988). *Say Goodnight, Gracie.*
Fox, P. (1995). *The Eagle Kite.*
Little, J. (1984). *Mama's Going to Buy You a Mockingbird.*
Shura, M. F. (1988). *The Sunday Doll.*
Smith, D. B. (1973). *A Taste of Blackberries.*
White, E. B. (1952). *Charlotte's Web.*

About suicide in adolescence:
Arrick, F. (1980). *Tunnel Vision.*
Draper, S. M. (1994). *Tears of a Tiger.*
Grollman, E., & Johnson, J. (2001). *A Teenager's Book about Suicide: Helping Break the Silence and Preventing Death.*
Grollman, E., & Malikow, M. (1999). *Living when a Young Friend Commits Suicide.*

About experiencing the death of a sibling, peer, parent, grandparent, or other adult:
Adler, C. S. (1993). *Daddy's Climbing Tree.*
Agee, J. (1969). *A Death in the Family.*
Aiken, S. (2001) *Anna's Scrapbook: Journal of a Sister's Love.*
Blume, J. (1981). *Tiger Eyes.*
Brisson, P. (1999). *Sky Memories.*
Cleaver, V., & Cleaver, B. (1970). *Grover.*
Deedy, C. A. (1995). *The Last Dance.*
Dragonwagon, D. (1990). *Winter Holding Spring.*
Henkes, K. (1997). *Sun and Spoon.*
Henkes, K. (2003). *Olive's Ocean.*
Jukes, M. (1985). *Blackberries in the Dark.*
Lewis, C. S. (1976). *A Grief Observed.*
Martin, A. M. (1986). *With You and Without You.*
Park, B. (1995). *Mick Harte Was Here.*
Paterson, K. (1977). *Bridge to Terabithia.*
Richter, E. (1986). *Losing Someone You Love: When a Brother or Sister Dies.*
Rylant, C. (1992). *Missing May.*

(continued)

Selected Literature for Adolescents about Death, Dying, and Bereavement

About experiencing the death of a sibling, peer, parent, grandparent, or other adult: *(continued)*

Sims, A. M. (1986). *Am I Still a Sister?*

Tolstoy, L. (1960). *The Death of Ivan Ilych and Other Stories.*

About loss and coping as an adolescent:

Heegaard, M. E. (1990). *Coping with Death and Grief.*

McCaleb, J. (1998). *Our Hero, Freebird: An Organ Donor's Story.*

O'Toole, D. (1995). *Facing Change: Falling Apart and Coming Together Again in the Teen Years.*

Scrivani, M. (1991). *When Death Walks In.*

Stokes, J., & Oxley, P. (2006). *Out of the Blue: Making Memories Last When Someone Has Died.*

Traisman, E. S., & Sieff, J. (Comps.). (1995). *Flowers for the Ones You've Known: Unedited Letters from Bereaved Teens.*

Contact the **Centering Corporation** (P.O. Box 4600, Omaha, NE 68104-0600; 402-553-1200; fax 402-553-0507; www.centering.org; e-mail to Centeringcorp@aol.com) for additional information about death-related literature for adolescents, or to purchase any books listed here or in Appendix B.

(Andersen, 1998, p. 250). In fact, something important has happened, and it is not likely to escape the minds of Diana's children. It would be far better to initiate a constructive program that helps bereaved adolescents obtain accurate information about a loss and begin the process of interpreting and integrating that loss into their ongoing lives. Such a program should also help bereaved adolescents identify emotional and other responses to a death, express their feelings in safe and manageable ways, find their own ways of coping, take active roles in funeral practices and commemorate losses in constructive ways, and find ways to go on with healthy and productive living (Fitzgerald, 2000). Activity workbooks and journaling projects may be useful, either as adjuncts to other interventions or for adolescents who are most comfortable addressing their grief in private ways (e.g., Barber, 2003).

Counseling interventions with adolescents should be guided by two principles: (1) provide a safe environment in which the adolescent can explore difficulties; and (2) assist with the process of addressing the developmental and situational tasks that are often closely interrelated in adolescent bereavement (Calvin & Smith, 1986). This latter principle means that it must be the adolescent, not the counselor, who works out acceptable solutions to challenges in his or her own life. Educators can assist when they themselves understand the nature of bereavement, grief, and mourning. Recent research showing that "bereaved college students are at risk for decreased academic performance . . . academic difficulties that may result

Expressing grief and finding support can help a bereaved adolescent.

in attrition" (Servaty-Seib & Hamilton, 2006, pp. 230 & 233) provides empirical support for long-held clinical impressions. This research reinforces guidance for counselors offered by a number of authors (Balk, 1984; Cohen et al., 2006; Fitzgerald, 1998; Floerchinger, 1991; Gray, 1988; McNeil, Silliman, & Swihart, 1991; Valentine, 1996; Zinner, 1985). Programs of *postvention* (described in Chapter 12 for children) have been developed for adolescents at both the secondary (Hill & Foster, 1996) and postsecondary (Lerner et al., 2004; Rickgarn, 1994, 1996) levels.

Adolescents who are unwilling to talk to parents, counselors, or other adults may find it more congenial to address their death-related concerns in the context of a support group populated by peers with similar experiences (Tedeschi, 1996). By establishing a community of bereaved peers, groups of this sort dispel the stigma of being "different" or marked out by a death. This overcoming of isolation from others is important in all bereavement, but especially so in a developmental era like adolescence, in which struggles with identity and the need for peer validation is so characteristic. Support groups can provide important information to bereaved adolescents, offer help with tensions involving containing and expressing emotions, assist in confronting life's hard lessons, and confirm the fundamental message that it is only natural to experience grief in connection with a significant loss.

Many adolescents recognize that there can be positive outcomes even in the wake of intense tragedy, such as a deeper appreciation of life, greater caring for and stronger emotional bonds with others, and greater emotional strength (Oltjenbruns, 1991). Adults can help to encourage such outcomes in adolescents and can learn important lessons from them in their own lives.

❧ Summary

In this chapter, we explored interactions between adolescents and death within the contemporary American death system. We noted how the distinctive developmental tasks of early, middle, and late adolescence have a direct bearing on how adolescents relate to death. These tasks influence encounters with death among adolescents (we noted that adolescence is an era characterized by low death rates especially associated with human-induced deaths resulting from accidents, homicide, and suicide) and attitudes of adolescents toward death (which generally combine a strong emphasis on the present and a tendency to resist recognition of the personal significance of death). We described issues that confront adolescents who are coping with life-threatening illness and dying, as well as those encountered by adolescents who are coping with bereavement and grief. We gave special attention to issues related to suicide, homicide, and violence in adolescent life. Finally, we suggested ways to help adolescents who are coping with death and bereavement.

Glossary

Adolescence: the era in human development occurring between childhood and adulthood; often characterized by the developmental task of achieving individuation and the establishment of a more or less stable sense of personal identity; for Erikson this era is distinguished by striving to achieve the virtue of fidelity or faithfulness (to self, ideals, and others); not necessarily coextensive with the teenage years

Developmental eras in adolescence: early, middle, and late adolescence

Early adolescence: a period dominated by the goal of achieving emotional separation from parents and the conflict of separation versus reunion

Late adolescence: a period dominated by the goal of achieving intimacy and commitment, and the conflict of closeness versus distance

Leading influences on adolescent understandings of death: ambiguities or tensions arising from biological, cognitive, social, and emotional factors

Middle adolescence: a period dominated by the goal of achieving competency, mastery, or control, and the conflict of independence versus dependence

Postvention: after-the-fact interventions for individuals affected by traumatic loss

Questions for Review and Discussion

1. Did you have any experiences like those described in the vignette near the beginning of this chapter during your high school years? If so, what did the administrators, teachers, parents, and other students at your school do to cope with those experiences?

2. What sorts of death-related losses have you experienced in your own adolescence, and what did they mean to you? What helped you to cope with them? What help did you want or need but failed to find?

3. During your own adolescence, have you been seriously ill or have you experienced an important loss? If so, what were your most significant concerns about that illness or loss? Or perhaps you know an adolescent who has been in such a situation. If so, what were his or her most significant concerns?

4. What would you recommend to adults as ways they could help adolescents cope with death? Think about how your recommendations would differ (if at all) for different adolescents or different losses.

Suggested Readings

General resources on adolescents, their development, and death include:

Corr, C. A., & Balk, D. E. (Eds.). (1996). *Handbook of Adolescent Death and Bereavement.*
Corr, C. A., & McNeil, J. N. (Eds.). (1986). *Adolescence and Death.*
Kalergis, M. M. (1998). *Seen and Heard: Teenagers Talk about Their Lives.*
Offer, D., Ostrov, E., & Howard, K. I. (1981). *The Adolescent: A Psychological Self-Portrait.*

For life-threatening illness in adolescence, consult:

Krementz, J. (1989). *How It Feels to Fight for Your Life.*
Pendleton, E. (Comp.). (1980). *Too Old to Cry, Too Young to Die.*

Bereavement and grief in adolescence are explored in the following:

Balk, D. E. (Ed.). (1991b). Death and Adolescent Bereavement [Special issue]. *Journal of Adolescent Research, 6*(1).
Baxter, G., Bennett, L., & Stuart, W. (1989). *Adolescents and Death: Bereavement Support Groups for Secondary School Students* (2nd ed.).
Fitzgerald, H. (2000). *The Grieving Teen: A Guide for Teenagers and Their Friends.*
Fry, V. L. (1995). *Part of Me Died, Too: Stories of Creative Survival among Bereaved Children and Teenagers.*
Grollman, E. A. (1993). *Straight Talk about Death for Teenagers: How to Cope with Losing Someone You Love.*
Sjöqvist, S. (Ed.). (2006). *Still Here with Me: Teenagers and Children on Losing a Parent.*

Teaching adolescents about death or helping them to cope with death is examined in:

Fairchild, T. N. (Ed.). (1986). *Crisis Intervention Strategies for School-Based Helpers.*
Fiorini, J. J., & Mullen, J. A. (2006). *Counseling Children and Adolescents through Grief and Loss.*
Fitzgerald, H. (1998). *Grief at School: A Guide for Teachers and Counselors.*
Stevenson, R. G. (Ed.). (2001). *What Will We Do? Preparing a School Community to Cope with Crises* (2nd ed.).
Stevenson, R. G., & Stevenson, E. P. (Eds.). (1996b). *Teaching Students about Death: A Comprehensive Resource for Educators and Parents.*
Turner, M. (2006). *Talking with Children and Young People about Death and Dying* (2nd ed.).

Suicide and life-threatening behavior among adolescents and children are explored in the following:

Cobain, B. (2007). *When Nothing Matters Anymore: A Survival Guide for Depressed Teens.*
Klagsbrun, F. (1976). *Too Young to Die: Youth and Suicide.*
Lester, D. (1993). *The Cruelest Death: The Enigma of Adolescent Suicide.*
Orbach, I. (1988). *Children Who Don't Want to Live: Understanding and Treating the Suicidal Child.*
Peck, M. L., Farberow, N. L., & Litman, R. E. (Eds.). (1985). *Youth Suicide.*
Pfeffer, C. R. (Ed.). (1986). *The Suicidal Child.*

Pfeffer, C. R. (Ed.). (1989). *Suicide among Youth: Perspectives on Risk and Prevention.*

Rubel, B. (1999). *But I Didn't Say Goodbye: For Parents and Professionals Helping Child Suicide Survivors.*

Stillion, J. M., & McDowell, E. E. (1996). *Suicide across the Life Span: Premature Exits* (2nd ed.).

Selected Web Resources

Some useful search terms include: ADOLESCENTS AND DEATH; CAUSES OF DEATH IN ADOLESCENCE; DEVELOPMENTAL TASKS IN ADOLESCENCE; HOMICIDE AND ADOLESCENTS; SUICIDE AND ADOLESCENTS

Visit the book companion website for *Death & Dying, Life & Living, Sixth Edition,* at academic.cengage.com/psychology/corr for all URLs and live links to the following *organizational and other Internet sites:*

Adolescent Directory On-Line, Center for Adolescence and Family Studies, Indiana University

American School Counselors Association

Boulden Publishing

Centering Corporation

Compassion Books

YOUTH.ORG

CHAPTER 14

Young and Middle-Aged Adults

© David H. Wells/Corbis

Objectives of This Chapter

◆ To illustrate some issues that often arise for young and middle-aged adults within the contemporary American death system

◆ To consider the distinctive developmental tasks of young and middle-aged adults

◆ To describe typical encounters with death in the United States during adulthood

◆ To explore death-related attitudes during the adult years

◆ To identify key issues for young and middle-aged adults who are coping with life-threatening illness and dying

◆ To explore central issues for young and middle-aged adults who are coping with bereavement and grief: in relationship to the death of a child, spouse, life partner, sibling, peer, friend, parent, or grandparent

An Orthodox Archbishop Faces His Mother's Death

My mother died of cancer over a period of three years. She was operated on unsuccessfully. The doctor told me about it and then added: "But of course you will not say anything to your mother."

I said: "I will." And I did.

I remember how I came to her and said to her that her doctor had rung and that the operation was not successful. We kept silent for a moment and then my mother said: "And so I shall die."

I said: "Yes."

And then we stayed together in complete silence, communing without any words. I don't think that we thought thoughts. We faced something that had entered life and made all the difference to life. It was not a shadow. It was not an evil. It was not a terror. It was the ultimate. And we had to face this ultimate without yet knowing what this ultimate would unfold itself into. We stayed as long as we felt we had to stay. And then life continued.

But two things happened as a result. The one is that at no moment was either my mother or I walled up within a lie, forced into a comedy, deprived of any help. At no moment had I to come into my mother's room with a smile that was untrue, or say words that were untrue. At no moment were we to play a comedy of life conquering death, of illness waning, of things being better than they were, when we both knew they were not. At no moment were we deprived of one another's help. There were moments when my mother felt she needed help. She would then ring the bell and I would come and we would speak of her dying, of my bereavement.

She loved life. She loved it deeply. A few days before she died she said that she would be prepared to live 150 years in suffering, but to live. She loved us. She grieved over separation: "Oh, for the touch of a vanished hand and the sound of a voice that is still."

And then there were other moments when I felt the pain of it, and I would come and speak of it to my mother. And she would give me her support and help me face her death. This was a deep and true relationship. There was nothing of a lie in it....

There was another side. . . . Because death could come at any moment, and it would be too late to put right something that had gone wrong, all life has to be at every moment an expression, as perfect and complete as possible, of a relationship that is one of reverence and love. Only death can make things that seem to be small and insignificant into signs that are great and significant. The way you prepare a cup of tea on a tray, the way you put cushions behind the back of a sick person, the way your voice sounds, the way you move—all that can be an expression of all there is in a relationship.

If there is a false note, if there is a crack, if something has gone wrong, it must be repaired now, because there is the inevitable certainty that later it may be too late. Death confronts you with the truth of life, with a sharpness and a clarity that nothing else can convey. (A. Bloom [Metropolitan of Souvozh], "Death and Bereavement," in A. Walker & C. Carras [Eds.], *Living Orthodoxy in the Modern World*, pp. 85–107. Reprinted by permission of St. Vladmir's Seminary Press. 575 Scarsdale Rd., Crestwood, NY 10707.)

🍎 Young and Middle-Aged Adults, Developmental Tasks, and Death

Young and middle adulthood is a period of some 40 years, stretching from the close of adolescence in the early twenties to the beginning of older adulthood in the mid-60s. Many view these years as the longest single era in human development and describe it as the "prime of life." Others now prefer to speak of this lengthy period in life as including two 20-year generational cohorts and two distinguishable eras—*young adulthood* (roughly ages 21 or 22–45) and *middle adulthood* or middle age (ages 45–65). According to Erikson (1963, 1968; see also Cavanaugh & Blanchard-Fields, 2005; Papalia, Sterns, et al., 2006), the principal *normative developmental task in young adulthood* is to achieve *intimacy* (versus the danger of isolation), while the *major task for development in middle adulthood* is *generativity* (versus the danger of stagnation or self-absorption).

Despite notable differences among themselves, young and middle-aged adults share many issues arising from new elements in family relationships, work roles, and an evolving set of death-related concerns. Among some of the special challenges faced by many of these adults is their role as *middle-escents* or *members of the sandwich generation*—individuals situated in terms of developmental eras between their younger counterparts (children and adolescents), on one hand, and their older predecessors (older adults), on the other. Nevertheless, because a large number of variables impact the lives of young and middle-aged adults during their lengthy adulthood, and because many developmental aspects of adulthood have not been well or broadly studied, it is wise to be cautious in making generalizations about these adult humans and their experiences.

In general, young and middle adulthood is a period of exploring and exploiting the identity established in earlier stages of development through choices about one's lifestyle, relationships, and work (Kail & Cavanaugh, 2006; Newman & Newman, 2005; Papalia, Sterns, et al., 2006). Decisions made in the vitality of young adulthood chart much of the remaining course of human life in terms of relationships, vocation, and lifestyle. Those decisions enable humans to know themselves in much fuller ways than were possible during adolescence. In middle age, one typically conserves and draws on personal, social, and vocational resources that were established earlier. The transition in midlife from young to middle adulthood can be focused on what is past and gone (youth and its distinctive opportunities), or it can lead to a renewed appreciation of life as one achieves a new understanding of one's self and determines how to live out the remainder of one's life. Once depicted as a tumultuous crisis, *the midlife transition* is now generally thought of as a more or less calm transition in which individual perceptions of responses to events are central (Hunter & Sundel, 1989).

Within the broad division between early and middle adulthood, Levinson (1978) distinguished several "seasons" or qualitatively distinct eras in human development, with boundary zones, periods of transition, and characteristic issues. In *young adulthood*, this involves an early transition from preadulthood, a novice phase in which one enters the adult world and is involved in "forming a dream," an internal transition at about age 30, and a period of "settling down." Similarly, *middle adulthood* can be depicted in terms of another novice or introductory period, an internal transition around age 50, and a concluding period, followed by a further transition into older adulthood. The boundary between young and middle adulthood for Levinson is the celebrated midlife transition, during which the individual reappraises the past and terminates young adulthood, modifies the life structure and initiates middle adulthood, and seeks to resolve four principal polarities: tensions between young/old, destruction/creation, masculine/feminine, and attachment/separateness.

It is only fair to note that much of the original research on adulthood has been confined to male subjects. However, in a later, posthumously published study, Levinson (1996) reported results from detailed interviews with 45 women conducted in the period 1980–1982. This study examined three groups of young adult women: homemakers, women with careers in the corporate-financial world, and women with careers in academia. As a result of this study, Levinson (1996, p. 36) concluded that the "alternating sequence of structure building-maintaining periods and transitional periods holds for both women and men." This is the schema of developmental seasons he identified in earlier studies of male adults.

Gilligan (1982) was among the first prominent researchers to argue that the course of human development in females is likely to differ in significant ways from that of their male counterparts. For example, both male and female adults can find themselves caught between pressures from older and younger developmental cohorts (parents and/or children). Still, responses to issues facing the sandwich generation can be expected to differ in important ways for males and females. For example, when care is needed for an elderly relative or an ill child, adult males historically would mainly have been expected to provide economic and logistical support, whereas responsibility for practical hands-on care and nurturing would have been assigned to adult females. For many in this generation, this is still the case.

It has been argued that these traditional divisions of roles by gender are no longer accurate for many people in contemporary American society, in part because many women have assumed new responsibilities outside the home in the workforce. Nevertheless, significant differences are still likely to exist between men and women, resulting largely from the ongoing influence of gender splitting or differences in the social roles and responsibilities that are assigned to males and females. Many women who work outside the home are expected to assume a "second shift" or double burden in which men may help out more but do not generally assume responsibility for domestic chores and caregiving. Thus, Levinson (1996) concluded that thorough descriptions of adult life need to take into account both developmental and gender factors. The point is that common aspects in adult development may coexist with differences arising from gender, historical variables, and other factors.

❦ Encounters with Death during Young and Middle Adulthood

Deaths and Death Rates among Young and Middle Adults

Adults between the ages of 25–64 make up 52.5 percent of the total population of the United States. In 2004, this group experienced 568,624 deaths (see Table 14.1), which is 23.7 percent of the nearly 2.4 million deaths in the United States that year.

TABLE 14.1
Number of Deaths during Young and Middle Adulthood, by Age, Race or Hispanic Origin,[a] and Gender: United States, 2004

	Ages 25–34			Ages 35–44		
	Both Sexes	Males	Females	Both Sexes	Males	Females
All origins[b]	40,868	28,359	12,509	85,362	53,677	31,685
Caucasian Americans, total	29,275	20,584	8,691	64,040	41,215	22,825
Non-Hispanic Caucasian Americans	23,397	16,098	7,299	55,543	35,253	20,290
African Americans	9,925	6,684	3,241	18,474	10,700	7,774
Hispanic Americans[c]	5,959	4,547	1,412	8,546	5,973	2,573
Asian or Pacific Island Americans[d]	973	630	343	1,654	1,015	639
American Indians and Alaskan Natives[e]	695	461	234	1,194	747	447

	Ages 45–54			Ages 55–64		
	Both Sexes	Males	Females	Both Sexes	Males	Females
All origins[b]	177,697	111,163	66,534	264,697	158,032	106,665
Caucasian Americans, total	135,719	86,266	49,453	214,171	128,575	85,596
Non-Hispanic Caucasian Americans	123,037	77,741	45,296	198,842	119,171	79,671
African Americans	36,710	21,756	14,954	43,490	25,352	18,138
Hispanic Americans[c]	12,628	8,451	4,177	15,198	9,246	5,952
Asian or Pacific Island Americans[d]	3,529	2,096	1,433	4,963	2,893	2,070
American Indians and Alaskan Natives[e]	1,739	1,045	694	2,073	1,212	861

[a]Data for specified groups other than Caucasian Americans and African Americans should be interpreted with caution because of inconsistencies between reporting race and/or Hispanic origin on death certificates and on censuses and surveys.

[b]Figures for origin not stated are included in "all origins" but not distributed among specified origins.

[c]Includes all persons of Hispanic origin of any race.

[d]Includes Chinese, Filipino, Hawaiian, Japanese, and other Asian or Pacific Islander.

[e]Includes Aleuts and Eskimos.

Source: Based on Miniño et al., 2007.

Table 14.1 provides *numbers of deaths* in 2004 according to ten-year age groupings from ages 25–64 by sex, race, and Hispanic origin. It is obvious that overall numbers of deaths rise rapidly throughout this 40-year period. Further, as shown in Table 14.2, an even steeper increase is found in *death rates* for young and middle adults, which rise by a factor of nearly 9 times during adulthood (from 102.1 deaths per 100,000 for

TABLE 14.2

Death Rates (per 100,000) during Young and Middle Adulthood, by Age, Race or Hispanic Origin,[a] and Gender: United States, 2004

	Ages 25–34			Ages 35–44		
	Both Sexes	Males	Females	Both Sexes	Males	Females
All origins[b]	102.1	139.5	63.5	193.5	243.6	143.5
Caucasian Americans, total	92.9	127.0	56.8	179.8	229.1	129.5
Non-Hispanic Caucasian Americans	95.9	130.9	60.3	185.9	235.7	136.0
African Americans	179.3	252.3	112.3	322.3	397.0	256.0
Hispanic Americans[c]	78.2	109.2	40.9	138.7	184.2	88.2
Asian or Pacific Island Americans[d]	38.6	50.9	26.8	72.2	91.3	54.2
American Indians and Alaskan Natives[e]	147.4	188.8	102.9	256.3	321.2	191.6

	Ages 45–54			Ages 55–64		
	Both Sexes	Males	Females	Both Sexes	Males	Females
All origins[b]	427.0	543.5	314.3	910.3	1,128.8	707.4
Caucasian Americans, total	394.0	504.0	285.4	863.5	1,065.9	671.8
Non-Hispanic Caucasian Americans	400.8	510.5	292.9	875.1	1,076.4	683.8
African Americans	744.8	954.9	564.1	1,499.6	1,960.8	1,128.6
Hispanic Americans[c]	313.5	417.8	208.3	684.0	874.0	511.3
Asian or Pacific Island Americans[d]	190.9	241.9	145.8	435.5	545.3	339.9
American Indians and Alaskan Natives[e]	438.7	543.5	340.0	878.9	1,067.3	704.0

[a]Data for specified groups other than Caucasian Americans and African Americans should be interpreted with caution because of inconsistencies between reporting race and/or Hispanic origin on death certificates and on censuses and surveys.

[b]Figures for origin not stated are included in "all origins" but not distributed among specified origins.

[c]Includes all persons of Hispanic origin of any race.

[d]Includes Chinese, Filipino, Hawaiian, Japanese, and other Asian or Pacific Islander.

[e]Includes Aleuts and Eskimos.

Source: CDC, National Vital Statistics System, National Center for Health Statistics, Mortality Statistics Branch (http://www.cdc.gov/nchs/datawh/statab/unpubd/mortabs.htm); Miniño et al., 2007.

those 25–34 years of age in 2004 to 910.3 for those 55–64 years of age). These patterns of rapid increase in numbers of deaths and death rates apply across the board to all segments of the adult population in our society, as well as to male and female adults, and to Caucasian-American, Hispanic-American, African-American, Asian and Pacific Island American, and American-Indian adults.

Notable features of changing mortality patterns in the United States during adulthood can be highlighted in three comparisons. First, middle adults die in much larger numbers and at higher rates than do young adults. In 2004 almost twice as many Americans died in middle age as in young adulthood. This increase occurred in a middle-aged population that was more than 28 percent smaller than the population of young adults. Second, each successive ten-year cohort of adults experiences a larger number of deaths and a higher death rate. Third, the very high infant death rates for the population as a whole (695.0 per 100,000, as discussed in Chapter 12) are not exceeded until the final ten-year cohort in middle adulthood (those 55–64 years of age) with death rates of 910.3 per 100,000.

Leading Causes of Death among Young and Middle Adults

Table 14.3 shows that the five leading causes of death change in interesting ways with age during adulthood. For all young adults taken as a group (ages 25–44), accidents were by far the leading cause of death in 2004. Together with cancer and diseases of the heart, these three causes accounted for just over 50 percent of all deaths in this 20-year cohort. Suicide and homicide were the next two leading causes of death in this overall group, but in different ways. That is, suicide and homicide were relatively more significant during the first half of this era (ages 25–34), whereas cancer and heart disease became more important during the second half of the era (ages 35–44). This shift signals a decline during young adulthood in the relative significance of human-induced deaths (especially those arising from suicide and homicide) and a parallel rise in the relative significance of degenerative diseases (such as cancer and heart disease)—trends that continue throughout the remainder of the human life course.

During middle adulthood (ages 45–65), cancer and heart disease accounted for 56 percent of all deaths in our society in 2004, followed at a great distance by accidents and a series of degenerative diseases (chronic lower respiratory diseases, diabetes mellitus, cerebrovascular diseases, and chronic liver disease and cirrhosis). Among cancer deaths in adults, leading causes for both sexes are cancer of the respiratory and intrathoracic organs (lung cancer), followed by prostate and colon/rectum cancer for males, and by breast and colon/rectum cancer for females.

Rates for accidental death throughout early and middle adulthood are lower than those in adolescence, but types of accidents other than those involving motor vehicles become increasingly more significant as causes of death throughout adulthood. Death rates for homicide decline during adulthood, although death rates from suicide remain roughly steady.

During the 1980s, a new factor appeared in encounters with death—human immunodeficiency virus (HIV) and acquired immune deficiency syndrome (AIDS)—and soon became especially significant during young adulthood and middle age (see Chapter 20). By 1994, HIV infection was the leading cause of death for young adults

TABLE 14.3
Numbers of Deaths and Death Rates (per 100,000) during Young and Middle Adulthood for the Five Leading Causes of Death in Specified Age Groups, Both Genders, All Races: United States, 2004

Rank	Ages 25–34 Cause of Death	Number	Rate	Ages 35–44 Cause of Death	Number	Rate
...	All causes	40,868	102.1	All causes	85,362	193.5
1	Accidents (unintentional injuries)	13,032	32.6	Accidents (unintentional injuries)	16,471	37.3
	Motor vehicle accidents	7,036	17.6	Motor vehicle accidents	6,663	15.1
	All other accidents	5,996	15.0	All other accidents	9,808	22.2
2	Intentional self-harm (suicide)	5,074	12.7	Malignant neoplasms (cancer)	14,723	33.4
3	Assault (homicide)	4,495	11.2	Diseases of the heart	12,925	29.3
4	Malignant neoplasms (cancer)	3,633	9.1	Intentional self-harm (suicide)	6,638	15.0
5	Diseases of the heart	3,163	7.9	Human immunodeficiency virus (HIV) disease	4,826	10.9

Rank	Ages 45–54 Cause of Death	Number	Rate	Ages 55–64 Cause of Death	Number	Rate
...	All causes	177,697	427.0	All causes	264,697	910.3
1	Malignant neoplasms (cancer)	49,520	119.0	Malignant neoplasms (cancer)	96,956	333.4
2	Diseases of the heart	37,556	90.2	Diseases of the heart	63,613	218.8
3	Accidents (unintentional injuries)	16,942	40.7	Chronic lower respiratory diseases	11,754	40.4
	Motor vehicle accidents	6,276	15.1			
	All other accidents	10,666	25.7			
4	Chronic liver disease and cirrhosis	7,496	18.0	Diabetes mellitus	10,780	37.1
5	Intentional self-harm (suicide)	6,906	16.6	Cerebrovascular diseases	9,966	34.3

Source: CDC, National Vital Statistics System, National Center for Health Statistics, Mortality Statistics Branch (http://www.cdc. gov/nchs/datawh/statab/unpubd/mortabs.htm); Miniño et al., 2007.

25 to 44 years of age, accounting for some 30,260 deaths (Singh et al., 1995). By 2004, however, HIV infection had fallen to become the sixth leading cause of death during young adulthood (following accidents, cancer, diseases of the heart, suicide, and homicide), with 6,294 deaths (Miniño et al, 2007). That decline of nearly 80 percent in deaths among young adults in a period of just 11 years is due to many factors, such as better education about HIV and AIDS, more effective prevention measures, and

better care for infected persons. In 2004, even though HIV infection remained the eighth leading cause of death for those 45–54 years of age (causing 4,422 deaths), it was no longer among the ten leading causes of death for those 55–64 years of age.

Two Variables in Deaths of Young and Middle Adults: Gender and Race

Tables 14.1 and 14.2 indicate contrasts by gender and race in number of deaths and death rates among adults in the United States. For gender, the main difference is that adult males die far more frequently and at much higher rates than females do in our society. Both male and female young adults (ages 25–44) experience significant numbers of deaths from accidents, HIV infection, and homicide, but males are more prone to heart disease and suicide than females, whereas the influence of cancer as a cause of death appears much earlier among females than males. As males and females proceed into middle adulthood (ages 45–64), degenerative diseases become more prominent as leading causes of death in both groups.

In both young and middle adults, there is a much larger *number* of deaths among Caucasian Americans than among African Americans, Hispanic Americans, Asian and Pacific Island Americans, and American Indians. However, African Americans (and, to a lesser extent, American Indians) experience much higher death *rates* than Caucasian Americans. In all of these racial and cultural groups, males greatly exceed females in both absolute numbers of deaths and death rates. In terms of causes of death, HIV infection and homicide are more typical causes of death among African Americans, whereas suicide is more prevalent among Caucasian Americans.

❦ Attitudes toward Death among Young and Middle Adults

Some features of adult encounters with death are particularly significant in shaping attitudes toward death—especially during middle adulthood. The years of the late twenties and early thirties are likely to be times of more stability in self-understanding compared to adolescence. As a result, anxiety about one's own death and defenses against that realization appear to be a less prominent feature of young adulthood than of adolescence. Of course, this may change if new or different encounters with death generate new threats and anxieties. Also, general patterns of death-related attitudes begin to alter for many persons in our society as they move into middle adulthood.

For example, typical encounters with death during adulthood are likely to increase as the next-older generation begins to experience higher death rates. The death of the Archbishop's mother described in the vignette near the beginning of this chapter is an example of events that are likely to confront a middle-aged adult in the United States today. This, together with issues arising from their developing children, is what is meant when we speak of the *sandwich generation,* a group that often feels trapped by new and different pressures arising simultaneously from both the older and younger generations that surround it on either developmental front.

In the case of younger adults, death-related worries and concerns are most likely to relate to the deaths of others. However, as one progresses developmentally and, more significantly, as one learns from one's own life experiences, one typically encounters a newly personalized sense of mortality (Doka, 1988). This recognition occurs particularly in two ways: through encounters with the deaths of parents, peers, siblings, and spouses, often for the first time in one's life and especially as a result of natural causes; and through one's own newly emerging realization of oneself as a mortal creature who could die at any time and who will die someday.

Peers, siblings, or a spouse can die at any time, but in adulthood it is more likely that they will die of natural causes (such as heart attack, cancer, or stroke). When that happens, bereaved adults cannot easily dismiss such deaths as the result of ill fortune or external forces—both of which might, in principle, be avoided. Similarly, when adults begin to sense the limits of their bodily capacities or to recognize problems associated with aging or lifestyle, their personal sense of invulnerability must diminish. As a result, a shift begins in perspective from time lived to time left to live (Neugarten, 1974). In so doing, adults begin to make a retrospective assessment of their achievements, to realize that they have already passed through half or two-thirds of average life expectancy, to appreciate that the future does not stretch endlessly ahead without any real possibility of a horizon or end point, and to entertain prospective thoughts of retirement and eventual death. This can lead to a reappraisal of personal values and priorities, which may result in an enriched capacity for love and enjoyment and a richer, more philosophical sense of meaning in one's life—or it may have less positive results such as a dissatisfaction with one's past and potential accomplishments in life (Jacques, 1965). In short, the implications of death play a prominent role in the reevaluation of life and self that characterizes middle age.

As young and middle-aged adults turn to thoughts of their own death, they are likely to think of what that will mean for their children, family members, or significant others, as well as for the vocational and other creative projects that have occupied so much of their time and energy since becoming adults.

To all of this, HIV infection and AIDS have added the lethal specter of an infectious disease, but one whose shadow has changed significantly in form and power since the 1990s. Someone once said to us: "There was a world before the discovery of AIDS, and there is a world after the discovery of AIDS. But things will never be the same after the discovery of AIDS." If so, then life is irrevocably altered for adults and many others. Moreover, the terrorist attacks on the World Trade Center and the Pentagon in September 2001, subsequent warfare in Afghanistan, and, in particular, both the war in Iraq in 2003 and the ongoing struggle that has followed each have had a special impact on many mature adults. Older members of the military reserve and National Guard who were called up for some of these war and peacekeeping situations because of their special skills are in a different situation from many younger volunteers already serving on active duty. And the hundreds of firefighters and police officers who lost their lives or worked as rescuers at the World Trade Center were all adults in their active middle years.

In recent years, in other words, a number of new death-related perils have been presented to young and middle adults. Some (such as issues related to nuclear threats or to the environment) are shared with all who inhabit the planet. Others (such as those involving war, alcoholism, or drug abuse) apply mainly to individuals in specific localities or roles. Still others (such as the deaths of significant age-mates from natural causes and the implications of an emerging sense of personal mortality) are particularly relevant to those in the long middle years of life. In general, however, one might say that death-related events often confront young adults with frustration and disappointment, even as they take on a very personal tone for middle adults with interpersonal implications for their loved ones.

🐦 Young and Middle Adults Who Are Coping with Life-Threatening Illness and Dying

Coping as a Young Adult

If the basic developmental task in young adulthood is that of achieving intimacy, then, as Cook and Oltjenbruns (1998) suggested, life-threatening illness and dying challenge the needs of young adults to develop intimate relationships, express their sexuality, and obtain realistic support for their goals and future plans. "*Intimacy* involves the ability to be open, supportive, and close with another person, without fear of losing oneself in the process. The establishment of intimacy with a significant other implies the capacity for mutual empathy, the ability to help meet one another's needs, the acceptance of each other's limitations, and the commitment to care deeply for the other person" (Cook & Oltjenbruns, 1998, p. 329). In short, intimacy depends on a sense of one's own identity and trust in the other.

To achieve quality in living, young adults who are seriously ill or dying still need to pursue and maintain intimacy. In general, an inability to develop intimate relationships results in isolation. As we saw in Chapter 6, abandonment and isolation are often the principal concerns of individuals who are coping with dying.

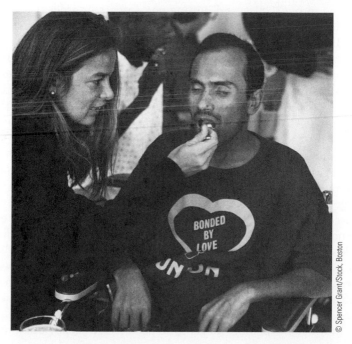

A young adult helps a peer who is close to death.

Thus, life-threatening illness and dying directly challenge the main developmental task of young adulthood. As a result, when there is difficulty in achieving or maintaining intimacy, all concerned should reexamine barriers (such as death-related fears or lack of information about the person's disease) and consider what may be gained by renewed efforts to risk sharing in a pressured and precious time.

Many couples express their intimacy most naturally through *sexuality*. Not confined to sexual intercourse, sexuality includes a broad range of thoughts, feelings, and behaviors. Such expressions of sexuality in the lives of seriously ill and dying adults should be fostered (Lamb, 2001). To do so may involve decisions about grooming or dressing, a gentle touch or caress, open discussion of physical and psychological needs, and other aspects of feeling positive about oneself. Nonjudgmental attitudes, privacy, and efforts to adapt to changes brought about by disease and treatment (e.g., mastectomy or colostomy) can all be helpful in this area.

For young adults, a life-threatening illness may threaten *goals and future plans* in many areas, such as getting married, having children, and pursuing educational or vocational aspirations. If so, young adults must reevaluate their plans and determine what may be appropriate in their new situation. They may appreciate assistance from those who can clarify the realities of the situation while also supporting their autonomy and decision-making processes. In this way, one respects efforts to satisfy important personal and developmental needs while also recognizing constraints on former hopes and dreams.

Coping as a Middle-Aged Adult

According to Erikson (1963, 1968), the principal developmental task for middle-aged adults is the pursuit of *generativity*. In terms of life-threatening illness and dying, this means that the needs of the dying at midlife involve reevaluating one's life, continuing in one's roles, and putting one's affairs in order (Cook & Oltjenbruns, 1998). Reassessment, conservation, and preparation are characteristic activities of all middle-aged adults. They involve "stock-taking" (Butler & Lewis, 1982), efforts to sustain generativity as an alternative to self-indulgence and stagnation (Erikson, 1963), and a need to prepare for the future and to carry out one's responsibilities to others. Awareness of a life-threatening illness and challenges involved in coping with dying are likely to heighten, rather than to thwart, these developmental processes.

In middle adulthood, questions of *reevaluation* relate to the meaning and direction of one's life. Such questions become more, not less, poignant and urgent under the dual stimuli of illness and maturation. One person might more vigorously pursue a creative, vocational, or personal project established in young adulthood in recognition of new pressures that may now threaten its completion. Another midlife adult might decide to change earlier projects and to strike out in new directions or relationships. In either case, the individual might experience grief over what he or she has not attained, along with some overshadowing awareness of other losses yet to come.

However they choose to look toward a future that may now be perceived as more clouded and less extensive than it was before, middle-aged adults who are coping with life-threatening illness or dying can be expected to consider the prospects for *continuation or enduring value* in the legacies that they have been establishing for the future. Again, they may strive more diligently to achieve such goals, alter their form in ways that appear more satisfying or more achievable, or choose to settle for what has already been achieved. Insofar as possible, it would be desirable to support constructive processes of generativity in ill and dying midlife adults by enabling them to continue to take part in meaningful roles and relationships in suitable ways.

Looking to the future within a context of life-threatening illness or dying, and in light of developmental tasks of middle adulthood, typically leads midlife adults to strive to *put their affairs in order.* Most often, this involves an effort to continue to meet responsibilities to those whom they love and to ensure such obligations are met after the individual dies. Life-threatening illness and dying threaten one's ability to meet such commitments but need not render them completely impossible. With support, one can strive to influence the future to the degree possible or to arrange for others to assume specific responsibilities on one's behalf. This can take the form of making a will, disposing of property, or conveying important wishes and messages. In this regard, activities such as those involved in planning one's own funeral and burial arrangements can represent a healthy vitality in continuing to fulfill prized roles and an ability to minimize post-death disruptions or burdens on others.

❦ Young and Middle Adults Who Are Coping with Bereavement and Grief

Members of an aging, sandwich generation often find themselves beset with death-related losses on all sides. Young and middle-aged adults may suffer a full range of deaths, including those of their parents and grandparents; their spouses or life partners, siblings, peers, and friends; their children; and themselves. This is itself distinctive in some respects: children and most adolescents do not experience the deaths of their own children, and most elderly adults have already experienced the deaths of their parents. What is most characteristic of bereavement in young and middle adults is the very real potential for so many kinds of death-related losses.

Even the birth of a child who is impaired in some way may present adult parents with losses, challenges, and opportunities that they must meet (see Personal Insights 14.1). Each loss is difficult in its own way. However, research by Sanders (1979) showed that bereavement in adults is usually impacted most significantly by the death of a child, a spouse, and a parent—in that order. This finding is consistent with a familiar saying among bereaved adults, who report that "the death of my parent is the death of my past; the death of my spouse is the death of my present; the death of my child is the death of my future." What bereavement means to adults can be seen in the following analyses of different types of deaths encountered during adulthood and in what some bereaved adults have written about their experiences (see Focus On 14.1).

Death of a Child

Fetal Death Along with some adolescent parents, many young adults experience the death of a child in the uterus or during the birthing process. In general, these may be called *fetal deaths,* a category that includes what are popularly termed miscarriages, stillbirths, or spontaneous abortions. Fetal deaths are usually distinguished

Welcome to Holland

I am often asked to describe the experience of raising a child with a disability—to try to help people who have not shared that unique experience to understand it, to imagine how it would feel. It's like this. . . .

When you're going to have a baby, it's like planning a fabulous vacation trip—to Italy. You buy a bunch of guidebooks and make your wonderful plans. The Coliseum. The Michelangelo David. The gondolas in Venice. You may learn some handy phrases in Italian. It's all very exciting.

After months of eager anticipation, the day finally arrives. You pack your bags and off you go. Several hours later, the plane lands. The stewardess comes in and says, "Welcome to Holland."

"Holland?!?" you say. "What do you mean, Holland?? I signed up for Italy! I'm supposed to be in Italy. All my life I've dreamed of going to Italy."

But there's been a change in the flight plan. They've landed in Holland and there you must stay.

The important thing is that they haven't taken you to a horrible, disgusting, filthy place, full of pestilence, famine and disease. It's just a different place.

So you must go out and buy new guidebooks. And you must learn a whole new language. And you will meet a whole new group of people you would never have met.

It's just a different place. It's slower-paced than Italy, less flashy than Italy. But after you've been there for a while and you catch your breath, you look around . . . and you begin to notice that Holland has windmills . . . Holland has tulips. Holland even has Rembrandts.

But everyone you know is busy coming and going from Italy . . . and they're all bragging about what a wonderful time they had there. And for the rest of your life, you will say, "Yes, that's where I was supposed to go. That's what I had planned."

The pain of that will never, ever, ever go away . . . because the loss of that dream is a very, very significant loss.

But . . . if you spend your life mourning the fact that you didn't get to Italy, you may never be free to enjoy the very special, the very lovely things . . . about Holland.

Source: From "Welcome to Holland," by E. P. Kingsley. Copyright © 1987 Emily Perl Kingsley. Reprinted by permission.

from elective abortions. Fetal deaths may take place at various times during gestation or (as perinatal deaths) during the birthing process. Although data are not readily available on all forms of fetal death, one source has reported that "each year in the United States, out of an estimated 4.4 million *confirmed* pregnancies, there are more than half a million miscarriages, and twenty-nine thousand stillbirths" (Davis, 1991, xiii; italics in original).

Selected Descriptions of Bereavement Experiences during Young and Middle Adulthood

ABOUT THE DEATH OF A CHILD:

Ash, L. (2004). *Life Touches Life: A Mother's Story of Stillbirth and Healing.*

Bramblett, J. (1991). *When Good-Bye Is Forever: Learning to Live Again after the Loss of a Child.*

Crider, T. (1996). *Give Sorrow Words: A Father's Passage through Grief.*

Daher, D. (2003). *And the Passenger was Death: The Drama and Trauma of Losing a Child.*

DeFord, F. (1997). *Alex, the Life of a Child.*

Evans, R. P. (1993). *The Christmas Box.*

Fleming, D. (2005). *Noah's Rainbow: A Father's Emotional Journey from the Death of His Son to the Birth of His Daughter.*

Guest, J. (1976). *Ordinary People.**

Koppelman, K. L. (1994). *The Fall of a Sparrow: Of Death and Dreams and Healing.*

Kotzwinkle, W. (1975). *Swimmer in the Secret Sea.**

Leach, C. (1981). *Letter to a Younger Son.*

Schrauger, B. (2001). *Walking Taylor Home.*

Simonds, W., & Rothman, B. K. (Eds.). (1992). *Centuries of Solace: Expressions of Maternal Grief in Popular Literature.*

Smith, A. A. (1974). *Rachel.*

Smith, G. H. (2006). *Remembering Garrett.*

Stinson, R., & Stinson, P. (1983). *The Long Dying of Baby Andrew.*

Wagner, S. (1994). *The Andrew Poems.*

ABOUT THE DEATH OF A SPOUSE, LIFE PARTNER, SIBLING, PEER, OR FRIEND:

Brothers, J. (1990). *Widowed.*

Caine, L. (1975). *Widow.*

Didion, J. (2005). *The Year of Magical Thinking.*

Elmer, L. (1987). *Why Her, Why Now: A Man's Journey through Love and Death and Grief.*

Goshen-Gottstein, E. (2002). *Surviving Widowhood.*

Graham, L. (1990). *Rebuilding the House.*

Kaimann, D. S. (2002). *Common Threads: Nine Widows' Journeys through Love, Loss and Healing.*

Lewis, C. S. (1976). *A Grief Observed.*

Roberts, B. K. (2003). *Death without Denial, Grief without Apology: A Guide for Facing Death and Loss.*

Smith, H. I. (1996). *Grieving the Death of a Friend.*

Walter, C. A. (2003). *The Loss of a Life Partner: Narratives of the Bereaved.*

Wertenbaker, L. T. (1957). *Death of a Man.*

Wray, T. J. (2003). *Surviving the Death of a Sibling: Living through Grief when an Adult Brother or Sister Dies.*

(continued)

Selected Descriptions of Bereavement Experiences during Young and Middle Adulthood

ABOUT THE DEATH OF A PARENT:

Anderson, R. (1968). *I Never Sang for My Father.**
De Beauvoir, S. (1973). *A Very Easy Death.*
Donnelly, K. F. (1987). *Recovering from the Loss of a Parent.*
Jury, M., & Jury, D. (1978). *Gramps: A Man Ages and Dies.*
March, A. (2007). *Dying into Grace: Mother and Daughter . . . a Dance of Healing.*
Nouwen, H. (2005). *In Memoriam.*
Smith, H. I. (1994). *On Grieving the Death of a Father.*
Smith, H. I. (2003). *Grieving the Death of a Mother.*

ABOUT ONE'S OWN STRUGGLES WITH LIFE-THREATENING ILLNESS:

Armstrong, L., & Jenkins, S. (2000). *It's Not about the Bike: My Journey Back to Life.*
Broyard, A. (1992). *Intoxicated by My Illness, and Other Writings on Life and Death.*
Hanlan, A. (1979). *Autobiography of Dying.*
Simmons, P. (2002). *Learning to Fall: The Blessings of an Imperfect Life.*
Tolstoy, L. (1960). *The Death of Ivan Ilych and Other Stories.**
*Titles marked with an asterisk are fiction.

Some have claimed that fetal death experiences have minimal impact on the parents and do not generate a significant grief reaction. Parents have been offered false consolation: "Now you have a little angel in heaven" or "You can always have another child." Such easy dismissal of the losses in a fetal death reflects ignorance and the discomfort of outsiders. It is often bolstered by an erroneous claim that there could not be much grief when there had not been real bonding with the infant. In fact, during pregnancy most parents begin to actively reshape their lives and self-concepts to accommodate the anticipated baby. Such parents observe the movements of the fetus in the womb with the aid of new imaging technologies, explore potential names for the baby, plan accommodations, and develop dreams.

When the death occurs in the uterus, it is often important to complete a process of bonding that is already under way in order to enhance opportunities for productive grief and mourning (Lamb, 1988). Parental grief associated with fetal or infant death is a reality that is related not to the length of a baby's life but to the nature of the attachment (Borg & Lasker, 1989; DeFrain et al., 1986; Gamino & Cooney, 2002; Kohn et al., 2000; Lafser, 1998; Peppers & Knapp, 1980). We must recognize the depth of the parents' grief and how they cope with their losses (Allen & Marks, 1993; Ash, 2004; Gray & Lassance, 2002); otherwise, the grief is disenfranchised (see Chapter 10).

Thus, programs have emerged in which parents and other family members are permitted (if they wish to do so) to see and hold their dead infant, name the child, take pictures (Gough, 1999; Johnson et al., 1985; Reddin, 1987; Siegel et al., 1985), retain other mementos (such as a blanket, name tag, or lock of hair), obtain information from a postmortem examination, and take part in rituals that validate the life and the loss. Such practices provide opportunities to interact with the baby, share experiences, and strengthen a realistic foundation for mourning. Implementing such practices requires attention to detail and sensitivity to individual preferences. The key is to understand the meaning of the loss for the parents and then to provide appropriate support. The aim is to affirm that the child and his or her abbreviated life were real and have value, and to honor the needs of those bereaved by the death.

In cases of elective abortion when the parents feel unable or unwilling to bring the baby to term, or in cases of infant adoption, when the child is given over shortly after birth to be raised by others, one often experiences a lingering sense of loss and grief (Doane & Quigley, 1981; Peppers, 1987). When one chooses (deliberately or ambivalently) to abort, even if one believes that the fetus is not yet a human child, one often feels a sense of a loss that must be mourned. To opt for adoption, even when convinced that one is really not able to rear this child, may also leave one with feelings of pain or regret. Neither elective abortion nor adoption need result in grief that incapacitates. It is wrong, however, to assume that these are easy, painless decisions and to dismiss out of hand the implications for parents of events and decisions that close off opportunities involving what is or would become their biological offspring.

Neonatal and Other Infant Deaths After birth, the principal causes of death during infancy present contrasting scenarios for parents and significant others. On one hand, congenital malformations, disorders related to short gestation and low birth weight, newborns affected by maternal complications of pregnancy, and respiratory distress syndrome (RDS) may involve a struggle for life, the intervention of professionals and advanced technology prior to the death, and lingering implications of genetic origins and other feelings of parental responsibility. In such circumstances, the death of the infant is likely to occur in an institutional context, when the parents are perhaps excluded or may not always be able to be present. On the other hand, sudden infant death syndrome (SIDS) will likely involve none of these factors, since it is the prototype of an encounter whose first symptom is death, as well as a death arising from an unknown cause that mostly occurs at home and for which parents often feel guilty in terms of what they did or did not do (see Focus On 12.1; Corr et al., 1991; DeFrain et al., 1991; Horchler & Morris, 2003).

When neonatal and other infant deaths are encountered, they most often have in common the untimely and perhaps unheralded death of a vulnerable individual (Delgadillo & Davis, 1990). Even though pregnancy, the birthing process, and infancy are known to be risky times for the offspring, we commonly believe that tiny babies should not die. Thus, it is often said in the wake of such a death that "it's just not fair." Nevertheless, the hard fact is that "none of us is guaranteed long life, only a lifetime" (Showalter, 1983, p. x).

The specific impact of various types of infant deaths will depend on diverse factors that enter into the mode of death and the situation of the bereaved. For

Courtesy of Carol Kinghorn-Landry

"See! I will not forget you, . . . I have carved you on the palm of my hand" (Isaiah 49:15).

example, the death of an infant in a neonatal intensive care unit can be an excruciating experience for professionals and parents alike. The experience may be even more difficult if there is conflict between professional care providers and family members (or between family members themselves) about care goals (Stinson & Stinson, 1983). Some bereaved mothers may prefer to remain on a maternity ward because of the staff's expertise in postpartum care, whereas others may wish to be relocated in order not to be confronted with happy parents interacting with newborn babies.

In most cases involving the death of an infant, a variety of issues arise for the parents and others involved. These issues include feelings of responsibility, loss of the idealized baby, loss of a part of oneself and one's future, lack of memories and rituals of mourning, and lack of social or professional support (Davis, 1991; Picard, 2002). Even when support is offered, it may not match the parents' needs or be available for as long as they require (Brabant et al., 1995).

The death of an infant and the unique ways in which surviving parents may experience and express their grief responses may create or add to existing strains on parental relationships (Bramblett, 1991; Schwab, 1990). In addition, single parents face special challenges when they must cope with an infant's death on their own (Wyler, 1989). Most of these bereaved parents display amazing resilience in finding ways to go on with productive living (Knapp, 1986; Miles, n.d.). Such parents deserve the best that can be offered in terms of information (e.g., about the nature of the infant's death and about parental loss and grief), professional support, and contact with those who have had similar experiences (Brabant et al., 1995; Donnelly, 1982; Johnson, 1987; Klass, 1988; Schiff, 1977). In many cases, key areas of decision making involve whether (and, if so, when) to consider undertaking another pregnancy and how to help subsequent children relate to the older sibling who died before they were born (Schwiebert, 2003, 2007; Schwiebert & Kirk, 1986). In all cases, it is important to help bereaved parents identify their own needs and not to overburden them with criticisms or expectations of others.

Deaths during Childhood, Adolescence, and Young Adulthood A child, adolescent, or young adult (who is still a child to his or her parents in many ways) can die in many ways—for example, through some sort of accident (often involving a motor vehicle), as a result of homicide or suicide, through natural causes, or even through social conflict, terrorism, or war (as in the conflicts in Afghanistan and Iraq). Typically, these deaths take place suddenly and without much warning or opportunity for preparation; often they involve trauma. In all cases, these deaths involve multiple dimensions for parents and other bereaved adults: loss of the life of the child, loss of what was or is a part of the self, loss of the hopes and dreams that the child represents, and a search for meaning (Klass, 1999; Wheeler, 2001).

Pain associated with the death of a child is often extraordinarily deep, pervasive, and enduring (Davies et al., 1998; Murphy et al., 2003; Talbot, 2002). Charles Dickens (1848/1963, p. 274) recognized this fact in his novel *Dombey and Son* when he put the following exclamation into the mouth of a bereaved father: "And can it be that in a world so full and busy, the loss of one weak creature makes a void in any heart, so wide and deep that nothing but the width and depth of vast eternity can fill it up!" Only a few years earlier than Dickens, Ralph Waldo Emerson (1970, p. 165) made a similar point after the death of his son, when he wrote in his journal on January 28, 1842, "sorrow makes us all children again." Much the same is evident both in a novel centered on a long-past but not-forgotten experience of the death of a child, *The Christmas Box* (Evans, 1993), and in a prizewinning book of poems by a bereaved mother, *The Andrew Poems* (Wagner, 1994; see Personal Insights 14.2). All of the resources that an individual and a family can command are required to cope with such a deep and intimate experience (Rosof, 1994).

A special problem for parents who have experienced the death of a child arises from simple, everyday questions like "How many children do you have?" The difficulty is partly a matter of how the bereaved parent should view his or her own identity ("Am I still a parent?" "What does this death mean for me?") and partly an issue of how much of one's personal life one might or should be willing to disclose to the person who posed the question. Above all, the challenge is how to be faithful to the deceased child and to his or her memory. Bereaved parents meet this challenge often and in different ways, but not so easily as it may seem to those who have not been bereaved (see Personal Insights 14.3).

When the child's death has come about by some form of more or less deliberate behavior (e.g., suicide or homicide), by inadvertence (e.g., accidents), by irresponsible behavior (such as drunken driving), or by war and terrorism (as in Afghanistan or Iraq), elements of responsibility, anger against the person or persons who are thought to be responsible, guilt, or blame (by oneself or by others) may enter into the bereavement experience (Conrad, 1997; Stetson, 2002). Such elements can be expected to add to the burdens of parental grief and mourning (Bolton, 1995; Chance, 1994; Matthews & Marwit, 2004). Despite all of the difficulties involved in parental bereavement, however, there are many things that professional care providers and others can do to be helpful, and bereaved parents have taken part in formulating guidelines for how professionals might help others in similar situations from the initial notification of a death through care of the body and the funeral (Janzen et al., 2004).

Shelly Wagner: The Tie

At night, I imagine
lying on my side next to him,
my arm under his head,
whispering in his ear,
smoothing the child-sized red tie
that lies on his chest
like an upside-down
exclamation mark.
I put off buying him
men's clothing,
but for Easter he wanted a tie—
a red one
and a navy blue blazer.
Now, just under six years old,
he is buried wearing it forever—
as old a man
as he will ever be.
At night,
lying next to my husband,
I back into
the curved question mark
of his body
and ask,
"What is Andrew like now?"
He always whispers,
"His coat and tie are the same."

Source: From *The Andrew Poems,* by S. Wagner, p. 36. Copyright © 1994 Shelley Wagner. Reprinted with permission from Texas Tech University Press.

Guilt in Parental Bereavement Guilt is in part the conviction that one has done wrong by violating some principle or responsibility. Guilt may be realistic and well founded or unrealistic and unjustified (Stearns, 1985). Typically associated with guilt are lowered self-esteem, heightened self-blame, and a feeling that one should make retribution for the supposed wrong. Guilt is by no means exclusive to parental bereavement, but it is almost always—at least initially—a prominent part of such bereavement.

Miles and Demi (1984, 1986) argued that guilt in parental bereavement arises from feelings of helplessness and responsibility. These feelings lead parents to ask how their past and present actions and feelings might have contributed to the child's death. Inevitable discrepancies between ideal standards and actual performance can lead to guilt feelings. How that works itself out in individual cases depends on

How Many Children Do You Have?

It is early fall and I am standing in line at the grocery store. As I turn around to check the items in my cart, the woman behind me notices that I am very pregnant. "Is this your first child?" she asks innocently. Tears form in my eyes as I try to decide what to answer. If I say no, this will lead to the inevitable question: "How many children do you have?" Am I up for the possible reaction to my answer? Am I ready to bring up old feelings and memories? That day, I decide yes.

I turn to the woman and say, "This is my second child. My first child, my son, died in October of 1985 of Sudden Infant Death Syndrome." She puts her hand on my shoulder and tells me how sorry she is. She asks me some questions about our son and about SIDS. I appreciated so much the opportunity to talk about our son, Brendan, and SIDS, even to a complete stranger!

Unfortunately, that is not always the response I receive. Many times people will mumble something unintelligible and walk away. That is okay, too. I understand how difficult it is to hear about a baby dying—no one likes to hear about that.

Responses among bereaved parents will differ when they are asked how many children they have. In most cases, I will tell people I have a son who died, and two daughters.

There have been situations when I haven't mentioned Brendan. This is okay—it doesn't mean I don't love him or that I deny that he ever existed. It doesn't mean that I am a bad mother. What it does mean, is that, for the moment, I choose not to share Brendan. Early in my bereavement, I told everyone about Brendan's life and death. More than twelve years later, I have learned to cope with his absence and do not feel the need to mention him every time I meet someone new.

There are many ways in which my family and I keep his memory alive. As bereaved parents, we decide what is right for each of us. When we choose to mention our deceased children, we may make some people uncomfortable, but we may also have the opportunity to educate others. If we choose not to mention our deceased children, that does not mean that we deny them or that we should feel guilty. The only correct choice is what feels right to the bereaved parent.

Source: Maruyama, N. L. (1998). How many children do you have? *Bereavement Magazine, 12*(5), p. 16. Reprinted with permission from Bereavement Publishing, Inc., 4765 N. Carefree Circle, Colorado Springs, CO 80917; 888-604-4673.

parental, situational, personal, and societal variables. At least six potential sources of guilt may apply to bereaved parents:

1. *Death causation guilt,* related to the belief that the parent either contributed to or failed to protect the child from the death

2. *Illness-related guilt,* related to perceived deficiencies in the parental role during the child's illness or at the time of death

3. *Parental role guilt,* related to the belief that the parent failed to live up to self-expectations or societal expectations in the overall parental role

4. *Moral guilt,* related to the belief that the child's death was punishment or retribution for violating a moral or religious standard

5. *Survival guilt,* related to violating the standard that a child should outlive his or her parents

6. *Grief guilt,* related to the behavioral and emotional reactions at the time of or following the child's death—that is, feeling guilt about how one acted at or after the time of the child's death

In the case of a bereaved parent, one must identify and address any of these elements of guilt that might appear in the overall bereavement experience. Each needs to be attended to in the mourning process.

Gender and Role Differences in Parental Bereavement   Fathers and mothers are different; married, unmarried, and divorced parents are different. Each bereaved individual is distinguished by his or her gender, role(s), and personal characteristics. Each of these distinguishing factors may and likely will influence the bereavement experience (Schwab, 1990). For example, according to traditional gender-based roles in American society, expression of strong feelings was sanctioned for females but discouraged for males. Similarly, wives were expected to remain at home, while husbands went out to work. Although such gender-based roles do not apply in all relationships and are changing in many areas of society, factors like these may encourage different types of grief experiences for mothers and fathers (e.g., Davies et al., 1998, 2004). Even simply because they are two different individuals, at any given time spouses may be coping with loss and grief in different ways and may not be available to support each other as they otherwise do in healthy marital relationships (Schatz, 1986; Simonds & Rothman, 1992). Consequently, it is important for bereaved parents to try to be tolerant of and patient with each other (Rosenblatt, 2000, 2001). Assistance from empathetic friends, other bereaved parents (e.g., through a support group like The Compassionate Friends), or an experienced counselor may be helpful.

As gender expectations are altered, as social roles change, and as individual differences are permitted freer expression, responses to bereavement are likely to be affected. A single parent and a surviving couple will be alone in different ways after the death of their child. Divorced or widowed parents whose child dies may face competing demands from grief and surviving children. A young parent and a grandparent may not always be able to help each other in mourning. We must appreciate the many factors that enter into individual experiences of parental bereavement during adulthood.

Death of a Spouse, Life Partner, Sibling, Peer, or Friend

Pair relationships can be very important in human life. Among adults, pair relationships may be established and carried over from childhood or adolescence, or newly formed during the adult years. Such relationships may be of many types; those involving marital ties are not the only model. One may have special bonds with many other adults, such as a brother or sister, other relative, friend, co-worker, lover, or life partner (heterosexual, gay, or lesbian). The relationship may be overt or hidden, continuous or intermittent, satisfying or complicated, healthy or abusive. There are perhaps as many variables in adult-to-adult relationships as there are in the individuals involved and in the ways they interact.

The dimensions of an adult's bereavement occasioned by the death of someone who is also an adult will depend, in the first place, on the intimacy and significance of the roles that the deceased person played in that individual's life. For example, the sibling relationship is typically the longest and most enduring familial relationship. Where that relationship is especially close, the death of one sibling may involve both his or her loss and the loss of an important part of the surviving sibling's identity (see Personal Insights 14.4 and 14.5). Multiple siblings may react quite differently to the death of their brother or sister (Van Riper, 1997).

In spousal or other intimate friendships, two individuals are likely to have established a relationship that gradually becomes an important and enduring part of their identity (Sklar & Hartley, 1990; Smith, 1996, 2001). The deceased individual is no longer alive to receive love, his or her contributions to the relationship go unfulfilled, the comforting presence to which one formerly turned for love and solace is no longer available, and plans that the couple had made for the future may now go unrealized (Caine, 1999; Kaimann, 2002). Some of Al Joyner's experiences after the death of his wife, FloJo, reflect issues encountered by many bereaved adult spouses (see Personal Insights 14.6).

Another important factor in this type of bereavement has to do with the cause of the death and the circumstances in which it occurred. This is evident when an adult is confronted with the death of a significant other adult as a result of suicide

PERSONAL INSIGHTS 14.4

Cokie Roberts on the Death of Her Sister

At some point during Barbara's illness I began preparing myself for a different vision of my old age. Without really thinking about it, I had always assumed we'd occupy adjacent rockers on some front porch, either literally or figuratively. Now one of those chairs would be empty. Intellectually I understood that. But every time some new thing happens that she's not here for, emotionally it hits me all over again—that sense of charting new territories without the map of my older sister.

And here's what I didn't expect at all—not only was I robbed of some part of my future, I was also deprived of my past. When a childhood memory needed checking, all my life I had simply run it by Barbara. Now there's no one to set me straight. My mother and brother can help some. My brother and I have, in fact, grown a good deal closer since our sister died; after all, without him, I would not only not have a sister, I would not be a sister. But Tommy didn't go to school with me, share a room with me, grow up female with me. Though I love him dearly, he is not my sister.

There it is. For all of the wonderful expressions of sisterhood from so many sources, for all of the support I both receive and provide, for all of the friendships I cherish, it's not the same. I only had one sister.

Source: Roberts, 1998, pp. 16–17.

Jon Davis on the Death of His Brother

I had a brother and he died. I didn't cause it; I couldn't stop it. He got on his motorcycle and rode away. A car turned in front of him and that began his dying. How terrible for everyone involved. Do I sound bitter? I felt the usual guilts: Did I love him enough? Did I show it?

It happened eleven years ago and what I remember: Looking out at the lawn, September and a breeze; watching him ride—flash of red gas tank, brown leather jacket; the sound of the bike; what we said, which I recall as a kind of gesture, the sound of *what are you doing,* some dull rhythm and *see you later.*

The phone call. The drive to the hospital. I think I drove but I can't be sure. We drove the wrong way down a one-way street and I remember feeling responsible. I cried most of the time. I knew he was dying. My brother's girlfriend asked me *Why are you crying?* And I couldn't say or else I sobbed *It's bad I know it's bad.*

Then we were taken into a green room and told he was dead. I curled on a red plastic chair. My body disappeared or seemed to. I was looking for my brother; a nurse called me back: *Your family needs you.* I came back.

But why am I telling you this? Because I want you to love me? To pity me? To understand I've suffered and that excuses my deficiencies? To see how loss is loss and no elegy, no quiet talk late at night among loved ones who suddenly feel the inadequacy of their love and the expression of that love can take it away? Or give it back? Perhaps even loss is lost?

My brother is gone and the world, you, me, are not better for it. There was no goodness in his death. And there is none in this poem, eleven years later and still confused. An attempt, one might say, to come to terms with his death as if there were somewhere to come to, as if there were terms. But there is nowhere to come to; there are no terms. Just this spewing of words, this gesture neither therapy nor catharsis nor hopelessness nor consolation. Not elegy but a small crumb. An offering.

or homicide. Such deaths are challenging and difficult. Similar difficulties in bereavement have been noted when members of the military have died during the conflicts in Iraq and Afghanistan. For some, the social context of the loss is problematic because they have questioned the appropriateness of the American role in those situations. More importantly for many, however, their loss is hard because these deaths have often occurred in traumatic ways and have frequently involved not just young adults in the regular military, but also older members of the military reserves and National Guard (both male and female), many of whom had spouses and children.

The Death of Florence Griffith Joyner and Its Aftermath

Florence Griffith Joyner, known to friends and fans as "FloJo," died unexpectedly on September 21, 1998, at the age of 38 (Gregorian, 1998).

FloJo was known for her athletic abilities and flamboyant style. She set new world records in track while winning three gold medals and a silver medal at the Olympic Games in Seoul in 1988.

FloJo's husband, Al Joyner, and his sister, Jackie Joyner-Kersee, experienced the sudden death of their mother at the age of 37 as a result of cerebrospinal meningitis. But Al said that tragic event did not prepare them for FloJo's death (Brennan, 1998).

On September 21, 1998, Al woke at 6:30 A.M. to the sounds of the bedroom alarm clock. When he went to wake his wife, in bed with their 7-year-old daughter, Mary, Al experienced what he later said was "the most hopeless moment of my life" (Brennan, 1998, p. 5E).

A postmortem examination determined that FloJo had died in her sleep of an epileptic seizure.

Several weeks after FloJo's death, Al was reported to have said: "If Mary were not here, I really think I would do something stupid. I feel like I have nothing to live for, until I think of her" (Brennan, 1998, p. 5E).

Al also said that he has not had his wife's mobile telephone service disconnected. In fact, from time to time he calls that number just to hear the voice of Florence on the answering tape saying, "This is Florence. I can't talk to you right now. Please leave a message."

Death of a fellow adult—a spouse, life partner, sibling, peer, or friend—can change the world, the other, and the self for a bereaved adult (as well as for children and others who may also be involved) (Rodger et al., 2007). The death of only one person like this can entail many emotional, social, financial, spiritual, and other losses. It can also precipitate renewed struggles with identity (DiGiulio, 1989; Golan, 1975). Much will depend on how the death occurred, on the perspective of the survivor, and on social norms. For example, if it was an ex-spouse who died, is the bereaved individual to be thought of and recognized as a widow or widower (Campbell & Silverman, 1996; Kohn & Kohn, 1978; Stillion, 1985)? And will considerations arise about the possibility of remarriage or other forms of new relationships (Bishop & Cain, 2003)?

Death of a Parent or Grandparent

Young and middle adults typically emancipate themselves in some measure from parental and family bonds. For example, they may move away from parental influences, either geographically or psychosocially. Usually, but not always, they reestablish new relationships with parents, grandparents, and other family members,

© AP Photo/Rusty Kennedy

FloJo's excellent health but sudden death complicated the mourning for those who loved her.

revising the relationships that characterized their childhood. In any case, adults have unique relationships—simple, ambivalent, or complicated though they may be—with their own parents and grandparents throughout their adult lives. These members of an older generation often are sources of advice, support, and assistance to their adult children and grandchildren. Sometimes they become individuals who need to be cared for by their adult children (Comer, 2006).

In our society, most adults expect their parents and grandparents to precede them in death, and in fact this is the most common form of bereavement during adult life. Nevertheless, when such deaths do occur, they often are difficult experiences for those left behind (Horowitz et al., 1984; Moss & Moss, 1983, 2007; Myers, 1986). They involve the loss of a lifelong relationship, full of shared (playful and sorrowful) experiences. The surviving adult may have devoted much time and energy to the care of the older person who has now died (e.g., Collier, 2003). An individual like this may also perceive the death as the removal of a "buffer" or source of generational "protection" against his or her own personal death (Akner & Whitney, 1993; Angel, 1987). Literature on experiences following the death of a mother or father (e.g., Lutovich, 2001; Smith, H.I., 1994, 2003), as well as more specific situations involving motherless daughters (Edelman, 1994), fatherless daughters (Simon, 2001), and fatherless sons (Chethik, 2001), describes special complications that may apply to each of these bereavement situations. Sometimes, the death may be perceived as the completion of a long, full life or as a release from suffering. Just as easily, however, it may involve lost opportunities or unfinished business and a failure to experience certain developmental or situational milestones by the deceased, the bereaved adult, or that person's children. For example, following the death of a parent or grandparent the adult child no longer has an opportunity to renew or extend relationships with the deceased person on an adult-to-adult basis. Difficult and important issues may be left unresolved. In these and other ways, the death of a parent almost inevitably gives his or her adult children a "developmental push," which most often alters their sense of themselves and through which they may feel with additional force their own finitude or the weight of their own responsibility as members of the now-oldest living generation (Umberson, 2003). Finally, the death of a parent of one partner has also been shown to have multiple impacts, not just on that individual, but also on various practical matters and shifting issues of closeness/intimacy versus distance in couple relationships (Rosenblatt & Barner, 2006).

🍂 Summary

In this chapter, we explored many aspects of interactions between young and middle-aged adults and death within our society. We noted how the distinctive developmental tasks of young adulthood (striving to achieve intimacy versus isolation) and middle age (striving to achieve generativity versus stagnation) have a direct bearing on how adults relate to death. These tasks influence encounters with death among young and middle adults (we noted an accelerating increase in death rates involving diseases of the heart and cancer) and attitudes of these adults toward death (special concerns about the deaths of others in young adults and the appearance of a newly personalized sense of mortality in middle adults). We also explored some of the main concerns that arise when young and middle adults are coping with life-threatening illness and dying. Finally, we reviewed many typical types of bereavement encounters that adults may experience and some of their implications.

Glossary

Developmental eras in adulthood: young adulthood and middle adulthood
Fetal death: death resulting from miscarriage, stillbirth, or spontaneous abortion
Generativity: maintaining productivity in one's life and projects; typically involves reassessing or reevaluating the meaning and direction of one's life, conserving or considering prospects for continuation or enduring value in one's legacies, and preparation through efforts to put one's affairs in order
Intimacy: the ability to be open, supportive, and close with another person, without fear of losing oneself in the process
Midlife transition: the transition from young to middle adulthood; may be more or less calm or tumultuous
Normative developmental tasks in adulthood: to achieve intimacy (versus the danger of isolation) in young adulthood; to pursue generativity (versus the danger of stagnation or self-absorption) in middle adulthood
The sandwich generation: adults who experience pressures from both older and younger generations

Questions for Review and Discussion

1. Think back to the situation described in the vignette near the beginning of this chapter. What types of losses were the Archbishop and his mother coping with? If you were a friend, how would you try to help?

2. What sorts of death-related losses are most typical in adulthood, and what do such losses usually mean to adults?

3. Think about some of the losses you have experienced as an adult. How did you cope with them?

4. Do you know an adult who has experienced significant death-related losses? What were those losses like for that person? What did you do or what could you have done to help?

Suggested Readings

Concerning life-threatening illness in adulthood, consult:

Cousins, N. (1979). *Anatomy of an Illness as Perceived by the Patient: Reflections on Healing and Regeneration.*

Frank, A. W. (2002). *At the Will of the Body: Reflections on Illness.*

Bereavement and grief in adulthood are explored in several ways: in terms of the death of a child:

Bolton, I. (1995). *My Son, My Son: A Guide to Healing after a Suicide in the Family.*

Chance, S. (1994). *Stronger than Death.*

Corr, C. A., Fuller, H., Barnickol, C. A., & Corr, D. M. (Eds.). (1991). *Sudden Infant Death Syndrome: Who Can Help and How.*

Davis, D. L. (1991). *Empty Cradle, Broken Heart: Surviving the Death of Your Baby.*

DeFrain, J., Ernst, L., Jakub, D., & Taylor, J. (1991). *Sudden Infant Death: Enduring the Loss.*

DeFrain, J., Martens, L., Story, J., & Stork, W. (1986). *Stillborn: The Invisible Death.*

Donnelly, K. F. (1982). *Recovering from the Loss of a Child.*

Gray, K., & Lassance, A. (2002). *Grieving Reproductive Loss: A Healing Process.*

Horchler, J. N., & Morris, R. R. (2003). *The SIDS and Infant Death Survival Guide: Information and Comfort for Grieving Families and Friends and Professionals Who Seek to Help Them* (3rd ed.).

Ilse, S. (1989). *Miscarriage: A Shattered Dream.*

Johnson, S. (1987). *After a Child Dies: Counseling Bereaved Families.*

Klass, D. (1988). *Parental Grief: Solace and Resolution.*

Klass, D. (1999). *The Spiritual Lives of Bereaved Parents.*

Kohn, I., Moffit, P-L., & Wilkins, I. A. (2000). *A Silent Sorrow: Pregnancy Loss— Guidance and Support for You and Your Family* (rev. 2nd ed.).

Lafser, C. (1998). *An Empty Cradle, a Full Heart: Reflections for Mothers and Fathers after Miscarriage, Stillbirth, or Infant Death.*

Limbo, R. K., & Wheeler, S. R. (1998). *When a Baby Dies: A Handbook for Healing and Helping* (2nd ed.).

Osmont, K., & McFarlane, M. (1986). *Parting Is Not Goodbye.*

Rando, T. A. (Ed.). (1986a). *Parental Loss of a Child.*

Rosenblatt, P. C. (2000). *Parent Grief: Narratives of Loss and Relationship.*

Rosenblatt, P. C. (2001). *Help Your Marriage Survive the Death of a Child.*

Rosof, B. D. (1994). *The Worst Loss: How Families Heal from the Death of a Child.*

Stetson, B. (2002). *Living Victims, Stolen Lives: Parents of Murdered Children Speak to America.*

Talbot, K. (2002). *What Forever Means after the Death of a Child: Transcending the Trauma, Living with the Loss.*

Tedeschi, R. G. (2003). *Helping Bereaved Parents: A Clinician's Guide.*

In terms of the death of a spouse, life partner, sibling, peer, or friend:

Campbell, S., & Silverman, P. R. (1996). *Widower: What Happens when Men Are Left Alone.*

Lewis, C. S. (1976). *A Grief Observed.*

Smith, H. I. (2001). *Friendgrief: An Absence Called Presence.*

Stroebe, W., & Stroebe, M. S. (2003). *Bereavement and Health: The Psychological and Physical Consequences of Partner Loss.*

White, P. G. (2006). *Sibling Grief: Healing after the Death of a Sister or Brother.*

In terms of the death of the adult's parent or grandparent:

Akner, L. F., with C.V. Whitney. (1993). *How to Survive the Loss of a Parent: A Guide for Adults.*

Angel, M. D. (1987). *The Orphaned Adult.*

Chethik, N. (2001). *FatherLoss: How Sons of All Ages Come to Terms with the Deaths of Their Dads.*

Edelman, H. (1994). *Motherless Daughters: The Legacy of Loss.*

Gilbert, A., & Kline, C. B. (2006). *Always Too Soon, Voices of Support for Those Who Have Lost Both Parents.*

Lutovich, D. S. (2001). *Nobody's Child: How Older Women Say Good-bye to Their Mothers.*

Myers, E. (1986). *When Parents Die: A Guide for Adults.*

Simon, C. (2001). *Fatherless Women: How We Change after We Lose Our Dads.*

Smith, H. I. (1994). *On Grieving the Death of a Father.*

Smith, H. I. (2003). *Grieving the Death of a Mother.*

Selected Web Resources

Some useful search terms include: ADULTS AND DEATH; CAUSES OF DEATH IN ADULTHOOD; DEVELOPMENTAL TASKS IN ADULTHOOD; "SANDWICH" GENERATION

Visit the book companion website for *Death & Dying, Life & Living, Sixth Edition,* at academic.cengage.com/psychology/corr for all URLs and live links to the following *organizational and other Internet sites:*

Bereaved Parents of the USA

Candlelighters Childhood Cancer Foundation

The Compassionate Friends

CHAPTER 15
Older Adults

© Photodisc/Getty Images

Objectives of This Chapter

- ◆ To identify distinctive developmental tasks of older adults
- ◆ To describe typical encounters with death among older adults in the United States today
- ◆ To explore death-related attitudes among older adults

- ◆ To identify key issues for older adults who are coping with life-threatening illness and dying
- ◆ To explore central issues for older adults who are coping with bereavement and grief
- ◆ To examine issues related to suicide among older adults

❦ Lives Crowned by Love

He calls her Miss America. Sometimes she calls him John, the name of her deceased husband. . . . Francis Eldridge is 92. Marie Franzen is 97. Both lived full and happy lives before they met nine years ago. Francis was married to his Edyth for 58 years. Marie was married to John for 64.

Neither was looking to begin again when they were introduced during lunch at the . . . Senior Center. . . . Instead they became soul mates. Francis remembers what happened later, at Marie's home. "She was having trouble lifting a window," he says. "I went by to fix it and never left."

They decided against marriage, but after a month Francis moved into Marie's . . . bungalow. . . . Francis loved Marie's cooking. Her beef stew, Hungarian goulash and stuffed cabbage pushed his weight up to a robust 175 pounds.

Then Marie was diagnosed with Alzheimer's. But as long as Francis was around, Marie eventually found the words she intended to say.

Everything changed in March of 1999 when Francis developed a severe case of pneumonia that landed him in the . . . Medical Center for three weeks.

He was released from the hospital too weak to take care of himself and Marie. He moved in with his daughter, Sylvia Whitney . . . Marie moved into Crystal Oaks [a nursing home].

"He was happy to be with me, but he missed her so much," says Whitney. "I would take him to visit her once or twice a week, but he kept losing weight. Marie is the only woman—besides my mother—that my dad ever cared about."

As Francis shriveled, Marie languished. "He dropped to 114 pounds; she was lost," says Whitney. Out of desperation, she moved Francis to Crystal Oaks to live with Marie.

Francis is back up to 137 pounds. No one expects Marie's Alzheimer's to go away, but she now has longer stretches of clarity.

"You don't know what your feelings can do to your body," says Francis as he and Marie soak up the sun on a green metal bench in front of Crystal Oaks. They come here each morning after breakfast to hold hands and say hello to all who pass. . . .

The two are teasing each other about their dancing when Francis' black wrist watch begins to talk. "Ten forty-two," it says in a monotone. This is followed by a recording of a crowing rooster. Francis and Marie are both legally blind. They depend on the rooster to tell them when to go inside.

They shuffle along the polished floors until they come to the large water fountain they use as a landmark. "When we find the fountain, we've found our room," says Marie.

Inside, she has a collection of teddy bears. Friends bring them as gifts, and Marie keeps them for a while before passing them on to visitors and friends. But the small white bear dressed in blue never leaves the room. It was a gift from Francis.

When they melt into Marie's single bed for their daily noontime rest, the bear is there too. They will spend the next hour wrapped in each other's arms, Miss America and her darling John. (*Source:* "Lives Crowned by Love" by Jamie Francis, p. 1D in the Floridian, *St. Petersburg Times,* March 9, 2001, Reprinted by permission.)

❦ Older Adults, Developmental Tasks, and Death

Older adults—those who are 65 years of age and older—represented approximately 12.4 percent of the total population of the United States in 2004. Because older adults are a growing portion of America's population whose number is expected to rise from around 36.3 million in 2004 to 63.5 million in 2025, some have spoken of the *graying of America*. In many societies, these older adults would be thought of as the repository of social wisdom, but America's youth-oriented society does not typically take this view. Thus, the position of older adults is more ambiguous and less honored by much of our society.

With the emergence of a body of gerontological and geriatric knowledge about older adults, much has been learned about the developmental tasks and other issues that distinguish them from other members of American society. In particular, it has been recognized that aging is not identical with pathology. Becoming an older adult is often marked by a variety of biological, psychological, and social changes—but the majority of older adults in the United States are living vigorous, productive, and satisfying lives (Cavanaugh & Blanchard-Fields, 2005; Cox, 2000; Papalia, Sterns, et al., 2006). NBC news correspondent Tom Brokaw (1998) has called older adults in our society *The Greatest Generation,* and former President Jimmy Carter (1998) has written about *The Virtues of Aging.* One notable example of achievement by an older American occurred on October 29, 1998, when John Glenn—the first American to orbit the earth on February 20, 1962—went back into space at the age of 77 after successful careers in the military, as an astronaut, and as a United States senator.

The belief that to be old is always to be frail and weak is inaccurate: Senator John Glenn at age 77 returned to space after 36 years.

Nevertheless, American society often gives evidence of what Butler (1969) called *ageism,* which he (1975, p. 12) defined as "a process of systematic stereotyping of and discrimination against people because they are old." In fact, it is wrong, unfair, and potentially harmful to older adults when they are casually lumped together, when their lives are devalued, and when appreciation is lacking for what they have in common with all other human beings. Against this stereotyping, it is desirable to acknowledge the shared humanity, the significant human values, the potential contributions they might still make, and the great diversity to be found in this portion of the population (see Issues for Critical Reflection #12). If it is true that "human beings are more alike at birth than they will ever be again" (Stillion, 1985, p. 56), then it should also be true that human beings are most unalike in older adulthood, in view of the many years in which each individual has had to work out his or her long story.

Research on *late adulthood* has demonstrated that it is not appropriate to speak of "old age" without qualification. In fact, older adults are neither a static nor a monolithic segment of the population (Erikson et al., 1986; Havighurst, 1972). As one researcher has reported, "old people do not perceive meaning in aging itself, so much as they perceive meaning in being themselves in old age. Thus . . . [the central issue is] how old people maintain a sense of continuity and meaning that helps them cope with change" (Kaufman, 1986, pp. 13–14).

In Erikson's (1959) original schematization, the last era in the human life course was called *senescence*. This term had been used earlier by Hall (1922) to designate the entire last half of human life. The word itself identifies the process of

---

ISSUES FOR CRITICAL REFLECTION
#12 Two Old Women: Do Older Adults Still Have Anything to Contribute?

It is sometimes assumed that old age necessarily leads to incapacity and increasing dependence on others. This belief is not limited to contemporary culture. In cultures living near the Arctic Circle, tribes sometimes abandoned elderly persons who were considered no longer able to contribute to the needs of the group. Velma Wallis (2004) in her book *Two Old Women* develops an Alaskan Athabaskan legend that she learned from her mother.

Wallis' tale begins by describing a tribe in which there are two old women who are viewed by tribal members as complaining, demanding, and not contributing to the needs of the society. They are seen as merely a burden on the tribe's scarce resources. When the tribe faces starvation during a particularly harsh winter, the leader of the tribe decides to leave behind the two old women.

Wallis continues her tale:

The two old women sat old and small before the campfire with their chins held up proudly, disguising their shock. . . . They stared ahead numbly as if they had not heard the chief condemn them to a certain death—to be left alone to fend for themselves in a land that understood only strength. Two weak old women stood no chance against such a rule. (p. 7)

But this is only the beginning of Wallis' story. The two old women do not simply descend into loneliness, despair, and death. Instead, their dire situation calls forth from them resources—psychological, physical, intellectual, and spiritual—that they hardly knew they had, and they survive, even flourish. A year later, the tribe encounters the old women once more when the tribe's condition is again very precarious. The two old women offer some of the food from the stores they have accumulated through their own labor and resourcefulness. In the end, the tribe and the two old women realize that they are each able to help the other. Thus, the two women and the tribe come to recognize that old age need not always lead to incapacity and dependence, but rather can lead to a new level of *inter*-dependence from which *all* can benefit.

growing old, and thus by transference designates older adults themselves. Unfortunately, *senescence* is etymologically linked to the terms *senile* and *senility,* which now designate not merely the condition of being old but the presence of cognitive impairment often mistakenly associated with old age. This linkage between normative developmental eras and pathology is generally not accurate and thus undesirable (Madey & Chasteen, 2004). Perhaps to avoid such implications, Erikson later (1963, 1982) spoke about this period as the era of *maturity* or one in which human development is "completed."

Different developmental theorists describe *the principal developmental task of older adulthood* in similar ways. Erikson (1963, 1982) described this task as involving *the achievement of ego integrity versus despair or disgust,* Maslow (1968) spoke of *self-actualization,* and Birren (1964) wrote about *reconciliation.* In each of these languages, the principal developmental work of old age involves the attainment of an inner sense of wholeness (Cavanaugh & Blanchard-Fields, 2005; Papalia, Sterns, et al., 2006). Successfully resolving earlier developmental tasks and coming to terms with one's past helps older adults achieve the balance and harmony in this wholeness (integrity means being whole or undivided), which emerges from a process of introspection, self-reflection, and reminiscence that Butler (1963) called *life review* (compare Hendricks, 1995; Woodward, 1986).

In this process of heightened interiority, past experiences are spontaneously brought to consciousness, reviewed and assessed, and perhaps reinterpreted or reintegrated. The aim is to resolve old conflicts and to achieve a new sense of meaning, both as an accounting to oneself of one's past life and as a preparation for death. If this process is successful, it results in integrity and wisdom (Erikson & Erikson, 1981). If not, it yields a sense of despair because one is not satisfied with what one has done with one's life and does not feel that sufficient time or energy remains to alter directions and compensate for the ways in which one has lived.

Customarily, older adults in our society have been thought of as those who are 65 years of age or older (perhaps in part because many faced a social marker of mandatory retirement at that age). In the 21st century, however, the situation is more complicated than this. For example, persons reaching age 65 in the United States in 2004 had an estimated average life expectancy of an additional 18.7 years (20.0 years for females; 17.1 years for males) and that such averages have been trending upward in recent years (Miniño et al., 2007). In fact, the portion of those in the very oldest segment of our society, our centenarians, is projected to grow most rapidly of all during the first half of the 21st century (see Figure 15.1 and Gertner, 2001; see also Issues for Critical Reflection #13).

In short, many older adults in our society—especially those in the 65- to 74-year-old age group—possess relatively good health, education, purchasing power, and free time—and are politically active (Neugarten, 1974; Thorson, 2000a). This suggests the need to draw important distinctions within older adults between the "young old" (those 65–74 years of age), the "old" or "old old" (those 75–84 years of age), and the "oldest old" or "very old" (those 85 years of age and older) (Settersten, 2002). Some have spoken of the very old as the "frail elderly," but that is a health category, not a developmental designation—older adults of any age (as well as younger persons) may or may not be frail. In any event, there clearly are different social cohorts among older adults and distinctive developmental tasks in this evolving population (Rocke & Cherry, 2002).

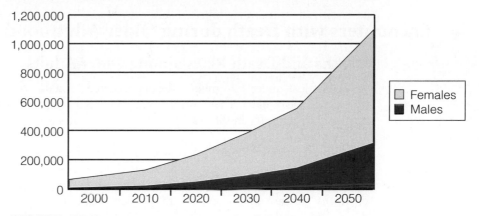

FIGURE 15.1

Actual and Projected Centenarian Populations by Gender, United States, 2000–2050. *Source:* U.S. Bureau of the Census, National Population Projections, 2001.

ISSUES FOR CRITICAL REFLECTION

#13 What Can You Do to Increase Your Life Expectancy?

- Have a pool of "good" genes (choose your parents wisely!).
- Keep your blood pressure low; take an aspirin a day.
- Participate in regular exercise and maintain your weight.
- Avoid a diet high in protein and high in saturated fats; limit coffee drinking.
- Do not smoke cigarettes or use other tobacco products; avoid secondhand smoke.
- Limit your use of alcohol products to not more than two drinks per day.
- Avoid excessive exposure to the sun.
- Practice effective stress management techniques and maintain a good sense of humor.
- Engage in rewarding hobbies.
- Enjoy many friends (of all age groups) and share gratifying activities with them.

Consult the book *Living to 100: Lessons in Living to Your Maximum Potential at Any Age* (Perls et al., 2000) and check the quiz at the website www.livingto100.com to see how you are doing in this regard.

If you could increase your life expectancy substantially (perhaps even reach age 100 or older):

- What would you want to do?
- What would be your goals?
- How would you plan to support yourself financially?
- What health problems would you anticipate?
- With whom would you want to live?
- Where would you choose to live?
- What living facilities would you desire?

Encounters with Death during Older Adulthood

Deaths and Death Rates among Older Adults

A total of just under 1.76 million deaths occurred in 2004 among those who were 65 years of age or older. That represented about 73.2 percent of the nearly 2.4 million deaths in the country in the year in a group that makes up 12.4 percent of the total U.S. population.

Table 15.1 provides an overview of numbers of deaths in the United States in 2004 for three groups of older adults: individuals 65–74 years of age, 75–84 years of age, and 85 years and older. By comparing these data, one can see that *numbers of deaths* increase significantly from 399,666 deaths among those 65–74 years of age to 684,230 deaths among those 75–84 years of age, and then decline slightly to 671,773 deaths among the much smaller population of those 85 years of age and older. This curve continues the general pattern of a steady and rapid increase in numbers of deaths throughout the whole of adulthood in American society, at least up to age 85 and older.

Similar patterns are true of *death rates* among older adults (see Table 15.2). In 2004, very high overall death rates of 2,164.6 per 100,000 among individuals who were 65–74 years of age rose to exceptional heights of 13,823.5 per 100,000 among persons who were 85 years of age or older. Similar increases in death rates appeared in all segments of the older adult population. All of these figures are greatly in excess of the overall mortality rate in the United States, which was 816.5 per 100,000 in 2004. In short, death is very much a part of the life of older adults in American society. Since human beings are mortal and cannot live indefinitely, the longer one lives, the closer one comes to the limit of the human life course.

Leading Causes of Death among Older Adults

Table 15.3 identifies the five leading causes of death (along with numbers of deaths and death rates for each of those causes) for three age groupings among individuals in our society who were 65 years of age or older in 2004. All of these leading causes of death for older adults in our society are chronic or degenerative diseases. This pattern extends throughout older adulthood: as in young and middle adulthood, degenerative diseases are increasingly prominent as leading causes of death among older adults, whereas human-induced deaths and communicable diseases decline in relative significance. In general, leading causes of death are essentially the same for both male and female older adults, with only minor differences in their relative significance.

Nevertheless, other causes of death among older adults are also of interest. For example, numbers of accidental deaths among the oldest members of our society (13,457 deaths among those 75–84 years of age and an additional 13,447 deaths among those 85 years of age and older) contrast with just 8,116 accidental deaths among individuals 65–74 years of age. Similarly, accidental death rates of 276.7 per 100,000 among individuals 85 and older are much higher than similar rates for individuals 75–84 years of age (103.7) and those 65–74 years of age (44.0). In brief, accidental deaths are increasingly prominent among older adults as they age. Nevertheless, it is important to note that accidental deaths related to motor

TABLE 15.1
Number of Deaths, Ages 65 and Older, by Age, Race or Hispanic Origin,[a] and Gender, United States, 2004

	Ages 65–74 Years			Ages 75–84 Years			Ages 85 & Older		
	Both Sexes	Males	Females	Both Sexes	Males	Females	Both Sexes	Males	Females
All origins[b]	399,666	222,891	176,775	684,230	333,669	350,561	671,773	226,650	445,123
Caucasian Americans, total	338,262	190,123	148,139	609,660	299,342	310,318	613,740	207,589	406,151
Non-Hispanic Caucasian Americans	317,606	178,642	138,964	582,454	285,752	296,702	593,382	200,357	393,025
African Americans	51,682	27,555	24,127	61,379	27,695	33,684	47,300	14,548	32,752
Hispanic Americans[c]	20,420	11,279	9,141	26,879	13,397	13,482	19,937	7,090	12,847
Asian or Pacific Island Americans[d]	7,393	3,988	3,405	10,816	5,486	5,330	9,230	3,989	5,241
American Indians and Alaska Natives[e]	2,329	1,225	1,104	2,375	1,146	1,229	1,503	524	979

[a]Data for specified groups other than Caucasian Americans and African Americans should be interpreted with caution because of inconsistencies between reporting race and/or Hispanic origin on death certificates and on censuses and surveys.

[b]Figures for origin not stated are included in "all origins" but not distributed among specified origins.

[c]Includes all persons of Hispanic origin of any race.

[d]Includes Chinese, Filipino, Hawaiian, Japanese, and other Asian or Pacific Islander.

[e]Includes Aleuts and Eskimos.

Source: CDC, National Vital Statistics System, National Center for Health Statistics, Mortality Statistics Branch (http://www.cdc.gov/nchs/datawh/statab/unpubd/mortabs.htm); Miniño et al., 2007.

vehicles are far less frequent among older adults than all other accidental deaths (7,421 versus 27,599). By contrast, accidental falls are the leading cause of nonfatal injuries among older adults, and thus are often the source of death and debilitation among such individuals (National Safety Council, 2007; Tideiksaar, 2002). In terms of overall *numbers,* homicide, suicide, and HIV infection do not appear among the ten leading causes of death for older adults, although until quite recently the highest *rates* of suicide in the whole of American society had for many years been found among persons age 85 and older. In 2004, the suicide rate for that population was 16.4 per 100,000, exceeded only by the rate for individuals 45–54 years of age

TABLE 15.2
Death Rates (per 100,000), Ages 65 and Older, by Age, Race or Hispanic Origin,[a] and Gender: United States, 2004

	Ages 65–74 Years			Ages 75–84 Years			Ages 85 & Older		
	Both Sexes	Males	Females	Both Sexes	Males	Females	Both Sexes	Males	Females
All origins[b]	2,164.6	2,644.8	1,761.4	5,275.1	6,394.3	4,521.8	13,823.5	15,031.1	13,280.3
Caucasian Americans, total	2,120.4	2,584.0	1,723.6	5,272.8	6,384.8	4,514.4	14,010.1	15,250.7	13,450.9
Non-Hispanic Caucasian Americans	2,152.5	2,617.9	1,752.0	5,337.1	6,461.5	4,571.1	14,191.1	15,489.2	13,609.6
African Americans	2,982.6	3,818.3	2,386.1	6,170.4	7,710.3	5,300.0	13,338.5	14,452.5	12,896.9
Hispanic Americans[c]	1,607.5	1,994.3	1,297.2	3,926.7	4,791.6	3,329.6	9,483.8	9,932.8	9,253.0
Asian or Pacific Island Americans[d]	1,124.7	1,363.4	933.2	3,055.3	3,766.3	2,558.2	8,881.7	10,118.2	8,125.8
American Indians and Alaskan Natives[e]	1,930.1	2,196.8	1,700.9	3,972.8	4,584.2	3,533.4	7,362.6	7,923.8	7,093.7

[a]Data for specified groups other than Caucasian Americans and African Americans should be interpreted with caution because of inconsistencies between reporting race and/or Hispanic origin on death certificates and on censuses and surveys.

[b]Figures for origin not stated are included in "all origins" but not distributed among specified origins.

[c]Includes all persons of Hispanic origin of any race.

[d]Includes Chinese, Filipino, Hawaiian, Japanese, and other Asian or Pacific Islander.

[e]Includes Aleuts and Eskimos.

Source: CDC, National Vital Statistics System, National Center for Health Statistics, Mortality Statistics Branch (http://www.cdc.gov/nchs/datawh/statab/unpubd/mortabs.htm); Miniño et al., 2007.

(16.6 per 100,000) and closely followed by the rate for individuals 75–84 years of age (16.3 per 100,000) (see Table 17.1 in Chapter 17).

Two Variables in Deaths of Older Adults: Gender and Race

Tables 15.1 and 15.2 also reveal contrasts by gender in number of deaths and death rates among older adults. At first, males die in larger numbers than females, but that changes as individuals reach 75 years of age and older. Because more American females live to an advanced age than males, there are more of them to die among the "oldest old" in our society. Thus, in 2004 there were 94,562 more deaths in the

TABLE 15.3
Numbers of Deaths and Death Rates (per 100,000) during Older Adulthood for the Five Leading Causes of Death in Specified Age Groups, Both Genders, All Races: United States, 2004

Rank	Ages 65–74			Ages 75–84		
	Cause of Death	Number	Rate	Cause of Death	Number	Rate
...	All causes	399,666	2,164.6	All causes	684,230	5,275.1
1	Malignant neoplasms (cancer)	139,417	755.1	Diseases of the heart	195,379	1,506.3
2	Diseases of the heart	99,999	541.6	Malignant neoplasms (cancer)	166,085	1,280.4
3	Chronic lower respiratory diseases	28,390	153.8	Cerebrovascular diseases	50,092	386.2
4	Cerebrovascular diseases	19,901	107.8	Chronic lower respiratory diseases	47,568	366.7
5	Diabetes mellitus	16,093	87.2	Diabetes mellitus	22,945	176.9

Rank	Ages 85 & Older		
	Cause of Death	Number	Rate
...	All causes	671,773	13,823.5
1	Diseases of the heart	237,924	4,895.9
2	Malignant neoplasms (cancer)	80,345	1,653.3
3	Cerebrovascular diseases	60,545	1,245.9
4	Alzheimer's disease	39,790	818.8
5	Chronic lower respiratory diseases	29,239	601.7

Source: CDC, National Vital Statistics System, National Center for Health Statistics, Mortality Statistics Branch (http://www.cdc.gov/nchs/datawh/statab/unpubd/mortabs.htm); Miniño et al., 2007.

oldest group of American females (those 85 years of age and older) than among females 75–84 years of age. Similarly, death rates for males remain consistently higher throughout older adulthood than those for females.

In terms of other subgroups among older adults, numbers of deaths climb sharply among "young old" and "old old" Caucasian Americans before falling slightly among those 85 years of age and older. This trend reflects a crossover effect in which the population of the "oldest old" who remain alive in our society is less numerous than any other ten-year age group. Much smaller numbers of deaths among Hispanic-American, African-American, Asian and Pacific Island American, and American-Indian older adults rise only modestly at first in these age groups and then decline in relatively steeper fashion. In all these groups, death rates rise steadily throughout older adulthood, and males have higher death rates than their female counterparts.

❦ Attitudes toward Death among Older Adults

There is general and long-standing agreement in the research literature that older adults are significantly less fearful of death than younger persons (e.g., Bengtson et al., 1977; Catt et al., 2005; Cicirelli, 2002). Of course, "fear of death" is not an uncomplicated notion (as we saw in Chapter 3), and older adults may differ among themselves in this regard. Also, variables that tend to reduce or threaten quality of life in older adults, such as poor physical and mental health, being widowed, or being institutionalized, appear likely to be inversely associated with fear of death (Marshall, 1975; Swenson, 1961; Templer, 1971). Nevertheless, many studies (such as Kastenbaum, 1967; Matse, 1975; Saul & Saul, 1973) have shown that older adults often talk about aging and death (see Personal Insights 15.1), even within fairly restrictive institutional environments that may not encourage such discussions.

PERSONAL INSIGHTS 15.1

Jenny Joseph: Warning

When I am an old woman
I shall wear purple
With a red hat which doesn't go, and doesn't suit me.
And I shall spend my pension on brandy and summer gloves
And satin sandals, and say we've no money for butter.
I shall sit down on the pavement when I'm tired
And gobble up samples in shops and press alarm bells
And run my stick along the public railings
And make up for the sobriety of my youth.
I shall go out in my slippers in the rain
And pick the flowers in other people's gardens
And learn to spit.

You can wear terrible shirts and grow more fat
And eat three pounds of sausages at a go
Or only bread and a pickle for a week
And hoard pens and pencils and beermats and things in boxes.

But now we must have clothes that keep us dry
And pay our rent and not swear in the street
And set a good example for the children.
We must have friends to dinner and read the papers.

But maybe I ought to practice a little now?
So people who know me are not too shocked and surprised
When suddenly I am old, and start to wear purple.

Source: "Warning" from *Selected Poems,* Bloodaxe Books Ltd. © Jenny Joseph 1992. Reprinted by permission of John Johnson (Authors' Agent) Limited.

Kalish (1985a) proposed three explanations for the relatively low level of fear of death among older adults: (1) they may accept death more easily than others because they have been able to live long, full lives; (2) they may have come to accept their own deaths as a result of a socialization process through which they repeatedly experience the deaths of others; and (3) they may have come to view their lives as having less value than the lives of younger persons and thus may not object so strenuously to giving them up. For any of these reasons, death may seem to an older adult to represent less of a threat than, for example, debility, isolation, or dependence. As a result, most older adults want to die at home, without pain, and without becoming a burden on their families.

❦ Older Adults Who Are Coping with Life-Threatening Illness and Dying

Four specific needs of older adults who are coping with life-threatening illness or dying have been identified by Cook and Oltjenbruns (1998, p. 346): "maintaining a sense of self, participating in decisions regarding their lives, being reassured that their lives still have value, and receiving appropriate and adequate health care services."

Maintaining a Sense of Self

Preserving and affirming the value in the identity established in one's developmental work throughout life is an important task for individuals involved in transitions and reassessments like those that characterize developmental work in older adulthood. One's sense of integrity is founded on one's self-concept and self-esteem. As we have already noted, in older adults this reassessment is typically pursued through the processes of *life review*—reflection, reminiscence, and reevaluation (Kaufman, 1986).

For older adults who are coping with life-threatening illness or dying, these processes need not be eliminated, although they may be curtailed by distress, lack of energy or ability to concentrate, absence of social support, and what often appear to be societal tendencies to devalue aging and older adults. Against these inhibiting factors, family and professional caregivers can encourage life review activities in a number of ways. For example, they can directly participate by listening and serving as sounding boards or by providing stimuli such as photographs and prized mementos. Enabling older adults who are ill or dying to remain at home or to retain and express their individuality within an institution is another way of affirming the person's uniqueness and value. Hospice programs often encourage older adults who are ill or dying to identify achievable goals in craftwork or other ways of making tangible gifts to give to others. Passing on such gifts or valued personal items can be a cherished activity in itself and a way of leaving behind an enduring legacy. Accepting such gifts with warmth and appreciation is not an expression of a wish for the death of an older adult but rather an act of affection.

Copyright © Stefan Verwey

Participating in Decisions about Their Lives

In Western society, autonomy or the ability to be in charge of one's own life is a prized value for many individuals. This may be particularly true for older adults, who may already have experienced a number of losses and who are often concerned with issues related to dependence. Older adults often want to continue to take part in decisions about their own lives, insofar as that is possible. They may have a very broad and active role in such decision making, or that role might be highly constrained and largely symbolic. Nevertheless, it will usually be regarded as important and should be sustained as much as possible, as former President Jimmy Carter has pointed out (see Personal Insights 15.2).

Fostering autonomy may require delicate negotiations between a specific older adult, his or her family members, and professional care providers (Norlander & McSteen, 2001). For example, many older adults desire to remain in their own homes at the end of their lives (Gott et al., 2004). For such individuals, the decision to enter a long-term care facility may become a matter of contention between older adults and other family members; in some cases, it may lead to a kind of

Jimmy Carter, on Aging and Facing Death

We are not alone in our worry about both the physical aspects of aging and the prejudice that exists toward the elderly, which is similar to racism or sexism. What makes it different is that the prejudice also exists among those of us who are either within this group or rapidly approaching it. When I mentioned the title of this book to a few people, most of them responded, "Virtues? What could possibly be good about growing old?" The most obvious answer, of course, is to consider the alternative to aging. But there are plenty of other good answers—many based on our personal experiences and observations. . . .

Perhaps the most troubling aspect of our later years is the need to face the inevitability of our own impending physical death. For some people, this fact becomes a cause of great distress, sometimes with attendant resentment against God or even those around us. . . .

We can either face death with fear, anguish, and unnecessary distress among those around us or, through faith and courage, confront the inevitable with equanimity, good humor, and peace. When other members of my family realized that they had a terminal illness, the finest medical care was available to them. But each chose to forego elaborate artificial life-support systems and, with a few friends and family members at their bedside, they died peacefully. All of them retained their life-long character and their personal dignity. During the final days of their lives they continued to enjoy themselves as well as possible and to reduce the suffering and anguish of those who survived. My older sister Gloria was surrounded by her biker friends and talked about Harley-Davidsons and their shared pleasures on the road. Her funeral cortege, in fact, was a hearse preceded by thirty-seven Harley-Davidson motorcycles. Until the end, my brother Billy and my mother retained their superb sense of humor, and my youngest sister, Ruth, was stalwart in her faith as an evangelist.

Rosalynn and I hope to follow in their footsteps, and we have signed living wills that will preclude the artificial prolongation of our lives.

Source: Carter, 1998, pp. 8–9, 82, 85–86.

learned helplessness when the older adult's wishes are not supported or validated (Solomon, 1982).

As a culture, American society has long valued individualism and autonomy. However, it is only lately that our society has gradually come to realize—in theory, at least—the need that older adults in particular have for autonomy and the values that it represents. Thus, according to the Patient Self-Determination Act, which went into effect in 1991, individuals who are admitted to a health care facility must be informed of their rights to fill out a living will or health care proxy, grant someone their durable power of attorney in health care matters, or otherwise have their wishes about treatment recorded and respected (Annenberg Washington Program, 1993; Cate & Gill, 1991). This procedure contributes to positive mental health and general satisfaction with life (Rodin & Langer, 1977). In other words, encouraging older adults to participate in decision making about their own lives works against premature psychosocial and even physical decline and death—in older adults who may have felt beset by loss of control and other external or internal pressures that undermine autonomy and quality of life and that foster hopelessness, helplessness, and "giving up" (Maizler et al., 1983; Schulz, 1976; Verwoerdt, 1976).

Being Reassured That Their Lives Still Have Value

As already noted, in a youth-oriented society, ageism can foster discrimination against and devaluation of the lives of older adults. Combined with losses that such older adults may have experienced, such as those involved in retirement or in bodily functioning, this attitude may encourage older persons to depreciate their own value and sense of worth. Life-threatening illness or dying may compound this process of devaluation by older adults and others. Reduced contacts with significant others may lead to isolation and justified or unjustified concerns about social death even when physical death is not imminent. At least for some older adults, a lasting dimension of quality of life involves the possibility or impossibility of expressing one's sexuality and sexual needs (Verwoerdt et al., 1969; Weinberg, 1969). Sexuality may take the form of sexual intercourse, but often it involves no more than simple touching or hugging, as we saw in the vignette near the beginning of this chapter.

The hospice philosophy, with its emphasis on life and maximizing present quality in living, points the way to an antidote to this sort of devaluation of the lives of elderly persons. Conveying to older adults—even those who are coping with life-threatening illness and dying—that their lives are still valued and appreciated, that they are important to and have much to teach others, and that they can still find satisfaction in living can enhance their sense of self-worth. Simple things like not talking down to older adults, or not assuming deafness or incompetence on their part, can do much to foster self-esteem and dignity. Showing family members how to be involved in constructive ways in the life and care of an older adult who is ill or dying can improve present quality in living and diminish feelings of guilt or frustration for all concerned (Kaufman, 1986).

Receiving Appropriate and Adequate Health Care

Studies conducted many years ago in both the United States (Sudnow, 1967) and Great Britain (Simpson, 1976) demonstrated that older adults who were brought to hospital emergency rooms in critical condition were likely to receive care that was not as thorough or vigorous as that provided to younger persons. This finding raises questions of equity and issues of decision making that may often be difficult, particularly for those who are critically ill, dying, vulnerable, and perhaps alone or not fully competent (Matulonis, 2004; Sheehan & Schirm, 2003). Constructive lessons drawn from the life-affirming orientation of hospice programs, as well as positive developments in geriatric medicine and in gerontological specializations in other fields such as nursing, social work, and law, can do much to change

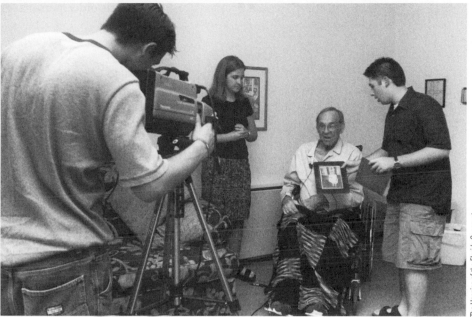

Recording precious memories can be a valuable part of a lifetime legacies project.

this situation (e.g., Karp & Wood, 2003). Older adults who are coping with life-threatening illness or dying have helped to create and support societal health care and welfare systems. In return, such systems should address their health care needs appropriately. Through political action and organizations such as AARP (formerly, the American Association of Retired Persons), older adults are mobilizing to try to ensure that these needs are addressed.

❦ Older Adults Who Are Coping with Bereavement and Grief

Most older adults encounter many occasions for bereavement (Hansson & Stroebe, 2006). We illustrated some of these in the vignette near the beginning of this chapter. Not all of these losses are directly associated with death. However, death-related losses alone offer a broad array of challenges for many elderly persons in the form of the deaths of spouses, life partners, siblings, friends, and peers; the deaths of "very old" parents who may have lived to such advanced old age that their children have now reached "young old" status; the deaths of adult children; and the deaths of grandchildren or great-grandchildren. In addition, there is the special poignancy of the death of a pet or companion animal when its owner is an older adult, as well as the possible impact of physical disability or psychosocial impoverishment. In fact, as Kastenbaum (1969) noted, older adults are likely to experience losses in greater number, variety, and rapidity than any other age group. Consequently, older adults are often exposed to *bereavement overload*, a situation in which they do not have the time or other resources needed to process their grief and mourn one significant loss effectively before another occurs. For such older persons, grief is a constant companion.

Illness, Disability, and Loss

Older adults may be grieving as a result of the many "little deaths" that they have experienced throughout life or in later adulthood. Among these are losses associated with illness of various sorts. Not every older adult experiences such losses, but many live with one or more illness-related burden. For example, high blood pressure and constriction or obstruction in the arteries are common in many older adults, as are certain forms of cancer (lung and prostate cancer in males; lung and breast cancer in females). Even when these conditions are not fatal, they may restrict quality of life. Chronic health problems, such as those involved in arthritis, emphysema, and diabetes, have similar effects.

Some long-term degenerative diseases, such as Alzheimer's and Parkinson's diseases or amyotrophic lateral sclerosis (often called "Lou Gehrig's disease" in the United States), have special import for losses in older adults. These diseases may manifest themselves in ways that are physical (e.g., through pain or loss of muscle control), psychological (e.g., through confusion), social (e.g., through loss of mobility, institutionalization, and limited capacity for social exchanges), or spiritual (as in questions about the meaning of one's life and the goodness of a universe in which these losses occur). They affect both the individual person—for example, an older adult with Alzheimer's disease who may be aware of his or her declining mental function (Larson & Shadlen, 2004; Rauschi, 2001; Taylor, 2006)—and those who love and must care for a person who may become unable to perform even the most basic activities of daily living (Bell & Troxel, 2003; Comer, 2006; Kapust, 1982; Mace & Rabins, 1999). (For the impact on caregivers of these sorts of diseases, see Cox & Monk, 1993; Delgado & Tennstedt, 1997a; and Owen et al., 2001.) Often, these diseases generate the very special problems of complicated or "ambiguous" loss (Boss, 1999) and psychosocial death involved in what Toynbee (1968a, p. 266) has termed "the premature death of the spirit in a human body that still remains physically alive." These issues stand alongside very difficult problems of decision making, appropriate modes of care, and costs.

Less dramatic, but still significant in terms of well-being, are the accumulated losses or deficits that older adults often experience in effective functioning. These can include sensory and cognitive impairments, oral and dental problems, loss of energy, reduced muscle strength, diminished sense of balance, and problems related to osteoporosis, arthritis, or sexual functioning. Specific losses like these and their combined effect on an individual older adult can reduce quality in living and generate regret on the part of that person, family members, and care providers for what has been lost.

The Death of a Spouse, Life Partner, Sibling, Friend, or Other Significant Peer

Surviving the death of a spouse, sibling, life partner, friend, or other significant peer is a common experience in older adulthood (Bennett & Bennett, 2001; Carr, Nesse, & Wortman, 2005; Walter, 2003). The individual who has died may be a marriage partner, a brother or sister, an individual of the same or opposite sex with whom one has lived for some time and formed a stable relationship, or a special friend or peer. One problem for some older adults (particularly among the "very old" group) may be the loss through death or incapacitation of most or all of the members of one's family of origin. Survivors of losses of this type constitute a special group of "lonely oldies" whose particular form of loneliness and deprivation may not be assuaged even by the joy they find in the presence and attention of members of younger generations.

In general, sustaining roles and relationships is crucial for most older adults who are bereaved. The most important of these roles and relationships may include companionship, someone with whom one can talk, someone with whom to share burdens, pleasures, and sexual gratification, and someone to offer presence and care in the future as one's own needs increase (Lopata, 1996; Lund, 1989). When the relationship with the partner is such that their lives are closely interwoven, "the loss of one partner may cut across the very meaning of the other's existence" (Raphael, 1983, p. 177). Of course, most relationships with a partner are complicated in some ways and are not without conflict. Still, every older adult experiences multiple losses in the death of a significant peer, and those who have experienced the death of a spouse or life partner may be at higher risk during the following year for increased morbidity and mortality (from illness or suicide, for example) (Glick et al., 1974; Stroebe & Stroebe, 2003).

The death of a spouse or close companion in late adulthood often generates bereavement experiences of separation and deprivation involving grief (including yearning, pain, and anger), isolation, and loneliness (D'Epinay et al., 2003; Worden, 2002). In our society, the burdens of survival following the death of a spouse most often fall upon women (Hurd & Macdonald, 2001). In the United States, women outlive men on the average, and women most often marry men who are their own age or older. In addition, widowers are more likely than widows to remarry (Carey, 1979), partly because of the relative availability of potential spouses for elderly males (and the opposite for elderly females). However, many widowers are resilient, and it is not the case that all older adults who are widowed wish to marry again (Moore & Stratton, 2002). In any event, emotional ties to the deceased are likely to persist, and memories may be cherished by both sexes (Moss & Moss, 1984). Thus, it may not be so much the experience of bereavement as its expression that is influenced by gender roles.

Both in place of or as a supplement to other forms of social support, self-help groups (Lund et al., 1985; Yalom & Vinogradov, 1988) and Widow-to-Widow programs (Silverman, 1969, 1986, 2004) have been found to be very helpful for older adults who are bereaved, as we saw in Chapters 10 and 11. Social interventions of this type typically serve the full range of bereaved persons who have experienced certain kinds of losses (not only those evaluated as "high risk") and do so on a foundation of shared experience. Through these interventions, individuals who have had similar bereavement experiences can share feelings and problems. They can also encourage each other to regain control in living by evaluating options and alternatives represented in the lives of the others. Also, older adults who are bereaved can obtain helpful information about loss, grief, and living.

The Death of an Adult Child

To a parent, one's offspring always remains one's child in some important ways despite his or her age. In the United States, as average life expectancy increases, it becomes increasingly likely that middle-aged and elderly parents may experience the deaths of an *adult child*. For example, many young adults in their twenties and thirties who die in accidents or from communicable diseases and individuals in their forties, fifties, and sixties who die of degenerative diseases may leave behind a surviving parent (Rando, 1986b). In fact, one study (Moss et al., 1986) reported that as many as 10 percent of elderly persons with children had experienced the death of a child when the parent was 60 years of age or older.

For such a parent, the grief felt at this type of loss may be combined with special developmental complications (Blank, 1998; Brubaker, 1985; Moss et al., 1986). For example, surviving parents may feel that the death of an adult child is an untimely violation of the natural order of things, in which members of the older generation are expected to die before the younger (see Personal Insights 15.3). Such parents may experience survivor guilt and wish to have died in place of their child. In addition, there may be special hardships if the adult child had assumed certain responsibilities as helper or care provider for the parent. After the death, these needs will have to be met in some other way, and the parent may face an increased likelihood of institutionalization or of diminished social contacts. How family legacies will be carried forward is less certain. The parent may also join to his or her own sense of loss added regret and grief for the pain that the spouse or children of the adult child are experiencing. In all too many cases, the older survivor may be obliged to take over the care of surviving grandchildren (Hayslip & Goldberg-Glen, 2000).

The Death of a Grandchild or Great-Grandchild

If it is more likely that children and adolescents will have living grandparents and great-grandparents because of increased life expectancy among older adults, then it is also more likely that these older adults will experience the death of one of their grandchildren or great-grandchildren. This area of bereavement is not well studied, even though it is recognized that cross-generational relationships between grandchildren and grandparents can involve special bonds of intimacy (Wilcoxon, 1986).

Grandparents have been described as *forgotten grievers* (Gyulay, 1975), both connected to and distanced from events involving the fatal illness, death, or bereavement of a grandchild. The grief and mourning of such grandparents responds to their own losses, to the losses experienced by their son or daughter, and to the losses experienced by the grandchild. Such grief may contain elements of hurt over such an "out of sequence" death, anger at parents who perhaps did not seem to take adequate care of the grandchild, guilt at their own presumed failure to prevent the loss or death, and resentment at God for letting such tragic events occur (Galinsky, 1999; Reed, 2000). All of these reactions may be complicated in a situation in which there is unwillingness to acknowledge certain causes of death (such as suicide or HIV infection) or to discuss openly the circumstances of the death. Finally, there may be conflicts between grandparents and one or more surviving parent—for example, when members of the older or younger generation blame the others for

Lament of a Man for His Son

Son, my son!
I will go up to the mountain
And there I will light a fire
To the feet of my son's spirit,
And there will I lament him;
Saying,
O my son,
What is my life to me, now you are departed!

Son, my son,
In the deep earth
We softly laid thee in a Chief's robe,
In a warrior's gear.
Surely there,
In the spirit land
Thy deeds attend thee!
Surely,
The corn comes to the ear again!

But I, here,
I am the stalk that the seed-gatherers
Descrying empty, afar, left standing
Son, my son!
What is my life to me, now you are departed?

a perceived failure to prevent the death or when grandparents are drawn into or otherwise affected by disputes between the surviving parents.

Loss of a Pet or Companion Animal

We discussed pet loss in Chapter 10, but it is important to note that loss of a pet or companion animal can be of great and special importance in the lives of older adults (Peretti, 1990; Sable, 1995). Companion animals can be sources of unconditional love, as well as objects of care and affection in the lives of many older adults. Some of these animals protect and aid the handicapped. In recent years, others have become welcome visitors in many nursing homes, long-term care facilities, and other institutions. In these roles, companion animals can relieve loneliness, contribute to a sense of purpose, and enhance self-esteem (Rynearson, 1978).

When an older adult's companion animal dies, it becomes immediately obvious that the key point is the relationship with that animal, rather than its intrinsic value (Lagoni et al., 1994). Such a loss can represent a major bereavement for an elderly person who may otherwise have only limited social contacts (Quackenbush, 1985; Shirley & Mercier, 1983; Toray, 2004) and thus should not be dismissed as insignificant. Similar losses and grief may occur when an older adult is no longer able to care for an animal, cannot pay for veterinary services it needs, cannot take it along when relocating to new living quarters or to an institution, or must have a sick or feeble animal euthanized (Kay et al., 1988). Older adults may also be concerned about what will happen to a prized pet if they should die.

🐦 Suicide among Older Adults

Although suicide is no longer among the ten leading causes of death for older adults in our society, it was the cause of death for 5,198 individuals 65 years of age and older in the United States in 2004 (Miniño et al., 2007; McIntosh, 2006). These deaths among older adults represent 16 percent of all deaths by suicide in the United States in 2004, an unusual proportion since older adults make up only 12.4 of the total population in our society. This number of suicide deaths in this relatively small segment of the population means that very high rates of suicide in the United States are found among the oldest members of our society. In 2004, those rates were 16.3 per 100,000 among those who were 75–84 years of age and 16.4 per 100,000 among those who were 85 years of age and older (Miniño et al., 2007; McIntosh, 2006). This last figure has declined since 2000, when it was 19.4 per 100,000 (see Table 17.1), but suicide rates for all older adults in our society are considerably higher than the rate of 11.1 suicides per 100,000 for the U.S. population as a whole or the rate of 10.4 suicides per 100,000 among individuals 15–24 years of age. Among older adults, Caucasian-American males are by far the most likely to take their own lives. In general, older adults are less likely to attempt suicide than their younger counterparts, but far more deliberate once they have chosen their course. Older adults are unlikely to ask for help that might interfere with or alter their decision, and they are unlikely to fail to complete the suicidal act once they have undertaken the attempt (Butler & Lewis, 1982; Farberow & Moriwaki, 1975; McIntosh, 1985). Therefore, any indicators of suicidal tendencies on the part of older adults should be taken seriously and evaluated carefully.

The single most significant factor associated with suicidal behavior in older adults is *depression* (Leenaars et al., 1992; Osgood, 1992). Another important variable may be institutionalization in a long-term care facility (Osgood et al., 1991). Older adults may begin to contemplate suicide when the *life review* process results in a sense of despair about the meaning of their lives; when they experience physical or mental debility; when they experience the death of a spouse or other significant person (especially a person on whom they had been dependent for care and support); or when confinement in an institution seems to undermine control over their lives. In these circumstances, some may come to consider suicide an acceptable alternative to continued living under what appear to them to be unsatisfactory conditions (Segal et al., 2004). Other factors—such as the impact of an unwanted layoff or retirement on males whose identity had hitherto been greatly dependent on their vocational roles (a factor that is increasingly likely to impact women as they move into similar vocational roles), previous dependency on a now-deceased female caretaker (Campbell & Silverman, 1996; Kohn & Kohn, 1978), or social isolation—appear to account for much higher rates (rising with age) of male than female suicides among older adults (Miller, 1979; Osgood, 1992).

In American society, there are a number of obstacles to interventions designed to minimize the likelihood of suicidal behavior among older adults. Some of these obstacles arise from efforts to apply interventions that have been successful with younger persons in ways that are inappropriate to the developmental situation of older adults. For example, claims that suicide is a permanent solution to a temporary problem apply more aptly to impulsive decisions by adolescents than to decisions arising from an older adult's long deliberation. Equally, advice to concentrate on a promising future or to consider interpersonal obligations to others seems better suited to younger persons than to older adults with less rosy expectations and diminished social relationships. Again, arguing that suicide terminates life prematurely and cuts short a full life is less obviously relevant to a person in old age. Also, some argue that efforts intended to thwart suicidal behavior in older adults are inappropriate assaults on the autonomy of older adults, although others make a vigorous case that too-ready tolerance of suicide among older adults may reflect lack of interest in the lives of such individuals (Moody, 1984; Osgood, 1992).

In the end, suicidal behavior among older adults needs to be understood within the broad physical, psychosocial, and developmental situation of older adults in American society (Osgood, 2000). Particular attention must be paid to social attitudes associated with ageism, a devaluation of worth and meaning in the lives of older adults, and an unresponsiveness to the needs of older adults. Significant changes in these and other sociocultural factors will be required to alter suicidal behavior in older adults.

🍎 Summary

In this chapter, we explored many aspects of interactions between older adults and death in our society. We saw that the distinctive developmental tasks of older adulthood (striving to achieve ego integrity versus despair) have a direct bearing on how older adults relate to death. These tasks influence encounters with death among older adults (we noted high death rates mainly brought about by long-term degenerative diseases) and attitudes of older adults toward death (in general, manifesting less anxiety than younger persons). We noted the importance for older adults who are coping with life-threatening illness and dying to maintain a sense of self, participate in decisions regarding their lives, be reassured that their lives still have value, and receive appropriate and adequate health care services. We considered that older adults may find themselves coping with bereavement and grief as a result of illness, disability, and loss; the death of a spouse, life partner, sibling, or other significant peer; the death of an adult child; the death of a grandchild or great-grandchild; or the loss of a pet or companion animal. We also observed that high rates of suicide among older adults are strongly associated with depression.

Glossary

An adult child: an individual who is an adult, but also the living child of an older parent

Ageism: Butler's term for the systematic stereotyping of and discrimination against people because they are old

Bereavement overload: Kastenbaum's phrase for a situation in which individuals (especially older adults) do not have the time or other resources needed to process their grief and mourn one significant loss effectively before another occurs

Developmental eras in older adulthood: most often, older adults (elderly persons, golden-agers, senior citizens) or "the old" are treated as if they were a single developmental cohort; recently, however, some writers have begun to make distinctions in older adulthood between the "young old" (those 65–74 years of age), the "old old" (those 75–84 years of age), and the "oldest old" or "very old" (those 85 years of age and older), even though these are properly chronological rather than developmental distinctions

Developmental tasks in late adulthood: conceptualized by Erikson as involving a tension between "ego integrity" versus "despair"; successfully resolving this polarity is said to lead to the virtues of "renunciation and wisdom"

Ego integrity: Erikson's term to describe the attainment of an inner sense of wholeness; also described as "self-actualization" or "reconciliation"

Forgotten grievers: a term sometimes applied to grandparents who experience a double loss over the death of a grandchild and over the losses experienced by that child's parent(s) (their son or daughter)

The "graying" of America: a term designating the fact that older adults are a growing portion of the U.S. population

Late adulthood: an alternative phrase for "older adulthood"

Life review: a process of introspection, heightened interiority, self-reflection, and reminiscence, designed to resolve old conflicts and achieve a new sense of meaning as means to achieve integrity, account to oneself for one's past life, and prepare for death (Butler)

Maturity: the term that Erikson substituted for "senescence" to designate the concluding period in the human life course; now more commonly replaced by "older adulthood" or "late adulthood"

Normative developmental task of older adulthood: the achievement of ego integrity (versus despair or disgust; according to Erikson); self-actualization (Maslow); reconciliation (Birren)

Older adulthood: an era in the human life course that follows "middle adulthood" or "middle age"; sometimes called "late adulthood"; includes those who are

65 years of age or older; encompasses distinctions within this era between the "young old," the "old old," and the "very old"

Senescence: Erikson's original term for the last era in the human life course; replaced by the term *maturity*

Suicide among older adults: in recent years older adults in the United States have had the highest rate of suicide among all developmental groups; this behavior is frequently very deliberate and often associated with depression

Questions for Review and Discussion

1. Think back to the situation of the elderly couple described in the vignette near the beginning of this chapter. What types of losses did they experience? How did those losses affect them? How did they help each other?

2. Do you know an older adult who has experienced significant death-related losses? What were those losses like for that person? How did you or could you help such a person?

Suggested Readings

On aging and older adults, consult:

Butler, R. N. (1975). *Why Survive? Being Old in America.*

Erikson, E. H., Erikson, J. M., & Kivnick, H. (1986). *Vital Involvements in Old Age.*

Nouwen, H., & Gaffney, W. J. (1990). *Aging: The Fulfillment of Life.*

Perls, T. T., Silver, M. H., & Lauerman, J. F. (2000). *Living to 100: Lessons in Living to Your Maximum Potential at Any Age.*

Thorson, J. A. (2000a). *Aging in a Changing Society.*

Thorson, J. A. (Ed.). (2000b). *Perspectives on Spiritual Well-Being and Aging.*

On death, loss, and older adults, consult:

Campbell, S., & Silverman, P. (1996). *Widower: When Men Are Left Alone.*

Carr, D., Nesse, R., & Wortman, C. (Eds.). (2005). *Spousal Bereavement in Late Life.*

Doka, K. J. (Ed.). (2002b). *Living with Grief: Loss in Later Life.*

Galinsky, N. (1999). *When a Grandchild Dies: What to Do, What to Say, How to Cope.*

Hansson, R. O., & Stroebe, M. S. (2006). *Bereavement in Late Life: Coping, Adaptation and Developmental Influences.*

Hurd, M., & Macdonald, M. (2001). *Beyond Coping: Widows Reinventing Their Lives.*

Leenaars, A. A., Maris, R. W., McIntosh, J. L., & Richman, J. (Eds.). (1992). *Suicide and the Older Adult.*

Lopata, H. Z. (1996). *Current Widowhood; Myths and Realities.*

Lund, D. A. (1989). *Older Bereaved Spouses: Research with Practical Applications.*

Norlander, L., & McSteen, K. (2001). *Choices at the End of Life: Finding Out What Your Parents Want before It's Too Late.*

Osgood, N. J. (1992). *Suicide in Later Life: Recognizing the Warning Signs.*

Osgood, N. J., Brant, B. A., & Lipman, A. (1991). *Suicide among the Elderly in Long-Term Care Facilities.*

Reed, M. L. (2000). *Grandparents Cry Twice: Help for Bereaved Grandparents.*

Stroebe, W., & Stroebe, M. S. (2003). *Bereavement and Health: The Psychological and Physical Consequences of Partner Loss.*

Walter, C. A. (2003). *The Loss of a Life Partner: Narratives of the Bereaved.*

Selected Web Resources

Some useful search terms include: AGEISM; CAUSES OF DEATH IN OLDER ADULTS; DEVELOPMENTAL TASKS IN OLDER ADULTS; EGO INTEGRITY; GRAYING OF AMERICA; LATE ADULTHOOD; OLDER ADULTHOOD; PET LOSS; SENESCENCE; SUICIDE AND OLDER ADULTS; SURVIVOR GUILT

Visit the book companion website for *Death & Dying, Life & Living, Sixth Edition,* at academic.cengage.com/psychology/corr for all URLs and live links to the following *organizational and other Internet sites:*

Administration on Aging, U.S. Department of Health and Human Services

American Association of Retired Persons (AARP)

The Center for Practical Bioethics

Ethnic Elders Care

Living to 100

National Institute of Aging

SeniorNet

Widowed Persons Service (WPS)

PART SIX

Legal, Conceptual, and Moral Issues

❧ In Chapters 16 through 19, we address legal, conceptual, moral, religious, and philosophical issues that are directly related to dying, death, and bereavement. Issues related to the law, suicide, assisted suicide and euthanasia, and questions of ultimate meaning are brought together here because they pose vital conceptual and moral challenges. In addressing these issues, one must undertake two parallel tasks: first, to *understand* the facts and implications of the situation at hand, along with the options that are available; second, to *choose* one's values and a particular course of action within the situation.

We begin with *legal issues* because the law is the most explicit framework of rules and procedures that a society establishes within its death system. In Chapter 16 we describe what the American legal system requires or permits before, at the time of, and after death. These discussions include advance directives for health care; definition, determination, and certification of death; organ, tissue, and body donation; and disposition of one's body and property.

In Chapter 17, we seek to clarify the concept of *suicide*, provide data about some common patterns in suicidal and life-threatening behavior, describe some perspectives that may help to explain this behavior, discuss its impact on bereaved survivors, suggest constructive ways to intervene to minimize the likelihood of a completed suicide, introduce the concept of rational suicide, and identify selected religious views about suicide.

In Chapter 18, we clarify the concepts of *assisted suicide and euthanasia,* describe moral and religious arguments that have been advanced to favor or oppose such activities, and illustrate what they might mean for social policy through examples taken from the Netherlands and the state of Oregon.

In Chapter 19, we address questions of ultimate values by examining *the meaning and place of death in human life.* Many religious and philosophical perspectives seek answers to these questions. Such perspectives are frameworks within which both individuals and particular societies approach death-related experiences. We also explore in this chapter reports about near-death experiences and their interpretation.

CHAPTER 16

Legal Issues

Organ & Tissue Donation
Share your life... USA 32

© AP Photo/U.S. Postal Service

Objectives of This Chapter

◆ To describe the origin and nature of formal legal systems as they relate to death-related events

◆ To explain the nature and role of advance directives for health care

◆ To explore legal issues associated with definition, determination, and certification of death

◆ To examine topics related to organ, tissue, and body donation

◆ To review subjects related to disposition of one's body and one's property or estate

🐾 Donor Husband, Donor Father

It was October 28, 1992, and Kenneth Moritsugu, M.D., M.P.H., was returning to his home in Silver Spring, Maryland, from Baltimore. He had taken his aunt and sister, visiting from Hawaii, on a day trip to visit art museums and the Inner Harbor—a mammoth shopping complex along the waterfront. His wife, Donna Lee, had elected to stay home.

As the three approached the end of their commute, traffic slowed. An accident had taken place, they thought. A long, tedious drive lay ahead as every car strained to advance.

As they approached the scene of the accident, Dr. Moritsugu looked out his window. He noticed the similarities in the wrecked vehicle and the car at home, the one Donna Lee drove. Panic set in as he realized the crushed vehicle on the road was in fact his wife's.

At the hospital, he learned Donna Lee was brain dead and would never recover.

"Several years before, we had talked about what we should do when the other died," Dr. Moritsugu recalled. "We had both said we wanted to donate. When the concept was brought up in that deepest, darkest moment, the memory of that conversation came back to me, and I had the privilege of carrying out her wishes. Because of her, many other individuals are surviving today."

A year later, Dr. Moritsugu, Assistant Surgeon General of the United States and Medical Director of the Federal Bureau of Prisons of the U.S. Department of Justice, began a personal crusade to encourage organ and tissue donation. . . .

[Dr. Moritsugu] has suffered the bittersweet solace of donation not only once, but twice.

In 1996 Dr. Moritsugu's 22-year-old daughter, Vikki Lianne, was struck by an automobile while crossing the street. She, too, was declared brain dead and her organs donated.

It was only later that Dr. Moritsugu learned that Vikki Lianne and his older daughter, Erika Elizabeth, had made the commitment to donate their organs shortly after their mother's death. They had learned how much the donations had meant to others, and they had seen the comfort it had brought their family.

"It makes me proud," Dr. Moritsugu said. "We talk about donation as affecting one person, but there are ripples. Each donation affects so many more people—family, friends, colleagues." Dr. Moritsugu is quick to point out that he should not be credited for the donations. "I didn't do anything," he noted. "I was just someone who happened to be there. They [Donna Lee and Vikki Lianne] are the ones who made the miracle."

Through Donna Lee:

- ◆ A marine biologist engaged in research on the effects of environmental pollution received a new heart.
- ◆ A 35-year-old diabetic hospital custodian received a kidney and pancreas.
- ◆ An 11-year-old child on dialysis, failing in school, received the other kidney. He is now making straight As and is on his way to college.
- ◆ A retired schoolteacher received a new liver.

- A young retarded woman who had lost her sight due to an accident received a cornea, while the other cornea provided new vision to a 49-year-old government worker.

Through Vikki Lianne:

- A mother of five received a new heart.
- A widow with four children received a lung.
- A 59-year-old man, an active volunteer with a local charitable organization, received a liver.
- A widower with one daughter received a kidney.
- A married, working father of several children received the other kidney.
- A 26-year-old man and a 60-year-old woman received her corneas.

(*Source:* Benenson, E. [1988]. Donor husband, donor father: UNOS board member Kenneth Moritsugu looks beyond tragedy to serving others. *UNOS Update.* [Special edition, Spring], 26. Reprinted with permission.)

American Society and Its Laws

Every society develops a more or less formal system of law to serve its interests as a community and to promote the welfare of its members. Such a system may include both written and unwritten rules and procedures. These rules and procedures reflect values upheld by a society, as well as ways in which it organizes itself to implement those values.

Any such system of societal rules and procedures is likely to function most effectively when social values are well established and when it is responding to familiar events. It may be less effective when there is a lack of consensus about social values, when the values are in flux, or when social changes and progress pose new problems not easily addressed by existing legal frameworks. In recent years in the United States, challenges to the legal system have arisen from all three of these circumstances: there is disagreement in our heterogeneous population about some social values, other social values appear to be in transition, and new challenges have arisen from new circumstances and from new medical procedures and technology.

Our federal system assigns certain obligations (such as foreign relations and defense) to the national government and reserves most other responsibilities to the authority of the individual states and their subordinate entities. For most issues related to death, dying, and bereavement, state law governs what is to be done and how it is to be done. This results in different laws and procedures applying in different states. Some states might even have no legislation on a given subject. Thus, this chapter can only address legal issues and structures in a general way. Individuals should seek competent legal advice that is appropriate to their particular situations.

The establishment of *legislation* is often a slow and complicated process subject to political pressures, competing interests, and social circumstances. When values in society are changing or when there is no consensus on social values, the process of embodying and codifying those values in legislation may not go forward easily.

Difficult cases may frustrate a society in its process of determining how to implement its values. This is particularly true in cases that involve fast-moving advances in medical technology and procedures.

When no specific legislation covers a specific subject, decisions must still be made in individual cases. One way this is done is by drawing on precedents set by prior court decisions. Such prior decisions and precedents constitute *case law*.

When neither the legislature nor the courts in their prior decisions have addressed a topic, the legal system turns to *common law*. Originally, this was a set of shared values and views drawn from English and early American legal and social history. In practice, it is typically represented in a more formal way by the definitions contained in standard legal dictionaries, such as *Black's Law Dictionary* (Garner, 2004).

It is important to be clear about which type(s) of legal rules and procedures apply to any given issue. The principles set forth here constitute the broad legal and social framework within which a large spectrum of moral, social, and human issues is addressed in American society. This legal framework is an important part of the contemporary American death system, but only one such component. Some death-related issues, such as cemetery regulations and cultural or religious rituals, are not directly addressed by the legal system. Other issues, such as assisted suicide and euthanasia (see Chapter 18), have challenged our legal system and remain wholly or partly outside its framework.

❦ Advance Directives for Health Care

The phrase *advance directives* applies to a wide range of instructions that one might make orally or set down in writing about actions that one would or would not want to be taken if one were somehow incapacitated and unable to join in making decisions (Burnell, 2008; Haman, 2004; Shenkman & Klein, 2004; Williams, 1991). Of course, any advance directive depends on an individual's willingness to address ahead of time the implications of death for his or her life and the lives of his or her family members and friends. Many people are reluctant to consider issues of this sort, perhaps because they involve contemplating the implications of one's own mortality. Our vignette near the beginning of this chapter makes clear that Donna Lee and Vikki Lianne Moritsugu had at least discussed organ donation with some family members before their untimely deaths.

Since 1991, the Patient Self-Determination Act has required that individuals being admitted to a health care institution that receives federal Medicare or Medicaid funds be informed of their right to accept or refuse treatment and to execute an advance directive (Zucker, 2007). Such individuals must also be told about the options available to them to implement those rights (Urich, 2001). Even so, many do not exercise their right to complete an advance directive—but that, too, is within their rights.

Some advance directives are intended to come into force at the time of one's death—for example, directives on organ and tissue donation, the disposition of one's body, or the distribution of one's estate. We discuss those directives later in this chapter. First, we consider advance directives concerned with decisions about treatment before death, such as living wills, durable powers of attorney in health care matters, and the "Five Wishes" document.

Living Wills

Living wills were originally developed in the early 1970s as a means whereby persons who were competent decision makers could express their wishes to professional care providers, family members, and friends about interventions that they might or might not wish to permit in the event of a terminal illness. In particular, living wills set forth a set of prior instructions for situations in which a terminal illness has left an individual unable to make or to express such decisions.

Originally, living wills had no legal standing and could take any form. A "living will" was simply any sort of document through which an individual could express various wishes about treatment prior to death. The common threads of these early living wills were: (1) a concern about the possibility or likelihood of finding oneself in a situation in which one would be unable to take part in making important decisions; and (2) a concern about the context of dying in which one might be in an unfamiliar or alien environment, among strangers or others who might have their own individual or professional views of what should or should not be done, and who might not understand, appreciate, or agree with the wishes of the person who wrote the living will.

In response to concerns of this sort, early living wills usually combined a desire expressed by those who composed and signed them; a request that the desire be given serious consideration by those providing care to the signers; and an effort to share responsibility for certain decisions made in specified situations. For this last point, living wills could be understood as an effort by those who composed them to protect health care providers from accusations of malpractice, as well as from civil liability or criminal prosecution. However we interpret their context, living wills represent a desire to promote individual autonomy in death-related matters by thinking ahead about issues of life and death, formulating one's views concerning important decisions, and communicating them to others.

In the absence of legal standing or requirements, individuals and organizations could formulate living wills any way they wished. Early efforts to standardize the form and language of living wills typically focused on a directive to withhold or withdraw treatments that merely prolong dying when one is in an incurable or irreversible condition with no reasonable expectation of recovery, and a directive to limit interventions in such circumstances to those designed to provide comfort and relieve pain.

Note that living wills characteristically do not call for direct killing or active euthanasia. Most often, they explicitly state: "I am not asking that my life be directly taken, but that my dying be not unreasonably prolonged." Most living wills are primarily intended to refuse certain kinds of cure-oriented interventions ("artificial means" and "heroic measures") when they are no longer relevant ("futile care," that is, care that can no longer be expected to produce a cure), to request that dying be permitted to take its own natural course, and to ask that suffering associated with life-threatening illness be mitigated with effective palliative care, even if such palliative care should have a collateral or side effect of hastening the actual moment of death.

The broad legal context for living wills is the well-established *right to privacy* and the right of competent decision makers to give or withhold informed consent, to accept or refuse interventions even when that might affect the timing of the individual's death (Alderman & Kennedy, 1997; Annas, 2004; President's Commission, 1982, 1983a, 1983b; Rozovsky, 1990; Smith, 2002).

In 1976, the California legislature enacted the first "natural death" or "living will" legislation. Since then, similar legislation (sometimes with local variations) has been passed in all 50 states and the District of Columbia. Typically, such legislation: (1) specifies the conditions under which a competent adult is authorized to sign a document of this type; (2) stipulates the form that such a document must take to have legal force; (3) defines what sorts of interventions can or cannot be refused—for example, interventions undertaken with a view toward cure, which may or may not include hydration or nutrition; (4) authorizes oral or written repudiation of the signed document by the signer at any time; (5) requires that professional care providers either cooperate with the document's directives or withdraw from the case and arrange for alternative care (consenting to do so is thus legally protected, whereas failure to do so is theoretically subject not merely to potential malpractice liability but also to penalties that could extend in principle to loss of professional licensure); and (6) stipulates that death resulting from actions authorized by the legislation is not to be construed for insurance purposes as suicide.

A presidential commission (President's Commission, 1982) and other agencies have proposed models for legislation on this subject. These proposals typically: (1) relate to all competent adults and mature minors—not only those who are dying; (2) apply to all medical interventions and do not limit the types of interventions that may be refused; (3) permit the designation of a *substitute or surrogate decision maker* in a manner similar to that described in the following section; (4) require health care providers to follow the directives of the individual and incorporate sanctions for those who do not do so; and (5) stipulate that palliative care be continued for those who refuse other interventions. This model goes beyond the scope of early living wills and incorporates features now more typical of durable powers of attorney.

Historically, living wills have not been without their limitations or potential difficulties (see Issues for Critical Reflection #14). Like any documents written down in advance of a complex and life-threatening situation, living wills may not anticipate every relevant feature that may arise. Partly for this reason, their significance and force may be subject to interpretation or dispute among the very family members and professional care providers whom they seek to guide.

Durable Powers of Attorney in Health Care Matters

Because of limitations and potential difficulties associated with living wills, some have preferred an alternative approach. One alternative is found in state legislation that authorizes a *durable power of attorney for the making of decisions in health care matters.* "Power of attorney" is a well-established legal doctrine whereby one individual authorizes another individual (or group of individuals) to make decisions and take actions on behalf of the first individual in specific circumstances or for a specified period of time. For example, a power of attorney might authorize an individual to sign a contract on my behalf to close the sale of a house at a time when I am not available to do so. Historically, a power of attorney or authorization to act in place of some individual continued only while that person remained competent. A "durable" power of attorney is one that endures until it is revoked; that is, it continues in force even (or especially) when the individual who authorized the

#14 What Are Some Criticisms of Living Wills?

Although living wills are intended to and have been claimed to preserve an individual's autonomy, some have argued that they fail to accomplish this. Fagerlin and Schneider (2004) found at least seven problems with living wills, and they argued that these problems were so significant that public policy should not support their use. The problems they identified were:

- Most (up to 80 percent) Americans do not have them, apparently for several reasons, such as: (1) people do not know about living wills; (2) they doubt that they need them; (3) they believe that living wills will not change the treatment they receive; or (4) they find these documents to be incompatible with their cultural traditions (see Chapter 5 on this last point).
- People cannot be certain about what sorts of treatment they will want in the future and may change their mind when confronted with different circumstances.
- A living will is often not able to make clear just what a person's wishes are about the sorts of treatment he or she desires, often because those desires are stated in terms so general that they are of little help, or because desires become so specific that they overwhelm the ability of the person signing them to understand all the specifics.

- The living will may get "lost" and not be available when it is needed.
- The persons interpreting the living will often may not do so accurately in terms of the signer's actual wishes.
- Living wills cannot be shown actually to alter patient care.
- Living wills represent a significant cost to society without providing the desired benefit.

Although these are serious difficulties with living wills and at least some of them have been recognized to be such for some time, even Fagerlin and Schneider do not argue that living wills should be abolished, nor do others who recognize the existence of some of these problems. Thus, Swartzberg (2004, p. 3) argued: "Do I still advise you to have one? Yes I do, simply on the chance that it might do some good. The act of writing the [living] will may help you to understand your own wishes now, as well as providing some guidance for your family." In addition, all of these writers argue that the difficulties with living wills make it even more important to appoint a health care surrogate with durable power of attorney. This latter action, if carried out along with careful, updated communication between the individual and his or her surrogate, should alleviate many of the problems associated with living wills.

designation is no longer able to act as a competent decision maker. A durable power of attorney in health care matters (sometimes called a "health care proxy") is one that is concerned with issues of health care.

Advocates argue that a durable power of attorney has two significant advantages over other written or oral directives, such as a living will. First, it empowers a surrogate or substitute decision maker to make decisions on behalf of an individual in any and all circumstances that the document covers. Second, the surrogate decision maker can be instructed to refuse all interventions, to insist on all interventions, or to approve some interventions and reject others. The first advantage attempts to minimize problems arising from changing circumstances and competing interpretations of written documents; the second allows the person authorizing the surrogate—and the surrogate—some degree of freedom in choosing which interventions to accept and which to refuse.

Durable powers of attorney in health care matters were first authorized in the state of California in 1985. Similar legislation has since been approved in nearly all states and the District of Columbia. Sample documents and booklets explaining durable powers of attorney in health care matters are available from the American Bar Association, AARP, and many local sources, such as hospitals, long-term care facilities, and hospice programs. Note that to be effective any durable power of attorney must satisfy the legislative requirements of the legal jurisdiction within which it is to be enforced. Competent legal advice should be sought to confirm this. Interested parties are usually advised (wherever possible) to complete both a state-authorized living will (providing general guidance to decision makers) and an appropriate durable power of attorney for health care (authorizing discretion within those guidelines on the part of a health care agent or substitute decision maker).

Five Wishes

In 1997, the Florida Commission on Aging with Dignity created a new document called "Five Wishes" that combines many of the best elements of living wills and durable powers of attorney in health care matters. This document is specifically designed to be easy to understand, simple to use, personal in character, and thorough. As the cover page of the document says, it "is a gift to your family members and friends so that they won't have to guess what you want." "Five Wishes" asks the person filling out the document to express his or her wishes about the following issues and provides guidance in relation to each of them: (1) the person I want to make health care decisions for me when I can't make them for myself; (2) the kind of medical treatment I want or don't want if I am close to death, in a coma, or have permanent and severe brain damage and am not expected to recover from that situation, or am in another condition under which I do not wish to be kept alive; (3) how comfortable I want to be; (4) how I want people to treat me; and (5) what I want my loved ones to know.

Because of widespread interest in "Five Wishes," a cooperative effort was undertaken with the American Bar Association (www.abanet.org/aging) to develop a revised version structured to meet the legal requirements of other jurisdictions. At this writing, 6 million copies of the "Five Wishes" document have been distributed. It is valid in 38 states and the District of Columbia; elsewhere it can be used to help individuals offer guidance to their care providers. The entire "Five Wishes" document, along with a video and accompanying booklet (Aging with Dignity, 2001), can be obtained for a nominal fee from Aging with Dignity (P.O. Box 1661, Tallahassee, FL 32302-1661; tel. 888-5-WISHES [888-594-7437] or 850-681-2010) or ordered from its website, www.agingwithdignity.org. There also is a version in Spanish, "Cinco Deseos."

🍎 Definition, Determination, and Certification of Death

The central issues that relate to death itself and the time at which it occurs are definition, determination, and certification of death.

Definition of Death

Definition of death reflects the fundamental human and social understanding of the difference between life and death. This distinction underlies all issues related to determination and certification of death. These issues all involve approaches designed to identify whether the condition that society has defined as death exists. Above all, determination of death must be based on a definition that discriminates between real and only apparent death. This definition is essential to be as clear as possible about who is to be included among those who are alive or dead. It would be just as wrong to treat the dead as if they were living as it would be to treat the living as if they were already dead. The dead are no longer alive; the living are not yet dead.

The difference between being alive and being dead is of course a profoundly important one. Aristotle called death a kind of destruction or perishing involving a change from being to nonbeing (see *Physics,* bk. V, ch. 1; *Metaphysics,* bk. XI, ch. 11). He meant that death involves a change in the very substance of the being. When a human being dies an important consequence follows: there is no longer a human being present—instead, there is only a dead body or a corpse. Because the corpse is still an object deserving honor and respect, it is not simply to be discarded in a cavalier or thoughtless manner. However, it is also important not to confuse the remains with a living human person (Nabe, 1981). That is why two distinct things can be said after a death of a loved one: "These are the hands that held and caressed me" and "Everything that was essential to the person whom I knew and loved is no longer here."

How can we define the condition that we call death, the condition that is the opposite of life? Here is one answer:

> An individual who has sustained either (1) irreversible cessation of circulatory and respiratory functions, or (2) irreversible cessation of all functions of the entire brain, including the brain stem, is dead. (President's Commission, 1981, p. 73)

That definition was codified in the Uniform Determination of Death Act (UDDA; reprinted in Iserson, 1994, p. 611) and has since been adopted (as such or in a closely modified form) by many state legislatures.

Several points in the UDDA are critical:

1. It speaks of "an individual," not "a person," because whether a person is present is precisely the issue.

2. It requires *irreversible*—not merely temporary or reversible—cessation of the designated functions.

3. It recognizes the possibility of situations in which external interventions mask or hide the precise status of respiratory and circulatory functions—in

which it may be unclear whether the individual is actually sustaining those functions spontaneously or is even capable of doing so.

4. In such circumstances, the UDDA requires evaluation of the capacities of the central nervous system—which is the body's command and control center—because the definition recognizes that under normal circumstances, the life of the central nervous system ends shortly (a matter of a few minutes) after respiratory and circulatory functions are brought to a halt.

5. Finally, and most important, in such circumstances, it concludes that irreversible cessation of all functions of the brain and brain stem (which controls autonomic activities, such as respiration and circulation) is the condition understood as death.

Some have proposed that the irreversible loss of the capacity for bodily integration and social interaction is sufficient to define the death of a human being (Veatch, 1975, 1976). If so, neocortical or upper brain activity (excluding lower brain or brain stem activity) would be definitive of the presence or absence of human life (Karakatsanis & Tsanakas, 2002). In this case, a human person could be considered to be dead even when bodily or vegetative functioning remained. In other words, this proposal would regard the presence of a "persistent vegetative state" as the equivalent of death (Gervais, 1986).

Critics have charged that this proposal could lead, in the extreme, to a situation in which society would be asked to bury a body that demonstrated no upper brain function but in which there was spontaneous respiratory and circulatory function (Ramsey, 1970; Walton, 1979, 1982). More realistically, this situation would call not for immediate burial but for the removal of artificial support, including artificial means of providing nutrition and hydration, on the grounds that the individual was no longer alive *as a human being*. All of these decisions depend on a concept or definition of death; if one conceded that the individual was alive and still proposed to remove artificial support, one would be advocating the withdrawal of an intervention that is no longer relevant to restoring the individual to a state of health or some form of euthanasia (see Chapter 18).

Both the UDDA and the proposal from the President's Commission also include the following sentence: "A determination of death must be made in accordance with accepted medical standards."

Determination of Death

Determination of death has to do with deciding whether death has actually occurred, establishing the conditions under which it took place, evaluating the manner of the death, and confirming whether further investigation is required. This process is similar to the work of referees in organized sports. Those involved in determination of death are expected to contribute expertise about the subject and good judgment in applying their expertise to individual cases. Like referees, those who determine that death has occurred do not make the rules. Their role is to apply tests or criteria in an expert manner to arrive at the best decisions possible. They may also help to develop new and better ways of determining death.

Traditional tests applied to determine whether someone has died are well known. In times past one might hold a feather under an individual's nostrils to observe whether it moved when he or she exhaled or inhaled. Sometimes a mirror was used in a similar way to see whether moisture contained in exhalations from a warm body condensed on its cool surface. One could also place one's ear on the chest to listen for a heartbeat or touch the body at certain points to feel for arterial pulsation. Over time, more sensitive and discriminating tests have been developed. For example, stethoscopes make possible a more refined way of listening for internal body sounds.

In all cases, the tests used to determine death depend on established procedures and available technology. These tests vary from place to place and from time to time (Shrock, 1835). The complex testing procedures of a highly developed society are not likely to be available in the rudimentary health care system of an impoverished country, just as the advanced technology of a major urban medical center is not likely to be found in a sparsely populated rural area. Determination of death is closely related to the state of the art or prevailing community practices in a particular setting. Although they can vary, procedures to determine death in American society are clearly adequate for the vast majority of deaths.

Still, as might be expected, determination of death is inevitably subject to human limitations and fallibility. In particular, modern medicine has in some ways made it more difficult to determine the meaning of *any* tests used to determine whether or not death (in a meaningful sense) has occurred. We know that cells, tissues, and organs can be kept functioning in laboratory conditions (in petri dishes, etc.) outside the body of a live human being. Advanced life support systems also can continue to support the functioning of bodily organs when it is uncertain whether or not they are doing anything other than this. That is, advanced life support systems can continue the functioning of cells, tissues, and organs within a human body when it is uncertain whether or not that body is still a live human being in any meaningful sense.

Questions of this sort led a committee of the Harvard Medical School (Ad Hoc Committee, 1968) to develop the following criteria for irreversible coma as a basis for certifying that death has occurred:

1. *Unreceptivity and unresponsivity.* Neither externally applied stimuli nor inner need evokes awareness or response.

2. *No movements or breathing.* Observation over a period of at least one hour does not disclose spontaneous muscular movement, respiration, or response to stimuli. For individuals on respirators, one must turn off the machine for a specified period and observe for any effort to breathe spontaneously.

3. *No reflexes.* A number of reflexes that can normally be elicited are absent. For example, pupils of the eye will be fixed, dilated, and not responsive to a direct source of light. Similarly, ocular movement (which normally occurs when the head is turned or when ice water is poured into the ear) and blinking are absent.

4. *Flat electroencephalogram.* The electroencephalograph (EEG) is a machine that monitors minute electrical activity in the upper brain (cerebrum). A flat EEG reading suggests the absence of such activity. The Harvard Committee indicated that the EEG has its primary value in confirming the determination that follows from the previous three criteria.

The Harvard Committee added "all of the above tests shall be repeated at least 24 hours later with no change" (p. 338).

To apply the *Harvard criteria* properly, one must exclude two special conditions: hypothermia, in which the temperature of the body has fallen below 90 degrees Fahrenheit; and the presence of central nervous system depressants, such as barbiturates. In both of these special conditions, the ability of the body to function may be masked or suppressed in such a way as to yield a false negative on the Harvard Committee's tests.

The first three of the Harvard Committee's criteria are essentially sophisticated and modernized restatements of tests that have traditionally been employed in determination of death. The fourth criterion adds an additional criterion in a confirmatory role—not as an independent test in its own right. Requiring that all four tests be repeated after a 24-hour interval indicates the committee's desire to proceed with great care in this important matter.

The limits of the committee's work are clear in its own stipulation: "We are concerned here only with those comatose individuals who have no discernible central nervous system activity" (p. 337). In other words, these criteria are not intended to be applied to all determinations of death. Rather, they represent an effort to define "irreversible coma." A negative outcome resulting from a careful application of the Harvard criteria (two sets of four tests each, separated by a 24-hour period) is intended to demonstrate the presence of irreversible coma, and irreversible coma is to be understood as a new indicator that death has occurred.

The President's Commission (1981, p. 25) observed that the phrase "irreversible coma" may be misleading here since any coma is a condition of a living person, whereas "a body without any brain functions is dead and thus beyond any coma." This observation reminds us of the difficulty of being clear about language and concepts in matters of this sort.

There would have been no need for criteria of the kind proposed by the Harvard Committee if irreversible coma had not become an object of some puzzlement in modern society. In times past, individuals in irreversible coma would simply have begun to deteriorate. There would have been no way to sustain even the limited functioning that they had or seemed to have. More recently, interventions resulting from advances in modern medical technology have made it possible to sustain the reality or the appearance of vital bodily functioning. The Harvard criteria are intended to identify situations in which life only appears to continue and to equate such situations with death.

Since the Harvard criteria first appeared in 1968, their implementation in some circumstances has been modified and additional or alternative tests, such as cerebral angiograms to test for blood flow in the brain, have sometimes been employed. That modification is only to be expected as experts develop new tests and devise new ways to evaluate whether individuals are alive. In fact, various approaches to determination of death might or might not all relate to the same definition of death. That is because determination of death is a separable matter from the more fundamental question of definition of death.

Certification of Death: Death Certificates, Coroners, and Medical Examiners

Most people in North America and in other developed countries die under the care of a physician—for example, while they are in health care institutions (such as hospitals or long-term care facilities) or in organized hospice or home care programs. In such circumstances, a physician or other authorized person usually determines the time and cause of death, together with other significant conditions. That information is recorded on a form called a *death certificate,* which is then signed or certified by the physician or other authorized person (Iserson, 1994).

Death certificates are the basis for much of the record keeping and statistical data concerning mortality and health in modern societies. They serve a broad range of public and private functions, such as claiming life insurance and other death benefits, disposition of property rights, and the investigation of crime.

The U.S. Standard Certificate of Death (see Figure 16.1) and most state certificates of death are a single-page form containing the following categories of information: personal information about the deceased and the location of his or her death; the names of his or her parents, together with the name and address of the person who provided this and the previous information; causes and conditions of death; certification of death, along with the signature of and information about the certifier; and information about disposition of the body (whether by burial, cremation, removal, etc.), together with the signature of a funeral director. When completed, a death certificate is delivered to a local (usually county) registrar, who signs the form, records it, and provides a permit for disposition of the body.

Every death certificate classifies the *manner of death* in four basic categories: natural, accidental, suicide, or homicide. This system of classification is known as the "NASH" system, based on the first initials of these four terms. In addition, some deaths may be categorized as "undetermined" or "pending investigation." Deaths come under the jurisdiction of a coroner or medical examiner if the person who died was not under the care of a physician, if the death occurred suddenly, if there is reason to suspect foul play, and in all cases of accidents, suicide, or homicide (Iserson, 1994). The function of a coroner or medical examiner is to investigate the circumstances and causes of such deaths.

Coroners and medical examiners are empowered to take possession of the body (or to release it to family members for donation or other forms of disposition), to arrange for various types of investigations (such as autopsies), and to hold an inquest or coroner's jury, which is a quasi-judicial proceeding designed to determine the cause of a death. The term *coroner* goes back to medieval times in England, where it identified the representative of the crown (*corona* in Latin). Originally, the coroner's function was to determine whether the property of the crown—that is, the deceased—had been unlawfully appropriated or killed. In modern societies, coroners are usually individuals who have been elected to office. They are not normally required to have any special qualifications other than being adult citizens of their elective jurisdiction. Many—but not all—coroners or deputy coroners in the United States, especially in rural areas, are funeral directors. By contrast, *medical examiners* are appointed to their positions and are required to be qualified medical doctors (usually forensic pathologists). Some states have eliminated the office of coroner and have replaced that role with medical examiners. Other states continue to maintain a coroner system in rural areas, often with medical examiners in large, urban centers.

❦ Organ, Tissue, and Body Donation

Death is the prerequisite for many forms of anatomical gifts that involve the donation of human organs, tissues, or an entire body, although living donors can donate kidneys and portions of their other organs, along with some tissues. Some background will help to clarify these complex subjects.

U.S. STANDARD CERTIFICATE OF DEATH

LOCAL FILE NO.   STATE FILE NO.

NAME OF DECEDENT — For use by physician or institution

To Be Completed/Verified By: FUNERAL DIRECTOR

1. DECEDENT'S LEGAL NAME (Include AKA's if any) (First, Middle, Last)			2. SEX	3. SOCIAL SECURITY NUMBER

4a. AGE-Last Birthday (Years)	4b. UNDER 1 YEAR		4c. UNDER 1 DAY		5. DATE OF BIRTH (Mo/Day/Yr)	6. BIRTHPLACE (City and State or Foreign Country)
	Months	Days	Hours	Minutes		

7a. RESIDENCE-STATE	7b. COUNTY		7c. CITY OR TOWN

7d. STREET AND NUMBER		7e. APT. NO.	7f. ZIP CODE	7g. INSIDE CITY LIMITS? • Yes • No

8. EVER IN US ARMED FORCES? • Yes • No	9. MARITAL STATUS AT TIME OF DEATH • Married • Married, but separated • Widowed • Divorced • Never Married • Unknown	10. SURVIVING SPOUSE'S NAME (If wife, give name prior to first marriage)

11. FATHER'S NAME (First, Middle, Last)	12. MOTHER'S NAME PRIOR TO FIRST MARRIAGE (First, Middle, Last)

13a. INFORMANT'S NAME	13b. RELATIONSHIP TO DECEDENT	13c. MAILING ADDRESS (Street and Number, City, State, Zip Code)

14. PLACE OF DEATH (Check only one: see instructions)

IF DEATH OCCURRED IN A HOSPITAL: • Inpatient • Emergency Room/Outpatient • Dead on Arrival
IF DEATH OCCURRED SOMEWHERE OTHER THAN A HOSPITAL: • Hospice facility • Nursing home/Long term care facility • Decedent's home • Other (Specify):

15. FACILITY NAME (If not institution, give street & number)	16. CITY OR TOWN, STATE, AND ZIP CODE	17. COUNTY OF DEATH

18. METHOD OF DISPOSITION: • Burial • Cremation • Donation • Entombment • Removal from State • Other (Specify):	19. PLACE OF DISPOSITION (Name of cemetery, crematory, other place)

20. LOCATION-CITY, TOWN, AND STATE	21. NAME AND COMPLETE ADDRESS OF FUNERAL FACILITY

22. SIGNATURE OF FUNERAL SERVICE LICENSEE OR OTHER AGENT	23. LICENSE NUMBER (Of Licensee)

To Be Completed By: MEDICAL CERTIFIER

ITEMS 24-28 MUST BE COMPLETED BY PERSON WHO PRONOUNCES OR CERTIFIES DEATH	24. DATE PRONOUNCED DEAD (Mo/Day/Yr)	25. TIME PRONOUNCED DEAD

26. SIGNATURE OF PERSON PRONOUNCING DEATH (Only when applicable)	27. LICENSE NUMBER	28. DATE SIGNED (Mo/Day/Yr)

29. ACTUAL OR PRESUMED DATE OF DEATH (Mo/Day/Yr) (Spell Month)	30. ACTUAL OR PRESUMED TIME OF DEATH	31. WAS MEDICAL EXAMINER OR CORONER CONTACTED? • Yes • No

CAUSE OF DEATH (See instructions and examples)

32. PART I. Enter the chain of events--diseases, injuries, or complications--that directly caused the death. DO NOT enter terminal events such as cardiac arrest, respiratory arrest, or ventricular fibrillation without showing the etiology. DO NOT ABBREVIATE. Enter only one cause on a line. Add additional lines if necessary.

Approximate interval: Onset to death

IMMEDIATE CAUSE (Final disease or condition ------> resulting in death)   a. _____ Due to (or as a consequence of): _____

Sequentially list conditions, if any, leading to the cause listed on line a. Enter the UNDERLYING CAUSE (disease or injury that initiated the events resulting in death) LAST   b. _____ Due to (or as a consequence of): _____

c. _____ Due to (or as a consequence of): _____

d. _____

PART II. Enter other significant conditions contributing to death but not resulting in the underlying cause given in PART I.

33. WAS AN AUTOPSY PERFORMED? • Yes • No
34. WERE AUTOPSY FINDINGS AVAILABLE TO COMPLETE THE CAUSE OF DEATH? • Yes • No

35. DID TOBACCO USE CONTRIBUTE TO DEATH? • Yes • Probably • No • Unknown	36. IF FEMALE: • Not pregnant within past year • Pregnant at time of death • Not pregnant, but pregnant within 42 days of death • Not pregnant, but pregnant 43 days to 1 year before death • Unknown if pregnant within the past year	37. MANNER OF DEATH • Natural • Homicide • Accident • Pending Investigation • Suicide • Could not be determined

38. DATE OF INJURY (Mo/Day/Yr) (Spell Month)	39. TIME OF INJURY	40. PLACE OF INJURY (e.g., Decedent's home; construction site; restaurant; wooded area)	41. INJURY AT WORK? • Yes • No

42. LOCATION OF INJURY: State: City or Town:
Street & Number: Apartment No.:   Zip Code:

43. DESCRIBE HOW INJURY OCCURRED:	44. IF TRANSPORTATION INJURY, SPECIFY: • Driver/Operator • Passenger • Pedestrian • Other (Specify)

45. CERTIFIER (Check only one):
• Certifying physician-To the best of my knowledge, death occurred due to the cause(s) and manner stated.
• Pronouncing & Certifying physician-To the best of my knowledge, death occurred at the time, date, and place, and due to the cause(s) and manner stated.
• Medical Examiner/Coroner-On the basis of examination, and/or investigation, in my opinion, death occurred at the time, date, and place, and due to the cause(s) and manner stated.

Signature of certifier: _____

46. NAME, ADDRESS, AND ZIP CODE OF PERSON COMPLETING CAUSE OF DEATH (Item 32)

47. TITLE OF CERTIFIER	48. LICENSE NUMBER	49. DATE CERTIFIED (Mo/Day/Yr)	50. FOR REGISTRAR ONLY- DATE FILED (Mo/Day/Yr)

To Be Completed By: FUNERAL DIRECTOR

51. DECEDENT'S EDUCATION-Check the box that best describes the highest degree or level of school completed at the time of death.	52. DECEDENT OF HISPANIC ORIGIN? Check the box that best describes whether the decedent is Spanish/Hispanic/Latino. Check the "No" box if decedent is not Spanish/Hispanic/Latino.	53. DECEDENT'S RACE (Check one or more races to indicate what the decedent considered himself or herself to be)
• 8th grade or less	• No, not Spanish/Hispanic/Latino	• White • Black or African American • American Indian or Alaska Native (Name of the enrolled or principal tribe) _____
• 9th - 12th grade; no diploma	• Yes, Mexican, Mexican American, Chicano	• Asian Indian • Chinese • Filipino
• High school graduate or GED completed	• Yes, Puerto Rican	• Japanese • Korean • Vietnamese
• Some college credit, but no degree	• Yes, Cuban	• Other Asian (Specify) _____
• Associate degree (e.g., AA, AS)	• Yes, other Spanish/Hispanic/Latino (Specify) _____	• Native Hawaiian • Guamanian or Chamorro • Samoan
• Bachelor's degree (e.g., BA, AB, BS)		• Other Pacific Islander (Specify) _____
• Master's degree (e.g., MA, MS, MEng, MEd, MSW, MBA)		• Other (Specify) _____
• Doctorate (e.g., PhD, EdD) or Professional degree (e.g., MD, DDS, DVM, LLB, JD)		

54. DECEDENT'S USUAL OCCUPATION (Indicate type of work done during most of working life. DO NOT USE RETIRED).

55. KIND OF BUSINESS/INDUSTRY

FIGURE 16.1
U.S. Standard Certificate of Death

Retrieved May 4, 2005, from www.cdc.gov/nchs/data/dvs/DEATH11-03final-ACC.pdf.

Background: Tissue Typing, Immunosuppression, and Organ Donation

The modern era of *organ and tissue donation* began in the 1950s, when a combination of advances in knowledge, technology, pharmacology, and practice made it possible for biomedical scientists and clinicians to transplant specific organs and tissues from one individual to another (Dowie, 1988; Fox & Swazey, 1974, 1992; Herrick, 2004; Murray, 2001; Tilney, 2003). One key advance involved learning how to classify or type and compare human tissues so as to achieve the greatest likelihood of success in matching the biological characteristics of donor and recipient. Another major breakthrough—which has been called "the most notable development in this area"—occurred when an immunosuppressant medication (cyclosporine) was developed in the mid-1970s and approved for commercial use in November 1983. Effective immunosuppression prevents the recipient's immune system from attacking and rejecting transplanted organs as foreign material. These advances made transplantation of human organs and tissues a real option for transplant recipients to save or enhance the quality of their lives.

Major organs that can currently be transplanted are listed in the top line of Table 16.1. They include individual kidneys and hearts; entire livers, pancreas, intestines, and lungs, or portions thereof; and joint transplants of a kidney/pancreas or heart/lung.

Tissue Donation

Human tissues are donated and transplanted for a wide variety of purposes. For example, skin grafts are used for burn and accident victims, heart valves and aortic patch grafts sustain heart functioning, saphenous and femoral veins are used in cardiac bypass surgery, eye and ocular components can restore or improve sight, and bone and connective tissue grafts make possible periodontal and trauma reconstructions, as well as orthopedic and neurosurgical procedures such as spinal fusions. Because blood and fat cells are removed during the processing of donated tissues, there is usually no problem of rejection after transplantation. Also, many *transplantable human tissues* can be sterilized, frozen, and kept in storage often for many years. It has been estimated that approximately 95 percent of all deaths in our society—mostly those that occur suddenly and unexpectedly as a result of cardiac death—could lead to tissue donation (versus only 5 percent leading to organ donation) and that each donation of human tissue could be life-enhancing for up to 70 individuals. A further estimate is that more than 900,000 human tissue transplants are accomplished each year in the United States (Donate Life America, www.shareyourlife.org). Two distinctive forms of tissue transplantation are *xenotransplantation*, or transplantation from animals to humans, which has been successful in cases involving heart valves taken from pigs, and *skin donation from living donors after certain forms of bariatric or weight-loss surgery*. Despite all this, tissue donation and transplantation is generally not well understood or appreciated by the general public (Youngner et al., 2005).

Body Donation

It is also possible to donate entire bodies for medical education and research. There are, however, some significant differences between organ or tissue donation and body donation both as to the need for donated bodies and as to the ways in which they

TABLE 16.1

Number of Candidates on the National Transplant Waiting List as of November 30, 2007, by Organ, Gender, Age, and Race or Ethnicity[a]

Number	Kidney	Liver	Pancreas	Kidney Pancreas	Intestine	Heart	Heart-Lung	Lung	Total
Total:[b]	73,909	16,704	1,643	2,299	227	2,687	106	2,276	97,400
By Gender:									
Females	31,013	6,756	825	991	93	685	61	1,383	40,765
Males	42,936	9,956	818	1,308	134	2,002	45	893	56,687
By Age:									
<1 year	6	69	20	1	33	17	0	2	100
1–5 yrs	129	239	39	0	98	84	0	12	506
6–10 yrs	146	172	3	0	21	53	8	33	419
11–17 yrs	502	244	7	2	23	78	10	87	925
18–34 yrs	8,164	812	246	423	22	261	33	315	9,916
35–49 yrs	21,882	3,111	895	1,333	11	518	36	512	27,169
50–64 yrs	31,015	9,986	422	536	15	1,287	19	1,130	43,701
65+	12,081	2,072	11	4	0	389	0	185	14,683
By Race or Ethnicity:									
White	28,941	11,922	1,354	1,540	141	1,943	72	1,870	46,186
Black	25,649	1,168	163	397	42	439	13	215	27,659
Hispanic	12,972	2,657	97	278	36	223	15	137	16,136
Asian	4,892	813	16	37	4	53	2	31	5,782
American Indian/Alaska Native	810	82	6	23	3	11	1	6	914
Pacific Islander	470	25	3	16	1	9	1	5	516
Multiracial	457	76	5	10	1	11	2	12	562
Unknown	0	2	0	0	0	1	0	0	3

[a]Some patients are registered at more than one transplant center for the same organ. This table only counts individual transplant candidates.

[b]Totals may be less than the sums because of patients included in multiple categories.

Source: Based on OPTN data as of November 30, 2007. Retrieved on December 6, 2007, from www.unos.org. This work was supported in part by Health Resources and Services Administration contract 234-2005-370011C. The content is the responsibility of the authors alone and does not necessarily reflect the views or policies of the Department of Health and Human Services, nor does mention of trade names, commercial products, or organizations imply endorsement by the U.S. Government.

should (or should not) be prepared. Individuals who wish to make a gift of their bodies for these purposes after death should confirm arrangements in advance with its intended recipients and follow required procedures (Iverson, 1990). These recipients might include the anatomy departments of medical or dental schools, state or regional agencies that serve this purpose, or organizations like the International Institute for the Advancement of Medicine (www.iiam.org; tel. 800-486-4426), which has "Gift of Body" procedures in ten states. Institutions receiving donated bodies typically have special procedures for disposing of their remains once such bodies have been used for educational or research purposes (e.g., Reece & Ziegler, 1990).

Why There Is a Need for Organ Donation and Transplantation

The growing need for *transplantable human organs* arises from nonfunctioning or poorly functioning organs in potential recipients. Also, with better screening practices and diagnostic techniques, individuals who might benefit from transplantation are now being identified earlier and more effectively than they would have been previously. In addition, transplant centers have improved their technical abilities to transplant major organs (Frist, 1989, 1995; Maier, 1991; Starzl, 1992).

Recognizing these developments, Congress enacted the *National Organ Transplant Act* (*NOTA*) in 1984. Among other things, NOTA established the national *Organ Procurement and Transplantation Network* (*OPTN*) to facilitate the procurement and distribution of scarce organs in a fair and equitable way by matching donated organs with potential recipients (Prottas, 1994). The *United Network for Organ Sharing* (*UNOS*; www.unos.org) currently administers the OPTN under contract to the Division of Transplantation in the U.S. Department of Health and Human Services. NOTA also established the Scientific Registry of Transplant Recipients to measure the success of transplantation by tracing recipients from time of transplant to failure of organ (graft) or patient death.

The need for organ transplantation is evident from Table 16.1, which provides data on the number of transplant candidates on the National Transplant Waiting List in the United States as of November 30, 2007, by gender, age, and race or ethnicity. Among these candidates, most are waiting for kidneys and livers, approximately 58 percent are males, 42 percent are females, the largest numbers by age are individuals 50–64 years of age followed by those 35–49 years old, and the largest numbers by race or ethnicity are Caucasian Americans (whites) and African Americans (blacks). The number of candidates on lists like these increases constantly. Nevertheless, approximately 18 candidates on the National Transplant Waiting List die every day in the United States because no suitable organs become available for transplantation. In 2006, 6,706 transplant candidates (approximately 7 percent of the total at that time) were removed from the waiting list because of death.

Figure 16.2 shows that the need for organ donation and transplantation has grown substantially from 1988 through 2006. This figure reflects end-of-year data for numbers of patient candidates on the National Transplant Waiting List, the number of transplants accomplished in each of those years, and the numbers of donors from whom organs were recovered in each year. In brief, the number of patient candidates on the list has increased by over 500 percent during this 19-year period, while numbers of transplants and donors have increased approximately 130 percent

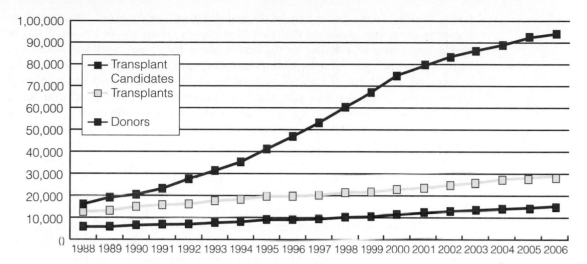

FIGURE 16.2

Transplant Candidates, Organ Transplants, and Organ Donors, United States, 1988–2006

Source: Based on published and unpublished OPTN data from United Network for Organ Sharing as of November 30, 2007. Published data retrieved on December 6, 2007, from www.unos.org; unpublished data provided in personal communication on December 18, 2007. This work was supported in part by Health Resources and Services Administration contract 234-2005-370011C. The content is the responsibility of the authors alone and does not necessarily reflect the views or policies of the Department of Health and Human Services, nor does mention of trade names, commercial products, or organizations imply endorsement by the U.S. Government.

and 150 percent, respectively. In other words, while there has been a notable growth in the need for transplantable organs during this period, the United States has seen only a much slower increase in the availability of these organs.

As a result, *the single largest obstacle to organ transplantation today is the scarcity of transplantable organs.* Because there would be no organ transplantation if there were no organ donation, it is useful to look more closely at some facts about organ donation and at efforts to increase the numbers of donated organs.

Who Can Donate

Organ donation is only possible when: (1) the organ in question is not uniquely vital to the donor's health; or (2) the donor is already dead when the organ is retrieved from his or her body. The former condition applies to living donors, whereas the latter applies to nonliving or deceased donors. The *Uniform Anatomical Gift Act* (*UAGA*; reprinted in Iserson, 1994, pp. 615–618)—enacted in 1968, with amendments in 1987, and passed with only slight variations by all of the state legislatures in the United States—allows persons to make known before their deaths their wishes about the donation of their organs. To do this, the act designates who may execute an anatomical gift; who may receive such donations and for what purposes; how such an anatomical gift may be authorized, amended, or revoked; and the rights and duties at death of an individual or organization to whom such a gift is made. Under the provisions of the UAGA, individuals who are of sound mind and 18 years of age or older can donate all or any part of their bodies, with the gift to take effect at the time of their deaths, and to be made for the purposes of health care education, research, therapy, or transplantation.

Living Donors *Living donors* may be *directed donors* whose donation is made to help a specific transplant candidate that they have chosen (Hamilton & Brown, 2002) or *nondirected donors* who donate for the benefit of any transplant candidate who might be in need of their gift. All living donors can offer replaceable materials (such as blood or blood products), one of a pair of twinned organs (such as a kidney), or a portion of certain organs (such as a liver, pancreas, intestine, or lung). (A very small number of living donors can be multiple-organ donors, as when someone donates a kidney and a segment of a pancreas.) Consent to donate is obtained directly from potential living donors, after a suitable screening and evaluation process to determine that they understand the procedure that will be undertaken, are consenting freely, are a good tissue match to the potential recipient, are likely to be able to withstand the donation process, and can be expected to cope effectively with the aftermath of the experience however that might work out (The Authors for the Live Organ Donor Consensus Group, 2000).

The number of individuals agreeing to become living donors has been growing in recent years and seems to reflect an increased willingness among such individuals to offer a part of their bodies for transplantation—whether or not they are related by blood or marriage to a potential recipient. In 1988, living donors represented only about 31 percent of all organ donors, whereas in 2006 they were just over 45.6 percent of all donors. In 2001, the total number of living donors surpassed that of nonliving donors for the first time, although a significant increase in nonliving donors in 2004 reversed that situation. In 2006, 6,731 living donors provided organs for approximately 23.3 percent of all transplants.

Living donation has many advantages. The donor's medical history is known and can be investigated in advance of donation, an extensive evaluation of the donor and the organ in question can be conducted prior to donation, consent to donate is obtained directly from the potential donor rather than from a substitute decision maker, the organ is removed under elective conditions, and the donated organ is out of the body only a very short period, which is preferable because shorter time outside the body (ischemic time) maximizes the efficacy of the organ. Living donation has also made possible the development of imaginative strategies to facilitate organ donation and transplantation. For instance, it is now possible for a potential living donor who might desire to donate to a particular individual (transplant candidate A), but who is not biologically compatible with transplant candidate A, to arrange to donate to a second individual (transplant candidate B) with whom he or she is biologically compatible, in return for which a potential living donor who is incompatible with transplant candidate B will donate to transplant candidate A (with whom he or she is biologically compatible). So-called swapping donations like this, and even more complex stratagems of a similar type, demonstrate the flexibility made possible by living organ donors. Finally, a promise is typically made to potential living donors that, if at any time in the future their decision to donate might compromise their health status—for example, if they donated one kidney and then later discovered that their other kidney was failing—they would be put at the head of the list for an appropriate organ transplant.

Nonliving or Deceased Donors Individuals who have died prior to donation and the subsequent recovery of their organs can donate multiple organs and tissues, as we saw in the vignette near the beginning of this chapter. In 2006 in the United States, there were 14,755 nonliving donors. In each case, however, it is crucial that conditions preceding, at the time of, and immediately following the death do not damage the organs or otherwise render them unsuitable for transplantation. This means that organs must be recovered shortly after the death of an otherwise healthy donor and before they have begun to deteriorate (the time frame depends on the particular organ in question). Nonliving donors are also the source of almost all tissue donation.

There are two primary types of *nonliving or deceased donors*: those who have suffered brain death and those who have suffered cardiac death. In the vast majority of cases, a nonliving organ donor will have died suddenly and often traumatically of a cerebrovascular incident (e.g., a stroke or cerebral hemorrhage) or of an external blow to the head (e.g., as a result of an accident, homicide, or suicide). Typically, such individuals appear in an emergency department or other critical care situation where external support is initiated to stabilize their bodily functions and provide time for medical investigation and diagnosis. Later, these individuals will be pronounced dead, most often on the basis of clinical examinations including tests involving arterial blood flow, and will be said to have experienced *brain death* or *death by a neurological event*. This form of nonliving donation is called *donation after brain death*. At that point, external support will be continued, not to keep the dead individual "alive" (a contradiction in terms), but to sustain bodily functions for a limited period in order to determine whether or not donation has been authorized and, if so, to preserve the quality of the organs that might eventually be transplanted. If donation is not authorized or after appropriate organs (and tissues) are recovered, external support will be removed and procedures for handling any dead body will apply.

A second group of nonliving donors is composed of individuals in persistent vegetative states or other conditions who have not experienced brain death and are not expected to do so. These individuals do display ventilatory and circulatory functioning, but it is not known whether such functioning is an artifact of the external support they are receiving (e.g., via respirators) or an ability they retain in their own right. To test which alternative applies in any given case, one must remove the external support to find out if a specific individual can continue such functioning on his or her own.

For many individuals in our society who are in this condition—quite apart from any issues of potential organ donation—competent decision makers (such as next of kin or other individuals who are authorized to act as substitute decision makers by such documents as durable powers of attorney in health care matters) may decide that there is no useful purpose served by continuing external support.

With the permission of a competent decision maker in these circumstances, medical personnel may withdraw external support and things would be allowed, as is said, "to take their natural course." That is, the individual in question either will continue life-sustaining functioning on his or her own or will be allowed to die. If the individual does die, he or she will be said to have experienced *cardiac death* and, if a competent decision maker authorizes *donation after cardiac death*, specified organs would be removed (Steinbrook, 2007; Zamperetti et al., 2003). Interestingly, a procedure much like this form of nonliving donation would have been the most common route to organ donation for nonliving donors prior to the advent of brain-death legislation. Since that time, donation after cardiac death has been practiced in some, but not all, areas of the United States. However, it has received renewed emphasis in recent years.

The 14,755 nonliving donors in the United States in 2006 represented approximately 54.4 percent of all organ donors in that year. Among these were 7,377 donors who had experienced brain death (91.9%) and 647 who had experienced cardiac death (8.1%). Together, these donors provided organs for nearly 77 percent of all transplants in that year. Most transplants come from nonliving donors because they can donate six to eight major organs along with ocular components and other tissues that can affect the lives of a large number of recipients (as we saw in the vignette near the beginning of this chapter), while most living donors can only donate one of a pair of organs or a portion of an organ to a single recipient.

Authorizing Donation: Principles and Procedures

Living donors may decide to donate on their own, they may be asked to do so by a family member, friend, or some other person, or they may be guided by health care professionals in considering the relative advantages and disadvantages of their decision both for themselves and for a potential transplant recipient. Things are a bit more complicated in the case of nonliving donors.

Historically, the American death system has not generally recognized a policy found in some other countries of "presumed consent" for donation of major organs (whereby organs can be retrieved unless there is a written directive to the contrary from the decedent or next of kin that specifically refuses donation). As a result, in our society authorization for donation must be sought from an appropriate source in accordance with the requirements of the Uniform Anatomical Gift Act and state legislation (Wendler & Dickert, 2001). This can occur in one of two ways.

Donor Rights Legislation and First-Person Consent Historically, in most jurisdictions in the United States even a formal declaration of a desire to donate made by an individual prior to death and communicated in an appropriate way would not override a negative decision by a surrogate decision maker or next of kin. The reasoning behind this is twofold: (1) the view that once a person has died, he or she no longer owns his or her body; and (2) the practical reality that outsiders (such as organ procurement organizations and hospitals) would usually be unwilling to enter into conflicts between family members on a matter of this degree of sensitivity when there is typically only a relatively short time for its resolution. More recently, many states have passed "donor rights" legislation establishing "first-person consent" registries open to enrollment by individuals 18 years of age or older. An individual giving *first-person consent* has made a legally binding decision that does not require additional witnesses or family consent to authorize organ and tissue donation in the event of death. Family members remain involved in various ways: donation is explained to them, their questions are answered, and they are offered support; they provide a current medical/social history about the individual who died; and they are offered follow-up information and bereavement support.

Authorization for Donation by Next-of-Kin When an individual has not satisfied the conditions required for first-person consent and has not given notice that he or she did not wish to donate, authorization for donation is normally sought from that person's next of kin. Under the UAGA, organ donation from a nonliving donor may be authorized by a health care surrogate; the donor's spouse; an adult son or daughter; either parent; an adult brother or sister; a legal guardian; or any other person authorized or under obligation to dispose of the body. In principle, the order of priority in this list of persons is important; actual notice of opposition on the part of an individual of the same or a prior class would prevent a donation. Thus, a surviving spouse's decisions about donation would take precedence over those of the decedent's parents or adult children, whereas decisions authorized by a health care surrogate would take precedence over those of any relative.

After a determination of death has been made by health care professionals who are not part of an organ recovery or transplant team, an effort will be made to inform family members of their loved one's death and give them time to absorb that fact before issues associated with donation are raised. Subsequently, an approach will be made to family members to provide support, present information about donation and transplantation, offer the opportunity for donation, and permit next of kin to consider decisions about donation (Albert, 1994). If the donation decision is favorable, external support will be continued while the donor is evaluated, a search for appropriate recipients is undertaken, arrangements are made for organ recovery and transportation, and a potential recipient is prepared to receive a transplant (Siebert, 2004).

In seeking authorization for donation from family members, the National Donor Family Council (NDFC) and others have recommended that this approach be framed as "offering the opportunity of donation," not as "requesting donation," since when one asks for or requests something from family members in these circumstances that may be perceived as asking to take one more thing away from them and as implying that if family members were to deny such a request the requestor would have failed in his or her initiative. By contrast, it is thought that "offering the opportunity of donation" puts the family members back in charge of at least one aspect of a most difficult situation in which they have little else to control (Corr, 2005). (The NDFC and many others have also recommended that talk about "harvesting" of organs is inappropriate and should be replaced with language about "recovering" organs, and that the phrase "cadaver donors" or "cadaveric donors" should be replaced by talk of "nonliving donors" or "deceased donors" because the rejected language is offensive to donor family members.) Offering the opportunity of donation is meant to respect whatever decision a potential donor family might make; even a decision not to donate does not take away from the care embodied in this offer. In fact, the only failure would be not even to offer such an opportunity. Imagine the horror and sadness felt by family members who have reported that they had wanted to respect their loved one's wishes to donate but simply did not think of it in this time of great confusion, or family members who recognized too late that they would have wanted to make a decision to donate, but nobody mentioned it at the time!

Under a government regulation called the Medicare and Medicaid "Conditions of Participation for Organ, Tissue, and Eye Donation" that went into effect in 1998, all hospitals that receive Medicare or Medicaid funding must: (1) have a memorandum of agreement with their local or regional organ, tissue, and eye banks concerning organ donation; (2) report to their local or regional *Organ Procurement Organization (OPO)* all patients whose deaths are imminent or who have died in the hospital; (3) permit the OPO to determine the suitability or eligibility of such patients for donation; and (4) arrange for trained personnel (such as members of the OPO's staff or hospital personnel who have been trained by the OPO for this purpose) to offer the opportunity to donate (U.S. Department of Health and

Human Services, 1998, 2000). As might be expected, trained procurement professionals (often working with ICU nurses) have been shown to be most effective in introducing the opportunity for donation (Evanisko et al., 1998; Siminoff et al., 1995). Still, it is recognized that individuals cannot and should not be coerced to donate organs, either their own or those of a deceased relative, and that equal respect should be given both to decisions to donate and to decisions not to donate.

The "Conditions of Participation" regulation has the goal of seeking to increase the number of donated organs. In addition, its purpose is to ensure that family members will be given an appropriate opportunity to know about and consider donation at a time when they have been victimized by the death of a loved one and when so little else is within their control. Many have reported that helping others by making a "gift of life" was the single positive aspect in this difficult experience, a way of continuing the legacy of the donor's life and finding some measure of solace in their own bereavement (Personal Insights 16.1; Cowherd, 2004).

Conversations about the recovery of transplantable tissues from nonliving donors may be part of the overall discussion of organ donation. More often, they occur independently, frequently in the form of a telephone conversation rather than a face-to-face interaction. In the former instance, a procurement coordinator or donation advocate from an OPO might be the principal professional in the discussion; in the latter instance, a staff member from a specialized eye or tissue bank might fill that role.

Efforts to Increase Organ and Tissue Donation

In recent years there have been many efforts to educate the public about organ and tissue donation and transplantation, to broaden criteria for acceptable donors, to encourage more living donors, to try to obtain more organ donors from the estimated 10,500–13,800 potential donors among the approximately 1 million people who die in U.S. hospitals annually (Sheehy et al., 2003), and to obtain more tissue donors from those who die suddenly and unexpectedly most often outside of hospitals. For example, word of mouth and public education projects have sought to dispel myths about donation by emphasizing facts such as the following: "brain-dead" individuals cannot return to life; donor families incur no costs to donate; human organs and tissues cannot legally be bought or sold in the United States; organ and tissue donation usually have no substantive effect on desired funeral practices, other than the possibility of a brief delay; donation and transplantation are encouraged and supported (or at least not opposed) by nearly all religious communities in the United States; members of some minority groups whom research has shown to have lower rates of donation than the general population (Callender et al., 1991; Wheeler & Cheung, 1996) are most likely to find a close tissue match with other members of similar groups and gene pools; and a large and growing number of individuals on the National Transplant Waiting List are in desperate need of a transplanted organ. Public education efforts are reflected in messages like the following: "Don't take your organs to heaven . . . heaven knows we need them here!"; or "Jerry Orbach gave his heart and soul to acting, and the gift of sight to two New Yorkers." (The latter message comes from The Eye Bank of New York [www.eyedonation.org; 212-742-9000] and refers to the well-known actor on Broadway and in the television series "Law and Order," who made provisions for eye donation before his death in 2004.)

The Best Part of the Worst Day of My Life

I want to tell you about a woman who enriched the lives of everyone who knew her, and who, through her foresight, is even now enriching the lives of people she never even met. I want to tell you about my late wife Carolyn.

Carolyn was a cheerful person, and an optimist. She had boundless energy, and she loved life and all it had to offer. I was the cautious one who worried. Carolyn usually assumed that things would turn out all right, and they generally did.

That's why it took me by surprise about 7 years ago when she came home with a new driver's license and told me that she had registered as a donor. "If I die," she told me, "I want to help people."

Until that moment, I never had any problem with the idea of organ donation.

In my mind, it had always been something that happened to other people. Carolyn's statement forced me to think about the possibility of her death, and how I would feel about donating her organs.

I was uncomfortable, and I told her this. In fact, I asked her to change her mind. She smiled slyly, "It's my body, and this is what I want!" I was disturbed, and I said, "OK, if it's on your license, then that's fine, because I don't think I could make that decision."

Up to this point, everything on her side had been light and joking. Now she became serious, "Doug," she told me, "no matter what is on my license, if anything happened to me, you would have to give your consent. That's why I'm telling you."

I remember my reply very clearly. "Carolyn, do you realize what you're asking me? On what would be the worst day of my life, you're asking me to undergo that additional ordeal?" But, she was adamant. I was surprised how strongly she felt about it. I had initially thought it was a whim, but it was clearly something that she had given a lot of thought, and in the end, I had to promise.

That was 7 years ago, and in the meantime, I thought about it myself to the point where I realized that I agree with her. Having moved to Maryland, last January I went to get a new driver's license, and after a moment's hesitation, I, too, signed up to be a donor. Like a little boy, when I got home I proudly showed Carolyn my new license with the words DONOR/YES. It's strange to me now to remember how big her smile was, but that's the way Carolyn was with things that she cared deeply about.

Just two short months later, the worst day of my life arrived. On Friday, March 23rd I was in Louisville, Kentucky, helping my mother make funeral arrangements for my grandmother who had died the day before. Just before noon, I got a call that Carolyn had collapsed at work and been rushed to the hospital with a massive heart attack. I was able to speak to her briefly, giving me hope, but ninety minutes later, after a brave struggle, she died.

Shortly afterwards, talking to my father by phone, he relayed the question that I hoped I'd never have to answer. Did I want Carolyn to be a donor?

(continued)

The Best Part of the Worst Day of My Life

At that moment I realized the great gift that Carolyn had given me with our conversation of 7 years ago. I didn't have to think. I knew. She wanted to help others, and I wanted that too. I gave my consent.

Then there were two things I had to do. One filled me with sorrow, but the other buoyed my spirit. I knew that I had to get myself back to Maryland to see Carolyn and spend some time with her, and, I knew that I had to hold myself together so that I could make the arrangements for her to be a tissue donor.

I think we've all heard it said that the body of a dead loved one doesn't really matter. The body is not the person; it's just an empty vessel. I can tell you that the time I spent with Carolyn there in the basement of the hospital, I felt very differently. It's true that it wasn't animated with her fabulous spirit, but this was the body of my wife, my soul-mate, my best friend. It's how I had known her all our life together. If this was just an empty vessel, then I wouldn't care what was done with it. But I did care—very much.

I still felt so much love for Carolyn, and I knew that I could express this to her through the loving and respectful disposition of her body. And it was so important to her that her body be used to improve the lives of others. Making the arrangements for her to be a tissue donor was an act done out of love: her love of life, our love for the unknown people who would be helped, and my love for her.

Most people are familiar with organ donation, such as a heart or a kidney. Before the day Carolyn died, I, like most people, had never heard of tissue donation. Carolyn told me, "If I die, I want to help people." Sadly, her death has come to pass, but the sorrow I feel over the loss of Carolyn is lightened by the knowledge that people have been helped. Already, two people have had their sight restored, and two others have received either life-saving or life-prolonging heart valve transplants.

If I could speak to these people, I would tell them two things. First, this gift you have received was given to you with great love by Carolyn and by me. Always know that wherever you are, there are two beings who love you profoundly. Second, please don't ever feel guilty about what you have received. Nothing could save Carolyn. You have given me a great gift by making it possible for something life-affirming to come out of her death.

On March 23rd [2001], my beloved Carolyn died. It has been a great source of comfort to me to know that through her compassion and her wisdom, two people are living richer lives, two people are leading longer lives, and, perhaps, somewhere, a family has been spared the anguish that nothing could spare mine. We must all take responsibility to spread the word about donation among our friends and colleagues so that people in need are helped, and so that families in grief can benefit from the comfort that donation brings. Perhaps for them, it will be like it was for me: the best part of the worst day of my life.

Douglas Harrell

Other educational efforts have encouraged potential donors to sign, date, and have witnessed a *donor card*. Donor cards can be obtained from the federal government's Division of Transplantation (tel. 888-90-SHARE; www.organdonor.gov) or local, regional, or national organizations, such as Donate Life America (tel. 800-355-SHARE; www.shareyourlife.org), UNOS (800-355-SHARE; www.unos.org), or the National Kidney Foundation (NKF; 800-622-9010; www.kidney.org). Many states also have a donor card on the reverse side of their automobile driver's licenses or computer registration systems through which one may indicate willingness to donate at the time of obtaining or renewing a driver's license. As we noted earlier, however, first-person consent or donor's rights registries are now replacing "intent to donate" registries in most states. The goal of all these efforts and systems is to sensitize the public to the need for transplantable organs and tissues, to encourage dialogue about donation among family members, and to have a readily accessible way to determine either intent or a prior decision to donate when death occurs.

However, many of these approaches—apart from registering first-person consent—are not sufficient on their own. It is also not appropriate to include wishes about donation in one's last will and testament, because wills are generally not officially read for some time after a death and thus are not a good vehicle for this time-sensitive purpose. What those who wish to be organ or tissue donors should do is discuss this matter with their next of kin. As the slogan says: "Share your life. Share your decision." The reason for this is to involve family members in one's decision, to prepare them in case a donation situation should arise, and to guide them when they need to follow one's wishes and authorize donation. *Historically, an absence of legislation authorizing first-person consent registries and lack of discussion among family members about their wishes have been the most significant barriers to donation.* Therefore, for those who wish to donate: (1) report your decision to donate on a first-person consent registry; and (2) convey your wishes in clear and unambiguous ways to your next of kin.

Research on factors that seem to influence family members in making decisions to donate organs (e.g., Siminoff et al., 2001; Sque et al., 2005) and tissue (e.g., Rodrigue et al., 2003) has suggested that family members who authorize donation are more knowledgeable about brain death, more likely to have discussed donation previously, more likely to know the deceased's wishes about donation, and had more favorable attitudes and beliefs about donation compared with family members who did not consent to donation. Family members who authorize donation often reported that they were approached in a caring manner and provided with both information and time to make their decision. Research on members of minority groups who have been less willing than the general population to donate organs found that African Americans generally expressed distrust of physicians and the health care system and had not previously had family discussions about organ donation (Minniefield et al., 2001), whereas culturally specific information about organ failure rates and organ donation could increase donation among Native Americans when presented by knowledgeable individuals from within the culture (Danielson et al., 1998). Still, some have suggested that there will never be enough organs available to provide transplants to all patients who need one (Sheehy et al., 2003).

In April 2003, the Department of Health and Human Services launched the Organ Donation Breakthrough Collaborative (www.organdonationnow.org), a new effort to increase access to transplantable organs. Previous national data indicated

Make your wishes about organ and tissue donation known to your family members.

© Dennis McDonald/Alamy

that organs have been recovered from only about 46 percent of potential donors, although many large hospitals have average donation rates that are well above this figure (200 hospitals had provided 50 percent or more of eligible organ donors in the United States). The goal of the Organ Donation Breakthrough Collaborative is to identify and share with other institutions practices that can be replicated from hospitals in the United States that have already achieved organ donation rates of 75 percent or greater. This and other initiatives led to a major increase of more than 24 percent in the number of nonliving donors from 2003 to 2006. Achieving an average donation rate of 75 percent in the 200 largest hospitals in the United States (and then extending that effort to other hospitals) could save or enhance thousands of additional lives each year.

Caring for Family Members at the Time of Donation and Afterwards

Explaining "first-person consent" to family members as an expression of their loved one's desire to donate and involving them in the process, or offering family members of other nonliving donors the opportunity to authorize donation of human organs and tissues from the body of their loved ones, is essentially a way of caring for such individuals (Jacoby et al., 2005). Many of these family members have reported that this opportunity enabled them to:

- ◆ Act in accordance with the previously expressed or perceived wishes and values of their loved one who has died
- ◆ Give some meaning to the death of their loved one
- ◆ Find some good or solace for themselves in a time of great difficulty
- ◆ Help others in need by offering something of benefit to another as a free gift of love
- ◆ Act upon their generally favorable attitudes toward donation

As such, offering the opportunity of donation should be accompanied by a comprehensive program of bereavement-centered care for potential donor families, donor family members who have authorized donation, family members in "first-person consent" situations, and living donors—both before and after a death or donation. Principles underlying appropriate practices have been set forth in a "Bill of Rights for Donor Families" (see Focus On 16.1) and other publications (Holtkamp, 2002; Maloney & Wolfelt, 2001). In addition, the National Donor Family Council (Corr & the Members of the Executive Committee of the National Donor Family Council, 2001) has made available a quarterly newsletter (*For Those Who Give and Grieve*), a booklet with the same name (now in its third edition in English, plus a Spanish edition), and numerous other booklets and brochures on a variety of subjects, such as brain death, and the death of a young child, an adult child, and a spouse or lifetime companion (contact the NDFC at 800-622-9010 or www.donorfamily.org). Also, since January 1995 a National Donor Family Quilt, entitled "Patches of Love" and consisting of individually designed 8-inch quilt squares, has become an effective way for donor families to commemorate their loved ones, participate in an international program of memorialization, and contribute to public awareness and education about tissue and organ donation (Corr, 2001b; National Kidney Foundation, 2007).

At the national level, the NDFC and its parent organization, the National Kidney Foundation (NKF), have worked cooperatively with the federal government's Division of Transplantation and other organizations to sponsor the annual National Donor Recognition Ceremonies and the biennial Transplant Games. The Donor Recognition Ceremonies have helped to recognize and validate the difficult decisions made by organ and tissue donors and their families (note the "Gift of Love, Gift of Life" inscription and medal on the photo of Karen Musto's gravestone on p. 482; see also Musto, 1999). The Transplant Games have demonstrated some of the successes of organ transplantation and the rich lives that many transplant recipients have achieved (e.g., Klug & Jackson, 2004). For these recipients, the NKF has also published two valuable booklets: *Waiting for a Transplant* (2002)

Bill of Rights for Donor Families

Families have the right:
1. To a full and careful explanation about what has happened to their loved one, his or her current status, and his or her prognosis.
2. To be full partners with the health care team in the decision-making process about the care and support given to their loved one and to themselves.
3. To a full and careful explanation about how the (impending) death of their loved one was or will be determined with appropriate reference to the concepts of cardiac and/or brain death.
4. To be given opportunities to be alone with their loved one during his or her care and after his or her death occurs. This should include offering the family an opportunity to see, touch, hold or participate in the care of their loved one, as appropriate.
5. To be cared for in a manner that is sensitive to the family's needs and capacities by specially trained individuals.
6. To be informed if their loved one had previously indicated an intent to donate organ and/or tissues and their family's responsibility to honor that decision.
7. To be given the opportunity to make organ and tissue donation decisions on behalf of their loved one, where appropriate and in accordance with applicable laws. The health care provider should include this opportunity in the normal continuum of care, after death has been determined and the family has had sufficient time to acknowledge that death has occurred.
8. To receive information in a manner that is suited to the family's needs and capacities about the need for organ and tissue donation, the conditions and processes of organ and tissue donation and the implications of organ and tissue donation for later events, such as funeral arrangements, viewing of the body and related practices.
9. To be provided with time, privacy, freedom from coercion, confidentiality and (if desired) the services of an appropriate support person (e.g., clergyperson) and other resources (e.g., a second medical opinion, advice from significant others or the services of an interpreter for those who speak another language), which are essential to optimal care for the family.
10. To have opportunities to spend time alone with their loved one before and/or after the process of removing donated organs and/or tissues, and to say their 'goodbyes' in a manner that is appropriate to the present and future needs of the family and consistent with their cultural and religious identity (e.g., asking the family if they want handprints, footprints, a lock of hair, etc.).
11. To be assured that their loved one will be treated with respect throughout the process of removing donated organs and/or tissues.
12. To receive basic written information from Organ Procurement Organizations (OPOs) and tissue banks either at the time of consent or in the days immediately following that decision. At a minimum, this written material should include a copy of the signed consent form(s), information on how

(continued)

Bill of Rights for Donor Families

the organs and tissues may be used and instructions on how to follow up with the OPO or tissue bank in case concerns arise.

13. To receive timely information that is suited to the family's needs and capacities about which organs and/or tissues were or were not removed and why.

14. To receive timely information regarding how any donated organs and/or tissues were used, upon request and whenever possible. If desired, families should be given an opportunity to exchange communications with individual recipients and/or recipient family members. Upon request, donor families should also be given accurate updates on the condition of the recipients.

15. To be assured that the donor family will not be burdened with any expenses arising from organ and/or tissue donation, and to be given assistance in resolving any charges that might be erroneously addressed to the family.

16. To receive ongoing bereavement follow-up support for a reasonable period of time. Such support might take the form of: the name, address and telephone number of a knowledgeable and sensitive person with whom they can discuss the entire experience; an opportunity to evaluate their experience through a quality assurance survey; free copies of literature about organ and tissue donation; free copies of literature about bereavement, grief and mourning; opportunities for contact with another donor family; opportunities to take part in a donor or bereavement support group; and/or the services of a skilled and sensitive support person.

◆ THIS DOCUMENT is intended to represent the rights and legitimate expectations of families of loved ones who die and who are (or may be considered) potential organ and/or tissue donors. This document is also intended to serve as a guide for services that are (or should be) offered to such families.

◆ THE TERM "FAMILY" identifies legal next-of-kin but is also intended to embrace other individuals who may have a significant relationship with a potential or actual organ and/or tissue donor, whether through biological, matrimonial, legal or affectional ties.

◆ THE TERM "DONOR FAMILY" identifies family members who may be or have already been approached to give consent for organ and/or tissue donation from the body of a loved one after death has occurred.

◆ THIS DOCUMENT does not address the situation of living persons who are contemplating or have consented to organ and/or tissue donation during their lifetime.

◆ ALL EXPLANATIONS mentioned in this document should be provided by a knowledgeable and sensitive person in a private, face-to-face conversation whenever possible in a manner suited to the family's needs. These explanations may need to be repeated or supplemented more than one time, and have to meet state and/or federal requirements and regulations.

Source: From C. A. Corr, L. G. Nile, and other members of the National Donor Family Council of the National Kidney Foundation, Inc. Copyright © 2004. Reprinted with permission from the National Kidney Foundation.

As her memorial attests, Karen Musto was an organ donor.

KAREN L. MUSTO
SEPT. 28, 1964
NOV. 18, 1991
LOVING DAUGHTER AND SISTER
Gift of love, Gift of life

(left and right) Courtesy of Barbara Musto

and *From Illness to Wellness: Life after Transplantation* (2004a). In addition, the NDFC and the NKF have been leaders in developing *National Communications Guidelines* concerning communications between all who are involved in donation and transplantation (NKF, 2004b). The goals of these guidelines are to ensure that donor families and living, nondirected donors can obtain appropriate information about the consequences of their decisions to donate; to enable transplant recipients to express thanks for the gifts they have received; and to guide professionals in their roles in facilitating such communications. Research by Albert (1998, 1999) has suggested that: (1) appropriate contacts between donor family members and transplant recipients can benefit all involved, and (2) sound ethical considerations can facilitate such contacts.

❦ Disposition of One's Body and Property

Disposition of Dead Bodies

Apart from body donation, there are a number of issues that are concerned with disposition of dead bodies. State and local regulations provide a general framework for the disposition of such bodies that is principally concerned with recording vital statistics, giving formal permission for burial or some other form of disposition, preventing bodies or institutions that handle bodies from becoming a source of contamination or a threat to the health of the living, protecting the uses of cemetery land, and governing processes of disinterment or exhumation. Beyond that, regulation of body disposition is essentially a matter of professional practice, social custom, and good taste.

For example, as we indicated in Chapter 11, there is no general legal requirement that bodies be embalmed following a death, although this is common practice among many groups in the United States. Embalming is legally required when bodies are to be transported via common carrier in interstate commerce. It may also be mandated when disposition of a body does not occur promptly and when refrigeration is not available. In other circumstances, the practice of embalming is mainly undertaken to permit viewing of the body prior to or as part of funeral ceremonies. Similarly, concrete grave liners and other forms of individual vaults that are used as the outer liners for caskets in the graves at many cemeteries are typically required not by law but by the cemeteries themselves to prevent settling of the ground and thus to minimize costs of grounds keeping and other maintenance activities in the cemetery.

Disposition of Property: Probate

After a death, it is necessary to distribute property owned by the deceased to others. In general, disposition of personal property is governed by the laws of the state where a person lived at the time of death, whereas disposition of real estate (land and the structures built on it) is governed by the laws of the state where the real estate is located. The process of administering and executing these functions is called *probate*, a term deriving from a Latin word (*probare*, "to prove") that has to do with proving or verifying the legitimacy of a will.

In the American death system, probate courts supervise the work of a decedent's personal representative who is charged to carry out necessary post-death duties (Atkinson, 1988; Bove, 2005). That representative is called an *executor* if he or she has been named by the decedent in a will or an *administrator* if appointed by the court. Such a representative is responsible for making an inventory and collecting the assets of the estate; notifying parties who may have claims against the estate of the decedent; paying debts, expenses, and taxes; winding up business affairs; arranging for the preparation of necessary documents; managing the estate during the process; distributing the decedent's remaining property to those entitled to receive it; and closing the estate (Dukeminier et al., 2005). Charges levied against the estate may include a commission for the personal representative; fees charged by attorneys, accountants, or others who assist in administering the estate; and court costs. Many individuals seek to reduce these costs, along with the time consumed by the probate process, by arranging their affairs in ways that minimize involvements with or complexities for the probate process, as we will discuss later in relationship to trusts and other will substitutes.

Wills and Intestacy

Individuals who die without a valid will are said to have died *intestate* or without a testament stating their wishes. In every state, there are laws governing how the estate of an intestate individual will be distributed. These rules vary from state to state but are generally based on assumptions made by state legislators as to how a typical person would wish to distribute his or her property (Atkinson, 1988; Bove, 2005). For example, a surviving spouse and children are likely to be regarded as preferred heirs, and the decedent's descendants are likely to be given precedence over parents, other ancestors, or their descendants. In the case of an intestate individual with no one who qualifies as an heir under the intestacy statute, the estate *escheats* or passes to the state.

Individuals can gain some measure of control over the distribution of their property through estate planning and a formal statement of their wishes, commonly called a *will*. Each state has regulations on how a will must be prepared and submitted to the probate process. Such regulations are intended to communicate the importance that the state attaches to the process of drawing up a will and to provide an evidentiary basis for proving during the probate process that the document really is the decedent's will and does actually represent his or her intentions. For example, wills are to be drawn up, signed, and dated by adults *(testators)* who are of "sound mind," who are not subject to undue influence, and whose action is witnessed by the requisite number (as provided by state law) of individuals who do not have a personal interest in the will whereby they would benefit from the disposition of the estate for which it provides. In general, through their wills individuals are free to dispose of their property as they wish, subject to exceptions (such as community property laws relating to marriages) that have been enacted by most states to protect certain close family members from total disinheritance.

Holographic wills—those that are handwritten and unwitnessed—are acceptable in many states. However, state law varies greatly on this matter, and wills of this sort may be unreliable if they do not include specific, required language, or if the meaning of their language is ambiguous.

In general, professional legal assistance is usually recommended to draw up and execute a formal, written will in order to ensure that the document does convey its intended meaning and will have legal effect, notwithstanding changes in the testator's circumstances.

Wills can be changed at any time before the testator's death, assuming that the individual remains of sound mind and gives evidence of intent to make the change. This can be accomplished through a supplementary document called a *codicil*, which leaves the previous document intact while altering one or more of its provisions; through a new will that revokes the previous document either explicitly or implicitly; through a formal revocation process that does not establish a new will; or through some physical act, such as divorce, subsequent marriage, or marriage followed by the birth of a child. The most recent, valid will governs disposition of the decedent's estate. There are many published resources on these subjects, both for legal professionals and for lay readers (e.g., Clifford & Jordan, 2006; Esperti & Peterson, 1999; Hughes & Klein, 2001; Magee & Ventura, 1998).

In addition, some (e.g., Baines, 2001, 2006; Turnbull, 2005) have recently sought to renew an ancient tradition by advocating for *ethical wills*, moral statements that do not have legal force but through which individuals seek to put their values on paper in order to pass them on to others.

Trusts and Other Will Substitutes

It is both possible and legal to seek to avoid the expense and delay of the probate process by *transferring assets during one's life*. For example, with the exception of certain limited circumstances in which death is imminent, one can simply make an irrevocable and unconditional *gift* of property in which full control of the gift is conveyed to the recipient at the time the gift is made. Such gifts can now be made by individuals in amounts as high as $11,000 per year per donee (the receiver of such a gift) without incurring any federal tax liability. Similarly, ownership of real estate (land and the structures built on it) can be directly and immediately transferred through a written *deed*. Both gifts and deeds surrender ownership and benefit of the object of the gift or deed, although some states permit *revocable deeds* or other conditions under which the transfer is not as absolute. Gifts and deeds may reduce the size of an estate that is presented for probate or considered for tax purposes.

Alternatively, one can make *transfers effective at death* that convey possession and complete ownership rights to another person upon the death of the current owner of the property, even though the current owner retains many benefits from and control over the property until his or her death. For example, *joint tenancy with right of survivorship* amounts to an arrangement for transfer of property at death through a form of co-ownership. Under this arrangement, two or more parties possess equal rights to the property during their mutual lifetimes. When one party dies, his or her rights dissolve, and the rights of the survivor(s) automatically expand to include that person's previous ownership rights. This process can continue until the last survivor acquires full and complete ownership of the entire property interest. At each stage in the process nothing is left unowned by a living person, and nothing is therefore available to pass through the probate process. Joint tenancy with right of survivorship usually avoids delay in getting assets to survivors, but it does not necessarily reduce tax liability.

Life insurance policies are another familiar social vehicle through which assets are transferred from one person to another at the time of the first person's death. Such insurance policies depend on a contractual agreement in which premium payments made by the policyholder result in a payment of benefits to a specified beneficiary by an insurance company upon the death of the insured. Many life insurance policies provide considerable flexibility to the insured as to how the monetary value of the policy can be employed during his or her lifetime, including the power to change beneficiaries before death. Benefits from life insurance policies are not included as taxable assets in the estate of the insured, although they clearly add to the property or estate of the beneficiary.

A *trust* is one of the most adaptable and efficient ways of preserving one's assets from probate. One makes a trust by transferring property to a trustee (usually a third party, such as an officer of a corporation or a bank), with instructions on its management and distribution (Abts, 2002; Esperti & Peterson, 1999; Esperti et al., 2001). Trustees are legally bound to use the trust property for the benefit of the beneficiaries according to the terms provided in the trust instrument or imposed by law. Typically, the maker of the trust retains extensive use and control over the property during his or her life.

Usually, upon the death of the person who established the trust (the *settlor*), the property is distributed to designated beneficiaries without becoming part of the estate in probate. However, a trust can be established that stipulates other circumstances for distribution of property. For example, a trust might stipulate that the settlor's surviving spouse receives a life estate in the income from the trust assets, with the principal to be distributed to children upon the death of the spouse. Rights to amend or revoke the trust can be retained by the person who established the trust. In addition to these *testamentary trusts*, one can also establish *living trusts*, which are essentially set up for the benefit of the trustor—for example, in case he or she is incapacitated and unable to act on his or her own behalf. Couples often set up revocable living trusts in which they are both trustees for each other's trust to insure that property passes directly from one trust to the other upon a death and that one trustee can act for the other when that person is unable to do so. Living trusts are also useful for single adults with no dependents and minimal assets.

Estate and Inheritance Taxes

Two basic types of taxes follow upon a death: estate taxes and inheritance taxes. *Estate taxes* are imposed on and paid from the decedent's estate. They could be described as taxes not on property itself but on the transfer of property from a decedent to his or her beneficiaries. This occurs before all remaining assets in the estate are distributed to heirs or beneficiaries. By contrast, *inheritance taxes* are imposed on individuals who receive property through inheritance.

Federal estate tax law applies uniformly throughout the United States. Among many other changes, the Economic Growth and Tax Relief Reconciliation Act of 2001 exempts from federal taxes an unlimited amount of property that is donated to charity, together with other property in an individual's estate valued at $2 million in the year 2006. (This amount is doubled in the case of an estate of a couple. For an individual, this amount is scheduled to rise to $3.5 million in 2009 until this tax is automatically repealed in its entirety in 2010—although this law has a "sunset" provision whereby estate taxes will be reinstated in 2011 unless Congress and the president take further action on this matter. There have already been some attempts within Congress to increase the amounts exempted from federal estate tax or to do away with this tax altogether, even though it is estimated that the vast majority of estates—as many as 97 to 98 percent in 2001—were already exempt from its taxable burden.) Also, one can transfer to a surviving spouse an unlimited amount of property without estate taxes. However, such a transfer may only have the effect of postponing or deferring rather than avoiding taxes, since property transferred in this way that remains in the spouse's possession at the time of his or her death will become part of that individual's estate. Federal gift taxes exempt a cumulative amount of $1 million from 2002 onward, and rates gradually fall from 50–35 percent in 2010.

In addition, most states have estate and/or inheritance taxes. These taxes vary from state to state and may impose different rates on those who are more closely or more distantly related to the decedent. Thus, it is sound and prudent policy for those faced with potential estate and/or inheritance taxes to seek the advice of experts in order to minimize any tax burden that might arise.

❦ Summary

In this chapter, we surveyed legal issues that arise before, at, and after the death of a human being in the United States. In particular, we first considered advance directives for health care (living wills, durable powers of attorney in health care matters, and "Five Wishes"). Next, we examined issues associated with definition, determination, and certification of death. We then explored organ, tissue, and body donation. Finally, we reviewed subjects related to disposition of one's body and one's property or estate.

Glossary

Advance directives: instructions from an individual about actions that the individual would or would not want to be taken if he or she were somehow incapacitated and unable to join in making decisions; originally, these were informal statements made orally or in writing; currently, they are more formally codified in living wills and durable powers of attorney

Artificial means: external interventions or supports used to sustain life or bodily functioning

Body donation: making a gift of a human body for research or educational purposes

Case law: legal precedents arising from court decisions

Common law: shared values and views drawn from English and early American legal and social history; now, typically represented by definitions contained in standard legal dictionaries

Conditions of Participation: federal regulations under which hospitals that receive Medicare or Medicaid funding must cooperate in specified ways to facilitate organ donation

Coroner: originally, the representative of the crown in England; currently in the United States, an elected official authorized to investigate the circumstances and causes of death of individuals who were not under the care of a physician at the time of death, who died suddenly, who died under suspicious conditions, or who died as a result of accidents, suicide, or homicide

Death certificate: a legal document recording time and cause of death, along with other significant information

Definition of death: a statement of the conditions under which an individual is understood to be dead

Determination of death: the process (or its result) by which competent authorities employ tests or criteria to decide whether death has actually occurred

Donor card: a document whereby individuals can indicate their willingness to donate organs and/or tissues in the event of their deaths; in some states, these cards are printed on the reverse side of automobile driver's licenses

Durable powers of attorney in health care matters: a form of advance directives through which an individual can authorize another individual to make decisions and take actions on his or her behalf under specific circumstances; applies in particular to issues involving health care; continues in force (until or unless revoked by its maker) even when the individual who authorized it is no longer able to act as a competent decision maker; sometimes called a "health care proxy"

Estate taxes: taxes levied by the federal government or a state government on the assets of a person who has died

"Five Wishes": a type of advance directive developed in Florida that combines elements of living wills and durable powers of attorney in health care matters in a form that is intended to be easy to understand, simple to use, personal in character, and thorough

The Harvard criteria: tests developed by a committee at the Harvard Medical School to determine the existence of irreversible coma

Health care proxy: see durable powers of attorney in health care matters; can also refer to the individual designated as a substitute or surrogate decision maker

Inheritance taxes: taxes levied by the federal or a state government on the assets that a beneficiary inherits from the estate of someone who has died

Intestate: the condition of an individual who dies without leaving a valid will or other legally qualified statement as to how he or she wishes to distribute his or her estate or property

Living donor: an individual who donates replaceable materials, one of a pair of twinned organs, or a portion of certain organs for transplantation, research, or educational purposes

Living wills: a form of advance directives originally intended to refuse certain cure-oriented interventions ("artificial means" or "heroic measures") that are no longer desired by an individual; living wills often asked that dying be permitted to take its own natural course and that suffering associated with life-threatening illness be mitigated with effective palliative care

Medical examiner: a qualified medical doctor (usually a forensic pathologist) who has been appointed to replace a coroner, especially in large, urban centers

NASH system: a fourfold classification system for identifying manner of death (natural, accidental, suicide, or homicide)

Natural death legislation: legislation authorizing living wills or durable powers of attorney in health care matters

Nonliving donors: individuals who have experienced brain death or cardiac death prior to donation and the subsequent recovery of one or more of their organs or tissues for transplantation, research, or educational purposes; also called *deceased donors*

NOTA: the National Organ Transplant Act, enacted by Congress in 1984 to regulate the procurement and transplantation of human organs

OPO: an organ procurement organization; one of the authorized local or regional agencies that implements procedures to offer the opportunity of organ donation and to recover donated organs

OPTN: the Organ Procurement and Transplantation Network, a system established by the NOTA to facilitate the procurement and distribution of scarce human organs in a fair and equitable way by matching donated organs with potential transplant recipients

Organ donation: making a gift of a human organ for medical, research, or educational purposes

Organ and tissue transplantation: using a donated human organ or tissue to save the life or improve the quality of the life of a transplant recipient

Probate: the legal system of administering and executing distribution of personal property and real estate after a death; proving or verifying the legitimacy of a will (where such exists) or carrying out estate law

Right to privacy: affirmed by the U.S. Supreme Court as an individual's right to be left alone and to refuse interventions, even at risk of death, that do not promise significant benefit to the person

Substitute or surrogate decision maker: an individual authorized to act by a durable power of attorney in health care matters

Tissue donation: making a gift of human tissue for medical, research, or educational purposes

Transplantable human organs: kidneys, hearts, and livers, pancreas, intestines, and lungs in whole or in part

Transplantable human tissues: skin, heart valves, saphenous and femoral veins, eye and ocular components, bone, tendons, and ligaments

Trusts: legal arrangements to preserve one's assets from probate by transferring their ownership to a trustee with instructions for their management and distribution to a beneficiary; "living trusts" serve the interests of those who establish them; "testamentary trusts" typically control distribution of assets at death

UAGA: the Uniform Anatomical Gift Act, originally enacted by Congress in 1968 to establish criteria under which human organs can be donated; the act was amended in 1987

UNOS: the United Network for Organ Sharing, a private corporation that administers the OPTN under contract to the Division of Transplantation in the U.S. Department of Health and Human Services

Xenotransplantation: transplantation across species, that is, from animals to humans, as in the transplantation of heart values obtained from pigs

Questions for Review and Discussion

1. Which of the available advance directives (living wills; durable powers of attorney; "Five Wishes") discussed in this chapter seems to you most desirable for situations in which you might be unable to participate in decision making about your medical treatment? Why?

2. Why is it difficult in some cases in contemporary American society to decide whether someone is dead? Why is it important to make such a decision?

3. What are your views about donating your body's organs or tissues for transplantation after your death? What about donating the organs or tissues of someone you love? What about living donation? What feelings, beliefs, and values led you to these views?

4. Have you thought about disposition of your body and/or property if you should die? What have you done about these matters, what do you think you should or might do, or why have you done nothing?

Suggested Readings

Two unusual resources on legal and other issues related to dead bodies are:

Iserson, K. V. (1994). *Death to Dust: What Happens to Dead Bodies?*
Roach, M. (2003). *Stiff: The Curious Lives of Human Cadavers.*

Concerning rights to privacy, informed consent, and advance directives, see:

Alderman, E., & Kennedy, C. (1997). *The Right to Privacy.*
Burnell, G. M. (2008). *Freedom to Choose; How to Make End-of-life Decisions on Your Own Terms.*
Cebuhar, J. K. (2006). *Last Things First, Just in Case … : The Practical Guide to Living Wills and Durable Powers of Attorney for Health Matters.*
Haman, E. A. (2004). *How to Write Your Own Living Will.*

Haman, E. A. (2006). *Complete Living Will Kit (+ CD-ROM): How to Write Your Own Living Will.*

Shenkman, M. M., & Klein, P. S. (2004). *Living Wills and Health Care Proxies: Assuring That Your End-of-Life Decisions Are Respected.*

Urich, L. P. (2001). *The Patient Self-Determination Act: Meeting the Challenges in Patient Care.*

Urofsky, M. I. (1994). *Letting Go: Death, Dying, and the Law.*

Williams, P. G. (1991). *The Living Will and the Durable Power of Attorney for Health Care Book, with Forms* (rev. ed.).

Concerning organ and tissue donation and transplantation, consult:

Caplan, A. L., & Coelho, D. H. (Eds.). (1999). *The Ethics of Organ Transplants: The Current Debate.*

Green, R. (1999). *The Nicholas Effect: A Boy's Gift to the World.*

Holtkamp, S. (2002). *Wrapped in Mourning: The Gift of Life and Organ Donor Family Trauma.*

Kaserman, D. L., & Barrett, A. H. (2002). *The United States Organ Procurement System: A Prescription for Reform.*

Maloney, R., & Wolfelt, A. D. (2001). *Caring for Donor Families: Before, During and After.*

Munson, R. (2004). *Raising the Dead: Organ Transplants, Ethics, and Society.*

Parr, E., & Mize, J. (2001). *Coping with an Organ Transplant: A Practical Guide to Understanding, Preparing for, and Living with an Organ Transplant.*

Price, D. (2001). *Legal and Ethical Aspects of Organ Transplantation.*

Schwartz, T. P. (2005). *Organ Transplants: A Survival Guide for the Entire Family—The Ultimate Teen Guide.*

Tilney, N. L. (2003). *Transplantation: From Myth to Reality.*

Veatch, R. M. (2002). *Transplantation Ethics.*

Youngner, S. J., Anderson, M. W., & Schapiro, R. (Eds.). (2005). *Transplanting Human Tissue: Ethics, Policy, and Practice.*

Concerning estate planning and disposition of property, consult:

Abts, H. W. (2002). *The Living Trust: The Failproof Way to Pass Along Your Estate to Your Heirs Without Lawyers, Courts, or the Probate System* (3rd ed.).

Atkinson, T. E. (1988). *Handbook of the Law of Wills and Other Principles of Succession* (2nd ed.).

Bove, A. A. (2005). *Complete Guide to Wills, Estates, and Trusts* (3rd ed.).

Chambers, J. S. (2005). *The Easy Will and Living Will Kit* (+ CD-ROM).

Clifford, D. (2007). *Make Your Own Living Trust* (+ CD-ROM).

Clifford, D., & Jordan, C. (2006). *Plan Your Estate* (8th ed.).

Dukeminier, J., Johanson, S. M., Lindgren, J. M., & Sitkoff, R. H. (2005). *Wills, Trusts, and Estates* (7th ed.).

Esperti, R. A., & Peterson, R. L. (1992). *The Living Trust Revolution: Why America Is Abandoning Wills and Probate.*

Esperti, R. A., & Peterson, R. L. (1999). *Protect Your Estate: Definitive Strategies for Estate and Wealth Planning from the Leading Experts.*

Esperti, R. A., Peterson, R. L., & Cahoone, D. (2001). *The Living Trust Workbook: How You and Your Legal Advisor Can Design, Fund, and Maintain Your Living Trust Plan, and Secure Your Family's Future* (rev. ed.).

Hughes, T. E., & Klein, D. (2001). *A Family Guide to Wills, Funerals, and Probate: How to Protect Yourself and Your Survivors* (2nd ed.).

Magee, D. S., & Ventura, J. (1998). *Everything Your Heirs Need to Know: Organizing Your Assets, Family History, Final Wishes* (3rd ed.).

On ethical wills, see:

Baines, B. K. (2001). *The Ethical Will Writing Guide and Workbook: Preserving Your Legacy of Values for Tour Family and Community.*

Baines, B. K. (2006). *Ethical Wills: Putting Your Values on Paper* (2nd ed.). See also the website: www.ethicalwill.com.

Selected Web Resources

Some useful search terms include: ADVANCE DIRECTIVES; CORONER; DEFINITION OF DEATH; DETERMINATION OF DEATH; DURABLE POWER OF ATTORNEY IN HEALTH CARE; ETHICAL WILLS; "FIVE WISHES"; HEALTH CARE PROXY; INHERITANCE TAXES; INTESTATE; LIVING DONORS; LIVING WILLS; MEDICAL EXAMINER; NONLIVING OR DECEASED DONORS; ORGAN AND TISSUE DONATION AND TRANSPLANTATION; PROBATE; WILLS; XENOTRANSPLANTATION

Visit the book companion website for *Death & Dying, Life & Living, Sixth Edition,* at academic/cengage.com/psychology/corr for all URLs and live links to the following *organizational and other Internet sites:*

Aging with Dignity

American Society of Law, Medicine, and Ethics (ASLME)

Division of Transplantation, U.S. Department of Health and Human Services

Donate Life America

Ethical Wills

National Donor Family Council (NDFC)

National Kidney Foundation (NKF)

Organ Donor Breakthrough Collaboration

United Network for Organ Sharing (UNOS)

CHAPTER 17

Suicide and Life-Threatening Behavior

© Jeremy Bernard/Indexstock

Objectives of This Chapter

◆ To clarify the meaning of suicide and life-threatening behavior

◆ To describe some common patterns in suicidal behavior

◆ To identify psychological, biological, and sociological factors that might help to understand or explain suicidal behavior

◆ To explore the impact of suicide on those who are bereaved by such an act

◆ To describe warning signs for suicide and interventions that individuals or social groups can undertake to reduce the likelihood of a completed suicide or at least to minimize suicidal behavior

◆ To address the morality of suicide and briefly study several religions' views of suicide

🍂 Two Completed Suicides

Ernest Hemingway

When he died on July 1, 1961, Ernest Hemingway was 62 years old and a successful journalist and writer. Best known for his novels, such as *The Sun Also Rises* (1926), *A Farewell to Arms* (1929), and *For Whom the Bell Tolls* (1940), Hemingway won the Pulitzer Prize for his novella, *The Old Man and the Sea* (1952), and two years later he was awarded the Nobel Prize for literature. The image that he presented to the public was that of a writer, hunter, and sportsman characterized by courage and stoicism—the classic macho male. In his private life, however, Hemingway was subject to severe depression and paranoia. In the end (like his father), he used a shotgun to complete his own suicide (Lynn, 1987). This is a notoriously deliberate and effective means of committing suicide. Perhaps it was foreshadowed in the words of a character in *For Whom the Bell Tolls* (1940, p. 468), who said, "Dying is only bad when it takes a long time and hurts so much that it humiliates you."

Sylvia Plath

Sylvia Plath (1932–1963) was an American poet and novelist. She is best known for her novel *The Bell Jar* (1971), which was first published in England under an assumed name

Ernest
Hemingway
(1899–1961).

in January 1963, only a month before her death. This book has an autobiographical quality in its description of a woman caught up in a severe crisis who attempts suicide. Like the author's poetry, *The Bell Jar* emphasizes conflicts that result from family tensions and rebellion against the constricting forces of society.

The death of Plath's father when she was 8 years old was a significant event in her life, as was what Alvarez (1970, p. 7) called her "desperately serious suicide attempt" in 1953 (in which she used stolen sleeping pills, left a misleading note to cover her tracks, and hid behind firewood in a dark, unused corner of a cellar). Plath also survived a serious car wreck

Sylvia Plath
(1932–1963).

during the summer of 1962, in which she apparently ran off the road deliberately. In one of her own poems, Plath (1964) seems to describe these events in the following way*:

I have done it again.
One year in every ten
I manage it—

A sort of walking miracle . . .
I am only thirty.
And like the cat I have nine times to die.

This is Number Three. . . .

In December 1962, Plath separated from her husband—the British poet Ted Hughes, whom she had married in June 1956—and moved to London with her two children, Freda and Nicholas. Early on the morning of February 11, 1963, Plath died.

In the days before her death, Plath's friends and her doctor had been concerned about her mental state. Her doctor had prescribed sedatives and had tried to arrange an appointment for her with a psychotherapist. But Plath convinced them that she had improved and could return to her apartment to stay alone with her children during the night of February 10–11. A new Australian *au pair* (an in-home child care provider) was due to arrive at 9 A.M. on the morning of Monday, February 11, to help with the children and housework.

---

*Excerpted from "Lady Lazarus" in *Ariel* by Sylvia Plath. Copyright © 1963 by Ted Hughes. Copyright renewed. Reprinted by permission of HarperCollins Publishers, Inc. and Faber & Faber Ltd.

When the *au pair* arrived and could raise no response at the door of the building, she went to search for a telephone to call the agency that employed her to confirm that she had the right address. After returning and trying the door again, and then calling her employer a second time, the woman came back to the house at about 11 A.M. and was finally able to get into the building with the aid of some workmen. Smelling gas, they forced open the door of the apartment and found Plath's body, still warm, together with a note asking that her doctor be called and giving his telephone number. The children were asleep in an upstairs room, wrapped snugly in blankets against the cold weather and furnished with a plate of bread and butter and mugs of milk in case they should wake up hungry before the *au pair* arrived—but their bedroom window was wide open, protecting them from the effects of the gas.

Apparently, at about 6 A.M., Plath had arranged the children and the note about calling her doctor, sealed herself in the kitchen with towels around the door and window, placed her head in the oven, and turned on the gas (Stevenson, 1989). A neighbor downstairs was also knocked out by seeping gas and thus was not awake to let the *au pair* into the building when she arrived.

After Plath's death, Alvarez (1970, p. 34) wrote: "I am convinced by what I know of the facts that this time she did not intend to die." However that may be, interest in Plath's life, chronic suicidality, and death continues long after her death (e.g., Gerisch, 1998; Lester, 1998).

Suicide: Individuality and Perplexity

For many people, behavior that appears to involve a deliberate intention to end one's life is puzzling (Marcus, 1996). First, such behavior seems to challenge values that are widely held, including the value of human life. Second, the motivations or intentions behind suicidal behavior frequently seem to be enigmatic or incomprehensible. For those reasons, when a death occurs by suicide, there is often a desperate search for a note, an explanation, or some elusive meaning that must have been involved in the act. Typically, however, there is no single explanation or meaning in all of the individuality and complexities that typify *suicidal and life-threatening behavior*. Thus, Jamison (1999, p. 73) wrote: "Each way to suicide is its own: intensely private, unknowable, and terrible. Suicide will have seemed to its perpetrator the last and best of bad possibilities, and any attempt by the living to chart this final terrain of a life can be only a sketch, maddeningly incomplete." That may be the most tantalizing aspect of it all.

Note that we have already studied some issues related to suicide: in our discussion of death rates and leading causes of death in Chapter 2, and as related to adolescents and the elderly in Chapters 13 and 15. Also, we will discuss assisted suicide, euthanasia, and intentionally deciding to end a human life in Chapter 18.

What Is Suicide?

I can become dead by killing myself. If so, I do something to cause my own death, or I do not do something to prevent my own death. No one else is involved in the actions that bring about my death. Hemingway's and Plath's deaths are good examples of this. No one else was present, and no one else acted to bring about these deaths. This is part of the meaning of *suicide*: an individual acts to cause his or her own death.

However, this is not enough by itself to make a death a suicide. Someone might engage in an action that accidentally causes his or her death. For example, a sky diver whose parachute does not open engages in an action that causes his or her own death, but that death is not a suicide. What is missing is the *intention* to die.

Thus, for death to be a suicide, the person carrying out the act must have the *intention* that the act results in death. But determining the intention of someone—even of ourselves—is seldom easy, and suicidal behavior often turns out to be a particularly ambiguous and ambivalent sort of behavior. The intentions of those who engage in suicidal behavior are varied. They may include attempts at revenge (as may be the case in suicide bombers), to gain attention, to end some form of perceived suffering, or to end one's life—or, perhaps, some combination of one or more of these and other intentions.

Partly because of this ambiguity in intentions, it is not always clear whether a specific situation should be described as a suicide. We can see that in the case of Sylvia Plath and in Alvarez's comment that "this time she did not intend to die." Suppose someone has been warned about a diabetic condition and cautioned to monitor his or her diet. If that person fails to do so and dies in a diabetic coma, was the death caused intentionally? What if someone drove too rapidly for road conditions and died when his or her car crashed into a bridge abutment at high speed with no brake marks on a clear, dry day? Can one unconsciously act to end one's life (do unconscious intentions even exist) (Farberow, 1980)? *Suicidologists* struggle with questions like these and disagree about how to answer them.

Uncertainty about whether a particular act was a suicidal one has important consequences for anyone studying this subject. For example, it may have social significance if certain acts are not included among those classified as suicidal because one is uncertain about them. If so, then statistical data on the number of deaths resulting from suicidal behavior will at best be inaccurate (Evans & Farberow, 1988).

Data on suicide may be inaccurate for other reasons, too. For example, authorities may be reluctant to call a death a suicide in order to give the decedent and his or her survivors the benefit of the doubt and to protect family members from guilt and the social stigma often attached to suicide. Family members themselves and those concerned with their welfare may resist labeling a death as a suicide. For reasons like these, it has been suggested that the actual number of deaths due to suicide may be at least twice the number recorded (O'Carroll, 1989). If so, the impact of suicide on individual lives and on society may be seriously misunderstood.

Further, difficulties in recognizing someone's actual intentions may contribute to our failing to recognize suicidal behavior when confronted by it. If we do not believe that someone's intention is to end up dead, or if that person does not express or even denies such an intention, we may pay less attention to that person. Thus, certain forms of life-threatening behavior are sometimes discounted on the grounds that they are *only* a "cry for help" (Farberow & Shneidman, 1965). At a minimum, though, the case of Sylvia Plath shows that life-threatening acts are a desperate way to seek help, and even a cry for help can have lethal consequences, whether or not they were fully foreseen or intended. It is, therefore, important to try to get a clear understanding of suicidal and life-threatening behavior and to become familiar with common patterns of such behavior in our society.

🍒 Some Common Patterns in Suicidal Behavior

In 2004, suicide (designated as "intentional self-harm" in the new international classification system) was the 11th leading cause of death in the United States, accounting for 32,439 deaths and a death rate of 11.1 per 100,000 (McIntosh, 2006; Miniño et al., 2007). That amounts to 89 suicides per day or 1 suicide every 16 minutes in our society. During the decade of the 1990s, suicide had been the eighth or ninth leading cause of death in our society, overall numbers of suicide deaths had fluctuated between 30,000 and 31,000 (even while the total population in the United States grew by about 10 percent), and death rates from suicide had declined from 12.4 per 100,000 in 1990 to 10.7 in 1999 (see Table 17.1 for data on suicide rates during the 12-year period from 1993 to 2004). Thus the 2004 data on numbers of deaths and death rates from suicide represent a modest increase in numbers and rates of suicide by contrast with recent years, but also a slight comparative decline in the relative status of suicide as a leading cause of death. Nevertheless, for some years now the United States has had one of the lowest suicide rates (in the bottom third) in the world (Seltzer, 1994).

If we compare suicide to homicide as a cause of death in our society, in 2004 there were 17,357 deaths caused by homicide, or 15,082 more deaths from suicide

TABLE 17.1
Suicide Rates per 100,000 Population by Age: United States, 1993–2004

Age	1993	1994	1995	1996	1997	1998	1999	2000	2001	2002	2003	2004
5–14	0.9	0.9	0.9	0.8	0.8	0.8	0.6	0.8	0.7	0.6	0.6	0.7
15–24	13.5	13.8	13.3	12.0	11.4	11.1	10.3	10.4	9.9	9.9	9.7	10.4
25–34	15.1	15.4	15.4	14.5	14.3	13.8	13.5	12.8	12.8	12.6	12.7	12.7
35–44	15.1	15.3	15.2	15.5	15.3	15.4	14.4	14.6	14.7	15.3	14.9	15.1
45–54	14.5	14.4	14.6	14.9	14.7	14.8	14.2	14.6	15.2	15.7	15.9	16.6
55–64	14.6	13.4	13.3	13.7	13.5	13.1	12.4	12.3	13.1	13.6	13.8	13.8
65–74	16.3	15.3	15.8	15.0	14.4	14.1	13.6	12.6	13.3	13.5	12.7	12.3
75–84	22.3	21.3	20.7	20.0	19.3	19.7	18.3	17.7	17.4	17.7	16.4	16.3
85+	22.8	23.0	21.6	20.2	20.8	21.0	19.2	19.4	17.5	18.0	16.9	16.4
65+	19.0	18.1	18.1	17.3	16.8	16.9	15.9	15.3	15.3	15.6	14.6	14.3
Total	12.1	12.0	11.9	11.6	11.4	11.3	10.7	10.7	10.8	11.0	10.8	11.1
Men	19.9	19.8	19.8	19.3	18.7	18.6	17.6	17.5	17.6	17.9	17.6	17.7
Women	4.6	4.5	4.4	4.4	4.4	4.4	4.1	4.1	4.1	4.3	4.3	4.6
Whites	13.1	12.9	12.9	12.7	12.4	12.4	11.7	11.7	11.9	12.2	12.1	12.3
Nonwhites	7.1	7.2	6.9	6.7	6.5	6.2	6.0	5.9	5.6	5.5	5.5	5.8
Blacks	7.0	7.0	6.7	6.5	6.2	5.7	5.6	5.6	5.3	5.1	5.1	5.2

Source: McIntosh, 2006; Miniño et al., 2007.

than from homicide. That is, more Americans killed themselves than were killed by others—a pattern that has been true for some time. In 2004 there were also many more deaths from suicide than from the 13,063 deaths associated with human immunodeficiency virus (HIV) infection. In fact, there were more deaths from suicide in 2004 than there were from homicide and HIV combined. By contrast, there were 44,933 deaths from motor vehicle accidents in the United States in 2004, or 12,494 more of these accidental deaths than those from suicide.

Some common patterns in completed suicides in the United States have been dramatized by Dr. John L. McIntosh (see McIntosh, 2006 at www.suicidology.org; for additional data, consult http://mypage.iusb.edu/~jmcintos/) in the following ways for the year 2004: an average of 1 person killed himself or herself every 16.2 minutes; an average of 1 elderly person killed himself or herself about every 101 minutes; an average of 1 young person (15–24 years of age) killed himself or herself just over every 2 hours and 2 minutes. McIntosh has also estimated that there are 25.1 attempts at suicide for every completed suicide in our society, which would represent about 811,000 suicide attempts in the United States in 2004. Among young people, there may be as many as 100 to 200 attempts for every completed suicide, whereas there may be only 4.1 attempts for every completed suicide among the elderly. In general, suicide rates are highest among the divorced, separated, and widowed; lowest among the married. Moreover, McIntosh has also estimated that each completed suicide intimately affects at least 6 other people, or a total of more than 194,000 persons in 2004. Based on a total of 754,570 completed suicides from 1980 through 2004, that would mean the overall number of survivors of suicide in the United States is 4.5 million or 1 of every 65 Americans.

Men carry out a completed suicide more frequently than do women, by a ratio of more than 3.7:1 in 2004. However, it is also noteworthy that women attempt suicide more frequently than do men, by an estimated ratio of approximately 3:1. The risk of attempted, but nonfatal, suicide is greatest among females and the young.

In terms of methods, firearms are the main instruments used to carry out suicide among both men and women. In the United States in 2004, 51.6 percent of all suicides (16,750 deaths) employed firearms as the mechanism to cause death. Approximately 58 percent of all men who died by suicide in 2004 used firearms, with hanging (including strangulation and suffocation) as the second most common means. Among females, poisoning has been the most common method of suicide since 2001, while about 33 percent of females used firearms to complete their suicides in 2004.

Although suicide is sometimes portrayed as an urban phenomenon, the highest rates of suicide in the United States actually occurred in 2004 in the Mountain region (16.9 per 100,000), by contrast with a rate of only 7.9 in the Middle Atlantic region and 8.1 in the East North Central area. The largest numbers of suicides in 2004 took place in the South Atlantic region (6,610 deaths), while the smallest numbers occurred in the New England region (1,201 deaths). Among the states, Alaska (23.6) was the only state with a suicide rate exceeding 20.0 per 100,000 in 2004 (followed by Montana and Nevada with rates of 18.9), while the District of Columbia (6.0) and New York state (6.2) had the lowest suicide rates in that year. Of course, annual fluctuations in state levels of suicide combined with some relatively small populations can result in highly variable data from year to year.

A particularly disturbing aspect of suicidal behavior is its frequency among young persons. Between 1960 and 1990, suicide rates more than doubled among individuals who were 15–24 years of age, although similar rates in this group have since declined from 13.3 per 100,000 in 1995 to 10.4 per 100,000 in 2004 (see Chapter 13 for a fuller discussion of youth suicide). In 2004 suicide was the third leading cause of death among 15- to 24-year-olds (following accidents and homicide), accounting for 4,316 deaths. This figure represented approximately 13.3 percent of all deaths from suicide in 2004 and about 12.9 percent of all deaths among individuals 15–24 years of age (McIntosh, 2006; Miniño et al., 2007). In the same year, suicide was the sixth leading cause of death among 5- to 14-year-olds, accounting for 264 deaths.

Both absolute numbers and death rates for suicide increase as one moves from adolescence through young adulthood and early middle adulthood (see Table 17.1). For example, among those 25–34 years of age in 2004, suicide was the second leading cause of death, accounting for 5,046 deaths (12.2 percent of all deaths in this age group) and a death rate of 12.6 per 100,000 (Miniño et al., 2007). By contrast, in the 45- to 54-year-old age group, suicide was the fifth leading cause of death, accounting for 6,308 deaths (only 3.7 percent of all deaths in this age group) and a death rate of 15.7 per 100,000. Among the elderly, however—individuals 65 years old and over—suicide declines in status to only the 11th leading cause of death, accounting for 5,198 deaths (only 0.3 percent of all deaths in this age group). Still, the highest rates of suicide are found among the elderly—especially among elderly white males and others over 85 years of age (see Table 17.1, as well as Chapter 15 for more on suicide among the elderly). In fact, although individuals 65 years of age and older constituted only 10.8 percent of the population in 2004, they experienced 16 percent of all deaths by suicide.

In relation to ethnicity, Caucasian Americans most frequently complete a suicidal action; just over 90 percent of all suicide deaths in 2004—a total of 29,251 deaths—involved Caucasian Americans (McIntosh, 2006; Miniño et al., 2007). Among males, Caucasian Americans (with 23,081 suicide deaths in 2004 and a death rate of 19.6 per 100,000) are most at risk for suicide, whereas nonwhite males accounted for only 2,485 deaths by suicide. Among females, 6,170 Caucasian Americans died of suicide in 2004 (for a death rate of 5.1 per 100,000) by contrast with only 703 suicide deaths among all nonwhite females.

In general, African Americans have much lower mortality rates from suicide than Caucasian Americans (5.2 versus 12.3 per 100,000 in 2004). This is true even among young persons, where Caucasian-American youths complete far more suicides than African-American youths (just the opposite of the situation in homicide deaths). However, suicide among African Americans reaches a peak among young adults, and suicide rates are increasing among young African-American males, even more rapidly than among young white males (Utsey et al., 2007). Among African Americans in 2004, 1,655 males died of suicide versus only 364 females, resulting in a difference in mortality rates of 9.0 versus 1.8 deaths per 100,000 in these two groups.

For 2004 the National Center for Health Statistics reported a total of 122,416 deaths from all causes among Hispanic Americans (Miniño et al., 2007), but only 2,207 of these deaths (1,840 males and 367 females) resulted from suicide (for a suicide death rate of 5.3 per 100,000). This contrasts with 30,232 deaths by suicide among non-Hispanic individuals in 2004. Still, all reports on deaths by suicide are dependent on available data, and several authors (such as Duarté-Vélez & Bernal, 2007) have noted that among Hispanic Americans (and African Americans) many deaths that are suicides may not be reported as such (e.g., they may be reported as accidents or homicides). Not surprisingly, numbers of suicide deaths among white non-Hispanics in 2004 were nearly 14 times higher than those attributed to Hispanic Americans.

Among Asian and Pacific Island Americans, there were 765 deaths by suicide in 2004 for a death rate of 5.6 per 100,000 (McIntosh, 2006). There are many differences in this very diverse population (Else et al., 2007; Leong et al., 2007). For example, Lester (1994) reported that among Asian Americans in his study, Japanese Americans had the highest suicide rates, whereas Filipino Americans had the lowest. Lester also reported that Asian-American women had a relatively higher suicide rate compared to men than women in other ethnic groups, and Chinese and Japanese Americans showed a relatively greater increase in suicidal behavior as they aged. As a rule, Asian-American suicide rates are highest among the elderly (McIntosh & Santos, 1981a).

It is commonly claimed that there are high suicide rates among American Indians. According to the best available data (McIntosh, 2006), there were 404 deaths by suicide among American Indians in 2004, for a death rate of 12.9 per 100,000. This rate is more than double that of the three other minority groups in our society that we have mentioned. However, it is only slightly higher than the rate of 12.3 for overall Caucasian-American suicides and does not justify the commonly heard claim that suicide rates among American Indians are extraordinarily high. Critics of that claim (e.g., Thompson & Walker, 1990; Van Winkle & May, 1986) have asserted that it is based on small numbers of suicides over short time spans and among small population bases. (This dispute reveals in another form our dependence on data and statistics to try to understand suicide mortality rates.) In fact, Webb and Willard (1975) determined that there is no single common American Indian pattern for suicides, and Thompson and Walker (1990) argued that suicide rates in the various tribes seem most closely related to suicide rates in their surrounding populations. If that is correct, then American Indian rates of suicide should be compared to rates among others in the areas in which the American Indians live. Thus, no overall statistic for American Indian suicide rates is really reliable, since such rates vary markedly from area to area and tribe to tribe (Alcántara & Gone, 2007; McIntosh, 1983).

Still, this myth persists and even influences beliefs among American Indians themselves. Thus, Levy and Kunitz (1987, p. 932) reported that the Hopi have become concerned about suicide rates among themselves, even though "Hopi suicide rates are no higher than those of the neighboring counties." Furthermore, they found no evidence that Hopi suicide rates are increasing. This finding does not suggest that there should be no concern about suicide rates in any particular American Indian group, but only that such rates need to be understood in context if we are to appreciate them properly.

The only generalization about American Indians that does appear to be valid is that suicide in this group is largely a phenomenon of young males, since suicide rates among the elderly are low in this cultural group (McIntosh & Santos, 1981b; Thompson & Walker, 1990).

With these data about common patterns in suicidal behavior in hand, we can now examine some of the leading interpretations of this behavior—psychological, biological, and sociological—that have been offered to help understand suicide. In each case, part of the work of these interpretations has been to try to elucidate the causes of (or, perhaps better, contributing factors to) suicide.

🍐 Efforts to Understand or Explain Suicidal Behavior

As we have suggested, acts of suicide produce an intense urgency in survivors to find an explanation—a reason for or a way of understanding this unsettling behavior. Although this pressure to find a reason is understandable, it is not an easy one to respond to with clarity.

For instance, when terrorists flew airplanes into the World Trade Center or when individuals killed themselves in an act of suicide bombing, many wanted to know why anyone would do such things. At first glance, it appeared that these and other self-destructive and murderous acts were the product of distorted fanatical religious beliefs. However, this cannot be an adequate explanation of what such individuals have done. As Ariel Merari (who heads the Political Violence Research Center at Tel Aviv University and who has studied terrorist violence extensively) argues, there are many religious believers (from all religions) who hold distorted and fanatical beliefs but who do not engage in such behaviors (Martin, 2001).

Merari then looked for other reasons for these acts. First, he noticed that such behavior is not limited to religious believers. Soldiers in World Wars I and II and Japanese pilots during World War II also performed suicidal acts that bore similarities to those in the events of September 11. Second, Merari found that what these people had in common was they belonged to organizations that encouraged them to do these things. In particular, he claims that groups that get members to engage in suicidal/murderous acts share three characteristics: (1) they build up motivation to overcome ambivalence and perform the act; (2) they provide group pressure to stick to the mission; and (3) they get a direct commitment from the individual to perform the act. This last element includes identifying the individual before the group as a "living martyr" and having the individual identify himself (until recently, these acts have nearly always been performed by males) this way, for instance, by writing letters to family members in which he identifies himself as such. Having publicly proclaimed himself as having accepted this role, it is difficult to back out.

Whether or not this explanation is adequate, it demonstrates the difficulty and complexity of providing a single explanation of suicide. Perhaps that is why the three general types of explanations that follow have been offered to help us understand suicide.

Psychological Explanations of Suicide

Leenaars (1990) identified three major forms that psychological explanations of suicide have taken. The first of these is based on Freud's psychoanalytic theory. Freud argued that suicide is *murder turned around 180 degrees* (Litman, 1967) and suggested that it is related to the loss of a desired person or object. Psychologically, the person at risk comes to identify himself or herself with the lost person. He or she feels anger toward this lost object of affection and wishes to punish (even to kill) the lost person. However, since the individual has identified his or her self with this object of affection, the anger and its correlated wish to punish become directed against the self. Thus, self-destructive behavior is the result.

A second psychological approach sees the problem as *essentially cognitive in nature.* In this view, clinical depression (suicide is highly correlated with depression)

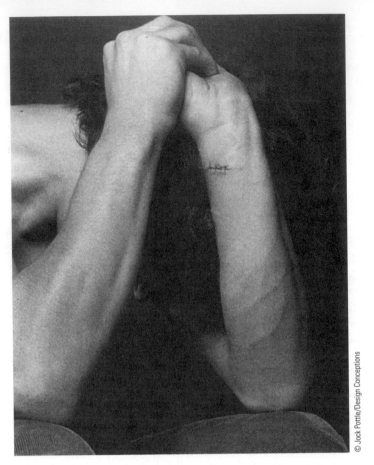
© Jack Pottle/Design Conceptions

Suicidal behavior is often closely linked to depression.

is believed to be an important contributing factor, especially when it is associated with hopelessness (see Gotlib & Hammen, 2002; Kessler et al., 2005). The central issue here is that negative evaluations are a pervasive feature of the suicidal person's worldview. The future, the self, the present situation, and the limited number of possible options envisioned by the individual are all viewed as undesirable. Along with these evaluations, impaired thinking is present: such thinking is "often automatic and involuntary . . . characterized by a number of possible errors, some so gross as to constitute distortion" (Leenaars, 1990, p. 162). This way of looking at things may help to understand what has come to be called "suicide by cop" (Lindsay & Lester, 2004) or behavior in which a police officer is provoked by an individual to cause that person's death.

A third psychological theory claims that *suicidal behavior is learned.* This theory contends that as a child the suicidal individual learned not to express aggression outward but rather to turn it back on the self. Again, depression is noted as an important factor, now the result of negative reinforcement from the environment for a person's actions. Furthermore, this depression (and its associated suicidal or life-threatening behavior) may even be seen as being positively reinforced—that is, rewarded by those around the individual. It might be argued, for example, that

Ernest Hemingway's depression, as mentioned earlier, was positively reinforced by the example of his father's own suicide (Slaby, 1992). In any event, this theory views the suicidal individual as poorly socialized and maintains that constructive cultural evaluations of life and death have not been learned.

Jamison (1999)—a psychiatrist who had herself once attempted suicide—argued that psychopathology is "the most common element in suicide" (p. 100). In particular, she focused on the relationships between "mood disorders, schizophrenia, borderline and antisocial personality disorders, alcoholism, and drug abuse." She believes that these mental illnesses play a (and perhaps *the*) significant role in accounting for suicidal acts. She also described genetic and brain chemistry abnormalities (discussed next), and related these to psychopathological factors. In that discussion, she reiterated her view that even when these other factors are taken into account, they are of most significance when associated with mental illness.

These psychological theories need not be seen as incompatible, of course. Putting them together helps bring our overall understanding of suicide and suicidal behavior more sharply into focus. Since suicide is a complex behavior, it probably makes most sense to see it as arising (at least often) from a complex basis.

Biological Explanations of Suicide

Some studies have sought to discover whether there are biological explanations for suicidal behavior (e.g., Roy, 1990). These have typically focused on biological explanations relating to either neurochemical or genetic factors. Some theorists believe that there may be a disturbance in the levels of certain neurochemicals found in the brain, such as a reduction in the level of serotonin (a chemical related to aggressive behavior and the regulation of anxiety) in suicidal individuals. However, such studies have not made clear whether such a decrease is associated with depression, suicidal behavior, or the violent outward or inward expression of aggression.

Other studies (Egeland & Sussex, 1985; Roy, 1990; Wender et al., 1986) have suggested that some predispositions to suicidal behavior may be inherited. For example, a study of adopted children in Denmark looked at the biological families of adopted children diagnosed with "affective disorder" who had completed suicide (Wender et al., 1986). More of these persons who showed signs of "affective disorder" and had completed a suicide had relatives who showed the same signs and actions than was the case for a control group. However, it is uncertain from this study exactly what it is that may be inherited. Perhaps the inherited element is an inability to control impulsive behavior, not suicidal behavior in itself.

Thus, it has not yet been demonstrated that biological factors can be related clearly to suicidal behavior. Nevertheless, continued research into biological explanations of suicide may eventually yield helpful information to add to what is already known about other factors contributing to suicidal behavior.

Sociological Explanations of Suicide

The oldest and best-known attempt to offer an explanation of suicide comes from the work of a French sociologist, Emile Durkheim (1951; Selkin, 1983), originally published in France at the end of the 19th century. Durkheim argued that no psychological condition *by itself* invariably produces suicidal behavior. Instead, he believed that suicide can be understood as an outcome of the relationship of the individual to his or her society, with special emphasis on ways in which individuals are or are not *integrated* and *regulated* in their relationships with society. Durkheim's analysis has been criticized, but his book remains a classic in the literature on suicide (Douglas, 1967; Lester, 2000; Maris, 1969). In it, he identified three primary sorts of relationships between individuals and society as conducive to suicidal behavior, and he made brief reference to the possibility of a fourth basic type of suicide.

Egoistic Suicide   The first of these relationships may result in what Durkheim called *egoistic suicide,* or suicide involving more or less isolated individuals. It has been shown that the risk of suicide is diminished in the presence of a social group that provides some integration for the individual (especially in terms of meaning for his or her life). When such integration is absent, loses its force, or is somehow removed (especially abruptly), suicide becomes a more likely possibility.

Durkheim argued for this thesis in the case of three sorts of "societies"—religious society, domestic society, and political society. A *religious society* may provide integration (meaning) for its members in many ways—for example, by means of a unified, strong creed. A *domestic society* (e.g., marriage) also seems to be a factor that tends to reduce suicidal behavior by providing individuals with shared "sentiments and memories," thereby locating them in a kind of geography of meaning. In addition, a *political society* can be another vehicle that assists individuals in achieving social integration. When any of these societies—religious, domestic, or political—does not effectively help individuals to find meaning for their lives or when the society disintegrates or loses its influence, individuals may be thrown back on their own resources, may find them inadequate to their needs, and may become more at risk for suicidal or life-threatening behavior.

In short, Durkheim's thesis here is that whenever an individual experiences himself or herself in a situation wherein his or her society fails to assist that individual in finding his or her place in the world, suicidal behavior can result. Thus, egoistic suicide depends on an *under*involvement or *under*integration, a kind of disintegration and isolation of an individual from his or her society.

Altruistic Suicide   The second form of social relationship that is or may be related to suicide arises from an *over*involvement or *over*integration of the individual into his or her society. In this situation, the ties that produce the integration between the individual and the social group are so strong that they may result in *altruistic suicide* or suicide undertaken on behalf of the group. Personal identity may give way to identification with the welfare of the group, and the individual may find the meaning of his or her life (completely) outside of self. For example, in some strongly integrated societies, there are contexts in which suicide may be seen as a duty. In other words, the surrender of the individual's life may be demanded on behalf of what is perceived to be the welfare of the society.

Durkheim listed several examples found in various historical cultures that involve relationships of strong integration or involvement and that lead to suicidal behavior: persons who are aged or ill (the Eskimo); women whose husbands have died (the practice of *suttee* in India before the English came); servants of social chiefs who have died (many ancient societies). One might think also of persons who have failed in their civic or religious duties so as to bring shame on themselves, their families, or their societies—for example, the samurai warrior in Japanese society who commits ritual *seppuku*. Also, involvement in a religious cult led some Americans to altruistic suicide at the People's Temple in Georgetown in British Guyana (1978) and at the Heaven's Gate complex in California (1997), and there may be religious explanations that account in part for the events of 9/11 and similar acts since then.

Anomic Suicide Durkheim described a third form of suicide, *anomic suicide,* not in terms of integration of the individual into society but rather in terms of how the society *regulates* its members. All human beings need to regulate their desires (for material goods, for sexual activity, and so forth). To the extent that a society assists individuals in this regulation, it helps keep such desires under control. When a society is unable or unwilling to help its members in the regulation of their desires—for example, because the society is undergoing rapid change and its rules are in a state of flux—a condition of *anomie* is the result. (The term *anomie* comes from the Greek *anomia = a* [without] + *nomoi* [laws or norms], and means "lawlessness" or "normlessness.")

Anomie can be conducive to suicide, especially when it thrusts an individual suddenly into a situation perceived to be chaotic and intolerable. In contemporary American society, examples of this sort of suicide might involve adolescents who have been unexpectedly rejected by a peer group, some farmers who find that economic and social forces outside their control are forcing them into bankruptcy and taking away both their livelihood and their way of life, or middle-aged employees who have developed specialized work skills and who have devoted themselves for years to their employer only to be suddenly thrown out of their jobs and economically dislocated. For such individuals, *under*regulation or a sudden withdrawal of control may be intolerable because of the absence of (familiar) principles to guide them in living.

Fatalistic Suicide Durkheim only mentions a fourth type of suicide, called fatalistic suicide, in a footnote in his book, where it is described as the opposite of anomic suicide. Fatalistic suicide derives from *excessive regulation* of individuals by society—for example, when one becomes a prisoner or a slave. These are the circumstances of "persons with futures pitilessly blocked and passions violently choked by oppressive discipline" (1951, p. 276). Durkheim did not think that this type of suicide was very common in his own society, but it may be useful as an illustration of social forces that lead an individual to seek to escape from an *over-controlling* social context.

❦ Suicide: An Act with Many Determinants and Levels of Meaning

In a way similar to Durkheim's claim that suicidal behavior cannot be understood solely by studying the psychology of those who engage in such behavior, Menninger (1938, p. 23) wrote, "Suicide is a very complex act, and not a simple, incidental, isolated act of impulsion, either logical or inexplicable." Both of these theorists saw a completed suicide as an outcome of *many* causes, not only one. Shneidman (1980/1995), Douglas (1967), and others (such as Breed, 1972) also have suggested that a variety of elements may enter into suicidal behavior.

One popular way to reflect the complexity of suicidal behavior is to think of it as involving three elements: *haplessness* (being ill fated or unlucky), *helplessness,* and *hopelessness.* Shneidman (1980/1995) took this understanding forward to a still more complex and precise account by thinking of the factors that lead to suicide in terms of three main components and a triggering process: (1) *inimicality,* or an unsettled life pattern in which one acts against one's own best interests; (2) *perturbation,* or an increased psychological disturbance in the person's life; (3) *constriction,* which appears in *tunnel vision* and *either/or thinking,* and which represents a narrowing of the range of perceptions, opinions, and options that occur to the person's mind; and (4) the idea of *cessation,* of resolving the unbearable pain of disturbance and isolation by simply ending it or being out of it.

These characterizations of suicide can lead to an important conclusion in the search for an understanding of suicidal behavior. As we have noted, there is often a natural impulse among students of suicidal behavior and bereaved family members to look for *the* cause of a suicide. This need can be illustrated in the efforts of many people to find a suicide note that they hope might explain what has happened. In fact, however, there usually is no such single cause. Suicide is most often an act with many determinants and levels of meaning. It may arise from a context of many sorts of causes, among which biological, psychological, and social factors are surely prominent (Lester, 1992, 2003; Maris, 1981, 1988; Maris et al., 1992). In fact, one expert on suicide notes wrote that "in order to commit suicide, one cannot write a meaningful suicide note; conversely, if one could write a meaningful note, one would not have to commit suicide" (Shneidman, 1980/1995, p. 58).

❦ The Impact of Suicide

In addition to the individual who dies or who puts his or her life in jeopardy, a suicidal act always affects other people. Reports in the literature from the 1970s and ongoing communications from counselors, therapists, and members of suicide support or bereavement self-help groups have indicated that *survivors of the person who has died from suicide* almost always have a difficult time dealing with that death (e.g., Cain, 1972; Wallace, 1973). The common theme in these reports is that the aftereffects of suicide intensify experiences of anger, sadness, guilt, physical complaints, and other dimensions of grief found in all loss and bereavement. Thus, Lindemann and Greer (1972, p. 67) wrote: "The survivors of a suicide are likely to get 'stuck' in their grieving and to go on for years in a state of cold isolation, unable to feel close to others and carrying always with them the feeling that they are set apart or under the threat of doom."

More recent reports have questioned the adequacy of this account of bereavement following a suicide (e.g., Barrett & Scott, 1990; Dunne et al., 1987; Jordan, 2001; Nelson & Frantz, 1996; Silverman et al., 1994). In particular, it has been noted that most of the published studies on this subject have had significant methodological weaknesses (McIntosh, 1987). The size of the study groups has been small. Persons who participate in these studies have often come from clinical sources, from support groups, and from college students (and each of these groups may have people who are atypical in one way or another). For obvious reasons, participants in most studies have been volunteers. Thus, large numbers of survivors who are not members of this kind of group or who have refused to participate (and who may in fact make up the largest group of survivors) have not been studied (Van Dongen, 1990). Also, there have been few comparison studies in which survivors of someone who committed suicide are compared to other bereaved persons (Hauser, 1987). Those studies that have made some comparison between different groups of survivors have yielded inconclusive results (Demi & Miles, 1988; McIntosh, 1987).

Most researchers (such as Barrett & Scott, 1990; Calhoun et al., 1986; Demi & Miles, 1988; Hauser, 1987) themselves warn against making generalizations on the basis of their work. Still, actual empirical study is important to correct impressions that arise from "clinical observation, intellectual conjecture, and theoretical speculation" (Barrett & Scott, 1990, p. 2). Only such study can prevent us from making false generalizations or from stereotyping suicide survivors and thus increasing the difficulty of their mourning by placing expectations on them that they may or may not meet.

Thus, what we can say about the nature of the mourning process for suicide survivors and how it differs from that process for other survivors is still somewhat tentative. Perhaps one of the clearest statements on this subject comes from the work of Barrett and Scott (1990). They pointed out that suicide survivors at least have *more types of issues* to deal with than do other survivors. The survivors of someone's suicide must cope with: (1) the tasks anyone has *after the death of someone to whom one has been close;* (2) tasks related to a death that *arises from some cause other than a natural one* and is often therefore *perceived to have been a death that was avoidable;* (3) tasks associated with *a sudden death;* and finally (4) tasks due to *the suicidal nature of the death,* such as the repudiation of life-affirming values and abandonment issues that it seems to imply.

Some aspects of these tasks are present in the mourning process of suicide survivors more frequently than in the mourning of persons bereaved as a result of other types of death. Blame (of others or of oneself) and guilt (the response to a sense of being at fault), a sense of being rejected by the deceased, and perhaps especially significant, a search for an explanation for why the person acted to end his or her life often play heightened roles in the lives of these mourners (Dunn & Morrish-Vidners, 1988; Lukas & Seiden, 2007; Reed & Greenwald, 1991; Silverman et al., 1994; Van Dongen, 1990, 1991).

Although some have claimed that suicide survivors are themselves subject to self-destructive and suicidal thoughts and actions, other studies have reported that these survivors found a strong deterrent to such actions in realizing how devastating another suicide in the family would be for fellow survivors (Dunn & Morrish-Vidners, 1988; Van Dongen, 1990).

Not all suicide survivors will have to deal with these tasks to the same extent. Some evidence indicates that it is the degree of emotional attachment to the deceased that matters most here (as with all mourning), as much as or even more than the formal nature (parent, sibling, friend) of the relationship (Barrett & Scott, 1990; Reed & Greenwald, 1991), or the type of death. Not surprisingly, however, children may face special problems in understanding and making sense of a parent's suicide (Requarth, 2006; see also Personal Insights 17.1).

Life with Dad, a True Story by Reyna Paez, Age 9

Seven years ago, there was a two year old girl. Her father had committed suicide. She had asked where he was a lot but her Mom lied and said, "He died in a car accident." Her Mom had cried a lot since that had happened.

Another year later, she had spent the night at her Grandparents and they put her slippers by the bedside so she could wear them the next day. But the next day the slippers were gone! Her Grandparents thought and thought about where they had gone. Then her Grandma got an idea. She said, "What if her Dad took the slippers!?" Her Grandpa said, "Maybe, we'll see if the slippers are there tomorrow and if they are there he must have taken them!" The next day they looked by the bedside and the slippers were in the exact same place!

When it was her birthday they were in a car driving to her party. The little girl's Grandparents thought she was talking to herself. Her Grandma asked, "Who are you talking to?" The girl said, "My Daddy." They were confused. When they got to the party they told her Mom what had happened. Her Mom thought that was weird. She asked her daughter if she was really talking to her Dad. The girl said straight up, "Yup, I was talking to him the whole time. He was sitting right next to me."

When she was four, she headed off to pre-school. Everyday she would bring a blanket that was given to her by her Dad. She called the blanket "KyKy," and she also would squeeze it tight all the time at school. At school they had nap time, and the girl didn't like nap time so she just thought about her Dad and cuddled with her blanket.

The next year her Mom was with another guy. The girl cried because she didn't know him. But after awhile she got to know him and later began to call him Dad.

When she was six her Mom and new Dad said, "You are going to have a baby sister!" The girl was so happy. Then one day her Mom had the baby. After the baby was born, the girl got to hold her. The girl kissed her new baby sister. Every night the girl would tell her about her Dad when nobody was there.

Then in the third grade, the girl told her class that her Dad had died. One day a classmate teased the girl about not having a Dad. The girl didn't say anything, and she just walked away. The boy said, "Sorry," but she said, "There is no way I can forgive you."

After school one day, when she was eight, the girl was told how her Dad died. The girl was a bit excited to hear how but she was mostly scared to know because her family was keeping it a secret for six years! "Well," her Mom said, "I'm going to tell you how your Dad died. He died by taking his own life, he grabbed an object and killed himself." The girl burst into tears.

The next day her Mother called the school counselor to talk with the girl. The counselor pulled her out of class and walked with her to her counseling room. The counselor gave her a bear just in case. They talked about what had happened and the girl felt much better. After that talk the girl wasn't sad to talk about her Daddy ever again.

Although there are few longitudinal studies of survivors of another's suicide, one study of elderly survivors indicated that whereas many mourners of other sorts of death begin to experience a change in their mourning around six months, these survivors take longer to reach that first change. Even after two and a half years, suicide survivors rated their mental health differently than did the survivors of natural deaths or other types of sudden death (Farberow et al., 1992).

Barlow and Coleman (2003) studied the role of the family in the mourning process of suicide survivors. They found that families that were able to form a "healing alliance" were better able to cope with the aftereffects of a suicide, while the inability to form such an alliance made the grief process more difficult. Healing alliances included watching the responses to the suicide of other family members and allowing other family members to grieve in their own ways. The watchful waiting was motivated by both a fear of another suicide and the need emotionally to take care of each other.

This pattern was reflected also in how family members communicated with each other about the suicide. Some talked openly among themselves about it whereas others guarded what they said around each other. And some families simply did not talk about the suicide among themselves, often to protect emotionally vulnerable family members. However, Barlow and Coleman (2003) found that this response, along with one in which a family member assigned guilt or blame for the suicide to another member of the family, resulted in a breakdown or even severing of familial relationships. This complicated the grief process.

Another issue affecting the mourning of survivors of another's suicide is the interaction of these survivors with persons outside of the family. Some studies indicate that these survivors find less helpful support than do other survivors (Dunn & Morrish-Vidners, 1988; Rudestam, 1987). Rudestam (1987) noted that in one study 84 percent of funeral directors who were interviewed said that people reacted differently to suicide survivors. Such studies imply that suicide survivors may be a good example of persons experiencing disenfranchised grief (see Chapter 10).

Part of the difficulty for such survivors concerns the social rules governing how to behave in this situation. Not only are there fewer social rules to guide people, but the rules that do exist seem to constrain behavior more than those rules governing other mourning situations (Calhoun et al., 1986; Dunn & Morrish-Vidners, 1988; Van Dongen, 1990). Another complicating factor is that the survivors themselves seem often to withdraw from others and do not reach out for or readily accept other people's support (Dunn & Morrish-Vidners, 1988). Thus, survivors may experience the stigmatization associated with suicide intrapsychically as much as socially (Allen et al., 1993; Rudestam, 1987).

As we have noted, however, mourning is a process in which people need a support system. If one is to cope adequately with mourning a suicide, then communication, or at least the nonjudgmental presence of others, can be helpful (Bolton, 1995; Chance, 1994; Dunn & Morrish-Vidners, 1988; Jordan & McMenamy, 2004). For all survivors of suicide, the American Association of Suicidology offers a survivor's page on its website (www.suicidology.org) which makes available a great deal of information and resources, including a quarterly newsletter, *Surviving Suicide*, and *A Handbook for Survivors of Suicide* (Jackson, 2003). See also, Survivors of Suicide (www.survivorsofsuicide.com).

Another issue of concern around suicide involves what have been called *cluster* or *copycat* suicides. There is no agreement about how to define such suicides (Davies, 1993; Gould et al., 1990). To the extent that a set of suicides can be seen as being formed by more than chance, such sets occur more frequently among 15- to 19- and 20- to 24-year-olds and perhaps among 45- to 64-year-olds (Gould et al., 1990). However, careful study of such events is still in development. Although it may be the case that some adolescents are influenced by the experience of an earlier suicide, either directly (by actually knowing someone who has committed suicide) or indirectly (by knowing of a suicide from the media or from other people's accounts), the adolescents who have committed suicide following earlier suicides and who have been carefully studied share other attributes that are at least as likely to account for their behavior as this contact (Davidson et al., 1989). Those attributes include substance abuse, mental illness, losing a girlfriend or boyfriend, witnessing or using violence themselves, damaging themselves physically, being more easily offended, attending more schools, moving more frequently, and having more than two adults who served as parents (Davidson et al., 1989).

🐛 Suicide Intervention

In this section we focus on *suicide prevention*. However, because one cannot really prevent very determined acts of suicide, it is better to speak here of *intervention aimed at reducing the likelihood of a completed suicide* (Jobes, 2006; Shneidman, 1971; Silverman & Maris, 1995). Many programs have been developed throughout the United States and in other countries to work toward this goal, often using the techniques of *crisis intervention* (consult local crisis intervention programs in your area or contact the American Association of Suicidology's National Suicide Prevention Lifeline, which is staffed 24 hours per day, seven days per week by trained counselors, at 1-800-SUICIDE [784-2433] or 1-800-273-TALK [8255]). Such programs minister to the needs of persons who feel themselves to be in crisis or who sense an inclination toward suicide. Over decades of work, much has been learned about how persons like this behave. In turn, much has been learned about how others can assist such people—that is, about how to intervene constructively in cases of suicidal or life-threatening behavior (Seiden, 1977).

First, mistaken impressions about suicidal behavior must be confronted (see Table 17.2). For instance, many people believe that suicidal persons do not talk about their intentions, that suicide is the result of a sudden impulse, and that mentioning suicide to someone who is emotionally upset may make a suggestion to that person that he or she had not previously entertained. It has long been recognized that these are all erroneous beliefs (Maris, 1981).

People who are thinking about killing themselves most often *do* talk about this. One estimate claims that 80 percent of persons who are inclined toward suicide communicate their plans to family members, friends, authority figures (such as physicians or clergy), or telephone intervention programs (Hewett, 1980, p. 23). For these reasons, it has been said that most suicidal people desperately want to live or are at least ambivalent about choosing between life and death; they are simply unable to see alternatives to their problems.

TABLE 17.2
Facts and Fables about Suicide

These Statements Are *Not* True	These Statements *Are* True
Fable: People who talk about suicide don't commit suicide.	**Fact:** Of any ten persons who kill themselves, eight have given definite warnings of their suicidal intentions. Suicide threats and attempts *must* be taken seriously.
Fable: Suicide happens without warning.	**Fact:** Studies reveal that the suicidal person gives many clues and warnings regarding his suicidal intentions. Alertness to these cries for help may prevent suicidal behavior.
Fable: Suicidal people are fully intent on dying.	**Fact:** Most suicidal people are undecided about living or dying, and they "gamble with death," leaving it to others to save them. Almost no one commits suicide without letting others know how he is feeling. Often this "cry for help" is given in "code." These distress signals can be used to save lives.
Fable: Once a person is suicidal, he is suicidal forever.	**Fact:** Happily, individuals who wish to kill themselves are "suicidal" only for a limited period of time. If they are saved from self-destruction, they can go on to lead useful lives.
Fable: Improvement following a suicidal crisis means that the suicidal risk is over.	**Fact:** Most suicides occur within about three months following the beginning of "improvement," when the individual has the energy to put his morbid thoughts and feelings into effect. Relatives and physicians should be especially vigilant during this period.
Fable: Suicide strikes more often among the rich—or, conversely, it occurs more frequently among the poor.	**Fact:** Suicide is neither the rich man's disease nor the poor man's curse. Suicide is very "democratic" and is represented proportionately among all levels of society.
Fable: Suicide is inherited or "runs in a family."	**Fact:** Suicide does not run in families. It is an individual matter and can be prevented.
Fable: All suicidal individuals are mentally ill, and suicide is always the act of a psychotic person.	**Fact:** Studies of hundreds of genuine suicide notes indicate that although the suicidal person is extremely unhappy, he is not necessarily mentally ill. His overpowering unhappiness may result from a temporary emotional upset, a long and painful illness, or a complete loss of hope. It is circular reasoning to say that "suicide is an insane act," and therefore all suicidal people are psychotic.

Source: From Shneidman and Farberow, 1961, for the U.S. Government Printing Office, PHS Publication No. 852.

Suicide rarely occurs without warning. It is seldom an action that erupts from nowhere. It is often thought out well in advance and carefully planned. Frequently, a suicidal person gives many clues about his or her intentions (see Focus On 17.1). These clues may or may not be verbal. They might include giving away beloved objects, making changes in eating or sleeping habits, or even displaying a sense of calmness after a period of agitation (calmness because a *decision* has finally been made about what to do).

Asking someone if he or she is thinking about attempting suicide is not planting an idea that would otherwise not have occurred to the person. Individuals who are depressed or who are severely agitated most likely have already thought about killing themselves. Many suicidologists believe that almost all human beings think about the possibility of suicide at one time or another. Thus, suicide is not an infrequently encountered idea. If the person does not volunteer information about suicidal thoughts or plans, the simplest way to discover this is to ask.

Once suicidal intentions are noticed, intervention can take many forms (Hatton & Valente, 1984; Rudd et al., 2001; Westefeld et al., 2006; Yufit & Lester, 2005). Some practical ways to help suicidal people are summarized in Focus On 17.2. First, one should note that many suicidal intentions are not long lasting. A primary goal may be to help the person work through a relatively short-term crisis period. That is a basic strategy employed by all crisis intervention programs.

FOCUS ON 17.1

Warning Signs of Suicide

A person at risk for suicidal behavior most often will exhibit warning signs:

I	Ideation	Expressed or communicated ideation
		o Threatening to hurt or kill him/herself, or talking of wanting to hurt or kill him/herself; and/or
		o Looking for ways to kill him/herself by seeking access to firearms, available pills, or other means; and/or
		o Talking or writing about death, dying or suicide, when these actions are out of the ordinary
S	Substance Abuse	Increased substance (alcohol or drug) use
P	Purposelessness	No reason for living; no sense of purpose in life
A	Anxiety	Anxiety, agitation, unable to sleep or sleeping all the time
T	Trapped	Feeling trapped (like there's no way out)
H	Hopelessness	Hopelessness
W	Withdrawal	Withdrawal from friends, family and society
A	Anger	Rage, uncontrolled anger, seeking revenge
R	Recklessness	Acting reckless or engaging in risk activities, seemingly without thinking
M	Mood Change	Dramatic mood changes

Source: American Association of Suicidology.

Some Practical Ways to Help Suicidal Persons

◆ Take the person seriously; be available to get involved and to listen.

◆ Allow the person to express his or her feelings and try to accept the person for what he or she is; be empathetic, calm, and nonjudgmental.

◆ Don't be afraid to speak openly about suicide; ask questions like "Have you ever thought about hurting or killing yourself?" You can also offer concrete examples of what leads you to believe the person is close to suicide.

◆ Express your concern for the person by listening attentively, maintaining eye contact, moving closer to the person, and touching the person or holding his or her hand, if that seems appropriate.

◆ Don't debate with the person whether suicide is right or wrong or whether the person's feelings are good or bad; an argumentative or lecturing posture will distance you from the person.

◆ Never challenge a potentially suicidal person to complete the act; don't dare him or her to do it.

◆ Find out if the person has a specific plan to carry out a suicidal action or has taken concrete steps to prepare to do so (such as gaining access to the means that might be used to end his or her life).

◆ Point out constructive alternatives that are available, but do not offer glib reassurance; stress that suicide is most often a permanent solution for temporary problems.

◆ Take action by removing the means (such as firearms or stockpiled pills) that the person might use to end his or her life.

◆ Remind the person that although he or she is ultimately responsible for his or her actions, help is available, people do care, and you will try to make connections with helping resources.

◆ Get help from people or agencies that are knowledgeable about intervening in crises and preventing suicide.

◆ Until you can get such help, try to stay with the person and not leave him or her alone; if you must leave, ask the person to make a contract with you or promise not to take any further steps to end his or her life until you can get help or can return to address the situation further.

◆ Do not allow yourself to promise confidentiality or to be sworn to unconditional secrecy; such commitments should be contingent on a contract that the person not act before certain conditions that you set (such as seeking professional help) are met.

Source: Based on guidelines from the American Association of Suicidology and the Depression and Bipolar Support Alliance.

To help suicidal persons it is critical to listen to them. Paying attention to and being present for someone who is suffering is an essential step toward helping that person. Others really must hear the feelings being expressed to try to understand what this person needs. Part of the listening process is to hear suicidal remarks for what they are and to recognize the several levels or dimensions that each remark may contain. Most crisis intervention workers insist that *every* suicidal remark must be taken seriously.

Once such a remark is heard, the actual intentions and plans should be evaluated. The more the person has thought about suicide, and the more he or she has worked out actual plans for suicide, the more seriously must the remarks be taken. A remark like "Sometimes I just feel like killing myself" with no follow-up is less serious than remarks that indicate someone's having thought out when and how he or she intends to accomplish the act. The situation becomes even more serious when actual steps have been taken to prepare to implement the plan.

In general, changes in affect are significant. If someone has been depressed but now seems suddenly much lighter in emotional tone, this is not necessarily a time for reduced concern (Farberow, 1983). Suicidal actions actually increase when people are coming out of depression. In such circumstances, they may finally have the requisite energy to act. Similarly, a change toward agitation can signal a crisis.

In listening, attention must be paid to what the person says. This usually means that one should not engage in the process of evaluating in a judgmental way (from one's own point of view) what the person believes or feels. What looks like a problem from the suicidal person's point of view *is* a problem for that person. Telling such individuals that their problems are insignificant is not likely to be of much help. It is more likely to sound as though we are not really hearing them or are unwilling to appreciate the magnitude of the problems that they believe themselves to be facing. Not surprisingly, they may then turn away from us.

Many suicidal persons experience "tunnel vision," a process in which the individual perceives only a very narrow range of possible solutions for resolving the crisis. From this perspective, suicide may seem to be the only available solution. One way to help is to point out other, constructive options for resolving the crisis, such as drawing on inner resources not previously recognized or turning to external resources available in the community that might help with the crisis (whether they might be emotional, physical, financial, spiritual, or other types).

Finally, specific action is necessary. Getting some particular agreement can be helpful, such as to the following questions: will you agree *not* to do anything until I get there; will you go with me to talk to a counselor; will you promise not to harm yourself until after you next see your therapist? It is also usually important not to let the person be alone or to have access to the means intended to be used to commit suicide. In many cases, the involvement of a trained professional will be essential (Leenaars et al., 1994). Call 1-800-273-TALK (8255) or 1-800-SUICIDE (784-2433) for assistance or a referral from the National Suicide Prevention Lifeline.

One last word on behalf of those involved in suicide or crisis intervention: some who work in this field have pointed out that in the end no one can really take responsibility for someone else's life. If a person is seriously determined to end his or her life, ordinarily someone else cannot prevent that event—short of essentially "jailing" the person. Although guilt is a frequently encountered response to suicide, suicide is, finally, an action over which others have little control. It is an option for human beings.

We should also add that a number of writers (e.g., Lester, 2003, 2006a, 2006b; Werth, 1996, 1999b) have argued that at least in some cases suicide can be a rational and morally acceptable action for some people, while others have disagreed (e.g., Feldman, 2006; Leenaars, 2006; see also Issues for Critical Reflection #15). For example, the philosopher, Seneca (1932, vol. 1, p. 239), offered the following views on this subject:

> But life, as you know, needn't always be held fast. It isn't in living, but in living well, that the good consists. Hence the philosopher-adept [i.e., the wise person] lives as long as he ought, and not as long as he can. . . . The quality of life, not its length, is always his thought. If he encounters a throng of troubles fatal to peace of mind, he sets himself free. . . . It matters not a whit to him whether he procures his end or accepts it, whether it comes slowly or quickly. . . . To die soon or die late matters nothing: to die badly or die well is the important point. But to die well is to escape the risk of living badly.

ISSUES FOR CRITICAL REFLECTION
#15 Can Suicide Ever Be a Morally Appropriate Act?

One issue that has been discussed since ancient times is whether suicide can ever be a morally appropriate act. In part, the answer to this question hinges on whether one believes that suicide can ever be a "rational" act. As we have seen, depression, ambivalence, and other powerful emotions play central roles in much suicidal behavior. This leads some to argue that suicide is always or almost always an "irrational" act (Jamison, 1999). If this is in fact the case, then it would influence how we are to view the moral status of suicide.

However, others have argued that there may be lucid, rational, even morally appropriate motives for suicide (Lester, 2003; Werth, 1996, 1999b). Rollin (1985) agreed with this view, at least under some circumstances. She wrote, "The real question is, does a person have a right to depart from life when he or she is nearing the end and has nothing but horror ahead?" (Humphry, 1992, p. 14). Rollin views suicide as a legitimate form of "self-deliverance." This position is based on an assertion that the legitimate scope of an individual's autonomy should include a "right to die" or a right to end one's life (Fox et al., 1999; Hillyard & Dombrink, 2001; Humphry &

Clement, 1998; Meisel & Cerminara, 2004). In fact, it is not illegal to commit suicide in any jurisdiction in the United States. This suggests that for many people in our society suicide lies legitimately within the range of the individual's autonomy.

Other societies also think of suicide as appropriate under some types of conditions. Social, political, and moral contexts may be held to demand the suicide of an individual for the sake of the good of the society or the family (see the discussion of altruistic suicide in this chapter). However, most arguments supporting the moral appropriateness of suicide require at least that the person engaged in such an action be rational when the action is undertaken.

Arguments opposed to the morality of suicide assume that anyone engaged in such an action is not rational or that there are other overriding moral values that come into play. For instance, as we discuss elsewhere in this chapter, almost all religions oppose taking one's own life. This may be because they believe that the individual's life does not belong to him or her alone (it belongs ultimately to God) or because a sacred writing forbids it.

As a result, Seneca and other writers argue that it is not universally appropriate to intervene to prevent a suicide and that it might equally be acceptable to assist a person who seeks to carry out a *rational suicide.*

❧ Religious Views of the Moral Appropriateness of Suicide

Although it is impossible to describe in any simple way a given religious tradition's view on suicide, the following statements offer a sampling of religious positions.

Judaism

"For Judaism, human life is 'created in the image of God.' . . . The sanctity of human life prescribes that, in any situation short of self-defense or martyrdom, human life be treated as an end in itself. . . . Even individual autonomy is secondary to the sanctity of human life and therefore, a patient is not permitted to end his or her life" (Feldman & Rosner, 1984, p. 106). Notice the exceptions given here.

Christianity

The *Declaration on Euthanasia* from the Roman Catholic tradition in Christianity includes the following statement: "Intentionally causing one's own death, or suicide, is . . . equally as wrong as murder; such an action on the part of a person is to be considered as a rejection of God's sovereignty and loving plan. Furthermore, suicide is also often a refusal of love for self, the denial of the natural instinct to live, a flight from the duties of justice and charity owed to one's neighbor, to various communities, or to the whole of society" (Sacred Congregation for the Doctrine of the Faith, 1982, p. 512). This last point is reinforced by Smith (1986, p. 64), arguing out of the Anglican tradition: "In any context suicide is a social act . . . because selfhood is so social, suicide cannot be simply a matter of private right. . . . As a child of God the Christian must relate all choices to that relationship." He also argues (in the context of suicide because of medical circumstances, but this argument might be extended to all suicidal contexts), "the great difficulty with supposed altruistic suicide, on medical grounds, is that it ignores the guilt felt by others and the desertion of them that is involved."

Islam

The *Qur'an* contains the following relevant passages: "Do not with your own hands cast yourselves into destruction" (2, 195) and "Do not destroy yourselves . . . he that does that through wickedness and injustice shall be burned in fire" (4, 29). However, Rahman (1987, p. 126) reports, "The only way a Muslim can and is expected to freely give and take life is 'in the path of Allah,' as a martyr in jihad or holy war. According to a Hadith a person who dies defending self, family, and property (by extension also the country) against aggression is also a martyr."

Hinduism

"Hinduism condemns suicide as evil when it is a direct and deliberate act with the intention voluntarily to kill oneself for self-regarding motives. Subjectively, the evil resides in the act as the product of ignorance and passion; objectively, the evil encompasses the karmic consequences of the act which impede the progress of liberation." This view is modified, however, under some circumstances: "Hinduism permits selective recourse to suicide when it is religiously motivated. . . . The whole of Hindu discipline is an exercise in progressive renunciation, and continuous with that, *suicide is the supreme act of renunciation*. For the sage, it is the death of death" (Crawford, 1995, pp. 68, 71).

Buddhism

"The standard Buddhist attitude towards suicide is that it is a futile, misguided act motivated by the desire for annihilation . . . the affirmation of nirvana cannot be a choice against life." Again, however, under some circumstances, suicide might be acceptable to Buddhists: "Bodhisattvas who sacrifice themselves are not choosing against life but displaying a readiness to lay down their lives in the service of their fellow man. They do not seek death for its own sake, but accept that death may come, so to speak, in the course of their duty" (Keown, 1995, pp. 58, 59).

❧ Summary

In this chapter, we explored some of the many dimensions and implications of suicide and life-threatening behavior. We sought to clarify the concept of suicide and to emphasize the many elements that may enter into a completed suicide. We also described some common patterns in suicidal behavior, and we examined psychological, biological, and sociological efforts to explain such behavior. We gave special attention to the impact on someone who survives the suicide of another person. In addition, we identified warning signs for suicide, along with interventions that individuals and society might initiate to minimize suicidal behavior. Finally, we reported statements from five major religious traditions as to whether suicide could ever be considered a morally appropriate action.

Glossary

Altruistic suicide: suicide undertaken on behalf of one's social group; a sociological category in which suicide is said to arise from an overinvolvement or overintegration of an individual into his or her society

Anomic suicide: suicide undertaken when society is unable or unwilling to help its members in regulating their desires; a sociological category in which suicide is said to arise from social underregulation or sudden withdrawal of social control; *anomia* = *a* [without] + *nomoi* [laws or norms], thus "lawlessness" or "normlessness"

Arguments that favor suicidal behavior: generally depend on concepts like rational suicide

Arguments that oppose suicidal behavior: generally depend on psychological concerns (e.g., that such behavior is most often motivated by treatable depression or ambivalence) or religious beliefs (e.g., that life ultimately belongs to God or that suicide is forbidden by some sacred writing)

Completed suicide: a situation in which someone has deliberately ended his or her life

Egoistic suicide: suicide undertaken when society fails to help individuals find meaning in their lives so that they (often suddenly) find themselves alone or isolated; a sociological category in which suicide is said to arise from underinvolvement or underintegration of an individual from his or her society

Either/or thinking: constricted thought processes in which one can only envision continuing in a painful condition or escaping that condition by ending one's life

Explanations of suicide: efforts to understand or account for suicidal behavior; in general, these look to psychological, biological, or sociological factors

Fatalistic suicide: suicide undertaken when an individual seeks to escape from an overcontrolling social context; a sociological category in which suicide is said to arise from excessive regulation of individuals by society

Haplessness: describes persistently ill-fated or unlucky behavior

Helplessness: an inability to assist or take care of oneself

Hopelessness: a condition in which one has no positive expectations for his or her future

Inimicality: an unsettled life pattern in which one acts against one's own best interests

Life-threatening behavior: actions that put one's life at risk, whether or not they actually end it; a more general phrase than "suicidal behavior"

Perturbation: heightened psychological disturbance in a person's life

Rational suicide: the ending of one's life as a result of motives that are thought to be lucid, rational, and morally appropriate; a view that the legitimate scope of one's autonomy and self-determination should include the right to end one's life; sometimes described as a legitimate form of "self-deliverance"

Suicidal behavior: actions that have a high risk of ending one's life

Suicide: the deliberate or intentional ending of one's own life; sometimes called intentional self-harm

Suicide intervention: efforts made to reduce the likelihood of completed suicides or at least to minimize suicidal behavior

Suicide prevention: since very determined acts of suicide quite often cannot be prevented, suicidologists prefer to speak of "intervention" rather than "prevention"

Suicidology and suicidologists: the scientific study of suicide and suicidal behavior; individuals who study suicidal behavior, intervene to minimize such behavior, or treat its aftereffects

Survivors of suicide: a phrase usually used to refer to individuals who experience the aftereffects of the suicide of another; not ordinarily used to refer to individuals who attempt to end their lives but who do not succeed in their attempts

Tunnel vision: a condition of constricted thinking in which one can only envision few or limited options; a narrowing of one's range of perceptions, opinions, and options

Questions for Review and Discussion

1. This chapter began with examples of two individuals who ended their own lives: Ernest Hemingway and Sylvia Plath. Using what you have learned about suicide, what similarities and differences do you see in these two actions?

2. Have you ever thought about ending your life? Has anyone you know and care about reported to you thoughts about ending his or her life? What was going on in your life (or in the other person's life) that led to such thoughts or that helped you (or the other person) get past that point? What might you (or someone else) have done to help a person with such thoughts get past that point?

3. Have you ever known someone who ended his or her life by suicide? What was your response to that action? Think about how other people reacted to that action. How were these responses like what we learned about grief and mourning in Chapter 9? How were they different?

Suggested Readings

Dunne, E. J., McIntosh, J. L., & Dunne-Maxim, K. (Eds.). (1987). *Suicide and Its Aftermath: Understanding and Counseling the Survivors.*

Evans, G., & Farberow, N. L. (Eds.). (1988). *The Encyclopedia of Suicide.*

Hawton, K., & Van Heeringen, K. (2000). *The International Handbook of Suicide and Attempted Suicide.*

Jacobs, D. G. (1999). *The Harvard Medical School Guide to Suicide Assessment and Intervention.*

Jamison, K. R. (1999). *Night Falls Fast: Understanding Suicide.*

Jobes, A. A. (2006). *Managing Suicidal Risk: A Collaborative Approach.*

Leenaars, A. A., Maltsberger, J. T., & Neimeyer, R. A. (1994). *Treatment of Suicidal People.*

Leenaars, A. A., & Wenckstern, S. (Eds.). (1991). *Suicide Prevention in the Schools.*

Leong, F. T. L., & Leach, M. M. (Eds.). (2007). Ethnicity and Suicide in the United States. [Special issue]. *Death Studies, 31*(5).

Lester, D. (1992). *Why People Kill Themselves* (3rd ed.).

Lukas, C., & Seiden, H. M. (2007). *Silent Grief: Living in the Wake of Suicide* (rev. ed.).

Maris, R. W. (1981). *Pathways to Suicide: A Survey of Self-Destructive Behaviors.*

Maris, R. W. (Ed.). (1988). *Understanding and Preventing Suicide.*

Maris, R. W., Berman, A. L., & Silverman, M. M. (2000). *Comprehensive Textbook of Suicidology.*

Poland, S. (1989). *Suicide Intervention in the Schools.*

Rudd, M. D., Joiner, T., & Rajab, M. H. (2001). *Treating Suicidal Behavior: An Effective, Time-Limited Approach.*

Shneidman, E. S. (1980/1995). *Voices of Death.*

Shneidman, E. S. (1985). *Definition of Suicide.*

Silverman, M. M., & Maris, R. W. (1995). *Suicide Prevention: Toward the Year 2000.*

Smolin, A., & Guinan, J. (1993). *Healing after the Suicide of a Loved One.*

Yufit, R. I., & Lester, D. (2005). *Assessment, Treatment and Prevention of Suicidal Behavior.*

Selected Web Resources

Some useful search terms include: ALTRUISTIC SUICIDE; ANOMIC SUICIDE; EGOISTIC SUICIDE; FATALISTIC SUICIDE; LIFE-THREATENING BEHAVIOR; RATIONAL SUICIDE; SUICIDE; SUICIDOLOGY; SURVIVORS OF SUICIDE

Visit the book companion website for *Death & Dying, Life & Living, Sixth Edition,* at academic.cengage.com/psychology/corr for all URLs and live links to the following *organizational and other Internet sites:*

American Association of Suicidology

American Foundation for Suicide Prevention

Depression and Bipolar Support Alliance

International Association for Suicide Prevention (IASP)

Metanoia (counseling, especially related to suicide)

The Samaritans International

Suicide and Life-Threatening Behavior **(published by Guilford Press)**

The Suicide and Mental Health Association International (SMHAI)

Survivors of Loved One's Suicides (SOLOS)

Survivors of Suicide

CHAPTER 18

Assisted Suicide and Euthanasia: Intentionally Ending a Human Life

© Topham/The Image Works

Objectives of This Chapter

◆ To examine conceptual and moral issues related to the intentional ending of a human life

◆ To define *assisted suicide* and *euthanasia*, and to distinguish them from other modes of intentionally ending a human life

◆ To differentiate assisted suicide and euthanasia by considering *agency* (who acts?)

and *intent* (what goals guide decision making?)

◆ To explore the morality of assisted suicide and euthanasia by examining philosophical arguments and the perspectives of several world religions on these topics

◆ To discuss recent social policies on these subjects in the Netherlands and in the state of Oregon

🐦 Terri Schiavo

On February 25, 1990, Terri Schiavo was 26 years old and had been married to Michael Schiavo for 6 years. She had not signed either a living will or a durable power of attorney. On that day, Terri's heart stopped (apparently as a consequence of an eating disorder), and her brain was deprived of oxygen. From that date forward, Terri was in a coma, and some (including several physicians) believed that she was in a persistent vegetative state. The National Institute of Neurological Disorders and Stroke defines a persistent vegetative state as one in which persons "have lost their thinking abilities and awareness of their surroundings, but retain noncognitive function and normal sleep patterns. . . . Spontaneous movements may occur, and the eyes may open in response to external stimuli. They may even occasionally grimace, cry or laugh" (Anonymous, 2003, p. 4A). Terry showed many of these symptoms, and that fact eventually led to a legal battle between her husband (who was her court-appointed legal guardian) and her parents. On one hand, after several years of rehabilitative efforts Michael Schiavo came to believe that Terri would never recover. He said she told him before her heart attack that she would not want to be kept alive by artificial means. On that basis, since 1998 he repeatedly asked a local circuit court to order the removal of a tube that had been surgically implanted in her stomach to provide (1) hydration, (2) nutrition, and (3) medications. On the other hand, Terri's parents and siblings (who believed that she still had some cognitive function and at least limited potential for improved quality of life) repeatedly blocked Michael's requests by various legal means.

In February of 2000, a Florida circuit court judge ruled that the implanted tube (technically, a gastrostomy tube, but commonly called a "feeding tube") could be removed. That was done on April 24, 2001. However, on April 26, 2001, a different

Terri Shiavo

Florida circuit court judge ordered physicians to reinstate the stomach tube while Terri's parents pursued a lawsuit against Michael (Ulferts & Lindberg, 2003, p. 1A). In November of 2002, the first judge again ordered the tube removed, but stayed implementation of his order until a state appeals court upheld it and the Florida Supreme Court declined to review the decision of the appeals court. The tube was then removed for a second time on October 15, 2003.

A group of opponents to this action and supporters of the parents' view began a round-the-clock vigil outside the hospice facility in which Terri was receiving care. At this point, after receiving many calls and e-mails from around the country opposing the removal of Terri's stomach tube, the Florida legislature stepped in and very quickly (without holding the usual hearings or taking testimony from experts) passed "Terri's Law." This bill gave the governor of Florida, Jeb Bush, the authority to order the stomach tube to be reinserted; that was done on October 21, 2003. (A poll in December 2003 showed that 65 percent of Florida voters were opposed to this law [Smith, 2003, pp. 1A, 21A]. However, a set of disability rights groups and others supported the governor's action [*Times* Staff Writer, 2004, p. 3B].)

In May of 2004, a Florida circuit court judge ruled Terri's Law to be a violation of the Florida constitution. The governor appealed, but the Florida appellate court passed the issue directly to the Florida Supreme Court. In August of 2004, arguments were heard by that court, which ruled unanimously in September that Terri's Law was an unconstitutional violation of the separation of powers in our governmental system. The same court subsequently refused to reconsider that decision. In December 2004, the governor of Florida requested a review of that decision by the U.S. Supreme Court, but that request was turned down without comment in January 2005.

On February 25, 2005, the original local judge gave permission to remove the stomach tube. That was done on March 18. Subsequently, the U.S. Congress passed and President Bush signed a bill to allow a federal court to review the case. In response to a request from Terri Schiavo's parents for such a review, a federal district judge declined to order the stomach tube reinserted. That ruling was sustained by the Eleventh U.S. Circuit Court of Appeals, after which the U.S. Supreme Court again declined to hear the case. Additional local court rulings prohibited the state of Florida from reinserting the stomach tube or taking Terri into state custody. The Florida Supreme Court refused to overturn these rulings, and the federal district court, the Eleventh U.S. Circuit Court of Appeals, and the U.S. Supreme Court once again declined to intervene.

Terri Schiavo finally died on March 31, 2005, more than 15 years after the heart attack that had begun her long saga. Her death has been followed by a flood of books and other publications by her husband, her family of origin, lawyers, bioethicists, and other commentators (e.g., Caplan et al., 2006; Colby, 2006; Eisenberg, 2005; Gibbs & DeMoss, 2006; Gostin, 2005; Lynne, 2005; The Schiavo Case, 2005; Schiavo & Hirsh, 2006; Terri's Family et al., 2006; Werth, 2006).

❦ Situating the Issues

The issues addressed in this chapter concern decisions made in certain specific situations intentionally to end a human life. People in our society may be led to or compelled to make such decisions as a consequence of advances that are used to extend the length of human lives. For example, beginning in the second half of the 20th century, modern technology has kept many individuals alive who clearly would have died in earlier times. Such persons include those unable to breathe on their own and many persons with severe brain trauma or with progressive debilitating diseases who would have died when respirators or nasogastric feeding tubes were unavailable. In addition, chemotherapy, radiation therapy, organ and tissue transplants, and many other techniques have extended the lives of many persons. This is a widely admired outcome of modern medicine.

However, these technologies not only have made possible the continuation of someone's living but sometimes have increased the depth, length, and degree of that individual's suffering. In certain instances, the life continued by these techniques has been felt by some to be demeaning and demoralizing as well as filled with suffering. When contemporary therapies are unable effectively to handle these aspects of people's dying, some have argued that death is to be preferred to continuing such a dying.

How often this issue needs to be confronted is a matter of dispute. Hospice philosophy (see Chapter 8) would argue that inadequate care is being provided when someone experiences a demeaning dying process filled with suffering. That is, hospice philosophy suggests that it is seldom necessary that anyone with a life-threatening illness should be faced with the question of whether death is to be preferred to this present existence. That may be true. However, hospice care is not (yet) available to everyone who is dying, and there are a (perhaps small) number of situations in which even hospice or palliative care is unable successfully to handle the suffering being experienced. In these situations, the question of the desirability of choosing to end a life may still arise.

The basic question examined in this chapter is: Is it ever appropriate to choose to end rather than to continue a human life? If this question is answered affirmatively, then other questions arise out of that response. These questions include: In what way is it appropriate to become dead, and who may properly be involved in the process of someone's becoming dead? In addressing such questions, we look for some basis on which they might appropriately be answered, and we enter a path that compels us to think explicitly about the morality of intentionally ending a human life.

In the United States, questions such as these have been most closely associated with assisted suicide and euthanasia. We discuss these issues here because they have become matters of intense debate in our society in recent years and because they are often associated with a degree of conceptual and moral confusion that hinders such debate. Our principal aim in this chapter is to clarify the concepts of assisted suicide and euthanasia, and to help sort out arguments made on behalf of or against such ways of deciding to end a human life.

❧ Deciding to End a Human Life: Who Acts?

One key issue in deciding to end a human life is the matter of *agency*. Put briefly, the question is: *Who acts?* In both assisted suicide and euthanasia, at least two individuals are always involved. The difference is in the role that these individuals play in bringing about the ultimate outcome.

Assisted Suicide: Who Acts?

In all cases of assisted suicide, like all other instances of suicide, an individual ends his or her own life. The classic portrait of a suicidal act is one in which an individual obtains a lethal means and uses it to cause his or her own death. We should add that we will assume here that the person engaging in this act is under no coercion from someone else to engage in that act. Such coercion fundamentally alters the situation from the one we are discussing here. As a form of suicide, then, *assisted suicide* follows this same pattern. The difference is that now the suicide is deliberately assisted. That is, in assisted suicide the means used to end the life of one person are obtained from and with the cooperation of a second individual who understands that the first person intends to use those means to end his or her life. In cases of assisted suicide, the first person performs the act that ends his or her own life. No other individual commits this act. If a gun is used to kill the person, the person pulls the trigger. If a lethal drug is injected, the person injects himself or herself. No one else need even be present when this action takes place.

Euthanasia: Who Acts?

The situation is quite different when an individual is asked to act in some way (to commit or forego an action) to end the life of another person. Suppose that a person is suffering physically or emotionally and would prefer to be dead. That person might call upon some other individual to act in such a way as to end the first person's life. The action of the second individual is critical to what is meant by the term *euthanasia*. Euthanasia occurs when at least two people are involved and one of those persons dies because some other individual intends that person to die and acts in such a way as to bring about that outcome.

To be more precise, euthanasia properly refers to a situation in which the intention of the second individual who contributes to the death of the first person embodies an attempt to end the suffering of that first person. Whether that suffering must already be present (e.g., the person is in great suffering right now) or may be expected to be present in the future is, as we note later, a matter of some dispute. What is not in dispute in all cases of euthanasia is that the individual who does not die is the principal agent involved in bringing about the death.

Discussions of euthanasia frequently make use of *a distinction concerning whether the death is accomplished with or without the permission of the person who dies.* If the person who dies asked for or assented to his or her death, this is *voluntary euthanasia* (Downing, 1974; Gruman, 1973); the will of the person who dies is known. If the will of the person who dies remains unknown, then it is *nonvoluntary euthanasia.* For example, the person might be unconscious or unable to make plain his or her choice for some other reason (think of a person who has had a severe stroke). Or a person such as a child or someone intellectually or emotionally disabled might be incompetent to make such a decision. If a second individual somehow intentionally contributes to the death of this sort of person, it is nonvoluntary euthanasia.

A third possibility (in theory, at least) is one in which the wishes of the person are known—he or she wants to be kept alive—but someone else decides to end that life anyway. Perhaps this could be called "involuntary euthanasia." However, to act *against* someone's wishes is more like homicide than like a "good death" (see our discussion of the meaning of the term *euthanasia* next), so one might not want to associate this possibility with the term *euthanasia* in any way.

Some argue that a person who is acutely suffering, by the very fact of that suffering, has diminished capacity to make difficult decisions. If that were true, one might be uncomfortable following the directions of a person in severe physical or emotional pain. Choosing to cooperate in a person's death is an irreversible decision; in the face of that irrevocability, one would want to be as certain as possible that the person's own choice was clearly and competently presented.

So far, we have carefully distinguished between assisted suicide and euthanasia by indicating who the agent is who performs (or fails to perform) an act that results in the death. However, we acknowledge that there are situations in which the usefulness of this distinction is less obvious than our discussion indicates. Consider three possibilities. First, suppose you are able to carry out an act that results in your death. Now suppose you ask someone else to provide you with the means to carry out this act and that individual agrees to provide the means for you to kill yourself. That is *assisted suicide.* Second, now suppose you could perform such an action, but you ask someone else to perform it. Suppose what that individual does next is done out of compassion and results in your death. That is *euthanasia.* Third, now suppose you are unable to perform the action yourself (you are paralyzed for instance). Then if someone else performs the action that produces your death, it can be less clear whether that action is an assisted suicide or an act of euthanasia. You would kill yourself if you could (but you cannot because of your paralysis); thus the other individual acts in your place because of your inability to carry out the act.

What this means is perhaps best described as follows. Assisted suicide and euthanasia belong on opposite ends of a continuum. At one end of the continuum, it is obvious that you (with means provided by another individual) kill yourself. At the other end of the continuum, someone else kills you. In between these will be a variety of situations that lie closer to one end or the other of the continuum. However, these situations will less easily be assigned to the category of assisted suicide or euthanasia.

This lack of certainty matters most when we begin to think about the morality of certain sorts of acts. Also, this lack of certainty suggests that any attempt to reason adequately about the morality of these issues must be subtle enough to take note of the relevant differences between these various sorts of cases.

❧ Deciding to End a Human Life: What Is Intended?

Another key issue in discussions about deciding to end a human life is *the nature of the act itself.* One helpful element in characterizing the nature of the act is the *intention* that underlies it.

Assisted Suicide: What Is Intended?

The phrase *assisted suicide* applies to a wide range of actions in which one person intentionally acts to end his or her life and secures assistance from another individual to achieve that result. Assisted suicide occurs only when: (1) one person *intentionally* acts to obtain assistance in ending his or her life from a second individual; (2) the second individual *intentionally* acts to provide the necessary assistance to bring about the death of the first person *with full awareness of how that assistance is to be used;* and (3) the first person *intentionally* uses the assistance provided to carry out his or her own self-destruction (or what some call "self-deliverance"). The role of intent is evident in all aspects of the assistance that defines assisted suicide.

The assistance provided in an assisted suicide could be the means used to produce the death (e.g., a gun or a drug), the environment or place in which the act occurs, emotional support, or some combination of these elements. Whether someone needs such forms of assistance is usually related to the person's ability to obtain the required means. Situations that are not instances of assisted suicide include ones in which a person is able on his or her own to buy a gun and use it to end his or her life or to go to a physician's office and get a prescription for a particular medication, then go to a pharmacist and get that prescription filled, and then use that medication to end his or her own life. Only if the person buying the gun or requesting the medication (explicitly or implicitly) informs the seller or the physician/pharmacist that he or she intends to use the gun or the medication to end his or her life, and the seller or health care provider *acts in concurrence with that intention,* could these situations be regarded as instances of *assisted* suicide.

When a person asks a physician to help end his or her life—for example, by prescribing medications that only physicians can order—this marks out a special kind of assisted suicide called *physician-assisted suicide.* In view of the special professional authority accorded to physicians in our society and their access to certain means that can be used in ending a human life, physician-assisted suicide is the type of assisted suicide that has received most public attention in recent years. However, the physician in this situation does nothing to the person when the action is taken that ends the life of the person. As we noted previously, this absence of participation in the lethal act in most situations clearly marks off physician-assisted suicide from cases of euthanasia. In physician-assisted suicide, the physician provides (indirectly, if giving the person a prescription) only the means (and perhaps emotional support)—as was typical in Dr. Kevorkian's early cases (see Focus On 18.1).

Other individuals may also provide such means. For example, a friend or relative might have access to medications or to weapons that could be used for suicidal acts and might provide them to help a person end his or her life. Whenever

Dr. Jack Kevorkian burns a cease-and-desist order in April 1997 in Detroit.

© AP Photo/Carlos Osorio

Dr. Jack Kevorkian

During the 1990s, Dr. Jack Kevorkian helped to bring to public attention a number of issues associated with assisted suicide and euthanasia. A retired pathologist, Kevorkian publicly announced in 1990 his willingness to assist individuals to end their own lives (Betzold, 1993). Later that year, Kevorkian was involved in the assisted suicide of Janet Adkins, 54, of Portland, Oregon. While asking others to join him in these activities, Kevorkian insisted that he would do what he thought right in what he viewed as matters of self-determination and choice, regardless of individual or community opposition.

The assistance that Kevorkian provided at first took the form of a "suicide machine" through which individuals could control the administration of a series of eventually lethal drugs. Later, Kevorkian simply began providing instructions through which individuals could bring about their deaths in other ways. It appears that Kevorkian took pains to ensure that he was not present when an individual undertook the action that resulted in death or, at least, that he took no active role in that action. For whatever reasons, prosecutors found it impossible to convict Kevorkian of assisted suicide or any other substantial legal wrongdoing. Subsequently, one retrospective examination of their autopsy reports (Roscoe et al., 2000) claimed that only 17 of the first 69 persons whom Kevorkian helped kill were actually terminally ill or had less than six months to live, although most had chronic, often painful life-threatening illnesses (5 appeared to have no significant physical disease).

In late 1998, Kevorkian acknowledged being present at or involved in about 130 deaths (*St. Petersburg Times,* 1998). Then, Kevorkian videotaped his own direct involvement in bringing about the death of Thomas Youk, a 52-year-old man with advanced amyotrophic lateral sclerosis (ALS or Lou Gehrig's disease). A videotape from September 15, 1998, showed Youk agreeing to this act of euthanasia and signing what Kevorkian said was a consent form. Another videotape from September 17 showed Kevorkian injecting Youk with two chemicals that caused his death (Werth, 2001). On Sunday, November 22, an edited version of these videotapes was shown on the CBS television show *60 Minutes.*

On November 25, the prosecutor in Oakland County, Michigan, charged Kevorkian with first-degree murder and criminal assisted suicide. This occurred after Kevorkian challenged the prosecutor to charge him within a week. It also followed the defeat in early November by Michigan voters of a ballot referendum approving of assisted suicide. Although the prosecutor had been elected after a pledge not to waste more public funds in futile prosecutions of Kevorkian, he is reported to have regarded the public showing of the videotape as demonstrating an obvious violation of law that he could not ignore.

At trial in March 1999, Kevorkian acted as his own lawyer. After the charge of assisted suicide was withdrawn, the judge ruled that testimony of Thomas Youk's family members would be prohibited as irrelevant to

(continued)

Dr. Jack Kevorkian

the remaining charges of murder. Subsequently, Kevorkian rested his case without calling himself or any other witnesses for the defense. On March 26, the jury found Kevorkian guilty of second-degree murder and delivering a controlled substance.

On April 13, 1999, Kevorkian was sentenced to 10–25 years in prison for murder and 3–7 years for delivery of a controlled substance. In handing down these sentences, the judge is reported to have said to Kevorkian that, "This trial was not about the political or moral correctness of euthanasia. It was about you, sir. It was about lawlessness. It was about disrespect for a society that exists because of the strength of the legal system. No one, sir, is above the law. No one" (*St. Louis Post-Dispatch*, 1999, p. A1). The judge agreed to allow these sentences to run concurrently but refused to release Kevorkian on bail, and his subsequent appeals were rejected. Kevorkian did not fulfill a pledge he once made to starve himself to death. With time off for good behavior, he was granted a parole on June 1, 2007, conditioned in part on his pledge not to assist others in the future to end their lives.

there is a mutual (explicit or implicit) understanding of a suicidal intention, the involvement of these other individuals in deciding to end a person's life constitutes an instance of assisted suicide but not physician-assisted suicide.

Euthanasia: What Is Intended?

The intention to end a human life is also central in cases of euthanasia. There is some confusion and disagreement about what is meant by "euthanasia" (to what it refers) in many contemporary discussions. Etymologically, *euthanasia* comes from the Greek (*eu* = "good" + *thanatos* = "death") and literally means a "good death." Since few would oppose a good death for themselves or others, the real question is what might be involved in bringing about such a death, even when acting for benevolent motives. Clearly, it would not be a good death if whatever is done or not done were not guided by a beneficent or well-meaning intention. A malevolent intention would define some form of homicide.

However, this description is incomplete. Euthanasia properly refers to a situation in which the individual who contributes to the death of another person *intends to end the suffering of that second person.* That suffering might already be present (the person is in great suffering right now), or it might be expected to be present in the future (think of someone in the early stages of Lou Gehrig's disease or Alzheimer's disease). Note that this understanding of euthanasia does not limit it to situations in which someone is close to death. Some people would further limit the use of the term *euthanasia* to these latter situations—that is, they hold that a person must be close to death for euthanasia to be at issue. In this view, if the person were not near death, we would be discussing homicide or manslaughter, not euthanasia. This viewpoint led some to criticize the actions of Dr. Jack Kevorkian (see Focus On 18.1) on the grounds that some of those whom he helped end their lives had not previously been actively dying or near death.

Active versus Passive Euthanasia

Another distinction frequently encountered in discussions of the morality of euthanasia concerns the means by which the ending of a suffering person's life will occur. Here some draw a distinction between active and passive euthanasia. *Actively doing something to end suffering by ending a human life* is often called *active euthanasia*. In situations of this type, one deliberately commits an act (for benevolent motives) that in itself causes the death. This definition allows little room for ambiguity.

The case is a bit more complex when we turn to *passive euthanasia*. Two alternatives often come up in this discussion: the first of these alternatives refers to *withholding* (not supplying) some intervention necessary to sustain life; the latter alternative involves *withdrawing* (taking away) some intervention that is currently in place and may be helping to sustain life. Those who see no moral difference between these two alternatives often speak of "foregoing" some intervention, which seems to include either withholding (not initiating some intervention) or withdrawing (taking away some intervention) that may be necessary to sustain life (Lynn, 1986). In practice, some individuals in our society and many health care providers have been concerned that the act of withdrawing is not passive. (In part, their concern may also be about their legal responsibilities that would be involved in stopping or removing some existing intervention.) Acting to withdraw an intervention seems to involve doing something to take away the existing intervention. This appears to be so even if the result does not in itself end the life but only removes an obstacle that is or may be blocking the natural processes of dying leading to death.

Because of the uncertainty we just noted, this distinction between active and passive euthanasia is not always as clear or helpful as we might like it to be. If the person who is ill is able to walk away from the care provider, that person can simply refuse any treatment offered, and in our system is *legally* allowed to do so as an expression of what is now a well-established *right of privacy* (Alderman & Kennedy, 1997; Annas, 2004). In addition, we do not typically describe such walking away as *immoral*. If a care provider offers you a form of treatment that he or she believes is necessary to sustain your life (say, hemodialysis or chemotherapy) and you refuse it and never return to receive it, this is not an example of an illegal (or to many minds, an immoral) act. Your personal autonomy includes the right to make such a choice.

This issue may appear to be more obscure when someone is unable to walk away (because he or she is too weak or is bedridden, paralyzed, etc.). For someone who has a life-threatening illness and who is in a medical care institution—willingly or not—to refuse apparently necessary treatment to sustain his or her life raises questions for many persons about the legitimacy of that refusal. In these circumstances, in many eyes, to refuse the chemotherapy or the treatment for one's burns carries a nuance of choosing to die that is not as clear in the situation described in the previous paragraph. That is, it may appear to be a request for someone else to help one to die and is thus an instance of passive euthanasia.

To recognize what is really going on in these situations, however, once more we must understand the *intentions* of the person who refuses the treatment and those of the caregiver. The person who walks away may or may not intend to die; if he or she does have that intention, then this may be part of a *suicidal* act. The person who cannot walk away may or may not intend to die; if he or she does have this intention, the refusal of treatment may be a request for *passive euthanasia*. Simply refusing treatment, *in and of itself*, need be neither an instance of suicide nor a request for passive euthanasia. A person might refuse treatment simply because it has become too burdensome (physically, psychologically, financially, etc.). Everything hinges on the intentions of the persons involved. It is suicide or euthanasia only when the person who refuses some treatment does this *in order to die*, and, if another person is involved, only when that person also *intends for death to occur*.

Extraordinary versus Ordinary Means

Another distinction often introduced in discussions about ending a human life is that between *extraordinary and ordinary means of treatment*. The point of this distinction is to argue that there is no moral obligation to provide extraordinary means of treatment. Many have made this claim; for instance, Roman Catholic ethicists (e.g., McCormick, 1974) have long argued that care providers have no such moral obligation.

Several criteria are offered to help implement this distinction. *Ordinary means of treatment* are those that: (1) have outcomes that are predictable and well known; (2) offer no unusual risk, suffering, or burden for either the person who is being treated or others; and (3) are effective. *Extraordinary means of treatment* fail to meet one or more of these criteria. Extraordinary means may have outcomes that are not predictable or well known, as in the case of some experimental procedures. Such procedures may not have been widely used or studied, so that one cannot be certain what will happen when one embarks on their use in particular cases. Or it may be that a procedure itself puts the patient at risk or imposes undue burdens on those who would assist the patient. That is, the procedure may have a broad range of outcomes, some of which make the person worse off than he or she was before. The side effects, for instance, of a treatment might produce more suffering than the person was undergoing before the treatment began. An extraordinary means of treatment might even produce effects that are worse than the disease. Since the outcome of using such means is unpredictable, one might have little confidence that they will in fact be helpful in dealing either with the person's symptoms or disease. That is, the actual effectiveness of an extraordinary means of treatment may be uncertain, too.

What counts as ordinary and extraordinary means cannot be determined independently of an individual person's context. What might be ordinary treatment in one situation could be extraordinary in another. There is no list of treatments that can—purely on their own—be determined to be ordinary in this moral sense, and another list of treatments that can be determined to be extraordinary. Whether a specific treatment is ordinary or extraordinary must be decided in terms of a particular person's situation.

It is important not to confuse this *moral* distinction between ordinary and extraordinary means with an empirical distinction between that which is routine or familiar and that which is not. What is *medically* ordinary may not also be *morally* ordinary in the context of this discussion. For example, the use of ventilators and respirators is quite common in many hospitals and long-term care facilities. That does not determine their moral status according to the ordinary/extraordinary distinction. Similarly, in recent years various forms of artificial feeding have become common, especially for individuals in various forms of temporary coma or in the more serious condition described as a permanent or persistent vegetative state (PVS). Artificial nutrition and hydration for individuals in persistent vegetative states is a form of medical treatment commonly delivered as special liquid formulas through a feeding tube implanted directly into the stomach. Many bioethicists and moral theologians have suggested that such medical interventions may be or become (after sufficient time has enabled specialists to confirm the diagnosis of PVS)

ISSUES FOR CRITICAL REFLECTION
#16 Pope John Paul II on Artificial Feeding for Individuals in Permanent Vegetative States

On March 22, 2004, Pope John Paul II spoke to an international congress on life-sustaining treatments and the vegetative state. In that speech, the Pope first spoke of the importance of arriving at a correct diagnosis of such a state in any individual case. Then, arguing that individuals in these states retain their "intrinsic value and personal dignity," he went on:

> This important congress . . . is dealing with a very significant issue: the clinical condition called the *vegetative state*. . . . The person in a vegetative state, in fact, shows no evident sign of self-awareness or of awareness of the environment, and seems unable to interact with others or to react to specific stimuli. . . . Moreover, not a few of these persons, with appropriate treatment and with specific rehabilitation programs, have been able to emerge from a vegetative state.

On the basis of these assertions, the Pope went on to discuss the moral ramifications of treating persons in a permanent or persistent vegetative state. He asserted that "the administration of water and food, even when provided by artificial means, always represents a natural means of preserving life, not a medical act." As a result, the Pope claimed that such administration is always morally required.

Two American bioethicists (Shannon & Walter, 2004) observed that this statement represents "a major reversal of the moral tradition of the Catholic church." Further, these commentators pointed out that the moral claim as to what is obligatory or required seems to be based again on an unclear distinction between "natural" and "artificial" treatments. One of the most difficult issues in discussions of the morality of treating persons in these states lies in determining just what counts as natural versus clinical or medical treatment. This distinction in turn has been related—often in tenuous ways—to the moral distinction between ordinary and extraordinary treatments. As Shannon and Walter wrote:

> [T]he primary determinant of whether the intervention is morally ordinary or extraordinary is not how the intervention—whether a medical therapy or some other kind of intervention—is classified. Historically, the determinant has been the effect on the patient. Thus the fact that some intervention is considered a "natural means" . . . does not determine the moral or obligatory status of the intervention. (pp. 9–10)

examples of extraordinary means. If so, in this view their removal could become morally optional (see, however, Issues for Critical Reflection #16). But again, that would need to be assessed on an individual basis with full understanding of the particular situation.

These issues can be seen historically in three celebrated cases:

◆ In April of *1975*, Karen Ann Quinlan at the age of 21 slipped into a comatose state, apparently as a result of ingesting alcohol and some tranquilizers at a party; eventually, Karen Ann's parents were permitted by the New Jersey Supreme Court to have a respirator (which they regarded as having become an extraordinary intervention that would not restore Karen to health) removed on May 22, 1976—however, they did continue intravenous feeding and regular visits with her, and Karen did not die until June 11, 1985 (see Colen, 1976; Quinlan et al., 1977).

◆ In January of *1983*, Nancy Cruzan at the age of 26 experienced severe brain damage from a lack of oxygen following an automobile accident; after a lengthy court battle that reached both the Missouri and the U.S. Supreme Courts, Nancy's parents and sister were permitted to act on her behalf to remove artificial nutrition and hydration delivered through a tube implanted directly into her stomach, after which she died in a matter of days on December 26, 1990 (see Colby, 2002).

◆ In February of *1990*, Terri Schiavo at the age of 26 entered into the situation described in the vignette near the beginning of this chapter. She died on March 31, 2005.

Note that none of these women had completed a written advance directive (a document not even available to Karen Ann Quinlan in 1975) to communicate her wishes about end-of-life care.

In general, then, if the therapy proposed for use or already in use is an extraordinary means of treatment according to the criteria listed here, then most moralists agree that there is no moral obligation to use it. Individuals may choose not to begin (withhold) the use of such a therapy, or they may choose to terminate (withdraw) its use with no moral culpability attached to that decision.

This brings the discussion back to issues associated with euthanasia. The distinction between extraordinary and ordinary means is often employed in the following way. Many would hold that not to begin to use or to stop using extraordinary means of treatment is not to be engaged in decisions about euthanasia. In this view, questions about euthanasia arise only when one is trying to decide whether to use ordinary means of treatment. Those who argue in favor of euthanasia will suggest that in some situations

Nancy Cruzan's grave marker.

there is no moral requirement to use ordinary means of treatment. Those who argue against euthanasia will suggest that in this situation (or in all situations) morally one must use the ordinary means of treatment under discussion; otherwise, one would be intending to end a human life.

🍂 Deciding to End a Human Life: Moral Arguments

We turn next to issues relating to the morality of intentionally ending a human life. Some have argued that intentionally doing something to end someone's life and intentionally not doing something to sustain that life ought to be distinguished morally. For instance, many people hold that active euthanasia is morally unacceptable. Their argument is that in active euthanasia the agent (the cause) of death is a person, the agent intends to bring about the death, and it is morally unacceptable for one person to deliberately kill another (in the circumstances under consideration in this chapter). However, many of these same people argue that passive euthanasia can, under some circumstances, be morally appropriate. Their argument here is that in passive euthanasia the agent (the cause) of death is a disease process—no person directly causes the death of another or intends to do so—and thus this is morally acceptable.

Not everyone accepts these claims. Some argue that in either case, another human being is involved, and whether that person commits an act to cause the death or omits an action that could prevent the death is morally irrelevant. In either case, so this argument goes, that person is involved in the occurrence of the death and is aware that death may likely follow from the action or omission whatever he or she may be intending, so the two situations are morally equivalent. People who think this way believe that if passive euthanasia is morally acceptable, so too must active euthanasia be morally acceptable. They also believe that if active euthanasia is morally unacceptable, then passive euthanasia must be morally unacceptable.

Arguments in Support of Intentionally Ending a Human Life

Prevention of Suffering An argument to support the moral acceptability of assisted suicide and euthanasia is that suffering is evil. Therefore, one function of caregivers is to prevent and, if possible, end suffering. Hence, actions involving assisted suicide and euthanasia to achieve such a goal would be permissible. Again, one could take this argument to its extreme and urge that *all* suffering is evil, and therefore that one ought *always* to strive to end *any* suffering—but probably few would hold this view. From slogans supporting physical exercise as a means to health ("no pain, no gain"), to the realization that success in most valued endeavors (such as intellectual growth, emotional maturity, artistic creativity) involves some suffering, the conclusion seems to follow that some suffering can have consequences that are good. Therefore, at least as a means to some desired good end, suffering cannot automatically be taken as something to be eliminated altogether. Thus, one is forced to evaluate particular instances of suffering rather than to issue blanket condemnations (Cassell, 1991; Nabe, 1999). This conclusion, of course, may leave us uncertain about what to do in a particular instance.

Enhancement of Liberty Another argument sometimes used to support assisted suicide and euthanasia arises based on the value placed on human liberty. Most Americans believe that liberty is good. That is, they value being free from external coercion when making decisions about themselves and their lives. In other words, many people value autonomy—a word that literally means being able to make law *(nomos)* for oneself *(auto)* (Childress, 1990). Such individuals disvalue interference from others in matters that they believe to be their own affair. This position supports the rights of individuals to decide what to do about their own suffering. On this view, if someone so disvalues the suffering that he or she is experiencing, and that individual prefers that his or her life end, that decision ought to be supported. In short, those who value autonomy must seriously consider the view that it is the suffering person's right as an autonomous agent to make that decision and others ought not to interfere with it (see Kaplan, 1999; Werth, 1999b). This is the view that Dr. Kevorkian—correctly or incorrectly—consistently stressed.

There are two difficulties with accepting this argument as definitive. One is that it presupposes that one can tell when someone is acting autonomously. However, someone who is experiencing severe pain or emotional trauma may not be completely free of coercion. The pain or emotional suffering itself may be so affecting the person that any decision made under its influence is *not,* in fact, autonomous. It is not always easy to decide about this. However, one position to guard against is the belief that such pain or trauma is *always* a coercive factor in someone's ability to make rational decisions. Even with severe suffering, it may be possible that the person is still an autonomous agent. Individuals involved in the lives of people who are experiencing severe suffering must find ways—really listening to such a person is a step in this direction—to decide what is happening in the particular person and the concrete situation.

Still, even if the person is autonomous, that does not automatically decide what *others* ought to do in the face of his or her autonomy. Difficult moral dilemmas often involve conflicts between autonomous persons. Individuals may decide autonomously that they want their lives to end, but that may come into conflict with the autonomous decisions of others. Remember that assisted suicide and euthanasia always involve (at least) two persons. One person's autonomous decision to have his or her life ended may conflict with another person's autonomous decision not to participate in that sort of event. Further, a decision to engage in assisted suicide or euthanasia seldom involves only the persons who are directly associated with the particular event of this one death. Typically, these decisions have broader social effects or repercussions. So even if someone's decision to end his or her life is autonomous, the acting out of that decision will inevitably affect others, and that, too, should be taken into account.

Quality of Life Another argument relevant to this discussion depends on *the value assigned to quality of life.* This argument holds that it is not *life as such* that is good, but rather *a certain form of life.* Most Americans do not concern themselves with life as such on a purely biological level; for example, they are perfectly willing to kill bacteria, viruses, pesky mosquitoes, and so forth. Rather, this argument maintains that we are properly concerned primarily with specific forms of life. In particular, some urge that we ought to be concerned specifically with what we understand to be *human* forms of life.

This argument compels its supporter to clarify what counts as human life. Some people hold that life in certain forms, such as those that involve high levels of suffering or lack of individual autonomy (e.g., life in a persistent vegetative state) are inhuman or undignified and therefore not worth living. If such situations are intolerable, then when individuals say, "I wouldn't want to live like that," the argument is that death or ending a life is to be preferred to those situations.

This argument depends on asserting that some form of life is so disvalued that it is less valuable than death. Widespread agreement about this is unlikely. For example, a powerful videotape (*Please Let Me Die*, 1974; compare Kliever, 1989; Platt, 1975; White & Engelhardt, 1975) depicts a young man who was burned over 67 percent of his body and was subjected to excruciatingly painful baths each day to prevent infection. The young man requested that his treatments be discontinued and that he be allowed to die. It has been argued that the young man and those around him could learn from his suffering; others have insisted that he was clearly competent and should have had the right to reject unwanted and painful interventions. Clearly, what one person counts as unbearable suffering someone else may not. However, there are also moral questions focused around someone's deciding that someone else's suffering is bearable or unbearable. It could be argued (though not everyone would agree even on this point) that each of us is in the best position to decide what is for us unbearable suffering and therefore no one else is in a position (and certainly not a better position than we are) to make such a judgment.

Arguments against Intentionally Ending a Human Life

Preservation of Life One argument used to show that intentionally ending a human life is morally inappropriate is that it violates the caregiver's (and society's) *commitment to the preservation of life.* According to this argument, it is part of the caregiver's role as a provider of care to preserve life. Thus, if a caregiver deliberately behaves in such a way that the death of the person for whom he or she has been caring will result, then that caregiver has behaved immorally. That is, the person has not fulfilled in an appropriate manner his or her role as a provider of care.

This argument holds that life is good, that there is a *sanctity* to life. If so, we ought to preserve and support life whenever we can. A qualified form of this view might contend that life is valuable, but it is not the *preeminent* value. That is, it does not take precedence over *all* other values in *all* instances. As has been said, human life is sacred but not absolute in its value. If this is the view one holds, it will not be possible to decide whether assisted suicide and euthanasia are morally acceptable (or even desirable) in some instances merely by appealing to the sanctity of life.

Slippery Slope Arguments Another argument used against the morality of assisted suicide and euthanasia is a *slippery slope argument.* It contends that once a decision is made to end someone's life for whatever reason, then one will have moved onto a slippery slope upon which it is all too easy to slide toward ending other people's lives for other reasons. If it is too difficult to stop once one has begun to act in these ways, this argument contends that it is better not to begin at all—at least until some way of knowing where to stop has been established. However, it is not clear that the slide down this slope is inevitable. In many parts of our lives, we are able to make careful distinctions between one sort of situation and another. Why not here?

Additional Arguments Others argue against assisted suicide and euthanasia for the following reasons: medicine is at best an uncertain science. Wrong diagnoses and prognoses are made. Also, medicine moves quickly sometimes and nearly always with some degree of unpredictability. New therapies and new cures are discovered at unknown moments. So when one contemplates ending a person's life, there is always the possibility of a misdiagnosis or of the appearance of a new cure or therapy that might ease or even end that person's suffering. Furthermore, some suggest that assisted suicide and euthanasia may undermine the trust that is essential to the physician/patient relationship or that they may detract from the role of the physician as healer and preserver of life.

These arguments have some weight. If that were not so, probably no one would ever have thought to advance them. Whether these arguments are persuasive in showing that one ought never to engage in assisted suicide and euthanasia depends on *how much* weight one gives to them. Human wisdom is always imperfect; if one waits for complete certainty in any moral matter, one will seldom act at all. But not to decide is to decide. If one chooses not to engage in assisted suicide and euthanasia, one might simply allow suffering to continue. Doing so involves its own danger. If a person's suffering is allowed to continue because of moral uncertainty or unclarity, there is a risk of becoming inured or hardened to suffering.

Further, although it is true that a new therapy or cure may come along at any time, it is not certain that such a discovery will help all persons with the particular disease or condition at issue. They may have progressed too far in the course of the disease, or their condition may involve other problems that the new therapy or cure can do nothing about. Thus these issues are relevant but not necessarily decisive.

❦ Deciding to End a Human Life: Some Religious Perspectives

For many persons, religious teachings are important sources of beliefs about the morality of intentionally ending a human life. Therefore, it may help to study some of religious teachings related to these issues.

Most religious traditions are themselves complex. For example, it is not possible to state *the* Christian view of intentionally ending a human life because there are disagreements among Christians themselves about this issue. Such disagreements can be found in almost all religious traditions. Because there is a danger of stereotyping persons and beliefs when only brief summaries of religious traditions are given, the following discussions should be understood as no more than abbreviated introductions to some of the unique beliefs in each tradition. These are some (not all) of the beliefs that might have an impact on how believers in that tradition think about the morality of euthanasia.

Judaism

Jewish teachings come from the Hebrew scriptures (what most Christians call the Old Testament), from oral traditions (the *Mishnah*), from commentaries on these earlier sources (the *Talmuds*), and from the decisions of rabbis throughout the centuries on specific situations. Important Jewish beliefs related to the morality of decisions to end a human life include the following: many Jews believe that God created and thus owns a person's body (Bleich, 1979). Thus, a person is caretaker of his or her body but has no right to do with it whatever he or she chooses. A second belief held by many Jews is that life is of infinite value, independent of its quality (Davis, 1994). Based on this view, the duty to preserve life is held to take precedence over almost all other human duties. Orthodox and Conservative Jews often find these to be the most significant teachings related to assisted suicide and euthanasia, and on their basis find these acts morally unacceptable.

However, many Reform Jews (who are often more oriented toward secular Western moral views) hold that autonomy and self-determination are also values of primary importance. On this basis, these Jews often assert that it is individuals who have ultimate control over their bodies. Insofar as that is so, Reform Jews may be less critical of some forms of suicide and euthanasia.

Active euthanasia seems to be universally condemned by all Jewish groups (Rosner, 1979). Support for this condemnation is often traced to a teaching from the *Mishnah* (Shabbat, 23:5):

> They do not close the eyes of a corpse on the Sabbath, nor on an ordinary day at the moment the soul goes forth. And he who closes the eyes of a corpse at the moment the soul goes forth, lo, this one sheds blood. (Neusner, 1988, p. 207)

Using this statement from the *Mishnah* as its basis, the *Babylonian Talmud* (Tract Sabbath, p. 353) argued that one must not hasten death:

> The rabbis taught: Who closes the eyes of a dying man is like a murderer, for it is the same as a candle which is about to go out. If a man lays a finger on the dying flame, it immediately becomes extinguished, but if left alone would still burn for a little time. The same can be applied to the case of an expiring man; if his eyes were not closed, he would live a little longer, and hence it is like murder. (Rodkinson, 1896, p. 353)

Moses Maimonides (1949), a 12th-century Jewish physician/philosopher regarded by many Jews as a significant voice on moral issues, used a similar image:

> One who is in a dying condition is regarded as a living person in all respects. . . . He who touches him is guilty of shedding blood. To what may he be compared? To a flickering flame, which is extinguished as soon as one touches it. Whoever closes the eyes of the dying while the soul is about to depart is shedding blood. One should wait a while; perhaps he is only in a swoon. (*The Code of Maimonides,* Book 14, The Book of Judges, Chapter 4, paragraph 5)

Thus, most Jews find only passive euthanasia to be morally acceptable, if they accept it at all.

Christianity

Christianity has three major branches: the Orthodox churches, Roman Catholicism, and Protestantism. These three branches themselves are complex. For example, there is no Protestant church as such, but rather dozens of Protestant denominations, all independent of each other. Although this complexity should always be kept in mind, Christians do share some basic beliefs, values, and practices.

Christians also share several beliefs with Judaism and Islam. Among these is the belief that since human life comes from God, it is inherently valuable, indeed sacred. However, Christians are also likely to emphasize that only God has absolute, ultimate value; human life does not. Christians identify the sacredness of this life in its bearing and manifesting the image and purpose of the Creator (Breck, 1995; Flannery, 1982). Christians also locate human dignity in considering each person to be an image of God (Cohen, 1996).

Uniquely Christian features arise from several other notions. As a Trinitarian faith, ultimate reality is understood by Christianity to be irreducibly relational (Harakas, 1993). Human beings are made for community with God and with each other; as Cicely Saunders (1970, p. 116) put it: "We belong with all other men (and) we belong with God also."

This essential interpersonal component of our humanness is also said to be revealed in the life of Jesus. Compassion and love for God and for his fellow human beings were central characteristics of Jesus' way of life. Much of his ministry involved healing, reducing the suffering of others. Since Christians are called to be an image of Christ, they too are to heal and, where that is not possible, to suffer with (be compassionate toward) others.

Some Christians hold that suffering is part of God's plan for all humans, whereas others find this belief difficult to fit with Jesus' emphasis on healing others (Breck, 1995). Suffering may be redemptive (bring individuals closer to each other and to God), but Christians are not required merely to accept it. One Christian document said of physical suffering that "human and Christian prudence suggest for the majority of sick people the use of medicines capable of alleviating or suppressing pain" (Sacred Congregation for the Doctrine of the Faith, 1982, p. 514). Christianity also teaches that we need not see ourselves as alone in our suffering; "in Jesus God was identified with (our) brokenness and suffering . . . God in Christ . . . has owned suffering for himself by undergoing it . . . thus the sufferer is not alone" (Smith, 1986, p. 7).

Christianity also has an eschatological emphasis. This means that human life's "ultimate value and meaning lie outside itself, beyond the limits of earthly existence" (Breck, 1995, p. 325). Harakas (1993, p. 540) echoes this point: Christianity "does not see any of the strivings of this world as ultimate."

What this means for the issues under discussion in this chapter is that many Christians oppose any intentional killing either of oneself or of others. Staying with, providing the necessary care to alleviate suffering, being compassionate toward each other: these are the desired goals for Christians faced with their own or someone else's death.

Islam

"Islam" means submission (to the will of Allah). Important Muslim beliefs include the following: Allah alone is God, and since Allah creates everything that exists, He is therefore the owner of every life. Thus, Muslims share with many Jews and Christians the belief that God alone may decide when a person's life is to end. Since suffering is used by Allah to remind human beings of their misdeeds and to lead them closer to Allah, to interfere with a person's suffering may also interfere with Allah's plan for that person (Hamel, 1991; Larue, 1985).

A Muslim's whole (public and private) life is ideally to be governed by Islamic law *(Shari'a)*. All Muslims accept the *Qur'an* and the *sunna* (practices and teachings) of Mohammed as sources of this law (Kelsay, 1994). Although there is no clearly stated position by Islamic leaders on assisted suicide or euthanasia (Islam has no definitive hierarchy to issue such a statement), the general impression is that they would be disapproved. A *sura* (chapter) in the *Qur'an* (4:29) reads: "Do not destroy yourselves." Many commentators take this to refer not only to suicide, but also to one Muslim killing another.

A statement from a 1981 conference in Kuwait is also relevant here:

> The doctor is well advised to realize his limit and not transgress it. If it is scientifically certain that life cannot be restored, then it is futile to diligently [maintain] the vegetative state of the patient by heroic means. . . . It is the process of life that the doctor aims to maintain and not the process of dying. In any case, the doctor shall not take positive measures to terminate the patient's life. (*Islamic Code of Medical Ethics,* First International Conference on Islamic Medicine, 1981, p. 10)

Hinduism

Hinduism is more like a cluster of various religious traditions than a single religion. As a group of various traditions, Hinduism has no central teaching authority or hierarchy. What most Hindus share is respect for the *Vedas* (scriptures, some of which may have been written as much as 3,500 years ago). Hindus may believe in creator gods, or they may believe that all reality is founded on Brahman, an impersonal, featureless entity from which rises all that is as waves rise from the ocean.

Many Hindus believe that most individuals will be reincarnated again and again, passing through death and rebirth through many lifetimes. The cause of these rebirths lies in one's *karma,* the actions one performs. One reaps inevitably and inexorably what one sows in one's actions. Thus, some Hindus believe that illness (life-threatening illness in particular) is an effect of one's karma and must be suffered through to pay one's karmic debt (Crawford, 1995). If so, to end life before it has run its natural course may interfere with the process of working off this debt. Assisted suicide and euthanasia would interfere with the karmic process and are thus undesirable.

However, other Hindus argue that this is a misunderstanding of karma (Crawford, 1995). If ending a human life interferes with the karmic process, then extending a human life through medical intervention interferes with that process, too. However, Hindus have developed a rich medical tradition (Ayurvedic medicine), and people who follow that tradition do not believe that it is inappropriate to alleviate someone's suffering and even to heal life-threatening disease. In this view, one is not interfering with the effects of karma if one seeks or provides treatment, or even perhaps ends a life.

Hinduism also emphasizes that one ought to avoid violence whenever possible. The Hindu term for this practice is *ahimsa. Ahimsa* is grounded in the view that life is sacred. Mohandas Gandhi taught that ahimsa is a central feature of a Hindu view of life. He explained what is meant by this term as follows: "*Ahimsa* does not simply mean non-killing. *Himsa* means causing pain to or killing any life out of anger, or from a selfish purpose, or with the intention of injuring it. Refraining from so doing is *ahimsa*" (quoted in Crawford, 1995, p. 115).

At first glance, the teaching on ahimsa seems to argue against assisted suicide and active euthanasia. But the intention in active euthanasia is to end suffering, not produce it. Gandhi (1980) himself used an example suggesting that intentionally ending a life might be compatible with the doctrine of ahimsa: "Should my child be attacked with rabies and there was no helpful remedy to relieve his agony, I should consider it my duty to take his life" (p. 84).

Thus, Hindu attitudes toward the intentional ending of human life are likely to be as diverse as Hinduism itself. One can locate teachings arguing against such actions and teachings supporting their use in some circumstances.

Buddhism

Buddhism differs from theistic religions in holding that there is no god who is creator of all that is. Its core doctrines include the beliefs that every action performed has consequences for the individual who performs it (karma), that one of the effects of one's actions (one's karma) is to cause one to be reincarnated again and again, and that life as we know it here is filled with suffering, so salvation lies ultimately in ending the cycle of rebirths. The Buddha also taught an eightfold path that helps one along the way to salvation. One of the precepts in this path is the rule never to kill a living creature. It is largely from this rule that Buddhist teaching on the intentional ending of human life is derived.

Because Buddhism holds that life is a basic good (in part because it is only in life—especially in a human life—that one may reach salvation), intentionally to end such a life is unacceptable (Keown, 1995). Some of the earliest scriptures of Buddhism offer teachings as to how Buddhist monks ought to live their lives. Some commentators use these teachings as a basis for Buddhist ethics in general (not only for monks) (Keown, 1995). In the *Vinaya-Pitaka* (Book of Discipline), the Buddha is reported to have said:

> Whatever monk should intentionally deprive a human being of life or should look about so as to be his knife-bringer, or should praise the beauty of death, or should incite (anyone) to death, saying, 'Hullo there, my man, of what use to you is this evil, difficult life? Death is better for you than life,' or who should deliberately and purposefully in various ways praise the beauty of death or incite (anyone) to death: he also is one who is defeated, he is not in communion. (Horner, 1949, vol. 1, pp. 125–126)

The reference to being someone's "knife-bringer" could be understood as referring to either assisted suicide or active euthanasia. A monk who engages in such activity has failed in his religious/moral responsibilities (is defeated) and is to be excommunicated.

Although individual autonomy is also an important value in Buddhist thought (Becker, 1990), it cannot override the principle that life is a basic good. Preferring death to life is never morally acceptable (Keown, 1995).

Compassion *(karuna)* is a central virtue in Buddhism (Lecso, 1986), and thus to ease the suffering of someone is appropriate. This means that when someone is near death, one may use drugs that may have the effect of suppressing respiration and even lead to death. Also, one may legitimately not start or may remove therapies that simply prolong someone's dying. These are acts of compassion. However, one must not do this intending to cause death. What is forbidden is the intentional killing of someone.

Euthanasia, Assisted Suicide, and Social Policy

Euthanasia Practices and Legislation in the Netherlands

In the Netherlands euthanasia is technically illegal, but for many years it has also been familiar in practice (De Wachter, 1989, 1992; Thomasma et al., 1998). In this context, euthanasia is defined as "the administration of drugs with the explicit intention of ending the patient's life, at the patient's explicit request" (Van der Maas et al., 1996, p. 1700). In 1984, the Royal Dutch Medical Association issued guidelines for this practice that were later endorsed by a government-appointed commission on euthanasia. The guidelines are: "(1) the patient must be a mentally competent adult; (2) the patient must request euthanasia voluntarily, consistently, and repeatedly over a reasonable time, and the request must be documented; (3) the patient must be suffering intolerably, with no prospect of relief, although the disease need not be terminal; and (4) the doctor must consult with another physician not involved in the case" (Angell, 1996, p. 1676). Physicians in the Netherlands who practice euthanasia under these guidelines have not been subject to criminal sanctions for many years. Apparently, no moral or legal distinction is drawn in the Netherlands between this form of active euthanasia and assisted suicide (Swarte & Heintz, 1999).

In November 2001, new legislation—"The Dutch Termination of Life on Request and Assisted Suicide (Review Procedures) Act"—went into effect. According to an official "question and answer" pamphlet on the subject (Anonymous, 2001b; see also more recent documents of a similar nature, such as the Netherlands Ministry of Health, Welfare and Sport, and the Netherlands Ministry of Justice, n.d.; the Netherlands Ministry of Foreign Affairs, n.d.), this legislation incorporated in the Dutch criminal code "a special ground for exemption from criminal liability," which provides that "doctors who terminate life on request or assist in a patient's suicide can no longer be prosecuted, provided they satisfy the statutory due care criteria and notify death by non-natural causes to the appropriate regional euthanasia review committee" (Anonymous, 2001b, p. 4). In other words, under the new legislation when a doctor carries out euthanasia or assisted suicide in accordance with the legislative criteria and has reported his or her actions correctly, and when a regional review committee (composed of at least one lawyer, one physician, and an ethicist) has decided on the basis of that report that the physician has acted with due care, the Public Prosecution Service will not be informed, and no further action will be taken. Only when a review committee finds that a doctor has failed to satisfy the statutory due care criteria will the case be referred to the public prosecutor for possible prosecution.

According to official documents, "the basic principle underlying the legislation is that patients have no absolute right to euthanasia and doctors no absolute duty to perform it" (Anonymous, 2001b, p. 6). Thus, approximately two-thirds of all requests for euthanasia in the Netherlands are refused, and one hospice doctor could say that his attitude toward this legislation and the practices that it sanctions was one of "peaceful coexistence and respectful nonparticipation" (Z. Zylicz, in a discussion at the meeting of the International Work Group on Death, Dying, and Bereavement, June 13, 2001).

Although official studies of euthanasia practices in the Netherlands had been conducted in 1990, 1995, and 2001 (Onwuteaka-Philipsen et al., 2003), implementation of the new Euthanasia Act called for additional research. As a result of their examination of deaths under this legislation, Van der Heide and colleagues (2007, p. 1957) reported that,

> In 2005, of all deaths in the Netherlands, 1.7% were the result of euthanasia and 0.1% were the result of physician-assisted suicide. These percentages were significantly lower than those in 2001, when 2.6% of all deaths resulted from euthanasia and 0.2% from assisted suicide. Of all deaths, 0.4% were the result of the ending of life without an explicit request by the patient. Continuous deep sedation was used in conjunction with possible hastening of death in 7.1% of all deaths in 2005, significantly increased from 5.6% in 2001.

This study concluded that, "The Dutch Euthanasia Act was followed by a modest decrease in the rates of euthanasia and physician-assisted suicide. The decrease may have resulted from the increased application of other end-of-life care interventions, such as palliative sedation." A separate study (Rietjens et al., 2007, p. 220) reported that "ending life without an explicit request of the patient seems to be a part of medical end-of-life practices in the Netherlands as well as other countries," practices that are said mainly to apply to incompetent, terminally ill patients without opening the door to the acceptance of other forms of ending life.

Those who favor the Dutch policies and practices note that all citizens of the Netherlands enjoy a high standard of living, full health insurance, a home physician, and generous retirement and social services. Nevertheless, the population of the Netherlands is aging, and the government recognizes that dying patients may request euthanasia for reasons of pain, degradation, and the longing to die with dignity. Advocates also draw attention to the fact that euthanasia accounts for only a small fraction of all deaths in the Netherlands and that it is performed in less than a third of cases when a request is made. It is further argued that this type of euthanasia is performed "almost entirely on those who were terminally ill; 87 percent of the patients were expected to die within a week, and another 12 percent in a month" (Angell, 1996, p. 1676). In addition, advocates note that in cases when there was no explicit request, factors such as a previous discussion of the subject, present lack of competency, or discussions with other physicians, nurses, or family members had influenced the decision. Finally, advocates of euthanasia in the Netherlands observe that reporting of these cases has increased from about 18 percent in 1990 to over 80 percent in 2005 (Van der Heide et al., 2007; Van der Wal et al., 1996). Thus, the authors of the 1995 studies contend, "in our view, these data do not support the idea that physicians in the Netherlands are moving down a slippery slope" (Van der Maas et al., 1996, p. 1705). They add, "A large majority of Dutch physicians consider euthanasia an exceptional but accepted part of medical practice." Family members involved in these practices apparently also find them acceptable (Georges et al., 2007; Swarte et al., 2003).

Opponents of these practices and policies (such as Hendin, 1995, 1997, 2002; Hendin et al., 1997) generally describe them as rife with danger and not possessing adequate safeguards. They seize on what they see as "the gradual extension of assisted suicide to widening groups of patients after it is legally permitted for patients designated as terminally ill" (Hendin et al., 1997, p. 1720), failures of the guidelines and problems of underreporting despite the implementation since 1991 of a notification procedure (see Van der Wal et al., 1996), and "the documentation of cases in which patients who have not given their consent have their lives ended by physicians" (p. 1721).

Because their populations, social services, and health care systems are so dissimilar, Angell (1996, p. 1677) noted that "it is virtually impossible to draw any meaningful comparisons" between the Dutch experience and practices in the United States. She added, "until recently, physician-assisted dying has been considered in the United States to be quite different" from accepted practices in end-of-life care. However, "support for decriminalizing assisted suicide has been growing, whereas support for euthanasia remains weak," perhaps because "euthanasia can be involuntary, where suicide, by definition, must be voluntary," and assisted suicide may be considered to be less liable to abuse than euthanasia.

Assisted Suicide Legislation and Practices in Oregon

In 1994, the citizens of the state of Oregon approved, by a narrow margin of just 51 percent to 49 percent, a "Death with Dignity Act" (DWDA). The provisions of the act—which became effective in October of 1997—stipulate the conditions under which a terminally ill, adult resident of Oregon is permitted to request that a physician provide a prescription for lethal medication that an individual can use to end his or her life (Reagan, 2000). The act only applies to patients with a diagnosed terminal illness and a prognosis of less than six months to live. To comply with the act, several procedures must be followed. These include a requirement that a physician ensure that the patient is making this request voluntarily. This is accomplished by requiring that the patient make two oral requests separated by at least 15 days and that he or she sign a written request in the presence of two witnesses. The prescribing physician must also inform the patient of his or her diagnosis, prognosis, available options (such as comfort care, hospice care, and pain control), and the right to withdraw the request at any time. In addition, the prescribing physician must refer the patient to a consulting physician to confirm the diagnosis and prognosis, and to determine that the patient is capable (able to make and communicate health care decisions). Psychiatric illness or depression that might impair judgment must be ruled out. Further, the prescribing physician must request (but may not require) the patient to notify his or her next of kin of the prescription request. Physicians must report all prescriptions for lethal medications to the Oregon Department of Human Services and must inform pharmacists of the prescribed medication's intended use.

It is important to be clear that the act only authorizes voluntary self-administration of lethal medications prescribed by a physician for the purpose of ending one's life; euthanasia or situations in which a physician or other person directly administers a medication to end another's life is specifically prohibited. Although the DWDA makes clear that physicians and health care systems are under no obligation to participate in its implementation, those physicians and patients who adhere to the requirements of the act are protected from criminal prosecution, and the choice to end one's life in this way cannot affect the status of a patient's health or life insurance policies. The DWDA stipulates that a death under these conditions does not constitute suicide, mercy killing, or homicide under the law.

The DWDA also requires the collection of information and the publication by the Oregon Department of Human Services (DHS) of an annual report on its implementation. Currently, extensive annual reports are available on the DHS website (http://egov.oregon.gov/DHS/ph/pas) for the first 8 years' experiences with the DWDA, together with a brief summary and two tables for year nine. In the eighth annual report on this subject, the DHS (2006, p. 7) provided the following comment on terminology:

The Death with Dignity Act allows terminally ill Oregon residents to obtain and use prescriptions from their physicians for self-administered, lethal medications. Under the Act, ending one's life in accordance with the law does not constitute suicide. However, we use the term "physician-assisted suicide" because it is used in medical literature to describe ending life through the voluntary self-administration of lethal medications prescribed by a physician for that purpose. The Death with Dignity Act legalizes PAS, but specifically prohibits euthanasia, where a physician or other person directly administers a medication to end another's life.

The DHS also has published on its website *The Oregon Death with Dignity Act: A Guidebook for Health Care Professionals* (The Task Force to Improve the Care of Terminally-Ill Oregonians, 2005), an extensive document whose various sections are updated periodically.

Those supporting the Oregon DWDA have argued that quality in living, personal choice or autonomy, and quality in medical decision making are the important values to be considered in this matter (e.g., Annas, 1994, 2004; Quill & Battin, 2004). Opponents generally describe such practices and policies as rife with danger and not possessing adequate safeguards, especially those to protect vulnerable patients from coercion of various sorts (e.g., Foley & Hendin, 2002; see also Issues for Critical Reflection #17). In the period since the DWDA came into effect, only a small number of persons in Oregon have requested and even fewer have carried out physician-assisted suicide (PAS) (Oregon Department of Human Services, 2007; see Table 18.1). That number peaked in 2003, remained relatively stable in 2004 and 2005, and increased somewhat in 2006. The 46 DWDA deaths in 2006 constitute a ratio of 14.7 per 10,000 overall deaths in Oregon.

Given the relatively small numbers of individuals involved, annual variations among those who have taken advantage of the Death with Dignity Act in Oregon are unavoidable. Still, it is important to understand the characteristics of those who seek out PAS (Tolle et al., 2004; Wineberg & Werth, 2003). For example, it has been noted that the median age of patients who used PAS in 2006 was 74 compared to 67 for those using PAS in preceding years. More broadly, the Oregon Department of Human Services (2006, p. 12) noted certain demographic patterns across the first eight years of its reports. For example:

> Males and females have been equally likely to take advantage of the DWDA. Divorced and never-married persons were more likely to use PAS than married and widowed residents. A higher level of education has been strongly associated with the use of PAS; Oregonians with a baccalaureate degree or higher were 7.9 times more likely to use PAS than those without a high school diploma.

In addition, individuals with certain terminal illnesses are most likely to use PAS. In 2006 the leading illnesses among these individuals were cancer, amyotrophic lateral sclerosis (ALS), and HIV/AIDS. Over the nine-year history of the act's implementation, the ratio of DWDA deaths to all deaths resulting from the same underlying illness was highest for three conditions: amyotrophic lateral sclerosis (ALS) (271.5 per 10,000 decedents dying from the same disease), HIV/AIDS (233.5), and malignant neoplasms (41.6) (Oregon Department of Human Services, 2007). Finally, in 2006 in Oregon all but one of the individuals who took advantage of physician-assisted suicide had some form of health insurance and most (76%, down from 87% previously) were enrolled in hospice care. Of the 46 total PAS deaths in 2006, 93 percent died at home.

ISSUES FOR CRITICAL REFLECTION

#17 What Have Been Some Legal Challenges to the Oregon "Death with Dignity Act"?

The Oregon "Death with Dignity Act" authorizing physician-assisted suicide has proved to be controversial among at least some Americans (Werth & Wineberg, 2005). Part of the controversy lies in the act's having raised questions about where the authority to legalize physician-assisted suicide (and perhaps implicitly other forms of assisted suicide and euthanasia) lies—at the federal level or with the states. From the outset, several groups went to court to prevent the implementation of the act. In 1997, the U.S. Supreme Court ruled that although there is no "right to die" in the U.S. Constitution, states have the constitutional right to make laws that provide for physician-assisted suicide. Meanwhile, an attempt to repeal the law was placed on the ballot in Oregon in November of 1997, only to be rejected by a vote of 60 to 40 percent.

On November 6, 2001, the Attorney General of the United States announced that Oregon's Death with Dignity Act violated federal drug laws. Accordingly, he issued a directive authorizing the government to cancel the federal license of physicians to prescribe what are called controlled substances or "scheduled drugs" if they are used to provide assistance in dying. The practical effect of

that action would be to make it difficult, if not impossible, to implement the Oregon legislation. However, in November 2001 a federal district court judge issued a temporary injunction to halt that action, and in April 2002 the same judge made the injunction permanent, ruling that the Attorney General did not have the authority to interfere with state laws governing the practice of medicine.

In May of 2004, a three-judge panel of the Ninth U.S. Circuit Court of Appeals rejected the government's appeal of those decisions. The panel's ruling held that the so-called "Ashcroft Directive" cannot be enforced because it violates the clear language of the Controlled Substances Act, runs contrary to the legislative intent of Congress, and disregards the limits of the Attorney General's lawful authority. In August 2004 a majority of that federal appeals court's 25 full-time judges voted to refuse to reconsider that decision. Subsequently, the U.S. Supreme Court ruled 6–3 on January 17, 2006, that the Attorney General does not have the authority to regulate medical practice, a responsibility left to the states, and that the Oregon DWDA does not violate the intent of Congress when it passed the 1970 Controlled Substances Act to regulate illicit drug dealing and trafficking.

Multiple concerns appear to have motivated most of those who completed an act of PAS under the Oregon initiative. The leading concerns of those who died under the act across all 9 years of its implementation have been reported to include loss of autonomy, a decreasing ability to participate in activities that made life enjoyable, and loss of dignity. Fear of intractable physical pain had not seemed to have been a central motivation in these actions in previous years, but it increased in 2006 from 22 percent to 48 percent.

TABLE 18.1

Numbers of Prescriptions Written and Individuals Who Died under the Oregon Death with Dignity Act (DWDA), 1998–2006

	Number of Prescriptions Written under the DWDA	Number of Individuals Who Ingested Lethal Medications and Died
2006	65	46
2005	64	38
2004	60	37
2003	68	42
2002	58	38
2001	44	21
2000	39	27
1999	33	27
1998	24	16
Total	455	292

Note: Individuals who received prescriptions under the DWDA may have died of their illnesses before they could act on those prescriptions; some received a prescription in one year but did not act on it immediately to ingest lethal medications and thus died in a subsequent year.

Source: Oregon Department of Human Services, 2007; http://egov.oregon.gov/DHS/ph/pas (accessed December 10, 2007).

Beyond this, it has been suggested that the availability of PAS may have led to efforts to improve end-of-life care in Oregon through other modalities. For example,

A request for PAS can be an opportunity for a medical provider to explore with patients their fears and wishes around end-of-life care, and to make patients aware of other options. Often once the patient's concerns have been addressed by the provider, he or she may choose not to pursue PAS. The availability of PAS as an option in Oregon also may have spurred Oregon doctors to address other end-of-life care options more effectively. In one study, Oregon physicians reported that, since the passage of the Death with Dignity Act in 1994, they had made efforts to improve their knowledge of the use of pain medications in the terminally ill, to improve their recognition of psychiatric disorders such as depression, and to refer patients more frequently to hospice. (Oregon Department of Human Services, 2005, p. 17)

🐛 Prospects for the Future

The issues discussed in this chapter are unlikely to be easily resolved or to disappear in the future. In fact, as medical technology advances, more and more people may find themselves in situations wherein they seriously question the quality of life offered by continued medical interventions, either for themselves or for others about whom they care. Also, health care providers may find themselves in situations in which those for whom they are caring ask for assistance in ending their lives (Emanuel et al., 2000). It is already clear that especially difficult challenges appear in cases involving: (1) individuals who are not regarded as competent to make any formal decision on these or other matters (such as infants, children, or the mentally ill); (2) those who once were thought to be competent but who did not then make known their wishes about conditions under which they might want to continue or end their lives (such as those in an irreversible coma or persistent vegetative state); and (3) when the issues involve assisted suicide, active euthanasia, or the removal not only of external support (e.g., a respirator), but also of artificially assisted nutrition and hydration (Lynn, 1986).

It is also likely that issues related to assisted suicide and euthanasia will be presented to society as some individuals seek to have their views prevail over others in individual situations and as efforts are made to legitimize widespread practice in some form of public policy (as in euthanasia practices in the Netherlands or assisted-suicide legislation in Oregon).

Whether or not American society at large adopts policies or practices that favor assisted suicide and/or euthanasia, decisions about these matters will continue to be made in individual circumstances. That is, situations will arise in which individuals cannot avoid deciding whether to (help) end the life of another and, if so, how. This means, also, that *someone will decide*. Some are most concerned about this latter point—who will or ought to decide whether assisted suicide and/or euthanasia are to be provided. However, although the question of identifying appropriate decision makers is significant, the grounds for making moral decisions are the most fundamental matter. In addition, questions of who will carry out these decisions (physician, family member, etc.)—whatever the grounds and whoever the decision maker may be—will need to be addressed, as will what kind of psychological or social impact such actions might create on others (Werth, 1999a).

❦ Summary

In this chapter, we examined issues related to intentionally ending a human life, with special attention to assisted suicide and euthanasia. We sought to define these two concepts and the central ideas with which they are linked. In this process, we first focused on two key issues: the agent who takes the decisive action and the intention behind whatever action is taken. During this discussion, we explored the distinction between voluntariness and nonvoluntariness, contrasts between ending a life actively or passively, and the difference between extraordinary and ordinary means of treatment.

Then our focus shifted to arguments for and against intentionally ending a human life, arguments drawn from general moral or philosophical premises, as well as from perspectives arising from five of the world's great religions. In presenting these arguments and perspectives, we recognized that none of them was without potential objection and that easy answers to the issues addressed were unlikely for most people. However, this does not mean that no answers of any sort are available. Obviously, many people have diverse positions on various aspects of this subject. Thoughtful positions in this complex conceptual and moral arena of human life require careful and sustained reflection.

Finally, we suggested that these topics are likely to grow in importance for individual decision makers and for social policy. To that end, we looked briefly at legislation governing euthanasia practices in the Netherlands and physician-assisted suicide in Oregon. Our primary concern throughout this discussion has been to help individuals think about this subject as clearly as possible before they are forced to confront it in their own lives.

Glossary

Active euthanasia: taking direct action to end suffering by ending the life of a suffering person

Assisted suicide: actions in which one person intentionally acts to end his or her life and secures assistance from another individual who intends to help the first person achieve that result

The Dutch Termination of Life on Request and Assisted Suicide (Review Procedures) Act: legislation that went into effect in November 2001 in the Netherlands to provide a special exemption from criminal liability for physicians who terminate life on request or assist in a patient's suicide in accordance with the due care and notification criteria set forth in the law

Euthanasia: literally, the word means "a good death"; mainly used now to refer to situations in which one individual contributes to the death of another person in order to end the suffering of that second person

Extraordinary means of treatment: interventions to sustain life that do not have predictable and well-recognized outcomes; that offer unusual risks, suffering, or burdens for the person being treated or for others; and that may not be effective; such interventions are thought to be optional (not mandatory) in some systems of moral theology and bioethics

Nonvoluntary euthanasia: euthanasia performed when the wishes of the person who dies are unknown

Ordinary means of treatment: interventions to support life that have predictable and well-recognized outcomes; that offer no unusual risk, suffering, or burden for the person being treated or for others; and that are effective; such interventions are thought to be obligatory in some systems of moral theology and bioethics

Oregon "Death with Dignity Act": legislation that went into effect in October 1997 in the state of Oregon specifying the conditions under which a terminally ill, adult resident of the state is permitted to request that a physician provide a prescription for lethal medication that an individual can use to end his or her life; commonly described as authorizing physician-assisted suicide

Passive euthanasia: allowing someone to die by either not doing (withholding) or omitting (withdrawing) some action that is necessary to sustain life

Physician-assisted suicide: a form of assisted suicide in which it is a physician who intentionally provides the assistance that a person needs and uses to end his or her life

Voluntary euthanasia: euthanasia performed at the request of the person who dies

Questions for Review and Discussion

1. In this chapter, we suggested that humans put value on such things as freedom, privacy, persons, religious traditions, life, self-respect, justice, and a good life. Which of these are most important to you? Why? Which, if any, of these would you be willing to sacrifice to preserve some other more important value(s)? Why? Relate your responses to these questions to the issue of deciding whether to assist someone who is incurably ill to die.

2. Would you be willing to assist someone who was thinking about ending his or her life if: (1) that person was not dying (i.e., any disease condition that the person had would not cause his or her death); (2) that person was suffering great emotional distress; and (3) that person was in great pain that could not be relieved? What are the values you hold that lead you to your responses to these questions?

3. In this chapter, we described arguments to support the moral appropriateness of assisted suicide and euthanasia, and arguments against their moral appropriateness. Which of these arguments do you find most compelling? Which are least persuasive to you? Why?

4. Would you support a law allowing physicians to undertake actions that might be thought to involve euthanasia and/or assisted suicide? Why would you support or not support such laws?

Suggested Readings

Battin, M. P. (Ed.). (1994). *The Least Worst Death: Essays in Bioethics on the End of Life.*

Battin, M. P. (1996). *The Death Debate: Ethical Issues in Suicide.*

Battin, M. P., Rhodes, R., & Silvers, A. (Eds.). (1998). *Physician Assisted Suicide: Expanding the Debate.*

Beauchamp, T. L. (Ed.). (1996). *Intending Death: The Ethics of Assisted Suicide and Euthanasia.*

Beauchamp, T. L., & Childress, J. F. (2001). *Principles of Biomedical Ethics.*

Camenisch, P. F. (Ed.). (1994). *Religious Methods and Resources in Bioethics.*

Colby, W. H. (2002). *Long Goodbye: The Deaths of Nancy Cruzan.*

Colby, W. H. (2006). *Unplugged: Reclaiming Our Right to Die in America.*

Doka, K. J., Jennings, B., & Corr, C. A. (Eds.). (2005). *Living with Grief: Ethical Dilemmas at the End of Life.*

Emanuel, L. L. (1998). *Regulating How We Die: The Ethical, Medical, and Legal Issues Surrounding Physician Assisted Suicide.*

Foley, K. M., & Hendin, H. (Eds.). (2002). *The Case against Assisted Suicide: For the Right to End-of-Life Care.*

Hamel, R. (1991). *Choosing Death: Active Euthanasia, Religion, and the Public Debate.*

Jamison, S. (1995). *Final Acts of Love: Families, Friends, and Assisted Dying.*

McKhann, C. F. (1999). *A Time to Die: The Place for Physician Assistance.*

Post, S. (Ed.). (2004). *Encyclopedia of Bioethics* (3rd ed.).

Weir, R. F. (Ed.). (1997). *Physician-Assisted Suicide.*

Werth, J. L. (Ed.). (1999b). *Contemporary Perspectives on Rational Suicide.*

Selected Web Resources

Some useful search terms include: ACTIVE EUTHANASIA; ARTIFICAL FEEDING; ARTIFICAL NUTRITION AND HYDRATION; ASSISTED SUICIDE; DEATH WITH DIGNITY ACT; EUTHANASIA; NONVOLUNTARY EUTHANASIA; PASSIVE EUTHANASIA; PERSISTENT (OR PERMANENT) VEGETATIVE STATE; PHYSICIAN-ASSISTED SUICIDE; VOLUNTARY EUTHANASIA

Visit the book companion website for *Death & Dying, Life & Living, Sixth Edition,* at academic.cengage.com/psychology/corr for all URLs and live links to the following *organizational and other Internet sites:*

American Journal of Bioethics (published by Taylor and Francis, Ltd.)

American Society for Bioethics and Humanities (ASBH)

American Society of Law, Medicine, and Ethics (ASLME)

The Center for Bioethics and Culture (CBC)

Center for Clinical Ethics in Health Care, University of Buffalo

Center for Ethics in Health Care, Oregon Health and Sciences University

The Center for Practical Bioethics

Compassion in Dying

Ethics in Medicine, School of Medicine, University of Washington

The Hastings Center

Kennedy Institute of Ethics, Georgetown University

CHAPTER 19

The Meaning and Place of Death in Life

Objectives of This Chapter

◆ To explore issues related to the meaning of death

◆ To examine several religious and philosophical ideas about the afterlife and the meaning of death

◆ To discuss the content and interpretation of near-death experiences

◆ To consider the place of death in human life

❦ The Buddha on the Place of Death in Human Experience

The following tale is drawn from Buddhist scriptures. It occurs in various forms; the one we present here draws on several sources.

A young woman named Gotami had a son. But when he had barely begun to walk, he died. Overcome by grief, she carried the dead boy from one house to another, begging people if they had some medicine for her son. At one house, an old man told her that there was one person who could give her medicine, Gautama (the Buddha).

Gotami went to the Buddha, and asked him for medicine for her dead child. He told her that he did know of such a medicine. She was to gather a little mustard seed from each house in the village that had not been touched by death. She went from house to house, but all in vain: nowhere did she find a family that had not known death.

She now began to think to herself: "I thought that my son alone had been overtaken by this thing which people call death. But I was wrong. This happens to everyone" (paraphrased from Burtt, 1955, pp. 45–46). She now understood that everything that exists is impermanent and eventually passes away.

After giving her son over to the funeral rites, Gotami returned to the Buddha. He asked her if she had brought the medicine he required. She told him no, that she knew now that all people die. The Buddha said to her: "All living beings resemble the flame of these lamps, one moment lighted, the next extinguished." (Ballou, 1944, p. 143)

❦ The Meaning of Death

Questions Raised by the Fact of Human Mortality

Almost all human beings eventually come up against an inescapable fact about themselves and the persons they love: they are mortal. For many persons, as for Gotami in the previous vignette, this fact raises questions of meaning: Why are we born? What is the meaning of our having lived? What is the impact of our death on the value and significance of our life? In short, what is the relationship between life and death? Are they simple opposites so that where there is death, there can be no life (Terkel, 2001)? Or is their relationship more complex than this?

These questions form part of our human reality. As the Buddha told Gotami, the fact of eventual death is common to all forms of life. But human beings can think about or reflect on this fact and its implications before the event. That ability to know in advance that one will die is perhaps unique to human beings. Awareness of death is especially sharpened when our security is threatened, for example when we are confronted by school shootings such as those at Virginia Tech University in April 2007(see Chapter 4 and Issues for Critical Reflection #18).

In fact, issues related to the meaning of death and its place in human life have been claimed to underlie almost all human activity. For instance, Socrates said that "those who really apply themselves in the right way to philosophy are directly and of their own accord preparing themselves for dying and death" (Plato, 1961, p. 46; *Phaedo*, 64a), and he argued that this implied that everything human beings do in life is finally to be evaluated by testing it against the fact of their mortality. If he

On April 16, 2007, a student at Virginia Tech University began shooting, and when he stopped, 33 people—students, faculty, and the shooter—were dead. Afterward, analysis of these events often focused on how universities (and implicitly, the rest of society) could provide more "security" from such deadly events. This response was probably unavoidable and certainly understandable. But it also brought into focus what some have claimed is an inevitable component of being a human person: anxiety about death. As Russ Federman, the director of counseling and psychological services at the University of Virginia said in an interview two days later: "We would like to think that violence and tragedy is [sic.] avoidable . . . we would like to think . . . so we can feel less anxious about life." But of course, this is always in some degree an illusion. Total security from violence and tragedy—including death—cannot be realized.

Our desire for security from the threats to our very existence arises on several levels. On the surface, there are questions about what society can do to protect its citizens from violence and "meaningless" death. To the extent that society can with reasonable means achieve such protection, those means should be pursued and encouraged. They will always, however, be limited in their effectiveness; no society can protect *every* citizen in *every* situation from *every* threat of death.

But at a deeper level, our insecurity in the face of violence reveals what philosophers and religious teachers have often described as an inescapable condition of being human: we are, as Martin Heidegger (1962) put it, beings onto death. In most of our everyday lives, we are able to keep this condition below the surface of our awareness. However, when we are forcibly confronted with that inevitability (as an event like the one at Virginia Tech can do), almost everyone experiences some anxiety facing that very inevitability. And there is nothing civil society can do to alleviate this *essential* insecurity about our being. To deal with this anxiety, we need something other than civil laws or civic responses: here philosophy and religion must go to work, if anything is to help.

Confronted by this essential truth about ourselves, we often respond in one of two ways. We may experience an anxiety that almost overwhelms us. Or we may take notice of the reality that our lives will one day come to an end and recognize that this makes every moment of our lives precious. In other words, when we face the inevitability of our death authentically, in that same moment the preciousness of our lives is also realized in a profound way. Thus, as we have suggested throughout this text, our death and the preciousness of our life are wholly intertwined.

was right about this, then everything we have considered in this book (e.g., how to treat dying and bereaved persons or the place of assisted suicide and euthanasia in human life, in fact all reflective actions related to death and dying) originates from more basic questions about the meaning of mortality. For instance, to say that people should care for dying persons in one way rather than in another way finds part of its justification in beliefs about death. If one believes that death is always and everywhere to be disvalued, and if one holds that death is the greatest evil known, this belief is likely to affect how one faces and deals with dying persons. If one believes that there can be something worse than death, that too will influence how one acts in these situations.

Possible Responses to These Questions

As human beings have reflected on questions raised by death, they have responded in many different ways (e.g., Becker, 1973; Grof & Halifax, 1978). The ancient Chinese Yin/Yang symbol at the beginning of this chapter provides one response to these questions. It suggests that life (represented by the light portion of the symbol—the Yang) and death (represented by the dark portion of the symbol—the Yin) interpenetrate each other; the Yin overlaps and intrudes into the space of the Yang and vice versa. More than this, at the very *center* of the Yin is the Yang, and again, vice versa. Thus, this symbol suggests that wherever there is life, there is death, and wherever there is death, there is life.

Another response to these questions has involved the attempt to understand just what happens after death (Adams, 2004; Toynbee et al., 1976). Art, popular culture (Bertman, 1991; Bolton, 2007), folk tales (Gignoux, 1998), anthropology (Reynolds & Waugh, 1977), literature (Enright, 1983; Weir, 1980), philosophy (Carse, 1980; Choron, 1963, 1964), religion (Chidester, 1990; Johnson & McGee, 1998; Obayashi, 1992), and theology (Gatch, 1969; Mills, 1969; Rahner, 1973) have all provided suggestions related to this question. Indeed, some of the best thinking ever done by humans has focused on such issues. Socrates and Albert Camus, Paul of Tarsus and Muhammad, the writer of *Ecclesiastes* and the writer of the *Bhagavad Gita;* in the work of such people can be found examples of attempts to address the disturbing implications of death in human life.

❦ Death: A Door or a Wall?

Feifel (1977a) simplified (perhaps overly so) how humans are likely to think of death when he wrote that death can be portrayed as either a door or a wall. He meant that when one looks at death, one can ask oneself what one sees. Is death simply the cessation of life? Is it the case that where death intrudes, life is irrevocably lost? If so, death is something that all will come up against, and it will mean the end of everything that one does or can know. It is a wall into which one crashes and through which one cannot pass.

However, some people believe that death is a stage along life's way. It is a river to cross, a stair to climb, a door through which to pass. If this is one's view, then death may be seen not as the irrevocable opposite to life but rather as a passage from one sort (or stage) of life to another.

Most people hold one or the other of these beliefs. Of course, these ideas and beliefs may be unconscious or not thought through clearly. But if one is (for example) afraid of death, that fear is based on some notion of the meaning of death, such as "I will never see loved ones again," or "I will never experience a sunset like that again," or "I will be punished for my sins," or "I may be reborn into a life of poverty." Since most of us have some sort of reaction to the fact of death—happiness or sadness, fear or anticipation—we also have some beliefs about its meaning.

It is also the case, however, that the evaluation one makes of death is not tied in any obvious way to whether one sees it as a door or as a wall (Nabe, 1982). One can think of death as a wall and evaluate that as good: for example, at least all suffering is over. One can see death as a door and evaluate that as evil: for example, it may bring eternal torment or a shadowy, shallow form of life. And, of course, some would see death as a wall as something evil, and death as a door as something good. The point is only that how one thinks of death philosophically is tied in some important way to how one values it.

❦ Alternative Images of an Afterlife

Exploring some of the principal alternative religious or philosophical images that human beings have employed to try to understand how death and life are related enriches our own thinking about these questions. To begin this process, we examine several of these images and their intended responses to the questions: is *this life* all there is, and is death the irrevocable loss of any sort of life? Now, as soon as we begin this study, it becomes clear that human beings have tried to respond to these questions in quite an astonishing array of ways (Toynbee, 1968b). Thus, we can only briefly consider here several of the best known of these ways.

Greek Concepts of the Afterlife

More than 400 years before the birth of Christ, the philosopher Socrates lived in the city-state of Athens. When he was 70 years old, some of Socrates' critics brought charges against him for not believing in the official state gods and for corrupting

Socrates accepts his death sentence and calmly drinks the fatal poison while his friends weep.

© North Wind Picture Archives

the youth by teaching them to challenge the beliefs of their elders. Socrates was found guilty of these charges and condemned to death.

After these actions by the jury, Socrates described what death meant to him. He said he believed that humans cannot *know* what death means in terms of our continued existence. Instead, he maintained that all people are left with *beliefs* on this point. On this most pressing question, Socrates contended that we can only make a choice to believe on less than demonstrative proof.

Socrates finally was content not to decide just what death means for our continued existence. Perhaps that was in part due to the options he presented for what death might involve. (Look at what he told the jurors about this, in Personal Insights 19.1.) If death is either a permanent sleep (unconsciousness) or a form of life in which one meets old friends and can make new ones, then death need not appear to be frightening or threatening.

But these scenarios do not exhaust the possibilities. Another ancient Greek, Homer, provided a different, less happy description of the afterlife. At one point in Homer's *Odyssey*, Odysseus calls up another Greek hero (Achilles) from his afterlife in *Hades*. Achilles says about that life, "No winning words about death to me. . . . By god, I'd rather slave on earth for another man—some dirt-poor tenant farmer who scrapes to keep alive—than rule down here over all the breathless dead" (Homer, 1996, p. 265). Achilles says this because Hades is described as an unhappy place; the dead have no sense or feeling and are mere "phantoms."

A third view found in ancient Greek sources is that of the *immortality of the soul*. This view appears in the writings of Plato, who sometimes represented human beings as made up of two parts, a body (earthly, mortal) and a soul (immortal). Plato went on to offer arguments intended to prove the inherent immortality of the soul. For Plato, souls are essentially immortal, deathless by their very nature. Nothing can cause a soul not to be; thus it must exist forever. Because humans (and all bodies that move "of themselves"—that is, animals) are in part souls, death must mean only the separation of the body and the soul. It does not mean the end of the soul.

PERSONAL INSIGHTS 19.1

Socrates' Thoughts about the Meaning of Death

This thing that has come upon me must be a good; and those of us who think that death is an evil must needs be mistaken. . . . For the state of death is one of two things: either the dead man wholly ceases to be and loses all consciousness or . . . it is a change and a migration of the soul to another place. And if death is the absence of all consciousness, and like the sleep of one whose slumbers are unbroken by any dreams, it will be a wonderful gain. . . . For it appears that all time is nothing more than a single night. But if death is a journey to another place, and what we are told is true—that all who have died are there—what good could be greater than this? . . . What would you not give to converse with Orpheus and Musaeus and Hesiod and Homer? . . . It would be an inexpressible happiness to converse with [heroes such as these] and to live with them and to examine them.

Source: Plato, 1948, pp. 47–48; *Apology,* 40b–41a.

Greek thought provided one major strand of Western beliefs about the relationship of life and death. Another major strand came from the Judeo-Christian tradition and its biblical scriptures.

Some Western Religious Beliefs

Many different beliefs about an afterlife are expressed in the Hebrew and Christian scriptures. Bailey (1978) found the following notions associated with an afterlife in those texts:

1. "Immortality" is sometimes associated only with divine beings (1 Timothy 6:16).
2. Sometimes "deathlessness" is seen as being given by the gods to specific human beings (e.g., Enoch in Genesis 5:24 and Elijah in 2 Kings 2:1–12).
3. An afterlife might be related to a phantomlike existence, a sort of "diminished life." (Compare Achilles' description of Hades noted earlier.) Some people have found this view present in Saul's consultations with a witch, who calls up Samuel from the afterworld (see 1 Samuel 28).
4. Ongoing life after death is often related to what one leaves behind at one's death, such as one's children.

Actually, the notion of the individual surviving death is only rarely encountered in the Hebrew scriptures. If there is a notion of ongoing life after death, it is found in the community and in one's specific descendants: I may die, but my community will go on. I may die, but my children and my children's children will go on. It is the community's life that is important, and it is the ongoing life of the familial line that is significant (Bowker, 1991).

In fact, it is even uncertain whether the Greek notion of a soul discussed earlier is found in the Hebrew scriptures. The Hebrew word often translated as "soul" *(nepesh)* means most simply "life." It is necessarily tied up with a body. Thus, at death, the *nepesh* ceases to exist because it is no longer bound up with a particular body. Eichrodt (1967) reports that various images are used: at death, the *nepesh* "dies; at the same time it is . . . feasible to think of it leaving a man at death, though this does not mean that one can ask where it has gone! . . . It is described as having been taken or swept away" (p. 135). He added: "In no instance does there underlie the use of *nepes* [a] conception of an immortal *alter ego.* . . . Equally remote from the concept . . . is the signification of a numinous substance in Man who survives death" (p. 140). If this is correct, then the notion of an immortal soul is not part of the original Judaic tradition. In fact, Eichrodt (1967) holds that this idea entered Judaic thought much later, under the influence of Hellenic (Greek) culture.

The Hebrew scriptures provided another image of an afterlife—the image of resurrection. This image grows out of the Judaic belief that the human being is not a combination of two different sorts of entities, a body and a soul; each of us is rather an integrated whole. To be a human being is not to be a soul entombed in a body as Plato claimed in some of his dialogues; it is to be a living-body. Life in this view cannot be understood *except* as embodied. (Islam sometimes teaches this precept, too; see Muwahidi, 1989, pp. 40–41). Thus, if there is to be a life after death, it must be an embodied life. That is what *resurrection* means: it refers to the "raising up" of a human being as a living-body. This raising up would require a new action by God—namely, a re-creation of the human being.

Western religion has also often associated an afterlife with the concepts of *heaven and hell*. These concepts are well developed in Islam. According to Islam, at a Last Judgment each individual's behavior while living in this world will be judged. If a person submits to Allah ("Islam" means "to submit"), rewards will be waiting after death. If a person rebels against Allah, punishments will be waiting. These rewards or punishments are often described vividly:

> For those that fear the majesty of their lord there are two gardens . . . planted with shady trees. . . . Each is watered by a flowering spring. . . . Each bears every kind of fruit. . . . They shall recline on couches lined with thick brocade . . . there shall wait on them immortal youths with bowls and ewers and a cup of purest wine. . . . And theirs shall be the dark-eyed houris, chaste as hidden pearls . . . those [who are cursed] shall dwell amongst scorching winds and seething water: in the shade of pitch-black smoke. (*Qur'an*, 1993, 55:35–56:55)

Similar concepts can be identified in Christianity, in Hinduism, and in some forms of Buddhism.

Islam has other beliefs that are of interest here. Sakr (1995) and Smith and Haddad (2002) reported that for Islam there is a form of life in the grave. The soul of the person who has died is believed to visit the grave regularly to receive reward or punishment. The "grave is a center of transformation, a center of molding, a center of reshaping, a center of preparation, and a place of resynthesis" (Sakr, 1995, p. 59).

Other cultures, however, have quite different beliefs.

Islamic men carry a coffin in the courtyard of a mosque.

© David Lees/Corbis

Some African Beliefs

The continent of Africa contains many cultures, and the philosophical and theological beliefs of the people in these various cultures have not been extensively described or studied. However, some preliminary generalizations have been made (Mbiti, 1970).

In general, for many of these people, the power that makes life possible is everywhere the same—in plants, in animals, and in human beings (Opoku, 1978, 1987). So human life is part of nature, and it is a constant cyclic process of becoming (as is nature). This process does have certain distinguishing moments or turning points in it: birth, adolescence, marriage, and death. But each of these crises only marks a particular point in the process of becoming. Those in the community who are alive are in one stage; those who are the "living-dead" (that is, those who are not living as we are here) are simply in a further stage. The community contains both the living and the living-dead. The living-dead are not thought of as being in another world; they are only in a different part of this world. The transition to this other part of the world is sometimes symbolized as a land journey, often including the crossing of a river, perhaps because rivers form natural boundaries between one part of the natural world and another part. This view typically does not include a notion of a heaven (a life of bliss) or of a hell (a life of torment).

The living-dead, in this view, are quasi-material beings. As ancestors, they are prized and respected. Their lives are ones of serenity and dignity, given over to concern for the well-being of the living members of their families and clans. Thus the family extends into this other world.

These are images drawn from a people living in close contact with nature. There is no notion of a pale, empty afterlife, as seen in Homer. Nor is there a notion of resurrection or of heaven or hell. The afterlife as it is portrayed here is a simple, natural continuation of the life we know. There *are* differences, just as living in the desert on this side of the river is different from living in the forest on the other side of the river. However, the life of the living-dead is not a wholly foreign existence. It is not a threatening one, quite different from fear of the dead that has been said to be found in some "primitive" religions (Frazer, 1977).

Some African Americans share this sort of belief. Sullivan (1995) reported that for such persons the dead and the living have reciprocal functions that create a unified whole. For these persons, to "pass on" is to be involved in "movement." It is a change in form whereby one moves on to the world of the ancestors.

Hindu and Buddhist Beliefs

When Westerners think about the philosophical and theological beliefs of the people of the Indian subcontinent, perhaps the notion that most often springs to mind is *reincarnation.* (A variety of terms are associated with this idea: *transmigration of souls, metempsychosis, rebirth;* we treat these terms here as if they are interchangeable.) This is a very ancient idea, one that can sometimes be found in Western thought, too. For example, ideas like this are found in some of Plato's dialogues. However, the idea of reincarnation is certainly older than Plato's writings (the fourth century BCE).

Devout Hindus release a dead body into the sacred river Ganges in India.

The first writings that discuss the idea of reincarnation go back at least to the seventh century BCE. One Hindu scripture (the *Katha Upanishad*) contains the following passage (Radhakrishnan & Moore, 1957, pp. 45–46):

The wise one . . . is not born, nor dies.
This one has not come from anywhere, has not become anyone.
Unborn, constant, eternal, primeval, this one
Is not slain when the body is slain.
If the slayer think to slay,
If the slain think himself slain,
Both these understand not.
Know thou the self *(atman)* as riding in a chariot,
The body as the chariot. . . .
He . . . who has not understanding,
Who is unmindful and ever impure,
Reaches not the goal,
But goes on to transmigration. . . .
He . . . who has understanding,
Who is mindful and ever pure,
Reaches the goal
From which he is born no more . . .

This passage expresses several important characteristics of a Hindu view of the human being. Humans are essentially an unborn, undying soul *(atman)*. This soul is repeatedly incarnated in bodies (and not necessarily always in human bodies, but also in "lower" forms). What body the soul is incarnated into depends on what one has done in previous lives. "Unmindfulness," "impurity," and a lack of understanding about the nature of reality will lead to transmigration of the soul from one body or one sort of body to another. But transmigration necessarily brings with it suffering, so the goal is to end transmigration, or rebirth. Perhaps one of the clearest statements of this view is found in the *Bhagavad Gita*. It contains the teachings of the lord Krishna (a god) to a human being (Arjuna). Arjuna is agonized about the killing that occurs in war, but Krishna tells him:

> Wise men do not grieve for the dead or for the living. . . . Never was there a time when I was not, nor thou . . . nor will there ever be a time hereafter when we shall cease to be. . . . Just as a person casts off worn-out garments and puts on others that are new, even so does the embodied soul cast off worn-out bodies and take on others that are new. (Radhakrishnan, 1948, pp. 102–108)

If this is so, then what does it tell people about how to live their lives here? Krishna answers:

> Endowed with a pure understanding, firmly restraining oneself, turning away from sound and other objects of sense and casting aside attraction, and aversion. . . . Dwelling in solitude, eating but little, controlling speech, body, and mind . . . taking refuge in dispassion . . . casting aside self-sense, force, arrogance, desire, anger, possession, egoless, and tranquil in mind, he becomes worthy of becoming one with *Brahman*. (Radhakrishnan, 1948, p. 370)

In other words, right living can lead to an end of the rebirths and to complete peace or union with a transcendent reality.

After death, three possibilities exist: (1) the *atman* may be in one of the heavens, awaiting rebirth; (2) the *atman* is immediately reborn; or (3) the *atman* is in a state of eternal bliss with Brahman (the transcendent reality), having achieved liberation from the cycle of rebirths.

Buddha's parinirvana (death).

A Buddhist Perspective in a Book for Children

First Snow (Coutant, 1974) is a book about a young girl named Liên who has recently come with her family from Vietnam to live in a small town in New England. Liên is impatiently waiting to experience snow for the first time when she overhears her parents say, "Grandmother is dying." No one really answers Liên when she asks, "What does it mean that Grandmother is dying?" Finally, one day her grandmother tells Liên to go out into the garden and hold her hand up to heaven to discover for herself what dying means. When a snowflake lands on her finger, Liên appreciates it as a tiny, fleeting thing that is both beautiful and delicate. Then when the sun causes the edges of the snowflake to burst into a thousand tiny rainbows, it changes to a drop of water and falls on the ground where it nourishes a tiny pine tree. All of this affirms Liên's Buddhist beliefs that life and death are but two parts of the same thing.

The founder of Buddhism (Siddhartha Gautama) was raised as a Hindu but eventually found its practices and beliefs unacceptable. After years of spiritual struggle, he experienced an awakening (thus becoming the Buddha—the enlightened one). As the *Buddha*, he taught that all is impermanence; nothing (not even a soul) exists in some eternal, unchanging condition (see Personal Insights 19.2 for an expression of this viewpoint in a death-related book for children). This fact produces suffering for everything that is aware of it. For human beings, "birth is suffering; sickness is suffering; death is suffering; sorrow and lamentation, pain, grief and despair are suffering; association with the unpleasant is suffering; dissociation from the pleasant is suffering; not to get what one wants is suffering" (Rahula, 1974, p. 93). As long as one fails to recognize this fact—and to confront and transcend it—one will live again and again, reincarnated into one suffering body after another. In this condition of ignorance about the true, impermanent nature of all reality, death is an evil because it only leads to rebirth into another life of suffering. Ideally, by transcending desire, one can escape the wheel of rebirths, achieving *nirvana,* a state beyond desire and thus beyond suffering, a state serene and peaceful (Radhakrishnan & Moore, 1957).

A Common Concern in Images of an Afterlife

The various notions we have described about what happens after death range from a permanent sleep (unconsciousness) through re-creation in an embodied form (resurrection), and on to a "blowing out" or a condition of absolute stillness. Some of these pictures seem threatening: a hell involving punishment or a Hades as it is described in Homer. Some seem attractive: meeting old companions or eternal joy in a heavenly state. Some provide a sense of peace: a surcease from a constant round of suffering. Each notion is likely to affect how one lives one's life here and now, and how one evaluates death.

In the United States in the 21st century, many persons no longer hold the typical religious beliefs of earlier times. The modern, scientific worldview has convinced many people that they are simply natural bodies. On that basis, it seems to many that when our bodies no longer function, then we simply are no more. Death means extinction.

How this view is likely to affect one's evaluation of death is not obvious. In a sense, it is an unthreatening view because there is no suffering after death, although of course, death means the loss of everything one has valued and loved. If this life is seen as basically good, then its loss is likely to be held to be an unhappy event. Death may then be only feared and hated—and denied. This may be one source of death denial.

In the face of uncertainty, people seek evidence. They would like to know what death means in terms of ongoing existence. Yet Socrates seems to have been correct; we cannot *know*. We must choose some picture of what death means and make do with it. For all of us, religious and nonreligious alike, faith is the only possible route here.

Near-Death Experiences

Or is faith the only possible route? Moody's (1975) book *Life after Life* drew attention to a set of phenomena reported by many people. Often, the phenomena were interpreted as providing evidence that there is a life after death and what that life might be like. However, these interpretations are controversial. To understand the issues involved, we look first at the general pattern of these phenomena and then at some of the competing interpretations.

What Are Near-Death Experiences?

Those whom Moody interviewed provided similar, but not identical, reports of their experiences. Typically, these persons reported out-of-body experiences in which they felt themselves to be in a peaceful and quiet state. During these experiences they often related that they were aware of their surroundings and heard themselves being pronounced clinically dead. At the same time, they frequently had unusual sensory encounters: hearing loud noises or auditory sensations, being in a dark tunnel, coming into contact with others, meeting a being of light, reviewing their own lives, and approaching a border or limit of some type. Often, people who had these experiences were hesitant to share them with others for fear of being disbelieved or ridiculed. When encouraged to share, however, they noted difficulties in communicating what appeared to them to be overwhelming, beyond words, and indescribable. They also typically reported that this experience had changed their lives, leaving them content, joyful, and no longer afraid of death.

Moody (1975) pointed out that these reports were not all identical. Still, he thought there were sufficient similarities on the main points that it was worth paying attention to the phenomena being reported. Other writers recorded similar phenomena and attempted to describe what they considered the key components of the "near-death experience" (NDE). For example, Ring (1980) examined a set of 102 cases, in which 60 percent reported a feeling of peace and a sense of well-being. Some in this sample reported "a sense of detachment from one's physical body" (p. 45) and a sense of "entering the darkness" (p. 53). A few described an appearance of light, with 10 percent telling of "entering the light" (p. 60). Similarly, Sabom (1982) concluded that the most common features in the cases that he examined were a sense of calm and peace, bodily separation, being dead, and "returning" to life. Other writers (such as Blackmore, 1993; Fenwick & Fenwick, 1995; Greyson, 1999, 2005; Moody, 1988) provided further portraits of NDEs or have made efforts to define their essential characteristics.

In an effort to bolster the so-called archetypal NDE and control for cultural bias, others set out to broaden the field of investigation. For example, some looked for reports from individuals who had experienced some type of trauma but who were not near death (Owens et al., 1990; Stevenson et al., 1989); others recorded interviews with individuals who were dying, underwent an NDE experience, recovered to communicate it to others, and then did die (Osis & Haraldsson, 1997); and still others sought NDE reports from outside North America (e.g., Lorimer, 1989; Van Lommel et al., 2001). Atwater (1992) and Greyson and Bush (1992) also reported near-death experiences that were distressing or frightening.

Interpreting the Meaning of Near-Death Experiences

The most common interpretative claim made by those who report having had an NDE is the assertion that they had been dead and then had returned to life. Supporters of this claim believe that NDEs provide conclusive evidence of the existence of an afterlife—into which the NDE is thought to have offered a brief glimpse. This is the view of Elisabeth Kübler-Ross in the foreword to Moody's (1975) book.

On the contrary, some people might argue with Socrates that beliefs about the afterlife are in principle restricted to the realm of faith and are not issues on which empirical evidence can be demonstrative. As Kelly (2001, p. 230) reported, "most scientific investigators of NDEs have virtually ignored this question [of whether human consciousness survives the death of the physical body], concentrating instead on less controversial activities such as describing the aftereffects of NDEs or speculating about the physiological mechanisms that might underlie them." Such scientists seem to hold such views as: survival after death is nonsensical; interpretations favoring post-death survival on grounds of NDEs are unsound and incapable of controlled replication; and NDEs most likely are artifacts of the unusual situations in which they occur, for example, arising physiologically from anoxia (being without oxygen for a time) or chemical imbalances associated with anesthesia and surgical procedures (Nuland, 1994). In short, NDEs are essentially hallucinations (Siegel, 1992).

In fact, the claim that some persons were at one time dead and are now alive to report an NDE is awkward. If what it means to be dead is to be *irreversibly* without biological life, then such persons were not dead. Perhaps they were almost dead, or near dead, or their experiences occurred during a set of processes that often lead to death. For example, they might have been *clinically dead* where that phrase means they met some criteria used to decide when death has occurred. However, the connection between meeting such medical criteria and being dead is unclear; the two need not be identical. For instance, because someone shows no external signs of consciousness does not mean that person is having no experiences. *Unconscious* in this context means little more than "not showing signs of consciousness"; it does not mean no consciousness is present.

Kelly and her colleagues (2000) drew attention to three particular features of NDEs: "enhanced mental processes at a time when physiological functioning is seriously impaired; the experience of being out of the body and viewing events going on around it as from a position above; and the awareness of remote events not accessible to the person's ordinary senses" (p. 513). None of these features on its own is conclusive in settling the dispute as to whether NDEs can offer an expectation of an afterlife or are merely hallucinations. However, Kelly (2001) concluded that their convergence suggests the survival hypothesis "may be worthy of closer, more serious consideration—both as a framework for generating empirical research and as a candidate explanation for phenomena observed—than it has so far received from researchers" (p. 246). But note this qualification: "We emphasize, however, that near-death experiences can provide only *indirect* evidence of the continuation of consciousness after death: because the persons having these experiences have lived to report them, they were therefore not dead, however close they may have been to that condition" (Kelly et al., 2000, p. 518). And Moody has said: "I am a complete skeptic regarding the possibility that science as we know it or any sort of conventionally established methodological procedures will be able to get evidence of life after death or to come to some sort of rational determination of this question" (Kastenbaum, 1995, p. 95).

None of this rules out other lines of evidence that might support beliefs about an afterlife. However, they have not been studied extensively, and when they have been studied, the evidence is at best ambiguous. Socrates' dictum seems to stand: we do not, and perhaps cannot, know what happens after death. We must take a stand—even those who are agnostic are under the same practical compulsion—on less than complete proof. This central fact of our humanness—our mortality—remains a mystery.

❧ The Place of Death in Human Life

Now that we have considered several images of what happens after death, it is useful to ask: What conclusions can we draw from these images for the meanings of our lives as we live them in this temporal, physical world?

Afterlife Images and Life Here and Now

One might argue that what we do here in this life influences what will happen to us after death. This becomes an argument meant to persuade us to behave in one way rather than another in order to reap benefits in an afterlife. Certain forms of Christianity, Islam, Hinduism, and Buddhism make suggestions like this. They contend that what we do here and now has desirable or undesirable consequences (for us) after death.

But even if one holds no such ideas, one can still make ties between what happens after death and life in the world now. For instance, if death is permanent extinction, then perhaps humans ought to live life to the fullest and seek to get as much experience as they can. Or, again, if death means extinction, one might hold that this eliminates the value of everything we know and do in our lives: all is vanity. Also, death can mean an end to suffering, as Hindus and Buddhists claim; it eliminates "the heartache and the thousand natural shocks that flesh is heir to" (*Hamlet*, III, i: 62). In this sense, death might be courted, even welcomed.

Some have gone beyond this to maintain the "conviction that in the last analysis all human behavior of consequence is a response to the problem of death" (Feifel, 1977a, xiii). If that seems too bold or too broad a thesis, then at least it can be said that we humans are able to make of death an important steering force in the way we interpret its place in our lives. If so, "appreciation of finiteness can serve not only to enrich self-knowledge but to provide the impulse to propel us forward toward achievement and creativity" (Feifel, 1977a, p. 11).

Efforts to Circumvent or Transcend Death

Many people have tried to circumvent death and have gone about it in a variety of ways. Another way to say this is that people have sought to find a way to continue after they die what they have found valuable in their lives. Lifton (1979) pointed to several such forms of what he called *symbolic immortality*. The main varieties that he described are biological, social, natural, and theological immortality. That is, one's life (and the values one finds in life) might be continued through one's biological descendants. Or it could be continued in what one has created—a painting, a garden, a book—or perhaps in the lives of others one has touched—students, patients, clients, friends. Some people have sought a continuation of their lives after their own deaths in the natural world around them. In this view, one's body returns to the ground (dust to dust), wherein its components dissolve and are reorganized into new life. And as we have seen earlier, other people have looked for immortality in the form of an afterlife and reunion with or absorption into the divine. Furthermore, some have favored a program of *cryonics* in which one's entire body or perhaps just one's head would be frozen at the moment of death and maintained in that state until a time comes (or so they hope) when they could be thawed out and the cause of their death cured by future generations.

Attempts to circumvent death reveal a meaning for that irrevocable, unavoidable moment: it produces suffering. If anything is valued in this life, death threatens that value. It means the loss (at least for now) of persons we have loved, places we have enjoyed, music, a stunning sunrise, or the feeling of material (soil, paper and ink, the bow on the strings) coming into form through our labor.

If this is the meaning we find for death, inevitably it will influence how we live and how we treat each other. It teaches us that life is precious. So we entitled this book *Death and Dying, Life and Living*. It seems that whatever meaning we find for death, to look at death leads us to realize the fragility and the value of life. Indeed, perhaps death makes possible the value of life. A life (as we know life here) that went on indefinitely might become unbearable. Why do anything today, when there are endless tomorrows in which to do it?

Ultimately, the meaning any individual finds for death will be his or her own. In this sense, each individual is alone in facing his or her own death. But there is a history—thousands of years long—and a cultural diversity among persons with whom one can enter into dialogue. Each person can enter into this dialogue to gain help in choosing how to live his or her own life and how to make sense of his or her own death and the deaths of those for and about whom he or she cares. Each individual can also contribute to the history of human debate about the meaning and place of death in human life. This book is but one voice in that ongoing dialogue.

🍂 Summary

In this chapter, we engaged in a reflection on the meaning and place of death in human life. We considered questions that human beings have raised about death and responses offered, on one hand, by religious and philosophical perspectives, and, on the other, by students of near-death experiences. The lesson we drew is that each person is both free and responsible to determine for himself or herself the stand that he or she will take in the face of death.

Glossary

Atman: the unborn, undying self (in Hindu writings)

Cryonics: a practice in which one's body (or sometimes just the head) is frozen at the time of death and held in that state until a time comes when, it is hoped, it could be thawed and the cause of death cured by future generations

Hades: the kingdom of the dead in Homer's *Odyssey;* the place where one goes after death according to some ancient Greek thought; a dreary place

Heaven and hell: places of reward or punishment, respectively, after death according to some Western religions

Immortality of the soul: a view originating in ancient Greek thought according to which the soul or essential element in a human does not die; it simply separates from the body at death and lives on eternally

Living-dead: a view found in some African thought according to which the human community consists of both the living and the living-dead or those individuals who are no longer living here, but are living in some different part of the world; as ancestors they continue to have concerns for the well-being of their descendants

Near-death experiences (NDEs): phenomena arising from reports by individuals who have experienced out-of-body experiences or a sense of detachment from their bodies; efforts have been made to classify the common characteristics of these experiences; interpretations of their meaning have varied, and some are controversial

Nepesh: a Hebrew word for "soul," implying an inextricable involvement with a body, such that when the body dies the *nepesh* also ceases to exist

Nirvana: a goal in Buddhism; a serene and peaceful state, beyond desire and suffering (which leads to rebirth)

Reincarnation: literally, to be reborn or reinserted in a body; an ancient concept found both in Greek thought and Hindu writings; allied notions include *transmigration* of souls and *metempsychosis*, which imply movement of souls from body to body

Symbolic immortality: Lifton's term for efforts made to transcend or circumvent death through biological, social, natural, or theological accounts of continuity

Questions for Review and Discussion

1. This chapter reviewed several notions of what happens after death. These included: (1) immortality of the soul; (2) resurrection of the body; (3) life continued in a place of bliss (heaven) or torture (hell) or exceeding boredom (the Greek Hades); (4) rebirth (transmigration or reincarnation of the soul); (5) a life much like this one only somewhere else; and (6) permanent peace and stillness (nirvana, extinction). Which of these views are you inclined toward? How might your response to this question affect how you live your life? How might it influence how you treat someone else who is dying?

2. This chapter discussed near-death experiences. What is your assessment of what such experiences can or do tell us about what happens to us after we die?

Suggested Readings

For religious, philosophical, spiritual, and other perspectives on death-related issues, see:

Badham, P., & Badham, L. (Eds.). (1987). *Death and Immortality in the Religions of the World.*

Berger, A., Badham, P., Kutscher, A. H., Berger, J., Perry, M., & Beloff, J. (Eds.). (1989). *Perspectives on Death and Dying: Cross-Cultural and Multi-Disciplinary Views.*

Chidester, D. (1990). *Patterns of Transcendence: Religion, Death, and Dying.*

Cox, G. R., & Fundis, R. J. (Eds.). (1992). *Spiritual, Ethical and Pastoral Aspects of Death and Bereavement.*

Doka, K. J., with Morgan, J. D. (Eds.). (1993). *Death and Spirituality.*

Gignoux, J. H. (1998). *Some Folk Say: Stories of Life, Death, and Beyond.*

Goss, R. J., & Klass, D. (2005). *Dead but Not Lost: Grief Narratives in Religious Traditions.*

Johnson, C. J., & McGee, M. G. (Eds.). (1998). *How Different Religions View Death and Afterlife.*

Kauffman, J. (Ed.). (1995). *Awareness of Mortality.*

Klass, D. (Ed.). (2006). Death, grief, religion, and spirituality [Special issue]. *Omega, Journal of Death and Dying,* 53(1–2).

Morgan, J. D., & Laungani, P. (Eds.). (2002). *Death and Bereavement around the World: Vol. 1, Major Religious Traditions.*

Obayashi, H. (Ed.). (1992). *Death and Afterlife: Perspectives of World Religions.*

Reynolds, F. E., & Waugh, E. H. (Eds.). (1977). *Religious Encounters with Death: Insights from the History and Anthropology of Religion.*

Issues related to near-death experiences are examined in:

Fenwick, P., & Fenwick, E. (1995). *The Truth in the Light: An Investigation of Over 300 Near-Death Experiences.*

Kellehear, A. (1996). *Experiences near Death: Beyond Medicine and Religion.*

Moody, R. A. (1975). *Life after Life.*

Moody, R. A. (1988). *The Light Beyond.*

Osis, K., & Haraldsson, E. (1997). *At the Hour of Death* (3rd ed.).

Ring, K. (1980). *Life at Death: A Scientific Investigation of the Near-Death Experience.*

Ring, K. (1984). *Heading toward Omega: In Search of the Meaning of the Near-Death Experience.*

Sabom, M. B. (1982). *Recollections of Death: A Medical Investigation.*

Selected Web Resources

Some useful search terms include: IMMORTALITY OF THE SOUL; NEAR-DEATH EXPERIENCES; REINCARNATION; RESURRECTION OF THE BODY

Visit the book companion website for *Death & Dying, Life & Living, Sixth Edition,* at academic.cengage.com/psychology/corr for all URLs and live links to the following *organizational and other Internet sites:*

American Cryonics Society

Association for Clinical Pastoral Education

Association for Professional Chaplains

BELIEVE: Religious Information Source (multiple topics)

International Association for Near-Death Studies

***Journal of Near-Death Studies* (published by Springer Science + Business Media B.V.)**

Near-Death Experiences and the Afterlife

PART SEVEN

An Example of a Specific Disease Entity

In this book, we examined a large and what may seem to be an overwhelming number of issues related to dying, death, and bereavement. In so doing, we focused our discussions on several central themes:

◆ The components of **death-related experiences,** that is, death-related: (a) *encounters,* (b) *attitudes,* and (c) *practices*

◆ *Gender, racial, and cultural* influences on death-related experiences

◆ *Death systems* in our society and in other parts of the world

◆ *Efforts to cope* with dying and bereavement

◆ *Ways to help* others and ourselves in coping with dying and bereavement

◆ *Developmental* influences on death-related experiences

◆ Some important *lessons about life and living*

◆ *Moral and spiritual values* related to death, dying, and bereavement

In the earlier portions of this book we covered these issues in general ways. In so doing, we mentioned a wide variety of causes of death, disease entities, and contexts in which dying, death, and bereavement are encountered. What we offer now is an extended portrait of one specific disease entity to help us integrate as many of these issues as possible. The disease entity chosen for this purpose must provide both an example of as many of our central themes as possible and a test case of their power to illuminate human interactions with death.

We recognize there are several life-threatening diseases which might serve this purpose. To do so, the disease needs to have sufficient complexity in its realization and a sufficiently lengthy dying trajectory to allow these issues to emerge. So a sudden dying (say from a heart attack, suicide, or a car accident) would not serve very well as the sort of paradigm we seek to achieve our purpose here.

We have chosen for Chapter 20 one particular disease entity. Some readers might prefer to choose some other disease entity to develop a different portrait of how the issues in this book are realized and integrated in specific ways. We encourage such efforts and would be interested to learn what the portrait would look like for disease entities such as influenza, lung or breast cancer, Lou Gehrig's disease, or Alzheimer's disease.

In the meantime, we proceed in Chapter 20 to explore how the issues raised throughout this book are realized in the particular context of one specific disease entity: HIV infection and AIDS.

CHAPTER 20

Illustrating the Themes of This Book

Only men, women and children get AIDS

A project of the 4th District American Advertising Federation and Cathy Robinson's Friends Together

Find out more at www.friendstogether.org

© Friends-Together, Inc./www.friendstogether.org

❦ Prologue

This chapter differs in important ways from those that have preceded it. In previous chapters, we examined how dying, death, and bereavement are experienced in a wide variety of contexts. As we did so, we emphasized a number of central themes, including:

◆ The components of **death-related experiences**, that is, death-related: (a) *encounters*, (b) *attitudes*, and (c) *practices*

◆ *Gender, racial, and cultural* influences on death-related experiences

◆ *Death systems* in our society and in other parts of the world

◆ *Efforts to cope* with dying and bereavement

- *Ways to help* others and ourselves in coping with dying and bereavement
- *Developmental* influences on death-related experiences
- Some important *lessons about life and living*
- *Moral and spiritual values* related to death, dying, and bereavement

In this chapter we show how these themes come together and get played out in *one specific context.* That is, instead of studying these themes in general contexts, here we examine many of these central themes in relationship to one specific disease entity: infection with the human immunodeficiency virus (HIV) and acquired immunodeficiency syndrome (AIDS). Our primary goal is to provide an illustration of how these central themes reveal themselves in the context of this specific disease. In other words, the framework of the entire book becomes the explicit structure for this final chapter.

We selected HIV infection and its end state, AIDS, when we developed this chapter for the first edition of this book because at that time they had begun to have a significant impact on American consciousness. But more than that, HIV and AIDS were perceived as unique in several ways. HIV was a *communicable disease* leading to significant numbers of deaths in a society in which this was infrequent. In addition, AIDS was also perceived then as an inevitably fatal disease—one which threatened quickly to become a major threat to the entire human community.

Of course, many things have changed since that time. Public attention has waned as the media have paid less attention to HIV/AIDS. More importantly, HIV and AIDS are now less prominent than they once were as a cause of death in the United States and many other developed countries—even though they remain the underlying causes of thousands of deaths annually in our society and they brought about an estimated total of over 2 million deaths around the world in 2007 (UNAIDS, 2007). In short, HIV and AIDS remain a serious threat to human life both in the technologically advanced nations and even more so in those less technologically advanced. Moreover, even where the impact of HIV and AIDS is much like that of a chronic disease, they most often become a life-changing condition affecting quality of life significantly. Also, even in areas of the world where treatment of HIV and AIDS has had great effect, there is still much that is needed by way of prevention. Thus, HIV and AIDS remain good examples of the central themes developed in this book.

Objectives of This Chapter

The principal objectives of this chapter are:

- To provide an extended example of how the central themes of this book come together in the experience of one specific disease entity in our society

- To offer an overview of experiences with HIV and AIDS in the United States and around the world

🍎 Coming to Terms: A Reflection on the Life and Death of My Mother

My name is Ronald Porter, and I am a 20-year-old college student. In 1996, my 43-year-old mother, Melba Q. Porter, died due to the HIV/AIDS virus. I was 12 years old. Since that time, I have had to cope with two of the most tragic occurrences that can happen in the life of any individual. First, the loss of a dearly loved parent; and second, confronting the stigma associated with losing that parent to a socially stereotyped disease such as AIDS.

My life's journey can be divided into three sections: before, during, and after my mother's death. Before her sickness, I lived with my mother and father just outside of Washington, D.C. We enjoyed many wonderful moments together. Around 1990, my mother and father separated. It is during this time that we believe that she contracted the HIV virus through sexual contact. I lived with my mother for some time, and I remember watching her health gradually deteriorate, and not knowing why. She did try to tell me that she was HIV positive, but I broke down emotionally because I could not understand the news. I just thought it meant that my mother was going to die. After seeing my reaction, my mother told me that she only had cancer, and that she would be alright. I went on to believe that my mother was suffering from the more easily accepted disease—cancer. My mother carried the burden of her secret for my sake, not having the chance to prepare and educate me as I believe

Courtesy of Ronald Porter

Ronald Porter (as a child) and his mother.

that she had attempted to do that day. My family either concealed or denied the truth. I question whether their motives were for their sake or mine. I suppose that things were easier for everyone to cope with when left unspoken.

The final years of my mother's life were very difficult. She began living with my grandmother in Washington, D.C., and I moved outside of Baltimore with my father and aunt. It was around this time that I began to lose touch with my mother. She was isolated and shunned by some and withdrew herself from others. She was very sad and constantly told me that she was going to die. I would later understand this sadness as depression brought about by the stigma that surrounds HIV/AIDS. In January 1996, my mother came to visit me and my father in Baltimore. At the time she was very ill, suffering from diarrhea and a constant cough. I remember asking her if she was having trouble breathing, and she said, "Yes." My father and my aunt rushed her to the hospital. I did not understand what was happening. My mother stayed in the hospital for over a month. I visited only four times. The final visit, February 14, 1996, she was unconscious and on a respirator. She died soon after we left the hospital. No one was with her when she died. This lack of support during her final days has left me with a sense of guilt that will probably stay with me for the rest of my life.

After my mother's death, my family rarely talked about her, or how she died. I went through my teenage years constantly wondering what had caused her illness. I had a feeling it was AIDS, but I was afraid to ask due to the stigma. I was also afraid that I might have the disease. However, fear caused me not to discuss my feelings with anyone because I thought they might think my family was dirty. I also did not feel comfortable trying to discuss the issue with my family.

I had so many memories of my wonderful mother, who deeply enriched my life, but there were so many things that I still did not know. I did not start asking questions until my freshman year of college. My reaction to the confirmation of my mother's illness filled me with anger. I did not understand why no one had talked to me about the disease. I also did not understand why no one tried to give her the support she needed. I believe that if she were given more love she may have lived longer. I suspect that the stigma that comes with HIV/AIDS prevented my mother from reaching out to her own family and certainly believe that it prevented my family from giving her the support she needed. It has bothered me to know that the stigma surrounding HIV/AIDS often further complicates the effects of the disease. Sadly, the remnants of stigma still loom in my family and are illustrated by the fact that I have discussed the death of my mother more with my friends at college than with my actual family.

Nevertheless, I have had to come to an understanding. My experiences in understanding my mother's illness and expressing a rekindled love for my mother have begun to lend understanding to my feelings of anger and guilt. I believe that each one of us has the responsibility to let individuals living with HIV/AIDS know that they are no less than human and deserving of love, respect, and support. Through understanding my mother's experiences I have learned to celebrate the beautiful life of my mother and focus on the many gifts she brought to those around her. (Reprinted by permission of Ronald K. Porter.)

❦ Encounters with Death and Disease

Reports about a New Disease in the United States

AIDS was first brought to public attention in the United States through a report on June 5, 1981, in the *Morbidity and Mortality Weekly Report,* a publication of the U.S. Centers for Disease Control (CDC). The report (CDC, 1981a; see also

Gottlieb, M. S., et al., 1981) described five young men who had been admitted to hospitals in the Los Angeles area with an unusual type of pneumonia. Prior to that time, the pneumonia in question (which is caused by a commonly occurring protozoan, *Pneumocystis carinii*) had mainly been seen in individuals with immune system deficiencies—for example, in newborns or in adults treated with immunosuppressive drugs.

Shortly thereafter, another group of young men in New York City were reported to have *Pneumocystis carinii* pneumonia and a hitherto rare form of cancer. The cancer (*Kaposi's sarcoma*) is a tumor of blood vessel tissue in the skin or internal organs that had previously been found in relatively benign forms and only among elderly Italian and Jewish men of Mediterranean descent (CDC, 1981b; Gottlieb, G. J., et al., 1981; Hymes et al., 1981). Between June and August of 1981, the CDC (1981c) reported 110 of these unusual cases, all involving otherwise healthy males who were homosexual. All of these men were dying quite rapidly at a relatively young age (15–52 years old) of infectious diseases that were otherwise seldom fatal in America.

As these reports continued to appear, they were soon supplemented by information about similar occurrences of unusual life-threatening conditions and deaths in other groups of people, such as hemophiliacs, Haitian immigrants, intravenous drug users, children in families in which one or both parents had the disease, and heterosexual partners (female or male) of persons with the disease.

Identifying the New Disease Syndrome: AIDS

Three points soon became clear. First, despite their differences, it was realized that all of the reports involved *a common syndrome*—a clinical entity or recognizable pattern of manifestations arising from an underlying cause that was as yet unknown. Second, the pattern pointed to *a deficiency in the immune systems* of those experiencing this syndrome. In other words, the syndrome suggested there were problems involving the specific systems that normally defend the body against foreign invaders. When these systems do not function properly, those involved fall victim to internal forces and external invaders that normally are not troublesome for those with healthy immune systems. Third, there seemed to be no common genetic or natural basis for this syndrome, which suggested that the deficiency in the immune systems of these individuals had somehow been *acquired*. As a result, it was concluded that affected individuals had an *acquired immunodeficiency syndrome* or *AIDS*.

Because the underlying cause of AIDS remained unknown in the early years of the epidemic, the CDC could not explain why so many different individuals were experiencing immune dysfunction. By the early 1990s, however, the CDC (1992a) had learned a great deal about this syndrome and implemented a new definition of AIDS. It was now defined as a situation in which individuals had a CD4+ T-lymphocyte (often called *T-cells* for short) count of less than 200 per microliter (a normal count is around 1,000 per microliter). Note that this definition is based on a biological or laboratory marker rather than a clinical finding. That is, a diagnosis of the syndrome could now be made even if an individual displayed no overt symptoms associated with the syndrome. There were two important consequences of this change in the diagnosis of AIDS: (1) individuals were able to be diagnosed much earlier so that understandings of average length of survival of people with the disease changed as persons living with AIDS were seen to live much longer than had been previously expected and (2) more cases of AIDS were identified, particularly among women and children whose disease had often gone unrecognized when clinicians interpreted AIDS primarily through clinical manifestations most often found in adult males. (A side effect of the new understandings of AIDS was that the focus of the CDC was expanded and it was renamed the Centers for Disease Control and Prevention, even though it is still widely referred to as the CDC.)

Putting all of this together, we now know that AIDS is a condition in which an individual's immune system has become so dysfunctional that the person falls victim to *opportunistic infections* or unusual diseases and is therefore at heightened risk of dying.

Identifying the Cause of the New Disease Syndrome: HIV

The fact that AIDS appeared in a large number of individuals with *hemophilia* provided an important, early clue concerning the nature of the underlying cause of this syndrome. Hemophiliacs already had one life-threatening disease in the form of a blood clotting disorder that made them susceptible to internal and external bleeding problems. To combat their bleeding problems, hemophiliacs typically receive transfusions of blood or blood products. Perhaps the transfusions were themselves somehow contaminated with an unknown agent that caused AIDS?

Those who supply blood in the United States and in other industrialized countries make many efforts to ensure the purity of the blood and blood products that they collect and provide for transfusion. For example, our blood system *screens* potential donors and *filters* the blood that they donate to remove potential contaminants. But some wondered whether there was an as-yet-unidentified contaminant that was neither recognized nor removed by these procedures from donated blood and blood products. For instance, only *sterilization* of such blood and blood products would kill a microscopic virus.

Furthermore, although AIDS had once been referred to as "Gay Related Immune Disorder" (GRID) and although other adults with this syndrome might have transmitted its causal agent to each other through sexual activity, the same could hardly apply to infants and young children. It would seem that infants with AIDS, in particular, were very likely somehow to have acquired the agent that was producing their immune disorder from their mothers before, at the time of, or shortly after their births. The obvious question thus became: what sort of causal agent could be transmitted in all of these ways—from mother to child, via direct sexual behavior, and indirectly through transfused blood and blood products?

Ultimately, the answer was that *AIDS was caused by a virus,* one that eventually came to be called the human immunodeficiency virus (HIV). Intensive research by French and American scientists identified that virus in 1983 (see Grmek, 1990). Soon scientists were also able to identify and test for *antibodies* manufactured by human immune systems in their fight to repel this foreign agent. Antibody testing is still the main screening test for HIV infection. It is accomplished in several ways, for example, the inside of the cheek may be scraped with a special tool to obtain mucosal cells for testing or blood may be drawn from a vein. These specimens are then sent to a laboratory, which runs the test, and it can take up to two weeks to get the results. More recently, rapid HIV tests have become available that can yield results in about an hour.

However, it may take the immune system of a person infected with HIV several weeks or months to manufacture such antibodies. In most persons they show up by three months after infection occurs, but in some atypical cases they can take six months to a year to appear after infection. Thus, it is usually recommended that someone who may have been infected should wait for several weeks or up to three months before having the antibody test. If that first test is negative, it is recommended that a second test be done at six months after the date of the possible infection. What this means is that individuals who are unaware of their HIV status or whose bodies have not had time to develop antibodies that would register in a test may still be infected with the virus and be capable of transmitting it to others. The CDC (2006c) estimates that 24–27 percent of those infected with the disease in the United States do not know that they are infected (see also, National HIV Testing Resources, www.hivtest.org).

HIV in the Body

The ways in which HIV operates in the body of an infected person—a person who is said to be *HIV positive*—are complicated and multifaceted (Alcamo, 2003). In general, HIV primarily attacks a special kind of white blood cell called a helper T4 lymphocyte. These T4 cells are the ones that organize the body's immune response to a large variety of infections and disease organisms. Under normal circumstances, the T4 is precisely the type of cell that would be among the principal enemies of HIV. HIV also appears to attack macrophages, another form of white blood cells that migrate to all parts of the body to provide protection from disease. Infected macrophages may spread HIV to cells of the central nervous system (the brain and spinal cord), thereby producing dementia and other sorts of mental disorders that are often seen in AIDS.

HIV is a *retrovirus* whose genetic material is RNA instead of the usual DNA. When the virus enters the affected cell, it acts through an enzyme called reverse transcriptase to turn the virus' RNA into DNA. It then integrates this new viral DNA into the chromosomes of the cell, begins to replicate or produce new copies of itself, and eventually spreads throughout the body to infect new cells. In these ways, the HIV further weakens or destroys the immune system of the infected individual. If this is permitted to go on unchecked, the result is a general, overall weakening of the body's ability to function effectively, and an increasing vulnerability to the opportunistic infections and other life-threatening challenges that the body will no longer be able to resist effectively. In many cases, this means that an individual in the advanced phase of HIV infection is likely to encounter a series of infections, medical and nutritional interventions to contain these infections, and eventually, reinfections. Each of these infections represents its own relatively unpredictable assault from one or more of a variety of possible sources; each counterattack may involve a mobilization of one's remaining natural defenses along with whatever resources are available from modern medicine.

Recent Encounters with HIV/AIDS-Related Death and Disease in the United States

Following the introduction in the mid-1990s of new therapies to fight the disease, deaths associated with HIV/AIDS dropped dramatically in the United States. Since that time, however, annual numbers of AIDS-related deaths have remained relatively stable. For example, during the most recent five-year period for which data are available as this is written, Table 20.1 shows an overall decline of just under 4 percent among these deaths, with significant up ticks in 2003 and 2004. As a result of declines in these deaths since the mid 1990s, HIV and AIDS are ranked as only the 20th leading cause of death in our society in 2004. That is a major achievement. Still, the cumulative total of these deaths continues to climb in the United States.

Unfortunately, there has been no decline in the numbers of individuals who are newly infected with HIV (see Table 20.2). As a result, the cumulative total of those infected with HIV has increased each year. Thus, the CDC estimates that 425,910 persons were living with AIDS in the United States in 2005. As a result, the overall effect of improved therapeutic interventions and better overall care has been twofold: (1) it has held down (but not eliminated) the numbers of AIDS-related deaths in our society, and (2) it has prolonged the lives of many individuals by providing a "substantial increase in survival after AIDS diagnosis" (CDC, 2006c, p. 589) so that more and more people are living with HIV in the United States.

TABLE 20.1
Estimated Numbers of Deaths of Persons with AIDS, by Year of Death and Race/Ethnicity, 2001–2005 and Cumulative, United States[a]

Race/Cumulative Ethnicity	Year of Death					
	2001	2002	2003	2004	2005	Total[a]
White, not Hispanic	5,239	5,153	5,263	5,137	5,006	235,879
Black, not Hispanic	9,085	8,927	9,077	9,302	8,562	211,559
Hispanic	2,436	2,306	2,774	2,664	2,444	77,125
Asian/Pacific Islander	99	93	88	113	97	3,383
American Indian/Alaska Native	79	84	75	85	81	1,657
Total[b]	16,980	16,641	17,404	17,453	16,316	530,756

[a]Includes persons who died of AIDS, from the beginning of the epidemic through 2005.

[b]Includes persons of unknown race or multiple races. Cumulative total includes 3,462 persons of unknown race or multiple races. Because column totals were calculated independently of the values for the subpopulations, the values in each column may not sum to the column total.

Source: CDC, 2006a.

TABLE 20.2
Estimated Numbers of Persons Living with AIDS by Year, by Age and Race/Ethnicity, United States, 2001–2005

	2001	2002	2003	2004	2005
Age at End of Year (yrs)					
<13	2,536	2,298	1,990	1,660	1,373
13–14	616	684	745	784	769
15–19	1,265	1,488	1,712	1,981	2,290
20–24	3,766	3,931	4,343	4,743	5,431
25–29	13,037	12,746	12,819	13,238	14,286
30–34	37,348	35,690	34,054	32,413	31,157
35–39	71,132	70,438	68,558	65,670	64,132
40–44	75,045	80,913	86,831	92,074	96,211
45–49	58,856	65,356	72,017	78,204	86,211
50–54	36,046	41,722	47,370	53,967	60,766
55–59	17,045	20,422	24,498	28,788	34,383
60–64	8,168	9,839	11,459	13,495	15,771
≥65	6,653	7,856	9,311	11,023	13,131
Race/Ethnicity					
White, not Hispanic	124,399	130,545	136,546	142,989	150,673
Black, not Hispanic	141,918	152,606	163,788	174,609	188,077
Hispanic	59,471	63,897	68,427	72,913	78,901
Asian/Pacific Islander	2,825	3,161	3,538	3,904	4,356
American Indian/ Alaska Native	1,170	1,268	1,378	1,480	1,595
Total[a]	331,512	353,384	375,707	398,029	425,910

[a]Includes persons of unknown race or multiple races. Because column totals were calculated independently of the values for the subpopulations, the values in each column may not sum to the column total.

Source: CDC, 2006a.

Differential Encounters with HIV and AIDS in the United States

Next, we examine differential encounters with HIV and AIDS in recent years among selected population subgroups in the United States. Here the data identify significant racial, ethnic, gender, transmission category, and age differences among those who become infected with HIV and die of AIDS in the United States today.

Racial and Ethnic Differences According to the CDC (2006a), African Americans accounted for 49 percent of all HIV/AIDS cases diagnosed in 2005. In that year, "rates of HIV/AIDS cases were 72.8 per 100,000 in the black population, 28.5 per 100,000 in the Hispanic population, 10.6 per 100,000 in the American Indian/Alaska Native population, 9.0 per 100,000 in the white population, and 7.6 per 100,000 in the Asian/Pacific Islander population" (CDC, 2006a, p. 6). During the period from 2001 through 2005 the estimated number of deaths of persons with AIDS decreased among whites and blacks while remaining stable among other racial and ethnic groups.

Gender Differences According to CDC (2006a), during the period from 2001–2005 "the estimated number of HIV/AIDS cases increased approximately 2% among males and decreased 17% among females. In 2005, males accounted for 74% of all HIV/AIDS cases among adults and adolescents" (p. 6). Despite this good news concerning a recent decrease of HIV/AIDS cases among females, this still means that they now constitute roughly one-quarter of all individuals with HIV/AIDS, an increase of about 40 percent in their relative share since the 1980s and early 1990s. Moreover, during the period 2001–2005 when AIDS-related deaths among males declined by nearly 4 percent, they only declined about 1 percent among females. As a result, a CDC report (2006b, p. 587) has stated that, "Today women account for approximately one quarter of all new HIV/AIDS diagnoses and, in 2002, HIV infection was the leading cause of death for black women aged 25–34 years."

Transmission Category Differences From 2001 through 2005, the CDC (2006a, p. 6) reports that "the estimated number of HIV/AIDS cases increased among men who have sex with men (MSM)." This is particularly unfortunate because during the early years of the epidemic males in this category experienced high rates of infection and deaths. As a result, many modified their behaviors, and both infection and death rates declined. It now appears that younger men in this category have forgotten some of the lessons their elders had learned.

During this same period, HIV/AIDS cases decreased among injection drug users, heterosexual adults and adolescents, and children. Consequently, "MSM (49%) and persons exposed through high-risk heterosexual contact (32%) accounted for 81% of all HIV/AIDS cases diagnosed in 2005" (CDC 2006a, p. 6; "high-risk heterosexual contact" is heterosexual contact with a person known to have, or to be at high risk for, HIV infection). For males, these transmission categories, along with injection drug use, are the principal causes of AIDS-related deaths; for females, injection drug use and high-risk heterosexual contact are the main causes of AIDS-related deaths.

Age Differences "The largest number of HIV/AIDS cases occurred among persons aged 35–39 years and accounted for 16% of all HIV/AIDS cases diagnosed in 2005" (CDC, 2006a, p. 6). Similarly, the largest number of AIDS-related deaths in 2005 occurred among adults age 35–55, although no age group in our society is completely safe from this disease, even the elderly. In particular, Oliviero (2004) revealed that many women older than 50 know little about how HIV is spread, making them more vulnerable to infection. Personal Insights 20.1 offers an example of one woman who would never have imagined she could test positive for HIV at the age of 55 in 1991 (see also Emlet, 2004, 2006).

Jane Fowler: Why Me?

Early in January 1991, shortly after returning home to Kansas City from a happy Christmas holiday, Jane Fowler found in her accumulated mail a letter that declined her application for new health insurance. The letter said that her blood test had disclosed a significant abnormality and indicated that her physician would be notified.

When she called the company, they declined on grounds of confidentiality to explain the nature of the abnormality. Then, when she visited her doctor, she was told that the insurance company claimed that she had tested positive for HIV! A second, anonymous test at a local health care facility confirmed that diagnosis.

Jane was stunned. She was 55, had lived a conventional life, did not do drugs, and had lived monogamously with her husband for 23 years until they separated in 1982. After her divorce, Jane reported that she did sleep with a few men—men who were her own age, recently divorced, and not strangers. One of these men, Jim, had been a close friend all her adult life.

Jane retreated from her diagnosis into a period of self-imposed isolation. . . .

But she didn't actually feel sick. She says she wouldn't have known she was infected without the insurance company's test. A journalist, Jane researched HIV and found that the initial infection is often followed by a brief period of flulike symptoms. Sure enough, she recalled such symptoms in early 1986 and was able to confirm visits to her doctor at that time with those complaints.

After suffering from annoying skin conditions and becoming a compulsive hand washer to fight germs, by the middle of 1991 Jane retired, telling her friends that she wanted to reduce her stress and protect her health. But in fact, "I withdrew because I lacked the courage to face possible discrimination, rejection, and intolerance. I became a recluse over the next four years."

At one point, Jane contacted her friend, Jim, after confirming from her diaries that they had spent a happy New Year's Eve together five years earlier and had unprotected sex that night. He denied being infected and hung up, calling back later, angry that she might have discussed her disease with mutual friends and that she had given his name (and those of her other sexual partners) to the local health department. Jim never directly admitted that he was infected, acknowledged that he might have been the source of Jane's infection, or said he was sorry. He died in 1995.

Jim's death helped Jane to rethink her reactions to her illness and to overcome her isolation. She decided to acknowledge her predicament publicly and to speak about HIV to those who are not infected. Jane wanted especially to talk about HIV prevention and, in particular, risks involving those her own age.

Source: Based on Fowler, 2000.

Subpopulations at Risk To summarize, HIV infection and AIDS-related deaths are especially prevalent among men who have sex with men, individuals (male or female) who engage in high-risk heterosexual behavior, and injecting drug users (despite declining numbers in this population). More broadly, it is clear that this disease in the United States and its associated deaths are gradually, but increasingly, becoming experiences of women, persons of color (Dean et al., 2005), and members of younger generations who may not remember the deadlier, early days of the epidemic.

Encounters with HIV and AIDS around the World

Of course, HIV and AIDS are not only encountered in the United States. To appreciate the worldwide impact of HIV and AIDS, we must recognize that they have "brought about a global epidemic far more extensive than what was predicted even a decade ago" (UNAIDS, 2001a, p. 4; see also Piot et al., 2001). In this section, we examine encounters with HIV and AIDS around the world. We do so in the first place because of the horrific scale of this *pandemic* (worldwide epidemic) and the heavy toll it has taken on both individuals and communities around the world. A second reason for attending to experiences with HIV and AIDS around the world is because it is in their own interests for Americans and others to become concerned about the implications of this disease. When HIV and AIDS destabilize societies, they become a threat to both human and national security. This threat is compounded in areas where there already are poor employment prospects, economic insecurity, endemic poverty, political instability, mobile or displaced populations, famine, and conflict or war. Thus, in 2000 the Clinton administration formally designated AIDS as *a threat to U.S. national security* because it could "topple foreign governments, touch off ethnic wars and undo decades of work in building free-market democracies abroad" (Gellman, 2000, p. A1). A national intelligence estimate in January 2000 is reported to have identified dramatic declines in life expectancy as the strongest risk factor for "revolutionary wars, ethnic wars, genocides and disruptive regime transitions" in developing states (Gellman, 2000, p. A8). Clearly, the United States is not likely to remain untouched by the effects of HIV/AIDS around the world.

In December 2007, UNAIDS (a joint project of several United Nations bodies, including the World Health Organization and the World Bank; 2007, p. 4) described the global HIV/AIDS pandemic in the following way: "Every day, over 6800 persons become infected with HIV and over 5700 persons die from AIDS, mostly because of inadequate access to HIV prevention and treatment services." Accordingly, UNAIDS estimated that in 2007 approximately 33.2 million persons around the world were living with HIV/AIDS (see Table 20.3)—4.2 million more than in 2001. Among these were 2.5 million children under 15 years of age and 15.4 million women. In the same year, UNAIDS estimates that 2.5 million people (including 420,000 children) were newly infected with HIV. In addition, UNAIDS estimated that the international community experienced 2.1 million deaths, including the deaths of 330,000 children, related to HIV/AIDS during 2007. Tens of millions of people have died as a result of HIV and AIDS since the worldwide epidemic first began to be noticed in the late 1970s and early 1980s. Currently, HIV and AIDS are the primary cause of death in Africa (Hunter, 2003; Iliffe, 2006; Kalipeni et al., 2003) and a leading cause of death worldwide. (Additional and ongoing information about HIV and AIDS in countries

TABLE 20.3
Regional HIV/AIDS Estimated Statistics and Features, during 2007

Region	Epidemic Started	Adults and Children Living with HIV/ AIDS	Adults and Children Newly Infected with HIV	Adult Prevalence (%)	Adult and Child Deaths during 2006
Sub-Saharan Africa	late 1970s– early 1980s	22,500,000	1,700,000	5.0	1,600,000
Middle East and North Africa	late 1980s	380,000	35,000	0.3	25,000
South and South- east Asia	late 1980s	4,000,000	340,000	0.3	270,000
East Asia	late 1980s	800,000	92,000	0.1	32,000
Oceania (Australia New Zealand, & Islands)	late 1970s– early 1980s	75,000	14,000	0.4	1,200
Latin America	late 1970s– early 1980s	1,600,000	100,000	0.5	58,000
Caribbean	late 1970s– early 1980s	230,000	17,000	1.0	11,000
Eastern Europe and Central Asia	early 1990s	1,600,000	150,000	0.9	55,000
Western and Central Europe	late 1970s– early 1980s	760,000	31,000	0.3	12,000
North America	late 1970s– early 1980s	1,300,000	46,000	0.6	21,000
Total		33,200,000	2,500,000	0.8	2,100,000

Source: UNAIDS, 2007.

around the globe can be obtained from UNAIDS through its many publications and its Web site, www.unaids.org.)

Encounters with HIV/AIDS have varied in different parts of the world (see Table 20.3). For example, the epidemic began at different times in different regions of the world, starting as early as the late 1970s in some areas, but not until the late 1980s in other regions, and still later in Eastern Europe and Central Asia. In terms of people living with HIV/AIDS in 2007 and newly infected individuals in that year, the largest numbers are found in Sub-Saharan Africa and in South and Southeast Asia. Sub-Saharan Africa and the Caribbean have the highest adult prevalence rates of HIV infection. By contrast with other regions, women are disproportionately impacted in Sub-Saharan Africa, North Africa and the Middle East, South and Southeast Asia, and the Caribbean. Also, there are clear regional differences in principal modes of transmission for adults living with HIV/AIDS: heterosexual transmission is dominant in Sub-Saharan Africa, injecting drug use in Eastern Europe and Central Asia, and men who have sex with men in the South Pacific Ocean countries of Australia and New Zealand.

As UNAIDS (2007) has reported, "Sub-Saharan Africa remains the most seriously affected region, with AIDS remaining the leading cause of death there" (p. 4). An estimated 68 percent of all adults and children who are living with HIV around the world live in Sub-Saharan Africa, and approximately 76 percent of all adult and child deaths due to AIDS in 2007 occurred in that region. Furthermore, "Unlike other regions, the majority of people living with HIV in sub-Saharan Africa (61%) are women" (p. 15). In southern Africa, in particular, the Republic of South Africa, an advanced country in many respects by comparison with its regional neighbors, "is the country with the largest number of HIV infections in the world .... [and] in Swaziland, approximately one in four (26%) adults (15–24 years) are infected with HIV" (p. 16). For all of these reasons, as early as 2001 the CDC (2001, p. 436) noted that, "In the countries most affected in Africa, life expectancy has declined by 10 years and infant death rates have doubled."

It is important to acknowledge that declines in HIV prevalence rates seem to have begun in some sub-Saharan African countries and there is evidence that other countries in this region and elsewhere may be approaching a plateau in such rates. These changes, resulting in large part from increased access to treatment (including the expanded provision of antiretroviral treatment), as well as better provision of care, have been highly beneficial in recent years for many individuals and communities around the world. Still, these improvements began quite late and from a very low starting level in many countries. They also require a sustained effort on the part of many members and agencies within each society. In addition, they depend not just on drugs, but also on substantial changes in attitudes and behaviors among very large population groups.

Two key groups—women and youth—are important indicators of what is likely to happen in the near future with HIV infection and AIDS around the world. For women, "the estimated 15.4 million [13.9–16.6 million] living with HIV in 2007 numbered 1.6 million more than the 13.8 million [12.7–15.2 million] in 2001" (UNAIDS, 2007, p. 8). For youth, "In many regions of the world, new HIV infections are heavily concentrated among young people (15–24 years of age). Among adults 15 years and older, young people accounted for 40% of new HIV infections in 2006. ... [As a result,] the future course of the world's HIV epidemics hinges in many respects on the behaviours young people adopt or maintain, and the contextual factors that affect those choices." (UNAIDS, 2006, pp. 3 & 8).

HIV and AIDS affect communities around the world in many ways. Households lose breadwinners and care providers, children lose parents, and families are forced to apply earnings, savings, and other assets to expenditures for health care and funerals. Those who are ill or impoverished may have no one to care for them. Some who are infected or impacted by AIDS are forced to turn to commercial sex that may in turn increase their risk of transmitting or contracting HIV. Governments and businesses experience lower productivity through the loss of skilled employees to death or absenteeism, even as they face mounting costs for health care and the training of new employees. Health care, social services, and education systems become overburdened. Women are most often required to care for sick relatives or bear other family burdens, girls are removed from school to assist in that work, and teacher shortages occur. Basic food production is undermined when HIV/AIDS takes the health or lives of workers with critical expertise or of unskilled workers in labor-intensive processes.

In its summary of the global situation, UNAIDS (2004, p. 3) offered the following comment that is still quite relevant:

> AIDS is an extraordinary kind of crisis; it is both an emergency and a long-term development issue. Despite increased funding, political commitment and progress in expanding access to HIV treatment, the AIDS epidemic continues to outpace the global response. No region of the world has been spared. The epidemic remains extremely dynamic, growing and changing character as the virus exploits new opportunities for transmission.

In a more recent report, UNAIDS (2007, p. 4) described the worldwide HIV/AIDS epidemic more succinctly: "The HIV pandemic remains the most serious of infectious disease challenges to public health."

❦ Death-Related Attitudes Concerning HIV and AIDS

Early Confusion and Fear

Just over ten years after the first reports of the new disease, the CDC (1992b, p. 142) commented: "The recognition of a disease and its emergence as a leading cause of death within the same decade is without precedent." Not surprisingly, many became frightened by the changes that seemed to be occurring around them so quickly. Some defended our national blood supply system as safe long after it had become clear to many hemophiliacs and others receiving transfusions of infected blood and blood products that it was not. Others found it difficult to believe that it would require substantial funding and a major mobilization of our health system to care for those who became infected and were dying, as well as to prevent additional infections or at least minimize the likelihood of additional infections as much as possible. Critics like Shilts in his book, *And the Band Played On* (1987), argued that the government was indifferent to a major public health tragedy and too slow in responding in ways that were necessary.

Early responses of fear and ignorance all too often led to social stigma and outright discrimination (Sontag, 1989). Many ill persons were treated badly in the workplace, in schools, in matters of housing, and even by some health care personnel. Some infected persons internalized a sense of stigma, hiding their HIV status or even isolating themselves socially (and this is still a problem in some cases, as is evident in the vignette near the beginning of this chapter).

Attitudes and HIV Transmission

Identification of the HIV virus had many consequences. It quickly became clear that the virus can only be transmitted from one human to another and that it is not spread through casual contact (e.g., through using a telephone, sharing eating utensils, or touching and hugging an infected person). The primary routes of transmission through which HIV is spread are: (1) through having unprotected vaginal, anal, or oral sex with an infected person (and thus exchanging semen, vaginal fluid, or blood); (2) through sharing needles or syringes with an infected person (and

© Stefan Verwey

thus exchanging even microscopic quantities of blood); and (3) from mother to child through blood or breast milk.

A new and lethal disease whose cause was initially not known, but one that is most often directly associated with sexual behavior and sharing needles for illicit drug use, was disturbing to many. For some, it was all too easy to make moral judgments about individuals whom they thought were engaged in immoral behaviors. Here, attitudes inserted themselves in hurtful ways. For example, in Kokomo, Indiana, one child (*Ryan White*) became a symbol for many who were denied the right to attend school in the early 1980s because some thought he was a danger to his classmates (White & Cunningham, 1991). In fact, as a hemophiliac who had contracted AIDS from tainted blood products that are required to sustain his life, a child like this with a compromised immune system was actually at much greater risk of acquiring opportunistic infections from his peers. Another example of negative attitudes appeared when the family of Clifford and Louise Ray discovered that their three hemophiliac sons had been infected with HIV. Although they had expected support from their small-town community in Arcadia, Florida, when they tried to enroll their sons in regular school classes in 1986, they experienced ugly protests, death threats, and had their house burned down by unknown persons (Buckley, 2001).

Attitudes like these are uninformed and reprehensible. They harmed those who had been sickened by the newly discovered viral agent. Never really justifiable, such attitudes were even more unsustainable when it was learned that the new disease was being contracted by newborn infants and hemophiliacs. Punishment or claims of moral misbehavior could hardly be held to be appropriate for newborn infants or for hemophiliacs who already had one life-threatening disease.

Overall, the CDC (2006b, p. 587) has noted "the widespread belief that AIDS is no longer a problem or a severe disease in the United States." In fact, "HIV/AIDS remains a potentially deadly chronic disease" (p. 588). The difficulty is that, "Complacency, stigma, and discrimination persist and all decrease motivation among persons and communities to adopt risk-reduction behaviors, get tested for HIV, and access prevention and treatment services" (p. 587). (For one example of the complexities of attitudes within a particular subgroup in American society, see Focus On 20.1.) While research by Herek, Capitanio, and Widaman (2002) has shown that overt stigma seen in the early years of the epidemic has declined, these authors point out that stigma persists in such forms as discomfort with persons who are HIV positive, blaming them for their disease, and misapprehensions concerning casual social contact with such individuals.

Global Attitudes toward HIV and AIDS

Attitudes have had significant impact on the encounters with HIV and AIDS that have occurred globally. Local attitudes and behaviors influenced by specific cultures have led to many individuals in specific countries becoming infected by HIV. Most often, these attitudes and behaviors involve *sexual behavior*. In heterosexual transmission, this typically reflects lack of access to condoms; religious, cultural, or psychological influences that work against their use; sexual coercion and violence experienced by women and girls; and situations in which females are unable to control the terms on which they have sex (all of which are found in Sub-Saharan Africa and elsewhere). Among men who have sex with men, HIV infection is facilitated in some regions (such as Latin America) by religious and cultural prohibitions against acknowledging homosexual behavior and against taking appropriate precautions. In other regions (including the industrialized countries of Western Europe and North America), because "few young gay men have seen friends die of AIDS, and some mistakenly view antiretrovirals as a cure, there is growing complacency about the HIV risk" (UNAIDS, 2001a, p. 9). In all forms of sexual transmission, multiple sexual partnerships and large sexual networks facilitate HIV infection.

In other areas, such as Central and Eastern Europe, infection rates are relatively low but climbing alarmingly, arising largely from *injecting drug use* and the difficult, large-scale social changes occurring in these countries. Here, HIV is threatening to spread to the general population through the sexual partners of injecting drug users, growing prostitution, and high levels of sexually transmitted infections.

Attitudes of Some African-American Leaders concerning HIV and AIDS

HIV and AIDS have presented peculiar and difficult challenges to many subcultures. This can be seen in the example of one principal American minority group, the African-American community. While this community has experienced some of the largest rates of infection and deaths from the disease, it has also suffered from uncertain responses by some community leaders to the disease. Thus, Cohen (1999) contended that since the beginning of the epidemic African-American political organizations and leaders, African-American media, and African-American religious leaders have often been reticent or ineffective in assisting members of their community to deal with the disease.

More recently, an African-American columnist, Bill Maxwell, wrote about the role of African-American churches in dealing with HIV and AIDS. Maxwell believes that it is the church that often provides structure for the African-American community. However, he argued that it has largely failed to do so in the instance of HIV and AIDS. He wrote (Maxwell, 2007, p. 3P):

> Of the more than 85,000 black churches in the United States, only a handful . . . are actively involved in this important work. The others have descended into denial, ignorance and homophobia . . . Although the infection rates for blacks are dropping nationwide, the statistics remain grim . . . while blacks are roughly 13 percent of the nation's population, they account for 54 percent of new AIDS cases. Black women between 25 and 44 are more likely to die of AIDS than any other illness.

By contrast with this depiction of failed leadership in the African-American community, at least one prominent African-American religious and political leader has sought to draw the attention of the community to the harmful consequences of ignoring HIV and AIDS. Reverend Jesse Jackson has worked in very public ways to promote HIV testing. To reinforce the importance and the necessity of this testing, Jackson has himself publicly taken the test (Savage, 2000). Democratic senator and presidential candidate Barack Obama also publicly took the same test.

Attitudes of governments and their leaders in some countries have also played key roles in helping or hindering the spread of the epidemic. For example, UNAIDS (2001a, p. 19) noted that "most countries in Africa—and indeed worldwide—lost valuable time because AIDS was not fully understood and its significance as a new epidemic was not grasped." In one astonishing example, the president of South Africa, Thabo Mbeki, stunned an international AIDS conference in 2000 by questioning whether HIV causes AIDS and by proposing theories about this disease that had long been dismissed in the global scientific community (Clifton, 2000).

🍂 Death-Related Practices Concerning HIV and AIDS

Minimizing the Risk of Acquiring HIV

In light of early knowledge about AIDS, health educators sought to provide accurate information and foster healthy attitudes and practices concerning HIV and AIDS among members of the public and professional health care providers. In so doing, the American death system slowly began to function in constructive ways to warn, educate, and protect citizens against this lethal disease. One example of these early efforts occurred when the Surgeon General of the United States, Dr. C. Everett Koop (1988), mailed to every household in the country (something never done before) a brochure, "Understanding AIDS."

As the nature of AIDS, its underlying viral cause, and its principal routes of transmission became clearer, recommendations for more specific action followed. Health authorities began to recommend that *the most effective ways to prevent HIV infection* are: (1) not having vaginal, anal, or oral sex with an infected person; (2) having sex only with a mutually monogamous person who is known not to be infected and who is known not to share needles or syringes with anyone; (3) not injecting nonprescribed drugs; (4) not sharing needles or syringes for any reason (even injecting vitamins, steroids, tattooing, or body piercing); and (5) not engaging in activities that involve exchange of blood, semen, vaginal fluids, or breast milk. Further, *the risk of HIV infection can be reduced* by: (6) using a latex condom *every* time during vaginal, anal, or oral sex; (7) cleaning needles and syringes with chlorine bleach and water if more effective prevention is not available; and (8) using barrier protection such as latex gloves when coming into contact with blood or fluids that could contain blood.

However, strenuous efforts to teach people how to prevent HIV infection have not always proved successful. Many who know how the virus is transmitted are unwilling or unable to take the steps needed to prevent infection. Some decline to remain sexually abstinent, to practice *safer sex* techniques, and to avoid injecting drugs or sharing unsterile needles and syringes. Others wrongly believe that they will not get infected if they have unprotected sex only once with a partner whose HIV status is unknown or if they share an unsterile needle only once. But a single exposure can result in infection, even if it does not always do so.

The need for continuing education has been emphasized in recent years, when some people have come to believe that becoming infected is no longer life threatening because there now are medications available to control it. Here, faulty attitudes undermine necessary practice. Such attitudes ignore the drastic life changes necessary to cope with medications used to fight HIV infection and others to minimize the harmful effects of AIDS itself. In addition, these attitudes fail to take into account that these medications have difficult and dangerous side effects, do not work for everyone, and are unlikely to work permanently. Thus, it has become apparent that there is still a great and ongoing (and unless a vaccine or cure is found will always be) need for continuing public education about HIV and AIDS. (Some Internet, telephone, and journal resources for information about AIDS and HIV are listed in Focus On 20.2.)

Some Ongoing Resources on HIV and AIDS

TELEPHONE NUMBERS AND WEBSITES:

- AIDS Education and Training Centers, Health Resources and Services Administration, U.S. Department of Health and Human Services: 410-955-7634; http://hab.hrsa.gov/educating.htm
- American Foundation for AIDS Research: 323-857-5900; www.amfar.org
- Canadian AIDS Society: 613-230-3580; www.cdnaids.ca
- Canadian HIV/AIDS Clearinghouse (a project of the Canadian Public Health Association): 613-725-3434; in Canada, 877-999-7740; www.cpha.ca
- CDC National HIV/AIDS Hotline: 800-342-2437; 800-344-7432 (Spanish); www.cdc.gov/hiv
- Elizabeth Glaser Pediatric AIDS Foundation: 888-499-HOPE (4673); 310-314-1459; www.pedaids.org
- National AIDS Clearinghouse (a project of the National Prevention Information Network, National Center for HIV, STD, and TB Prevention): 800-458-5231; www.cdcnpin.org
- National Association on HIV Over Fifty: 816-421-5263; www.hivoverfifty.org
- National Minority AIDS Council: 202-483-6622; www.nmac.org
- National Native American AIDS Prevention Center: 510-444-2051; www.nnaapc.org
- Positive Education, Inc.: 813-831-4159; www.pos-ed.org
- UNAIDS: www.unaids.org

JOURNALS:

- *A&U* (America's AIDS Magazine), Art & Understanding, Inc., www.aumag.org
- *HIV Plus*, Liberation Publications, Inc., www.hivplusmag.com
- *Journal of Acquired Immune Deficiency Syndromes and Human Retrovirology*, Lippincott-Raven Publishers, www.jaids.com
- *Journal of the International Association of Physicians in AIDS Care*, Medical Publications Corp., www.iapac.org
- *POZ* and *POZ en Español*, POZ Publishing, www.poz.com

Interventions to Fight HIV Infection

With the virus identified, scientists are able to trace the HIV virus itself in its various strains and mutations, and to measure the so-called *viral load* in the blood of a person who is *HIV positive* (i.e., who has acquired the virus). This makes possible a wide range of interventions intended to respond either to symptoms typically associated with HIV/AIDS or to the viral infection itself. These include nutritional strategies to strengthen the body's overall health, as well as medical treatments (usually some drugs) to respond to the presence or threat of specific symptoms and opportunistic infections. In response to HIV infection itself, a series of *combination therapies* (also called *HAART* or *highly active antiretroviral therapy*) came into use by clinicians from the mid-1990s onward. These therapies involve the use of several drugs in precise combinations. At first, these combinations meant that persons infected with the HIV would have to take many pills per day, at different times, some with food and some without. But by 2006, the Federal Drug Administration (Anonymous, 2006a) had approved for use a capsule containing three drugs to be taken once a day. For some persons, that would be all that was necessary to contain the virus. For others, there might be a need to combine that one capsule with other antiretroviral products (Anonymous, 2006a).

While the success of HAART can be applauded, these combination therapies or drug cocktails are quite expensive and often have significant side effects (see Issues for Critical Reflection #19). Those side effects include hepatotoxicity, hyperglycemia, hyperlipidemia, lactic acidosis, lipodsystrophy, and osteoporosis (Anonymous, 2005). Also, it should be noted that although the number of medications needed each day to combat HIV has become smaller in many cases, the medications needed to deal first with the side effects of these medications and then with the opportunistic infections to which the HIV virus makes its host vulnerable can make a day coping with the HIV virus and/or AIDS complex and difficult.

Another factor producing difficulty in treating HIV infection is that the virus is able to mutate and eventually to become resistant to the drugs used against it. In fact, by the end of 2001 it appeared that many if not most HIV-infected persons had developed at least some virus strains resistant to some of the available drugs. In

---

ISSUES FOR CRITICAL REFLECTION
#19 What Are Some of the Difficulties Involved in Living with HIV Disease?

Since the advent of the many drugs available to treat HIV disease, an impression has grown among some people that this disease is no longer a serious concern. However, this impression is inaccurate. There is much evidence to show that infection with the HIV virus and AIDS are both major disruptions of one's life and are ultimately life threatening. One author who has pointed this out is the playwright Harvey Fierstein (2003, p. A-25). Here is what he wrote on this topic:

The truth is that AIDS is not fun. It's not sexy or manageable. AIDS is a debilitating, deform-ing, terminal and incurable disease. HIV drugs can bring on heart, kidney and liver disease, as well as a host of daily discomforts . . . most of my friends who are on drug cocktails . . . spend mornings in the bathroom throwing up or suffering from diarrhea. They spend afternoons at doctor's appointments, clinics and pharmacies. And they spend endless evenings planning their estates and trying to make ends meet because they are not well enough to support themselves and their new [HIV] drug habit. And those are just the friends for whom the drugs work. For many women the cocktails are nothing but a drain on finance, internal organs and stamina.

addition, treatment is complicated because even when the viral load in the blood-stream of a person living with AIDS can no longer be measured, scientists have learned that the HIV virus has not been eradicated. It is merely in remission—it may be hiding in the body's tissues and organs, it can return in force, and there may still be a risk of transmitting this undetectable HIV. Thus, many are concerned that high expectations for these combination therapies may soon no longer be met and that it may no longer be possible to postpone or prevent many additional deaths from HIV infection.

Nevertheless, deaths and death rates dropped dramatically as the new combination therapies came into effect. For example, overall deaths associated with HIV in the United States declined by over 25 percent from 1995–1996 and by another 42 percent from 1996–1997. Additional successes have been achieved in minimizing transmission of the HIV from mother to child (CDC, 2006d) and in developing diagnostic and screening tests that have rendered safe blood and blood products used for transfusion and treatment of hemophilia and coagulation disorders.

For the future, the CDC (2006b) has recommended a scaling up of traditionally effective interventions along with a series of new strategies to combat HIV infection and AIDS. These include: (1) public health partnerships of individuals, communities, religious and business organizations, governmental agencies, and mental health services to address stigma and discrimination, as well as to support research, prevention, treatment, care, and rehabilitative services for persons affected by HIV/AIDS; (2) increased access to voluntary HIV testing to prevent transmission and make possible early interventions of care; (3) provision of culturally and contextually appropriate prevention messages to help avoid contracting or transmitting the infection; (4) integrated prevention programs combining HIV, sexually transmitted disease, viral hepatitis, mental health, and substance abuse services; (5) improved monitoring of new HIV infections; and (6) development of new prevention technologies.

Global Practices Related to HIV and AIDS

Countries have responded to the threats arising from HIV/AIDS epidemics in various ways (Buchanan & Cernada, 1998). Sadly, some have misunderstood the threat of this disease, while others have tried to ignore the implications of HIV and AIDS—perhaps hoping that the peril would go away or its consequences would not be very severe if their causes were disregarded. However, many countries have coped in admirable ways by integrating HIV/AIDS into larger developmental strategies and programs, such as efforts to reduce poverty, strengthen health care and social services, and carry out campaigns of public education, risk reduction, and intervention. As the CDC (2001, p. 437) has observed, "Even countries with modest resources have demonstrated that the epidemic can be stabilized or reversed. In these countries, successful programs have included strong, high-level political leadership for HIV prevention, a national program plan, adequate funding, and strong community involvement."

Efforts directed specifically at HIV/AIDS include prevention measures (such as AIDS education, condom promotion, needle exchange, and drug treatment such as oral maintenance on methadone), counseling and testing, treatment and prevention of opportunistic infections, palliative care for pain and symptom relief in ill persons, and care for orphans. Because UNAIDS (2001a, p. 11) has estimated that "conservatively nine-tenths of HIV-positive individuals worldwide do not know they are infected," it has recommended voluntary testing services on the proven premise that "finding out their infection status could expand their basket of HIV prevention options." In more prosperous countries, antiretroviral therapies have also been used with great success to forestall death and improve quality of life, but the costs and other requirements of such interventions make them difficult for most areas of the world.

There have been regional success stories in coping with HIV/AIDS around the world. For example, Uganda is an African country that used to have the highest rates of infection in the region. But through an intensive prevention program for behavior change, condom promotion, and voluntary HIV counseling and testing, Uganda reduced the adult HIV prevalence rate from around 14 percent in the early 1990s to 8 percent in 2000. Similarly, in Australia a program for exchanging needles and syringes is slowing the increase in HIV prevalence among injecting drug users.

Wherever achievements have been made, they need to be duplicated in every part of the world and sustained, especially in countries in which the epidemic started late or remains confined to specific groups. As UNAIDS (2001a, p. 19) has noted, "Once HIV has become firmly established in the general population, most new infections occur in the majority of adults who do not have a specially high number of partners. This means that prevention campaigns have to be expanded greatly, making them harder and costlier, though still very worthwhile." As the scale of the epidemic increases, the scale of the action necessary to make a difference also increases—from efforts to reduce the number of new infections to programs offering care and treatment for people living with HIV/AIDS to efforts to minimize the impact on orphans, other survivors, families, and communities.

The United Nations noted that epidemics such as HIV/AIDS bring out both the best and the worst in people: "They trigger the best when individuals group together in solidarity to combat government, community and individual denial, and to offer support and care to people living with HIV and AIDS. They bring out the worst when individuals are stigmatized and ostracized by their loved ones, their family and their communities, and discriminated against individually as well as institutionally" (UNAIDS, 2001c, p. 1).

❦ Coping with HIV/AIDS and Helping

Because HIV infection and AIDS are evolving phenomena, they demand continual changes in the ways in which we think about, understand, and respond to them. As we have noted, the virus itself is constantly changing, both in its behavior within the infected person's body and genetically over time. HIV infection has also constantly changed in terms of the groups most affected by it. As a result, coping with HIV infection and AIDS taxes not only the resources of an infected person, but also those of local, national, and international communities. In this section, we describe these different forms of coping with HIV and AIDS. Examining HIV/AIDS from these perspectives serves as a way to help organize the bewildering amount of information—and uncertainty—arising from human experiences with HIV infection and AIDS.

Coping with HIV/AIDS and Helping by Individuals

As with any life-threatening situation, there are two groups of persons who are drawn into *coping with HIV infection and AIDS as individuals.* These two groups are *those who are infected themselves* and *those who are not infected but who are affected* because someone they know or love is infected (in the vignette near the beginning of this chapter, Ronald Porter falls into the latter category and his mother into the former). In some situations, these two groups are joined in one individual: a person who must cope with his or her own infection while also being affected by and forced to cope with the effects of an infection in another person, such as a family member or a friend. This reinforces what we learned in earlier chapters: life-threatening illnesses have impacts on many individuals (not only those who are suffering from the illness) and in different ways.

Individuals Who Are Infected with HIV *Those who are infected* see their lives changed dramatically in many ways: physically, emotionally, socially, economically, and spiritually. HIV infection does not result merely in minor changes because it impacts so much of an individual's life. First, the person is confronted with his or her mortality in a

One man comforts another at an exhibition of the AIDS quilt.

© Glen Korengold/Stock, Boston

way similar to all who face a life-threatening illness. In the early years, HIV infection was taken to mean that death was near. Subsequently, it became clear that the situation is a good deal more ambiguous. Even before treatments were developed, the health of some infected persons was less impacted than that of others; not all of them moved quickly toward death. With the development of combination therapies and other interventions, the length of time between infection and death has typically lengthened, as much as 20 years and longer (CDC, 2006c; Schackman et al., 2006). This has led some to claim that HIV infection should be seen as a chronic, rather than an acute, disease. In turn, this has been taken by many to mean that it need not be life threatening if it is treated appropriately.

Still, the period after being infected is hardly a return to "normalcy." For instance, many infected individuals find their typical days punctuated by the need to keep careful track of large numbers of medications with or without food on a strict schedule. Along with the disease itself, these medications, especially after they have been used for many years, have short-term and long-term side effects, ranging from nausea, vomiting, and diarrhea to much more severe effects as we noted above (Sherman, 2001). In addition, because the drugs used to treat HIV infection are themselves so toxic, it is uncertain that the infection can be controlled indefinitely. What this means is that HIV infection is still likely eventually to end in death for at least many infected persons.

Life changes in other ways, too. The types of social stigma and outright discrimination against those who are infected with HIV and perhaps have developed AIDS that we described in early responses of fear and ignorance have not completely disappeared (Herek et al., 2002). Problems in obtaining adequate housing, appropriate health care, health insurance and benefits, and fair treatment in schools and in the workplace have not completely gone away. Also, some infected persons, as is evident in the vignette near the beginning of this chapter, have internalized a sense of stigma, hiding their HIV status or even isolating themselves socially. Of course, any form of discrimination, arising from others or from oneself, can interfere with the ability of an infected person to receive needed support from others. The inclusion of HIV infection under the Americans with Disabilities Act has—at least theoretically—undermined some forms of economic and residential discrimination, even if they have not been entirely eliminated. And although in the early stages of the epidemic some health care workers were fearful of being infected themselves, scrupulous adherence to the principles of *universal precautions* in clinical practice minimizes the possibility of infection (not only with HIV, but also with hepatitis B and other infectious agents).

Economically, costs associated with HIV infection can be staggering for individuals. The medications associated with combination therapies alone can average *$2,100* a month (Schackman et al., 2006). Persons who have the symptoms associated with AIDS typically meet *monthly (at least)* with a physician. At some point in the course of the infection, such persons are likely to be hospitalized—again, typically more than once. Although fortunate individuals have much of this health care covered by their insurance, insurers are reluctant to provide such coverage. In addition, many infected persons have no insurance. Loss of one's insurance is a possibility, for instance, if one is unable to work and so is no longer covered by an employer's insurance plan. Although insurers are required by law to make available continued coverage under these circumstances, its cost is often prohibitive.

HIV infection increasingly is found among poorer members of society, in both the United States and elsewhere. Medicare or Medicaid often provides care for such persons in our society, but that care is then vulnerable to the variability in those systems. Thus, whether one has one's own insurance or is being cared for under social programs, one's financial situation is likely to become more fragile after becoming infected with HIV.

The infected person's life is impacted in other ways, too. Pet ownership becomes a possible danger. (This is more evidence that living beings—other humans and pets—are typically more of a danger to infected persons than infected persons are to those around them.) Because house pets can carry disease agents to which human beings are vulnerable, HIV-infected persons are advised to be wary of being around and handling such animals. A long list of suggestions about the interactions of HIV-infected persons and household pets is found in the July 2001 draft of guidelines for prevention of opportunistic infections in persons infected with HIV published by the U.S. Public Health Service and Infectious Diseases Society of America (Masur et al., 2001).

This same document includes warnings about the risk to HIV-infected persons from certain foods: raw or undercooked foods, grapefruit, soft cheeses, and foods from deli counters—indeed any food in which there may be some potentially untreated infectious agent or that might interact unfavorably with a medication. Water can also contain such agents, so there are warnings about exposing oneself to untreated water. Given these latter warnings, travel to developing countries is also an activity that puts HIV-infected persons at increased risk.

All of us are at some risk from these sorts of encounters with potential disease-causing pathogens. For most of us, however, our healthy immune systems protect us from a wide range of these dangers. HIV-infected persons with compromised immune systems must pay especially close attention to such pathogens because of their heightened risk of acquiring opportunistic infections. Thus, activities that noninfected persons can more or less take for granted become activities HIV-infected persons must evaluate very carefully.

Children who have been infected with the virus also experience many of the life changes just described and some others unique to their status as children. Since U.S. courts have ruled that being infected with HIV is not a legitimate reason to keep children out of schools, there has been a lessening of academic discrimination against such children. In part, this results from the legal requirement to keep such diagnostic information private. Still, as a child develops the symptoms of AIDS, it can become more and more difficult to maintain this privacy.

Many children infected with the virus live in homes of persons who are themselves infected. The parents of these children may be too ill to provide proper care for them. As a result, many of these children end up in foster care or in the homes of other family members, notably grandparents or even great-grandparents (see Caliandro & Hughes, 1998; Joslin & Harrison, 1998; Linsk & Mason, 2004; Murphy, 2006; www.hivoverfifty.org). When the parents of infected children die, if there is no family member who is willing or able to deal with the challenges such a child presents, it may be quite difficult for the child—now an orphan—to be adopted. Although some families have been willing to adopt these children—and two persons of the same gender have formed some of these families—many more infected children are not adopted and become subject to the difficulties associated with overworked courts and social agencies.

Many Uninfected Individuals Are Also Affected by HIV In addition to those who are themselves infected with HIV, *people who are coping with the infection of others* see their lives changed, too (e.g., Cadell & Marshall, 2007). Uninfected children, spouses, partners, parents, grandparents, and others may all be challenged as they live with and try to care for those who are infected by HIV. Clearly, HIV infection of others can be economically, emotionally, socially, and spiritually challenging for the care provider.

I HAVE AIDS
PLease hug me

J.Keeler

I can't make you sick

AIDS HOT LINE FOR KIDS
CENTER FOR ATTITUDINAL HEALING
19 MAIN ST., TIBURON, CA 94920, (415) 435-5022

Courtesy of the Center for Attitudinal Healing

Children with AIDS need understanding, love, and care.

Early in the history of AIDS, many persons experienced the deaths of one after another of their friends, until they were vulnerable to "grief overload" (Nord, 1997). This experience has declined somewhat among gay men, a group most heavily affected by HIV infection in the United States. However, as we have noted, it seems to be erupting again in a new generation of gay men, some of whom ignore or are unfamiliar with the experiences of the first generation facing AIDS. This can also be a problem in those minorities that today are experiencing the onslaught of the disease—that is, African Americans and Hispanic Americans.

It is only fair to add that throughout the history of the HIV/AIDS epidemic in our society, many Americans have faced their own deaths or the deaths of loved ones with courage and heroism. Those who provide care, as professionals, volunteers, family members, or friends, have often set shining examples for the rest of us. (A sampling of books describing personal accounts of coping with HIV and AIDS is given in the Suggested Readings at the end of this chapter.)

For example, when *Elizabeth Glaser* hemorrhaged during the delivery of her first child in 1981, she was transfused with blood that no one knew was infected with the HIV. Several years later, when Ariel became sick, it was realized that she had AIDS and must have become infected through breast feeding. At that point, Elizabeth learned that she also was HIV positive and that her second child, Jake, had become infected in the uterus before she learned of her HIV status (Glaser & Palmer, 1991). Ariel and Elizabeth have died, although Jake is still alive at this writing. Well before her death Elizabeth helped to co-found the national Pediatric AIDS Foundation (now the Elizabeth Glaser Pediatric AIDS Foundation, 2950 31st Street, Suite 125, Santa Monica, CA 90405; tel. 310-314-1459; www.pedaids.org), which has played a major role in encouraging research on pediatric AIDS and maternal transmission issues.

Coping with HIV/AIDS and Helping at the Community Level

A disease that can have such powerful impacts on individuals' lives also has a potentially dramatic impact on the life of formal and informal communities. *Local communities that are coping with this disease* have responded in a variety of ways. For example, at one early point in the United States AIDS was most often found in gay males, many of whom had had a high number of sexual partners. When that community realized the threat and was educated about harm prevention, behaviors changed dramatically. Similarly, the extreme ignorance, fear, and anger that stigmatized infected persons and those living with AIDS have declined in many parts of our society.

In many communities, people come together to raise public awareness about efforts that are needed to prevent HIV infection and AIDS.

© Joseph Sohm/ChromoSohm Inc./Corbis

Americans have often found it difficult to cope with HIV/AIDS when they are associated with injecting drug use or sexual practices of which the public at large does not understand or approve. That association has often inhibited programs that provide clean needles to addicts and other harm reduction interventions. This situation is particularly complicated in some parts of the United States (especially certain large metropolitan areas) where HIV infection is most often found among vulnerable people (including ethnic minorities) who are poor and marginalized, who experience discrimination and social exclusion, who may be missed by prevention campaigns, or who may be deprived of access to treatment for their injecting drug use.

In many American communities, the first priority in coping with HIV/AIDS has been to provide health care for sick people. Often, this has involved the development of medical and nursing expertise in addressing the challenges and complexities of a new disease entity, as well as the provision of home care, hospital, and hospice services. As the disease evolved and new interventions were developed, requirements for care extended over time and costs increased greatly (e.g., for new medications). Also, coordination between health care and social service agencies has always been a challenge.

Without a cure for HIV, communities quickly realized the importance of education in preventing infection and treating the disease. Many communities undertook campaigns to increase awareness, knowledge, and sensitivity about HIV among the general public, professionals, and groups deemed to be at high risk for infection. Other communities sent informed persons into schools, churches, health care facilities, and businesses to provide accurate information about HIV and AIDS. For example, the AIDS Service Association of Pinellas (a division of The Hospice of the Florida Suncoast; tel. 727-328-3260, www.ASAPservices.org) offers a broad range of case management and support services for those infected or affected by HIV/AIDS, as well as a speaker's bureau, which provides information to various groups and institutions in the community, and a library of more than 4,000 volumes related to HIV infection, with computer and Internet access, that is open to the public and to those who might have special concerns for themselves or for those they love.

To minimize sexual transmission of HIV and other diseases, some communities have provided (often free) condoms in schools and public places. With a similar goal in mind, a few communities have also provided sterile needles to injecting drug users. Providing condoms and sterile needles is controversial, although it has been shown to be effective in reducing the spread of the disease.

Because HIV infection, as we have noted, often strains the financial resources of infected persons, many have needed to turn to their local communities for assistance. For example, if infected persons become unable to work or to pay for health insurance, they may need financial assistance from a variety of public and private agencies. Some community programs help infected persons pay for health insurance or for the deductible amounts associated with that insurance. Other programs may help to pay for medications—which can cost as much as $25,200 a year—both for drugs fighting the virus infection itself and for drugs to fight the opportunistic diseases that often accompany HIV infection (Schackman et al., 2006).

Another area in which community assistance is often needed is housing for infected persons. People living with HIV/AIDS need safe, dependable, and affordable housing. Appropriate housing for such persons improves their quality of life, encourages successful compliance with complicated medical regimens, improves access to critically needed health care opportunities, and can support the desire of family members to stay together. The response of one community to housing problems experienced by HIV-infected persons is described in Focus On 20.3.

Care for families and children affected by HIV infection can take other forms. For example, both the illness itself and the financial burdens that it generates may make it impossible for parents to provide back-to-school supplies or traditional meals and presents at holidays like Thanksgiving and Christmas. A holiday program in many communities provides support for these important events.

Funding for community programs can come from a variety of sources. Federal grants, private donations, and grants from state and local governments all play a role. Medicare and Medicaid programs also provide some funds for these community activities. However, fund-raising is a continuous, ongoing necessity for any community agency seeking to provide programs for those infected and affected by HIV. Such fund-raising is difficult when economic times are hard or when other worthwhile causes seem more pressing.

FOCUS ON 20.3

Doorways: An Interfaith AIDS Residence Program

In 1988, religious, business, and other community leaders in metropolitan St. Louis, Missouri, joined together to create an independent, interfaith, nonprofit corporation to meet the housing needs of people living with HIV/AIDS. Eligibility for acceptance into Doorways' programs is based on criteria such as a medically confirmed diagnosis of HIV/AIDS and an attending physician, a need for a place to live, and a willingness to participate in case management services and community resources.

Doorways offers four types of housing services:

- *The Residential Program* provides 65 apartments for low-income individuals and families (with rent assessed on a sliding scale) located in various St. Louis apartment buildings.
- *The Own Home Program* provides emergency, transitional, short-term, or ongoing rent, mortgage, and utility subsidies to individuals and families who would otherwise be unable to stay in their own homes.
- *The Clearinghouse* maintains a list of property managers and available rental units, and provides housing advocacy, placement assistance, and outreach to people living with HIV/AIDS.
- *The Supportive Housing Facility* is a licensed residential care facility that provides furnished private rooms (with bath, phone, and individually controlled heating and cooling); nursing care with IV infusion therapy; assistance with bathing, dressing, and other activities of daily living; laundry, housekeeping, food and nutrition services; and social and recreational services.

(continued)

Doorways: An Interfaith AIDS Residence Program

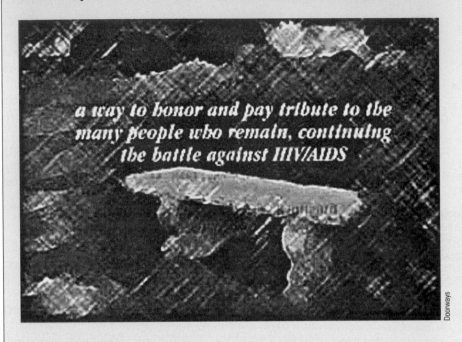

a way to honor and pay tribute to the many people who remain, continuing the battle against HIV/AIDS

Doorways

Doorways also established the *St. Louis AIDS Memorial Garden.* People can purchase a brick to be placed in the garden to memorialize those who have died from the disease or workers who have assisted such individuals and their loved ones. (See photo above.)

Additional information about these programs can be obtained from Doorways at 4385 Maryland Avenue, St. Louis, MO, 63108-2703; tel. 314-535-1919; info@doorwaysmo.org.

What this discussion shows is that HIV infection and AIDS can make significant demands on communities. Some are better able to cope with those demands than others. Some simply have greater resources to be tapped; others have private or public social agencies already in place that have taken on the responsibility of dealing specifically with this disease.

We also see here, once again, a *death system* at work (see Chapter 4). Although HIV infection and AIDS are no longer an instantaneous death sentence, they are still life-threatening and life-affecting diseases. Because of the large numbers of persons who are infected—and still becoming infected—and because infected persons require continuous and expensive care, HIV and AIDS will continue to strain community resources. They demand creative, compassionate responses, and they do this in a social and political environment in which there are many barriers and competing demands.

Coping with HIV/AIDS and Helping at the National Level

In considering *coping with HIV and AIDS at the national level,* we begin with the CDC's estimate that 425,910 persons were living with HIV/AIDS in the United States at the end of 2005 (see Table 20.2). Further, since the beginning of the epidemic through December 2005, 530,756 people in the United States have died as a result of HIV infection and AIDS (see Table 20.1). (Additional and ongoing information about HIV/AIDS in the United States can be obtained from the CDC through its many publications and its website, www.cdc.gov/hiv.)

In the early years of the epidemic (and perhaps still in some ways today), many members of affected communities, as well as many knowledgeable clinicians and scientists, believed that the American government and the public at large did not appreciate the scale of the disaster that had befallen the United States and was not exhibiting the political will to respond appropriately. Today, U.S. efforts to cope with HIV/AIDS have clearly changed, even though one could debate whether they have changed enough or in the right ways.

Still, the United States has seen many effective programs designed to educate the public about HIV and AIDS and to show what can be done to prevent infection. For example, a major federal AIDS funding bill was named in honor of Ryan White to support services for those infected with the HIV. Further, many legislative jurisdictions have mandated that every woman diagnosed as pregnant be offered HIV testing and counseling with subsequent treatment if she is infected.

As a result of these and many other community and national initiatives, Valdiserri (2002) has made the interesting point that the HIV/AIDS epidemic in the United States has had the positive side effective of actually strengthening public health and public health systems in our society.

❧ Lessons and Values

Several constructive lessons and positive values have been implicit in our explorations of death-related experiences with HIV and AIDS (and actually throughout this entire book). These lessons and values can help to point up things to be kept in mind as we look to the future.

As we indicated in Chapter 1, because life and death, living and dying, are inexorably intertwined, learning about death, dying, and bereavement is also a way of learning about life and living. This chapter has demonstrated that lesson well. Consider, for example, the four themes that we identified in Chapter 1: control/limitation, individual persons/community, vulnerability/resilience, quality in living/the search for meaning. In pointing up these four themes, we suggested they would underlie many of the subjects addressed throughout this book, and we have seen them quite explicitly at work in this chapter.

For instance, the appearance of HIV and AIDS in the 1980s and 1990s reminded us that we human beings are finite and limited creatures. When it first appeared, we did not know what the nature of this new disease entity was. And even now, well into the first decade of the 21st century, there is much that we still do not know about this virus and its effects. All of this reminds us of our *limitations*, even as we acknowledge that there are many things about HIV/AIDS that we can influence and some that we can at least partly *control*.

In this chapter, we also learned what HIV and AIDS have meant for *individuals* (both those infected and those affected by this disease entity) and *communities* in the United States and around the world. Persons, societies, nations, and the global village have all been forced to confront and try to cope with the challenges of HIV/AIDS, even as many have reached out in efforts to help those most affected.

Our *vulnerability* to the deaths, losses, and suffering wrought by HIV and AIDS has been all too apparent, but at the same time there have been many fine examples of courage and *resilience* in the ways people have responded to and lived with the scourge of the HIV/AIDS pandemic.

In the end, encounters with HIV and AIDS have shown the importance of *quality in living*, of trying to enable as many as possible to live as well as they can in the shadow of this disease entity, and to join with them as we all engage in *the human search for meaning*.

Two commentators identify lessons to be learned from encounters with HIV/AIDS in other words:

> In all its horror AIDS, like leprosy, is another disease—no more no less. It is not symbolic of anything. There are no "victims," because there is no crime. There are no "innocents," because there are no "guilty," and there is no blame, because there has been no intention to cause harm. There are only sick men, women and children, all of whom need our help. (Shenson, 1988, p. 48)

> I often wonder how other children without AIDS learn to appreciate life. That's the best part about having AIDS. (The words of an 11-year-old child in Wiener et al., 1994, p. 13.)

As we have seen, HIV and AIDS challenge us as individuals, as members of society, and as participants in a global community to look again at our beliefs, feelings, values, and behaviors associated with dying, death, and bereavement. As we do so, information must replace ignorance and reasoned judgment must replace irrational decisions in all aspects of individual behavior, interpersonal relations, public policy, and the provision of care, education, and research. The reason for this is that each person who is living with HIV infection or dying with AIDS is, in the end, like all of the rest of us: most fundamentally, he or she is a person. And he or she is a person living with suffering.

In the last sentence of his novel, *The Bridge of San Luis Rey*, Thornton Wilder (1927/1986, p. 148) wrote: "There is a land of the living and a land of the dead and the bridge is love, the only survival, the only meaning." As health care providers, as spiritual guides, as members of social communities, as friends, as family members, and finally, simply as fellow human beings, we must care about and for persons with HIV infection and AIDS, just as we must do so for all of those who are coping with dying, death, and bereavement. Not to do so is to risk the loss of our own best selves, our humanness. In caring for others, we care for ourselves—as individuals, as members of our own societies, and as people in the worldwide community—and we become fully who we are—human beings.

🐦 Summary

In this chapter, we used one specific disease entity to illustrate the central themes in this book. We examined death-related encounters, attitudes, and practices related to the HIV/AIDS epidemic in the United States and around the world. In terms of *death-related encounters*, we explored how AIDS and HIV first appeared during the 1980s and 1990s in our society, as well as how they came to be identified and understood. We pursued this account of encounters with HIV/AIDS by examining more recent data concerning individuals in our society who are living with or have died from this disease entity. That led us to a profile of distinctive effects this disease entity has had on different racial and ethnic, gender, transmission category, and age groups in the United States and in other countries around the globe.

In terms of *death-related attitudes*, we examined early confusion and fear, attitudes related to transmission of the HIV, and global attitudes toward HIV and AIDS. In relationship to *death-related practices*, we noted how individuals and health educators have taken action to minimize the risk of transmission of the HIV, how scientists, clinicians, and organizations have developed programs to fight HIV infection, and how countries around the world have struggled with local epidemics of HIV/AIDS.

Our next major topic was *coping and helping*, by individuals (both those who are infected with the virus and those who are affected by the disease), by communities, and at the national level. Much of this involved societal death systems as they (slowly) roused themselves to recognize and respond to the threat of HIV/AIDS. We have been at pains to describe the broad outlines of this disease entity both because of its horrific scope in our own society and around the world, and because of its implications for the security of communities and nations around the world.

In conclusion, we took note of lessons learned from the HIV/AIDS epidemic/pandemic and some of the positive values that have shown through its difficult history. And we saw again that HIV and AIDS provide a lived model that simultaneously illustrates and reflects many of the central themes and patterns we have discussed throughout this book.

Glossary

AIDS: an acronym for Acquired Immunodeficiency Syndrome (or Acquired Immune Deficiency Syndrome); the end state of HIV infection defined by a T-cell count of less than 200 per microliter; a condition in which the body's immune system is unable to fight off many opportunistic infections and other harmful conditions

Combination therapies: the use of several drugs in precise combinations to fight HIV infection; developed in the mid-1990s; typically including reverse transcriptase inhibitors (drugs that interrupt early stages of HIV replication and thus interfere with the ability of the HIV virus to replicate itself and infect new cells), protease inhibitors (drugs that disable a protein that the HIV virus uses to replicate itself), and fusion inhibitors (drugs that prevent the HIV from entering cells)

Elizabeth Glaser: a woman who became infected with the HIV virus from a blood transfusion in 1981 when she hemorrhaged during the delivery of her first child; she died on December 3, 1994, at the age of 47; she co-founded the Elizabeth Glaser Pediatric AIDS Foundation

HAART: an acronym for Highly Active Antiretroviral Therapy; a combination therapy

Hemophilia: a blood clotting disorder that makes individuals susceptible to internal and external bleeding problems; in the past, hemophiliacs often acquired the HIV virus through transfusions of contaminated blood or blood products

HIV: an acronym for Human Immunodeficiency Virus; a retrovirus that acts through an enzyme to turn its RNA into DNA, replicates itself in infected host cells, and spreads throughout the body

HIV positive: the condition of being infected with the HIV virus

Kaposi's sarcoma: a cancer of blood vessel tissue in the skin or internal organs; found in many individuals with AIDS

Opportunistic infection: an external or internal threat to bodily health often found in individuals with compromised or dysfunctional immune systems

Pandemic: a worldwide or global epidemic

Pneumocystis carinii: a pneumonia caused by a commonly occurring protozoan mainly seen in individuals with immune system deficiencies; an opportunistic infection in many individuals with AIDS

Retrovirus: a type of virus whose genetic material is RNA; when a retrovirus enters an affected cell, it acts through an enzyme called reverse transcriptase to turn its RNA into DNA, integrates this new viral DNA into the chromosomes of the cell, begins to replicate or produce new copies of itself, and eventually spreads throughout the body to infect new cells

Ryan White: a boy who became infected with HIV through contaminated blood or blood products in the early 1980s, and experienced stigma and discrimination (he died on April 8, 1990, at the age of 18); a major federal AIDS care funding bill has been named in his honor

Safer sex: sexual practices intended to minimize the transmission of HIV and other infectious agents

Syndrome: a clinical entity or recognizable pattern of manifestations arising from an unknown underlying cause

T-cells: T-lymphocyte cells; a special type of white blood cell in the immune system that normally organizes the body's response to infections and disease organisms

Universal precautions: clinical practices that minimize the possibility of accidents and contamination with infectious agents

Viral load: the amount of HIV in the body of an individual who is HIV positive

Questions for Review and Discussion

1. Read once again the vignette near the beginning of this chapter. Try to imagine how HIV infection might come into your family. Think about the burdens it imposes on those who are affected as well as those who are infected. If it did come into your family, what specific issues might you have to deal with? How might

you cope with such issues? What complicates these experiences when death results from HIV/AIDS?

2. Many (perhaps most) people in the United States report that they know how HIV is transmitted and what should be done to prevent acquiring that virus. Many Americans also report that they are not doing what is necessary to prevent transmission and acquisition of HIV. Do you know what is involved in the transmission and acquisition of HIV? Are you doing what is necessary to prevent transmission/acquisition of HIV? Why or why not?

3. In your judgment, what is the most important thing that each of us as individuals should do to help individuals who are already infected with HIV and/or who have AIDS? In your judgment, what is the most important thing that society should do to help individuals who are already infected with HIV and/or who have AIDS? Are you doing such things? Is society doing such things? Why or why not?

Suggested Readings

Historical and personal accounts can be found in:

Ashe, A., & Rampersad, A. (1993). *Days of Grace: A Memoir*.

Banish, R. (2003). *Focus on Living: Portraits of Americans with HIV and AIDS*.

Bush, J. (2007). *Ana's Story: A Journey of Hope*.

Cameron, E. (2005). *Witness to AIDS*.

Donnelly, K. F. (1994). *Recovering from the Loss of a Loved One to AIDS*.

Fisher, M. (1994). *Sleep with the Angels: A Mother Challenges AIDS*.

Garfield, C. A., with C. Spring & D. Ober. (1995). *Sometimes My Heart Goes Numb: Love and Caring in a Time of AIDS*.

Glaser, E., & Palmer, L. (1991). *In the Absence of Angels: A Hollywood Family's Courageous Story*.

Holleran, A. (2006). *Grief: A Novel*.

Johnson, E. "Magic," with W. Novak. (1992). *My Life*.

Jones, C. (1994). *Living Proof: Courage in the Face of AIDS*.

Louganis, G., with E. Marcus. (1995). *Breaking the Surface*.

Monette, P. (1988). *Borrowed Time: An AIDS Memoir*.

Monette, P. (1992). *Becoming a Man: Half a Life Story*.

Monette, P. (1995). *Last Watch of the Night: Essays Too Personal and Otherwise*.

Newman, L. (Ed.). (1995). *A Loving Testimony: Remembering Loved Ones Lost to AIDS*.

Ruskin, C. (1988). *The Quilt: Stories from the NAMES Project*.

Selwyn, P. A. (1998). *Surviving the Fall: The Personal Journey of an AIDS Doctor*.

Shilts, R. (1987). *And the Band Played On: Politics, People, and the AIDS Epidemic*.

Wilshire, S. F. (1994). *Seasons of Grief and Grace: A Sister's Story of AIDS*.

Wooten, J. T. (2004). *We Are All the Same: A Story of a Boy's Courage and a Mother's Love*.

Introductions to and analyses of HIV infection and AIDS can be found in:

Barnett, T., & Whiteside, A. (2006). *AIDS in the Twenty-First Century: Disease and Globalization* (rev. ed.).

Behrman, G. (2004). *The Invisible People: How the U.S. Has Slept through the Global AIDS Pandemic, the Greatest Humanitarian Catastrophe of Our Time.*

Buchanan, D., & Cernada, G. (Eds.). (1998). *Progress in Preventing AIDS?: Dogma, Dissent and Innovation—Global Perspectives.*

Doka, K. J. (1997). *AIDS, Fear, and Society: Challenging the Dreaded Disease.*

Fan, H., Conner, R. F., & Villarreal, L. P. (2004). *AIDS: Science and Society* (4th ed.).

Frumkin, L. R., & Leonard, J. M. (1997). *Questions & Answers on AIDS* (3rd ed.).

Gifford, A. L., Lorig, K., Laurent, D., & González, V. (1997). *Living Well with HIV and AIDS.*

Gostin, L. O. (Ed.). (2004). *The AIDS Pandemic: Complacency, Injustice, and Unfulfilled Expectations.*

Grmek, M. D. (1990). *History of AIDS: Emergence and Origin of a Modern Pandemic.*

Hoffman, M. A. (1996). *Counseling Clients with HIV Disease: Assessment, Intervention, Prevention.*

Iliffe, J. (2006). *The African AIDS Epidemic: A History.*

Irwin, A., Millen, J., & Fallows, D. (2003). *Global AIDS: Myths and Facts, Tools for Fighting the AIDS Pandemic.*

Kalipeni, E., Craddock, S., Oppong, J. R., & Ghosh, J. (Eds.). (2003). *HIV and AIDS in Africa: Beyond Epidemiology.*

Klitzman, R., & Bayer, R. (2005). *Mortal Secrets: Truth and Lies in the Age of AIDS.*

Koop, C. E. (1988). *Understanding AIDS.*

Nord, D. A. (1997). *Multiple AIDS-Related Loss: A Handbook for Surviving a Perpetual Fall.*

O'Neill, J. F., Selwyn, P. A., & Schietinger, H. (2003). *A Clinical Guide to Supportive and Palliative Care for HIV/AIDS.*

Seligson, M. R., & Peterson, K. E. (Eds.). (1992). *AIDS Prevention and Treatment: Hope, Humor, and Healing.*

Sontag, S. (1989). *AIDS and Its Metaphors.*

Volberding, P. A., & Aberg, J. A. (Eds.). (1999). *The San Francisco General Hospital Handbook of HIV Management: A Guide to the Practical Management of HIV-Infected Patients.*

For special issues concerning women, children, the elderly, the workplace, and other policy matters, consult:

Boyd-Franklin, N., Steiner, G. L., & Boland, M. G. (Eds.). (1995). *Children, Families, and HIV/AIDS: Psychosocial and Therapeutic Issues.*

Emlet, C. A. (Ed.). (2004). *HIV/AIDS and Older Adults: Challenges for Individuals, Families, and Communities.*

Hunter, N. D., & Rubenstein, W. B. (Eds.). (1992). *AIDS Agenda: Emerging Issues in Civil Rights.*

Krieger, N., & Margo, G. (Eds.). (1994). *AIDS: The Politics of Survival.*

Luna, G. C. (1997). *Youths Living with HIV: Self-Evident Truths.*

Roth, N. L., & Fuller, L. K. (1998). *Women and AIDS: Negotiating Safer Practices, Care, and Representation.*

Rubenstein, W. B., Eisenberg, R., & Gostin, L. O. (1996). *The Rights of People Who Are HIV Positive: The Authoritative ACLU Guide to the Rights of People Living with HIV Disease and AIDS.*

Terl, A. H. (1992). *AIDS and the Law: A Basic Guide for the Nonlawyer.*
Wiener, L. S., Best, A., & Pizzo, P. A. (Comps.). (1994). *Be a Friend: Children Who Live with HIV Speak.*

Selected Web Resources

Some useful search terms include: ACQUIRED IMMUNODEFICIENCY SYNDROME (OR ACQUIRED IMMUNE DEFICIENCY SYNDROME); AIDS; AIDS AND COMBINATION THERAPIES; HAART (HIGHLY ACTIVE ANTIRETROVIRAL THERAPY); HIV (OR HUMAN IMMUNODEFICIENCY VIRUS); KAPOSI'S SARCOMA; LIPODYSTROPHY; PNEUMOCYSTIS CARINII; PROTEASE INHIBITORS; RETROVIRUS; REVERSE TRANSCRIPTASE INHIBITORS; RYAN WHITE PROGRAM; T-CELLS; UNIVERSAL PRECAUTIONS; VIRAL LOAD

Visit the book companion website for *Death & Dying, Life & Living, Sixth Edition,* at academic.cengage.com/psychology/corr for all URLs and live links to the following *organizational and other Internet sites:*

AIDS Education Global Information System

Canadian AIDS Society

Centers for Disease Control and Prevention

Elizabeth Glaser Pediatric AIDS Foundation

HIV/AIDS Bureau, U.S. Department of Health and Human Services

National Association of People with AIDS

National Association on HIV Over Fifty

UNAIDS

Epilogue

Calendar Date Gives Mom Reason to Contemplate Life
by Elizabeth Vega-Fowler

I used to think life's defining moments were dramatic, like a speeding train that hits you head on and throws you forward.

This week, however, I changed my mind.

I decided that progress in life can more often be measured in inches, not miles. All those heavenly epiphanies are really the accumulation of everyday wisdom breaking through the surface.

All this was prompted by a date on my calendar.

Somewhere in my mind June 9 registered as familiar. It took a few moments for me to realize the significance. It was the four-year anniversary of my daughter's death.

Gabrielle was born with a malignant brain tumor. In truth, she was terminally ill before birth.

She was 16 days old when she died in her father's arms.

Even today I marvel at the brevity of her life.

Her father, brothers, 8-year-old Christopher and 6-year-old Joey, and I decided that if we couldn't give her longevity, we could give her quality.

So in 16 days, she smelled flowers and tasted cotton candy. She felt the sun on her face and heard countless lullabies. Even though we knew it was only a matter of time before we had to let her go, we opened ourselves up to knowing her.

Despite her medical condition—a condition doctors said left her with only one-fourth of her brain—my daughter responded in kind.

She would look into our eyes and without a word would communicate volumes of love.

Once she took every ounce of her strength and lifted a tiny wavering hand to touch my face.

When Gabrielle died quietly at home, I thought that my life had changed forever.

Time has taught me otherwise.

My daughter's death didn't place me on a new path but rather allowed me to experience things I had missed before. In fact, everything looked the same. It just felt different.

It was this journey—continuing along every day without her—that changed me and is still changing me.

The beginning was the most arduous.

For a time, I was enraged at God. Like a town crier I shouted "Unfair" through the streets.

I cried gallons of tears. Tears I never even knew I had.

I learned grieving was not just an emotional experience. It was a physical one. My arms throbbed with the need to hold her.

My heart really hurt from the emptiness.

I had a perpetual lump in my throat for years.

Seeing the date brought another simple realization.

Instead of the torrential sorrow of years past, this June 9 brought a gentle melancholy. There is a definite sadness of what will never be—birthday parties, frilly dresses, first dates and prom.

I know that loss will always be there.

But there in the midst of it is something else—memories of a sweet little girl whose death taught me everything that was important about life.

Like the power of magnolia blossoms and unconditional love, and how the joy of knowing another human being far outweighs the void that is left when they're gone.

There is also the new knowledge that this state called grief is not a final destination but rather a continuous journey that changes me in a thousand small ways—slowly and mysteriously.

I don't know exactly where I will end up. I just know that somehow without even realizing it I found peace along the way.

SOURCE: Elizabeth Vega-Fowler, 1998.
Reprinted by permission.

APPENDIX A

Selected Literature for Children: Annotated Descriptions

Picture and Coloring Books for Preschoolers and Beginning Readers

Anonymous. (2004). *My Always Sister Coloring Book.* St. Paul, MN: A Place to Remember (1885 University Ave., Suite 110, 55104; www.aplacetoremember.com; tel. 800-631-0973 or 651-645-7045). Callie the bunny talks about learning that his new baby sister is sick and must stay in the hospital. One day, Callie's Daddy tells him that his new sister has died, and they have a funeral with music. Callie experiences many emotions and draws a picture of how he feels.

Bartoli, J. (1975). *Nonna.* New York: Harvey House. A boy and his younger sister, with good memories of their grandmother, are permitted to participate in her funeral, burial, and the division of her property among family members so that each receives some memento of her life.

Blackburn, L. B. (1987). *Timothy Duck: The Story of the Death of a Friend.* Omaha, NE: Centering Corporation. Timothy Duck tries to understand his reactions to the death of a friend and how the adults are overlooking the needs of his friend's sister. Sharing his questions and concerns with his mother and with his best friend is helpful.

Blackburn, L. B. (1991). *I Know I Made It Happen: A Gentle Book about Feelings.* Omaha, NE: Centering Corporation. Many young children believe they must somehow be responsible when bad things happen. Here, adults explain that bad things don't happen because of a child's words or wishes. It helps to share bad feelings and to know you're not at fault. Also, the adults suggest positive things children can do when someone becomes ill or after an accident, a death, or a divorce.

Boulden, J. (1989). *Saying Goodbye.* Weaverville, CA: Boulden Publishing (P.O. Box 1186, 96093-1186). This activity book tells a story about death as a natural part of life, the feelings that are involved in saying good-bye, and the conviction that love is forever, while allowing the child-reader to draw pictures, color images, or insert thoughts on its pages.

Breebaart, J., & Breebaart, P. (1993). *When I Die, Will I Get Better?* New York: Peter Bedrick Books. Fred and Joe are rabbit brothers who live in the woods. When Joe does not get out of bed one morning, Doctor Owl says he has a high fever but will get better. But Joe dies and neighbors help prepare things—the mole family digs the grave, Beaver makes the coffin, and Fred talks to Hedgehog about his feelings. At the burial, Fred reads a letter to Joe, puts Joe's favorite things into the coffin, and promises to play in the nearby field every day. Afterwards, Fred wants to be alone and is angry, but gradually he and his parents begin to feel better with the support of their friends. Five-year-old Joeri created the text for this book after his younger brother, Remi, died, and guided their father, Piet, in writing it down and drawing the illustrations.

Brown, M. W. (1958). *The Dead Bird.* Reading, MA: Addison-Wesley. Some children find a wild bird that is dead, touch its cold body, bury it in a simple ceremony, and return to the site each day to mourn ("until they forgot"). Sadness need not last forever; life can go on again. An early classic.

Buscaglia, L. (1982). *The Fall of Freddie the Leaf: A Story of Life for All Ages.* Thorofare, NJ: Slack. Photographs of leaves on a tree in the park are accompanied by text in which one leaf (Freddie) asks another (Daniel) to explain their anticipated fall from the tree and the meaning of life. Fear of dying is compared to fear of the unknown and to natural changes in the seasons. Life itself is its own purpose and death is a kind of comfortable sleep (a metaphor that can easily mislead children).

Carlstrom, N. W. (1990). *Blow Me a Kiss, Miss Lilly.* New York: Harper & Row. Sara's best friend is her neighbor across the street, an old lady named Miss Lilly. When Miss Lilly is unexpectedly taken to the hospital and dies, Sara cries, looks for the light in her house, and is lonely. In spring, Sara finds happiness in Miss Lilly's garden and in her conviction that Miss Lilly is blowing her a kiss.

Carney, K. L. (1997-2001). *Barklay and Eve Activity and Coloring Book Series.* Dragonfly Publishing Co., Wethersfield, CT (277 Folly Brook Boulevard, Wethersfield, CT 06109; 860-257-7635). This series includes eight titles: Book 1, *Together We'll Get through This!*; Book 2, *Honoring Our Loved Ones: Going to a Funeral*; Book 3, *What is the Meaning of Shiva?*; Book 4, *Our Special Garden: Understanding Cremation*; Book 5, *What IS Cancer, Anyway?*; Book 6, *Everything Changes, but Love Endures: Explaining Hospice to Children*; Book 7, *Precious Gifts: Katie Coolican's Story*; Book 8, *They're Part of the Family: Barklay and Eve Talk to Children about Pet Loss.* Each book tells a story and offers drawings to color or blank spaces to draw pictures about a loss-related topic that adults may find difficult to discuss with children. In each book, two curious Portuguese water dogs learn lessons like: loss and sadness do happen; those events are not their fault; it is OK to have strong feelings as long as they are expressed in constructive ways; and "we can get through anything with the love and support of family and friends" (Book 1, p. 5). The books and other items are available from the website www.barklayandeve.com. An outstanding series.

Carson, J. (1992). *You Hold Me and I'll Hold You.* New York: Orchard Books. When her Daddy's Aunt Ann dies, a little girl thinks about her parents' divorce and other losses she has experienced. During the memorial ceremony, the girl watches all the people and everything that happens. She wonders how sorry she will have to get. Being held and holding others is comforting.

Clardy, A. F. (1984). *Dusty Was My Friend: Coming to Terms with Loss.* New York: Human Sciences. Benjamin is 8 years old when his friend Dusty is killed in an automobile accident. As Benjamin struggles to understand his reactions to this tragic event, his parents allow him to express his thoughts and feelings, mourn his loss, remember the good times he shared with Dusty, and go on with his own life.

Cohn, J. (1987). *I Had a Friend Named Peter: Talking to Children about the Death of a Friend.* New York: Morrow. The children's section of this book describes Beth's reactions when a car kills her friend, along with helpful ways her parents and teacher respond to Beth, her classmates, and Peter's parents. An adult section tries to prepare adults to assist children in coping with death.

Connolly, M. (1997). *It Isn't Easy.* New York: Oxford University Press. When his 9-year-old brother is killed in a car accident, a little boy is sad, lonely, and angry. As he ponders many good memories of his brother, he gradually gets used to being an only child—but it isn't easy.

Czech, J. (2000). *The Garden Angel: A Young Child Discovers a Grandparent's Love Grows Even after Death.* Omaha, NE: Centering Corporation. After her grandpa dies, 8-year-old Camilla remembers all of his gardening activities. That year she plants the new garden herself, dresses a scarecrow with his old clothes, and spreads his old quilt behind it like wings.

Dean, A. (1992). *Meggie's Magic.* New York: Viking Penguin. After 8 year old Meggie's illness and death, her parents and sister feel sad and lonely. But one day when Meggie's sister goes to their special place, she finds it still filled with the magical qualities of the games they used to play and she realizes that Meggie's magic still remains inside each of them.

De Paola, T. (1973; Rev. ed. 1998). *Nana Upstairs and Nana Downstairs.* New York: Putnam's; revised edition with new full color illustrations by the author. Tommy loves to visit his great-grandmother ("Nana Upstairs"). When told she has died, he doesn't believe it until he sees her empty bed. A few nights later, Tommy sees a falling star and his mother suggests it might represent a kiss from Nana who is now "upstairs" in a new way. Later, an older Tommy repeats the experience and interpretation after the death of "Nana Downstairs" (his grandmother).

Dodge, N. C. (1984). *Thumpy's Story: A Story of Love and Grief Shared by Thumpy, the Bunny.* Springfield, IL: Prairie Lark Press (P.O. Box 699, Springfield, IL 62705). In picture book, coloring book, and workbook formats (in both English and Spanish), a rabbit tells a simple story about the death of his sister and its effects on their family.

Doleski, T. (1983). *The Hurt*. Mahwah, NJ: Paulist Press. Justin is hurt by an angry insult from his friend, but he doesn't share his feelings with anyone. He takes The Hurt into his room, like a big, round, cold, hard stone, but it just gets bigger and bigger and bigger. It is ruining everything until he finally tells Daddy. As he gradually lets it go, The Hurt gets smaller and smaller until at last it goes away.

Duckworth, L. (2003). *Ragtail Remembers: A Story That Helps Children Understand Feelings of Grief*. Omaha, NE: Centering Corporation. A mouse is sad, lonely, and angry when he learns that his friend, Old Tim the cat, is dead. Ragtail wishes Old Tim would come back, but as he learns what dead means, he begins to come to terms with his loss and he makes a new friend.

Ewart, C. (2003). *The Giant*. New York: Walker & Co. Before she died, a young girl's mother said that a giant would look after her. As the seasons pass on the family farm, the girl misses her mother and searches for the giant. Her hardworking Pa says there is no such thing as a giant, but the girl keeps searching everywhere until she finally realizes that her tall, strong Pa is the giant looking after her.

Fassler, D., & McQueen, K. (1990). *What's a Virus, Anyway? The Kids' Book about AIDS*. Burlington, VT: Waterfront Books. Just a few words or pictures on each page leave room for coloring, drawing, and shared discussion so that parents and teachers can begin to talk about AIDS with young children.

Fassler, J. (1971). *My Grandpa Died Today*. New York: Human Sciences. David's grandfather has tried to prepare the boy for his impending death, but when it actually happens David still needs to mourn his loss. He does find comfort in a legacy of many good memories of his grandfather and in the knowledge that his grandfather does not want him to be afraid to live and enjoy life.

Fox, M. (1994). *Tough Boris*. New York: Harcourt Brace. Boris von der Borch is a huge, tough, scruffy, greedy, fearless, and scary pirate—just like all pirates. But when his parrot dies, Boris cries and cries—just like all pirates, and everyone else. A simple story and pictures give children permission to experience and express their grief.

Gant, L. G. (2003). *Never Say Goodbye*. Nashville, TN: Tommy Nelson. An old rabbit (Netta) tells a beloved young rabbit (Hannah) that Netta has to "go away." That evokes a flood of questions from Hannah. Netta calmly replies to each question, displaying her conviction that "God has made me a new home" and that even in death they will always be connected.

Greenlee, S. (1992). *When Someone Dies*. Atlanta: Peachtree Publishers. This book explores changes and reactions that people typically experience when someone close to them dies. It encourages sharing tears with someone you love, writing a letter to the person who died, and keeping a special part of that person in our hearts.

Gryte, M. (1988). *No New Baby: For Siblings Who Have a Brother or Sister Die before Birth*. Omaha, NE: Centering Corporation. Also in Spanish as *No Tenremos Un Nuevo Bebé*. A young child describes her reactions when the anticipated birth of a new sibling does not happen. Grandma picks up a young bud off the ground and uses it to explain that while most buds keep growing and become flowers, some don't, like this one. The girl realizes that something like this happened to their baby. Grandma says no one is to blame and we do not always have answers.

Harris, A. (1965). *Why Did He Die?* Minneapolis, MN: Lerner. The death of a friend's grandfather leads a mother to explain to her young son that death is something that happens when someone's body, like an engine in a car, no longer works. They discuss aging, the life cycle, memories, and quality of life.

Harris, R. H. (2001). *Goodbye Mousie*. New York: Margaret K. McElderry Books (Simon & Schuster). A boy finds it hard to believe that his pet Mousie has died. Over time, he comes to understand that Mousie is dead and will not be coming back. The boy shares his grief with his father and mother. Together they prepare a shoebox in which they bury Mousie.

Hazen, B. S. (1985). *Why Did Grandpa Die? A Book about Death*. New York: Golden. Molly cannot accept it when her much-loved Grandpa dies suddenly. She feels frightened, awful, and misses Grandpa very much, but cannot cry. Only after a long time is Molly finally able to acknowledge that Grandpa will not come back, to cry, and to realize that Grandpa still is available to her through pictures, in her memories, and in stories shared with her family.

Heegaard, M. E. (1988). *When Someone Very Special Dies*. Minneapolis, MN: Woodland Press (99 Woodland Circle, 55424; 612-926-2665). A story line about loss and death encourages children to share their thoughts and feelings through coloring and drawing in this activity book.

Hemery, K. M. (1998). *The Brightest Star*. Omaha, NE: Centering Corporation. Molly and her parents used to go to the beach, wait until it was very dark, and look at the stars. After Mommy died, Molly is especially troubled when Ms. Baylor asks the children to draw a picture of their families for the open house at school. Daddy helps by taking Molly to the beach and pointing out the brightest star, which reminds her of her mother's love.

Hemery, K. M. (2000). *Not Just a Fish*. Omaha, NE: Centering Corporation. Marybeth thinks her goldfish, Puffer, is the best pet fish in the world because he always listens to her and watching him makes her feel calm and peaceful. So Marybeth is shocked when she finds Puffer floating upside down in his bowl. Even though people tell Marybeth they are sorry Puffer had died, they also say he was "just a fish" and that makes her angry. Then her father flushes Puffer down the toilet before Marybeth can bury him! Only Aunt Lizzie understands Marybeth's loss and helps by arranging a memorial service with music, a few words from Marybeth about Puffer, and a heart-shaped pin with a fish painted on it.

Hesse, K. (1993). *Poppy's Chair*. New York: Scholastic. Leah visits her grandparents every summer, but this time things are different: Poppy has died. Leah remembers things she did with Poppy but is still afraid to look at his pictures. One evening, Leah finds Gramm half asleep in Poppy's chair. They sit together, share their grief and plans for the future, and help each other feel a little better.

Hodge, J. (1999) *Finding Grandpa Everywhere: A Young Child Discovers Memories of a Grandparent*. Omaha, NE: Centering Corporation. A little boy realizes that Grandpa is dead, not "lost" as the adults keep saying. But he consoles himself and his Grandma with this thought: Grandpa always said "to do something for someone you have to put a little of yourself into it." So memories of Grandpa and his love live on everywhere the boy looks.

Holmes, M. M. (2000). *A Terrible Thing Happened*. Washington, DC: Magination Press. Sherman Smith is a raccoon who saw a terrible thing happen. He is afraid and tries not to think about it, but something inside still bothers him. At different times, he has stomach and headaches, feels sad or nervous, and isn't hungry, can't sleep, or has bad dreams. Often he is angry and gets into trouble at school. Ms. Maple listens to Sherman and helps him understand his feelings. Talking to her and drawing pictures enables Sherman to vent his feelings.

Horn, G. (White Deer of Autumn). (1992). *The Great Change*. Hillsboro, OR: Beyond Words Publishing, Inc. (20827 NW Cornell Road, Suite 500, 97124-9808; 800-284-9673). A Native-American grandmother explains to her 9-year-old granddaughter, Wanba, that death is not the end, but the Great Change—a part of the unbreakable Circle of Life in which our bodies become one with Mother Earth while our souls or spirits endure.

Johnson, J., & Johnson, M. (1982; Rev. ed., 2004). *Where's Jess?* Omaha, NE: Centering Corporation. A book to help young children cope with infant sibling death by exploring topics like what "death" means, remembering the dead child, and the value of tears.

Jordan, M. K. (1989). *Losing Uncle Tim*. Morton Grove, IL: Albert Whitman. When Uncle Tim becomes infected with HIV, develops AIDS, and dies, his nephew looks for solace through an idea they had once discussed: "Maybe Uncle Tim is like the sun, just shining somewhere else."

Joslin, M. (1998). *The Goodbye Boat*. Grand Rapids, MI: Eerdmans. Simple pictures and few words describe friendships and loving, loss and grief, and the idea that when a boat is gone from view it is surely sailing somewhere new.

Kantrowitz, M. (1973). *When Violet Died*. New York: Parents' Magazine Press. After the death of their pet bird, Amy, Eva, and their friends have a funeral with poems, songs, punch, and even humor. It's sad to think that nothing lasts forever, but then Eva recognizes that life can go on in another way through an ever-changing chain of life involving the family cat, Blanche, and her kittens.

Keckler, B. (2006). *My Friend, Matilda*. Indianapolis, IN: Eagle Creek Publications (P.O. Box 781166, 46278; 866-870-9904; www.eaglecreekpubs.com). Chris's best friend is a golden retriever named Matilda. She loves Chris unconditionally during all his problems and transitions in life, including as he becomes sick and when he dies. Brief, rhyming text and colorful illustrations speak of the value of friendship during difficult times.

Kent, J. (1975). *There's No Such Thing as a Dragon*. New York: Golden Books. One morning when he wakes, Billy Bixbee finds a small dragon in his room, but his mother says, "There's no such thing as a dragon!" During the day, the dragon eats Billy's pancakes and grows larger and larger. It even chases after a bakery truck, carrying the house on its back like a shell on a snail. When Mr. Bixbee comes home, Billy tries to explain

APPENDIX A   615

what has been happening, but his mother still wants to insist that there is no such thing as a dragon. When Billy says, "There IS a dragon" and pats it on its head, that makes the dragon happy and it immediately starts getting smaller. When it was kitten-size again, Mother says, "I don't mind dragons THIS size. . . .Why did it have to grow so BIG?" Billy answers, "I'm not sure . . . but I think it just wanted to be noticed."

Krasny, L., & Brown, M. (1998). *When Dinosaurs Die: A Guide to Understanding Death*. Boston: Little, Brown. A cartoon format introduces young children to issues of death and loss.

Ladwig, T. (Illus.) (1997). *Psalm Twenty-Three*. Grand Rapids, MI: Eerdmans. The familiar text of this psalm, comparing God to a loving shepherd, is here accompanied by forceful and moving illustrations depicting the world of love and fear faced by an urban, African-American family.

Lanton, S. (1991). *Daddy's Chair*. Rockville, MD: Kar-Ben Copies, Inc. (800-4-KARBEN). After his father's death, Michael does not want anyone to sit in Daddy's chair, so it will be ready for him when he comes back. Mommy explains what it means to be sick and die, as well as the Jewish customs involved in sitting shiva. Sharing memories of Daddy gradually enables Michael to allow the chair to be used again.

London, J. (1994). *Liplap's Wish*. San Francisco: Chronicle Books. As a rabbit named Liplap builds the winter's first snow bunny, he remembers and misses his Grandma. He finds comfort in an old Rabbit's tale that his grandmother used to tell about how, long ago, when the First Rabbits died, they became stars in the sky that even now come out at night, watch over us, and shine forever in our hearts.

Loring, P., & Johnson, J. (1994). *Lucy Lettuce: A Head of Her Time*. Omaha, NE: Centering Corporation. The experiences of a head of lettuce illustrate what grief is like and suggest that the lid of sorrow can be lifted. Some of the lessons Lucy realizes are: "Her life would never be the same. She would always have part of her heart missing. She would get tossed around now and then. Her person lived on in her memory and in the new part of her that was her heart. . . . Now that she had finally reached this place in her life she could go out and nurture others. Life was still good, after all." The book also suggests a recipe for a visual demonstration of this grief story.

Lucado, M. (1992, 2000). *Just In Case You Ever Wonder*. Nashville: Thomas Nelson. This little tale (published in board book and other formats) gives words to parents to tell their children how much they love them and how special they are to God.

MacGregor, C. (1999). *"Why Do People Die?": Helping Your Child Understand—with Love and Illustrations*. Secaucus, NJ: Carol Publishing Group. Explains dying and death as a process in which our bodies wear out and just stop working. When that happens, it is normal to be sad and OK to cry. Then there often will be a funeral, a ceremony, a burial, and a time when friends celebrate the life of the person who died and try to comfort each other. Some religious views are mentioned, as are memories that live on within us and times when our grief returns for a while.

McIntyre, B. B. (2000). *Jungle Journey: Grieving and Remembering Eleanor the Elephant*. Traverse City, MI: Traverse Publishing Co. (P.O. Box 4054, 49685; 231-929-0015; info@traversepublishing.com). Each of the animals reacts in its own way to the death of their beloved Eleanor the Elephant who had protected them while they slept. As they mourn, they find ways to work together to continue their jungle journey. Sharing fears and bad dreams makes them less scary.

Mellonie, B., & Ingpen, R. (1983). *Lifetimes: A Beautiful Way to Explain Death to Children*. New York: Bantam. Multiple examples affirm that "there is a beginning and an ending for everything that is alive. In between is living. . . . So, no matter how long they are, or how short, lifetimes are really all the same. They have beginnings, and endings, and there is living in between."

Muñoz-Kiehne, M. (2000). *Since My Brother Died/ Desde Que Murió Mi Hermano*. Omaha, NE: Centering Corporation. With text in both English and Spanish, a child wonders if a brother's death is only a dream or if anything could have been done to keep him from dying. The child reports sadness in the family as well the child's own physical reactions (headaches and stomachaches). Afraid of forgetting this brother, the child begins to paint, with simple watercolor illustrations gradually turning into rainbows and the confidence that life can go forward.

O'Toole, D. (1988). *Aarvy Aardvark Finds Hope*. Burnsville, NC: Compassion Books (477 Hannah Branch Road, 28714). Designed to be read aloud, this story is about how Aarvy Aardvark comes to terms with the loss of his mother and brother. Many animals offer unhelpful advice to Aarvy; only one friend, Ralphy Rabbit, who really listens to Aarvy as the two of them share their losses, is truly helpful.

Prestine, J. S. (193). *Someone Special Died.* Torrance, CA: Fearon Teacher Aids/Frank Schaeffer Publications (23740 Hawthorne Blvd., 90505-5927). A young girl reacts to the death of someone special. She discusses death with her mother, explains how she feels, and plans a scrapbook to remember good times shared with the person who died.

Puttock, S., & Bartlett, A. (2001). *A Story for Hippo: A Book about Loss.* New York: Scholastic Press. Brightly colored artwork depicts the friendship between Hippo and Monkey. Hippo is the oldest animal and best storyteller in the jungle; Monkey is the funniest. Together they eat cabbages, play games, and tell stories. One day, Hippo tells Monkey that it is time for her to die. Monkey is sad: who will tell wonderful stories, play games, and laugh at his jokes? When Monkey promises not to forget her, Hippo says "that will be part of my happily ever after." After Hippo dies, Monkey is very sad, but finally Little Chameleon insists that Hippo's stories still need to be told—and a new friendship begins.

Raschka, C. (2007). *The Purple Balloon.* New York: Schwartz & Wade. The premise for this book is that children who draw their feelings when they become aware of their impending death often draw a blue or purple balloon, released and floating free. Here balloon images first depict the death of an elderly person before turning to a dying youngster. The text says, "Good help makes leaving easier" and offers suggestions for those who want to help make dying less difficult.

Rylant, C. (1995/1997). *Dog Heaven* and *Cat Heaven.* New York: Blue Sky Press. Vivid acrylic illustrations and charming story lines in these two books describe the delights that dogs and cats might hope to find in their own special heavens.

Schlitt, R. S. (1992). *Robert Nathaniel's Tree.* Maryville, TN: Lightbearers Publishers (P.O. Box 5895, 37802-5895). A child tells about the things he likes, including getting ready for a new baby. But the baby dies, and then there is much that he does not like. Later, he likes caring for Robert Nathaniel's memorial tree and being his big brother—"even if he didn't come home."

Schwiebert, P. (2003). *We Were Gonna Have a Baby, but We Had an Angel Instead.* Portland, OR: Grief Watch (2116 NE 18th Avenue, 97212; 503-284-7426; www. griefwatch.com). Bright, colored drawings and just a single sentence on each page allow a young boy to tell how he excited he was as he anticipated the birth of the new baby. But something happened; the baby died and everyone is sad. The boy makes clear that having the baby would have been more fun than missing him.

Schwiebert, P. (2007). *Someone Came before You.* Portland, OR: Grief Watch. Vivid artwork and simple text describe a mommy and a daddy who love each other very much but desperately want to have a child with whom to share their love. They are excited during the pregnancy but greatly saddened when the baby dies. In time, their hearts are able to stretch enough to enable them to have a new baby—YOU! Through this book and in other ways, they share the memory of that prior baby with you.

Shriver, M. (1999). *What's Heaven?* New York: Golden Books. This book reflects the author's discussions with her 5- and 6-year-old daughters when their great-grandmother, Rose Fitzgerald Kennedy, died. It suggests that heaven is a place without hurts where your soul goes when you die.

Simon, J. (2001). *This Book Is for All Kids, but Especially My Sister Libby. Libby Died.* Austin, TX: Idea University Press. Five-year-old Jack struggled to understand the death of his young sister. This book reproduces his questions and comments, along with dramatic, colorful illustrations.

Stull, E. G. (1964). *My Turtle Died Today.* New York: Holt, Rinehart & Winston. When a pet turtle dies, a boy and his friends bury it and talk about what this means. They conclude that life can go on in another way through the newborn kittens of their cat, Patty. Much of this is sound, but the book also poses two questions that need to be addressed with care: Can you get a new pet in the way that one child has a new mother, and do you have to live—a long time—before you die?

Varley, S. (1992). *Badger's Parting Gifts.* New York: Mulberry Books. Badger is old and knows he must die, but he is not afraid. He worries about his friends. They are sad when he dies but find consolation in the special memories he left with each of them and in sharing those memories with others.

Viorst, J. (1971). *The Tenth Good Thing about Barney.* New York: Atheneum. A boy tries to think of ten good things to say when his pet cat dies. At first, he can only think of nine: Barney was brave and smart and funny and clean; he was cuddly and handsome and he only once ate a bird; it was sweet to hear him purr in my ear; and sometimes he slept on my belly and kept it warm. Out in the garden, he realizes the tenth good thing is that "Barney is in the ground and he's helping grow flowers."

Warburg, S. S. (1969). *Growing Time.* Boston: Houghton Mifflin. When his aging collie, King, dies, Jamie's father gets him a new puppy. At first, Jamie is not ready for the new dog, but after he is allowed to express his grief, he finds it possible to accept the new relationship.

Weir, A. B. (1992). *Am I Still a Big Sister?* Newtown, PA: Fallen Leaf Press (P.O. Box 942, 18940). This is the story of a young girl's concerns through the illness, hospitalization, death, and funeral of her baby sister, and the subsequent birth of a new brother.

Wilhelm, H. (1985). *I'll Always Love You.* New York: Crown. A boy and his dog grow up together, but Elfie grows old and dies while the boy is still young. Afterward, family members regret not telling Elfie they loved her. But the boy did so every night and he realizes that his love for her will continue even after her death. He doesn't want a new puppy right away, even though he knows that Elfie will not come back and there may come a time when he will be ready for a new pet.

Winsch, J. L. (1995). *After the Funeral.* Mahwah, NJ: Paulist Press. This book seeks to normalize reactions people have after a death, like crying and feeling sad or scared. It says, "Everyone handles sadness in their own way." It also recommends sharing feelings and affirms a hope in everlasting life.

Woodson, J. (2000). *Sweet, Sweet Memory.* New York: Hyperion Books for Children. When Grandpa dies, a young African-American girl named Sarah and her grandmother are consoled by stories and funny memories of him, as well as by recalling what he always said, "The earth changes . . . Like us it lives, it grows. Like us . . . a part of it never dies. Everything and everyone goes on and on."

Yeomans, E. (2000). *Lost and Found: Remembering a Sister.* Omaha, NE: Centering Corporation. A young girl recounts the confusing experiences she and her parents have after her sister dies, but she also realizes many ways in which she still feels her sister's love. So Paige isn't "lost" forever; she is right there in their hearts, and the girl knows where to find her.

Zeifert, H. (2001). *Ode to Humpty Dumpty.* Boston: Houghton Mifflin. Following the model of the original verses, this book uses rhyming text and large images to pick up the story after Humpty's great fall. When all the king's horses and men cannot put Humpty back together again, citizens try to help without success. Then, the king's faithful servant, Norma Jean Foote, encourages the community to create monuments, engage in activities, and sing an ode to help them cope with their grief, cheer up the king, and memorialize the fallen Humpty.

Zolotow, C. (1974). *My Grandson Lew.* New York: Harper & Row. When 6-year-old Lewis wonders why his grandfather has not visited lately, his mother says she didn't tell him that his grandfather had died because he had never asked. The boy says he hadn't needed to ask; grandfather just appeared. Son and mother share warm memories of someone they both miss: Lewis says, "He gave me eye hugs"; his mother concludes, "Now we will remember him together and neither of us will be so lonely as we would be if we had to remember him alone."

Storybooks and Other Texts for Primary School Readers

Adams, G. (2006). *Lessons from Lions: Using Children's Media to Teach about Grief and Mourning* + CD. Little Rock, AR: Center for Good Mourning, Arkansas Children's Hospital (800 Marshall Street, Slot 690, 72202). This booklet explains how to use ten slides from Disney's *The Lion King* (1994) to encourage discussions with children or adults about grief and mourning. Three unhelpful reactions following a loss are: (1) running away from the problem, the pain, and those who know and love you best; (2) pretending the bad thing never happened—living as if the past doesn't matter; and (3) treating your feelings, experiences, and story as a big secret—never telling anyone about them. The positive lesson is: By not making any of these three mistakes, we can keep the person with us in our hearts.

Al-Chokhachy, E. (1999). *The Angel with the Golden Glow.* Marblehead, MA: Penny Bear Publishing (Six Elmwood Rd., 01945; 877-887-2828 or 781-639-2828; www.pennybear.org). An angel is chosen to be born as a special child, one who cannot do what other children do, but who gives his family healing in the brief time he is with them. According to this book, the role of angel children like this is one of bringing love, joy, hope, and healing to their families.

Al-Chokhachy, E. (2002). *How Can I Help, Papa?: A Child's Journey through Loss and Healing.* Gloucester, MA: Works of Hope Publishing (149 Eastern Ave., 01930; 877-887-2828; www.WorksofHope.com). A

9-year-old girl experiences happy times with her grandfather, his illness, and his death.

Alexander, A. K. (2002). *A Mural for Mamita/Un Mural Para Mamita*. Omaha, NE: Centering Corporation. A young girl, her family, and their whole neighborhood plan a fiesta to celebrate the life of her grandmother who recently died after a long illness. Mamita was well known and greatly loved as the proprietor of the local bodega or store. The girl's special contribution to the celebration is a brilliant mural painted on the side of the bodega. The text of this book appears in both English and Spanish.

Alexander, S. (1983). *Nadia the Willful*. New York: Pantheon Books. After Nadia's older brother dies, her father in his grief decrees that no one in his kingdom may speak of this death. Nadia helps her family, particularly her father, deal with their grief by willfully talking about her brother.

Alexander-Greene, A. (1999). *Sunflowers and Rainbows for Tia: Saying Goodbye to Daddy*. Omaha, NE: Centering Corporation. A 10-year-old African-American girl named Tia describes how she and other family members feel when her Daddy dies suddenly. Tia tells about her sadness and grief, along with her fears that Mama might also die and leave the children alone. She explains how people came over to the house to share their love for Daddy, support her family, and bring food. Being involved in many of the preparations for the funeral and taking part in the funeral itself helps Tia, especially when she is allowed to bring Daddy's favorite sunflowers to the ceremony and a big rainbow comes shining.

Arnold, C. (1987). *What We Do When Someone Dies*. New York: Franklin Watts. This book provides information about death-related feelings, concepts, and beliefs, but gives most attention to disposition of the body, funeral customs, and memorial practices.

Atkins, J. (1999). *A Name on the Quilt: A Story of Remembrance*. New York: Atheneum Books for Young Readers. After Uncle Ron's death, Lauren, her family, and friends reminisce as they gather together to make a panel in his memory for the AIDS Memorial Quilt. Sharing stories about Ron comforts them all.

Barreras, C. (1998). *Hope in Heaven*. Folsom, CA: Hope in Heaven (P.O. Box 874, 95763). This slim booklet tries to show how one might talk about the possibility of death to a child with a life-threatening illness. It insists the child is important and is loved, and promises that no one will give up the fight, even while admitting that things do not always turn out as we might wish. The remainder of the text affirms God's presence and the expectation of heaven.

Barron, T. A. (2000). *Where Is Grandpa?* New York: Philomel Books. After Grandpa dies, family members share memories. When a boy wants to know where Grandpa is now, they agree Grandpa is in heaven and that "heaven is any place where people who love each other have shared some time together." The thought that Grandpa is way off in the Never Summer range of the Rockies that they used to look at together "as far as we can possibly see" from the tree house they built comforts the boy.

Boritzer, E. (2000). *What Is Death?* Santa Monica, CA: Veronica Lane Books (513 Wilshire Blvd. #282, 90401; 800-651-1001). The third in a series by this author (following *What Is God?* and *What Is Love?*), this book seeks to introduce children to the concept of death and to some of its implications, using examples of customs and beliefs from various religions and cultures.

Bosak, S. V. (2003). *Something to Remember Me By* (also available in Spanish and French). Toronto: The Communication Project (9 Lobraico Lane, Whitechurch-Stouffville, Ontario, L4A 7X5 Canada; 905-640-8914; www.somethingtorememberme by.org). A little girl loves to visit and share activities with her grandmother. One day Grandmother says she wants to give the girl something to remember her by and tells her that the cedar chest at the foot of the bed will be hers some day. Grandmother says the same thing every time the girl visits from that day forward and each time she also gives the girl a small gift. As the girl grows and asks why grandmother is giving her all these things, grandmother says, "Because everyone wants to be remembered." Then, on the day that grandmother moves out of her house, she gives the girl the cedar chest and the girl gives her a photo of the two of them with their names written on the back. These legacies reflect and nourish their love.

Boulden, J., & Boulden, B. (1992). *Uncle Jerry Has AIDS*. Weaverville, CA: Boulden Publishing (P.O. Box 1186, 96093-1186; tel. 800-238-8433). This activity book allows children at about grade level 3–4 to explore issues, attitudes, and emotions that might arise when a loved one has AIDS.

Bunting, E. (1982). *The Happy Funeral*. New York: Harper & Row. Two young Chinese-American girls are puzzled when their mother says they will have a "happy funeral" for their grandfather. At the funeral, food is provided for the journey to the other side, play money is burned, people cry and give speeches, and a marching band plays. After the ceremony, a small candy is provided to "sweeten the sorrow" of the mourners. In the end, the children realize that although no one was happy that their grandfather died, his good life and everyone's fond memories of him did make for a happy funeral.

Bunting, E. (1999). *Rudi's Pond*. New York: Clarion. While Rudi is sick, his friend and classmates send cards and make a big "GET WELL RUDI" banner for his hospital room. After Rudi dies, the children write poems and make a memorial pond in the schoolyard that attracts a beautiful hummingbird.

Bunting, E. (2000). *The Memory String*. New York: Clarion. Laura's grief three years after her mother's death is still vivid, and she is having trouble accepting her new stepmother, Jane. Laura consoles herself with a string of buttons going back three generations in her family, but especially with the buttons from Mom's prom and wedding dresses and from the nightgown she was wearing when she died. When the string breaks, the 43 buttons are scattered all over the yard. Laura, Dad, and Jane find all but one button. Dad suggests to Jane that they substitute a twin for the missing button, but Laura overhears Jane wisely saying, "It's like a mother. No substitute allowed" (p. 25). When Jane does find the missing button, Laura asks her to help restring her buttons.

Carrick, C. (1976). *The Accident*. New York: Seabury Press. Christopher's dog, Bodger, is accidentally killed when he runs in front of a truck. Christopher is angry at the driver, at his father for not being mad at the driver, and at himself for not paying attention and letting Bodger wander across the road as they walked. Christopher's parents bury Bodger too quickly the next morning, before he can take part, but anger dissolves into tears when he and his father join together to erect a marker at Bodger's grave.

Coerr, E. (1977). *Sadako and the Thousand Paper Cranes*. New York: Putnam's. This book is based on a true story about a Japanese girl who died of leukemia in 1955 as one of the long-term results of the atomic bombing of Hiroshima (which occurred when Sadako was 2 years old). In the hospital, a friend reminds Sadako of the legend that the crane is supposed to live for a thousand years and that good health will be granted to a person who folds 1,000 origami paper cranes. With family members and friends, they begin folding. Sadako died before the project was finished, but her classmates completed the work, and children all over Japan have since contributed money to erect a statue in her memory.

Cohn, J. (1994). *Molly's Rosebush*. Morton Grove, IL: Albert Whitman & Co. Molly is eagerly waiting for the birth of her new baby sibling when her mother experiences a miscarriage. Her father explains that not all babies are strong enough to be born. Her Grandma helps by comparing this death to a flower bud that doesn't blossom.

Coleman, P. (1996). *Where the Balloons Go*. Omaha, NE: Centering Corporation. When Corey asks where balloons go as they fly up into the sky, Grandma suggests that perhaps their destination is a lovely Balloon Forest. Later, after Grandma becomes sick and dies, Corey wishes that his balloons could carry him up to the Balloon Forest to see Grandma, but he settles for attaching a message of his love to a balloon and releasing it.

Copeland, K. M. (2005). *Mama's Going to Heaven Soon*. Minneapolis, MN: Augsburg Fortress. Vivid colors and minimal text in this storybook for young readers describe reactions of two children when their Mama becomes ill and their Daddy says she will soon go to heaven to live with God and the angels. Mama will be gone forever, but she will always love her children. Remembering her love and talking about feelings with Daddy can help.

Corley, E. A. (1973). *Tell Me about Death, Tell Me about Funerals*. Santa Clara, CA: Grammatical Sciences. A young girl and her father talk about her grandfather's recent death. They avoid euphemisms while discussing guilt, abandonment, and choices about funerals, burial, cemeteries, and mausoleums. At one point, we are treated to a child's delightful misunderstanding about the "polarbears" who carry the casket.

Coutant, H. (1974). *First Snow*. New York: Knopf. A young girl who has come to America from Vietnam with her family is eager to experience snow for the first time, but puzzled to hear her parents say "Grandmother is dying." No one explains what it means to be dying until Liên is told to catch a snowflake on her finger. The snowflake is a tiny, fleeting thing, beautiful and delicate. When the sun causes the edges of the snowflake to burst into a thousand tiny rainbows, it changes to a drop of water and falls on the ground where it nourishes a tiny pine tree. This affirms Liên's Buddhist beliefs that life and death are but two parts of the same thing.

Dickerson, J. G. (1995). *Grandpa's Berries: A Story to Help Children Understand Grief and Loss.* Johnstown, PA: Cherubic Press. During a visit with her grandparents, Alice notices a single, orange-gold berry on a golden raspberry bush that Grandma says had never done well. The berry tastes wonderful, and Grandpa says she can have the bush all for her own. Later, after Grandpa's death, Alice finds the little bush is also dead. As they share their grief, Alice's mother reminds her that she will never forget the special taste of those berries even though now they are gone. The same will be true for Grandpa: "The remembering will become easier until one day you'll notice that all that's left is the sweetness that you remember. Just like the berries."

DiSunno, R., Zimmerman, S., & Ruffin, P. (2004). *Jeremy Goes to Camp Good Grief.* Westhampton Beach, NY: East End Hospice (481 Westhampton-Riverhead Road, P.O. Box 1048, 11978; www.eeh.org). Jeremy takes part in a week-long, summer day camp for children who have experienced the death of someone they love. During the week, Jeremy learns to give words to his grief, and he begins to understand how the loss has changed his family. Along with his new friends, he comes to understand that he is not alone in his grief.

Donnelly, E. (1981). *So Long, Grandpa.* New York: Crown. At 10, Michael witnesses his grandfather's deterioration and eventual death from cancer. The story follows Michael's reactions to these events and shows how his grandfather had helped prepare him by taking him to an elderly friend's funeral.

Douglas, E. (1990). *Rachel and the Upside Down Heart.* Los Angeles: Price Stern Sloan. After Rachel's daddy died when she was 4 years old, she is sad and has to move from a house in Kentucky with a yard, green grass, and two dogs to a noisy apartment in New York City. Mommy says Daddy will always be in Rachel's heart, so she begins to draw hearts but can only make them upside down. Later, Rachel finds some new friends and some of her hearts are upside up. Finally, when a new friend's father dies, Rachel is able to talk to the new friend and help him with his loss.

Evarts, D. M. (1998). *The Butterfly Bush: A Story about Love.* Omaha, NE: Centering Corporation. Grandma gave Lindsay a pot of sticks for her birthday. It was a butterfly bush they planted together. But nothing happened and Lindsay soon forgot the bush. Each year after that, Grandma gave Lindsay beautiful, expensive gifts for her birthday.

Lindsay always thanked Grandma for these gifts but then would run off to open other presents or be with her friends while Grandma went out to visit the butterfly bush. One year, Grandma died before Lindsay's birthday, but not before mailing her a small package. It contains a lovely locket with two pictures inside: one of Grandma holding Lindsay as a small child, the other of a mass of beautiful purple flowers. Lindsay runs out to the woods where she finds the butterfly bush is now more than 15 feet tall and covered all over with beautiful flowers and butterflies. Years later, Grandma Lindsay gives her granddaughter a pot of sticks on her birthday.

Evenson, I. (1999). *Serafina's Silver Web.* Richmond, VA: Noah's Children, Inc. (6954 Forest Hill Avenue, 23225; 804-327-8417; www.noahschildren.org). A dying boy develops a special relationship with a spider who takes him on many magical adventures, including a trip around the world. When Peter tells Serafina he is frightened of death, she says he need not be because "death is a journey. There is nothing for you to be afraid of. . . . You simply leave your body behind and continue your life without it" (p. 30). One day, Serafina tells Peter, "My time here on earth is up. I have fulfilled my purpose and must now return to where I came from" (p. 33). She leaves her old body behind and departs Peter's world, but soon they are reunited as spirits on a new journey.

Farrington, L. & Weil, J. C. (1993). *And Peter Said Goodbye.* Woodside, CA: Enchanté Publishing (P.O. Box 620471, 94062; 800-473-2363). After his Grandpa moves to California and is killed in a car accident, Peter is left behind in the care of a neighbor while his parents go to the funeral. Only a magical character, Mrs. Murgatroyd, seems to understand. Through Mrs. Murgatroyd's enchanted paints, Peter visits the funeral in a dream and finds within himself ways to accept the death and say goodbye.

Ferguson, D. (1992). *A Bunch of Balloons.* Omaha, NE: Centering Corporation. This book begins as a story about a child who loves to play with balloons. One day when the string slips out of his hand, the child loses his balloon. Then the book shifts to the reader, who may also have lost someone or something. Many different grief reactions that the reader may be experiencing are described and two pages offer blank balloons within which to write or draw what has been lost and what is still left.

Goble, P. (1993). *Beyond the Ridge.* New York: Aladdin/ Simon & Schuster. At her death, while her family members prepare her body according to their custom, an elderly Plains Indian woman experiences the afterlife believed in by her people. She makes the long climb up a difficult slope to see the Spirit World beyond the ridge.

Godfrey, J. (1996). *The Cherry Blossom Tree: A Grandfather Talks about Life and Death.* Minneapolis: Augsburg Fortress. A cherry tree planted by Grandpa and 5-year-old Harriet is covered with pink blossoms each year on his birthday. After the tree falls, Grandpa says, "It was very, very old, and time for it to die." He adds, "Everything that is born has to die sometime. . . . And that makes us sad. But death is a new beginning, like waking up after a long sleep." He says that everyone who loves God can go and be with him when they die in a new and different place called heaven.

Goldman, L. (1997). *Bart Speaks Out: An Interactive Storybook for Young Children about Suicide.* Los Angeles: Western Psychological Services. Provides words for children to use to discuss the sensitive topic of suicide.

Goldman, L. (2006). *Children Also Grieve: Talking about Death and Healing.* Philadelphia, PA: Jessica Kingsley Publishers. This book combines a story told by a dog named Henry and his questions to readers, a section for making a memory book, a glossary of grief words, and advice for caring adults. Henry's story uses photographs and text to tell about the sadness that follows Grandfather's death. He explains what death means, what grief is like, things to do when you are sad or scared, and ways to feel a bit better, while offering blank spaces for readers to respond to questions.

Graeber, C. (1982). *Mustard.* New York: Macmillan. An elderly cat with a heart condition must avoid stress. But one day Mustard runs outside and gets into a fight with another animal, leading to a heart attack and his death. After Father buries the cat, Alex donates Mustard's dishes and some money to the animal shelter. Because he is preoccupied with sadness, Alex declines (for now) a well-meaning offer of a new pet.

Grollman, E., & Johnson, J. (2006). *A Complete Book about Death for Kids.* Omaha, NE: Centering Corporation. The three main parts of this book address death and feelings, funerals and cemeteries, and cremation, respectively. Most pages have two photos and a few simple sentences directed to child readers and adults who might interact with those children. The authors are well-known experts in this field who are sensitive to the needs of children and insightful in how to address those needs.

Hanks, B. H. (1996). *Green Mittens from Grandma: A Gentle Story about a Child's Grief.* Omaha, NE: Centering Corporation. While Grandma makes green mittens for a young girl, she talks about when she was a little girl and the girl's mother was small. After Grandma dies, people come to the house and there is a funeral. The girl misses her Grandma, recalls things she had said and done, and holds tight to her green mittens. She knows memories of Grandma and the mittens will stay with her always.

Hanson, R. (2005). *A Season for Mangoes.* New York: Clarion. In Jamaica, Sareen is concerned about participating in her first sit-up, a ritual in which villagers share food and tell stories to celebrate the life of her recently deceased grandmother. Sharing stories about Nana's passion for mangoes helps ease Sareen's sadness.

Heegaard, M. E. (2001). *Saying Goodbye to Your Pet: Children Can Learn to Cope with Grief.* Minneapolis: Fairview Press. This activity book has checklists and pages on which to draw or color, to help 5- to 12-year-old children learn to express their feelings and cope with the loss or death of a pet.

Hemery, K. M. (2001). *The Healing Tree.* Omaha, NE: Centering Corporation. One day Baba Marta tells Sammy a story about the oak tree in her backyard with a long bare strip on its trunk where there is no bark. Baba says that when she was a little girl her mamma became very sick and died. Baba just wanted to be alone, so she went to the swing under the tree where she had shared many good times with her mother. When a storm came up, Baba didn't want to leave that special place. Her Papa rushed out, grabbed Baba, and ran to the porch with her just before lightning struck the tree and tore off one of its massive branches. The next day, Papa explained that they were all just like the tree: in pain from losing a big part of their family. Like the tree, he said, we will heal and go on living, but life will be different and forever changed. After telling her story, Baba explains to Sammy that her Papa was right; she did go on to enjoy love, laughter, and a good life.

Hewett, J. (1987). *Rosalie.* New York: Lothrop, Lee & Shepard. Rosalie is an aging dog who enjoys an important role in the life of a child. When Rosalie was 16 years old, Cindy's veterinarian told her that Rosalie would be nearly 100 years old if she was a person! Now, Rosalie is in poor health, deaf, and less active than she used to be, but Cindy and her friends enjoy visiting and playing with Rosalie. They love and care for Rosalie even as she still gives love to Cindy and all around her.

Holmes, M. M. (1999). *Molly's Mom Died* and *Sam's Dad Died*. Omaha, NE: Centering Corporation. Each of these two books contains just a dozen pages in which Molly and Sam each tell about how things are different after a parent has died, how they feel now, and what they can do to feel better.

Hopkinson, D. (2001). *Bluebird Summer*. New York: Greenwillow Books/HarperCollins. Every summer, Meg and her little brother Cody visit Grandpa's farm. Now that Grandma has died, they all miss her and have much to mourn. One thing they specially miss is her wonderful garden of flowers and vegetables, as well as the bluebirds that used to visit regularly to enjoy their favorite plants. Then the children decide to replace the weeds and grass that have sprung up with a new garden in memory of Grandma. Above all, they will install a new birdhouse to encourage the bluebirds to return.

Hucek, M.W. (2002). *Lilacs for Grandma*. Omaha, NE: Centering Corporation. Megan has a special hiding place under an old lilac bush in her grandmother's yard. Both Grandmother (when she was a child) and Megan enjoyed that special place. But when Grandmother tells Megan she is very sick and getting ready to die, she asks Megan to bring her a bouquet each morning when the lilacs bloom and promises to enjoy them even when she is no longer able to talk. After Grandmother dies, Megan brings a bouquet of lilacs to grave as "a kiss for you Grandma, to send you on your way" (p. 20).

Johnson, J. (1998). *Remember Rafferty: A Book about the Death of a Pet . . . for Children of All Ages* (Rev. ed.). Omaha, NE: Centering Corporation. Rafferty is a sheepdog who becomes ill and has to be euthanized. A neighbor, Miss Bertie, who lives with Rafferty's friend, a cat named Four-Eyes, helps by sharing stories of the deaths of other pets and validating the importance of such losses. Mom also encourages the child to make a book about memories of Rafferty. The moral: pet loss is important to children and they need to mourn such losses. The book also contains two pages of suggestions for adults and eight pages for a memorial scrapbook.

Johnson, J. (2001). *The Very Beautiful Dragon*. Omaha, NE: Centering Corporation. Two young boys are scared when they first encounter a dragon; they become even more frightened when they see it again on other occasions. It isn't enough for them to be shown there actually is no dragon present. What really helps is a neighbor who teaches the boys to confront their fears and get to know what scares them. That's the way to face down one's dragons and recognize one's own strengths and power. The *Beautiful Dragons and Other Fears Workbook* accompanies this title.

Johnson, J., & Johnson, M. (2001). *Tell Me, Papa: A Gentle Explanation for Children about Death and the Funeral* (Rev. ed.). Omaha, NE: Centering Corporation. A discussion between children and a grandparent leads to explanations of death, funerals, and saying goodbye.

Kadono, E. (1999). *Grandpa's Soup*. Grand Rapids, MI: Eerdmans. After his wife's death, an old man finds that making her meatball soup and sharing it with friends eases his loneliness. While singing the song his wife used to guide her soup making, the old man gradually adds more ingredients as he progresses from smaller to larger pots and better and better tasting soup to share with his newfound friends (three mice, a cat, a dog, and some children).

Keough, P. (2001). *Remembering Our Baby: A Workbook for Children Whose Brother or Sister Dies before Birth*. Omaha, NE: Centering Corporation. This workbook is for young children whose brother or sister dies before birth. It includes pages designed to encourage writing and drawing to help share thoughts and feelings. The book starts with finding out about the new baby who is to join the family and then learning about the death. Also included are questions about these events and suggestions of things to do to remember the baby.

Klein, L. (1995). *The Best Gift for Mom*. New York: Paulist Press. Jonathan doesn't remember his dad who died when he was a baby. So Jonathan is uncomfortable when his classmates talk about both of their parents and he can only mention his hardworking Mom. After Mom tells him lots of stories about his Dad, including the only two songs Dad knew to sing when he put Jonathan to bed ("Taps" and "Silent Night"), Jonathan joins a glee club at school and plans a special gift for Mom. At the Christmas concert, Jonathan sings a solo rendition of "Silent Night" as a surprise present for Mom and then writes a letter to his father.

Krementz, J. (1981; republished by Knopf, 2004) *How It Feels When a Parent Dies* and (1989; paperback by Simon & Schuster, 1991) *How It Feels to Fight for Your Life*. Boston: Little, Brown. Short essays by children and adolescents (7–16 years old) describe their individual reactions to life-threatening illnesses and/or the death of a parent. A photograph of its author accompanies each essay.

Krisher, T. (1992). *Kathy's Hats: A Story of Hope*. Morton Grove, IL: Albert Whitman. Kathy loved hats. She had a woolen hat as an infant, a sun bonnet, a velvet hat with a veil for dress-up, a straw boater for Easter, and so on. But after being diagnosed with cancer and her hair falls out, she is upset at having to wear a stupid hat. Her mother tells Kathy to put on her "thinking cap": "My mother said that the most important thing about a person is the way she thinks about things." So Kathy attaches pins to her cap, and one day her whole class wears caps to school to celebrate because the doctors told Kathy the cancer had gone away.

Landalf, H. (2000). *Getting Used to Candy*. Omaha, NE: Centering Corporation. A year after her mother died, a girl still resents it when her father buys a new car (called "Candy" because it is red and shiny like the candy apples you get on Halloween) and begins to date a new girlfriend. But with time, tears, laughter, and hugs, they share sadness and loneliness, and the girl begins to get used to Candy.

Lee, V. (1972). *The Magic Moth*. New York: Seabury. Maryanne, 5-year-old Mark-O's 10-year-old sister, dies as a result of an incurable heart disease. Mark-O is helped to make sense of this experience by the metaphor of a moth as it experiences a transition from one mode of life to another.

Lowden, S. G. (1993). *Emily's Sadhappy Season*. Omaha, NE: Centering Corporation. Before he died, Emily's Daddy helped her become a good baseball player. After he died Emily and Mom are alone. Emily's grief is confusing and complex. She is afraid that playing baseball might have caused Daddy's death, and she worries that now Mom might die. In time, Mom encourages Emily to teach her to play baseball. Mom says they will feel "sadhappy": happy remembering the fun times they had with Daddy, but sad because he is not with them.

Maple, M. (1992). *On the Wings of a Butterfly: A Story about Life and Death*. Seattle: Parenting Press. Lisa, a child dying of cancer, and Sonya, her caterpillar friend, share insights and experiences as Lisa approaches her death and Sonya prepares for her transformation into a Monarch butterfly.

Marshall, B. (1998). *Animal Crackers: A Tender Book about Death and Funerals and Love*. Omaha, NE: Centering Corporation. Nanny would hide animal crackers in her house for her grandchildren. After Nanny becomes forgetful, she goes to live in a nursing home and eventually dies. But the children have fond memories of sharing good times with Nanny and of her "Nanny crackers."

McLaughlin, K. (2001). *The Memory Box*. Omaha, NE: Centering Corporation. A young boy is mad at Grandpa for dying when he had promised to take the boy fishing. Mommy agrees the boy will miss doing some things with Grandpa, but she tells him to hold onto his good memories of all they shared. Making a memory box and putting special objects into it help the boy continue this special relationship.

McNamara, J. W. (1994). *My Mom Is Dying: A Child's Diary*. Minneapolis, MN: Augsburg Fortress. An illustrated diary format offers an imaginary record of Kristine's conversations with God while her mother is dying. Author's notes identify Kristine's reactions and suggest how they could become a basis for talking with children.

Miles, M. (1971). *Annie and the Old One*. Boston: Little, Brown. A 10-year-old Navajo girl is told it will be time for her grandmother "to go to Mother Earth" when her mother finishes weaving a rug. Annie secretly tries to unravel and delay the weaving, until the adults realize what is going on. Her grandmother explains that we are all part of a natural cycle. When Annie realizes she cannot hold back time, she is ready herself to learn to weave.

Miller, M. (1987). *My Grandmother's Cookie Jar*. Los Angeles: Price Stern Sloan. Grandma has a special cookie jar shaped like an Indian head. The jar is a little scary to her granddaughter, but not when Grandma removes its headdress and takes out a cookie. As they share cookies each evening, Grandma tells stories of Indian people of long ago. The stories make Indian ways, pride, and honor come alive for the little girl. After Grandma dies, Grandfather gives the jar to the girl and tells her it is full of Grandma's love and her Indian spirit heritage. Some day, he says, the girl will have her own children and will put cookies in the jar. And the girl knows that when she tells Grandma's stories with each cookie, she will be keeping Grandma's spirit alive and the spirit of those who went before her.

Mills, J. C. (2004). *Gentle Willow: A Story for Children about Dying* (2nd ed.). Washington, DC: Magination Press. Amanda is a squirrel who becomes upset when she learns that her tree-friend, Gentle

Willow, is dying. The Tree Wizards explain that, while they can give Gentle Willow their love and some medicines to help her feel stronger and more comfortable, they cannot make her all better. Even so, they point out the many gifts that Gentle Willow has given to Amanda over the years—which are now memories in Amanda's mind. One day, Gentle Willow begins to cry and tells Amanda she is afraid to face this change. Amanda just listens, stays close, and tells Gentle Willow the comforting story of a caterpillar that changed into Yellow Butterfly.

Mills, L. (1991). *The Rag Coat*. Boston: Little, Brown. After Papa gets sick and dies, Minna can't start school; she has to stay home and help Mama make quilts to support the family. Later Minna wants to go to school but doesn't have a winter coat. She is elated when the "Quilting Mothers" make her a coat out of scraps of old materials and have it ready for Sharing Day. At first, the children tease her about her rag coat, but not after she explains the stories behind each scrap that she selected.

Morning, B. (1994). *Grandfather's Shirt*. Omaha, NE: Centering Corporation. Grandfather loves working in his garden and teaching his buddy, Peter, to help him. When Grandfather gets sick and goes to the hospital, Peter and his parents share special memories of Grandfather. After Grandfather's death, Dad tells Peter that the two of them "are the seeds Grandfather left behind when he died. Grandfather lives forever through us and our memory of him." Peter finds comfort in Grandfather's old baseball cap and especially in his musty old gardening shirt, which the boy wears as he tends the garden.

Napoli, D. J. (2002). *Flamingo Dream*. New York: Greenwillow Books. After her father gets sick and dies from cancer, a young girl draws on her memories of good times with him to make a book with words and pictures. Above all, she looks back on their trip to Florida and the pink flamingoes they saw there.

Newman, L. (1995). *Too Far Away to Touch*. New York: Clarion. Uncle Leonard is Zoe's favorite relative. He takes her to special places, tells her jokes, and makes her laugh; but now he is sick and has less energy (gradually, we learn that he has AIDS). When he takes Zoe to a planetarium one day, he explains that if he dies he will be like the stars, "too far away to touch, but close enough to see." Then the lesson is confirmed at the seashore as they again watch the night sky and witness a shooting star.

Old, W. (1995). *Stacy Had a Baby Sister*. Morton Grove, IL: Albert Whitman. Stacy liked her baby sister sometimes, but not always. The baby took up a lot of her parents' time and Stacy was jealous until one night she woke up to find that the baby died from SIDS. Stacy wonders if she caused the baby to die and if she will get SIDS. She also has trouble sleeping until she talks with her parents about it.

Olívíero, J. (1995). *Som See and the Magic Elephant*. New York: Hyperion Books for Children. This story of a little girl who helps her great-aunt prepare for death draws on an original Thai folktale. Som See seeks out a charm in the form of a great white elephant who brings good luck to all who touch his trunk. When the quest succeeds, Som See's great-aunt finds peace and is ready now for her journey.

Parker, M. B. (2002). *Jasper's Day*. New York & Toronto: Kids Can Press (2250 Military Road, Tonawanda, NY 14150; www.kidscanpress.com). On Jasper's day, Riley and his parents let their dog sleep late, feed him his favorite foods, take him for a ride, get him ice cream, and bring him to visit Grandma. But this isn't Jasper's birthday. He is stiff with arthritis, ill with cancer, and he sleeps a lot. This is the day for Jasper to go to the clinic before his pain pills wear off. There the veterinarian will give him a shot, and his death will be quick and gentle. Afterwards, the family buries Jasper's body in the backyard and Riley plans a memory book of Jasper's life.

Peavy, L. (1981). *Allison's Grandfather*. New York: Charles Scribners' Sons. While her friend Allison's grandfather is dying, Erica asks questions we might all ask: Is he ready to die? Would she be told if her own grandfather was dying? When Allison's grandfather does die, Erica's mother is able to be there and hold his hand, and then tell Erica about what it was like.

Pellegrino, M. W. (1999). *I Don't Have an Uncle Phil Anymore*. Washington, DC: Magination Press. Following the unexpected death of his uncle, a boy and his extended family attend the funeral while he thinks about what this will mean for all of them. In the end, he throws a sparkle blue ball up toward heaven and catches it as he used to do when he played with Uncle Phil.

Peterkin, A. (1992). *What about Me?* Washington, DC: Magination Press. Laura is two years older than her brother, Tom, and likes helping to care for him. As they grow older, they often play together and sometimes quarrel. One day Aunt Ann tells Laura that Tom is sick and in the hospital. Laura misses Tom, feels responsible for his illness, and worries that he might die. All too often, their parents and other adults seem to focus only on Tom, thereby ignoring Laura's needs. Finally, Laura's parents and the doctor explain Tom's illness to her, let them play together, and take her out for a special treat.

Pitzer, S. (2001). *Grandfather Hurant Lives Forever*. Omaha, NE: Centering Corporation. Grigor loves to spend time with his grandfather who teaches him about their Armenian history and how to weave a rug. Their warm relationship is disturbed when grandfather becomes sick and enters a hospital. When Grigor visits, grandfather says, "I will always be with you." But grandfather dies and Grigor feels betrayed, angry, and unable to cry. Not until Grigor returns to the rug shop does he realize that grandfather lives on in him and in this special place.

Plourde, L. (2003). *Thank You, Grandpa*. New York: Dutton Children's Books. Over the years, a girl and her grandfather enjoy walking in the woods together. They share discoveries of a bird, a bee sipping nectar, a sneaky snake, a squirrel waving his tail at them, a butterfly, and a mouse. One day they find a dead grasshopper and the girl asks, "What can we do?" Grandpa says: "We can say thank you and good-bye." In time, Grandpa becomes too old to walk and one day the girl finds herself walking alone. When she finds a dandelion, she says to herself: "Thank you, Grandpa, for our walks. You kept me steady when I wasn't so steady. You let me run ahead when I was ready to run ahead. Thank you for sharing spiderweb tears and firefly flashes. But most of all, thank you for teaching me the words I need to say. . . . Grandpa, I love you and I'll miss you. But I will never forget you. Thank you and good-bye."

Powell, E. S. (1990). *Geranium Morning*. Minneapolis, MN: CarolRhoda Books. Two children—Timothy, whose father died suddenly in an accident, and Frannie, whose mother is dying—struggle with strong feelings, memories, guilt ("if onlys"), and some unhelpful adult actions. In sharing their losses, the children help each other; Frannie's father and her mother (before she dies) are also helpful.

Rappaport, D. (1995). *The New King*. New York: Dial Books for Young Readers. Young Prince Rakoto commands court officials to bring his dead father back to life, but they cannot. Then a Wise Woman explains that when the earth was new God gave the first human couple a choice. God said, "One day you must die. When it is your turn, do you want to die like the moon or like a banana tree?" The moon starts out like a sliver, grows bigger and bigger until it is full, then gets smaller and smaller until at last it disappears, only later to begin to grow all over again. By contrast, the banana tree grows and sends forth shoots. When the tree finally dies, the shoots keep growing until they are big enough and strong enough to send out their own shoots. At first, the man wanted to die like the moon so as to come back to life and live forever, but the woman persuaded him that it would be better to live, love, and die, while one's children carry on—and thus to find a way of living forever by giving life to others. Appreciating his father's legacy, Prince Rakoto "ruled with love and justice as his father had taught him, and he passed his father's lessons on to his children."

Raschka, C. (2007). *The Purple Balloon*. New York: Schwartz & Wade (Random House). The author explains that children who draw their feelings when they become aware of their impending death often draw a blue or purple balloon, released and floating free. Here the balloon images first depict the death of an elderly person before turning to a dying youngster. The text says, "Good help makes leaving easier" and offers suggestions for those who want to help make dying not be so hard.

Reeder-Bey, V., & Wilburn, A. M. (2000). *My Grandma has AIDS: Annisha's Story*. La Jolla, CA: Agouron Pharmaceuticals. Forceful artwork and 14 pages of text tell a simple story about a young girl's grandma who has AIDS. Grandma does not look sick, she takes her medicines, and she does all of the things with Annisha that any loving grandmother would. Annisha knows that she "cannot get AIDS by loving my grandma or by doing any of the other things we do together" (p. 9), so she tells her friends to be nice and help people with AIDS.

Romain, T. (1999). *What on Earth Do You Do when Someone Dies?* Minneapolis: Free Spirit Publishing (217 Fifth Ave. North, Suite 200, 55401-1299; tel. 612-338-2068; www.freespirit.com). This little pocketbook poses questions about death and offers suggestions for constructive responses. The questions concern topics like feelings and other reactions to death, funeral and memorial rituals, cremation and burial, and saying goodbye. The suggestions encourage talking to someone you love and trust, taking care of your anger, keeping a journal, and finding ways to honor the person who died.

Roper, J. (2001). *Dancing on the Moon.* Cheverly, MD: SIDS Educational Services (2905 64th Avenue, 20785; 877-935-6839). Carly is 5 years old and jealous over all the attention paid to the new baby when he comes home. But when Nigel dies suddenly, everyone is sad and Carly wants very much to bring him back home. In her dream, she imagines flying to the moon to find Nigel. Even though Carly can't bring Nigel back with her, she realizes that he is inside her heart and they will never again be apart.

Rosen, M. (2004). *Michael Rosen's Sad Book.* Cambridge, MA: Candlewick Press. Michael Rosen pretends to be happy when he is sad "because I think people won't like me if I look sad." Michael is sad because his son, Eddie, died. Sometimes he wants to talk about this and sometimes not. Sometimes he does crazy things because life just isn't the same as it used to be. Michael knows that being sad isn't the same as being bad, so he tries to figure out ways of being sad that don't hurt so much. He also tries to do one thing each day that involves a good time—it can be anything so long as it doesn't make anyone else unhappy. Memories of Eddie and good times seem to help. Bright illustrations illuminate a spare, achingly honest text.

Russo, M. (1996). *Grandpa Abe.* New York: Greenwillow Books. Soon after Sarah's first birthday, her grandmother marries Abe and she gets a new grandfather. Then Sarah and Abe share many happy times together until Abe dies when she is 9 years old. Sarah knows Abe enriched her life in many ways.

Sanford, D. (1985). *It Must Hurt a Lot: A Book about Death and Learning and Growing.* Milwaukie, OR: Multnomah Press. After Joshua's dog Muffin is hit by a car and dies, he is very angry and hurts a lot. He doesn't want another puppy; he wants Muffin! And he doesn't understand why his friend acts funny when he comes over to play the next day and never once mentions Muffin, or why his brother yells at him when he cries. Joshua hurts for many weeks, crying himself to sleep each night and feeling more alone than he ever felt in his life. But gradually Joshua finds that he is experiencing some big internal changes that lead him to discover six special secrets—insights that comfort him and could help others.

Santucci, B. (2002). *Anna's Corn.* Grand Rapids, MI: Eerdmans. Grandpa taught Anna to hear the music of the wind breathing through the dry corn stalks, and he gave her a few kernels of corn to keep for her own. After his death, Anna is reluctant to keep her promise to Grandpa to plant her seeds next spring because she fears they will then be gone forever. Mama explains that the seeds won't be gone; they'll just be different. One day in fall, after Anna plants the seeds and the corn has grown, Anna once again hears the song that she had shared with Grandpa, and she takes some new seeds to plant next spring.

Schwiebert, P., & DeKlyen, C. (1999). *Tear Soup: A Recipe for Healing after Loss.* Portland, OR: Grief Watch (2116 NE 18th Avenue, 97212; 503-284-7426; www.tearsoup.com). See Personal Insights 10.2 in Chapter 10.

Scrivani, M. (1994/1996). *I Heard Your Mommy Died* and *I Heard Your Daddy Died.* Omaha, NE: Centering Corporation. These two slim booklets offer an empathic approach to a child whose parent has died. The child's feelings and needs are recognized and affirmed. Suggestions are offered for expressing strong feelings in constructive ways and for things a child can do for self help. Permission is given to go on with living and loving, even while the child remembers the deceased parent.

Shreve, S. (1979). *Family Secrets: Five Very Important Stories.* New York: Knopf. Five stories involve the death of a family dog, divorce, a neighbor boy who hanged himself, an aging grandmother, and cheating at school. The stories are short, about 10–11 pages in length; each is illustrated with two pencil sketches. In each story, the concerns and reactions to the events described by the narrator, a young boy named Sammy, are typical of a child his age and would form a good basis for discussion between adults and children.

Simon, N. (1979). *We Remember Philip.* Chicago: Whitman. When the adult son of an elementary school teacher dies in a mountain climbing accident, Sam and other members of his class observe how Mr. Hall is affected by his grief. In time, the children persuade Mr. Hall to share with them a scrapbook and other memories of his son, and they plant a tree as a class memorial.

Simon, N. (1986). *The Saddest Time.* Morton Grove, IL: Albert Whitman. This book describes three moving situations: (1) Michael faces the death of his Uncle Joe who has been sick for some time; (2) the children at Fleetwood School cope with the death of Teddy Baker, who was hit by a car and killed as he rode his bicycle; and (3) Emily confronts the death of her Grandma in the hospital. In each case, the children are confused, sad, frightened, and angry, even as they are comforted by good memories, receive support from those around them, and seek out constructive things to do.

Stillwell, E. (1998). *Sweet Memories*. Omaha, NE: Centering Corporation. Here are a dozen different, hands-on, craft activities through which children can preserve memories of loved ones who have died.

Stolz, M. (1991). *King Emmett the Second*. New York: Greenwillow. Emmett is a boy who lives in an apartment in New York City, has a collection of images of pigs and objects shaped like pigs, and has his very own live pig (King Emmett) who lives upstate on a farm. One day, Emmett's parents tell him they are moving to a house in a small town in Ohio, and they admit that his pig has been slaughtered. Emmett is angry about both of these events. He is sure he will never like Ohio or anything else about the new home, and he will not want a new pet. But gradually he adapts, makes friends, and ultimately agrees to accept a pet from the animal shelter. The new dog is named King, but officially he will be called King Emmett the Second.

Tamberrino, S. S. (2001). *Grunt*. Omaha, NE: Centering Corporation. Grunt is an old dog, now blind, in pain, and sick with cancer and arthritis. A boy and his Dad agree it will be best for Grunt to be euthanized. Still, it isn't easy to carry out that decision, to take Grunt in the car to the veterinarian's office and hold him on the table while the shot takes effect. They bury Grunt in a box in the back yard under a big oak tree and then just sit together for a long while as they talk about happy times with Grunt and warm memories of a good dog.

Temes, R. (1992). *The Empty Place: A Child's Guide through Grief*. Far Hills, NJ: New Horizon Press (P.O. Box 669, 07931). Both text and drawings in this book reflect the emptiness and other reactions a 9-year-old boy feels in his life and in his heart after his big sister dies. Sharing his grief with his babysitter helps because one of her brothers had also died much earlier. Betsy is a good role model for the boy, and she gives him permission to do many things he needs to do to cope with his loss.

Tiffault, B. W. (1992). *A Quilt for Elizabeth*. Omaha, NE: Centering Corporation. When Elizabeth was 8 years old, her Daddy got sick and died. Elizabeth got angrier and angrier. One day, Grandma suggests that together they sew a patchwork quilt out of swatches of material from their old clothes. Each square of fabric has a story to tell and memories to recall as it binds the quilt and their lives together.

Traisman, E. S. (1994). *A Child Remembers*. Omaha, NE: Centering Corporation. This is a "write-in memory book for bereaved children," a resource that permits its owner to describe a special person who died and their relationship. Issues mentioned include getting the news, the funeral or memorial service, going back to school, coping with feelings, addressing unfinished business, and ways to honor the life of the person who died.

Trunz, D. M. (2004). *Laughter in the Wind*. Lakewood, CO: Cheerful Cherub (www.cheerfulcherub.com). This book follows a caterpillar named Bernadette through her metamorphoses into a butterfly. Coping with these changes helps Bernadette face death. In each case, as her physical form changes, her soul remains unchanged.

Turner, B. J. (1996). *A Little Bit of Rob*. Morton Grove, IL: Albert Whitman. After the death of her big brother, Lena and her parents are unable to mention his name as they try to be strong and avoid crying. Several weeks later, they take their boat out crabbing again in an effort to resume some of the activities they shared with Rob. In doing so and by sharing his old sweatshirt, they are finally able to speak about Rob and to realize they will always have their memories of him to comfort them.

Vajentic, A., & Neuer, N. V. (1993). *Remembering: Explaining Organ and Tissue Donation; Loss, Grief and Hope*. Cleveland, OH: Academy Graphic Communication (1000 Brookpark Rd., 44109-5824). In two parts, this booklet offers a basic explanation of organ and tissue donation, together with some comments on loss and grief.

Vigna, J. (1991). *Saying Goodbye to Daddy*. Morton Grove, IL: Albert Whitman. Clare is scared, lonely, and angry after her father is killed in a car accident. Her mother and grandparents help her recall Sam, the hamster who died, cope with her grief, get through the funeral, and recollect good memories.

Vogel, R. H. (2002). *The Snowman* (Rev. ed.). Omaha, NE: Centering Corporation. Two brothers are building their first snowman since their Dad died. Talking about their father's illness and how he died helps answer some of 8-year-old Buddy's questions. It also lets 12-year-old Tommy release some of his internal anger and guilt. Using Dad's old pipe, hat, and favorite scarf, the two boys finish the snowman and share good memories of Dad.

Wallace-Brodeur, R. (1995). *Goodbye, Mitch*. Morton Grove, IL: Albert Whitman. When Michael's cat, Mitch, stops eating, his Mom says the veterinarian believes Mitch has an inoperable tumor. They agree to try to keep Mitch comfortable and let him find his own way. It isn't easy for Michael, but being with Mitch, crying, and finally just holding him in a blanket when he dies somehow feels good, too.

Weigelt, U. (2003). *Bear's Last Journey*. New York: North-South Books. All the forest animals are concerned when they learn that Bear is sick. Bear explains he will have to say good-bye to each of his friends because he is dying. He adds that no one really knows what it means to be dead; some say one simply sleeps, while Bear and others believe that one goes to heaven. The little fox is frustrated: he wants to know now what will happen, and he is angry when Bear dies. Sharing memories of Bear and some of his things helps the little fox and other animals.

Wood, R. (2004). *Now Caitlin Can: A Donated Organ Helps a Child Get Well*. El Dorado, AR: Abc Press (rwood@seark.net). Freddie's little sister was born with kidney problems. When Caitlin was old enough and had gained enough weight, she was able to receive a transplanted kidney. That changed Caitlin's life and made it possible for her to do many things that she had previously been unable to do.

Wood, S. (1998). *Mama Mockingbird*. Omaha, NE: Centering Corporation. When one of her sons dies, Mama Mockingbird is so grief stricken that she loses her beautiful singing voice. On her journey to find her song again, she seeks help from an owl, a fish, and an eagle. Ultimately, the eagle draws on his own encounters with loss to teach her to trust life and honor its cycles.

Wrenn, E. (2001). *The Christmas Cactus*. Omaha, NE: Centering Corporation. As Christmas nears, Nana is in the hospital and Megan cannot feel joy. When they prepare to visit, Megan asks her father if Nana is dying. He says, "We never know for sure when someone will die. . . .So what we need to do is tell the people we love just how much we love them, every chance we get." As a present for Nana, Megan brings a Christmas cactus, and Nana explains that a Christmas cactus waits all year for the one season when it blooms. "Well, I think our lives are like that. We live and grow for a whole lifetime. And then, at the end of our lives, we bloom. We become something very different and wonderful." So Nana asks Megan to take care of the plant and when it blooms to think of her. She did and that made Christmas good.

Zebrowski, M. (2002). *Babka's Serenade*. Omaha, NE: Centering Corporation. Babka shared magical stories with her granddaughter (Pipchin) in her garden, stories that Babka had told Mama when she was a girl. After Babka dies, the girl cannot imagine not seeing her anymore, and it is hard when Mama and Daddy sell her house. In spring, the girl decides to build Babka's garden in their backyard. Her parents help, so the girl can visit that special place any time she wishes. There she smells the flowers and thinks of Babka and her stories.

Zotovich, K. D. (2000). *Good Grief for Kids: A Journal to Help Children Cope with Their Grief during Times of Loss*. Los Osos, CA: Journal Keepers (P.O. Box 6173, 93412; www.journalkeepers.com). This activity book provides a lengthy section intended to help children 6–12 years of age write, color, and draw about losses they have experienced, as well as a dozen pages for adults offering guidelines and resources for helping.

Selected Literature for Adolescents: Annotated Descriptions

Literature for Middle School Readers

Adler, C. S. (1990). *Ghost Brother*. New York: Houghton Mifflin. After his older brother and father both die in a car accident, Wally desperately wants to live up to his brother's memory. Whenever Wally needs extra support or brotherly advice, his ghost brother appears to give it to him. As summer ends, Wally enters a skateboarding contest in his brother's memory, and it helps him get back on his feet.

Adler, C. S. (1993). *Daddy's Climbing Tree*. New York: Clarion. Shortly after her cat is accidentally killed and the family moves from their former home (the one Daddy inherited and the only home 11-year-old Jessica had ever known), Daddy dies in a road accident. Jessica refuses to believe that her father is really dead, but there is nowhere to turn to avoid all the people and their expressions of sympathy. So she takes her 6-year-old brother, Tycho, and sets out to walk through the state park to their old home where she imagines Daddy must be hiding in his favorite climbing tree. The journey is difficult, but when she is high up in the tree she finally accepts that Daddy is dead and Mom does love her.

Aiken, S. (2001). *Anna's Scrapbook: Journal of a Sister's Love*. Omaha, NE: Centering Corporation. When Anna was 8 years old, her baby sister, Amelia, was born. Anna loved Amelia and they shared many good times together. But one day, when she was a preschooler, Amelia had an accidental fall and died. Anna's grief was profound, as was the grief of the adults in her family. After the funeral, Anna kept a diary, which fills most of the remainder of this book. In the diary, Anna writes about her grief and then describes a scrapbook of memories and photos of Amelia. Blank pages at the end of the book allow readers to make their own similar scrapbooks.

Armstrong, W. (1969). *Sounder*. New York: Harper & Row (reprinted in paperback in 1972 & 2005). Only the dog has a proper name in this tale of an African-American sharecropper family in the late 19th century. After the father is arrested for stealing a ham to feed his family, their coon hound is shot and disappears. Angry and grieving, the oldest son searches relentlessly for the dog and then for his father, who is in a prison labor camp. The boy grows, takes on the farm work, and is taught to read by a white teacher. Eventually, the dog returns (but is too injured to hunt); later the father comes back (hurt by an explosion in a prison quarry), only to die soon after. This is a story of a harsh life in hard times for people "born to lose," as the devout mother says.

Arrick, F. (1980). *Tunnel Vision*. Scarsdale, NY: Bradbury. After Anthony hangs himself at 15, his family, friends, and teacher feel bewildered and guilty. There is no easy resolution for such feelings, but important questions are posed: What should be done in the face of serious problems? Where should one turn for help?

Bernstein, J. E. (1977). *Loss: And How to Cope with It*. New York: Clarion. This book provides wise advice for young readers about how to cope with loss. Topics include: what happens when someone dies; children's concepts of death; feelings in bereavement; living with survivors; handling feelings; specific types of deaths (e.g., parents, grandparents, friends, pets); traumatic deaths (suicide or murder); and legacies for survivors.

Blume, J. (1981). *Tiger Eyes*. Scarsdale, NY: Bradbury. After her 34-year-old father is killed during a holdup of his 7-Eleven store in Atlantic City, Davey (age 15), her mother, and her younger brother all react differently and are unable to help each other in their grief. They relocate to live temporarily with Davey's aunt in Los Alamos but eventually decide to move back to New Jersey to rebuild their lives.

Boulden, J., & Boulden, J. (1994). *The Last Goodbye I.* Weaverville, CA: Boulden Publishing (P.O. Box 1186, 96093-1186). This activity book offers exercises designed for children at about grade levels five through eight to process feelings and issues that surround death. It is also available in a Spanish version.

Brisson, P. (1999). *Sky Memories.* New York: Delacorte. While her mother struggles with cancer and before she dies, Emily (age 10) and Mom develop a ritual to celebrate and commemorate their relationship. Together they gather "sky memories," mental pictures of the ever-changing sky in all its variety and wonder. The sky seems to reflect the phases of Mom's illness and the vitality of her soul.

Buck, P. S. (1948). *The Big Wave.* New York: Scholastic. After a tidal wave kills his family and all the fishing people on the shore, Jiya chooses to live with his friend Kino's poor family instead of being adopted by a rich man. Years later, Jiya marries Kino's sister and decides to move back to the seaside with his new bride. Loss is universal and inevitable, but life is stronger than death.

Calvert, P. (1994). *Writing to Richie.* New York: Charles Scribner's Sons. David and his brother, Richie, live with foster parents, the best ones they have had yet. Unfortunately, Richie has bad food allergies and dies from a reaction to a food additive. Worse yet, the foster parents now accept a new child to take Richie's place. However, this "tomboy" girl ultimately helps David cope with his brother's death.

Cleaver, V., & Cleaver, B. (1970). *Grover.* Philadelphia: Lippincott. When Grover was 11, his mother became terminally ill and took her own life to "spare" herself and her family the ravages of her illness. His father cannot face the facts of this death or the depth of his grief; he tries to hold his feelings inside and convince his son it was an accident. Issues posed include whether one must endure life no matter what suffering it holds; whether religion is a comfort; and how one should deal with grief.

Coburn, J. B. (1964). *Annie and the Sand Dobbies: A Story about Death for Children and Their Parents.* New York: Seabury Press. When young Danny encounters the deaths of both his toddler sister from a respiratory infection and his dog after it runs away from home and is found frozen to death, a neighbor uses imaginary characters to suggest that the deceased are safe with God.

Crawford, B. B., & Lazar, L. (1999). *In My World: A Journal for Young People Facing Life-Threatening Illness.* Omaha, NE: Centering Corporation. This journal format is designed to help teenagers who are coping with a life-threatening illness make a record of their lives and give expression to thoughts, feelings, and worries that they may find difficult to share with family members and friends.

Deedy, C. A. (1995). *The Last Dance.* Atlanta, GA: Peachtree. Ninny and Bessie are close friends from childhood, extending throughout their lives together and even after Ninny's death. As children, they would sneak out at night to visit the graveyard where Ninny's grandparents were buried. Before his death, they used to visit the graveyard with Ninny's grandfather, Oppa, who taught them to tell stories, sing, and dance. Oppa said, "Those we love are never really gone as long as their stories are told." After Oppa's death, Ninny and Bessie pledge to each other that when one dies, the other will come to the graveyard and dance. Thus, they shared a rich life and their love endured even after death.

Dragonwagon, C. (1990). *Winter Holding Spring.* New York: Atheneum/Simon & Schuster. At first, nothing is the same for 11-year-old Sarah and her father after her mother dies. Each is in great pain, but gradually they begin to share their experiences and their memories of Sarah's mother. Eventually, they realize together that "nothing just ends without beginning the next thing at the same time" (p. 11). Each season somehow contains its successor; life and love and grief can continue together, for winter always holds spring. And Sarah knows that "love is alive in me and always will be" (p. 31).

Farley, C. (1975). *The Garden Is Doing Fine.* New York: Atheneum. While dying of cancer, Corrie's father inquires about his beloved garden. Corrie can't tell him the garden is dead nor can she lie. Instead, she searches for reasons to explain why a good person like her father would die. She also tries to bargain with herself and with God to preserve her father's life. A wise neighbor helps Corrie see that even though there may be no reasons for her father's death, she and her brothers are her father's real garden. The seeds that he has planted in them will live on, and she can let go without betraying him.

Fox, P. (1995). *The Eagle Kite.* New York: Orchard Books. Liam Cormac struggles to make sense of things when his father develops AIDS, moves out of their home, and eventually dies. Liam is confused, puzzled by the half-truths he is told, and unable to understand the different reactions of his mother and aunt. Eventually, Liam recalls a day when he was flying his eagle kite and came upon his father embracing another man. He realizes his father is gay and comes to terms with this by sharing it with his father and later telling his mother what he had seen.

Frank, A. (1993). *The Diary of a Young Girl.* New York: Bantam. A young girl's classic record of her thoughts about events when she and her family had to hide from the Nazis in Amsterdam during World War II because they were Jewish.

Fuqua, J. S. (2004). *The Willoughby Spit Wonder.* Cambridge, MA: Candlewick Press. It is 1953 in Norfolk, Virginia. The Korean War has just ended and Carter Johnston's father is dying. To inspire his father to fight to remain alive, Carter decides to emulate Prince Namor, the Sub-Mariner, a comic book superhero who can both fly in the air and breathe under water. Carter's goal is to swim from their home in Willoughby Spit, Virginia, across Hampton Roads. Carter makes desperate efforts to do the impossible and overcome the inevitable, even as his father tries to remain cheerful while his illness weakens him and tries to prepare his children for when he is gone.

Gignoux, J. H. (1998). *Some Folk Say: Stories of Life, Death, and Beyond.* New York: FoulkeTale Publishing. Here are 38 legends, retold in prose and poetry, used by different cultures to come to terms with the reality of death and hopes for life beyond the grave. The stories are grouped under five headings: origins of death; balancing life and death; lessons for life; after death; and reconciliation with death. Brief comments introduce each section and follow each story. The book also has eight dramatic illustrations. A treasury of global culture to stimulate the imagination; good for working with children.

Girard, L. W. (1991). *Alex, the Kid with AIDS.* Morton Grove, IL: Albert Whitman. Alex, the new kid in the fourth-grade class, is treated differently and left out of some activities because he has AIDS. As Michael comes to appreciate Alex's weird sense of humor, they become friends. Their teacher realizes that Alex needs to be treated as a member of the class, not as someone odd or special.

Greene, C. C. (1976). *Beat the Turtle Drum.* New York: Viking. This book describes 13-year-old Kate and 11-year-old Joss' warm, loving family. When Joss is abruptly and unexpectedly killed in a fall from a tree, the family is flooded with grief. Conveying

this sense of the many dimensions of bereavement is the book's strong point.

Heegaard, M. E. (1990). *Coping with Death and Grief.* Minneapolis, MN: Lerner Publications. This book describes change, loss, and death as natural parts of life, provides information and advice about coping with feelings, and suggests ways to help oneself and others who are grieving.

Hemery, I. M. (2005). *Sunflower Promise.* Omaha, NE: Centering Corporation. Willow and Davy are best friends in a small town in Ohio in 1948. One day, Davy accidentally tears the big, cloth sunflower off Willow's new hat. She is furious and refuses to play with Davy even though he promises to make it up to her some day. After Willow punches Davy on the arm, his bruises don't go away. He becomes tired and misses school. Willow worries when Davy gets sicker and goes to the hospital for testing. Will he never get better? Did she cause it? In the end, Davy dies, but not before arranging a surprise for Willow to fulfill his promise: a gorgeous crop of sunflowers in the field where they used to play.

Henkes, K. (1997). *Sun and Spoon.* New York: Greenwillow Books (Puffin, 1998). After his grandmother's death, 10-year-old "Spoon" Gilmore searches for something special of hers to keep. At grandfather's house, Spoon finds the deck of cards Gram used when they played triple solitaire, each card with a unique image of the sun. Without asking, Spoon takes the deck. A few days later, Spoon learns these cards are a source of solace to Pa, who thinks he misplaced them. In time, Spoon puts the cards back, and Pa takes their reappearance as a sign from Gram. When Spoon confesses he had taken them, Pa understands, gives Spoon the cards to keep, and shows him a drawing of her hand that Gram made when she was Spoon's age. On the drawing, she inscribed a large capital letter "M" and smaller lowercase letters "a-r-t-h-a" with the legend "M is always for Martha" (her name). Spoon then discovers that the lines on his palm also make a large "M," which he takes as a special sign from Gram.

Henkes, K. (2003). *Olive's Ocean.* New York: Harper Collins. After Olive Barstow's accidental death, her mother brings a page from her journal to 12-year-old Martha Boyle. Olive's three hopes puzzle Martha: to become a writer, to see a real ocean, and to become friends with Martha, "the nicest person in my whole entire class" (p. 5). Martha hardly knew Olive, but Martha also secretly wants to be a writer, and the next day her family is off to visit her grandmother who lives by the shore of the Atlantic Ocean. Martha spends her vacation thinking about many things: Olive, her aging grandmother (who calmly said, "Who knows, this might be our last summer together."), her relations with her parents and siblings, her plans to be a writer, and her emerging feelings for boys. Finally, she decides to bring a small jar of seawater—Olive's ocean—back to Olive's mother. That leads to a near-drowning experience (death can happen to anyone at any time). Back home Mrs. Barstow has moved away, so Martha says goodbye by writing Olive's name in water on the steps of her old house.

Hurd, E. T. (1980). *The Black Dog Who Went into the Woods*. New York: Harper & Row. One day, Benjamin, the youngest child, tells the others that Black Dog must have gone into the woods to die. The other children in the family and their parents don't believe Benjamin. They search all over for the dog even though they know she is deaf and can't hear them. Eventually, Benjamin says: "I don't think we should look for Black Dog anymore. . . . Black Dog doesn't want us to look for her" (p. 11). Father agrees: "Benjamin understands better than any of us. Animals sometimes do go into the woods, or someplace, by themselves when they know it is time for them to die" (p. 14). Later, each family member has a dream about an event shared with Black Dog, a dream in which they believe she came to say goodbye to each of them, but especially to Benjamin "because he could still talk to her" (p. 31).

Jukes, M. (1985). *Blackberries in the Dark*. New York: Dell Yearling. Everything seems so different when Austin comes to visit his Grandma on the farm after Grandpa died. In previous summers, Austin and his Grandpa would do things together, like go fishing or pick blackberries in the dark and eat them for dinner. This summer, Austin had looked forward to Grandpa teaching him to fly-fish. Still, when Grandma joins Austin at the stream, they help each other learn to fly-fish, pick blackberries together, and begin some new traditions of their own.

LeShan, E. (1976). *Learning to Say Good-by: When a Parent Dies*. New York: Macmillan. This book offers advice to bereaved children and the adults around them on a broad range of topics, including what grief is like; the importance of honesty, trust, sharing, and funerals; fear of abandonment and guilt; accepting the loss of the deceased; maintaining a capacity for love; and meeting future changes.

Little, J. (1984). *Mama's Going to Buy You a Mockingbird*. New York: Viking Kestrel. Jeremy and his younger sister, Sarah, only learn that their father is dying from cancer by overhearing people talk. They experience many losses, large and small, that accompany his dying and death, often made worse by lack of information and control over their situation. They clearly need support from others.

Mann, P. (1977). *There Are Two Kinds of Terrible*. New York: Doubleday/Avon. Robbie's broken arm is one kind of terrible—but it ends. His mother's death leaves Robbie and his "cold fish" father with no conclusion. They are together, but each grieves alone until they begin to find ways to share their suffering and their memories.

McCaleb, J. (1998). *Our Hero, Freebird: An Organ Donor's Story*. Chattanooga, TN: Tennessee Donor Services (651 E. 4th St., Suite 402, 37403; 423-756-5736). This spiral-bound book is a memorial to Chuck Foster, who died of an aneurysm and became an organ donor in 1996 just before he was to enter eighth grade. Words, pictures, and art from his classmates, along with letters from his transplant recipients and some of their family members, speak about Chuck and about organ donation.

Napoli, D. J. (2003). *The Bravest Thing*. New York: Scholastic (Dutton Children's Books, 1995). Ten-year-old Laurel loves animals. Even after her pet newt and a rabbit die, she struggles to get a new rabbit and arrange for her to breed. All but one baby rabbit from two litters dies, saved only because Laurel feeds it by hand. When the new rabbit is six months old and needs to be separated from his mother, Laurel gives him to her best friend. During all of these events, Laurel learns one day that Mom's long telephone calls with her sister are because Aunt Lizzie is being treated for bronchial cancer.

Park, B. (1995). *Mick Harte Was Here*. New York: Knopf (Random House Bullseye Books, 1996). This is Phoebe Harte's story about the death of her brother, Mick, killed when he was hit by a truck while riding his bicycle without a helmet. Phoebe had a bad argument with Mick that morning and later refused when he asked her to ride his bike home for him after school. Phoebe relates many memories from her relationship with Mick and describes her profound grief after his death. Phoebe and her parents are each alone in their grief. She wants very much to know where Mick is now; eventually she decides that if Mick is with God (as people keep saying) and God is everywhere, then Mick is everywhere, too. Mick's body is cremated, there is a memorial service with lots of funny stories about Mick, Phoebe speaks about bike safety at a school assembly, and she prints the following in the fresh concrete at the new soccer field bleachers: "M-I-C-K H-A-R-T-E W-A-S H-E-R-E."

Paterson, K. (1977). *Bridge to Terabithia*. New York: Crowell. Jess and Leslie have a special, secret meeting place in the woods, called Terabithia. When Leslie is killed one day in an accidental fall, the magic of their play and friendship is disrupted. Jess mourns the loss of this special relationship, is supported by his family, and ultimately is able to initiate new relationships that will share friendship in a similar way with others.

Potok, C. (1998). *ZEBRA and Other Stories*. New York: Knopf. Six stories by this renowned storyteller focus on youngsters facing grief, trauma, and change. Each story is named for its protagonist. "Zebra" (a nickname for Adam Martin Zebrin), who has an injured hand from a car accident, is positively influenced in many ways by an art teacher who lost an arm in Vietnam. "B.B." is a girl facing multiple issues—her little brother died, her Mom gives birth to a new brother, and her Dad has threatened to leave them because he cannot face the possibility of another ill/dying child. "Moon" has anger management problems but is touched by a boy from Pakistan who has been rescued from a sweatshop and brought to the U.S. to expose such evils only to be killed (accidentally?) on returning home—there is a memorial service for Ashraf at Moon's high school. "Nava," whose Dad's life was saved by a comrade after a firefight in Vietnam, is bothered by a schoolmate who tries to involve her in drugs and eventually must fight to defend herself. "Isabel" is a 14-year-old girl struggling with intrusive dreams after her father and little brother are tragically killed in a car accident and further challenged a year later when her mother announces that she will remarry and Isabel will have a 15-year-old sister who lost her mother to breast cancer. "Max" is a young boy who experiences an aircraft crash in his schoolyard and whose life is overshadowed by stories about his Uncle Max who died in Vietnam.

Richter, E. (1986). *Losing Someone You Love: When a Brother or Sister Dies*. New York: Putnam's. Fifteen adolescents describe their reactions to a wide variety of experiences of sibling death.

Rofes, E. E. (Ed.), and the Unit at Fayerweather Street School. (1985). *The Kids' Book about Death and Dying, by and for Kids*. Boston: Little, Brown. The result of a class project, this book describes what its 11- to 14-year-old authors learned about a wide range of death-related topics, making clear what children want to know about these subjects and how they want adults to talk to them. One main lesson is that "a lot of the mystery and fear surrounding death has been brought about by ignorance and avoidance" (p. 111). Another lesson is expressed in the hope "that children can lead the way in dealing with death and dying with a healthier and happier approach" (p. 114).

Romond, J. L. (1989). *Children Facing Grief: Letters from Bereaved Brothers and Sisters*. St. Meinrad, IN: Abbey Press. Each of the 18 children (ages 6–15) record here what it was like to experience the death of a brother or sister. Helpful comments from young people who have been there in grief.

Rudin, C. (1998). *Children's Books about the Holocaust: A Selective Annotated Bibliography*. Bayside, NY: The Holocaust Resource Center & Archives, Queensborough Community College, CUNY (718-225-1617). An annotated guide to literature for children from grade four onwards, with lists of biography and memoirs, fiction, nonfiction, and reference works, as well as indexes by grade, title, and subject.

Russell, B. T. (1996). *Last Left Standing*. Boston: Houghton Mifflin. After his older brother is killed by a train, it's as if Josh is "in another dimension" (as a friend tells him on p. 64). Josh isolates himself and roams the nearby orange groves. He wants to "go back to the way things were before . . ." (p. 78). One day, Josh comes across a cabin in the woods and meets an old woman (Mattie) and a girl (Beth Ann) who live there and had known Toby. Josh doesn't tell them about Toby's death because he doesn't want to acknowledge it or talk about it with others. Then he cannot tell his parents about the cabin, and everything becomes more difficult. Josh wants to help Mattie and Beth Ann like Toby did, but the loss of Beth Ann's special pet seems to be the catalyst that enables him to face the truth at last.

Rylant, C. (1992). *Missing May*. New York: Orchard Books. After Summer's mother dies when she is 6 years old, no one really wants her. Finally, Uncle Ob and Aunt May take her back with them to their rusty old trailer in Deep Water, West Virginia, and love her deeply. When May dies suddenly when Summer is 12, she and Ob have a hard time coping. Summer worries about Ob and is irritated at the support he seems to be getting from Cletus, a strange neighboring boy. Summer wishes she could fix Ob's grief, and they try to contact May in the afterlife. In the end, a memory of May opens the floodgates, and Summer cries her heart out. That catharsis and Ob's love reminds them that May will always be with them.

Salloum, A. (1998). *Reactions: A Workbook to Help Young People Who are Experiencing Trauma and Grief*. Omaha, NE: Centering Corporation. This workbook allows bereaved youngsters to describe their experiences and think about their implications. The text offers prompts for writing, drawing, and answering questions. The effort is to legitimize different reactions people may have to loss. Its goal is to reflect on what has been learned from these exercises as one moves into the future.

Shura, M. F. (1988). *The Sunday Doll*. New York: Dodd, Mead. This is a complex and rich story of a 13-year-old girl whose parents exclude her from something terrible involving her older sister (the suicide of a boyfriend) and who is frightened by her Aunt Harriet's life-threatening "spells" (transient ischemia attacks). Like the Amish doll without a face, Emily learns that she has her own strengths and can choose which face to present to the world.

Sims, A. M. (1986). *Am I Still a Sister?* Louisville, KY: Accord, Inc. (1941 Bishop Lane #202, 40218-1941; 800-346-3087). When Alicia was four, her brother, Austin, died of a rare brain cancer. Some years later, she began writing letters to Austin. The letters record Alicia's thoughts and feelings, her memories of their short time together, her everyday activities, and her insistence that she still is a big sister. Alicia shares her letters so that other children will know they are not alone in their sadness.

Smith, D. B. (1973). *A Taste of Blackberries*. New York: HarperCollins. After Jamie dies from an allergic reaction to a bee sting, his best friend (the book's unnamed narrator) reflects on this unexpected event: Did it really happen, or is it just another of Jamie's pranks? Could it have been prevented? Is it disloyal to go on eating and living when Jamie is dead? He concludes that no one could have prevented this death, "some questions just don't have answers," and life can go on.

Smith, H. I., & Johnson, J. (2006). *What Does that Mean? A Dictionary of Death, Dying and Grief Terms for Grieving Children and Those Who Love Them*. Omaha, NE: Centering Corporation. Finding the right words to use in talking about loss and death is important. This book identifies more than 70 death-related words, explains how to pronounce them and what they mean, and offers guidance about how to use them correctly.

Sternberg, E., & Sternberg, B. (1980). *If I Die and When I Do: Exploring Death with Young People*. Englewood Cliffs, NJ: Prentice Hall. This book is the result of a nine-week middle school course on death and dying. The text mainly consists of drawings, poems, and statements by the students on various death-related topics, plus a closing chapter of 25 suggested activities.

Stickney, D. (1985). *Water Bugs and Dragonflies*. New York: Pilgrim Press. This story is about transformations—in life and between life and death. Thus, a water bug transformed into a dragonfly is no longer able to return to the underwater colony to explain what has happened. Each individual must wait for his or her own transformation to appreciate what it involves.

Stokes, J., & Oxley, P. (2006) *Out of the Blue: Making Memories Last When Someone Has Died*. Cheltenham, UK: Winston's Wish (www.winstonswish.org.uk). This little booklet comes from the leading English support program for grieving children and their families. Its 28 pages are filled with good ideas for commemorating the life of a loved one who has died.

Thomas, J. R. (1981). *The Comeback Dog*. New York: Clarion. Daniel is a 9-year-old boy who is angry because his dog died recently and his parents don't seem to care as much as he does about Captain's death. When he finds a dirty, wet, raggedy dog that is barely breathing, Daniel takes the dog home and talks the adults into letting him take care of her, even though they don't believe she will survive and want to euthanize her. With Daniel's care, Lady gradually grows stronger but doesn't begin to act like Captain. Lady doesn't become Daniel's friend and won't come near him if she doesn't have to. Almost three weeks after running away, Lady returns with porcupine quills all over her face. Daniel is angry with her, but Lady lets him help her, and now it seems that they might become friends.

Traisman, E. S. (1992). *Fire in My Heart, Ice in My Veins: A Journal for Teenagers Experiencing a Loss*. Omaha, NE: Centering Corporation. This book is intended to become a journal for teenagers who have had a loss. A line or two of text on each page and many small drawings offer age-appropriate prompts for this purpose.

Traisman, E. S., & Sieff, J. (Comps.). (1995). *Flowers for the Ones You've Known: Unedited Letters from Bereaved Teens*. Omaha, NE: Centering Corporation. In this support book for teens, unedited letters and poems written by bereaved peers are reproduced in various handwritten and print formats.

White, E. B. (1952). *Charlotte's Web*. New York: Harper. This is a classic story of friendship on two levels: that of a young girl named Fern who lives on a farm and saves Wilbur, the runt of the pig litter; and that of Charlotte, the spider, who spins fabulous webs that save an older and fatter Wilbur from the butcher's knife. In the end, Charlotte dies of natural causes, but her feats and her offspring live on.

Whitehead, R. (1971). *The Mother Tree*. New York: Seabury Press. Where do 11-year-old Tempe and her 4-year-old sister, Laura, turn for comfort in the early 1900s when their mother dies and Tempe is obliged to assume her mother's duties? To a temporary spiritual refuge in the large backyard tree of the book's title, and eventually to good memories of their mother that live on within them.

Wiener, L. S., Best, A., & Pizzo, P. A. (Comps.). (1994). *Be a Friend: Children Who Live with HIV Speak*. Morton Grove, IL: Albert Whitman. The vivid colors, drawings, and layout in this book seek to permit children living with HIV infection to speak in their own voices. The result is sometimes poignant, often charming, and always compelling. For example, one 11-year-old writes: "I often wonder how other children without AIDS learn to appreciate life. That's the best part about having AIDS" (p. 13).

Literature for High School Readers

Agee, J. (1969). *A Death in the Family*. New York: Bantam. This Pulitzer Prize-winning novel unerringly depicts the point of view of two children in Knoxville, Tennessee, in 1915, when they are told of the accidental death of their father. Agee skillfully portrays ways in which the children experience unusual events, sense strange tensions within the family, struggle to understand what has happened, and strive to work out their implications.

Barnouw, D., & Van der Stroom, G. (Eds.). (1989). *The Diary of Anne Frank: The Critical Edition*. Trans. A. J. Pomerans & B. M. Mooyaart-Doubleday. New York: Doubleday. This is a more sophisticated version (with commentaries) of this classic record of a young girl's life while hiding from the Nazis in occupied Holland during World War II. (See the entry earlier in this appendix under Frank, A.)

Bode, J. (1993). *Death Is Hard to Live With: Teenagers and How They Cope with Death*. New York: Delacorte. Teenagers speak frankly about how they cope with death and loss.

Boulden, J., & Boulden, J. (1994). *The Last Goodbye II*. Weaverville, CA: Boulden Publishing (P.O. Box 1186, 96093-1186; 800-238-8433). This activity book offers exercises designed for youngsters at grade levels 9–12 to process feelings and issues that surround death. It is similar to *The Last Goodbye I* but includes topics like suicide and not acting destructively that are appropriate to these older readers.

Carter, F. (1976). *The Education of Little Tree*. New York: Delacorte (paperback ed.; Albuquerque: University of New Mexico Press, 1986). After the death of his parents, the author is taken in at the age of 5 by his grandparents in the mountains of Tennessee during the 1930s. From his grandparents, Little Tree receives a rich, informal education as they teach him about living close to nature and The Way of the Cherokees. When one of the family dogs dies and we are told that "Granpa said everything you lost which you had loved give you that [bad, empty] feeling. He said the only way round it was not to love anything, which was worse because you would feel empty all the time" (p. 78). After the government places Little Tree in a harsh and unwelcoming Christian orphanage, he is finally allowed to return to his grandparents' home where he eventually experiences the deaths of Granpa and Granma. As they are dying, they tell him, "We will wait for you. Next time will be better. All is well" (p. 214). In the end, as Little Tree strikes out on his own to make his way west, one more dog dies and is buried—setting the animal free to run on ahead to catch up with Granpa.

Craven, M. (1973). *I Heard the Owl Call My Name*. New York: Dell. This novel describes a young Episcopal priest with a terminal illness. He is sent by his bishop to live with Native Americans in British Columbia, who believe that death will come when the owl calls someone's name. From them, the bishop hopes that the young priest will learn to face his own death.

Crawford, B. B., & Lazar, L. (1999). *In My World: A Journal for Young People Facing Life-Threatening Illness*. Omaha, NE: Centering Corporation. This book's format is designed to help teenagers who are coping with a life-threatening illness make a record of their lives and give expression to thoughts, feelings, and worries that they may find difficult to share with family members and friends.

Deaver, J. R. (1988). *Say Goodnight, Gracie*. New York: Harper & Row. When her close friend, Jimmy, is killed by a drunken driver in an automobile accident, Morgan is so disoriented by the extent of her loss that she is unable to face her feelings, attend Jimmy's funeral, or speak to his parents. Her own parents offer support and tolerate Morgan's withdrawal from the world, but it is not until a wise aunt intervenes that Morgan is able to confront her feelings in a way that leads her to more constructive coping and to decide to go on with living.

Draper, S. M. (1994). *Tears of a Tiger*. New York: Atheneum. Without any narrative, this book uses excerpts from official statements, newspaper articles, letters, diaries, homework, phone calls, and conversations to describe the aftermath of the death of Robert Washington, captain of the Hazelwood High School Tiger basketball team, in a fiery automobile accident. The car's driver, Andrew Jackson, cannot get over Rob's death and his feelings of guilt. Two other friends in the car do well, but Andy sinks gradually into a deeper and more desperate depression. Smiling on the surface, he offers lots of clues about his inner trauma, but his parents, friends, teachers, and even a psychologist do not realize what is happening until he eventually takes his own life.

Gipson, F. (1956). *Old Yeller*. New York: Harper & Brothers (reissued by HarperTrophy, 1990). An ugly, yellow stray dog becomes a close companion of 14-year-old Travis in Texas in the late 1800s and saves some members of his family from various dangers. But when the dog is bitten by a rabid wolf, Travis must kill him.

Greenberg, J. (1979). *A Season In-Between*. New York: Farrar. Carrie Singer, a seventh grader, copes with the diagnosis of her father's cancer in spring and his death that summer. She draws on the rabbinical teaching: turn scratches on a jewel into a beautiful design.

Grollman, E., & Johnson, J. (2001). *A Teenager's Book about Suicide: Helping Break the Silence and Preventing Death*. Omaha, NE: Centering Corporation. Brief text passages in boxes and ample space for readers to write or draw open up the topic of teenage suicide. There are writings by teens who have contemplated suicide or been affected by the suicide of someone else, as well as the authors' comments designed to dispel myths and throw light on a dark subject. The authors identify danger signals and warning signs, and they offer advice as to what a teen might do if he or she suspects a friend or family member is thinking about suicide.

Grollman, E., & Malikow, M. (1999). *Living when a Young Friend Commits Suicide*. Boston: Beacon Press. This book is intended to help adolescents by guiding them through typical reactions and questions after a friend completes a suicide. It offers suggestions for how to cope and how to help suicidal people. Also addressed are religious questions, popular misconceptions about suicide, and getting on with one's life. A final chapter lists helpful resources.

Guest, J. (1976). *Ordinary People*. New York: Viking. This impressive novel gradually reveals that Conrad Jarrett has many problems after his older brother drowns in a boating accident. Conrad's grief is compounded by the guilt he feels for not saving the life of his sibling. An overprotective father and a cold mother are little help, but a therapist eventually helps Conrad realize that he is not to blame for his brother's death because he lived through the accident.

Gunther, J. (1949). *Death Be Not Proud: A Memoir*. New York: Harper. An early biographical account of the author's 15-year-old son and his lengthy struggle with a brain tumor.

Hughes, M. (1984). *Hunter in the Dark*. New York: Atheneum. A boy with overprotective parents sets out to face life and death on his own by confronting threats at different levels: his leukemia and the challenge of going hunting in the Canadian woods for the first time.

Klagsbrun, F. (1976). *Too Young to Die: Youth and Suicide*. New York: Houghton Mifflin; paperback edition by Pocket Books, 1977. A clear, informed, and readable introduction to the myths and realities surrounding youth suicide, with useful advice for helpers. Other books on this subject include: W. Colman, *Understanding and Preventing Teen Suicide* (Chicago: Children's Press, 1990); D. B. Francis, *Suicide: A Preventable Tragedy* (New York: E. P. Dutton, 1989); S. Gardner & G. Rosenberg, *Teenage Suicide* (New York: Messner, 1985); M. O. Hyde & E. H. Forsyth, *Suicide: The Hidden Epidemic* (New York: Franklin Watts, 1986); J. Kolehmainen & S. Handwerk, *Teen Suicide: A Book for Friends, Family, and Classmates* (Minneapolis, MN: Lerner, 1986); J. M. Leder, *Dead Serious: A Book for Teenagers about Teenage Suicide* (New York: Atheneum, 1987); and J. Schleifer, *Everything You Need to Know about Teen Suicide* (rev. ed.; New York: The Rosen Publishing Group, 1991).

L'Engle, M. (1960). *Meet the Austins*. New York: Vanguard (Farrar Straus & Giroux, 1997). Maggie

Hamilton is 10 years old when she comes to live with the Austins. After her mother died of pneumonia, Maggie lived with her grandfather (but he had a heart attack) and then her father (only for a month before he was killed in a plane accident). Maggie is spoiled, self-centered, and a disruptive influence in the Austin family. Vicky (age 12) and her three siblings wish Maggie would go away. The book is largely about the adventures of a busy family while the girl is with them (and, eventually, of their desire to keep her), but the backdrop is the effect of her parents' deaths and her unsettled life on Maggie.

Lewis, C. S. (1976). *A Grief Observed*. New York: Bantam. The author, a celebrated British writer and lay theologian, recorded his experiences of grief on notebooks lying around the house. The published result is an unusual and extraordinary document, a direct and honest expression of one individual's grief that has helped innumerable readers by normalizing their own experiences in bereavement.

Martin, A. M. (1986). *With You and Without You*. New York: Holiday House; paperback by Scholastic. Family members (parents and four children) struggle to cope when the father is told that he will soon die as a result of an inoperable heart condition. Before his death, each member of the family tries to make the father's remaining time as good as possible; afterward, each strives to cope with their losses. One important lesson is that no one is ever completely prepared for a death; another is that each individual must cope in his or her own way.

Martin, C. (2004). *The Dead Don't Dance: A Novel of Awakening*. Nashville: WestBow Press. Dylan Styles and his wife, Maggie, live in a small town in rural South Carolina. Their expectations for the birth of their first child turn into tragedy when the baby dies at birth and Maggie is left comatose for many months. Eventually she recovers and there is a happy ending, but the real strength of this novel is how it conveys the pall that hangs over lives affected by grief, guilt, anger, and frustration. Dylan would end his own life if it weren't for the seemingly unlikely possibility that Maggie might recover. His friends, teaching a writing course at a local college, students, and a pregnant nursing aide named Amanda all help. Only after a terrible automobile accident involving Dylan's best friend and Amanda, during which her baby is born, is Dylan's faith restored and he can see a way forward.

Müller, M. (1998). *Anne Frank: The Biography*. Trans. R. Kimber & R. Kimber. New York: Metropolitan. A new exploration of the life and death of a young Jewish girl in occupied Holland during World War II.

O'Toole, D. (1995). *Facing Change: Falling Apart and Coming Together Again in the Teen Years*. Burnsville, NC: Compassion Books (477 Hannah Branch Road, 28714). The aim is to help adolescents understand loss, grief, and change, and think about how they might respond to those experiences.

Patz, N. (2003). *Who Was the Woman Who Wore the Hat?* New York: Dutton Books. The text, copies of old photographs, watercolors, and pencil drawings in this book are meant to evoke memories of the Holocaust and bring into sharp focus some of its realities. The theme is a meditation on a woman's hat that once was on display in the Jewish Historical Museum in Amsterdam. This unlabeled remnant is all that remains of a woman's life after the Nazis rounded up her and all of the other Jews in Amsterdam. It reminds the author that this unknown woman (and all of her peers) was a real person and that "except for the winds of chance, I might have been that woman."

Pendleton, E. (Comp.). (1980). *Too Old to Cry, Too Young to Die*. Nashville: Thomas Nelson. Thirty-five teenagers describe their experiences in living with cancer, including treatments, side effects, hospitals, parents, siblings, and friends.

Rawlings, M. K. (1939). *The Yearling*. New York: Charles Scribner's Sons (50th anniversary ed.; New York: Simon Pulse/Simon & Schuster, 1988). This Pulitzer Prize-winning novel is a tale of a boy and his parents eking out a bare subsistence living in rural Florida in the early 20th century where the struggle to survive overrides everything else. Young Jody's desire for a pet, something of his very own, is fulfilled by an orphaned fawn that he names Flag. There are many death-related events in Jody's life: all of his siblings have died; Old Slewfoot, the bear, kills their brood sow and is later killed by Pa; his father is bit by a rattler and almost dies, only later to become ill and frail; Jody's best friend, the crippled Fodder-wing, dies and is buried; wild animals are hunted and killed, and a plague causes other animal deaths; a pack of wolves kills their heifer calf; and as Flag grows he becomes a yearling, gets into the family's garden, and eats their precious crops. Finally, Jody's father orders him to kill the deer. He tries not to but ultimately must do so after Ma wounds the deer.

Rawls, W. (1961). *Where the Red Fern Grows: The Story of Two Dogs and a Boy*. Garden City, NY: Doubleday (reissued by Random House, 1997).

Billy Colman saves for two years to get $50 to buy two registered coonhound pups. He trains them, and together they hunt raccoons in the Ozarks of northeastern Oklahoma. There are numerous instances of hunting and killing coons, including one in which a boy trips, falls on an axe, and dies. There is also a contest won by Billy's dogs and a vicious fight with a mountain lion in which Billy's life is threatened, the lion is killed, and the male dog is mortally wounded. After Billy buries Old Dan, Little Ann refuses food and dies at her sibling's grave. The money the dogs have earned enables the family to leave the hills, but as they depart they are comforted by the sight of a sacred red fern that has grown up at the dogs' gravesite.

Scrivani, M. (1991). *When Death Walks In.* Omaha, NE: Centering Corporation. This little booklet tries to help teens explore the many facets of grief and how one might cope with them in productive ways.

Tolstoy, L. (1960). *The Death of Ivan Ilych and Other Stories.* New York: New American Library. The title story is a brilliant piece of world literature in which a Russian magistrate in the prime of his life is afflicted with a grave illness that becomes steadily more serious. As his health deteriorates, Ivan realizes that glib talk in college about mortality does not apply only to other people or humanity in general. He also discovers that many around him gradually withdraw and become more guarded in what they say to him; only one servant and his young son treat him with real compassion and candor.

Voigt, C. (1983). *Dicey's song.* New York: Atheneum. At 13, Dicey Tillerman has many responsibilities. Her father disappeared when she was 7 years old, and her mother is now institutionalized. Dicey brought her three younger siblings to live with Gram on the edge of Chesapeake Bay. For herself, Dicey wants to refinish an old sailboat, but she has to take care of the others. Often, she has to "hold on" to let others solve problems when she really wants to jump in herself. Gram and the children need love, trust, and courage to face their new beginnings and many challenges. Overshadowing everything are the losses they have all suffered. That becomes clear when Gram and Dicey fly up to Boston to be at Momma's bedside when she dies, after which they bring her ashes back to Maryland for burial in the yard.

References

Abrahamson, H. (1977). *The origin of death: Studies in African mythology.* New York: Arno Press.

Abts, H.W. (2002). *The living trust: The failproof way to pass along your estate to your heirs without lawyers, courts, or the probate system* (3rd ed.). New York: McGraw-Hill.

Achté, K., Fagerström, R., Pentikäinen, J., & Farberow, N. L. (1990). Themes of death and violence in lullabies of different countries. *Omega, Journal of Death and Dying, 20,* 193–204.

Ad Hoc Committee of the Harvard Medical School to Examine the Definition of Brain Death. (1968). A definition of irreversible coma. *Journal of the American Medical Association, 205,* 337–340.

Adamec, C. (2000). *When your pet dies: Dealing with your grief and helping your children cope.* Lincoln, NE: iUniverse.

Adams, C. A. (2003). *ABC's of grief: A handbook for survivors.* Amityville, NY: Baywood.

Adams, D. W., & Deveau, E. J. (1986). Helping dying adolescents: Needs and responses. In C. A. Corr & J. N. McNeil (Eds.), *Adolescence and death* (pp. 79–96). New York: Springer.

Adams, D. W., & Deveau, E. J. (1993). *Coping with childhood cancer: Where do we go from here?* (New rev. ed.). Hamilton, Ontario: Kinbridge.

Adams, D. W., & Deveau, E. J. (Eds.). (1995). *Beyond the innocence of childhood* (3 vols.). Amityville, NY: Baywood.

Adams, G. (2006). *Lessons from lions: Using children's media to teach about grief and mourning* + CD. Little Rock, AR: Center for Good Mourning, Arkansas Children's Hospital.

Adams, J. R. (2004). *Prospects for immortality: A sensible search for life after death.* Amityville, NY: Baywood.

Adler, B. (1979, March). You don't have to do homework in heaven! *Good Housekeeping,* 46.

Agee, J. (1969). *A death in the family.* New York: Bantam.

Aging with Dignity. (2001). *Next steps: Discussing and coping with serious illness.* Tallahassee, FL: Author.

Ahronheim, J., & Weber, D. (1992). *Final passages: Positive choices for the dying and their loved ones.* New York: Simon & Schuster.

Ajemian, I., & Mount, B. M. (Eds.). (1980). *The R. V. H. manual on palliative/hospice care.* New York: Arno Press.

Akner, L. F. (with Whitney, C. V.). (1993). *How to survive the loss of a parent: A guide for adults.* New York: Morrow.

Albert, P. L. (1994). Overview of the organ donation process. *Critical Care Nursing Clinics of North America, 6,* 553–556.

Albert, P. L. (1998). Direct contact between donor families and recipients: Crisis or consolation? *Journal of Transplant Coordination, 8*(3), 139–144.

Albert, P. L. (1999). Clinical decision making and ethics in communications between donor families and recipients: How much should they know? *Journal of Transplant Coordination, 9,* 219–224.

Albom, M. (1997). *Tuesdays with Morrie: An old man, a young man, and life's greatest lesson.* New York: Doubleday.

Alcamo, I. E. (2003). *AIDS: The biological basis* (3rd ed.). Boston: Jones & Bartlett.

Alcántara, C., & Gone, J. P. (2007). Reviewing suicide in Native American communities: Situating risk and protective factors within a transactional-ecological framework. *Death Studies, 31*(5), 457–477

Alderman, E., & Kennedy C. (1997). *The right to privacy.* New York: Vintage.

Aldrich, C. K. (1963). The dying patient's grief. *Journal of the American Medical Association, 184,* 329–331.

Alexander, A. K. (2002). *A mural for Mamita/Un mural para Mamita.* Omaha, NE: Centering Corporation.

Alexander, I. E., & Adlerstein, A. M. (1958). Affective responses to the concept of death in a population of children and early adolescents. *Journal of Genetic Psychology, 93,* 167–177.

Alexander-Greene, A. (1999). *Sunflowers and rainbows for Tia: Saying goodbye to Daddy.* Omaha, NE: Centering Corporation.

Allberg, W. R., & Chu, L. (1990). Understanding adolescent suicide: Correlates in a developmental perspective. *The School Counselor, 37,* 343–350.

Allen, A. (2007). *Vaccine: The controversial story of medicine's greatest lifesaver.* New York: Norton.

Allen, B. G., Calhoun, L. G., Cann, A., & Tedeschi, R. G. (1993). The effect of cause of death on responses to the bereaved: Suicide compared to accident and natural causes. *Omega, Journal of Death and Dying, 28,* 39–48.

Allen, M., & Marks, S. (1993). *Miscarriage: Women sharing from the heart.* New York: Wiley.

Allison, G. (2004). *Nuclear terrorism: The ultimate preventable catastrophe.* New York: Times Books.

Allumbaugh, D. L., & Hoyt, W. T. (1999). Effectiveness of grief counseling: A meta-analysis. *Journal of Counseling Psychology, 46,* 379–380.

Alperovitz, G. (1995). *The decision to use the atomic bomb and the architecture of an American myth.* New York: Knopf.

Alvarez, A. (1970). *The savage god: A study of suicide.* New York: Random House.

American Academy of Pediatrics (AAP), Committee on Bioethics and Committee on Hospital Care. (2000b). Palliative care for children. *Pediatrics, 106,* 351–357.

American Academy of Pediatrics (AAP), Committee on Communications. (1995). Media violence. *Pediatrics, 95,* 949–951.

American Academy of Pediatrics (AAP), Committee on Psychosocial Aspects of Child and Family Health. (2000a). The pediatrician and childhood bereavement. *Pediatrics, 105,* 445–447.

American Academy of Pediatrics (AAP), Hymel, K. P., & the Committee on Child Abuse and Neglect, National Association of Medical Examiners. (2006). Distinguishing sudden infant death syndrome from child abuse fatalities. *Pediatrics, 118,* 421–427.

American Academy of Pediatrics (AAP), Task Force on Infant Positioning and SIDS. (1992). Positioning and SIDS. *Pediatrics, 89,* 1120–1126.

American Academy of Pediatrics (AAP), Task Force on Infant Positioning and SIDS. (1996). Positioning and sudden infant death syndrome (SIDS): Update. *Pediatrics, 98,* 1216–1218.

American Academy of Pediatrics (AAP), Task Force on Infant Sleep Position and Sudden Infant Death Syndrome (2000a). Changing concepts of sudden infant death syndrome: Implications of infant sleeping environment and sleep position. *Pediatrics, 105,* 650–656.

American Academy of Pediatrics (AAP), Task Force on Sudden Infant Death Syndrome. (2005). The changing concept of sudden infant death syndrome: Diagnostic coding shifts, controversies regarding the sleeping environment, and new variables to consider in reducing risk. *Pediatrics, 116,* 1245–1255.

American Psychological Association. (1993). *Violence & youth: Psychology's response.* Summary Report of the American Psychological Association Commission on Violence and Youth, Vol. 1. Washington, DC: Author.

And We Were Sad, Remember? [Videotape]. (1979). Northern Virginia Educational Telecommunications Association. (Available from the National Audiovisual Center, Reference Department, National Archives and Records Service, Washington, DC 20409.)

Andersen, C. (1998). *The day Diana died.* New York: William Morrow.

Anderson, R. (1968). *I never sang for my father.* New York: Dramatists Play Service.

Anderson, R. N., & Smith, B. L. (2005). Deaths: Leading causes for 2002. *National Vital Statistics Reports, 53*(17). Hyattsville, MD: National Center for Health Statistics.

Angel, M. D. (1987). *The orphaned adult.* New York: Human Sciences.

Angell, M. (1996). Euthanasia in the Netherlands—good news or bad? *New England Journal of Medicine, 335,* 1676–1678.

Annas, G. J. (1994). Death by prescription: The Oregon initiative. *New England Journal of Medicine, 331,* 1240–1243.

Annas, G. J. (2004). *The rights of patients* (3rd ed.). Carbondale: Southern Illinois University Press.

Annenberg Washington Program. (1993). *Communications and the Patient Self-Determination Act: Strategies for meeting the educational mandate.* Washington, DC: Author.

Anonymous. (1957). *Read-aloud nursery tales.* New York: Wonder.

Anonymous. (1963). Medical ethics, narcotics, and addiction [Editorial]. (1963). *Journal of the American Medical Association, 185,* 962–963.

Anonymous. (1998, September 19). Listen. In A. Landers. *St. Louis Post-Dispatch,* p. D31.

Anonymous. (2001a). L.A. gangs are back. *Time, 158*(9), 46–49.

Anonymous. (2001b). *Q & A euthanasia 2001: A guide to the Dutch Termination of Life on Request and Assisted Suicide (Review Procedures) Act* (debated in the Senate of the States General on 10 April 2001). The Hague: Author.

Anonymous. (2002). Drawing a bead on terrorism: A survey of recent articles. *The Wilson Quarterly, 26*(3), 83–84.

Anonymous. (2003, October 28). Awake, but is she aware? *St. Petersburg Times,* p. 4A.

Anonymous. (2005, October). Side effects of anti-HIV medication. *AIDSinfo.* http://aidsinfo.nih.gov.

Anonymous. (2006a, July 12). FDA approves the first once-a-day three-drug combination tablet for treatment of HIV-1. *FDA News.* http://www.fda.gov/bbs/topics/NEWS/2006/NEW01408.htm.

Anonymous. (2006b, August). Ways to go. *National Geographic, 210*(2), p. 21.

Anonymous. (2007a, January 18). Corner turned in cancer battle? *St. Petersburg Times,* p. 1A.

Anonymous. (2007b, January 18). Five minutes until nuclear destruction. *St. Petersburg Times,* p. 4A. (See *Bulletin of the Atomic Scientists* at www.thebulletin.org/minutes-to-midnight/.)

Anonymous. (2007c, May 4). Putting female spin on smokes touches nerve. *St. Petersburg Times,* p. 3D.

Anthony, S. (1939). A study of the development of the concept of death [abstract]. *British Journal of Educational Psychology, 9,* 276–277.

Anthony, S. (1940). *The child's discovery of death.* New York: Harcourt Brace.

Anthony, S. (1972). *The discovery of death in childhood and after.* New York: Basic Books. (Revised edition of *The child's discovery of death*)

Ariès, P. (1962). *Centuries of childhood: A social history of family life* (R. Baldick, Trans.). New York: Random House.

Ariès, P. (1974a). The reversal of death: Changes in attitudes toward death in Western societies (V. M. Stannard, Trans.). *American Quarterly, 26,* 55–82.

Ariès, P. (1974b). *Western attitudes toward death: From the middle ages to the present* (P. M. Ranum, Trans.). Baltimore: Johns Hopkins University Press.

Ariès, P. (1981). *The hour of our death* (H. Weaver, Trans.). New York: Knopf.

Ariès, P. (1985). *Images of man and death* (J. Lloyd, Trans.). Cambridge, MA: Harvard University Press.

Arkin, W., & Fieldhouse, R. (1985). *Nuclear battlefields.* Cambridge, MA: Ballinger.

Armstrong, L., & Jenkins, S. (2001). *It's not about the bike: My journey back to life.* New York: Berkley Publishing Group.

Armstrong-Dailey, A., & Zarbock, S. (Eds.). (in press). *Hospice care for children* (3rd ed.). New York: Oxford University Press.

Arnold, B., Bruno, S. M., Corr, C. A., Eisemann, L., & Sunter, S. (2004a). *Bereavement program training series* (4 vols.). Largo, FL: The Hospice Institute of the Florida Suncoast.

Arnold, B., Bruno, S. M., Corr, C. A., Eisemann, L., & Sunter, S. (2004b). *Bereavement program development series* (2 vols.). Largo, FL: The Hospice Institute of the Florida Suncoast.

Arvio, R. P. (1974). *The cost of dying and what you can do about it.* New York: Harper & Row.

Ash, L. (2004). *Life touches life: A mother's story of stillbirth and healing.* Troutdale, OR: NewSage Press.

Ashe, A., & Rampersad, A. (1993). *Days of grace: A memoir.* New York: Knopf.

Ashenburg, K. (2004). *The mourner's dance: What we do when people die* (reprint ed.). New York: North Point Press.

Associated Press (2007, February 15). U.S., Britain get low marks on child welfare. *St. Petersburg Times,* p. 18A.

Associated Press. (2004, December 31). One-tenth of preschoolers too hefty. *St. Petersburg Times*, p. 7A.

Association for Children with Life-Threatening or Terminal Conditions and Their Families (ACT). (1995). *The ACT charter for children with life-threatening conditions and their families* (2nd ed.). Bristol, England: Author.

Atkinson, T. E. (1988). *Handbook of the law of wills and other principles of succession, including intestacy and administration of decedents' estates* (2nd ed.). St. Paul, MN: West Group.

Attig, T. (1981). Death education as care of the dying. In R. A. Pacholski & C. A. Corr (Eds.), *New directions in death education and counseling* (pp. 168–175). Arlington, VA: Forum for Death Education and Counseling.

Attig, T. (1986). Death themes in adolescent music: The classic years. In C. A. Corr & J. N. McNeil (Eds.), *Adolescence and death* (pp. 32–56). New York: Springer.

Attig, T. (1991). The importance of conceiving of grief as an active process. *Death Studies, 15,* 385–393.

Attig, T. (1996a). Beyond pain: The existential suffering of children. *Journal of Palliative Care, 12*(3), 20–23.

Attig, T. (1996b). *How we grieve: Relearning the world.* New York: Oxford University Press.

Attig, T. (2000). *The heart of grief: Death and the search for lasting love.* New York: Oxford University Press.

Attig, T. (2001). Relearning the world: Making and finding meanings. In R. A. Neimeyer (Ed.), *Meaning reconstruction and the experience of loss* (pp. 33–53). Washington, DC: American Psychological Association.

Atwater, P. M. H. (1992). Is there a hell? Surprising observations about the near-death experience. *Journal of Near-Death Studies, 10,* 149–160.

Auden, W. H. (1940). *Collected poems* (E. Mendelson, Ed.). New York: Random House.

Austin, M. (1930). *The American rhythm: Studies and reexpressions of Amerindian songs* (New & enlarged ed.). Boston: Houghton Mifflin.

The Authors for the Live Organ Donor Consensus Group. (2000). Consensus statement on the live organ donor. *Journal of the American Medical Association, 284,* 2919–2926.

Bachelor, P. (2004). *Sorrow and solace: The social world of the cemetery.* Amityville, NY: Baywood.

Bachman, J. G., Johnston, L. D., & O'Malley, P.M. (1986). *Monitoring the future: Questionnaire responses from the nation's high school seniors, 1986.* Ann Arbor: University of Michigan.

Bachman, R. (1992). *Death and violence on the reservation: Homicide, family violence, and suicide in American Indian populations.* New York: Auburn House.

Bacon, F. (1962). Of marriage and single life. In *Francis Bacon's Essays.* New York: Dutton. (Original work published 1625)

Bacon, J. B. (1996). Support groups for bereaved children. In C. A. Corr & D. M. Corr (Eds.), *Handbook of childhood death and bereavement* (pp. 285–304). New York: Springer.

Badham, P., & Badham, L. (Eds.). (1987). *Death and immortality in the religions of the world.* New York: Paragon House.

Bailey, L. (1978). *Biblical perspectives on death.* Philadelphia: Fortress Press.

Bailey, S. S., Bridgman, M. M., Faulkner, D., Kitahata, C. M., Marks, E., Melendez, B. B., et al. (1990). *Creativity and the close of life.* Branford, CT: The Connecticut Hospice.

Baines, B. K. (2001). *The ethical will writing guide and workbook: Preserving your legacy of values for your family and community.* Minneapolis: Josaba Ltd.

Baines, B. K. (2006). *Ethical wills: Putting your values on paper* (2nd ed.). Cambridge, MA: Perseus.

Baker, J. E., & Sedney, M. A. (1996). How bereaved children cope with loss: An overview. In C. A. Corr & D. M. Corr (Eds.), *Handbook of childhood death and bereavement* (pp. 109–129). New York: Springer.

Baker, J. E., Sedney, M. A., & Gross, E. (1992). Psychological tasks for bereaved children. *American Journal of Orthopsychiatry, 62,* 105–116.

Balk, D. E. (1984). How teenagers cope with sibling death: Some implications for school counselors. *The School Counselor, 32,* 150–158.

Balk, D. E. (1990). The self-concepts of bereaved adolescents: Sibling death and its aftermath. *Journal of Adolescent Research, 5,* 112–132.

Balk, D. E. (Ed.). (1991a). Death and adolescent bereavement [Special issue]. *Journal of Adolescent Research, 6*(1).

Balk, D. E. (1991b). Death and adolescent bereavement: Current research and future directions. *Journal of Adolescent Research, 6,* 7–27.

Balk, D. E. (1991c). Sibling death, adolescent bereavement, and religion. *Death Studies, 15,* 1–20.

Balk, D. E. (2004). Recovery following bereavement: An examination of the concept. *Death Studies, 28,* 361–374.

Balk, D. E., & Corr, C. A. (2001). Bereavement during adolescence: A review of research. In M. S. Stroebe, R. O. Hansson, W. Stroebe, & H. Schut (Eds.), *Handbook of bereavement research: Consequences, coping, and care* (pp. 199–218). Washington, DC: American Psychological Association.

Balk, D. E., & Hogan, N. S. (1995). Religion, spirituality, and bereaved adolescents. In D. W. Adams & E. J. Deveau (Eds.), *Beyond the innocence of childhood: Helping children and adolescents cope with death and bereavement* (Vol. 3, pp. 61–88). Amityville, NY: Baywood.

Balk, D., Wogrin, C., Thornton, G., & Meagher, D. (Eds.). (2007). *Handbook of thanatology: The essential body of knowledge for the study of death, dying, and bereavement.* Northbrook, IL: Association for Death Education and Counseling.

Ball, A. (1995). *Catholic book of the dead.* Huntington, IN: Our Sunday Visitor.

Ballou, R. O. (Ed.). (1944). *The Viking portable world library bible.* New York: The Viking Press.

Balmer, L. E. (1992). *Adolescent sibling bereavement: Mediating effects of family environment and personality.* Unpublished doctoral dissertation, York University, Toronto.

Bandura, A. (1980). The stormy decade: Fact or fiction? In R. E. Muuss (Ed.), *Adolescent behavior and society: A book of readings* (3rd ed.; pp. 22–31). New York: Random House.

Banish, R. (2003). *Focus on living: Portraits of Americans with HIV and AIDS.* Amherst: University of Massachusetts Press.

Banks, J., Marmot, M., Oldfield, Z., & Smith, J. P. (2006). Disease and disadvantage in the United States and in England. *Journal of the American Medical Association, 295,* 2037–2045.

Banks, R. (1991). *The sweet hereafter.* New York: HarperCollins.

Barber, E. (2003). *Letters from a friend: A sibling's guide for coping and grief.* Amityville, NY: Baywood.

Barlow, C. A., & Coleman, H. (2003). The healing alliance: How families use social support after a suicide. *Omega, Journal of Death and Dying, 47*(3), 87–201.

Barnard, D., Towers, A., Boston, P., & Lambrinidou, Y. (2000). *Crossing over: Narratives of palliative care.* Oxford: Oxford University Press.

Barnett, T., & Whiteside, A. (2006). *AIDS in the twenty-first century: Disease and globalization* (Rev. ed.). London: Palgrave Macmillan.

Barnickol, C. A., Fuller, H., & Shinners, B. (1986). Helping bereaved adolescent parents. In C. A. Corr & J. N. McNeil (Eds.), *Adolescence and death* (pp. 132–147). New York: Springer.

Barrett, H. C., & Behne, T. (2005). Children's understanding of death as the cessation of agency: A test using sleep versus death. *Cognition, 96,* 93–108.

Barrett, R. K. (1996). Adolescents, homicidal violence, and death. In C. A. Corr & D. E. Balk (Eds.), *Handbook of adolescent death and bereavement* (pp. 42–64). New York: Springer.

Barrett, R. K. (2006). Dialogues in diversity: An invited series of papers, advance directives, DNRs, and end-of-life care for African Americans. *Omega, Journal of Death and Dying, 52,* 249–261.

Barrett, T. W., & Scott, T. B. (1990). Suicide bereavement and recovery patterns compared with nonsuicide bereavement patterns. *Suicide and Life-Threatening Behavior, 29,* 1–15.

Battin, M. P. (Ed.). (1994). *The least worst death: Essays in bioethics on the end of life.* New York: Oxford University Press.

Battin, M. P. (1996). *The death debate: Ethical issues in suicide.* Upper Saddle River, NJ: Prentice Hall.

Battin, M. P., Rhodes, R., & Silvers, A. (Eds.). (1998). *Physician assisted suicide: Expanding the debate.* New York: Routledge.

Bauer, Y. (1982). *A history of the Holocaust.* New York: Franklin Watts.

Bauer, Y. (1986). Introduction. In E. Kulka, *Escape from Auschwitz* (pp. xiii–xvii). South Hadley, MA: Bergin & Garvey.

Baugher, R. (2001, March/April). How long (according to the media) should grief last? *Columbia Journalism Review,* 58–59.

Baxter, G., Bennett, L., & Stuart, W. (1989). *Adolescents and death: Bereavement support groups for secondary school students* (2nd ed.). Etobicoke, Ontario: Canadian Centre for Death Education and Bereavement at Humber College.

Beamer, L. (with Abraham, K.). (2002). *Let's roll!: Ordinary people, extraordinary courage.* Wheaton, IL: Tyndale House.

Bearison, D. J. (2006). *When treatment fails: How medicine cares for dying children.* New York: Oxford University Press.

Beauchamp, T. L. (Ed.). (1996). *Intending death: The ethics of assisted suicide and euthanasia.* Upper Saddle River, NJ: Prentice Hall.

Beauchamp, T. L., & Childress, J. F. (2001). *Principles of biomedical ethics.* New York: Oxford University Press.

Becker, C. B. (1990). Buddhist views of suicide and euthanasia. *Philosophy East and West, 40,* 543–556.

Becker, D., & Margolin, F. (1967). How surviving parents handled their young children's adaptations to the crisis of loss. *American Journal of Orthopsychiatry, 37,* 753–757.

Becker, E. (1973). *The denial of death.* New York: Free Press.

Becvar, D. S. (2003). *In the presence of grief: Helping family members resolve death, dying, and bereavement issues.* New York: Guilford Press.

Beder, J. (2005). Loss of the assumptive world—How we deal with death and loss. *Omega, Journal of Death and Dying, 50,* 255–265.

Behrman, G. (2004). *The invisible people: How the U.S. has slept through the global AIDS pandemic, the greatest humanitarian catastrophe of our time.* New York: Free Press.

Bell, V., & Troxel, D. (2003). *A dignified life: The Best Friends approach to Alzheimer's care, a guide for family caregivers* (Rev. ed.). Baltimore: Health Professions Press.

Bendann, E. (1930). *Death customs: An analytical study of burial rites.* New York: Knopf.

Benenson, E. (1998). Donor husband, donor father: UNOS board member Kenneth Moritsugu looks beyond tragedy to serving others. *UNOS Update* [Special edition, Spring], 26.

Bengtson, V. L., Cuellar, J. B., & Ragan, P. K. (1977). Stratum contrasts and similarities in attitudes toward death. *Journal of Gerontology, 32,* 76–88.

Benham, K. (2005, March 27). The good listener. *St. Petersburg Times,* p. 1E.

Benjamin, B. (1965). *Social and economic factors affecting mortality.* The Hague: Mouton.

Benjamin, D., & Simon, S. (2002). *The age of sacred terror.* New York: Random House.

Bennett, C. (1980). *Nursing home life: What it is and what it could be.* New York: Tiresias Press.

Bennett, K. M., & Bennett, G. (2001). "And there's always this great hole inside that hurts": An empirical study of bereavement in later life. *Omega, Journal of Death and Dying, 42,* 237–251.

Bensinger, J. S., & Natenshon, M. A. (1991). Difficulties in recognizing adolescent health issues. In W. R. Hendee (Ed.), *The health of adolescents* (pp. 381–410). San Francisco: Jossey-Bass.

Beresford, L. (1993). *The hospice handbook: A complete guide.* Boston: Little, Brown.

Berger, A., Badham, P., Kutscher, A. H., Berger, J., Perry, M., & Beloff, J. (Eds.). (1989). *Perspectives on death and dying: Cross-cultural and multi-disciplinary views.* Philadelphia: Charles Press.

Berkovitz, I. H. (1985). The role of schools in child, adolescent, and youth suicide prevention. In M. L. Peck, N. L. Farberow, & R. E. Litman (Eds.), *Youth suicide* (pp. 170–190). New York: Springer.

Berman, A. L. (1986). Helping suicidal adolescents: Needs and responses. In C. A. Corr & J. N. McNeil (Eds.), *Adolescence and death* (pp. 151–166). New York: Springer.

Berman, A. L. (1988). Fictional depiction of suicide in television film and imitation effects. *American Journal of Psychiatry, 145,* 982–986.

Berman, A. L., & Jobes, D. (1991). *Adolescent suicide: Assessment and intervention.* Washington, DC: American Psychological Association.

Bern Klug, M., DeViney, S., & Ekerdt, D. J. (2000). Variations in funeral-related costs of older adults and the role of pre-need funeral contracts and type of disposition. *Omega, Journal of Death and Dying, 41,* 23–38.

Bertman, S. L. (1974). Death education in the face of a taboo. In E. A. Grollman (Ed.), *Concerning death: A practical guide for the living* (pp. 333–361). Boston: Beacon Press.

Bertman, S. L. (1984). Children's and others' thoughts and expressions about death. In H. Wass & C. A. Corr (Eds.), *Helping children cope with death: Guidelines and resources* (2nd ed.; pp. 11–31). Washington, DC: Hemisphere.

Bertman, S. L. (1991). *Facing death: Images, insights, and interventions.* Washington, DC: Hemisphere.

Bertman, S. L. (Ed.). (1999). *Grief and the healing arts: Creativity as therapy.* Amityville, NY: Baywood.

Berzoff, J., & Silverman, P. (Eds.). (2004). *Living with dying: A comprehensive resource for health care professionals.* New York: Columbia University Press.

Bettelheim, B. (1977). *The uses of enchantment—The meaning and importance of fairy tales.* New York: Vintage Books.

Betzold, M. (1993). *Appointment with Doctor Death.* Troy, MI: Momentum Books.

Binkewicz, M. P. (2005). *Peaceful journey: A hospice chaplain's guide to end of life.* Ithaca, NY: Paramont Market Publishing.

Birren, J. E. (1964). *The psychology of aging.* Englewood Cliffs, NJ: Prentice Hall.

Bishop, S. L., & Cain, A. C. (2003). Widowed young parents: Changing perspectives on remarriage and cohabitation rates and their determinants. *Omega, Journal of Death and Dying, 47,* 299–312.

Blackhall, L. J., Murphy, S. T., Frank, G., Michel, V., & Azen, S. (1995). Ethnicity and attitudes toward patient autonomy. *Journal of the American Medical Association, 274,* 820–825.

Blackman, S. (1997). *Graceful exits: How great beings die.* New York: Weatherhill.

Blackmore, S. (1993). *Dying to live: Science and the near-death experience.* London: Grafton.

Blane, D. (1995). Social determinants of health: Socioeconomic status, social class, and ethnicity [Editorial]. *American Journal of Public Health, 85,* 903–905.

Blank, J. W. (1998). *The death of an adult child: A book for and about bereaved parents.* Amityville, NY: Baywood.

Blauner, R. (1966). Death and social structure. *Psychiatry, 29,* 378–394.

Bleich, J. D. (1979). The obligation to heal in the Judaic tradition: A comparative analysis. In F. Rosner & J. D. Bleich (Eds.), *Jewish bioethics* (pp. 1–44). New York: Sanhedrin Press.

Block, C. R. (1993). Lethal violence in the Chicago Latino community. In A. V. Wilson (Ed.), *Homicide: The victim/offender connection* (pp. 267–342). Cincinnati, OH: Anderson.

Bloom, A. (Metropolitan of Sourozh). (2000). Death and bereavement. In A. Walker & C. Carras (Eds.), *Living orthodoxy in the modern world* (pp. 85–107). Crestwood, NY: St. Vladimir's Seminary Press.

Blos, P. (1941). *The adolescent personality: A study of individual behavior.* New York: D. Appleton-Century-Crofts.

Blos, P. (1979). *The adolescent passage: Developmental issues.* New York: International Universities Press.

Bluebond-Langner, M. (1977). Meanings of death to children. In H. Feifel (Ed.), *New meanings of death* (pp. 47–66). New York: McGraw-Hill.

Bluebond-Langner, M. (1978). *The private worlds of dying children.* Princeton, NJ: Princeton University Press.

Bluebond-Langner, M. (1991). Living with cystic fibrosis: The well sibling's perspective. *Medical Anthropology Quarterly, 5*(2), 133–152.

Bluebond-Langner, M. (1996). *In the shadow of illness: Parents and siblings of the chronically ill child.* Princeton, NJ: Princeton University Press.

Bluebond-Langner, M., Belasco, J. B., Goldman, A., & Belasco. C. (2007). Understanding parents' approaches to care and treatment of children with cancer when standard therapy has failed. *Journal of Clinical Oncology, 25,* 2414–2419.

Bluebond-Langner, M., Lask, B., & Angst, D. B. (Eds.). (2001). *Psychosocial aspects of cystic fibrosis.* London: Arnold.

Bluebond-Langner, M., Perkel, D., & Goertzel, T. (1991). Pediatric cancer patients' peer relationships: The impact of an oncology camp experience. *Journal of Psychosocial Oncology, 9*(2), 67–80.

Blume, J. (1981). *Tiger eyes.* Scarsdale, NY: Bradbury.

Bolton, C., & Camp, D. J. (1987). Funeral rituals and the facilitation of grief work. *Omega, Journal of Death and Dying, 17,* 343–352.

Bolton, G. (Ed.). (2007). *Dying, bereavement and the healing arts.* Philadelphia: Jessica Kingsley.

Bolton, I. (1995). *My son, my son: A guide to healing after a suicide in the family* (Rev. ed.). Atlanta, GA: Bolton Press.

Bonanno, G. A. (2004). Loss, trauma and human resilience: Have we underestimated the human capacity to thrive after extremely aversive events? *American Psychologist, 59,* 20–28.

Bonanno, G. A. (2006). Is complicated grief a valid construct? *Clinical Psychology: Science and Practice, 13,* 129–134.

Borg, S., & Lasker, J. (1989). *When pregnancy fails: Families coping with miscarriage, stillbirth, and infant death* (Rev. ed.). New York: Bantam.

Borkman, T. (1976). Experiential knowledge: A new concept for the analysis of self-help groups. *Social Service Review, 50,* 445–456.

Boss, P. (1999). *Ambiguous loss: Learning to live with unresolved grief.* Cambridge, MA: Harvard University Press.

Bosticco, C., & Thompson, T. L. (2005). Narratives and story telling in coping with grief and bereavement. *Omega, Journal of Death and Dying, 51,* 1–16.

Bottrell, M. M., O'Sullivan, J. E., Robbins, M. A., Mitty, E. L., & Mezey, M. D. (2001). Transferring dying nursing home residents to the hospital: DON perspectives on the nurse's role in transfer decisions. *Geriatric Nursing, 22,* 313–317.

Bove, A. A. (2005). *Complete guide to wills, estates, and trusts* (3rd ed.). New York: Owl Books.

Bowen, M. (1991). Family reactions to death. In F. Walsh & M. McGoldrick (Eds.), *Living beyond loss: Death in the family* (pp. 164–175). New York: Norton.

Bowker, J. (1991). *The meanings of death.* Cambridge, England: Cambridge University Press.

Bowlby, J. (1961). Processes of mourning. *International Journal of Psychoanalysis, 42,* 317–340.

Bowlby, J. (1969–80). *Attachment and loss* (3 vols.). New York: Basic Books.

Bowman, L. E. (1959). *The American funeral: A study in guilt, extravagance and sublimity.* Washington, DC: Public Affairs Press.

Boyd-Franklin, N., Steiner, G. L., & Boland, M. G. (Eds.). (1995). *Children, families, and HIV/AIDS: Psychosocial and therapeutic issues.* New York: Guilford.

Brabant, S. (1996). *Mending the torn fabric: For those who grieve and those who want to help them.* Amityville, NY: Baywood.

Brabant, S., Forsyth, C., & McFarlain, G. (1995). Life after the death of a child: Initial and long term support from others. *Omega, Journal of Death and Dying, 31,* 67–85.

Bradach, K. M., & Jordan, J. R. (1995). Long-term effects of a family history of traumatic death on adolescent individuation. *Death Studies, 19,* 315–336.

Brady, E. M. (1979). Telling the story: Ethics and dying. *Hospital Progress, 60,* 57–62.

Bramblett, J. (1991). *When good-bye is forever: Learning to live again after the loss of a child.* New York: Ballantine.

Braun, K. L., Tanji, V. M., & Heck, R. (2001). Support for physician-assisted suicide: Exploring the impact of ethnicity and attitudes toward planning for death. *Gerontology, 41*(1), 51–60.

Braun, K., Pietsch, J., & Blanchette, P. (Eds.). (2000). *Cultural issues in end-of-life decision making.* Thousand Oaks, CA: Sage.

Braun, M. L., & Berg, D. H. (1994). Meaning reconstruction in the experience of bereavement. *Death Studies, 18,* 105–129.

Breck, J. (1995). Euthanasia and the quality of life debate. *Christian Bioethics, 1,* 322–337.

Breed, W. (1972). Five components of a basic suicide syndrome. *Life-Threatening Behavior, 2,* 3–18.

Brennan, C. (1998, November 5). Al Joyner can't escape memories of FloJo. *USA Today,* p. 5E.

Brent, S. (1978). Puns, metaphors, and misunderstandings in a two-year-old's conception of death. *Omega, Journal of Death and Dying, 8,* 285–294.

Brent, S. B., & Speece, M.W. (1993). "Adult" conceptualization of irreversibility: Implications for the development of the concept of death. *Death Studies, 17,* 203–224.

Brodman, B. (1976). *The Mexican cult of death in myth and literature.* Gainesville: University of Florida Press.

Brokaw, T. (1998). *The greatest generation.* New York: Random House.

Brothers, J. (1990).*Widowed.* New York: Simon & Schuster.

Brown, E., with B. Warr. (2007). *Supporting the child and the family in paediatric palliative care.* Philadelphia: Jessica Kingsley.

Brown, J. E. (1987). *The spiritual legacy of the American Indian.* New York: Crossroad.

Brown, J. H., Henteleff, P., Barakat, S., & Rowe, C. J. (1986). Is it normal for terminally ill patients to desire death? *American Journal of Psychiatry, 143,* 208–211.

Brown, M.W. (1958). *The dead bird.* Reading, MA: Addison-Wesley.

Browning, C. R. (2004). *The origins of the final solution: The evolution of Nazi Jewish policy, September 1939–March 1942.* Lincoln: University of Nebraska Press.

Broyard, A. (1992). *Intoxicated by my illness, and other writings on life and death* (A. Broyard, Comp. & Ed.). New York: Clarkson Potter.

Brubaker, E. (1985). Older parents' reactions to the death of adult children: Implications for practice. *Journal of Gerontological Social Work, 9,* 35–48.

Bruner, J. S. (1962). *The process of education.* Cambridge: Harvard University Press.

Bryant, C. D. (Ed.). (2003). *Handbook of death and dying* (2 vols.). Thousand Oaks, CA: Sage.

Bryer, K. B. (1979). The Amish way of death: A study of family support systems. *American Psychologist, 34,* 255–261.

Buchanan, D., & Cernada, G. (Eds.). (1998). *Progress in preventing AIDS? Dogma, dissent and innovation—global perspectives.* Amityville, NY: Baywood.

Bucholz, J. A. (2002). *Homicide survivors: Misunderstood grievers.* Amityville, NY: Baywood.

Buchwald, A. (2006). *Too soon to say goodbye.* New York: Random House.

Buckley, S. (2001, September 2). Slow change of heart. *St. Petersburg Times,* pp. 1A, 8A–9A.

Buckman, R. (1992a). *How to break bad news: A guide for health care professionals.* Baltimore: Johns Hopkins University Press.

Buckman, R. (1992b). *I don't know what to say: How to help and support someone who is dying.* New York: Vintage Books.

Buell, J. (2006). *The emotional first aid manual.* Mission Viejo, CA: Innovations Press.

Bühler, C. (1968). The general structure of the human life cycle. In C. Bühler & F. Massarik (Eds.), *The course of human life: A study of goals in the humanistic perspective* (pp. 12–26). New York: Springer.

Bumiller, E. (2001, November 12). Honoring lost lives from some 80 nations in memorial for world. *The New York Times,* p. B10.

Bunting, E. (1982). *The happy funeral.* New York: Harper & Row.

Burnell, G. M. (2007). *Freedom to choose: How to make end-of-life decisions on your own terms.* Amityville, NY: Baywood.

Burns, S. B. (1990). *Sleeping beauty: Memorial photography in America.* Altadena, CA: Twelvetrees Press.

Burtt, E. A. (1955). *The teachings of the compassionate Buddha.* New York: New American Library.

Busch, K. G., Zagar, R., Hughes, J. R., Arbit, J., & Bussell, R. E. (1990). Adolescents who kill. *Journal of Clinical Psychology, 46,* 472–485.

Bush, J. (2007). *Ana's story: A journey of hope.* New York: HarperCollins.

Butler, C. L., & Lagoni, L. S. (1996). Children and pet loss. In C. A. Corr & D. M. Corr (Eds.), *Handbook of childhood death and bereavement* (pp. 179–200). New York: Springer.

Butler, R. N. (1963). The life review: An interpretation of reminiscence in the aged. *Psychiatry, 26,* 65–76.

Butler, R. N. (1969). Age-ism: Another form of bigotry. *The Gerontologist, 9,* 243–246.

Butler, R. N. (1975). *Why survive? Being old in America.* New York: Harper & Row.

Butler, R, N., & Lewis, M. I. (1982). *Aging and mental health* (3rd ed.). St. Louis, MO: Mosby.

Byock, I. (1996). The nature of suffering and the nature of opportunity at the end of life. *Clinics in Geriatric Medicine, 12,* 237–252.

Byock, I. (1997). *Dying well: The prospect for growth at the end of life.* New York: Putnam.

Byock, I. (2004). *The four things that matter most: A book about living.* New York: Free Press.

Cade, S. (1963). Cancer: The patient's viewpoint and the clinician's problems. *Proceedings of the Royal Society of Medicine, 56,* 1–8.

Cadell, S., & Marshall, S. (2007). The (re)construction of self after the death of a partner to HIV/AIDS. *Death Studies, 31,* 537–548.

Cain, A. (Ed.). (1972). *Survivors of suicide.* Springfield, IL: Bannerstone House.

Caine, L. (1975).*Widow.* New York: Bantam Books.

Caine, L. (1999). *Being a widow.* New York: Penguin Books.

Calhoun, L. G., & Tedeschi, R. G. (Eds.). (1999). *Facilitating posttraumatic growth: A clinician's guide.* Mahwah, NJ: Lawrence Erlbaum Associates.

Calhoun, L. G., & Tedeschi, R. G. (Eds.). (2006). *The handbook of posttraumatic growth: Research and practice.* Mahwah, NJ: Lawrence Erlbaum Associates.

Calhoun, L. G., Abernathy, C. B., & Selby, J.W. (1986). The rules of bereavement: Are suicidal deaths different? *Journal of Community Psychology, 14,* 213–218.

Caliandro, G., & Hughes, C. (1998). The experience of being a grandmother who is the primary caregiver for her HIV-positive grandchild. *Nursing Research, 47,* 17–113.

Callanan, M., & Kelley, P. (1992). *Final gifts: Understanding the special awareness, needs, and communications of the dying.* New York: Poseidon Press.

Callender, C. O., Hall, L. E., Yeager, C. L., Barber, J. B., Dunston, G. M., & Pinn-Wiggins, V. W. (1991). Organ donation and blacks: A critical frontier. *New England Journal of Medicine, 325,* 442–444.

Calvin, S., & Smith, I. M. (1986). Counseling adolescents in death-related situations. In C. A. Corr & J. N. McNeil (Eds.), *Adolescence and death* (pp. 215–230). New York: Springer.

Camenisch, P. F. (Ed.). (1994). *Religious methods and resources in bioethics.* Boston: Kluwer.

Cameron, E. (2005). *Witness to AIDS.* London: I. B. Taurus.

Campbell, G. R. (1989). The political epidemiology of infant mortality: A health crisis among Montana American

Indians. *American Indian Culture and Research Journal, 13,* 105–148.

Campbell, S., & Silverman, P. R. (1996). *Widower: When men are left alone.* Amityville, NY: Baywood.

Canine, J. D. (1999). *What am I going to do with myself when I die?* Stamford, CT: Appleton & Lange.

Cantor, R. C. (1978). *And a time to live: Toward emotional well-being during the crisis of cancer.* New York: Harper & Row.

Caplan, A. L., & Coelho, D. H. (Eds.). (1999). *The ethics of organ transplants: The current debate.* Buffalo, NY: Prometheus.

Caplan, A. L., McCartney, J. J., & Sisti, D. A. (Eds.). (2006). *The case of Terri Schiavo: Ethics at the end of life.* Buffalo, NY: Prometheus.

Carey, R. G. (1979). Weathering widowhood: Problems and adjustment of the widowed during the first year. *Omega, Journal of Death and Dying, 10,* 263–274.

Carlson, L. (1998). *Caring for the dead: Your final act of love.* Hinesburg, VT: Upper Access.

Carmack, B. J. (2003). *Grieving the death of a pet.* Minneapolis, MN: Augsburg Fortress.

Carr, B. A., & Lee, E. S. (1978). Navajo tribal mortality: A life table analysis of the leading causes of death. *Social Biology, 25,* 279–287.

Carr, C. (2002). *The lessons of terror.* New York: Random House.

Carr, D., Nesse, R., & Wortman, C. (Eds.). (2005). *Spousal bereavement in late life.* New York: Springer.

Carrick, C. (1976). *The accident.* New York: Seabury Press.

Carse, J. P. (1980). *Death and existence: A conceptual history of mortality.* New York: Wiley.

Carson, U. (1984). Teachable moments occasioned by "small deaths." In H. Wass & C. A. Corr (Eds.), *Childhood and death* (pp. 315–343). Washington, DC: Hemisphere.

Carter, B. S., & Levetown, M. (Eds.). (2004). *Palliative care for infants, children, and adolescents: A practical handbook.* Baltimore: Johns Hopkins University Press.

Carter, B., & McGoldrick, M. (Eds.). (1988). *The changing family life cycle: A framework for family therapy* (2nd ed.). New York: Gardner Press.

Carter, J. (1998). *The virtues of aging.* New York: Library of Contemporary Thought/Ballantine.

Cassarett, D. J., Hirschman, K. B., & Henry, M. R. (2001). Does hospice have a role in nursing home care at the end of life? *Journal of the American Geriatrics Society, 49,* 1493–1498.

Cassell, E. J. (1985). *Talking with patients: Vol. 1, The theory of doctor-patient communication; Vol. 2, Clinical technique.* Cambridge, MA: MIT Press.

Cassell, E. J. (1991). *The nature of suffering and the goals of medicine.* New York: Oxford University Press.

Cassileth, B. R., Zupkis, R. V., Sutton-Smith, K., & March, V. (1980). Information and participation preferences among cancer patients. *Annals of Internal Medicine, 92,* 832–836.

Cate, F. H., & Gill, B. A. (1991). *The Patient Self-Determination Act: Implementation issues and opportunities.* Washington, DC: The Annenberg Washington Program.

Catt, S., Blanchard, M., Addington-Hall, J., Zis, M., Blizard, R., & King, M. (2005). Older adults' attitudes to death, palliative treatment and hospice care. *Palliative Medicine, 19*(5), 402–410.

Cavanaugh, J. C., & Blanchard-Fields, F. (2005). *Adult development and aging* (5th ed.). Belmont, CA: Thomson Wadsworth.

Cebuhar, J. K. (2006). *Last things first, just in case . . . : The practical guide to living wills and durable powers of attorney for health matters.* West Des Moines, IA: Murphy Publishing.

Center for the Advancement of Health. (2004). Report on bereavement and grief research [Special Issues]. *Death Studies, 28*(6).

Centers for Disease Control (CDC). (1981a). *Pneumocystis* pneumonia—Los Angeles. *Morbidity and Mortality Weekly Report, 30,* 250–252.

Centers for Disease Control (CDC). (1981b). Kaposi's sarcoma and *Pneumocystis* pneumonia among homosexual men—New York City and California. *Morbidity and Mortality Weekly Report, 30,* 305–308.

Centers for Disease Control (CDC). (1981c). Follow-up on Kaposi's sarcoma and *Pneumocystis* pneumonia. *Morbidity and Mortality Weekly Report, 30,* 409–410.

Centers for Disease Control (CDC). (1992a). 1993 revised classification system for HIV infection and expanded surveillance case definition for AIDS among adolescents and adults. *Morbidity and Mortality Weekly Report, 41,* No. RR-17.

Centers for Disease Control and Prevention (CDC). (1992b). *HIV/AIDS Surveillance Report,* Vol. 4(1). Atlanta: U.S. Department of Health and Human Services, Centers for Disease Control and Prevention.

Centers for Disease Control and Prevention (CDC). (2001). The global HIV and AIDS epidemic, 2001. *Morbidity and Mortality Weekly Report, 50*(21), 434–439.

Centers for Disease Control and Prevention (CDC). (2006a). *HIV/AIDS Surveillance Report, 2005.* Vol. 17. Atlanta: U.S. Department of Health and Human Services, Centers for Disease Control and Prevention. Also available at: http://www.cdc.gov/hiv/topics/surveillance/resources/reports/.

Centers for Disease Control and Prevention (CDC). (2006b). Twenty-five years of HIV/AIDS—United States, 1981–2006. *Morbidity and Mortality Weekly Report, 55*(21), 585–589.

Centers for Disease Control and Prevention (CDC). (2006c). Epidemiology of HIV/AIDS—United States, 1981–2005. *Morbidity and Mortality Weekly Report, 55*(21), 589–592.

Centers for Disease Control and Prevention (CDC). (2006d). Reduction in perinatal transmission of human immunodeficiency virus—United States, 1985–2005. *Morbidity and Mortality Weekly Report, 55*(21), 592–597.

Centers for Disease Control and Prevention (CDC). (2006e). National Vital Statistics System, National Center for Health Statistics, Mortality Statistics Branch. Unpublished mortality data available at: http://www.cdc.gov/nchs/datawh/statab/unpubd/mortabs.htm.

Chambers, J. S. (2005). *The easy will and living will kit* (+ CD-ROM). Naperville, IL: Sphinx Publishing.

Chance, S. (1994). *Stronger than death: When suicide touches your life—A mother's story.* New York: Avon.

Chappell, B. J. (2001). My journey to the Dougy Center. In O. D. Weeks & C. Johnson (Eds.), *When all the friends have gone: A guide for aftercare providers* (pp. 141–154). Amityville, NY: Baywood.

Chen, P. W. (2006). *Final exam: A surgeon's reflections on mortality.* New York: Knopf.

Chethik, N. (2001). *FatherLoss: How sons of all ages come to terms with the deaths of their dads.* New York: Hyperion Books.

Chidester, D. (1990). *Patterns of transcendence: Religion, death, and dying.* Belmont, CA: Wadsworth.

Childers, P., & Wimmer, M. (1971). The concept of death in early childhood. *Child Development, 42,* 1299–1301.

Childress, J. F. (1990). The place of autonomy in bioethics. *Hastings Center Report, 20*(1), 12–17.

Choron, J. (1963). *Death and Western thought.* New York: Collier Books.

Choron, J. (1964). *Death and modern man.* New York: Collier Books.

Christ, G. H. (2000). *Healing children's grief: Surviving a parent's death from cancer.* New York: Oxford University Press.

Christ, G. H., Siegel, K., & Christ, A. E. (2002). Adolescent grief: "It never really hit me . . . until it actually happened." *Journal of the American Medical Association, 288,* 1269–1278.

Christakis, N., & Iwashyna, T. (2003). The health impact of hospice care on families: A matched cohort study of hospice use by decedents and mortality outcomes in surviving, widowed spouses. *Social Science and Medicine, 57*(3), 465–475.

Churn, A. (2003). *The end is just the beginning: Lessons in grieving for African Americans.* New York: Broadway Books.

Cicirelli, V. G. (2002). *Older adults' views on death.* New York: Springer.

Clark, D. (Ed). (2002). *Cicely Saunders – founder of the hospice movement. Selected letters 1959–1999.* Oxford, UK: Oxford University Press.

Clark, D. (2007). End-of-life care around the world: Achievements to date and challenges remaining. In C. M. Parkes (Ed.), "Hospice heritage": In memory of Dame Cicely Saunders [Special issue]. *Omega, Journal of Death and Dying, 56,* 101–110.

Clark, D., Small, N., Wright, M., Winslow, M., & Hughes, N. (2005). *A bit of heaven for the few?: An oral history of the modern hospice movement in the United Kingdom.* Lancaster, United Kingdom: Observatory Publications.

Clark, J., & Cheshire, A. (2004). RIP by the roadside: A comparative study of roadside memorials in New South Wales, Australia, and Texas, United States. *Omega, Journal of Death and Dying, 48,* 203–222.

Clark, J., & Franzmann, M. (2006). Authority from grief, presence and place in the making of roadside memorials. *Death Studies, 30,* 579–599.

Clayton, P. J. (1973). The clinical morbidity of the first year of bereavement: A review. *Comprehensive Psychiatry, 14,* 151–157.

Clayton, P. J. (1974). Mortality and morbidity in the first year of widowhood. *Archives of General Psychiatry, 30,* 747–750.

Clayton, P. J., Herjanic, M., Murphy, G. E., & Woodruff, R. A. (1974). Mourning and depression: Their similarities and differences. *Canadian Psychiatric Association Journal, 19,* 309–312.

Cleckley, M., Estes, E., & Norton, P. (Eds.). (1992). *We need not walk alone: After the death of a child* (2nd ed.). Oak Brook, IL: The Compassionate Friends.

Clements, P. T., Vigil, G. J., Manno, M. S., Henry, G. C., Wilks, J., Das, S., et al. (2003). Cultural perspectives of death, grief, and bereavement. *Journal of Psychosocial Nursing, 41*(7), 18–26.

Clifford, D. (2007). *Make your own living trust* (+ CD-ROM). Berkeley, CA: Nolo Press.

Clifford, D., & Jordan, C. (2006). *Plan your estate* (8th ed.). Berkeley, CA: Nolo Press.

Clifton, C. E. (2000). Mbeki fails to break the silence. *Positively Aware, The Journal of Test Positive Aware Network, 11*(5), 54–55.

Cobain, B. (2007). *When nothing matters anymore: A survival guide for depressed teens* (rev. & updated ed.). Minneapolis: Free Spirit Publishing.

Coffin, M. M. (1976). *Death in early America: The history and folklore of customs and superstitions of early medicine, burial and mourning.* Nashville, TN: Thomas Nelson.

Cohen, C. B. (1996). Christian perspectives on assisted suicide and euthanasia: The Anglican tradition. *Journal of Law, Medicine and Ethics, 24,* 369–379.

Cohen, C. J. (1999). *The boundaries of blackness: AIDS and the breakdown of black politics.* Chicago: The University of Chicago Press.

Cohen, J. A., Mannarino, A. P., & Deblinger, E. (2006). *Treating trauma and traumatic grief in children and adolescents.* New York: Guilford.

Cohen, M. N. (1989). *Health and the rise of civilization.* New Haven, CT: Yale University Press.

Colby, W. H. (2002). *Long goodbye: The deaths of Nancy Cruzan.* Carlsbad, CA: Hay House.

Colby, W. H. (2006). *Unplugged: Reclaiming our right to die in America.* New York: American Management Association.

Coleman, J. C. (1978). Current contradictions in adolescent theory. *Journal of Youth and Adolescence, 7,* 1–11.

Colen, B. D. (1976). *Karen Ann Quinlan: Dying in the age of eternal life.* New York: Nash.

Collett, L., & Lester, D. (1969). The fear of death and the fear of dying. *Journal of Psychology, 72,* 179–181.

Collier, A. K. (2003). *Still with me: A daughter's journey of love and loss.* New York: Simon & Schuster.

Collins, C. O., & Rhine, C. D. (2003). Roadside memorials. *Omega, Journal of Death and Dying, 47,* 221–244.

Colorado Collaboration on End-of-Life Care. (n.d.). *Five themes for caring: Spiritual care giving guide.* Denver, CO: Author.

Combs, C. C., & Slann, M. (2002). *Encyclopedia of terrorism.* New York: Facts on File.

Comer, J. (2006). *When roles reverse: A guide to parenting your parents.* Charlottesville, VA: Hampton Roads Publishing Co.

Comstock, G. A., & Paik, H. (1991). *Television and the American child.* San Diego, CA: Academic Press.

Conger, J. J., & Peterson, A. C. (1984). *Adolescence and youth: Psychological development in a changing world* (3rd ed.). New York: Harper & Row.

Connor, S. R. (1998). *Hospice: Practice, pitfalls, and promise.* Bristol, PA: Taylor & Francis.

Connor, S. R. (2007). Development of hospice and palliative care in the United States. In C. M. Parkes (Ed.), "Hospice heritage": In memory of Dame Cicely Saunders [Special issue]. *Omega, Journal of Death and Dying, 56,* 89–99.

Connor, S. R., Pyenson, B., Fitch, K., Spence, C., & Iwasaki, K. (2007). Comparing hospice and nonhospice patient survival among patients who die within a three-year window. *Journal of Pain and Symptom Management, 33,* 238–246.

Conrad, B. H. (1997). *When a child has been murdered: Ways you can help the grieving parents.* Amityville, NY: Baywood.

Contro, N., Larson, J., Scofield, S., Sourkes, B., & Cohen, H. (2002). Family perspectives on the quality of pediatric palliative care. *Archives of Pediatric and Adolescent Medicine, 156*(1), 14–19.

Cook, A. S., & Dworkin, D. S. (1992). *Helping the bereaved: Therapeutic interventions for children, adolescents, and adults.* New York: Basic Books.

Cook, A. S., & Oltjenbruns, K. A. (1998). *Dying and grieving: Lifespan and family perspectives* (2nd ed.). Fort Worth, TX: Harcourt Brace.

Corace, B. (2000, July/August). End-of-life care: A personal reflection. *Innovations in end-of-life care, 2*(4), 81–82. M. Z. Solomon, A. L. Romer, K. S. Heller, & D. E. Weissman (Eds.). Larchmont, NY: Mary Ann Liebert Publishers. Retrieved September 5, 2001, from http://www2.edc.org/lastacts/archives/archivesJuly00/ reflections.asp#Corace.

Cordesman, A. H. (2005). *The challenge of biological terrorism.* Washington, DC: Center for Strategies and International Studies.

Corless, I. B. (2001). Bereavement. In B. R. Ferrell & N. Coyle (Eds.), *Textbook of palliative nursing* (pp. 352–362). New York: Oxford University Press.

Corless, I. B., & Foster, Z. (Eds.). (1999). The hospice heritage: Celebrating our future [Special issue]. *The Hospice Journal, 14* (3/4).

Corley, E. A. (1973). *Tell me about death, tell me about funerals.* Santa Clara, CA: Grammatical Sciences.

Corr, C. A. (1978). A model syllabus for death and dying courses. *Death Education, 1,* 433–457.

Corr, C. A. (1980).Workshops on children and death. *Essence, 4,* 5–18.

Corr, C. A. (1981). Hospices, dying persons, and hope. In R. A. Pacholski & C. A. Corr (Eds.), *New directions in death education and counseling: Enhancing the quality of life in the nuclear age* (pp. 14–20). Arlington, VA: Forum for Death Education and Counseling.

Corr, C. A. (1984a). Helping with death education. In H. Wass & C. A. Corr (Eds.), *Helping children cope with death: Guidelines and resources* (2nd ed.; pp. 49–73).Washington, DC: Hemisphere.

Corr, C. A. (1984b). A model syllabus for children and death courses. *Death Education, 8,* 11–28.

Corr, C. A. (1991). Should young children attend funerals? What constitutes reliable advice? *Thanatos, 16*(4), 19–21.

Corr, C. A. (1992a). A task-based approach to coping with dying. *Omega, Journal of Death and Dying, 24,* 81–94.

Corr, C. A. (1992b). Teaching a college course on children and death: A 13-year report. *Death Studies, 16,* 343–356.

Corr, C. A. (1992c). *Someone you love is dying: How do you cope?* Houston, TX: Service Corporation International.

Corr, C. A. (1993a). Coping with dying: Lessons that we should and should not learn from the work of Elisabeth Kübler-Ross. *Death Studies, 17,* 69–83.

Corr, C. A. (1993b). The day we went to Auschwitz. *Omega, Journal of Death and Dying, 27,* 105–113.

Corr, C. A. (1995a). Children and death: Where have we been? Where are we now? In D. W. Adams & E. J. Deveau (Eds.), *Beyond the innocence of childhood: Factors influencing children and adolescents' perceptions and attitudes toward death* (Vol. 1, pp. 15–28). Amityville, NY: Baywood.

Corr, C. A. (1995b). Children's understandings of death: Striving to understand death. In K. J. Doka (Ed.), *Children mourning, mourning children* (pp. 3–16). Washington, DC: Hospice Foundation of America.

Corr, C. A. (1995c). Death education for adults. In I. B. Corless, B. B. Germino, & M. A. Pittman (Eds.), *A challenge for living: Dying, death, and bereavement* (pp. 351–365). Boston: Jones & Bartlett.

Corr, C. A. (1995d). Entering into adolescent understandings of death. In E. A. Grollman (Ed.), *Bereaved children and teens: A support guide for parents and professionals* (pp. 21–35). Boston: Beacon Press.

Corr, C. A. (1996). Children and questions about death. In S. Strack (Ed.), *Death and the quest for meaning: Essays in honor of Herman Feifel* (pp. 317–338). Northvale, NJ: Jason Aronson.

Corr, C. A. (1998a). Developmental perspectives on grief and mourning. In K. J. Doka & J. D. Davidson (Eds.), *Living with grief: Who we are, how we grieve* (pp. 143–159). Washington, DC: Hospice Foundation of America.

Corr, C. A. (1998b). Enhancing the concept of disenfranchised grief. *Omega, Journal of Death and Dying, 38,* 1–20.

Corr, C. A. (2000a). Using books to help children and adolescents cope with death: Guidelines and bibliography. In K. J. Doka (Ed.), *Living with grief: Children, adolescents, and loss* (pp. 295–314). Washington, DC: Hospice Foundation of America.

Corr, C. A. (2000b).What do we know about grieving children and adolescents? In K. J. Doka (Ed.), *Living with grief: Children, adolescents, and loss* (pp. 21–32). Washington, DC: Hospice Foundation of America.

Corr, C. A. (2001a, July). Restructuring relationships: Four examples. *Journeys: A Newsletter to Help in Bereavement, 1,* 3.

Corr, C. A. (2001b). Some reflections on the National Donor Quilt. *For Those Who Give and Grieve, 9*(4), 6.

Corr, C. A. (2002a). Revisiting the concept of disenfranchised grief. In K. J. Doka (Ed.), *Disenfranchised grief: New directions, challenges, and strategies for practice* (pp. 39–60). Champaign, IL: Research Press.

Corr, C. A. (2002b). Coping with challenges to assumptive worlds. In J. Kauffman (Ed.), *Loss of the assumptive world: A theory of traumatic loss* (pp. 127–138). New York: Brunner-Routledge.

Corr, C. A. (2002c). Teaching a college course on children and death for 22 years: A supplemental report. *Death Studies, 26,* 595–606.

Corr, C. A. (2002d). Helping adolescents cope with long-term illness and death. *The Prevention Researcher, 9*(2), 6–8.

Corr, C. A. (2003a). Loss, grief, and trauma in public tragedy. In M. Lattanzi-Licht & K. J. Doka (Eds.), *Living with grief: Coping with public tragedy* (pp. 63–76). Washington, DC: Hospice Foundation of America.

Corr, C. A. (2003b). Death education for adults. In I. Corless, B. B. Germino, & M. A. Pittman (Eds.), *A challenge for living: Dying, death, and bereavement* (2nd ed.; pp. 43–60). New York: Springer.

Corr, C. A. (Ed.). (2004a). Death-related literature for children [Special issue]. *Omega, Journal of Death and Dying, 48*(4).

Corr, C. A. (2004b). Bereavement, grief, and mourning in death-related literature for children. *Omega, Journal of Death and Dying, 48,* 337–363.

Corr, C. A. (2004c). Grandparents in death-related literature for children, *Omega, Journal of Death and Dying, 48,* 383–397.

Corr, C. A. (2004d). Pet loss in death-related literature for children. *Omega, Journal of Death and Dying, 48,* 399–414.

Corr, C. A. (2004e). Spirituality in death-related literature for children. *Omega, Journal of Death and Dying, 48*(4), 365–381.

Corr, C. A. (2004f). Teaching courses on death, dying, and bereavement. In G. R. Cox & T. B. Gongaware (Eds.), *The sociology of death and dying: A teaching resource* (2nd ed.; pp. 23–32). Washington, DC: American Sociological Association.

Corr, C. A. (2005). Organ donation: Ethical issues and issues of loss and grief. In K. J. Doka, B. Jennings, & C. A. Corr (Eds.). (2005). *Living with grief: Ethical dilemmas at the end of life* (pp. 251–266). Washington, DC: Hospice Foundation of America.

Corr, C. A. (2007a). Anticipatory grief and mourning: An overview. In K. J. Doka (Ed.), *Living with grief: Before and after a death* (pp. 5–20). Washington, DC: Hospice Foundation of America.

Corr, C. A. (2007b). Parents in death-related literature for children, *Omega, Journal of Death and Dying, 54,* 237–254.

Corr, C. A. (in press, a). Death-related literature for children and adolescents: Selected, annotated, and with guidelines and resources for adults. In A. Armstrong-Dailey & S. Zarbock (Eds.). (in press). *Hospice care for children* (3rd ed.). New York: Oxford University Press.

Corr, C. A. (in press, b). Siblings and child friends in death-related literature for children, *Omega, Journal of Death and Dying.*

Corr, C. A., & Balk, D. E. (Eds.). (1996). *Handbook of adolescent death and bereavement.* New York: Springer.

Corr, C. A., & Corr, D. M. (Eds.). (1983). *Hospice care: Principles and practice.* New York: Springer.

Corr, C. A., & Corr, D. M. (Eds.). (1985a). *Hospice approaches to pediatric care.* New York: Springer.

Corr, C. A., & Corr, D. M. (1985b). Situations involving children: A challenge for the hospice movement. *Hospice Journal, 1,* 63–77.

Corr, C. A., & Corr, D. M. (1985c). Pediatric hospice care. *Pediatrics, 76,* 774–780.

Corr, C. A., & Corr, D. M. (1988). What is pediatric hospice care? *Children's Health Care, 17,* 4–11.

Corr, C. A., & Corr, D. M. (1992a). Adult hospice day care. *Death Studies, 16,* 155–171.

Corr, C. A., & Corr, D. M. (1992b). Children's hospice care. *Death Studies, 16,* 431–149.

Corr, C. A., & Corr, D. M. (Eds.). (1996). *Handbook of childhood death and bereavement.* New York: Springer.

Corr, C. A., & Corr, D. M. (1998). Key elements in a framework for helping grieving children and adolescents. *Illness, Crisis, and Loss, 6*(2), 142–160.

Corr, C. A., & Corr, D. M. (2000). Anticipatory mourning and coping with dying: Similarities, differences, and suggested guidelines for helpers. In T. A. Rando (Ed.), *Clinical dimensions of anticipatory mourning: Theory and practice in working with the dying, their loved ones, and their caregivers* (pp. 223–251). Champaign, IL: Research Press.

Corr, C. A., & Corr, D. M. (2003a). Death, dying, and bereavement in the United States of America. In J. D. Morgan & P. Laungani (Eds.), *Death and bereavement around the world, Vol. 2: The Americas* (pp. 37–55). Amityville, NY: Baywood.

Corr, C. A., & Corr, D. M. (2003b). Sudden infant death syndrome. In C. D. Bryant (Ed.), *Handbook of death and dying* (Vol. 1, pp. 275–283). Thousand Oaks, CA: Sage.

Corr, C. A., & Corr, D. M. (2003c). Death education. In C. D. Bryant (Ed.), *Handbook of death and dying* (Vol. 1, pp. 292–301). Thousand Oaks, CA: Sage.

Corr, C. A., & Corr, D. M. (2007a). Culture, socialization, and dying. In D. E. Balk, C. Wogrin, G. Thornton, & D. Meagher. (Eds.), *ADEC handbook of thanatology* (pp. 3–9). Northbrook, IL: Association for Death Education and Counseling.

Corr, C. A., & Corr, D. M. (2007b). Historical and contemporary perspectives on loss, grief, and mourning. In D. E. Balk, C. Wogrin, G. Thornton, & D. Meagher. (Eds.), *ADEC handbook of thanatology* (pp. 131–142). Northbrook, IL: Association for Death Education and Counseling.

Corr, C. A., & Doka, K. J. (2001). Master concepts in the field of death, dying, and bereavement: Coping versus adaptive strategies. *Omega, Journal of Death and Dying, 43,* 183–199.

Corr, C. A., & McNeil, J. N. (Eds.). (1986). *Adolescence and death.* New York: Springer.

Corr, C. A., & the Members of the Executive Committee of the National Donor Family Council. (2001). The National Donor Family Council and its Giving, Grieving, Growing™ program. *Progress in Transplantation, 11,* 255–260.

Corr, C. A., & the Staff of the Dougy Center. (1991). Support for grieving children: The Dougy Center and the hospice philosophy. *American Journal of Hospice and Palliative Care, 8*(4), 23–27.

Corr, C. A., Corr, K. M., & Ramsey, S. M. (2004) Alzheimer's disease and the challenge for hospice. In K. J. Doka (Ed.), *Living with grief: Alzheimer's disease* (pp. 227–243). Washington, DC: Hospice Foundation of America.

Corr, C. A., Doka, K. J., & Kastenbaum, R. (1999). Dying and its interpreters: A review of selected literature and some comments on the state of the field. *Omega, Journal of Death and Dying, 39,* 239–259.

Corr, C. A., Fuller, H., Barnickol, C. A., & Corr, D. M. (Eds.). (1991). *Sudden infant death syndrome: Who can help and how.* New York: Springer.

Corr, C. A., Morgan, J. D., & Wass, H. (Eds.). (1994). *Statements about death, dying, and bereavement by the International Work Group on Death, Dying, and Bereavement.* London, Ontario: King's College.

Corr, C. A., Nabe, C. M., & Corr, D. M. (1994). A task-based approach for understanding and evaluating funeral practices. *Thanatos, 19*(2), 10–15.

Cosby, B., & Poussaint, A. F. (2007). *Come on, people: On the path from victims to victors.* Nashville, TN: Thomas Nelson.

Counts, D. R., & Counts, D. A. (Eds.). (1991). *Coping with the final tragedy: Cultural variation in dying and grieving.* Amityville, NY: Baywood.

Cousins, N. (1979). *Anatomy of an illness as perceived by the patient: Reflections on healing and regeneration.* New York: Norton.

Cousins, N. (1989). *Head first: The biology of hope.* New York: E. P. Dutton.

Coutant, H. (1974). *First snow.* New York: Knopf.

Cowell, A. (2007, February 4). Deadly bird flu confirmed in British turkeys. *The New York Times,* p. 10.

Cowherd, R. (2004). *Healing the spirit: Inspirational stories of organ and tissue donors and their families.* Virginia Beach, VA: LifeNet Donor Memorial Foundation.

Cox, C., & Monk, A. (1993). Hispanic culture and family care of Alzheimer's patients. *Health and Social Work, 18*(2), 92–100.

Cox, G. R., & Fundis, R. J. (Eds.). (1992). *Spiritual, ethical and pastoral aspects of death and bereavement.* Amityville, NY: Baywood.

Cox, G. R., Bendiksen, R. A., & Stevenson, R. G. (Eds.). (2004a). *Complicated grieving and bereavement: Understanding and treating people experiencing loss.* Amityville, NY: Baywood.

Cox, G. R., Bendiksen, R. A., & Stevenson, R. G. (Eds.). (2004b). *Making sense of death: Spiritual, personal, and pastoral aspects of dying and bereavement.* Amityville, NY: Baywood.

Cox, H. G. (2000). *Later life: The realities of aging* (5th ed). Upper Saddle River, NJ: Prentice Hall.

Crase, D. R., & Crase, D. (1976). Helping children understand death. *Young Children, 32*(1), 21–25.

Crase, D. R., & Crase, D. (1984). Death education in the schools for older children. In H. Wass & C. A. Corr (Eds.), *Childhood and death* (pp. 345–363). Washington, DC: Hemisphere.

Craven, J., & Wald, F. S. (1975). Hospice care for dying patients. *American Journal of Nursing, 75,* 1816–1822.

Craven, M. (1973). *I heard the owl call my name.* New York: Dell.

Crawford, S. C. (1995). *Dilemmas of life and death: Hindu ethics in a North American context.* Albany, NY: State University of New York Press.

Cremation Association of North America. (2007). Retrieved May 5, 2007, from http://www.cremationassociation.org.

Crenshaw, D. A. (1995). *Bereavement: Counseling the grieving throughout the life cycle.* New York: Crossroad.

Crider, T. (1996). *Give sorrow words: A father's passage through grief.* Chapel Hill, NC: Algonquin Books.

Crissman, J. K. (1994). *Death and dying in central Appalachia: Changing attitudes and practices.* Urbana: University of Illinois Press.

Crowder, L. (2000). Chinese funerals in San Francisco Chinatown: American Chinese expressions in mortuary ritual performance. *Journal of American Folklore, 113*(450), 451–463.

Crowe, D. M. (2004). *Oskar Schindler: The untold account of his life, wartime activities and the true story behind the list.* Boulder, CO: Westview Press.

Czarnecki, J. P. (1989). *Last traces: The lost art of Auschwitz.* New York: Atheneum.

Czech, D. (1990). *Auschwitz chronicle, 1939–1945.* New York: Holt.

D'Epinay, C. J. L., Cavalli, S., & Spini, D. (2003). The death of a loved one: Impact on health and relationships in very old age. *Omega, Journal of Death and Dying, 47,* 265–284.

Daher, D. (2003). *And the passenger was death: The drama and trauma of losing a child.* Amityville, NY: Baywood.

Daley, K. C. (2004). Update on sudden infant death syndrome. *Current Opinion in Pediatrics, 16*(2), 227–232.

Dane, B. O. (1996). Children, HIV infection, and AIDS. In C. A. Corr & D. M. Corr (Eds.), *Handbook of childhood death and bereavement* (pp. 51–70). New York: Springer.

Danforth, L. M. (1982). *The death rituals of rural Greece.* Princeton, NJ: Princeton University Press.

Danielson, B. L., LaPree, A. J., Odland, M. D., & Steffens, E. K. (1998). Attitudes and beliefs concerning organ donation among Native Americans in the upper Midwest. *Journal of Transplant Coordination, 8,* 153–156.

Davidson, G.W. (1975). *Living with dying.* Minneapolis, MN: Augsburg Fortress.

Davidson, G.W. (1984). *Understanding mourning: A guide for those who grieve.* Minneapolis, MN: Augsburg Fortress.

Davidson, L. E., Rosenberg, M. L., Mercy, J., & Franklin, J. (1989). An epidemiologic study of risk factors in two teenage suicide clusters. *Journal of the American Medical Association, 262,* 2687–2692.

Davidson, L., & Gould, M. S. (1989). Contagion as a risk factor for youth suicide. In *Alcohol, Drug Abuse, and Mental Health Administration, Report of the secretary's task force on youth suicide* (Vol. 2, pp. 88–109). Washington, DC: U.S. Government Printing Office.

Davies, B. (1998). *Shadows in the sun: The experiences of sibling bereavement in childhood.* Washington, DC: Taylor & Francis.

Davies, B., & Howell, D. (1998). Special services for children. In D. Doyle, G.W.C. Hanks, & N. MacDonald (Eds.), *Oxford textbook of palliative medicine* (2nd ed.; pp. 1077–1084). New York: Oxford University Press.

Davies, B., Brenner, P., Orloff, S., Sumner, L., & Worden, J. W. (2002). Addressing spirituality in pediatric hospice and palliative care. *Journal of Palliative Care, 18*(1), 59–67.

Davies, B., Deveau, E., deVeber, B., Howell, D., Martinson, I., Papadatou, D., et al. (1998). Experiences of mothers in five countries whose child died of cancer. *Cancer Nursing, 21*(5), 301–311.

Davies, B., Gudmundsdottir, M., Worden, J. W., Orloff, S., Sumner, L., & Brenner, P. (2004). "Living in the dragon's shadow": Fathers' experiences of a child's life-limiting illness. *Death Studies, 28,* 111–135.

Davies, B., Reimer, J. C., Brown, P., & Martens, N. (1995). *Fading away: The experience of transition in families with terminal illness.* Amityville, NY: Baywood.

Davies, D. (1993). Cluster suicide in rural western Canada. *Canadian Journal of Psychiatry, 38,* 515–519.

Davies, R. E. (1999). The Diana community nursing team and paediatric palliative care. *British Journal of Nursing, 8,* 506–511.

Davis, C. G., & Nolen-Hoeksema, S. (2001). Loss and meaning: How do people make sense of loss? *American Behavioral Scientist, 44,* 726–741.

Davis, C. G., Wortman, C. B., Lehman, D. R., & Silver, R. C. (2000). Searching for meaning in loss: Are clinical assumptions correct? *Death Studies, 24,* 497–540.

Davis, D. L. (1991). *Empty cradle, broken heart: Surviving the death of your baby.* Golden, CO: Fulcrum.

Davis, D. S. (1994). Method in Jewish bioethics. In P. F. Camenisch (Ed.), *Religious methods and resources in bioethics* (pp. 109–126). Dordrecht, Germany: Kluwer.

Davis, J. (1995). The bait. In J. Davis, *Scrimmage of appetite* (pp. 12–13). Akron, OH: The University of Akron Press.

Dawidowicz, L. S. (1975). *The war against the Jews 1933–1945.* New York: Holt, Rinehart & Winston.

De Beauvoir, S. (1973). *A very easy death* (P. O'Brian, Trans.). New York: Warner. (Original work published 1964)

De Vries, B., & Roberts, P. (Eds.). (2004). Expressions of grief on the World Wide Web [Special issue]. *Omega, Journal of Death and Dying, 49*(1).

De Vries, B., & Rutherford, J. (2004). Memorializing loved ones on the World Wide Web. *Omega, Journal of Death and Dying, 49,* 5–26.

De Wachter, M.A.M. (1989). Active euthanasia in the Netherlands. *Journal of the American Medical Association, 262,* 3315–3319.

De Wachter, M.A.M. (1992). Euthanasia in the Netherlands. *Hastings Center Report, 22*(2), 23–30.

Dean, H. D., Steele, C. B., Satcher, A. J., & Nakashima, A. K. (2005). HIV/AIDS among minority races and ethnicities in the United States, 1999–2003. *Journal of the National Medical Association, 97*(7 Suppl.), S5–12.

Deaton, R. L., & Berkan, W. A. (1995). *Planning and managing death issues in the schools: A handbook.* Westport, CT: Greenwood Press.

DeFord, F. (1997). *Alex, the life of a child*. Nashville, TN: Thomas Nelson.

DeFrain, J., Ernst, L., Jakub, D., & Taylor, J. (1991). *Sudden infant death: Enduring the loss*. Lexington, MA: Lexington Books.

DeFrain, J., Martens, L., Story, J., & Stork, W. (1986). *Stillborn: The invisible death*. Lexington, MA: Lexington Books.

DeGregory, L. (2000, October 29). Final wish granted. *St. Petersburg Times*, p. 5F.

Delgadillo, D., & Davis, P. (1990). *When the bough breaks*. San Diego, CA: San Diego County Guild for Infant Survival.

Delgado, M., & Tennstedt, S. (1997a). Making the case for culturally appropriate community services: Puerto Rican elders and their caregivers. *Health and Social Work, 22*(4), 246–255.

Delgado, M., & Tennstedt, S. (1997b). Puerto Rican sons as primary caregivers of elderly parents. *Social Work, 42*(2), 125–134.

Demi, A. S., & Miles, M. S. (1987). Parameters of normal grief: A Delphi study. *Death Studies, 11*, 397–412.

Demi, A. S., & Miles, M. S. (1988). Suicide bereaved parents: Emotional distress and physical health problems. *Death Studies, 12*, 297–307.

Demmer, C. (2003). A national survey of hospice bereavement services. *Omega, Journal of Death and Dying, 47*, 327–341.

DeNavas-Walt, C., Proctor, B. D., & Mills, R. J. (2004). U.S. Census Bureau, Current population reports, P60-226, *Income, poverty and health insurance coverage in the United States: 2003*. Washington, DC: U.S. Government Printing Office.

Des Pres, T. (1976). *The survivor: An anatomy of life in the death camps*. New York: Oxford University Press.

Detmer, C. M., & Lamberti, J. W. (1991). Family grief. *Death Studies, 15*, 363–374.

Deutsch, H. (1937). Absence of grief. *Psychoanalytic Quarterly, 6*, 12–22.

DeVoe, J. F., Peter, K., Kaufman, P., Miller, A., Noonan, M., Snyder, T. D., et al. (2004). *Indicators of School Crime and Safety, 2004*. (NCES 2005-002/NCJ 205290) Washington, DC: U.S. Departments of Education and Justice.

DeVoe, J. F., Peter, K., Kaufman, P., Ruddy, S. A., Miller, A. K., Planty, M., et al. (2003). *Indicators of School Crime and Safety, 2003*. (NCES 2004-004/NCJ 201257) U.S. Departments of Education and Justice. Washington, DC: U.S. Government Printing Office.

Diamant, A. (1994, October). Special report: Media violence. *Parents Magazine*, 40–41, 45.

Dickens, C. (1963). *Dombey and son* (E. Johnson, Ed.). New York: Dell. (Original work published 1848)

Dickinson, G. E. (2006). Teaching end-of-life issues in US medical schools: 1975–2005. *American Journal of Hospice and Palliative Medicine, 23*, 197–204.

Didion, J. (2005). *The year of magical thinking*. New York: Knopf.

DiGiulio, R. C. (1989). *Beyond widowhood: From bereavement to emergence and hope*. New York: Free Press.

Din-Dzietham, R., & Hertz-Picciotto, I. (1998). Infant mortality differences between whites and African Americans: The effect of maternal education. *American Journal of Public Health, 88*(4), 651–656.

Disaster Mortuary Operational Response Team (DMORT). (1998). *Team member handbook*. USA: Author.

Doane, B. K., & Quigley, B. Q. (1981). Psychiatric aspects of therapeutic abortion. *Canadian Medical Association Journal, 125*, 427–432.

Doka, K. J. (1988). The awareness of mortality in midlife: Implications for later life. *Gerontology Review, 2*, 1–10.

Doka, K. J. (Ed.). (1989a). *Disenfranchised grief: Recognizing hidden sorrow*. Lexington, MA: Lexington Books.

Doka, K. J. (1989b). Disenfranchised grief. In K. J. Doka (Ed.), *Disenfranchised grief: Recognizing hidden sorrow* (pp. 3–11). Lexington, MA: Lexington Books.

Doka, K. J. (1993a). *Living with life-threatening illness: A guide for patients, families, and caregivers*. Lexington, MA: Lexington Books.

Doka, K. J. (1993b). The spiritual needs of the dying. In K. J. Doka & J. D. Morgan (Eds.), *Death and spirituality* (pp. 143–150). Amityville, NY: Baywood.

Doka, K. J. (Ed.). (1995). *Children mourning, mourning children*. Washington, DC: Hospice Foundation of America.

Doka, K. J. (1996a). The cruel paradox: Children who are living with life-threatening illnesses. In C. A. Corr & D. M. Corr (Eds.), *Handbook of childhood death and bereavement* (pp. 89–105). New York: Springer.

Doka, K. J. (Ed.). (1996b). *Living with grief after sudden loss: Suicide, homicide, accident, heart attack, stroke*. Washington, DC: Hospice Foundation of America.

Doka, K. J. (1997). *AIDS, fear, and society: Challenging the dreaded disease*. Washington, DC: Taylor & Francis.

Doka, K. J. (Ed.). (2000). *Living with grief: Children, adolescents, and loss*. Washington, DC: Hospice Foundation of America.

Doka, K. J. (Ed.). (2002a). *Disenfranchised grief: New directions, strategies, and challenges for practice*. Champaign, IL: Research Press.

Doka, K. J. (Ed.). (2002b). *Living with grief: Loss in later life*. Washington, DC: Hospice Foundation of America.

Doka, K. J. (2003). The death awareness movement: Description, history, and analysis. In C. D. Bryant (Ed.), *Handbook of death and dying* (Vol. 1, pp. 50–56). Thousand Oaks, CA: Sage.

Doka, K. J. (Ed.). (2007a). *Living with grief: Before and after the death*. Washington, DC: Hospice Foundation of America.

Doka, K. J. (2007b). Challenging the paradigm: New understandings of grief. In K. J. Doka (Ed.). (2007). *Living with grief: Before and after the death* (pp. 87–102). Washington, DC: Hospice Foundation of America.

Doka, K. J. (Ed.). (2007c). *Death, dying and bereavement* (4 vols.). New York: Routledge. [Vol. 1, The human encounter with death; Vol. 2, Developmental perspectives; Vol. 3, Illness, dying and death; Vol. 4, Loss and grief.]

Doka, K. J. (with Morgan, J. D.). (Eds.). (1993). *Death and spirituality*. Amityville, NY: Baywood.

Doka, K. J., Jennings, B., & Corr, C. A. (Eds.). (2005). *Living with grief: Ethical dilemmas at the end of life*. Washington, DC: Hospice Foundation of America.

Donnelley, N. H. (1987). *I never know what to say*. New York: Ballantine.

Donnelly, K. F. (1982). *Recovering from the loss of a child*. New York: Macmillan.

Donnelly, K. F. (1987). *Recovering from the loss of a parent*. New York: Dodd, Mead.

Donnelly, K. F. (1988). *Recovering from the loss of a sibling*. New York: Dodd, Mead.

Donnelly, K. F. (1994). *Recovering from the loss of a loved one to AIDS*. New York: Fawcett Columbine.

Douglas, J. D. (1967). *The social meanings of suicide*. Princeton, NJ: Princeton University Press.

Douglas, M. (1970). *Natural symbols.* New York: Random House.

Dowie, M. (1988). *"We have a donor": The bold new world of organ transplanting.* New York: St. Martin's Press.

Downing, A. B. (Ed.). (1974). *Euthanasia and the right to death: The case for voluntary euthanasia.* London: Peter Owen.

Doyle, D., Hanks, G.W.C., Cherny, N. I., & Calman, K. (Eds.). (2003). *Oxford textbook of palliative medicine* (3rd ed.). New York: Oxford University Press.

Duarté-Vélez, Y. M., & Bernal, G. (2007). Suicide behavior among Latino and Latina adolescents; Conceptual and methodological issues. *Death Studies, 31*(5), 435–455.

DuBoulay, S. (1984). *Cicely Saunders: The founder of the modern hospice movement.* London: Hodder & Stoughton.

Dukeminier, J., Johanson, S. M., Lindgren, J. M., & Sitkoff, R. H. (2005). *Wills, trusts, and estates* (7th ed.). Rockville, MD: Aspen Systems Corp.

Dula, A. (1994). African American suspicion of the healthcare system is justified: What do we do about it? *Cambridge Quarterly of Healthcare Ethics, 3,* 347–357.

Dumont, R., & Foss, D. (1972). *The American view of death: Acceptance or denial?* Cambridge, MA: Schenkman.

Duncan, J., Spengler, E., & Wolfe, J. (2007). Providing pediatric palliative care. *MCN, American Journal of Maternal Child Nursing, 32,* 279–287.

Dundes, A. (1989). *Little Red Riding Hood: A casebook.* Madison: University of Wisconsin Press.

Dunlop, R. J., & Hockley, J. M. (1998). *Hospital based palliative care teams: The hospital-hospice interface* (2nd ed.). Oxford: Oxford University Press.

Dunn, R. G., & Morrish-Vidners, D. (1988). The psychological and social experience of suicide survivors. *Omega, Journal of Death and Dying, 18,* 175–215.

Dunne, E. J., McIntosh, J. L., & Dunne-Maxim, K. (Eds.). (1987). *Suicide and its aftermath: Understanding and counseling the survivors.* New York: Norton.

Dunsmore, J. C., & Quine, S. (1995). Information support and decision making needs and preferences of adolescents with cancer: Implications for health professionals. *Journal of Psychosocial Oncology, 13*(4), 39–56.

Durkheim, E. (1951). *Suicide: A study in sociology* (J. A. Spaulding & G. Simpson, Trans.). Glencoe, IL: Free Press. (Original work published 1897)

Durkheim, E. (1954). *The elementary forms of religious life* (J. W. Swaine, Trans.). London: Allen & Unwin. (Original work published 1915)

Dutton, Y. C., & Zisook, S. (2005). Adaptation to bereavement. *Death Studies, 29,* 877–903.

Dwyer, T., Ponsonby, A.-L., Blizzard, L., Newman, N. M., & Cochrane, J. A. (1995). The contribution of changes in the prevalence of prone sleeping position to the decline in sudden infant death syndrome in Tasmania. *Journal of the American Medical Association, 273,* 783–789.

Eckert, P. (2007, January 15). Experts see bird flu challenge to US health system. Reuters Health Information. Available at: http://www.nlm.nih.gov/medlineplus/news/fullstory_43839.htm.

Edelman, H. (1994). *Motherless daughters: The legacy of loss.* Reading, MA: Addison-Wesley.

The Editors of *New York* Magazine. (2001). *September 11, 2001: A record of tragedy, heroism, and hope.* New York: Abrams.

Education Development Center. (2003). *The initiative for pediatric palliative care curriculum.* Newton, MA: Author.

Egan, K. A. (1998). *A patient-family value based end-of-life care model.* Largo, FL: Hospice Institute of the Florida Suncoast.

Egan, K. A., & Labyak, M. J. (2001). Hospice care: A model for quality end-of-life care. In B. R. Ferrell & N. Coyle (Eds.), *Textbook of palliative nursing* (pp. 7–26). New York: Oxford University Press.

Egeland, J., & Sussex, J. (1985). Suicide and family loading for affective disorders. *Journal of the American Medical Association, 254,* 915–918.

Ehlers, A. (2006). Understanding and treating complicated grief: What can we learn from posttraumatic stress disorder? *Clinical Psychology: Science and Practice, 13,* 135–140.

Eichrodt, W. (1967). *Theology of the Old Testament,* Vol. 2. (J. A. Baker, Trans.). Philadelphia: Westminster.

Eisenberg, J. B. (2005). *Using Terri: The religious right's conspiracy to take away our rights.* San Francisco: HarperSanFrancisco.

Eisenbruch, M. (1984). Cross-cultural aspects of bereavement. II: Ethnic and cultural variations in the development of bereavement practices. *Culture, Medicine and Psychiatry, 8,* 315–347.

Elias, N. (1991). On human beings and their emotions: A process-sociological essay. In M. Featherstone, M. Hepworth, & B. S. Turner (Eds.), *The body: Social process and cultural theory* (pp. 103–125). London: Sage.

Elison, J. (2007, January 29). The stage of grief no one admits to: Relief. *Newsweek,* p. 18.

Elison, J., & McGonigle, C. (2003). *Liberating losses: When death brings relief.* Cambridge, MA: Perseus.

Elkind, D. (1967). Egocentrism in adolescence. *Child Development, 38,* 1025–1034.

Ellershaw, J., & Wilkinson, S. (2003). *Care of the dying: A pathway to excellence.* Oxford, UK: Oxford University Press.

Elliot, G. (1972). *The twentieth century book of the dead.* New York: Random House.

Elmer, L. (1987). *Why her, why now: A man's journey through love and death and grief.* New York: Bantam.

Else, I.R.N., Andrade, N. N., & Nahulu, L. B. (2007). Suicide and suicidal-related behaviors among indigenous Pacific Islanders in the United States. *Death Studies, 31*(5), 479–501.

Emanuel, E. J., Fairclough, D. L., & Emanuel, L. L. (2000). Attitudes and desires related to euthanasia and physician-assisted suicide among terminally ill patients and their caregivers. *Journal of the American Medical Association, 284,* 2460–2468.

Emanuel, L. L. (1998). *Regulating how we die: The ethical, medical, and legal issues surrounding physician assisted suicide.* Cambridge, MA: Harvard University Press.

Emerson, R. W. (1970). *The journals and miscellaneous notebooks of Ralph Waldo Emerson* (Vol. 8, pp. 1841–1843). (W. H. Gilman & J. E. Parsons, Eds.). Cambridge, MA: Belknap Press of Harvard University Press.

Emlet, C. A. (2006). "You're awfully old to have *this* disease": Experiences of stigma and ageism in adults 50 years and older living with HIV/AIDS. *The Gerontologist, 46,* 781–790.

Emlet, C. A. (Ed.). (2004). *HIV/AIDS and older adults: Challenges for individuals, families, and communities.* New York: Springer.

Emswiler, M. A., & Emswiler, J. P. (2000). *Guiding your child through grief.* New York: Bantam.

End-of-Life Nursing Education Consortium (ELNEC). (2003). *Advancing palliative care in pediatric nursing: ELNEC—Pediatric palliative care.* Duarte, CA: American Association of Colleges of Nursing and City of Hope National Medical Center.

Engel, G. L. (1961). Is grief a disease? A challenge for medical research. *Psychosomatic Medicine, 23,* 18–22.

Enright, D. J. (Ed.). (1983). *The Oxford book of death.* New York: Oxford University Press.

Erikson, E. H. (1959). Identity and the life cycle: Selected papers. *Psychological Issues, 1,* 1–171.

Erikson, E. H. (1963). *Childhood and society* (2nd ed.). New York: Norton. (Original edition published 1950)

Erikson, E. H. (1968). *Identity: Youth and crisis.* London: Faber & Faber.

Erikson, E. H. (1982). *The life cycle completed: A review.* New York: Norton.

Erikson, E. H., & Erikson, J. M. (1981). On generativity and identity: From a conversation with Erik and Joan Erikson. *Harvard Educational Review, 51,* 249–269.

Erikson, E. H., Erikson, J. M., & Kivnick, H. (1986). *Vital involvements in old age.* New York: Norton.

Eron, L. D. (1993). *The problem of media violence and children's behavior.* New York: Guggenheim Foundation.

Esperti, R. A., & Peterson, R. L. (1992). *The living trust revolution: Why America is abandoning wills and probate.* New York: Viking.

Esperti, R. A., & Peterson, R. L. (1999). *Protect your estate: Definitive strategies for estate and wealth planning from the leading experts.* New York: McGraw-Hill.

Esperti, R. A., Peterson, R. L., & Cahoone, D. (2001). *The living trust workbook: How you and your legal advisor can design, fund, and maintain your living trust plan, and secure your family's future* (Rev. ed.). New York: Penguin.

Evanisko, M. J., Beasley, C. L., & Brigham, L. E. (1998). Readiness of critical care physicians and nurses to handle requests for organ donation. *American Journal of Critical Care, 7,* 4–12.

Evans, G., & Farberow, N. L. (Eds.). (1988). *The encyclopedia of suicide.* New York: Facts on File.

Evans, J. (1971). *Living with a man who is dying: A personal memoir.* New York: Taplinger.

Evans, R. P. (1993). *The Christmas box.* Salt Lake City, UT: Steinway.

Everett, H. (2002). *Roadside crosses in contemporary memorial culture.* Denton: University of North Texas Press.

Ewald, P. W. (1994). *Evolution of infectious diseases.* New York: Oxford University Press.

Ewalt, P. L., & Perkins, L. (1979). The real experience of death among adolescents: An empirical study. *Social Casework, 60,* 547–551.

Fagerlin, A., & Schneider, C. E. (2004). Enough: The failure of the living will. *Hastings Center Report, 34*(2), 30–42.

Fairchild, T. N. (Ed.). (1986). *Crisis intervention strategies for school-based helpers.* Springfield, IL: Charles C Thomas.

Fales, M. (1964). The early American way of death. *Essex Institution Historical Collection, 100*(2), 75–84.

Fallowfield, L. J., Jenkins, V. A., & Beveridge, H. A. (2002). Truth may hurt but deceit hurts more: Communication in palliative care. *Palliative Medicine, 16,* 297–303.

Fan, H., Conner, R. F., & Villarreal, L. P. (2004). *AIDS: Science and society* (4th ed.). Boston: Jones & Bartlett.

Fanestil, J. (2006). *Mrs. Hunter's happy death: Lessons on living from people preparing to die.* New York: Doubleday.

Farberow, N. L. (1983). Relationships between suicide and depression: An overview. *Psychiatria Fennica Supplementum, 14,* 9–19.

Farberow, N. L. (Ed.). (1980). *The many faces of suicide: Indirect self-destructive behavior.* New York: McGraw-Hill.

Farberow, N. L., & Moriwaki, S. Y. (1975). Self-destructive crises in the older person. *The Gerontologist, 15,* 333–337.

Farberow, N. L., & Shneidman, E. S. (Eds.). (1965). *The cry for help.* New York: McGraw-Hill.

Farberow, N. L., Gallagher-Thompson, D., Gilewski, M., & Thompson, L. (1992). Changes in grief and mental health of bereaved spouses of older suicides. *Journal of Gerontology, 47,* 357–366.

Farrell, J. J. (1980). *Inventing the American way of death: 1830–1920.* Philadelphia: Temple University Press.

Faulkner, A. (1993). *Teaching interactive skills in health care.* London: Chapman & Hall.

Faulkner, W. (1930). *As I lay dying.* New York: Random House.

Feifel, H. (Ed.). (1959). *The meaning of death.* New York: McGraw-Hill.

Feifel, H. (1963). Death. In N. L. Farberow (Ed.), *Taboo topics* (pp. 8–21). New York: Atherton.

Feifel, H. (1977a). Preface and introduction: Death in contemporary America. In H. Feifel (Ed.), *New meanings of death* (pp. xiii–xiv, 4–12). New York: McGraw-Hill.

Feifel, H. (Ed.). (1977b). *New meanings of death.* New York: McGraw-Hill.

Feldman, D. B. (2006). Can suicide be ethical? A utilitarian perspective on the appropriateness of choosing to die. *Death Studies, 30,* 529–538.

Feldman, D. M., & Rosner, F. (Eds.). (1984). *Compendium on medical ethics* (6th ed.). New York: Federation of Jewish Philanthropies of New York.

Fenwick, P., & Fenwick, E. (1995). *The truth in the light: An investigation of over 300 near-death experiences.* New York: Berkley Books.

Ferrell, B. R., & Coyle, N. (Eds.). (2005). *Textbook of palliative nursing* (2nd ed.). New York: Oxford University Press.

Ferris, F. D., Balfour, H. M., Bowen, K., Farley, J., Hardwick, M., Lemontagne, C., et al. (2002). *A model to guide hospice palliative care.* Ottawa, Canada: Canadian Hospice Palliative Care Association.

Field, D., Hockey, J., & Small, N. (Eds.). (1997). *Death, gender and ethnicity.* New York: Routledge.

Field, M. J., & Berhman, R. E. (Eds.). (2003). *When children die: Improving palliative and end-of-life care for children and their families.* Washington, DC: National Academies Press.

Field, M. J., & Cassel, C. K. (Eds.). (1997). *Approaching death: Improving care at the end of life.* Washington, DC: National Academies Press.

Field, N. P. (Ed.). (2006). Continuing bonds in adaptation to bereavement: I. Theoretical and empirical foundations; II. Clinical and cultural considerations. [Special Series.] *Death Studies, 30*(8 & 9).

Fierstein, H. (2003, July 31). The culture of disease. *The New York Times,* p. A-25.

Figley, C. R. (1999). *Traumatology of grieving.* New York: Brunner/Mazel.

Fingerhut, L. A., & Kleinman, J. C. (1989). Mortality among children and youth. *American Journal of Public Health, 79,* 899–901.

Fingerhut, L. A., Kleinman, J. C., Godfrey, E., & Rosenberg, H. (1991). Firearm mortality among children, youth, and young adults 1–34 years of age, trends and current status: United States, 1979–88. *Monthly Vital Statistics Report, 39*(11), Suppl. Hyattsville, MD: National Center for Health Statistics.

Fiorini, J. J., & Mullen, J. A. (2006). *Counseling children and adolescents through grief and loss.* Champaign, IL: Research Press.

First International Conference on Islamic Medicine. (1981). Islamic Code of Medical Ethics. (Reprinted in *Choosing death; Active euthanasia, religion, and the public debate,* p. 62, by R. Hamel, Ed., 1991, Philadelphia: Trinity Press International)

Fisher, M. (1994). *Sleep with the angels: A mother challenges AIDS.* Wakefield, RI: Moyer Bell.

Fitzgerald, H. (1992). *The grieving child: A parent's guide.* New York: Simon & Schuster.

Fitzgerald, H. (1995). *The mourning handbook: A complete guide for the bereaved.* New York: Fireside.

Fitzgerald, H. (1998). *Grief at school: A guide for teachers and counselors.* Washington, DC: American Hospice Foundation.

Fitzgerald, H. (1999). *Grief at work: A manual of policies and practices.* Washington, DC: American Hospice Foundation.

Fitzgerald, H. (2000). *The grieving teen: A guide for teenagers and their friends.* New York: Simon & Schuster.

Fitzgerald, H. (2003). *Grief at school: A training guide.* Washington, DC: American Hospice Foundation.

Flannery, A. (Ed.). (1982). *Vatican Council II: More postconciliar documents.* Grand Rapids, MI: Eerdmans.

Fleming, D. (2005). *Noah's rainbow: A father's emotional journey from the death of his son to the birth of his daughter.* Amityville, NY: Baywood.

Fleming, S. J. (1985). Children's grief: Individual and family dynamics. In C. A. Corr & D. M. Corr (Eds.), *Hospice approaches to pediatric care* (pp. 197–218). New York: Springer.

Fleming, S. J., & Adolph, R. (1986). Helping bereaved adolescents: Needs and responses. In C. A. Corr & J. N. McNeil (Eds.), *Adolescence and death* (pp. 97–118). New York: Springer.

Fleming, S., & Balmer, L. (1996). Bereavement in adolescence. In C. A. Corr & D. E. Balk (Eds.), *Handbook of adolescent death and bereavement* (pp. 139–154). New York: Springer.

Floerchinger, D. S. (1991). Bereavement in late adolescence; Interventions on college campuses. *Journal of Adolescent Research, 6,* 146–156.

Fogarty, J. A. (2000). *The magical thoughts of grieving children: Treating children with complicated mourning and advice for parents.* Amityville, NY: Baywood.

Foley, K. M., & Hendin, H. (Eds.). (2002). *The case against assisted suicide: For the right to end-of-life care.* Baltimore: Johns Hopkins University Press.

Folta, J. R., & Deck, E. S. (1976). Grief, the funeral, and the friend. In V. R. Pine, A. H. Kutscher, D. Peretz, R. C. Slater, R. DeBellis, R. J. Volk, et al. (Eds.), *Acute grief and the funeral* (pp. 231–240). Springfield, IL: Charles C Thomas.

Forbes, H. (1927). *Gravestones of early New England and the men who made them, 1653–1800.* Boston: Houghton Mifflin.

Ford, G. (1979). Terminal care from the viewpoint of the National Health Service. In J. J. Bonica & V. Ventafridda (Eds.), *International symposium on pain of advanced cancer: Advances in pain research and therapy* (Vol. 2, pp. 653–661). New York: Raven Press.

Foster, Z., Wald, F. S., & Wald, H. J. (1978). The hospice movement: A backward glance at its first two decades. *New Physician, 27,* 21–24.

Fowler, J. P. (2000, July/August). Why me? I learned the hard way that you don't have to be young to get hit with HIV. *Modern Maturity, 43*(4), 58–63, 76.

Fox, E., Kamakahi, J. J., & Capek, S. M. (1999). *Come lovely and soothing death: The right to die movement in the United States.* New York: Twayne.

Fox, J. A. (2007). Why they kill. Retrieved May 17, 2007, from latimes.com/news/opinion/la-oe-fox17apr17,0,6739883.story?coll5la-opinion-rightrail.

Fox, J. A., & Levin, J. (2005). *Extreme killing: Understanding serial and mass murder.* Thousand Oaks, CA: Sage.

Fox, J. A., & Levin, J. (2006). *The will to kill: Explaining senseless murder.* Boston: Pearson/Allyn and Bacon.

Fox, R. C., & Swazey, J. P. (1974). *The courage to fail: A social view of organ transplants and dialysis.* Chicago: University of Chicago Press.

Fox, R. C., & Swazey, J. P. (1992). *Spare parts: Organ replacement in American society.* New York: Oxford University Press.

Fox, S. S. (1988a). *Good grief: Helping groups of children when a friend dies.* Boston: The New England Association for the Education of Young Children.

Fox, S. S. (1988b, August). Helping child deal with death teaches valuable skills. *Psychiatric Times,* 10–11.

Francis, D., Kellaher, L., & Neophytou, G. (2005). *The secret cemetery.* Oxford, UK: Berg Publishers.

Francis, J. (2001, March 9). Lives crowned by love. *St. Petersburg Times,* p. 1D.

Francis, V. M. (1859). *A thesis on hospital hygiene.* New York: J. F. Trow.

Frank, A. W. (1995). *The wounded storyteller: Body, illness, and ethics.* Chicago: University of Chicago Press.

Frank, A. W. (2002). *At the will of the body: Reflections on illness* (new Afterword). Boston: Houghton Mifflin.

Frankl, V. (1984). *Man's search for meaning.* New York: Simon & Schuster.

Frazer, J. G. (1977). *The fear of the dead in primitive religion.* New York: Arno Press.

Freeman, S. J. (2005). *Grief and loss: Understanding the journey.* Belmont, CA: Wadsworth.

French, S. (1975). The cemetery as cultural institution: The establishment of Mount Auburn and the "rural cemetery" movement. In D. E. Stannard (Ed.), *Death in America* (pp. 69–91). Philadelphia: University of Pennsylvania Press.

Freud, A. (1958). Adolescence. *Psychoanalytic Study of the Child, 13,* 255–268.

Freud, S. (1959a). Mourning and melancholia. In J. Strachey (Ed. & Trans.), *The standard edition of the complete psychological works of Sigmund Freud* (Vol. 14, pp. 237–258). London: Hogarth Press. (Original work published 1917)

Freud, S. (1959b). *New introductory lectures on psycho-analysis.* In J. Strachey (Ed. & Trans.), *The standard edition of the complete psychological works of Sigmund Freud* (Vol. 22, pp. 1–182). London: Hogarth Press. (Original work published 1933)

Freud, S. (1959c). Thoughts for the time on war and death. In J. Strachey (Ed. & Trans.), *The standard edition of the complete psychological works of Sigmund Freud* (Vol. 14, pp. 273–300). London: Hogarth Press. (Original work published 1915)

Freyer, D. R. (2004). Care of the dying adolescent: Special considerations. *Pediatrics, 113,* 381–388.

Friedman, E. H. (1980). Systems and ceremonies: A family view of rites of passage. In E. A. Carter & M. McGoldrick (Eds.), *The family life cycle: A framework for family therapy* (pp. 429–460). New York: Gardner Press.

Friedrich, M. J. (1999). Hospice care in the United States: A conversation with Florence Wald. *Journal of the American Medical Association, 281,* 1683–1685.

Friel, M., & Tehan, C. B. (1980). Counteracting burn-out for the hospice care-giver. *Cancer Nursing, 3,* 285–293.

Frist, W. H. (1989). *Transplant: A heart surgeon's account of the life and death dramas of the new medicine.* New York: Atlantic Monthly Press.

Frist, W. H. (1995). *Grand rounds and transplantation.* New York: Chapman & Hall.

Fristad, M. A., Cerel, J., Goldman, M., Weller, E. B., & Weller, R. A. (2001). The role of ritual in children's bereavement. *Omega, Journal of Death and Dying, 42,* 321–339.

Frumkin, L. R., & Leonard, J. M. (1997). *Questions & answers on AIDS* (3rd ed.). Los Angeles: Health Information Press.

Fry, V. L. (1995). *Part of me died, too: Stories of creative survival among bereaved children and teenagers.* New York: Dutton Children's Books.

Fulton, R. (1961). The clergyman and the funeral director: A study in role conflict. *Social Forces, 39,* 317–323.

Fulton, R. (1978). The sacred and the secular: Attitudes of the American public toward death, funerals, and funeral directors. In R. Fulton & R. Bendiksen (Eds.), *Death and identity* (Rev. ed.; pp. 158–172). Bowie, MD: Charles Press.

Fulton, R. (1995). The contemporary funeral: Functional or dysfunctional? In H. Wass & R. A. Neimeyer (Eds.), *Dying: Facing the facts* (pp. 185–209). Washington, DC: Taylor & Francis.

Fulton, R. (2003). Anticipatory mourning: A critique of the concept. *Mortality, 8,* 342–351.

Fulton, R. L., & Bendiksen, R. (1994). *Death and identity* (3rd ed.). Philadelphia: Charles Press.

Fulton, R., & Fulton, J. (1971). A psychosocial aspect of terminal care: Anticipatory grief. *Omega, Journal of Death and Dying, 2,* 91–100.

Fulton, R., & Gottesman, D. J. (1980). Anticipatory grief: A psychosocial concept reconsidered. *British Journal of Psychiatry, 137,* 45–54.

Furman, E. (Ed.). (1974). *A child's parent dies: Studies in childhood bereavement.* New Haven, CT: Yale University Press.

Furman, R. A. (1973). The child's capacity for mourning. In E. J. Anthony & C. Koupernik (Eds.), *The child in his family: Vol. 2. The impact of disease and death* (pp. 225–231). New York: Wiley.

Furth, G. M. (1988). *The secret world of drawings: Healing through art.* Boston: Sigo Press.

Gaes, J. (1987). *My book for kids with cansur: A child's autobiography of hope.* Aberdeen, SD: Melius & Peterson.

Galea, S., Ahern, J., Tardiff, K., Leon, A. C., & Vlahov, D. (2002). Drugs and firearm deaths in New York City, 1990–1998. *Journal of Urban Health: Bulletin of the New York Academy of Medicine, 79*(1), 70–86.

Galinsky, N. (1999). *When a grandchild dies: What to do, what to say, how to cope.* Houston, TX: Gal In Sky Publishing (P.O. Box 70976, Houston, TX 77270).

Gallagher-Allred, C., & Amenta, M. (Eds.). (1993). Nutrition and hydration in hospice care: Needs, strategies, ethics. [Special issue] *Hospice Journal, 9*(2/3).

Gambetta, D. (Ed.). (2006). *Making sense of suicide missions* (Rev. ed.) Oxford, UK: Oxford University Press.

Gamino, L. A., & Cooney, A. J. (2002). *When your baby dies through miscarriage or stillbirth.* Minneapolis: Augsburg Fortress.

Gandhi, M. (1980). *All men are brothers: Autobiographical reflections.* New York: Continuum.

Gans, J. E. (1990). *America's adolescents: How healthy are they?* American Medical Association, Profiles of Adolescent Health Series. Chicago: American Medical Association.

Garber, B. (1983). Some thoughts on normal adolescents who lost a parent by death. *Journal of Youth and Adolescence, 12,* 175–183.

Garciagodoy, J. (1998). *Digging the days of the dead: A reading of Mexico's Dias de muertos.* Boulder: University Press of Colorado.

Garfield, C. A. (1976). Foundations of psychosocial oncology: The terminal phase. In J. M. Vaeth (Ed.), *Breast cancer: Its impact on the patient, family, and community* (pp. 180–212). Basel, Switzerland: Karger.

Garfield, C. A. (with Spring, C., & Ober, D.). (1995). *Sometimes my heart goes numb: Love and caring in a time of AIDS.* San Francisco: Jossey-Bass.

Garner, B. A. (2004). *Black's law dictionary* (8th ed.). St. Paul, MN: West Group.

Garrett, L. (1995). *The coming plague: Newly emerging diseases in a world out of balance.* New York: Penguin.

Garrison, C. Z., Lewinsohn, P. M., Marstellar, F., Langhinrichsen, J., & Lann, I. (1991). The assessment of suicidal behavior in adolescents. *Suicide and Life-Threatening Behavior, 21,* 329–344.

Gartley, W., & Bernasconi, M. (1967). The concept of death in children. *Journal of Genetic Psychology, 110,* 71–85.

Gatch, M. McC. (1969). *Death: Meaning and mortality in Christian thought and contemporary culture.* New York: Seabury Press.

Gaylin, W., & Jennings, B. (2003). *The perversion of autonomy: The uses of coercion and constraints in a liberal society* (2nd ed.). Washington, DC: Georgetown University Press.

Geddes, G. E. (1981). *Welcome joy: Death in Puritan New England.* Ann Arbor, MI: UMI Research Press.

Gelfand, D. E., Balcazar, H., Parzuchowski, J., & Lenox, S. (2001). Mexicans and care for the terminally ill: Family, hospice, and the church. *American Journal of Hospice and Palliative Care, 18,* 391–396.

Gellman, B. (2000, April 30). White House ranks AIDS as a threat to national security. *St. Louis Post-Dispatch,* pp. A1, A8.

Georges, J-J., Onwuteaka-Philipsen, B. D., Muller, M. T., van der Wal, G., van der Heide, A., & Van der Maas, P. J. (2007). Relatives' perspective on the terminally ill patients who died after euthanasia or physician-assisted suicide: A retrospective cross-sectional interview study in the Netherlands. *Death Studies, 31,* 1–15.

Gerisch, B. (1998). "This is not death, it is something safer": A psychodynamic approach to Sylvia Plath. *Death Studies, 22,* 735–761.

Gertner, J. (2001). Are you ready for 100? *Money, 30*(4), 98–106.

Gervais, K. G. (1986). *Redefining death.* New Haven, CT: Yale University Press.

Gibbs, D. C., & DeMoss, B. (2006). *Fighting for dear life: The untold story of Terri Schiavo and what it means for all of us.* Minneapolis: Bethany House.

Gibson, P. (1994). Gay male and lesbian youth suicide. In G. Remafedi (Ed.), *Death by denial: Studies of suicide in gay and lesbian teenagers* (pp. 15–68). Boston: Alyson.

Gifford, A. L., Lorig, K., Laurent, D., & González, V. (1997). *Living well with HIV and AIDS.* Palo Alto, CA: Bull Publishing.

Gignoux, J. H. (1998). *Some folk say: Stories of life, death, and beyond.* New York: FoulkeTale Publishing.

Gilbert, A., & Kline, C. B. (2006). *Always too soon, Voices of support for those who have lost both parents.* Emeryville, CA: Seal Press.

Gilbert, K. R. (1996). "We've had the same loss, why don't we have the same grief?" Loss and differential grief in families. *Death Studies, 20,* 269–283.

Gilbert, K. R. (2002). Taking a narrative approach to grief research: Finding meaning in stories. *Death Studies, 26,* 223–239.

Gilbert, K. R., & Murray, C. I. (2007). The family, larger systems, and death education. In D. E. Balk C. Wogrin, G. Thornton, & D. Meagher. (Eds.), *ADEC handbook of thanatology* (pp. 345–353). Northbrook, IL: Association for Death Education and Counseling.

Gilbert, M. (1993). *Atlas of the Holocaust* (2nd rev. printing). New York: William Morrow.

Gill, D. L. (1980). *Quest: The life of Elisabeth Kübler-Ross.* New York: Harper & Row.

Gilligan, C. (1982). *In a different voice: Psychological theory and women's development.* Cambridge, MA: Harvard University Press.

Gillon, E. (1972). *Victorian cemetery sculpture.* New York: Dover.

Glannon, W. (2002). Extending the human life span. *Journal of Medicine and Philosophy, 27*(3), 339–354.

Glaser, B., & Strauss, A. (1965). *Awareness of dying.* Chicago: Aldine.

Glaser, B., & Strauss, A. (1968). *Time for dying.* Chicago: Aldine.

Glaser, E., & Palmer, L. (1991). *In the absence of angels: A Hollywood family's courageous story.* New York: Putnam's.

Glick, I., Weiss, R., & Parkes, C. (1974). *The first year of bereavement.* New York: Wiley.

Glover, J. (1999). *Humanity: A moral history of the twentieth century.* London: Jonathan Cape.

Goble, P. (1993). *Beyond the ridge.* New York: Aladdin/Simon & Schuster.

Golan, N. (1975). Wife to widow to woman. *Social Work, 20,* 369–374.

Goldberg, S. B. (1973). Family tasks and reactions in the crisis of death. *Social Casework, 54,* 398–405.

Golden, T. R. (1996). *Swallowed by a snake: The gift of the masculine side of healing.* Kensington, MD: Golden Healing Publishing.

Goldman, A. (1998). Life threatening illnesses and symptom control in children. In D. Doyle, G.W.C. Hanks, & N. MacDonald (Eds.), *Oxford textbook of palliative medicine* (2nd ed.; pp. 1033–1043). New York: Oxford University Press.

Goldman, A., Hain, R., & Lieben, S. (Eds.). (2005). *Oxford textbook on pediatric palliative care.* Oxford: Oxford University Press.

Goldman, C. (2002). *The gifts of caregiving: Stories of hardship, hope and healing.* Minneapolis, MN: Fairview Press.

Goldman, L. (1999). *Life and loss: A guide to help grieving children* (2nd ed.) New York: Routledge.

Goldman, L. (2001). *Breaking the silence: A guide to helping children with complicated grief—suicide, homicide, AIDS, violence and abuse* (2nd ed.). New York: Brunner-Routledge.

Goldman, L. (2004). *Raising our children to be resilient: A guide to helping children cope with trauma in today's world.* New York: Routledge.

Goldman, L. (2006). *Children also grieve: Talking about death and healing.* Philadelphia: Jessica Kingsley Publishers.

Goldscheider, C. (1971). *Population, modernization, and social structure.* Boston: Little, Brown.

Goldscheider, F., & Goldscheider, C. (1999). *The changing transition to adulthood: Leaving and returning home.* Thousand Oaks, CA: Sage.

Golubow, M. (2001). *For the living: Coping, caring and communicating with the terminally ill.* Amityville, NY: Baywood.

Goodman, R. F., & Fahnestock, A. H. (Eds.). (2002). *The day our world changed: Children's art of 9/11.* New York: Harry N. Abrams.

Goody, J. (1962). *Death, property, and the ancestors: A study of the mortuary customs of the LoDagaa of West Africa.* Stanford, CA: Stanford University Press.

Gordon, A. K. (1974). The psychological wisdom of the Law. In J. Riemer (Ed.), *Jewish reflections on death* (pp. 95–104). New York: Schocken.

Gordon, A. K. (1986). The tattered cloak of immortality. In C. A. Corr & J. N. McNeil (Eds.), *Adolescence and death* (pp. 16–31). New York: Springer.

Gordon, A. K., & Klass, D. (1979). *They need to know: How to teach children about death.* Englewood Cliffs, NJ: Prentice Hall.

Gorer, G. (1965a). The pornography of death. In G. Gorer, *Death, grief, and mourning* (pp. 192–199). Garden City, NY: Doubleday.

Gorer, G. (1965b). *Death, grief, and mourning.* Garden City, NY: Doubleday.

Goshen-Gottstein, E. (2002). *Surviving widowhood.* Hewlett, NY: Gefen Publishing.

Goss, R. J., & Klass, D. (2005). *Dead but not lost: Grief narratives in religious traditions.* Walnut Creek, CA: AltaMira Press.

Gostin, L. O. (2005). Ethics, the constitution, and the dying process: The case of Theresa Marie Schiavo. *Journal of the American Medical Association, 293,* 2403–2407.

Gostin, L. O. (Ed.). (2004). *The AIDS pandemic: Complacency, injustice, and unfulfilled expectations.* Chapel Hill, NC: University of North Carolina Press.

Gotlib, I. H. & Hammen, C. L. (Eds.). (2002). *Handbook of depression.* New York: Guilford Press.

Gott, M., Seymour, J., Bellamy, G., Clark, D., & Ahmedzai, S. (2004). Older people's views about home as a place of care at the end of life. *Palliative Medicine, 18*(5), 460–461.

Gottfried, R. S. (1983). *The black death: Natural and human disaster in medieval Europe.* New York: Free Press.

Gottlieb, G. J., Ragaz, A., Vogel, J. V., Friedman-Kien, A., Rywkin, A. M., Weiner, E. A., et al. (1981). A preliminary communication on extensively disseminated Kaposi's sarcoma in young homosexual men. *American Journal of Dermatopathology, 3,* 111–114.

Gottlieb, M. S., Schroff, R., Schanker, H. M., Weisman, J. D., Fan, P. T., Wolf, R. A., et al. (1981). Pneumocystic carinii pneumonia and mucosal candidiasis in previously healthy homosexual men: Evidence of a new acquired cellular immunodeficiency. *New England Journal of Medicine, 305,* 1425–1431.

Gough, M. L. (1999). Remembrance photographs: Caregiver's gift for families of infants who die. In S. L. Bertman (Ed.), *Grief and the healing arts: Creativity as therapy* (pp. 205–216). Amityville, NY: Baywood.

Gould, M. S., Wallenstein, S., Kleinman, M. H., O'Carroll, P., & Mercy, J. (1990). Suicide clusters: An examination of age-specific effects. *American Journal of Public Health, 80,* 211–212.

Gourevitch, P. (1998). *We wish to inform you that tomorrow we will be killed with our families: Stories from Rwanda.* New York: Farrar Straus & Giroux.

Grabowski, J. A., & Frantz, T. (1993). Latinos and Anglos: Cultural experiences of grief intensity. *Omega, Journal of Death and Dying, 26*(4), 273–285.

Graeber, C. (1982). *Mustard.* New York: Macmillan.

Graham, B. (with Nussbaum, J.). (2004). *Intelligence matters: The CIA, the FBI, Saudi Arabia, and the failure of America's war on terror.* New York: Random House.

Graham, L. (1990). *Rebuilding the house.* New York: Viking Penguin.

Gray, K., & Lassance, A. (2002). *Grieving reproductive loss: A healing process.* Amityville, NY: Baywood.

Gray, R. E. (1987). Adolescent response to the death of a parent. *Journal of Youth and Adolescence, 16,* 511–525.

Gray, R. E. (1988). The role of school counselors with bereaved teenagers: With and without peer support groups. *The School Counselor, 35,* 188–193.

Grayling, A. C. (2006). *Among the dead cities: The history and moral legacy of the WWII bombing of civilians in Germany and Japan.* New York: Walker.

Green, R. (1999). *The Nicholas effect: A boy's gift to the world.* Sebastopol, CA: O'Reilly & Associates.

Greenberg, B. S., & Parker, E. B. (Eds.). (1965). *The Kennedy assassination and the American public: Social communication in crisis.* Stanford, CA: Stanford University Press.

Gregorian, V. (1998, September 22). Track superstar Flo-Jo is found dead at 38. *St. Louis Post-Dispatch,* p. A1.

Greiner, K. A., Perera, S., & Ahluwalia, J. S. (2003). Hospice usage by minorities in the last year of life: Results from the National Mortality Followback Survey. *Journal of the American Geriatrics Society, 51,* 970–978.

Greyson, B. (1999). Defining near-death experiences. *Mortality, 4,* 7–22.

Greyson, B. (2005). "False positive" claims of near-death experiences and "false negative" denials of near-death experiences. *Death Studies, 29,* 145–155.

Greyson, B., & Bush, N. E. (1992). Distressing near-death experiences. *Psychiatry, 55,* 95–110.

Grmek, M. D. (1990). *History of AIDS: Emergence and origin of a modern pandemic* (R. C. Maulitz & J. Duffin, Trans.). Princeton, NJ: Princeton University Press.

Grof, S., & Halifax, J. (1978). *The human encounter with death.* New York: Dutton.

Grollman, E. A. (1967). Prologue: Explaining death to children. In E. A. Grollman (Ed.), *Explaining death to children* (pp. 3–27). Boston: Beacon Press.

Grollman, E. A. (1977). *Living when a loved one has died.* Boston: Beacon Press.

Grollman, E. A. (1980). *When your loved one is dying.* Boston: Beacon Press.

Grollman, E. A. (1990). *Talking about death: A dialogue between parent and child* (3rd ed.). Boston: Beacon Press.

Grollman, E. A. (1993). *Straight talk about death for teenagers: How to cope with losing someone you love.* Boston: Beacon Press.

Grollman, E. A. (1995). *Caring and coping when your loved one is seriously ill.* Boston: Beacon Press.

Grollman, E. A. (Ed.). (1981). *What helped me when my loved one died.* Boston: Beacon Press.

Groopman, J. (2004). *The anatomy of hope: How people prevail in the face of illness.* New York: Random House.

Grove, S. (1978). I am a yellow ship. *American Journal of Nursing, 78,* 414.

Groves, B. M., Zuckerman, B., Marans, S., & Cohen, D. J. (1993). Silent victims: Children who witness violence. *Journal of the American Medical Association, 269,* 262–264.

Gruman, G. J. (1973). An historical introduction to ideas about voluntary euthanasia, with a bibliographic survey and guide for interdisciplinary studies. *Omega, Journal of Death and Dying, 4,* 87–138.

Gubrium, J. F. (1975). *Living and dying at Murray Manor.* New York: St. Martin's Press.

Guest, J. (1976). *Ordinary people.* New York: Viking.

Gunther, J. (1949). *Death be not proud.* New York: Harper.

Guthke, K. S. (1999). *The gender of death: A cultural history in art and literature.* New York: Cambridge University Press.

Gutman, I., & Berenbaum, M. (Eds.). (1994). *Anatomy of the Auschwitz death camp.* Bloomington: Indiana University Press.

Guzman, B. (2001). *The Hispanic population: Census 2000 brief.* Washington, DC: U.S. Census Bureau.

Gyulay, J. E. (1975). The forgotten grievers. *American Journal of Nursing, 75,* 1476–1479.

Habenstein, R. W., & Lamers, W. M. (1962). *The history of American funeral directing* (Rev. ed.). Milwaukee, WI: Bulfin.

Habenstein, R. W., & Lamers, W. M. (1974). *Funeral customs the world over* (Rev. ed.). Milwaukee, WI: Bulfin.

Haley, J. D. (2001). *How to write comforting letters to the bereaved: A simple guide for a delicate task.* Amityville, NY: Baywood.

Hall, E. T. (1966). *The hidden dimension.* Garden City, NY: Doubleday.

Hall, G. S. (1904). *Adolescence: Its psychology and its relationship to physiology, anthropology, sociology, sex, crime, religion and education* (2 vols.). New York: D. Appleton.

Hall, G. S. (1922). *Senescence: The last half of life.* New York: D. Appleton.

Haman, E. A. (2004). *How to write your own living will.* Naperville, IL: Sphinx Publishing.

Haman, E. A. (2006). *Complete living will kit (+ CD-ROM): How to write your own living will.* Naperville, IL: Sphinx Publishing.

Hamel, R. (Ed.). (1991). *Choosing death: Active euthanasia, religion, and the public debate.* Philadelphia: Trinity Press International.

Hamilton, B. E., Miniño, A. M., Martin, J. A., Kochanek, K. D., Strobino, D. M., & Guyer, B. (2007). Annual summary of vital statistics: 2005. *Pediatrics, 119,* 345–360.

Hamilton, M. M., & Brown, W. (2002). *Black and white and red all over: The story of a friendship.* New York: Public Affairs.

Hampson, R. (2006, October 5). Amish community unites to mourn slain schoolgirls. *USA Today,* p. 3A.

Haney, C. A., Leimer, C., & Lowery, J. (1997). Spontaneous memorialization: Violent death and emerging mourning ritual. *Omega, Journal of Death and Dying, 35,* 159–171.

Hanlan, A. (1979). *Autobiography of dying.* Garden City, NY: Doubleday.

Hansen, A. (2004). *Responding to loss: A resource for caregivers.* Amityville, NY: Baywood.

Hanson, J. C., & Frantz, T. T. (Eds.). (1984). *Death and grief in the family.* Rockville, MD: Aspen Systems Corp.

Hanson, W. (1978). Grief counseling with Native Americans. *White Cloud Journal of American Indian/Alaska Native Mental Health, 1*(2), 19–21.

Hansson, R. O., & Stroebe, M. S. (2006). *Bereavement in late life: Coping, adaptation and developmental influences.* Washington, DC: American Psychological Association.

Harakas, S. S. (1993). An Eastern Orthodox approach to bioethics. *The Journal of Medicine and Philosophy, 18,* 531–548.

Harmer, R. M. (1963). *The high cost of dying.* New York: Collier Books.

Harmer, R. M. (1971). Funerals, fantasy and flight. *Omega, Journal of Death and Dying, 2,* 127–135.

Harper, B. C. (1994). *Death: The coping mechanism of the health professional* (Rev. ed.). Greenville, SC: Swiger Associates.

Harris, E. (1998). *Pet loss.* St. Paul, MN: Llewellyn.

Harvey, J. (1995). *Embracing their memory: Loss and the social psychology of storytelling.* Boston: Allyn & Bacon.

Harvey, J. (1998). *Perspectives on loss: A sourcebook.* Philadelphia: Brunner/Mazel.

Hassl, B., & Marnocha, J. (2000). *Bereavement support group program for children* (2nd ed.). Philadelphia: Accelerated Development.

Hatton, C. L., & Valente, S. M. (Eds.). (1984). *Suicide: Assessment and intervention* (2nd ed.). Norwalk, CT: Appleton-Century-Crofts.

Hauser, M. J. (1987). Special aspects of grief after a suicide. In Dunne, E. J., McIntosh, J. L., & Dunne-Maxim, K. (Eds.), *Suicide and its aftermath: Understanding and counseling the survivors* (pp. 57–70). New York: Norton.

Havighurst, R. J. (1953). *Human development and education.* New York: Longmans, Green.

Havighurst, R. J. (1972). *Developmental tasks and education* (3rd ed.). New York: McKay.

Hawton, K., & Van Heeringen, K. (2000). *The international handbook of suicide and attempted suicide.* New York: Wiley.

Hayslip, B., & Goldberg-Glen, R. (2000). *Grandparents raising grandchildren: Theoretical, empirical, and clinical perspectives.* New York: Springer.

Hayslip, B., & Peveto, C. A. (2004). *Shifts in attitudes toward death, dying, and bereavement.* New York: Springer.

Hazell, L. V. (2001). Disaster mortuary operational response teams (DMORT). *The Forum, 27*(6), 5, 8.

The Heart of the New Age Hospice [Videotape]. (1987). Houston: The University of Texas at Houston, Health Sciences Center.

Hebert, L. E., Scherr, P. A., Bienias, J. L., Bennett, D. A., & Evans, D. A. (2003). Alzheimer disease in the U. S. population: Prevalence estimates. *Archives of Neurology, 60,* 1119–1122.

Hedtke, L., & Winslade, J. (2004). *Re-membering lives: Conversations with the dying and the bereaved.* Amityville, NY: Baywood.

Heidegger, M. (1962). *Being and time* (Rev. ed.) (J. Macquarrie & E. S. Robinson, Trans.). San Francisco: HarperSanFrancisco.

Heiney, S. P., Dunaway, N. C., & Webster, J. (1995). Good grieving—an intervention program for grieving children. *Oncology Nursing Forum, 22,* 649–655.

Heinz, D. (1999). *The last passage: Recovering a death of our own.* New York: Oxford University Press.

Hemingway, E. (1926). *The sun also rises.* New York: Scribner.

Hemingway, E. (1929). *A farewell to arms.* New York: Scribner.

Hemingway, E. (1940). *For whom the bell tolls.* New York: Scribner.

Hemingway, E. (1952). *The old man and the sea.* New York: Scribner.

Henderson, K. (2005). *While they're at war: The true story of American families on the homefront.* New York: Mariner Books.

Henderson, M. L., Hanson, L. C., & Reynolds, K. S. (2003). *Improving nursing home care of the dying: A training manual for nursing home staff.* New York: Springer.

Hendin, H. (1995). Selling death and dignity. *Hastings Center Report, 25*(3), 19–23.

Hendin, H. (1997). *Seduced by death: Doctors, patients and the Dutch Cure.* New York: Norton.

Hendin, H. (2002). The Dutch experience. *Issues in Law & Medicine, 17,* 223–246.

Hendin, H., Rutenfrans, C., & Zylicz, Z. (1997). Physician-assisted suicide and euthanasia in the Netherlands: Lessons from the Dutch. *Journal of the American Medical Association, 277,* 1720–1722.

Hendricks, J. (1995). *The meaning of reminiscence and life review.* Amityville, NY: Baywood.

Herek, G. M., Capitanio, J. P., & Widaman, K. F. (2002). HIV-related stigma and knowledge in the United States: Prevalence and trends, 1991–1999. *American Journal of Public Health, 92,* 371–377.

Herrick, C. B. (2004). *The best he had to offer: The Ron Herrick story.* Available from 605 Dunn Road, Belgrade, ME 04917; tel. 207-495-3325; cherrick@prexar.com.

Hersey, J. (1948). *Hiroshima.* New York: Bantam.

Hewett, J. (1980). *After suicide.* Philadelphia: Westminster Press.

Hilden, J. M., & Tobin, D. R. (with Lindsey, K.). (2003). *Shelter from the storm: Caring for a child with a life-threatening condition.* Cambridge, MA: Perseus.

Hill, D. C., & Foster, Y. M. (1996). Postvention with early and middle adolescents. In C. A. Corr & D. E. Balk (Eds.), *Handbook of adolescent death and bereavement* (pp. 250–272). New York: Springer.

Hillyard, D., & Dombrink, J. (2001). *Dying right: The death with dignity movement.* New York: Routledge.

Himelstein, B. P., Hilden, J. M., Boldt, A. M., & Weissman, D. (2004). Pediatric palliative care. *New England Journal of Medicine, 350,* 1752–1762.

Hinde, A. (1998). *Demographic methods.* London: Arnold.

Hinds, P. S., Drew, D., Oakes, L. L., Fouladi, M., Spunt, S. L., Church, C., & Furman, W. L. (2005). End-of-life care preferences of pediatric patients with cancer. *Journal of Clinical Oncology, 23,* 9146–9154.

Hines, P. (1986). Afro American families. In M. McGoldrick, P. Hines, E. Lee, & N. Garcia-Preto, Mourning rituals: How cultures shape the experience of loss. *The Family Therapy Networker, 10*(6), 32–33.

Hinton, J. (1963). The physical and mental distress of the dying. *Quarterly Journal of Medicine,* New Series, *32,* 1–21.

Hinton, J. (1984). Coping with terminal illness. In R. Fitzpatrick, J. Hinton, S. Newman, G. Scambler, & J. Thompson (Eds.), *The experience of illness* (pp. 227–245). London: Tavistock Publications.

Hirayama, K. K. (1990). Death and dying in Japanese culture. In J. K. Parry (Ed.), *Social work practice with the terminally ill: A transcultural perspective* (pp. 159–174). Springfield, IL: Charles C Thomas.

Hockey, J. L., Katz, J., Small, N., & Hockey, J. (Eds.). (2001). *Grief, mourning and death rituals.* New York: Open University Press.

Hodge, E. (1998). *Write through loss and grief: A guide to recovery through writing.* Bairnsdale, Victoria, Australia: BW Publications.

Hoess, R. (1959). *Commandant of Auschwitz: The autobiography of Rudolf Hoess* (C. FitzGibbon, Trans.). Cleveland, OH: World Publishing.

Hoff, B. (1983). *The Tao of Pooh.* New York: Penguin.

Hoffman, A. (1996). *Counseling clients with HIV disease: Assessment, intervention, and prevention.* New York: Guilford.

Hogan, N. S., & Balk, D. E. (1990). Adolescent reactions to sibling death: Perceptions of mothers, fathers, and teenagers. *Nursing Research, 39,* 103–106.

Hogan, N. S., & DeSantis, L. (1992). Adolescent sibling bereavement: An ongoing attachment. *Qualitative Health Research, 2,* 159–177.

Hogan, N. S., & DeSantis, L. (1994). Things that help and hinder adolescent sibling bereavement. *Western Journal of Nursing Research, 16,* 132–153.

Hogan, N. S., & Greenfield, D. B. (1991). Adolescent sibling bereavement symptomatology in a large community sample. *Journal of Adolescent Research, 6,* 97–112.

Holinger, P. C., Offer, D., Barter, J. T., & Bell, C. C. (1994). *Suicide and homicide among adolescents.* New York: Guilford.

Holland, J. M., Currier, J. M., & Neimeyer, R. A. (2006). Meaning reconstruction in the first two years of bereavement: The role of sense-making and benefit-finding. *Omega, Journal of Death and Dying, 53,* 175–191.

Holleran, A. (2006). *Grief: A novel.* New York: Hyperion.

Holloway, K. F. C. (2003). *Passed on: African American mourning stories, a memorial.* Durham, NC: Duke University Press.

Holtkamp, S. (2002). *Wrapped in mourning: The gift of life and organ donor family trauma.* New York: Taylor & Francis.

Homer. (1996). *The odyssey* (R. Fagles, Trans.). New York: Penguin.

Hooyman, N. R., & Kramer, B. J. (2006). *Living through loss: Interventions across the life span.* New York: Columbia University Press.

Hopmeyer, E., & Werk, A. (1994). A comparative study of family bereavement groups. *Death Studies, 18,* 243–256.

Horchler, J. N., & Morris, R. R. (2003). *The SIDS and infant death survival guide: Information and comfort for grieving families and friends and professionals who seek to help them* (3rd ed.). Hyattsville, MD: SIDS Educational Services, Inc.

Horn, G. (White Deer of Autumn). (1992). *The great change.* Hillsboro, OR: Beyond Words Publishing.

Horner, I. B. (Trans.). (1949). *The book of discipline (Vinaya-Pitaka),* Vol. 1. London: Luzac.

Horowitz, M. J., Weiss, D. S., Kaltreider, N., Krupnick, J., Marmar, C., Wilner, N., et al. (1984). Reactions to the death of a parent. *Journal of Nervous and Mental Disease, 172,* 383–392.

Hostetler, J. A. (1994). *Amish society* (4th ed.). Baltimore: Johns Hopkins University Press.

Howarth, G. (1996). *Last rites: The work of the modern funeral director.* Amityville, NY: Baywood.

Howarth, G., & Leaman, O. (Eds.). (2001). *Encyclopedia of death and dying.* New York: Routledge.

Howell, D. A. (1993). Special services for children. In D. Doyle, G.W.C. Hanks, & N. MacDonald (Eds.), *Oxford textbook of palliative medicine* (pp. 718–725). New York: Oxford University Press.

Hoyert, D. L., Singh, G. K., & Rosenberg, H. M. (1995). Sources of data on socioeconomic differential mortality in the United States. *Journal of Official Statistics, 11,* 233–260.

Huff, S. M., & Orloff, S. (Eds.). (2004). *Interdisciplinary clinical manual for pediatric hospice and palliative care.* Alexandria, VA: Children's Hospice International.

Hughes, T. (1994). *Collected poems.* New York: Knopf.

Hughes, M. (1995). *Bereavement and support: Healing in a group environment.* Washington, DC: Taylor & Francis.

Hughes, T. E., & Klein, D. (2001). *A family guide to wills, funerals, and probate: How to protect yourself and your survivors.* New York: Facts on File/Checkmark Books.

Hultkrantz, A. (1979). *The religions of the American Indians* (M. Setterwall, Trans.). Berkeley: University of California Press.

Humphry, D. (1992). *Final exit: The practicalities of self-deliverance and assisted suicide for the dying.* New York: Dell.

Humphry, D., & Clement, M. (1998). *Freedom to die: People, politics, and the right-to-die movement.* New York: St. Martin's Press.

Hunter, E. [aka Ed McBain]. (2005). *Let's talk: A story of cancer and love.* London: Orion.

Hunter, N. D., & Rubenstein, W. B. (Eds.). (1992). *AIDS agenda: Emerging issues in civil rights.* New York: New Press.

Hunter, S. (2003). *Black death: AIDS in Africa.* London: Palgrave Macmillan.

Hunter, S., & Sundel, M. (Eds.). (1989). *Midlife myths: Issues, findings, and practice implications.* Newbury Park, CA: Sage.

Hurd, M., & Macdonald, M. (2001). *Beyond coping: Widows reinventing their lives.* Halifax, Nova Scotia: Pear Press.

Hurwitz, C. A., Duncan, J., & Wolfe, J. (2004). Caring for the child with cancer at the close of life: "There are people who make it, and I'm hoping I'm one of them." *Journal of the American Medical Association, 292,* 2141–2149.

Huston, A. C., Donnerstein, E., Fairchild, H., Feshbach, N. D., Katz, P. A., Murray, J. P., et al. (1992). *Big world, small screen: The role of television in American society.* Lincoln: University of Nebraska Press.

Huxley, A. (1939). *After many a summer dies the swan.* New York: Harper & Brothers.

Hyland, L., & Morse, J. M. (1995). Orchestrating comfort: The role of funeral directors. *Death Studies, 19,* 453–474.

Hymes, K. B., Greene, J. B., Marcus, A., et al. (1981). Kaposi's sarcoma in homosexual men: A report of eight cases. *Lancet, 2,* 598–600.

Iliffe, J. (2006). *The African AIDS epidemic: A history.* Athens, OH: Ohio University Press.

Ilse, S. (1989). *Miscarriage: A shattered dream.* Wayzatta, MN: Pregnancy and Infant Loss Center. Long Lake, MN: Wintergreen Press.

Imber-Black, E. (1991). Rituals and the healing process. In F. Walsh & M. McGoldrick (Eds.), *Living beyond loss: Death in the family* (pp. 207–223). New York: Norton.

Infeld, D. L., Gordon, A. K., & Harper, B. C. (Eds.). (1995). *Hospice care and cultural diversity.* Binghamton, NY: Haworth Press.

Ingles, T. (1974). St. Christopher's Hospice. *Nursing Outlook, 22,* 759–763.

Ingram, P. (1992). The tragedy of Tibet. *Contemporary Review, 261,* 122–125.

The Initiative for Pediatric Palliative Care (IPPC). (2003). *The initiative for pediatric palliative care curriculum.* Newton, MA: Author.

Institute of Medicine. (1986). *Confronting AIDS: Directions for public health, health care, and research.* Washington, DC: National Academies Press.

Institute of Medicine. (2004). *Preventing childhood obesity: Health in the balance.* Washington, DC: National Academies Press.

International Work Group on Death, Dying, and Bereavement. (1993). Palliative care for children: Position statement. *Death Studies, 17,* 277–280. (Reprinted in *Statements about death, dying, and bereavement by the International Work Group on Death, Dying, and Bereavement,* pp. 17–19, by C. A. Corr, J. D. Morgan, & H. Wass, Eds., 1994, London: King's College.

International Work Group on Death, Dying, and Bereavement. (2006). Caregivers in death, dying, and bereavement situations. *Death Studies, 30,* 649–663.

Irion, P. E. (1991). Changing patterns of ritual response to death. *Omega, Journal of Death and Dying, 22,* 159–172.

Irish, D. P., Lundquist, K. F., & Nelson, V. J. (Eds.). (1993). *Ethnic variations in dying, death, and grief: Diversity in universality.* Washington, DC: Taylor & Francis.

Irwin, A., Millen, J., & Fallows, D. (2003). *Global AIDS: Myths and facts, tools for fighting the AIDS pandemic.* Cambridge, MA: South End Press.

Isenberg, N., & Burstein, A. (Eds.). (2003). *Mortal remains: Death in early America.* Philadelphia: University of Pennsylvania Press.

Iserson, K. V. (1994). *Death to dust: What happens to dead bodies?* Tucson, AZ: Galen Press.

Iserson, K. V., & Iserson, K. Y. (1999). *Grave words: Notifying survivors about sudden, unexpected death.* Tucson, AZ: Galen Press.

Iverson, B. A. (1990). Bodies for science. *Death Studies, 14,* 577–587.

Iwashyna, T., & Chang, V. (2002). Racial and ethnic differences in place of death: United States. 1993. *Journal of American Geriatrics Society, 50,* 1113–1117.

Iyasu, S., Randall, L. L., Welty, T. K., Hsia, J., Kinney, H. C., Mandell, F., et al. (2002). Risk factors for sudden infant death syndrome among Northern Plains Indians. *Journal of the American Medical Association, 288,* 2717–2723.

Jackson, C. O. (Ed.). (1977). *Passing: The vision of death in America.* Westport, CT: Greenwood Press.

Jackson, E. N. (1963). *For the living.* Des Moines, IA: Channel Press.

Jackson, E. N. (1984). The pastoral counselor and the child encountering death. In H. Wass & C. A. Corr (Eds.), *Helping children cope with death: Guidelines and resources* (2nd ed.; pp. 33–47). Washington, DC: Hemisphere.

Jackson, J. (2003). *A handbook for survivors of suicide.* Washington, DC: American Association of Suicidology.

Jackson, M. (1980). The Black experience with death: A brief analysis through Black writings. In R. A. Kalish (Ed.), *Death and dying: Views from many cultures* (pp. 92–98). Farmingdale, NY: Baywood.

Jacobs, D. G. (1999). *The Harvard Medical School guide to suicide assessment and intervention.* San Francisco: Jossey-Bass.

Jacobs, L. G., Bonuck, K., Burton, W., & Mulvihill, M. (2002). Hospital care at the end of life: An institutional assessment. *Journal of Pain and Symptom Management, 24*(3), 291–298.

Jacobs, S. (1999). *Traumatic grief: Diagnosis, treatment, and prevention.* Washington, DC: Taylor & Francis.

Jacoby, L. H., Breitkopf, C. R., & Pease, E. A. (2005). A qualitative examination of the needs of families faced with the option of organ donation. *Dimensions of Critical Care Nursing, 24,* 183–189.

Jacques, E. (1965). Death and the mid-life crisis. *International Journal of Psychoanalysis, 46,* 502–514.

Jaffe, C., & Ehrlich, C. H. (1997). *All kinds of love: Experiencing hospice.* Amityville, NY: Baywood.

Jamison, K. R. (1999). *Night falls fast: Understanding suicide.* New York: Knopf.

Jamison, S. (1995). *Final acts of love: Families, friends, and assisted dying.* New York: Tarcher/Putman.

JanMohamed, A. B. (2004). *The death-bound-subject: Richard Wright's archaeology of death.* Durham, NC: Duke University Press.

Janoff-Bulman, R. (1992). *Shattered assumptions: Towards a new psychology of trauma.* New York: Free Press.

Janzen, L., Cadell, S., & Westhues, A. (2004). From death notification through the funeral: Bereaved parents' experiences and their advice to professionals. *Omega, Journal of Death and Dying, 48,* 149–164.

Jeffreys, J. S. (2005). *Helping grieving people when tears are not enough: A handbook for care providers.* New York: Brunner-Routledge.

Jenkins, P. (2003). *Images of terror: What we can and can't know about terrorism.* New York: Aldine de Gruyter.

Jennings, B., Ryndes, T., D'Onofrio, C., & Baily, M. A. (2003). Access to hospice care: Expanding boundaries, overcoming barriers. *Hastings Center Report, Special Supplement, 33*(2), S11–S12.

Jesse, G., Taylor, M., & Kurent, J. E. (2002). *A clinician's guide to palliative care.* Oxford, England: Blackwell.

Jewett, C. L. (1982). *Helping children cope with separation and loss.* Harvard, MA: Harvard Common Press.

Jobes, A. A. (2006). *Managing suicidal risk: A collaborative approach.* New York: Guilford.

John Paul II, Pope. (2004). Care for patients in a "permanent" vegetative state. *Origins, 33*(43), 737, 739–740.

Johnson, C. J., & McGee, M. G. (Eds.). (1998). *How different religions view death and afterlife* (2nd ed.). Philadelphia: Charles Press.

Johnson, C., & Weeks, O. D. (2001). How to develop a successful aftercare program. In O. D. Weeks & C. Johnson (Eds.), *When all the friends have gone: A guide for aftercare providers* (pp. 5–23). Amityville, NY: Baywood.

Johnson, E. "Magic" (with Novak, W.). (1992). *My life.* New York: Random House.

Johnson, J. (1999). *Keys to helping children deal with death and grief.* Hauppauge, NY: Barron's Educational Series.

Johnson, J., Johnson, S. M., Cunningham, J. H., & Weinfeld, I. J. (1985). *A most important picture: A very tender manual for taking pictures of stillborn babies and infants who die.* Omaha, NE: Centering Corporation.

Johnson, M. (2006). *The dead beat: Lost souls, lucky stiffs, and the perverse pleasures of obituaries.* New York: HarperCollins.

Johnson, S. (1987). *After a child dies: Counseling bereaved families.* New York: Springer.

Johnson, S. (1998). *Who moved my cheese? An amazing way to deal with change in your work and in your life.* New York: Putnam's.

Jonah, B. A. (1986). Accident risk and risk-taking behaviour among young drivers. *Accident Analysis and Prevention, 18,* 255–271.

Jones, B. (1967). *Design for death.* Indianapolis, IN: Bobbs-Merrill.

Jones, C. (1994). *Living proof: Courage in the face of AIDS.* New York: Abbeville Press.

Jones, E. O. (1948). *Little Red Riding Hood.* New York: Golden Press.

Jones, J. H. (1992). *Bad blood: The Tuskegee syphilis experiment.* New York: Simon & Schuster.

Jones, S. (2004). 404 not found: The internet and the afterlife. *Omega, Journal of Death and Dying, 49,* 83–88.

Jonker, G. (1997). The many facets of Islam: Death, dying and disposal between orthodox and historical convention. In C. M. Parkes, P. Laungani, & B. Young (Eds.), *Death and bereavement across cultures* (pp. 147–165). London: Routledge.

Jordan, J. & McMenamy, J. (2004). Interventions for suicide survivors: A review of the literature. *Suicide and Life-Threatening Behavior, 34,* 337–339.

Jordan, J. R. (2001). Is suicide bereavement different? A reassessment of the literature. *Suicide and Life-Threatening Behavior, 31,* 91–102.

Jordan, J. R., & Neimeyer, R. A. (2003). Does grief counseling work? *Death Studies, 27,* 765–786.

Jordan, J. R., & Neimeyer, R. A. (2007). Historical and contemporary perspectives on assessment and intervention. In D. E. Balk, C. Wogrin, G. Thornton, & D. Meagher. (Eds.), *ADEC handbook of thanatology* (pp. 213–225). Northbrook, IL: Association for Death Education and Counseling.

Joseph, J. (1992). *Selected poems*. Newcastle-upon-Tyne, England: Bloodaxe Books.

Joslin, D., & Harrison, R. (1998). The "hidden patient": Older relatives raising children orphaned by AIDS. *Journal of the American Medical Women's Association, 53*, 65–71, 76.

Jozefowski, J. T. (1999). *The Phoenix phenomenon: Rising from the ashes of grief*. Northvale, NJ: Jason Aronson.

Jung, C. G. (1970). The stages of life. In H. Read, M. Fordham, & G. Adler (Eds.), *The collected works of Carl G. Jung* (2nd ed.; Vol. 8). Princeton, NJ: Princeton University Press. (Original work published 1933)

Jupp, P. C. (2006). *From ashes to dust: The history of cremation in Britain*. London: Palgrave Press.

Jurich, A. P., & Collins, O. P. (1996). Adolescents, suicide, and death. In C. A. Corr & D. E. Balk (Eds.), *Handbook of adolescent death and bereavement* (pp. 65–84). New York: Springer.

Jury, M., & Jury, D. (1978). *Gramps: A man ages and dies*. Baltimore: Penguin.

Kail, R. V., & Cavanaugh, J. C. (2006). *Human development: A lifespan view* (4th ed.). Belmont, CA: Thomson Wadsworth.

Kaimann, D. S. (2002). *Common threads: Nine widows' journeys through love, loss and healing*. Amityville, NY: Baywood.

Kalergis, M. M. (1998). *Seen and heard: Teenagers talk about their lives*. New York: Stewart, Tabori & Chang.

Kalipeni, E., Craddock, S., Oppong, J. R., & Ghosh, J. (Eds.). (2003). *HIV and AIDS in Africa: Beyond epidemiology*. Oxford, UK: Blackwell Publishing.

Kalish, R. A. (1985a). Death and dying in a social context. In R. H. Binstock & E. Shanas (Eds.), *Handbook of aging and the social sciences* (2nd ed.; pp. 149–170). New York: Van Nostrand.

Kalish, R. A. (1985b). The horse on the dining-room table. In *Death, grief, and caring relationships* (2nd ed.; pp. 2–4). Pacific Grove, CA: Brooks/Cole.

Kalish, R. A. (Ed.). (1980). *Death and dying: Views from many cultures*. Farmingdale, NY: Baywood.

Kalish, R. A., & Goldberg, H. (1978). Clergy attitudes toward funeral directors. *Death Education, 2*, 247–260.

Kalish, R. A., & Goldberg, H. (1980). Community attitudes toward funeral directors. *Omega, Journal of Death and Dying, 10*, 335–346.

Kalish, R. A., & Reynolds, D. K. (1981). *Death and ethnicity: A psychocultural study*. Farmingdale, NY: Baywood. (Originally published, Los Angeles: Andrus Gerontology Center, 1976)

Kane, B. (1979). Children's concepts of death. *Journal of Genetic Psychology, 134*, 141–153.

Kaplan, K. J. (1999). Right to die versus sacredness of life [Special issue]. *Omega, Journal of Death and Dying, 40*(1).

Kapust, L. R. (1982). Living with dementia: The ongoing funeral. *Social Work in Health Care, 7*(4), 79–91.

Karakatsanis, K. G., & Tsanakas, J. N. (2002). A critique on the concept of brain death. *Issues in Law and Medicine, 18*(2), 127–141.

Karp, N., & Wood, E. (2003). *Incapacitated and alone: Health care decision-making for the unbefriended elderly*. Washington, DC: American Bar Association.

Kaserman, D. L., & Barrett, A. H. (2002). *The United States organ procurement system: A prescription for reform*. Washington, DC: AEI Press.

Kashurba, G. J. (2006). *Quiet courage: The definitive account of Flight 93 and its aftermath*. Somerset, PA: SAJ Publishing.

Kassis, H. (1997). Islam. In H. Coward (Ed.), *Life after death in world religions* (pp. 48–65). Maryknoll, NY: Orbis Books.

Kastenbaum, R. (1967). The mental life of dying geriatric patients. *The Gerontologist, 7*(2), Pt. 1, 97–100.

Kastenbaum, R. (1969). Death and bereavement in later life. In A. H. Kutscher (Ed.), *Death and bereavement* (pp. 28–54). Springfield, IL: Charles C Thomas.

Kastenbaum, R. (1972). On the future of death: Some images and options. *Omega, Journal of Death and Dying, 3*, 306–318.

Kastenbaum, R. (1973, January). The kingdom where nobody dies. *Saturday Review, 56*, 33–38.

Kastenbaum, R. (1977). Death and development through the lifespan. In H. Feifel (Ed.), *New meanings of death* (pp. 17–45). New York: McGraw-Hill.

Kastenbaum, R. (1989a). Ars moriendi. In R. Kastenbaum & B. Kastenbaum (Eds.), *Encyclopedia of death* (pp. 17–19). Phoenix, AZ: Oryx Press.

Kastenbaum, R. (1989b). Cemeteries. In R. Kastenbaum & B. Kastenbaum (Eds.), *Encyclopedia of death* (pp. 41–45). Phoenix, AZ: Oryx Press.

Kastenbaum, R. (1995). Raymond A. Moody, Jr.: An *Omega* interview. *Omega, Journal of Death and Dying, 31*, 87–98.

Kastenbaum, R. (2000). *The psychology of death* (3rd ed.). New York: Springer.

Kastenbaum, R. (Ed.). (2003). *Macmillan encyclopedia of death and dying* (2 vols.). New York: Macmillan.

Kastenbaum, R. J. (2004a). *On our way: The final passage through life and death*. Berkeley, CA: University of California Press.

Kastenbaum, R. J. (2004b). Death writ large. *Death Studies, 28*, 375–392.

Kastenbaum, R. J. (2006). *Death, society, and human experience* (9th ed.). Boston: Allyn and Bacon.

Kastenbaum, R., & Aisenberg, R. (1972). *The psychology of death*. New York: Springer.

Kastenbaum, R., & Thuell, S. (1995). Cookies baking, coffee brewing: Toward a contextual theory of dying. *Omega, Journal of Death and Dying, 31*, 175–187.

Katzenbach, J. (1986). *The traveler*. New York: Putnam's.

Kaufert, J. M., & O'Neil, J. D. (1991). Cultural mediation of dying and grieving among Native Canadian patients in urban hospitals. In D. R. Counts & D. A. Counts (Eds.), *Coping with the final tragedy: Cultural variation in dying and grieving* (pp. 231–251). Amityville, NY: Baywood.

Kauffman, J. (2004). *Guidebook on helping persons with mental retardation mourn*. Amityville, NY: Baywood.

Kauffman, J. (Ed.). (1995). *Awareness of mortality*. Amityville, NY: Baywood.

Kauffman, J. (Ed.). (2002). *Loss of the assumptive world: A theory of traumatic loss*. New York: Brunner-Routledge.

Kaufman, K. R., & Kaufman, N. D. (2006). And then the dog died. *Death Studies, 30*, 61–76.

Kaufman, S. R. (1986). *The ageless self: Sources of meaning in late life*. Madison: University of Wisconsin Press.

Kaufman, S. R. (2006). *And a time to die: How American hospitals shape the end of life*. Chicago: University of Chicago Press.

Kavanaugh, R. E. (1972). *Facing death*. Los Angeles: Nash.

Kay, W. J., Cohen, S. P., Nieburg, H. A., Fudin, C. E., Grey, R. E., Kutscher, A. H., et al. (Eds.). (1988). *Euthanasia of the companion animal: The impact on pet owners, veterinarians, and society*. Philadelphia: Charles Press.

Kean, T. H., & Hamilton, L. H. (2006). *Without precedent: The inside story of the 9/11 Commission.* New York: Knopf.

Keating, D. (1990). Adolescent thinking. In S. S. Feldman & G. R. Elliott (Eds.), *At the threshold: The developing adolescent* (pp. 54–89). Cambridge, MA: Harvard University Press.

Keister, D. (2004). *Stories in stone: The complete guide to cemetery symbolism.* Layton, UT: Gibbs Smith.

Kellehear, A. (1996). *Experiences near death: Beyond medicine and religion.* New York: Oxford University Press.

Kelly, E. W. (2001). Near-death experiences with reports of meeting deceased people. *Death Studies, 25,* 229–249.

Kelly, E. W., Greyson, B., & Stevenson, I. (2000). Can experiences near death furnish evidence of life after death? *Omega, Journal of Death and Dying, 40,* 513–519.

Kelly, O. (1975). *Make today count.* New York: Delacorte Press.

Kelly, O. (1977). Make today count. In H. Feifel (Ed.), *New meanings of death* (pp. 182–193). New York: McGraw-Hill.

Kelsay, J. (1994). Islam and medical ethics. In P. F. Camenisch (Ed.), *Religious methods and resources in bioethics* (pp. 93–107). Dordrecht, Germany: Kluwer.

Kemp, C. E. (1999). *Terminal illness: A guide to nursing care.* Philadelphia: Lippincott Williams & Wilkins.

Keneally, T. (1982). *Schindler's list.* New York: Simon & Schuster.

Kenyon, B. L. (2001). Current research in children's conceptions of death: A critical review. *Omega, Journal of Death and Dying, 43,* 63–91.

Keown, D. (1995). *Buddhism and bioethics.* New York: St. Martin's Press.

Kephart, W. M. (1950). Status after death. *American Sociological Review, 15,* 635–643.

Kerbel, M. R. (2000). *If it bleeds, it leads: An anatomy of television news.* Boulder, CO: Westview Press.

Kessler, D. (2000). *The needs of the dying: A guide for bringing hope, comfort, and love to life's final chapter.* New York: Perennial Currents.

Kessler, D. (2001). *A question of intent: A great American battle with a deadly industry.* New York: Public Affairs.

Kessler, D. (2004). The extraordinary ordinary death of Elisabeth Kübler-Ross. *American Journal of Hospice and Palliative Medicine, 21,* 415–416.

Kessler, R. C., Berglund, P., Demler, O., Jin, R., Merikangas, K. R., & Walters, E. E. (2005). Lifetime prevalence and age-of-onset distributions of DSM-IV disorders in the national comorbidity survey replication. *Archives of General Psychiatry, 62,* 593–602.

King, A. (1990). A Samoan perspective: Funeral practices, death and dying. In J. K. Parry (Ed.), *Social work practice with the terminally ill: A transcultural perspective* (pp. 175–189). Springfield, IL: Charles C Thomas.

Kirk, W. G. (1993). *Adolescent suicide: A school-based approach to assessment and intervention.* Champaign, IL: Research Press.

Kissane, D.W., & Bloch, S. (2002). *Family focused grief therapy: A model of family-centered care during palliative care and bereavement.* Philadelphia: Open University Press.

Kitagawa, E. M., & Hauser, P. M. (1973). *Differential mortality in the United States: A study in socioeconomic epidemiology.* Cambridge, MA: Harvard University Press.

Klagsbrun, F. (1976). *Too young to die: Youth and suicide.* New York: Houghton Mifflin.

Klass, D. (1982). Elisabeth Kübler-Ross and the tradition of the private sphere: An analysis of symbols. *Omega, Journal of Death and Dying, 12,* 241–261.

Klass, D. (1985a). Bereaved parents and the Compassionate Friends: Affiliation and healing. *Omega, Journal of Death and Dying, 15,* 353–373.

Klass, D. (1985b). Self-help groups: Grieving parents and community resources. In C. A. Corr & D. M. Corr (Eds.), *Hospice approaches to pediatric care* (pp. 241–260). New York: Springer.

Klass, D. (1988). *Parental grief: Solace and resolution.* New York: Springer.

Klass, D. (1999). *The spiritual lives of bereaved parents.* Philadelphia: Taylor & Francis.

Klass, D. (Ed.). (2006). Death, grief, religion, and spirituality [Special issue]. *Omega, Journal of Death and Dying, 53*(1–2).

Klass, D., & Hutch, R. A. (1985). Elisabeth Kübler-Ross as a religious leader. *Omega, Journal of Death and Dying, 16,* 89–109.

Klass, D., & Shinners, B. (1983). Professional roles in a self-help group for the bereaved. *Omega, Journal of Death and Dying, 13,* 361–375.

Klass, D., Silverman, P. R., & Nickman, S. L. (Eds.). (1996). *Continuing bonds: New understandings of grief.* Washington, DC: Taylor & Francis.

Klevins, R. M., et al., for the Active Bacterial Care surveillance (ABCs) MRSA Investigators. (2007). Invasive methicillin-resistant *staphylococcus aureus* infections in the United States. *Journal of the American Medical Association, 298,* 1763–1771.

Klicker, R. L. (2000). *A student dies, a school mourns: Dealing with death and loss in the school community.* Philadelphia: Accelerated Development.

Kliever, L. D. (Ed.). (1989). *Dax's case: Essays in medical ethics and human meaning.* Dallas, TX: Southern Methodist University.

Klitzman, R., & Bayer, R. (2005). *Mortal secrets: Truth and lies in the age of AIDS.* Baltimore: The Johns Hopkins University Press.

Klug, C., & Jackson, S. (2004). *To the edge and back: My story from organ transplant survivor to Olympic snowboarder.* New York: Carroll & Graf.

Knapp, R. J. (1986). *Beyond endurance: When a child dies.* New York: Schocken.

Kochanek, K. D., & Hudson, B. L. (1994). Advance report of final mortality statistics, 1992. *Monthly Vital Statistics Report, 43*(6), Suppl. Hyattsville, MD: National Center for Health Statistics.

Koenig, B. A., & Gates-Williams, J. (1995). Understanding cultural difference in caring for dying patients. *Western Journal of Medicine, 163*(3), 244–249.

Kohn, I., Moffit, P-L., & Wilkins, I. A. (2000). *A silent sorrow: Pregnancy loss—Guidance and support for you and your family* (Rev. 2nd ed.). New York: Brunner-Routledge.

Kohn, J. B., & Kohn, W. K. (1978). *The widower.* Boston: Beacon Press.

Komro, K. A. (1999). Adolescents' access to firearms: Epidemiology and prevention. *Journal of Health Education, 30*(5), 290–296.

Koocher, G. (1973). Childhood, death, and cognitive development. *Developmental Psychology, 9,* 369–375.

Koocher, G. P. (1974). Talking with children about death. *American Journal of Orthopsychiatry, 44,* 404–411.

Koocher, G. P., & O'Malley, J. E. (1981). *The Damocles syndrome: Psychosocial consequences of surviving childhood cancer.* New York: McGraw-Hill.

Koocher, G. P., O'Malley, J. E., Foster, D., & Gogan, J. L. (1976). Death anxiety in normal children and adolescents. *Psychiatria clinica, 9,* 220–229.

Koop, C. E. (1988). *Understanding AIDS*. HHS Publication No. (CDC) HHS-88–8404, U.S. Department of Health and Human Services. Washington, DC: U.S. Government Printing Office.

Koppelman, K. L. (1994). *The fall of a sparrow: Of death and dreams and healing*. Amityville, NY: Baywood.

Kotzwinkle, W. (1975). *Swimmer in the secret sea*. New York: Avon.

Kozol, J. (1995). *Amazing grace*. New York: Crown.

Kramer, K. (2005). You cannot die alone: Dr. Elisabeth Kübler-Ross (July 8, 1926–August 24, 2004). *Omega, Journal of Death and Dying, 50*, 83–101.

Kraybill, D. B. (2001). *The riddle of Amish culture* (Rev. ed.). Baltimore: Johns Hopkins University Press.

Kreicbergs, U., Valdimarsdóttir, U., Onelöv, E., Henter, J.-I., & Steineck, G. (2004). Talking about death with children who have severe malignant disease. *New England Journal of Medicine, 351*, 1175–1186.

Krementz, J. (1989). *How it feels to fight for your life*. Boston: Little, Brown.

Krieger, N., & Margo, G. (Eds.). (1994). *AIDS: The politics of survival*. Amityville, NY: Baywood.

Krizek, B. (1992). Goodbye old friend: A son's farewell to Comiskey Park. *Omega, Journal of Death and Dying, 25*, 87–93.

Krugman, P. (2001, February 24). Fowl play badmouthing the economy. *St. Petersburg Times*, p. 16A.

Krumholz, H. M., Phillips, R. S., Hamel, M. B., Teno, J. M., Bellamy, P., Broste, S. K., et al., for the SUPPORT Investigators. (1998). Resuscitation preferences among patients with severe congestive heart failure: Results from the SUPPORT Project. *Circulation, 98*, 648–655.

Kübler-Ross, E. (1969). *On death and dying*. New York: Macmillan.

Kübler-Ross, E. (1983). *On children and death*. New York: Macmillan.

Kübler-Ross, E. (1997). *The wheel of life: A memoir of living and dying*. New York: Scribner.

Kuhl, D. (2002). *What dying people want: Practical wisdom for the end of life*. New York: Public Affairs.

Kulka, E. (1986). *Escape from Auschwitz*. South Hadley, MA: Bergin & Garvey.

Kurtz, D. C., & Boardman, J. (1971). *Greek burial customs*. Ithaca, NY: Cornell University Press.

Kushner, H. S. (1981). *When bad things happen to good people*. New York: Avon.

Kushner, H. W. (2002). *Encyclopedia of terrorism*. Thousand Oaks, CA: Sage.

Lack, S. A., & Buckingham, R. W. (1978). *First American hospice: Three years of home care*. New Haven, CT: Hospice.

Laderman, G. (2003). *Rest in peace: A cultural history of death and the funeral home in twentieth century America*. New York: Oxford University Press.

Lafser, C. (1998). *An empty cradle, a full heart: Reflections for mothers and fathers after miscarriage, stillbirth, or infant death*. Chicago: Loyola Press.

Lagoni, L., Butler, C., & Hetts, S. (1994). *The human-animal bond and grief*. Philadelphia: W. B. Saunders.

LaGrand, L. E. (1980). Reducing burnout in the hospice and the death education movement. *Death Education, 4*, 61–76.

LaGrand, L. E. (1981). Loss reactions of college students: A descriptive analysis. *Death Studies, 5*, 235–247.

LaGrand, L. E. (1986). *Coping with separation and loss as a young adult: Theoretical and practical realities*. Springfield, IL: Charles C Thomas.

LaGrand, L. E. (1988). *Changing patterns of human existence: Assumptions, beliefs, and coping with the stress of change*. Springfield, IL: Charles C Thomas.

LaGrand, L. E. (1997). *After-death communication: Final farewells*. St. Paul, MN: Llewellyn.

LaGrand, L. E. (1999). *Messages and miracles: Extraordinary experiences of the bereaved*. St. Paul, MN: Llewellyn.

LaGrand, L. E. (2001). *Gifts from the unknown: Using extraordinary experiences to cope with loss and change*. St. Paul, MN: Llewellyn.

LaGrand, L. E. (2006). *Love lives on: Learnings from the extraordinary encounters of the bereaved*. New York: Berkley Books.

Lamb, J. M. (Ed.). (1988). *Bittersweet . . . hellogoodbye*. Belleville, IL: SHARE National Office.

Lamb, M. (2001). Sexuality. In B. R. Ferrell & N. Coyle (Eds.), *Textbook of palliative nursing* (pp. 309–315). New York: Oxford University Press.

Lamberti, J.W., & Detmer, C. M. (1993). Model of family grief assessment and treatment. *Death Studies, 17*, 55–67.

Lamers, E. P. (1986). Books for adolescents. In C. A. Corr & J. N. McNeil (Eds.), *Adolescence and death* (pp. 233–242). New York: Springer.

Lamers, E. P. (1995). Children, death, and fairy tales. *Omega, Journal of Death and Dying, 31*, 151–167.

Lamm, M. (2000). *The Jewish way in death and mourning* (Rev. ed.). Middle Village, NY: Jonathan David.

Lamm, M. (2004). *Consolation: The spiritual journey beyond grief*. Philadelphia: The Jewish Publication Society.

Landay, D. S. (1998). *Be prepared: The complete financial, legal, and practical guide for living with a life-challenging condition*. New York: St. Martin's Press.

Landry, S. (1999a, June 15). He wanted you to know. *St. Petersburg Times*, p. 1D.

Landry, S. (1999b, June 22). His message transcends death. *St. Petersburg Times*, p. 3D.

Lang, A. (Ed.). (1904). *The blue fairy book*. New York: Longman's Green.

Lang, L. T. (1990). Aspects of the Cambodian death and dying process. In J. K. Parry (Ed.), *Social work practice with the terminally ill: A transcultural perspective* (pp. 205–211). Springfield, IL: Charles C Thomas.

Langbein, H. (1994). *Against all hope: Resistance in the Nazi concentration camps 1938–1945* (H. Zohn, Trans.). New York: Paragon House.

Laqueur, W. (2003). *No end to war: Terrorism in the twenty-first century*. New York: Continuum.

Lareca, A. M., Silberman, W. K., Vernberg, E.M., & Roberts, M. C. (Eds.). (2002). *Helping children cope with disasters and terrorism*. Washington, DC: American Psychological Association.

Largo, M. (2006). *Final exits: The illustrated encyclopaedia of how we die*. New York: Harper.

Larson, D. G. (1993). *The helper's journey: Working with people facing grief, loss, and life-threatening illness*. Champaign, IL: Research Press.

Larson, D. G., & Hoyt, W. T. (2007a). The bright side of grief counseling: Deconstructing the new pessimism. In K. J. Doka (Ed.), *Living with grief: Before and after the death* (pp. 157–174). Washington, DC: Hospice Foundation of America.

Larson, D. G., & Hoyt, W. T. (2007b). What has become of grief counseling? An evaluation of the empirical foundations of the new pessimism. *Professional Psychology: Research and Practice, 38*, 347–355.

Larson, E. B., & Shadlen, M. F. (2004). Survival after initial diagnosis of Alzheimer disease. *Annals of Internal Medicine, 6,* 501–509.

Larue, G. A. (1985). *Euthanasia and religion: A survey of the attitudes of world religions to the right to die.* Los Angeles: The Hemlock Society.

Lattanzi, M. E. (1983). Professional stress: Adaptation, coping, and meaning. In J. C. Hanson & T. T. Frantz (Eds.), *Death and grief in the family* (pp. 95–106). Rockville, MD: Aspen Systems Corp.

Lattanzi, M. E. (1985). An approach to caring: Caregiving concerns. In C. A. Corr & D. M. Corr (Eds.), *Hospice approaches to pediatric care* (pp. 261–277). New York: Springer.

Lattanzi, M. E., & Hale, M. E. (1984). Giving grief words: Writing during bereavement. *Omega, Journal of Death and Dying, 15,* 45–52.

Lattanzi-Licht, M. E. (1996). Helping families with adolescents cope with loss. In C. A. Corr & D. E. Balk (Eds.), *Handbook of adolescent death and bereavement* (pp. 219–234). New York: Springer.

Lattanzi-Licht, M. E (2007). Religion, spirituality, and dying. In D. E. Balk C. Wogrin, G. Thornton, & D. Meagher. (Eds.), *ADEC handbook of thanatology* (pp. 11–17). Northbrook, IL: Association for Death Education and Counseling.

Lattanzi-Licht, M. E., & Doka, K. J. (Eds.). (2003). *Living with grief: Coping with public tragedy.* Washington, DC: Hospice Foundation of America.

Lattanzi-Licht, M. E., Mahoney, J. J., & Miller, G.W. (1998). *The hospice choice: In pursuit of a peaceful death.* New York: Simon & Schuster.

Lauderdale, D. S., & Kestenbaum, B. (2002). Mortality rates of elderly Asian American populations based on Medicare and Social Security data. *Demography, 39*(3), 529–540.

Lazar, A., & Torney-Purta, J. (1991). The development of the subconcepts of death in young children: A short-term longitudinal study. *Child Development, 62,* 1321–1333.

Lazarus, R. S., & Folkman, S. (1984). *Stress, appraisal, and coping.* New York: Springer.

Lazenby, R., with Cupp, K., Higgs, S., Maglalang, O., Massey, L., Sangalang, T., Thomas, C., & Turnage, N. (2007). *April 16th: Virginia Tech remembers.* New York: Plume.

Leach, C. (1981). *Letter to a younger son.* New York: Harcourt Brace Jovanovich.

Lecso, P. A. (1986). Euthanasia: A Buddhist perspective. *Journal of Religion and Health, 25,* 51–57.

Lee, P.W.H., Lieh-Mak, F., Hung, B.K.M., & Luk, S. L. (1984). Death anxiety in leukemic Chinese children. *International Journal of Psychiatry in Medicine, 13,* 281–290.

Leenaars, A. A. (1990). Psychological perspectives on suicide. In D. Lester (Ed.), *Current concepts of suicide* (pp. 159–167). Philadelphia: Charles Press.

Leenaars, A. A. (2006). People who have committed a certain sin ought to be dead. *Death Studies, 30,* 539–553.

Leenaars, A. A., & Wenckstern, S. (Eds.). (1991). *Suicide prevention in the schools.* Washington, DC: Hemisphere.

Leenaars, A. A., & Wenckstern, S. (1996). Postvention with elementary school children. In C. A. Corr & D. M. Corr (Eds.), *Handbook of childhood death and bereavement* (pp. 265–283). New York: Springer.

Leenaars, A. A., Maltsberger, J. T., & Neimeyer, R. A. (1994). *Treatment of suicidal people.* Washington, DC: Taylor & Francis.

Leenaars, A. A., Maris, R.W., McIntosh, J. L., & Richman, J. (Eds.). (1992). *Suicide and the older adult.* New York: Guilford.

Leininger, M. (1995). *Transcultural nursing: Concepts, theories, and practices* (2nd ed.). New York: McGraw-Hill.

Leong, F.T.L., & Leach, M. M. (Eds.). (2007). Ethnicity and suicide in the United States. [Special issue]. *Death Studies, 31*(5).

Leong, F.T.L., Leach, M. M., Yeh, C., & Chou, E. (2007). Suicide among Asian Americans: What do we know? What do we need to know? *Death Studies, 31*(5), 417–434.

Lerner, M. (1970). When, why, and where people die. In O. Brim, H. Freeman, S. Levine, & N. Scotch (Eds.), *The dying patient* (pp. 5–29). New York: Russell Sage Foundation.

Lerner, M. D., Volpe, J. S., & Lindell, B. (2003). *A practical guide for crisis response in our schools: A comprehensive school crisis response plan* (5th ed.). Commack, NY: The American Academy of Experts in Traumatic Stress.

Lerner, M. D., Volpe, J. S., & Lindell, B. (2004). *A practical guide for university crisis response: A comprehensive crisis response plan for colleges and universities.* Commack, NY: The American Academy of Experts in Traumatic Stress.

LeShan, E. (1976). *Learning to say good-by: When a parent dies.* New York: Macmillan.

LeShan, L. (1964). The world of the patient in severe pain of long duration. *Journal of Chronic Diseases, 17,* 119–126.

Lester, D. (1992). *Why people kill themselves* (3rd ed.). Springfield, IL: Charles C Thomas.

Lester, D. (1993). *The cruelest death: The enigma of adolescent suicide.* Philadelphia: Charles Press.

Lester, D. (1994). Differences in the epidemiology of suicide in Asian Americans by nation of origin. *Omega, Journal of Death and Dying, 29,* 89–93.

Lester, D. (1998). The suicide of Sylvia Plath: Current perspectives. [Special issue] *Death Studies, 22*(7).

Lester, D. (2000). The social causes of suicide: A look at Durkheim's *Le Suicide* one hundred years later. *Omega, Journal of Death and Dying, 40,* 307–321.

Lester, D. (2003). *Fixin' to die: A compassionate guide to committing suicide or staying alive.* Amityville, NY: Baywood.

Lester, D. (2006a). Can suicide be a good death? *Death Studies, 30,* 511–527.

Lester, D. (2006b). Can suicide be a good death? A reply. *Death Studies, 30,* 555–560.

Lesy, M. (1973). *Wisconsin death trip.* New York: Pantheon.

Levi, P. (1986). *Survival in Auschwitz and the reawakening: Two memoirs* (S. Woolf, Trans.). New York: Simon & Schuster.

Levin, A. (2006, October 6). Grief travels through Amish country. *USA Today,* p. 4A.

Levin, A., & Hall, M. (2006, October 5). Shooter's relatives: No recall of being molested. *USA Today,* p. 3A.

Levinson, D. J. (1978). *The seasons of a man's life.* New York: Knopf.

Levinson, D. J. (1996). *The seasons of a woman's life.* New York: Knopf.

Leviton, D. (Ed.). (1991a). *Horrendous death, health, and well-being.* Washington, DC: Hemisphere.

Leviton, D. (Ed.). (1991b). *Horrendous death and health: Toward action.* Washington, DC: Hemisphere.

Levy, J. E., & Kunitz, S. J. (1987). A suicide prevention program for Hopi youth. *Social Science and Medicine, 25,* 931–940.

Lewis, B. (2003). *The crisis of Islam: Holy war and unholy terror.* New York: Modern Library.

Lewis, C. S. (1976). *A grief observed.* New York: Bantam Books.

Lewis, O. (1970). *A death in the Sanchez family.* New York: Random House.

Ley, D.C.H., & Corless, I. B. (1988). Spirituality and hospice care. *Death Studies, 12,* 101–110.

Lieberman, A. F., Compton, N. C., Van Horn, P., & Ippen, C. G. (2003). *Losing a parent to death in the early years: Guidelines for the treatment of traumatic bereavement in infancy and early childhood.* Washington, DC: Zero To Three Press.

Liegner, L. M. (1975). St. Christopher's Hospice, 1974: Care of the dying patient. *Journal of the American Medical Association, 234,* 1047–1048. (Reprinted in 2000 in Vol. 284, p. 2426.)

Lifton, R. J. (1964). On death and death symbolism: The Hiroshima disaster. *Psychiatry, 27,* 191–210.

Lifton, R. J. (1967). *Death in life: Survivors of Hiroshima.* New York: Random House.

Lifton, R. J. (1979). *The broken connection.* New York: Simon & Schuster.

Lifton, R. J. (1982). *Indefensible weapons: The political and psychological case against nuclearism.* New York: Basic Books.

Lifton, R. J. (1986). *The Nazi doctors: Medical killing and the psychology of genocide.* New York: Basic Books.

Lifton, R. J., & Mitchell, G. (1995). *Hiroshima in America: Fifty years of denial.* New York: Putnam's.

Limbo, R. K., & Wheeler, S. R. (1998). *When a baby dies: A handbook for healing and helping* (2nd ed.). La Crosse, WI: Lutheran Hospital—La Crosse, Inc.

Lindemann, E. (1944). Symptomatology and management of acute grief. *American Journal of Psychiatry, 101,* 141–148.

Lindemann, E., & Greer, I. M. (1972). A study of grief: Emotional responses to suicide. In A. C. Cain (Ed.), *Survivors of suicide* (pp. 63–69). Springfield, IL: Charles C Thomas. (Reprinted from *Pastoral Psychology,* 1953, 4, 9–13)

Lindsay, M., & Lester, D. (2004). *Suicide by cop: Committing suicide by provoking police to shoot you.* Amityville, NY: Baywood.

Lindstrom, T. (2002). "It ain't necessarily so" . . . Challenging mainstream thinking about bereavement. *Family and Community Health, 25,* 11–21.

Linenthal, E. T. (2001). *The unfinished bombing: Oklahoma City in American memory.* New York: Oxford University Press.

Linn, E. (1986). *I know just how you feel . . . Avoiding the clichés of grief.* Incline Village, NV: Publisher's Mark.

Linsk, N. L., & Mason, S. (2004). Stresses on grandparents and other relatives caring for children affected by HIV/AIDS. *Health and Social Work, 29,* 127–136.

Lipman, A. G., Kenneth, C., Jackson, I., & Tyler, L. S. (Eds.). (2000). *Evidence-based symptom control in palliative care: Systemic review and validated clinical practice guidelines for 15 common problems in patients with life-limiting disease.* Binghamton, NY: Haworth Press.

Lipstadt, D. (1993). *Denying the Holocaust: The growing assault on truth and memory.* New York: Free Press.

Litman, R. E. (1967). Sigmund Freud on suicide. In E. S. Shneidman (Ed.), *Essays in self-destruction* (pp. 324–344). New York: Science House.

Lloyd-Williams, M. (Ed.). (2003). *Psychosocial issues in palliative care.* New York: Oxford University Press.

Loftin, C., McDowall, D., Wiersema, B., & Cottey, T. J. (1991). Effects of restrictive licensing of handguns on homicide and suicide in the District of Columbia. *New England Journal of Medicine, 325,* 1615–1620.

Lonetto, R. (1980). *Children's conceptions of death.* New York: Springer.

Lonetto, R., & Templer, D. I. (1986). *Death anxiety.* Washington, DC: Hemisphere.

Long, K. A. (1983). The experience of repeated and traumatic loss among Crow Indian children: Response patterns and intervention strategies. *American Journal of Orthopsychiatry, 53*(1), 116–126.

Longaker, C. (1998). *Facing death and finding hope: A guide to the emotional and spiritual care of the dying.* New York: Doubleday.

Lopata, H. Z. (1996). *Current widowhood: Myths and realities.* London: Sage.

Lorimer, D. (1989). The near-death experience: Cross-cultural and multi-disciplinary dimensions. In A. Berger, P. Badham, A. H. Kutscher, J. Berger, M. Perry, & J. Beloff (Eds.), *Perspectives on death and dying: Cross-cultural and multidisciplinary views* (pp. 256–267). Philadelphia: Charles Press.

Louganis, G. (with Marcus, E.). (1995). *Breaking the surface.* New York: Random House.

Lukas, C., & Seiden, H. M. (2007). *Silent grief: Living in the wake of suicide* (Rev. ed.). Philadelphia: Jessica Kingsley.

Luna, G. C. (1997). *Youths living with HIV: Self-evident truths.* Binghamton, NY: Haworth Press.

Lund, D. A. (1989). *Older bereaved spouses: Research with practical applications.* Washington, DC: Hemisphere.

Lund, D. A. (2000). *Men coping with grief.* Amityville, NY: Baywood.

Lund, D. A., Dimond, M., & Juretich, M. (1985). Bereavement support groups for the elderly: Characteristics of potential participants. *Death Studies, 9,* 309–321.

Lustig, A. (1977). *Darkness casts no shadow.* New York: Inscape.

Lutovich, D. S. (2001). *Nobody's child: How older women say good-bye to their mothers.* Amityville, NY: Baywood.

Lynch, T. (1997). *The undertaking: Life studies from the dismal trade.* New York: Penguin.

Lynn, J. (Ed.). (1986). *By no extraordinary means: The choice to forgo life-sustaining food and water.* Bloomington: Indiana University Press.

Lynn, J., & Harrold, J. (1999). *Handbook for mortals: Guidance for people facing serious illness.* New York: Oxford University Press.

Lynn, J., Schuster, J. L., & Kabcenell, A. (2000). *Improving care for the end of life: A sourcebook for health care managers and clinicians.* New York: Oxford University Press.

Lynn, K. S. (1987). *Hemingway.* New York: Simon & Schuster.

Lynne, D. (2005). *Terri's story: The court ordered death of an American woman.* Medford, OR: WND Books.

Mace, N. L., & Rabins, P. V. (1999). *The 36-hour day: A family guide to caring for persons with Alzheimer disease, related dementing illnesses, and memory loss in later life* (3rd ed.). Baltimore: Johns Hopkins University Press.

Maciejewski, P. K., Zhang, B., Block, S. D., & Prigerson, H. G. (2007). An empirical examination of the stage theory of grief. *Journal of the American Medical Association, 297,* 716–723.

Mack, A. (Ed.). (1974). *Death in American experience.* New York: Schocken.

Mack, S. (2004). *Janet and me: An illustrated story of love and loss.* New York: Simon & Schuster Paperbacks.

MacMillan, I. (1991). *Orbit of darkness.* San Diego, CA: Harcourt Brace Jovanovich.

MacPherson, M. (1999). *She came to live out loud: An inspiring family journey through illness, loss, and grief.* New York: Scribner.

Maddox, R. J. (1995).*Weapons for victory: The Hiroshima decision fifty years later.* Columbia, MO: University of Missouri Press.

Madey, S. F., & Chasteen, A. L. (2004). Age-related health stereotypes and illusory correlation. *International Journal of Aging and Human Development, 58,* 109–126.

Magee, D. (1983). *What murder leaves behind: The victim's family.* New York: Dodd, Mead.

Magee, D. S., & Ventura, J. (1998). *Everything your heirs need to know: Organizing your assets, family history, final wishes* (3rd ed.). Chicago: Dearborn Financial Publishing.

Mahoney, M. C. (1991). Fatal motor vehicle traffic accidents among Native Americans. *American Journal of Preventive Medicine, 7,* 112–116.

Maier, F. (1991). *Sweet reprieve: One couple's journey to the frontiers of medicine.* New York: Crown.

Maimonides, M. (1949). *The code of Maimonides (Mishneh Torah): Book Fourteen, The Book of Judges* (A. M. Hershman, Trans.). New Haven, CT: Yale University Press.

Maizler, J. S., Solomon, J. R., & Almquist, E. (1983). Psychogenic mortality syndrome: Choosing to die by the institutionalized elderly. *Death Education, 6,* 353–364.

Malinowski, B. (1954). *Magic, science, and religion and other essays.* New York: Doubleday.

Maloney, R., & Wolfelt, A. D. (2001). *Caring for donor families: Before, during and after.* Fort Collins, CO: Companion Press.

Mandelbaum, D. (1959). Social uses of funeral rites. In H. Feifel (Ed.), *The meaning of death* (pp. 189–217). New York: McGraw-Hill.

Mandell, H., & Spiro, H. (Eds.). (1987). *When doctors get sick.* New York: Plenum.

Mann, T. C., & Greene, J. (1962). *Over their dead bodies: Yankee epitaphs and history.* Brattleboro, VT: Stephen Greene Press.

Mann, T. C., & Greene, J. (1968). *Sudden and awful: American epitaphs and the finger of God.* Brattleboro, VT: Stephen Greene Press.

Manning, D. (1979). *Don't take my grief away from me: How to walk through grief and learn to live again.* Hereford, TX: In-Sight Books.

Manning, D. (2001). *The funeral: A chance to teach, a chance to serve, a chance to heal.* Oklahoma City, OK: In-Sight Books.

Mannino, J. D. (1996). *Grieving days, healing days.* Englewood Cliffs, NJ: Prentice Hall.

March, A. (2007). *Dying into grace: Mother and daughter . . . a dance of healing.* Cambridge, MA: Quantum Lens Press.

Marcus, E. (1996). *Why suicide? Answers to 200 of the most frequently asked questions about suicide, attempted suicide, and assisted suicide.* San Francisco: HarperCollins.

Maris, R. W. (1969). *Social forces in urban suicide.* Homewood, IL: Dorsey Press.

Maris, R. W. (1981). *Pathways to suicide: A survey of self-destructive behaviors.* Baltimore: Johns Hopkins University Press.

Maris, R. W. (1985). The adolescent suicide problem. *Suicide and Life-Threatening Behavior, 15,* 91–109.

Maris, R. W. (Ed.). (1988). *Understanding and preventing suicide.* New York: Guilford.

Maris, R. W., Berman, A. L., & Silverman, M. M. (2000). *Comprehensive textbook of suicidology.* New York: Guilford.

Maris, R. W., Berman, A. L., Maltsberger, J. T., & Yufit, R. I. (Eds.). (1992). *Assessment and prediction of suicide.* New York: Guilford.

Marks, A. S., & Calder, B. J. (1982). *Attitudes toward death and funerals.* Evansville, IL: Northwestern University, Center for Marketing Sciences.

Marks, R., & Sachar, E. (1973). Undertreatment of medical inpatients with narcotic analgesics. *Annals of Internal Medicine, 78,* 173–181.

Marmot, M. (2004). *The status syndrome: How social standing affects our health and longevity.* New York: Times Books.

Marmot, M., & Wilkinson, R. G. (Eds.). (2005) *Social determinants of health* (2nd ed.). New York: Oxford University Press.

Marshall, J. R. (1975). The geriatric patient's fears about death. *Postgraduate Medicine, 57*(4), 144–149.

Marta, S. Y. (2003). *Healing the hurt, restoring the hope: How to guide children and teens through times of divorce, death, and crisis with the RAINBOWS approach.* Emmaus, PA: Rodale Books.

Martikainen, P., & Valkonen, T. (1996). Mortality after the death of a spouse: Rates and causes of death in a large Finnish cohort. *American Journal of Public Health, 36,* 1087–1093.

Martin, G. (2003). *Understanding terrorism: Challenges, perspectives, and issues.* Thousand Oaks, CA: Sage.

Martin, S. T. (2001, November 29). Willing to kill and die, but why? *St. Petersburg Times,* pp. 1D, 3D.

Martin, T. L., & Doka, K. J. (1996). Masculine grief. In K. J. Doka (Ed.), *Living with grief after sudden loss: Suicide, homicide, accident, heart attack, stroke* (pp. 161–171). Washington, DC: Hospice Foundation of America.

Martin, T. L., & Doka, K. J. (1998). Revisiting masculine grief. In K. J. Doka & J. D. Davidson (Eds.), *Living with grief: Who we are, how we grieve* (pp. 133–142). Washington, DC: Hospice Foundation of America.

Martin, T. L., & Doka, K. J. (2000). *Men don't cry, women do: Transcending gender stereotypes of grief.* Philadelphia: Brunner/Mazel.

Martinson, I. M. (Ed.). (1976). *Home care for the dying child.* New York: Appleton-Century-Crofts.

Martinson, I. M., Davies, E. B., & McClowry, S. G. (1987). The long-term effects of sibling death on self-concept. *Journal of Pediatric Nursing, 2,* 227–235.

Maruyama, N. L. (1998). How many children do you have? *Bereavement Magazine, 12*(5), 16.

Masera, G., Spinetta, J. J., Jankovic, M., Ablin, A. R., D'Angio, G. J., Van Dongen-Melman, J., et al. (1999). Guidelines for assistance to terminally ill children with cancer: A report of the SIOP working committee on psychosocial issues in pediatric oncology. *Medical and Pediatric Oncology, 32,* 44–48.

Maslow, A. (1968). *Toward a psychology of being* (2nd ed.). Princeton, NJ: Van Nostrand.

Maslow, A. (1971). *The farther reaches of human nature.* New York: Viking Penguin.

Masur, H., Kaplan, J. E., & Holmes, K. K. (2001). July, 2001: Draft/2001 USPHS/IDSA. Guidelines for the Prevention of Opportunistic Infections in Persons Infected with Human Immunodeficiency Virus, p. 49.

Matchett, W. F. (1972). Repeated hallucinatory experiences as a part of the mourning process among Hopi Indian women. *Psychiatry, 35,* 185–194.

Mathews, L. L., & Servaty-Seib, H. L. (2007). Hardiness and grief in a sample of bereaved college students. *Death Studies, 31,* 183–204.

Matse, J. (1975). Reactions to death in residential homes for the aged. *Omega, Journal of Death and Dying, 6,* 21–32.

Matthews, L. T., & Marwit, S. J. (2004). Examining the assumptive world views of parents bereaved by accident, murder, and illness. *Omega, Journal of Death and Dying, 48,* 115–136.

Matthews, W. (1897). Navaho legends. *Memoirs of the American Folk-Lore Society,* Vol. 5. New York: G. E. Stechert.

Matulonis, U. A. (2004). End of life issues in older patients. *Seminars in Oncology, 31*(2), 274–281.

Mauk, G.W., & Weber, C. (1991). Peer survivors of adolescent suicide: Perspectives on grieving and postvention. *Journal of Adolescent Research, 6*, 113–131.

Maurer, A. (1964). Adolescent attitudes toward death. *Journal of Genetic Psychology, 105*, 75–90.

Maurer, A. (1966). Maturation of the conception of death. *Journal of Medical Psychology, 39*, 35–41.

Maxwell, B. (2007, February 11). Black churches must address HIV/AIDS. *St. Petersburg Times*, p. 3P.

May, G. (1992). For they shall be comforted. *Shalem News, 16*(2), 3.

Mayer, R. A. (1996). *Embalming: History, theory, and practice* (2nd ed.). Norwalk, CT: Appleton & Lange.

Mazanec, P., & Tyler, M. K. (2003). Cultural considerations in end of-life care. *American Journal of Nursing, 103*, 50–58.

Mbiti, J. S. (1970). *African religion and philosophy*. Garden City, NY: Doubleday Anchor.

McCaffery, M., & Beebe, A. (1989). *Pain: Clinical manual for nursing practice*. St. Louis, MO: Mosby.

McCallum, D. E., Byrne, P., & Bruera, E. (2000). How children die in hospital. *Journal of Pain and Symptom Management, 20*, 417–423.

McCord, C., & Freeman, H. P. (1990). Excess mortality in Harlem. *New England Journal of Medicine, 322*, 173–177.

McCormick, R. (1974). To save or let die. *Journal of the American Medical Association, 224*, 172–176.

McCown, D. E., & Davies, B. (1995). Patterns of grief in young children following the death of a sibling. *Death Studies, 19*, 41–53.

McCue, J. D. (1995). The naturalness of dying. *Journal of the American Medical Association, 273*, 1039–1043.

McCue, K., & Bonn, R. (1996). *How to help children through a parent's serious illness*. New York: St. Martin's Press.

McGinnis, J. M., & Foege, W. H. (1993). Actual causes of death in the United States. *Journal of the American Medical Association, 270*, 2207–2212.

McGinnis, J. M., & Foege, W. H. (2004). The immediate vs the important [Editorial]. *Journal of the American Medical Association, 291*, 1263–1264.

McGoldrick, M. (1988). Women and the family life cycle. In B. Carter & M. McGoldrick (Eds.), *The changing family life cycle: A framework for family therapy* (2nd ed.; pp. 29–68). New York: Gardner Press.

McGoldrick, M., & Gerson, R. (1985). *Genograms in family assessment*. New York: Norton.

McGoldrick, M., & Gerson, R. (1988). Genograms and the family life cycle. In B. Carter & M. McGoldrick (Eds.), *The changing family life cycle: A framework for family therapy* (2nd ed.; pp. 164–189). New York: Gardner Press.

McGoldrick, M., & Walsh, F. (2004). A time to mourn: Death and the family life cycle. In F. Walsh & M. McGoldrick (Eds.), *Living beyond loss: Death in the family* (2nd ed.; pp. 27–46). New York: Norton.

McGoldrick, M., Pearce, J. K., & Giordano, J. (Eds.). (1982). *Ethnicity and family therapy*. New York: Guilford.

McGrath, P. A. (1998). Pain control. In D. Doyle, G.W.C. Hanks, & N. MacDonald (Eds.), *Oxford textbook of palliative medicine* (pp. 1013–1031). New York: Oxford University Press.

McGuffey, W. H. (1866). *McGuffey's new fourth eclectic reader: Instructive lessons for the young* (Enlarged ed.). Cincinnati, OH: Wilson, Hinkle.

McIntosh, J. L. (1983). Suicide among Native Americans: Further tribal data and considerations. *Omega, Journal of Death and Dying, 14*, 215–229.

McIntosh, J. L. (1985). Suicide among the elderly: Levels and trends. *American Journal of Orthopsychiatry, 56*, 288–293.

McIntosh, J. L. (1987). Research, therapy, and educational needs. In Dunne, E. J., McIntosh, J. L., & Dunne-Maxim, K. (Eds.), *Suicide and its aftermath: Understanding and counseling the survivors* (pp. 263–277). New York: Norton.

McIntosh, J. L. (2006). *U.S.A. suicide: 2004 official final data* (rev. 15 December). Washington, DC: American Association of Suicidology.

McIntosh, J. L., & Santos, J. F. (1981a). Suicide among minority elderly: A preliminary investigation. *Suicide and Life-Threatening Behavior, 11*, 151–166.

McIntosh, J. L., & Santos, J. F. (1981b). Suicide among Native Americans: A compilation of findings. *Omega, Journal of Death and Dying, 11*, 303–316.

McKhann, C. F. (1999). *A time to die: The place for physician assistance*. New Haven, CT: Yale University Press.

McNeil, J. N. (1986). Talking about death: Adolescents, parents, and peers. In C. A. Corr & J. N. McNeil (Eds.), *Adolescence and death* (pp. 185–201). New York: Springer.

McNeil, J. N., Silliman, B., & Swihart, J. J. (1991). Helping adolescents cope with the death of a peer: A high school case study. *Journal of Adolescent Research, 6*, 132–145.

McNurlen, M. (1991). Guidelines for group work. In C. A. Corr, H. Fuller, C. A. Barnickol, & D. M. Corr (Eds.), *Sudden Infant Death Syndrome: Who can help and how* (pp. 180–202). New York: Springer.

McQuay, J. (1995). Cross-cultural customs and beliefs related to health crises, death, and organ donation/transplantation: A guide to assist health care professionals understand different responses and provide cross-cultural assistance. *Critical Care Nursing Clinics of North America, 7*(3), 581–594.

McWhorter, G. (2003). *Helping activities for children in grief: Activities suitable for support groups with grieving children, preteens and teens*. Roanoke, TX: Author (1713 Bellechase Drive, Roanoke, TX 76262; tel. 817-379-5544; griefactivities@aol.com).

Mead, M. (1973). Ritual and social crisis. In J. D. Shaughnessy (Ed.), *The roots of ritual* (pp. 87–101). Grand Rapids, MI: Eerdmans.

Meisel A., & Cerminara, K. L. (2004). *The right to die: The law of end-of-life decision-making*. New York: Aspen.

Meltzer, M. I., Cox, N. J., & Fukuda, K. (1999). Modeling the impact of pandemic influenza in the United States: Implications for setting priorities for intervention/Background paper. Emerging infectious diseases. Available at: http://www.cdc.gov/ncidod/eid/vof5no5/meltzer.htm.

Melzack, R. (1990, February). The tragedy of needless pain. *Scientific American*, 27–33.

Melzack, R., & Wall, P. D. (1991). *The challenge of pain* (3rd ed.). New York: Penguin.

Melzack, R., Mount, B. M., & Gordon, J. M. (1979). The Brompton mixture versus morphine solution given orally: Effects on pain. *Canadian Medical Association Journal, 120*, 435–438.

Melzack, R., Ofiesh, J. G., & Mount, B. M. (1976). The Brompton mixture: Effects on pain in cancer patients. *Canadian Medical Association Journal, 115*, 125–129.

Menninger, K. (1938). *Man against himself*. New York: Harcourt, Brace & World.

Meshot, C. M., & Leitner, L. M. (1993). Adolescent mourning and parental death. *Omega, Journal of Death and Dying, 26,* 287–299.

Metzgar, M. M., & Zick, B. C. (1996). Building the foundation: Preparation before a trauma. In C. A. Corr & D. M. Corr (Eds.), *Handbook of childhood death and bereavement* (pp. 245–264). New York: Springer.

Metzger, A. M. (1979). A Q-methodological study of the Kübler-Ross stage theory. *Omega, Journal of Death and Dying, 10,* 291–302.

Meyer, R. E. (Ed.). (1992). *Cemeteries and gravemarkers: Voices of American culture.* Logan, UT: Utah State University Press.

Michalczyk, J. J. (Ed.). (1994). *Medicine, ethics, and the Third Reich: Historical and contemporary issues.* Kansas City, MO: Sheed & Ward.

Michel, L., & Herbeck, D. (2001). *American terrorist: Timothy McVeigh and the Oklahoma City bombing.* New York: Regan Books.

Miles, M. (1971). *Annie and the old one.* Boston: Little, Brown.

Miles, M. S. (n.d.). *The grief of parents when a child dies.* Oak Brook, IL: The Compassionate Friends.

Miles, M. S., & Demi, A. S. (1984). Toward the development of a theory of bereavement guilt: Sources of guilt in bereaved parents. *Omega, Journal of Death and Dying, 14,* 299–314.

Miles, M. S., & Demi, A. S. (1986). Guilt in bereaved parents. In T. A. Rando (Ed.), *Parental loss of a child* (pp. 97–118). Champaign, IL: Research Press.

Miletich, L. (2001). Defining the essence of aftercare. In O. D. Weeks & C. Johnson (Eds.), *When all the friends have gone: A guide for aftercare providers* (pp. 25–34). Amityville, NY: Baywood.

Miller, J., Engelberg, S., & Broad, W. (2001). *Germs: Biological weapons and America's secret war.* New York: Simon & Schuster.

Miller, M. (1979). *Suicide after sixty: The final alternative.* New York: Springer.

Miller, M. (1987). *My grandmother's cookie jar.* Los Angeles: Price Stern Sloan.

Miller, P. J., & Mike, P. B. (1995). The Medicare hospice benefit: Ten years of federal policy for the terminally ill. *Death Studies, 19,* 531–542.

Miller, R. A. (2002). Extending life: Scientific prospects and political obstacles. *Milbank Quarterly, 80,* 155–174.

Mills, L. O. (Ed.). (1969). *Perspectives on death.* Nashville, TN: Abingdon.

Mindel, C. H., Habenstein, R.W., & Wright, R. (1988). *Ethnic families in America: Patterns and variations* (3rd ed.). New York: Elsevier.

Miniño, A. M., Heron, M. P., Murphy, S. L., & Kochanek, K. D. (2007). Deaths: Final data for 2004. *National Vital Statistics Reports, 55*(19). Hyattsville, MD: National Center for Health Statistics.

Minnich, H. C. (1936a). *Old favorites from the McGuffey readers.* New York: American Book Company.

Minnich, H. C. (1936b). *William Holmes McGuffey and his readers.* New York: American Book Company.

Minniefield, W. J., Yang, J., & Muti, P. (2001). Differences in attitudes toward organ donation among African Americans and whites in the United States. *Journal of the National Medical Association, 93,* 372–379.

Minow, N. N., & LaMay, C. L. (1995). *Abandoned in the wasteland: Children, television and the First Amendment.* New York: Hill & Wang.

Mitchell, L. (1977). *The meaning of ritual.* New York: Paulist Press.

Mitford, J. (1963). *The American way of death.* New York: Simon & Schuster.

Mitford, J. (1998). *The American way of death revisited.* New York: Knopf.

Mitterand, F. (1998). Foreword. In M. de Hennezel, *Intimate death: How the dying teach us to live* (pp. vii–x, C. B. Janeway, Trans.). New York: Knopf.

Mofenson, L., Taylor, A. W., Rogers, M., Campsmith, M., Ruffo, N. M., Clark, J., Lampe, M. A., Nakashima, A. K., & Sansom, S. (2006). Reduction in perinatal transmission of HIV infection—United States, 1985–2005. *Mortality and Morbidity Weekly Report, 55*(21), 592–597.

Moffat, M. J. (1982). *In the midst of winter: Selections from the literature of mourning.* New York: Vintage.

Mokdad, A. H., Marks, J. S., Stroup, D. F., & Gerberding, J. L. (2004). Actual causes of death in the United States, 2000. *Journal of the American Medical Association, 291,* 1238–1245.

Monat, A., & Lazarus, R. S. (Eds.). (1991). *Stress and coping: An anthology* (3rd ed.). New York: Columbia University Press.

Monette, P. (1988). *Borrowed time: An AIDS memoir.* San Diego, CA: Harcourt Brace Jovanovich.

Monette, P. (1992). *Becoming a man: Half a life story.* San Diego, CA: Harcourt Brace Jovanovich.

Monette, P. (1995). *Last watch of the night: Essays too personal and otherwise.* San Diego, CA: Harcourt Brace.

Monroe, B., & Kraus, F. (Eds.). (2004). *Brief interventions with bereaved children.* Oxford, UK: Oxford University Press.

Montgomery, J., & Fewer, W. (1988). *Family systems and beyond.* New York: Human Sciences Press.

Moody, H. R. (1984). Can suicide on grounds of old age be ethically justified? In M. Tallmer, E. R. Prichard, A. H. Kutscher, R. DeBellis, M. S. Hale, & I. K. Goldberg (Eds.), *The life-threatened elderly* (pp. 64–92). New York: Columbia University Press.

Moody, R. A. (1975). *Life after life.* Covington, GA: Mockingbird Books. (Reprinted New York: Bantam, 1976).

Moody, R. A. (1988). *The light beyond.* New York: Bantam.

Moore, A. J., & Stratton, D. C. (2002). *Resilient widowers: Older men speak for themselves.* New York: Springer.

Moos, R. H., & Schaefer, J. A. (1986). Life transitions and crises: A conceptual overview. In R. H. Moos & J. A. Schaefer (Eds.), *Coping with life crises: An integrated approach* (pp. 3–28). New York: Plenum.

Morgan, E., & Morgan, J. (2001). *Dealing creatively with death: A manual of death education and simple burial* (14th rev. ed.). Hinesburg, VT: Upper Access.

Morgan, J. D. (Ed.). (2001). *Social support: A reflection of humanity.* Amityville, NY: Baywood.

Morgan, J. D., & Laungani, P. (Eds.). (2002). *Death and bereavement around the world: Vol. 1, Major religious traditions.* Amityville, NY: Baywood.

Morgan, J. D., & Laungani, P. (Eds.). (2003). *Death and bereavement around the world: Vol. 2, Death and bereavement in the Americas.* Amityville, NY: Baywood.

Morgan, J. D., & Laungani, P. (Eds.). (2004). *Death and bereavement around the world: Vol. 3, Death and bereavement in Europe.* Amityville, NY: Baywood.

Morgan, J. D., & Laungani, P. (Eds.). (2005). *Death and bereavement around the world, Vol. 4, Death and bereavement in Asia, Australia, and New Zealand.* Amityville, NY: Baywood.

Morgan, R. (2006). *Flight 93 revealed: What really happened on the 9/11 "Let's Roll" flight*. New York: Carroll & Graf.

Morgan, R., & Murphy, S. B. (2000). Care of children who are dying of cancer. *New England Journal of Medicine, 342*, 347–348.

Moroney, R. M., & Kurtz, N. R. (1975). The evolution of long-term care institutions. In S. Sherwood (Ed.), *Long-term care: A handbook for researchers, planners, and providers* (pp. 81–121). New York: Spectrum.

Morrison, R. S., Maroney-Galin, C., Kralovec, P. D., & Meier, D. E. (2005). The growth of palliative care programs in United States hospitals. *Journal of Palliative Medicine, 8*, 1127–1134.

Morrison, R. S., & Meier, D. E. (2004). Palliative care. *New England Journal of Medicine, 350*, 2582–2590.

Morse, S. S. (Ed.). (1993). *Emerging viruses*. New York: Oxford University Press.

Moss, F., & Halamanderis, V. (1977). *Too old, too sick, too bad: Nursing homes in America*. Germantown, MD: Aspen Systems Corp.

Moss, M. S., & Moss, S. Z. (1983). The impact of parental death on middle-aged children. *Omega, Journal of Death and Dying, 14*, 65–75.

Moss, M. S., & Moss, S. Z. (1984). Some aspects of the elderly widow(er)'s persistent tie with the deceased spouse. *Omega, Journal of Death and Dying, 15*, 195–206.

Moss, M. S., & Moss, S. Z. (2007). Death of a parent of an adult child. In K. J. Doka (Ed.), *Living with grief: Before and after a death* (pp. 255–269). Washington, DC: Hospice Foundation of America.

Moss, M. S., Lesher, E. L., & Moss, S. Z. (1986). Impact of the death of an adult child on elderly parents: Some observations. *Omega, Journal of Death and Dying, 17*, 209–218.

Mount, B. M., Jones, A., & Patterson, A. (1974). Death and dying: Attitudes in a teaching hospital. *Urology, 4*, 741–747.

Mueller, J. (2006a). *Overblown: How politicians and the terrorism industry inflate national security threats, and why we believe them*. New York: Free Press.

Mueller, J. (2006b). Is there still a terrorist threat? The myth of the omnipresent enemy. *Foreign Affairs, 85*(5), 2–8.

Munet-Vilaró, F. (1998). Grieving and death rituals of Latinos. *Oncology Nursing Forum, 25*(10), 1761–1763.

Munson, R. (1993). *Fan mail*. New York: Dutton.

Munson, R. (2004). *Raising the dead: Organ transplants, ethics, and society*. New York: Oxford University Press.

Murphy, S. A., Johnson, L. C., & Lohan, J. (2003). Challenging the myths about parents' adjustment after the sudden, violent death of a child. *Journal of Nursing Scholarship, 35*(4), 359–364.

Murphy, T. (2006, October). Meet the grandparents. *Poz: Health, Life and HIV, #128*.

Murray, J. E. (2001). *Surgery of the soul*. Sagamore Beach, MA: Science History Publications/USA.

Musto, B. (1999, January 19). Karen's gift. *Women's World*, 39.

Muwahidi, A. A. (1989). Islamic perspectives on death and dying. In A. Berger, P. Badham, A. H. Kutscher, J. Berger, M. Perry, & J. Beloff (Eds.), *Perspectives on death and dying: Cross-cultural and multi-disciplinary views* (pp. 38–54). Philadelphia: Charles Press.

Myers, E. (1986). *When parents die: A guide for adults*. New York: Viking Penguin.

Myers, J. (2000). Is there a youth gang epidemic? *The Education Digest, 66*(3), 34–39.

Nabe, C. M. (1981). Presenting biological data in a course on death and dying. *Death Education, 5*, 51–58.

Nabe, C. M. (1982). "Seeing as": Death as door or wall. In R. A. Pacholski & C. A. Corr (Eds.), *Priorities in death education and counseling* (pp. 161–169). Arlington, VA: Forum for Death Education and Counseling.

Nabe, C. M. (1987). Fragmentation and spiritual care. In C. A. Corr & R. A. Pacholski (Eds.), *Death: Completion and discovery* (pp. 281–286). Lakewood, OH: Association for Death Education and Counseling.

Nabe, C. M. (1999). A caregiver's quandary: How am I to evaluate and respond to the other's suffering? *Omega, Journal of Death and Dying, 39*, 71–91.

Nadeau, J. (1998). *Families make sense of death*. Thousand Oaks, CA: Sage.

Nader, K. O. (1996). Children's exposure to traumatic experiences. In C. A. Corr & D. M. Corr (Eds.), *Handbook of childhood death and bereavement* (pp. 201–220). New York: Springer.

Nagy, M. A. (1948). The child's theories concerning death. *Journal of Genetic Psychology, 73*, 3–27. (Reprinted with some editorial changes as "The child's view of death" in *The meaning of death*, pp. 79–98, by H. Feifel, Ed., 1959, New York: McGraw-Hill)

Nakaya, A. C. (Ed.). (2005). *Juvenile crime: Opposing viewpoints*. Detroit: Greenhaven/Thomson Gale.

Naparstek, B. (2005). *Invisible heroes: Survivors of trauma and how they heal*. New York: Bantam.

National Center for Health Statistics (NCHS). (2004, October 6). Prevalence of overweight and obesity among adults: United States, 1999–2002. *NCHS Health E-Stats*. Hyattsville, MD: Author.

National Commission on Terrorist Attacks. (2004). *The 9/11 Commission report: Final report of the National Commission on Terrorist Attacks upon the United States*. New York: Norton.

National Ethics Committee, Veterans Health Administration. (2007). The ethics of palliative sedation as a therapy of last resort. *American Journal of Hospice and Palliative Medicine, 23*, 483–491.

National Hospice and Palliative Care Organization (NHPCO). (2000). *Compendium of pediatric palliative care*. Alexandria, VA: Author.

National Hospice and Palliative Care Organization (NHPCO). (2001). *Hospice care in nursing facilities: An educational resource for effective partnerships in end-of-life care* (2 vols.). Alexandria, VA: Author.

National Hospice and Palliative Care Organization (NHPCO). (2003). *Education and training curriculum for pediatric palliative care*. Alexandria, VA: Author.

National Hospice and Palliative Care Organization (NHPCO). (2004). *Caring for kids: How to develop a home-based support program for children and adolescents with life-threatening conditions*. Alexandra, VA: Author.

National Hospice and Palliative Care Organization (NHPCO). (2006a). *NHPCO's facts and figures—2005 findings*. Alexandria, VA: Author. From http://www.nhpco.org.

National Hospice and Palliative Care Organization (NHPCO). (2006b). *Standards of practice for hospice programs*. Alexandria, VA: Author.

National Hospice and Palliative Care Organization (NHPCO). (2007a). Facts and figures: Hospice care in America, November 2007 edition. Alexandria, VA: Author. Retrieved November 30, 2007, from http://www.nhpco.org/research.

National Hospice and Palliative Care Organization (NHPCO). (2007b). *Jewish ritual, reality and response at the end of life: A guide to caring for Jewish patients and their families.* Arlington, VA: Author.

National Hospice and Palliative Care Organization (NHPCO) & the Center to Advance Palliative Care in Hospitals and Health Systems. (2001). *Hospital-hospice partnerships in palliative care: Creating a continuum of service.* Alexandria, VA: National Hospice and Palliative Care Organization.

National Institute of Allergy and Infectious Diseases (NIAID). (2005, April 5). Focus on TB. Tuberculosis in history. A killer returns: The face of the epidemic. Retrieved on January 28, 2007, from http://www3.niaid.nih.gov/news/focuson/tb/research/history/historical_killer.htm.

National Kidney Foundation. (2002). *Waiting for a transplant.* New York: Author.

National Kidney Foundation. (2004a). *From illness to wellness: Life after transplantation.* New York: Author.

National Kidney Foundation. (2004b). *National communications guidelines regarding communication among donor families, transplant candidates/recipients, non-directed living donors, and health care professionals* (2nd ed.). New York: Author.

National Kidney Foundation. (2007). *Patches of love: The National Donor Family Quilt.* New York: Author.

National Research Council. (1993). *Losing generations: Adolescents in high-risk settings.* Washington, DC: National Academies Press.

National Safety Council. (2007). *Injury facts: 2007 edition.* Itaska, IL: Author.

Neaman, J. S., & Silver, C. G. (1983). *Kind words: A thesaurus of euphemisms.* New York: Facts on File.

Neimeyer, R. A. (1998). *Lessons of loss: A guide to coping.* New York: McGraw-Hill.

Neimeyer, R. A. (2000). Searching for the meaning of meaning: Grief therapy and the process of reconstruction. *Death Studies, 24,* 541–558.

Neimeyer, R. A. (2007). Meaning breaking, meaning making: Rewriting stories of loss. In K. J. Doka (Ed.), *Living with grief: Before and after a death* (pp. 193–208). Washington, DC: Hospice Foundation of America.

Neimeyer, R. A. (Ed.). (1994). *Death anxiety handbook: Research, instrumentation, and application.* Washington, DC: Taylor & Francis.

Neimeyer, R. A. (Ed.). (2001). *Meaning reconstruction and the experience of loss.* Washington, DC: American Psychological Association.

Neimeyer, R. A., & Van Brunt, D. (1995). Death anxiety. In H. Wass & R. A. Neimeyer (Eds.), *Dying: Facing the facts* (3rd ed.; pp. 49–88). Washington, DC: Taylor & Francis.

Neimeyer, R. A., Wittkowski, J., & Moser, R. P. (2004). Psychological research on death attitudes: An overview and evaluation. *Death Studies, 28,* 309–340.

Nelson, B. J., & Frantz, T. T. (1996). Family interactions of suicide survivors and survivors of non-suicidal death. *Omega, Journal of Death and Dying, 33,* 131–146.

The Netherlands Ministry of Foreign Affairs. (n.d.). *Q & A euthanasia: A guide to the Dutch Termination of Life on Request and Assisted Suicide (Review Procedures) Act.* The Hague: Author.

The Netherlands Ministry of Health, Welfare and Sport, and The Netherlands Ministry of Justice. (n.d.). *Euthanasia: The Netherlands' new rules.* The Hague: Author.

Neugarten, B. L. (1974). Age groups in American society and the rise of the young-old. *Annals of the American Academy of Political and Social Science, 415,* 187–198.

Neugarten, B. L., & Datan, N. (1973). Sociological perspectives on the life cycle. In P. B. Baltes & K. W. Schaie (Eds.), *Lifespan developmental psychology: Personality and socialization* (pp. 53–69). New York: Academic Press.

Neusner, J. (Trans.). (1988). *The Mishnah: A new translation.* New Haven, CT: Yale University Press.

New England Primer. (1962). New York: Columbia University Press. (Original work published 1727)

Newell, C. (1989). *Methods and models in demography.* New York: Wiley.

Newman, B. M., & Newman, P. R. (2005). *Development through life: A psychosocial approach* (9th ed.). Belmont, CA: Thomson Wadsworth.

Newman, K. S. (2004). *Rampage: The social roots of school shootings.* New York: Basic Books.

Newman, L. (Ed.). (1995). *A loving testimony: Remembering loved ones lost to AIDS.* Freedom, CA: Crossing Press.

Nichols, M. P. (1995). *The lost art of listening.* New York: Guilford.

Noack, D. (1999). Controversial photo draws support from readers. *Editor and Publisher, 132*(26), 8.

Noppe, I. C. (2007). Historical and contemporary perspectives on death education. In D. E. Balk, C. Wogrin, G. Thornton, & D. Meagher. (Eds.), *ADEC handbook of thanatology* (pp. 329–343). Northbrook, IL: Association for Death Education and Counseling.

Noppe, I. C., & Noppe, L. D. (1997). Evolving meanings of death during early, middle and later adolescence. *Death Studies, 21,* 253–275.

Noppe, I. C., & Noppe, L. D. (2004). Adolescent experiences with death: Letting go of immortality. *Journal of Mental Health Counseling, 26,* 146–167.

Noppe, I. C., Noppe, L. D., & Bartell, D. (2006). Terrorism and resilience: Adolescents' and teachers' responses to September 11, 2001. *Death Studies, 30,* 41–60.

Noppe, L. D., & Noppe, I. C. (1991). Dialectical themes in adolescent conceptions of death. *Journal of Adolescent Research, 6,* 28–42.

Noppe, L. D., & Noppe, I. C. (1996). Ambiguity in adolescent understandings of death. In C. A. Corr & D. E. Balk (Eds.), *Handbook of adolescent death and bereavement* (pp. 25–41). New York: Springer.

Nord, D. A. (1997). *Multiple AIDS-related loss: A handbook for surviving a perpetual fall.* Washington, DC: Taylor & Francis.

Norlander, L., & McSteen, K. (2001). *Choices at the end of life: Finding out what your parents want before it's too late.* Minneapolis, MN: Fairview Press.

Nouwen, H. (1972). *The wounded healer: Ministry in contemporary society.* Garden City, NY: Doubleday.

Nouwen, H. (1994). *Our greatest gift: A meditation on dying and caring.* New York: HarperCollins.

Nouwen, H. (2005). *In memoriam.* Notre Dame, IN: Ave Maria Press.

Nouwen, H., & Gaffney, W. J. (1990). *Aging: The fulfillment of life.* New York: Doubleday.

Novack, D. H., Plumer, R., Smith, R. L., Ochitill, H., Morrow, G. R., & Bennett, J. M. (1979). Changes in physicians' attitudes toward telling the cancer patient. *Journal of the American Medical Association, 241,* 897–900.

Novick, P. (1999). *The Holocaust in American life.* Boston: Houghton Mifflin.

Noyes, R., & Clancy, J. (1977). The dying role: Its relevance to improved patient care. *Psychiatry, 40,* 41–47.

Nuland, S. B. (1994). *How we die: Reflections on life's final chapter.* New York: Knopf.

Nussbaum, K. (1998). *Preparing the children: Information and ideas for families facing terminal illness and death.* Kodiak, AK: Gifts of Hope Trust.

O'Carroll, P.W. (1989). A consideration of the validity and reliability of suicide mortality data. *Suicide and Life-Threatening Behavior, 19,* 1–16.

O'Connor, P. (1999). Hospice vs. palliative care. *The Hospice Journal, 14,* 123–137.

O'Hara, K. (2006). *A grief like no other: Surviving the violent death of someone you love.* New York: Marlowe & Company.

O'Neill, J. F., Selwyn, P. A., & Schietinger, H. (2003). *A clinical guide to supportive & palliative care for HIV/AIDS.* Washington, DC: U.S. Department of Health and Human Services, Health Resources and Services Administration, HIV/AIDS Bureau.

O'Toole, D. (1995). *Facing change: Falling apart and coming together again in the teen years.* Burnsville, NC: Compassion Books.

Obayashi, H. (Ed.). (1992). *Death and afterlife: Perspectives of world religions.* Westport, CT: Praeger.

Offer, D. (1969). *The psychological worlds of the teenager.* New York: Basic Books.

Offer, D., & Offer, J. B. (1975). *From teenage to young manhood: A psychological study.* New York: Basic Books.

Offer, D., & Sabshin, M. (1984). Adolescence: Empirical perspectives. In D. Offer & M. Sabshin (Eds.), *Normality and the life cycle: A critical integration* (pp. 76–107). New York: Basic Books.

Offer, D., Ostrov, E., & Howard, K. I. (1981). *The adolescent: A psychological self-portrait.* New York: Basic Books.

Offer, D., Ostrov, E., Howard, K. I., & Atkinson, R. (1988). *The teenage world: Adolescents' self-image in ten countries.* New York: Plenum.

Oken, D. (1961).What to tell cancer patients: A study of medical attitudes. *Journal of the American Medical Association, 175,* 1120–1128.

Oliver, S. L. (1998). *What the dying teach us: Lessons on living* (Rev. ed.). Binghamton, NY: Haworth Press.

Oliviero, H. (2004, December 21). Study: Older women are naïve about HIV. *St. Petersburg Times,* p. 4S.

Olshansky, S. J., Passaro, D. J., Hershow, R. C., Layden, J., Carnes, B. A., Brody, J., et al. (2005). A potential decline in life expectancy in the United States in the 21st century. *New England Journal of Medicine, 352,* 1138–1145.

Olson, L. M., & Wahab, S. (2006). American Indians and suicide: A neglected area of research. *Trauma, Violence, and Abuse, 7*(1), 19–33.

Olson, L. M., Becker, T. M., Wiggins, C. L., Key, C. R., & Samet, J. N. (1990). Injury mortality in American Indian, Hispanic, and non-Hispanic White children in New Mexico, 1958–1982. *Social Science and Medicine, 30,* 479–486.

Oltjenbruns, K. A. (1991). Positive outcomes of adolescents' experience with grief. *Journal of Adolescent Research, 6,* 43–53.

Oltjenbruns, K. A. (1996). Death of a friend during adolescence: Issues and impacts. In C. A. Corr & D. E. Balk (Eds.), *Handbook of adolescent death and bereavement* (pp. 196–215). New York: Springer.

Onwuteaka-Philipsen, B. D., van der Heide, A., Koper, D., Keij-Deerenberg, I., Rietjens, J. A., Rurup, M. L., et al. (2003). Euthanasia and other end-of-life decisions in the Netherlands in 1990, 1995, and 2001. *Lancet, 362,* 395–399.

Opie, I., & Opie, P. (1969). *Children's games in street and playground: Chasing, catching, seeking, hunting, racing, dueling, exerting, daring, guessing, acting, and pretending.* Oxford, UK: Oxford University Press.

Opoku, K. A. (1978).*West African traditional religion.* Singapore: Far Eastern.

Opoku, K. A. (1987). Death and immortality in the African religious heritage. In P. Badham & L. Badham (Eds.), *Death and immortality in the religions of the world* (pp. 9–21). New York: Paragon House.

Orbach, I. (1988). *Children who don't want to live: Understanding and treating the suicidal child.* San Francisco: Jossey-Bass.

Oregon Department of Human Services. (2005). *Seventh annual report on Oregon's Death with Dignity Act.* From http://egov.oregon.gov/DHS/ph/pas.

Oregon Department of Human Services. (2006). *Eighth annual report on Oregon's Death with Dignity Act.* From http://egov.oregon.gov/DHS/ph/pas.

Oregon Department of Human Services. (2007). *Ninth annual report on Oregon's Death with Dignity Act.* Retrieved December 14, 2007, from http://egov.oregon.gov/DHS/ph/pas.

Orloff, S., & Huff, S. (Eds.). (2003). *Home care for seriously ill children: A manual for parents* (3rd ed.). Alexandria, VA: Children's Hospice International.

Osgood, N. J. (1992). *Suicide in later life: Recognizing the warning signs.* New York: Lexington.

Osgood, N. J. (2000). Elderly suicide [Special issue]. *Omega, Journal of Death and Dying, 42*(1).

Osgood, N. J., Brant, B. A., & Lipman, A. (1991). *Suicide among the elderly in long-term care facilities.* New York: Greenwood Press.

Osis, K., & Haraldsson, E. (1997). *At the hour of death* (3rd ed.). Norwalk, CT: Hastings House.

Osmont, K., & McFarlane, M. (1986). *Parting is not goodbye.* Portland, OR: Nobility Press.

Osofsky, J. D. (Ed.). (2004). *Young children and trauma.* New York: Guilford.

Osterweis, M., Solomon, F., & Green, M. (Eds.). (1984). *Bereavement: Reactions, consequences, and care.* Washington, DC: National Academies Press.

Owen, J. E., Goode, K. T., & Haley, W. E. (2001). End of life care and reactions to death in African-American and white family caregivers of relatives with Alzheimer's disease. *Omega, Journal of Death and Dying, 43*(4), 349–361.

Owens, J. E., Cook, E. W., & Stevenson, I. (1990). Features of "near-death experience" in relation to whether or not patients were near death. *The Lancet, 336,* 1175–1177.

The Oxford English Dictionary. (1989). (2nd ed.; 20 vols.) (J. A. Simpson & E.S.C. Weiner, Eds.). Oxford, England: Clarendon Press.

Papadatou, D. (1989). Caring for dying adolescents. *Nursing Times, 85,* 28–31.

Papadatou, D. (2000). A proposed model of health professionals' grieving process. *Omega, Journal of Death and Dying, 41,* 59–77.

Papalia, D. E., Olds, S. W., & Feldman, R. D. (2005). *A child's world: Infancy through adolescence with LifeMAP CD-ROM and PowerWeb* (10th ed.). Boston: McGraw-Hill.

Papalia, D. E., Olds, S. W., & Feldman, R. D. (2006). *Human development with LifeMAP CD-ROM and PowerWeb* (10th ed.). Boston: McGraw-Hill.

Papalia, D. E., Sterns, H., & Feldman, R. D., & Camp, C. (2006). *Adult development and aging* (3rd ed.). Boston: McGraw-Hill.

Pape, R. A. (2005). *Dying to win: The strategic logic of suicide terrorism.* New York: Random House.

Parkes, C. M. (1970a). The first year of bereavement: A longitudinal study of the reaction of London widows to the death of their husbands. *Psychiatry, 33,* 444–467.

Parkes, C. M. (1970b). "Seeking" and "finding" a lost object: Evidence from recent studies of reaction to bereavement. *Social Science and Medicine, 4,* 187–201.

Parkes, C. M. (1975a).What becomes of redundant world models? A contribution to the study of adaptation to change. *British Journal of Medical Psychology, 48,* 131–137.

Parkes, C. M. (1975b). Determinants of outcome following bereavement. *Omega, Journal of Death and Dying, 6,* 303–323.

Parkes, C. M. (1987). Models of bereavement care. *Death Studies, 11,* 257–261.

Parkes, C. M. (1993). Bereavement as a psychosocial transition: Processes of adaptation to change. In M. Stroebe, W. Stroebe, & R. O. Hansson (Eds.), *Handbook of bereavement: Theory, research, and intervention* (pp. 91–101). New York: Cambridge University Press.

Parkes, C. M. (1996). *Bereavement: Studies of grief in adult life* (3rd ed.). New York: Routledge.

Parkes, C. M. (Ed.). (2006a). Symposium on complicated grief. [Special issue] *Omega, Journal of Death and Dying, 52*(1).

Parkes, C. M. (2006b). Part I. Introduction to a symposium. *Omega, Journal of Death and Dying, 52,* 1–7.

Parkes, C. M. (2006c). *Love and loss: The roots of grief and its complications.* New York: Routledge.

Parkes, C. M. (2007a). Complicated grief: The debate over a new DSM-V diagnostic category. In K. J. Doka (Ed.), *Living with grief: Before and after a death* (pp. 139–151). Washington, DC: Hospice Foundation of America.

Parkes, C. M. (Ed.). (2007b). "Hospice heritage": In memory of Dame Cicely Saunders [Special issue]. *Omega, Journal of Death and Dying, 56*(1).

Parkes, C. M., & Weiss, R. (1983). *Recovery from bereavement.* New York: Basic Books.

Parkes, C. M., Laungani, P., & Young, B. (Eds.). (1997). *Death and bereavement across cultures.* New York: Routledge.

Parkes, C. M., Relf, M., & Couldrick, A. (1996). *Counseling in terminal care and bereavement.* Leicester, England: BPS Books.

Parkes, C. M., Stevenson-Hinde, J., & Marris, P. (Eds.). (1993). *Attachment across the life cycle.* New York: Routledge.

Parks, G. (1971). *Gordon Parks: Whispers of intimate things.* New York: Viking.

Parr, E., & Mize, J. (2001). *Coping with an organ transplant: A practical guide to understanding, preparing for, and living with an organ transplant.* New York: Avery/Penguin Putnam.

Parry, J. K. (Ed.). (1990). *Social work practice with the terminally ill: A transcultural perspective.* Springfield, IL: Charles C Thomas.

Parry, J. K., & Ryan, A. S. (Eds.). (1995). *A cross-cultural look at death, dying, and religion.* Chicago: Nelson-Hall.

Parsons, T. (1951). *The social system.* New York: Free Press.

Partridge, E. (1966). *A dictionary of slang and unconventional English.* New York: Macmillan.

Pastan, L. (1978). *The five stages of grief.* New York: Norton.

Paterson, D. S., Trachtenberg, F. L., Thompson, E. G., Belliveau, R. A., Beggs, A. H., Darnall, R., Chadwick, A. E., Krous, H. F., & Kinney, H. C. (2006). Multiple serotonergic brainstem abnormalities in sudden infant death syndrome. *Journal of the American Medical Association, 296,* 2124–2132.

Pattison, E. M. (1977). *The experience of dying.* Englewood Cliffs, NJ: Prentice Hall.

Pawelczynska, A. (1979). *Values and violence in Auschwitz: A sociological analysis* (C. S. Leach, Trans.). Berkeley: University of California Press.

Peabody, F. W. (1927). The care of the patient. *Journal of the American Medical Association, 88,* 877–882. (Reprinted as a monograph by Harvard University Press in the same year.)

Peck, M. L., Farberow, N. L., & Litman, R. E. (Eds.). (1985). *Youth suicide.* New York: Springer.

Pendleton, E. (Comp.). (1980). *Too old to cry, too young to die.* Nashville, TN: Thomas Nelson.

Peppers, L. G. (1987). Grief and elective abortion: Breaking the emotional bond. *Omega, Journal of Death and Dying, 18,* 1–12.

Peppers, L. G., & Knapp, R. J. (1980). *Motherhood and mourning: Perinatal death.* New York: Praeger.

Peretti, P. O. (1990). Elderly-animal friendship bonds. *Social Behavior and Personality, 18,* 151–156.

Perls, T. T., Silver, M. H., & Lauerman, J. F. (2000). *Living to 100: Lessons in living to your maximum potential at any age.* New York: Basic Books.

Pfeffer, C. R. (1986). *The suicidal child.* New York: Guilford.

Pfeffer, C. R. (Ed.). (1989). *Suicide among youth: Perspectives on risk and prevention.* Washington, DC: American Psychiatric Press.

Pfeffer, C. R., Jiang, H., Kakuma, T., Hwang, J., & Metsch, M. (2002). Group intervention for children bereaved by the suicide of a relative. *Journal of the American Academy of Child and Adolescent Psychiatry, 41,* 505–513.

Piaget, J. (1998). *The equilibration of cognitive structures: The central problem of intellectual development* (T. A. Brown & K. J. Thampy, Trans.). Chicago: University of Chicago Press.

Piaget, J., & Inhelder, B. (1958). *The growth of logical thinking from childhood to adolescence* (A. Parsons & S. Milgram, Trans.). New York: Basic Books.

Picard, C. (2002). Family reflections on living through sudden death of a child. *Nursing Science Quarterly, 25,* 242–250.

Pike, M. M., & Wheeler, S. R. (1992). *Bereavement support group guide: Guidebook for individuals and/or professionals who wish to start a bereavement, mutual, self-help group.* Covington, IN: Grief, Ltd.

Piot, P., Bartos, M., Ghys, P. D., Walker, N., & Schwartlander, B. (2001). The global impact of HIV/AIDS. *Nature, 410,* 968–973.

Piper, F. (1994). The number of victims. In I. Gutman & M. Berenbaum (Eds.), *Anatomy of the Auschwitz death camp* (pp. 61–76). Bloomington: Indiana University Press.

Pitch of Grief. [Videotape]. (1985). Newton, MA: Newton Cable Television Foundation and Eric Stange.

Planchon, L. A., Templer, D. I., Stokes, S., & Keller, J. (2002). Death of a companion cat or dog and human bereavement: Psychosocial variables. *Society & Animals, 10,* 93–105.

Plath, S. (1964). *Ariel.* New York: Harper & Row.

Plath, S. (1971). *The bell jar.* New York: Harper & Row.

Plato. (1948). *Euthyphro, Apology, Crito* (F. J. Church, Trans.). New York: Macmillan.

Plato. (1961). *The collected dialogues of Plato including the letters* (E. Hamilton & H. Cairns, Eds.). New York: Bollingen Foundation.

Platt, A. (1995). The resurgence of infectious diseases. *World Watch, 8*(4), 26–32.

Platt, M. (1975). Commentary: On asking to die. *Hastings Center Report, 5*(6), 9–12.

Player, T. A., Skipper, H. D., & Lambert, J. (2002). A global definition of terrorism. *Risk Management, 49*(9), 60.

Please Let Me Die. [Videotape]. (1974). Galveston: University of Texas Medical Branch.

Plepys, C., & Klein, R. (1995). *Health status indicators: Differentials by race and Hispanic origin* (10). Washington, DC: National Center for Health Statistics.

Plopper, B. L., & Ness, M. E. (1993). Death as portrayed to adolescents through Top 40 rock and roll music. *Adolescence, 28,* 793–807.

Podell, C. (1989). Adolescent mourning: The sudden death of a peer. *Clinical Social Work Journal, 17,* 64–78.

Poe, E. A. (1948). *The letters of Edgar Allan Poe* (2 vols.). (J. W. Ostrom, Ed.). Cambridge, MA: Harvard University Press.

Poland, S. (1989). *Suicide intervention in the schools.* New York: Guilford.

Polednak, A. P. (1990). Cancer mortality in a higher-income Black population in New York State: Comparison with rates in the United States as a whole. *Cancer, 66,* 1654–1660.

Popovic, J. R., & Kozak, L. J. (2000). National hospital discharge survey: Annual summary, 1998. *Vital and Health Statistics, 13*(148). Hyattsville, MD: National Center for Health Statistics.

Post, S. (Ed.). (2004). *Encyclopedia of bioethics* (3rd ed.). New York: Macmillan Reference USA

Pound, L. (1936). American euphemisms for dying, death, and burial: An anthology. *American Speech, 11,* 195–202.

Powell-Griner, E. (1988). Differences in infant mortality among Texas Anglos, Hispanics, and Blacks. *Social Science Quarterly, 69,* 452–467.

President's Commission for the Study of Ethical Problems in Medicine and Biomedical and Behavioral Research. (1981). *Defining death: A report on the medical, legal, and ethical issues in the determination of death.* Washington, DC: U.S. Government Printing Office

President's Commission for the Study of Ethical Problems in Medicine and Biomedical and Behavioral Research. (1982). *Making health care decisions: A report on the ethical and legal implications of informed consent in the patient-practitioner relationship. Vol. 1, Report; Vol. 3, Studies on the foundation of informed consent.* Washington, DC: U.S. Government Printing Office.

President's Commission for the Study of Ethical Problems in Medicine and Biomedical and Behavioral Research. (1983a). *Deciding to forego life-sustaining treatment: A report on the ethical, medical, and legal issues in treatment decisions.* Washington, DC: U.S. Government Printing Office.

President's Commission for the Study of Ethical Problems in Medicine and Biomedical and Behavioral Research. (1983b). *Summing up: Final report on studies of the ethical and legal problems in medicine and biomedical and behavioral research.* Washington, DC: U.S. Government Printing Office.

Preston, R. J., & Preston, S. C. (1991). Death and grieving among northern forest hunters: An East Cree example. In D. R. Counts & D. A. Counts (Eds.), *Coping with the final tragedy: Cultural variation in dying and grieving* (pp. 135–155). Amityville, NY: Baywood.

Preston, S. H. (1976). *Mortality patterns in national populations: With special reference to recorded causes of death.* New York: Academic Press.

Preston, S. H., & Haines, M. R. (1991). *Fatal years: Child mortality in late nineteenth-century America.* Princeton, NJ: Princeton University Press.

Preston, S. H., Heuveline, P., & Guillot, M. (2001). *Demography: Measuring and modeling population processes.* Oxford, England: Blackwell.

Price, D. (2001). *Legal and ethical aspects of organ transplantation.* Cambridge, UK: Cambridge University Press.

Prigerson, H. G., & Maciejewski, P. K. (2006). A call for sound empirical testing and evaluation of criteria for complicated grief proposed for DSM-V. *Omega, Journal of Death and Dying, 52,* 9–19.

Prigerson, H. G., Vanderwerker, L. C., & Maciejewski, P. K. (in press). A case for inclusion of prolonged grief disorder in *DSM.* In M. S. Stroebe, R. O. Hansson, W. Stroebe, & H. A. Schut (Eds.), *Handbook of bereavement research and practice: 21st century perspectives.* Washington, DC: American Psychological Association Press.

Prothero, S. (2001). *Purified by fire: A history of cremation in America.* Berkeley: University of California Press.

Prothrow-Stith, D., & Spivak, H. R. (2004). *Murder is no accident: Understanding and preventing youth violence in America.* San Francisco: Jossey-Bass.

Prottas, J. (1994). *The most useful gift: Altruism and the public policy of organ transplants.* San Francisco: Jossey-Bass.

Puckle, B. S. (1926). *Funeral customs: Their origin and development.* London: Laurie.

Purtillo, R. B. (1976). Similarities in patient response to chronic and terminal illness. *Physical Therapy, 56,* 279–284.

Quackenbush, J. (1985). The death of a pet: How it can affect pet owners. *Veterinary Clinics of North America: Small Animal Practice, 15,* 305–402.

Quill, T. E. (1996). *A midwife through the dying process: Stories of healing and hard choices at the end of life.* Baltimore: Johns Hopkins University Press.

Quill, T. E. (2007). Legal regulation of physician-assisted death—The latest report cards. *New England Journal of Medicine, 356,* 1911–1913.

Quill, T. E., & Battin, M. P. (2004). *Physician-assisted dying: The case for palliative care and patient choice.* Baltimore: Johns Hopkins University Press.

Quindlen, A. (1994). *One true thing.* New York: Random House.

Quinlan, J., Quinlan, J., & Battelle, P. (1977). *Karen Ann: The Quinlans tell their story.* Garden City, NY: Doubleday.

[*Qur'an.*] Koran. (1993). (N. J. Dawood, Trans.). London: Penguin.

Raddatz, M. (2007). *The long road home: A story of war and family.* New York: G. P. Putnam's Sons.

Radhakrishnan, S. (1948). *The Bhagavadgita: With an introductory essay, Sanskrit text, English translation and notes.* New York: Harper & Brothers.

Radhakrishnan, S., & Moore, C. (1957). *A sourcebook in Indian philosophy.* Princeton, NJ: Princeton University Press.

Radin, P. (1973). *The road of life and death: A ritual drama of the American Indians.* Princeton, NJ: Princeton University Press.

Raether, H. C. (Ed.). (1989). *The funeral director's practice management handbook.* Englewood Cliffs, NJ: Prentice Hall.

Rahman, F. (1987). *Health and medicine in the Islamic tradition: Change and identity.* New York: Crossroad.

Rahner, K. (1973). *On the theology of death* (C. H. Henkey, Trans.). New York: Seabury Press.

Rahula, W. (1974). *What the Buddha taught.* New York: Grove Press.

Ramsey, P. (1970). *The patient as person: Explorations in medical ethics.* New Haven, CT: Yale University Press.

Randall, F., & Downie, R. (2006). *The philosophy of palliative care: Critique and reconstruction.* Oxford, UK: Oxford University Press.

Randall, F., & Downie, R. S. (1999). *Palliative care ethics: A companion for all specialties* (2nd ed.). Oxford: Oxford University Press.

Rando, T. A. (1984). *Grief, dying, and death: Clinical interventions for caregivers.* Champaign, IL: Research Press.

Rando, T. A. (Ed.). (1986a). *Parental loss of a child.* Champaign, IL: Research Press.

Rando, T. A. (1986b). Death of the adult child. In T. A. Rando (Ed.), *Parental loss of a child* (pp. 221–238). Champaign, IL: Research Press.

Rando, T. A. (Ed.). (1986c). *Loss and anticipatory grief.* Lexington, MA: Lexington Books.

Rando, T. A. (1988a). Anticipatory grief: The term is a misnomer but the phenomenon exists. *Journal of Palliative Care, 4*(1/2), 70–73.

Rando, T. A. (1988b). *How to go on living when someone you love dies.* New York: Bantam.

Rando, T. A. (1993). *Treatment of complicated mourning.* Champaign, IL: Research Press.

Rando, T. A. (1996). Complications in mourning traumatic death. In K. J. Doka (Ed.), *Living with grief after sudden loss: Suicide, homicide, accident, heart attack, stroke* (pp. 139–159). Washington, DC: Hospice Foundation of America.

Rando, T. A. (Ed.). (2000). *Clinical dimensions of anticipatory mourning: Theory and practice in working with the dying, their loved ones, and their caregivers.* Champaign, IL: Research Press.

Raphael, B. (1983). *The anatomy of bereavement.* New York: Basic Books.

Rauschi, T. M. (2001). *A view from within: Living with early onset Alzheimer's.* Albany, NY: Northeastern New York Chapter of the Alzheimer's Disease and Related Disorders Association.

Rawson, H. (1981). *A dictionary of euphemisms and other doubletalk.* New York: Crown.

Reagan, B. (2000). *The Oregon Death with Dignity Act: A guidebook for health care providers.* Portland: Center for Ethics in Health Care, Oregon Health & Science University.

Reddin, S. K. (1987). The photography of stillborn children and neonatal deaths. *Journal of Audiovisual Media in Medicine, 10*(2), 49–51.

Reder, P. (1969). *Epitaphs.* London: Michael Joseph.

Reece, R. D., & Ziegler, J. H. (1990). How a medical school (Wright State University) takes leave of human remains. *Death Studies, 14,* 589–600.

Reed, M. D., & Greenwald, J. Y. (1991). Survivor-victim status, attachment, and sudden death bereavement. *Suicide and Life-Threatening Behavior, 21,* 385–401.

Reed, M. L. (2000). *Grandparents cry twice: Help for bereaved grandparents.* Amityville, NY: Baywood.

Rees, W. D. (1972). The distress of dying. *British Medical Journal, 2,* 105–107.

Reid, J. K., & Reid, C. L. (2001). A cross marks the spot: A study of roadside death memorials in Texas and Oklahoma. *Death Studies, 25,* 341–356.

Reitlinger, G. (1968). *The final solution: The attempt to exterminate the Jews of Europe 1939–1945* (2nd rev. ed.). London: Vallentine, Mitchell.

Requarth, J. (2006). *After a parent's suicide: Helping children heal.* Sebastopol, CA: Healing Hearts Press.

Reynolds, F. E., & Waugh, E. H. (Eds.). (1977). *Religious encounters with death: Insights from the history and anthropology of religion.* State College: Pennsylvania State University Press.

Rhodes, R. L., Teno, J. M., & Connor, S. R. (2007). African American bereaved family members' perceptions of the quality of hospice care: Lessened disparities, but opportunities. *Journal of Pain and Symptom Management, 34,* 472–479.

Richardson, L. (2006). *What terrorists want: Understanding the enemy, containing the threat.* New York: Random House.

Rickgarn, R. L. V. (1994). *Perspectives on college student suicide.* Amityville, NY: Baywood.

Rickgarn, R. L. V. (1996). The need for postvention on college campuses: A rationale and case study findings. In C. A. Corr & D. E. Balk (Eds.), *Handbook of adolescent death and bereavement* (pp. 273–292). New York: Springer.

Rietjens, J. A. C., Bilsen, J., Fischer, S., van der Heide, A., van der Maas, P. J., Miccinessi, G., Norup, M., Onwuteaka-Philipsen, B. D., Vrakking, A. M., & van der Wal, G. (2007). Using drugs to end life without an explicit request of the patient. *Death Studies, 31,* 205–221.

Ring, K. (1980). *Life at death: A scientific investigation of the near-death experience.* New York: Coward, McCann & Geoghegan.

Ring, K. (1984). *Heading toward omega: In search of the meaning of the near-death experience.* New York: Morrow.

Roach, M. (2003). *Stiff: The curious lives of human cadavers.* New York: Norton.

Roberts, B. K. (2003). *Death without denial, grief without apology: A guide for facing death and loss.* Troutdale, OR: NewSage Press.

Roberts, C. (1998). *We are our mothers' daughters.* New York: William Morrow.

Roberts, P. (2004). The living and the dead: Community in the virtual cemetery. *Omega, Journal of Death and Dying, 49,* 57–76.

Rochlin, G. (1967). How younger children view death and themselves. In E. A. Grollman (Ed.), *Explaining death to children* (pp. 51–85). Boston: Beacon Press.

Rocke, C., & Cherry, K. E. (2002). Death at the end of the 20th century: Individual processes and developmental tasks in old age. *International Journal of Aging and Human Development, 54*(4), 315–333.

Rodger, M. L., Sherwood, P., O'Connor, M., and Leslie, G. (2007). Living beyond the unanticipated sudden death of a partner: A phenomenological study. *Omega, Journal of Death and Dying, 54,* 107–133.

Rodgers, L. S. (2004). Meaning of bereavement among older African American widows. *Geriatric Nursing, 25*(1), 10–16.

Rodin, J., & Langer, E. J. (1977). Long-term effects of a control-relevant intervention with the institutionalized aged. *Journal of Personality and Social Psychology, 35,* 879–902.

Rodkinson, M. L. (Trans.). (1896). *New edition of the Babylonian Talmud*, Vol. 2. New York: Talmud Publishing.

Rodrigue, J. R., Scott, M. P., & Oppenheim, A. R. (2003). The tissue donation experience: A comparison of donor and nondonor families. *Progress in Transplantation, 13*(4), 1–7.

Rollin, B. (1985). *Last wish*. New York: Warner Books.

Romano-Dwyer, L., & Carley, G. (2005). Schoolyard conversations: Influencing suicide talk in an elementary school community. *Social Work Education, 24*, 245–250.

Romanoff, B. D., & Terenzio, M. (1998). Rituals and the grieving process. *Death Studies, 22*, 697–711.

Romanoff, B. D., & Thompson, B. E. (2006). Meaning construction in palliative care: The use of narrative, ritual, and the expressive arts. *American Journal of Hospice and Palliative Medicine, 23*, 309–316.

Romond, J. L. (1989). *Children facing grief: Letters from bereaved brothers and sisters*. St. Meinrad, IN: Abbey Press.

Ropp, L., Visintainer, P., Uman, J., & Treloar, D. (1992). Death in the city: An American childhood tragedy. *Journal of the American Medical Association, 267*, 2905–2910.

Roscoe, L. A., Egan, K. A., & Schonwetter, R. S. (2004). Creating an academic-community provider partnership in hospice, palliative care, and end-of-life studies. *Cancer Control, 11*, 397–403.

Roscoe, L. A., Melphurs, J. E., Dragovic, L. J., & Cohen, D. (2000). Dr. Jack Kevorkian and cases of euthanasia in Oakland County, Michigan, 1990–1998. *New England Journal of Medicine, 343*, 1735–1736.

Rosen, E. J. (1998). *Families facing death: A guide for health care professionals and volunteers* (Rev ed.). San Francisco: Jossey-Bass.

Rosen, H. (1986). *Unspoken grief: Coping with childhood sibling loss*. Lexington, MA: Lexington Books.

Rosenberg, C. E. (1987). *The care of strangers: The rise of America's hospital system*. New York: Basic Books.

Rosenblatt, P. C. (1983). *Bitter, bitter tears: Nineteenth-century diarists and twentieth-century grief theories*. Minneapolis: University of Minnesota Press.

Rosenblatt, P. C. (2000). *Parent grief: Narratives of loss and relationship*. Philadelphia: Brunner/Mazel.

Rosenblatt, P. C. (2001). *Help your marriage survive the death of a child*. Philadelphia: Temple University Press.

Rosenblatt, P. C. (2007). Grief: What we have learned from cross-cultural studies. In K. J. Doka (Ed.), *Living with grief: Before and after a death* (pp. 123–136). Washington, DC: Hospice Foundation of America.

Rosenblatt, P. C., & Barner, J. R. (2006). The dance of closeness-distance in couple relationships after the death of a parent. *Omega, Journal of Death and Dying, 53*, 277–293.

Rosenblatt, P. C., & Wallace, B. R. (2005a). Narratives of grieving African-Americans about racism in the lives of deceased family members. *Death Studies, 29*, 217–235.

Rosenblatt, P. C., & Wallace, B. R. (2005b). *African American grief*. New York: Brunner-Routledge.

Rosenblatt, P. C., Walsh, P. R., & Jackson, D. A. (1976). *Grief and mourning in cross-cultural perspectives*. Washington, DC: Human Relations Area Files.

Rosenthal, N. R. (1986). Death education: Developing a course of study for adolescents. In C. A. Corr & J. N. McNeil (Eds.), *Adolescence and death* (pp. 202–214). New York: Springer.

Rosenthal, T. (1973). *How could I not be among you?* New York: George Braziller.

Rosenwaike, I., & Bradshaw, B. S. (1988). The status of death statistics for the Hispanic population of the Southwest. *Social Science Quarterly, 69*, 722–736.

Rosenwaike, I., & Bradshaw, B. S. (1989). Mortality of the Spanish surname population of the Southwest: 1980. *Social Science Quarterly, 70*, 631–641.

Rosner, F. (1979). The Jewish attitude toward euthanasia. In F. Rosner & J. D. Bleich (Eds.), *Jewish bioethics* (pp. 253–265). New York: Sanhedrin Press.

Rosof, B. D. (1994). *The worst loss: How families heal from the death of a child*. New York: Henry Holt.

Ross, C. B., & Baron-Sorenson, J. (2007). *Pet loss and human emotion: A guide to recovery*. Philadelphia: Brunner-Routledge.

Ross, C. P. (1980). Mobilizing schools for suicide prevention. *Suicide and Life-Threatening Behavior, 10*, 239–243.

Ross, C. P. (1985). Teaching children the facts of life and death: Suicide prevention in the schools. In M. L. Peck, N. L. Farberow, & R. E. Litman (Eds.), *Youth suicide* (pp. 147–169). New York: Springer.

Ross, E. S. (1967). Children's books relating to death: A discussion. In E. A. Grollman (Ed.), *Explaining death to children* (pp. 249–271). Boston: Beacon Press.

Roth, N. L., & Fuller, L. K. (1998). *Women and AIDS: Negotiating safer practices, care, and representation*. Binghamton, NY: Haworth Press.

Rowland, D. T. (2003). *Demographic methods and concepts*. New York: Oxford University Press.

Rowling, L. (2003). *Grief in school communities: Effective support strategies*. Philadelphia: Open University Press.

Roy, A. (1990). Possible biologic determinants of suicide. In D. Lester (Ed.), *Current concepts of suicide* (pp. 40–56). Philadelphia: Charles Press.

Rozovsky, F. A. (1990). *Consent to treatment: A practical guide* (2nd ed.). Boston: Little, Brown. (Also see 1994 Supplement.)

Rubel, B. (1999). *But I didn't say goodbye: For parents and professionals helping child suicide survivors*. Kendall Park, NJ: Griefwork Center.

Rubenstein, W. B., Eisenberg, R., & Gostin, L. O. (1996). *The rights of people who are HIV positive: The authoritative ACLU guide to the rights of people living with HIV disease and AIDS*. Carbondale: Southern Illinois University Press.

Rubin, B., Carlton, R., & Rubin, A. (1979). *L.A. in installments: Forest Lawn*. Santa Monica, CA: Hennessey & Ingalls.

Ruby, J. (1987). Portraying the dead. *Omega, Journal of Death and Dying, 19*, 1–20.

Ruby, J. (1991). Photographs, memory, and grief. *Illness, Crisis and Loss, 1*, 1–5.

Ruby, J. (1995). *Secure the shadow: Death and photography in America*. Cambridge, MA: MIT Press.

Ruccione, K. S. (1994). Issues in survivorship. In C. L. Schwartz, W. L. Hobbie, L. S. Constine, & K. S. Ruccione (Eds.), *Survivors of childhood cancer: Assessment and management* (pp. 329–337). St. Louis, MO: Mosby.

Rudd, M. D., Joiner, T., & Rajab, M. H. (2001). *Treating suicidal behavior: An effective, time-limited approach*. New York: Guilford.

Rudestam, K. E. (1987). Public perceptions of suicide survivors. In E. J. Dunne, J. L. McIntosh, & K. Dunne-Maxim (Eds.), *Suicide and its aftermath: Understanding and counseling the survivors* (pp. 31–44). New York: Norton.

Rudin, C. (Comp.). (1998). *Children's books about the Holocaust: A selective annotated bibliography*. Bayside, NY: The Holocaust

Resource Center and Archives, Queensborough Community College.

Rudman, M. K., Gagne, K. D., & Bernstein, J. E. (1993). *Books to help children cope with separation and loss*, Vol. 4. New Providence, NJ: R. R. Bowker. (Vol. 1 [1978] and Vol. 2 [1989] by Bernstein alone; Vol. 3 by Bernstein & Rudman)

Ruskin, C. (1988). *The quilt: Stories from the NAMES Project.* New York: Pocket Books.

Ryan, C., & Ryan, K. M. (1979). *A private battle.* New York: Simon & Schuster.

Rynearson, E. (2001). *Retelling violent death.* New York: Brunner-Routledge.

Rynearson, E. K. (1978). Humans and pets and attachment. *British Journal of Psychiatry, 133,* 550–555.

Sable, P. (1995). Pets, attachment and well being across the life cycle. *Social Work, 40,* 334–341.

Sabom, M. B. (1982). *Recollections of death: A medical investigation.* New York: Harper & Row.

Sacred Congregation for the Doctrine of the Faith. (1982). Declaration on euthanasia. In A. Flannery (Ed.), *Vatican Council II: More postconciliar documents* (pp. 510–517). Grand Rapids, MI: Eerdmans.

Sageman, M. (2004). *Understanding terror networks.* Philadelphia: University of Pennsylvania Press.

St. Louis Post-Dispatch. (1995, January 12). Breast cancer death rate drops dramatically, but not for blacks, p. A5.

St. Louis Post-Dispatch. (1999, April 14). Judge assails "lawlessness" of Kevorkian, gives him 10–25 years, p. A1.

St. Petersburg Times. (1998, November 28). Kevorkian is charged in killing, released, pp. A1, A12.

St. Petersburg Times. (2001a, February 23). For first time, rape found to be war crime, p. 2A.

St. Petersburg Times. (2001b, October 1). Brian Sweeney's last message, p. 10A.

St. Petersburg Times. (2001c October 6). Foreign officials seek out their own, p. 12A.

Sakr, A. H. (1995). Death and dying: An Islamic perspective. In J. K. Parry & A. S. Ryan (Eds.), *A cross-cultural look at death, dying, and religion* (pp. 47–73). Chicago: Nelson-Hall.

Salcido, R. M. (1990). Mexican-Americans: Illness, death and bereavement. In J. K. Parry (Ed.), *Social work practice with the terminally ill: A transcultural perspective* (pp. 99–112). Springfield, IL: Charles C Thomas.

Sanders, C. M. (1979). A comparison of adult bereavement in the death of a spouse, child and parent. *Omega, Journal of Death and Dying, 10,* 303–322.

Sanders, C. M. (1989). *Grief: The mourning after.* New York: Wiley.

Sanders, C. M. (1992). *Surviving grief . . . and learning to live again.* New York: Wiley.

Sanders, M. A. (Ed.). (2007). *Nearing death awareness: A guide to the language, visions, and dreams of the dying.* Philadelphia: Jessica Kingsley.

Saul, S. R., & Saul, S. (1973). Old people talk about death. *Omega, Journal of Death and Dying, 4,* 27–35.

Saunders, C. M. (1967). *The management of terminal illness.* London: Hospital Medicine Publications.

Saunders, C. M. (1970). Dimensions of death. In M.A.H. Melinsky (Ed.), *Religion and medicine: A discussion* (pp. 113–116). London: Student Christian Movement Press.

Saunders, C. M. (1976). The challenge of terminal care. In T. Symington & R. L. Carter (Eds.), *Scientific foundations of oncology* (pp. 673–679). London: William Heinemann.

Saunders, C. M. (2003). *Watch with me: Inspiration for a life in hospice care.* Sheffield, England: Mortal Press.

Saunders, C. M. (Ed.). (1990). *Hospice and palliative care: An interdisciplinary approach.* London: Edward Arnold.

Saunders, C. M., & Kastenbaum, R. (1997). *Hospice care on the international scene.* New York: Springer.

Saunders, C. M., & Sykes, N. (Eds.). (1993). *The management of terminal malignant disease* (3rd ed.). London: Edward Arnold.

Saunders, C. M., Baines, M., & Dunlop, R. (1995). *Living with dying: A guide to palliative care* (3rd ed.). New York: Oxford University Press.

Savage, T. (2000, October/November). Jesse's campaign. *HIV Plus* (11).

Schackman, B. R., Gebo, K. A., Walensky, R. P., Losina, E., Muccio, T. Sax, P. E., Weinstein, M. C., Seage, G. R., Moore, R. D., & Freedberg, K. A. (2006). The lifetime cost of current immunodeficiency virus care in the United States. *Medical Care, 44*(11), 990–997.

Schaefer, D., & Lyons, C. (2002). *How do we tell the children? A step-by-step guide for helping children two to teen cope when someone dies* (3rd ed.). New York: Newmarket.

Schatz, W. H. (1986). Grief of fathers. In T. A. Rando (Ed.), *Parental loss of a child* (pp. 293–302). Champaign, IL: Research Press.

Schechter, D. S., Coates, S. W., & First, E. (2002). Observations of acute reactions of young children and their families to the World Trade Center attacks. *Zero to Three, 22,* 9–13.

Scheper-Hughes, N. (1992). *Death without weeping: The violence of everyday life in Brazil.* Berkeley: University of California Press.

The Schiavo Case. (2005). *Hastings Center Report, 35*(3), 16–27.

Schiavo, M., & Hirsh, M. (2006). *Terri: The truth.* New York: Dutton.

Schiff, H. S. (1977). *The bereaved parent.* New York: Crown.

Schiff, H. S. (1986). *Living through mourning: Finding comfort and hope when a loved one has died.* New York: Viking Penguin.

Schilder, P., & Wechsler, D. (1934). The attitudes of children toward death. *Journal of Genetic Psychology, 45,* 406–451.

Schneider, J. M. (1980). Clinically significant differences between grief, pathological grief, and depression. *Patient Counseling and Health Education, 2,* 161–169.

Schrauger, B. (2001). *Walking Taylor home.* Nashville, TN: Thomas Nelson.

Schultz, N.W., & Huet, L. M. (2000). Sensational! Violent! Popular! Death in American movies. *Omega, Journal of Death and Dying, 42,* 137–149.

Schulz, R. (1976). Effect of control and predictability on the physical and psychological well-being of the institutionalized aged. *Journal of Personality and Social Psychology, 33,* 563–573.

Schulz, R., & Aderman, D. (1974). Clinical research and the stages of dying. *Omega, Journal of Death and Dying, 5,* 137–144.

Schuurman, D. (2003). *Never the same: Coming to terms with the death of a parent.* New York: St. Martin's Press.

Schwab, R. (1990). Paternal and maternal coping with the death of a child. *Death Studies, 14,* 407–422.

Schwartz, C. L., Hobbie, W. L., Constine, L. S., & Ruccione, K. S. (Eds.). (1994). *Survivors of childhood cancer: Assessment and management.* St. Louis, MO: Mosby.

Schwartz, M. (1999). *Morrie: In his own words.* New York: Walker. (Originally published in 1996 by the same publisher as *Letting go: Morrie's reflections on living while dying.*)

Schwartz, T. P. (2005). *Organ transplants: A survival guide for the entire family—The ultimate teen guide.* Lanham, MD: Scarecrow Press.

Schwiebert, P. (2003). *We were gonna have a baby, but we had an angel instead.* Portland, OR: Grief Watch (2116 NE 18th Avenue, Portland, OR 97212; 503-284-7426; www.griefwatch.com).

Schwiebert, P. (2007). *Someone came before you.* Portland, OR: Grief Watch.

Schwiebert, P., & DeKlyen, C. (1999). *Tear soup: A recipe for healing after loss.* Portland, OR: Grief Watch.

Schwiebert, P., & Kirk, P. (1986). *Still to be born: A guide for bereaved parents who are making decisions about the future.* Portland, OR: Perinatal Loss.

Scott, S. (2000). Grief reactions to the death of a divorced spouse revisited. *Omega, Journal of Death and Dying, 41,* 207–219.

Seale, C. (1998). *Constructing death: The sociology of dying and bereavement.* Cambridge, England: Cambridge University Press.

Segal, D. L., Mincic, M. S., Coolidge, F. L., & O'Riley, A. (2004). Attitudes toward suicide and suicidal risk among younger and older persons. *Death Studies, 28,* 671–678.

Seiden, R. H. (1977). Suicide prevention: A public health/public policy approach. *Omega, Journal of Death and Dying, 8,* 267–276.

Seligson, M. R., & Peterson, K. E. (Eds.). (1992). *AIDS prevention and treatment: Hope, humor, and healing.* Washington, DC: Hemisphere.

Selkin, J. (1983). The legacy of Emile Durkheim. *Suicide and Life-Threatening Behavior, 13,* 3–14.

Seltzer, F. (1994, April/June). Trend in mortality from violent deaths: Suicide and homicide, United States, 1960–1991. *Statistical Bulletin,* 10–18.

Selwyn, P. A. (1998). *Surviving the fall: The personal journey of an AIDS doctor.* New Haven, CT: Yale University Press.

Selye, H. (1978a, October). On the real benefits of eustress. *Psychology Today,* 60–61, 63–64, 69–70.

Selye, H. (1978b). *The stress of life* (Rev. ed.). New York: McGraw-Hill.

Seneca, L. A. (1932). *Seneca's letters to Lucilius* (2 vols.) (E. P. Barker, Trans.). Oxford: Clarendon Press.

Servaty-Seib, H. L., & Hamilton, L. A. (2006). Educational performance and persistence of bereaved college students. *Journal of College Student Development, 47,* 225–234.

Servaty-Seib, H. L., & Pistole, M. C. (2007). Adolescent grief: Relationship category and emotional closeness. *Omega, Journal of Death and Dying, 54,* 147–167.

Settersten, R. A. (Ed.). (2002). *Invitation to the life course: Toward new understandings of later life.* Amityville, NY: Baywood.

Shachtman, T. (2006). *Rumspringa: To be or not to be Amish.* New York: North Point Press.

Shakoor, B., & Chalmers, D. (1991). Co-victimization of African-American children who witness violence and the theoretical implications of its effect on their cognitive, emotional, and behavioral development. *Journal of the National Medical Association, 83,* 233–238.

Shannon, T. A., & Walter, J. J. (2004, April 16). Artificial nutrition, hydration: Assessing papal statement. *National Catholic Reporter, 40*(24), 9–10. (See also http://natcath.org/NCR_Online/archives2/2004b/041604/041604i.php.)

Shapiro, E. (1995). Grief in family and cultural context: Learning from Latino families. *Cultural Diversity and Mental Health, 1*(2), 159–176.

Shapiro, E. R. (1994). *Grief as a family process: A developmental approach to clinical practice.* New York: Guilford.

Shaw, E. (1994). *What to do when a loved one dies: A practical and compassionate guide to dealing with death on life's terms.* Irvine, CA: Dickens Press.

Sheehan, D. K., & Schirm, V. (2003). End-of-life care of older adults. *American Journal of Nursing, 103,* 48–58.

Sheehy, E., Conrad, S. L., Brigham, L. E., Luskin, R., Weber, P., Eakin, M., et al. (2003). Estimating the number of potential organ donors in the United States. *New England Journal of Medicine, 349,* 667–674.

Shen, W. W. (1986). The Hopi Indian's mourning hallucinations. *Journal of Nervous and Mental Disease, 174*(6), 365–367.

Shenkman, M. M., & Klein, P. S. (2004). *Living wills and health care proxies: Assuring that your end-of-life decisions are respected.* Teaneck, NJ: Law Made Easy Press.

Shenson, D. (1988, February 28). When fear conquers: A doctor learns about AIDS from leprosy. *New York Times Magazine,* pp. 35–36, 48.

Shephard, D. A. E. (1977). Principles and practice of palliative care. *Canadian Medical Association Journal, 116,* 522–526.

Sherman, D.W. (2001). Patients with Acquired Immune Deficiency Syndrome. In B. R. Ferrell & N. Coyle (Eds.), *Textbook of palliative nursing* (pp. 467–500). New York: Oxford University Press.

Shield, R. R. (1988). *Uneasy endings: Daily life in an American nursing home.* Ithaca, NY: Cornell University Press.

Shilts, R. (1987). *And the band played on: Politics, people, and the AIDS epidemic.* New York: St. Martin's Press.

Shine, T. M. (2000). *Fathers aren't supposed to die: Five brothers reunite to say good-bye.* New York: Simon & Schuster.

Shirley, V., & Mercier, J. (1983). Bereavement of older persons: Death of a pet. *The Gerontologist, 23,* 276.

Shneidman, E. S. (1971). Prevention, intervention, and postvention of suicide. *Annals of Internal Medicine, 75,* 453–458.

Shneidman, E. S. (1973a). *Deaths of man.* New York: Quadrangle.

Shneidman, E. S. (1973b). Suicide. *Encyclopedia Britannica* (14th ed.; Vol. 21, pp. 383–385). Chicago: William Benton.

Shneidman, E. S. (1980/1995). *Voices of death.* New York: Harper & Row/Kodansha International.

Shneidman, E. S. (1981). *Suicide thoughts and reflections, 1960–1980.* New York: Human Sciences Press.

Shneidman, E. S. (1983). Reflections on contemporary death. In C. A. Corr, J. M. Stillion, & M. C. Ribar (Eds.), *Creativity in death education and counseling* (pp. 27–34). Lakewood, OH: Forum for Death Education and Counseling.

Shneidman, E. S. (1985). *Definition of suicide.* New York: Wiley.

Shneidman, E. S., & Farberow, N. L. (1961). *Some facts about suicide* (PHS Publication No. 852). Washington, DC: U.S. Government Printing Office.

Showalter, J. E. (1983). Foreword. In J. H. Arnold & P. B. Gemma, *A child dies: A portrait of family grief* (pp. ix–x). Rockville, MD: Aspen Systems Corp.

Shrock, N. M. (1835). On the signs that distinguish real from apparent death. *Transylvanian Journal of Medicine, 13,* 210–220.

Shulman, W. L. (Ed.). (2005). *Association of Holocaust organizations: Directory.* Bayside, NY: The Holocaust Resource Center and Archives, Queensborough Community College.

Siebert, C. (2004). *A man after his own heart: A true story.* New York: Crown.

Siegel, K., & Weinstein, L. (1983). Anticipatory grief reconsidered. *Journal of Psychosocial Oncology, 1,* 61–73.

Siegel, M. (Ed.). (1997). *The last word:* The New York Times *book of obituaries and farewells—A celebration of unusual lives.* New York: William Morrow.

Siegel, R. (1982). A family-centered program of neonatal intensive care. *Health and Social Work, 7,* 50–58.

Siegel, R. K. (1992). *Fire in the brain.* New York: Dutton.

Siegel, R., Rudd, S. H., Cleveland, C., Powers, L. K., & Harmon, R. J. (1985). A hospice approach to neonatal care. In C. A. Corr & D. M. Corr (Eds.), *Hospice approaches to pediatric care* (pp. 127–152). New York: Springer.

Sife, W. (2005). *The loss of a pet* (3rd ed.). New York: Howell Book House.

Sifton, E. (2003). *The serenity prayer: Faith and politics in time of peace and war.* New York: Norton.

Siggins, L. (1966). Mourning: A critical survey of the literature. *International Journal of Psychoanalysis, 47,* 14–25.

Silver, R. L., & Wortman, C. B. (1980). Coping with undesirable life events. In J. Garber & M. E. P. Seligman (Eds.), *Human helplessness: Theory and applications* (pp. 279–340). New York: Academic Press.

Silverman, E., Range, L., & Overholser, J. (1994). Bereavement from suicide as compared to other forms of bereavement. *Omega, Journal of Death and Dying, 30,* 41–51.

Silverman, M. M., & Maris, R.W. (1995). *Suicide prevention: Toward the year 2000.* New York: Guilford.

Silverman, P. R. (1969). The widow-to-widow program: An experiment in preventive intervention. *Mental Hygiene, 53,* 333–337.

Silverman, P. R. (1978). *Mutual help groups: A guide for mental health workers.* Rockville, MD: National Institute of Mental Health.

Silverman, P. R. (1980). *Mutual help groups: Organization and development.* Newbury Park, CA: Sage.

Silverman, P. R. (1986). *Widow to widow.* New York: Springer.

Silverman, P. R. (2000). *Never too young to know: Death in children's lives.* New York: Oxford University Press.

Silverman, P. R. (2004). *Widow to widow: How the bereaved help one another* (2nd ed.). New York: Routledge.

Silverman, P. R. (2007). Helping built on personal experience. In K. J. Doka (Ed.), *Living with grief: Before and after a death* (pp. 175–191). Washington, DC: Hospice Foundation of America.

Silverman, P. R., & Worden, J. W. (1992a). Children and parental death. *American Journal of Orthopsychiatry, 62,* 93–104.

Silverman, P. R., & Worden, J. W. (1992b). Children's understanding of funeral ritual. *Omega, Journal of Death and Dying, 25,* 319–331.

Silverman, P. R., Nickman, S., & Worden, J. W. (1992). Detachment revisited: The child's reconstruction of a dead parent. *American Journal of Orthopsychiatry, 62,* 494–503.

Simeone, W. E. (1991). The Northern Athabaskan potlatch: The objectification of grief. In D. R. Counts & D. A. Counts (Eds.), *Coping with the final tragedy: Cultural variation in dying and grieving* (pp. 157–167). Amityville, NY: Baywood.

Siminoff, L. A., Arnold, R. M., Caplan, A. L., Virnig, B. A., & Seltzer, D. L. (1995). Public policy governing organ and tissue procurement in the United States. *Annals of Internal Medicine, 123,* 10–17.

Siminoff, L. A., Gordon, N., Hewlett, J., & Arnold, R. M. (2001). Factors influencing families' consent for donation of solid organs for transplantation. *Journal of the American Medical Association, 286,* 71–77.

Simmons, P. (2002). *Learning to fall: The blessings of an imperfect life.* New York: Bantam.

Simon, C. (2001). *Fatherless women: How we change after we lose our dads.* New York: Wiley.

Simon, N. (1979). *We remember Philip.* Chicago: Whitman.

Simonds, W., & Rothman, B. K. (Eds.). (1992). *Centuries of solace: Expressions of maternal grief in popular literature.* Philadelphia: Temple University Press.

Simone, P. M., & Dooley, S. W. (1994). Multidrug-resistant tuberculosis, 1994. CDC, Division of Tuberculosis Elimination. Available at: http://www.cdc.gov/nchstp/tb/pubs/mdrtb.htm.

Simpson, M. A. (1976). Brought in dead. *Omega, Journal of Death and Dying, 7,* 243–248.

Singh, G. K., & Yu, S. M. (1995). Infant mortality in the United States: Trends, differentials, and projections, 1950 through 2010. *American Journal of Public Health, 85,* 957–964.

Singh, G. K., Mathews, T. J., Clarke, S. C., Yannicos, T., & Smith, B. L. (1995). Annual summary of births, marriages, divorces, and deaths: United States, 1994. *Monthly Vital Statistics Report, 43*(13). Hyattsville, MD: National Center for Health Statistics.

Sjöqvist, S. (Ed.). (2006). *Still here with me: Teenagers and children on losing a parent* (M. Myers, Trans.). Philadelphia: Jessica Kingsley.

Skidelsky, R. (2004). The killing fields. *New Statesman, 26,* pp. 18–21.

Sklar, F., & Hartley, S. F. (1990). Close friends as survivors: Bereavement patterns in a "hidden" population. *Omega, Journal of Death and Dying, 21,* 103–112.

Slaby, A. (1992). Creativity, depression, and suicide. *Suicide and Life-Threatening Behavior, 22,* 157–166.

Slaughter, V., & Lyons, M. (2003). Learning about life and death in early childhood. *Cognitive Psychology, 46,* 1–30.

Sloane, D. C. (1991). *The last great necessity: Cemeteries in American history.* Baltimore: Johns Hopkins University Press.

Smith, A. A. (1974). *Rachel.* Wilton, CT: Morehouse-Barlow.

Smith, A. C. (2003, December 7). Voters: Schiavo law was bad move. *St. Petersburg Times,* pp. 1A, 21A.

Smith, D. H. (1986). *Health and medicine in the Anglican tradition: Conscience, community, and compromise.* New York: Crossroad.

Smith, D.W.E. (1995). Why do we live so long? *Omega, Journal of Death and Dying, 31,* 143–150.

Smith, G. H. (2006). *Remembering Garrett.* New York: Carroll & Graf.

Smith, H. I. (1994). *On grieving the death of a father.* Minneapolis, MN: Augsburg Fortress.

Smith, H. I. (1996). *Grieving the death of a friend.* Minneapolis, MN: Augsburg Fortress.

Smith, H. I. (1999). *A decembered grief: Living with loss when others are celebrating.* Kansas City, MO: Beacon Hill Press of Kansas City.

Smith, H. I. (2001). *Friendgrief: An absence called presence.* Amityville, NY: Baywood.

Smith, H. I. (2003). *Grieving the death of a mother.* Minneapolis, MN: Augsburg Fortress.

Smith, H. I. (2004a). *Grievers ask: Answers to questions about death and loss.* Minneapolis, MN: Augsburg Fortress.

Smith, H. I. (2004b). *When a child you love is grieving.* Kansas City, MO: Beacon Hill Press of Kansas City.

Smith, H. I. (2004c). *GriefKeeping: Learning how long grief lasts.* New York: Crossroads.

Smith, H. I., & Jeffers, S. L. (2001). *ABC's of healthy grieving: Light for a dark journey.* Shawnee Mission, KS: Shawnee Mission Medical Center Foundation.

Smith, H. I., & Johnson, J. (2006). *What does* that *mean? A dictionary of death, dying and grief terms for grieving children and those who love them.* Omaha, NE: Centering Corporation.

Smith, I. (1991). Preschool children "play" out their grief. *Death Studies, 15,* 169–176.

Smith, I. (2000). *A tiny boat at sea.* Portland, OR: Author (3254 SE Salmon, Portland, OR 97214).

Smith, J. D. (2002). *Right-to-die policies in the American states: Judicial and legislative innovation.* New York: LFB Scholarly Publishing.

Smith, J. I., & Haddad, Y. Y. (2002). *The Islamic understanding of death and resurrection.* New York: Oxford University Press.

Smith, S. A. (2000). *Hospice concepts: A guide to palliative care in terminal illness.* Champaign, IL: Research Press.

Smolin, A., & Guinan, J. (1993). *Healing after the suicide of a loved one.* New York: Simon & Schuster.

Solomon, K. (1982). Social antecedents of learned helplessness in the health care setting. *The Gerontologist, 22,* 282–287.

Solomon, M. Z., Sellers, D. E., Heller, K. S., Dokken, D. L., Levetown, M., Rushton, C., Truog, R. D., & Fleischman, A. R. (2005). New and lingering controversies in pediatric end-of-life care. *Pediatrics, 116,* 872–883.

Sontag, S. (1978). *Illness as metaphor.* New York: Farrar, Straus & Giroux.

Sontag, S. (1989). *AIDS and its metaphors.* New York: Farrar, Straus & Giroux.

Sorlie, P. D., Backlund, E., & Keller, J. B. (1995). U.S. mortality by economic, demographic, and social characteristics: The National Longitudinal Mortality Study. *American Journal of Public Health, 85,* 949–956.

Soto, A. R., & Villa, J. (1990). Una platica: Mexican-American approaches to death and dying. In J. K. Parry (Ed.), *Social work practice with the terminally ill: A transcultural perspective* (pp. 113–127). Springfield, IL: Charles C Thomas.

Sourkes, B. M. (1995). *Armfuls of time: The psychological experience of the child with a life-threatening illness.* Pittsburgh: University of Pittsburgh Press.

Sourkes, B. M. (1996). The broken heart: Anticipatory grief in the child facing death. *Journal of Palliative Care, 12*(3), 56–59.

Speece, M. W., & Brent, S. B. (1984). Children's understanding of death: A review of three components of a death concept. *Child Development, 55,* 1671–1686.

Speece, M. W., & Brent, S. B. (1996). The development of children's understanding of death. In C. A. Corr & D. M. Corr (Eds.), *Handbook of childhood death and bereavement* (pp. 29–50). New York: Springer.

Spiegel, D. (1993). *Living beyond limits: New hope and help for facing life-threatening illness.* London: Vermilion.

Spiegelman, V., & Kastenbaum, R. (1990). Pet Rest Cemetery: Is eternity running out of time? *Omega, Journal of Death and Dying, 21,* 1–13.

Spinetta, J. J., & Deasy-Spinetta, P. (1981). *Living with childhood cancer.* St. Louis, MO: Mosby.

Spinetta, J. J., & Maloney, L. J. (1975). Death anxiety in the outpatient leukemic child. *Pediatrics, 56,* 1034–1037.

Spinetta, J. J., Rigler, D., & Karon, M. (1973). Anxiety in the dying child. *Pediatrics, 52,* 841–849.

Sprang, G., & McNeil, J. (1995). *The many faces of bereavement: The nature and treatment of natural, traumatic, and stigmatized grief.* New York: Bruner/Mazel.

Sque, M., Long, T., & Payne, S. (2005). Organ donation: Key factors influencing families' decision-making. *Transplant Proceedings, 37,* 543–546.

Stahlman, S. D. (1996). Children and the death of a sibling. In C. A. Corr & D. M. Corr (Eds.), *Handbook of childhood death and bereavement* (pp. 149–164). New York: Springer.

Stambrook, M., & Parker, K. C. (1987). The development of the concept of death in childhood: A review of the literature. *Merrill Palmer Quarterly, 33,* 133–157.

Stannard, D. E. (1977). *The Puritan way of death: A study in religion, culture, and social change.* New York: Oxford University Press.

Stanworth, R. (2003). *Recognizing spiritual needs in people who are dying.* New York: Oxford University Press.

Staples, B. (1994). *Parallel time: Growing up in black and white.* New York: Pantheon.

Starr, P. (1982). *The social transformation of American medicine.* New York: Basic Books.

Starzl, T. L. (1992). *The puzzle people: Memoirs of a transplant surgeon.* Pittsburgh, PA: University of Pittsburgh Press.

Staton, J., Shuy, R., & Byock, I. (2001). *A few months to live: Different paths to life's end.* Washington, DC: Georgetown University Press.

Staudacher, C. (1991). *Men and grief.* Oakland, CA: New Harbinger Publications.

Stearns, A. K. (1985). *Living through personal crisis.* New York: Ballantine.

Stearns, A. K. (1988). *Coming back: Rebuilding lives after crisis and loss.* New York: Random House.

Stedeford, A. (1978). Understanding confusional states. *British Journal of Hospital Medicine, 20,* 694–704.

Stedeford, A. (1979). Psychotherapy of the dying patient. *British Journal of Psychiatry, 135,* 7–14.

Stedeford, A. (1984). *Facing death: Patients, families and professionals.* London: William Heinemann.

Stedeford, A. (1987). Hospice: A safe place to suffer? *Palliative Medicine, 1,* 73–74.

Steinbach, U. (1992). Social networks, institutionalization, and mortality among elderly people in the United States. *Journal of Gerontology, 47,* S183–S190.

Steinbrook, R. (2007). Organ donation after cardiac death. *New England Journal of Medicine, 357,* 209–213.

Stetson, B. (2002). *Living victims, stolen lives: Parents of murdered children speak to America.* Amityville, NY: Baywood.

Stevens, M. M. (1993). Family adjustment and support. In D. Doyle, G.W.C. Hanks, & N. MacDonald (Eds.), *Oxford textbook of palliative medicine* (pp. 707–717). New York: Oxford University Press.

Stevens, M. M. (1998). Psychological adaptation of the dying child. In D. Doyle, G.W.C. Hanks, & N. MacDonald (Eds.), *Oxford textbook of palliative medicine* (2nd ed.; pp. 1046–1055). New York: Oxford University Press.

Stevens, M. M., & Dunsmore, J. C. (1996a). Adolescents who are living with a life-threatening illness. In C. A. Corr & D. E. Balk (Eds.), *Handbook of adolescent death and bereavement* (pp. 107–135). New York: Springer.

Stevens, M. M., & Dunsmore, J. C. (1996b). Helping adolescents who are coping with a life-threatening illness, along with their siblings, parents, and peers. In C. A. Corr & D. E. Balk (Eds.), *Handbook of adolescent death and bereavement* (pp. 329–353). New York: Springer.

Stevens, R. (1989). *In sickness and in wealth: American hospitals in the twentieth century.* New York: Basic Books.

Stevenson, A. (1989). *Bitter fame: A life of Sylvia Plath.* Boston: Houghton Mifflin.

Stevenson, I., Cook, E. W., & McClean-Rice, N. (1989). Are persons reporting "near-death experiences" really near death? A study of medical records. *Omega, Journal of Death and Dying, 20,* 45–54.

Stevenson, R. G. (2004). Where have we come from? Where do we go from here? Thirty years of death education in schools. *Illness, Crisis and Loss, 12,* 231–238.

Stevenson, R. G. (Ed.). (2001). *What will we do? Preparing a school community to cope with crises* (2nd ed.). Amityville, NY: Baywood.

Stevenson, R. G., & Cox, G. R. (Eds.). (2007). *Perspectives on violence and violent death.* Amityville, NY: Baywood.

Stevenson, R. G., & Stevenson, E. P. (1996a). Adolescents and education about death, dying, and bereavement. In C. A. Corr & D. E. Balk (Eds.), *Handbook of adolescent death and bereavement* (pp. 235–249). New York: Springer.

Stevenson, R. G., & Stevenson, E. P. (Eds.). (1996b). *Teaching students about death: A comprehensive resource for educators and parents.* Philadelphia: The Charles Press.

Stewart, M. F. (1999). *Companion animal death: A practical and comprehensive guide for veterinary practice.* Woburn, MA: Butterworth-Heinemann Medical.

Stillion, J. M. (1985). *Death and the sexes: An examination of differential longevity, attitudes, behaviors, and coping skills.* Washington, DC: Hemisphere.

Stillion, J. M., & McDowell, E. E. (1996). *Suicide across the life span: Premature exits* (2nd ed.).Washington, DC: Taylor & Francis.

Stillion, J. M., McDowell, E. E., & May, J. (1989). *Suicide across the life span: Premature exits.* Washington, DC: Hemisphere.

Stinson, R., & Stinson, P. (1983). *The long dying of Baby Andrew.* Boston: Little, Brown.

Stoddard, S. (1992). *The hospice movement: A better way of caring for the dying* (Rev. ed.). New York: Vintage.

Stokes, J. A. (2004). *Then, now and always—Supporting children as they journey through grief: A guide for practitioners.* Cheltenham, England: Winston's Wish.

Stokes, J., & Crossley, D. (1995). Camp Winston: A residential intervention for bereaved children. In S. C. Smith & M. Penells (Eds.), *Interventions with bereaved children* (pp. 172–192). London: Jessica Kingsley Publications.

Storey, P. (1996). *Primer of palliative care* (2nd ed.). Glenview, IL: American Academy of Hospice and Palliative Medicine.

Strasburger, V. C. (1993). Children, adolescents, and the media: Five crucial issues. *Adolescent Medicine: State of the Art Review, 4,* 479–493.

Straub, S. H. (2000). *Death without notice.* Amityville, NY: Baywood.

Straub, S. H. (2004). *Pet death.* Amityville, NY: Baywood.

Strickland, A. L., & DeSpelder, L. A. (1995). Communicating about death and dying. In I. B. Corless, B. B. Germino, & M. A. Pittman (Eds.), *A challenge for living: Dying, death, and bereavement* (pp. 37–51). Boston: Jones and Bartlett.

Stroebe, M. S., Hansson, R. O., Stroebe, W., & Schut, H. (Eds.). (2001). *Handbook of bereavement research: Consequences, coping, and care.* Washington, DC: American Psychological Association Press.

Stroebe, M. S., Hansson, R. O., Stroebe, W. & Schut, H. A. (Eds.). (2007). *Handbook of bereavement research and*

practice: 21st century perspectives. Washington, DC: American Psychological Association Press.

Stroebe, M., & Schut, H. (1999). The dual process model of coping with bereavement: Rationale and description. *Death Studies, 23,* 197–224.

Stroebe, M., & Schut, H. (2005). To continue or relinquish bonds: A review of consequences for the bereaved. *Death Studies, 29,* 477–494.

Stroebe, W., & Stroebe, M. S. (2003). *Bereavement and health: The psychological and physical consequences of partner loss.* Cambridge, UK: Cambridge University Press.

Sudnow, D. (1967). *Passing on: The social organization of dying.* Englewood Cliffs, NJ: Prentice Hall.

Sugar, M. (1968). Normal adolescent mourning. *American Journal of Psychotherapy, 22,* 258–269.

Sullivan, L. (1991). Violence as a public health issue. *Journal of the American Medical Association, 265,* 2778.

Sullivan, M. A. (1995). May the circle be unbroken: The African-American experience of death, dying, and spirituality. In J. K. Parry & A. S. Ryan (Eds.), *A cross-cultural look at death, dying, and religion* (pp. 160–171). Chicago: Nelson-Hall.

Sumner, L. H., Kavanaugh, K., & Moro, T. (2006). Extending palliative care into pregnancy and the immediate newborn period: State of the practice of perinatal palliative care. *Journal of Perinatal and Neonatal Nursing, 20,* 113–116.

Supportive Care of the Dying: A Coalition for Compassionate Care. (1997). *Living and healing during life-threatening illness: Executive summary.* Portland, OR: Author.

The SUPPORT Principal Investigators. (1995). A controlled trial to improve care for seriously ill hospitalized patients: The Study to Understand Prognoses and Preferences for Outcomes and Risks of Treatments (SUPPORT). *Journal of the American Medical Association, 274,* 1591–1598.

Swanson, D. A., & Siegel, J. S. (2004). *The methods and materials of demography* (2nd ed.). New York: Academic Press.

Swarte, N., & Heintz, A. (1999). Euthanasia and physician-assisted suicide. *Annals of Medicine, 31,* 364–371.

Swarte, N., van der Lee, M., van der Born, J., van den Bout, J., & Heintz, A. (2003). Effects of euthanasia on the bereaved family and friends: A cross sectional study. *British Medical Journal, 327,* 189–192.

Swartzberg, J. (2004). Do living wills work? *UC Berkeley Wellness Letter, 20*(11), 3.

Swenson, W. M. (1961). Attitudes toward death in an aged population. *Journal of Gerontology, 16,* 49–52.

Tagliaferre, L., & Harbaugh, G. L. (1990). *Recovery from loss: A personalized guide to the grieving process.* Deerfield Beach, FL: Health Communications.

Talbot, K. (2002). *What forever means after the death of a child: Transcending the trauma, living with the loss.* New York: Brunner-Routledge.

Tanner, J. G. (1995). Death, dying, and grief in the Chinese-American culture. In J. K. Parry & A. S. Ryan (Eds.), *A cross-cultural look at death, dying, and religion* (pp. 183–192). Chicago: Nelson-Hall.

The Task Force to Improve the Care of Terminally-Ill Oregonians. (2005). *The Oregon Death with Dignity Act: A guidebook for health care professionals* (current edition). Retrieved on February 23, 2007, from http://egov.oregon.gov/DHS/ph/pas.

Tatelbaum, J. (1980). *The courage to grieve.* New York: Lippincott & Crowell.

Taylor, D. H., Ostermann, J., Van Houtven, C. H., Tulsky, J. A., & Steinhauser, K. (2007). What length of hospice use maximizes reduction in medical expenditures near death in the US Medicare program? *Social Science and Medicine, 65,* 1466–1478.

Taylor, R. (2006). *Alzheimer's from the inside out.* Baltimore: Health Professions Press.

Tedeschi, R. G. (1996). Support groups for bereaved adolescents. In C. A. Corr & D. E. Balk (Eds.), *Handbook of adolescent death and bereavement* (pp. 293–311). New York: Springer.

Tedeschi, R. G. (2003). *Helping bereaved parents: A clinician's guide.* New York: Routledge.

Tedeschi, R. G., & Calhoun, L. G. (1995). *Trauma and transformation: Grieving in the aftermath of suffering.* Thousand Oaks, CA: Sage.

Tedeschi, R. G., & Calhoun, L. G. (2007). Grief as a transformative struggle. In K. J. Doka (Ed.), *Living with grief: Before and after a death* (pp. 107–121). Washington, DC: Hospice Foundation of America.

Tedeschi, R. G., Park, C. L., & Calhoun, L. G. (Eds.). (1998). *Posttraumatic growth: Positive changes in the aftermath of crisis.* Mahwah, NJ: Lawrence Erlbaum Associates.

Templer, D. (1970). The construction and validation of a death anxiety scale. *Journal of General Psychology, 82,* 165–177.

Templer, D. (1971). Death anxiety as related to depression and health of retired persons. *Journal of Gerontology, 26,* 521–123.

Teno, J. M., Clarridge, B. R., Casey, V., Welch, L. C., Wetle, T., Shield, R., et al. (2004). Family perspectives on end-of-life care at the last place of care. *Journal of the American Medical Association, 291,* 88–93.

Terkel, S. (2001). *Will the circle be unbroken?: Reflections on death, rebirth, and hunger for a faith.* New York: New Press.

Terl, A. H. (1992). *AIDS and the law: A basic guide for the nonlawyer.* Washington, DC: Taylor & Francis.

Terri's Family, Schindler, M., Schindler, R., Vitadona, S. S., & Schindler, B. (2006). *A life that matters: The legacy of Terri Schiavo—A lessons for us all.* New York: Warner Books.

Thomas, N. (2001). The importance of culture throughout all of life and beyond. *Holistic Nursing Practice 15*(2), 40–46.

Thomasma, D. C., Kimbrough-Kushner, T., Kimsma, G. K., & Ciesielski-Carlucci, C. (1998). *Asking to die: Inside the Dutch debate about euthanasia.* Boston: Kluwer Academic.

Thompson, J. W., & Walker, R. D. (1990). Adolescent suicide among American Indians and Alaska natives. *Psychiatric Annals, 20,* 128–133.

Thompson, N. (Ed.). (2002). *Loss and grief: A guide for human service practitioners.* London: Palgrave Macmillan.

Thorson, J. A. (1995). *Aging in a changing society.* Belmont, CA: Wadsworth.

Thorson, J. A. (2000a). *Aging in a changing society.* Philadelphia: Brunner/Mazel.

Thorson, J. A. (Ed.). (2000b). *Perspectives on spiritual well-being and aging.* Springfield, IL: Charles C Thomas.

Thorson, J. A., Powell, F. C., & Samuel, V. T. (1998). African and Euro-American samples differ little in scores on death anxiety. *Psychological Reports, 83,* 623–626.

Thurman, H. (1953). *Meditations of the heart.* New York: Harper & Row.

Tibbetts, E. (2000). Learning to value every moment. *Innovations in end-of-life care, 2*(4), 78–79. M. Z. Solomon, A. L. Romer, K. S. Heller, & D. E. Weissman (Eds.). Larchmont, NY: Mary Ann Liebert Publishers. Retrieved September 5, 2001, from http://www2.edc.org/lastacts/archives/archivesJuly00/reflections.asp#Tibbetts.

Tideiksaar, R. (2002). *Falls in older people: Prevention and management* (3rd ed.). Baltimore: Health Professions Press.

Tilney, N. L. (2003). *Transplantation: From myth to reality.* New Haven, CT: Yale University Press.

Times Staff Writer. (2004, July 14). Groups for disabled side with Schiavo. *St. Petersburg Times,* p. 3B.

Tobin, D. (1999). *Peaceful dying: The step-by-step guide to preserving your dignity, your choice, and your inner peace at the end of life.* Cambridge, MA: Perseus.

Tolle, S. W., Tilden, V. P., Drach, L. L., Fromme, E. K., Perrin, N. A., & Hedberg, K. (2004). Characteristics and proportion of dying Oregonians who personally consider physician-assisted suicide. *Journal of Clinical Ethics, 15,* 111–118.

Tolstoy, L. (1960). *The death of Ivan Ilych and other stories* (A. Maude, Trans.). New York: New American Library. (Original work published 1884)

Tomer, A., & Eliason, G. (1996). Toward a comprehensive model of death anxiety. *Death Studies, 20,* 343–366.

Tong, K. L., & Spicer, B. J. (1994). The Chinese palliative patient and family in North America: A cultural perspective. *Journal of Palliative Care, 10*(1), 26–28.

Toray, T. (2004). The human-animal bond and loss: Providing support for grieving clients. *Journal of Mental Health Counseling, 26,* 244–259.

Toray, T., & Oltjenbruns, K. A. (1996). Children's friendships and the death of a friend. In C. A. Corr & D. M. Corr (Eds.), *Handbook of childhood death and bereavement* (pp. 165–178). New York: Springer.

Toynbee, A. (1968a). The relation between life and death, living and dying. In A. Toynbee, A. K. Mant, N. Smart, J. Hinton, S. Yudkin, E. Rhode, et al., *Man's concern with death* (pp. 259–271). New York: McGraw-Hill.

Toynbee, A. (1968b). Traditional attitudes towards death. In A. Toynbee, A. K. Mant, N. Smart, J. Hinton, S. Yudkin, E. Rhode, et al., *Man's concern with death* (pp. 59–94). New York: McGraw-Hill.

Toynbee, A., Koestler, A., et al. (1976). *Life after death.* New York: McGraw-Hill.

Travis, S. S., Loving, G., McClanahan, L., & Bernard, M. (2001). Hospitalization patterns and palliation in the last year of life among residents in long term care. *The Gerontologist, 41*(2), 153–160.

Trozzi, M., & Massimini, K. (1999). *Talking with children about loss: Words, strategies, and wisdom to help children cope with death, divorce, and other difficult times.* New York: Penguin Putnam.

Tschann, J., Kaufmann, S., & Micco, G. (2003). Family involvement in end-of-life hospital care. *Journal of the American Geriatrics Society, 51,* 835–840.

Tucker, J. B. (2001). *Scourge: The once and future threat of smallpox.* New York: Atlantic Monthly Press.

Turnbull, S. B. (2005). *The wealth of your life: A step-by-step guide for creating your ethical will.* Wrenham, MA: Benedict Press (www.yourethicalwill.com).

Turner, M. (2006). *Talking with children and young people about death and dying* (2nd ed.). Philadelphia: Jessica Kingsley.

Turner, R. E., & Edgley, C. (1976). Death as theatre: A dramaturgical analysis of the American funeral. *Sociology and Social Research, 60,* 377–392.

Tuzeo-Jarolmen, J. (2006). *When a family pet dies: A guide to dealing with children's loss.* Philadelphia: Jessica Kingsley.

Twomey, J. (2001, May 19). Youth crime: It's not what you think. *St. Petersburg Times,* p. 14A.

Twycross, R. G. (1976). Long-term use of diamorphine in advanced cancer. In J. J. Bonica & D. Albe-Fessard (Eds.), *Advances in pain research and therapy* (Vol. 1, pp. 653–661). New York: Raven Press.

Twycross, R. G. (1979a). The Brompton cocktail. In J. J. Bonica & V. Ventafridda (Eds.), *International symposium on pain of advanced cancer: Advances in pain research and therapy* (Vol. 2, pp. 291–300). New York: Raven Press.

Twycross, R. G. (1979b). Overview of analgesia. In J. J. Bonica & V. Ventafridda (Eds.), *International symposium on pain of advanced cancer: Advances in pain research and therapy* (Vol. 2, pp. 617–633). New York: Raven Press.

Twycross, R. G. (1982). Principles and practice of pain relief in terminal cancer. *Cancer Forum, 6,* 23–33.

Twycross, R. G. (1994). *Pain relief in advanced cancer.* New York: Churchill Livingstone.

Twycross, R. G. (2003). *Introducing palliative care* (3rd ed.). Oxford, England: Radcliffe Medical Press.

Twycross, R. G., & Lack, S. A. (1989). *Oral morphine: Information for patients, families and friends.* Beaconsfield, England: Beaconsfield Press.

Twycross, R. G., & Wilcock, A. (2002). *Symptom management in advanced cancer* (3rd ed.). Oxford, England: Radcliffe Medical Press.

U.S. Bureau of the Census. (1975). *Historical statistics of the United States, colonial times to 1970, bicentennial edition* (2 parts).Washington, DC: U.S. Government Printing Office.

U.S. Bureau of the Census. (1998). *Statistical abstract of the United States, 1998* (118th ed.). Washington, DC: U.S. Government Printing Office.

U.S. Census Bureau. (2004). *Statistical abstract of the United States, 2004–2005* (124th ed.).Washington, DC: U.S. Government Printing Office.

U.S. Census Bureau. (2005). *Statistical abstract of the United States, 2006* (125th ed.). Washington, DC: U.S. Government Printing Office.

U.S. Congress. (1986). *Indian health care.* Washington, DC: U.S. Government Printing Office.

U.S. Department of Health and Human Services, Health Care Financing Administration. (1998). Medicare and Medicaid programs; hospital conditions of participation; identification of potential organ, tissue, and eye donors and transplant hospitals' provision of transplant-related data. *Federal Register, 63,* 33856–33874.

U.S. Department of Health and Human Services, Health Resources and Services Administration and Health Care Financing Administration. (2000). *Roles and training in the donation process: A resource guide.* Rockville, MD: Authors.

U.S. Department of Health and Human Services. (2001a). *The Surgeon General's call to action to prevent and decrease overweight and obesity.* Washington, DC: U.S. Government Printing Office.

U.S. Department of Health and Human Services. (2001b). *Youth violence: A report of the Surgeon General.* Washington, DC: U.S. Government Printing Office.

U.S. Department of Health and Human Services. (2004). *The health consequences of smoking: A report of the Surgeon General.* Washington, DC: U.S. Government Printing Office.

Uhlenberg, P. (1980). Death and the family. *Journal of Family History, 5,* 313–320.

Ulferts, A. C., & Lindberg, A. (2003, October 15). Schiavo's family ends legal fight. *St. Petersburg Times,* pp. 1A, 5A.

Umberson, D. (2003). *Death of a parent: Transition to a new adult identity.* New York: Cambridge University Press.

UNAIDS. (2001a). AIDS epidemic update: December 2000. Geneva, Switzerland: Author.

UNAIDS. (2001b). AIDS epidemic update: December 2001. Geneva, Switzerland: Author.

UNAIDS. (2001c). HIV/AIDS: Global crisis—global action. Geneva, Switzerland: Author.

UNAIDS. (2004). *2004 report on the global AIDS epidemic: Executive summary.* Geneva, Switzerland: Author.

UNAIDS. (2006). AIDS epidemic update: December 2006. Geneva, Switzerland: Author. Also available at www.unaids.org.

UNAIDS. (2007). *2007 AIDS epidemic update.* Geneva, Switzerland: Author.

United Network for Organ Sharing (UNOS). (2004, August 1). *2004 annual report of the U.S. Scientific Registry of Transplant Recipients and the Organ Procurement and Transplantation Network: Transplant data 1994–2003.* Rockville, MD: HHS/HRSA/OSP/DOT and UNOS. From http://www.optn.org/AR2004.

United Network for Organ Sharing (UNOS). (2007). http://www.unos.org. Retrieved December 6, 2007.

Until We Say Goodbye. [Videotape]. (1980).Washington, DC: WJLA-TV.

Urich, L. P. (2001). *The Patient Self-Determination Act: Meeting the challenges in patient care.* Washington, DC: Georgetown University Press.

Urofsky, M. I. (1994). *Letting go: Death, dying and the law* (Rev. ed.). Norman, OK: University of Oklahoma Press.

Utsey, S. O., Hook, J. N., & Stannard, P. (2007). A re-examination of cultural factors that mitigate risk and promote resilience in relation to African American suicide: A review of the literature and recommendations for future research. *Death Studies, 31*(5), 399–416.

Vachon, M.L.S. (1987). *Occupational stress in the care of the critically ill, the dying, and the bereaved.* Washington, DC: Hemisphere.

Vachon, M.L.S. (1997). Recent research into staff stress in palliative care. *European Journal of Palliative Care, 4,* 99–103.

Vachon, M.L.S. (2007). Caring for the professional caregivers: Before and after the death. In K. J. Doka (Ed.), *Living with grief: Before and after a death* (pp. 311–330). Washington, DC: Hospice Foundation of America.

Valdiserri, R. O. (Ed.). (2002). *Dawning answers: How the HIV/AIDS epidemic has helped to strengthen public health.* New York: Oxford University Press.

Valente, S. M., & Saunders, J. M. (1987). High school suicide prevention programs. *Pediatric Nursing, 13*(2), 108–112, 137.

Valente, S. M., & Sellers, J. R. (1986). Helping adolescent survivors of suicide. In C. A. Corr & J. N. McNeil (Eds.), *Adolescence and death* (pp. 167–182). New York: Springer.

Valentine, L. (1996). Professional interventions to assist adolescents who are coping with death and bereavement. In C. A. Corr & D. E. Balk (Eds.), *Handbook of adolescent death and bereavement* (pp. 312–328). New York: Springer.

Van der Heide, T., Onwuteaka-Philipsen, B. D., Rurup, M. L., Buiting, H. M., van Delden, J.J.M., Hanssen-de Wolf, J. E., Janssen, A.G.J.M., Pasman, H.R.W., Rietjens, J.A.C., Prins, C.J.M., Deerenberg, I. M., Gevers, J.K.M., van der Maas, P. J., and van der Wal, G. (2007). End-of-life practices in the Netherlands under the Euthanasia Act. *New England Journal of Medicine, 356,* 1957–1965.

Van der Maas, P. J., Van der Wal, G., Haverkate, I., de Graaff, C.L.M., Kester, J.G.C., Onwuteaka-Philipsen, B. D., et al. (1996). Euthanasia, physician-assisted suicide, and other medical practices involving the end of life in the Netherlands, 1990–1995. *New England Journal of Medicine, 335,* 1699–1705.

Van der Wal, G., Van der Maas, P. J., Bosma, J. M., Onwuteaka-Philipsen, B. D., Willems, D. L., Haverkate, I., et al. (1996). Evaluation of the notification procedure for physician-assisted death in the Netherlands. *New England Journal of Medicine, 335,* 1706–1711.

Van der Zee, J., Dodson, O., & Billops, C. (1978). *The Harlem book of the dead.* Dobbs Ferry, NY: Morgan & Morgan.

Van Dongen, C. J. (1990). Agonizing questioning: Experiences of survivors of suicide victims. *Nursing Research, 39,* 224–229.

Van Dongen, C. J. (1991). Experiences of family members after a suicide. *Journal of Family Practice, 33,* 375–380.

Van Gennep, A. (1961). *The rites of passage* (M. B. Vizedom & G. L. Caffee, Trans.). Chicago: University of Chicago Press.

Van Lommel, P., van Wees, R., Meyers, V., & Elfferich, I. (2001). Near-death experience in survivors of cardiac arrest: A prospective study in the Netherlands. *The Lancet, 358,* 2039–2045.

Van Riper, M. (1997). Death of a sibling: Five sisters, five stories. *Pediatric Nursing, 23,* 587–593.

Van Winkle, N. W., & May, P. A. (1986). Native American suicide in New Mexico, 1957–1979: A comparative study. *Human Organization, 45,* 296–309.

Veatch, R. M. (1975). The whole-brain-oriented concept of death: An outmoded philosophical formulation. *Journal of Thanatology, 3*(1), 13–30.

Veatch, R. M. (1976). *Death, dying, and the biological revolution: Our last quest for responsibility.* New Haven, CT: Yale University Press.

Veatch, R. M. (2002). *Transplantation ethics.* Washington, DC: Georgetown University Press.

Veninga, R. (1985). *A gift of hope: How we survive our tragedies.* New York: Ballantine Books.

Vernick, J., & Karon, M. (1965). Who's afraid of death on a leukemia ward? *American Journal of Diseases of Children, 109,* 393–397.

Verwoerdt, A. (1976). *Clinical geropsychiatry.* Baltimore: Williams & Wilkins.

Verwoerdt, A., Pfeiffer, E., & Wang, H. S. (1969). Sexual behavior in senescence. *Geriatrics, 24,* 137–154.

Victoria Hospice Society, Cairns, M., Thompson, M., & Wainwright, W. (2003). *Transitions in dying and bereavement: A psychosocial guide for hospice and palliative care.* Baltimore: Health Professions Press.

Viorst, J. (1986). *Necessary losses.* New York: Simon & Schuster.

Volberding, P. A., & Aberg, J. A. (Eds.). (1999). *The San Francisco General Hospital handbook of HIV management: A guide to the practical management of HIV-infected patients.* Boca Raton, FL: CRC Press-Parthenon Publications.

Volkan, V. (1970). Typical findings in pathological grief. *Psychiatric Quarterly, 44,* 231–250.

Volkan, V. (1985). Complicated mourning. *Annual of Psychoanalysis, 12,* 323–248.

Voyich, J. M., Braughton, K. R., Sturdevant, D. E., Whitney, A. R., Saïd-Salim, B., Porcella, S. F., Long, R. D., Dorward, D. W., Gardner, D. J., Kreiswirth, B. N., Musser, J. M., & DeLeo, F. R. (2005). Insights into mechanisms used by *Staphylococcus aureus* to avoid destruction by human neutrophils. *The Journal of Immunology, 175*(6), 3907–3919.

Waechter, E. H. (1971). Children's awareness of fatal illness. *American Journal of Nursing, 71,* 1168–1172.

Waechter, E. H. (1984). Dying children: Patterns of coping. In H. Wass & C. A. Corr (Eds.), *Childhood and death* (pp. 51–68). Washington, DC: Hemisphere.

Wagner, S. (1994). *The Andrew poems.* Lubbock: Texas Tech University Press.

Waldrop, D. P., Tamburlin, J. A., Thompson, S J., & Simon, M. (2004). Life and death decisions: Using school-based health education to facilitate family discussion about organ and tissue donation. *Death Studies, 28,* 643–657.

Walker, A. C., & Balk, D. E. (2007). Bereavement rituals in the Muscogee Creek tribe. *Death Studies, 31,* 633–652.

Walker, J. S. (2004). *Three Mile Island: A nuclear crisis in historical perspective.* Berkeley: University of California Press.

Wall, P. (2002). *Pain: The science of suffering.* New York: Columbia University Press.

Wall, P. D., & Melzack, R. (Eds.). (1994). *Textbook of pain* (3rd ed.). New York: Churchill Livingstone.

Wallace, S. E. (1973). *After suicide.* New York: Wiley-Interscience.

Wallis, C. L. (1954). *Stories on stone: A book of American epitaphs.* New York: Oxford University Press.

Wallis, V. (2004). *Two old women: An Alaska legend of betrayal, courage and survival.* New York: Perennial/HarperCollins.

Walsh, F., & McGoldrick, M. (1988). Loss and the family life cycle. In C. J. Falicov (Ed.), *Family transitions: Continuity and change over the life cycle* (pp. 311–336). New York: Guilford.

Walsh, F., & McGoldrick, M. (Eds.). (2004a). *Living beyond loss: Death in the family* (2nd ed.). New York: Norton.

Walsh, F., & McGoldrick, M. (2004b). Loss and the family: A systemic perspective. In F. Walsh & M. McGoldrick (Eds.), *Living beyond loss: Death in the family* (2nd ed.; pp. 3–26). New York: Norton.

Walter, C. A. (2003). *The loss of a life partner: Narratives of the bereaved.* New York: Columbia University Press.

Walter, T. (1999). *On bereavement: The culture of grief.* Buckingham, England: Open University Press.

Walton, D. N. (1979). *On defining death: An analytic study of the concept of death in philosophy and medical ethics.* Montreal, Quebec, Canada: McGill-Queen's University Press.

Walton, D. N. (1982). Neocortical versus wholebrain conceptions of personal death. *Omega, Journal of Death and Dying, 12,* 339–344.

Ward, L. (2003). Race as a variable in cross cultural research. *Nursing Outlook, 51,* 120–125.

Wass, H. (1984). Concepts of death: A developmental perspective. In H. Wass & C. A. Corr (Eds.), *Childhood and death* (pp. 3–24). Washington, DC: Hemisphere.

Wass, H. (2003). Children and media violence. In R. Kastenbaum (Ed.), *Macmillan encyclopedia of death and dying* (Vol. 1, pp. 133–139). New York: Macmillan.

Wass, H. (2004). A perspective on the current state of death education. *Death Studies, 28,* 289–308.

Wass, H., & Cason, L. (1984). Fears and anxieties about death. In H. Wass & C. A. Corr (Eds.), *Childhood and death* (pp. 25–45). Washington, DC: Hemisphere.

Wass, H., & Corr, C. A. (Eds.). (1984). *Childhood and death.* Washington, DC: Hemisphere.

Wasserman, H., & Danforth, H. E. (1988). *The human bond: Support groups and mutual aid.* New York: Springer.

Wasserman, J., Clair, J. M., & Ritchey, F. J. (2006). Racial differences in attitudes toward euthanasia. *Omega, Journal of Death and Dying, 52,* 263–287.

Waters, C. M. (2001). Understanding and supporting African Americans' perspectives of end-of-life care planning and decision making. *Qualitative Health Research, 11*(3), 385–398.

Watson, M., Lucas, C., Hoy, A., & Back, I. (Eds.). (2005). *The Oxford handbook of palliative care.* New York: Oxford University Press.

Waugh, E. (1948). *The loved one.* Boston: Little, Brown.

Weaver, R. R., & Rivello, R. (2007). The distribution of mortality in the United States: The effects of income (inequality), social capital, and race. *Omega, Journal of Death and Dying, 54,* 19–39.

Webb, J. P., & Willard, W. (1975). Six American Indian patterns of suicide. In N. L. Farberow (Ed.), *Suicide in different cultures* (pp. 17–33). Baltimore: University Park Press.

Webb, M. (1997). *The good death: The new American search to reshape the end of life.* New York: Bantam.

Webb, N. B. (Ed.). (1999). *Play therapy with children in crisis: Individual, group, and family treatment* (2nd ed.). New York: Guilford.

Webb, N. B. (Ed.). (2002). *Helping bereaved children: A handbook for practitioners* (2nd ed.). New York: Guilford.

Webb, N. B. (Ed.). (2004). *Mass trauma and violence: Helping families and children cope.* New York: Guilford.

Webster, B. D. (1989). *All of a piece: A life with multiple sclerosis.* Baltimore: Johns Hopkins University Press.

Wechsler, H., Davenport, A., Dowdall, G., Moeykens, B., & Castillo, S. (1994). Health and behavioral consequences of binge drinking in college: A national survey of students at 140 campuses. *Journal of the American Medical Association, 272,* 1672–1677.

Weeks, O. D. (2001). Ritualistic downsizing and the need for aftercare. In O. D. Weeks & C. Johnson (Eds.), *When all the friends have gone: A guide for aftercare providers* (pp. 187–197). Amityville, NY: Baywood.

Weeks, O. D., & Johnson, C. (Eds.). (2001). *When all the friends have gone: A guide for aftercare providers.* Amityville, NY: Baywood.

Weese-Mayer, D. E. (2006). Sudden infant death syndrome: Is serotonin the key factor? *Journal of the American Medical Association, 296,* 2143–2144.

Wehrle, P. F., & Top, F. H. (1981). *Communicable and infectious diseases* (9th ed.). St. Louis, MO: Mosby.

Weinberg, J. (1969). Sexual expression in late life. *American Journal of Psychiatry, 126,* 713–716.

Weiner, I. B. (1985). Clinical contributions to the developmental psychology of adolescence. *Genetic, Social, and General Psychology Monographs, 111*(2), 195–203.

Weir, R. F. (Ed.). (1980). *Death in literature.* New York: Columbia University Press.

Weir, R. F. (Ed.). (1997). *Physician-assisted suicide.* Bloomington: Indiana University Press.

Weisman, A. D. (1972). *On dying and denying: A psychiatric study of terminality.* New York: Behavioral Publications.

Weisman, A. D. (1977). The psychiatrist and the inexorable. In H. Feifel (Ed.), *New meanings of death* (pp. 107–122). New York: McGraw-Hill.

Weisman, A. D. (1984). *The coping capacity: On the nature of being mortal.* New York: Human Sciences Press.

Weisman, M.-L. (1982). *Intensive care: A family love story.* New York: Random House.

Weizman, S. G. (2005). *About mourning: Support and guidance for the bereaved.* Beachwood, OH: Sunrise Publications.

Welch, K. J., & Bergen, M. B. (2000). Adolescent parent mourning reactions associated with stillbirth or neonatal death. *Omega, Journal of Death and Dying, 40,* 435–451.

Weller, E. B., Weller, R. A., Fristad, M. A., Cain, S. E., & Bowes, J. M. (1988). Should children attend their parent's funeral? *Journal of the American Academy of Child and Adolescent Psychiatry, 27,* 559–562.

Wender, P., Ketu, S., Rosenthal, D., Schulsinger, F., Ortmann, J., & Lunde, I. (1986). Psychiatric disorders in the biological and adoptive families of adopted individuals with affective disorders. *Archives of General Psychiatry, 43,* 923–929.

Wendler, D., & Dickert, N. (2001). The consent process for cadaveric organ procurement: How does it work? How can it be improved? *Journal of the American Medical Association, 285,* 329–333.

Wentworth, H., & Flexner, S. B. (Eds.). (1967). *Dictionary of American slang* (with supplement). New York: Crowell.

Wertenbaker, L. T. (1957). *Death of a man.* New York: Random House.

Werth, J. L. (1996). *Rational suicide: Implications for mental health professionals.* Washington, DC: Taylor & Francis.

Werth, J. L. (1999a). The role of the mental health professional in helping significant others of persons who are assisted in death. *Death Studies, 23,* 239–255.

Werth, J. L. (Ed.). (1999b). *Contemporary perspectives on rational suicide.* Philadelphia: Taylor & Francis.

Werth, J. L. (2001). Using the Youk-Kevorkian case to teach about euthanasia and other end-of-life issues. *Death Studies, 25,* 151–177.

Werth, J. L. (Ed.). (2006). Implications of the Theresa Schiavo case and end-of-life decisions [Special issue]. *Death Studies, 30*(2).

Werth, J. L., & Blevins, D. (Eds.). (2006). *Psychosocial issues near the end of life: A resource for professional care providers.* Washington, DC: American Psychological Association.

Werth, J. L., & Wineberg, H. (2005). A critical analysis of criticisms of the Oregon Death with Dignity Act. *Death Studies, 29,* 1–27.

Weseen, M. H. (1934). *A dictionary of American slang.* New York: Crowell.

Westberg, G. (1971). *Good grief.* Philadelphia: Fortress Press.

Westefeld, J. S., Button, C., Haley, J. T., Kettmann, J. J., Macconnell, J., Sandil, R., & Tallman, B. (2006). College student suicide: A call to action. *Death Studies, 30,* 931–956.

Westerhoff, J. H. (1978). *McGuffey and his readers: Piety, morality, and education in nineteenth-century America.* Nashville, TN: Abingdon.

Westphal, M. (1984). *God, guilt, and death.* Bloomington: Indiana University Press.

Wheeler, I. (2001). Parental bereavement: The crisis of meaning. *Death Studies, 25,* 51–66.

Wheeler, M. S., & Cheung, A.H.S. (1996). Minority attitudes toward organ donation. *Critical Care Nurse, 16,* 30–35.

White, E. B. (1952). *Charlotte's web.* New York: Harper.

White, P. G. (2006). *Sibling grief: Healing after the death of a sister or brother.* Lincoln, NE: iUniverse.

White, R. B., & Engelhardt, H. T. (1975). A demand to die. *Hastings Center Report, 5*(3), 9–10, 47.

White, R., & Cuningham, A. M. (1991). *Ryan White: My own story.* New York: Dial Press.

Whitfield, J. M., Siegel, R. E., Glicken, A. D., Harmon, R. J., Powers, L. K., & Goldson, E. J. (1982). The application of hospice concepts to neonatal care. *American Journal of Diseases of Children, 136,* 421–424.

Whitney, S. (1991). *Waving goodbye: An activities manual for children in grief.* Portland, OR: The Dougy Center.

Wiener, L. S., Best, A., & Pizzo, P. A. (Comps.). (1994). *Be a friend: Children who live with HIV speak.* Morton Grove, IL: Albert Whitman.

Wiesel, E. (1960). *Night* (S. Rodway, Trans.). New York: Avon.

Wilcoxon, S. A. (1986). Grandparents and grandchildren: An often neglected relationship between significant others. *Journal of Counseling and Development, 65,* 289–290.

Wilder, T. (1986). *The bridge of San Luis Rey.* New York: Harper & Row. (Original work published 1927)

Wilhelm, H. (1985). *I'll always love you.* New York: Crown.

Wilkes, E., Crowther, A.G.O., & Greaves, C.W.K.H. (1978). A different kind of day hospital—For patients with preterminal cancer and chronic disease. *British Medical Journal, 2,* 1053–1056.

Wilkes, E., et al. (1980). *Report of the working group on terminal care of the standing subcommittee on cancer.* London: Her Majesty's Stationery Office.

Willans, J. H. (1980). Nutrition: Appetite in the terminally ill patient. *Nursing Times, 76,* 875–876.

Williams, P. G. (1991). *The living will and the durable power of attorney for health care book, with forms* (Rev. ed.). Oak Park, IL: P. Gaines.

Willinger, M. (1995). Sleep position and sudden infant death syndrome [Editorial]. *Journal of the American Medical Association, 273,* 818–819.

Willinger, M., James, L. S., & Catz, D. (1991). Defining the sudden infant death syndrome (SIDS): Deliberations of an expert panel convened by the National Institute of Child Health and Human Development. *Pediatric Pathology, 11,* 677–684.

Wilshire, S. F. (1994). *Seasons of grief and grace: A sister's story of AIDS.* Nashville, TN: Vanderbilt University Press.

Wineberg, H., & Werth, J. L. (2003). Physician-assisted suicide in Oregon: What are the key factors? *Death Studies, 27,* 501–518.

Wolfe, J., Grier, H. E., Klar, N., Levin, S. B., Ellenbogen, J. M., Salem-Schatz, E., et al. (2000a). Symptoms and suffering at the end of life in children with cancer. *New England Journal of Medicine, 342,* 326–333.

Wolfe, J., Klar, N., Grier, H. E., Duncan, J., Salem-Schatz, S., Emanuel, E. J., et al. (2000b). Understanding of prognosis among parents of children who died of cancer: Impact on treatment goals and integration of palliative care. *Journal of the American Medical Association, 284,* 2469–2475.

Wolfe, T. (1940). *You can't go home again.* New York: Harper & Brothers.

Wolfelt, A. (1996). *Healing the bereaved child: Grief gardening, growth through grief and other touchstones for caregivers.* Fort Collins, CO: Companion Press.

Wolfelt, A. (2004a). *The understanding your grief support group guide: Starting and leading a bereavement support group.* Fort Collins, CO: Companion Press.

Wolfelt, A. (2004b). *When your pet dies: A guide to mourning, remembering and healing.* Fort Collins, CO: Companion Press.

Wolfelt, A. (2005a). *Companioning the bereaved: A soulful guide for counselors and caregivers.* Fort Collins, CO: Companion Press.

Wolfelt, A. (2005b). *Healing grief at work: 100 practical ideas after your workplace is touched by loss.* Fort Collins, CO: Companion Press.

Wolfelt, A., & Yoder, G. (2005). *Companioning the dying: A soulful guide for counselors and caregivers.* Fort Collins, CO: Companion Press.

Wolfenstein, M. (1966). How is mourning possible? *Psychoanalytic Study of the Child, 21,* 93–123.

Wolfenstein, M., & Kliman, G. (Eds.). (1965). *Children and the death of a president.* Garden City, NY: Doubleday.

Woodson, R. (1976). The concept of hospice care in terminal disease. In J. M. Vaeth (Ed.), *Breast cancer* (pp. 161–179). Basel, Switzerland: Karger.

Woodward, K. (1986). Reminiscence and the life review: Prospects and retrospects. In T. R. Cole & S. A. Gadow (Eds.), *What does it mean to grow old? Reflections from the humanities* (pp. 135–161). Durham, NC: Duke University Press.

Wooten, J. T. (2004). *We are all the same: A story of a boy's courage and a mother's love.* New York: Penguin.

Wooten-Green, R. (2001). *When the dying speak: How to listen to and learn from those facing death.* Chicago: Loyola Press.

Worden, J. W. (1982). *Grief counseling and grief therapy: A handbook for the mental health practitioner.* New York: Springer.

Worden, J. W. (1996). *Children and grief: When a parent dies.* New York: Guilford.

Worden, J. W. (2002). *Grief counseling and grief therapy: A handbook for the mental health practitioner* (3rd ed.). New York: Springer.

World Health Organization (WHO). (1990). *Cancer pain relief and palliative care.* WHO Technical Report Series 804. Geneva, Switzerland: Author.

World Health Organization (WHO). (1998). *Cancer pain relief and palliative care in children.* Geneva, Switzerland: Author.

Worswick, J. (2000). *A house called Helen: The development of hospice care for children* (2nd ed.). New York: Oxford University Press.

Wortman, C. B., & Silver, R. C. (1989). The myth of coping with loss. *Journal of Clinical Consulting Psychology, 57,* 349–357.

Wortman, C. B., & Silver, R. C. (2001). The myths of coping with loss revisited. In M. S. Stroebe, R. O. Hansson, W. Stroebe, & H. Schut (Eds.), *Handbook of bereavement research: Consequences, coping, and care* (pp. 405–429). Washington, DC: American Psychological Association.

Wray, T. J. (2003). *Surviving the death of a sibling: Living through grief when an adult brother or sister dies.* New York: Three Rivers Press.

Wright, L. (2006). *The looming tower: Al-Qaeda and the road to 9/11.* New York: Knopf.

Wright, R. H., & Hughes, W. B. (1996). *Lay down body: Living history in African-American cemeteries.* Detroit: Visible Ink Press.

Wrobel, T. A., & Dye, A. L. (2003). Grieving pet death: Normative, gender, and attachment issues. *Omega, Journal of Death and Dying, 47,* 385–393.

Wrobleski, A. (1984). The suicide survivors grief group. *Omega, Journal of Death and Dying, 15,* 173–183.

Wyler, J. (1989). Grieving alone: A single mother's loss. *Issues in Comprehensive Pediatric Nursing, 12,* 299–302.

Wyschogrod, E., & Caputo, J. D. (1998). Postmodernism and the desire for God: An Email exchange. *Cross Currents, 48*(3), 293–310.

Yalom, I. D. (1995). *The theory and practice of group psychotherapy* (4th ed.). New York: Basic Books.

Yalom, I. D., & Vinogradov, S. (1988). Bereavement groups: Techniques and themes. *International Journal of Group Psychotherapy, 38,* 419–446.

Yaukey, D., & Anderton, D. L. (2001). *Demography: The study of human population* (2nd ed.). Long Grove, IL: Waveland Press.

Yeung, W. (1995). Buddhism, death, and dying. In J. K. Parry & A. S. Ryan (Eds.), *A cross-cultural look at death, dying, and religion* (pp. 74–83). Chicago: Nelson-Hall.

Yin, P., & Shine, M. (1985). Misinterpretations of increases in life expectancy in gerontology textbooks. *The Gerontologist, 25,* 78–82.

Young, B., Dixon-Woods, M., Windridge, K. C., & Heney, D. (1999). Partnership with children. *British Medical Journal, 319,* 778–780.

Young, B., Dixon-Woods, M., Windridge, K. C., & Heney, D. (2003). Managing communication with young people who have a potentially life threatening chronic illness: A qualitative study of patients and parents. *British Medical Journal, 326,* 305.

Youngner, S. J., Anderson, M. W., & Schapiro, R. (Eds.). (2005). *Transplanting human tissue: Ethics, policy, and practice.* New York: Oxford University Press.

Yufit, R. I., & Lester, D. (2005). *Assessment, treatment and prevention of suicidal behavior.* Hoboken, NJ: John Wiley & Sons.

Zaheer, K. (2007, January 8). Future flu pandemic could be "very scary." U. S. Reuters Health Information. Available at: http://www.nlm.nih.gov/medlineplus/news/fullstory_43531.html.

Zambelli, G. C., & DeRosa, A. P. (1992). Bereavement support groups for school-age children: Theory, intervention, and case example. *American Journal of Orthopsychiatry, 62,* 484–493.

Zamperetti, N., Bellomo, R., & Ronco, C. (2003). Defining death in non-heart beating organ donors. *Journal of Medical Ethics, 29*(3), 182–185.

Zanger, J. (1980, February). Mount Auburn Cemetery: The silent suburb. *Landscape,* 23–28.

Zeitlin, S. J., & Harlow, I. B. (2001). *Giving a voice to sorrow: Personal responses to death and mourning.* New York: Perigee (Penguin).

Zerwekh, J. V. (1983). The dehydration question. *Nursing 83, 13,* 47–51.

Zerwekh, J. V. (1994). The truth-tellers: How hospice nurses help patients confront death. *American Journal of Nursing, 94,* 31–34.

Zerzan, J., Stearns, S., & Hanson, L. (2000). Access to palliative care and hospice in nursing homes. *Journal of the American Medical Association, 284,* 2489–2494.

Zielinski, J. M. (1975). *The Amish: A pioneer heritage.* Des Moines, IA: Wallace-Homestead.

Zielinski, J. M. (1993). *The Amish across America* (Rev. ed.). Kalona, IA: Amish Heritage Publications.

Zimmerman, J. (2005). *From the heart of a bear: True stories of the faith and courage of children facing life-threatening illness.* Des Moines, IA: Lazarus Publishing.

Zinner, E. S. (Ed.). (1985). *Coping with death on campus.* San Francisco: Jossey-Bass.

Zinner, E. S., & Williams, M. B. (1999). *When a community weeps: Case studies in group survivorship.* Philadelphia: Brunner/Mazel.

Zipes, J. (1983). *The trials and tribulations of Little Red Riding Hood: Versions of the tale in sociocultural context.* South Hadley, MA: Bergin & Garvey.

Zisook, S., & DeVaul, R. A. (1983). Grief, unresolved grief, and depression. *Psychosomatics, 24,* 247–256.

Zisook, S., & DeVaul, R. A. (1984). Measuring acute grief. *Psychiatric Medicine, 2,* 169–176.

Zisook, S., & DeVaul, R. A. (1985). Unresolved grief. *American Journal of Psychoanalysis, 45,* 370–379.

Zlatin, D. M. (1995). Life themes: A method to understand terminal illness. *Omega, Journal of Death and Dying, 31,* 189–206.

Zorza, V., & Zorza, R. (1980). *A way to die.* New York: Knopf.

Zucker, A. (2007). Ethical and legal issues and end-of-life decision making. In D. E. Balk C. Wogrin, G. Thornton, & D. Meagher. (Eds.), *ADEC handbook of thanatology* (pp. 103–112). Northbrook, IL: Association for Death Education and Counseling.

Zulli, A. P. (2001). The aftercare workers and support group facilitation. In O. D. Weeks & C. Johnson (Eds.), *When all the friends have gone: A guide for aftercare providers* (pp. 199–213). Amityville, NY: Baywood.

Name Index

Hyland, L., 291
Hymes, K. B., 576

Iliffe, J., 583, 608
Ilse, S., 424
Imber-Black, E., 240
Infectious Diseases Society of America, 597
Infeld, D. L., 200
Ingles, T., 155
Ingpen, R., 348, 616
Ingram, D. A., 79
Inhelder, B., 332, 374
The Initiative for Pediatric Palliative Care, 199, 207, 361
Institute of Medicine, 40, 109
International Association for Near-Death Studies, 570
International Association for Suicide Prevention (IASP), 520
International Association of Pet Cemeteries and Crematories, 260, 278, 290
International Cemetery and Funeral Association, 290
International Institute for the Advancement of Medicine, 468
International Order of the Golden Rule, 290
International Work Group on Death, Dying, and Bereavement, 173, 338, 542
Irion, P. E., 291
Irish, D. P., 125
Irwin, A., 608
Isenberg, N., 60
Iserson, K. V., 71, 285, 286, 292, 314, 460, 464, 469, 489
Iserson, K. Y., 71
Iverson, B. A., 468
Iwashyna, T., 105, 109, 186
Iyasu, S., 118

Jackson, C. O., 60
Jackson, D. A., 126
Jackson, E. N., 296, 381
Jackson, I., 205
Jackson, J., 509, 589
Jackson, M., 112
Jackson, S., 479
Jacobs, D. G., 519
Jacobs, L. G., 202
Jacobs, S., 247
Jacoby, L. H., 479
Jacques, E., 406
Jaffe, C., 205
Jakub, D., 424
Jamison, K. R., 495, 503, 515, 519
Jamison, S., 550
JanMohamed, A. B., 125
Janoff-Bulman, R., 243–244
Janzen, L., 415
Jeffers, S. L., 277
Jenkins, P., 74
Jenkins, S., 135, 412
Jenner, E., 37
Jennings, B., 144, 200, 550

Jesse, G., 205
Jesus, 220, 539
Jewett, C. L., 354
Jewish Funeral Directors of America, 290
Job, 253
Jobes, A. A., 510, 519
Jobes, D., 387
Johanson, S. M., 490
John Paul II, Pope, 532
Johns, E., 3, 5, 8
Johnson, "Magic." *See* Johnson, E.
Johnson, C., 302–303, 315
Johnson, C. J., 555, 569
Johnson, E., 607
Johnson, J., 348, 349, 350, 360, 391, 413, 615, 616, 622, 623, 635, 637
Johnson, M., 88, 615, 623
Johnson, S., 132, 414, 424
Joiner, T., 519
Jonah, B. A., 374
Jones, B., 54–55
Jones, C., 607
Jones, E. O., 4
Jones, J. H., 111
Jones, S., 302
Jonker, G., 56
Jordan, C., 484, 490
Jordan, J., 509
Jordan, J. R., 222, 270, 370, 384, 506
Jordan, M. K., 615
Joseph, J., 436
Joslin, D., 597
Joslin, M., 615
Joyner, A., 419, 421
Joyner, F. G. (FloJo), 419, 421, 422
Joyner, M., 421
Joyner-Kersee, J., 421
Jozefowski, J. T., 227
Jukes, M., 391, 633
Jung, C. G., 317
Jupp, P. C., 287, 314
Jurich, A. P., 387
Jury, D., 135, 412
Jury, M., 135, 412

Kabcenell, A., 205
Kadono, E., 623
Kail, R. V., 317, 364
Kaimann, D. S., 411
Kalergis, M. M., 365, 395
Kalipeni, E., 583, 608
Kalish, R. A., xxi, xxviii, xxx, 1, 14, 103, 107, 110, 112, 114, 115, 125, 136, 291, 437
Kane, B., 330
Kantrowitz, M., 615
Kaplan, K. J., 535
Kapust, L. R., 442
Karakatsanis, K. G., 461
Karon, M., 336
Karp, N., 441
Kaserman, D. L., 490
Kassis, H., 56

Kastenbaum, R., 5, 15, 56, 64–65, 68–69, 84, 127, 139, 149–150, 200, 243, 260, 300, 301, 318, 321, 332, 333–334, 345, 436, 441, 448, 566
Katz, J., 125
Katzenbach, J., 345
Kaufert, J. M., 120
Kauffman, J., 244, 258, 569
Kaufman, K. R., 259
Kaufman, N. D., 259
Kaufman, S. R., 188, 206, 429, 437, 440
Kaufmann, S., 111
Kavanaugh, R. E., 223
Kay, W. J., 446
Kean, T. H., 68
Keating, D., 374
Keckler, B., 615
Keister, D., 302, 315
Kellaher, L., 315
Kellehear, A., 569
Kelley, P., 171, 178
Kelly, E. W., 565, 566
Kelly, O., 13, 86, 135
Kelsay, J., 540
Kemp, C., 159, 178
Keneally, T., 93
Kennedy, C., 530
Kennedy, E. (Senator), 90
Kennedy Institute of Ethics, Georgetown University, 551
Kennedy, J. B., 257
Kennedy, J. F. (President), 90, 257, 299
Kenneth, C., 205
Kenyon, B. L., 332
Keough, P., 349, 623
Keown, D., 517, 541
Kephart, W. M., 285, 292
Kerbel, M. R., 88
Kessler, D., 40, 133, 139
Kessler, R. C., 501
Kestenbaum, B., 114
Kevorkian, J., xxv, 527–529, 530, 535
King, A., 116, 144
King's University College Centre for Education about Death and Bereavement, 15
Kingsley, E. P., 410
Kirk, P., 414
Kirk, W. G., 387
Kissane, D.W., 240
Kitagawa, E. M., 22
Kivnick, H., 449
Klagsbrun, F., 395, 637
Klass, D., 138, 146, 147, 231, 250, 309, 312, 360, 414, 415, 424, 569
Klebold, D., 73
Klein, D., 484, 490
Klein, L., 349, 623
Klein, P. S., 455, 490
Klein, R., 109
Kleinman, J. C., 383, 385

Klevins, R. M., 30
Klicker, R. L., 357, 360
Kliever, L. D., 536
Kliman, G., 299
Kline, C. B., 425
Klitzman, R, 608
Klug, C., 479
Knapp, R. J., 412, 414
Kochanek, K. D., 20, 326
Koenig, B. A., 112
Koerner, Dr. & Mrs. S., 10–11
Kohn, I., 412, 424
Kohn, J. B., 421, 447
Kohn, W. K., 421, 447
Kolehmainen, J., 637
Komro, K. A., 385
Koocher, G. P., 330, 334, 339, 379
Koop, C. E., 590, 608
Koppelman, K. L., 411
Kotzwinkle, W., 411
Kozak, L. J., 202
Kozol, J., 327
Kramer, B. J., 211
Krasny, L., 347, 616
Kraus, F., 360
Kraybill, D. B., 45, 60, 334
Kreicbergs, U., 346
Krementz, J., 395, 623
Krieger, N., 608
Krisher, T., 624
Krishna, 562
Krizek, B., 273
Krugman, P., 88
Krumholz, H. M., 183
Kübler-Ross, E., 5, 91, 137–140, 150–151, 178, 221, 351, 565
Kuhl, D., 178
Kulka, E., 80
Kunitz, S. J., 500
Kurent, J. E., 205
Kurtz, D. C., 125
Kurtz, N. R., 190–191
Kushner, H. S., 235, 267, 276
Kushner, H. W., 93
Kutscher, A. H., 569

Labyak, M. J., 185
Lack, S. A., 158, 197
Laderman, G., 314
Ladwig, T., 616
Lafser, C., 412, 424
Lagoni, L., 261, 347, 354, 446
LaGrand, L. E., 173, 232, 371, 372
LaMay, C. L., 90
Lamb, J. M., 412
Lamb, M., 408
Lambert, J., 74
Lamberti, J. W., 240
Lambrinidou, Y., 135
Lamers, E. P., 335, 390
Lamers, W. M., 285, 286
Lamm, M., 267, 299
Landalf, H., 624
Landay, D. S., 178
Landry, S., 18, 19
Lang, A., 4, 336
Lang, L. T., 115

Owens, J. E., 565
The Oxford English Dictionary, 48, 85, 188, 201, 212, 213, 321, 364
Oxley, P., 392, 635

Paez, R., xxv, 508
Paik, H., 89
Pain.com (website), 179
Palmer, L., 599, 607
Papadatou, D., 173, 376, 380
Papalia, D. E., 317, 321, 399, 428, 430
Pape, R. A., 77
Parents of Murdered Children (POMC), 94, 305–306, 308, 316
Parents Without Partners, Inc., 308
Park, B., 391, 633
Parker, E. B., 299
Parker, K. C., 328, 332
Parker, M. B., 348, 625
Parkes, C. M., 126, 162, 178, 211, 218, 222–223, 226, 227, 230, 234, 236, 243, 246, 247, 248, 249, 250, 305
Parks, G., 294
Parr, E., 490
Parry, J. K., 125
Parsons, T., 64
Partnership for Parents/Padres Compadres (website), 199, 207
Partridge, E., 86
Pastan, L., 226
Pasteur, L., 37, 189
Paterson, K., 634
Patterson, K., 391
Pattison, E. M., 32, 42, 138, 173, 182
Patz, N., 638
Paul of Tarsus, 555
Pawelczynska, A., 80, 93
Peabody, F. W., 155
Pearce, J. K., 125
Peavy, L., 625
Peck, M. L., 386 395
Pediatric AIDS Foundation. *See* Elizabeth Glaser Pediatric AIDS Foundation
Pellegrino, M. W., 625
Pendleton, E., 395, 638
Pennsylvania Dutch Country Welcome Center, 61
Peppers, L. G., 412, 413
Peretti, P. O., 445
Perkins, L., 371
Perl, E. K., 410
Perls, T. T., 431, 449
Perry, M., 569
Peterkin, A., 625
Peterson, A.C., 364
Peterson, K. E., 608
Peterson, R. L., 484, 490
Petloss.com (website), 278
Peveto, C. A., 111, 125
Pfeffer, C. R., 356, 395
Phipps, W., 58
Piaget, J., 332–333, 373–374
Pietsch, J., 125

Pike, M. M., 305
Piot, P., 583
Piper, F., 81
Pistole, M. C., 380
Pitzer, S., 626
Pizzo, P. A., 609, 636
Planchon, L. A., 260
Plath, S., 493–495, 519
Plato, 10, 553, 557, 558, 560
Platt, A., 28
Platt, M., 536
Player, T. A., 74
Plepys, C., 109
Plopper, B. L., 375
Plourde, L., 349, 626
Podell, C., 370
Poe, E. A., 240–241
Poland, S., 388, 519
Polednak, A. P., 109
Popovic, J. R., 202
Porter, M. Q., 574
Porter, R., 574–575, 595
Positive Education, Inc., 591
Post, S., 550
Potok, C., 634
Pound, L., 85
Poussaint, A. F., 125
Powell, E. S., 349, 626
Powell, F. C., 50
Powell-Griner, E., 109
President's Commission for the Study of Ethical Problems in Medicine and Biomedical and Behavioral Research, 171, 456, 457, 460, 461, 463
Prestine, I. S., 617
Preston, R. J., 122
Preston, S. C., 122
Preston, S. H., 19, 20, 23
Price, D., 490
Prigerson, H. G., 221, 246, 247
Proctor, B. D., 23
Promoting Excellence in End-of-Life Care (website), The Practical Ethics Center at the University of Montana, 207
Prothero, S., 287, 315
Prothrow-Stith, D., 386
Prottas, J., 468
Puckle, B. S., 281
Puff Daddy, 375
Purtillo, R. B., 133
Puttock, S., 347, 617

Quackenbush, J., 446
Quigley, B. Q., 413
Quill, T. E., 178, 201, 545
Quindlen, A., 135
Quine, S., 376, 379
Quinlan, J., 533
Quinlan, K. A., 533

Rabins, P. V., 178, 442
Raddatz, M., 80
Radhakrishnan, S., 561, 562, 563
Radin, P., 125
Raether, H. C., 285, 291

Rahman, F., 516
Rahner, K., 555
Rahula, W., 563
Rajab, M. H., 519
Rampersad, A., 112, 607
Ramsey, P., 461
Randall, F., 205
Rando, T. A., 214, 218, 224, 234, 240–241, 242, 247, 250, 265, 269, 275, 277, 424, 444
Raphael, B., 250, 376, 443
Rappaport, D., 626
Raschka, C., 348, 617, 626
Rauschi, T. M., 135, 442
Rawlings, M. K., 638
Rawls, W., 638
Rawson, H., 85
Ray, C., 587
Ray, L., 587
Reagan, B., 544
Reagan, N., 257
Reagan, R. (President), 257, 299
Reddin, S. K., 413
Reder, P., 301
Reece, R. D., 468
Reed, M. D., 507
Reed, M. L., 444, 450
Reeder-Bey, V., 349, 626
Rees, W. D., 182
Reid, C. L., 266, 282
Reid, J. K., 266, 282
Reimer, J. C., 178
Reitlinger, G., 80, 93
Relf, M., 178
Requarth, J., 356, 507
Reynolds, D. K., 103, 107, 110, 112, 114, 115
Reynolds, F. E., 555, 569
Rhine, C. D., 284
Rhodes, R., 550
Rhodes, R. L., 200
Richardson, L., 74, 78
Richman, J., 449
Richter, E., 391, 634
Rickgarn, R.L.V., 389, 393
Rietjens, J.A.C., 543
Riley, K., 564, 569
Rinpoche, K. L. *See* Ling Rinpoche, K.
Rivello, R., 22
Roach, M., 314, 489
Roberts, B. K., 411
Roberts, C., 419
Roberts, C. C., 47
Roberts, P., 302
Rochlin, G., 335
Rocke, C., 430
Rodger, M. L., 421
Rodgers, L. S., 99, 113
Rodin, J., 440
Rodkinson, M. L., 538
Rodrigue, J. R., 477
Roesel, D., 112
Rofes, E. E., 634
Rollin, B., 515
Romain, T., 626
Romano-Dwyer, L., 350

Romanoff, B. D., 166, 291
Romond, J. L., 340, 634
Roper, J., 627
Ropp, L., 384
Roscoe, L. A., 200, 528
Rosen, E. J., 133, 167, 169, 178
Rosen, H., 341
Rosen, M., 349, 627
Rosenberg, C. E., 188–189, 206
Rosenberg, G., 637
Rosenberg, H. M., 22
Rosenblatt, P. C., 24, 113, 125, 126, 222, 418, 422, 424
Rosenthal, N. R., 390
Rosenthal, T., 135, 141
Rosenwaike, I., 102
Rosner, F., 516, 538
Rosof, B. D., 415, 424
Ross, C. B., 260
Ross, C. P., 388, 389
Ross, E. S., 334
Roth, N. L., 608
Rothman, B. K., 411, 418
Rowland, D. T., 19
Rowling, L., 357
Roy, A., 503
Royal Dutch Medical Association, 542
Rozovsky, F. A., 171, 456
Rubel, B., 389, 396
Rubenstein, W. B., 608
Rubin, D., 301
Ruby, J., 302, 315
Ruccione, K. S., 339
Rudd, M. D., 512, 519
Rudestam, K. E., 509
Rudin, C., 347, 634
Rudman, M. K., 347
Ruffin, P., 621
Ruskin, C., 607
Russell, B. T., 634
Russo, M., 627
Rutherford, J., 302
Ryan, A. S., 125
Ryan, C., 135
Ryan, J., 129–130, 133, 154, 156, 177, 181, 187, 190, 194, 195, 204
Ryan, K. M., 135
Ryan, M., 129–130, 133, 149, 154, 156, 177, 181
Rylant, C., 391, 617, 634
Rynearson, E. K., 242, 259, 445

S.C.D.F. *See* Sacred Congregation for the Doctrine of the Faith
Sable, P., 445
Sabom, M. B., 565, 569
Sabshin, M., 365
Sachar, E., 182
Sacred Congregation for the Doctrine of the Faith (S.C.D.F.), 516, 539
Sageman, M., 77
St. Louis Post-Dispatch, 109, 255, 529
St. Petersburg Times, 67, 68, 80, 528

Subject Index

Alaskan Athabaskan legend, 429
Alaskan Natives, 124. *See also* American Indians and Native Alaskans
Alcoholic beverages, dangers of, 37, 39, 40
Alfred P. Murrah Federal Building. *See* Murrah (Alfred P.) Federal Building (Oklahoma City)
All-inclusiveness (as sub-concept within the concept of death), 330, 359
Almshouses, 188
Altruistic suicide, 504–505, 517. *See also* Suicide, sociological explanations of
Alzheimer's disease. *See* Disease, Alzheimer's
Ambivalence, 387–388, 389, 496, 501, 510, 515, 518
American Indians and Native Alaskans, 97, 117–123, 124
  adolescent death rates, 368
  adolescent deaths, 367
  and AIDS, 579–581
  and alcoholism, 118–119
  attitudes toward death, 119–120
  and automobile accidents, 118–119
  and caring for the dying, 119, 120–121
  causes of death, 118
  child death rates, 325
  child deaths, 322
  and communication issues, 119–120
  death rates, age-adjusted, 102, 118
  death-related practices, 120–123
  deaths, numbers of, 102, 118, 579
  diversity within, 99, 117
  encounters with death, 118–119
  and expressing grief, 122
  and funerals, 122–123
  infant mortality rates, 118
  living with AIDS, 580–581
  middle adult death rates, 402
  middle adult deaths, 401
  and mourning, 121–122
  older adults' death rates, 434
  older adults' deaths, 433
  and post-death rituals, 122–123
  and poverty, 119
  resident U.S. population, 100, 118
  and sudden infant death syndrome (SIDS), 118
  and suicide, 118, 119, 500
  and survivor actions and the postdeath journey, 120
  and trained interpreters, 120–121
  and view of life and death as circular or interwoven, 119, 121
  young adult death rates, 402
  young adult deaths, 401
American Journal of Bioethics (journal), 551
The American Rhythm (book), 445
Americans with Disabilities Act, 596
Amish, 35, 45–47, 48, 57, 58
Amyotrophic lateral sclerosis. *See* Disease, amyotrophic lateral sclerosis
Anabaptist movement, 45
Analgesia/analgesics, 158, 182
Anatomical gifts. *See* Organ and tissue donation
Ancestor worship, 115
The Andrew Poems (book), 224, 415, 416
And the Band Played On (book), 586

And We Were Sad, Remember? (video), 320
Anesthesia, 158
Anger, 134, 161. *See also,* Dying, stages in; Stages, in coping with dying
Animism, 332, 358
Annie and the Old One (children's book), 121
Anniversaries and reactions to loss and bereavement, 236, 273
Anomic suicide, 505, 517. *See* Suicide, sociological explanations of
Anomie, 505
Antibiotics, 28, 38
Antibodies. *See* AIDS; HIV
Anticipatory grief. *See* Grief, anticipatory
Anticipatory mourning. *See* Mourning, anticipatory
Antigone (play), 293
Anxiety, 50. *See also* Death, anxiety; Separation, anxiety
"Arbeit macht frei" ("Work makes one free"), Nazi slogan at Auschwitz, 81
Arguments favoring/opposing suicidal behavior, 517–518. *See also* Suicide, rational
Ariel (book), 494
Ars moriendi (art of dying well), 56, 59
Artificial feeding, 532, 548
Artificialism, 332, 358
Artificial means, 456, 488, 532
"Ashcroft Directive," 546. *See also* "Death with Dignity Act" challenges to/criticisms of
Asian and Pacific Island Americans, 97, 113–117, 124
  adolescent death rates, 368
  adolescent deaths, 367
  and AIDS, 579–581
  and ancestor worship, 115
  attitudes toward death, 114–115
  attitudes toward funerals, 115
  causes of death, 114
  child death rates, 325
  child deaths, 322
  and communication issues, 114–115
  deaths, numbers of, 102, 114
  death rates, age-adjusted, 102, 114
  death-related practices, 115–117
  and decision-making, 115
  diversity within, 99, 114
  encounters with death, 114
  and funeral rituals, 116–117
  and gravesite visits, 117
  infant mortality rates, 114
  living with AIDS, 580
  middle adult death rates, 402
  middle adult deaths, 401
  and mourning customs, 115
  older adults' death rates, 434
  older adults' deaths, 433
  and physician-assisted suicide, 115
  resident U.S. population, 100, 113–114
  and suicide, 500
  young adult death rates, 402
  young adult deaths, 401
As I Lay Dying (book), 35
Assault. *See* Homicide
Assistant Surgeon General of the U.S., 453

Assisted suicide, 10, 11, 512–551. *See also* Suicide; Euthanasia
  defined, 526–527, 549
  distinguished from euthanasia, 526
  legislation and practices in Oregon, 544–547
  moral arguments for and against, 534–537
  by physicians, 527
  practices and legislation in the Netherlands, 542–544
  religious perspectives on, 537–542
  what is intended, 526–530
  who acts, 525
Assumptive world(s), 243–244.
Athabaskan legend, 429
Atman (soul), 561–562, 568
Atomic bombing, 82–83
Attachments, 143, 145–146, 164–165, 210–211, 212, 218, 248
  interpersonal, 143, 145, 164
  with social groups, 143, 146, 165
Attitudes, death-related, 16, 44–61
  in adolescence, 372–376
  and African Americans, 110–112
  and American Indians and Native Alaskans, 119–120
  and Asian or Pacific Island Americans, 114–115
  in childhood, 334–336
  as component of death-related experiences, 16, 44, 49
  defined, 48
  five dominant patterns in the West, 55–56
  and Hispanic Americans, 103–104
  and HIV/AIDS, 586–589
  influence humans can exert over, 54–55
  interactions with encounters, 48, 49
  interactions with practices, 49, 63–64
  in middle adults, 405–407
  in older adults, 436–437
  variation in, 54
  in young adults, 405–407
Auschwitz (Oswiecim), 81–82
Autonomy, 144, 456, 535
Autopsy, 464
  virtual, 7
Average life expectancy, 25–26, 40, 41
Avoidability of death, 330, 332
Awareness contexts, 136–137
Ayurvedic medicine, 540

Babylonian Talmud (Jewish scripture), 538
"Back to Sleep" campaign, 324. *See also,* Sudden Infant Death Syndrome (SIDS)
Bad news, breaking, 171–172
Balkans, 79–80
Barbaro (race horse), xxiv, 259
Bargaining, 138, 225. *See also,* Dying, stages in; Grief, stages of; Stages, in coping with dying
Bariatric surgery, and tissue donation, 466
The Bell Jar (book), 493
Beltway Snipers, 75
Bereaved parents. *See* Adult child, death of; Adults, and death of a child
Bereaved persons
  helping, 262–268, 275–276
  lessons for, 262

and terrorism, 74–78. *See also* Terrorism
traumatic, 242–245, 249
two-sidedness of, 208
unexpected, 242
universality, 330–331, 358, 359
vicarious, 87–89
violent, 218
and war and genocide, 79–80. *See also* War
and genocide
and what will happen to me after, 53
Death announcements, 88
Death-awareness movement, 5
Death Anxiety Handbook, 50
Death certificate, 464, 465. *See also* U.S.
Standard Death Certificate
Death-denying society, 91
Death education, 3, 5, 6–13. *See also*
Education (about death, dying, and
bereavement)
A Death in the Family (book), 350
The Death of Ivan Ilych (novella), 375
Death rates, 19–25, 41
in adolescence, 21, 367–368
and African Americans, 102, 107
and American Indians and Native Alaskans,
102, 118
and Asian and Pacific Island Americans,
102, 114
and Caucasian Americans, 102
in childhood, 21, 324–325, 326
and class or societal differences, 22–23
and gender, 22
and Hispanic Americans, 101–102
and infants, 23–24, 325
among middle adults, 21
and mothers, 24
among older adults, 21
in U.S. (2004), age-adjusted, 19–20
in U.S. (2004), crude or unadjusted, 19, 20
in U.S. (1900 versus 2004), 21
among young adults, 21
Death-related attitudes. *See* Attitudes toward
death
Death-related concerns and responses, 51–54
Death-related encounters. *See* Encounters
with death
Death-related experiences, 16
Death-related language, 86–87, 92
Death-related practices. *See* Practices,
death-related
Death Studies (journal), 61
Death system, 9, 63–67, 92, 602
defined, 64
elements and functions, 65
and natural disasters, 66
and September 11, 2001, 67–69
"Death with Dignity Act" (DWDA) (Oregon
legislation), 544–547, 549 challenges
to/criticisms of, 546
Deaths
in adolescence, 367
in childhood, 322–323, 324–325
combat, 70
and gender, 20–21
among middle adults, 400–403
among older adults, 432, 433
overall numbers in U.S. (2004), 19

preventable, 39
among young adults, 400–403
Deceased donors. *See* Nonliving donors;
Organ and tissue donors
"Declaration on Euthanasia" (statement), 516
Deed (of property), 485
Defense mechanisms, 137, 142
Definition of death, 460–461
Degenerative disease. *See* Disease, degenerative
Dehydration, 159
Delayed grief reactions, 245. *See also* Grief,
complicated
Dementia. *See* Disease, dementia
Demographic statistics, 19
Denial, 138, 140, 225. *See also*, Dying, stages
in; Grief, stages of; Stages, in coping
with dying
Dependence, physical, 159, 176
Depression, 138, 140, 163, 215, 221, 225, 381,
446. *See also*, Dying, stages in; Grief,
and depression; Grief, stages of; Stages,
in coping with dying
Determination of death, 461–463
Development
of attitudes, 334–336, 374–376
cognitive, 328–334, 373–374
eras in human, 318
Developmental conflicts and virtues,
317–318
Developmental perspectives on death-related
subjects, 317–318
"Developmental push," 422
Developmental situation, 11, 218
Developmental tasks
in adolescence, 318, 365–366
in childhood, 318, 320–321, 358
in middle adulthood, 318, 399–400
in older adulthood, 318, 430
in young adulthood, 318, 399–400
*Diagnostic and Statistical Manual of Mental
Disorders* (DSM; book), 243, 247
Diet, 39–40
Dignity, 144
Disability, 442
Disaster, 66, 218, 370
Disaster Mortuary Operational Response
Team (DMORT), 291
Disbelief, 221. *See also* Grief, stages of
Discomfort, being comfortable with one's
own, 1661
Disease
AIDS. *See* AIDS
Alzheimer's, 27, 32, 136, 187, 191, 103, 199,
203, 257, 435, 442, 529
amyotrophic lateral sclerosis (ALS; motor
neuron or "Lou Gehrig's disease"), 32,
199, 203, 442, 528, 529, 545
anthrax, 37
biomedical model of, 37–38
bird flu, 28, 29
cancer, 18, 27, 28, 30–31, 32, 39, 102, 114,
118, 158, 187, 199, 203, 325–326, 337,
369–370, 376, 403, 435, 442, 545
cerebrovascular, 27, 28, 114, 376, 403, 435
cholera, 37
chronic. *See* Disease, degenerative
chronic liver disease and cirrhosis, 118, 403

chronic lower respiratory diseases, 27, 28,
102–103, 376, 403, 435
chronic obstructive pulmonary (COPD).
See Disease, chronic lower respiratory
diseases
communicable, 26, 32, 37, 573
cystic fibrosis, 337, 379
degenerative, 28, 32, 573
dementia, 136, 199, 203, 258
diabetes mellitus, 27, 118, 403, 435, 442
encephalitis, 28, 37
epidemics, 27,29
germ theory of, 189
heart, 27, 28, 40, 102, 114, 118, 187, 199,
203, 326, 369, 376, 403, 435
Human immunodeficiency virus. *See* HIV
influenza and pneumonia, 27, 28, 103, 376
infectious. *See* Disease, communicable
Lou Gehrig's disease. *See* Disease,
amyotrophic lateral sclerosis
lung, 199, 203
malaria, 37
malignant neoplasms. *See* cancer
meningitis, 28
MRSA (methicillin-resistant
Staphylococcus aureus), 30
multiple sclerosis, 32
muscular dystrophy, 32
neoplastic. *See* Cancer
Parkinson's, 32, 442
smallpox, 37
tuberculosis, 28, 29
typhoid, 37
understanding of, 189
Disenfranchised grief and mourning.
See Grief, disenfranchised; Mourning,
disenfranchised
Disenfranchisement, 259, 275
Disintegration, occasioned by death, 296–298
Dislocation of populations, 10
Disorganization and despair, 222, 223. *See also*
Mourning, phases in
Disposition (disposal) of dead bodies,
286–288, 313, 482–483
Disposition of property/estate, 483–486
Distrust of the medical community, 111–112
Divorce, 212
DMORT team. *See* Disaster Mortuary
Operational Response Team
Dombey and Son (book), 415
Donation
of human bodies, 285, 287–288, 466, 468, 487
of human organs. *See* Organ and tissue
donation
of human tissue. *See* Organ and tissue
donation
Donor card. *See* Organ donor card
Donors. *See* Organ and tissue donation
Don't Take My Grief Away from Me (book), 264
Doomsday Clock, 83
The Dougy Center: The National Center for
Grieving Children and Families, 356, 361
Dual process model (of mourning).
See Mourning, processes in
Durable power(s) of attorney in health care
matters, 457–459, 471, 487. *See also*
Advance directives

"The Dutch Termination of Life on Request and Assisted Suicide (Review Procedures) Act," 542, 549
DWDA. *See* "Death with Dignity Act"
Dying, 127–208
  in adolescence, 376–380
  attitudes toward, 51–52, 53
  awareness contexts, 136–137, 150
  in childhood, 336–340
  coping with, 133–134, 137–150
  distinguished from death, 127, 128–129
  fear of, 35
  four dimensions of care, 156–167, 176–177
  how communities can help persons who are coping with, 180–207
  how persons can help persons who are coping with, 153–179
  in middle adulthood, 408–409
  my own, 51
  in older adulthood, 437–441
  persons as living human beings, 127, 128
  phases in coping with, 148–149, 161
  recognizing and responding to the needs of, 181–184
  of someone else, 53–54
  stages in, 137–141, 150
  and suicidal tendencies, 163
  tasks in, 142–149, 150
  trajectories, 32–33, 41, 134, 136, 150
  when begins, 127
  in young adulthood, 407–408

Ecclesiastes (scripture), 555
"Economic Growth and Tax Relief Reconciliation Act," 472
Education (about death dying and bereavement), 2–15 *See also,* Death education
  for adolescents, 390
  for children, 346–349
  for college students, 3
  for the community, 12, 303
  concerns leading to, 5–6
  dimensions of, 8–10, 13–14
  how conducted, 6–8
  lessons about living from, 12–13, 603–604
  formal or planned, 6–7, 14
  goals, 10–11
  about HIV/AIDS, 590, 593, 600
  informal or unplanned, 7–8, 14
  about suicide, 388–389
  and teachable moments, 8, 14
Education and Training Curriculum for Pediatric Palliative Care (book), 199
Ego integrity, 430, 448
Egoistic suicide, 504, 518. *See* Suicide, sociological explanations of
"Either/or" thinking (in suicidal behavior), 506, 518. *See also,* Suicide, psychological explanations of
Electroencephalogram (EEG), 462
Elizabeth Glaser Pediatric AIDS Foundation, 599, 605
Embalming, 285, 313
Emotion, 213
Emotional relocation of the deceased in mourning, 227, 228. *See also* Mourning, tasks in

Empathy, 156, 162, 165
Encephalitis. *See* Disease, encephalitis
Encounters with death, 9, 16, 17–43
  among adolescents, 366–372
  and African Americans, 107–110
  and American Indians and Native Alaskans, 118–119
  and Asian or Pacific Island Americans, 114
  as component of death-related experiences, 16
  in childhood, 321–327
  factors associated with changes in, 36–41, 42
  and Hispanic Americans, 101–103
  interactions with death-related attitudes, 49
  interactions with death-related practices, 49, 63–64
  among middle adults, 400–405
  among older adults, 432–435
  among young adults, 400–405
End-of-life care, 204. *See also* Hospice deficiencies in, 181–184
Enriched remembrance (in mourning), 232, 233, 248
Entertainment programs. *See* Media
Entombment, 286, 313
Epidemic, 10, 27–28, 29
Epitaph, 26, 301
Erikson's model (of human development). *See* Development human
Escheat, 483
Estate taxes. *See* Taxes
Ethical wills, 484
Ethnic cleansing, 79. *See also* War and genocide
Eulogies, 59
Euphemisms, 84–86, 92, 350
Euthanasia, 10, 11, 521–551. *See also* Assisted suicide
  active versus passive, 530–531, 549
  and assisted suicide in Oregon, 544
  defined, 529, 549
  distinguished from homicide, 529
  distinguished from assisted suicide, 526, 545
  and extraordinary/ordinary means, 531–534, 549
  involuntary, 525–526
  moral arguments for and against, 534–537
  of pets, 85, 260
  practices and legislation in the Netherlands, 542–544
  religious perspectives on, 537–541
  voluntary versus nonvoluntary, 525, 549–550
  what is intended, 529–530
  who acts, 525–526
Exaggerated grief reactions, 245. *See also* Grief, complicated
Executor (in probate court proceedings), 483
Exercise, 253–255. *See* Needs of bereaved persons
Extermination camps, 81
Extraordinary or paranormal experiences (in bereavement), 232, 273
Extraordinary means of treatment, 531–534, 549. *See also* Euthanasia, and extraordinary/ordinary means
Facilitating uncomplicated grief. *See* Grief counseling

Fairy tales, 335–336
Family/families, 248
  and African Americans, 110–111
  and changing encounters with death, 38–39, 41. *See also* Encounters with death, factors associated with changes in
  changing nature of, 38–39, 191, 238–240
  coping with dying, 167–169
  developmental life cycle, 239
  and grief/mourning, 238–240
  and Hispanic Americans, 103
  and hospice, 185–186, 187
  systems, 238–239
Famine, 10
A Farewell to Arms (book), 493
Fatalistic suicide, 505, 518. *See* Suicide, sociological explanations of
Fear, 50, 342
Feeding tube, 522–523. *See also* Gastrostomy tube
Feelings. *See* Emotion
Females and death. *See* Gender differences
Feminine grief. *See* Grief and gender; Mourning and gender
Fetal death, 409–410, 412–413, 423
"Final solution," 80
Finality of death, 330, 332
Firearms
  and homicide, 72–73
  misuse, 39–40
  and suicide, 498
First Nation Peoples, 99, 100, 102, 124. *See also* American Indians and Native Alaskans
"Five Wishes," 459, 487. *See also* Advance directives
Fixed end points in bereavement, 233–234. *See also* Mourning, outcomes of
Flight #175 (on September 11, 2001), 68
Florida Supreme Court, 523
Focal theory, 382
Forbidden death. *See* Death, as forbidden
Foregoing an intervention, 530. *See* Euthanasia, active versus passive
Forest Lawn Memorial Park (cemetery), 300, 301
"Forgotten grievers," 444, 448
For Those Who Give and Grieve (book and newsletter), 479
For Whom the Bell Tolls (book), 493
From Illness to Wellness: Life after Transplantation (booklet), 482
Funeral director(s), 35,85. *See also* Funeral services practitioner(s); Disaster Mortuary Operational Response Team (DMORT)
Funeral services personnel/practitioner(s), 85, 284–285
Funerals/funeral services, 35, 313
  and African Americans, 112–113
  and American Indians and Native Alaskans, 122–123
  and Amish, 46
  and Asian and Pacific Island Americans, 116–117
  and children, 355–356
  a happy funeral, 96–97
  and Hispanic Americans, 105–106

Hispanic Americans *(Continued)*
    resident U.S. population, 99–101
    and suicide, 499–500
    and variations in mourning, 106–107
    young adult death rates, 402
    young adult deaths, 401
HIV (Human Immunodeficiency Virus), 28,
        29, 32, 545, 573–609
    and adolescents, 370, 585
    and African Americans, 579–581
    and American Indians and Native Alaskans,
        579–581
    and antibiodies, 577–578
    and Asian and Pacific Island Americans,
        579–581
    and blood or blood products, 577
    in the body, 578
    and Caucasian Americans, 579–580
    as cause of AIDS, 577
    in childhood, 339–340, 577, 580, 583, 585,
        587, 599
    as chronic versus acute disease, 32, 595
    and combination therapies, 590–591, 592,
        595, 605–606
    coping with
        by communities, 599–602
        by individuals, 595–599
        at the national level, 603
    and courage/heroism, 598
    and death-related attitudes, 586–589
    and death-related practices, 590–594
    deaths of persons around the world, 583–584
    deaths of persons in U.S., 579
    decline in numbers of deaths (1995–1997),
        593
    defined, 577, 606
    distinguished from AIDS, 605
    early recognition of, 9, 577
    economic costs, 596
    education, 590
    and exposure category differences, 581
    and funding for care and community
        programs,
    and gender differences, 577, 581, 585
    global impact of, 583–586
    and grief overload, 598. *See also*
        Bereavement overload
    and HAART (Highly Active Antiretroviral
        Therapy), 592, 606. *See also* HIV,
    combination therapies
    and hemophilia/hemophiliacs, 606
    and Hispanic Americans, 579–581
    and hospice, 187, 199, 600
    individuals infected/affected, 595–599
    and injecting drug use, 588
    interventions to fight, 591–593
    and lessons about life and living, 603–604
    and middle adults, 580, 581
    mutation of, 592–593
    number of persons around the world
        infected with, 583–584
    number of persons around the world
        estimated as newly infected (2007),
        583–584
    and older adults, 582
    and opportunistic infections, 578, 592, 597
    positive, 578, 591

and racial and ethnic differences, 581
    resistance to drugs, 592
    resources for information about, 591
    a retrovirus, 578
    side effects of treatment, 592
    stigma, 257, 574–575, 586, 596
    testing for, 577–578
    transmission, 586–588
    and universal precautions, 606
    and viral load, 591, 606
    ways to prevent/reduce risk of infection
        by, 590
    worldwide regional statistics, 584
    and young adults, 403–404, 580, 581
Hive of affect, 141
HIV Plus (magazine), 591
Holistic care, 182, 185
The Holocaust, 80–82, 83, 92
Holographic wills, 484
Holy war. *See* Jihad
Home
    as location of wake or visitation and
        funeral, 35
    as place of dying and death, 34–36
Home care, 204. *See also* Home health care
        programs
    for dying children and their families, 353
Home health care programs, 194–195, 203, 204
    and care of dying, 195
Homicide, 71–74, 92
    and adolescents, 72, 369–370, 383–386
    as leading cause of death among individuals
        15–24 years of age, 71
    and children, 326
    and death, 71
    distinguished from euthanasia, 529
    and family members, 72, 384
    and firearms, 72, 384
    and gangs, 385
    and gender differences, 72
    and Hispanic Americans, 103
    and the media, 72, 88
    as a public health crisis, 386
    and school shootings, 72, 89, 384
    survivors, 74
    victims (primary and secondary), 383–384
    and young adults, 72, 404
Homosexuality/homosexuals, 80, 387, 577,
        581, 588
Hope, 137, 143, 147–148, 150, 171, 174–175,
        177, 225
Hopelessness (in suicidal behavior), 502, 506,
        518. *See also*, Suicide, psychological
        explanations of
Horrendous death, 84
"The Horse on the Dining-Room Table," xxi,
        xxviii–xxx, 1, 14, 136
Hospice, 36, 183, 195–200, 203, 204
    bereavement follow-up care/programs, 200,
        304–305, 313
    and care of the dying, 195–199, 203
    characteristics of persons served in U.S.,
        198–199
    and children or adolescents, 199–200, 203,
        353–354, 358. See also Children's
        Project on Palliative/Hospice Services
        (ChiPPS)

day care, 196
    deaths while under hospice care in U.S., 198
    defined, 184
    and end-of-life care, 195–200, 203, 204
    funding and reimbursement, 197–198
    Helpline, 197
    historical development of, 196–197
    and HIV/AIDS, 187, 199, 600
    home care teams, 196
    and hospital support teams, 196
    inpatient facilities, 196
    and interdisciplinary teamwork, 186
    Medicare benefit, 197–198
    and older adults, 198
    and palliative care, 301–303
    patient and family as unit of care, 185
    philosophy and principles, 183–187, 204,
        524
    as a program of care, 204
    and recent research reports, 200
    and staff support, 187
    teen volunteers in, 376–377, 382
    volunteers, 186, 199
Hospitals, 188–190, 202, 204
    and acute care, 190, 203
    and care for the dying, 188–190
    as contributors to health care, 37–38
    as location of death, 34–35
Hostage to fortune, 210
House/Senate Joint Inquiry into Intelligence
        Community Activities Before and After
        the Terrorist Attacks of September, 11,
        2001, 68
Human Immunodeficiency Virus. *See* HIV
Human-induced death, 69–84
    and accidents, 69–71. *See also* Accidents
    and The Holocaust, 80–82. *See also* The
        Holocaust
    and homicide, 71–74. *See also* Homicide
    and the Nuclear Era, 82–84. *See also* The
        Nuclear Era
    and terrorism, 74–78. *See also* Terrorism
    and war and genocide, 79–80. *See also* War
        and genocide
Hurricane Katrina (August, 2005), xxiii, 66,
        242, 328
Hurricane Rita (September, 2005), 242, 328
Hydration, 253–255. *See* Needs of bereaved
        persons

I'll Always Love You (children's book), 260
Illegal or illicit drugs, dangers of, 37, 39, 40
Illness, Crisis & Loss (journal), 61
Illustrating the themes of this book, 572–609
Immortality of soul, 557, 558, 568. *See also*
        Symbolic immortality
Immunosuppression, 466
Indicators of School Crime and Safety
        (U.S. Departments of Education and
        Justice annual reports), 72
Individuals, 12. *See also* Lessons about life
        and living
Industrialization, 36–37, 41. *See also*
        Encounters with death, factors
        associated with changes in
Inevitability (as sub-concept within the
        concept of death), 330–331, 359

Memorial photographs/photography, 302
Memorial sculpture, 301–302
Memorial services, 288, 291, 313
Memorial societies, 288–289
Memorialization. *See* Memorial activities
Meningitis. *See* Disease, meningitis
Metaphysics (book), 460
Metempsychosis, 560, 568. *See also*
    Reincarnation
Microbial agents (as cause of communicable
    diseases and death), 37, 39
Middle adulthood, 397–425
    defined, 318, 399
    major developmental task in, 318, 399–400
    and gender, 400
    and generativity, 318, 399
    "seasons" or eras in, 399
Middle adults (or Middle-aged adults)
    and attitudes toward death, 405–407
    books about bereavement experiences of,
        411–412
    books about helping children cope with
        death, 350
    causes of death, 403–405
    coping with bereavement and grief, 409–422
    coping with life-threatening illness and
        dying, 408–409
    and death of a child, 409–410, 412–414
    and death of a parent or grandparent,
        421–423
    and death of a spouse, life partner, sibling,
        peer, or friend, 418–421
    death rates, 400–403
    deaths of, 400–403
    and developmental tasks, 399–400
    and encounters with death, 400–405
    gender and role differences, 405, 418
    guidelines for communications with
        adolescents about death, 390
    guidelines for using death-related resources
        to help children, 351
    as members of the sandwich generation,
        399, 405, 409
    and midlife transition, 399, 405, 423
    and personalized sense of mortality, 406
    responsibilities for helping children,
        345–346
    talking to children about death, 346
Middle knowledge, 140
Midlife transition, 399, 423
Military reserve, 406, 420
Miscarriage, 409–410, 412–413
Mishnah (Jewish oral traditions), 537–538
Missouri Supreme Court, 533
Mormons, 35
Mortality (journal), 61
Mortality rates. *See* Death rates
Mortician, 85. *See also* Funeral director
Mount Auburn Cemetery, 300
Mourning, 9, 220–242, 349
    and African Americans, 112–113
    and American Indians and Native Alaskans,
        121–123
    anticipatory, 240–242, 247
    and Asian and Pacific Island Americans,
        115–117
    complicated, 248

and continuing bonds, 231–232, 248
defined as coping with loss and grief, 220
disenfranchised, 257–259, 275
dual process model of, 229–230
external, public, or interpersonal aspects,
    220, 249
and families, 238–240
and fixed end points, 234
and gender, 236–237
as grief work, 220–222, 248, 249
and grieving, 220, 248
and grieving styles, 236–237
helping with, 252–316
and Hispanic Americans, 105–107
internal, private, or intrapersonal aspects,
    220, 249
interpretations or theories of, 220–233,
    248
Jewish rituals in, 299
and meaning reconstruction, 230–231
among middle adults, 409–422
among older adults, 441–447
and opportunities for growth and
    transformation, 234–236
outcomes of, 231, 233–236, 249
phases in, 222–224, 248
as potentially transformative, 233–236
processes in, 229–233, 248
and suicide, 506–510
tasks in, 222, 226–229, 248–249
and World Wide Web, 302
among young adults, 409–422
Movies, 89–90, 375
Murrah (Alfred P.) Federal Building
    (Oklahoma City), 75
Music, and death-related themes, 375
Muslims, 56
Mustard (children's book), 260
Mutual aid/help, 268, 305, 309
Mutual pretense. *See* Awareness contexts
My Book for Kids with Cansur (child's book),
    346
My Grandmother's Cookie Jar (children's
    book), 121

Nagasaki, Japan, 82–83
Narratives (in mourning), 231. *See also*
    Storytelling (in mourning)
"NASH" system (for classifying manner of
    death), 464, 488
Nasogastric tube, 524. *See also* Feeding tube
National Commission on Terrorist Attacks,
    68, 69
National Communications Guidelines
    (booklet), 482
National Donor Family Council (NDFC), 473,
    479–482
National Donor Family Quilt, 479
National Donor Recognition Ceremonies,
    479
National Guard, 406, 420
National Health and Nutrition Examination
    Survey (1999–2002), 40
National HIV Testing Resources, 578
National Kidney Foundation, 477, 479, 482
"National Organ Transplant Act" (NOTA),
    468, 488

National Suicide Prevention Lifeline, 510,
    514. *See also* Suicide, interventions to
    minimize likelihood of; Suicide, ways
    to help
National Transplant Waiting List, 467, 468, 474
Native Americans, 99, 124. *See also* American
    Indians and Alaskan Natives
Natural death legislation, 457
Natural disaster(s), 66
Nazis, 80, 82
Near-death experiences (NDEs), 564–566, 568
    descriptions of, 564–565
    interpreting the meaning of, 565–566
Nearing death awareness, 171, 177
Needs of bereaved persons, 253–255, 275
Neonatal deaths, 413–414
Neoplastic disease. *See* Disease, cancer
Nepesh (Hebrew term for "soul" or "life"),
    558, 568
The Netherlands, 542–544
New England Journal of Medicine, 40
New England Primer (book), 58
New England Puritans. *See* Puritans
New Haven Burying Ground (cemetery), 300
New Jersey Supreme Court, 533
"New normals" (in bereavement), 223, 236,
    249
New Orleans, 66
News reports. *See* Media
Newsworthy events, 88
Next-of-kin, and authorization for organ/
    tissue donation, 472
Nickel Mines Amish School, xxiii, 47
9/11. *See* September 11, 2001
Nirvana, 148, 563, 568
Noncorporeal continuation (as sub-concept
    within the concept of death), 330, 331,
    358, 359
Nonfunctionality (as sub-concept within
    the concept of death), 330, 331, 342,
    358, 359
Nonliving donors, 469, 470–472, 488. *See also*
    Organ and tissue donors
Nonvoluntary euthanasia. *See* Euthanasia
    voluntary versus nonvoluntary
Normalization (of bereavement experiences),
    265, 273
NOTA. *See* National Organ Transplant Act
Notification of death, 22, 71
The nuclear era, 82–84, 92
Nuclear threats/warfare, 10, 83
Nurses and nurse's aides, 35, 191–192
Nursing homes, 34, 190, 204. *See also*
    Long-term care facilities
Nutrition, 253–255. *See* Needs of bereaved
    persons

Obesity, 40
Obituaries, 88
Odyssey (book), 557, 568
Oklahoma City bombing, 75
Older adulthood, 426–451
    defined, 318, 428–431
    developmental eras within, 430, 448
    major developmental task in, 318, 430
    and gender, 433, 434–435
    and ego integrity, 318, 430

common patterns in, 497–500
completed, 518
"by cop," 502
as a cry for help, 496
deaths and death rates, 497
defined, 495–496, 497, 518
and depression, 446, 501–502
many determinants and levels of meaning,
505–506
education about, 388–389
efforts to understand or explain,
501–506, 518
as an effort to escape stressful situations,
387
and "either/or" thinking, 506, 518
and ethnicity, 499–500
facts and fables about, 510–511
and gay/lesbian youths, 387
and gender differences, 387, 498
and guilt, 507
impact on survivors of person who died,
498, 506–510
individuality and perplexity of, 495
and institutionalization, 446–447
and (over/under) integration, 504–505
and intention, 496
interventions to minimize likelihood of,
388–389, 510–514, 518
as leading cause of death, 497
as learned behavior, 502–503
methods, 498
National Suicide Prevention Lifeline, 510,
514
notes, 506
and older adults, 446–447, 448, 499
as permanent solution to temporary
problem, 389
physician assisted, 527, 549
prevention. See Suicide, interventions to
minimize likelihood of
psychological explanations of, 501–503
and race/ethnicity, 499–500
rates, 497
rational, 514–515, 518
and (over/under) regulation, 505
religious views of, 516–517
and social integration/regulation, 503–504
sociological explanations of, 503–505
and stigma, 257
survivors of the suicide of another person,
498, 506–510, 518
tendencies, 163
and terrorism, 76–78
and "tunnel vision," 506, 514, 518
as urge to escape from stressful life
situation, 387
and warning signs, 512
ways to help, 512–514
and young persons, 499
Suicide and Life-Threatening Behavior
(journal), 520
Suicidologists/suicidology, 496, 518
The Sun Also Rises (book), 493
*Sunflowers and Rainbows for Tia: Saying
Goodbye to Daddy* (children's book), 113
Sunna (practices and teachings of
Mohammed), 540

Support groups for the bereaved, 305–312,
313, 314
for adolescents, 393
for children, 356
help outside the group, 312
helping factors in, 310–312
hospice, 305
leadership in, 309–301
principles and practices, 306, 309–310
Support organizations. See Bereavement,
support organizations
"The SUPPORT (Study to Understand
Prognoses and Preferences for
Outcomes and Risks of Treatments)"
project, 182–184
The Surgeon General of the U.S., 590
Surrogate decision maker, 457, 458–459,
471, 488. See also Advance directives;
Durable powers of attorney in health
care matters; Living wills
Surviving Suicide (newsletter), 509
Survivor guilt, 444
Survivor(s), 236, 244, 249
Survivors of the Shoah Visual History
Foundation, 82
Suspected awareness. See Awareness contexts
Suttee, 504
Symbolic immortality, 567, 568
Sympathy cards, 85
Symptoms of grief. See Grief, signs or
manifestations
Syndrome, defined, 576, 606

Taboo topics, 5, 85
Talmud (Jewish scriptural writings), 537
Tame death. See Death, tame
Tasks
in adolescence, 365–366
affective, 265, 275
behavioral, 266, 276
in childhood, 358
cognitive, 264–265, 276
in coping with dying, 142–149, 151
in coping with loss and grief. See Tasks, in
mourning
developmental, 317–318, 358
distinguished from needs, 142
and funerals, 292–299
as guidelines for helping persons who are
coping with dying, 167–170
helping bereaved persons with, 263–268
human and professional, 155–156
in middle adults, 399–400
in mourning, 222, 224, 226–229
in mourning, for bereaved children, 343–344
in older adults, 428–430
physical, 143
psychological, 143–144
social, 143, 144–146
spiritual, 143, 146–148, 165
for survivors of suicide, 507
valuational, 267–268, 276
in young adults, 399–400
"Tattered cloak of immortality" (in childhood
and adolescence), 372
Taxes, estate and inheritance, 486, 487, 488
T-cells, 576, 606. See also HIV/AIDS

Teachable moments, 8, 347. See also
Education (about death dying and
bereavement)
Teamwork, interdisciplinary, 182, 186, 204
Tear Soup (book), 213, 263, 310
Teenagers. See Adolescents
Teen volunteers (in hospice), 376–377, 382
Television and death/violence, 87, 88, 91, 328
"Terri's law," 523
Terrorism, 10, 74–78, 83, 92
Terrorists, 77–78, 501
Thanatology, 5, 85. See also Death-awareness
movement
Therapy, grief. See Grief, therapy
Three Mile Island (Pennsylvania), 83
Tiger Eyes (children's book), 271
"Time heals," 234. See also Mourning,
outcomes of
Tissue donation, 466, 488. See Organ and
tissue donation
Tissue donors. See Organ and tissue donors
Tissue typing, 466
Titration of drugs, 158
Tobacco products, use and dangers of, 18, 37,
39–40. See also Cigarettes; Smoking
Touch, 162
Trajectories. See Dying, trajectories
Transcendence, 143, 147–148, 177. See also
Tasks, spiritual
Transfers (of property) effective at death, 485
Transmigration (of souls), 560, 562, 568. See
also Reincarnation
Transplantable human organs, 466, 467, 488
Transplantable human tissues, 489
Transplantation, of human organs and tissue,
466–469
candidates for, 467
need for/obstacle to, 467–469
Transplant Games. See U.S. Transplant Games
Traumatic loss(es). See Loss(es), traumatic
Trinity test site (New Mexico), 82
Trusts, 484–486, 489
Tsunami in Asia (December 2004), 66, 87,
242, 327
Tuberculosis. See Disease, tuberculosis;
Disease, MRSA
"Tunnel vision" (in suicidal behavior), 506,
518. See also, Suicide, psychological
explanations of
Tuskegee syphilis study, 111
Two Old Women (book), 429

UAGA. See "Uniform Anatomical Gift Act"
UDDA. See "Uniform Determination of Death
Act"
"Understanding AIDS" (Surgeon General's
brochure), 590
Understandings of death
development in childhood, 328–334
influenced by ambiguities/tensions during
adolescence, 374–375
Undertaker, 85. See also Funeral director
Unfinished business, 52, 138
Unhelpful messages (addressed to the
bereaved), 255–257
"Uniform Anatomical Gift Act" (UAGA), 489,
469, 472, 489